Operations M

Improving Customer Service

Operations Management
Improving Customer Service

Richard J. Schonberger
University of Washington
and
Schonberger & Associates, Inc.

Edward M. Knod, Jr.
Western Illinois University

Fourth Edition

Homewood, IL 60430
Boston, MA 02116

Sponsoring editor: *Richard T. Hercher, Jr.*
Project editor: *Lynne Basler*
Production manager: *Bette K. Ittersagen*
Cover designer: *Lucy Lesiak Design*
Artist: *Precision Graphics*
Compositor: *J. M. Post Graphics, Corp.*
Typeface: *10/12 Palatino*
Printer: *R. R. Donnelley & Sons Company*

Library of Congress Cataloging-in-Publication Data

Schonberger, Richard.
    Operations management: improving customer service / Richard
J. Schonberger, Edward M. Knod, Jr. — 4th ed.
        p.   cm.
    Includes bibliographical references and index.
    ISBN 0-256-08240-5 — ISBN 0-256-09881-6 (International ed.)
    1. Production management.   I. Knod, Edward M.
TS155.S3244   1991
658.5—dc20   90–44669

Printed in the United States of America
    2   3   4   5   6   7   8   9   0   DOC   7   6   5   4   3   2   1

Preface

Businesses exist to serve customers. We thought so when we wrote the third edition of this book, subtitled *Serving the Customer*. That theme re-aimed operations management (OM) at a target that had been largely ignored by OM practitioners as well as by academics in business and engineering schools.

In the past, customer concern was the purview of sales and marketing. The rest of the firm was insulated. Not today. Operations is a hotbed of customer awareness, and many of the newer and better concepts of OM aim squarely at improving service to the customer—which today means the next process, plus all the "hand-offs" in the customer chain leading to the final user.

We chose the subtitle, *Improving Customer Service*, for this, our fourth edition, because the book is crammed with lore on how a firm should drive itself toward improvement—in the eyes of the customer. That is the book's theme, and it fits the mind-set of the world's best companies.

It isn't hard to see that the customer service idea has caught fire: "King Customer" was the cover story of *Business Week's*, March 12, 1990 issue. The story proclaimed, in bold print, "At companies that listen hard and respond fast, bottom lines thrive." It went on to note the flurry of recently published business books that have "customer" in the title.

That doesn't mean, of course, that customer-driven activity has pushed aside narrower, short-term, "protect-your-turf" behaviors throughout OM and the business world. Glitzy advertising and indifferent service still are more common than genuine dedication to serve and improve. But customers wise up fast. If there's a provider offering substance rather than show, that provider wins the business—and allegiance.

MORE SPECIFICALLY

What do we mean by "substance"? What's "in the eyes of the customer" that operations management can do something about? Quality, quality, and quality. We have two chapters on the subject (Chapters 4 and 15), and most of the rest of the chapters weave in more quality thinking—because that is the customer's foremost concern.

The customer has several other concerns, which we tick off in Chapter 1—and follow up on in later chapters. These concerns include designing the product or service for the customer—and for ease of making or providing. There has been a virtual revolution in design concepts in recent years, and we think it is time that operations management studies took note of it (as we do in Chapter 3).

Treating suppliers as partners rather than adversaries is another dramatic change taking place in business; we give the topic its due in Chapter 7.

Hot new topics and techniques added in this edition include:

- Theory of constraints—except that we turn it around, fix it up, and present it as the *theory of response,* which better suits the theme of improving customer service (Chapter 8).
- Controlling *causes* of cost. We explain the power of the direct visual system, as compared with trying to control performance via periodic cost and productivity reports (Chapters 15 and 16).
- Our treatment of cost control and productivity management also includes *activity-based costing,* since it requires joint analysis by both accountants and operations managers (Chapter 16).
- *Focus* on customers and products, not functions. This is a major theme in the facility layout materials in Chapter 18; the point is stressed in many other chapters as well.

Topics emphasized because we think they should or will be hot include:

- *Principles of operations management.* The 17-item list from the third edition is retained, but with improved wording and stronger emphasis on services (Chapter 1); the relevant principle is restated where appropriate throughout the book.
- *Off-line buffer stock,* which allows slashing lead times, but without increasing risk (Chapter 8).
- *Contained costing,* an important by-product of getting the resources into focused plants-in-a-plant and cells (Chapter 18).

FOR THE INSTRUCTOR

We've made the book more logical and teachable, following the guidance of our own customers—the instructors. For example, demand management and forecasting have been combined (new Chapter 5); "capacity planning and master scheduling" is changed to *master planning* in Chapter 6, which has been made more "service-sector friendly"; location planning has been expanded, including a new matrix technique (Chapter 18).

IN GENERAL

We are careful to point out, especially in opening chapters, that the current turbulence in operations management is not a regional phenomenon. In fact, what is happening on the North American continent was inspired by withering global competition, at first from Japan. Now new ideas for improved operations management are springing up around the globe.

The aim in this textbook is to prescribe and explain—in simple, understandable language—what works, and, where necessary, what doesn't work. This is what academic people call a *normative* (as opposed to a descriptive) approach.

Earlier editions offered mainly stand-alone chapters, which allowed instructors to omit some chapters to fit time available in the course. This edition, on the other hand, is highly integrative. For instance, topics such as quality, quick response (just-in-time), customer-as-next-process, and employee involvement are treated in nearly all chapters. The service sector is prominent in all chapters as well. Can the chapters still stand alone? Well, yes. Leaving out a chapter, or part of one, simply means less intensive coverage of a certain topic, such as flexible response or quality improvement.

We owe special thanks to Professors Jay Bandyopadhyay, Central Michigan University; Sohail S. Chaudhry, Loyola University of Chicago; Keith Denton, Southwest Missouri State University; Ike C. Ehie, Southwest Missouri State University; John Haehl, Sonoma State University; John Milleville, University of Colorado, Denver; Jerry Murphy, Portland State University; David Osborne, Abilene Christian University; Taeho Park, San Jose State University; James A. Pope, Old Dominion University; Rhae M. Swisher, Jr., Troy State University; and Norman Ware, University of Louisville. Their thorough, incisive reviews and recommendations led us to alter the book's arrangement of topics as well as alerting us to gaffes, omissions, and key trends that deserve prominence in the book.

Please let us know what you like and don't like about the fourth edition. We value your opinion.

Richard J. Schonberger
Edward M. Knod, Jr.

Note to the Student

Operations is the front line. It is where services are delivered, where goods are made—and where most people work. Regardless of what career you choose (or end up in), you will rub elbows all the time with operating people. You may even spend your career, or part of it, in operations yourself. *Operations Management* explains what you need to know as a manager in operations or in dealing with operating people.

You will find the material realistic and up-to-date. Some of it is so current that average firms don't know about the concepts yet—but the best companies do. By understanding the concepts, you'll have an edge.

Operations management (OM) is partly a technical subject. You will find easy-to-grasp material intermingled with topics that require careful study. We suggest that you adjust your pace of study accordingly. For example, don't expect to get by just by marking certain passages with a highlighter—to be reviewed quickly later. You should slow down and work through examples on paper and with a calculator part of the time.

One thing more. You'll be happy to hear that OM is mostly common sense—a commodity that most of us appreciate (and that many of us feel we possess).

We hope you enjoy your OM studies; we know you'll benefit from them. Good luck!

R.J.S.
E.M.K.

Contents in Brief

Contents

Contents

Introduction to Operations Management

The operating end of a business is where products are made and services provided, where most of the money is spent, and where most of the people work. How should operations be managed? This book addresses that question. Part One introduces operations management and details the key issues.

Chapter 1 sets forth the theme of this book: Operations should be dedicated to improving service to customers. A set of principles is available to help operations managers accomplish that end. Chapter 2 continues the introduction by examining operations strategy and environment and by defining functions that operations managers perform.

CHAPTER 1
**Operations Management:
Customers, Principles, and Managers**

CHAPTER 2
**Operations Management:
Strategy, Environment, and Functions**

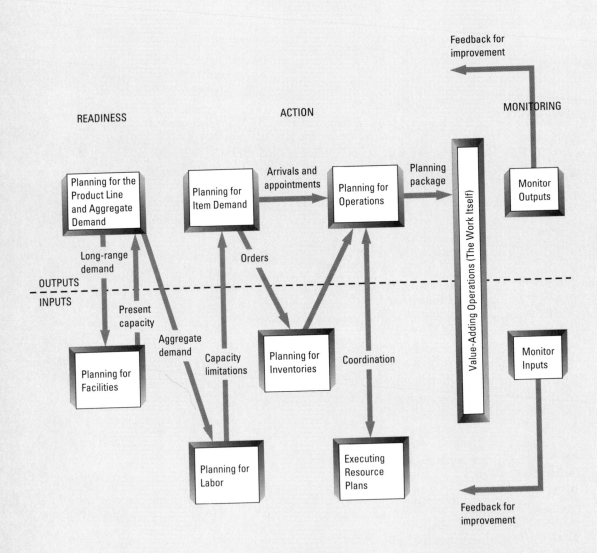

READINESS

ACTION

MONITORING

Feedback for improvement

Planning for the Product Line and Aggregate Demand

Long-range demand

OUTPUTS

INPUTS

Present capacity

Planning for Facilities

Aggregate demand

Planning for Item Demand

Arrivals and appointments

Planning for Operations

Planning package

Value-Adding Operations (The Work Itself)

Monitor Outputs

Orders

Capacity limitations

Planning for Inventories

Coordination

Planning for Labor

Executing Resource Plans

Monitor Inputs

Feedback for improvement

Operations Management: Customers, Principles, and Managers

Just what is **operations management (OM)**? First, its focus is on the operating end of a business, where resources are transformed into goods and services and where inputs become outputs. Second, the emphasis is on *management*, an iterative cycle of planning, implementing, and monitoring for continuing improvement.

All organizations have operations. Manufacturing companies conduct operations in a factory, hospital operations occur in admissions and examining rooms as well as in surgery, banks and public accounting firms operate out of offices, restaurant operations take place on counters and tables, and supermarkets and other retailers perform operations throughout the entire store.

Despite differences in format or in specific goods and services provided, certain observations regarding the management of operations in any organization began to emerge and then crystallize during the 1980s. Specifically:

- Operations should be performed with the overriding goal of improving service to customers.
- A normative approach to operations management, based on a guiding philosophy of continual improvement, is essential for success.
- Principles—with proven applicability—exist to guide the management of operations.
- Revision in our thinking about just who the operations managers *should be* opens the door to new career patterns.

Chapter 1 expands on those observations.

CONNECTIONS WITH CUSTOMERS

Most of us are familiar with the supplier-to-customer connection in the retail setting. For one thing, we've been customers. We have needs and expectations about how those needs should be met, and we convey those feelings in the form of requirements when we purchase goods and services. Whether in a bank, hardware store, or optometrist's office, the opportunity for face-to-face meetings and real-time discussions generally results in a more satisfying relationship. The oft-heard question "May I help you?" is a comforting reminder that the supplier-customer connection is a close one. And should we suffer a momentary lapse in memory, television and radio advertisers remind us that they constantly strive to give the *customer* center stage.

Maintaining a close supplier-customer connection sounds fine for retailers, and perhaps even for sales and marketing in general. It is time to realize that the same focus is every bit as applicable to operations management. We've seen what happens when connections aren't so close.

Supplier-Customer Separation: Formula for Trouble

What happens when there is no close connection between supplier and customer? First, consider services. Janitorial services, for example, are often performed with the customer out of sight, after the customer's working hours. Design services present an even greater problem. Not only is the customer not around, but design occurs weeks or months before a prototype is *produced*, and maybe even years before a retail customer *tries out* the finished product.

Let's look even closer at goods production. Where are the customers for goods produced in our factories? Across a continent or an ocean? How much time elapses between production and consumption? Whether we speak of goods or services, distance and time separation in the supplier-customer connection invites trouble.

Further, there seems to be a human tendency to react to the problem by pulling back from instead of reaching out to the customer. Even grocery store clerks, almost eyeball to eyeball with customers, are susceptible:

> Question: "What's your job?"
> Answer: "I run the cash register and sack groceries."
> Question: "But isn't your job to serve the customer?"
> Answer: "I suppose so, but my job description doesn't say that."

Even in grocery stores the operations *management* system is hard pressed to maintain a customer focus. In manufacturing, where time and distance make it much easier to stay in the background, the operations management challenge is proportionately greater. The almost certain consequences of inadequate contact with customers are obvious: lost orders and contracts, declining revenue, closed plants, loss of jobs, and economic decline.

The Customer: The Next Process

Against that bleak backdrop, there nevertheless is cause for cheer. For one thing, industry has come up with a potent new concept of the **customer**: *The customer is the next process, or where the work goes next.*[1] This slogan has become popular among manufacturing people in leading industrial companies. It packs power because it counters the common attitude that only sales, not manufacturing, can be customer oriented.

The next-process concept has its roots in the worldwide quality movement. It has become familiar to not only managers but also production and indirect labor in many major companies. As part of training in quality improvement, these companies are telling test equipment operators that their customer is the packer who packs what was just tested; the companies tell foundry people that their customer is the milling machine operator who mills the casting from the

---

[1]This phrase is attributed to the late Kaoru Ishikawa, a Japanese authority on quality.

foundry. The message applies to all service people as well: A buyer's customer is someone in the department to whom the purchased item goes; a cost accountant's customer is a manager who uses the accounting information to make a decision, and a product design engineer's customer is production—where the design will be manufactured. Thus the next-process concept makes it clear that *every* employee, not just the salesperson, has a customer. It is also clear that throughout operations management, people not only *have* customers, they *are* customers. Let's turn our attention to what customers want.

What Customers Want

Gabriel Pall, former director of the IBM Quality Institute, suggests that a customer's *requirement* has three components:

1. A statement of recognized need.
2. The expected manner in which that need should be met.
3. Some idea of benefits that will accrue from meeting the need.[2]

He goes on to assert that a requirement represents a *recipient or customer* view of a good or service. A **specification**, on the other hand, is the provider's or supplier's view of the good or service. The "spec" is the provider's target. Thus, from the provider's viewpoint, what customers want is specifications that accurately reflect their requirements. Good communication, available in close provider-customer connections, helps create such specifications, increasing suppliers' ability to provide the right things.

What else do customers want? As consumers, we have a constantly changing list of items on our personal requirements list. Some are recurring, while others are one-time needs. The same is true of business and industrial consumers. More meaningful than simple lists of required things, however, are common customer wants—universal requirements that apply regardless of service or good, industry or company, person or organization. Figure 1–1 shows the common customer requirements.

Customers want to deal with providers who offer *high* levels of quality, flexibility (to change such things as volume, specifications, and products), and service. They also want providers to offer *low* costs (passed on as low prices), *short* lead times (or response times), and *little or no* variability (deviation from target). The six customer requirements dictate, to some extent, the topics and concepts presented in this book, for a well-conceived operations management system must attempt to provide goods and services that meet all six of these attributes.

Be careful not to view Figure 1–1 as a list of potential trade-offs. For example,

[2]Gabriel A. Pall, *Quality Process Management* (Englewood Cliffs, N.J.: Prentice-Hall, 1987), pp. 18–19 (TS 157.P35).

FIGURE 1–1
Customer Requirements

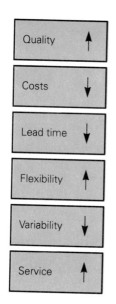

customers don't want to settle for *either* high quality *or* low costs; they want both. They don't want increased flexibility *or* shorter lead times; they want both. While customers seek goods and services that satisfy all six requirements, are providers capable of delivering all at the same time? Until recently, the trade-off viewpoint prevailed.

In general, this book's position regarding trade-offs may be summed up as follows: Weak companies are confronted everywhere they turn by trade-offs that appear to be clear opposites; improving companies develop immunities to some of the trade-offs that once plagued them; and world-class companies—those recognized for excellence in providing *all six* customer wants—have gained the upper hand over trade-off obstacles.

An equally important point about Figure 1–1 is that it should not be seen as a static list of customer wants; the arrows are meaningful. They signify that customers want—*and expect*—improvement along the six dimensions; *higher* quality, *better* service, and so forth. Motorola, winner of the 1988 Malcolm Baldridge National Quality Award (large-company category), operates with a philosophy that "the company that is satisfied with its progress will soon find that its customers are not."

At about this point, the reader—especially one with a few years of working experience—might begin to wonder if the ideas we've presented regarding customer service are just textbook talk. In short, the reader may wonder, Have any real-world managers bought into this view? Is it a fad, or is it likely to catch on? We address those issues next.

Improving Customer Service: Fact or Fantasy?

Fads are best judged through hindsight, and perhaps *serving the customer* will fail to stick as a core mission in many companies. We hope it thrives, because it's a persuasive viewpoint—one that benefits the provider as well as the user.

Plenty of companies *have* jumped on the customer-service bandwagon—at least in words. Consider the following examples:

- Toyota's Lexus LS 400, unveiled in August 1989, marked the company's entry into the luxury car market. As early as April 1985, chief developmental engineer Ichiro Suzuki sent 20 design engineers on a five-month mission to Southern California. The mission? Find out what customers want in a luxury car and then design the car.[3]

- Katherine Hudson, vice president of Information Systems at Eastman Kodak, defines her job as knowing what information other Kodak managers need and making sure that they have it so that they, in turn, can deliver products to their customers in a timely fashion. "I treat the other managers as my customers," she says.[4]

- John Akers, chairman and CEO of IBM, speaking of the company's growth slowdown of the mid-1980s, said, "We took our eye off the ball." That "ball" is the customer and the customer's changing tastes. As he leads the company on the most radical cultural change in its history, Akers's goal is for IBM to become "the world's champion in meeting the needs of our customers."[5]

- Sony Chairman Akio Morita loves his company's products. He takes a different one home to "play with" each week. "That's how I find

[3]Alex Taylor III, "Here Come Japan's New Luxury Cars," *Fortune,* August 14, 1989, pp. 62–66.
[4]Lisa J. Moore and Marc Silver, "A Baker's Dozen of Jobs for the Needs of the '90s," *U.S. News and World Report,* September 25, 1989, pp. 62–71.
[5]Joel Dreyfuss, "Reinventing IBM," *Fortune,* August 14, 1989, pp. 30–39.

what we should improve. . . . The product should be *loved* by the customers. That's how we can enrich their lives."[6]

Managers who talk like Suzuki, Hudson, Akers, and Morita are growing in number; other examples will be mentioned throughout this book. Like Hudson, they reconize their fellow employees as customers in the next-process sense. In support of their views, a rapidly expanding body of knowledge has emerged in the last few years that documents the goal of improving customer service as a hallmark of operations in world-class companies. For those companies, it seems not to be a fad or gimmick. It's the way operations ought to be managed.

The next section looks more closely at how operations management should be approached.

APPROACHING OPERATIONS MANAGEMENT: PHILOSOPHY AND PRINCIPLES

At one time, subjects like operations management—and business studies in general—were thought to be vocational and therefore questionable for inclusion in university curricula. Universities were supposed to educate and enrich the mind, not train in how to repeat what was already being done. No doubt there are some who have doubts about the educational value of business studies; we'll not debate the matter. There is a related issue, however, that is worth addressing here: Is contemporary thinking in operations management becoming more educational and less vocational? Restating in academic language, should our approach to OM be more normative—emphasizing what *should* be? Or should the approach be a descriptive one—emphasizing simply what the current practice *is*?

A Normative Approach to OM

We believe that a highly normative approach to the study of operations management is needed, and we suggest as much throughout the book. Despite our intent, there *is* plenty of description in the chapters ahead. That description, however, is couched in presentations of what is wrong with practices in the field (or with theories in books) and discussion of what the cure is—that is, what *works*.

According to the old saying, the only thing certain about the future is change. Case evidence suggests that perhaps the most significant factor in loss of competitive position is managers who don't acknowledge change and maintain a state of readiness to deal with it. When performance declines, the prudent manager should suspect that past practices are part of the problem and need to be altered.

---

[6]"Japan Goes Hollywood," A *Newsweek* Business Report; *Newsweek*, October 9, 1989, pp. 62–67.

An even more prudent manager will seek to *prevent* problems from occurring in the first place. A course that prevents trouble is the true one, the one that ought to be followed. In recent years some basic *principles of operations management* have emerged to help steer a firm along a true course.

Principles of Operations Management

Over the past decade, as the customer-service viewpoint took root, top companies began to adopt surprisingly similar new practices in operations management. The new practices, in turn, are founded on a common set of customer-serving, competitive guidelines, or principles. Those principles of operations management are listed in Figure 1–2.

The principles serve as a foundation for *any* organization, just as blocking and passing serve as fundamentals for *any* team in a variety of team sports. Operations strategies that emerge from a company's current business plan are comparable to the sports team's game-plan for a particular opponent; in both cases, execution of the specific plan depends on the strength of the foundation.

The principles of operations management have a commonsense ring to them. Nevertheless, they tend to be violated repeatedly in company after company, as discussed below.

Get to Know the Customer and the Competition. The customer, whether final consumer or next process, is the object of the first and most important principle.

FIGURE 1–2
Principles of Operations Management

1. Get to know the customer and the competition.
2. Cut work in process (waiting lines), throughput times, flow distances, and space.
3. Cut setup and changeover times.
4. Produce and deliver at the customer's use rate (or a smoothed representation of it); decrease cycle interval and lot size.
5. Cut the number of suppliers to a few good ones.
6. Cut the number of components in a product or service.
7. Make it easy to make/provide goods or services without error—the first time.
8. Convert multipath flows to single-channel lanes; create cells and flow lines.
9. Arrange the workplace to eliminate search time.
10. Cross-train for mastery of multiple skills.
11. Record and retain output volume, quality, and problem data at the workplace.
12. Ensure that line people get first crack at problem-solving—before staff experts.
13. Maintain and improve present equipment and human work before thinking about new equipment.
14. Look for simple, cheap, movable equipment.
15. Automate incrementally when process variability cannot otherwise be reduced.
16. Seek to have plural rather than singular work stations, machines, cells, and flow lines for each product, service, or customer.
17. Become dedicated to continual, rapid improvement.

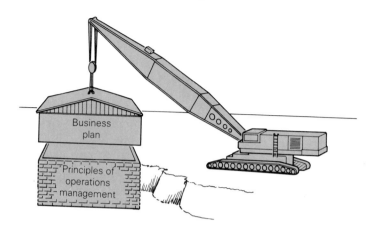

All other principles tend to follow naturally from this first one, because they are more specific about how to better serve the customer.

Any obstacles in the way of better understanding, communication, and coordination with the customer need to be struck down. Even the obstacle of geography, such as a customer located miles away, must be dealt with. Globe Metallurgical, supplier of additives to steel mills and foundries, sends its factory operators on buses to customer plants where they get to know their counterparts. That paves the way for quick and easy communication—operator to operator—when the mill or foundry has a problem or when Globe people have questions about customer needs. Globe's strong customer focus contributed to its being named the United States' first (1988) recipient of the Malcolm Baldrige quality prize in the small business category.[7]

Getting to know the competition is vital as well. While applicability of this principle in sales and marketing is clear (for competitive pricing, etc.), we are talking about its importance in operations management. Not knowing the strengths of the competition—their ability to deliver better quality or to offer quicker response, for example—leads to complacency and decline. *Having* such information, on the other hand, helps motivate a company's people to make necessary improvements. Part of competitive analysis is keeping informed about product and process innovations in order to better direct the firm's improvement efforts.

Cut Work in Process (Waiting Lines), Throughput Times, Flow Distances, and Space. The four parts of this principle are closely related. Keeping work in process as low as possible—by striving to keep in-baskets and waiting lines empty, for example—allows each job or customer to be processed or served without delay. That shortens **throughput time**, the time needed to transform resources into goods and services. Cutting flow distance by moving process stages closer together also makes it easier to reduce throughput times and work in process. It shrinks operating space as well.

---

[7]"Quality through Consistency: Globe Metallurgical Makes Improvements Quickly," *Target*, Fall 1989, pp. 4–12.

In factories, **work in process (WIP)** takes the form of in-process inventory—jobs waiting their turn on a machine or waiting for assembly. It is possible to cut throughput time and flow distance without reducing WIP. For example, a firm can store an extra supply of foam packing material cheaply across town but receive and use foam directly from its packing materials supplier every day; the stored foam is there for emergency use if the supplier has a problem. That practice seems sound. But it has been more common, oddly enough, for firms to have the supplier deliver each day to the remote warehouse and then have its own truck fetch from there. The common practice causes throughput time—when the foam is made (by the supplier) to when it is used—to increase. Operating costs associated with the additional delays for extra handling and transport, another set of shipping documents, and so forth, also increase.

Competition is the best cure for problems of long waits and throughput times. In some Western cities, supermarkets have policies and procedures for limiting checkout lines. When one supermarket limits line length to three people, competitors are forced to learn how to do the same thing. On a global scale, part of the political turbulence in Soviet Bloc countries has to do with citizens' demands for the kinds of service enjoyed in countries with free competition. Accustomed to waiting in lines for hours to buy a few grocery items (and not necessarily the specific things they want or need), many Eastern Europeans got their first taste of competitive customer service in late 1989 when travel restricitons were eased and they were allowed to venture across and outside of the Iron Curtain.

Competition has also forced Western manufacturers to learn how to shorten waiting lines, speed throughput, cut WIP, and reduce space. In this case, the competitive impetus came from Japan, which had developed the quick-response system known as *just-in-time production*. Today, the competition for quick response is widespread—in every industry and nearly all corners of the globe.

Cut Setup and Changeover Times. If you want to run a program on your personal computer, you must first get set up. When turning on the machine, you have to boot the disk, which, on your older model, takes 39 seconds. Then you make a menu selection (29 seconds). Next, you instruct the computer to read disk drive A (10 seconds). Then you call the desired program into memory (22 seconds). After a total of 1 minute and 40 seconds of setup, you are ready to perform useful work. Not so long, perhaps, but what if you needed to switch from a word-processing program to a spreadsheet? Would you have to go through another setup (reboot)? And then perhaps another, to use a database program?

Whether we refer to a personal computer or a manufacturing plant, **setup time** or **changeover time** is the time it takes to go from useful output in one mode to useful output in the second. With your computer, excess setup time may be a mild annoyance or it could seriously detract from your productivity.

In manufacturing, machine setup and production-line changeover time is a very real concern—it can eat up enormous amounts of capacity and can result in long production runs between changeovers. This causes inventories and lead times to serve the customer to grow, along with costs. Until recently, industry paid little heed to such costs.

Once changeover time reduction is elevated to a basic goal, a lot can be accomplished. For example, a 3M plant near Chicago making paper backing rolls for masking tape reduced setup time on a 30-year-old cutting machine from 222 to 17 minutes; a reduction of over 92 percent!

Produce and Deliver at the Customer's Use Rate (or a Smoothed Representation of It); Decrease Cycle Interval and Lot Size. Until about 1950, the U.S. Postal Service delivered to residences twice a day. Good service, right? But when frequency dropped to once a day, load *size* increased and the Postal Service had to put mail carriers into vehicles. The increased **cycle interval**—time between deliveries, in this case—meant worse service and a whole new expense for bulk-handling vehicles.

We can see parallels in factories, where increased cycle interval is typically accompanied by increased **lot size**—the quantity produced or transported in one cycle. The urge to pile containers higher on pallets just to reduce the number of delivery trips is an example. Less frequent trips, however, mean worse service among departments and necessitate larger, more costly bulk-handling equipment. Sometimes it seems that factories were designed more for forklift trucks than for production.

Today's emphasis on small, frequent production lots and deliveries has yielded diverse benefits. For example, Harley-Davidson has reduced its number of forklift trucks from 50 to 6 in its motorcycle assembly plant. Further, Harley is now able to produce some of every motorcycle model daily in a mixed-model assembly sequence that is roughly equal to the daily sales for each model. Formerly, production of each model—and every component going into those models— was in large lots, with cycle intervals ranging from many days to many weeks. Such long cycle intervals forced even longer-ranged (and thus more uncertain) demand forecasts. The results were large, costly inventories based on fallible forecasts—and a dim outlook for Harley.

Cut the Number of Suppliers to a Few Good Ones. Virtually every buyer of industrial materials knows the rule of thumb: For protection, have several suppliers for every purchased item. Today's new rule of thumb is to find one or perhaps two *good* suppliers and nurture them until they are almost like family. The long-term payoff is "clannish" loyalty, which offers its own kind of protection. Other benefits include lower prices, better quality, and reliable delivery because the supplier can gain economies of scale and concentrate on meeting customers' specific quality and schedule needs.

Cut the Number of Components in a Product or Service. NCR designers were able to reduce the number of purchased components for a new model of cash register from 110 to 15. Bill Sprague, a member of the design team, was shown in a *Business Week* article in a striking pose: He was blindfolded, assembling a cash register. It took him less than two minutes![8] Nearly all manufacturers in

---

[8]Otis Port, "The Best-Engineered Part Is No Part at All," *Business Week,* May 8, 1989, p. 150.

the electrical and electronics industry—as well as the entire auto industry—have adopted the same parts-reducing design approaches favored by NCR. In the service sector, successful fast-food chains are past masters at keeping the number of components low.

Make It Easy to Make/Provide Goods or Services without Error—The First Time. This principle is supported by a full set of concepts and practices broadly known as **total quality (TQ)** or **total quality management (TQM)**. A core concept in TQM is the management of quality at every stage of operations, from planning and design through self-inspection, to continual process monitoring for improvement opportunities.

In the past, neglect of quality managment and in-process control led to large inspection staffs for sorting bad output from good, typically in late production stages, and shipping the rejects off to large rework departments. In services, many managers' job descriptions could be accurately stated as "review and redo." Over the past decade, the phrase "Do it right the first time," has caught on as a long-overdue solution.

Convert Multipath Flows to Single-Channel Lanes; Create Cells and Flow Lines. This principle attacks the foundation of familiar bureaucratic statements like "This office is responsible for that job," or "Our department processes those forms." Just sending one's work on to the next department is a weak practice. Specifically *where* that work will be processed within the department—and by *whom*—is too uncertain and too variable. In short, multipath flows mean poor provider-customer connections.

To ensure good coordination, error prevention, and problem resolution, the customer at the next process should be known and familiar—a real partner or team member. A dependable line for work to flow along is needed. Those are reasons why some insurance companies are breaking up underwriting and claims-processing departments and reorganizing into teams, and why factories and their support offices are organizing cells and flow lines by the way the paperwork and production flows.

Arrange the Workplace to Eliminate Search Time. As we have seen, Harley-Davidson has been able to implement mixed-model production with short cycle intervals and small lot sizes. Those benefits were due in part to Harley's attention to the workplace arrangement principle as well. The company arranged motorcycle assembly line stations so that all parts for all models were within reach and in exact, known, color-coded positions. The improved layout eliminated both search time and setup time and, in short, made the mixed-model assembly sequence possible. Many feel that Harley-Davidson has wrought a minor miracle by surviving in the very competitive motorcycle business. Clearly, sound principles of operations management helped bring about that miracle.[9]

---

[9]"How Harley Beat Back the Japanese," *Fortune,* September 25, 1989, pp. 155–164.

In any organization, the precise placement of tools, materials, supplies, and other resources cuts time-wasting motions and search activities for humans. It also opens up possibilities for robotic assembly, for robots are not good at searching or reaching long distances.

Cross-Train for Mastery of Multiple Skills. Some years ago, when banks began to expand their product line, a customer might have had to go to one window to write a personal check, another to get traveler's checks, and still another to make a credit card transaction. Now bank tellers are cross-trained to perform several kinds of transactions. This offers better service to the customer and permits more flexible staffing with fuller utilization of tellers' time. The same concepts apply in all lines of work.

Some formal versions of this principle are tied to the pay system: skill-based pay and pay for knowledge, for example. Programs of that type have caught on even in some unionized companies with histories of rigid work rules. Usually skill-based pay systems require tests of mastery for each skill learned.

A brief note in passing: Application of this cross-training principle makes the creation of cells and good flow lines easier to obtain (Principle number 8). In general, experience has shown the principles of operations management to be mutually supportive, as we would expect them to be.

Record and Retain Output Volume, Quality, and Problem Data at the Workplace. Large staff departments—engineering, maintenance, inventory control, quality, and so on—need something to do. Sending data to them from where goods are produced and services are provided keeps them busy. The data processing industry is happy to provide the data transfer equipment. But there is a price to be paid for detaching the data from the work itself. If line operators and supervisors are to feel a sense of responsibility, they must have some ownership of the data about their performance; they *need* it to make decisions.

Ensure that Line People Get First Crack at Problem Solving—before Staff Experts. The previous principle continues here. Staff experts *do* need data in order to apply their special talents in solving problems, but it is best to let the line people have first chance. Line people become general practitioners who refer only the tough problems to staff specialists.

Maintain and Improve Present Equipment and Human Work before Thinking about New Equipment. In our technological society, we seem to have developed a blind spot: We can't wait to acquire the new machine, often without even evaluating the low-cost options, namely upgrading the present machine and its operator. The U.S. Navy took the World War II vintage battleship *Missouri* out of mothballs, and the *Missouri* plies the seas today. The same concept is becoming popular in factories. Further, after years of skimping on maintenance budgets— and the resulting deterioration of machinery—maintenance is enjoying renewed respect. Companies are initiating **total preventive maintenance (TPM)** programs in which machine operators learn to spend some time every day checking and fixing the little things that go wrong and could grow into big problems.

Look for Simple, Cheap, Movable Equipment. As product life cycles shorten—in some portions of the electronics industry, products roll over in less than a year—factories must become more flexible and factory equipment more mobile. Also, in line with the second principle, improvement shrinks space requirements; if machines and other resources are mobile, moving them closer together to close space gaps is one of the more attractive improvements. It also goes along with cutting WIP inventory.

Automate Incrementally When Process Variability Cannot Otherwise Be Reduced. Humans are inherently variable, and variability stands in the way of serving the customer. Automation, therefore, is progress. However, often the easy and cheap way to progress is to improve and tighten up human operators' slack habits and bad practices and stave off the cost of automation as long as the cheaper improvements keep coming.

Seek to Have Plural Rather than Singular Workstations, Machines, Cells, and Flow Lines for Each Product, Service, or Customer. Busy toll bridges and highways follow this principle; they have 5, 10, 20, or more toll stations. Technologically it would be feasible to have just one toll station for each lane of traffic; motorists could cast their coins at 55 or 65 miles per hour. We know what would happen, however: A technological failure or a traffic accident would bring toll-taking to a standstill, and traffic would pile up for miles. The driving public cannot be treated that way.

Material processed on large singular pieces of equipment suffers the same risk of work stoppage, which unravels our best plans. Thus, this principle calls for multiple paths through the processes. There are numerous other reasons for the "plurality" concept; these will be presented in later chapters.

Become Dedicated to Continual, Rapid Improvement. The slow pace of improvement in recent decades, when the news media was proclaiming a productivity crisis, has given way to elevated worldwide standards of performance. Perhaps we're beginning to recognize complacency as the enemy that it is. A company's ability to marshal the entire work force in the cause of continual improvement is the key to achieving a rapid, never-ending rate of improvement. The previous 16 principles provide the right climate for that to become a reality.

Without cluttering things up too much, we reintroduce the 17 principles of operations management at appropriate places throughout the book. Their purpose is to provide an integrating theme for the book and to serve as reminders of points made in this introductory chapter. They are not necessarily complete or perfectly stated; time may reveal others and further refine the existing ones. Their common thread is their support of a grand operations strategy of *continual improvement in the eyes of the customer.*

Philosophy of Continual Improvement

In late 1989, Motorola issued a series of advertisements in selected business periodicals. This series, titled *The Power of Belief,* shared the company's philosophy of operations. The first ad contained the following passage:

> Our formula is a simple one:
> First, banish complacency.
> Second, set heroic goals that compel new thinking.
> Finally, "raise the bar" as you near each goal. Set it out of reach all over again.[10]

Undeniably, Motorola's ad professed a philosophy of continual improvement. This came from a company that was *already* a leader in meeting the needs of its customers; that had (since 1981) *already* experienced a 100-fold improvement in quality; that was *already* recognized as a world-class competitor. Shouldn't Motorola have gotten off the improvement kick, realizing that most of the gain had already been attained? Shouldn't Motorola have let other, less competitive companies worry about improvement? Perhaps the general question is "When does improvement end?"

The answers to the three questions are *no, no,* and *never.* If a company is able to acquire "the precious habit of improvement" (to use Dr. Joseph Juran's excellent phrase), it would be gross mismanagement to let the habit lapse. For most firms, merely acquiring the habit is the challenge of the moment.

Thus far, we have emphasized the importance of the customer by looking at provider-customer connections, and have discussed both philosophy and principles for successful operations management. Now it's time to turn our attention to the operations managers. Who are they? Can job satisfaction and a rewarding career be found in OM?

OPERATIONS MANAGERS

The 17 principles of operations management tell what to look for, what to strive for, and how to manage operations effectively. The managers who should be guided by the principles are:

1. *The employee making the product or providing the service.* In any enterprise, every employee is a manager of the immediate workplace, which consists of materials, tools, equipment, space, and documents. In the best companies, every employee has a role in improving the management of those resources and of the products they produce.

---

[10]See, for example, the September, 1989, issue of *Inc.,* pp. 50–51.

The role involves problem solving, process control, and better service to the customer.

That has importance for upper managers and staff advisors. It means that one of their more important tasks is to manage the training and reward system to bring out the potential of line employees to become involved in improvement. Good managers are teachers.

> **PRINCIPLE:** Ensure that line people get first crack at problem solving—before staff experts.

2. *First-line supervisors and foremen.* Their proper role is more than directly supervising people; it is managing mixtures of human and physical resources in order to provide better service and better products. Supervisors are close partners with their subordinates in a common task.

3. *Upper-level managers, such as department heads and general foremen.* We've already defined their training and reward system duties. Another role is to serve as focal points for coordinating the support staff of experts, whose skills back up the direct efforts of line employees to solve problems and make improvements.

4. *Staff experts.* These include designers, buyers, purchasing agents, hirers, trainers, industrial engineers, manufacturing engineers, schedulers, maintenance technicians, management accountants, inspectors, programmers, and analysts. Most organizations overrely on staff experts, because line employees' mindpower has not been solidly tapped. Still, staff expertise will always be needed. The role of staff people is to plan for change and respond expertly to assist line employees.

Personal Satisfaction in an OM Job

The above four categories define the people needed to run the operations end of the business. Probably you see yourself (or will, or have in the past) among the groups. Perhaps you see yourself positively, perhaps not. What are the positive features of a good experience in an OM job or career?

The best OM system is one that provides two-way benefits: You contribute to high rates of improvement for the company, and the company's system provides high levels of personal satisfaction for you. For most people, making improvements and solving problems yield feelings of fulfillment and satisfaction. Similarly, the feeling of having made things better for a customer is rewarding to most. Thus, the book's emphasis on improvement and service to the customer is not just for the company's sake. It's for our sake as jobholders.

Careers in OM

Too often, organizations have a way of stifling initiative and settling for a no-change way of life. We are proposing a better way, one that provides chances for meaningful, satisfying assignments or careers in operations for everyone from line employees to operations executives. As we shall see, the meaningful way emphasizes product-oriented forms of organization.

Getting properly organized is not enough, however. Some means of preventing people from going stale seems necessary—if improvement really is to be continual. The best antidote to going stale seems to be learning new jobs and making small or large changes in job assignments now and then.

Along corridor walls in a Haworth (office furniture) plant in Michigan and an Imprimis (computer data storage systems) plant in Minnesota are large assignment boards. They list every line employee's name and the job rotation plan for the year out. In those and other companies that are making formal use of job rotation, one main reason is for each employee to acquire an understanding of more and more of the processes involved in producing a family of subproducts. The increased knowledge may then be channeled toward continual improvement of the subproducts. Job rotation—or cross-career migration—is just as vital in supervisory, staff expert, and higher management positions. The same reason—breadth of understanding in order to fuel the improvement effort—applies.

Will the career-migration concept spread to the point where accountants join sales teams, buyers become programmers, and engineers do a hitch as line supervisors? It is already happening. Calcomp (maker of computer-driven plotters) has a program of moving senior design engineers into line supervisory positions. Hewlett-Packard routinely moves technical and professional people, and line employees too, from one kind of job to another. IBM has a long-standing tradition of repeatedly retraining people throughout their careers.

In older industries more set in their ways, most companies do not yet practice cross-careering to such an extent, but the trend is in that direction. Further, it is not just another management fad. The companies doing it see it as part of a way of life—a way that features continual improvement and orientation to the customer. That way of life is not viewed as just an option. An elevated standard of performance in an increasingly competitive world seems to require it.

PRINCIPLE: Cross-train for mastery of multiple skills.

There is a message for you, the reader—if you work for a well-managed company. Regardless of your main career interest, you are likely to find your way into one or more operations management positions. It doesn't matter whether you are a fast-track manager, a staff expert, a supervisor, or a production or service employee on the firing line. Operations needs *you*—and you need at least *some* operations experience—if you are to become a capable and contributing member of your customer-serving, continually improving organization.

OPERATIONS
NEEDS
YOU!

**And you need
at least some
operations experience.**

SUMMARY

The operations end of a business is where resources are transformed into goods and services. Proper management of operations demands that close provider-customer connections be maintained, for separation in time or distance invites trouble in the form of poor feedback and misunderstandings. Every employee has a customer; it is the next process, or where the work goes next.

Customer requirements include needs and expectations about how those needs will be met. Specific—but universal—customer requirements include higher quality, lower costs, shorter lead times, increased flexibility to change volumes and products, decreased variability in output, and increased levels of service. Customers are not interested in trading one requirement off for improvement in another; they want them all, and will find a supplier that can deliver. On the supplier/provider side, strong companies have overcome traditional trade-off reasoning.

Providers' specifications, the targets of operations, must accurately mirror customer requirements in all six of these dimensions. Recent pronouncements and actions of world-class companies suggest that putting the customer on center stage *is* a real, ongoing phenomenon, not just a fad or gimmick.

Operations management has become more normative, that is, more capable of prescribing what *should* be done and what *works* rather than offering a menu of what *could* be done. A key component in the normative approach to OM is the emergence of 17 principles that serve to guide managers on a path of continual improvement.

These principles (as presented in Figure 1–2) are: Get to know the customer and the competition; cut work in process, throughput times, flow distance, and space; cut setup and changeover times; produce and deliver at the customer's use rate, and decrease cycle interval and lot size; cut the number of suppliers to a few good ones; cut the number of components in a product or service; make it easy to avoid error—the first time; convert multipath flows to single-channel lanes; arrange the workplace to eliminate search time; cross-train for mastery of multiple skills; record and retain operating data at the workplace; give line personnel first crack at problem-solving; maintain and improve present equipment and human work before thinking about new; look for simple, cheap, movable equipment; automate incrementally when process variability cannot otherwise be reduced; seek to have plural work stations, machines, cells, and flow lines for each product, service, or customer; and become dedicated to continual, rapid improvement.

Operations managers who carry out the normative principles are department managers, staff specialists, line supervisors, and line employees. Satisfaction from an OM job comes from making continual improvements.

Careers in OM, whether for the line employee, staff expert, or higher manager, call for job rotation and career changes. The idea is for everyone to learn more and more about the functions of the next process, the prior process, or a process twice removed. Knowledge of needs in other processes is a catalyst for generating unending streams of ideas for continual improvement and better service to the customer.

KEY WORDS

Note: Key words, which are listed in their order of appearance in the chapter, are collected into a glossary at the end of the book. The glossary provides short definitions.

| Operations management | Customer Specification | Throughput time Work in process (WIP) |

Setup time	Total quality (TQ)	Total preventive
Changeover time	Total quality	maintenance
Cycle interval	management	(TPM)
Lot size	(TQM)	

REFERENCES

The reference list at the end of each chapter provides limited help for further research. (It does not necessarily include books cited within the chapter.) The book lists are intended to lead you to the parts of the library that hold material on a given topic. Thus, a list might include one book with a management (HD) Library of Congress call number, one with an industrial engineering (T or TA) number, one with a management accounting (HF) number, and so forth. That will guide you to the right shelf, where there are likely to be other books on the same topic. Also included are lists of magazines, journals, and professional societies useful for people interested in operations management.

For more recent books, U.S. Library of Congress call numbers are given. *These may or may not be valid for your library.* There has been a nationally organized effort to standardize Library of Congress call numbers in university and college libraries, but it has not been in operation long.

Books

Dertouzos, Michael L., Richard K. Lester, and Robert M. Solow. *Made in America: Regaining the Productive Edge.* Cambridge, Mass.: The MIT Press, 1989 (HC110.I52M34).

Hall, Robert W. *Attaining Manufacturing Excellence.* Homewood, Ill.: Dow Jones-Irwin, 1987 (TS155.H355).

Hayes, Robert H., and Steven C. Wheelwright. *Restoring our Competitive Edge: Competing through Manufacturing.* New York: John Wiley & Sons, 1984 (HD9725.H39).

Peters, Thomas J., and Robert H. Waterman, Jr. *In Search of Excellence.* New York: Harper & Row, 1982 (HD70.U5.P424).

Reich, Robert B. *The Next American Frontier.* New York: Times Books, 1983 (JK467.R45).

Schonberger, Richard J. *World Class Manufacturing: The Lessons of Simplicity Applied.* New York: The Free Press, 1986 (HD31.S3385).

Shetty, Y. K., and Vernon M. Buehler, eds. *Competing through Productivity and Quality.* Cambridge, Mass.: Productivity Press, 1988 (HC110.I52C655).

Starr, Martin K., ed. *Global Competitiveness: Getting the U.S. Back on Track.* New York: W. W. Norton & Co., 1988 (HD41.G58).

Suzaki, Kiyoshi. *The New Manufacturing Challenge: Techniques for Continuous Improvement.* New York: The Free Press, 1987 (HD9720.5.S98).

Periodicals/Societies

National Productivity Review.
Operations Management Review (Operations Management Society).
Target (Association for Manufacturing Excellence).

REVIEW QUESTIONS

1. What organizational obstacles sometimes stand in the way of relating to one's customer?
2. What is profound about the sentence, "The customer is the next process."?
3. What is a requirement? A specification? What is the relationship between the two?
4. What are the six customer wants?
5. What is the world-class approach to trade-offs?
6. Serving the customer: fad or for real? Discuss.
7. What is meant by the phrase, "A normative approach to OM . . ."?
8. What are the principles of operations management? Will they affect the implementation of a company's business plan? Discuss.
9. Which principles of operations management most directly pertain to production costs?
10. Which principles of operations management most directly pertain to flexibility?
11. What characterizes a company's operations when it operates with a philosophy of continual improvement?
12. Identify the four types of operations managers and explain the role(s) of each type.
13. Is there a conflict between what's good for the company and what's good for its operations managers? Explain.
14. What is a good career pattern—that is, job assignments—for people in operations management? Does it depend on one's level in the organization?

PROBLEMS AND EXERCISES

Note: Some problems and exercises in this book have answers that are based almost solely on text materials. Others require thought and judgment that go beyond the book; in those cases, you should include reasons, assumptions, and outside sources of information. Answers to selected items are in Appendix D.

1. For each of the employee positions below, give an example of a next-process customer. Also give an example in which the listed employee would be the next-process customer.
   a. Assembler on a production line making kitchen cutlery.
   b. Product design engineer in a toy-manufacturing plant.
   c. Data-processing manager in a bank.
   d. Employee benefits counselor in a large law firm.
   e. Cost accountant for a department store chain.
   f. Economist employed by the Federal Reserve Board.

2. Arbor Nurseries, Inc., does a large business in planting trees for real estate developers, who invariably want service "right now." Which four principles of operations management must Arbor heed in order to be responsive to this customer want? Discuss.

3. Most of the equipment (automatic screw machines, grinding machines, boring machines, and so forth) are old and badly run down at North American Bearing Company. That leads to problems in holding tolerances and meeting specifications.
   a. What strategy do you recommend for correcting the situation? Refer to the relevant principles of operations management in your answer.
   b. Suggest a long-term strategy for "continual improvement" so that North American Bearing does not experience such problems in the future.

4. What are two examples of North American companies that generally have been successful in achieving both cost leadership and quality leadership? Discuss.

5. The food and restaurant division of a city health department is under pressure from the department director to improve its performance. The local newspaper has been running a series of exposés on filth in some popular restaurants and has criticized the health department for (a) infrequent inspections and (b) long delays in responding to written and telephone complaints about certain restaurants. The division, consisting of 5 inspectors, 20 clerical employees, and 5 managerial and supervisory employees, claims that it does not have enough staff and budget to be thorough, quick to respond, and make frequent visits at the same time. Select four principles of operations management that might help the division.

6. In the 1960s, companywide job announcements at Deere & Company's headquarters were regularly posted on bulletin boards in the information systems department. The department's policy was to encourage computer programmers and analysts to apply for jobs in marketing, production, and so forth. Is that policy outdated or up-to-date? Does it support or inhibit service to the customer? Does it relate to any of the 17 principles of OM? Discuss.

7. Following are functions or departments found in most businesses:

   Human resources
   Sales
   Design
   Management (cost) accounting

   a. Why should professionals in each of those departments have a thorough understanding of the operating end of the business?

   b. Describe a company program that will achieve the right amount of exposure of people in those four departments to operations.

8. The fastest-growing Western manufacturing companies of the past 10 years or so typically have assembled professional staffs composed of the cream of the crop from universities. Those professionals are innovative, competitive, and hard driving. Sometimes they tend to get so absorbed in new, exciting projects that they hesitate to take vacations or develop their personal lives. Those same companies, for all their success, have often done poorly at getting operating-level (factory-floor) employees involved in process improvements.

    Explain this paradox. What corrective actions are needed? (Note: The fast-growing companies in Japan—like Hitachi and NEC—also hire the cream of the crop from universities, yet they have highly involved operating employees.)

9. At one Imprimis plant, which manufactures disk drive products, automatic process-monitoring devices capture data from the assembly processes and put them into a computer system. Operators in the work centers plot summarized data (taken from computer terminals) by hand onto visual display charts, even though the computer system has full capability to print out impressive charts with color graphics. Why not use the color graphics? What principle of operations management seems to be the basis for this Imprimis practice?

10. Write a brief essay describing your career plan for the first five to ten years after you graduate. After you complete your essay, share it with a friend. Ask your friend to read the essay and answer the following question: "Does this essay tell you more about what I plan to *be*, or more about what I plan to *do*?"

11. Talk with a few friends who've been out of college for four or five years. Ask them about the importance of serving the customer in their work. Summarize your findings.

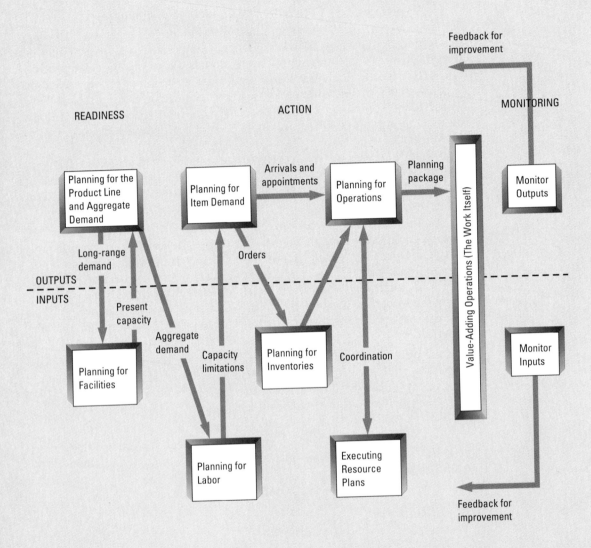

READINESS

ACTION

MONITORING

Feedback for improvement

Planning for the Product Line and Aggregate Demand

Long-range demand

Planning for Item Demand

Arrivals and appointments

Planning for Operations

Planning package

Value-Adding Operations (The Work Itself)

Monitor Outputs

OUTPUTS

INPUTS

Present capacity

Orders

Aggregate demand

Capacity limitations

Planning for Facilities

Planning for Inventories

Coordination

Monitor Inputs

Planning for Labor

Executing Resource Plans

Feedback for improvement

CHAPTER 2

Operations Management: Strategy, Environment, and Functions

FORMATION OF OPERATIONS STRATEGY

The Business Strategy Foundation
Distinctive Competency

STRATEGY SHAPING

Global and Regional Shaping
Local Shaping

**ORGANIZATIONAL ENVIRONMENT
FOR OPERATIONS MANAGEMENT**

Functions of the Organization
Specialization and Staffing Off
Organizational Structure: Charts and Linkages
The Process Approach: Operator Ownership
Types of Operations

OPERATIONS MANAGEMENT FUNCTIONS

Models of OM
Readiness, Action, and Monitoring for Improvement
Description of the Functions

Chapter 1 included a set of principles of operations management that serves as a foundation for any organization—a solid base upon which to build a business plan. But if all organizations strive to follow the principles, what differentiates one company from another? How does one business distinguish its goods and services from those of its competitors? Of more specific importance, what operations activities must a firm have to ensure that customers feel positively about its goods and services?

Answers to these questions are the subject of this chapter. First, we examine the formation and shaping of operations strategy. We then shift our concern to the implementation of that strategy by looking at the operations management environment, and finally we look at specific functions or activities that constitute *operations*.

FORMATION OF OPERATIONS STRATEGY

Dr. Kenichi Ohmae notes that in the formation of any business strategy, three key players must be taken into account: the corporation (or company) itself, the customers, and the competitors. Collectively, these form what Ohmae calls the *strategic triangle*.[1]

Managers should strive for a perspective that balances the three elements of the triangle. Strategy itself is necessary because of *competition*. Moreover, successful strategy ensures that *company* strengths match *customer* requirements. Thus, getting to know the customer and the competition certainly does have strategic implications.

PRINCIPLE: Get to know the customer and the competition.

Ohmae applies his strategic triangle concept to strategy at the overall *business* level. Since successful *operations* strategy evolves from the strategy of the complete business unit, we look first at business strategy.

The Business Strategy Foundation

It is common to view an organization as having three basic functions that must be managed. As Figure 2–1 shows, they are money, demand, and operations. Those are said to be *line* functions. They tend to be the first departments that form as an organization grows. They might be called *departments of finance, marketing,* and *operations;* or perhaps *accounting, sales,* and *production.*

To accomplish its aims, a business must plan strategy in all three of the basic

---

[1]Kenichi Ohmae, *The Mind of the Strategist: Business Planning for Competitive Advantage* (New York: Penguin Books, 1983), Chapter 8 (HD31.0485).

FIGURE 2–1

Basic or Generic (Line) Departments

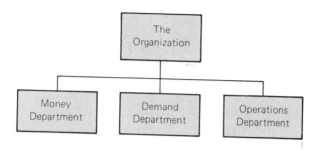

line functions. Each of the three functional strategies must support the overall business plan, and they must be compatible with one another. During the 1960s, 1970s, and into the early 1980s, managers of North American manufacturing companies developed financial and marketing strategies but neglected to pay attention to operations or production strategies.[2] Lack of that crucial third piece resulted in a serious decline of world market share of manufactured goods during the late 1970s and 1980s.

Thus we see that business strategies ought to deal with issues that affect the whole organization: employees, markets, customers, capital and financing, profitability, competition, public image, and so forth. Operations strategies should be consistent with business strategies, but their focus is narrower. Operations strategies concern operating resources (equipment, operating personnel and support staff, tools, information, and space); products; processes, methods, and systems; and output quality, cost, lead time, and flexibility.

Let's consider some examples. Suppose ABC Company executives decide on a business strategy that includes maintaining market share. That business strategy might be translated into an operations strategy of developing three new products that will utilize plant capacity as sales of present products X, Y, and Z continue to taper off.

Now, consider two companies, both manufacturers of shoelace extenders, which have the same key business strategy: rapid customer service. Company A has great trouble changing its machines over from processing 18-inch laces to the 24- or 28-inch varieties. Much downtime and defective output occur during and after the changeovers. Also, company A always seems to be out of the size and style that customers want most. To try to achieve its business objective of high customer service, company A builds increasingly larger inventories, trying to guess what customers will want next. Unfortunately, the large stock is high in defects, adding to company—and customer—woe.

Company B, on the other hand, has none of these deficiencies. It opted for an operations strategy consisting of methods improvements to reduce change-

---

[2]Elwood Buffa, *Meeting the Competitive Challenge: Manufacturing Strategy for U.S. Companies* (Homewood, Ill.: Dow Jones-Irwin, 1984), Chapter 1.

over times, frequent runs of small quantities of each size and style so that some of each type are available, and a process control program that keeps output quality high.

Although both companies have the same *business* strategy, company B's *operations* strategy will provide superior customer service. At times it seems that whole industries, or at least large segments, get into messes like company A's. The large, integrated U.S. steel manufacturers are an example.[3]

Despite some industrywide difficulties, a portion of the U.S. steel industry—the minimills—continued to thrive during the 1980s. Were their operations strategies very different from those of the larger, integrated producers? Indeed they were. For one thing, the minimills recognized the importance of developing distinctive competency.

Distinctive Competency

Bruce D. Henderson, respected consultant and authority on business strategy, recently alluded to the origin of strategy by referring to the 1934 work of Professor G. F. Gause of Moscow University. After a series of biological experiments, Gause postulated his principle of competitive exclusion: No two species that make their living the same way can coexist.[4]

Consider a town with three hospitals. The average citizen may see little difference among them. But an administrator or board member at one of the hospitals might explain—after expressing annoyance that the citizen didn't already know—that "we are the only hospital in the city with a fully certified burn care center," or perhaps, "We have the only neonatal care unit in the entire region." What the spokesperson is trying to do is identify the hospital's **distinctive competency**—strengths that set the organization apart from its competitors.

Distinctive competencies might be obvious to customers; fast service, very clean premises, and superior quality are examples. Less obvious factors, however, also qualify: things like expert maintenance, low operating costs, and effective research and development. All of the examples might help a firm satisfy one or more of the six customer requirements in some special or unique way. And that allows the firm to—in Professor Gause's terminology—make its living a little differently from its competitors. And that's needed for survival.

It is usually easier to develop and maintain distinctive competencies when strategy is *focused* on doing one or a few things well, thus avoiding diversification. Shouldice Hospital near Toronto is an example. It focuses on treating only patients whose single complaint is a hernia. Facility layout, medical staff, cafeteria, surgery and recovery rooms, and lounges all cater to that single type of patient. By doing numerous hernia repairs each year—and no other surgeries—

[3]John P. Hoerr, *And The Wolf Finally Came: The Decline of the American Steel Industry* (Pittsburgh: The University of Pittsburgh Press, 1988) (HD 9517.M85H64).

[4]Bruce D. Henderson, "The Origin of Strategy," *Harvard Business Review*, November–December 1989, pp. 139–43.

Shouldice doctors have become quite proficient. The common patient focus allows nurses to give better care to a greater number of patients, avoids the need for expensive equipment that diversified hospitals must have, and, of prime importance, results in higher-quality care. As evidenced by the relatively small number of patients needing repeat treatment of the same problems, Shouldice is ten times more effective than other hospitals.[5]

When a company is unable to sustain any distinctive competencies, the company goes under. On the other hand, when a company can be distinctively competent in several ways, it wows the world. Walt Disney Co., Hewlett Packard, McDonald's, and Toyota are examples. All four have dependably high quality. McDonald's and Toyota have very low production costs. H-P and Toyota have fanatically dedicated employees. H-P and Disney offer customer service that is unparalleled in their industries. Toyota and McDonald's have spectacular process efficiency and control, which leads to product uniformity. McDonald's provides extremely fast response to customer orders. Toyota is extremely flexible, well known for its ability to rapidly change machines and production lines from one component or car model to another.

An over-riding goal of operations management is to strategically guide the company in ways that will build distinctive competencies and thus invite business. The task demands full attention, for as we shall see next, environmental factors act to shape operations strategy.

STRATEGY SHAPING

Regardless of original strategic intent, companies often find themselves doing things they didn't plan on doing, but that are somehow required for survival. Global, regional, and local forces shape strategies of organizations and the operations management functions within.

Global effects are the most far-reaching, for they literally reach around the globe, touching us all. The global "shrinking" brought on by advances in communications and transportation makes that reach much easier. Regional comparisons, however, allow us to see how regional influences serve to create entirely different strategies even in the face of common global factors.

Global and Regional Shaping

The Great Depression that began in 1929 is an example of a global factor that shaped strategy. A more recent example is the Energy Crisis; crude oil prices rose more than fivefold in the first few years of the 1970s. Depending on their duration and severity, wars and natural disasters might also qualify as global

---

[5]William H. Davidow and Bro Uttal, "Service Companies: Focus or Falter," *Harvard Business Review*, July–August 1989, pp. 77–85.

shapers of strategy, as might sudden, large-scale shifts in political or economic alliances—the "opening" of the Iron Curtain, for example. World War II was perhaps the most pervasive global factor in recent history; evolution of business strategy among the world's industrial regions can be tied directly to its effects. Contemporary business and operations strategies were shaped by the outcome of the war along with conditions in the world's three great industrial regions: The United States and Canada, Japan, and Europe.

United States and Canada

Figure 2–2 shows the evolution of strategy changes in North America that took place between the 1940s and the early 1990s. The dashed arrow represents a possible future strategic mix. When World War II began, industry was mobilized to produce for the war effort; the service sector, including some professional sports, shrank, and production of many consumer goods—home appliances, rubber tires, and automobiles, for example—ground to a halt. Companies that had been innovation-oriented became production-oriented. Companies that had been customer service- or advertising-oriented became production-oriented. Industry became production-oriented. Production engineers and manufacturing managers were the "glamour boys" of industry.

FIGURE 2–2

Changing Strategic Focus—North America

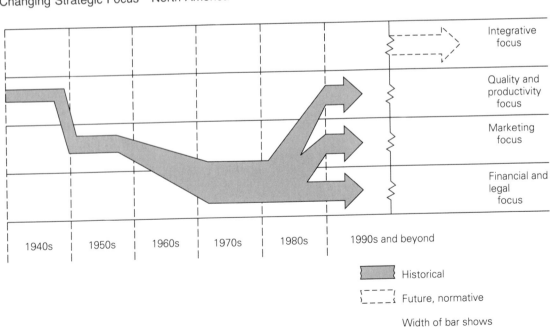

As a region, the United States and Canada did not have to be rebuilt after World War II. Production emphasis continued for a few years after the war, but generally just to fill consumer pipelines. At that point, the productivity focus ceased for many industrial companies. As Figure 2–2 shows, the transition from wartime production to peacetime marketing competition was relatively swift. The problem was too much industrial capacity, and marketing strategies—how to gain market share at the expense of one's competitor—became the dominant focus. Business colleges expanded marketing curricula, and marketing careers became important paths to advancement. Competition for market share led to a proliferation of options: models, styles, colors, and sizes.

The auto industry is the most visible example. As *The Wall Street Journal* put it, "For years, marketing departments in auto companies have demanded numerous options and different trim packages so that customers can practically design their own cars. Manufacturing executives usually agreed to the idea of options because it didn't add much to the amount of labor that went into a car."[6] While the options may not add much labor cost, they add a lot of inventory cost, because every option must be kept in stock. Further, there are significant extra costs for tooling (dies, fixtures, etc.) and setup time to change machines from one option to another. The very idea of mass production, for which the United States was at one time famous, is eroded when scores of options are allowed. (As Henry Ford said, "They can have any color they want, so long as it's black.")

Intensive marketing competition in the 1950s and 1960s produced winners and losers. The winners found themselves with a surfeit of cash to invest, and the losers were ready targets for takeover by cash holders. The era of mergers and conglomerates was launched. But we can think of it as the financial/legal era, because financial analysts and accountants were the new wizards seeking financially attractive marriage partners and legal experts were needed to tie the knots. Business schools responded with expanded finance and accounting curricula, and law schools turned out corporate lawyers. Figure 2–2 shows that the shifting strategy focus, from marketing to financial/legal, was gradual through the late 1950s and 1960s. By the early 1970s, marketing factors occupied a portion of strategic thinking, but financial and legal considerations clearly dominated North American business strategy.

All the Wall Street players had large "M&A" departments by the 1980s, busy setting up mergers and acquisitions. Typically, these deals were arranged purely for financial reasons; little or no thought was given to operational compatibility. Consider an example: James Ling parlayed a $4,000 stake in the late 1950s into the giant LTV conglomerate that at one time included such diverse subsidiaries as Wilson foods, Wilson sporting goods, Braniff Airlines, Jones and Laughlin Steel, Allied Radio, National Car Rental, Vought Helicopter, LTV Aerospace, Computer Technology, and many more. In 1970, Ling's LTV empire was collapsing, as were a number of other conglomerates. Many of the companies

---

[6]"U.S. Auto Makers are Having Trouble Adopting 'Kanban'," *The Wall Street Journal*, April 7, 1982, pp. 1, 32.

acquired in the 1960s had to be sold in the 1970s and 1980s to avoid total ruin. In 1986, LTV Corporation filed for Chapter 11 bankruptcy.

Why were so many conglomerates assembled with so little regard for operations compatibility? One reason was the lack of top corporate officers with operating experience. Wall Street certainly could offer no help in that area: Corporate suites—rich with production talent in the 1940s and early 1950s—had become dominated with financial/legal people. Basic understanding of how to deliver operations competencies (customer wants, if you will)—quality, productivity, on-time performance, innovativeness, and responsiveness—was lacking.

The 1970s and early 1980s was an era during which strategy decisions were made by managers who lacked the knowledge to make good ones. As Robert Reich puts it, our managerial innovations in recent years "have been based on accounting, tax avoidance, financial management, mergers, acquisitions, and litigation. They have been innovations on paper. Gradually, over the past 15 years, America's professional managers have become paper entrepreneurs."[7]

In the late 1970s, the North American news media openly declared a state of industrial crisis. The new leaders in excellence seemed to be Japan and West Germany; years of neglect in North American businesses had taken their toll. Western industrial corporations began sending study teams by the planeload to Japan to learn Japanese manufacturing techniques in order to meet the Japanese challenge. The year 1980 might accurately be called a year of discovery—discovery that some severe changes were needed.

Not until the mid-1980s, however, did enough "noise" arise to shake managers away from their myopic focus on short-term financial results. Continued poor performance relative to Japan and West Germany helped create that noise. The middle of the decade saw renewed emphasis in North America (actually, throughout the world) on operations strategy; things like quality, productivity, product and service design, and customer service became important again.[8] Concern for customer service, in the next-process sense, has had a fitting spinoff in the last few years. The phrase *serving the customer* has caused some refocus on marketing, where the *external* customer is king.[9] And rightly so; after all, good strategy should focus on all three areas.

Figure 2–2 shows the recent reemphasis on operations and marketing—without loss of focus in the financial/legal area. What about the future? The best outcome surely is one of *integrative focus*, which means a true blending of strategic interests; see the dashed arrow in Figure 2–2. There already is some evidence of that coming to pass. When operations gives first emphasis to customer service—the theme of this book—that brings operations strategy more closely in line with what we normally think of as marketing's focus.

Leading-edge companies are also altering their accounting and control systems. Costing systems are being remade to emphasize direct control of *causes*

---

[7]Robert B. Reich, *The Next American Frontier* (New York: Times Books, 1983), pp. 140–41 (JK467.R45).
[8]For example, see "The Push for Quality," *Business Week*, June 8, 1987, pp. 130–44.
[9]"Stalking the New Consumer," *Business Week*, August 28, 1989, pp. 54–62.

of costs—everywhere that costly activities take place—and deemphasize cost transactions and historical costs. The other key alteration is in performance measurement: the change is toward measuring what's important to customers and competitive advantage, rather than what the regulatory agencies require. Northern Telecom, for example, has developed new profit and loss reporting formats (P&Ls) for its business units. Although conventional P&Ls are still sent out to the regulators, the new P&Ls, which focus more on improvement in the eyes of the customer, are the ones actually used for managing the business units.

Japan

The general flow of Japanese business strategy since the 1940s, shown in Figure 2–3, has been quite different from that of the United States and Canada. Like other industrialized combatants, Japan focused on the production of war materials during the years of World War II. After the war, the productive capacity of Japan was devastated. The break in Figure 2–3 reflects those very lean years under postwar occupation when Japan struggled to regain its feet. Little need be said of strategy; survival was paramount.

In some ways, Japan was the worst off among industrialized countries and regions after the war. The country was small, crowded, and resource-poor. It faced not only the need to rebuild but also had to address a worldwide prewar

FIGURE 2–3

Changing Strategic Focus—Japan

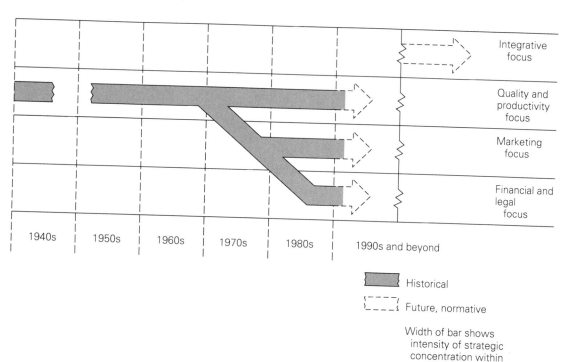

reputation as an exporter of shoddy goods. Industrywide consensus was that quality improvement should be the first priority.

That strategy was translated into a management training effort the likes of which has not occurred, even to present times, anywhere else in the world. Managers *at all levels* learned Western quality control techniques from Americans such as W. E. Deming and J. M. Juran in the early 1950s. Not satisfied to merely learn the tools, the Japanese mastered the habit of continual improvement. In the roughly three decades after World War II, Japan transformed itself into the nation with the *best*—rather than perhaps the worst—reputation for quality.

Japanese industry's *operations* strategy of quality improvement has been central to a *national* strategy of rapid growth in exports (there was no other way for Japan to finance its postwar rebuilding) and *corporate* strategies of rapid growth in market share. Figure 2–3 shows that consistent focus on quality and productivity—from the wreckage of the early 1950s to the beginning of the 1990s. The dedication has certainly paid off. A bonus of high quality is the avoidance of costly scrap, rework, and customer returns. Avoiding those costs improves productivity, stimulating exports and market-share growth even more. By pursuing the strategy of high quality and productivity for gaining market share and export business, Japan has assumed world leadership in high-volume repetitive (mass) production.

Other regional influences (unrelated to the war) are Japan's overcrowding and lack of natural resources, which led to a second important operations strategy: avoidance of waste or idleness of material resources. *Just-in-time (JIT)* production and Toyota's ingeniously simple *kanban* (card) system of managing work flow were perfected in response to this material-control operations strategy. This kind of resourcefulness improves productivity by reducing the material input component of product cost, sets off a chain reaction of problem solving to further improve productivity and quality, and compresses lead times.

By the early 1970s, Japan had begun to reap the rewards of its persistent focus on quality and productivity. The world's greatest market, the United States, began to exhibit an insatiable demand for Japanese goods: automobiles, consumer electronics, cameras, machine tools, and an endless list of component parts for these and other end-item products. Why? The Japanese products were thought to be better than their U.S.-made counterparts, *and they were cheaper*. Of course, any nation that relies heavily on exporting must develop sensitivities to the export markets. Thus, as shown in Figure 2–3, Japan's strategic focus expanded from quality and productivity to include marketing as well.

By 1989, Japan had become the wealthiest country in the world. Nine of the ten largest banks were Japanese, the Tokyo Stock Exchange was the world's largest, Japanese demand determined the price of U.S. Treasury bonds, and the Japanese supplied over 20 percent of all credit in the state of California. In short, Japan was *the key player* in world finances.[10]

---

[10]R. Taggart Murphy, "Power without Purpose: The Crisis of Japan's Global Financial Dominance," *Harvard Business Review*, March–April 1989, pp. 71–83.

As Japan was achieving all of this, its industrial strategy seems to have expanded along the following pecking order (from top priority down):

1. Improve quality of product and service.
2. Improve delivery performance and productivity.
3. Cut the costs associated with the first two steps.
4. Compete for increased market share based on results from the first three steps.
5. Take the profits obtained from steps 1 through 4 and move into financial arenas; fund creation of new products and services and compete there by returning to step 1.

The first three of these items relate to operations strategy, giving customers what they want; the fourth is marketing-oriented; and the fifth financial. Japan's success with this strategy offers some evidence that operations strategy is the "leg" that ought to be strengthened *first*. Ability to market is easier if you have something to sell—something people *want* to buy. And money from high market share creates a capital base from which to launch new rounds of excellence. As Figure 2–3 shows, the Japanese began with an operations-oriented strategy and they haven't wavered from it. They have, as they should have, broadened into a complete three-way strategy posture. Of course, an integrative strategy *ought* to drive Japan's future efforts to improve and excel.

Europe

Like Japan, Europe was devastated by World War II; some nations more than others. Unlike Japan, Europe had neither a quality image problem nor a severe shortage of natural resources. Instead, Europe's postwar industrial strategies were constrained by shortages of plant and skilled labor combined with small, fractionated markets and little labor mobility. Unlike Japan and to some extent North America, Europe is a land of diverse languages, customs, governments, currencies, and cultures. Much of Europe's postwar capacity was rebuilt to serve national markets, and its industrial strategies were shaped by widespread desire for stability and preservation of community and national traditions.

Europe as a region has had no comprehensive strategy other than turf protection for its members. Some believe the resulting sense of stability and security helped calm a region decimated by two world wars in the first half of the century and by the Cold War in the latter half. Others disagree; they claim the highly regulated European business—seldom extending much beyond national or even community borders—has created stagnation. West German economist Herbert Giersch, for example, refers to the business condition as "Eurosclerosis."[11] Figure 2–4 characterizes European strategy since the 1940s as rather stable; all three areas represented, but rather weakly, as shown by the narrow bands. There has been perhaps a bit more emphasis on operational aspects of quality and pro-

---

[11]Shawn Tully, "The Coming Boom in Europe," *Fortune*, April 10, 1989, pp. 108–14.

FIGURE 2–4
Changing Strategic Focus—Europe

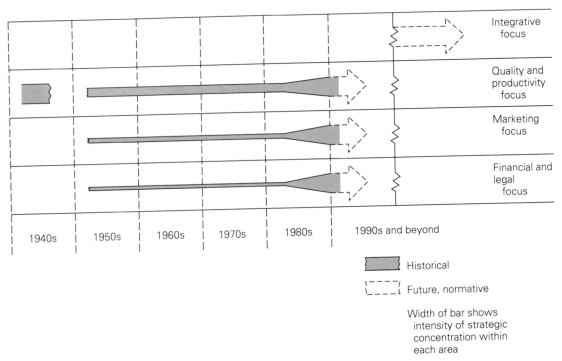

New Players, and Changing Old Ones

ductivity; but no large-scale, innovative attempts to improve operating performance, nor any strong effort to market beyond the immediate region. The operations strategy has favored flexible plants known as *job shops*.

Giersch and others conclude that structure has perhaps been Europe's biggest problem—too many players for the size of the region. Until recently, European business suffered from too much capacity, too little spending for research and development, and too many companies. The dominance of "mom and pop" stores in every industry from communications to travel to toy retailing has made unification difficult.[12]

Figure 2–4 shows the strategy becoming stronger in all areas in the late 1980s. As we shall see in the next section, the mid-1990s should see a healthy, competitive Europe.

New Players, and Changing Old Ones

If businesspeople agree on anything, it is that the international business strategy game is getting more exciting. That is certainly true for operations. Perhaps the most obvious of influences is the increasing number of global players to shape

---

[12]Ibid.

strategy. As recently as the mid-1980s, research on international industrial strategy could be limited to European, North American, and Japanese influences without much fear of omission.[13] Not so in the 1990s. Newly industrialized countries (NICs)—such as Brazil, Hong Kong, India, Malaysia, Mexico, South Korea, Taiwan, and Singapore—began to flex new industrial muscle in the late 1980s.

An example of how these new players affect operations strategy became apparent in the early 1980s when U.S. companies began to transfer their manufacturing operations overseas to Pacific Rim countries, retaining sales duties and service responsibility in the United States. The result was a transformation of the industrial firm into what *Business Week* has called "the hollow corporation."[14] Whether as individual countries or as members of newly defined economic regions, the presence of NICs will certainly continue to influence operations strategy in the next century.

Just as significant as the new nations, however, are major changes in the old players. Consider Europe. The "erasing" of internal borders among the 12-nation European Economic Community (EEC)—Belgium, Denmark, France, West Germany, Greece, Ireland, Italy, Luxembourg, Netherlands, Portugal, Spain, and United Kingdom—in 1992 creates an even more formidable global competitive force. Six other European nations—Austria, Finland, Iceland, Norway, Sweden, and Switzerland—all allied with the EEC under the European Free Trade Agreement (EFTA), sharing tariff-free trade but not the political commitments. Finally, add five Eastern European nations (Czechoslovakia, East Germany, Hungary, Poland, and Yugoslavia) that, with their emerging capitalistic tendencies, desire more trade with Western Europe. Should that 23-nation grand alliance form, the result could be a cohesive region with a $5 trillion economy![15] That opens the door to enormous economies of scale, a major competitive challenge—and opportunity—for producers elsewhere in the world.

The trade boom of the 1990s is projected by some economists to extend well into the 21st century. Import/export growth is part of the picture, but not all of it. Increasingly, multinational corporations (MNCs) make goods overseas rather than export from the home country. For example, Ford makes Escorts in Europe for sale in Europe, and Mitsubishi makes Eclipses in the United States for sale in North America. IBM, Coca-Cola, and 3M have long had manufacturing facilities in Europe; they are now being joined by companies like Whirlpool and International Paper—firms just starting to manufacture in Europe. Clearly, manufacturing and service operations strategy of many businesses is reflecting a strong desire to get close to the customer.

In addition to trade and "off-shore" production, companies sometimes simply buy in, even into a competing firm, to gain better access to customers. Japanese

---

[13]For example, see Kasra Ferdows, Jeffrey G. Miller, Jinichiro Nakane, and Thomas E. Vollmann, "Evolving Global Manufacturing Strategies: Projections into the 1990s," *International Journal of Operations and Production Management*, vol. 6, no. 4 (1985), pp. 5–14.
[14]"The Hollow Corporation," *Business Week*, March 3, 1986, pp. 57–85.
[15]"One Big European Economy Seems Less Like a Dream," *Business Week*, November 13, 1989, pp. 43–45.

and North American companies want in on the "Euroaction" (a new buzzword for the 21st century?), and began to woo European firms in the mid-1980s. North American automobile companies, for example, desiring a stronger *manufacturing* presence in Europe, conducted the "steamiest mating dances" (as *Forbes* put it) of all among the industry with European counterparts. Ford bought Britain's Jaguar in 1989; Chrysler owns Italy's Lamborghini, has an ownership stake in Maserati, and a marketing and service agreement with France's Renault; and General Motors owns Britain's Lotus. All the U.S. firms were courting Sweden's Saab.[16] In 1987 alone, U.S. businesses spent $20.9 billion to buy companies and build plants in Europe, 28 times the comparable figure for 1982.[17]

It is possible, of course, that mistakes are being repeated, that the new mergers and acquisitions—like so many in prior years—have been based solely on financial considerations, or perhaps marketing factors. It is too soon to judge the ultimate effect of the new alliances on operations strategies of the participants. It is clear, however, that old national barriers are tumbling. As the world continues to shrink, global and regional influences will have increased power as strategy shapers.

Other factors, more regional than global, shape corporate and operations strategies. National laws, policies, and regulations are especially influential: minimum wage, labor, immigration, tax, antitrust, liability, tariff, and patent laws; private versus public ownership; regulation of rates, routes, leases, and building permits; health, safety, and physical environment protection laws; and economic policies for stimulating business activity. Each of these factors is potent enough to have generated whole books about it.

For example, consider regional labor supply. U.S. immigration laws and policies result in nearly half a million legal immigrants and at least that many illegal ones per year. But the immigration "problem" is used (legally or illegally) in support of a labor-cost-saving strategy in many U.S. companies—from high-fashion clothing manufacturing in New York, to restaurants in Chicago, to construction in Texas, to auto refurbishing in California. Some labor economists feel that the United States will enjoy a labor cost advantage in the next decade because of the influx of immigrant labor, whose willingness to work at entry-level wages and perform less desirable tasks holds down the entire wage structure.

By contrast, Japan's low birth rate and low immigration portend long-run labor shortages and wage escalation as the work force ages. An operations strategy already undertaken by many Japanese manufacturers is to circumvent the labor supply and wage escalation problems by using robots. In the United States, robots perhaps are needed less for growth and productivity improvement than for quality reasons.

While European unemployment rates have been bouncing up and down, they may now be in a sustained downward cycle, because as national barriers come down, labor mobility increases. Eastern Europeans, anxious for opportunities,

---

[16]Jerry Flint, "Make Love, Not War," *Forbes*, October 2, 1989, pp. 46–48.
[17]Tully, "The Coming Boom in Europe," p. 110.

could relieve Northern Europe's projected labor shortages. Many observers believe, however, that European manufacturing will gradually move toward the southern parts of the continent. In Spain, for example, labor forces will continue to grow due to higher birth rates around the Mediterranean in the 1970s. And wages in Spain are about one-third less than in West Germany. For the immediate future, Europe's labor supply seems more like North America's than Japan's.

Local Shaping

Global factors affect us all. Regional factors affect whole countries or continents. What remain are local environmental influences, that is, factors that shape the strategies of particular industries, companies, or organizations. Figure 2–5 shows four kinds of local factors within the center circle along with regional and global factors in the outer circles.

The first local influence is community and supplier inputs. Community factors include labor supply and prevailing wages, tax rates, zoning, availability of utilities and transportation, and quality of life. Supplier factors concern materials, equipment, and services. Inputs that communities and suppliers are able to provide help shape strategic operating decisions, such as extent of vertical integration; plant size and location; and policies on subcontracting, shift work, and aggregate inventories.

The next local influence in Figure 2–5 is the nature of the products that the firm is in business to provide. The firm's line of goods and services is distinguishable by product technology, process technology, and stage in the product life cycle (introduction, growth, maturity, and decline). Innovative products require a research and development (R&D) strategy that will ensure a source of new product designs. Hard-to-make products require a strategy of high investing in process engineering and technology. Both product and process design strategies are changeable as the product line ages.

The third local influence in Figure 2–5 is demand. Demand for goods and services is generated by market forces and constrained by extent of competition. Demand factors are critical in the shaping of four key operations strategies, that is, strategies for design responsiveness, delivery responsiveness, quality, and cost. Most other operations strategies—plant location, aggregate inventories, R&D, and so forth—are also somewhat affected by demand factors.

The final local influence in Figure 2–5 is present capabilities. The operational capabilities of the work force and plant may be limited or flexible. In the just-in-time system, employees are quite flexible. That permits a quick-response operations strategy, because operators are moved around to wherever the work is. Existing management capabilities also affect operations strategies. In the early 1970s, large supermarket chains such as A&P and Kroger were considering optical scanning for grocery checkout. None decided to proceed with that far-reaching strategic change until the late 1970s. While immediate adoption was technologically feasible, the grocery industry had little experience in managing technological change, and caution was perhaps correct.

FIGURE 2–5
Environmental Influences on Business and Operations Strategies

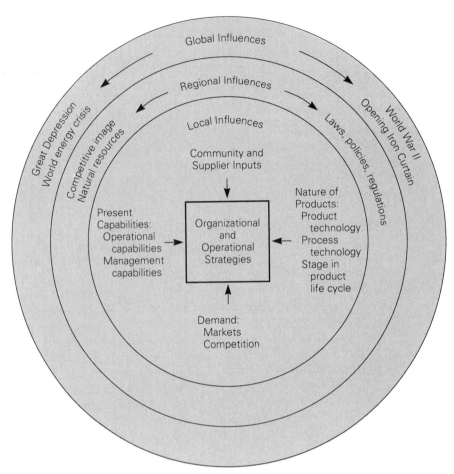

ORGANIZATIONAL ENVIRONMENT FOR OPERATIONS MANAGEMENT

We have seen that operations strategy should be integrated with other elements of overall business strategy. In much the same way, operations management activities must be carried out in harmony with other organizational functions; vital organizational linkages ought to be in place. Responsibilities that line managers must accept, and support that staff personnel must provide, are at the heart of those linkages.

The need for linkages and integration of the functions is partly an issue of structuring the organization properly. Besides *structure*, however, there is the matter of *responsibility* for results. The modern view is that line operators should assume primary responsibility for operating results—or, as it is often stated, they should have *ownership* of their processes. This *process* viewpoint is an effective way of warding off harmful bureaucratic tendencies and creating an environment for continually improving service to the customer.

In this section we address those issues and also examine how to ensure effective organizational linkages in different types of operating environments—for example, assembly lines, job operations, and construction project sites. First, however, we construct a framework for operations management within the organization as a whole.

Functions of the Organization

Earlier (Figure 2–1) we saw that the three primary or line functions of any organization are managing money, demand, and operations. But what about the other functions? As organizations grow, the demand for specialized skills increases and new departments are formed to advise and support the line departments. Those new departments are called *staff* departments, and they typically include personnel or human resources, quality control, engineering, purchasing, production control, and information systems.

Why should money, demand, and operations be basic but not, say, human resources or engineering? Consider this illustration. Suppose you buttonholed an employee at random coming out of a place of business and asked, "What is the purpose of this business?" The reply might well be, "To make a profit" (money), or "To satisfy a customer" (demand), or "To produce products or services" (operations). It is far less likely that the reply would be "To employ people" (a human resource function) or "To design products and services" (the engineering function). The last two may reasonably be considered as supportive—hence, staff rather than line.

Figure 2–6 shows the three basic functions as pieces of the total management pie. A gray area shows where managing operations overlaps with managing money on the one hand and managing demand on the other.

Finance and accounting concern managing money. That includes assessing proposals to invest money in operating resources. A goal is to fund proposals that will maximize return on investment or net dollar benefits. Managers of operating resources must do their own assessment, but from another angle. They deal with efficiency of the asset, detailed cost breakdown, and, above all, capability to meet customer requirements. Our focus is more on those factors and less on profitability for the organization as a whole.

The marketing function involves managing demand. That includes planning the mix of goods and services: which products, how many of each, and when they are to be available. The same questions face operations managers, but with a difference. In the marketing view, the question is "What products will the customer want?" From the operations standpoint, the question is "What customer demands are within our capacity to produce?"

FIGURE 2–6
The Total Management Pie

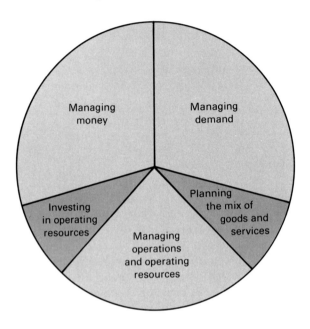

Specialization and Staffing Off

Managing the gray areas of Figure 2–6 is a special problem, one that is best handled by cross-functional teams. Two related phenomena—specialization and staffing off of responsibilities—are primary causes of problems in the gray areas.

Excessive specialization has been common in large organizations—that is, marketing managers pursue their own objectives, operations managers pursue their own (different) objectives, and the same tendencies hold true for finance and accounting managers. In his book *Theory Z,* William Ouchi argues that the specialization problem is acute in U.S. industry. Ouchi states: "In the United States we conduct our careers between organizations but within a single specialty. In Japan people conduct careers between specialties but within a single organization."[18]

Despite major changes in Western management thought and practice in the 1980s, the specialization problem is still acute, and ways of dealing with it are presented in later discussions. (It is worth noting that accredited schools of business in the United States and some in Canada require all students to learn about all of the pieces of the pie (Figure 2–6) regardless of whether they intend to specialize in one discipline or piece of the pie.)

---

[18]William Ouchi, *Theory Z: How American Business Can Meet the Japanese Challenge* (Reading, Mass.: Addison-Wesley Publishing, 1981), p. 83 (HD70.J3088).

Gaining concerted action among the demand, operations, and money elements is one problem; getting coordination among the subspecialties *within* OM is another. The OM subspecialties, or functions, is the next topic.

In very small firms, a single operations manager may direct virtually all of the organizational functions. In very large companies, especially goods producers, the operating manager may be responsible for the transformation and little else. What happened to all of the other functions? They were gradually "staffed off"—that is, staff specialists were hired to help plan and control.

The staff specialists start out working for the line manager; as they become more numerous, they cluster into new staff (advisory) departments of their own. Planning and monitoring progress may be staffed off to production control, engineering, and quality assurance departments. Purchasing, materials management, human resources, maintenance, and other departments may form to plan the resources in detail and execute the plans. One engineering department may plan fixed capacity and another have product design duties.

Figure 2–7 summarizes the types of operations management activities that are commonly staffed off. As the figure indicates, executive committees often plan and set policy in broad terms and staff departments perform and execute detailed planning.

However, staffing off has been carried too far. There is a strong movement among leading companies to reassign certain responsibilities, especially for qual-

FIGURE 2–7

Diffusion of Line Responsibilities (Staffing Off) as Organization Grows

Function	*Responsibility*
Transformation	Direct responsibility of line (service or factory employees and operating managers)
Planning operations and monitoring progress	Often staffed off wholly or partly to production control, engineering, and quality assurance groups
Scheduling end products and services	Usually staffed off to a master production scheduling group (which might include representatives of operations, production control, marketing, and finance)
Planning and controlling adjustable capacity (labor, materials, and tools)	Usually staffed off to an executive group for aggregate planning and to staff specialists (e.g., purchasing, human resources, and maintenance) for execution and control of plans
Planning fixed capacity (plant and equipment)	Usually staffed off to high-level finance/executive committee for decisions and to facilities planning/capital budgeting specialists for detailed planning
Demand planning	Usually staffed off to high-level executive committee for planning and to product development, marketing, and forecasting groups for execution of plans

ity and equipment maintenance, to operators and first-line supervisors. The reassigning of responsibilities is just one component—but an important one—in larger efforts to eliminate waste, improve quality, become customer-oriented, and generally be competitive with the world's best.

PRINCIPLE: Ensure that line people get first crack at problem solving—before staff experts.

Organizational Structure: Charts and Linkages

While there are no standard organization charts for operations and operations management, it is possible to draw a general chart showing key line and staff operations managers and their positions throughout the organization's structure. Figure 2–8 is such a chart.

Just as the president of the United States is commander-in-chief of the armed forces, the chief executive officer (CEO) of the firm is commander-in-chief of all operations managers. Below the CEO in Figure 2–8 are the four types of subordinate managers we have mentioned:

1. Line and staff department managers. The staff departments are product and process design, production and inventory control, human resources, quality assurance, and plant maintenance. The names are not standard, nor is the organizational breakdown shown in Figure 2–8. For example, process design sometimes is the shared purview of manufacturing engineering and industrial engineering departments.

2. Staff experts.

3. First-line supervisors.

4. Line employees who build the product or deliver the service.

Figure 2–8 does not show the complexity of the formal structure for large multidivisional companies. Big industry has tended to prefer organizing by functional rather than product division. The success of the IBM PC (personal computer), for which IBM created a nearly autonomous business unit, startled IBM—and plenty of other companies. Business units, focused factories, factories-within-factories, production lines, and cells all follow the idea of focusing on a narrow product or product family and on the customers for just those products.

IBM has led the parade, adopting the focused organizational concept from top to bottom. General Motors followed suit. The GM Assembly Division fell by the wayside in favor of more product-oriented divisions—even a brand-new product-oriented division called Saturn. In 1987, GM initiated the "radical step of 'dedicating' each assembly plant" to just one model of its newly designed midsize car.[19]

Benefits of the near-autonomous business unit have led to what General

---

[19]"Striking Back: GM Readies a New Mid-Size Line," *The Wall Street Journal*, May 1, 1987.

FIGURE 2–8

The Managers of Operations—Generalized Organization Chart

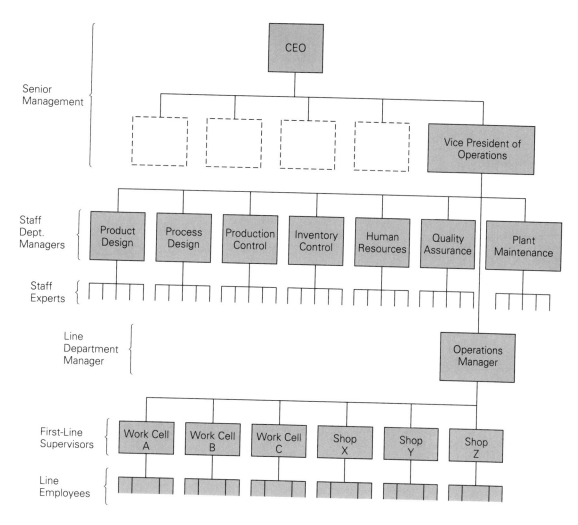

Electric Co. chairman Jack F. Welch calls the "big-company/small-company hybrid," an attempt to combine the best of both. The hybrids are created as corporate leaders hack away at bureaucracies, cut layers of management, push decision making down to lower levels, and streamline approval procedures.[20] In essence, little "companies" are created within corporate giants seeking the entrepreneurial spirit and flexibility that has proven successful in global competition during the 1980s. Rarely can organization charts show this.

The greatest weakness of organization charts, however, is their effect on

---

[20]"Is Your Company Too Big?" *Business Week,* March 27, 1989, pp. 84–94.

people—employees and customers. Charts pigeonhole people. In practice, the worst operations organization—as measured by service to customers—is the one with the "highest walls" between departments, between staff specialties, and between line employees. *Highest walls* has a more than figurative meaning. Companies actually are replacing rigid walls in offices with modest partitions. Some manufacturers are removing walls and restricting heights of shelving that otherwise might impede communications from one employee to the customer at the next process. In Chrysler's Sterling Heights, Michigan, plant, the maximum shelf height is 54 inches.

PRINCIPLE: Get to know the customer.

What the organization chart does not or cannot clearly show are the various kinds of wall-busting alliances—or *linkages*—that form in good companies: Committees, task forces, and teams; and cells, flow lines, and quality circles are among the more prevalent types.

Committees are found in poorly managed and well-managed companies alike, and complaining about committee work is a popular sport. A task force has a more definitive purpose: for example, many companies have formed task forces to plan the implementation of large-scale operations improvement efforts, like *just-in-time* manufacturing or *total quality management (TQM)*. The secret to effective committees and task forces is making sure that *all* affected functions—especially provider-customer linkages—are brought together and directed toward a common aim.

Teams are like task forces in that they have a rather clear purpose. But a task force usually breaks up after completing an assigned task (for example, developing a plan), while a team keeps getting new assignments. A potent kind of team that is becoming popular in leading companies is the product-development or design-build team. Product development may pass the baton on to an operations team.

Committees, teams, and task forces should be used selectively. On the other hand, cells, flow lines, and quality-circle-like groups are valuable just about anywhere operations are carried out, including staff support operations. By definition, a cell or flow line is a way of organizing that links makers and users machine to machine and "arm to arm." It is the key to directing operations toward serving the customer. Quality circles, if they are composed of maker-user pairs, also are customer serving.

We have been discussing the big picture—how the elements of the operating organizations link up. A related but narrower issue concerns responsibility—or "ownership"—of the processes where work is performed.

The Process Approach: Operator Ownership

At the action end of the business are the processes through which the work or clients pass. Who owns the processes? That may seem like an odd question. It's not. Companies from Motorola to Harley-Davidson to Florida Power and Light

FIGURE 2–9
Process Ownership

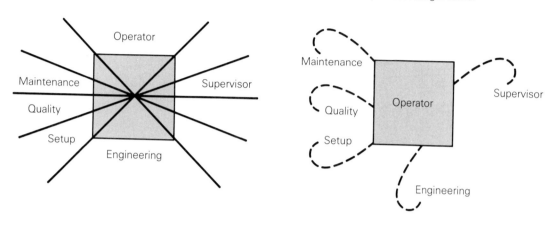

A. A process: Multiple owners

B. A process: Single owner

Defensive: "Don't let your process fail!"

consider "process ownership" a vital issue. The new belief in these companies is that every line employee should feel a sense of ownership of a process. That way of thinking contrasts with the ways of the past, when ownership of each process was divided among several parties: operator, supervisor, engineers, maintenance, trainers, quality control, and others.

Shifting ownership to the line employee starts with responsibility for quality. The best test of whether the line employee really has ownership of quality is when the inspectors disappear from the operations area, and any inspection that goes on is performed by the operator. The next element of ownership is maintenance and upkeep. The test is similar to that for quality: The operator "owns" the equipment when the operator, not maintenance, is doing preventive maintenance. Similarly, the line employee assumes process-related duties in data collection, data analysis, problem diagnosis, and some problem solving.

Figure 2–9A shows the divided-ownership pattern and 2–9B the single-ownership pattern. Those who share process ownership with the line employee in part A become true advisors and backstops in part B. When a problem is special enough to require help from support people, the dashed lines in part B are like hooks extended by the line employee.

A limitation of shared process ownership—and a severe one—is that if too many are in charge, no one is in charge. And no one is accountable for results. The pattern in Figure 2–9B clearly puts a single person or team in charge and appears to provide for accountability. Still, it shares a weakness with the pattern in Figure 2–9A. In both cases, the emphasis seems defensive. The message to the employee and support staff is, in effect: *Don't let your process fail!*

How can the accountability emphasis be shifted so it is offensive and oriented

FIGURE 2–10
Subproduct with Three Processes: Single-Person or Team Ownership

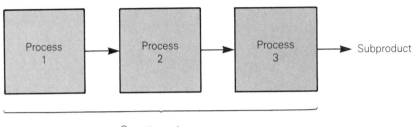

Offensive: '' Improve the way you make the product!''

toward continual improvement? One answer is to put first emphasis on products (services) or subproducts and second emphasis on the processes that produce them. Figure 2–10 shows three processes in a flow line or cell, with a subproduct as the output. The operations team of one, two, or three employees is challenged, in effect, to "improve the way you make the product." That, in turn, entails improving each process. Since the customer at the next process cares not about the prior process but only the product or service that emerges, priorities are straight.

Types of Operations

Implementation of operator process ownership ought to be a part of any organization's operations strategy. The specifics of carrying that out—along with decisions about what operations management tools and procedures to use—depend on types of operations.

For example, certain models and techniques apply to **continuous** or **repetitive operations**: this includes what some call *batch* production, for example, making one batch (of paint, chocolate chip cookies, chemicals) after another. Much goods manufacturing is of this type. At the opposite extreme are the fine arts and crafts. The artist and the craftsperson do nicely without the aid of operations management models and analytical techniques.

A builder is neither a repetitive producer nor an artist, although we often want our buildings to include some artful features. There is a need for better management of such semi-unique work. Large-scale endeavors of this type are known as **projects**, for example, construction projects and research and development (R&D) projects. If small scale, they are known as **jobs**, such as painting a room or performing surgery.

FIGURE 2–11
Three Types of Operations

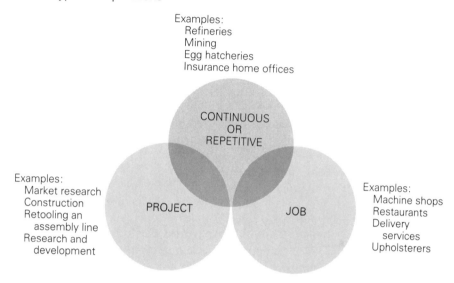

Examples:
   Refineries
   Mining
   Egg hatcheries
   Insurance home offices

CONTINUOUS
OR
REPETITIVE

Examples:
   Market research
   Construction
   Retooling an
      assembly line
   Research and
      development

PROJECT

JOB

Examples:
   Machine shops
   Restaurants
   Delivery
      services
   Upholsterers

   The three basic types of operation and examples are shown in Figure 2–11. The two overlapping zones are explained next, along with some terms that distinguish among the diverse processes and operations, products and services, and firms and industries.

Continuous and Repetitive

Four examples of continuous or repetitive operations are given in Figure 2–11: refineries, mining, egg hatcheries, and insurance home offices. Processing one type of insurance policy application or claim form can be a repetitive operation; the insurance example thus shows that service providers as well as goods producers may be classed as repetitive. Repetitive production of goods is far more common. High-volume production of goods is popularly called *mass production,* a term that is less useful in operations management than the terms *continuous* and *repetitive.*

   Refining and mining differ from egg hatching in an important way. Petroleum products and ores are materials that pour or flow. Egg hatcheries, of course, require procedures to ensure that the material does not pour! In statistics studies, things that pour are said to be *continuous variables* and may be counted in fractional parts. Things that do not pour are called *discrete variables* and are counted only in whole units.

   Firms that process materials that pour are often referred to simply as the **process industry** (short for *continuous-flow process*). Some industry members prefer the term **batch processing,** since the fluids often are mixed in batches in between flows through pipes. Liquids, gases, grains, flakes, and pellets, as well as mining of coal, metallic ores, and so forth, fit into the process industry. Makers of nails, toothpicks, pens, and even flashlight batteries sometimes consider themselves part of the process industry. Such products may be planned, scheduled, counted, and controlled by volume rather than by unit or piece. The process industry tends to be highly capital intensive. Refineries and chemical plants, for example, run with few employees. Labor is a small portion of product cost; plant and equipment (capital) is a large portion. There are relatively few day-to-day production control problems, but advance planning of fixed resources is extensive.

Repetitive production of discrete items is planned, scheduled, counted, and controlled by natural unit or piece. A wide variety of products are of this type. Some, such as eggs, require much handling but little processing. Others, such as chairs and circuit breakers, require extensive parts fabrication followed by assembly into finished goods (the *fabrication/assembly* industry). Discrete production operations tend to require more human assistance and less automation than continuous operations. Many products, such as spaghetti and aspirin, are in an early state of continuous flow (or batch) but are later chopped or formed into pieces and packaged in discrete units. The method of counting or measuring materials—continuously or discretely—is important in a few spots in this book. But continuous and repetitive are put together in one circle in Figure 2–11 because both have *little variety* as their main feature. Job operations, on the other hand, are characterized by *great variety*.

Job

Examples of job operations in Figure 2–11 are machine shops, restaurants, delivery services, and upholsterers. It is appropriate to include three service providers among the four examples because the service sector is mostly job-oriented. Repetitive processing of insurance forms, as discussed earlier, is an uncommon service industry exception. Job shops are also plentiful in the goods manufacturing sector. Some industrial job shops make special parts in small volumes for assembly into final products. Others repair equipment and make tooling.

Many job-oriented businesses are chaotic—nearly out of control. The main reason is an often bewildering variety of jobs; each customer wants something special or different. The management challenge is to reduce the complexity through such techniques as grouping customer requirements into common categories. That will be discussed further in later chapters.

Project

Projects are large scale. A single project typically takes months or years to complete. Repetitive production of a product may also run for months or years, but each unit is completed in minutes, hours, or days. Both job and project operations are low-volume endeavors (a project is usually unique—a unit of one), but projects are large and jobs are small.

Examples of projects in Figure 2–11 are a market research project, a construction project, a project for retooling an assembly line, and a research and development (R&D) project. In the project environment, the total number of projects is usually small, but each is composed of a large, diverse mix of small jobs or activities to be planned and controlled.

Continuous/repetitive is shown overlapping with the two other circles in Figure 2–11. The overlap zone on the left includes the special case of the large project that is ordered in multiple units. An example would be an order for 25 destroyer escorts by the Navy. The overlap zone on the right might include a large-quantity job order. For example, a welding business might receive an order to perform 500 identical welds; this is a job with some characteristics of repetitive production. The multiple-unit project or job is nice, because every unit need not be treated as a separate order; planning and control cost per unit goes down. The planning and control effects deserve further comment.

Planning and Control Requirements

The three types of operations described differ mainly in *variety* of models processed and *size* of the operation needed to produce the unit or units. The variety/size combinations are important for our purposes, because each of the three resulting types of operation calls for a different set of planning and control techniques. The specific techniques are taken up throughout the book. In general,

1. Continuous and repetitive operations require elaborate advance planning but are comparatively easy to control. Simple, inflexible rules and rather rigid standards of performance will suffice. The advantages of this type of production are many, and it is natural for any company to want either to become more continuous or repetitive or to streamline its operations in order to enjoy some of the advantages of continuous operations.

2. Job-oriented operations vary from job to job. Waiting lines are common, and priority-ordering schemes are needed. Excess resources must be on hand to handle short-run changes.

3. Project-oriented operations change as the project progresses, and large numbers of operations are in progress at any given time. Planning and control of sequence of operations are critical.

OPERATIONS MANAGEMENT FUNCTIONS

In the late 1950s and early 1960s, textbooks like this had titles such as *Industrial Management* or *Manufacturing Management*, reflecting a focus on manufacturing industries. Later, the term *production management* became more common. Realization that many of the production concepts and techniques were also applicable to the provision of *services* ushered in the name **production/operations management (POM)**, or simply **operations management (OM)**.

Today, there is wide recognition that operations management principles ought to govern activities anywhere in any kind of organization, including government, other services, and manufacturing. But within an organization, *any* organization, what activities or elements typically *are* associated with operations and governed by operations management principles? This section addresses that question.

Models of OM

Figure 2–12 shows the classic inputs-transformation-outputs model. Resource inputs are consumed by transformation processes where value-adding operations are performed to yield output goods and services. At one time, operations management studies treated inputs, transformations, and outputs as three more or less independent topics. That chopped-up approach has given way to the integrated process view: world-class companies pay great heed to how input sources, transformations, and outputs are linked.

Any **model**—mental, verbal, mathematical, graphical, and pictorial are a few types—is a representation of some reality. Simple models, like that in Figure 2–12, aren't very thorough; they needn't be, for their usefulness lies in their simplicity. They provide a quick, overall view of the big picture. In fact, commonsense management goes something like this: Make a mental model of the situation (a likeness of the reality), sketch or graph it if you can, then think it through and decide on a plan of action. Sometimes, however, more detail is needed; perhaps a more realistic model is required.

As a model is changed to more accurately represent reality, it usually gets more complicated. For example, the three elements in Figure 2–12 subdivide. Many kinds of inputs exist—transformations occur at whole-product or at component levels, and in different locations—and several kinds of outputs are provided to meet customers' diverse needs and wants. Additionally, a complete picture requires that the *management* of operations be included; things like strategy, policies, budgets, plans and controls, measures and rewards, and procedures.

Operations management activities are diverse: Quality planning and control, plant maintenance, demand forecasting, job scheduling, purchasing, and labor force planning are but a few of the OM subfunctions. They may not seem to be closely related, but they are! Within any process, *all* OM functions are concerned with either managing the value-adding operations (producing outputs) or managing the resources used in operations (input management).

FIGURE 2–12
Inputs-Transformation-Outputs Model

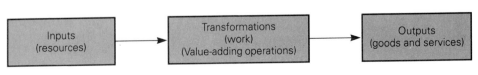

There is a reason for keeping in mind the distinction between outputs (goods and services) and inputs (operating resources). A brief story may help to illustrate. One of the authors worked for a time in various planning and analysis jobs for the U.S. Navy. The jobs sometimes included interviews with managers of shore-based commands. The meetings generally began with a commanding officer or department head stating the command's mission, which was always "Support the fleet." Placards on desks or walls proclaimed the same simple message. Keeping this message in prominent view helped avoid mixing up priorities in the vast bureaucratic organization that is the U.S. Navy. The thousands of people in these shore-based commands were to understand that they served the fleet, not the other way around. They served the fleet largely by helping to provide resource inputs, but the resources people were the first to go if there was a budget cut or if they served poorly.

When the distinction between resource inputs and outputs is widely understood, responsibility assignments are clearer and working relationships among company personnel are likely to be more harmonious. There is less chance of an upset foreman needing to ask a plant engineer or buyer, "Wait a minute—aren't *you* supposed to be helping *me*?"

In expanding Figure 2–12 into a more realistic model of OM, the output/input distinction is of prime importance, as may be seen in Figure 2–13—a functional model of OM. It shows how the OM functions are related; those functions concerned with outputs are *above* the dashed line, and those concerned with inputs are *below* it. In a general way, Figure 2–13 reveals organizational **productivity**—the ratio of output goods and services to input resources required to provide those goods and services.

The OM functions (in blocks) are connected by arrows that stand for certain key information flows. Not shown in Figure 2–13 are informational links with other major functions, such as marketing and finance. To show them would require a complicated grand model of information linkages. Ties to other sectors are discussed in appropriate places in the book.

The functional model fully applies to the manufacture of goods. It also pertains to businesses that provide services, except that in the service sector inventory management is a lesser function. The service itself cannot be stored (inventoried), but all services use supplies, a lesser type of inventory: Janitorial services consume wax and soap, educational services consume paper and chalk, counseling services consume forms. (Note: Some kinds of services yield a tangible good—a report, tax statement, or milkshake, for example—but they are delivered immediately rather than stored for future sale.)

Readiness, Action, and Monitoring for Improvement

Vertically, the functions group into time-related zones of *readiness, action, and monitoring for improvement*. Notice that the left side and center of Figure 2–13 focus heavily on planning; long-range planning within the *readiness* zone, and

FIGURE 2–13

Functional Model of Operations Management

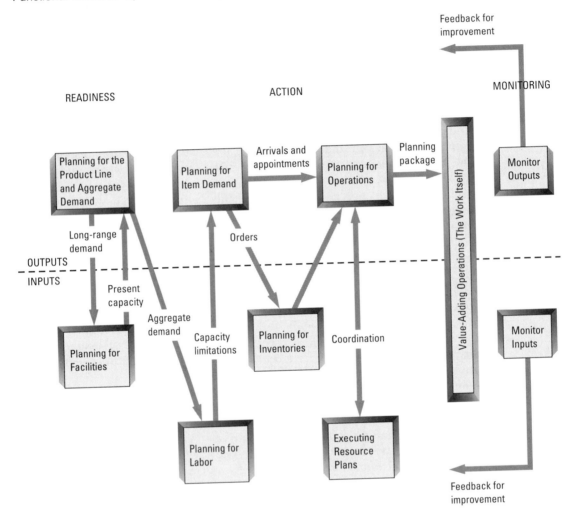

more immediate planning—scheduling, for example—in the *action zone*. As its name implies, the readiness zone is for getting ready. Plans for the product line; facilities, or fixed capacity; and to some extent aggregate demand are strategic in nature. They are approved infrequently and their implementation often takes years. Generally, Parts One and Two of the text address readiness zone functions. Also, Chapter 18 in Part Five addresses facility planning within a context of looking ahead for improvement opportunities.

The center zone is the action zone. In the sequence shown by the arrows, planning becomes more detailed and complete. The reader who has been in industry a few years might see an inconsistency here, thinking something like, How can this be an *action* zone with planning still going on? Shouldn't all the planning be over *before* the action starts? Well, that's the way things *used to be.* No longer. Remember the customer wants? *Shorter lead times. Flexibility.* Competitive companies have realized that the planning-action cycle *can and should* occur rapidly; long cycles mean that too much waste exists in the action zone. Adherence to several of the principles of operations management shortens time requirements (see principles 2, 3, 9, and 11, for example).

At the right side of the action zone in Figure 2–13 we find execution of resource plans. The double-ended arrow between execution and operations planning addresses the close coordination required in the planning-action cycle. Collectively, the action zone functions are directly involved with the flow of goods and services. They culminate in a *planning package:* operations design information dispatched to the work force so that transformations may begin. Part Three of this text, Translating Demand into Planning Orders, describes action zone functions in more detail.

Between the action zone and monitoring for improvement lies the band labeled "Value-Adding Operations (The Work Itself)." Don't let its narrowness suggest that nothing much goes on, for this little band is what all of the readiness and action functions have been leading up to. Here is where the goods and services—the things that customers want—come into being. *Do* let the narrowness suggest short transformation (**throughput time** or **lead time**): elapsed time, including delays, to transform resources into outputs, for that is what ought to happen. In Part Four of the text, Translating Planned Orders into Outcomes, we examine the management of operations in a variety of environments.

The final zone in Figure 2–13 is *monitoring for improvements.* It includes measurements of outputs and inputs that provide data for comparing *actual* outputs and resource usage with *planned* values. Measurement data are fed back to planners, who make decisions about process changes. The continual improvement idea forces changes to occur, even when things seem to be going well. Since measurement is closely related to planning for outputs and inputs, the monitoring function is partially covered in Part Four. Also, Part Five, Areas for Continuing Improvement, focuses directly on the topic of improvement.

The prudent operations manager ought to view these zones from left to right with this thought in mind: If the left zone is done correctly, then the zone to the right is much easier. For example, sufficient attention to the preparation steps in the *readiness* zone makes activities within the *action* zone go smoother. Likewise, diligence within the *action* phase makes value-adding operations more successful, thereby allowing *monitoring functions* to worry less about corrections and concentrate more on continual improvement.

Description of the Functions

Each of the blocks in Figure 2–13, along with some basic terms, are briefly introduced in this section. At this point, our aim is to get a general idea of how the functions of operations management are related; more detailed treatment of the topic comes in later chapters.

Planning for the Product Line and Aggregate Demand

Planning for the product line and aggregate demand, at the upper-left portion of the functional model, are what set operations management in motion. Design and development of a line of goods and services for which there will be sufficient demand—and for which the firm has distinctive competency in providing—are the aims. **Product planning** specifies types of goods and services, and **aggregate demand forecasting** predicts quantities. Aggregate demand covers both long-range and medium-range horizons, and the long-range component feeds facility planning.

Planning for Facilities

Long-range demand, the downward arrow from product line and aggregate demand planning, determines requirements for **facilities** or **fixed capacity**—plant and equipment that is generally unalterable for months or even years. Unless long-range forecasts indicate adequate aggregate customer demand, capital expenditures for facilities make no sense. The upward-pointing arrow, *present capacity*, indicates that choices of facilities set constraints on the array of goods and services that can be provided. Also, once plant and equipment are set, demand is needed. The company's response ought to be the development of products that generate demand. Facilities are a crucial component in determining distinctive competency.

Planning for Labor

Aggregate demand for the medium range is shown as an arrow pointing down and to the right in Figure 2–13. That demand triggers planning for labor; a resource that takes the form of *adjustable capacity*. Recruiting, overtime, shift work, cross-training, reassignments, and layoffs occur as labor force adjustments are carried out, to ensure a work force appropriate to meet demand for goods and services. Although acquisition of skilled labor may take longer, generally labor planning occurs within the medium-range planning period.

The *capacity limitations* arrow pointing upward from labor planning illustrates that labor force characteristics directly affect item demand planning within the action zone. For example, the ability to change item plans rapidly should customer preferences so dictate is heavily dependent on the flexibility of the work force.

PRINCIPLE: Cross-train for mastery of multiple skills.

Planning for Item Demand (Customers and Orders)

Aggregate demand must be broken down into **item demands**—demands for specific models, sizes, styles, and colors of goods or specific types of services. Demand for a single item is the sum of actual (in-hand) customer orders and forecasted customer orders. Operations responds to item demands with the creation of a *master production schedule* for products or an *appointment schedule or book* for services. In either case, the schedule is a plan for the timed completions of each separate *output*: a main product or customer service.

For some services there is little need for inventories; the arrival of a customer or the mere existence of an appointment is enough to trigger operations planning. The *arrivals and appointments* arrow depicts that flow. When inventories are required, forecasted or actual orders (contained in the master schedule or appointment book) set in motion activities to order needed materials, as shown by the arrow labeled *orders*. Inventories result from those orders.

Planning for Inventories

For some goods producers, *inventory planning* is a major activity. Master-scheduled items (the main outputs) divide into subassemblies and then into component parts (inputs), which must be planned for availability at the right times and in the right amounts.

Planning for Operations (Processes, Schedules, and Controls)

Every fabricated part or assembly and every step in providing a service might be planned as a separate order. One or more processes will provide for the completion of the order in the form of output goods and services. Orders may be scheduled and controlled as jobs, batches, tasks, project activities, or repetitive production runs. Figure 2–13 shows three arrows entering the planning for operations block: customer arrival or appointment data, item inventory plans, and resource availability information. As the arrow pointing to the right indicates, the result of operations planning is the *planning package*.

Executing Resource Plans

Operating resources—plant, equipment, tools, labor, and materials—have life cycles. They are acquired, deployed, maintained or stored, and eventually disposed of. In the case of labor, we might prefer the terms *hiring, assigning, training,* and *releasing*. The *executing resource plans* block in Figure 2–13 reflects activities that attend to all four of these life-cycle stages. The two-headed arrow between resource planning and operations planning signifies the need for resource deployment to dovetail with operations scheduling.

Monitoring Outputs and Inputs

When the planning package is released to the organization, transformation of inputs into outputs begins. As the work proceeds, monitoring of both outputs and inputs occurs. Monitoring serves two purposes. First, actual output is compared with planned output: Is the customer getting what was requested? Occasionally, plans or execution activities go awry and revised plans are needed to get things back on track. When things are going fine, the second purpose for monitoring comes into play: sustaining continual improvement efforts.

Feedback for improvement occurs in both outputs and inputs. For inputs, there might be feedback on waste, idleness, safety, or pollution. In the output loop, the aim is to improve what customers receive—things like quality, timely delivery, and good service. Of the two, the upper, or output, feedback loop is more vital. Ends take precedence over means.

The functional model in Figure 2–13 is general enough to apply to any operations management environment, though not always in the same way. Throughout this book, presentations of operations management topics will be tied back to the functional model. Each chapter begins with that chapter's topic highlighted and appropriately positioned on a copy of the functional model of operations management.

Part One has introduced the field of operations management and clearly positioned the goal of improved customer service as our major aim. In Part Two, we look more closely at customer needs and expectations and broaden, perhaps, our thinking about demand.

SUMMARY

The proper role of strategy in any business is to serve the *customers* and defend the *company* against its *competition*. Strategies for each of the three line functions—money, demand, and operations—should support a company's overall business plan and must be compatible with one another. In the 1960s, 1970s, and early 1980s, many North American manufacturers developed financial (money) and marketing (demand) strategies, but neglected operations strategy. The result was a serious decline in world market share during the late 1970s and 1980s.

Operations strategies are concerned with operating resources; products and services; operating processes; and output quality, cost, lead time, and flexibility. Companies with similar business strategies may have widely different operations strategies, each striving to attain *distinctive competency*, its own unique way of making a living.

Regardless of original intent, companies find that they must change business and operations strategies as global, regional, and local forces act to shape strategic plans. Global factors, such as the Great Depression of the 1930s and the opening of the Iron Curtain in the late 1980s, pervasively affect business strategies. World War II, however, was perhaps the most significant recent global shaper of business and operations strategies, especially among the world's three great industrial regions: the United States and Canada, Japan, and Europe.

In the United States and Canada, strategic emphasis on production during the 1940s (the war years) gave way to a marketing focus in the 1950s and early 1960s, and then to a financial and legal focus in the later 1960s, 1970s, and 1980s. The mid- to late 1980s witnessed a rebirth of concern for operations strategy in North America and the rest of the world as well. There is evidence—changing accounting and control systems and new measures of performance, for example—that future strategic emphasis ought to be *integrative*, blending the concerns of money, market, and operations.

Japan was devastated by World War II and faced a major rebuilding effort in the late 1940s and 1950s. Also, it had to overcome an image of shoddy export goods. The Japanese environment of overcrowding and lack of resources encouraged an operations strategy of waste avoidance, including wastes of poor-quality goods, idle inventories, and inefficiency. That operations strategy resulted in high-quality and low-cost goods, meeting the national and corporate strategies of rapid export growth and necessitating development of marketing strategies. Today, Japan is an international financial power, poised to make good use of an integrative strategic focus in the years to come.

Europe also had to rebuild after World War II, but it had neither Japan's bad-quality image nor its lack of natural resources. Thus, Europe rebuilt its traditional industrial base composed of smaller, more regional (less international) companies. Lack of unification across the continent promoted relatively narrow strategies in the decades after World War II. In the late 1980s and early 1990s, however, events such as formation of the European Economic Community and the opening of the Iron Curtain (reuniting Eastern and Western Europe) shook Europe and the rest of the world. For perhaps the first time in history, a unified Europe—competing with integrated strategies—is a possibility.

Increasingly, other global and regional variables must be factored into strategy formation. Newly industrialized countries, changing operations and marketing strategies of existing multinational corporations, and regional factors such as national laws and labor supplies all serve to influence strategy.

Local influences on strategy include community and supplier factors, the nature of a company's product line, the competitive climate, and present capacity and capability to produce. These factors shape a company's strategies for plant location, R&D, competitive response, technology, and so forth.

Just as operations strategy must fit within business strategy, operations activities must be carried out in harmony with the rest of the organization. Organizational structure is one influence on operations; another is the issue of responsibility for the results of operations—the output goods and services. As organizations grow, line functions of demand, money, and operations are augmented with staff departments, but staffing off of key line responsibilities to remote specialists can be carried too far.

Organizational charts don't show key "wall-busting" alliances and linkages that get provider-supplier pairs together, making good customer service happen. Committees, task forces, teams, flow lines, work cells, and quality circles all can help operating units link up with one another. Operator ownership of operating processes is the final step in keeping priorities straight.

Implementation of operations strategy depends partly on the type of operation: continuous or repetitive, job, or project. Within any type, however, OM's chief concern is with value-adding processes that create outputs, although management of operating resources (inputs) is necessary to ensure that transformations are productive.

The functional model of operations management identifies three major groups of OM activities: those associated with *readiness, action,* and *monitoring for improvement.* The model is general, and will apply to any operations management environment; it serves as a general outline for the remainder of this book.

KEY WORDS

Distinctive competency
Continuous operations
Repetitive operations
Projects
Jobs
Process industry
Batch processing
Production/operations
  management (POM)

Operations
  management (OM)
Model
Productivity
Throughput time (lead
  time)

Product planning
Aggregate demand
  forecasting
Facilities (fixed
  capacity)
Item demand

REFERENCES

Books

Greene, James H., ed. *Production and Inventory Control Handbook*. 2nd ed. New York: John Wiley & Sons, 1986 (TS155.p74).

Malabre, Alfred L., Jr. *Understanding the New Economy*. Homewood, Ill.: Dow Jones-Irwin, 1989 (HB171.M323).

McNair, Carol J., William Mosconi, and Thomas F. Norris. *Beyond the Bottom Line: Measuring World Class Performance*. Homewood, Ill.: Dow Jones-Irwin, 1989 (HF5686.M3M38).

Moody, Patricia J., ed. *Strategic Manufacturing: Dynamic New Directions for the 1990s*. Homewood, Ill.: Dow Jones-Irwin, 1990 (HD9725.S73).

Ohmae, Kenichi. *The Mind of the Strategist*. New York: McGraw-Hill, 1982 (HD31.O485).

Sheth, Jagdish, and Golpira Eshghi., eds. *Global Operations Perspectives*. Cincinnati: South-Western, 1989.

Wallace, Thomas A., and John R. Dougherty, eds. *APICS Dictionary*, 6th ed. Falls Church, Va.: American Production and Inventory Control Society, 1987.

Periodicals/Societies

Business Periodicals Index, an index of articles published in a limited number of business magazines and journals.

Engineering Index, an index of articles published on engineering in a large number of periodicals.

Interfaces (Institute for Management Science), a journal aimed at the interface between management scientist and practitioner.

Journal of Operations Management (Operations Management Society), a practitioner and academic journal.

Production and Inventory Management (American Production and Inventory Control Society), a practitioner's journal.
Technical Book Review Index.

REVIEW QUESTIONS

1. Identify and explain the roles of Ohmae's three key players in business strategy.
2. What is the likely fate of an organization that has no distinctive competencies? Why?
3. Give examples of global environmental shapers of organizational strategies.
4. How has the strategic focus changed in the United States and Canada since World War II?
5. Why did many of the conglomerates put together in the 1960s begin to crumble in the 1970s and 1980s?
6. What is an *integrative focus* in business strategy? What evidence exists to suggest that use of such a focus is increasing?
7. What are the differences in World War II's effects on Japanese and European versus North American industrial strategies?
8. What has been the Japanese priority list (or pecking order) for economic progress in the half-century since World War II?
9. How does the term *Eurosclerosis* characterize business strategy in Europe since World War II?
10. How have the emergence of NICs and changing practices of MNCs affected the way operations strategy is carried out?
11. Discuss possible roles of Europe as a world-class competitor within the next decade and beyond.
12. How does a regional factor such as labor supply shape strategy?
13. What are four major types of *local* influences on industrial strategies?
14. Why must operations be carried out in harmony with the rest of the organization?
15. How might staffing off and specialization negatively affect service to the customer?
16. What elements of a well-organized OM function does the formal organizational chart omit?
17. What is the difference between process ownership and subproduct ownership?
18. Explain the main differences among the three types of operations in Figure 2–11.

19. What is a model? How does the functional model of operations (Figure 2–13) relate to organizational productivity?

20. Operations management activities may be grouped into three time-related zones. What are they and what is the purpose of each?

21. What is the role of the *planning package* in operations?

22. What is meant by the term *value-adding operations*? Of what significance are they to the functional model of OM?

23. Examine Figure 2–13. Briefly describe the purpose of each item in the figure.

PROBLEMS AND EXERCISES

1. What are the distinctive competencies of the following organizations? Discuss.
   a. Holiday Inn.
   b. U.S. Marines.
   c. Boeing.
   d. Procter & Gamble.

2. The Great Depression, World War II, the oil shock of 1973, and the opening of the Iron Curtain in 1989 are cited in this chapter as global shapers of corporate strategy. Other, lesser factors that have had effects on strategies are listed below. Discuss each one. Is it a global, regional, or local factor? What has been its impact on strategy?
   a. Pollution control legislation.
   b. The Korean conflict.
   c. Desegregation laws.
   d. The Vietnam War.

3. What are the key local environmental influences on each of the following? Discuss.
   a. The typical department store.
   b. The typical commercial bus line.
   c. The typical lawn service.
   d. Your phone company.

4. One element of First City Bank's operations strategy is the opening of 15 new cash transaction machines in locations around the area.
   a. What business strategy does this operations strategy most likely support? Express that business strategy in one sentence.
   b. With which principle of operations management does this strategy seem most consistent? Explain.

5. Classic Wooden Toy Company's business strategy includes "responding more quickly to changes in sales patterns for our different toy models." Develop an operations strategy to support that business strategy, taking care not to violate the principles of operations management. Explain your answer.

6. Consolidated Enterprises has three main manufacturing businesses: (1) a fiberglass business in which products are made to customers' specifications, usually in small quantities; (2) a snow blower and lawn mower business in which several models of each product are made, a business in which Consolidated is an industry leader; and (3) a manmade fiber business in which tuberous plants are converted into thread. What type of production (continuous, job, etc.) would apply to each business? Explain.

7. Following are various types of organizations. For each, try to determine the main kind of operation: repetitive or continuous, job, or project. Discuss each.

Medical clinic	Cafeteria	Commercial fishing
Crane manufacturing	Book printing	Grocery checkout
Auditing	Petroleum refining	Farming
Architecture	Purchasing	Mowing grass on campus
Shoe repair	Bottling	Law practice
Radio manufacturing	Construction	Welding shop

8. Why does operations management tend to be more highly developed in repetitive than in job or project operations?

9. As organizations grow, their productive character may change, for example, from batch or job-shop (custom) to repetitive or from project to repetitive. Describe how this might happen for a type of organization of your choice. Also describe the accompanying changes in the management of operations; that is, why would different kinds of planning and control models be called for?

10. What kinds of organization/industry need extremely long-range demand forecasting? Why? What kinds need extremely short-range forecasting? Why?

11. Do you put planning packages together for your own life's activities (trips, school assignments, meals, dates, etc.)? Describe each element of the planning package in terms of one of your activities.

12. News stories about businesses sometimes include statements such as "The firm is operating at 80 percent of capacity." What kind of planning results in the rate of capacity use? How may the rate be measured? Find a news story that discusses rate of capacity use, and summarize what you learn (or surmise) about this kind of planning. (Alternatively, telephone a local manufacturing firm to learn what you can about how it sets its capacity use rate.)

13. In Japan, business colleges are rare and the M.B.A. degree perhaps still does not exist. How is this characteristic of Japan's educational system related to the specialization issue?

14. How does competition affect operations management? Consider, for example, some of the most successful firms in the highly competitive fast-food, lodging, and grocery industries. What do the successful firms do in operations management that their less successful competitors (maybe some that went under!) do not?

15. Think of five diverse examples of nonprofit organizations. For each, describe what its three line management functions (money, demand, and operations management) would consist of.

16. What are the main inputs (operating resources) and outputs, and which OM functions (see Figure 2–13) are most important, in
    a. A company such as United Parcel Service?
    b. A fire department?

17. What three OM functions (see Figure 2–13) are most important to the successful operation of
    a. A videotape rental store?
    b. A bicycle repair shop?
    c. A manufacturer of fence posts?
    d. A coal mine?

18. Think of cases in which you were given exaggerated delivery promises on goods you had ordered. Why is it so common for the sellers to be unable to say with reasonable accuracy when goods will arrive? Think especially of reasons pertaining to the management of operating resources (capacity).

19. W. Edwards Deming, America's famous quality control expert who is in his 90s and still going strong, says that the manager's job is to *design systems.* If that is so, why not just use "canned" systems and not even hire lower and middle managers?

PART TWO

Customer Needs and Expectations: New Ideas about Demand

Customer requirements are the driving force for operations. No longer content to take what's available, customers are expanding their expectations and the competitive organization must respond. Innovative products and services, and continual improvement in the processes that create them, are addressed in Chapter 3.

Perhaps the fundamental lesson for business and industry—maybe for all organizations—during the 1980s was the dominating importance of quality in company and national competitiveness. Chapter 4 looks at the planning component of quality management.

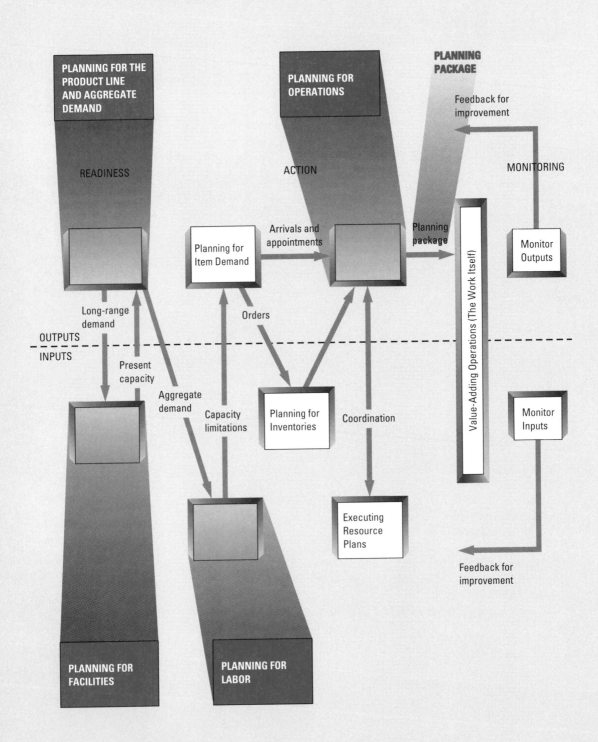

PLANNING FOR THE PRODUCT LINE AND AGGREGATE DEMAND

PLANNING FOR OPERATIONS

PLANNING PACKAGE

READINESS

ACTION

Feedback for improvement

MONITORING

Long-range demand

Planning for Item Demand

Arrivals and appointments

Planning package

Monitor Outputs

OUTPUTS

INPUTS

Present capacity

Orders

Value-Adding Operations (The Work Itself)

Aggregate demand

Capacity limitations

Planning for Inventories

Coordination

Monitor Inputs

Executing Resource Plans

Feedback for improvement

PLANNING FOR FACILITIES

PLANNING FOR LABOR

CHAPTER 3

Product, Service, and Process Planning

SIMPLIFYING PROCESS TECHNOLOGY

Processes and Operations
Process Elimination
Work Element Elimination
Quick Setup
Preautomation

LOW-GRADE PROCESS AUTOMATION

HIGH TECHNOLOGY

Data Capture and Transfer
Robotics
Programmable Robots for Flexible Automation
Numerically Controlled Machines
Computer-Integrated Manufacturing

JUSTIFYING AUTOMATION AND OTHER IMPROVEMENT PROJECTS

CASE STUDY: LINCOLN ELECTRIC COMPANY

Imagine an *ideal* company. Such a firm would be *completely* flexible—capable of instantaneous changes in structure, personnel skills, tools and equipment, operating and marketing plans, financial arrangements, and so forth. Flawless designs and perfect processes to transform those designs into output goods and services would exist. The primary beneficiaries of such a situation? Customers.

In an environment so flexible, there would be no delays, no waiting; setup times, purchasing lead times, training times, and the like would all be insignificant. There would be no need to forecast, or do much (if any) planning at all. The ideal company would exist in a state of constant readiness, able to meet demand—even demand for *new* goods and services—whenever it arose.

We could continue, describing the consistently perfect quality, lowest possible prices, and outstanding service that customers would enjoy. Such an exercise in fantasy is perhaps not totally frivolous, for it gives some sense of the direction in which firms ought to be moving. Regardless of the realities that prevent attaining the ideal, our aim should be to continually move a little closer to giving customers what they want.

We start by providing good products and services. In this chapter, the spotlight is on the planning or design of those products and services and on the processes that create them—portions of the readiness and action zones in the model of operations management. At the outset, let's make two important points: First, experience has shown that for good results, product and service planning *and* process planning must be concurrent activities; thus it is fitting that they be considered together. Second, any discussion of operating processes must address transformation technologies and the people who manage and apply those technologies.

INNOVATION AND THE PRODUCT OR SERVICE LINE

We often see biological system metaphors used in connection with organizational survivability; for example, dinosaurs didn't adapt so they died out, and companies that can't—or won't—adapt face the same fate. The common ground between modern organizations and the welfare of prehistoric creatures lies within the broad subject area of *change or transition.* Indeed, innovation *is* change, and is a requirement for organizational survival. Management of change is challenging, especially in regard to product-line transitions.

A story is told that in 1882, panic arose when astronomers predicted that a comet would crash into the earth, causing great havoc. Entrepreneurs—ever ready to offer customer service—began to market "anti-comet" pills, with an accompanying guarantee that consumption would prevent any comet-related calamity to one's person. The pills, obviously a scientific breakthrough, necessitated rapid creation of production facilities and marketing distribution channels. Demand for the pill lasted no longer than the comet threat. We can only wonder if the entrepreneurs made a successful product-line transition (to snake-oil elixir, perhaps?).

Products and services have finite life cycles; some—like anti-comet pills—are extremely short. Fashion fads, toys, and novelty items may last just one season. Clearly, providers of those items must stress innovation; new product development and smooth transition to production of the new goods are high-priority missions. Some transitions are upheavals, like buggy whips to throttles, propellers to jet engines, and slide rules to pocket calculators. Others are slight but pivotal transitions, like microwave popcorn, pump-your-own gasoline, and programmed instruction.

What about providers of products and services with very long life cycles? Is innovation also a high-priority mission for them? Competition for the consumer's attention and money ensures that it is. A few years before the anti-comet pills, another scientific breakthrough product—one that has outlasted the pills by more than a century—made its appearance: Alexander Graham Bell's telephone of 1876 allowed humans to converse beyond the natural range of the human voice and ear, and the telephone is still used for that purpose. Innovations over the last century, however, have clearly improved not only the product (the phone itself), but also the service that goes along with telephone usage. Customers want and expect their telephone *systems* to do much more than allow two-way conversation, and phone manufacturers as well as companies offering telephone-related services have kept innovation a high-priority goal. The laboratories of AT&T, for example, have long been renowned for their research output.

In spite of their fine research labs, companies like AT&T and DuPont have been faced with problems of keeping up with the competition in recent years. Those companies and many others have been reexamining their research strategies. One issue under scrutiny is the big-breakthrough approach ("go for the bomb") versus a continual succession of small improvements. This is a general issue that applies to both product and process innovation.

Real business innovation certainly includes technological breakthroughs— new products, services, and techniques—when they occur, but is more often the result of modest, incremental improvements to existing products, services, and operations (the "tinkerer's tool box"). Sometimes the tinkering lowers cost, sometimes it improves quality, sometimes it simplifies processes to permit faster service, and sometimes it yields a new, lucrative, spinoff product.

Michiyuki Uenohara, research director at NEC Corporation, says that innovation is "the result of tiny improvements in a thousand places."[1] John P. McTague, vice president for research at Ford Motor Co., elaborates on the point, saying, "The cumulation of a large number of small improvements is the surest path, in most industries, to increasing your competitive advantage."[2]

PRINCIPLE: Become dedicated to continual, rapid improvement.

Transitions in product and service lines are risky. They put into motion plans for facilities (fixed capacity) that can be altered only at great expense. Because

---

[1]Neil Gross, "A Wave of Ideas, Drop by Drop," *Business Week Special Report on Innovation in America,* June 16, 1989, pp. 22–30.
[2]Otis Port, "Back to Basics," *Business Week Special Report on Innovation in America,* June 16, 1989, pp. 14–18.

facilities are so costly, their actual or pending existence influences further innovations and developments to current product and service lines.

The reason that companies so often push unwanted products and models into the marketplace (leaving sales with the burden) is not just the impossibility of guessing demand. Existing facilities exert their own pressure to develop and make product models that fit the limited capabilities of those facilities. The point is reflected in the diagram that opens this chapter, showing arrows going both ways between planning for the product line and planning for facilities: Each influences the other.

RESEARCH STRATEGIES

While existing facilities act as a constraint on *what* products emerge from research and development (R&D), the greater issue is *whether* to commit to R&D at all. The question is, does R&D pay off?

An analysis by *Business Week* sheds some light on the question. The analysis reveals that firms with the best performances—in sales per employee and in overall profit margin—in their industries are also the ones with the greatest per-employee level of R&D spending.[3] Do we interpret that to mean that successful

---

[3]Anthony J. Parisi, "How R&D Spending Pays Off," *Business Week*, June 16, 1989, pp. 177–79.

companies simply have more money to spend on R&D? Or is it that spending for R&D leads to success? The latter seems the safer conclusion: Emulate the good companies, including their commitment to research and development of products and services.

Research strategies and commitments, therefore, beg our attention. We'll consider how research commitment relates to organization size, product life cycle, and organizational character; and also the uncertainties that determine the direction to which the research effort is aimed.

TABLE 3–1
R&D Expenditures

Industries	Percentage of Annual Sales Spent on Company-Financed R&D (1988)
Computer software and services	13.3
Health care: drugs and research	10.0
Computer systems design	9.2
Semiconductors	8.9
Computers	8.2
Health care: medical products and services	6.2
Electrical & electronic instruments	5.9
Telecommunictions	5.7
Data-processing services	5.0
Electronics	4.8
Leisure-time equipment (toys, sporting goods, etc.)	4.6
Aerospace	4.1
Chemicals	3.6
All-Industry Composite	**3.4**
General manufacturing	3.3
Automotive	3.2
Machine and hand-tool manufacturing	1.9
Housing and construction	1.9
Consumer products	1.6
Metals and mining	1.2
Service industries: composite	1.2
Containers and packaging	1.0
Paper and forest products	1.0
Nonbank financial services	0.8
Food	0.7
Fuel	0.7

Source: "R&D Scoreboard, 1988," *Business Week*, June 16, 1989, pp. 180–232. Obtained by *Business Week* from Standard & Poor's Compustat Services, Inc.

Research Commitment

Table 3–1 shows R&D expenditures as a percentage of sales in several U.S. industries. As might be expected, computer and medical products and services rank highest. Firms in those industries spend about 15 times more than those at the bottom of the list. Note that the goods and services of the top-spending industries require extensive design and development, while those of the lower-spending industries—food, fuel, forest and mining products, and so forth—require little; they are sold almost as they are obtained from nature. Also, with the exception of health care and computer-related services, service providers spend relatively little on R&D, as evidenced by the low figure for composite services. As services become more competitive, that may change.

Research strategies concern the extent and type of research as well as the source of research expertise. Expenditures for R&D range from massive for a corporation like General Motors, which spent over $4.7 billion for R&D in 1988, to meager for, say, the cemetery business.

Do larger companies spend more on R&D? Table 3–2 shows that within the health care industry, large companies do indeed spend the largest sums on drugs and research. On relative measures, however, the big spenders are the small firms. The data for 1988 put Alza, Amgen, and Centocor at or near the top of the entire 897 companies studied, both in R&D spending per employee and as a percentage of sales.

We should not conclude from Table 3–2 that old-line firms in the health care industry are complacent. Instead, the explanation is that for Amgen and other newly formed companies, the entire product line is new and in need of large cash infusions for R&D. At Pfizer and the other established firms, only a small percentage of products are new, cash-eating items; older products require far

TABLE 3–2

R&D in Health Care Industry (drugs and research)

Company	Sales (in millions of dollars)	R&D Expense (in millions of dollars)	R&D to Sales (%)	Industry Rank	R&D Expense per Employee (in thousands of dollars)	Industry Rank
Alza	$ 74.0	$ 29.4	39.7%	3	$ 45.6	4
Amgen	44.3	39.6	89.5	1	112.3	1
Centocor	55.2	33.8	61.3	2	78.7	2
Eli Lilly	4,069.7	540.8	13.3	8	20.3	8
Merck	5,939.5	668.8	11.3	12	20.9	7
Pfizer	5,385.4	472.5	8.8	17	11.6	17
SmithKline	4,749.0	495.1	10.4	14	11.9	16

Source: "R&D Scoreboard, 1988," *Business Week*, June 16, 1989, pp. 180–232. Obtained by *Business Week* from Standard & Poor's Compustat Services, Inc. (Data are shown for 7 of the 32 companies included in this survey category.)

less for R&D and more for production and promotion. In short, commitment to R&D often depends more on product life-cycle factors than it does on organization size.

Another influence on R&D commitment is competitive pressure. A prominent example is the U.S. government's reaction to the missile crisis of the 1960s. Congress was prompted to appropriate huge amounts of research money to close the Soviet-U.S. missile gap. Once the gap was closed, Congress saw fit to cut way back on research support.[4]

Still another factor in the direction that a firm's research takes is organizational character. There is room for both leaders and followers in most industries. Leaders may adopt aggressive or *offensive* product design strategies; followers may adopt *defensive* strategies; and those in between may make moderate commitments by *contracting* research or *licensing* other people's product designs as necessary.

The offensive strategy is to commit a lot of money to building a research team. The objective is to design and market products while competition is light or nonexistent. An offensive strategy may also have a short-run reason, such as product diversification. Large firms are better able to afford the risks of an offensive strategy, but many small firms have grown large by taking such risks; Xerox, Polaroid, 3M, and Texas Instruments are examples. In some industries—aerospace and electronics, for instance—nearly every firm sees the need for an offensive strategy. Other industries, such as railroads, seem to have a defensive research strategy.

Research Directions

We have considered research strategy in a broad sense. Narrower strategic factors include the uncertainties in carrying out successful research. In Figure 3–1, we see how three kinds of uncertainty may affect the direction of a firm's research effort.

The question in column 2 of the figure (Can we design it?) is the one most germane to this discussion. But that question is best viewed along with the equally important questions Can we make or provide it well? and Can we sell it? If the answer to all three questions is "Yes, easily," the new item is quickly designed and added to the product line at little cost. Where an answer is "Uncertain," more research is necessary to bring the product to market. For example, product design research is needed in the last four cases in the table, where there is uncertainty about designing the item. The product research should be intensive, following more than one research approach (concurrent or parallel approaches), if the product team believes the product can be easily made and marketed (case 5); and should be exploratory where uncertainty surrounds all three questions (case 8).

4"From 1961 to 1967 government-funded R&D increased 5.6 percent a year. . . . But from 1967 to 1975 the government R&D shrank 3 percent a year." Reported in "The Silent Crisis in R&D," *Business Week*, March 8, 1976, p. 90.

FIGURE 3–1

Research Strategies for Coping with Uncertainties

	Uncertainties			
Case	*Can We Design It?*	*Can We Make/Provide It Well?**	*Can We Sell It?†*	*Research Strategies*
1	Easily	Easily	Easily	Little research except for pilot testing and trial marketing
2	Easily	Easily	Uncertain	Intensive market research
3	Easily	Uncertain	Uncertain	Market research and process studies
4	Easily	Uncertain	Easily	Intensive process study
5	Uncertain	Easily	Easily	Intensive product design research using parallel approaches
6	Uncertain	Easily	Uncertain	Product design research and market research
7	Uncertain	Uncertain	Easily	Product design research and process study
8	Uncertain	Uncertain	Uncertain	Exploratory product design, process, and market research

*Uncertainty about making it calls for process research.
†Uncertainty about selling it calls for marketing research, which is not discussed in this book.
Source: Adapted from *Innovation: The Management Connection* by Robert O. Burns (Lexington, Mass.: Lexington Books, D. C. Heath and Company, Copyright 1975, D. C. Heath and Company).

While product research gets most of the glamour and publicity, process research—needed in cases 3, 4, 7, and 8—can be every bit as valuable strategically. Burger King, for example, developed the continuous-flow burger broiler and used that process technology for a time in its "broiled, not fried" advertising campaign.

We now turn from the broad strategic issues to concepts and techniques for getting the R&D job done—our topic for the remainder of the chapter.

MANAGING DESIGN AND DEVELOPMENT

Can creativity be managed? Can research "stars" exist within the corporate environment? The answer to these questons has traditionally been "Well, perhaps, but with much difficulty." Companies like Merck, 3M, and Rubbermaid (judged to be America's most innovative publicly held corporations in a recent *Fortune* survey) realize the urgency of acquiring and retaining innovative individuals. Allen Jacobson, CEO at 3M, offers two tips: First, he cautions managers against imposing too much of themselves ("You've got to sponsor your people's ideas"), and second, he urges researchers to put customers first ("Innovation works from understanding consumer needs").[5]

PRINCIPLE: Get to know the customer.

Historically, design engineers were aloof, often kept apart from other functional areas. Companies with successful R&D programs, however, have learned that design and development must blend with the activities of the rest of the company and its environment, especially those activities in (1) operations, (2) marketing and external customers, and (3) suppliers.

Integrating the Design Effort

People in the organization view product designers (or design engineers) with both admiration and annoyance. The admiration is for the designer's obvious talents and contributions to company success. The annoyance is over the detached way in which product design work is usually carried out. As they say, the design is "thrown over the wall" and operations has to try to produce or provide it. If it can't be done, design changes are required. (In manufacturing, they are called **engineering changes**, or **ECs**.) Still not producible? Second round of changes. And the cycle repeats.

Design and producibility problems are not restricted to manufacturing. In education, the design is the teacher's syllabus or instructor's manual. In the food industry, the design is a recipe, and anyone who has worked with recipes knows the kind that require the cook to do six things at once. The demands of the recipe often make a bad result likely.

The real problem, besides treating designers as isolates, has been that organizations lacked controls on design procedures and measures of effectiveness. In the 1980s, industry began intensifying the management of design. Seminars, books, and articles talk about designing for **producibility** (or **manufacturability**) and designing for automation, robotics, and quality. Restrictions are being imposed on designers, designers are teaming up with people in other functions, and design effectiveness is being measured in various ways.

Tightened design policies are being implemented with little rancor or finger pointing. Companies' attitude is "We finally have some techniques for managing the design function." Designers' reactions seems to be: "The organization is finally paying some attention to us."

Operations: The Next Process

The designer's "customer" is operations or, more likely, where operations planning is done. In manufacturing, one aspect of operations planning is *manufacturing engineering* (sometimes called *process engineering*). Manufacturing engineers

---

[5]"Leaders of the Most Admired," *Fortune*, January 29, 1990, pp. 40–54.

are equipment and automation experts. Machines—those now in use as well as any being considered—have limited capabilities. A certain machine may be able to cut aluminum but not brass, machine 14-mm. but not 18-mm. steel, or hold tolerances of 0.005 inches but not better. If the design is to be manufacturable, the designer must somehow acquire some of the manufacturing engineer's knowledge of machine capabilities—during design.

For a number of years, IBM has fed that kind of information to designers through a program called "early manufacturing involvement (EMI)." Under EMI, IBM assigns a manufacturing engineer to work in a development lab with product designers during a design project. More recently a number of companies, such as Deere and Company and Stanadyne Diesel, have adopted a more permanent solution: putting design engineering and manufacturing engineering under one manager. The single manager has full responsibility for ensuring close coordination. An even more profound and rapidly spreading approach is to form *design-build teams* composed of designers, engineers, other support people, and even line production employees.

Linkage with Marketing

The designer must also close ranks with the final, or external, customer, via marketing. Chrysler rescued itself from the grave largely by cost cutting. Design and marketing jointly played a central role. They developed a product line with a narrow range of options having broad appeal instead of the former practice of a broad range with narrow appeal. In other words, the new concept featured just a few standard design packages available to the customer.

For the Dodge Omni and Plymouth Horizon, some 8 million permutations of options (excluding colors) had been possible. The new design concept reduced the number of permutations to 42. Chrysler could then focus on making a small number of parts in very high volumes, which offered economies of scale and a narrower target for improving quality. As a result, the price Chrysler had to charge plunged in 1986 to $5,779, which was below that of almost all other cars sold in the United States.[6]

Eliminating options and reducing "part counts" can backfire if not done right. Customers' needs and wants are the foremost concern, and Detroit had been allowing options to proliferate because that seemed to be what customers wanted. Good design, however, allows high variety and small part counts; that is, a modest number of parts designed to fit together in many ways can yield a large number of end product variations (Legos, the toy construction blocks, come to mind). *Modular* design concepts also allow variety of end products while holding part counts down. For example, personal computer manufacturers offer a variety of compatible products—keyboard, mouse, extra memory, different screens, modems, and so forth—so that the consumer can tailor a system to meet personal needs and budgets.

---

[6]"Getting Smart: How U.S. Manufacturers Find Ways to Meet Japanese Competition in Specific Products," *The Wall Street Journal*, September 16, 1986.

Modularity is becoming a strong force in the automotive and major appliance industries as well. According to one report, Japanese automakers are talking about building networks of small market-driven factories that will allow construction of a car from just 37 snap-together parts. Each such factory would economically produce about 10,000 autos a year, versus a typical break-even volume of over 200,000 in today's auto plants.[7]

Interface with Suppliers

Design's third accommodation is with suppliers. Designers have major authority in choosing materials, which often is tantamount to choosing the supplier. Company policies, however, sometimes make it difficult for anyone but buyers in the purchasing department to interact directly with suppliers. (Under past purchasing practices, there was really little chance for either buyer or design engineer to interact with suppliers; there simply were too many suppliers. The movement to reduce number of suppliers per part number, discussed in Chapter 7, makes it reasonable to visit suppliers.) Now many companies are relaxing such policies. Designers need to visit supplier plants, perhaps along with buyers, in order to learn the suppliers' capabilities. Suppliers expect those visits, for they are usually a prerequisite to the supplier gaining certification, which, in turn, is needed to join the dwindling list of approved suppliers.

Top companies are not content to merely visit or certify their suppliers. They also seek **early supplier involvement**, which means inviting suggestions for making the supplied materials or components function better for the customer's intended uses. Often the supplier's designers work concurrently with the customer's. Furthermore, instead of the customer's specs being hurled "over the wall" to the supplier, the customer may specify only critical performance criteria to the supplier and let the supplier's engineers work out the detailed specifications. That practice makes sense only when coordination between supplier and customer are excellent; otherwise, thorough specifications are usually desirable.

Although effective management of design begins with integrating design with the rest of the business, it also includes techniques for effective design. Those topics are discussed next.

EFFECTIVE DESIGN

Getting designers in touch with the other parts of the business does much to ensure effective design. Strong design policies, goals, practices, and evaluation methods are additional ingredients in the recipe for good design management.

---

[7]Gary S. Vasilash, "How to Avoid Extinction," *Production*, October 1989, pp. 61–65.

FIGURE 3–2
Guidelines for Effective Design

General Guidelines
 1. Design to target cost.
 2. Minimize part counts or number of operations.
Quality Guidelines
 3. Ensure that customer requirements are known and unambiguous, and design to those requirements.
 4. Use standard materials, parts, and procedures with already-known quality.
 5. Design to process capability.
 6. Set tolerances and specifications that will not strain the capabilities of normal people and machines.
Producibility Guidelines (specific to manufacturing)
 7. Design parts to be easy to grasp.
 8. Design components and assemblies that are not overly heavy.
 9. Design shapes for ease of packing and unpacking.
 10. Design components that assemble or fasten together simply.
 11. Configure assemblies to avoid difficult angles and tight squeezes.

While the concepts of effective design seem still to be evolving, there is consensus on a few points. Figure 3–2 lists some of them in the form of guidelines. None are absolute. For example, jet engines are heavy by nature; they require hoists for installation in aircraft. *Lighter* engines, however, are still a good design objective.

General Guidelines

Two guidelines are general, the first being designing to target cost. In conventional practice, companies approve design projects based on *estimated* rather than *target* costs. There is a difference. A target cost is a basis for killing a bad project; that is, if design sees that the components or procedures specified in the design will exceed the target cost, which is carefully set based on target sales and profit, kill the project.

This guideline is not likely to increase chances of killing projects with good potential; rather, the explicit target cost has a positive motivational effect. Designers search, strive, and innovate until they *can* find a way to meet the target. With no targets for cost, designers are likely to set internal targets for themselves, such as how many exotic materials they can learn about and try out.

Guideline 2 is minimizing part counts, or in services, minimizing the number of operations. Having discussed this guideline to some degree, we simply note here that it is a general guideline in that it leads to lower cost, better quality, and easier production or service delivery.

PRINCIPLE: Cut the number of components in a product or service.

Design for manufacturing and assembly (DFMA) team at Digital Equipment Corp. designed a better mouse (computer accessory). New design cut screws from 7 to zero, assembly adjustments from 8 to zero, assembly time from 692 to 277 seconds; also cut material costs 47 percent, package costs 69 percent.

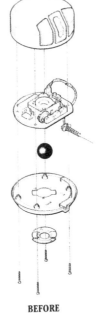

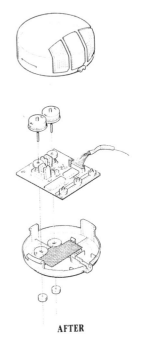

BEFORE   AFTER

Quality Guidelines

Guidelines 3 through 6 pertain particularly to quality.

Requirements

Guideline 3 is a good starting point in designing for quality: Find out customers' precise requirements or marketing's best estimates of them. Requirements may take the form of speed, brightness, smoothness, size, and so forth. Designers must be clear on the matter, because one of their jobs is to transform requirements into design specifications and tolerances.

This is *not* a minor issue. Since firms typically have failed to keep their designers in touch with customers, specs have often been based on guesswork or on specs designed for another customer or the average customer. As a result, suppliers often cite "ambiguous specifications" as the cause of a quality problem: "We produced to your specifications and then found you really didn't mean it" or "Your tolerances are impossible for anyone in the industry to achieve, so we just did things in the standard way."

Such complaints imply that the supplier is blaming the customer for not stating requirements clearly. While the customer surely deserves some blame, it is partly the supplier's fault. The third guideline says to the designer (or design-marketing team), "Don't wait for the customer to come to you. It's your job to know the requirements before proceeding." Following the guideline not only avoids quality problems; it is also an effective way to become a design partner with the customer, thus increasing the chance of continued business.

Standard Materials and Procedures

Guideline 4 states that the designer should favor standard materials, parts, and procedures. Nonstandard versions are risky because of lack of knowledge about their performance.

In 1981 to 1982, Xerox hired a consulting firm to assess its failures of the prior decade and chart a course of corrective action. One consultant observed that Xerox was loaded with bright engineers who, for lack of competition, focused their talents on developing machines with "incredibly complex technology." The consultant continued:

> Mere mortals could not develop these machines. The machines showed it. Everything inside a Xerox machine was special. You could not go out and use a normal nut. It had to be a specially designed nut. The concept of using as many standard parts as possible was not even thought of.[8]

The design complexities led to extensive field service to make sold copiers work right. The high cost of quality, as well as high costs of all special parts, opened the door to competition (which actually was good medicine for Xerox).

Now Xerox, along with many other companies, has firm policies on use of standard parts. Some apply the guideline quantitatively. For example, a copier manufacturer could set a limit of, say, 25 percent new parts in a new copier model, an opinion survey firm may limit the number of questions on a survey form, or a fast-food company may limit the number of allowable operations in a new process for delivering a new food item to a customer. While it might seem that such restrictions could stifle creativity or effectiveness, they may have the opposite effect: By not spending time designing new screws and locations for drill holes, or complex multistep forms or fast-food procedures, designers may have more time to be creative or thorough on what counts, and explore new materials, technologies, and competitors' procedures.

Process Capability

Guideline 5, designing to *process capability*, imposes two requirements on the designer. First, the designer is one of the parties *held responsible* if the design cannot easily be produced or provided using normal equipment, facilities, or service people (presuming those resources are properly maintained and capable). That responsibility extends to equipment in a supplier's company. These increased responsibilities lead to the second requirement: The designer must get familiar with process capabilities, including those of outside suppliers. (Process capability may be expressed quantitatively: See the discussion of the C_{pk} index in Chapter 15.)

Tolerances and Specifications That Don't Strain Capabilities

Guideline 6 is designing to the capabilities of "normal" machines and people. Companies that have tested their processes using *process capability study* techniques have often found that many tolerances cannot be met dependably, and

---

[8]Gary Jacobson and John Hillkirk, *Xerox: American Samurai* (New York: Macmillan, 1986), pp. 178–79.

some not at all, by existing machines. For manual tasks process capability is hard to test, since humans are very adaptable and some are more capable than others. Still, it is probably true that most specifications for human work are hard and sometimes impossible to achieve consistently. It is up to the designer to prescribe *realistic, attainable* tolerances and specifications.

Producibility Guidelines

The producibility guidelines apply to manual as well as automated processes, but in different ways. Manufacturers sometimes find that a product designed by these guidelines may be so simple to assemble manually that there is no point in automating. On the other hand, automation is complex and costly when the item's design is complex and "unfriendly" for processing by automated equipment. These *product design* guidelines nicely complement the *process design* guidelines discussed later in the chapter.

Easy to Grasp and Not Too Heavy

Guidelines 7 and 8 are related. Can two fingers grasp it easily, and lift it? If so, a common robot gripper would probably work. If grasping the part requires a difficult five-finger, arm-and-wrist contortion, with the right knee underneath to support the weight, finding an automated or robotic way of handling the part would be difficult.

Usually, what makes it easy for a human to grasp and lift also makes it easy for a robot, and vice versa. However, there are exceptions. For example, a robot can be equipped with suction-cup "fingers" to pluck cardboard lids off boxes of incoming materials. IBM uses such grippers in several of its newly robotized assembly plants.

Weight has been a problem in these early years of robotic assembly. Heavy-duty robots cost too much and incur high wear-and-tear costs. Thus, there is interest in trying to design lighter parts.

Easy to Pack

Traditionally, thought and care were applied only to the final pack, not to the many previous times the product or its components go in and out of containers. JIT, kanban, and robotics require exactness in containers and packing, and one element of the solution, according to guideline 9, is designing containers to fit the part. The other element where it makes sense is designing parts that have no odd protrusions or surfaces that inhibit precise, easy packing and unpacking.

Simple Assembly and Fastening
and Avoidance of Angles and Squeezes

Guidelines 10 and 11 concern fastening and assembly *difficulty*. Attention to those guidelines is a key reason why prices have plunged dramatically for hand calculators, clocks, radios, telephone sets, keyboards, and personal computers. Today those products fasten together with hardly any screws.

At one time screws and bolts were the preferred, indeed, almost universal, fasteners. Today's feeling is that, while bolts and screws are cheap and have excellent holding power, they are detrimental to manufacturability: They require too many "hands," too much fumbling, and too many wasted turns before the final, effective turn. Push it, snap it, clamp it, glue it—but don't screw it.

Simplified Design: An Example

In words alone, the producibility guidelines may seem valid but not critical. Example 3–1 illustrates their importance.

EXAMPLE 3–1   **DESIGN FOR PRODUCIBILITY AND ROBOTICS[9]**

Figure 3–3 shows an assembly diagram for a simple product. Redesign the assembly for producibility and robotics.

Solution
First, evaluate the present method in terms of the strict and well-defined requirements for assembly by a robot. Then simplify the design.

FIGURE 3–3
Assembly Using Common Fasteners

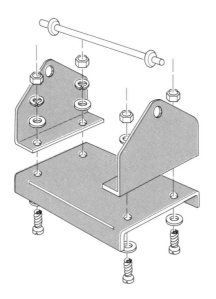

[9]Adapted from G. Boothroyd and P. Dewhurst, "Product Design . . . Key to Successful Robotic Assembly," *Assembly Engineering*, September 1986, pp. 90–93. Used with permission.

TABLE 3–3
Approximate Robotic Assembly Time—Bracket-and-Spindle Assembly

Part	Repeats	Time(s) (seconds)	Operation
Screw	4	12	Place in fixture
Washer	4	12	Place on screw
Base	1	3	Place on screws
Bracket	1	3	Position on base
Washer	2	6	Place on screw
Lock washer	2	6	Place on screw
Nut	2	12	Secure bracket (requires tool change)
Spindle	1	3	Insert one end in bracket (needs holding)
Bracket	1	3	Position on base and locate spindle
Washer	2	6	Place on screw
Lock washer	2	6	Place on screw
Nut	2	12	Secure bracket (requires tool change)
Totals	**24**	**84**	

Step 1: Robotic assembly. The robot starts by putting four bolts upright into four pods in a special fixture, one at a time. Then it puts a washer on each bolt. Next, the robot must position the base so the holes line up with the four bolts—a difficult alignment unless the holes are large. The robot's next tasks are to grab a bracket, position it, and secure it at each end with a washer, a lock washer, and a nut. Tightening the nuts requires that the robot return its ordinary gripper to the tool rack and fasten its "wrist" to a special nut-turning device; then, after the nuts are tight, switch back to the ordinary gripper.

Table 3–3 gives estimated times for the seven tasks described (some done more than

FIGURE 3–4
One-Piece Base and Elimination of Fasteners

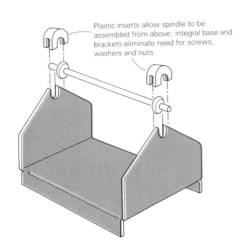

Plastic inserts allow spindle to be assembled from above; integral base and brackets eliminate need for screws, washers and nuts

FIGURE 3–5

Design for Push-and-Snap Assembly

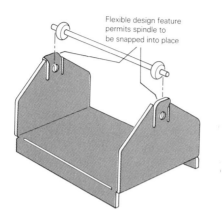

Flexible design feature
permits spindle to
be snapped into place

once), plus five more. The estimate of 12 seconds for assembling the two nuts may be optimistic. It assumes that bolts or nuts have special self-alignment features so threads will engage correctly and not bind or get cross-threaded.

The robot continues by inserting the spindle into one bracket hole and then moving the second bracket to receive the spindle. Since the robot has only one hand, it cannot hold the spindle and move the second bracket into place at the same time. It must move a fixture into place to hold up the spindle momentarily. Finally, the bracket is fastened down with washers and nuts.

The complete set of tasks includes insertions in several directions, requiring an elaborate, costly robot. The total assembly time is 84 seconds, of which 86 percent is fastening. Of the 24 parts in the assembly, 20 are just for fastening. Are all those bolts, nuts, and washers really necessary? Perhaps not. But they are common and cheap, and assembly designers routinely choose such means of fastening.

Step 2: Simplified design. One way to simplify the design is to look for simpler ways to fasten the brackets. But why fasten them? Isn't it possible to make the brackets and base as one piece? It is, as Figure 3–4 shows. In that design, plastic inserts secure the spindle; both spindle and inserts may be assembled from above, which allows use of a simpler, cheaper type of robot with no special grippers or holding fixtures. There are only 4 parts, and a robot could assemble them in, say, 12 seconds. That improves output and productivity by 600 percent (from 43 to 300 assemblies per hour).

There may be better solutions. If specifications permit, the spindle could be made from material that will bend or flex. Then a two-piece design, as in Figure 3–5, will be possible. Now assembly consists of just one step and one motion: Snap spindle downward into place. The simplest of robots may be used.

Now, however, the design has been made so simple that using a robot begins to seem like "overkill." If a robot were used, the parts would have to be presented to the robot on some sort of carrier—probably loaded by hand. Clearly it is just as easy—or even easier—to do the whole assembly by hand. Save the robot budget for tasks difficult for humans.

Formal Programs for Effective Design

The design guidelines complement and enhance programs for design effectiveness that are well established in industry. One older industry practice is a formal **design review**[10]—a series of formal meetings and studies aimed at identifying design defects and recommending design improvement. The design guidelines of Figure 3–2 are natural additions to a company's design review criteria. Some companies require a design review for all new products: computer software, manufactured goods, and services.

Design review is conducted by a team other than that assigned to the design project. In one approach, the design review team is composed of experts who have about the same skills as the design project group; they may be from another division, corporate headquarters, or an outside consulting firm. Alternatively, the design review team may be made up of "users"—people from operations, marketing, purchasing, quality, safety, and so forth who have to live with the design.

Another formal program directed toward effective design is **value engineering (VE)**, which is presented in Chapter 7 as a purchasing technique also known as *value analysis (VA)*. Example 3–1 resembles some of the examples in value engineering manuals from the 1960s. However, VA/VE has, as its main goal, reduction in cost, primarily material cost; improving producibility is considered a byproduct. Thus, while the techniques of VA/VE *could* have results like those in Example 3–1, they might not. To sum up, we may simply say that the techniques of VA/VE overlap the effective design guidelines presented in this chapter.

Measuring and Controlling Design Performance

The design guidelines in Figure 3–2 concern design activities. To close the loop, there must be measures and controls that are consistent with the guidelines. The exact wording and numerical targets for measurement must be worked out separately in every company. Thus, the following are just general measures of design effectiveness:[11]

Number of parts used or number of operations. A smaller number is preferred.

Percentage of standard parts or standard procedures used. This may be expressed as a target or a minimum percentage.

Use of existing manufacturing resources. The idea is to avoid new equipment and the need to hire or train for new skills.

---

[10]See John M. Groocock, *The Chain of Quality: Market Dominance through Product Superiority* (New York: John Wiley & Sons, 1986) pp. 133–40 (HF5415.157.G76).
[11]Adapted from David A. Waliszewski, "The JIT Starter Kit for Design Engineering," *Conference Proceedings, American Production and Inventory Control Society,* 1986, pp. 358–60.

Cost of first production run or service delivery. A low cost indicates that the design is realistic and producible or deliverable.

First-six-month cost of design changes. A low cost indicates thorough design.

First-year cost of field service and repair, returns, and warranty claims. A low cost indicates a design that does not exceed process capabilities.

Total product cost. This is an overall result of effective design and success in designing to target cost.

The above kinds of measures and controls close the design loop, allowing managers a means of assessing the quality and productivity of design and development activities. Perhaps most importantly, they suggest opportunities for improvement.

Consumer demand for new and improved goods and services creates a concurrent demand for new and improved transformation processes in operations and supporting functions. The next section addresses the role of process innovation in improvement efforts.

PROCESS INNOVATION: THE OTHER HALF OF IMPROVEMENT

Chapter 2 noted that in our rapidly changing world, every region or country has the same fears: How can we stay competitive? A popular answer is: Spend more on research and development. The theory is that more spending yields more inventions, which, in turn, translate into new goods and services that improve the economy and everyone's welfare.

But does the theory hold up? That is the question addressed in Figure 3–6, a collection of facts and comments gleaned from a *Business Week* report. (While it refers to the United States, similar concerns have been voiced in Canada, Britain, and other Western countries.)

Several points emerge from Figure 3–6. First, we see that invention does not necessarily lead to goods and services. Second, the United States (and other Western countries) are good at invention but not so adept at application; Japan, on the other hand, has excelled at application. Competitiveness depends not so much on how much is spent as on what the spending is for. Third, process innovation—essential for transforming inventions into marketable goods and services—is what is most lacking in Western countries such as the United States. Finally, the ideal global competitor (perhaps nonexistent in any single country today) is strong in *both* product invention and process innovation.

Other factors of concern in process innovations are *technology*, often in the form of automation, and the *people* who design and carry out process improvements (or get caught up in them). Interactions between these variables are considered next.

FIGURE 3–6

Competitiveness: From Invention to Useful Goods and Services

Facts

- America has 15 million companies; no other nation comes close.
- America has 5.5 million scientists and engineers, double the number of Japan.
- Americans have won more Nobel prizes than the rest of the world put together.
- America spends almost twice as much on R&D as Japan and Germany combined.

Comments

- "The Japanese would gladly give us all the Nobel prizes. . . . They're not worth a damn thing unless they're converted into products."

    H. John Caulfield, director of the Center for Applied Optics at the University of Alabama in Huntsville

- "The more inventive ideas the U.S. dreams up, the farther it will fall behind. Each one will be just another opportunity for a foreign rival to out-innovate a U.S. company in producing it. [Japan's] awesome machine for converting new scientific discovery into marketable products is living proof of that."

    Rustum Roy, director of the Science, Technology & Society Program at Pennsylvania State University

- "American companies don't like to build things—they like to make deals. . . . Our large organizations have become purchasing agents."

    C. Gordon Bell, R&D vice president of Ardent Computer Corp.

- ". . . we put twice the resources into product innovation as we do into process innovation. . . . Japan does just the opposite."

    Arden L. Bement, Jr., TRW's vice president of technical resources

Source: Otis Port, "Back to the Basics," *Business Week Special Report on Innovation in America*, June 16, 1989, pp. 14–18.

PROCESS TECHNOLOGY: PEOPLE AND AUTOMATION IN PERSPECTIVE

In 1947, the word *automation* was coined by John Diebold and D. S. Harder, to define any "self-powered, self-guiding and correcting mechanism," and was later extended to include all elements of the "automated factory." Another extension of the definition added office and clerical procedures.[12] People have made increasing use of machines to amplify human abilities since the dawn of recorded time; it certainly didn't start in the 1940s. Few words, however, have evoked as much emotion and socioeconomic discourse as "automation."

Recall from Chapter 2 that the post-World War II years emphasized production *quantity* in order to meet demand that had gone unsatisfied during the war. Automation fit the bill. In many ways, however, another war started—a war between people and machines.

---

[12]*The 1990 Information Please Almanac* (Boston: Houghton Mifflin Company, 1989), p. 551.

People and Machines

Between 1945 and 1955, U.S. industry suffered over 43,000 strikes.[13] Canada and England had similar labor strife. Japan, Germany, and other countries whose industrial capacity had been reduced to rubble during World War II had their own problems, including unemployment and politically induced labor agitation by Marxists, anarchists, and other groups.

Twentieth-century industrialists have rallied around a technological solution to the labor problem: Replace labor with machines—in other words, automate. How valid is that rationale today? Consider the following;

Strikes: A relatively minor problem throughout the industrial world today.

Human relationships: Much improved during the 1980s.[14]

Militant labor: Transformed into an "improvement engine" in a number of companies (notably in Japan).

Labor costs in manufacturing: Down from over 50 to about 15 percent since 1855.[15]

Labor availability: Competent, low-cost labor widely available "offshore."

Causes of process variability: Awareness of many causes other than labor, including ambiguous specifications for purchased materials and services, poor upkeep and maintenance, lack of quality control, and treatment of suppliers as adversaries.

Productivity and quality: New awareness of potent ways to simplify, cut wastes, upgrade processes, and improve quality with *existing* equipment.

In view of the above, why the automation fervor? Some say that automation is a necessary strategy for beating the competition. Ian Brammer, chief executive of the Australian Technology Transfer Council, calls it "extraordinary . . . [to consider] that techniques such as [computer-integrated manufacturing] are basic strategies. These never have been and never will be."[16]

Once we filter the rhetoric, we see that there *is* substance to the calls for automation and there *is* still a labor problem to which machines can respond. That problem is humans' inherent variability. It is hard for a person to perform a task the same way and in the same amount of time over and over again. Variability of method harms quality. Variability of cycle time (time needed to

---

[13]David F. Noble, *Forces of Production: A Social History of Industrial Automation* (New York: Alfred A. Knopf, 1984), p. 25.

[14]In October 1986, a Chicago seminar audience of about 400 people from many firms was asked, "How many of your companies have experienced improved labor relations in the past five years?" Nearly all hands went up. "How many have experienced worse relations?" Just one hand was raised.

[15]Patrick L. Romano, "Management Accounting: Change Is Needed in Accounting Systems for Advanced Manufacturing Environments," *Nexus*, Summer 1987, pp. 12–13.

[16]"The Resurgence of Western Manufacturing" (Keynote address, Value-Adding Manufacturing Conference, sponsored by Productivity, Inc., Chicago, October 1–3, 1986).

perform a task) hinders meeting schedules and dependably serving the customer.

Perhaps it is time to restate the link between competitive strategy and automation. The restatement is in the form of three axioms with three caveats:

1. *Process improvement* is an essential competitive strategy.

2. Automation is one tactic.
   Caveat 2.1: Automation is expensive. Less costly ways of improving processes ought to be sought first.

3. Humans' inherent variability makes automation more desirable.
   Caveat 3.1: Human variability has its good side, namely flexibility to react to change.
   Caveat 3.2: People have one attribute that makes them superior to any machine (aside from a few out of science fiction novels): brainpower. Without brainpower in the workplace, further process improvement would come to a halt.

With those points in mind, we may look critically at what industry has been doing about process improvement. First we examine human potential. Later in the chapter, we consider automation, along with other ways to improve process technology.

Unleashing Human Potential: Staff Cuts

The 1980s was a decade during which the phrase "lean and mean" helped market a growing health and fitness industry to baby boomers who were reaching the middle-age-spread years. It also described organizations, after a considerable reduction in the number of salaried managers and support staff personnel.

Financial deals—mergers, leveraged buyouts, corporate downsizing, and the like—caused many of the layoffs. Deliberate efforts to cut overhead, or *burden*, and reduce the hierarchical organizational levels (from 12 to 3 in some cases) were responsible for others. Unfortunately, experienced, trained, valuable human resources have been turned out to join the ranks of the unemployed; it takes time for them to become reemployed, learn new jobs, and turn productive again. Clearly, those are negative consequences for industry, the economy, and—most of all—the affected people.

There is, however, a positive side. The *functions* performed by the laid-off employees were generally unnecessary, wasteful, and unprofitable. (Recall the problems of staff specialization discussed in Chapter 2.) Companies found that legions of managers and staff personnel *inhibit* customer service and *prevent* attainment of human potential. Operating personnel weren't expected to make decisions, solve problems, and improve processes, and they weren't asked to; staff specialists were around to do that. Such an approach excluded line personnel—often the most knowledgeable people around.

PRINCIPLE: Ensure that line people get first crack at problem-solving—before staff experts.

Perhaps the invisible hand of free enterprise grasped the problem and made a needed correction. The resurgence of Xerox Corporation, as described in Figure 3–7, is a case in point. At Xerox and other companies that have followed similar paths, staff-size reductions have helped integrate successive stages of development. Rather than pass designs from one functional department to another (e.g., design engineering to drafting to detailing to manufacturing engineering

FIGURE 3–7

The Decline and Rise of Xerox

Xerox Corporation was the darling of Wall Street in the 1960s. Some veteran financial analysts claim that the Xerox 914 copier was the most successful product ever launched, and Xerox's stock prices soared.

In the 1970s, complacency set in. Sizable R&D expenditures in the copier division yielded poor results. Large projects ended up being canceled; a few new copier products were launched, but were not considered successes. While Xerox stood still, Canon, Kodak, and IBM entered the plain-paper copier business and became tough competitors. Xerox stock prices plunged.

What was the problem? According to chief executive David Kearns, the blue-collar work force could not be blamed. "Let's face it," he said. "The poor productivity of white-collar people puts blue-collar people out of work."*

Deborah Smith, vice president of personnel in Xerox's Business Systems Group, explained the growth of layers of management: "Somebody would do something out in the field and . . . would send a report into the region. The region had somebody who did nothing but check over . . . and consolidate all the materials. Headquarters would check it over, consolidate it some more, then send it up the line. You had checkers checking checkers. It was ridiculous."†

In late 1981, Xerox acted. Within one month, Xerox's work force had been trimmed by 2,000, including whole departments. The staff in Smith's department was halved. In 1982 and 1983, Xerox cut 13,923 more employees worldwide. Most of those were white-collar and indirect employees.

It cannot be proved that the staff reductions corrected Xerox's problems. It is clear, however, that Xerox is a strong performer again. Its 10-series copier was launched in late 1983. By the end of 1985, Xerox had sold or rented 750,000 units and regained 12 percentage points in its world share of the mid-range copier market.‡

Further, Xerox's top-of-the-line copier, the 9900, was developed by 300 to 350 people in only two and a half years. The new lean organization features fewer departments and approval levels as well as fewer people. Daniel W. Cholish, chief engineer for the project, says that in the past it would have taken 1,500 people and five years.§

The same problems—too many people in too many departments and layers—plagued Xerox's marketing organization as well. Product planners all over the world argued their points of view to copier division headquarters in Webster, New York. Much later, disputes went to corporate headquarters in Stamford, Connecticut, for further argument. What did get done took much too long, and product costs were too high.

*Gary Jacobson and John Hillkirk, *Xerox: American Samurai* (New York: Macmillan, 1986), Chap. 23.
†Ibid.
‡Ibid., p. 4.
§"Xerox Halts Japanese March," *The New York Times*, November 6, 1985.

to maintenance engineering), people attack them as an integrated team. The customer—the next process—is no longer very far away.

Staff cuts make the firm *lean*; reorganization of remaining resources helps make it *mean*. We consider those effects next.

Unleashing Human Potential: Circles, Cells, and Flexibility

We have seen how staff reductions help bridge gaps among staff specialties. Likewise, gaps among line operatives must be bridged in order to bring about line involvement in process improvement.

In the late 1970s, Western visitors to Japan were mesmerized by the apparent potency of *quality control circles.* Japan's QC circles contributed as many as 100 times more suggestions per employee than Western companies could elicit. In short order, quality circles (as most Westerners call them) were organized from Melbourne to Calcutta, Cape Town to Oslo, and Montevideo to Anchorage. The results were favorable, but not much more so than certain other programs, such as suggestion plans. It now seems clear that most quality circles were organized in a way that *avoided* a customer focus—that is, they excluded next processes. Figure 3–8 illustrates.

Part A of the figure shows two examples of a quality circle composed of five people in a single department. The first consists of four welders and a supervisor, while the second has four order-entry clerks and a supervisor. Those circles could meet every day and never hear a complaint about the quality of welds or errors in recording customer requirements. Also, the circles would not be inclined to discuss causes of delays in forwarding their outputs. Since their customers are not in the circles, the circles will discuss shared aggravations: room temperature, lighting, company recreation and benefits, work hours, and so forth. While all deserve to be discussed, they are only indirectly related to serving a customer.

Part B of Figure 3–8 shows how to organize quality circles for process improvement. This type of circle is hard to organize, because it requires moving people and equipment out of functional departments. Here an order-entry clerk is teamed up with the "customer" who processes the order at the first production operation: a saw operator. Their equipment—an order-entry terminal and a saw—are moved close together. Extension is accomplished by adding more maker-customer pairs from other departments: a welder and welding equipment, a grinder and grinding equipment, and a packer and packing tools and supplies.

The five operations become one, a **work cell** (or simply **cell**). The engineering term for the concept is **group technology**, because several technologies are grouped together.

In North America alone, hundreds of companies have organized thousands of work cells in recent years. Cells are rarely organized for the purpose of creating quality circles; rather, they are formed to eliminate bulk handling of stock across long distances, slash total inventories and delays, cut out many clerical transactions, eliminate potential scrap and rework, and greatly shorten throughput time.

FIGURE 3–8
Quality Circles: Incorrect and Correct Concept

A. Incorrectly organized: Quality circles composed of employees from same department or shop

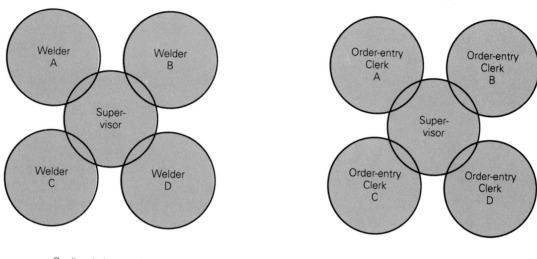

Quality circle — welding

Quality circle — order-entry

B. Correctly organized: Quality circle composed of a chain of
   provider-user pairs — formally organized into a work cell

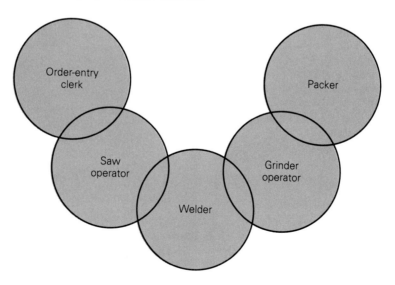

While most cells have been formed for reasons other than quality circles, one result is a group that can scarcely avoid some quality circle behaviors. The welder who closes a seam incompletely will very soon hear about it from the grinding machine operator at the adjacent workstation. The two are a team whether or not they care to be. A "bad pass" from the first team member to the second gets prompt attention. (The same effect is unlikely if the five people stay in dispersed departments and merely meet as a coordinating group now and then.)

PRINCIPLE: Get to know the customer.

The next step can be to formally sign up cell members as quality circles. Then they receive training in analyzing process variability, causes of defects, and other problems; additional discussion of quality circles occurs in Chapter 4.

In some manufacturing companies, cells, especially those composed of machines, are known as **flexible manufacturing systems (FMSs)** or **flexible manufacturing cells (FMCs)**. While at one time the two terms had different interpretations—FMSs were robot- and computer-driven, while FMCs were not—the

FIGURE 3–9
Flexible Manufacturing Systems (FMSs)

Defining Characteristic of FMS*		*Underlying Principle of Operations Management†*
A manufacturing process designed so that the production line may be rebalanced often, rapidly matching output to changes in demand.	→	Produce and deliver at the use rate (or a smoothed representation of it).
Involves mixed-model scheduling and multiskilled operators.	→	Cross-train for mastery of multiple skills.
Involves standardization of equipment for quick changeover times.	→	Cut setup and changeover times.
Involves design of the production line to allow workers to do more than one job.	→	Cross-train for mastery of multiple skills.
Involves design to cut down on transportation time between lines.	→	Cut work in process (waiting lines), throughput times, flow distances, and space.

And, *in practice,* an FMS provides *direct* support for the following principles:

Make it easy to make/provide goods or services without error—the first time.
Convert multichannel flows to single-channel lines.
Arrange the workplace to eliminate search time.
Seek to have plural rather than singular work stations, machines, cells, and flow lines for each product, service, or customer.

*Thomas F. Wallace and John R. Dougherty, *APICS Dictionary,* 6th. ed. (Falls Church, Va.: American Production and Inventory Control Society, 1987), p. 12.
†See Figure 1–2.

terms are sometimes used synonymously today. The definition of FMS in the dictionary of the American Production and Inventory Control Society suggests that the FMS/FMC concept has a promising future, for it *directly* supports several of the principles of operations management. Figure 3–9 illustrates.

The ideas behind FMS/FMC and work cells are powerful ones; they extend throughout production/operations management, and ought to extend throughout the company. Indeed, we shall learn more about them later in this book (Chapters 6 and 18), but we introduce them here for several reasons:

1. Cells and FMS/FMCs unleash human potential. The brainpower and flexibility of people, when freed from the confines of functional-area organization, are thought to be among the most effective of the process improvement tools.

2. Work cells and FMS/FMCs can be found in a wide range of organizational settings; from simple, small, human-paced flow lines in service-providing offices to large-scale, computer-controlled, robotic flow lines that manufacture automobiles. The central idea—*flexibility improves processes*—is common to all.

3. The flexibility built into cells and FMS/FMCs promotes readiness, the first "time zone" in operations management. Cells and FMS/FMCs link up successive operations, thus creating a fertile environment for better and more timely response to changes in customer requirements.

4. High technology is not a prerequisite for work cells and FMS/FMCs; in fact, it works the other way around. Cells and flexibility are often low-cost, low-tech avenues to process improvement. When—indeed, *if*—there is a need for high technology, it is cheaper and more effective when applied *after* cells and FMS/FMCs exist.

To summarize a bit: We have seen that process improvement does not demand highly technical equipment. Organizational efforts that get people-power going is the first step—maybe the only step that a company needs for awhile. Does automation follow? Not necessarily; simplification of process technology should be considered next.

SIMPLIFYING PROCESS TECHNOLOGY

Putting high-tech automation into processes is costly—costly to design, buy or build, operate, and maintain. It can also promote costly management mistakes, such as overproduction to "prove" that the new technology was needed. Therefore, the first priority is to try to simplify processes and escape, postpone, or at least reduce some of the costs of automation.

We will address simplification in four ways: (1) eliminating the need for an entire process, (2) eliminating steps, elements, or *operations*, (3) quick setup or changeover (a special case), and (4) what is known as *preautomation*.

Processes and Operations

Before discussing actual examples of process simplification, we need to clarify what we mean by doing away with a *process*, or an *operation*, and see how that affects output goods and services. Consider Figure 3–10; it might represent resources used by a large hospital in its campaign to get its employees to give up smoking.

Three processes, each consisting of four or five operations, are shown. Output from the data-collection process (A)—employee smoking history, for example—is fed to the statistical data analysis process (B); its output, in turn, goes to report preparation and distribution (C). We won't concern ourselves with where the reports go. We will look at operations within processes: The five in C have been improved; those in A are mixed, two improved and two needing attention; and process B—well, let's just say that much work is needed.

In this example, it would be nice if the hospital could improve operation 2 and eliminate operation 3 in process A, and eliminate process B entirely. Elimination of hospital-performed statistical analysis avoids any costs of improving

FIGURE 3–10

Processes vs. Operations

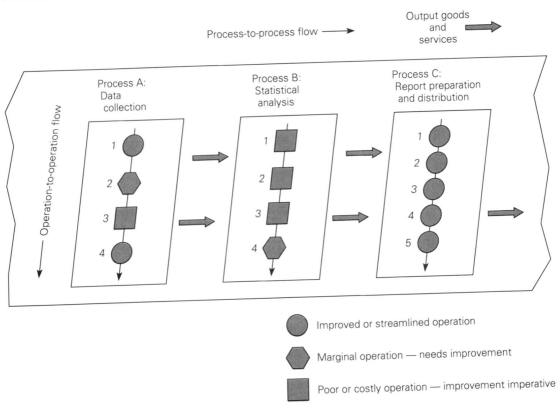

that process, and also removes bad effects of that process on output goods and services, a report in this case. Maybe an outside consulting firm could be hired to perform any statistical analysis the hospital needs.

Assume that operation 3 in process A involves conducting follow-up interviews of employees who failed to return a previously distributed questionnaire. Elimination of that operation would mean that data in the hospital's smoking report (and perhaps in future reports as well) would be limited to volunteer responses, a limitation that the hospital administrator might not oppose. The data-collection *process* would remain, however.

One final comment about our hospital: We can't assume that the report preparation and distribution *process* is needed simply because its *operations* are streamlined. If the process itself is needed, fine; but too many reports tend to foul the air more than tobacco smoke (especially when they get burned at the city dump). Process elimination might need to be considered.

Process Elimination

The ideal way to simplify process technologies is to do away with the process that requires the technology. Consider the following example.

Omark Industries, a medium-size company (now a subsidiary of Blount, Inc.) whose main product is saw chain, was one of the first North American companies to initiate just-in-time production. At Omark's saw chain plant in Guelph, Ontario, the first JIT efforts were on slashing machine setup times and production lot sizes, which led to large reductions in storage racks for holding the produced lots. Then machines were moved close together, filling the spaces where storage racks once stood. Packing machines together created several flow lines. The result: Manufacturing lead time (raw material to finished goods) dropped from 21 to 3 days.

At that point, JIT was stuck. The obstacle was the large central heat-treating department. (Heat treating hardens the saw chain blades so that they stay sharp longer.) The central heat-treating oven could not be integrated into the flow lines. A high-tech solution was considered: several small laser heat-treating stations put into the flow lines. Not feasible.

The next proposal was to replace the large heat-treating oven with several small ones, each positioned in the flow lines. Not necessary. Purchasing found a better solution: A suitable pretempered kind of steel that needed no heat treating. Thus, the Guelph plant eliminated the heat-treating process, including connected processes such as material handling, storage, work-order and move-ticket generation, and quality checking.

Work Element Elimination

The next best simplification approach is cutting out elements, or operations, of the process. An example is setup time reduction.

The Omark Guelph plant's successful effort to reduce machine setup time eliminated many work elements. For example, they drilled holes up through the bottom of 600-pound dies used in punch presses. Now operators attach an air hose to the die, and air goes down through the holes to raise the die slightly above the working surface. The operator then moves the die into place by hand, which avoids the need for a mobile crane, and several steps to bring it over and attach, hoist, move, lower, and detach the die. That simplification, plus a few more, cut setup time from *two or three hours to two minutes.*

There is almost no end to what industry needs to do in simplifying setup technology, because industry did hardly any in the past. Elaborate feasibility studies determined which machine to buy. However, most companies ran machines for their useful lives with virtually no modifications for quick setup. The assumption might have been that the machines' manufacturers knew best. Today, with just-in-time concepts forcing the issue, the belief is that equipment manufacturers design only for the general market and each machine buyer needs to modify the general-purpose machines for special uses.

For a particular customer, knobs and adjustment devices on general-purpose machines spell trouble. A descriptive slogan is: "If it can be adjusted, it will go out of adjustment." Even the cranks and knobs you don't need must be adjusted. That increases the number of things that can go wrong, yielding poor-quality output and frequent need to stop and readjust. The owner of a modern stereo or VCR, with all its buttons and knobs, knows exactly how that goes.

While modifying machines is important in setup time reduction, there is more to it. Some guidelines for quick setup are considered next.

Quick Setup

Recall from Chapter 1: *Setup or changeover time is from good production to good production.* In other words, setup is timed from the end of previous production to the start of *good* production—all checks for quality and further adjustments completed—on the next product. With that definition in mind, let us consider a few guidelines for improving setup or changeover; some are shown in Figure 3–11.

FIGURE 3–11
Guidelines for Quick, Error-Free Setup

1. The best setup is *no* setup—a machine or process dedicated to just one type of the product or service.
2. Perform all possible steps external to the machine's operation.
3. Store setup implements close by—clean and ready to go.
4. Remove or immobilize unneeded adjustment cranks, knobs, or buttons.
5. Outfit machine with guide tracks, glides, stops, and locator pins.
6. Standardize machines, jigs, fixtures, fasteners, and operations.
7. Load work-piece and tool holders externally.
8. Simplify all fasteners.
9. The operator leads the setup reduction project.
10. For expensive equipment, have plenty of setup people.

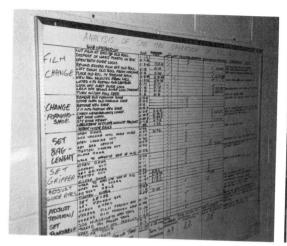
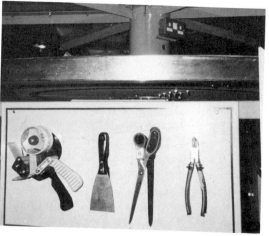

Quick setup at Microsoft Ireland in Dublin. Left: Detailed operator analysis for quick changeover of large packaging machine. Right: Setup tools positioned on *shadow board* at the machine.

Guideline 1 is for the ideal situation: when a single model (or a single type of customer) commands sufficient sales volume to warrant its own dedicated machine or process. In that case, there are *no* setups or process changes to worry about.

Guideline 2 is doing all possible setup steps while the process is engaged on its previous product, model, size, or color. That minimizes the time the process is stopped and nonproductive. Another way of stating this guideline is: Convert "internal" setup steps (while process is stopped) to "external" steps (while process is running on a prior job). For example, before a machine stops for the setup, fetch fixtures, cutting tools, adjustment tools, gauges, materials, supplies, and instructions, and put them close by.

Guideline 3, an extension of 2, could be reduced to "Be ready." Consider the pit crew at an Indianapolis 500 auto race: Crew members are at their stations with gas hoses, tires, and tire-changing devices in hand. Surgical teams in hospital operating rooms are similarly ready. Two factory examples are attaching hinged bolts to the machine or fixture so that they are always ready and keeping heavy fixtures, plates, or molds on hand in slings or chutes or on rollers.

Some equipment manufacturers advertise that their machines are designed for quick setup. Those claims can be only partially valid, however. The maker must design the machine with enough adjustments to appeal to users in different industries or market segments; then the machine can be produced in a certain volume in order to realize economies of scale. Therefore, according to guideline 4, since buyers have a limited range of uses for the machine, they should expect to devote some effort to immobilizing unneeded adjustment devices.

Guideline 5, on the other hand, calls for adding features. The additions are usually simple, cheap devices that make a guide path. The machine cannot be bought with all needed guidepath features because its maker cannot know what sizes and kinds of tool holders and work pieces will go into it.

Guideline 6 is standardizing all devices and procedures. This starts with the machine itself. Too many brands of computers, typewriters, drill presses, and operations expand exponentially the array of supporting tools, loaders, carriers, adjustment devices and sets of instructions needed. On a single machine, this guideline applies to such things as bolts: If all bolts are the same size, only one size of wrench is needed in machine setup.

Guideline 7 specifies having extra holders for the work piece and tools. Think of a fondue party where each person loads a backup fondue fork while having another fork already loaded in the hot oil.

Guideline 8 specifies simplifying all fasteners. Some examples are: Use simple clamps instead of bolts that require multiple turns; use tapered bolts that fit deeply into the hole, reducing the number of turns required; and use U-shaped washers, pear-shaped clamping holes, and cutaway threaded bolts and bolt holes to speed up washer and bolt installation (see Figure 3–12).

Guideline 9 calls for the operator to lead the project to cut setup time. At most of Omark's plants—as is traditional—engineers received the initial setup reduction training and led the projects. It soon became clear that machine operators could and should do the leading. The operator is the expert on the process, and most setup reduction requires experience and common sense, not an engineering degree.

Guideline 10 means throwing people at setup if the equipment is costly. The idea is to have plenty of people so that setup steps can be done in parallel instead of sequentially. A large crew handles pit stops in prestige auto races because the racing cars and the prize money are worth hundreds of thousands of dollars. Until recently, it was common in industry to assign only one or two people to set up a complex, expensive machine.

PRINCIPLE: Cut setup and changeover time.

FIGURE 3–12
Quick Washer and Bolt Installation

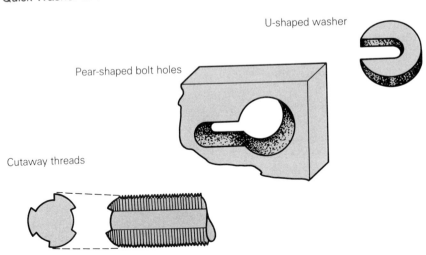

The 10 guidelines explain how to make setup easy for people to perform. Next we consider how to make it easy (or at least possible) for machines to perform a task.

Preautomation

Preautomation is what must be done to the work space to make it possible for a machine to work. Preautomation boils down to the *two Ps: propinquity* and *precision*.

Propinquity means "nearness." In preautomation, it means having all implements and work pieces within reach of the machine's mechanical or robotic device. When implements and pieces are not near the machine, automated conveyors could get them there. It is much better, however, to automate over short distances using the machine's own "arms" than via extenders, such as distance-spanning conveyors. Alternatively put, a company's automation capital is best spent on automating the process itself—where value is added to the product—rather than on the delays between value-added processes. Scenes of conveyors loaded with materials crisscrossing factories may dazzle the eye, but they often mask a faulty automation concept—too little attention to location.

Precision, the second "P," applies to placement of all implements and pieces—that is, the tools, fixtures, and work pieces must be in exact, known positions, or the machine's arm will reach and miss its target.

Preautomation is vital for both programmable automation, such as robots, and nonprogrammable "hard" automation. But preautomation can be daunting and expensive. If most machines and people are organized into departments by process (for example, a metal-stamping department), those departments and their resources must be almost totally taken apart and rearranged into cells and flow lines, which is how propinquity is achieved. This is costly as well as disruptive to established human relationships.

After relocation, the processes must be subjected to the severe discipline called for by the second "P," precision. Nonautomated work requires little workplace precision, because people are inherently flexible. Human eyes, hands, arms, legs, and feet compensate for lack of precision in the workplace. Since a machine lacks flexibility and sensory power, automation requires that time and money be spent on a massive campaign of workplace precision, including exact placement of parts boxes and tools.

Given all these difficulties, are robotic and highly automated factories feasible? Fortunately, we can sidestep the question because *anything that makes it easy for a machine to do something makes it easy for a human to do it.* In other words, the two Ps, if applied to manual operations, will eliminate long travel distances and wasteful search motions. Preautomation makes the human work force far more cost effective; therefore, preautomation is well worth doing *even if the automation is never installed.*

PRINCIPLE: Arrange the workplace to eliminate search time.

Actually, automation is unstoppable because the limits of human improvement will be reached sooner or later. A rational improvement approach is to install automation process by process. At a given process, the decision point is reached when human variability becomes a problem and human performance limits resist further improvement. A term for this is *problem-pull* automation as opposed to *technology-push* automation.

In this section, we considered tactics for simplifying process technologies, including preautomation. The next topic is the automation itself.

LOW-GRADE PROCESS AUTOMATION

While automation is expensive, some low-grade forms of it are less so. Examples are automatic tool changers, loaders and unloaders, machine start and stop devices, and fail-safe devices.

Automatic tool changers often are sold as a normal component of modern machines; older machines can have them added on. The other three examples usually are add-ons, and preferably added to machines already organized into machine cells.

Here's how it works. Suppose that a saw and a drill press have been moved together as two of the machines in a machine cell. A former saw operator now runs both machines, first sawing a piece and then drilling it; saw, then drill; saw, drill. Cells allow this—one person to work more than one process in the product flow—and cells eliminate bulk handling (and trips to stockrooms) between processes.

There are other low-cost ways to improve the process. The operator, if encouraged, may think of several, such as "How about an automatic feed on the saw? Then I could start the saw, and while the saw runs, I could clamp a sawed piece in the drill press."

The operator might also be able to recommend a machine start mechanism that will enhance safety as well as cut out manual steps. Here is an example:

> Clamp a piece to the saw's work surface, and go to the drill. With the operator at a safe distance from the saw blade and at the drill, the act of stopping the drill trips a switch to start the saw.
>
> Clamp a sawed piece under the drill, and go to the saw. The act of stopping the saw trips a switch to start the drill press.
>
> Repeat.

Similar mechanisms may be added to all the machines in a multiple-machine cell so that one operator can tend several machines in a circular route. This low-cost but potent form of low-grade automation was first perfected at Toyota and some of its key suppliers. Sometimes one operator tends as many as 15 machines.

The fourth type of low-grade automation is a fail-safe device. *Fail-safing* ensures that the work will not be passed on to the next process if it has some glaring defect or omission: a missing part, too many or two few screws, no instruction manual, no label, and so forth. "Electric eyes," limit switches, and weigh scales are among the devices that can make such checks.

Low-grade automation concepts have some uses in office and information processing work and in personal services; for example, operators using type-writers, point-of-sale terminals, dental equipment, data-entry equipment, and coffee machines. Simple modifications to such equipment can cut out and sim-plify changing, loading and unloading, and starting and stopping. In view of the high error rates in such work, the greatest need is probably for fail-safe devices. Top-notch fast-food franchisers make liberal use of fail-safing devices such as timing bells and lights for indicating that the pizza or fries have cooked long enough. On the other hand, in printing, copying, report preparation, and publishing, there is a notable lack of devices—such as sensitive page-weight scales—for checking for missing or duplicate pages.

PRINCIPLE: Automate incrementally when process variability cannot otherwise be reduced.

Despite the attractions of low-grade automation, many industries tend to skimp on it and eagerly embrace high technology, our next topic.

HIGH TECHNOLOGY

Processes that clearly have benefited from today's range of high-tech equipment include retail transaction processing, check processing, newsprinting, copying, cooking, welding, painting, and contour metal cutting. The large number of less-visible examples includes ultrasonic cleaning and laser surgery. There are also many more examples of high-tech processes with dubious track records. We begin our discussion with the more beneficial types of high-tech equipment.

Data Capture and Transfer

Electronic data processing is old enough to be considered mature technology, but computers are being linked to a variety of high-tech processes for data capture and transmission. For example, laser-based bar coding captures data on a retail or wholesale transaction, and microwave transmitters forward the data to a remote computer. Microwave transmission also enables banks to create funds transfer networks and national newspapers and magazines to be printed at scattered sites for quick delivery to local-area subscribers.

Other uses of high technology include facsimile copying (faxing), microwave cooking, laser welding, robotic painting, and numerically controlled (NC) con-tour metal cutting. The latter two technologies may be combined with computers and other technologies to create **computer-integrated manufacturing (CIM)**.

Robotics

After decades of talk, industry finally began to use robots in large numbers in the 1980s. Automobile manufacturers worldwide have installed thousands of robots. Recently, robots are being used for a far wider range of applications than the traditional welding and painting that had long seemed to be the limits of their use. When it began commercial production in September 1988, the Diamond-Star Motors plant in Bloomington–Normal, Illinois, was the most technically advanced auto assembly plant in the world. Some of its 470 robots do apply paint and sealant and weld unitized bodies together; but others install doors, hoods, tailgates, and windows. In final assembly, other robots perform tasks never automated before, including installation of instrument panels, tail lamps, windshields, front seats, wheels, and tires.

Despite apparent successes like Diamond-Star, light assembly work has been more easily adapted to robotics than has auto assembly. Several Japanese consumer electronics producers use robots extensively in assembling videocassette recorders, radios, and other products. Apple's Macintosh assembly plant was the first in the world to employ large numbers of robots for personal computer assembly. Two or three years later (around 1985), IBM began equipping its plants for robotic assembly. One milestone was IBM's Austin, Texas, plant which was the world's first all-robotic computer assembly plant to make the company's laptop PC Convertible computer.[17] That plant was able to employ simple, inexpensive up-and-down-motion robots because the product was designed for vertical layered assembly. Older products and some more complicated new ones cannot be assembled so simply. Multidirectional assembly requires multiaxis robots. The following box describes robots' axes of motion.

Robots can also be equipped with some humanlike sensory faculties that provide limited "search" capability. Sensory devices may allow the robot to select

---

Types of Robots

Robots are sometimes classified by number of axes of motion. A simple three-axis robot can go up-down, left-right, and in-out. The motions correspond to the X, Y, and Z axes in solid geometry. The three-axis robot often is used only for picking up a part or tool and placing it somewhere; hence, it is sometimes called a *pick-and-place* device or robot.

By one definition, a "real" robot must be more humanlike. It must have six axes of motion, much like a human shoulder-arm-elbow-wrist-finger assemblage (see Figure 3–13). Such a robot can sweep across perpendicular and horizontal axes and revolve, for example, turn a screw. Most heavy-duty robots are the six-axis type. A seven-axis robot also "walks" (moves on a track) to and from adjacent workstations.

FIGURE 3–13
Robot and Six Standard Movements

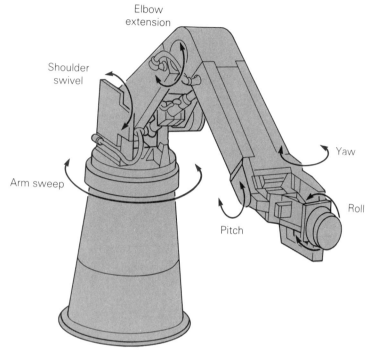

Reproduced with permission from Chris Voss, "Managing New Manufacturing Technologies," OMA Monograph 1, September 1986.

a screw from a jumbled box, move it to where a drilled hole is *supposed* to be, and gently search for the hole's exact location before inserting and tightening the screw.

Sensory-equipped robots are alluring but expensive. Often there is a cheaper solution: Put the object—screws, tools, or parts—into tubes, magazines, or "egg-crate" boxes oriented for easy grasp by the robot (or a person, for that matter); also, drill or locate the receiving holes precisely, and perhaps with tapered shapes for easier receipt of the incoming part. Search time is wasted time.

Programmable Robots for Flexible Automation

Since robots can be programmed to make a wide variety of products or product variations, they seem to fit the times. Popular books and articles assert that consumers are demanding one-of-a-kind variety; therefore, industry must invest

---

[17]"IBM's No-Hands Assembly Line," *Fortune*, September 1986, pp. 105–109.

FIGURE 3–14
Robot Selecting Display Screen

Courtesy of IBM Corporation

in *flexible automation*, including robots. So far, however, most of the world's robots are used in repetitive production; robotic production lines typically produce hundreds of thousands, even millions, of identical units per year. What's going on?

Actually, the programmability of robots generally *is* used on robotic production lines. A robot that selects component parts from a tray and assembles them must be programmed to reach to successive positions within the tray (see Figure 3–14). Another job commonly given to robots is that of placing boxes on a pallet with each pallet position different from the preceding one.

In the electronics industry, a common claim among robot users is that their robots will be reprogrammed for the next generation of product. Since electronic products have very short life cycles—sometimes only a year or two—that sounds like a real benefit. The temptation to replace the current generation of robots with a new, enhanced set next year could upset the prediction of reuse, however.

A greater benefit of robotic assembly lines may turn out to be "disaster recovery"—that is, when a product launched on the robot line fails in the marketplace, the line can be reprogrammed to produce something else. The rate of product failures is high, especially in electronics; examples are the Texas Instruments 99-4A home computer and IBM's PC jr.

Disaster recovery is poor with hard automation. In fact, some experts say that extensive hard automation in Detroit—multistation transfer lines making engines, transmissions, and so forth—is a key reason for the inflexibility and high costs that have plagued the auto industry. In contrast, according to a spokesperson at IBM's Austin plant, the robotic line can assemble "any electronic product that is no bigger than two feet by two feet . . . printers, other PCs—or toasters."[18]

Numerically Controlled Machines

Some of the above points apply generally to another type of flexible automation: **numerically controlled (NC) machines**. Think of the years of apprenticeship and experience needed to become a skilled machinist, someone who can transform blocks of metal into intricate parts to tolerances of 0.0001 inches. But NC machines cut metal (or wood or plastic) to form intricate parts automatically. The machines are numerical in that they are instructed digitally. Instructions used to be on punched paper tape; newer NC machines contain them in a computer program.

Some NC machines (and some non-NC machines as well) include rotary magazines holding various cutting tools. The computer program can select the proper tool and perform the cut (or drill, ream, bore, or broach); then it can turn the work piece, select another tool, and make a different cut. Continuing in this manner, the machine does all the setups and can produce a component that formerly had to be routed to several different machines performing different operations.

Some NC machines are fronted by a carousel holding several work pieces, such as castings, wood blocks, and hunks of plastic. The computer directs the machining of one component and then—with no human attention—may move another work piece forward and machine it.

NC machines originally were conceived for small-volume, high-variety pro-

---

[18]Ibid.

duction. Experts felt that in the age of flexible automation, NC machines would do the precision machining and robots the "mindless" loading, unloading, and assembly. For high-volume production, simpler, cheaper, and faster hard automation would do, since NC machines and robots are slow. So far, however, many NC machine applications have not followed this recipe—that is, many NC machines are making a narrow mix of parts. Whether this is cost effective depends on wage rates and availability of machinists, degree of precision required, machine reliability, and so forth. One factor that drives companies to use NC machines for narrow-mix production is the high cost of programming. Once a program is developed for machining a certain part, it may be reused to produce the same part intermittently at high volumes throughout the year.

NC machines seem to have made their biggest splash in contour metal cutting; examples are parabolic or other specially shaped structural members for aircraft. Conventional machines sometimes can do such machining, but highly skilled machinists—a scarce commodity—are required.

Like many technologies, NC machines have solved fewer problems than expected. Raw material imperfections, inevitable small programming errors, and variations in tool wear cause problems. In many cases, machinists or other technicians must still be on the scene or close by. Noble quotes a skilled NC machinist at a large aerospace plant on why NC machines still need tending:

> The engineers who design the fixtures have probably never worked in machine shops. The programmers are usually people who have a lot of computer experience but not people who've ever worked in a machine shop. . . . And the tooling and programming and production departments don't work together well. Every time something has to be changed, . . . all kinds of paper has to be filled out. . . . It takes so long . . . that the part gets behind schedule. . . . So usually they find some way of making an adjustment by manually moving the machine or changing the fixture or something so they can get around changing the program. A lot of time it involves changing the fixture or shimming a part, which is another problem, because the tools are not supposed to be altered on the fixtures.
>
> At any rate, the operator usually ends up the one who is responsible for trying to figure out how to correct all the mistakes that were made in tooling and programming and make the part work out right. It used to be that in most machine shops they had a little department where people could deburr (take the burrs off parts) after they're finished. Now that's developed into a whole thing where people are trying to repair the parts that have come off the machines. A lot of times they end up making kind of a crude part on a machine; then somebody outside the shop has to sand or file it or do whatever is necessary, or just put in on a conventional milling machine to get the dimensions that it was supposed to have in the first place.[19]

---

[19]David F. Noble, *Forces of Production: A Social History of Industrial Automation* (New York: Alfred A. Knopf, 1984), pp. 344–45.

The above quotation should be taken not as an indictment of the NC machine concept, but as an indication that the age of automation is still young and full of problems. The problems are gradually being solved (especially by breaking down the barriers from one specialty to another), however, and NC machines lie on the path of progress. Computer-integrated manufacturing, discussed next, is further along on that path.

Computer-Integrated Manufacturing

In a narrow sense, computer-integrated manufacturing (CIM) is a machine cell controlled by a microcomputer and assisted by one or more robots. Connecting two FMSs for automatic work flow requires a host computer and automated material handling. The handler commonly is an automated guided vehicle (AGV), which follows a current-carrying wire embedded in the floor or a stripe on the floor. That combination more clearly is CIM. Now we add *computer-assisted design (CAD)*, *computer-assisted engineering (CAE)*, and *computer-assisted process planning (CAPP)* to tell the FMSs what to make and how to make it. Two final enhancements to our CIM example are an automatic system for selecting and forwarding raw materials and another for sending on finished pieces.

Should the CIM system also include an *automatic storage and retrieval system (AS/RS)* to hold semifinished parts? Usually not. The AS/RS is a symptom of poor coordination among production stages. With the flexibility of NC machines and the central control of the computer, coordination should be good—that is, parts should be made at one stage only hours or a day or two before use at the next stage. Storing parts in an AS/RS makes sense only if they are to be kept in storage for, say, a week or more.

As we have mentioned, some early uses of flexible automation, including CIM, were for making large lots of a narrow range of certain parts—which meant paying for flexibility but not using it. An old but now partly discredited view may also enter the picture: Costly machines must be kept busy (highly utilized) whether or not demand exists. In those cases, an AS/RS may *seem* necessary for holding the glut of parts made well in advance of need. These conceptual problems of CIM use surely will be ironed out in the future.

The CIM concept is usually thought of in connection with machining. CIM is also being developed—but in a different way—for high-volume assembly. In high-volume assembly, there generally is a single flow path. The CIM computer need not be involved in complex routing, machine scheduling, parts storage, and machine utilization issues. Its jobs are simply to keep parts flowing to the assembly robots or hard-automated assembly stations and to adjust machines when models change. IBM, Hitachi, Apple, NEC, Northern Telecom, AT&T, and a number of other companies in electronics have developed CIM assembly systems. Some of their CIM-assembled products include small computers, keyboards, printers, line cards for telephone exchanges, and video- and audiocassette recorders.

JUSTIFYING AUTOMATION AND OTHER IMPROVEMENT PROJECTS

Automation is costly and raises break-even points. Therefore, it is hard to justify financially—no doubt about it. Some advocates have called for a certain degree of faith; they feel that financial justification should be replaced by acceptance of automation as inevitable. Some assert that automation is the only way for a high-wage society to compete. Perhaps that is true, but a number of industry's boldest automation projects have had technological troubles or have failed to earn a return on the capital invested.

On the other hand, many feel that worthy improvement projects, whether they involve automation or not, fail to survive company approvals simply because critical benefits are left out, or treated in an offhand manner as "intangibles." Consultant Michael O'Guin believes that economic analyses of improvement projects usually fail to accurately account for protection of "a company's market position." He presents a more thorough kind of economic justification that incorporates sales and market share, plus an overall weighting factor based on five key "customer-perceived quality" factors: consistency, lead time, personnel training, rate of product innovation, and sales engineering support. These vital competitive factors are rolled into a firm's traditional return-on-investment formulas.[20]

SUMMARY

Innovative people produce ideas for new and improved products, services, and processes. Product and service line planning includes research, design, and development. Technological breakthroughs are welcome, but a steady diet of small, continual improvements pays off over the long run.

Product and service development may be pursued via a number of research strategies. Leaders tend to adopt offensive strategies—to beat the competition to the marketplace, to control patents for possible licensing to other firms, and so forth. Followers tend to adopt the defensive strategy of letting others do the research and development. Research strategies may focus on new and improved processes. Product research tends to be more expensive than process research, since highly paid scientists and engineers are usually engaged in the former.

Tightened management of design and development is a strong industry trend. Designers are being brought into closer contact with the rest of the business. For example, manufacturing engineers are assigned to work with product designers, or both are placed under a single manager. The goal is for designers to become knowledgeable in process capabilities so that product designs are pro-

---

[20]Michael C. O'Guin, "A New Approach to Capital Justification," *P&IM Review with APICS News*, November 1989, pp. 35–36, 42.

ducible or deliverable. That knowledge must extend to outside suppliers' processes as well as in the designer's own company. Thus, designers often work with designers in a supplier's firm.

Designers also team up with marketing and the customer to better understand customer needs. One goal is to provide what the customer wants with fewer parts or operations that must be planned and controlled, thereby cutting costs and prices. Standardization and modular designs help make variety possible with fewer parts or operations.

Design practices are being controlled through policies or guidelines. General guidelines include designing to target cost and minimizing part counts or number of operations. Guidelines for improved product quality include ensuring known, unambiguous customer requirements; using materials with known quality; and setting specifications that do not strain machine or operator capabilities. Producibility guidelines include designing parts that are easy to grasp, not too heavy, shaped for ease of packing and unpacking, assemble easily, and avoid difficult angles or squeezes.

Producibility guidelines are useful in designing for automation and robotics or for facilitating manual assembly. Some feel that for assembly, screws and bolts, though cheap and easily available, often add many unnecessary steps and therefore should often be avoided in favor of snap-in or glued connections or one-piece constructions.

Formal programs for controlling design include value engineering (known as *value analysis* among purchasing people) and design review. Design reviews, required in some companies, are conducted by a separate group of experts who look for flaws and ways to improve the design.

To close the design loop, measures and controls are needed. The effective design guidelines can generally be quantified—for example, number of standard parts used in a design—and used as a control tool by management.

Advanced process technologies and automation can be costly, and high process costs can make products unappealing to the customer. As companies learn to elicit cooperation from employees, improvement strategies change: less emphasis on getting rid of labor and more options for employing people *and* machines in the cause of process improvement. Also, caution is necessary when considering automation, because technology can cut out the mindpower and high degree of flexibility that people possess.

In the 1980s many companies, such as Xerox, found that trimming layers of management and excess staff employees could pave the way for direct action and simple solutions to process problems. An effective catalyst is breaking up departments and reorganizing people into work cells, that is, lining up people and their machines the way the product flows. Each employee's customer (the next process) is thus nearby and must be directly and accurately served. The next step may be for the work cell to become a quality circle trained in process analysis techniques. In some companies, cells form flexible manufacturing systems or cells (FMS/FMC), which directly support a number of the principles of operations management, and provide a bridge—if needed—to high technology infusion.

While processes may be automated—usually at high cost—it is better to first look for ways to simplify them. One simplification is to eliminate the need for the process; for example, by using pretempered steel and avoiding the need for heat treatment in a furnace. Another simplification is to cut out work elements, which is the main aim in reducing time to set up a process. The best setup is *no* setup—a dedicated process. Quick setup calls for off-line preparation, immobilizing unneeded machine features and adding others, standardizing and simplifying tools and other implements, putting operators in charge of quick setup, and having plenty of setup people. Still another simplification is preautomation. Automation won't work unless everything is nearby and precisely placed (the two Ps: propinquity and precision). Preautomation also makes it easier for people to do the job efficiently and without error, often staving off the need to buy the automation.

In the same spirit, low-grade forms of automation can be effective: automatic tool changers, loaders and unloaders, start and stop devices, and fail-safe mechanisms. Each reduces the number of tasks that the machine tender must do, and fail-safe devices can catch human errors before the work moves onward.

High technology is hard to manage; sometimes it pays off and sometimes it just drains cash. Heavy-duty robots have found some productive application in welding, painting, and assembly. Smaller robots are coming into wide use in light assembly work, such as in electrical and electronic products. Seven-axis robots simulate human motions, and the more common six-axis robots do all but "walk." Sometimes cheaper three-axis "pick-and-place" devices have enough motions to be useful, particularly since their use forces more precision (preautomation) in placement of tools and materials.

There is a customer niche for flexible automation: programmable machines capable of making semicustom products in small quantities; robots and numerically controlled (NC) machines qualify. Many such machines are being used to gain precision but at the expense of flexibility, making large volumes of a narrow mix of parts. Still, if the product fails in the marketplace, the company can reprogram the machines to make something else—a form of disaster recovery protection.

NC machines can take over much of the work of skilled machinists. Nevertheless, machine tenders are sometimes needed because of program errors and variability in materials and conditions.

When NC machines are fed by computer-controlled robots, flexible manufacturing systems are formed. If two or more FMSs are combined with computer-assisted design, engineering, and process planning, the result is computer-integrated manufacturing (CIM). Another type of CIM is the computer-controlled robotic assembly line. Tight control of processes by a host computer can eliminate the need for stockrooms. Therefore, such high-tech automation as the automatic storage and retrieval system (AS/RS) may actually be rendered unnecessary by CIM technology.

Though costly, and often installed at the expense of people's jobs, automation has a role. It is more justifiable as the limits of human improvement are reached.

KEY WORDS

Engineering changes
(ECs)
Producibility
(manufacturability)
Early supplier
involvement
Design review

Value engineering (VE)
Cell (work cell)
Group technology
Flexible manufacturing
system (FMS)
Flexible manufacturing
cell (FMC)

Preautomation
Computer-integrated
manufacturing
(CIM)
Numerically controlled
(NC) machine

REFERENCES

Books

Frand, Erwin A. *The Art of Product Development.* Homewood, Ill.: Dow Jones-Irwin, 1989. (HF5415.153.F73).

Gibson, John E. *Managing Research and Development.* New York: John Wiley & Sons, 1981.

Klein, Janice A. *Revitalizing Manufacturing: Text and Cases.* Homewood, Ill.: Irwin, 1990 (HD9725.K57).

Schonberger, Richard J. *World Class Manufacturing: The Lessons of Simplicity Applied.* New York: Free Press, 1986 (HD31.S3385).

Shingo, Shigeo. *A Revolution in Manufacturing: The SMED System.* Stamford, Conn.: Productivity Press, 1985.

Shingo, Shigeo. *Non-Stock Production.* Stamford, Conn.: Productivity Press, 1988 (TS155.S45613).

Suzaki, Kiyoshi. *The New Manufacturing Challenge: Techniques for Continuous Improvement.* New York: The Free Press, 1987 (HD9720.5.S98).

Periodicals

Entrepreneur. *High Technology Business.*

REVIEW QUESTIONS

1. What is innovation? How does it relate to customer expectations?

2. How does the "tinkerer's toolbox" affect product, service, and process improvement?

3. What types of companies are most likely to pursue an offensive research strategy? Why?

4. How may a company's financial commitment to R&D be measured?

5. How does uncertainty affect R&D strategy?

6. What are two ways in which a firm can avoid the "over-the-wall" problem in product design and development?

7. What are the marketing issues in product designers' pursuit of part count reductions?

8. What connection, if any, should product designers have with suppliers of purchased parts and materials? Explain.

9. What are the guidelines for effective design?

10. How can managers determine the effectiveness of design and development activities?

11. What is the effect of ambiguous specs on quality?

12. Explain the meaning of *designing to target cost*.

13. When is designing for robotics also designing for human assemblers?

14. Why are bolts and screws sometimes thought to be poor types of fasteners?

15. What is a design review?

16. Which human weaknesses favor automation?

17. Which human strengths favor people over machines?

18. How do staff cuts and elimination of management levels tend to aid the cause of process improvement?

19. What are work cells and machine cells, and how can they stimulate process improvement?

20. What is a flexible manufacturing system or cell? What principles of operations management does it directly support?

21. Give *real* examples from the service sector (not from the book) of two ways to simplify process technology.

22. Why can't companies *buy* machines fully equipped for quick setup?

23. How does preautomation stave off the need for investing in automation?

24. How is low-grade automation different from high technology?

25. What is flexible automation, and how is it commonly misapplied?

26. How necessary is it for robots to have all the motion and sensory capabilities of humans?

27. Why don't NC machines totally eliminate the need for machine tenders?

28. What are the necessary components of computer-integrated manufacturing, and how can CIM reduce the need for automated storage?

29. What often-hidden factors should be given more emphasis in a proposal to spend capital on an improvement—automated or nonautomated?

PROBLEMS AND EXERCISES

1. You are the president of a company in serious financial trouble. Your production costs are higher than those of all your competitors. You realize that these costs must be cut drastically and that the measures used must include

layoffs of nonessential personnel. From your knowledge of organizational functions and departments, where would you look first for cuts? Think about this carefully; doesn't everyone supposedly cut costs by performing their jobs effectively? What does *nonessential* mean? Does the goal to cut *production* costs in this problem affect your answers?

2. The chapter made reference to Bell's invention of the telephone in 1876, and mentioned that more than a century of innovation transformed Bell's device into our contemporary telephone systems. List some of the major innovations in this evolution, in both products and telephone-related services. For each item on your list, indicate whether it was a technology breakthrough or a refinement (modest, perhaps) of existing technology.

3. What kind of research strategy do you think has been followed in each of the following industries in the past decade or two? Discuss tendencies in both product and process research.
    a. Major appliances.
    d. Home construction.
    b. Supermarkets.
    e. Physical fitness and health.
    c. Banking.
    f. Home entertainment.

4. Obtain the most recent copy of *Business Week's* annual R&D scoreboard (it typically is published in June for the preceding year). For one of the industry classifications, prepare a table similar to Table 3–2. Decide who are the better R&D companies and tell why you think so.

5. A chess clock is housed in a molded plastic case that is closed up in the rear with two flat plastic square plates. (Chess clocks contain two identical clocks, one for each player in a timed chess game.) The three pieces are represented below, along with a sample of the special screw that goes into the eight

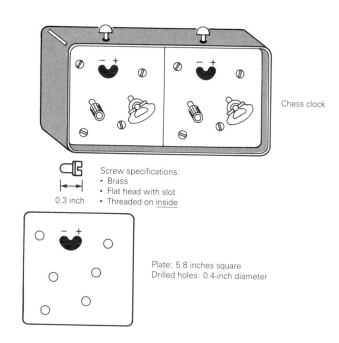

Chess clock

Screw specifications:
• Brass
• Flat head with slot
• Threaded on <u>inside</u>

0.3 inch

Plate: 5.8 inches square
Drilled holes: 0.4-inch diameter

drilled holes that fasten the clocks to the square plates. (Two other holes in the case and four holes and two "half-moons" in the squares are for clock adjustment. For purposes of this question, ignore them.)

Suggest two practical design improvements based on the guidelines in Figure 3–2. (Mention the specific guidelines you are using as the basis for your suggestions.)

6. Following are passages from an article on IBM's typewriter and keyboard factory:

> In the IBM Selectric System/2000 Typewriter, the new products are made with a layered design. The parts go together sequentially in one direction—from the bottom up—so that robots can do the job easily. There are many common fasteners [a limited number of different kinds], and nearly all screws were eliminated. Plastic molding offered many possibilities for more manufacturable designs.
>
> Detailed parts were combined wherever possible. Self-alignment reference points were designed for locating such things as posts and countersinks. Since robots are not efficient at finding a plug at the end of a wire, integrated packaging and solid connectors had to be used.
>
> The changes resulted in fewer parts and fewer adjustments. There are about 900 parts in the new typewriters, compared with 2,700 in the Selectric typewriter. The number of adjustments needed is down to six from 121 originally.[21]

The above description indicates use of some of the 11 guidelines for effective design listed in Figure 3–2. Which of these guidelines can you identify in the passage? Give brief explanations where required.

7. Faceplates that cover electrical wall outlets and wall switches fasten with one or two screws. Suggest a modification that would eliminate the need for screws. Would the benefits be significant? Explain. Can you offer any arguments *against* redesign to eliminate screws?

8. Play the role of dietician, fashion designer, architect, or financial portfolio designer. Describe the problems you can avoid with the proper degree of interaction with your suppliers.

9. At Monitor Manufacturing Company, product development engineers operate under a strict policy of frequent interaction with customers to ensure that designs match customer requirements. Still, customers view Monitor's designs as only average. What can the problem be?

10. When Mazda first came out with a rotary (Wankel) engine, there were serious performance problems. The public virtually quit buying the car, and Mazda's existence was threatened. Survival measures included sending design engineers all over Japan to sell cars. Besides cutting costs, what design engineering problem would this practice have helped deal with?

11. Tokyo Seating Company operates TRI-CON, a subsidiary manufacturing division in the United States. Some years ago, TRI-CON asked an American

[21]Mehran Sepehri, "IBM's Automated Lexington Factory Focuses on Quality and Cost Effectiveness," *Industrial Engineering,* February 1987, p. 66–74.

metal products company to bid on a contract to provide TRI-CON with metal seat pans for motorcycle seats. TRI-CON's "request for proposal" specified a steel gauge and little else. The American firm was uncomfortable with TRI-CON's minimal specifications and refused to bid. Why would TRI-CON say so little about the kind of seat pan it wanted?

12. GMF Robotics Corporation, a joint venture of General Motors and Fanuc of Japan, was the world's largest robot manufacturer in 1985. However, GMF laid off 30 percent of its work force in 1986, and industry analysts predicted that robot sales would fall 30 percent in 1987. Discuss the reasons for the falloff in sales of robots in industry, including comments about its effects on the economy.

13. As banks, retail stores, and manufacturers continue to adopt automated service production and equipment, how should company training programs change? How should wages and salaries be affected? Discuss, using examples.

14. Assume you are a manager preparing a financial justification for purchase and installation of a robot. You must include all costs and benefits regardless of their measurability. Make a complete list of all likely costs and benefits, separated into major and minor categories. Explain.

15. Seven bank tellers volunteered to form the bank's first quality circle. The human resources department conducted an attitude survey just before the quality circle was formed and again after it had been meeting for six months. The survey showed a dramatic improvement in morale and attitude. Further, the circle produced 38 suggestions in the six-month period. Is this quality circle well conceived? Do you think its results are excellent, or not?

16. Which of the following are examples of preautomation? Explain each of your choices.

    a. Placing all tools in labeled bins in a designated tool room.
    b. Moving all fixtures close to the machine.
    c. Designing inserts for material-handling containers to hold parts in designated locations.
    d. Moving similar machines together into functional (process) cells.
    e. Moving unlike machines together into product cells.
    f. Moving a die or mold storage rack out of a storage area and into the machine area.
    g. Installing simple roller conveyors between machines.

17. Following are three real examples of flexible manufacturing systems. Discuss whether each is being employed effectively. As much as possible, rank them in order of effectiveness.

    a. The FMS is composed of three 5-axis machining centers supplied with component parts and tools by five automatic guided vehicles (AGVs). The FMS produces a wide range of components, from cylinder heads to differential housings, in average lot sizes of 50. After machining, components go to a surface treatment robot station and a washing machine.

b. The FMS consists of eight machining centers with automatic tool changers and 90-tool magazines. It produces 531 different parts, usually in lots of 1. Four robot carriers move pallets holding up to 16 parts from one machining center to the next.

c. The FMS employs five 5-axis machining centers, each accessing at least 90 cutting tools. It includes an automatic storage/retrieval system, a 20-station pallet and part queue, three wire-guided vehicles, and a coordinate measurement machine for inspecting the parts. Production lot sizes range from 1 to 15 parts.

18. Which of the following is best suited for robotic assembly: (*a*) Assembling a clock consisting of a frame, faceplate, mechanism, backplate, and three screws; (*b*) assembling a clock into a plastic box, which requires inserting a bottom liner into the bottom box piece and then placing an instruction card, clock, and top liner on top; and (*c*) snapping the top box piece downward to engage with the bottom piece?

19. QuebecTron, Ltd., has a contract to assemble garage door remote controllers. It covers a two-year period with expected daily volume of 850 units. Purchased materials cost $8, and assembly labor averages $0.65 per unit. What are two strong arguments for installing a robotic assembly line and two strong arguments against doing so?

20. At Rocky Mountain tech, the basketball and skiing coaches have decided to employ the quality circle concept. Each circle will consist of the top five athletes on the team. The coaches' purpose is to try to tap their athletes' intelligence and thereby generate ideas that will improve the teams' effectiveness. Considering what makes quality circles work well or poorly, assess the likely results of the quality circle experiment for each coach.

21. Consider the setup steps commonly practiced by someone using an overhead projector in a lecture room. How could the setup be simplified and made more accurate?

22. Prison Production Company produces cord assemblies for electric lamps. Production is divided into four departments. The departments and their equipment are as follows: wire winding, four machines; rubber wire coating, two machines; plug molding, six machines; and cord assembly, five 3-person assembly lines. The board of directors has just approved a plan to automate some of the operations; cost cutting, better quality, and giving the prisoner-operators a more valuable factory experience are the main reasons. What do you suggest as the early steps in the plant conversions?

23. Would quality circles work well in improving performance of a hockey team? Of a group of students banding together to study? Discuss.

CASE STUDY   LINCOLN ELECTRIC COMPANY*

The Lincoln Electric Company is the world's largest manufacturer of welding machines and electrodes. Lincoln employs 2,400 people in two factories near Cleveland and about 600 in three factories in other countries. That does not include the field sales force of more than 200 persons. Lincoln's market share has been more than 40 percent of the U.S. market for arc-welding equipment and supplies, according to one estimate.

The main plant is in Euclid, Ohio, a Cleveland suburb. The plant layout is shown in Exhibit 1. There are no warehouses. Materials flow from the half-mile-long dock on the north side of the plant through the production lines to a very limited storage and loading area on the south. Materials used at each workstation are stored as close as possible to the workstation.

A plant just opened in Mentor, Ohio, houses some of the electrode production operations, which were removed from the main plant. The main plant is currently being enlarged by 100,000 square feet, and several innovative changes are being made in the manufacturing layout.

EXHIBIT 1
Lincoln Electric, Plant Layout

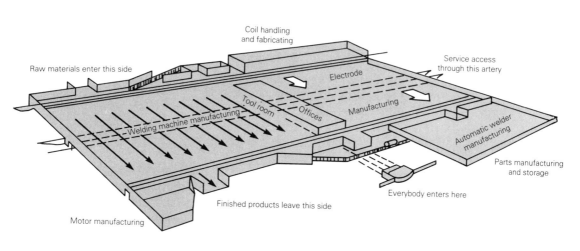

*Adapted from George A. Steiner, John B. Miner, and Edmund R. Gray, *Management Policy and Strategy; Text, Readings, and Cases,* © 1982, pp. 958–80. Used with permission of A. D. Sharplin, author of the case.

PRODUCTION AND MARKET INFORMATION

Products

The company's main products are electric welding machines and metal electrodes used in arc welding. Lincoln also produces electric motors ranging from
1 to 200 horsepower. Motors are about 8 to 10 percent of total sales.

The electric welding machines, some consisting of a transformer or motor
and generator arrangement powered by commercial electricity and others of an
internal combustion engine and generator, produce from 130 to over 1,000 am-
peres of electrical power. This current melts a consumable metal electrode, and
the molten material is transferred in a super-hot spray to the metal joint being
welded. Very high temperature and hot sparks are produced. Operators usually
must wear special eye and face protection, leather gloves, and often leather
aprons and sleeves.

Welding electrodes are of two basic types. The first is a coated "stick" electrode, usually 14 inches long and smaller than a pencil in diameter. The operator
holds these electrodes in a special insulated holder and must manipulate them
to maintain a proper arc width and pattern of deposition of the metal being
transferred. Stick electrodes are packaged in 6- to 50-pound boxes. The second
type of electrode consists of coiled wire, ranging in diameter from 0.035 to 0.219
inches. The wire is designed to be fed continuously to the welding arc through
a "gun" held by the operator or positioned by automatic positioning equipment.
The wire is packaged in coils, reels, and drums weighing from 14 to 1,000
pounds.

Manufacturing Processes

Electrode manufacturing is highly capital intensive. Metal rods bought from
steel producers are drawn or extruded down to smaller diameters. Then they
are cut to length and coated with pressed-powder "flux" for stick electrodes or
plated with copper (for conductivity) and spun into coils or spools for wire.
Some of Lincoln's wire, called *Innershield*, is hollow and filled with a material
similar to that used to coat stick electrodes. Lincoln is highly secretive about its
electrode production processes.

Welding machines and electric motors are made on a series of assembly lines.
Gasoline and diesel engines are purchased partly assembled, but almost all other
components are made from basic industrial products—for example, steel bars
and sheets and bare copper conductor wire—in the Lincoln factory. Components
such as gasoline tanks for engine-driven welders and steel shafts for motors and
generators are made by numerous small "factories within a factory." The shaft
for a certain generator, for example, is made from a raw steel bar by one operator
using five large machines, all running continuously. A saw cuts the bar to length,
a digital lathe machines different sections to varying diameters, a special milling
machine cuts a slot for a keyway, and so forth until a finished shaft is produced.

The operator moves the shafts from machine to machine and makes the necessary adjustments. Another operator punches, shapes, and paints sheet-metal cowling parts. One assembles steel laminations on a rotor shaft, then winds, insulates, and tests the rotors. Crane operators move finished components to the nearby assembly lines.

Market Information

Although advances in welding technology have been frequent, arc-welding products have hardly changed over the last 30 years. The most popular Lincoln electrode, the Fleetweld 5P, has been virtually the same since the 1930s. The most popular engine-driven welder in the world, the Lincoln SA-200, has been a gray-colored assembly, including a four-cylinder Continental "Red Seal" engine and a 200-ampere direct-current generator with two current control knobs for at least three decades. A 1980 model, SA-200, even weighs almost the same as the 1950 model. It seems likely that changes in the machines and techniques used in arc welding will be evolutionary, not revolutionary.

Lincoln and its competitors now market a wide range of general-purpose and specialty electrodes for welding mild steel, aluminum, cast iron, and stainless and special steels. Most of these electrodes are designed to meet the standards of the American Welding Society, a trade association. They are thus essentially the same in size and composition from one manufacturer to another. Every electrode manufacturer has a few unique products, but they typically constitute only a small percentage of total sales.

Lincoln's R&D expenditures recently have been less than 0.2 percent of sales. There is evidence that others spend several times as much as a percentage of sales.

Lincoln's market share has been between 30 and 40 percent for many years, and the welding products market has grown somewhat faster than industry in general. The market is highly price competitive. Variations in prices of standard products normally amount to only 1 or 2 percent. Lincoln's products are sold directly by its engineering-oriented sales force and indirectly through its distributor organization. Advertising costs amount to less than 0.25 percent of sales, one third as much as a major Lincoln competitor with whom the case writer checked.

A HISTORICAL SKETCH

In 1895, after being "frozen out" of the depression-ravaged Elliott-Lincoln Company, a maker of Lincoln-designed electric motors, John C. Lincoln took out his second patent and began to manufacture his improved motor. He opened his new business with $200 he had earned redesigning a motor for young Herbert Henry Dow, who later founded Dow Chemical Company.

Started during an economic depression and cursed by a major fire after only one year in business, Lincoln's company grew, but hardly prospered, through its first quarter-century. In 1906, John C. Lincoln incorporated and moved from his one-room, fourth-floor factory to a new three-story building he had erected in east Cleveland. He expanded his work force to 30, and sales grew to over $50,000 a year. John Lincoln was more an engineer and inventor than a manager, though, and it was to be left to another Lincoln to manage the company through its years of success.

In 1907, after a bout with typhoid forced him from Ohio State University in his senior year, James F. Lincoln, John's younger brother, joined the fledgling company. In 1914, with the company still small and in poor financial condition, he became the active head of the firm with the titles of general manager and vice president. John C. Lincoln remained president of the company for some years but became more involved in other business ventures and in his work as an inventor.

One of James Lincoln's early actions was to ask the employees to elect representatives to a committee that would advise him on company operations. The first year the advisory board was in existence, working hours were reduced from 55 per week, then standard, to 50 hours a week. In 1915, the company gave each employee a paid-up life insurance policy. A welding school, which continues today, was begun in 1917. In 1918, an employee bonus plan was attempted. It was discontinued, but the idea was to resurface and become the backbone of the Lincoln management system.

The Lincoln Electric Employees' Association was formed in 1919 to provide health benefits and social activities. It continues today and has assumed additional functions over the years. By 1923, a piecework pay system was in effect, employees got two-week paid vacations each year, and wages were adjusted for changes in the consumer price index. Approximately 30 percent of Lincoln's stock was set aside for key employees in 1914, and a stock purchase plan for all employees was begun in 1925.

The board of directors voted to start a suggestion system in 1929. The program is still in effect but cash awards, a part of the early program, were discontinued several years ago. Now suggestions are rewarded by additional "points," which affect year-end bonuses.

The legendary Lincoln bonus plan was proposed by the advisory board and accepted on a trial basis by James Lincoln in 1934. The first annual bonus amounted to about 25 percent of wages. There has been a bonus every year since.

By 1944, Lincoln employees enjoyed a pension plan, a policy of promotion from within, and continuous employment. Base pay rates were set by formal job evaluation, and a merit rating system was in effect. By the start of World War II, Lincoln Electric was the world's largest manufacturer of arc-welding products, with sales of $24 million.

Certainly since 1935—and probably for several years before that—Lincoln productivity has been well above the average for similar companies. Lincoln claims productivity levels of more than twice those for other manufacturers from 1945 onward. Information from other sources tends to support these claims.

James F. Lincoln died in 1965, and there was some concern that the Lincoln system would fall into disarray, profits would decline, and year-end bonuses would be discontinued. Quite the contrary: Each year since 1965 has seen higher profits and bonuses. Employee turnover is almost nonexistent except for retirements, and Lincoln's market share is stable.

COMPANY PHILOSOPHY

James F. Lincoln was the son of a Congregational minister, and Christian principles were at the center of his business philosophy. There is no indication that Lincoln attempted to evangelize his employees or customers—or the general public for that matter. The current board chairman, Mr. Irrgang, and the president, Mr. Willis, do not even mention the Christian gospel in their recent speeches and interviews.

Attitude toward the Customer

James Lincoln saw the customer's needs above all else. "When any company has achieved success so that it is attractive as an investment," he wrote, "all money usually needed for expansion is supplied by the customer in retained earnings. It is obvious that the customer's interests, not the stockholder's, should come first" [Lincoln, 1961, p. 119]. In 1947 he said, "Care should be taken . . . not to rivet attention on profit. Between 'How much do I get?' and 'How do I make this better, cheaper, more useful?' the difference is fundamental and decisive" ["You Can't Tell . . . ," p. 94]. Mr. Willis still ranks the customer as Lincoln's most important constituency.

Certainly Lincoln customers have fared well over the years. Lincoln quality has consistently been so high that Lincoln Fleetweld electrodes and SA-200 welders have been the standard in the pipeline and refinery construction industry, where price is hardly a criterion, for decades. The cost of field failures for Lincoln products was an amazing 0.04 percent in 1979. A Lincoln distributor in Monroe, Louisiana, says that he has sold several hundred of the popular AC-225 welders and, though the machine is warranted for only one year, he has never handled a warranty claim.

Attitude toward Stockholders

Stockholders are given last priority at Lincoln. This is a continuation of James Lincoln's philosophy: "The last group to be considered is the stockholders who own stock because they think it will be more profitable than investing money in any other way" [1961, p. 38]. Concerning division of the largess produced by incentive management, Lincoln writes, "The absentee stockholder also will get his share, even if undeserved, out of the greatly increased profit that the efficiency produces" [1961, p. 122].

Attitude toward Unionism and Employees

There has never been a serious effort to organize Lincoln employees. James Lincoln criticized the labor movement for "selfishly attempting to better its position at the expense of the people it must serve" [1961, p. 18]. Yet, he excused abuses of union power as "the natural reactions of human beings to the abuses to which management has subjected them" [1961, p. 76]. Lincoln stated that "Labor and management are properly not warring camps; they are parts of one organization in which they must and should cooperate fully and happily" [1961, p. 72].

The Lincoln attitude toward employees, reflected in the following quotations, is credited by many with creating the company's success [all taken from Lincoln, 1961]:

> The greatest fear of the worker, which is the same as the greatest fear of the industrialist in operating a company, is lack of income. . . . The industrial manager is very conscious of his company's need of uninterrupted income. He is completely oblivious, evidently, of the fact that the worker has the same need [p. 36].

> If money is to be used as an incentive, the program must provide that what is paid to the worker is what he has earned. The earnings of each must be in accordance with accomplishment [p. 98].

> Status is of great importance in all human relationships. The greatest incentive that money has, usually, is that it is a symbol of success. . . . The resulting status is the real incentive. . . . Money alone can be an incentive to the miser only [p. 92].

ORGANIZATION STRUCTURE

Lincoln has never had a formal organization chart. An open-door policy is practiced throughout the company, and personnel are encouraged to take problems to the person most capable of resolving them. Perhaps because of the quality and enthusiasm of the Lincoln work force, routine supervision is almost nonexistent. A typical production foreman, for example, supervises as many as 100 operators, a span of control that allows only infrequent operator-supervisor interaction.

Position titles and flows of authority do imply something of an organizational structure. For example, the vice president–sales and the vice president–electrode division report to the president, as do various staff assistants such as the personnel director and the director of purchasing. Using such implied relationships, it appears that production employees have two or, at most, three levels of supervision between themselves and the president.

PERSONNEL POLICIES

Recruitment, Selection, and Job Security

Every job opening at Lincoln is advertised on company bulletin boards, and any employee can apply for any job so advertised. External hiring is just for entry-level positions. People are selected by personal interviews—there is no aptitude or psychological testing. Not even a high school diploma is required except for engineering and sales positions, which are filled by graduate engineers. A committee of vice presidents and superintendents interviews candidates initially cleared by the personnel department. The supervisor with the job opening makes the final selection. In 1979, fewer than 300 of about 3,500 applicants interviewed by the personnel department were hired.

After one year, an employee is guaranteed not to be discharged except for misconduct. Each is guaranteed at least 30 hours of work each week. There has been no layoff at Lincoln since 1949.

Performance Evaluation and Compensation

Each supervisor formally evaluates all subordinates twice a year on "quality," "dependability," "ideas and cooperation," and "output." Employees who offer suggestions for improvement tend to receive high evaluations. Supervisors discuss individual performance marks with the employees concerned.

Basic wage levels for jobs at Lincoln are determined by a wage survey of similar jobs in the Cleveland area. Rates are adjusted quarterly with changes in the Cleveland area consumer price index. Insofar as possible, base wage rates are translated into piece rates. Practically all production employees and many others—for example, some forktruck drivers—are paid by piece rate. Once established, piece rates are never changed unless a substantive change in the way a job is done results from a source other than the person doing the job. Each December, a portion of annual profits goes to employees as bonuses. Since 1934, incentive bonuses have averaged about the same as annual wages and somewhat more than after-tax profits. The average bonus for 1979 was about $17,000. Individual bonuses are exactly proportional to merit-rating scores. For example, a person with a score of 110 gets 110 percent of the standard bonus as applied to his or her regular earnings.

Work Assignments and Employee Participation

Management has authority to transfer operators and to switch between overtime and short time as required. Supervisors have undisputed authority to assign specific parts to individual employees, who may have their own preferences due to variations in piece rates.

Participative management often connotes a relaxed, nonauthoritarian atmosphere. This is not the case at Lincoln. "We're very authoritarian around here," says Mr. Willis. James F. Lincoln stressed protecting management's authority. "Management in all successful departments of industry must have complete power," he said. "Management is the coach who must be obeyed. The men, however, are the players who alone can win the games" [1951, p. 228]. Despite this attitude, employees do participate in management at Lincoln.

Richard Sabo, manager of public relations, states: "The most important participative technique that we use is giving more responsibility to employees." Mr. Sabo says, "We give a high school graduate more responsibility than other companies give their foremen."

The advisory board, elected by the employees, meets with the chairman and the president every two weeks to discuss ways of improving operations. Every Lincoln employee has access to advisory board members, and answers to all suggestions are promised by the following meeting. Both Mr. Irrgang and Mr. Willis are quick to point out, though, that the advisory board only recommends actions. "They do not have direct authority," Mr. Irrgang says, "and when they bring up something that management thinks is not to the benefit of the company, it will be rejected" ["Incentive Management in Action . . ."].

Other Benefits

A plant cafeteria, operated on a break-even basis, serves meals at about 60 percent of usual costs. An employee association, to which the company does not contribute, provides disability insurance and social and athletic activities.

As to executive perquisites, there are none—crowded, uncarpeted austere offices; no executive washrooms or lunchrooms; and no reserved parking spaces. Even the company president pays for his own meals and eats in the cafeteria.

FINANCIAL MANAGEMENT

James F. Lincoln felt strongly that financing for company growth should come from within the company—through initial cash investment by the founders, retention of earnings, and stock purchases by those who work in the business.

Lincoln Electric Company does not borrow, and debt is limited to current payables. Even the new $20 million plant in Mentor, Ohio, was financed totally from earnings.

The pricing policy at Lincoln is succinctly stated by Mr. Willis: "At all times price on the basis of cost and at all times keep pressure on our cost." The SA-200 Welder, Lincoln's largest-selling portable machine, decreased in price from 1958 through 1965. According to Dr. C. Jackson Grayson of the American Productivity Center in Houston, Lincoln's prices in general have increased only one fifth as fast as the consumer price index since 1934. As a result, Lincoln is the undisputed price leader for the products it manufactures. Not even the major Japanese manufacturers, such as Nippon Steel for welding electrodes and Osaka Transformer for welding machines, have been able to penetrate the U.S. market.

Huge cash balances are accumulated each year preparatory to paying the year-end bonuses. Bonuses totaled $46.5 million for 1979. The money is invested in short-term U.S. government securities until needed.

EMPLOYEE PERFORMANCE AND ATTITUDES

Exceptional employee performance at Lincoln is a matter of record. The typical Lincoln employee earns about twice as much as other factory operators in the Cleveland area. Yet the labor cost per sales dollar at Lincoln, currently $0.235, is well below industry averages.

Sales per Lincoln factory employee currently exceeded $157,000. An observer at the factory quickly sees why this figure is so high. Each operator is proceeding busily and thoughtfully about his or her task. There is no idle chatter. Most take no coffee breaks. Many operate several machines and make a substantial component unaided. The supervisors are busy with planning and recordkeeping duties with hardly a glance at the many people they supervise. The manufacturing procedures appear efficient—no unnecessary steps, wasted motions, or wasted materials. Finished components move smoothly to subsequent workstations, and crane operators keep materials conveniently on hand.

The Appendix to this case summarizes interviews with two Lincoln employees.

CONCLUDING COMMENT

Richard Sabo, manager of publicity and educational services, suggests that appropriate credit for Lincoln's success be given to Lincoln executives, whom he credits with carrying out the following policies:

1. Management has limited research, development, and manufacturing to a standard product line designed to meet the major needs of the welding industry.

2. New products must be reviewed by manufacturing and all production costs verified before being approved by management.

3. Purchasing is challenged not only to procure materials at the lowest cost but to work closely with engineering and manufacturing to ensure implementation of the latest innovations.

4. Manufacturing supervisors and all others are held accountable for reduction of scrap, energy conservation, and maintenance of product quality.

5. Production control, material handling, and methods engineering are closely supervised by top management.

6. Material and finished goods inventory control, accurate cost accounting, and attention to sales costs, credit, and other financial areas have constantly reduced overhead.

7. Management has made cost reduction a way of life, and definite programs have been established in many areas, including traffic and shipping, where tremendous savings can result.

8. Management has established a sales department technically trained to reduce customer welding costs. That sales technique and other real customer services have eliminated nonessential frills and resulted in long-term benefits to all concerned.

9. Management has encouraged education, technical publishing, and long-range programs that have resulted in industry growth, thereby ensuring market potential for Lincoln Electric Company.

REFERENCES

"Incentive Management in Action: An Interview with William Irrgang, Chief Executive Officer, The Lincoln Electric Company," *Assembly Engineering,* March 1967. Reprinted by the Lincoln Electric Company, Cleveland, Ohio.

Lincoln, James F. *Incentive Management.* Cleveland, Ohio: Lincoln Electric Company, 1951.

———. *A New Approach to Industrial Economics.* New York: Devin-Adair Company, 1961.

"You Can't Tell What a Man Can Do—Until He Has the Chance." *Reader's Digest,* January 1947, pp. 93–95.

APPENDIX: EMPLOYEE INTERVIEWS

During the late summer of 1980, the case writer conducted numerous interviews with Lincoln employees. Typical questions and answers from those interviews are presented next. In order to maintain personal privacy, names are disguised.

I

Interview with Ed Sanderson, a 23-year-old high school graduate who had been with Lincoln four years and was a machine operator in the electrode division at the time of the interview.

Q: How did you happen to get this job?

A: My wife was pregnant and I was making three bucks an hour and one day I came here and applied. That was it. I kept calling to let them know I was still interested.

Q: Roughly what were your earnings last year, including your bonus?

A: $37,000.

Q: What have you done with your money since you have been here?

A: Well, we've lived pretty well and we bought a condominium.

Q: Have you paid for the condominium?

A: No, but I could.

Q: Have you bought your Lincoln stock this year?

A: No, I haven't bought any Lincoln stock yet.

Q: Do you get the feeling that the executives here are pretty well thought of?

A: I think they are. To get where they are today, they had to really work.

Q: Wouldn't that be true anywhere?

A: I think more so here because seniority really doesn't mean anything. If you work with a guy who has 20 years here and you have two months and you're doing a better job, you will get advanced before he will.

Q: Are you paid on a piece-rate basis?

A: My gang does. There are nine of us who make the bare electrode, and the whole group gets paid based on how much electrode we make.

Q: Do you think you work harder than workers in other factories in the Cleveland area?

A: Yes, I would say I probably work harder.

Q: Do you think it hurts anybody?

A: No, a little hard work never hurts anybody.

Q: If you could choose, do you think you would be as happy earning a little less money and being able to slow down a little?

A: No, it doesn't bother me. If it bothered me, I wouldn't do it.

Q: What would you say is the biggest disadvantage of working at Lincoln as opposed to working somewhere else?

A: Probably having to work shift work.

Q: Why do you think Lincoln employees produce more than workers in other plants?

A: That's the way the company is set up. The more you put out, the more you're going to make.

Q: Do you think it's the piece rate and the bonus together?

A: I don't think people would work here if they didn't know that they would be rewarded at the end of the year.

Q: Do you think Lincoln employees will ever join a union?

A: No.

Q: What are the major advantages of working for Lincoln?

A: Money.

Q: Are there any other advantages?

A: Yes, we don't have a union shop. I don't think I could work in a union shop.

Q: Do you think you are a career man with Lincoln at this time?

A: Yes.

II

Interview with Jimmy Roberts, a 47-year-old high school graduate who had been with Lincoln 17 years and was a multiple drill press operator at the time of the interview.

Q: What jobs have you had at Lincoln?

A: I started out cleaning the men's locker room in 1963. After about a year, I got a job in the flux department, where we make the coating for welding rods. I worked there for seven or eight years and then got my present job.

Q: Do you make one particular part?

A: No, there are a variety of parts I make—at least 25.

Q: Each one has a different piece rate attached to it?

A: Yes.

Q: Are some piece rates better than others?

A: Yes.

Q: How do you determine which ones you are going to do?

A: You don't. Your supervisor assigns them.

Q: How much money did you make last year?

A: $47,000.

Q: Have you ever received any kind of award or citation?

A: No.

Q: What was your merit rating last year?

A: I don't know.

Q: Did your supervisor have to send a letter—was your rating over 110?

A: Yes. For the past five years, probably, I made over 110 points.

Q: Is there any attempt to let others know . . . ?

A: The kind of points I get? No.

Q: Do you know what they are making?

A: No. There are some who might not be too happy with their points, and they might make it known. The majority, though, do not make it a point of telling other employees.

Q: Would you be just as happy earning a little less money and working a little slower?

A: I don't think I would—not at this point. I have done piecework all these years, and the fast pace doesn't really bother me.

Q: Why do you think Lincoln productivity is so high?

A: The incentive thing—the bonus distribution. I think that would be the main reason. The paycheck you get every two weeks is important too.

Q: Do you think Lincoln employees would ever join a union?

A: I don't think so. I have never heard anyone mention it.

A: What is the most important advantage of working here?

A: Amount of money you make. I don't think I would make this type of money anywhere else, especially with only a high school education.

Q: As a black person, do you feel that Lincoln discriminates, in any way, against blacks?

A: No. I don't think any more so than any other job. Naturally, there is a certain amount of discrimination, regardless of where you are.

Case Discussion Questions

1. To what degree is Lincoln Electric a just-in-time plant? Explain.

2. The case describes the plant layout and inventory conditions but does not comment on their contributions to Lincoln's success. What may we conclude about those contributions?

3. How important is labor flexibility in the way Lincoln operates?

4. While Lincoln Electric has much in common with some of the best Japanese manufacturing companies, it is rare for Japanese company to use piece rates (extra pay for extra output). Are piece rates a vital part of Lincoln's success? Discuss.

5. Comment on any weaknesses you can think of in the way Lincoln manages its operations.

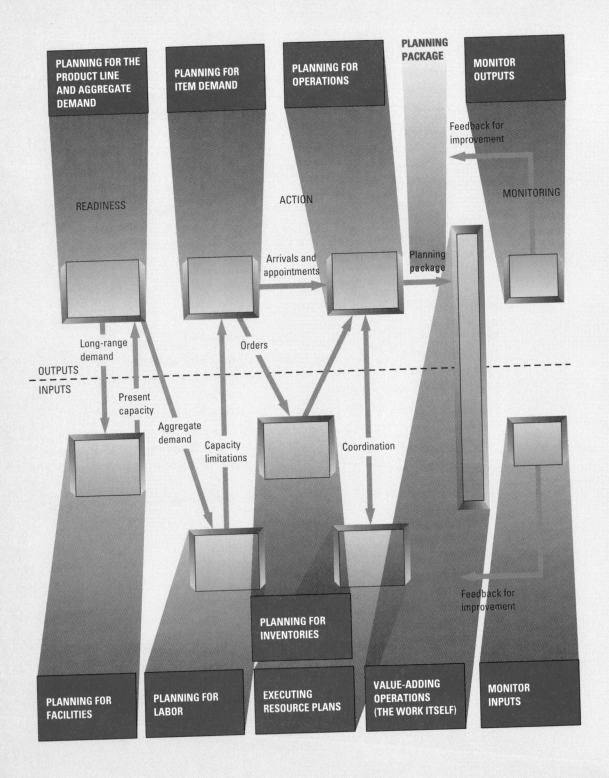

CHAPTER 4

Quality Management

Quality has been the most undermanaged of customer wants. In fact, the term *quality management* was rarely used until the 1980s; instead, the terms (and concepts) were *quality control* and, later, *quality assurance*. Further, until recently there was scant awareness that the object of quality is, firstly, the next process.

Quality management delves into every area of operations management—from planning the product line and facilities to scheduling and monitoring results. It is a part of all the other business functions (marketing, human resources, finance, etc.) as well. In fact, the quest for quality is a natural *common cause* for uniting the business functions.

Development of a body of knowledge on quality management has been largely due to the sustained efforts of certain quality pioneers. In this chapter, we examine some of their contributions, including a total system view of quality. Other topics include the various dimensions of quality, consumerism, competition, quality improvement teams, and quality costs. Chapter 15 presents more specifics on quality control and improvement techniques.

QUALITY: A GLOBAL CONCERN

The world seems to shrink as global competition grows and jolts one solid firm after another. Informed consumers are in a position to demand the best-quality goods and services offered by global companies. Low prices, short delivery lead times, and flexibility are in demand as well. In addition, consumers prowl the landscape seeking friendly, honest, and helpful services from service providers.

As consumers step up their demands, providers of goods and services are forced to respond with tightened management of quality. Is a quality revolution underway? Perhaps so.

The Quality Manifesto

On May 21, 1986, 25 past presidents of the American Society for Quality Control (ASQC) issued "The Quality Manifesto." It begins with a declaration of the proper role of quality in a world society and concludes with a call to action.

The declaration (see box) states the core beliefs that characterize the quality awakening of the 1980s (*awakening*, because as far as quality is concerned, society—including industry, government, and education—seems to have been asleep for years). Some of the declaration's main points are:

1. Quality is the key to pride, productivity, and profitability. By addressing quality first, the others logically follow.

2. Successful quality activities require managerial leadership, not just statements of commitment.

3. A consumer or customer orientation is basic, and customer satisfaction is *the* quality objective.

The Quality Manifesto Declaration

High quality is the key to pride, productivity, and profitability. The quality objective must be products and services that provide customer satisfaction. To be successful, the quality activities must be management-led and consumer-oriented. Management, labor, and government support for quality improvement is essential for effective competition in the global marketplace. Control of quality is a strategic business imperative essential to product and service process leadership.

Quality improvement, however, is more than a business strategy—it is a personal responsibility, part of our cultural heritage, and a key source of national pride. Quality commitment is an attitude, formulated in boardrooms and living rooms, visible on factory floors and service counters, expressed in concert halls and city halls, and demonstrated on playing fields and wheat fields. Quality demands a continuous improvement process with measurable individual, corporate, and national performance goals. Quality commitment must characterize the best of our relations with our fellow citizens and play a vital role in our search for global cooperation.

Excerpted from "The Quality Manifesto," *Quality Progress* 19, no. 7 (July 1986), pp. 14–15.

---

4. Management, labor, and government must all support quality improvement if a nation hopes to be an effective world competitor. Until the 1980s, *none* of the three gave just support to quality.

5. Quality control has strategic importance in achieving product and service leadership.

6. Quality improvement is a personal responsibility for all of us and is a continuous effort driven by measurable goals.

Despite the emotional appeal of "The Quality Manifesto," does anyone really take it seriously? Some companies do, as the following examples illustrate.

Quality First

- James L. Roberts, president and CEO of First Bank Milwaukee, believes enough in quality to have directed that *all* the bank's employees receive training in statistical process control.

- CEO James K. Batten of the Knight-Ridder newspaper chain, second largest in the United States, made "customer-driven excellence" a main company strategy. He has personally taken the message to each of the company's 30 papers, which range from the *Miami Herald* and *Philadelphia Enquirer* to the *Monrovia* (California) *News-Post*. One theme is that everyone has a customer—at the next process. "If the music critic misses his deadline, the editorial copy is delivered late, presses start late, the delivery trucks leave late, the newsboys start their routes late, and the customer gets his paper late."

Now Knight-Ridder people have more authority to serve the customer: Ad salespeople can rerun ads for unhappy customers, and circulation people can authorize sending out a replacement paper. Company headquarters approved several hundred thousand dollars to fix some technical problems at the St. Paul *Pioneer Press Dispatch:* Customers (readers) were angry that the comics and crossword puzzle weren't in the same places two days in a row.[1]

- More than 400 companies and governments have sent people to Florida Power and Light to learn about the utility's remarkable quality management program. Most of the company's 15,000 employees belong to one of its 1,900 quality teams.[2]

- Quality management was kicked off in the federal government with the signing of a Presidential Executive Order in February 1986. In implementing the order, the Internal Revenue Service sent 10,000 senior managers through quality training. Error rates involving tax deposits dropped tenfold in one year.[3]

- At Budgetel Inns, all new managers go through seven to nine weeks of training, which emphasizes quality backed up by a rigorous four-part inspection procedure. Stephen H. Marcus, CEO of the parent company, says, "Bad inspection scores are followed by lower occupancy rates like night follows day."[4]

- Nordstom (department stores) accepts all returns, General Electric and Procter & Gamble print free 800-numbers on their goods so customers can call and ask questions or complain, and at BIC the head of marketing and Mr. Bruno Bich (the product name was shortened) himself read and reply to about 1,000 customer letters per week.

These items point to an elevated level of interest in quality. They also suggest that there are a lot of ways to think about and provide quality. They involve both direct and indirect dealings with customers, as well as a host of methods used by providers of goods and services to improve quality. We've also seen a strong thread of high-level commitment as the driving force. While manufacturing companies can't reach out and touch the customer as easily as service providers can, manufacturers have their own ways of pushing for quality. Again, it's best for the push to come from the top.

At Corning Glass Works, for example, the quality concept affects and motivates every phase of company operations. To bring about the desired new pattern of behavior, CEO James R. Houghton appointed a highly respected senior vice president as director of quality, created a quality council, and set up a quality

---

[1]John Sedgwick, "Customers First," *Business Month,* June 1989, pp. 28–35.
[2]Gary Jacobson and John Hillkirk, "Crazy about Quality," *Business Month,* June 1989, pp. 71–75.
[3]Carolyn Burstein and Kathleen Sedlak, "The Federal Quality and Productivity Improvement Effort," *Quality Progress,* October 1988, pp. 38–41.
[4]Brad Stratton, "The Low Cost of Quality Lodging," *Quality Progress,* June 1988, pp. 49–53.

institute that has about 1,000 Corning employees in classes at any given time. The first class included the Corning senior management committee.[5]

Corning's level of commitment is not unusual among top manufacturing companies. Similar quality campaigns have taken place at Ford, Texas Instruments, IBM, Hewlett-Packard, 3M, Northern Telecom, and many others. Part of the reason for the startling turnabout in industry's attitude toward quality has to do with research on quality's potent effects. Typical is a study by Shetty showing that companies with better-quality products can charge more, with resulting higher profit margins.[6] Data show that improvement in product quality has a stronger relationship to increases in market share than does price.

In fact, quality's role as a necessary first step in improved competitive position, market share, revenue, and profitability is gaining acceptance. Figure 4–1 sums up the benefits of a total approach to quality management.

FIGURE 4–1

Benefits of Total Quality Management

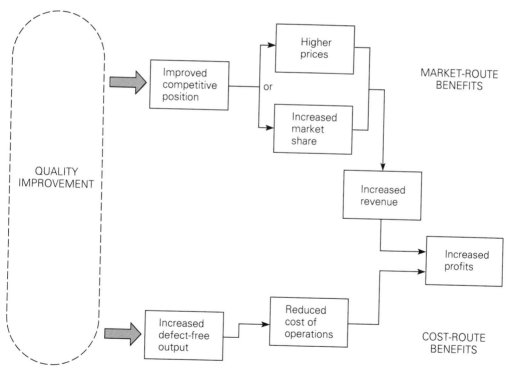

Source: Adapted from Gabriel Pall, *Quality Process Management* (Englewood Cliffs, N.J.: Prentice-Hall, Inc., 1987), Ch. 1.

---

[5]James R. Houghton, "The Old Way of Doing Things Is Gone," *Quality Progress*, September 1986, pp. 15–18.
[6]V.K. Shetty, "Product Quality and Competitive Strategy," *Business Horizons*, May–June 1987, pp. 46–52.

QUALITY: WHAT IS IT?

The preceding examples show a diversity of ways that companies are making their push for quality. Part of the reason for such diversity is the realization that quality is a complex subject, not defined in one sentence. From simple views of what quality is—such as meeting specifications—we now have broad definitions. Lack of a universal definition is not all bad; rather, it seems to make quality a more potent competitive weapon.

Quality: A Broad View

Professor David Garvin is one of the chief advocates of a broader view of quality. He suggests that there have been at least five groups of quality definitions: transcendent, product based, user based, manufacturing based, and value based. Garvin notes that scholars in philosophy, economics, marketing, and operations management have considered the subject, each group from a different vantage point and, no doubt, using the research methods, procedures, and databases of their respective disciplines.[7]

The variety of definitions helps explain the often-competing quality goals and plans within the organization. Marketing, with a customer view of quality, will debate operations' "do-it-right-the-first-time" definition. The debate is over not goals but different expectations as to the effects of better quality. Operations is coming to expect that better quality will lower costs, while in some firms marketing continues to see improved quality as a cost-increasing but market-share-gaining entity. Perhaps, as Garvin notes, the definition of quality should shift as goods and services move through design and transformation processes and toward the point of delivery.

Garvin identifies eight dimensions as a framework for considering quality:[8]

1. *Performance (grade of quality)*—an award-winning wine, the sound quality of a stereo.
2. *Features*—remote controls of home electronics items, a tavern that will have its patrons driven home.
3. *Reliability*—mail that always arrives on time, fire crackers that always fire.
4. *Conformance*—things that meet specifications, such as a car achieving promised mileage per gallon.
5. *Durability*—things that will stand up to abuse.
6. *Serviceability*—things that are easy to fix.
7. *Aesthetics*—things that are attractive or artful.
8. *Perceived quality*—something that has a mystique about it.

---

[7]David A. Garvin, "What Does 'Product Quality' Really Mean?" *Sloan Management Review*, Fall 1984, pp. 25–43.
[8]Ibid., pp. 29–30.

Garvin's eight dimensions were devised especially with manufacturing in mind (though by stretching meanings a bit, they can be made to apply to any service). But our concept of quality keeps expanding, along with growing concern about delivering it. With thanks to Garvin for opening our minds, we'll add a few more.

9. *Value*—none of the other dimensions directly gets at the customer's acute concern for good value: quality justifying the money spent.

10. *Responsiveness*—in human services, *time* is often the dominant way that people think about quality: How long the phone-in customer is kept on hold, how long the shopper waits for a clerk or to pay, how long it takes to get a repair done, and so forth. In manufacturing, time—quick response from process to process—has only recently been thought of as a dimension of quality. In recognition of customers' intense concern about *responsiveness* (as we'll call it, for clarity), a new body of strategic thought, called *time-based competition*, has emerged.[9]

11. *Humanity*—the quality of the service, or of delivery of goods, is not right without humanity in the delivery. That means sensitivity, not just a smile, and it includes courtesy, credibility (trustworthiness, having customers' best interests at heart), communication (keeping customers informed and listening to them), understanding (providing individualized attention, plunging beneath the surface to learn customers' real needs, recognizing the regular customer), and access (approachability and ease of contract).

12. *Security*—freedom from danger, risk, or doubt.

13. *Competency*—possession of the required skills and knowledge to provide the required services or goods.

    Numbers 10 through 13 are partially taken (and adapted) from research on what comprises service quality, which was based on focused interviews with people involved in providing retail banking, credit cards, securities brokerage, and product repair maintenance.[10]

Quality Improvement Never Ends

Each of the 13 dimensions of quality presents its own challenge. If a company is able to become outstanding in one of these dimensions, its task is to press on in making its service or product attractive in yet another dimension. For example, a certain fire department may be able to perform its main mission, putting out fires, with the best (performance, dimension 1). But its costs are

---

[9]See, for example, George Stalk, Jr., "Time—The Next Source of Competitive Advantage," *Harvard Business Review*, July–August 1988, pp. 41–51.

[10]Leonard L. Berry, Valerie A. Zeithaml, and A. Parasuramen, "Quality Counts in Services, Too," *Business Horizons*, May–June 1985, pp. 44–52.

high (value, dimension 9), and it doesn't do much fire prevention and community work (features, dimension 2). Its agenda for continual improvement should be clear.

QUALITY COMMITMENT: EVOLUTION OF AN IDEAL

The commitment to quality is rooted in the experience, research, and writings of several pioneers and leaders of the quality movement. They and the few audiences they could find in the 1950s, 1960s, and 1970s are owed a great debt for nurturing the quality ideal through some lean years. Five pioneering leaders of the quality movement warrant our attention (though many other names could be added): W. Edwards Deming, Joseph M. Juran, Armand V. Feigenbaum, Kaoru Ishikawa, and Philip B. Crosby. Notably, these individuals' thinking is not limited to the management of quality alone. All of them speak of companywide integration of purpose, need for work-life variety and versatility, and high regard for the human element.

W. Edwards Deming

W. Edwards Deming has been a Japanese hero for some 30 years while being relatively unknown in his native country. He began to gain recognition in the United States for his contributions to quality management on June 24, 1980. On that date, NBC broadcast "If Japan Can . . . Why Can't We?" That documentary highlights Deming's role in Japan's industrial ascendancy.

Japan named its top national prize for contributions to quality after Deming and first awarded the Deming Prize in 1951. Deming continued to travel to Japan over the next three decades, sharing his concepts on quality, competitive edge, and management in general.[11]

In recent years, Deming has traveled extensively, acquainting Western industry with his "14 points" for management (see box). He believes that while quality is everyone's job, management must lead the effort. Further, he states that his 14 points apply to both small and large organizations and in the service sector as well as in manufacturing.

Deming is an ardent proponent of training. He argues that everyone doing one's best simply isn't good enough, for one must first know what to do. According to Deming, there is no substitute for knowledge. Classic Deming may

---

[11]America's "discovery" of Deming has been traced to Clare Crawford-Mason, a television producer. Working on a documentary on the decline of American industry in the 1970s, Crawford-Mason heard of Deming's work in Japan and pursued her journalistic instincts. See Mary Walton, *The Deming Management Method* (New York: Dodd, Mead, 1986), Chap. 1 (HD38.W36).

Deming's 14 Points

1. Create constancy of purpose toward improvement of product and service with a plan to become competitive and to stay in business. Decide whom top management is responsible to.

2. Adopt the new philosophy. We are in a new economic age. We can no longer live with commonly accepted levels of delays, mistakes, defective materials, and defective workmanship.

3. Cease dependence on mass inspection. Require, instead, statistical evidence that quality is built in. (*Prevent* defects rather than *detect* defects.)

4. End the practice of awarding business on the basis of price tag. Instead, depend on meaningful measures of quality, along with price. Eliminate suppliers that cannot qualify with statistical evidence of quality.

5. Find problems. It is management's job to work continually on the system (design, incoming materials, composition of material, maintenance, improvement of machine, training, supervision, retraining).

6. Institute modern methods of training on the job.

7. The responsibility of foremen must be changed from sheer numbers to quality . . . [which] will automatically improve productivity. Management must prepare to take immediate action on reports from foremen concerning barriers such as inherited defects, machines not maintained, poor tools, fuzzy operational definitions.

8. Drive out fear, so that everyone may work effectively for the company.

9. Break down barriers between departments. People in research, design, sales, and production must work as a team, to foresee problems of production that may be encountered with various materials and specifications.

10. Eliminate numerical goals, posters, and slogans for the work force, asking for new levels of productivity without providing methods.

11. Eliminate work standards that prescribe numerical quotas.

12. Remove barriers that stand between the hourly worker and his right to pride of workmanship.

13. Institute a vigorous program of education and retraining.

14. Create a structure in top management that will push every day on the above 13 points.

W. Edwards Deming, *Quality Productivity, and Competitive Position* (Cambridge, Mass.: MIT, Center for Advanced Engineering Study, 1982), pp. 16–17.

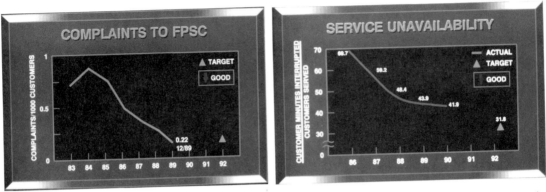

Two of the many quality improvement charts at Florida Power & Light, the first Western company to win Japan's Deming Prize.

be seen in the following excerpt from one of his (self-reported) communications to one organization's management:

> This report is written at your request after study of some of the problems that you have been having with production, high costs, and variable quality, which altogether, as I understand you, have been the cause of considerable worry to you about your competitive position . . . [M]y opening point is that no permanent impact has ever been accomplished in improvement of quality unless the top management carries out their responsibilities. These responsibilities never cease: they continue forever. No short-cut has ever been discovered. Failure of your own management to accept and act on their responsibilities for quality is, in my opinion, the prime cause of your trouble.[12]

Joseph M. Juran

Like Deming, Joseph M. Juran was a pioneer of quality education in Japan. He has also been known in the Western world for his textbooks and as editor-in-chief of *The Quality Control Handbook*. Like Deming, however, Juran was largely ignored by American management until the 1980s.

Juran's research has shown that over 80 percent of quality defects are *management controllable* and it is therefore management that most needs change. He published *Managerial Breakthrough* in 1964 as a guide for the solution of chronic quality problems.[13] To Juran, the breakthrough procedure is designed to gain and maintain improvements in quality. The sequence is as follows:

1. Convince others that a breakthrough is needed.
2. Identify the *vital few* projects (involves Pareto analyses, discussed in Chapter 15).

[12]W. Edwards Deming, *Quality, Productivity, and Competitive Position* (Cambridge, Mass.: MIT, Center for Advanced Engineering Study, 1982), p. 316.
[13]J. M. Juran, *Managerial Breakthrough* (New York: McGraw-Hill, 1964).

3. Organize for a breakthrough in knowledge.

4. Conduct an analysis to discover the cause(s) of the problem.

5. Determine the effect of the proposed changes on the people involved, and find ways to overcome resistance to these changes.

6. Take action to institute the changes, including training of all personnel involved.

7. Institute appropriate controls that will hold the new, improved quality level but not restrict continued improvement—perhaps through another breakthrough sequence.[14]

Juran's now-classic definition of quality is *fitness for use.* He intends those words to apply broadly, to include such properties as reliability, maintainability, and producibility; also, in certain situations, service response time, service availability, and price.

Juran defines quality management in terms of the *quality trilogy,* which consists of:

Quality planning.

Quality control.

Quality improvement.[15]

Proper quality planning results in processes capable of meeting quality goals under certain operating conditions. Quality control consists of measuring actual quality performance, comparing it with a standard, and acting on any difference. Juran believes that inherent planning deficiencies might result in chronic waste, and it is up to the control process to (initially) keep the waste from getting any worse. Finally, quality improvement is superimposed on quality control. Quality improvement means finding ways to do better than standard and breaking through to unprecedented levels of performance. The desired end results are quality levels that are even higher than planned performance levels.

Armand V. Feigenbaum

Armand V. Feigenbaum is best known for originating the concept of **total quality control (TQC)**. In his book *Total Quality Control* (first published in 1951 under an alternate title), Feigenbaum explains that quality must be attended to through all stages of the industrial cycle:

> . . . control must start with identification of customer quality requirements and end only when the product has been placed in the hands of a customer who remains satisfied. Total quality control guides the coordinated actions of people, machines, and information to achieve this goal.[16]

---

[14]For a detailed presentation of this sequence, see J. M. Juran and Frank M. Gryna, Jr., *Quality Planning and Analysis,* 2nd ed. (New York: McGraw-Hill, 1980), Chap. 5 (TS156.J86).
[15]J. M. Juran, "The Quality Trilogy," *Quality Progress* 19, no. 8 (August 1986), pp. 19–24.
[16]Armand V. Feigenbaum, *Total Quality Control,* 3rd ed. (New York: McGraw-Hill, 1983), p. 11 (TS156.F44).

To Feigenbaum, responsibility for TQC must be shared and should not rest with the quality assurance (QA) or quality control (QC) function alone. Feigenbaum also clarified the idea of **quality costs**, and he was among the first to argue that better quality is, in the long run, cheaper. He defines "hidden plant" as the proportion of plant capacity that exists in order to rework unsatisfactory parts. This proportion generally ranges from 15 to 40 percent of the plant's capacity.

Kaoru Ishikawa

Kaoru Ishikawa, the late Japanese quality authority, acknowledged Deming's and Juran's influence on his thinking. However, Ishikawa must be recognized for his own contributions. He originated **quality control circles** in both concept and practice. He also developed Ishikawa cause-effect charts, or "fishbone diagrams," so named because of their structural resemblance to the skeleton of a fish (discussed in Chapter 15). Like Deming, Juran, and Feigenbaum, Ishikawa also emphasizes quality as a way of management.

Ishikawa felt that there is not enough reliance on inputs to quality from

---

Ishikawa's Statistical Methods

I. Elemental Statistical Method
   A. Pareto analysis (vital few versus trivial many)
   B. Cause-and-effect diagram, also known as the *fishbone chart* (this, Ishikawa points out, is not a true statistical technique)
   C. Stratification
   D. Check sheet
   E. Histogram
   F. Scatter diagram
   G. Graph, and Shewhart process control chart

II. Intermediate Statistical Method
   A. Theory of sampling surveys
   B. Statistical sampling inspection
   C. Various methods of statistical estimation and hypothesis testing
   D. Methods of utilizing sensory tests
   E. Methods of experiment design

III. Advanced Statistical Method (using computers)
   A. Advanced experimental design
   B. Multivariate analysis
   C. Operations research methods

Source: Adapted from Kaoru Ishikawa, *What Is Total Quality Control? The Japanese Way*, trans. David J. Lu (Englewood Cliffs, N.J.: Prentice-Hall, 1985), Chap. XII (TS156.I8313).

nonspecialists. In 1968, he began using the term *companywide quality control (CWQC)* to differentiate the Japanese approach to TQC from the more specialized view attributed to Feigenbaum. The exchange of views has continued to evolve, and today the terms *TQC* and *CWQC* are used almost interchangeably.

Another significant contribution of Ishikawa is his work on taking much of the mystery out of the statistical aspects of quality assurance. Conforming to the belief that without statistical analysis there can be no quality control, Ishikawa divided statistical methods into three categories according to level of difficulty (see box).

The intermediate and advanced methods are for engineers and quality specialists and are beyond the scope of our discussion. The elemental statistical method, or the *seven indispensible tools* for quality control, however, are for everyone's use and should be mastered by all organization members. Ishikawa intends that to include company presidents, directors, middle managers, foremen, and line employees. His experience suggests that about 95 percent of *all* problems within a company can be solved with these tools. We will examine some of them in Chapter 15.

Ishikawa has reflected broadly on why Japanese industry has done better than Western industry at the quality game. In the West, he says, quality control has been delegated to a few staff specialists or consultants, and then only when things got badly out of hand. In Japan, however, the commitment to quality has been total and lasts throughout the company's life.

Philip B. Crosby

Philip B. Crosby, former corporate vice president and director of quality control at ITT Corp., is the developer of the **zero defects** concept and author of the popular book *Quality Is Free: The Art of Making Quality Certain*. In his book Crosby explains that quality is not a gift but is free. What costs money are all the things that prevent jobs from being done right the first time. When quality is made certain, an organization avoids these expenses.

Crosby proposes zero defects as the goal for quality. To any who find that goal too ambitious, he simply asks, "If not zero defects, then what goal would you propose?" One often-used figure is the acceptable quality level (AQL), which is used in acceptance inspection. Briefly, AQL allows a certain proportion of defective items. Crosby explains that an AQL is a commitment to produce a certain amount of imperfect material—before we start! He says that an AQL is not really a standard or target; it is simply acceptance of the status quo. The AQL idea is certainly out of step with a commitment to continuous improvement. Taking the consumer's view, Crosby makes his point bluntly:

> Consider the AQL you would establish on the product you buy. Would you accept an automobile that you knew in advance was 15 percent defective? 5 percent? 1 percent? One half of 1 percent? How about the nurses that care for newborn babies? Would an AQL of 3 percent on mishandling be too rigid?[17]

---

[17]Philip B. Crosby, *Quality Is Free: The Art of Making Quality Certain* (New York: McGraw-Hill, 1979), p. 146.

Crosby says that mistakes are caused by two things: lack of knowledge and lack of attention. Lack of knowledge, he argues, is measurable and can be attacked with tried and true means. Lack of attention, however, is an attitude problem and must be changed by the individual. The individual, in turn, has a better chance of making the change if commitment to zero defects exists.

QUALITY ASSURANCE

Today's level of interest in quality is a high point in the history of *quality assurance*, which once was exclusively in the hands of the craftsperson. The Industrial Revolution brought about the factory system and labor specialization, which served to increase output and decrease cost. That system also created a very long chain of quality, from one employee to another all the way to the end customer; the chain was bound to have weak links.

An early solution was to inspect after the product was made or the service provided. Inspection became a specialty. Inspectors identified defectives, which could be removed before passing the work on to the next process or to the end user. But relying on inspectors lets the maker off the hook, and concern for quality by operating people begins to erode. In many companies, quality fell apart. Consumers began to scream.

Consumerism

Increased public interest in product quality and safety began in the mid-1960s. Contributing to that interest were Ralph Nader, consumer federations, action-line columns in newspapers, and investigative TV and newspaper journalists. In 1965, the American Law Institute issued its "Restatement of the Law of Torts," which defined *strict liability*: making manufacturers liable for product defects even without proof of negligence.

Throughout the 1980s, physicians, accountants, attorneys, corporate directors, and volunteer members of civic organization boards increasingly became defendants in civil litigation. The mid-1980s was a time of liability insurance crisis in the United States.

Concern for safe consumption of goods and services also led to regulatory action. In 1972, the U.S. Congress passed the Consumer Product Safety Act, which aims at preventing hazardous or defective products from reaching the consumer. Most other Western countries have followed the same pattern. Some companies extended their product warranties in the 1970s and 1980s, but newspaper stories about massive product recalls seemed to say that quality on the warranty paper was not quality in fact. At the same time, in affluent nations large numbers of a new and demanding type of consumer were emerging: the consumer of average means, who prefers to do without rather than pay for second best. Neglected crafts such as handweaving, stone grinding of flour, and creation of stained-glass windows resurged. Consumers once again sought the quality of the earlier age of the craftsperson.

Competition

With higher demands for quality, North American industry went on the defensive. Industry tended to react to consumer complaints and legal and regulatory challenges as they occurred. But in the 1980s, the quality emphasis shifted to the offensive. The impetus was competition. A heavy amount of it came from Japan, where quality improvement has been spectacular. Competition also came from West Germany and certain other European countries where, for some products, quality has consistently been good for many years. We will consider quality management in Germany, Japan, and North America.

Quality in West Germany

Causes and effects in regard to West Germany's consistently high quality are not easy to pin down. Limprecht and Hayes cite fuzzy factors such as German determination to "get everything 'just right' " and insistence that "what goes out the door of their factories be as close to perfect as possible."[18] The authors argue, however, that those are not cultural traits. Rather, they are based on imitable industrial practices, one of which is managerial pursuit of technical strength. Technical strength serves as a marketing asset that is more enduring than the quick sale based on special options, colors, or styles. A second practice is an extensive apprenticeship system. In the German system, most young people go from school into a full-time, three-year apprentice program by age 16. Industry provides most of the training with the support of labor and government.

Quality in Japan

A massive effort to upgrade product quality has been going on in Japan since the late 1940s. Japan had lost the war and needed capital to rebuild its bombed-out industries and put people back to work. Lacking natural resources to sell, Japan could obtain capital only by exporting manufactured goods. But at that time, Japanese export goods were held in low regard by the rest of the world. As we have seen, U.S. experts (Deming, Juran, and others) accompanying Allied occupation forces began teaching quality control to the Japanese, and today nearly everyone, from production employee to chief executive officer, is knowledgeable in quality control techniques. The result is that Japan has become dominant in numerous quality-sensitive international markets. Good quality also avoids the high costs of rework, scrap, extra inventories, and warranty work; bad feelings and finger pointing within the firm; and loss of customers. These factors translate into lower prices for Japanese goods and a healthy environment for further improvements.

Quality in North America

It took awhile for North America to wake up. But awaken it did, instituting what has become a massive training effort, which commenced in about 1980. It

[18]Joseph A. Limprecht and Robert H. Hayes, "Germany's World-Class Manufacturers," *Harvard Business Review*, November–December 1982, pp. 137–45.

began in manufacturing and later spread to other sectors. Within a few years, it was not unusual to hear reports such as that made by the quality manager at F. D. Farnam, a supplier of gaskets and seals to the auto industry: He told a fall 1983 seminar audience in Chicago that in his company some production operators had been running formal training in statistical process control for other operators.

Thus, it appears that Western industry has launched its own assault on poor quality. Responsibilities and practices are changing in order to make the attack successful.

ORGANIZING FOR QUALITY IMPROVEMENT

As companies move beyond quality assurance to quality improvement, more resources need to be harnessed. One approach is to get people organized into groups to attack problems. Quality circles and small group improvement activities (SGIA) are the best known.

Quality Circles

The **quality circle** originated in Japan. It is a small work group that meets periodically to discuss ways to improve quality, productivity, or the work environment.

Membership in a circle generally is voluntary (sometimes with prudence dictating high rates of "volunteering") and may include supervisors. Usually the circles get formed through the efforts of a **facilitator**. The facilitator provides training in the concept, purpose, and techniques for process analysis and improvement. The techniques include process flowcharts, Pareto, fishbone, run diagrams, process control charts, and scatter diagrams (all discussed in Chapter 15). Members also learn how to make presentations on proposed improvements.

Some writers have suggested that quality circles in North America and Europe have been generally disappointing. Some circle programs have been halted. Of the many that still flourish, there are concerns that the projects center too much on matters only indirectly related to quality and productivity.

One explanation is that circles are unlikely to focus on quality until a companywide high commitment to quality is in place. Since many companies now have that commitment, perhaps quality circles are becoming more process improvement-oriented. Another explanation is that circles have been organized around groups who do the same thing, thus leaving their customers—the next process—out of the group. Still another view is that many Western circles have been given too much latitude in selecting their projects. In Japan, management or a committee assigns problems to circles. The circle then defines and refines the problem into projects. Analysis, solution, presentation, and implementation follow.

Small Group Improvement Activities (SGIA)

While proper management guidance can ensure that circles focus on process improvement, some companies prefer a different way of organizing the improvement effort: ad hoc (temporary) groups or project teams instead of a permanent quality circle. These ad hoc groups are called **small group improvement activities** or **SGIAs** (the name and concept appear to have come from Toyota). An SGIA is formed of operations people along with any needed technical support people. The SGIA is assigned a project, gives regular progress reports to management or a steering committee, and usually disbands when the project is completed. Some North American companies, disillusioned with the results of quality circle programs, have made a transition from circles to SGIA programs.

PRINCIPLE: Ensure that line people get first crack at problem solving—before staff experts.

QUALITY COSTS

The casual student of quality management might infer that the increased emphasis on quality sounds like "Damn the costs, let's do it." Nothing could be further from the truth! Better quality is less costly than inferior goods and services. Remember too that the customer wants *both* high quality and low price and businesses need low costs in order to price competitively. Let us take a closer look at quality costs.

Traditional Views

The pioneers of quality management have spelled out four categories of quality costs:

> Prevention costs.
> Appraisal costs.
> Internal failure costs.
> External failure costs.

Prevention and appraisal costs ensure and control quality; internal failure and external failure costs are losses from defective process output.

Figure 4–2 shows the usual view of how these costs change with quality level. The horizontal axis represents the quality level, q, ranging from $q = 0$ for 100 percent defective output to $q = 100$, or 0 percent defective. The term *defective* was generally taken to mean "not conforming to specification," though that meaning is now thought to be too narrow.

In the figure, failure costs decrease as quality improves while prevention and appraisal costs increase as quality improves. The sum is the total cost curve.

FIGURE 4–2
Quality Costs: Traditional Model

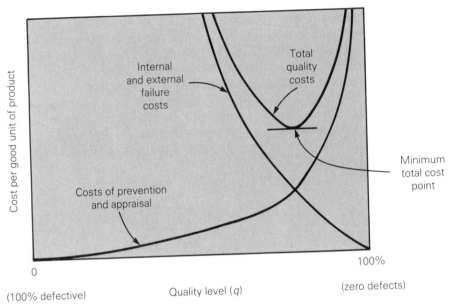

The minimum on the total cost curve is where its slope is zero, as shown. At that minimum, an additional investment in prevention should result in a failure reduction return of exactly the same amount. To the left of that point, prevention investment returns more than its value in reduction of failure costs. To the right, investment in additional improvement will not return its value in reduced costs associated with defectives and is therefore *economically* unjustifiable.

The model's portrayal of failure costs is sound, for these costs do go to zero as quality becomes perfect. A problem with the traditional model lies in the prevention and appraisal cost curve, which shows costs approaching infinity as perfect quality is neared. Infinite cost as the price of success does not sit well with continuing-improvement or zero-defects proponents.

The claim that quality improvement is economically unsound does not appeal to consumers either. It has been alleged that some companies "play the odds" by comparing potential liability damage costs of faulty products against the costs of preventing faulty products from being made in the first place. The traditional quality cost model seems to push managers into that mode of thinking. Now, however, there are challenges to the traditional quality cost model. One approach, considered next, addresses the way we view the quality improvement process itself.

Innovation versus Continual Improvement

In the traditional view, true improvement (or at least most of it), must come through innovative breakthroughs in technology. Indeed, improvement can and does occur this way, and often there *are* very high costs associated with development and acquisition of innovation-oriented technology. Industry is finding, however, that quality improvement depends *more* on smaller, inexpensive, but constantly occurring increments than on infrequent technology breakthroughs. The continual-improvement view affects the quality cost model.

Schneiderman suggests revision to the traditional model. He argues that quality cost functions must be viewed on the basis of *incremental* economics.[19] He points out that there is no mathematical requirement for the optimal value of total quality costs to occur at value of q less than 100 percent.

There may be no *optimal* value of total costs throughout the range of $q = 0$ percent to $q = 100$ percent. There may be a *minimum*, and this value might occur at $q = 100$ percent, as shown in Figure 4–3. In other words, Schneiderman argues that it does not really take infinite investment to continuously improve quality.

We might take the viewpoint even further. Figure 4–4 shows what might occur if prevention and appraisal costs become *lower* as quality improves. This may be possible for two reasons. First, an improving organization finally begins to make prevention a part of everyone's job, and it makes preventive activities simple, cheap, and routine to perform. Some of the preventive activities, such

FIGURE 4–3

Quality Costs: Total Cost Minimum at Zero Defects

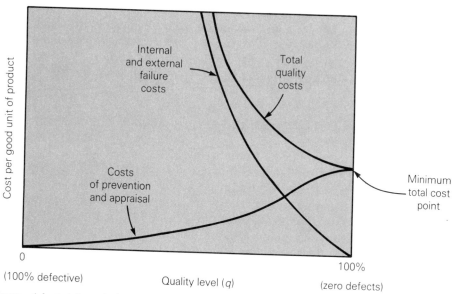

Source: Adapted from Arthur M. Schneiderman, "Optimum Quality Costs and Zero Defects: Are They Contradictory Concepts?" *Quality Progress* 19, no. 11 (November 1986), p. 29.

---

[19]Arthur M. Schneiderman, "Optimum Quality Costs and Zero Defects: Are They Contradictory Concepts?" *Quality Progress* 19, no. 11 (November 1986), pp. 28–31.

FIGURE 4–4
Quality Costs: Effects of Improvement through Simplification

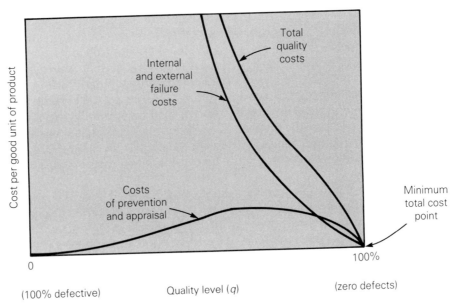

as clearing away chips or dust that could clog a mechanism, may even be performed mostly in off moments at *zero* extra cost. Second, the costs of both prevention and appraisal should fall over time, because such activities as oiling a machine, gauging, and checking specs can be simplified or cheaply automated; indeed, inspection itself—traditionally the main form of appraisal—is phased out as quality improvement makes inspection redundant.

Low-Cost Fail-Safing

A leading proponent of controlling processes by adding more and more simple, cheap controls is Shigeo Shingo, one of the key developers of JIT at Toyota. Shingo is the world's leading expert on the use of **fail-safing** (called *pokayoke* in Japanese—and in some Western companies as well). Fail-safing makes use of devices or strict procedures for doing a 100 percent check on a critical process characteristic. Shingo believes that fail-safing, along with self-inspection, are more effective even than the statistical tools of quality management: "It took 26 years for me to free myself completely from the spell of inductive statistics."[20]

The methods and uses of fail-safing are almost limitless. As an example, clerks in some beef sandwich shops are required to weigh a pile of beef for every

---

[20]Shigeo Shingo, *Zero Quality Control: Source Inspection and the Poka-yoke System*, trans. Andrew P. Dillon (Stamford, Conn.: Productivity Press, 1985), p. xv.

sandwich to ensure that the customer gets not too much nor too little (this is an example of a loose fail-safe procedure). To make it more fail-safe, add a bell that rings if the weight is out of spec limits. Of course, the clerk may choose to skip the scale entirely. It would not be easy to fail-safe around that possibility, but here's an off-the-wall idea for how it might be done, assuming the beef is weighed *on* the bun: Install an automatic device that squirts just the right amount of "special sauce"—but only if the scale reading is within spec. That simplifies the clerk's job and makes the scale a welcome device, rather than a policeman.

As the example suggests, fail-safing can, and usually does, deal with human failings, or, to depersonalize the issue, random mishaps. The best fail-safing is supportive of the human processor. In fact, fail-safing carries with it a revised assumption about people and work: Humans are variable creatures who deserve to be protected from their natural inclinations to be variable. In other words, let's consider a mishap to be a clear indication of a process weakness that needs to be fail-safed. In that spirit, operators may no longer feel any need to hide errors. That opens the door to active and willing involvement of operators in exposing and recording variation and mishaps—and in getting one more aggravation fail-safed.

PRINCIPLE: Make it easy to make/provide the goods or services without error.

Variation Stackup

Another slant on the view that quality should be improved continually goes by the term **variation stackup**—or, in engineering, **tolerance stackup**. Lawrence P. Sullivan has nicely articulated the concept. In his former position as an executive in quality management at Ford Motor Company, Sullivan preached the concept to Ford's suppliers and everyone else who would listen.

Tolerance stackup can happen when two or more parts that are good but near to specification limits are joined together. If part A is at the high side and part B at the low side of its spec limit, the result is bad quality of the assembly. Sullivan often cites the example of a car door. Say that 100 percent of door frames and doors are within their spec limits—zero defects is achieved. Still, a door that is on the small side can be matched with a frame on the large side. The result: gaps through which unwelcome weather pours in.

Variation stackup, the more general term, applies everywhere in the service sector: Commuters get to the bus stop a bit early or late, and the bus arrives a bit early or late. Sometimes the commuter is especially early and the bus especially late; result: angry commuter.

The best cure is reduction of process variability; for example, put enough slack in the bus schedule so that it rarely is late, and set a rule that a bus may never leave a bus stop early. Another cure is checking to avoid spec mismatches. One example is giving commuters a beeper that activates when the bus reaches a certain spot—at which time the commuter may dash from a comfortable building to the bus stop. An example in manufacturing is a common practice among bearing producers: They gauge all bearings and all bearing races and group them into separate feeder channels by size. Then machines assemble the smallest bearings to the smallest races, the largest to the largest, and so on. Earlier, all out-of-spec bearings and races would have been sent to the scrap bin so that those making it to the matching step in final assembly are "good." Over time, reduction of process variability will make them better.

The variation stackup problem is amplified in the mixing stages of continuous process production. Often several ingredients, not just two, are mixed together. Purities, specific gravities, and fineness of various liquid and solid ingredients may all be within spec, but on the high (or low) side. When mixed and processed, the result might be tacky rubber, cloudy glass, unstable chemicals, rough surfaces, crumbly pills, brittle plastic, or M&Ms that melt in the hands.

Taguchi's Approach to Quality Costs

Is it sufficient that quality management successfully controls processes, eliminates defects, and reduces variability? Japanese expert Genichi Taguchi says there is more—that cost must be injected into quality management. Taguchi's work generally was unknown in Western industry or even Japan until the mid-1980s.

Taguchi defines quality as the loss imparted to society from the time the product is shipped. This **social loss** determines a product's desirability: The smaller the loss, the more desirable the product. For Taguchi, social loss must affect quality cost management decisions; that is, investments in quality improvement should be compared to *savings to society* rather than to the firm alone. Ultimately society will reward (or penalize) the firm for its record of societal savings; thus, Taguchi's view is meant to be sound for business.

Briefly, Taguchi holds that there are unwelcome costs associated with *any* deviation of process performance from the quality characteristic's target value. Thus, he favors going beyond zero deviation from specs to continual reduction in variability.

The customer's loss from performance variation is approximately equal to the square of the deviation of the performance characteristic from its target value. This quadratic loss function may be defined as:

$$L = K(d)^2 \tag{4–1}$$

where

d = Distance from target to customer's tolerance limits
K = Loss constant, ideally made up of all internal and
     external costs (the four traditional costs)
L = Loss to customers from variation of the performance characteristic
     by amount d from target T (in monetary units)

FIGURE 4–5
Taguchi's Quality Loss Function

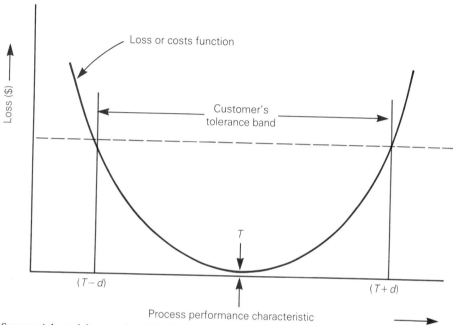

Source: Adapted from Arthur M. Schneiderman, "Optimum Quality Costs and Zero Defects: Are They Contradictory Concepts?" *Quality Progress* 19, no. 11 (November 1986), p. 29.

Figure 4–5 represents Taguchi's concept of social costs, or losses. The figure should be interpreted to show loss at any specified point during the product's life and not just immediately after delivery.

Like the quality pioneers discussed earlier, Taguchi is a student of management rather than of quality alone. His methods extend beyond the loss function mentioned here and are likely to receive attention through the remainder of the century.[21]

SUMMARY

Quality of goods and services is a global concern. Customers demand satisfaction and are increasingly willing to use worldwide shopping in order to obtain it.

---

[21]See Raghu N. Kackar, "Taguchi's Quality Philosophy: Analysis and Commentary," *Quality Progress*, December 1986, pp. 21–29; and Thomas R. Barker, "Quality Engineering by Design: Taguchi's Philosophy," *Quality Progress*, December 1986, pp. 32–42.

The quality revolution that began in the 1980s is changing the way quality is managed.

Commitment to quality has evolved. During its lean years (the 1950s, 1960s, and 1970s), the ideal was nurtured by pioneers in the field of quality management. Individuals such as Deming, Juran, Feigenbaum, Ishikawa, and Crosby are owed a debt by businesses and consumers alike. Although most of the early work in the quality management field was done by Americans, U.S. industry was not receptive. The Japanese deserve credit for initial implementation and subsequent improvement of quality management techniques.

Consumerism and competition have forced attention on quality assurance. The litigation wave of the mid-1980s was felt by providers of goods and services. The legal concept of strict liability coupled with consumer anger resulted in a liability insurance crisis. Competition from Germany and Japan also prompted North American managers to begin a movement to improve quality.

A universally accepted definition of quality has not been developed. Garvin's idea that quality has multiple dimensions suggests that quality can be a broad weapon for competition. The focus must be the customer.

The rate of process improvement may be speeded up by organizing people into quality circles or small group improvement activities (SGIAs) and giving them training in use of common process analysis tools. Circles seem to work best when there already is a companywide commitment to quality, when the circle includes the customer (next process), and when the circle is assigned problems rather than left free to select its own topics for study. An SGIA is a project team of line employees and technical support people: It is formed to study and solve a specific problem and is then disbanded.

Traditional views of quality costs are being challenged. Failure costs, resulting from defective output, are known to decrease as quality improves. Prevention and appraisal costs are now believed to also decrease with improving quality due to techniques such as fail-safing the process. Taguchi argues that managers must consider quality costs to *society* rather than just the firm; the customer's (society's) costs rise whenever there is variation from the desired production target.

KEY WORDS

Total quality control
  (TQC)
Quality cost
Quality control circles
Zero defects
Quality circle
Facilitator

Small group
  improvement activity
  (SGIA)
Fail-safing
Variation stackup
Social loss

REFERENCES

Books

Crosby, Philip B. *Quality Is Free.* New York: McGraw-Hill, 1979.

Deming, W. Edwards. *Out of the Crisis.* Cambridge, Mass.: MIT, Center for Advanced Engineering Study, 1986.

————. *Quality, Productivity, and Competitive Position.* Cambridge, Mass.: MIT, Center for Advanced Engineering Study, 1982.

Feigenbaum, Armand V. *Total Quality Control.* 3rd ed. New York: McGraw-Hill, 1983 (TS156.F44).

Garvin, David A. *Managing Quality: The Strategic and Competitive Edge.* New York: The Free Press, 1988 (HF5415.I57.G37).

Ishikawa, Kaoru. *Guide to Quality Control.* Tokyo: Asian Productivity Organization, 1972 (TS156.G82).

————. *What Is Total Quality Control?: The Japanese Way.* Translated by David J. Lu. Englewood Cliffs, N.J.: Prentice-Hall, 1985 (TS156.I8313).

Juran, J. M., and Frank M. Gryna, Jr., *Quality Planning and Analysis.* 2nd ed. New York: McGraw-Hill, 1980 (TS156.J86).

Shingo, Shigeo. *Zero Quality Control: Source Inspection and the Poka-yoke System.* Translated by Andrew P. Dillon. Stamford, Conn.: Productivity Press, 1985.

Walton, Mary. *The Deming Management Method.* New York: Dodd, Mead, 1986 (HD38.W36).

Periodicals/Societies

Journal of Quality Technology (American Society for Quality Control).

Quality Assurance.

Quality Engineering (American Society for Quality Control).

Quality Progress (American Society for Quality Control).

REVIEW QUESTIONS

1. How has global competition increased awareness of quality goods and services?

2. What is "The Quality Manifesto"? What are its main points?

3. What do we mean when we say that customer satisfaction is *the* quality objective?

4. Restate each of the 13 dimensions of quality in your own words.

5. What are the major contributions to the evolution of commitment to quality? Specifically, what have we received from Deming? Juran? Feigenbaum? Ishikawa? Crosby? What common beliefs do these experts apparently share?

6. How has consumerism affected quality assurance?

7. How have West Germany and Japan used quality as a competitive weapon? Have their tactics worked? What has been the North American response?

8. What is the role of quality circles? What does it take to make them produce maximal benefits?

9. How does the SGIA differ from the quality circle?

10. What is the traditional view of the costs associated with quality? How has that view been challenged by more recent thinking and experience?

11. What is Shingo's answer to the problem of controlling quality?

12. What is variation (tolerance) stackup? How can variation stackup be reduced?

13. What have been Taguchi's contributions to the concept of quality costs? Does society really lose anything when a spec's target value is not met? Why or why not?

PROBLEMS AND EXERCISES

1. Answer the following questions:
   a. What does quality mean to you?
   b. Are you satisfied with the goods and services you purchase?
   c. Could companies ensure better-quality goods and services?
   d. Should they?
   e. Why or why not?

   Has the material in this chapter changed any of your previously held ideas about quality?

2. Ask several friends the five questions listed in exercise 1. How do their responses compare with yours? Are your findings surprising? Discuss.

3. How do *you* determine quality in products? For example, how do you distinguish a "good" automobile (or barstool, topcoat, aspirin, or golfball) from a "bad" one? Does the item's price influence your thinking? What are society's "beliefs" regarding a relationship between price and quality? Are these beliefs realistic?

4. How do *you* determine quality in services? For example, how do you distinguish a "good" lawyer (or accountant, professor, athlete, or barber) from a "bad" one? Does the service's price—fee charged or salary received—have any influence on your thinking? Does society pay the same attention to price when judging the quality of services as it does in the case of products? Why or why not?

5. Briefly explain each of the 13 dimensions of quality as it applies to:
   a. One product of your choice.
   b. One service of your choice.

6. Suggest a fail-safe device that could be used at a popcorn stand to prevent too many unpopped kernels from ending up in customers' bags.

7. The manager of a large campus housing unit is considering gathering a group of residents together into a few quality circles or SGIAs. Which form of improvement team would you recommend? Discuss.

8. Suggest a fail-safing approach for each of the following:
   a. Forgetting to set the alarm clock.
   b. Missing appointments.
   c. Running out of gas.

9. Give two examples of tolerance stackup for a goods producer.

10. Give two examples of variation or tolerance stackup for a services provider.

Translating Demand into Planned Orders

An employee looking outward sees customer demand. But looking inward, the employee sees *orders*. In Part Three, we see how demand is translated into orders. First, there is the demand itself; Chapter Five explains the demand management function and demand forecasting techniques. Next come capacity planning and master scheduling in Chapter Six. Chapters Seven through Ten discuss breaking down the master schedule into plans and systems support for component inventory items and the management of materials.

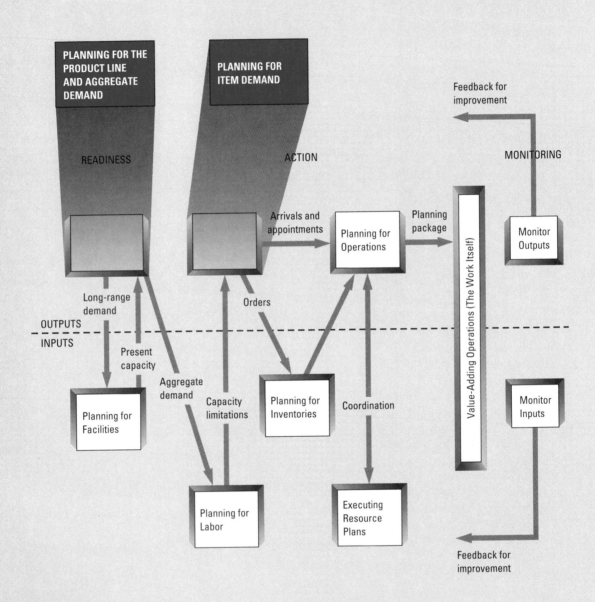

CHAPTER 5

Demand Management and Forecasting

SINGLE-PERIOD PATTERNLESS PROJECTION

Moving Average
Exponential Smoothing
Double Exponential Smoothing
Adaptive Smoothing
Forecasting by Simulation

ASSOCIATIVE PROJECTION

Leading Indicator
Correlation

SUPPLEMENT:
LEAST SQUARES AND CORRELATION COEFFICIENTS

How should the provider of services and goods deal with customer demand? Sit back and wait until the "whites of the eyes" of customers are in view, then scramble? Of course not. Demands are the lifeblood of an enterprise, and they deserve to be managed. Customer demand can even be manipulated—through promotional actions. However, our approach to demand management and forecasting is not so ambitious. It concerns *recognizing* all sources of demand, *planning* for demand, and *processing* demand. These demand management activities are a joint responsibility of marketing and operations.

DEMAND MANAGEMENT'S PLACE IN OM

The American Production and Inventory Control Society (APICS) defines **demand management** as:

> The function of recognizing and managing all of the demands for products to ensure that the master scheduler is aware of them. It encompasses the activities of forecasting, order entry, order promising, branch warehouse requirements, interplant orders, and service parts requirements.[1]

Although this definition has a manufacturing flavor, demand management applies in services as well. Insurance companies, government agencies, laundries, trucking, and schools have coordination problems between those who sell and promote and those who provide services and plan for resources. Demand management in services differs somewhat, since services do not involve external demands for service parts or interplant, branch warehouse, and international requirements for inventoriable products.

In either manufacturing or services, some sort of coordinator or master planning committee needs to take charge of demand management. A committee, with ties to both marketing and operations, is often best. In the absence of a strong link between the two functions at the demand management level, the likelihood of numerous errors and surprises is high.

While a coordinator or committee is basic, others also play key roles in demand management. Sales forces book orders, order-entry clerks (or order-entry computer routines) further process orders, product managers (or computers) forecast demand for orders not yet received, warehouses confirm or deny material availability, and traffic checks delivery dates against shipping capabilities. On the internal side are people who determine capacity, financial, and other limits on what is to be produced and delivered.

There are short-, medium-, and long-term purposes of demand management. The short-term question concerns **item demand**; that is, the organization needs to know what demands exist in the near future for its mix of goods and services—the items it makes or provides.

---

[1]Thomas F. Wallace and John R. Dougherty, *APICS Dictionary*, 6th ed. (Falls Church, Va.: American Production and Inventory Control Society, 1987), p. 8.

The medium term covers about 6 to 18 months in manufacturing, but often much less in the service sector. The purpose is to project aggregate demand so that productive capacity can be planned. In the medium term the plans particularly apply to labor, machine usage, and aggregate inventory; more on this in Chapter 6.

Long-term demand management affects planning for buildings, utilities, and equipment, which we focus on in Chapter 18. Long-term demand management also affects the introduction of new products and services and the phasing out of older ones—already treated in Chapter 3.

Medium- and long-term demand management decisions are made infrequently. The short-term product mix (item demand) activities, in contrast, keep a good many employees busy all the time—handling orders or guessing about orders not yet formally booked. Processing current orders is our next topic. Later we consider "guessing," more formally known as *forecasting*.

ORDER PROCESSING

When things are going well, operations is able to produce and deliver what marketing sells. To keep things going well, operations management must play an active role in processing customer orders. In most cases, it is poor policy for operations to simply put into backlog any orders that sales is able to scare up. Instead, there should be a well-devised order processing system. Central to the system is the *order promise*. In this section we discuss orders in general, examine the order processing sequence, and then look specifically at order promising.

Orders

Even when considered only as a noun and only within an operations context, the word *order* has multiple meanings. For example, there might be individual sales orders, consolidation of sales orders into a few batch orders (for total requirements of each item), scheduled production orders for major modules, planned orders for component parts, shop or work orders, purchase orders for component parts and raw materials, final assembly orders, and shipment orders. Each type of order may have its own numbering system and set of documentation. Clearly, in a manufacturing company, you will not necessarily get the response you are looking for when you inquire, "Where's my order?"

In the service sector, too, the customer order sometimes breaks down into subtypes. Consider, for example, a medical clinic. You, the patient, are an order; when you go to X-ray, an X-ray order number is assigned; when you go to the lab, several lab orders are created; when you are finished, there will be a billing order with its own number for total services rendered.

With these meanings in mind, we now turn our attention to the order processing sequence.

Order Processing Sequence

The sequence of order processing is shown in Figure 5–1. The processing usually begins and ends in functional areas other than operations. In between—the shaded portion—are operations management responsibilities.

The first step is *order booking:* An order is booked by sales. Second is **order entry**, which is really a subprocess in itself; it includes the *organizational* acceptance of the order into the order processing system. Order-entry activities might include:

Credit checks, especially for new customers.

Documentation of pertinent customer data, such as specifications.

Translation of what the customer wants into terms used by operations.

Determining whether the order can be filled from stock (if so, the process might skip directly to step 10).

Assignment of an internal order number.

The next seven steps are operations functions. Step 3 is *determining total requirements.* Orders by several customers for the same thing must be totaled. Additional translation might be required at this point, such as translation of sales catalog terminology into manufacturing part numbers. Some companies employ as many as three sets of part numbers, which are used with three different scheduling procedures: (1) the final assembly schedule—for assembly of finished end products, (2) the master production schedule—for production of major modules such as frames and engines, and (3) a schedule for the manufacture of service parts, interplant transfer parts, customer optional parts, and so forth.

Step 4, *order positioning,* accomplishes several things. First, a check is made to see if present schedules can accommodate new requirements. If so, the order or customer is positioned—placed—in the schedule. We might say that the order receives its third "acceptance," this time by the master schedule or appointment book.

If the schedule is full and the customer is willing to wait, the order is accepted and positioned at the tail end of a backlog. Some inventoriable items are made in advance to a forecast. The schedules for advance production are checked to see whether they will result in the goods requested by a customer at a desired future date.

Step 5 is the culmination of step 4. If the schedule can meet the customer order, an *order promise or reservation* notice goes to the customer. We will discuss the order promise step more fully a bit later.

In steps 6 through 8, customer identification is lost, and these steps are generally out of the realm of demand management. In step 6, *inventory planning,* accepted orders are divided into requirements for component parts. If the parts are not on hand, manufacture and purchase orders for parts are

FIGURE 5–1
The Order Processing Sequence

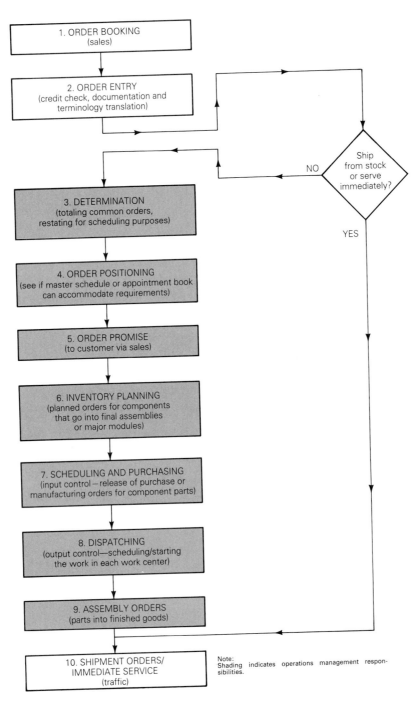

1. ORDER BOOKING
(sales)

2. ORDER ENTRY
(credit check, documentation and
terminology translation)

Ship
from stock
or serve
immediately?

NO

YES

3. DETERMINATION
(totaling common orders,
restating for scheduling purposes)

4. ORDER POSITIONING
(see if master schedule or appointment book
can accommodate requirements)

5. ORDER PROMISE
(to customer via sales)

6. INVENTORY PLANNING
(planned orders for components
that go into final assemblies
or major modules)

7. SCHEDULING AND PURCHASING
(input control—release of purchase or
manufacturing orders for component parts)

8. DISPATCHING
(output control—scheduling/starting
the work in each work center)

9. ASSEMBLY ORDERS
(parts into finished goods)

10. SHIPMENT ORDERS/
IMMEDIATE SERVICE
(traffic)

Note:
Shading indicates operations management responsibilities.

generated. The component parts orders do not easily tie to a given customer, because common parts go into various end items ordered by different customers. *Scheduling*, at a detailed level, and *purchasing* constitute step 7: Schedulers carefully release the parts manufacturing orders so as not to overload capacity; buyers release the purchase orders. *Dispatching* is step 8: Dispatchers control the priorities of parts orders as they queue up in the work centers to have certain operations done.

In step 9, *assembly orders*, the customer order reemerges as the basis for orders for the final assembly of end items (and accessories) into finished goods or end products. *Shipment orders*, geographically consolidated, or immediate service, constitute step 10.

Figure 5–1 makes order processing look complex. And indeed there is a complex approach to order processing, one in which several staff departments each do their own narrow set of order processing tasks. While most companies follow that approach, leading firms are switching over to simpler team and visual approaches that avoid some of the processing steps, written documents, and order numbers. We study both approaches in this book, while keeping an eye on the objective: quick, on-time completion of quality goods and services at a reasonable cost, with flexibility to respond to new orders or other customer needs.

Order Promising

Order promising means making a commitment to the customer to ship or deliver an order. Order promise by operations management also serves as its commitment to the partnership that marketing and operations should have. Speedy notice of order promise can provide salespeople with sound information for use in making any delivery arrangement, as well as nailing down the sale in the first place.

The only situation in which operations does not have an order promise function is the pure make-to-stock company. Here goods are made to a forecast and placed in distribution centers, and customer order processing is left to the marketing arm of the business. But few companies are strictly make-to-stock. Special large orders, orders for service parts, and so forth may be accepted. In that case, there should be a formal order promise procedure so that sales can give the customer some assurance that production is committed to meet the agreed-upon delivery date.

In client-oriented services, the order promise is known as an *appointment*. The order is not a legal promise; it just means that schedules have been checked and that, barring problems, the client should receive service at the appointed time. All parties realize that problems do occur and some services are going to be late. Just as obvious to all is that the firm with a good record of meeting appointments enhances its competitive position.

DEMAND FORECASTING

Actual customer orders are nice, but many a company has made its mark producing for "phantom customers"—those who do not order until the goods have already been made. Such make-to-stock companies produce to a demand forecast. It could be said that a demand forecast differs from actual orders only in that actual orders are more certain. Forecasts are unlikely to be correct, but actual orders are uncertain too, because they may be canceled or changed. Thus, the order processing steps explained above take place whether production is triggered by orders or by a forecast. Our discussion of demand forecasting in the rest of this chapter will proceed from the general—what-and-why questions—to specifics on forecast accuracy and forecasting techniques.

Components of Demand

The first what-and-why question is demand itself: What is it? Typically, the question is answered by reference to the *components of demand* and their behavior over time. A sequential set of observations of a variable, such as demand, taken at regular intervals is referred to as a **time series**. Viewing demand as a time series is useful in both historical analyses and future projections. The time-series approach may be used to examine demand for individual items or for groups of items, such as product families or classes of resources.

Time-series analysis of a demand stream begins by considering the components of demand as types of variations that occur in the series over time. The components are:

1. **Trend**, or slope, defined as the positive or negative shift in series value over a certain time period.
2. **Seasonal variation** or **seasonality**, usually occurring within one year and recurring annually.
3. **Cyclical pattern**, also recurring, but usually spanning several years.
4. **Random events**, which are of two types:
   a. Explained, such as effects of natural disasters or accidents.
   b. Unexplained, for which no *known* cause exists.[2]

The first three variations are shown in pure form in the three-year time series displayed in Figure 5–2. Figure 5–2A has only trend, in this case positive. Figure 5–2B shows seasonality, with the seasonal high occurring at the first quarter of each year and the seasonal low at the third quarter. Figure 5–2C shows a series with a three-year cycle, peaking at about the middle of year 2. Figure 5–2D shows how a time series might appear if it contained all three of the "pure" components along with some random events, shown as spikes.

---

[2]UFDs (unidentified flying demands).

FIGURE 5–2

Components of a Time Series

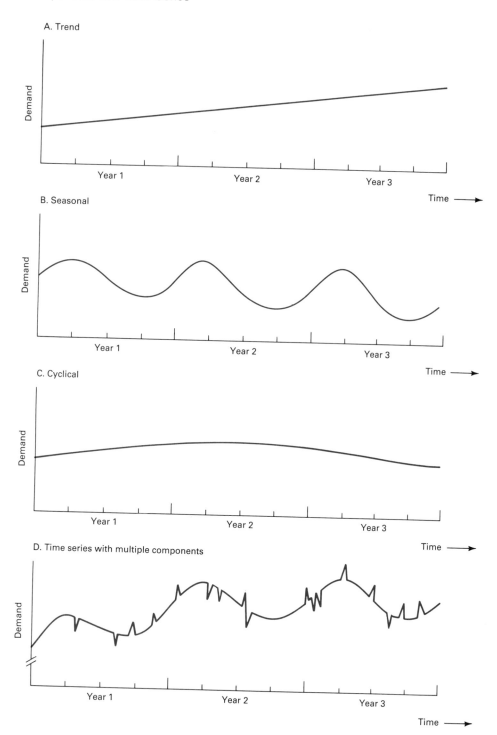

Forecasting models exist for use with time series containing any or all of the components. While caution is advised, many demand forecasts are rather simple extensions of past series behavior into the future. For example, suppose the demand for tow-truck and jump-start services has peaked in the winter season in the 10 years for which records exist. This seasonal component would be expected to continue and would affect the tow-truck firm's projections in planning service to troubled motorists in the future.

Having defined and examined demand and its components, our next task is to do the same for forecasting: What is it, and what are its purposes?

Types of Forecasts

Forecast and *forecasting* are popular words used in several ways. For example, if you ask a librarian for research materials on forecasting, you should expect to receive lore on *weather forecasting,* which is perhaps the most popular use of the term. If you look up forecasting in the library's subject card catalog, you will find mostly readings on *economic forecasting,* for example, on the forecasting of gross national product and disposable personal income. Economic forecasting has some bearing on the topic of this chapter. A third type is *technological forecasting,* which means predicting process and product breakthroughs. That is of some interest to us. A fourth, less common use of *forecasting* is in phrases such as "personnel forecast," "materials forecast," and "tool forecast." Those uses concern resources or means rather than products and services, or ends. While direct forecasting of resources may be done, an often better approach is to translate a product demand forecast into resource needs using conversion factors or standards. A fifth term, *sales forecasting,* is often used in the same way as the sixth term, **demand forecasting**. Of the two, demand forecasting is our term of choice, since it applies to services offered by not-for-profit institutions as well as sales-oriented enterprises.

Purposes of Demand Forecasting

The purposes of demand forecasting parallel the three purposes of demand management, but demand forecasting is more specific in that it helps plan both quantities and timing of:

1. Services provided or goods produced—in the short term.
2. Labor and inventories—in the medium term.
3. Facilities—in the long term.

Item forecasts must express demand in natural item units. Examples are tons of steel and gallons of diesel fuel in the process industries, and clients, or client hours, light bulbs, paper tablets, trucks, and so forth in discrete production industries. Both the forecast and the schedule are expressed in those terms.

Item forecasts are short term, from a few minutes for some fast foods to many months for some long-lead-time, heavy industrial products.

The medium term could cover just a few days for a firm that uses untrained labor and hires and lays off based on a few days' notice as demand rises and falls. Most firms adjust the labor force less often because of the cost of training labor. In that case, the medium-term forecast would extend several months or quarters into the future. Medium-term forecasts are often expressed in labor-hours' or machine-hours' worth of demand. Other units of measure, including dollars, are workable since they may be converted to labor, machine usage, and aggregate inventory.

Long-term forecasts for facilities—plant and equipment—may go 10 to 20 years into the future for plants that require extensive hearings, licenses, debate, and approvals. Nuclear power plants are one example. At the other extreme, the long-term forecast for a restaurant may need to extend only a couple of years out. Dollars are the preferred measure of long-term demand, but it usually is necessary to subdivide the total dollars into forecasts by type of product to indicate how the facility should be equipped—types of equipment, space, utilities, and so forth in each product area.

We have seen how the purposes of forecasting are affected by the time horizon. The complexity of forecasting, the next topic, depends on time horizon, plus another factor: type of industry or business.

Complexity of Forecasting

Competition affects the kind of forecast required. In some industries, there are competitive pressures to meet customer demand immediately: Services are provided on demand; deliveries from stock are the norm for auto replacement parts, consumer goods, and cafeteria foods. These are make-to-stock/ship-to-order businesses. They require complete advance preparation—everything from raw materials to finished goods based on demand forecasts.

At the other extreme are industries with very long manufacturing lead times, such as ships, locomotives, missiles, and heavy construction. These heavy-capital-goods firms are project-oriented, and they make to order. Such firms may maintain no inventories, not even raw materials. They need only long- and medium-term forecasting—as the basis for planning facilities and labor. Purchase of raw materials and production of goods are based on firm contracts rather than on forecasts.

Figure 5–3 illustrates the two extreme types of industry, plus two in between. As shown, it is customer lead time that dictates how many levels of forecasting are required.

The first in-between industry is in the class referred to as *job-oriented firms.* Such organizations, including foundries, hospitals, and restaurants, forecast for capacity and raw materials. These firms make to order, but from materials on hand.

The other in-between type of industry is that which produces components and plans capacity and raw materials based on forecasts. However, assembly

FIGURE 5–3
Demand Lead Times and Forecasts Required

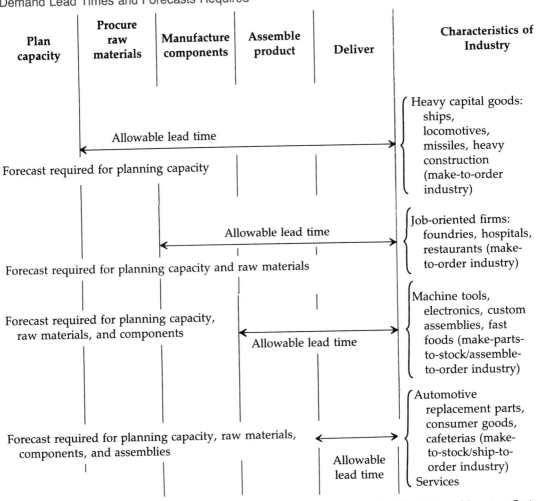

Source: An extension and adaptation of fig. 2–2 of G. W. Plossl and O. W. Wight, *Production and Inventory Control: Principles and Techniques,* © 1967, p. 16. Reprinted by permission of Prentice-Hall, Inc., Englewood Cliffs, New Jersey.

and shipment await firm customer ordering. Examples are machine tools, electronics, custom assemblies, and fast foods. (Fast-food restaurants often precook or preassemble ingredients based on forecasts.) These are assemble-to-order firms.

Figure 5–3 may imply that in a given firm up to four different types of forecasts could be required: one for facilities and labor, one for raw materials, one for components, and one for product assembly. Modern production and inventory control, based on just-in-time or time-phased material planning, is able to cut this to two or three forecasts: a long-term and a medium-term forecast for facilities and labor and a shorter-term forecast that links materials to components and, perhaps, to product assembly.

We have noted that competition forces industries such as consumer goods and cafeterias to make forecasts for all but final shipment or delivery. The risks and the costs are (1) being stuck with inventories of assembled products, components, and raw materials when forecasts are too high and (2) losing sales when forecasts are too low. Demand management walks a thin line between these two forecast-induced risks. In so doing, a principle sometimes called **delayed differentiation** can be selectively applied. At each stage of operations (assembly, components, etc.) and for each class of inventory items, look for a way to keep the item in the lower-cost or low-value-added state as long as possible. That is, delay transforming the standard item—say, resin—into a differentiated item, such as a plastic toy. The standard item retains possibilities of being made into any number of differentiated products.

Forecasting in Support Organizations

The common view seems to be that forecasting should be done by those with responsibility for final products/services. This would limit forecasting to items earning revenue. Or, for nonrevenue-producing organizations, forecasting would be restricted to major-mission items; for example, in social work, forecasting the number of eligible clients.

That view of forecasting is too narrow. *All* managers should forecast. Put another way, all staff services and nonrevenue items should be forecast in addition to forecasting for revenue and major-mission items. Example 5–1 may help to show why forecasting is necessary in support departments.

EXAMPLE 5–1   **APEX STEEL CABINET COMPANY**

O. R. Guy is the new president of Apex. One of his first acts is to create the department of management science and assign corporate forecasting to it. Corporate forecasting applies to the firm's revenue-earning products: its line of steel cabinets.

Management science department analysts arrive at a forecast of a 10 percent increase in total steel cabinet sales for next year. Mr. Guy informs key department heads that they may consider 10 percent increases their targets for planning departmental budgets. Protests come at Mr. Guy from several directions. Most notable are the following three:

1. *Engineering chief:* "O. R., I hate to protest any budget increase. But I'd rather wait until I need it. The engineering workload often goes down when cabinet sales go up. That's because marketing pressures us less for new product designs when sales are good. But then, in some years of good sales, we have a lot of new design and design modification work. This happens when several key products are in the decline phase of their life cycles. So you can see that our budget should not depend strictly on corporate sales."

2. *Personnel chief:* "We are the same way, O. R. The personnel workload depends more on things like whether the labor contract is up for renewal. Sure, we need to do more interviewing and training when corporate sales go up. But we have bigger problems when they go down. Layoffs and reassignments are tougher. Also, when sales go down, we may get more grievances."

3. *Marketing chief:* "Well, I hate to be the crybaby. But it's marketing that bears most of the load in meeting that 10 percent forecast sales increase. I was going to ask for a 20 percent budget increase—mainly for a stepped-up advertising campaign. I don't dispute the management science projection of a 10 percent sales increase. The market is there; we just need to spend more to tap it."

Based on those three comments, Mr. Guy rescinds his note about a 10 percent targeted budget increase. He then informs managers at all levels that they are expected to formally forecast their key workloads. This becomes the basis for their plans and budgets. The management science department is assigned to serve as adviser for those managers requesting help.

To explain what is meant by key workloads, Mr. Guy provides each manager with a simple forecasting plan developed by the chief of personnel. The plan is shown in Figure 5–4.

FIGURE 5–4
Forecasting Plan—Personnel Department, Apex Company

Workloads	*Forecast Basis*
1. Hiring/interviewing	Number of job openings—based on data from other departments Number of job applicants—based on trend projection and judgment
2. Layoffs and reassignments	Number of employees—based on data from other departments
3. Grievances	Number of stage 1, 2, and 3 grievances, estimated separately—based on trend projection and judgment
4. Training	Number of classroom hours Number of on-the-job training hours Both based on data from other departments
5. Payroll actions	Number of payroll actions—based on number of employees and judgment on impact of major changes
6. Union contract negotiations	Number of key issues—based on judgment
7. Miscellaneous—all other workloads	Not forecast in units; instead, resource needs are estimated directly based on trends and judgment

The plan in Figure 5–4 provides for forecasting *in units of demand* as much as possible. The alternative is to skip this step and directly plan for staff, equipment, and other resources. This is the approach taken for item 7 in Figure 5–4, miscellaneous workloads. Some of the same methods—trend projection and judgment—may be used in this approach. But this is not demand forecasting; it is supply, or resource, planning.

Planning resources directly rather than translating from a forecast of workload units is the easy way. But a more precise approach is to forecast demand in units. The standard time to produce one unit may be determined—very precisely if the product is a key one. Then the unit forecast may be multiplied by the standard time to give staffing needs. Also, the unit forecast may be multiplied by material factors, space factors, and so on to yield projected needs for other resources. The cost of all those resources then becomes the budget.

In the example, Mr. Guy is following a rational approach in requesting demand forecasts of all managers. It would be a mistake, however, to expect every manager to use extensive—and expensive—recordkeeping and historical data analysis. For lesser demands, a less formal approach should suffice.

Our discussion of types and sources of forecasting and influencing factors suggests that managers have discretion in deciding how much to forecast, how to forecast, what to use for reference data, and so forth. How is the exercise of this discretion evaluated? Quite simply, a forecast's accuracy serves as a simple but meaningful assessment of the people and procedures used to arrive at that forecast. Central to the concept of forecast accuracy is forecast error, considered next.

FORECAST ERROR

Forecast error has uses in item, product, product or capacity group, and industry demand management. There are several popular ways of measuring forecast error. All the techniques are after the fact; that is, a manager must wait one period—sometimes even longer—to unearth the error in the forecast. In this section we discuss measures of forecast error, compare item forecast error to aggregate forecast error, and study error as we project forecasts further into the future.

Measures of Forecast Error

In its basic form, **forecast error** is defined for a specific item in a given time period. Formally:

$$E_t = D_t - F_t \tag{5–1}$$

where

E_t = Error for period t

D_t = Actual demand that occurred in period t

F_t = Forecast for period t

Period t might refer to a certain hour, day, week, month, or whatever time period is most useful. Monthly, quarterly, and annual periods are popular in manufacturing. Many service organizations, however, might need to use weekly or even daily time periods. Typically, the interest is in some representative measure of forecast errors over several periods rather than for a single time period. Three such measures, mean absolute deviation, standard deviation, and mean absolute percent error, are considered next.

Mean Absolute Deviation

The **mean absolute deviation (MAD)** provides an accurate measure of the magnitude of forecast error. The MAD is the sum of the absolute values of the errors divided by the number of periods, that is,

$$\text{MAD} = \frac{\sum_{t=1}^{n} |E_t|}{n} \tag{5-2}$$

MAD's use of absolute values removes evidence of positive or negative forecast model bias, but its realistic expression of mean or average error magnitude makes it one of the most popular error measures.

Standard Deviation

The **standard deviation (SD)** is obtained by taking the square root of the mean error squared, with $n - 1$ in the denominator.

$$\text{SD} = \sqrt{\frac{\sum_{t=1}^{n} (E_t)^2}{n - 1}} \tag{5-3}$$

The standard deviation is useful in statistical analysis of forecast error data. If forecast errors are normally distributed, the standard deviation equals approximately 1.25(MAD). This relationship is explored later in the discussion of tracking signals.

Mean Absolute Percent Error

The **mean absolute percent error (MAPE)** directly relates forecast error to the target, actual period demand. It is calculated by dividing the absolute error for each period by the period demand, converting this ratio to a percentage, and computing the average of the percentage errors. We would show this as:

$$\text{MAPE} = \frac{\sum_{t=1}^{n} \left(\frac{|E_t|}{D_t}\right) \times 100\%}{n} \tag{5-4}$$

Because absolute values are used, the MAPE will not reveal model bias. Its advantage is that it gives demand managers a common percentage basis for comparing forecasting models.

Forecast Error: Examples

Figure 5–5 shows historical demand for an eight-period time series. The forecast is 10 for each period in the series. Data from the figure form the first three columns of Table 5–1. Column 4 is calculated using Equation 5–1. Columns 5, 6, and 7 (simple mathematical transformations of column 4) are used to compute the MAD, the SD, and the MAPE, as follows:

Mean absolute deviation (MAD)

(Equation 5–2): $$MAD = \frac{16}{8} = 2.00$$

Standard deviation (SD)

(Equation 5–3): $$SD = \sqrt{\frac{48}{7}} = \sqrt{6.86} = 2.62$$

Mean absolute percent error (MAPE)

(Equation 5–4): $$MAPE = \frac{210}{8} = 26.25\%$$

FIGURE 5–5

Historical Demand Series and Forecast Error

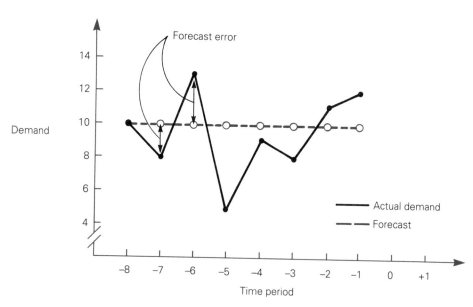

TABLE 5–1
Computations for Forecast Error Measures

(1)	(2)	(3)	(4)	(5)	(6)	(7)
				Absolute	Error	Absolute Percent
Period	Demand	Forecast	Error	Error	Squared	Error
(t)	(D_t)	(F_t)	(E_t)	$\lvert E_t \rvert$	$(E_t)^2$	$(\lvert E_t \rvert / D_t) \times 100\%$
−8	10	10	0	0	0	(0/10) × 100% = 0%
−7	8	10	−2	2	4	(2/8) × 100 = 25
−6	13	10	3	3	9	(3/13) × 100 = 23
−5	5	10	−5	5	25	(5/5) × 100 = 100
−4	9	10	−1	1	1	(1/9) × 100 = 11
−3	8	10	−2	2	4	(2/8) × 100 = 25
−2	11	10	1	1	1	(1/11) × 100 = 9
−1	12	10	2	2	4	(2/12) × 100 = 17
		Sum:	−4	16	48	210%

Forecast Error: Item versus Aggregate

As we have seen, history-based forecasting involves (1) analysis of historical demand data and (2) analysis of error. As we shall see later in this chapter, forecast errors are used to compare the abilities of various forecasting models to explain demand changes. The hazard for demand management is that inaccurate forecasts may lead to large overcommitment or undercommitment of resources. One way to reduce the risk is to rely on the lower error rates of group forecasts.

The result of forecasting for whole product or capacity groups is the **aggregate demand forecast**, which might be measured in pieces, pounds, and so on or converted into capacity units such as labor-hours, machine-hours, or appointment hours. Aggregate forecasts are useful in planning for adjustable capacity, such as work force and materials, in which the purpose is to adjust capacity to fit forecast aggregate demand.

Matching capacity to aggregate demand works well *only* if groups are set wisely (to be discussed in Chapter 6). The point here is that it *is* possible to rely on lower error rates of group forecasts. This concept is illustrated in Figure 5–6, which shows six items in a small group. These items could be members of a product family produced in a common work cell; this would imply that they share production resources. Figure 5–6 shows third-quarter actual demand, forecast, error, and absolute percent error for each item. The average error for the items as a group is 6.6 percent, while individual item errors range from 1.0 to 44.1 percent—a mean absolute percent error of 18.1 percent.

Caution is required in interpreting Figure 5–6. First, the figure may give the impression that a group forecast is merely the sum of item forecasts. However, that is *not* the best way. It is better to develop the forecast by examining trends, seasonality, and so forth *for the group as a whole*. The result is likely to be more accurate than the sum of item forecasts.

FIGURE 5–6

Item Forecast versus Group Forecast Accuracy

Item	(1) Third Quarter Actual	(2) Third Quarter Forecast	(3) Error [(1) − (2)]	(4) Absolute Percent Error [|(3)|/(1)]
Bracket	1,600	1,280	+320	20.0%
Doorknob	23,200	20,300	+2,900	12.5
Hinge	18,660	15,120	+3,540	19.0
Vise	22,210	32,010	−9,800	44.1
Tool case	7,960	7,880	+80	1.0
Grate	36,920	41,290	−4,370	11.8
Average item forecast error				18.1%
Group totals	110,550	117,880	−7,330	6.6%

Forecast Error: Near versus Distant Future

Forecasts are more accurate for shorter time periods. This makes intuitive sense and is shown by example in Figure 5–7. The demand forecast is set at 500 per week (column 2). Only a sample of weeks is included for illustration: 2, 5, 10, 15, 20, and 25. Cumulative demand forecast (column 3) is simply the number of weeks times the weekly forecast of 500; that is, column 3 = column 1 × column 2. Cumulative actual demand figures (column 4) were made up but are realistic. Cumulative absolute error (column 5) is actual (column 4) minus forecast (column 3). The result is a pattern of rising error as the forecast takes in more weeks of demand.

Knowing this does not mean that longer-term forecasting is futile. There must be such forecasts for capacity planning purposes. They must project as far into the future as the planning lead time for the given resource or unit of capacity.

FIGURE 5–7

Cumulative Forecast Error: Picture Frames

(1) Week Number	(2) Weekly Demand Forecast	(3) Cumulative Demand Forecast [(1) × (2)]	(4) Cumulative Actual Demand	(5) Cumulative Absolute Error [|(4) − (3)|]
2	500	1,000	1,162	162
5	500	2,500	2,716	216
10	500	5,000	5,488	488
15	500	7,500	8,110	610
20	500	10,000	11,250	1,250
25	500	12,500	14,010	1,510

Two useful principles follow from the knowledge that shorter forecasts are more accurate:

1. As time passes, forecasts should be refined by interjecting newer data and rolling the forecast over.
2. Different elements of the planning and control system should be based on a different type of forecast according to the degree of forecast accuracy required.

As an example of both points, some goods producers master schedule product modules and component parts based on projections of 52 weeks; they refine this schedule every month based on the latest revised forecasts plus actual orders. Final assembly of end products, as well as processing of drop-in customers, is based on shorter-term projection, perhaps only a few days or weeks. Scheduling for modules and components thus is based on forecasts containing more error than schedules for final assembly or customer/client arrivals.

At this point, armed with methods of determining forecast error, we consider demand forecasting sources, then techniques.

DEMAND FORECASTING SOURCES

In large, national corporations demand forecasting is often three-pronged, perhaps coordinated by a corporate planning department. This is shown in Figure 5–8. Marketing produces one set of forecasting figures. Economists look at how the economy is likely to affect the organization's demand, which gives another

FIGURE 5–8
Three Determinants of Demand Forecast

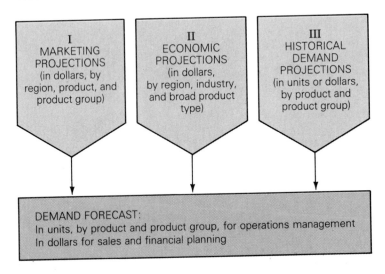

set of figures. Statisticians or computerized statistical routines project past demand trends, yielding a third set of figures. Then top management may review all three sets, and the "jury of executive opinion" may overrule them all. Executives may prefer to trust their own experience and judgment. Even so, the three sets of figures surely help to sharpen judgments about future demand.

The three major sources of demand projection data involve different techniques and have different uses. Figure 5–9 illustrates.

Marketing Projections

Marketing departments assemble demand projections, in dollars, based on sales projections, sales force estimates, test market results, and market research. A sales promotion has a major impact on short-term demand. Moving excessive inventory is one purpose of a sales promotion. Simply increasing cash inflow

FIGURE 5–9

Techniques of Demand Forecasting

			Forecast Horizon	
Forecast Basis	*Unit of Measure*	*Short Term*	*Medium Term*	*Long Term*
I. Marketing projections	$			
Sales promotions		Yes	No	No
Sales force estimates		Yes	Somewhat	No
Consumer surveys and test marketing		No	Yes	Yes
II. Economic projections	$	No	Yes	Yes
III. Historical demand projection	Items or $			
Multiperiod pattern projection (Mean, trend, seasonal)		Yes	Yes	Yes
Single-period patternless projection (Moving average, exponential smoothing, and simulation)		Yes	No	No
Associative projection (leading indicator and correlation)		Yes	Yes	Yes
		↑ Product scheduling	↑ Labor and inventory planning	↑ Facilities planning

Forecast purposes

and making short-term profits look good is another. Clearly the latter financial purpose can wreak havoc with schedules and resource availability. It is important that promotions be closely coordinated with operations planning, which is one of the roles of the master scheduling committee. Sales promotions usually do not extend beyond the near future. Therefore, as Figure 5–9 indicates, sales promotions generally have little effect on either medium- and long-term demand forecasting or labor and inventory planning.

Salespeople may be required to submit periodic sales estimates for their product lines and districts. The estimates are consolidated to yield product forecasts for the whole company. While sales force estimates are unlikely to be accurate on the whole, they are valued in particular cases because they enable salespeople to find out early about major orders. Such information contributes especially to short-term forecasting, but sometimes salespeople also glean demand data for medium-term forecasting and planning.

Consumer surveys and test marketing are helpful in finding out customers' buying plans or reactions to a new product or product idea. *Plans*, in this case, generally means next year or beyond, which affects medium- and long-term forecasts and capacity planning.

Economic Projections

Economic projections, shown next in Figure 5–9, are useful for medium- and long-term purposes. For example, any firm offering goods and services related to homemaking surely is interested in national economic projections for housing starts in the next few years. Economic projections range from educated guesses of an economist or panel of economists to computer projections based on mathematical equations. Economic forecasting based on sets of computer-processed mathematical equations is a field known as *econometrics*.

The econometrician builds forecasting models by such methods as statistical regression analysis. A simple approach is to use a single regression equation. For example, suppose that farm machinery demand is to be forecast. The econometrician tries out various possible causes of change in farm machinery expenditures. Past data on different sets of causal factors are put into a computer for regression tests. The set of causal factors that works best on past data may be used to forecast future demand. The forecast equations would have the causal variables (e.g., good crops, machinery prices, advertising) on the right side and the dependent variable (demand projection) on the left.

A single regression equation may not be accurate enough, because causes of demand may be complicated by interrelationships. For example, demand for machinery may indeed be affected by price and advertising, but price probably goes up when there are more advertising expenses. It may be prudent to set up and test factors that affect price, which will result in a second regression equation. Perhaps a third regression equation should be set up to test causal factors affecting advertising. This would result in a system of simultaneous regression equations, which could be solved to yield a forecast of farm machinery.

Historical Demand Projections

The final basis of forecasting shown in Figure 5–9 is historical demand projection. Eight techniques are grouped into three general categories. All of them rely on historical demand data. The first two general categories, multiperiod pattern and single-period projections, require time-series data. The associative projections, however, require that demand be tracked against some variable other than time. For operations management purposes, all the techniques express forecasts in units (or dollars converted to units).

Three of the techniques—mean, trend, and seasonal—are actually names of the time-series patterns that can be projected as many periods into the future as desired, but with decreasing accuracy. Hence, they are referred to as *multiperiod pattern projection techniques* and are useful for product scheduling and capacity planning.

The next three techniques—moving average, exponential smoothing, and simulation—do not seek to discover a pattern (except in advanced models); they merely react to recent demand changes. Thus, they are referred to as *single-period patternless techniques* and are used primarily for short-term product scheduling.

The last two techniques are leading indicator and correlation. These attempt to discover an association between demand and some other known factors. The time horizon may be short, medium, or long term (but with poor accuracy for the long term), and the technique may be usable for product scheduling or, in some cases, capacity planning.

All of the historical demand projection techniques rely on demand records. Larger firms that keep careful records are likely to have profuse data on past demand for goods and services. Minimal or no records at all might be the case, however, especially with small firms or smaller departments within organizations.

Where sufficient records don't exist, historical demand projections are still made but are totally judgmental. The manager uses experience to decide what future demand to expect. The inaccuracies possible in these rough forecasts could result in idle resources at some times and failure to meet demand at others. Recordkeeping is essential even for small firms. The high rate of failure among small businesses illustrates the danger of misjudging—really, mismanaging—demand.

Consideration of the historical forecasting models constitutes the remainder of this chapter. First are the three models used in multiperiod pattern projection.

MULTIPERIOD PATTERN PROJECTION

Mean, trend, and seasonal analysis forecasting models may be used to project a past demand pattern several periods into the future. They are often used in the **rolling-forecast** mode: redoing or rolling over the forecast at intervals—for example, every month, quarter, or year. The forecast horizon may be limited to weeks or months, or extend years into the future.

Mean and Trend

The simplest projection of a time series uses the arithmetic mean. When historical demand lacks trend and is not inherently seasonal, the simple mean may be suitable for forecasting. More often there is at least some upward or downward trend, which could even be projected as a curve. Figure 5–10 illustrates the mean and trend for a company that we shall call Data Services, Inc., which offers computer programming commercially.

Three years of past quarterly demand in hours of programmer time are plotted. A first impression might be that there is no strong trend, and a bit of study shows no seasonal pattern either. If a certain quarter's demand is high one year, it looks as likely to be low the next. The up-and-down movement seems random. Also, one would not consider programming to be a service having some sort of seasonal demand pattern. What should the forecast be for upcoming quarters in 1992? Perhaps the mean (which works out to be 437) is the best way to minimize forecast error for such a nondescript demand; see the level dashed line.

There's another possible interpretation: Looking at only the most recent data—say the last seven quarters—the trend is downward; see the "eyeball" projection slanting downward in Figure 5–10. Data Services's analysts may consider the projection to be valid for one or two quarters into 1992. They do *not* accept it for the longer term, since it is aiming toward out-of-business status! Presuming they know the business is strong enough to carry on and prosper, the analysts would look for a more realistic way to project the future.

For a better forecast, better demand data might help. Let us assume that 20 instead of 12 quarters of past demand data are available. The demand history is displayed in Figure 5–11. Quite a different pattern emerges. The long-run trend is definitely upward. With a straightedge, the eyeballed upward trend line is drawn and projected two years (eight quarters) into the future. The 1992 quarterly forecasts are now in the range of 500 programmer-hours instead of the 300 to 200 range resulting from the 7-quarter downward trend projection in Figure 5–10.

Another interpretation is that the 20-quarter demand data describe a slow curve. Figure 5–12 shows such a curve projected by the eyeball method through 1993. The 1992–93 forecast is now between the two previous straight-line forecasts. This projection is for a leveling off at about 450.

The curving projection looks valid; in other cases, a straight-line projection may look valid. In any event, the managers may use the graphic projection only to sharpen their own judgment. For example, Data Services's managers may have other information about their customers that leads them to a more optimistic forecast than the projected 450. Even where such outside information seems to overrule historical projection, the projection is worth doing. It is quick and simple.

Another method of trend projection is less quick, less simple, but more precise: mathematical projection using regression analysis. The least-squares technique of regression analysis, discussed in the chapter supplement, results in an equation of a straight line that best fits the historical demand data. To get a

FIGURE 5–10

Arithmetic Mean and Trend Projection—Data Services, Inc.

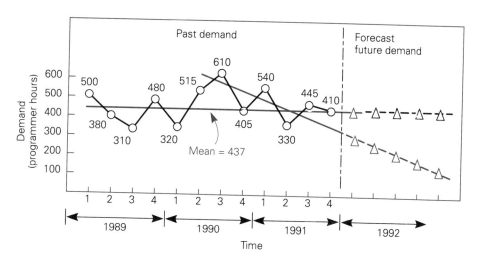

FIGURE 5–11

Twenty-Quarter Eyeball Trend—Data Services, Inc.

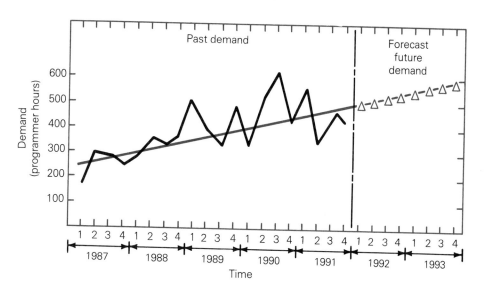

trend projection, we extend the line into the future. (The least-squares method may be modified to yield nonlinear projections as well.)

The accuracy of least squares is not its main value. Eyeballing is generally accurate enough for something so speculative as forecasting. But drawing graphs for eyeball projections is time-consuming, prohibitively so if there are a large

FIGURE 5–12
Twenty-Quarter Eyeball Curve—Data Services, Inc.

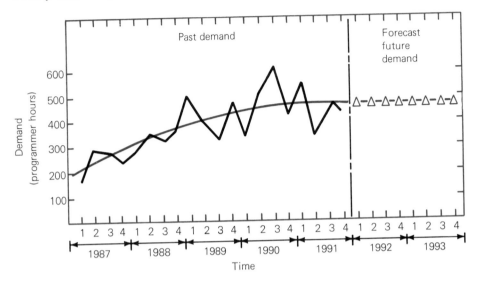

number of products to forecast. Least squares takes time to set up, but after that it goes fast, especially with a programmable calculator or computer. Computer-based forecasting routines have an extra benefit: They are usually able to print out mathematical formulas as approximations of the demand pattern, graphic projections, and tabular listings. Thus, least-squares regression is valued not for its forecasting accuracy but because it aids in routinizing some of the forecasting steps.

Seasonal

Oftentimes an item showing a trend also has a history of demand seasonality. In fact, perhaps most goods and services exhibit at least some seasonality. We'll examine the **seasonal index** method of building seasonality into a demand forecast.

Seasonal Index: An Example

A typical example of a seasonal industry is a moving company. How might a mover make use of seasonal indexes? Consider Figure 5–13, which shows four years of demand data, in van loads, for a hypothetical company we'll call Metro Movers.

Since a moving company experiences a heavy surge in demand for moving in June, July, and August (during school vacations), Metro groups its demand history into summer, fall, winter, and spring, rather than using the usual fiscal quarters (e.g., with third quarter consisting of July, August, and September).

FIGURE 5–13

Seasonal Demand History—Metro Movers

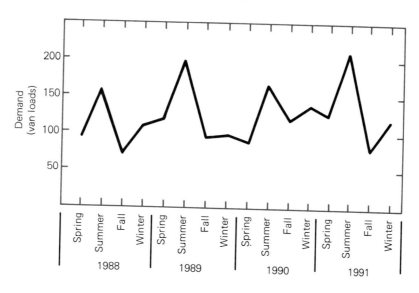

The first step is to scrutinize the demand graph. It is clear that summer demand is by far the highest in every year and fall demand is generally the lowest. The seasonal index measures how much higher and how much lower.

Figure 5–14 shows calculations of seasonal indexes for the 16 available past demands. (Note: Besides seasonality, it looks as though there is a slight upward trend over the last 16 quarters. We shall ignore the trend for now.) The third column in Figure 5–14 contains average seasonal demand figures, which are working figures that are needed to calculate the seasonal indexes in the last column. Each entry in column 3 is a four-period moving average, which is "centered" $1\frac{1}{2}$ months into the season. It includes demands going back six months and forward six months from that point. Thus, the first figure in column 3 is based on demands for the last $1\frac{1}{2}$ months of spring 1988; all of summer, fall, and winter 1988; and the first $1\frac{1}{2}$ months of spring 1989. So,

$$\frac{(90/2) + 160 + 70 + 120 + (130/2)}{4} = 115$$

This is a bit cumbersome, but it ensures that no one season is weighted more heavily than any other.

Column 4 is simply actual demand divided by the average for a season. For example, the first calculated index, for fall 1988, is 70 divided by 115, which is 0.61. In other words, fall 1988's demand was only 61 percent of the average seasonal demand.

FIGURE 5–14
Seasonal Index Calculations—Metro Movers

(1) Time	(2) Actual Demand	(3) Mean Seasonal Demand	(4) Seasonal Index [(2)/(3)]
Spring 1988	90		
Summer 1988	160		
Fall 1988	70	115	0.61
Winter 1988	120	125	0.96
Spring 1989	130	132	0.98
Summer 1989	200	132	1.52
Fall 1989	90	124	0.73
Winter 1989	100	114	0.88
Spring 1990	80	115	0.70
Summer 1990	170	125	1.36
Fall 1990	130	136	0.96
Winter 1990	140	147	0.95
Spring 1991	130	146	0.89
Summer 1991	210	138	1.52
Fall 1991	80		
Winter 1991	120		

FIGURE 5–15
Summary and Projection of Seasonal Indexes—Metro Movers

		Spring	Summer	Fall	Winter	
	1988			0.61	0.96	
Past	1989	0.98	1.52	0.73	0.88	
	1990	0.70	1.36	0.96	0.95	
	1991	0.89	1.52			
Future	1992	0.85	1.46	0.76	0.93	←Mean of each column

The last step is to rearrange the indexes by season to see if there is any pattern; see Figure 5–15. The three values for each season need to somehow be reduced to a single index. The index for fall is steadily rising, from 0.61 to 0.73 to 0.96. That is not sufficient reason to expect it to continue to rise, however, especially since the other seasons do not show trends. Thus, the projections of the seasonal indexes for 1992 are the means of each column.

Metro Movers may now use the seasonal indexes in fine-tuning its demand forecasts for each coming season. For example, suppose that Metro expects to move 480 vans of goods next year based on projection of the mean of past years' demands. It would be naive to divide 480 by 4 and project 120 vans in each season. Instead,

Divide 480 by 4 = 120 vans in an average season
120 × 0.85 = 102 vans forecast for spring 1992
120 × 1.46 = 175 vans forecast for summer 1992
120 × 0.76 = 91 vans forecast for fall 1992
120 × 0.93 = <u>112</u> vans forecast for winter 1992–93
Yearly total = 480

Seasonally Adjusted Trends

It takes a few more steps if the basic demand projection is an up or down trend instead of a level line. For example, assume that Metro again projects 1992 demand at 480 vans, this time based on historical projection of an upward trend of about 2.5 percent per quarter. The 480 is the sum of four quarterly demands at a 2.5 percent upward slope:

116—spring 1992

119—summer 1992

121—fall 1992

<u>124</u>—winter 1992–93

480

Basis: 480/4 = 120, the average seasonal value, applicable to mid-year; 1.25 percent less = 119, the projection for mid summer; and 2.5 percent less than 119 = 116, the projection for mid-spring. Fall and winter are calculated similarly.

Now the seasonal adjustments are:

116 × 0.85 = 99 vans forecast for spring 1992
119 × 1.46 = 174 vans forecast for summer 1992
121 × 0.76 = 92 vans forecast for fall 1992
124 × 0.93 = 115 vans forecast for winter 1992–93

A comparison of the last two cases, without trend and with trend, is given in Figure 5–16. The figure shows what might be expected: Trend effects, which are so important in the long run, tend to be overshadowed in the short run by seasonal (or other) influences.

Natural and Induced Cyclicity

Seasonal analysis is actually one form of cycle analysis. If a certain demand pattern were to recur, say, every five months, the basic seasonal method may be applied.

Sometimes, for an item whose demand is clearly seasonal, seasonal analysis should *not* be applied. This is generally true of items that are newly marketed or back in the market after interruption. The problem is the "pipeline" phenomenon: When the product hits the market, its demand may rise slowly and then spurt until the wholesale/retail pipeline is filled; the demand may go slack until consumers become fully aware of and respond to the product. A simple moving

FIGURE 5–16
Seasonal Adjustment of Level and Upward Projection—Metro Movers

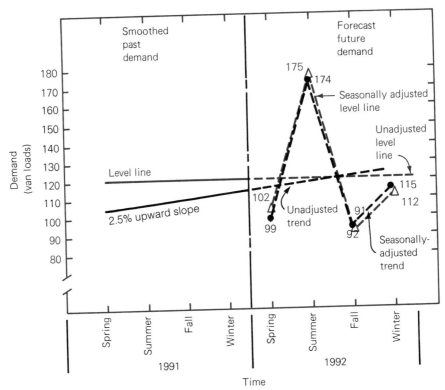

average (to be covered in the next section), unadjusted for seasonality, may be the best forecasting method during the transitional period. Later, when product demand has reached a steadier state, seasonal indexing refinements may be added.

Pipelining is an artificial situation. So is channel stuffing, which is inflating current sales totals—by various means—to meet some sort of goal. One version, well known in manufacturing circles, is called the *end-of-month push* (also *end-of-week*, *end-of-quarter*, and *end-of-year push*). The many companies (few were immune) falling into this pattern would relax in the early part of the period and then go into a frenzy at the end to meet the target. In a few cases, pressures to meet goals have driven people to desperate, sometimes illegal, acts; see the box entitled "Stuffing the Channel."

One company, Physio Control, a producer of a medical electronic product line, tried mightily to escape from its end-of-year demand-surge pattern. So far, they have been unable to do so because most of their customers, medical institutions, have money to spend at the end of the year and spend a lump of it on Physio's products.

In such cases, where channel stuffing is a fact of life, seasonal analysis can

Stuffing the Channel

"Hitting the number became a company-wide obsession. Although many high-tech manufacturers accelerate shipments at the end of the quarter to boost sales—a practice known as *stuffing the channel*—MiniScribe went several steps beyond that. On one occasion, an analyst relates, it shipped more than twice as many disk drives to a computer manufacturer as had been ordered; a former MiniScribe sales manager says the excess shipment was worth about $9 million. . . .

"Other accounting maneuvers, starting as far back as 1986, involved shipments of disk drives from MiniScribe's factory in Singapore. Most shipments went by air freight, but a squeeze on air-cargo space toward the end of each quarter would force some shipments onto cargo ships—which required up to two weeks for transit. On several occasions, says a former division manager, MiniScribe executives looking to raise sales changed purchase orders to show that a customer took title to a shipment in Singapore, when, in fact, title wouldn't change until the drives were delivered in the United States. . . .

"To avoid booking losses on returns . . . defective drives would be tossed onto a "dog pile" and booked as inventory, according to [a technician]. Eventually, the dog-pile drives would be shipped out again to new customers, continuing the cycle. Returns of defective merchandise ran as high as 15 percent in some divisions [according to the same technician]."

Andy Zipser, "How Pressure to Raise Sales Led MiniScribe to Falsify Numbers," *The Wall Street Journal*, Monday, September 11, 1989.

---

and should account for it. That should not stop people from attacking the problem directly in an effort to eliminate the causes of spikey demand patterns.

Summarizing the multiperiod pattern projections, keep in mind that their source is historical demand data described as time-series patterns. Finding the patterns can require some computations, but projecting them into the future is direct and simple. If there is evidence suggesting that future conditions will differ markedly from past ones, the pattern projection techniques should be avoided or used with extreme caution.

We now turn to single-period patternless projection.

SINGLE-PERIOD PATTERNLESS PROJECTION

The patternless projection techniques make no inferences about past demand data but merely react to the most recent demands. These techniques—the moving average, exponential smoothing, and simulation—typically produce a single value, which is the forecast for a single period into the future.

In practice, the single-period projection is often extended for several additional periods into the future. In the absence of trend and seasonality, extending the single value is appropriate and results in a rolling forecast. In each new period, the previous projection is dropped and the newly computed forecast becomes the new projection for periods in the new forecast horizon. It is like driving at night with headlights aimed 300 feet out, always reaching out another 300 feet as the car moves over the next stretch of pavement. These techniques are best suited to short-term forecasting for scheduling the product mix. The forecast period typically is a week, a month, or a quarter, and the forecast horizon may include one or several periods.

Moving Average

The **moving average**, which became widely used in the 1950s and 1960s, is simply the mean or average of a given number of the most recent actual demands. Formulas and explanations for the moving average technique are presented in the following box.

Moving Average: Formulas and Explanation

A general expression for the moving average forecasting model is:

$$F_t = \frac{\sum_{i=t-n}^{t-1} (D_i \times w_i)}{\sum_{i=t-n}^{t-1} w_i} \tag{5-5}$$

where

F_t = Moving average forecast for period t

n = Time span—number of demand periods included in the computed average

D_i = Actual demand for period i

w_i = Weight value given to data in period i

When different weights are used for the various data values, the computed forecast is referred to as the *weighted moving average*. Typically, higher weights are assigned to more recent periods. When the demand for each time period is weighted equally—usually with a weight of 1—we compute a *simple moving average* forecast. The sum of the weights—the denominator in Equation 5–5—will then equal the number of periods in the time span, n. The numerator is also simplified for simple moving averages, resulting in:

$$F_t = \frac{\sum\limits_{i=t-n}^{t-1} (D_i)}{n} \qquad (5\text{--}6)$$

The weighted moving average recognizes more important demands by assigning them higher weights. The advantages of weighting are somewhat offset, however, by the added burden of selecting weights: Just how much more important is last month's demand than that from two months ago? From three months ago? Fortunately, exponential smoothing (discussed in the next section) provides an easier way to achieve about the same results as weighted moving averaging. Therefore, we shall limit our discussion of moving average forecasting to the simple moving average model.

Like other time-series methods, the moving average smooths the actual historical demand fluctuations, as illustrated in Figure 5–17. The data are for our moving company, Metro, except this time the demand history is in weekly instead of quarterly increments.

Demands for the last 16 weeks are shown on the left in Figure 5–17, where -1 means one week ago, -2 means two weeks ago, and so forth. On the right in Figure 5–17 is a calculation of three-week moving averages. A sample calculation for week -15 is shown below the figure. That result, 9.0, smooths the peaks in demand that actually occurred in the first three periods (6, 8, and 13).

FIGURE 5–17
Demand Data and Moving Average—Metro Movers

Week	Demand (van loads)	Three-Week Moving Average
-16	6	
-15	8	
-14	13	9.0
-13	11	10.7
-12	11	11.7
-11	16	12.7
-10	11	12.7
-9	8	11.7
-8	7	8.7
-7	15	10.0
-6	10	10.7
-5	11	12.0
-4	5	8.7
-3	9	8.3
-2	12	8.7
-1	12	11.0

Sample calculation for weeks -16, -15, and -14: $\dfrac{6 + 8 + 13}{3} = 9.0$

In Figure 5–18, the three-week moving average for weeks -16, -15, and -14 is projected as the forecast for week -13. The result, 9.0, can be obtained from the general formula,

$$F_{-13} = \frac{\sum\limits_{i=t-n}^{t-1} (D_i)}{n}$$

$$= \frac{\sum\limits_{i=-13-3}^{-13-1} (D_i)}{n}$$

$$= \frac{\sum\limits_{i=-16}^{-14} (D_i)}{n}$$

$$= \frac{6 + 8 + 13}{3} = 9.0$$

Since actual demand in week -13 was 11, the forecast error is $11 - 9 = 2$. That is a shortage or underestimate of two vans for that week. The moving average for weeks -15, -14, and -13 then becomes the forecast for week -12. The

FIGURE 5–18
Three-Week Moving Average and MAD—Metro Movers

(1) Week	(2) Actual Demand	(3) Forecast Demand (Three-Week Moving Average)	(4) Forecast Error [(2) − (3)]	(5) Absolute Sum of Forecast Errors
-16	6			
-15	8			
-14	13			
-13	11	9.0	2.0	2.0
-12	11	10.7	0.3	2.3
-11	16	11.7	4.3	6.6
-10	11	12.7	-1.7	8.3
-9	8	12.7	-4.7	13.0
-8	7	11.7	-4.7	17.7
-7	15	8.7	6.3	24.0
-6	10	10.0	0.0	24.0
-5	11	10.7	0.3	24.3
-4	5	12.0	-7.0	31.3
-3	9	8.7	0.3	31.6
-2	12	8.3	3.7	35.3
-1	12	8.7	3.3	38.6

$$\text{MAD} = \frac{38.6}{13} = 3.0 \text{ vans per week}$$

forecast error is $11 - 10.7 = 0.3$. The process continues, the average moving (or rolling over) each week, dropping off the oldest week and adding the newest; hence, a moving average.

The three-period moving average forecast results in a forecast error (MAD) of 3.0 vans per week (see calculations at the bottom of Figure 5–18).[3]

Suppose we decide to try a different time span, say, six weeks. The six-week moving average, forecast errors, and MAD calculations are shown in Figure 5–19. The mean error of 2.4 is better than the previous 3.0 value. We could try other moving average time spans and perhaps further reduce the error. In a larger firm with many products, searching for the best time span is a job for the computer.

Moving average time spans generally should be long where demand is rather stable (e.g., for toilet tissue) and short for highly changeable demand (e.g., for houseplants). Most users of moving average are producers or sellers of durable goods, which tend to have stable demand patterns in the short run. Therefore, longer time spans—say, 6 to 12 periods—are common.

FIGURE 5–19

Six-Week Moving Average and MAD—Metro Movers

(1) Week	(2) Actual Demand	(3) Forecast Demand (Six-Week Moving Average)	(4) Forecast Error [(2) − (3)]	(5) Absolute Sum of Forecast Errors
−16	6			
−15	8			
−14	13			
−13	11			
−12	11			
−11	16			
−10	11	10.8	0.2	0.2
−9	8	11.7	−3.7	3.9
−8	7	11.7	−4.7	8.6
−7	15	10.7	4.3	12.9
−6	10	11.3	−1.3	14.2
−5	11	11.2	−0.2	14.4
−4	5	10.3	−5.3	19.7
−3	9	9.3	−0.3	20.0
−2	12	9.5	2.5	22.5
−1	12	10.3	1.7	24.2

$$\text{MAD} = \frac{24.2}{10} = 2.4 \text{ vans per week}$$

[3]Use of the MAD in this and other examples is arbitrary. Another measure of forecast error would work just as well.

FIGURE 5–20
Smoothing Effects of the Moving Average

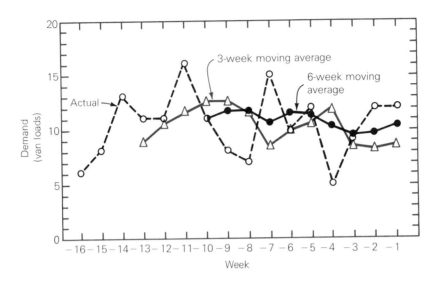

The time span resulting in the lowest MAD would be the best choice for actual use in forecasting future demand. But keep in mind that we provide it based on past data. As long as we think that the future will be similar to the past, this is fine. If we are sure that the future will be different, there is little point in expending much time analyzing past demand.

History-based forecasting analysis methods such as moving average attempt to wash out some of the forecast error from historical demand data. The effect is to produce a series of forecast values that are smoother—less variable—than the historical time series. These smoothing effects are illustrated in Figure 5–20 for the three-week and six-week data in the moving average example. The actual demand pattern, taken from Figure 5–17, exhibits some extreme high and low spikes. The three-week moving average data pattern, taken from Figure 5–18, has spikes that are much less pronounced. The six-week moving average data pattern, taken from Figure 5–19, is smoothed to look like gently rolling hills. Taken to the extreme, the 12 weeks of actual data would be smoothed to a single flat prediction line—no peaks or valleys—which is the mean (discussed earlier). The "correct" amount of smoothing—the correct moving average time span—is the one resulting in the least amount of error (smallest (MAD)).

Exponential Smoothing

Many firms that adopted the moving average technique in the 1950s saw fit to change to **exponential smoothing** in the 1960s and 1970s. Today it is perhaps the most popular forecasting technique.

Simple exponential smoothing smooths the historical demand time series.

However, it assigns a different weight to each period's data and thus, is really a weighted moving average. Weight values are obtained by selecting a smoothing coefficient, α, such that $0 \leq \alpha \leq 1.0$. A popular version of the exponential smoothing formula is given in Equation 5–7 as:

$$F_{t+1} = F_t + \alpha(D_t - F_t) \qquad (5–7)$$

where

$$F_{t+1} = \text{Forecast for period } t + 1$$
$$\alpha = \text{Smoothing constant}$$
$$D_t = \text{Actual demand for period } t$$
$$F_t = \text{Forecast for period } t$$

As we see from Equation 5–7, each smoothed average has two elements: the most recent demand, D_t (new information) and the historical smoothed average F_t (old information). The term in parentheses, $D_t - F_t$, is the forecast error for period t. Thus, the exponential smoothing forecast for a period may be thought of as the forecast for the preceding period adjusted by some fraction (α) of the forecast error; that is:

Next forecast = Last forecast + α(Last demand − Last forecast)

For example, assume that the last forecast was for 100 units but only 90 were demanded. If α is set at 0.2, the exponential smoothing forecast is:

$$\begin{aligned} \text{Next forecast} &= 100 + 0.2(90 - 100) \\ &= 100 + 0.2(-10) \\ &= 100 - 2 \\ &= 98 \end{aligned}$$

This forecast of two fewer units than the forecast for last period makes sense because the last period was overestimated. Thus, exponential smoothing results in lower forecasts where you have recently overestimated and in higher forecasts where you have underestimated. This is shown in Figure 5–21, again using Metro Movers as the example.

The data for Figure 5–21 come from Figure 5–17; α is set equal to 0.2. In exponential smoothing, there must be a startup forecast; in this case, it is 10.6 for week -5. Following the suggestions of Brown,[4] the startup value here is the simple mean of past demand data.

The underestimate for startup week -5 was slight: only 0.4 units. Multiplying that 0.4 by the 0.2 smoothing constant yields an adjustment of 0.1, rounded off. Adding that 0.1 to the old forecast of 10.6 yields 10.7 as the forecast for the next week, week -4.

In week -4, the 10.7 forecast exceeds actual demand of 5; the error is -5.7.

---

[4]Robert Goodell Brown, *Smoothing, Forecasting, and Prediction of Discrete Time Series* (Englewood Cliffs, N.J.: Prentice-Hall, 1963), p. 102 (TA168.B68).

FIGURE 5–21

Exponentially Smoothed Demand Forecasts—Metro Movers

(1)	(2)	(3)	(4)	(5)	(6)	(7)	
					Exponentially	*Absolute*	
			Forecast	*Smoothing*	*Smoothed*	*Sum of*	
	Actual		*Error*	*Adjustment*	*Forecast*	*Forecast*	
Week	*Demand*	*Forecast*	*[(2) − (3)]*	*[(0.2) × (Col. 4)]*	*[(3) + (5)]*	*Error*	
							Startup
−5	11	10.6	0.4	0.1	10.7		*phase*
−4	5	10.7	−5.7	−1.1	9.6	5.7 ⎫	
−3	9	9.6	−0.6	−0.1	9.5	6.3 ⎪	*Forecasting*
−2	12	9.5	2.5	0.5	10.0	8.8 ⎬	*phase*
−1	12	10.0	2.0			10.8 ⎭	

$$\text{MAD} = \frac{10.8}{4} = 2.7 \text{ vans per week}$$

That times 0.2 gives an adjustment of −1.1. Thus, the next forecast, for week −3, is cut back by −1.1 to 9.6. And so on.

Figure 5–21 results may be compared with the three-week moving average results in Figure 5–18. Moving average absolute forecast errors for the last four weeks from Figure 5–18 sum to 14.3 (7.0 + 0.3 + 3.7 + 3.3). Exponential smoothing forecast errors in Figure 5–21 are better at 10.8 (week −5 is not counted). However, this is by no means a fair comparison, since the number of demand weeks is so small and exponential smoothing has not run long enough for the artificial startup forecast to be "washed out." Yet it indicates the tendency for exponential smoothing to be more accurate than moving average forecasts.

In testing for the proper value of α, the mean absolute deviation is again helpful. Using past demand data, the MAD could be calculated for $\alpha = 0.1$, 0.2, . . . , 0.9. The α yielding the lowest MAD could then be adopted. It is common to use an α in the range of 0.1 to 0.3. The reason is the same as that mentioned earlier for using longer moving average time spans: Most larger firms using exponential smoothing are makers or sellers of durable goods having rather stable short-run demand patterns. A small α, such as 0.2, fits this situation well. A small α means a small adjustment for forecast error, and this keeps each successive forecast close to its predecessor. A large α—say, 0.7—would result in new forecasts that followed even large up-and-down swings of actual demand. This would be suitable for the less stable demand pattern of a luxury good or service.

It may appear that the next exponential smoothing forecast is always based solely on what happened last period with no regard for all preceding demand periods. Not so. Metaphorically, if the forecast for next period, F_t is the son, the father is F_{t-1}, the grandfather is F_{t-2}, the great-grandfather is F_{t-3}, and so forth. The current sibling, F_t, has inherited a portion, α, of the error attributable to the father, F_{t-1}; a smaller portion of the error attributable to the grandfather; and so forth.

Recall the manner in which weights are assigned in an exponential smoothing series. In a case where $\alpha = 0.2$, we would get the following results:

0.2 is the weight assigned to the F_{t-1} error.

$(0.2)(0.8)$ is the weight assigned to the F_{t-2} error.

$(0.2)(0.8)^2$ is the weight assigned to the F_{t-3} error.

$(0.2)(0.8)^3$ is the weight assigned to the F_{t-4} error.

In general, $(\alpha)(1 - \alpha)^{i-1}$ is the weight assigned to the F_{t-i} error.

The pattern of decreasing weights for $\alpha = 0.2$ is plotted in Figure 5–22. Also plotted are the calculated weights for $\alpha = 0.5$. The exponential smoothing weights extend back into the past indefinitely.

It is possible to construct a weighted moving average that closely approximates exponential smoothing. But why bother? The word *exponential* and the symbol α may frighten off those who don't "speak mathematics." But exponential smoothing is actually simpler and less expensive to perform than any moving average process. Exponential smoothing involves one small formula, while moving average requires adding all the past demands in the time span. A greater advantage of exponential smoothing over moving average is in data storage. Only the latest exponential smoothing forecast need be saved; in contrast, for moving average forecasting all the data in the most recent time span must be saved.

FIGURE 5–22
Weights for Moving Average and Exponential Smoothing

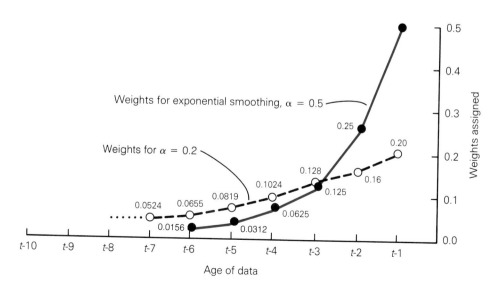

The main strengths of both exponential smoothing and moving average are that they are simple and automatic, making them suitable for computer programming. However, these are also weaknesses; that is, the methods are sometimes too simple, or crude—and sometimes too automatic, or inflexible. A cafeteria chain might be willing to turn over the demand forecasting for bread, salad, and desserts to a computer using a moving average method. But for expensive meat entrées, it might prefer to project demand by combining analysis techniques with a strong dose of judgment and experience. A business ought to devote more time and study to its most costly product.

Another weakness of exponential smoothing and moving average lies in the underlying assumption that the recent past is the best indicator of the future. That is often true. But sometimes the very fact that a product or service was recently demanded in large quantities means that less is likely to be demanded in the near future. In other words, buyers may become partly sated after a period of high demand and hold off for awhile, thereby causing a period of low demand.

Double Exponential Smoothing

The exponential smoothing method explained above is known as *single-order* exponential smoothing. However, this technique does not keep up with trends. For example, if there is a general upward trend in demand, the single-order exponential smoothing forecast will be consistently too low. *Double exponential smoothing,* which is a bit more complicated, includes an adjustment feature for bringing the forecast up (or down) to the trend line. (A further adjustment—which we shall not cover—allows for seasonality.) One form of double exponential smoothing has the following formula:

$$D_t = 2S_{t-1} - F_{t-2} \qquad (5\text{--}8)$$

where

D_t = Double exponential smoothing forecast for next period, t

S_{t-1} = Single-order exponential smoothing forecast for last period, $t-1$

F_{t-2} = Double exponential smoothing function for period before last, $t-2$

The value of S and F functions are obtained by:

$$S_t = S_{t-1} + \alpha(A_{t-1} - S_{t-1}) \qquad (5\text{--}9)$$

$$F_t = \alpha S_t + (1 - \alpha)F_{t-1} \qquad (5\text{--}10)$$

where

$$\alpha = \text{Smoothing constant}$$

$$A = \text{Actual demand}$$

Double exponential smoothing is demonstrated using data from the last six quarters for Data Services (from Figure 5–10), which, in programmer-hours, are: 610, 405, 540, 330, 445, and 410. For these six quarters, single-order and double

FIGURE 5–23

Double Exponentially Smoothed Demand Forecasts—Data Services, Inc.

(1) Period (t)	(2) (A)	(3) S (S_{t-1} + Col. 5)	(4) Single Exponential Smoothing Error [(2)−(3)]	(5) Smoothing Adjustment [(0.3)×(Col. 4)]	(6) F [(0.3)(S)+ (0.7)(F_{t-1})]	(7) D ($2S_{t-1}$− F_{t-2})	(8) Double Exponential Smoothing Error [(2)−(7)]
1	—		Assumed		565		
2	—	580			560		
3*	610	530	80	+24	551	595	15
4	405	554	−149	−45	552	500	−95
5	540	509	+31	+9	539	557	−17
6	330	518	−188	−56	533	466	−136
7	445	462	−17	−5	512	497	−52
8	410	457	−47	−14	496	391	15
Absolute error =			512				334

*Corresponds to third quarter 1990.

exponential smoothing calculations and their errors are shown in Figure 5–23. So that the double exponential smoothing forecast may be determined for third quarter, 1990, assumed S and F factors are given for the two preceding quarters. A smoothing constant, α, of 0.3 is used. The total absolute forecast error is 512 using single-order smoothing. The error is 334 for double exponential smoothing. Double exponential smoothing performs better, as it should, because there is a clear downward trend in actual demand over the six quarters.

Adaptive Smoothing

Adaptive smoothing allows for automatic adjustment of the smoothing coefficient, α, based on some function of the forecast error measurement. The most commonly used function is the **tracking signal**, which is calculated as follows:

$$\text{Tracking signal} = \frac{\text{Cumulative deviation}}{\text{MAD}}$$

$$= \frac{\text{RSFE}}{\text{MAD}}$$

where

RSFE = Running sum of the forecast error

An increase in the magnitude of the tracking signal usually reflects a continuing increase in forecast error in the same direction, either positively or negatively. This suggests the possibility of bias in the model, a condition we would want to correct. The unbiased model will have the RSFE constantly located around zero.

Recall from earlier discussion that when forecast errors are normally distributed, one standard deviation equals approximately 1.25 times the MAD. From the table of areas under the normal curve in Appendix A, we may obtain probabilities associated with various portions of a hypothetical tracking signal distribution assuming that no forecast model bias exists. The approximate probabilities are:

Area	Probability
0 ± 1 SD (or ± 1.25 MAD)	0.6826
0 ± 2 SD (or ± 2.50 MAD)	0.9545
0 ± 3 SD (or ± 3.75 MAD)	0.9972

Thus, the likelihood of the tracking signal exceeding a value of ±3.75 is *very* remote *if* the model is not biased. Continued tracking signal values with magnitudes less than 3.0—with some alternation in sign—usually denotes an unbiased forecasting model. A helpful rule of thumb is: Consider changing the smoothing constant when the tracking signal exceeds 4 for high-value items or 8 for low-value items. For example, if the cumulative deviation is 850 and the MAD is 100, the signal is 850/100 = 8.5, which is above the maximum. Forecast error is overly positive, that is, forecasts are too low. Other α values should be tested on recent data to see if the error may be reduced.

Forecasting by Simulation

Trend and seasonal analysis, moving average, and exponential smoothing are standard forecasting tools, especially for durable goods manufacturers. The techniques do not require a computer, but most firms have computerized them for efficiency reasons. The modern computer, however, provides the firm with computational power to run *forecasting simulations* involving several techniques. Forecasting simulation has the potential to surpass in accuracy any of the individual forecasting techniques.

In each simulated trial, the forecast values are subtracted from a set of actual demands from the recent past, giving simulated forecast error. The forecast method yielding the least error is selected by the computer, which uses it to make *just* the next period's forecast. For each successive forecast a new simulation is done, possibly based on a new technique. (In contrast, the search for a time span or a smoothing constant—for a moving average or exponential smoothing—is performed as an occasional review rather than every forecasting period.)

One ardent advocate of forecasting simulation is Bernard T. Smith. While inventory manager at American Hardware Supply,[5] Smith devised a forecast

---

[5]Bernard T. Smith, *Focus Forecasting: Computer Techniques for Inventory Control* (Boston: CBI Publishing, 1978) (HD55.S48).

simulation system that applied to 100,000 hardware products. In Smith's system, **focus forecasting**, each product is simulated every month for the next three months and seven forecast techniques are tested. Each is simple for buyers and other inventory people in the company to understand. For example, one of the seven forecasting techniques is a simple three-month sum (which is not quite the same as a three-month moving average). The simulation for that method uses historical demand data for only the past six months, which are grouped into two three-month demand periods.

To illustrate the simulation, let us assume that demand for giant-size trash bags was 500 in the last three-month period and 400 in the period before that. In a three-month-sum forecasting method, the latest three-month sum is the forecast for the next period. Therefore, the computer simulation treats 400 as the forecast for the three-month period in which actual demand was 500. The simulated forecast error is 500 − 400 = 100 trash bags. That forecast error is converted to a percent error so that it may be compared with six other computer-simulated methods for forecasting trash bags. The percent error is 1 − (400/500) = 0.20, or 20 percent.

Six other simple, easy-to-understand methods (including simple trend and simple seasonal) are simulated to see what percent error results. If the three-month-sum method turns out to have a lower percent error than the other six simulated methods, the computer uses that method to make the next forecast. The forecast would be 500 for the next three months, and for each of those months the forecast is simply 500/3 = 167 trash bags. The forecast rolls over (is recomputed) each month The computer prints out the forecast for each of the 100,000 items, but buyers may overrule the printed forecast if they disbelieve it.

ASSOCIATIVE PROJECTION

In all of the preceding techniques, demand is tracked over *time*. In associative projection, demand is tracked not against time but against some other known variable, perhaps student enrollment or inches of precipitation. The associative techniques are the *leading indicator* and *correlation.*

Leading Indicator

Changes in demand may be preceded by changes in some other variable. If so, the other variable is a **leading indicator**. The leading indicator is helpful if the patterns of change in the two variables are similar (i.e., they correlate) and if the lead time is long enough for action to be taken before the demand change occurs.

Few firms are able to discover a variable that changes with demand but leads it significantly. The reason probably is that demand for a given good or service usually depends on (is led by) a number of variables rather than one dominant variable. The search for such a variable can be costly and futile. Therefore, most of the work with leading indicators has centered on national economic forecasting instead of local demand forecasting. Nevertheless, the leading indicator should be part of the demand forecaster's tool kit, since it is a valued predictor in those cases where it can be isolated.

One story about leading indicators has been widely circulated. It is said that the Rothschild family reaped a fortune by getting advance news of Napoleon's defeat at Waterloo. Nathan, the Rothschild brother who lived in England, received the news via carrier pigeon. On that basis he bought depressed war-effort securities and sold them at a huge profit after the news reached England.[6]

The leading indicator in this case was news of the war, and it led prices of securities. The Rothschilds' astuteness was not in realizing this, for it was common knowledge; rather it was in their development of an information network with which to capitalize on that knowledge. A costly information system like that set up by the Rothschilds can provide highly accurate information rapidly. In contrast, personal judgment as a basis for action is cheap but tends to be less accurate and to be hindsight rather than foresight; that is, personal judgment often does not lead events.

In sum, leading indicators should have long lead times as well as accuracy. This requires good information systems. Example 5–2 demonstrates this.

| EXAMPLE 5–2 | **STATE JOBS SERVICE AND LEADING INDICATORS** |

Mr. H. Hand, manager of the Metro City office of the State Jobs Service, sees the need for better demand forecasting. The problem has been that surges in clients tend to catch the office offguard. Advance warning of demand is needed in order to plan for staff, desks, phones, forms, and even space.

One element of demand is well known: Many of the job seekers are there as a result of being laid off by Acme Industries, which is by far the largest employer in Metro City. Hand is able to obtain Acme records on layoffs over the past year. He plots the layoff data on a time chart, along with the Jobs Service office's data on job applicants, in Figure 5–24. The chart shows number of job applicants ranging from a high of 145 (period 8) to a low of 45 (period 20). Layoffs at Acme range from a high of 60 (periods 6 and 7) to a low of zero (several periods).

Plotting the points seems well worth the effort, because Hand notes a striking similarity in the shapes of the two plots. Further, the layoffs plot seems to lead the applicants plot. For example, the high of 145 applicants occurred two weeks after the high of 60 layoffs and the low of 45 applicants occurred two weeks after layoffs spiked downward to zero. Weeks 1, 3, 17, 21, and 22 are other places on the layoff plot in which a two-week lead appears; the lead is close to two weeks in weeks 11 through 15.

---

[6]One historian disputes this story, asserting that the Rothschilds made more money during the war than at its end and that the news was forwarded by a courier in a Rothschilds ship, not a carrier pigeon. See Virginia Cowles, *The Rothschilds: A Family of Fortune* (New York: Alfred A. Knopf, 1973), pp. 47–50 (HG1552.R8C66).

FIGURE 5–24

Layoffs at Acme and Job Applications at Jobs Service—with Time Scale

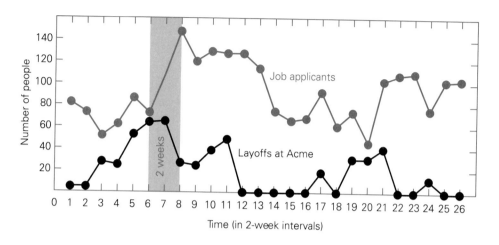

FIGURE 5–25

Correlation of Layoffs at Acme (T–2) with Demand at Jobs Service (T)

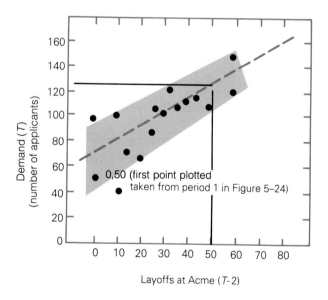

Does a two-week lead make sense, or could it be coincidence? Hand feels that it makes sense. He bases this on the impression that laid-off Acme people tend to live off their severance pay for a time—two weeks seems reasonable—before actively seeking other jobs. Hand therefore takes the final steps. First, he establishes an information system. This is simply an agreement that every two weeks Acme will release the number of its laid-off employees to the Jobs Service office. Second, he establishes a forecasting procedure based on that layoff information and the two-week lead pattern in Figure 5–24.

In establishing a forecasting procedure, Hand regraphs the data from Figure 5–24 into the form shown in Figure 5–25 (a scatter diagram); that is, layoffs at Acme for period $T-2$ matched with applicants at the Jobs Service office for period T constitute points that are plotted as the two axes of the graph. For example, the first point plotted is (0,50), which is taken from Figure 5–24, where for period 1 layoffs are 0 and two weeks later applicants are 50. Every other point is plotted in the same way. The points tend to go upward left to right, clustering around the dashed line (an "eyeball" regression line).

The dashed line is used for forecasting. Suppose, for example, that Hand learns today that Acme is laying off 50 people this week. In Figure 5–25 a solid vertical line extending from 50 to the dashed line and leftward yields a forecast demand of about 125. Thus, the procedure tells Hand to expect 125 applicants in two weeks.

Correlation

How good is Mr. Hand's leading indicator? By one measure—the supporting information system—it is very good! The layoff data from Acme are cheap to obtain and highly accurate. In terms of lead time, it is not so good. Two weeks' notice is not much for the purpose of adjusting resources on hand. In terms of validity, the leading indicator *seems* good, but how may we measure "good"? One answer is: Measure it by the correlation coefficient—our next topic.

Correlation means degree of association. The *correlation coefficient*, r, is a measure of degree of association. The value of r ranges from 1.0 for perfect correlation to 0.0 for no correlation at all to -1.0 for perfect negative correlation. In positive correlation, a rise in one attribute occurs along with a rise in the other; in negative correlation, a rise in one occurs along with a fall in the other. To calculate r, a number of pairs of values are needed. The chapter supplement provides a formula and sample calculations.

For the Jobs Service example, the correlation coefficient is quite good (about $+0.78$, calculations not given), which one can see by looking at Figure 5–25. The points tend to cluster along the broad, shaded band running upward at about a 30-degree angle. This is the pattern of a positive correlation. (Negative correlations go downward left to right.)

In the Jobs Service example, the amount of lead was determined visually. The two variables were plotted on the time scale in Figure 5–24, and brief inspection showed that the two curves were generally two weeks apart. Sometimes the amount of lead is hard to see, and where there are many potential leading indicators to check out, manual plotting and visual inspection become tedious. In such cases, computers may take over. It is simple for the computer to calculate r for a number of different lead periods. The one with the best r may then be selected.

What about a lead period of zero? That would exist where a pair of events occur at the same time.[7] Even if the correlation is perfect ($r = 1.0$), it *appears*

---

[7]The introductory statistics course usually focuses on this type of simple correlation—with no lead time.

that it is useless in forecasting. No lead time means no forewarning and, it might seem, no forecasting. This impression is not correct. Correlation with no lead *can* be valuable *if* the indicator (independent variable) is more predictable than is demand.

As an example, a phone company in a large city may know that new residential phone orders correlate nearly perfectly with new arrivals in the city—with no lead time. There is probably value in knowing this, because in most large cities careful studies are done to project population increases. Fairly reliable projections of new residences may be available. The phone company need not spend a lot of money projecting residential telephone installations; instead, it may use the city's data on new residences. For these reasons, most large firms are indeed interested in establishing good correlations, even without lead time.

Multiple regression/correlation is an extension of simple regression and correlation. In this method, multiple casual variables may be analyzed. The result is a formula with demand on the left side of the equal sign and each of the causal variables, properly weighted, on the right. For example, the phone company may look for predictors other than new residences, such as level of savings in local thrift institutions and amount of phone advertising. A multiple regression equation might be put together with three causal variables: new residences (N), savings (S), and advertising (A). Then computer processing using past data would yield the parameters for each variable. As an example, the equation for forecasting next month's demand (D) for phone installations might be:

$$D = 0.36N + 2.81S + 0.89A$$

Since advertising effects may take awhile, advertising perhaps should be analyzed as a leading indicator. Maybe it could be shown that advertising leads demand by one month. The revised multiple regression equation might appear as:

$$D = 0.41N + 2.70S + 0.88A_{t-1}$$

Much more has been done with multiple regression/correlation in economic forecasting than in demand forecasting. The method, which is complex and requires a computer, is beyond the scope of this book. The approach often has proved futile at the level of the firm; however, multiple regression frequently has been used for large utilities or public agencies, whose demand is likely to be affected by a number of broad socioeconomic variables.

SUMMARY

The responsibility for demand management is shared by marketing and operations. For goods producers, a master scheduling committee frequently coordinates demand management.

There are three purposes of demand management: short term, which deals with item demand; medium term, which projects aggregate demand for capacity groups; and long term, which is needed for planning facilities and equipment.

Long- and medium-term decisions are infrequent, but short-term demand management keeps people busy all the time processing orders.

There are many kinds of orders, several of which occur within the demand management function. Consequently, customer satisfaction depends on a carefully constructed and well-maintained order processing system. The order processing sequence begins and ends outside the typical operations function. Most of the sequence, however—specifically, total requirements determination, order positioning, order promise, inventory planning, scheduling and purchasing, dispatching, and assembly—is the responsibility of operations.

Order promising is the act of making a delivery commitment to the customer and to the rest of the producing organization. In client-oriented services, the appointment is the order promise.

Demand forecasting, or estimating future demand, is a major activity of demand management. It is essential because planning usually must begin long before actual customer orders are received. The demand that is to be forecast consists of long-, medium-, and short-term components in addition to noise. Viewing demand as a time series suggests analysis of the time series components of trend, seasonality, cyclical patterns, and random events. Analyses of historical time series data often justify using simple projections of past patterns as forecasts of future demand performance. Demand is more certain in the immediate future, for which there usually exist customer orders specifying needed goods and services.

Forecasting results may be evaluated by studying forecast error. For a given time period, error is equal to demand minus forecast. Typically, however, a measurement of error over multiple time periods is more useful than that for single periods. Several measures of forecast error exist, including mean absolute deviation, standard deviation, and mean absolute percentage error.

Aggregate demand forecasts are used for planning product or capacity groups. Error percentage for group forecasts is usually lower than an average of comparable figures for individual items.

Forecast accuracy deteriorates as we project into the more distant future. This suggests that as time passes older forecasts should be refined in light of more recent developments. Also, planning and control systems dependent on forecasts should be segmented according to the importance of forecast accuracy.

Like demand management, demand forecasting has short-, medium-, and long-term components. Three primary sources of demand forecasts are marketing, economic, and historical demand projections. Historical demand projection is greatly aided by accurate records of historical demand. Forecasting procedures are affected by industry and organizational variables such as required customer lead time, but *all* managers should forecast.

Demand forecasting often is based on projection of historical demand time series. Historical demand analysis addresses the simple mean, trend, and seasonality in time-series data.

Multiperiod pattern projection techniques are often used in a rolling-forecast mode. These techniques project the mean, trend, and seasonal components and are useful in short-, medium-, and long-term forecasting. The least-squares procedure for trend projection may be used when precision is desired or where there are many products or services to be forecast. Seasonal indexes are combined with trend to produce projections that are more sensitive to seasonal influences on demand. The multiperiod projection techniques are useful only when past demand patterns are expected to remain valid in the future. In the short run, forecast inaccuracies can stem from artificial conditions, such as "stuffing" distribution channels to make sales figures look good.

Single-period patternless projection tools include moving average, exponential smoothing, and simulation. Although they are most useful for short-term forecasts, they may be extended further into the future if certain conditions are met. A moving average is a mean of recent past demands, rolling over as time progresses. The number of periods used to compute the mean is the time span of the moving average forecast.

Exponential smoothing, perhaps the most popular of the single-period techniques, is really a form of weighted moving averaging. It is simple and inexpensive and has been shown to be accurate. The single or simple exponential smoothing forecast for a time period is the forecast for the last period plus some fraction (α) of the last period's forecast error. Double exponential smoothing does the same thing, but it adds a trend adjustment. Adaptive smoothing uses a tracking signal—a ratio of the running sum of forecast error to the MAD—to permit adjustment of α should forecast error become too large.

The widespread availability of microcomptuer-based forecasting software has resulted in computerization of much business forecasting. The computer is essential in forecasting by simulation, in which several forecasting models are studied simultaneously in the search for the best forecast.

In associative projection, demand is tracked against some variable other than time. Techniques include leading indicator and correlation. Attempts to isolate an association (correlation) between one known variable and demand are most productive if the predictor variable, X, can be shown to lead demand. The greater the correlation and the longer the lead time, the better the leading indicator as a forecasting aid. Correlation without lead may itself be useful, however, if the correlated variable is more predictable than demand. Multiple regression/correlation permits use of more than one independent or predictor variable.

While all of the historical techniques are potentially useful, demand forecasting is inherently imprecise. No amount of mathematical analysis can change that. Recently, the preference seems to be for the simple models, such as those discussed in this chapter.

KEY WORDS

Demand management	Seasonal variation	Forecast error
Item demand	(seasonality)	Mean absolute
Order entry	Cyclical pattern	deviation
Order promising	Random events	Standard deviation
Time series	Demand forecasting	Mean absolute percent
Trend	Delayed differentiation	error

Aggregate demand
   forecast
Rolling forecast
Seasonal index
Moving average

Exponential smoothing
Adaptive smoothing
Tracking signal
Focus forecasting

Leading indicator
Correlation
Multiple regression/
   correlation

SOLVED PROBLEMS

1. Historical demand data and forecasts exist for the eight-period time interval shown below:

Period	−8	−7	−6	−5	−4	−3	−2	−1
Demand	100	110	104	98	106	102	100	98
Forecast	104	102	104	100	100	104	103	102

Arrange the information in a table similar to Table 5–1. Compute the following measures of forecast error: MAD, SD, and MAPE. Plot the demand and forecasts as time series as in Figure 5–5.

Solution

The period, demand, and forecasts are shown in the first three columns of Table 5–2. The rest of the table is constructed like Table 5–1; it contains the computations necessary for determining the required error measures.

TABLE 5–2
Forecast Error Measures: Sample Problem

Period (t)	Demand (D_t)	Forecast (F_t)	Error (E_t)	Absolute Error $|E_t|$	Error Squared $(E_t)^2$	Absolute Percent Error $(|E_t|/D_t) \times 100\%$
−8	100	104	−4	4	16	4.00%
−7	110	102	8	8	64	7.27
−6	104	104	0	0	0	0.00
−5	98	100	−2	2	4	2.04
−4	106	100	6	6	36	5.66
−3	102	104	−2	2	4	1.96
−2	100	103	−3	3	9	3.00
−1	98	102	−4	4	16	4.08
		Sum:	−1	29	149	28.01%

$$\text{MAD (from Equation 5–2):} = \frac{29}{8} = 3.625$$

$$\text{SD (from Equation 5–3):} = \sqrt{\frac{149}{7}} = \sqrt{21.286} = 4.614$$

$$\text{MAPE (from Equation 5–4):} = \frac{28.01}{8} = 3.501$$

FIGURE 5–26
Demand and Forecast Plots: Sample Problem

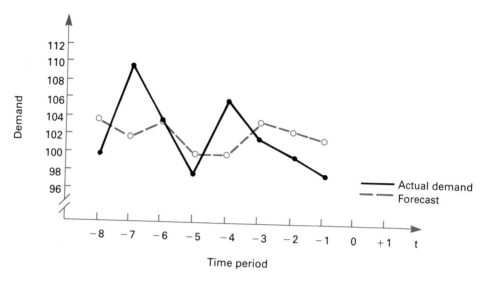

The actual historical demand and forecasts for the eight time periods are plotted in Figure 5–26.

2. Consider again the historical demand and forecast data in solved problem 1. Determine the running sum of the forecast error (RSFE) at the end of each period, and calculate the tracking signal after period −1.

Solution
The following table contains the given data, forecasts, and error calculations in the first five columns. The sixth contains the RSFE values at the end of each period. The tracking signal at the end of period −1 is calculated below the table.

Period (t)	Demand (D_t)	Forecast (F_t)	Error (E_t)	Absolute Error ($|E_t|$)	RSFE
−8	100	104	−4	4	−4
−7	110	102	8	8	4
−6	104	104	0	0	4
−5	98	100	−2	2	2
−4	106	100	6	6	8
−3	102	104	−2	2	6
−2	100	103	−3	3	3
−1	98	102	−4	4	−1
			Sum =	29	

$$\text{MAD} = \frac{29}{8} = 3.625$$

$$\text{Tracking signal} = \frac{\text{RSFE}}{\text{MAD}} = \frac{-1}{3.625} = -0.276$$

3. Following are historical demand data for 12 periods:

Period	−12	−11	−10	−9	−8	−7	−6	−5	−4	−3	−2	−1
Demand	40	42	41	44	40	39	39	41	45	41	38	40

a. Calculate simple moving average forecasts and mean absolute deviation for the data, using a time span of 4.
b. Plot the demand data and the forecast on a time axis.

Solution
The time periods and historical demand data are shown in the first two columns of the following table. Moving average forecasts are in column 3 and error terms are in columns 4 and 5. Sample calculations and MAD values appear below the table.

(1) Period (t)	(2) Demand (D_t)	(3) Simple Moving Average Forecast (F_t)	(4) Error (E_t)	(5) Absolute Error ($|E_t|$)
−12	40			
−11	42			
−10	41			
−9	44			
−8	40	41.75	−1.75	1.75
−7	39	41.75	−2.75	2.75
−6	39	41.00	−2.00	2.00
−5	41	40.50	0.50	0.50
−4	45	39.75	5.25	5.25
−3	41	41.00	0.00	0.00
−2	38	41.50	−3.50	3.50
−1	40	41.25	−1.25	1.25
			Sum =	17.00

Sample calculations:
Simple moving average (from Equation 5–6):

$$F_{-8} = \frac{\sum\limits_{i=t-n}^{t-1} (D_i)}{n} = \frac{\sum\limits_{i=-12}^{-9} (D_i)}{n}$$

$$= \frac{40 + 42 + 41 + 44}{4} = \frac{167}{4} = 41.75$$

$$\text{MAD} = \frac{17.0}{8} = 2.125$$

The plots of the 12 periods of historical demand data and the moving average forecast are shown in Figure 5–27. We see how the moving average technique smooths the peaks in the data.

FIGURE 5–27
Historical Demand Data and Moving Average Forecasts

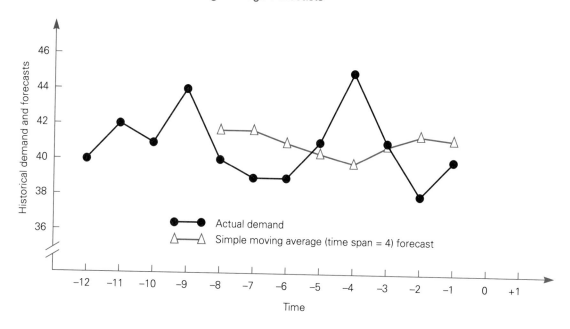

4. The first five periods of demand data from the solved problem 3 are shown in the following table. Using a smoothing coefficient, $\alpha = 0.3$, compute simple exponentially smoothed forecasts for periods -4 through -1. Initialize the procedure with a forecast value for period -5 of 41.

Period	-5	-4	-3	-2	-1
Demand	40	42	41	44	40

Solution

The data, forecasts, and absolute errors for the five-period interval are given in the following table. Sample calculations and the MAD follow.

Period (t)	Demand (D_t)	Exponentially Smoothed Forecast $(\alpha = 0.3)$ (F_t)	Error (E_t)	Absolute Error $(|E_t|)$
-5	40	41.000	-1.000	1.000
-4	42	40.700	1.300	1.300
-3	41	41.090	-0.090	0.090
-2	44	41.063	2.937	2.937
-1	40	41.944	-1.944	1.944
			Sum $=$	7.271

Sample calculations (from Equation 5–7):

$$F_{t+1} = F_t + \alpha(D_t - F_t)$$

$$F_{-4} = F_{-5} + \alpha(D_{-5} - F_{-5})$$

$$= 41 + 0.3\,(40 - 41)$$

$$= 41 + 0.3\,(-1)$$

$$F_{-4} = \underline{40.700}$$

$$F_{-3} = F_{-4} + 0.3\,(D_{-4} - F_{-4})$$

$$= 40.7 + 0.3\,(42 - 40.7)$$

$$= 40.7 + 0.3\,(1.3)$$

$$F_{-3} = 41.090$$

$$\text{MAD} = \frac{7.271}{5} = 1.454$$

5. Historical monthly demand data for the past two years follow:

Period	-24	-23	-22	-21	-20	-19	-18	-17	-16	-15	-14	-13
Demand	10	12	14	12	10	8	6	8	10	12	14	12

Period	-12	-11	-10	-9	-8	-7	-6	-5	-4	-3	-2	-1
Demand	10	8	6	8	10	12	14	12	10	8	6	8

a. Compute a single exponentially smoothed forecast for the 24 months. Initialize the forecasting model by setting the forecast for period $t = -24$ to a value of 10. Use a smoothing coefficient of $\alpha = 0.2$. Repeat the forecast using $\alpha = 0.8$. Calculate the MAD for each forecast.

b. Plot the historical data and the forecasts on a time axis. Discuss the form of the demand data. Is the simple exponential model suitable for these data? What effects does the value of α have on the behavior of the forecasting model?

Solution

The time periods and historical demand data are shown in columns 1 and 2. Exponential smoothing forecasts are given for $\alpha = 0.2$ in column 3 and error and absolute error (or deviation) in columns 4 and 5. The forecasts computed with $\alpha = 0.8$ are in column 6, and error measures for this model are in columns 7 and 8. Mean absolute deviation (MAD) values for the two models are shown following the table.

(1)	(2)	(3) Exponentially Smoothed Forecast ($\alpha = 0.2$)	(4)	(5)	(6) Exponentially Smoothed Forecast ($\alpha = 0.8$)	(7)	(8)
Period (t)	Demand (D_t)	($F_{t_{\alpha=0.2}}$)	Error ($E_{t_{\alpha=0.2}}$)	Absolute Error ($|E_{t_{\alpha=0.2}}|$)	($F_{t_{\alpha=0.8}}$)	Error ($E_{t_{\alpha=0.8}}$)	Absolute Error ($|F_{t_{\alpha=0.8}}|$)
−24	10	10.000	0	0	10.000	0	0
−23	12	10.000	2.000	2.000	10.000	2.000	2.000
−22	14	10.400	3.600	3.600	11.600	2.400	2.400
−21	12	11.120	0.880	0.880	13.520	−1.520	1.520
−20	10	11.296	−1.296	1.296	12.304	−2.304	2.304
−19	8	11.037	−3.037	3.037	10.461	−2.461	2.461
−18	6	10.429	−4.429	4.429	8.492	−2.492	2.492
−17	8	9.544	−1.544	1.544	6.498	1.502	1.502
−16	10	9.235	0.765	0.765	7.700	2.300	2.300
−15	12	9.388	2.612	2.612	9.540	2.460	2.460
−14	14	9.910	4.090	4.090	11.508	2.492	2.492
−13	12	10.728	1.272	1.272	13.502	−1.502	1.502
−12	10	10.983	−0.983	0.983	12.300	−2.300	2.300
−11	8	10.786	−2.786	2.786	10.460	−2.460	2.460
−10	6	10.229	−4.229	4.229	8.492	−2.492	2.492
−9	8	9.383	−1.383	1.383	6.498	1.502	1.502
−8	10	9.106	0.894	0.894	7.700	2.300	2.300
−7	12	9.285	2.715	2.715	9.540	2.460	2.460
−6	14	9.828	4.172	4.172	11.508	2.492	2.492
−5	12	10.663	1.337	1.337	13.502	1.502	1.502
−4	10	10.930	−0.930	0.930	12.300	−2.300	2.300
−3	8	10.744	−2.744	2.744	10.460	−2.460	2.460
−2	6	10.195	−4.195	4.195	8.492	−2.492	2.492
−1	8	9.356	−1.356	1.356	6.498	1.502	1.502
			Sums =	53.249			49.695

$$\text{MAD}_{\alpha=0.2} = \frac{\sum\limits_{-24}^{-1} |E_t|}{24} = \frac{53.249}{24} = 2.219$$

$$\text{MAD}_{\alpha=0.8} = \frac{\sum\limits_{-24}^{-1} |E_t|}{24} = \frac{49.695}{24} = 2.071$$

Plots of the demand data and the two forecasts are shown in Figure 5–28. First, a note of caution: The data were created solely to illustrate some aspects of exponential smoothing. Do not infer that either exponential smoothing model is appropriate in this case. As can be seen, the data are perfectly seasonal and both forecasts lag the demand, illustrating why simple exponential smoothing generally is not a good model for obviously seasonal data. The model with α

FIGURE 5–28

Historical Demand Data and Exponential Smoothing Forecasts

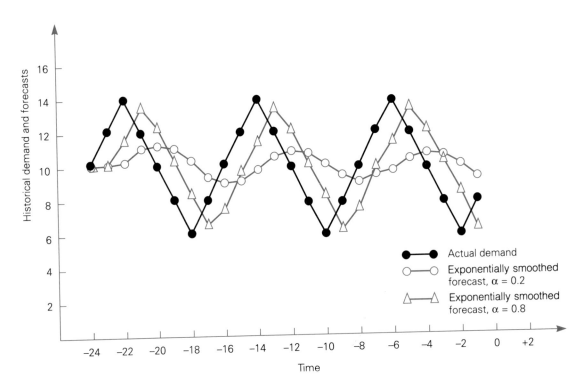

= 0.8, putting 80 percent weight on new information and 20 percent weight on old data, is more reactive to peaks in the data. The model with $\alpha = 0.2$ reverses the weight emphasis and tends to smooth out peaks, being less sensitive to variations in demand data.

REFERENCES

Books

Abraham, B. and J. Ledolter. *Statistical Methods for Forecasting*. New York: John Wiley & Sons, 1983 (QA279.2.A27).

Bails, Dale G., and Larry C. Peppers. *Business Fluctuations: Forecasting Techniques and Applications*. Englewood Cliffs, N.J.: Prentice-Hall, 1982 (HB3730.B25).

Box, G. E. P., and G. M. Jenkins. *Time Series Analysis, Forecasting, and Control*, Rev. ed. San Francisco: Holden-Day, 1976 (QA280.B67).

Chatfield, Christopher. *The Analysis of Time Series: An Introduction*, 3rd ed. London: Chapman and Hall, 1984 (QA280.C4).

Makridakis, Spyros G., and Steven C. Wheelwright. *Forecasting Methods for Management*, 5th ed. New York: John Wiley & Sons, 1989 (HD30.27.W46).

Smith, Bernard T. *Focus Forecasting: Computer Techniques for Inventory Control.* Boston: CBI Publishing, 1978.

Willis, Raymond E. *A Guide to Forecasting for Planners and Managers.* Englewood Cliffs, N.J.: Prentice-Hall, 1987 (HD30.27.W55).

Periodicals

Interfaces.
Journal of Forecasting.
Journal of the Operations Research Society.
Management Science.

REVIEW QUESTIONS

1. How does demand management differ for goods producers and service providers?

2. Why does the term *order* have different meanings to different people in a producing organization? Who is responsible for demand management?

3. In the order processing sequence, there are three "acceptances" of an order. Explain each, and tell how they differ.

4. In an order promise, who promises what to whom? How firm is that promise? What constitutes order promise in a service organization?

5. How does the ability to ship from stock affect the order processing sequence?

6. What are the purposes of demand management? How do they compare with the purposes of demand forecasting?

7. What is a time series? What are its principal components?

8. What are the measures of forecast error? Identify advantages and disadvantages for each measure.

9. What is the relationship between lead time for providing a product and requirements for demand forecasts?

10. If a manager told you, "I don't need to do demand forecasting," what arguments would you use to counter that statement?

11. Compare the accuracy of item and group forecasts. Explain.

12. Since forecast error is worse for distant future periods than for the near future, is it prudent to forecast *only* for the near term? Explain.

13. Marketing projections and economic projections are both done in dollars. How, then, do they differ?

14. What are the consequences for organizations that keep no demand records?

15. What does the term *historical demand pattern projection* mean?

16. When is a simple mean a suitable forecast? When would a trend forecast be preferable over the mean?

17. Is it permissible to make "eyeball projections"? Discuss. Under what conditions should the least-squares technique be used for trend projection?

18. Why is it sometimes difficult to decide whether to use the mean, straight-line trend, or curve trending as a forecast basis?

19. What is the purpose of calculating seasonal indexes? What is done with them?

20. How is one forecasting model compared with another in selecting a model for future use?

PROBLEMS AND EXERCISES

1. Think back on your experiences with physician appointments, and select the appointment system that worked best. What demand management activities must be taking place among the staff who served you in order for the system to work well? Explain.

2. Following is a list of organization types. Figure 5–3 shows that forecasts may be required for planning (*a*) facilities and adjustable capacity, (*b*) raw materials, (*c*) components, and (*d*) assemblies. Refer to the concepts presented in the figure to match up the listed organizations with the four purposes. Briefly explain your matchups.

Furniture manufacturing   Roller-skating rink
Clothing manufacturing   Natural gas distributor
Air conditioning/heating contractor Orthodontist
Highway construction   Church parish
Airframe manufacturing   Sound system manufacturing
Commercial printing   Small appliance manufacturing
Tractor manufacturing   Toy manufacturing

3. At Apex Steel Cabinet Company, personnel was the first department to separately forecast its key workloads (see Example 5–1). Mr. Guy, the president, wants key workload forecasting extended to other departments. Your assignment is to prepare logical workload lists and forecast bases, similar to Figure 5–4, for the following departments or sections: public relations, advertising, and data processing.

4. Planners at county hospital are preparing a staffing plan and budget for next quarter. The following listing is computer data on labor-hours in various departments for last quarter. The trouble is, the average forecast error looks very high. Is the forecast error too high, or could next quarter's computer forecast be useful as the basis for a quarterly staffing plan? Perform any necessary calculations, and discuss.

Department	Last-Quarter Labor-Hour Actual	Last-Quarter Labor-Hour Forecast
Anesthesia	208	130
Cardiopulmonary	175	210
Emergency	589	650
Obstetrics	391	380
Pathology	68	90
Physical therapy	71	110
Radiology	277	200
Surgery	950	810

5. At Henry, Henry, and Henry, Public Accountants, the administrative vice president is responsible for forecasting demand for professional accounting services. The forecast for the preceding six-month period (made six months prior to that) was 120 client-days of work per month. Actual demand turned out to be 130, 100, 150, 150, 90, and 80. Calculate the MAD, SD, and MAPE for the six-month time interval. From your calculations, what would you say about the pattern of error? Is it about what you expect? Why or why not?

6. Metro Auto Sales forecasts new-car demand 12 months into the future. The forecast is updated every month. Metro's supplier, a large U.S. auto maker, requires a 12-month forecast of total number of cars of all types so that it may plan equipment, space, labor, and so on in its manufacturing plants. It also requires a two-month forecast of numbers of each model. Internally Metro finds the forecast useful for staffing (new-car salespeople) and for ensuring the correct amount of lot space on lease. Metro and its new-car supplier clearly are practicing a number of the concepts and principles of demand forecasting discussed in the chapter. Your assignment is to discuss the principles and concepts that apply to this situation (as many as you can think of).

7. A study of forecast accuracy over a recent past time period for five products—A, B, C, D, and E—reveals the following:

Product	Forecast Error	Percent Error
A	−20	10%
B	−10	5
C	+20	8
D	−30	15
E	+40	12

Calculate the average percent error, first by item and second for the five items as a group. (Note: You will be able to make these calculations even without being given the raw data on forecast and actual demands.) Explain the resulting percent error for the group. Why are the item and group errors so different?

8. Following are the recent actual demands and forecasts for a "service part" (industry's term for a spare or replacement part).

Time (t)	−5	−4	−3	−2	−1
Actual demand	9	10	17	25	27
Forecast	10	12	15	19	25

   a. Calculate the MAD, SD, and MAPE.
   b. Plot the demand and forecasts on a graph similar to Figure 5–5. If you had to forecast the next two or three periods, what would your concerns be? Why?

9. Should the manager of a television or radio station forecast demand? Why or why not? What sort of demand are we talking about? (A brief interview with such a manager would be informative.)

10. In a certain time-sharing computer system, the quarterly number of "connects" or "logons" is one useful indicator of demand. Recent data are as follows:

	Quarter							
	−8	−7	−6	−5	−4	−3	−2	−1
Number of connects (in thousands)	8	9	11	10	11	13	16	12

What is your forecast for next quarter? Look for seasonality and trend. Explain.

11. Service part demands for lawn mower blades at Lawngirl Manufacturing Company, along with three-week and nine-week moving average data, are as follows:

	Week							
	−16	−15	−14	−13	−12	−11	−10	−9
Demand	800	460	630	880	510	910	420	740
Three-week moving average		630	657	673	767	613	690	650
Nine-week moving average					682	671	713	710

	Week							
	−8	−7	−6	−5	−4	−3	−2	−1
Demand	790	700	840	600	930	680	900	800
Three-week moving average	743	777	713	790	737	837	793	
Nine-week moving average	716	734	733	776				

a. For weeks −12 through −5, plot the raw demand data, the three-week moving average data, and the nine-week moving average data on one graph. Comment on the smoothing effects of the different time spans (note that the raw data constitute a one-week moving average).

b. Assuming a nonseasonal demand, what is the forecast for next week if a one-week moving average is used? If a three-week moving average is used? If a nine-week moving average is used?

c. Consider your answers from question *b* and the nature of the product: lawn mower blades. Which moving average time span seems best?

12. Recent monthly caseload in a public defender's office was:

January	February	March	April	May	June
180	100	90	110	110	120

July	August	September	October	November	December
140	170	150	160	160	170

a. Graph the demands as (1) a two-month moving average and (2) a six-month moving average. What do the graphs show about the smoothing effects of different moving average time spans?

b. Calculate a five-month moving average centered on June. Then use that value to calculate a seasonal index for June.

c. What factors would determine the usefulness of the seasonal index in question *b*?

13. Demand data and seven-month moving average data are as follows:

	Month											
	−12	−11	−10	−9	−8	−7	−6	−5	−4	−3	−2	−1
Actual demand	130	160	80	130	100	40	150	160	210	200	150	170
Seven-month moving average		133	121	107	113	117	124	141	144	154			

a. Compute a seasonal index applicable to next month.

b. If the trend projection, not adjusted for seasonality, is 168, what is the seasonally adjusted forecast for next month? Use the seasonal index from question *a* in your calculation.

c. If the product is *not* seasonal but the seven-month moving average time span is optimal, what should be the forecast for next month?

14. Computer Media, Inc., sells floppy disks, printer paper, and other computer items, which it reorders based on monthly exponential smoothing demand forecasts. Recent actual demand data, single-order exponential smoothing forecasts, and double exponential smoothing functions are as follows:

Month	Actual Demand	Single-Order Exponential Smoothing Forecast	Double Exponential Smoothing Function
January	—	—	150
February	140	164	
March	166		

a. If the smoothing constant is 0.3, what is the double exponential smoothing forecast for March? What are the forecast errors for the third month for (1) single-order exponential smoothing and (2) double exponential smoothing? What is the double exponential smoothing forecast for April?

b. What would be the double exponential smoothing forecast for April if the smoothing constant were 0.1 instead of 0.3?

c. Comparing your April results in questions a and b, would you say that the choice of smoothing constant makes much difference?

15. The stockroom manager at Citrus Life and Casualty Company forecasts use of office supplies by exponential smoothing using $\alpha = 0.3$. Three weeks ago, demand for letterhead envelopes and the forecast were both 12. Actual demands since then were 18 and 5 boxes, respectively. What is the forecast for next week?

16. The captain of the *Pescado Grande*, a sport-fishing boat that docks at Ensenada, Mexico, is trying to develop a plan for crew needs by day of the week. The basis is the number of paying customers per day. Following are data for the last three weeks:

	Monday	Tuesday	Wednesday	Thursday	Friday	Saturday	Sunday
Week −3	12	6	10	12	18	30	26
Week −2	9	4	5	8	22	32	34
Week −1	3	10	8	7	14	27	31

a. Calculate "seasonal" (daily) indexes for Sunday and Monday. Base the calculations on the appropriate seven-day average demand. What index should be used for planning the crew on Sunday and Monday of this week? Explain.

b. If the *average* number of paying customers per day next week is expected to be 16, how many should be forecast for Monday?

17. Huckleberry Farms, Inc., has three years of monthly demand data for its biggest seller, Huckleberry Jam. The planning director aims to use the following data for demand forecasting:

	Cases of Huckleberry Jam		
	Three Years Ago	Two Years Ago	Last Year
January	530	535	578
February	436	477	507
March	522	530	562

Cases of Huckleberry Jam

	Three Years Ago	Two Years Ago	Last Year
April	448	482	533
May	422	498	516
June	499	563	580
July	478	488	537
August	400	428	440
September	444	430	511
October	486	486	480
November	437	502	499
December	501	547	542

a. Calculate a six-month moving-average *forecast*. To which future time period is this forecast applicable?

b. Which of the following moving average time spans is best: three months, six months, or nine months? Prove your answer by calculating mean absolute deviations (MADs) using data *for the last 12 months only*. (If suitable computer facilities and software are available to you, use the full 36 months' data.)

c. If the most recent forecast—for December of last year—was 495, what is the next exponential smoothing forecast? Use $\alpha = 0.3$. To which future time period is this forecast applicable?

d. Which of the following alphas is best for exponential smoothing forecasting: 0.1, 0.3, or 0.5? Prove your answer by calculating MADs using monthly data *for the last three months only*. In each case, assume that 570 was the exponentially smoothed forecast for September of last year.

e. Although the given data are monthly, Huckleberry also needs a forecast for next quarter and next year. Manipulate the monthly data (that is, create new tables of data) to make them useful for a quarterly and annual forecast. Now compute a quarterly and annual moving average forecast using a three-period (*not* three months, in this case!) time span. Then compute a quarterly and annual exponential smoothing forecast using $\alpha = 0.3$ and assuming that the last-period forecast was (1) 1,596 for quarterly and (2) 5,990 for annual.

f. Plot the data on a scatter diagram with time as the horizontal axis (use graph paper or carefully create a substitute on ordinary lined paper). Use the eyeball trend projection method to produce a forecast (not adjusted for seasonality) for Huckleberry Jam for the next 12 months. You may use either a straight or curving line—whichever fits better. Write down each of the 12 forecast values. (If suitable computer facilities and software are available to you, verify your plotted trend line by processing the data on a computer.)

g. Most consumer products show some degree of demand seasonality. What kind of seasonality pattern would you expect for Huckleberry Jam? Why? *After responding to that question*, examine the three-year history to see if the data tend to follow your reasoning. You may find it helpful to plot the three sets of 12-month data on top of each other on a graph to see if there is a seasonality pattern. Now comment further on Huckleberry's demand patterns.

h. Select any 3 of the 12 months, and calculate seasonal indexes for those months for each year. Follow the method in Figure 5–14, modified so that the basis is a 12-month moving average. Now develop projected (next-year) seasonal indexes for each of the three months. (If suitable computer facilities and software are available to you, develop seasonal indexes for the full 12 months.)

i. Combine your results from g and h, that is, your trend projection with your seasonal indexes. What are your seasonally adjusted trend forecasts for next year?

18. Seal-Fine Sash Company has three years' quarterly demand data for its standard "bedroom" window unit. The production control manager uses the following data for demand forecasting:

	Number of Window Units		
	Three Years Ago	*Two Years Ago*	*Last Year*
Winter	190	215	401
Spring	147	210	510
Summer	494	755	925
Fall	773	1,088	1,482

a. Calculate the three-quarter moving average *forecast*. To what future time period does this moving average apply?

b. Which of the following moving average time spans is better: three quarters or four quarters? Prove your answer by calculating mean absolute deviations (MADs) using all 12 quarters of data. (If suitable computer facilities and software are available to you, process the data by computer rather than manually.) Do the MAD values seem to show that moving average is a suitable method for quarterly forecasting of Seal-Fine's window units? Explain.

c. If the most recent forecast—for fall of last year—was 1,550, what is the next exponential smoothing forecast? Use $\alpha = 0.2$. To what future time period is the forecast applicable?

d. Which of the following alphas is best for exponential smoothing forecasting: 0.1, 0.3, or 0.5? Prove your answer by calculating MADs using quarterly data *for the last three quarters only*. In each case, assume that 540 was the exponentially smoothed forecast for winter of last year. Do the MAD values seem to show that exponential smoothing is a suitable method for quarterly forecasting of Seal-Fine's window units? Explain.

e. Plot the data on a scatter diagram with time as the horizontal axis (use graph paper or carefully create a substitute on ordinary lined paper). Use the eyeball trend projection method to produce a forecast (not adjusted for seasonality) for the window units for the next four quarters. Now combine the data to yield yearly forecasts for the next three years. You may use either a straight or curving line, whichever fits best. Write down each forecast value. (If suitable computer facilities and software are available to you, verify your plotted trend line by processing the data by computer.)

f. What kind of seasonal demand pattern would you expect for Seal-Fine's product line? Explain. *After responding to that question,* examine the three-year history to see if the data tend to follow your reasoning. You may find it helpful to plot the three sets of quarterly data on top of each other on a graph to see if there is a pattern of seasonality. Now comment further on Seal-Fine's demand patterns.

g. Select any two of the four quarters and calculate seasonal indexes for those quarters for each year. Follow the method in Figure 5–14. Now develop projected (next-year) seasonal indexes for each of the two quarters. (If suitable computer facilities and software are available to you, develop seasonal indexes for all four quarters.)

h. Combine your four-quarter trend projection from question *e* with your seasonal indexes from *g*. What are your seasonally adjusted trend forecasts for next year?

19. Following are the last four months' demand data and exponential smoothing forecasts for the custom drapery department at a local department store. The data are in number of customer orders:

Month	Actual Demand	Forecast
−4	18	20
−3	6	18
−2	12	16
−1	9	15

a. Determine the mean absolute deviation of forecast error.
b. Calculate the tracking signal as of today. What does it suggest?

20. Q. R. Smith, owner-manager of Smith's Kitchens, Inc., sees some evidence that demand for kitchen cabinets is related to local tax mill rates, which are adjusted twice yearly. Following are recent data that Smith has collected:

	Half-Year Period									
	−10	−9	−8	−7	−6	−5	−4	−3	−2	−1
Cabinet demand	55	70	75	70	80	85	90	80	70	75
Mill rate	110	125	135	145	140	140	160	150	150	140

a. Develop a graph (scatter diagram) with cabinet demands (Y_t) on the vertical axis and mill rates three periods earlier (X_{t-3}) on the horizontal axis. Plot each combination of demand and mill rate three periods earlier (i.e., Y_t and X_{t-3}) on the graph. For example, the first point would be the demand, 70, for period −7 and the rate, 110, for period −10. Examine your graph. Is there enough association between demand and mill rates three periods (one-and-a-half years) earlier to be useful for forecasting? Explain.

b. Calculate the formula for the straight line of best fit for the data in question a. Using your formula along with the appropriate mill rate, what is the forecasted cabinet demand for the next six-month period?

c. Calculate the coefficient of correlation. Is your impression from question a confirmed?

21. The chief of planning at North American Hotels, Inc., suspects that convention business may be associated with productivity indexes and tourist business with weather. The following graphs show two of the chief's attempts to make these associations:

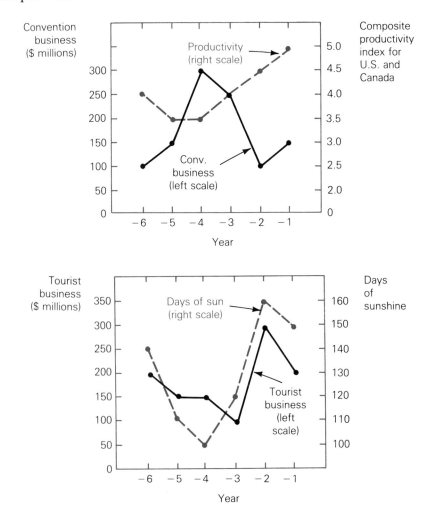

a. Based on your inspection of the productivity-convention business graph, what should the chief of planning conclude? Comment on the usefulness of the analysis for the hotel.

b. Based on your inspection of the sunshine-tourist business graph, what should the chief of planning conclude? Comment on the usefulness of the analysis for the hotel.

22. The safety division at Acme Manufacturing Company has written the following numbers of safety citations in the past seven months:

	Month						
	−7	−6	−5	−4	−3	−2	−1
Citations	71	63	60	58	61	40	42

a. Using the eyeball method, plot the data and project the number of citations that might be expected next month.

b. The chief safety inspector suspects that safety citations are related to number of new hires. She has collected the following data on new hires for the same seven months.

	Month						
	−7	−6	−5	−4	−3	−2	−1
New hires	40	31	27	33	10	25	25

Analyze the association between new hires and citations. Look for a leading indicator.

c. Calculate the formula for the straight line of best fit (line of regression) for the last seven months of citations. Use the formula to calculate the projected demand for the next two months.

d. Calculate the coefficient of correlation between new hires and citations. Make the same calculation but with new hires leading citations by one month. (Base the calculations on citations for months −6 to −1 and new hires for months −7 to −2.) Comment on the difference and on which type of associative forecast is more appropriate.

23. Anderson Theaters owns a chain of movie theaters. In one college town, there are several Anderson Theaters. Anderson wants to find out exactly what influence the college student population has on movie attendance. Student population figures have been obtained from local colleges. These, along with movie attendance figures for the past 12 months, are as follows:

	Month											
	1	2	3	4	5	6	7	8	9	10	11	12
Students*	8	18	18	18	15	9	11	6	17	19	19	13
Attendance*	14	15	16	12	10	8	9	7	11	13	14	17

*In thousands. The student figures are monthly averages.

a. What is the correlation coefficient?

b. Is this correlation analysis useful for Anderson Theaters? Discuss fully?

SUPPLEMENT

CHAPTER 5   **LEAST SQUARES AND CORRELATION COEFFICIENTS**

In this supplement we examine two related techniques. Both concern the straight line that most closely fits a set of plotted data points:

1. The least-squares technique, which yields an equation for the straight line of best fit (line of regression).
2. The correlation coefficient, which measures how well a given straight line or line of regression fits a set of plotted data points.

LEAST SQUARES

The general formula for a straight line is:

$$Y = a + bX$$

For any set of plotted data points, the least-squares method may be used to determine values for a and b in the formula that best fits the data points: a is the Y intercept, and b is the slope. Least-squares formulas for a and b follow, first in the general form and then in a simpler form for a special case.

General form:

$$a = \frac{\Sigma Y}{N} - b\left(\frac{\Sigma X}{N}\right)$$

$$b = \frac{N\Sigma XY - \Sigma X \Sigma Y}{N\Sigma X^2 - (\Sigma X)^2}$$

Special form (when $\Sigma X = 0$, i.e., an odd number of periods):

$$a = \frac{\Sigma Y}{N} \text{ and } b = \frac{\Sigma XY}{\Sigma X^2}$$

where

ΣY = Sum of Y-values for all plotted points

N = Total number of plotted points

ΣXY = Sum of product of X value and Y value for all plotted points

ΣX^2 = Sum of squares of X values for all plotted points

ΣX = Sum of X values for all plotted points

The least-squares technique is shown in Example S5–1 using the special form of the equation.

EXAMPLE S5–1	**LEAST-SQUARES TREND LINE—DATA SERVICES, INC.**

At Data Services, Inc., demand in the last seven quarters in programmer-hours was as follows: 510, 600, 400, 520, 340, 440, and 420. What is the trend line?

Solution

The following table simplifies computation of a and b values. The fourth quarter, in which demand was 520, is treated as the base period; it is numbered as period 0. The three previous periods are numbered -1, -2, and -3; the three succeeding periods are numbered $+1$, $+2$, and $+3$. The low numbers simplify calculation and, since their sum is zero—that is, $\Sigma X = 0$—the simpler least-squares equations apply. The Y values are the seven demand figures.

Y	X	X^2	XY	
510	-3	9	$-1,530$	
600	-2	4	$-1,200$	
400	-1	1	-400	
520	0	0	0	← Base period
340	$+1$	1	$+340$	
440	$+2$	4	$+880$	
420	$+3$	9	$+1,260$	
Sums = 3,230	0	28	-650	

FIGURE S5–1
Seven-Quarter Least-Squares Trend–Data Services, Inc.

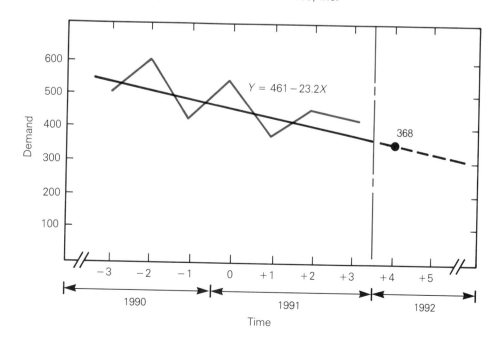

$Y = 461 - 23.2X$

Since $\qquad\qquad\qquad\qquad a = \Sigma Y/N$ and $b = \Sigma XY/\Sigma X^2,$

$$a = \frac{3{,}230}{7} = 461$$

$$b = \frac{-650}{28} = -23.2$$

The formula for the line of best fit is:

$$Y = 461 - 23.2X$$

The formula may be used to forecast, say, the next quarter. With the base or centermost period numbered 0, the next quarter is numbered $+4$. Then

$$Y = 461 - 23.2 (+4)$$

$$= 461 - 93$$

$$= 368 \text{ programmer-hours}$$

Figure S5–1 summarizes the results of the least-squares computations and the forecast for next quarter; note the very close pattern of the demand data here with that in Figure 5–10. Dates are added to the figure to make it agree with the dates for Figure 5–10 in the chapter. Clearly the least-squares trend is very nearly the same as the eyeball trend in Figure 5–10, as we would expect it to be.

CORRELATION COEFFICIENTS

The coefficient of correlation, r, ranges from ± 1.0 for perfect correlation to 0.0 for no correlation at all. An r of ± 1.0 applies to the case where all plotted points are on the straight line of best fit.

A widely used formula for r is:

$$r = \frac{\Sigma XY - \Sigma X \Sigma Y/N}{\sqrt{[\Sigma X^2 - (\Sigma X)^2/N] [\Sigma Y^2 - (\Sigma Y)^2/N]}}$$

Example S5–2, an extension of Example 5–2, demonstrates the formula.

EXAMPLE S5–2   **CORRELATION COEFFICIENT–STATE JOBS SERVICE**

Layoffs at Acme two weeks earlier are plotted against job applicants at the Jobs Service office. Figure 5–25 shows the correlation visually. What is the calculated coefficient of correlation, r?

FIGURE S5-2

Working Figures for Computing r—State Jobs Service

Number of Applicants (Y)	Layoffs at Acme (T − 2) (X)	Y^2	X^2	XY
50	0	2,500	0	0
60	0	3,600	0	0
80	25	6,400	625	2,000
65	20	4,225	400	1,300
110	50	12,100	2,500	5,500
145	60	21,025	3,600	8,700
115	60	13,225	3,600	6,900
125	25	15,625	625	3,125
120	20	14,400	400	2,400
120	35	14,400	1,225	4,200
110	45	12,100	2,025	4,950
70	0	4,900	0	0
60	0	3,600	0	0
65	0	4,225	0	0
90	0	8,100	0	0
55	0	3,025	0	0
70	20	4,900	400	1,400
45	0	2,025	0	0
100	30	10,000	900	3,000
105	30	11,025	900	3,150
105	40	11,025	1,600	4,200
70	0	4,900	0	0
95	0	9,025	0	0
100	10	10,000	100	1,000
Sums = 2,130	470	206,350	18,900	51,825

Solution

Figure S5–2 provides the necessary totals to solve for r. All X and Y values are taken from Example 5–2. Since there are 24 data items, $N = 24$. Calculation of r is as follows:

$$r = \frac{\Sigma XY - \Sigma X \Sigma Y/N}{\sqrt{[\Sigma X^2 - (\Sigma X)^2/N] [\Sigma Y^2 - (\Sigma Y)^2/N]}}$$

$$= \frac{51{,}825 - (2{,}130)(470)/24}{\sqrt{18{,}900 - (470)^2/24)(206{,}350 - (2{,}130)^2/24)]}}$$

$$= 0.78$$

An r of 0.78 is rather high. Layoffs at Acme may be considered a good leading indicator.

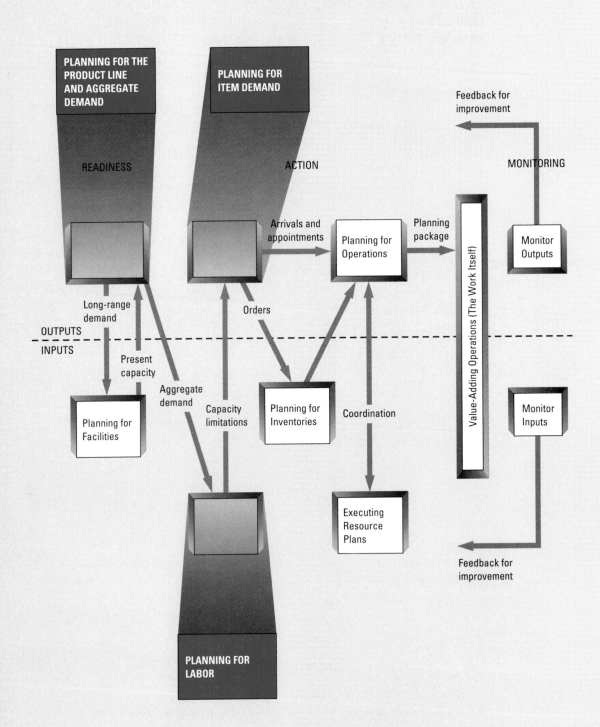

CHAPTER 6

Master Planning—for Capacity and Output

In this chapter, we turn our attention from studying demand (Chapter 5) to doing something about it—namely, developing a master plan. The broad purpose of **master planning** is matching aggregate demand with production capacity. The narrower purpose is steering the firm's capacity toward actual item demands that materialize over time; for a given planning horizon, the result is an **appointment book** or **master schedule** of customers, services, or goods to be processed.

AN INTRODUCTORY EXAMPLE

The central issue of this chapter can be looked at as two related questions: (1) What capacity is needed to meet aggregate demand? (2) Can unit (disaggregated) demand be met by planned capacity? These two questions are of central importance in any organization. We will see why via an example: a small, service-oriented business.

Master Planning—Photography Services

Consider a professional photographer who specializes in individual and family portraits. She shoots in her own studio and does her own developing and printing. Demand may be expressed as the number of customers or—perhaps more precisely—number of photos. But to the photographer, there is another, equally important way to state demand: demand for *capacity*.

The first capacity item might be the photographer's time, that is, her own expertise. There is demand for so many hours of studio time, developing time, packaging time, recordkeeping time, and so forth. Second, there is demand for so much paper, developing chemicals, film, and other supplies. Next are needs for certain tools and equipment, such as cameras, lights, backdrops, enlargers, drying racks, and light meters. Finally, there is the demand for the facility (studio) itself.

All these elements of capacity must be planned for if the photographer is to succeed in serving the customer. Further, each item is limited. The photographer's time is restricted to something less than 24 hours a day. The enlarger can handle only so many prints per hour. The studio is big enough for only certain group sizes, backdrops, and so forth. If our photographer can expect a relatively stable demand for her work, she may develop a relatively stable *capacity plan*.

But what if she desires to change her *business plan*, say, by expanding into event photography—weddings and other social or sporting events? Demand for photographs will grow, as will demand for capacity. That requires further capacity planning.

One thing that changes is the *kinds* of capacity to plan for. Event work places little demand on studio time, but it does create the need for travel and on-site shooting time. Further, event photography may require the purchase of faster lenses, battery packs, film winders, and other special equipment. Both event and portrait work, however, require capacity for developing and printing. Thus, we see that some capacity items are unique to each type of photography while others are common to both.

Another issue is the seasonality of event photography. Weddings, anniversaries, graduations, and proms tend to occur in May and June. Thus, additional capacity will be needed in those months. The photographer may consider buying more equipment, hiring assistants, and contracting out some developing and printing. On the other hand, she may choose simply to limit the amount of business she accepts, reasoning that any added springtime capacity will be unused during the rest of the year. She might wish to avoid the unpleasant task of dismissing assistants when there is not enough work. The point is that she has *options* in planning capacity.

The photographer's business plan, including goals, strategies, and policies, will affect her thinking about the capacity plan options. What she *wants to do* will influence what she *plans to do*.

In developing an *appointment book* (*master schedule*) for her firm, the photographer must consider demand for her services as well as her capacity to provide them. Total demand for all photography services (*aggregate demand*) will determine the load on her developing and printing capacity, as well as demand for billing and other clerical operations capacity. The mix of portrait and event photography (major subgroups of aggregate demand) will determine the capacity requirements for studio shooting and travel/site-shooting times, respectively. Finally, precise demand knowledge for specific capacity items, such as each type of film and each size of printing paper, will require forecasts of each type (item) of photography assignment, including number of shots, size and number of prints desired, and so forth. Actual customer bookings and ensuing print orders will most accurately help predict item capacity demand.

On the other side of the coin, the capacity plan the photographer selects will determine how much and what type of demand she can satisfy. Her appointment book might have to be revised, perhaps more than once, as she juggles demand and capacity, seeking a fit.

It is easy to see that inattention to demand for photography services might lead to investment in too much or too little capacity. Likewise, failure to consider capacity could lead to overbooking, promising more than can be delivered, or in general, creating an unrealistic master plan. Adverse effects may include delays, customer dissatisfaction, and lost business.

Several key points emerge from the above example. First, capacity is needed in order to meet demand. Second, the business plan influences capacity choices. Third, variation in product or service offerings (two types of photography service in this case) complicates capacity planning. Fourth, both demand and capacity plans are required in order to develop an initial, or trial, master schedule. Finally, one or more revisions might be required before the master schedule for a certain period can be set.

The focus of master planning in large corporations is similar to that for the photographer. In the next section, we examine a few terms and explore that focus further.

MASTER PLANNING: PURPOSE, DEFINITIONS, AND FOCUS

The master plan balances required capacity against customer demand; the plan results in a time-phased lineup of goods or services the firm expects to process. An aim of the capacity plan is to keep from over- or underusing capacity—keeping capacity utilization at the right level. Since capacity comes in several forms, discussion of this important aim carries over into other chapters: Production and inventory capacity is a topic of Chapter 8; advantages of under-capacity scheduling are examined in Chapters 11 and 16; detailed operation control and a computer-based routine known as *capacity requirements planning* are covered in Chapter 12; and finally, capacity utilization gets in-depth treatment in Chapters 14, 16, and 18.

Definitions

Capacity planning involves setting and adjusting capacity levels and usage. In complex cases there may be a need to plan or check capacity in stages, from coarse to refined—a series of steps called **resource requirements planning (RRP).** At a coarse level, a "first pass" check is made to see if the overall planned rate of output—the **production plan**—will strain key resources: labor, equipment, facility space, suppliers' capabilities, and, in some cases, money. A second round of resource planning—often called **rough-cut capacity planning**—checks whether a trial master schedule is sound prior to any attempt to implement that schedule. In manufacturing, such validation of a proposed master schedule can be complicated, requiring computer database manipulation. Further discussion of RRP comes later in this chapter. (Note: Usage of the terms *resource requirements planning* and *rough-cut capacity planning* is muddled, with some firms using *rough-cut* to mean the coarsest level of planning and others using it as we have, as a secondary check at the master scheduling stage. The American Production and Inventory Control Society (APICS), in an attempt to avoid some of the confusion, now uses the terms synonymously, based on the fact that the two procedures have much the same purpose.)

The APICS Dictionary also states that the **master production schedule (MPS)** "represents what the company plans to produce, expressed in specific configurations, quantities, and dates."[1] For services, we may call it an appointment

---

[1]Thomas F. Wallace and John R. Dougherty, *APICS Dictionary,* 6th ed. (Falls Church, Va.: American Production and Inventory Control Society, 1987), p. 18.

book, and substitute the word *provide* for *produce* in the definition; and we might call the production plan an operating plan.

With those few terms at our disposal, we may now explore five focal points for capacity planning and subsequent development of the master schedule. References to the photography (service sector) company, together with examples from manufacturing, will help us see what is involved.

Demand Focus

In Chapter 5, we distinguished between item forecasting and aggregate forecasting. The split may now be more fully explained. Item forecasts are needed for planning specific components, products, or services. Item forecasts, plus actual booked orders, make up the master schedule or appointment book. Forecasts of aggregate demand, by capacity group or product family, have the broader purpose of setting output rates and capacity, which become upper limits on the master schedule.

In Chapter 5, we also learned that group forecasts are more accurate than item forecasts. The challenge is to form meaningful groups. The groups make up units of capacity that can be separately staffed, subcontracted, set up, or inventoried.

Aggregate forecasts for group/family should go far enough into the future to account for seasonal and promotional surges. A forecast for a few weeks may be good enough for some services, especially if labor is unskilled and easy to hire. But for goods producers and skilled-labor services, such as those provided by the photographer in our example, the forecast and hiring plan must reach out several months. We consider the time focus next.

Medium-Term Planning Focus

Managers plan for short-, medium-, and long-term capacity. Our main interest in this chapter is with medium-term capacity, for which the planning horizon (outer limit) typically ranges from a few weeks to 18 months. Of course, the medium-term plan must fit into the long-term plan, and it also limits what can be done in the short term.

Consider our photographer, for example. Her supplies, such as film and paper, are short-term capacity items. Labor—hers and her assistants'—and facilities are different; it won't work to try to plan for them at the last minute. Recall from Chapter 3 that greater attention to readiness—increased flexibility, for example—usually reduces the required lead time, or planning time in this case. It is generally true, however, that regardless of the business's size, planning for medium-term items such as labor and equipment typically must occur well before intended usage.

For an electronics company, the business plan may call for shipment of 12,000 TV sets next quarter and a reduction in finished goods inventory by 2,000 units, yielding a net production plan of 10,000 TV sets for the quarter. As with the photography business, those are medium-term plans, in this case with a time horizon of several months.

Production Plan Focus

A company's medium-term business plan generally is a month-by-month or quarter-by-quarter plan for sales, production, shipments, research and development, customer service, and cash flow. Our interest is in the production plan segment.

The *production plan* (or operating plan) acts as a regulator. It regulates the production, inventories, backlogs, average waiting (for service) time, and expenses for purchasing and operating. Levels of inventories, backlogs and wait times in turn affect customer service, and operating expenses determine cash flow. Thus, the production plan is central in translating the business plan into action. (Note: *Product planning*, discussed in Chapter 3, refers to what the product line contains, while *production planning* concerns output rate.)

The production plan states the quantity of output in broad terms and by product family. For our photographer, the broad plan is the total number of engagements or photographs; the plan by product families is the number of event jobs and number of portrait jobs. In a consumer electronics company, TV sets might be one family and VCRs another. Output quantity may be stated in units or total dollar value processed. A steel company might use tons and a refinery gallons or barrels, again expressing output both by product family and in total volume.

Company strategy and policies are integral components of the business plan. What the company wants to do influences what it plans to do. Its targeted amount and type of demand and its selection of ways to provide capacity to meet demand are choices rather than givens. Our photographer, for example, could elect to shift strategies: Concentrate on event photography, and cease portrait work. Some manufacturing companies, such as IBM, have a no lay-off policy. The effects of strategy and policies on the production/capacity plan are discussed more fully in a later section.

Adjustable-Capacity Focus

As the term is usually used, capacity planning deals with capacity that is adjustable. **Adjustable capacity** refers to inputs that may be altered relatively easily over the medium-term planning horizon. Amount and schedules of labor, machine cycles, subcontracting, and inventory levels are examples. **Fixed capacity** refers to items that generally cannot be changed quickly or cheaply, such as buildings and capital equipment. Fixed-capacity alteration typically is part of long-range planning.

Our photographer really has only one fixed-capacity item: her studio. Relative to the rest of her business, a change in studio size would be a major event. Including planning, funding, design, construction, decorating, and so forth, a change in this resource could easily take a year or two. The remainder of her capacity items may be considered adjustable.

While machines are acquired based on long-term forecasts, the intensity of their use is an element of medium-term adjustable-capacity planning. The photographer might operate a developer for 2, 4, or 10 hours per day; a manufacturing plant might operate machinery 1, 2, or 3 shifts per day. One notable difference between the service and goods sectors in this regard, of course, is that services may not be stored in advance of demand. Finished-goods inventory is an element of adjustable capacity for goods-oriented companies only.

Output and Input Focus

Master planning focuses on both outputs and inputs. The master schedule is stated strictly in output terms: quantities of goods or services.

Capacity planning may be done partially in output terms (the production plan) and then converted into inputs (the capacity plan). For example, the photographer might convert demand for six portrait sessions into demand for 4 hours of studio time, 3 rolls of film, 2.5 hours of developing time, and so forth.

In a manufacturing company, a quarterly production plan for 10,000 television sets might be translated into a capacity plan for 5,000 labor-hours of TV assembly, 10,000 labor-hours of TV component subassembly, and so on. Machine capacity is obtained in a similar manner. For example, 10,000 molded plastic cabinets for the TV sets might be expressed as 2,500 machine cycles for an injection molding machine that forms 4 molds per cycle.

Sequence Overview

Figure 6–1 provides an overview of capacity planning and master scheduling. Inputs include aggregate demand forecasts, the business plan, and capacity strategy and policies. At the output end, the master schedule feeds inventory planning (Chapter 9) and operation control (Chapter 12).

Figure 6–1 is intended to show how capacity planning and master scheduling fit into the usual planning sequence; to an extent, it summarizes what we have covered thus far. Additional details, especially key feedback loops necessary for master schedule revisions, are explored later when we discuss master scheduling directly. The two boxes in Figure 6–1, "production/capacity plan" and "master schedule," are examined more closely in the next two sections.

PRODUCTION/CAPACITY PLANNING

The term *production/capacity planning* reminds us that we are referring to a plan that may be expressed in output terms (production plan) or in input terms (adjustable capacity). As Figure 6–1 shows, production/capacity planning is fed

FIGURE 6–1
Master Planning: Sequence Overview

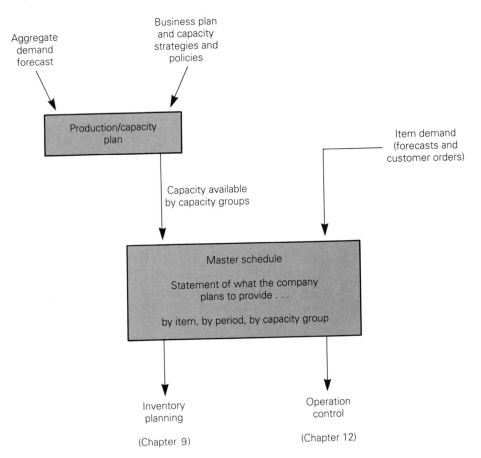

by an aggregate demand forecast, and the production/capacity plan, in turn, sets upper limits on the master schedule. Within limits imposed by the production/capacity plan, the contents of the master schedule are determined by item forecasts and actual customer orders.

Master schedules are also affected by the company's capacity strategies and policies, which place constraints on the production/capacity plan. Such constraints include:

1. Available facilities and present labor force.
2. Planned inventory levels.
3. Planned backlogs and waiting-line limitations.

If orders are processed on demand, backlogs are eliminated; item 3 may still partially apply since there usually will be some waiting lines from one process to the next. For service providers and make-to-order goods producers, the output is not inventoriable, ruling out item 2. But item 1, facilities and present labor, is always of concern.

To the extent that logical capacity groups—work cells, for example—exist, the aggregate forecast might be translated first into required number of processing hours in each cell and then into number of employees needed. If employees are free of restrictive job classifications and are cross-trained in all or most jobs in the cell, further subdivision by labor grouping is unnecessary.

PRINCIPLE: Cross-train for mastery of more than one job.

Thus, we see that the production/capacity planning process may be simplified. Strategies and policies, instrumental elements in production/capacity planning, are considered next.

Capacity Strategies

For our photographer, the seasonal nature of event photography makes capacity planning more difficult. She must develop a capacity strategy for responding to swings in demand. Assuming that she elects to forego event photography and stick with portrait photography and its greater demand stability, her capacity planning becomes simpler. Besides demand behavior, however, there are other factors that affect the production/capacity plan.

Capacity strategy often depends a great deal on the type of industry. Process industries tend to be capital intensive and thus are intent on achieving high utilization of machine capacity.[2] For example, petrochemical plants and steel mills run day and night if demand is sufficient.

Many other industries, especially services, tend to be labor intensive, so that capacity strategy centers on labor. A service business might have a strategy of cost leadership, in which case it may try to maintain only enough labor to meet current demand. This "bare-bones" labor-capacity strategy is known as **chase demand**: Hire when demand is good; lay off when demand is poor.

An alternative labor strategy is known as **level capacity**: Try to retain people through thick and thin. The lifetime (or career-time) employment policies of government agencies, large Japanese companies, and some American firms, such as 3M Corp., are examples. Level capacity is favored in labor-intensive operations when quality is a vital competitive factor. This is especially true if employees' skill qualifications are high or their skills are scarce.

The level-capacity strategy sometimes governs materials and backlogs as well as labor. When demand dips for a firm that makes to stock (an inventoriable product), inventory may be allowed to grow in order to keep capacity (labor)

---

[2]Sam G. Taylor, Samuel M. Steward, and Steven F. Bolander, "Why the Process Industries Are Different," *Production and Inventory Management* (Fourth Quarter 1981), pp. 9–24.

level. A make-to-order firm, in contrast, may let order backlogs instead of inventory grow to keep capacity level.

Consider, for example, the ABC brokerage company on Wall Street.[3] ABC handles transactions coming in from branch offices around the country, and Securities and Exchange Commission (SEC) regulations require all transactions to be settled within five days. The five days give ABC managers time to smooth out the daily volume fluctuations so that transaction-handling capacity will not be strained one day and underused the next. But stock market volume can swing dramatically overnight. For example, a rumor about a peace agreement might cause it to soar. This can tax capacity for processors of stock transactions. How would ABC cope with such sudden changes? Here are what two ABC managers might propose:

Manager A: Our capacity should be set at 12,000 transactions per day. This will allow us to meet demand most days. Last year we had a few hot periods when demand ran at 14,000–15,000 per day, and we probably will this year, too. We can handle those problems by overtime for a few days—until new clerks can be hired. Our labor turnover rate is high, so when transaction volume drops we can ease capacity down by not filling vacancies.

Manager B: I think we should keep capacity right at 17,000 transactions per day. That will be enough to handle the spurts in volume, which are very hard to predict.

Who is right? In this case both are—and here's the rest of the story—each is managing a different end of the business of handling the stock transactions. Manager A is in charge of cashiering: processing certificates, cash, and checks. Clerks and messengers with uncomplicated tasks are the work force. Manager B, on the other hand, runs order processing. The work force has higher skills: data entry, EDP, programming, and information analysis. Equipment is expensive, and lead times to change data processing procedures are long.

Manager A is advocating chase demand, which seems rational for his department. Manager B prefers a level-capacity strategy, which is logical for her department. Since low-skill labor from A's department cannot handle the work in B's department, each manager should have a separate capacity plan—rather than one plan covering the whole transaction-processing operation—and may be governed by a different capacity strategy.

Figure 6–2 outlines the two strategies. Firms tend to adopt the chase strategy when there are low-skill people doing jobs at low pay in a less than pleasant work environment. With low skill levels, training costs are low per employee but could be high per year, since turnover tends to be high. Turnover also means high hire-fire costs, and, along with low skills, contributes to high error rates.

---

[3]This example is adapted from W. Earl Sasser, R. Paul Olsen, and D. Daryl Wychoff, *Management of Service Operations* (Boston: Allyn & Bacon, 1978), pp. 303–05 (HD9981.5.S27).

FIGURE 6–2

Comparison of Chase Demand and Level-Capacity Strategies

	Chase Demand	Level Capacity
Labor skill level	Low	High
Wage rate	Low	High
Working conditions	Sweatshop	Pleasant
Training required per employee	Low	High
Labor turnover	High	Low
Hire-fire costs	High	Low
Error rate	High	Low
Type of budgeting and forecasting required	Short term	Long term

Forecasting and budgeting may be short term, since lead times for adding to or cutting the work force are short.

The level-capacity strategy has opposite features. Higher skills have to be attracted; thus, pay and working conditions must be better. High skills must be honed to suit more demanding jobs; hence, training costs per employee are high. The attractions of the job are meant to keep turnover and hire-fire costs low, and high labor skills hold down error rates. Forecasting and budgeting must be longer term, since hiring and training skilled people takes time.

The level strategy seems best from the outlook of the employee. But many businesses cannot compete that way. Thus, there are some industrial companies and lots of service industries—fast foods, hotels, amusement parks, and the like—that pay minimum wages and have most of the other characteristics of the chase strategy as well.

Policies: Translating Strategies into Action

Suppose our photographer has a chase-demand strategy. She might adopt a policy of promising finished photographs no later than 72 hours after pictures are taken. A companion policy for her strategy might call for extensive use of subcontracting for developing and printing. The effect of these policies is to translate her strategy into action. Other examples are:

A municipal power company may have a strategy of providing employee security in order to gain a stable work force (low turnover). This might translate into policies for absorbing surges in demand with little short-term hiring and layoffs. For example, one policy could be to maintain excess work force, especially linespeople and installers. Another might be to subcontract extraordinary maintenance, such as repairing downed lines.

A bowling proprietor's strategy might be one of of high capacity utilization. A supportive policy would be lower prices for daytime bowling.

A food wholesaler may have a strategy of very fast service to retail grocers. Supportive policies might include use of shift work, weekend hours, overtime, cross-trained employees for interdepartmental employee loans, and large inventories.

Any kind of organization might adopt a strategy of keeping a tight rein on internal service costs. One policy (not always sound) for this is to use service pools, for example, typing pools, motor pools, and labor pools. Small, start-up businesses operating out of Small Business Institute "incubators" must adopt a strategy of close cost control. They frequently share service pools as a "policy of necessity." In established companies, service pools usually seem less costly than assigning the service units to individual departments; however, service quality and response time may suffer.

The above examples point out common kinds of capacity policies. A more complete list follows:

Hiring and layoffs	Maintenance work as a filler
Overtime and extra shifts	Use of marginal facilities
Part-time and temporary labor	Renting space or tools
Cross-training and transfers (of people or work) among departments	Refusing, back-ordering, or postponing work
Service pools	Building inventories
Quick changeover techniques to make capacity flexible	Peak/off-peak price differences

Capacity policies (as well as underlying strategies) are set by top officers. They include high-level managers in operations, such as site manager, vice president of operations, chief production controller, and materials manager. Capacity policies may be expressed generally, such as "Avoid overtime and keep inventories low." Or, they may be expressed quantitatively, with minimums, maximums, or ranges, and may be priority ordered. For example, a set of priority-ordered policies aimed at maintaining a level permanent work force might be:

For insufficient demand:

1. Keep employees busy by building inventory—maximum of 10 percent buildup above predicted demand.

2. Lay off employees only after a 10 percent excess inventory is on hand.

For excess demand:

1. Use temporary labor for first 5 percent of excess demand.

2. Use overtime for next 5 percent.

3. Reduce customer service beyond that (refuse or postpone orders, offer partial shipments, etc.).

With such specific policies, production/capacity planning is straightforward; managers just follow the policies. Usually, however, a company will not hem itself in with such specific policies. For example, the famous "lifetime employment" of some Japanese firms is really not an explicit policy. The employee tends to have a lifetime (or career-time) commitment to a single company, but the company may or may not be able to retain the employee that long. Japan has a highly competitive economy, and each year many companies fail, putting employees out of work. More successful Japanese companies are often able to claim with pride that they have never had to lay off employees, as is true of a surprising number of North American companies. But Japanese companies do work very hard at avoiding layoffs, as is demonstrated by the Kawasaki motorcycle plant in Lincoln, Nebraska.

In the spring of 1981, Kawasaki built up a surplus of labor, largely because of productivity improvements. Later in the year, a recession severely cut motorcycle demand and killed off Kawasaki's entire snowmobile product line. The actions taken, in chronological order, were:

1. Assigned excess direct labor to essential support tasks, including modifying, moving, and installing equipment.
2. Assigned excess labor to maintenance work, such as painting, caulking, and minor remodeling.
3. In fall 1981, Kawasaki lent 11 of its excess employees to the city of Lincoln, where they worked for several months with Kawasaki paying wages and benefits.
4. The first layoffs—24 white-collar people—occurred in October.
5. In November, 16 blue-collar employees voluntarily took a six-month furlough with call-back rights.
6. In February 1982, 98 production employees were terminated.
7. In October 1982, the plant went to a four-day workweek to preserve jobs for the remaining work force.

Those actions were not governed by policy other than the general one of seeking to avoid layoffs in the face of insufficient demand. Actions of this kind tend to *look* as if they were policy based to the outside observer using hindsight. (Such is probably the case with much of what is referred to as *policy*.)

Capacity strategies and policies may guide any significant production/capacity planning problem. In addition, there are several practical tools that might fit specific situations. Learning-curve planning and group-based planning are examples that we will explore in this chapter. Other techniques include the transportation method and the linear decision rule. We will study the transportation method in Chapter 18; the linear decision rule is reserved for more advanced studies.

Learning-Curve Planning

As people learn, the time required for them to do a given task decreases. In industry this is known as the **learning-curve** phenomenon, and it applies not only to direct labor but also to those who support the direct-labor effort. More broadly, the learning curve is a foundation for the well-known economy-of-scale concept: Greater volumes yield lower unit costs.

Where the learning-curve effect is significant, planning of production rates and capacity should build on it. With learning effects, production rates may increase over time with no change in capacity level, or capacity levels may be cut over time without reducing production rates.

The learning-curve phenomenon was observed in airframe manufacturing as far back as 1925.[4] In later years, aircraft manufacturers found a dominant learning pattern—the 80 percent learning curve. The second plane required 80 percent as much direct labor as the first; the fourth 80 percent as much as the second; the tenth 80 percent as much as the fifth, and so forth. The rate of learning to assemble aircraft was 20 percent between doubled quantities.

FIGURE 6–3
80 Percent Learning Curve

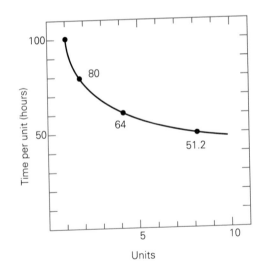

---

[4]The commander of Wright-Patterson Air Force Base was reported to have observed it in 1925. See Winfred B. Hirshmann, "Profits from the Learning Curve," *Harvard Business Review*, January–February 1964, p. 125–139.

An 80 percent learning curve appears graphically in Figure 6–3. Mathematically, the learning curve follows the general formula

$$Y = aX^b$$

(6-1)

where

$Y =$ Labor-hours per unit

$X =$ Unit number

$a =$ Labor-hours for first unit

$b = \dfrac{\text{Logarithm of learning-curve rate}}{\text{Logarithm of 2}}$

Learning Curves in Production/Capacity Planning

When using the learning curve for production–capacity planning, labor requirements are calculated over time, as Example 6–1 shows.

EXAMPLE 6–1   **LEARNING-CURVE PLANNING–BELLWEATHER ELECTRIC, INC.**

Bellweather has a contract for 60 portable electric generators. The labor-hour requirement for manufacturing the first unit is 100. With that as a given, Bellweather planners develop an aggregate capacity plan using learning-curve calculations. They use a 90 percent learning curve, based on previous experience with generator contracts.

Using formula 6–1, the labor requirement for the second generator is:

$$Y = aX^b$$
$$Y = (100)(2)^{\left(\frac{\log 0.9}{\log 2.0}\right)}$$
$$= (100)(2)^{-0.152}$$
$$= (100)(0.9)$$
$$= 90 \text{ hours}$$

This result for the second unit, 90, is expected, since for a 90 percent learning curve there is 10 percent learning between doubled quantities.

For the fourth unit,

$$Y = aX^b = 100(4)^{-0.152} = (100)(0.81) = 81$$

This result may be obtained more simply by

$$(100)(0.9)^2 = (100)(0.9)(0.9) = (100)(0.81) = 81$$

For the eight unit,

$$Y = aX^b = 100(8)^{-0.152} = (100)(0.729) = 72.9$$

This result is also obtained by

$$(100)(0.9)^3 = (100)(0.9)(0.9)(0.9) = (100)(0.729) = 72.9$$

FIGURE 6–4
Labor-Hour Requirements for Generator
Manufacturing—Bellweather Electric, Inc.

Generator Number	Labor-Hours Required	Cumulative Labor-Hours Required
1	100	100.0
2	90	190.0
3	84.6	274.6
10	70.5	799.4
20	63.4	1,460.8
30	59.6	2,072.7
40	57.1	2,654.3
50	55.2	3,214.2
60	53.7	3,757.4

This way of avoiding logarithms works for the 16th, 32nd, 64th, and so on units, that is for any unit that is a power of 2; but for the 3rd, 5th, 6th, 7th, 9th, and so forth units, the logarithmic calculation is necessary.

Figure 6–4 displays some of the results of the learning-curve-calculations. With those figures, Bellweather may assign labor based on the decreasing per-unit labor-hour requirements. For example, the 60th generator requires 53.7 labor-hours, which is only about half that required for the first unit. Completion of finished generators can be master scheduled to increase at the 90 percent learning-curve rate.

Learning Curves and Continuing Improvement

Learning-curve planning is most closely associated with production of large-scale items: airplanes, earthmovers, and so on. At first, no one is familiar with the work, and the production system needs to be debugged. As units are produced, improvements are natural. The learning curve may apply to any repetitive manufacturing—if the work climate is favorable for continuing improvement. In all too many companies, it is not. Labor may resist a productivity-enhancing idea, derogatorily calling it "speedup." Or, employees may resist changes in less vocal ways. In an entertaining book about his working life, Robert Schrank explains how employees tend to set their own informal output norms, or "bogeys," and enforce them through peer pressure.[5] Thus, the system is not allowed to learn.

It is easy to blame the employee or the union, but when we consider the many companies that do have a climate conducive to improvement, that explanation looks weak. In recent years, many companies have installed work systems

---

[5]Robert Schrank, *Ten Thousand Working Days* (Cambridge, Mass.: MIT Press, 1978) (HD8073.S34A37).

in which continuing improvement is part of every employee's job. Resulting rates of learning-driven productivity improvement are impressive.

PRINCIPLE: Become dedicated to continual, rapid improvement

Of course, nearly all companies enjoy some rate of improvement, which may suggest that firms could use the learning curve for labor-capacity planning, costing, budgeting, pricing, and so forth. But the learning curve fails as a planning aid unless improvements are measurable over each planning increment, such as each month or quarter. Companies performing poorly tend to get measurable improvements at model changeover time, when advanced equipment is bought and when plant expansion is undertaken. In between, the climate for improvement may be so poor that none takes place. How production systems may be designed so as to achieve *steady* improvement is a central issue in this book and is treated in most chapters. For now, let us return to capacity planning and examine group-based methods.

Group-Based Approach

To appreciate the value and uses of **group-based capacity planning**, we need to review a bit of a history. Following World War II, consumer waiting lists for refrigerators, washing machines, rubber tires, and so forth were often a year or two long. For the manufacturer, such order backlogs provided long planning lead times. During that era, the so-called *quarterly ordering system* came into use. The firm merely decided what items and components it would produce next quarter and thoroughly planned resource needs to fit that production.

While the quarterly ordering system directly concerns ordering of parts and raw materials, it also yields capacity plans. Also, planners need not settle for aggregate capacity plans; it is possible to convert "sure-thing" orders into highly detailed capacity plans down to the number of labor-hours on a given machine. For example, if it takes 15 minutes to spray paint one electric range and quarterly orders for ranges total 4,000, the number of paint-spraying hours for the quarter is:

$$4,000 \text{ ranges} \times 15 \text{ minute/range} \times 1 \text{ hour/60 minutes} = 1,000 \text{ hours}$$

At 40 hours per week, or 520 hours per 13-week quarter per employee, 1,000 hours equals 1.9 people (1,000/520) to run the paint sprayers. All other elements of adjustable capacity may be determined the same way and hiring, training, and so on planned accordingly.

The quarterly ordering system began to lose its effectiveness as postwar backlogs were whittled down and the consumer pipeline gradually filled up with goods. In the late 1950s and early 1960s, a new era of short backlogs and stiff competition emerged. Without the luxury of long backlogs, manufacturers had to turn to demand forecasting by capacity group.

One method of grouping is by product families—families having production rather than marketing commonality. For example, a sales catalog might have aluminum and wood doors and windows grouped together as a product family. But from a capacity planning viewpoint, it makes more sense to group all aluminum items separately from wood items.

Considering as a group all items requiring the same resources, using the same manufacturing technology, or passing through the same processes (same routing) are examples of sound group-based approaches. The existence of work cells makes the grouping easier. A purpose of group-based capacity planning is to have the right amount of labor on hand *in the aggregate.*

Let us briefly revisit our photographer at this point. Planning labor capacity is cut and dried at first, when she runs the firm herself. As the business expands, she needs more labor-hours for such things (capacity groups) as photography, developing, accounting, ordering/receiving supplies, marketing, and customer service. If every assistant she hires can perform all of these activities, her labor force will exemplify the ideal: a cross-trained, flexible work force. As we all know, however, such is usually not the case. She may plan for aggregate labor, but she must do so by considering the aggregate demand for each type of work. Perhaps she could use a variation on the method taken up next: group-based planning in a make-to-order business.

Capacity Groups in Make-to-Order Business

Capacity planning in a make-to-order business is made difficult by the lack of order lead time. Still, a quick and simple projection of recent demand data into the future is helpful—if orders can be backlogged. The method involves two steps:

1. Identify broad capacity groups or similar processes, following the principle that forecasts are more accurate for larger groupings.
2. Develop a production/capacity plan based on projection of recent total demand into the future and on backlog and lead-time policies.

Example 6–2 illustrates.

EXAMPLE 6–2   PRODUCTION/CAPACITY PLANNING—TAIL AND EXHAUST PIPE PLANT

The Hot Pipes Division of International Industries makes tailpipes and exhaust pipes for the aftermarket (that means replacement parts). Orders are small and diverse, and Hot Pipes does not retail its own brand name. Therefore, it is strictly a make-to-order plant.

Hot Pipes needs an aggregate capacity plan to cover a number of weeks. Fine-tuning is possible on a day-to-day basis; that is, Hot Pipes can do a limited amount of overtime work and labor borrowing on a daily basis, but the regular work force must be planned, hired, and trained in advance. Hot Pipes uses the two-step method:

Step 1: Tailpipes and exhaust pipes seem to be the two key groups that are logical for separate capacity plans: They are built in separate factory areas with different equipment and different labor skills. Capacity may be measured in *pieces* for both groupings.

Step 2: Figure 6–5 shows past demand for tailpipes on the left and two capacity options on the right. Option 1 provides for 1,800 pieces per week—100 fewer than the mean demand for the past 8 weeks. The deviations range from +700 to −1,400 pieces per week. Option 2 provides for 300 fewer pieces per week than option 1. The deviations range from +100 to −3,500 pieces per week. (Note: At Hot Pipes the positive deviations, e.g., +700, do *not* represent *idle* excess capacity. In such weeks of insufficient demand, the work force could be kept busy making standard lengths of pipe, performing maintenance, and so forth.)

Option 1 results in excess capacity in weeks 2 through 5. Option 2 results in excess capacity only in week 2.

Projected backlogs are the opposite. For option 1, the backlog reaches 1,400 pieces in week 7; that is nearly a one-week backlog at the planned production rate of 1,800 pieces per week. For option 2, the backlog reaches 3,500 pieces in week 7; that is over two weeks' backlog: 3,500 pieces/1,500 pieces per week = 2.3 weeks.

A backlog exceeding two weeks means a lead time greater than two weeks for Hot Pipes' customers. For its rather competitive industry, that may be unacceptable. Thus, Hot Pipes may decide to pay for the excess capacity of option 1 in order to keep planned backlogs and lead times down to within one week.

FIGURE 6–5

Capacity/Backlog Options for Tailpipes

Week	Recent Weekly Demand		Option 1: 1,800 Pieces per Week		Option 2: 1,500 Pieces per Week	
	Pieces	Cumulative Pieces	Cumulative	Deviation	Cumulative	Deviation
1	1,800	1,800	1,800	0	1,500	−300
2	1,100	2,900	3,600	+700	3,000	+100
3	1,800	4,700	5,400	+700	4,500	−200
4	1,950	6,650	7,200	+550	6,000	−650
5	2,300	8,950	9,000	+50	7,500	−1,450
6	2,800	11,750	10,800	−950	9,000	−2,750
7	2,250	14,000	12,600	−1,400	10,500	−3,500
8	1,200	15,200	14,400	−800	12,000	−3,200

$$\text{Mean demand} = \frac{15,200}{8} = 1,900 \text{ pieces per week}$$

Hot Pipe planners are aware that projecting future backlogs based on the past is fraught with error. The total pieces in the next eight weeks may be fairly close to the total (15,200 pieces) for the past eight weeks. But the week-by-week demand pattern is sure to be quite different. Thus, maximum backlogs can be much more or less than projected. Still, this simple method is helpful in planning, and flexibility (overtime, job transfers, etc.) in the short term can help correct for planning errors.

In this simplified example, we did not consider such options as extra shifts and subcontracting. Overtime, labor borrowing, and similar very short-range adjustments normally should *not* be considered in the production/capacity planning stage; those are measures to be taken only when capacity planning does not work out.

In this method, we assume that orders may be backlogged and worked off in later periods. Note that backlogs are carried forward by the cumulative totals.

In some firms, an unmet order is a lost order; backlogs are not carryable. This tends to be the case in transportation, restaurants, lodging, and similar service-on-demand businesses. Such industries may use a variation on the method of Example 6–2, in which demand is not cumulative. Therefore, negative deviations are lost sales, not backlogs.

Capacity Groups in a Make-to-Stock Plant

Production/capacity planning in a make-to-stock plant begins with the same two steps as in the make-to-order case: Identify capacity groups, and develop production rates to fit projected group demands. That may complete the plan, but more often the firm will add a third step: Refine the production rates to provide for desired inventory levels. Occasionally there is a fourth step: Further refine the plan by examining how production loads onto individual shops or departments. All four steps are presented in Example 6–3.

EXAMPLE 6–3 **PRODUCTION/CAPACITY PLANNING—ELECTRONICS PLANT**

Step 1: For production/capacity-planning purposes, Quark Electronics divides its productive processes into three product families or groups, identified simply as groups 1, 2, and 3. Each group covers a large number of produced items, including end products, subassemblies, and parts.

The reason for the division into three groups is seen in Figure 6–6. There are three dominant process-flow paths, or routings. They wind through the four shop areas and include 11 of the 16 work centers in the four shops. A few products do not exactly fit any of the three routings, but enough do to provide a solid basis for production/capacity planning, that is, groups large enough for decent forecast accuracy.

Next, Quark forecasts aggregate demand for each product group identified;

FIGURE 6–6
Common Routings—Quark Electronics

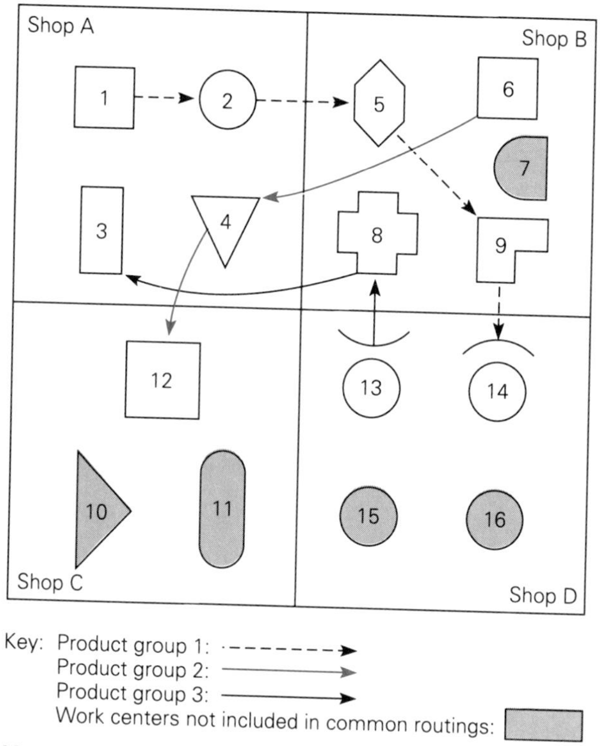
Shop A
Shop B
Shop C
Shop D
1
2
3
4
5
6
7
8
9
10
11
12
13
14
15
16
Key: Product group 1:
Product group 2:
Product group 3:
Work centers not included in common routings:

Note: Machines 13, 14, 15, and 16 are identical; thus 15 and 16 could be substituted for 13 and 14, if needed.

then both labor-hour and machine-hour requirements are roughly matched against product demand.

Step 2: Quark develops a production/capacity plan based on desired labor utilization. Figure 6–7 shows a forecast and a trial production plan for product group 1. The plan provides for an even 10,200-piece-per-week production rate for the 4 weeks covered by the forecast. All different kinds of pieces are counted. Still, Quark planners feel that pieces are a meaningful measure for producing a production/capacity plan. Product groups 2 and 3 should be similarly planned.

The plan appears to provide a good balance between forecast demand and planned production. They are equal at 40,800 cumulative pieces.

Step 3: Quark might want to refine the production/capacity plan to provide for desired inventory levels. Figure 6–7 shows beginning inventory of 14,000 pieces and an ending inventory (week 4) also of 14,000 pieces. Sometimes a change in inventory level is desired. For example, the firm may desire an inventory buildup, perhaps in anticipation of a seasonal or promotional surge in demand. If so, Quark would increase the planned production rate above the

FIGURE 6–7
Trial Production/Capacity Plan—Product Group 1

Pieces through Product Group 1

	Forecast		Trial Production Plan		
Week	Pieces per Week (000)	Cumulative	Pieces per Week (000)	Cumulative	Inventory
0	—	—	—	—	14.0
1	10.0	10.0	10.2	10.2	14.2
2	10.0	20.0	10.2	20.4	14.4
3	10.4	30.4	10.2	30.6	14.2
4	10.4	40.8	10.2	40.8	14.0

10,200 pieces per week shown in the trial production plan. To work off some inventory, it would decrease the planned rate.

Quark planners would also examine inventory levels for product groups 2 and 3. Production/capacity planning could stop there. But a more exacting plan may be derived by calculating effects on each shop, by labor-hours and by machine-hours; shop-level capacity planning is considered next.

Step 4: A detailed production/capacity plan requires converting group capacity into smaller-capacity units. Conversion factors are needed. If group capacity were in labor-hours (or machine-hours), historical percentages perhaps could be used to translate group hours into shop hours. In the case of Quark Electronics, group capacity is in pieces per week. Therefore, labor-hours and machine-hours per piece may serve as conversion factors. Those factors may be historical and not highly exact.

Figure 6–8 shows how such conversion factors may be used to convert planned pieces to labor-hours and machine-hours for each shop for week 1. Dividing planned pieces per week by the standard rates gives required labor-hours and machine-hours. Sample calculations are shown at the bottom of Figure 6–8 for the results in shop A, group 1.

After calculations are completed, total labor-hours and machine-hours may be summed for each shop. The totals are compared with single-shift shop capacities, and the difference is the shortage of labor-hours or machine-hours. (Shop capacities are based on number of people or machines times 40 hours' regular time per week less nonavailable time, such as break time and delay time.)

Few serious capacity problems are indicated by the results in Figure 6–8. The minus results show excess capacity, but only for shop A labor is this much of a concern. There is a greater amount of excess machine-hours, but this may be thought of as a normal margin for error, since machines constitute fixed capacity that cannot be added to on short notice.

Quark could deal with the 23 hours of excess labor in shop A by cutting the work force. Or, Quark planners could make out a revised production/capacity plan with more pieces in group 1, 2, or 3—whichever would cause the fewest additional labor-hours in the already overloaded shops B, C, and D.

The same procedure would extend to weeks 2, 3, and 4. A computer would ease the calculating burden. But it is not necessary to achieve a highly refined

FIGURE 6–8

Production Rate Converted to Labor-Hours and Machine-Hours—Quark Electronics

	Shop A	Shop B	Shop C	Shop D
Week 1: Labor-hours				
Group 1	⑤①	68		46
Group 2	36	58	83	
Group 3	50	80		40
Total labor-hours required	137	206	83	86
Labor-hour capacity	160	200	80	80
Shortage of labor-hours	−23	+6	+3	+6
Week 1: Machine-hours				
Group 1	④①	37		51
Group 2	29	29	21	
Group 3	50	20		27
Total machine-hours required	120	86	21	78
Machine-hour capacity	120	100	36	100
Shortage of machine-hours	0	−14	−15	−22

Sample calculations (for circled figures):
  Given:
    Standard labor rate in shop A = 200 pieces per hour
    Standard machine rate in shop A = 250 pieces per hour
    Trial production rate for group 1 = 10,200 pieces per week
  Therefore:
    Labor-hours required = 10,200/200 = 51
    Machine-hours required = 10,200/250 = 41

match between required and available capacity, since this is only an aggregate plan.

Simplified Production/Capacity Planning

What we have just reviewed is the kind of elaborate multistage capacity planning that was much admired in the 1970s. Some of today's leading-edge plants and offices have been able to greatly simplify capacity planning. Their strategy is to get focused and responsive. By focus, we mean reorganizing resources—people and equipment—into clusters that process a family of products, services, or customers. Figure 6–9 shows this for Quark Electronics; it is a rearrangement of Figure 6–6 such that each of the three main product families has its own cluster of resources (cells).

PRINCIPLE: Convert multipath flows to single-channel lanes: create cells and flow lines.

FIGURE 6–9
Cells—Quark Electronics

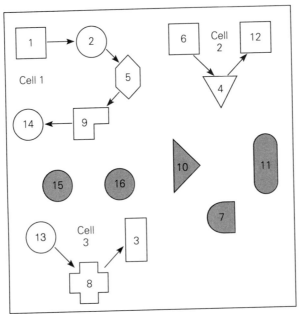

Note: Work centers not organized into cells are shaded.
Centers 15 and 16 are mobile, capable of quick replacement
for center 13 or 14.

For products having their own resources in cells, capacity planning requires just a simple check on whether the production plan is feasible. Say, for example, that cell 1 has sufficient capacity to produce 11,000 pieces per week. Since the trial plan shown in Figure 6–9 calls for production of 10,200 pieces per week, the plan is feasible.

That's it. There's no need to go through the kind of further detailed capacity analysis shown in Figure 6–8. Management emphasis shifts from capacity "by the numbers" to capacity responsiveness: flexible labor, quick-change equipment, dependability, and so forth—all supporting better service to the customer.

MASTER SCHEDULE

In professional services the costly, scarce resource is the time of the professional (e.g., tax advisor, physician, photographer). The appointment book schedules the client's use of that professional's time, and sometimes is subdivided by type of professional service; for example, our photographer's appointment book would treat portrait work differently than events, because more time and resources would be used up in event photography. Services other than the professional's time—billing, selling prints, and so forth—generally would not be noted in the appointment book.

Manufacturing is a bit more complicated. Some producers construct the master production schedule (MPS) around *major modules* of end products. The modules, such as a frame, a body, and an engine, consume a lot of time and resources in their manufacture and thus warrant careful scheduling well in advance; since they consume different resources, each module gets its own section of the MPS.

Basic Master Schedule: A Services Example

Before considering the complications in scheduling for factories, we'll examine the matchup between demand and capacity that results in a master schedule for a service. The service is management courses in a business school, Example 6–4.

EXAMPLE 6–4   **MASTER SCHEDULING IN DEPARTMENT OF MANAGEMENT—FUNK UNIVERSITY**

Each teaching department in the College of Business Administration at Funk University must prepare a master schedule consisting of one schedule for each course and covering the next few terms. The master schedule is prepared twice each term: One version is prepared based on preregistrations; an updated version is based on general registration data.

The master-scheduling steps are illustrated in Figure 6–10. There are eight blocks in the figure. The example is for one teaching department, the Department of Management. All other departments would follow the same steps, but the aggregate forecast groups (block 2) would be different. The Department of Management's courses—perhaps 30 to 40 offerings—cluster neatly into three capacity groups:

1. Quantitative/management information systems (MIS)/operations management (OM).

2. Behavioral/personnel.

3. General management/business policy.

Those groups are not intended to correspond to clusters of *demand* (though student demands may cluster that way). Rather, the purpose is to form natural units of *capacity;* that is, the courses in any given group should be similar enough to enable the group's faculty members to trade off on teaching assignments. The groupings shown would by no means be perfect. Someone whose specialty is personnel administration may, for example, have a secondary interest in general management instead of in behavior. Still, the groupings should be all right for the purpose, which is to arrive at a reasonable capacity plan for matching against total course requirements (block 6) in order to produce a trial master schedule of course offerings (block 7).

A capacity plan emerges from block 3. The unit of service in a teaching department has a rather invariable "standard time" requirement. For example, the standard 3-hour course takes 45 semester hours, or 30 quarter-hours of class time.

A control on the capacity plan is the budget (education plan) and strategies and policies (block 1). Policies generally exist regarding class sizes (i.e., faculty-student ratios), classroom space, teaching loads (per faculty member), use of teaching assistants, and utili-

FIGURE 6–10
Master Scheduling—Department of Management

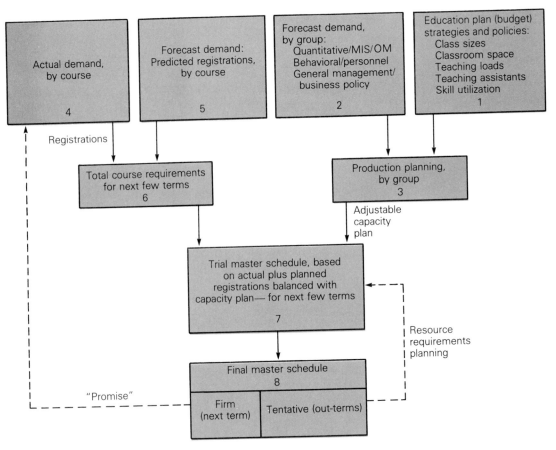

zation of faculty skills. The last has to do with the extent to which faculty will be assigned to teach in their strong versus weaker areas of expertise. Production planning (block 3) includes trade-off analysis, because the aggregate policies are in partial conflict with one another and also with the forecast group demands (block 2). The capacity plan, then, is a compromise.

While blocks 1 through 3 deal with aggregate demand and capacity, blocks 4 through 6 deal with unit demand course by course. Actual demand, consisting of registrations by course, comprises block 4. Block 5 is forecast demand: predicted registrations, by course, based on historical patterns plus other knowledge.

Next, in block 6, the chairperson assembles course requirements for the next few terms into a list. Then she matches this "shopping list" against what is available in the capacity plan. The result is the trial master schedule of course offerings for the next few terms. The feedback arrow from block 8 to block 7 of Figure 6–10, resource requirements planning, indicates *closed-loop control:* It makes the master schedule an accurate reflection of capacity to meet demands by adjusting the master schedule until scarce resource overloads are eliminated.

Finally, a master schedule emerges (block 8). It is firm for the current lead-time period, which is the upcoming term, and tentative for all future terms. When the master schedule is set within the department, Funk University's registrar sends out an "order promise" to students who have registered. The registrar either confirms or denies their registration for a given course. If denied, a substitute may be offered.

Matching Capacity and Demand: A Complex Case

Figure 6–10 contains the basics of master planning. Building on those basics, we end up with Figure 6–11 as the master planning model for the complex case of a manufacturer that fabricates and assembles in the job or batch mode.

Blocks 1 through 6 for a manufacturer are the same as for a service: 1, 2, and

FIGURE 6–11

Capacity-Demand Matching Process

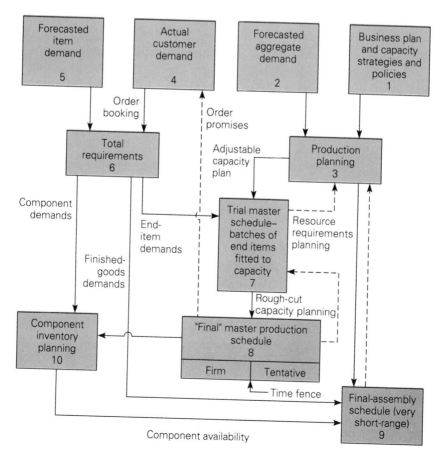

3 combine aggregate forecasts with overall business plans and policies to yield the production plan; 4, 5, and 6 bring in forecast and actual demands, item by item, to yield total requirements.

At block 6 in Figure 6–11, there *may* be a split into three different types of schedules, which need a bit of explanation: One schedule, the MPS, is for *end items*, which is industry's term for major capacity-consuming modules. The MPS usually smooths out lumpy demand streams and also may arrange production into reasonably sized lots. A second set of schedules is for component parts. Those schedules are based on demands for parts needed to meet the master production schedule, and also independently demanded component parts, such as service parts (or spare parts); see the arrows from blocks 6 and 8 to block 10 in Figure 6–11. A third and final stage of production is the work of combining already made modules and parts into finished goods (see the arrow from block 10 to block 9). Some firms put these activities into a separate schedule, because the final steps don't take long and consume different resources (often unskilled assembly labor) than the major modules do. In simpler cases, such as bicycle manufacturing, the final assembly schedule and master production schedule are one and the same.

Our main concern is with the master production schedule. A final MPS (block 8) emerges after suitable trials. The firm portion covers total lead time. Since lead time covers the period in which plans are in motion, schedules need to be more stable for that zone. Still, the "firm" schedule may be changed. A **time fence** separates the firm portion from the tentative portion. Penalties for changes far out in the future are slight; thus, changes in the tentative part of the master production schedule are to be expected.

Another dashed feedback line—block 8 to block 4—was mentioned in Chapter 5. It is the master scheduler's order promise. In industry, communication from production to sales traditionally has been poor. The sales staff bears the burden, because they cannot give the customer reliable delivery promises.

In some companies, life has been made a lot more pleasant for salespeople. Either the company has installed a complete information network that accurately calculates order completions, or it has simplified production and eliminated delays to the point where all jobs are done quickly and in a very predictable planned time period. In the latter case, salespeople can simply make promises based on firm order-promise policies, which are being called *rules of the game*.

PRINCIPLE: Make it easy to make/provide goods or services without error—the first time.

Master Scheduling in Make-to-Order Plants

A special case of master planning in manufacturing is make-to-order production. An example is a producer of precision turntables for recording studios—no production without a firm order. The bane of the make-to-order producer is lack of planning lead time. Recording studios order turntables and want them right

FIGURE 6-12

"Consuming" the Master Production Schedule

	Week				
	1	2	3	4	5
Turntable A:					
Master schedule	4	2	0	6	3
Actual demand	2	0	0	1	0
Available to promise	2	2	0	5	3
Turntable B:					
Master schedule	0	7	8	2	0
Actual demand	0	1	4	2	0
Available to promise	0	6	4	0	0

away. With no lead time, can a master production schedule extend far enough into the future to match demand with capacity reasonably well? The answer is yes. One approach is to use a flexible, customer-oriented procedure that involves what is called *consuming the master schedule.*

The method employs an MPS with three subdivisions: master schedule, actual demand, and available to promise. Figure 6–12 illustrates the three subdivisions for two models of turntable made to order. The procedure begins with the master schedule, based on forecasting. As orders are booked, the master scheduler enters the quantities in the actual demand row. *Available-to-promise* is the computed difference between master schedule and actual demand quantities.

In Figure 6–12, one of turntable A has been sold, for delivery (or completion) in week 4, and five are available to promise. In the same week, both master-scheduled units of turntable B have been sold, leaving none available to promise. The master schedule is said to be "consumed" by actual orders being booked by marketing. The master schedule keeps marketing informed about quantities available to promise so that the sales force will not overconsume the schedule.

The master scheduler revises the MPS periodically. For example, Figure 6–12 shows two of the four turntable As available to promise in week 1. If the firm *never* produces for inventory, the MPS would be revised at the last minute in order to produce just two, not four, of turntable A.

Resource Requirements Planning

The feedback loop from block 7 to block 3 in Figure 6–11 refers to *resource requirements planning (RRP).* The aim is to ensure that the production plan is not too ambitious for the resources that will be available. A second feedback loop, from block 8 to block 7, depicts *rough-cut capacity planning*—the application of resource requirements planning that serves as a gross check to see if the items in the master production schedule will overload a scarce resource. Typically, the scarce resource is an expensive machine, die, tool, or mold. It could also be an employee with a hard-to-get skill, such as a programmer for a numerically controlled machine, a tool and die maker, a welder, or a designer.

Resource planning can be reasonably accurate over a month or more but is too gross to show weekly resource requirements. Running an RRP check requires data that show how much of the scarce resource is required per unit of the end item to be built. For example, a plastics molder may have in its files a **bill of labor**, which states that an order for a certain kind of plastic fastener requires two hours of die-making labor. This is the type of conversion factor that was used in step 4 of Example 6–3; there the RRP concept was applied to check resource requirements for a proposed production/capacity plan. More commonly, resource requirements planning is associated with checking resource needs in the master production scheduling phase. We shall consider both a rough and a refined approach to resource requirements planning.

Rough-Cut Capacity Planning

Rough-cut capacity planning is a fast and simple approach to resource requirements planning. Rough-cut planning is usually done in monthly or quarterly time periods. The first step is to convert trial MPS quantities into workload requirements in the bottleneck work centers. The workloads may be stated in pieces, pounds, machine-hours, labor-hours, or (frequently) machine cycles per time period. The method is rough—that is, may overstate real needs just a bit—because there is no attempt to deduct inventories already on hand. The next step is to adjust the master production schedule if a bottleneck work center is overloaded. The adjustment usually consists of reducing the offending MPS quantity or moving some of it to a later time period. Example 6–5 illustrates rough-cut capacity planning.

EXAMPLE 6–5   **ROUGH-CUT CAPACITY PLANNING—MOLDED HOSES**

Ajax Rubber Company produces molded rubber hoses for the automotive industry. The master scheduler has prepared a trial MPS; a portion of it is shown in Figure 6–13.

In the hose-curing work center, cut lengths of extruded rubber are placed on mandrels that protrude from racks that roll into an oven for curing. The curing oven is the most critical bottleneck work center in the plant. The master scheduler wants to make sure that the MPS is not overstated for that oven, which has a maximum capacity of 2,700 rack loads per month. Although the MPS is stated in weeks, rough-cut capacity planning at Ajax is by month. One reason is that projected oven workloads cannot be accurate on a week-to-week basis because orders get rescheduled to earlier or later weeks; monthly totals, however, can be reasonably precise.

As Figure 6–13 shows, the total number of hoses in the trial MPS is 91,660 for month 1, 95,200 for month 2, and 94,990 for month 3. (Only a few of the hose types comprising the totals are shown.) The number of mandrels per rack depends on the hose model number, but it averages 34. For rough-cut purposes, that average is good enough to be used in converting hoses to rackloads of oven curing.

FIGURE 6–13
Trial MPS—Molded Hoses

End Item	Month 1	Month 2	Month 3
Hose 201XL	1,120	1,080	990
Hose 208S	600	300	410
⋮	⋮	⋮	⋮
Hose 618MM	870	1,050	1,100
Total hoses needing curing	91,660	95,200	94,990
Divided by conversion factor	34	34	34
Rack loads requiring curing	2,696	2,800	2,794
Capacity	2,700	2,700	2,700
Overload	−4	100	94

The conversion shows that the projected workload of 2,696 rack loads in month 1 is just below the capacity of 2,700, and in months 2 and 3 the projected workloads of 2,800 and 2,794 exceed capacity. The master scheduler sees that the trial MPS is not feasible. It appears that the hose quantities in the MPS should be reduced in months 2 and 3. Perhaps another of Ajax's plants can absorb the demand. If not, some of the projected hose demands (if they materialize) will probably be lost sales in the short term. But Ajax will be evaluating additional oven capacity as a longer-term solution.

Load Profile

For a more precise resource requirements plan, **load profiles** rather than simple conversion factors are used. A load (meaning *work*load) profile shows not only how much of a given resource is required, but when. However, like the rough-cut method, the profile does not deduct inventories already on hand or on order. Therefore, requirements might be overstated.

As an example, in assembly of mass spectrometers, a final test machine might be the scarce, or bottleneck, resource. The load profiles may show that one complete spectrometer of a certain type, model X, requires four hours of system test time on the second day prior to shipment. A complete load profile, showing time requirements for nonscarce as well as scarce resources, is portrayed in Figure 6–14 (only the processes, not the resources themselves, are shown). Other models of spectrometer would have different load profiles.

The profiles may exist as computer records or written data in a file cabinet. If the master production schedule calls for production of five of spectrometer model X, two of model Y, and three of model Z, the master scheduler may pull out the profiles and multiply the processing times by 5, 2, and 3, respectively. The result is a composite workload profile showing whether the MPS will over-load the scarce resource (the test machine). If so, the MPS quantities or timing may be changed.

FIGURE 6–14
Load Profile for Assembly of Mass Spectrometer, Model X

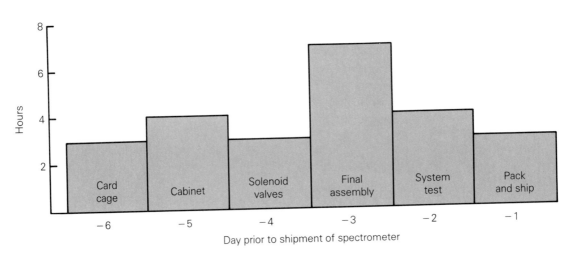

Day prior to shipment of spectrometer

MASTER PLANNING FOR REPETITIVE AND CONTINUOUS PRODUCTION

To complete our discussion of master planning, we must look briefly at the special case of high-volume repetitive or continuous production: spark plugs, small batteries, metals, chemicals, and so forth. Those industries often perform master planning in cumulative units rather than by orders, jobs, and lots. Steady use of the same production procedure month after month makes it possible to closely relate the master production schedule to production/capacity planning, including planned inventory and backlog levels. Also, the MPS may be related to elements of the firm's business plan, including the production budget and shipping forecast. Example 6–6 involves case data for a real company.[6]

EXAMPLE 6–6   **MASTER PLANNING FOR A CONTINUOUS PROCESSOR— PFIZER, INC.**

The Easton, Pennsylvania, plant of Pfizer, Inc., produces iron oxides used in paints, plastics, cosmetics, and other products. There are about 50 types of iron oxide products. Separate master schedules for each product are prepared quarterly, and totals are cumulative over a year's time. The graph in Figure 6–15 displays the schedule and other cumulative data for one of the 50 items.

---

[6]Example 6–6 is adapted from William L. Berry, Thomas E. Vollmann, and D. Clay Whybark, *Master Production Scheduling: Principles and Practice* (Falls Church, Va.: American Production and Inventory Control Society, 1979), pp. 23–35 (TS157.5B46x).

FIGURE 6–15

Cumulative Master Scheduling—Pfizer, Inc.

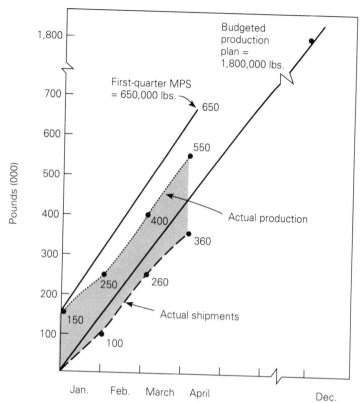

Note: Beginning Inventory = 150,000 pounds. Vertical distance in shaded zone = Inventory in pounds. Horizontal distance in shaded zone = Number of months supply of inventory.

Pfizer's business plan calls for 1,800,000 pounds of this type of iron oxide to be produced this year. This is Pfizer's budgeted production.

One quarter has passed at the time represented by Figure 6–15. Actual production and actual shipments have been plotted monthly, and the difference equals actual inventory. For example, at the end of February, cumulative actual production was 400,000 pounds and cumulative actual shipments totaled 260,000 pounds. The difference, 140,000, is the inventory on hand, which is represented graphically by the vertical distance between 400,000 and 260,000 in Figure 6–15. By the end of March, the inventory had grown to 550,000 − 360,000 = 190,000 pounds.

This quarter's actual production, at 550,000, is 100,000 pounds short of the master production schedule amount of 650,000. The reason for failing to meet the schedule could be production problems. But in this quarter the reason was that customer orders, reflected by shipments, were below the forecast, and the master scheduler took action monthly to decrease the MPS. (The decreased MPS amounts and the demand forecast are not shown in the graph.) Since the first-quarter master production schedule was too high, the second-quarter MPS would probably be adjusted downward.

SUMMARY

The capacity (resource inputs) needed for meeting customer demand must be planned for—a procedure known as master planning. The merger of the capacity plan with demand yields a master schedule or appointment book—a statement of what the company plans to provide. Capacity planning and master scheduling are integral parts of all business ventures, including small, entrepreneurial ones such as a photography business.

Meeting customer demand and utilizing capacity resources (not too much utilization or too little) are the aims of capacity planning and master scheduling. Capacity planning establishes, measures, and adjusts capacity limits or levels. The resource requirements plan converts the production plan into capacity needs for key resources. Determining whether the trial master schedule might overload scarce resources is referred to as rough-cut capacity planning.

We may understand the focus of master planning by making five key observations. First, the master scheduling focus is on item demand, while the capacity planning focus is on aggregate demand. Further, aggregate demand is forecast with capacity groups or dominant process routings in mind. Second, a medium-term planning horizon, typically a few weeks to 18 months, is used. Third, the production-plan part of the business plan—that part affected by capacity strategies and policies—states output quantities in broad terms and by product or service family. It translates the business plan into action. Fourth, capacity planning deals with adjustable capacity—those resource inputs that may be changed relatively easily over a medium-term horizon. Work force, inventories, and subcontracting are examples. Fifth, the focus is on input units of capacity and output units of product or service.

Production/capacity planning is governed by capacity strategies. A chase demand strategy permits responsive customer service, but at a cost of fluctuating capacity. A level-capacity strategy has opposite characteristics. Policies translate the chosen capacity strategies into action and, along with strategies, are set by top management.

Learning-curve planning is helpful in the case of large end products. As each unit is made, production time and costs tend to drop. The learning rate can be estimated and used in capacity planning and scheduling output and is a valued concept for managing improvement.

Companies with large order backlogs may plan capacity in detail for months into the future. However, with or without backlogs, capacity planning may be improved by centering it around product families or capacity groups. By taking this all the way—to reorganizing resources into cells, one for each family or group—some of the hazards, inaccuracies, and complexities of capacity planning are avoided.

In make-to-order plants, options for production/capacity planning for a given capacity group may be tested on recent demand data. Effects on backlogs and order lead times are revealed, and the plan that best fits the company may be selected.

In make-to-stock plants, production/capacity planning is also done by capacity groups. Based on demand forecasts, planners calculate the effect of a trial production rate on inventory levels and, in the complex case, on labor-hour and machine-hour requirements. The plan selected is the one that yields the closest approximation to desired inventory levels while staying within available capacity.

The master production schedule (MPS) is a statement of what the company plans to provide by item, by period, and by capacity group. The capacity plan places upper limits on MPS quantities, and sales bookings and item forecasts reveal the demands to be covered by the MPS. An order promise commits output to certain customers. This basic approach applies to service providers as well as goods producers.

Master schedule items are those that require large amounts of time and resources. Separate schedules may be developed for final assembly (which may take very little time) and for independently demanded component parts. In simple cases, the MPS is the same as the final assembly schedule.

Lack of planning lead time is the main problem in make-to-order plants, but an MPS based on forecasts can still work well. One approach is to "consume the MPS," by deducting actual customer orders as they arrive. MPS quantities not consumed are "available to promise."

Resource planning helps provide closed-loop control of the MPS by testing the MPS's effect on scarce resource capacity. If there are no overloads on scarce resources, the final MPS is released.

Master scheduling in continuous and repetitive production may involve cumulative graphical techniques. Graphs might show actual shipments, MPS quantities, and yearly budgeted quantities. Shipments can be watched to see whether master schedules should be changed.

KEY WORDS

Master planning
Appointment book
Master schedule
Capacity planning
Resource requirements
   planning (RRP)
Production plan

Rough-cut capacity
   planning
Master production
   schedule (MPS)
Adjustable capacity
Fixed capacity
Chase demand

Level capacity
Learning curve
Group-based capacity
   planning
Time fence
Bill of labor
Load profile

SOLVED PROBLEMS

1. A company wants to bid on a contract to produce 50 glider aircraft. In order to prepare a reasonable bid, it must determine the demand for assembly labor-hours. The first glider requires an estimated 700 direct-assembly labor-hours, and the company uses an 85 percent learning rate in its planning.

a. For the first five gliders, determine the direct-labor-hours required for each unit. Also, find the cumulative average number of direct-labor-hours for the five units.

b. How many direct-labor-hours will be required for the 50th glider according to the learning-curve plan?

Solution

a. The learning-curve plan for the first five gliders is as follows:

Unit Number	Direct-labor Hours	Cumulative Total	Cumulative Average
1	700.00	700.00	700.00
2	595.00	1295.00	647.50
3	541.04	1836.04	612.01
4	505.75	2341.79	585.45
5	479.97	2821.76	564.35

b. For the 50th glider, we may use formula 6–1 (logarithms to the base 10 are used, but the result is the same using natural logarithms):

$$Y = aX^b$$

$$= (700)(50)^{\left(\frac{\log\ 0.85}{\log\ 2.0}\right)}$$

$$= (700)(50)^{\left(\frac{-.07058}{.30103}\right)}$$

$$= (700)(50)^{-.2345}$$

$$= 700(.3996)$$

$$= 279.72 \text{ direct-labor-hours}$$

(An interesting point: After 50 gliders are assembled, the *average* direct-labor-hour requirement is about 357 hours—about half the time planned for the first glider.)

2. Jack Sharp, a recent college graduate, is embarking on an entrepreneurial career. He has started a consulting firm that specializes in helping small retail establishments and professional offices install microcomputer-based record-keeping. Realizing that the only resources he has to sell are his expertise and his workaholic nature, Jack has decided to plan on working about 280 hours per month. (Will all work and no play make Jack Sharp dull?) He is focusing on a certain market niche and has grouped his clients into three types: small retail outlets (such as shopping mall specialty stores, single-principal professional offices, and partnership professional offices). Jack estimates that time requirements for those clients will average 20, 40, and 50 hours, respectively.

Much telephone work and knocking on doors has resulted in a tentative client list for the next six months. Jack feels it is time to match customer demand with available capacity (his time) and develop a trial schedule. Our task is to help him. The demand for each job type is as follows:

Client Type	Time Required (Hours)	Demand—Customers/Month (months)					
		1	2	3	4	5	6
Retail store	20	4	—	6	3	4	2
Single professional	40	2	6	4	—	—	3
Multipartner professional	50	3	—	—	4	—	5

Solution

The following table shows Jack's capacity requirements by group (client type) for the six-month planning horizon as well as idle capacity or overload conditions:

Client Type	Demand—Resources/Month (hours per client × number of clients) (months)						Cumulative (for group)
	1	2	3	4	5	6	
Retail store	80	—	120	60	80	40	380
Single professional	80	240	160	—	—	120	600
Multipartner professional	150	—	—	200	—	250	600
Total capacity requirements (hours of time)	310	240	280	260	80	410	1,580
Capacity available	280	280	280	280	280	280	1,680
Idle capacity ("—" denotes overload)	−30	40	0	20	200	−130	100

For the total planning horizon, Jack has not overextended himself. He has 100 hours of idle, or excess, capacity. He may have to work a few more hours during the first month, if demand estimates are accurate. His problem is months 5 and 6. He might try to entice some customers to use his services a month earlier than planned. But schedules very far out have a way of changing—often several times—prior to when the originally scheduled dates become current.

REFERENCES

Books

Berry, William L.; Thomas E. Vollmann; and D. Clay Whybark. *Master Production Scheduling: Principles and Practice*. Falls Church, Va.: American Production and Inventory Control Society, 1979 (TS157.5.B46x).

Blackstone, John H., Jr., *Capacity Management*. Cincinnati: South-Western, 1989 (HD69.C3B63).

Orlicky, Joseph. *Material Requirements Planning*. New York: McGraw-Hill, 1975 (TS155.8.074).

Plossl, G. W., and O. W. Wight. *Production and Inventory Control: Principles and Techniques*. Englewood Cliffs, N.J.: Prentice-Hall, 1967 (HD55.P5).

Vollmann, Thomas E.; William Lee Berry; and D. Clay Whybark. *Manufacturing Planning and Control Systems*, 2nd ed. Homewood, Ill.: Dow Jones-Irwin, 1988.

Wight, Oliver W. *MRPII: Unlocking America's Productivity Potential*. Williston, Vt.: Oliver Wight Limited Publications, 1981 (TS161.W5x).

Periodicals/Societies

Decision Sciences (Decision Sciences Institute).

Journal of Operations Management (Operations Management Association).

Production and Inventory Management (American Production and Inventory Control Society).

(All of these periodicals contain numerous articles on capacity management.)

REVIEW QUESTIONS

1. What are the primary purposes of master planning?
2. Is capacity planning essential in small-business applications? Explain.
3. What is the focus of master planning?
4. What limits or constrains the production/capacity plan? How?
5. What limits or constrains the master schedule? How?
6. How can the master scheduler promote the goal of just the right use of capacity?
7. Is chase demand a capacity policy or a capacity strategy? Explain.
8. How do capacity plans for goods producers differ from those for services providers?
9. What determines whether a plant should have a single overall production/capacity plan or more than one plan?
10. Why might one department in a company follow chase demand and another in the same company follow level capacity?
11. What types of operating environments are best for using learning-curve planning? Why?
12. Why did the quarterly ordering system give way to group-based capacity planning?

13. Given the uncertainty of customer demand in make-to-order businesses, how can a business plan capacity intelligently?

14. In a make-to-order plant, how can a target inventory level (desired inventory after so many weeks) be translated into required machine-hours?

15. What is a time fence in master scheduling?

16. Why might a manufacturer have three separate schedules—a master production schedule, a component-parts schedule, and a final-assembly schedule?

17. Explain how a master schedule may be "consumed."

18. How does rough-cut capacity planning improve the validity of the master schedule?

19. What does the load-profile approach to RRP do that the rough-cut approach does not?

20. What is the effect of reducing lead time and increasing resource flexibility on analysis for master scheduling and capacity planning?

21. How does the graphical cumulative master scheduling approach help keep master schedules valid for the continuous processor?

PROBLEMS AND EXERCISES

1. Assume that you are president of a large company and have a strong aversion to laying off employees. Devise a multistep policy governing what your company would do if demand in certain product lines dropped, creating excess labor. Your last step should be employee terminations.

2. How has IBM been able to avoid laying off employees, given the competition and short life cycle of many products in the fast-changing computer and business machine industry? You may need to research the subject or interview IBM people to answer this question satisfactorily.

3. City Sod is a small business that sells and lays sod (rolled strips of grass). The owner has devised a forecasting procedure based on demand history from previous years plus projection of demand in recent weeks. The forecast for the next six weeks, in labor-hours of sod laying, is:

$$860 \quad 880 \quad 900 \quad 920 \quad 930 \quad 940$$

Currently City Sod has a staff of sod layers consisting of 4 crew chiefs and 15 laborers. A crew chief lays sod along with the laborers but also directs the crew. The owner has decided on the following staffing policies:
(1) A two-week backlog will be accumulated before adding staff.
(2) Plans are based on a 40-hour work week; overtime is used only to absorb weather or other delays and employee absence or resignations.

   (3)   The ideal crew size is one crew chief and four laborers.

        a.   Devise a hiring plan for the six-week period covered by the forecast. In your answer, assume a current backlog of 1,200 labor-hours of sod-laying orders.

        b.   Does City Sod follow more of a chase demand or level-capacity strategy of production planning? Explain.

4. Bright Way Janitorial Service (see the case study at the end of the chapter) is considering a shift from a level-capacity to a chase demand strategy of production/capacity planning. Bright Way managers know that chase demand would greatly simplify production/capacity planning. Explain why this is so. What new management problems would chase demand tend to create?

5. Iridion, Inc., has been awarded a contract to produce 200 of a new type of rail-driven passenger car for a large city. Based on Iridion's previous experience in guided rocket manufacturing, an 80 percent learning curve is planned for the passenger-car contract. The first passenger car takes 1,400 direct-labor-hours to make.

   a. If the city pays Iridion's accumulated direct-labor costs after the fourth unit, how many direct-labor-hours should the city expect to owe right after the fourth unit is produced?

   b. The actual direct-labor usage for the first eight units produced is as follows:

| 1,400 | 1,206 | 1,172 | 1,145 | 1,101 | 1,083 | 1,033 | 1,005 |

      Would you recommend that Iridion stay with its planning estimate of an 80 percent learning curve? Explain.

   c. Answer question *b* for the following changes in actual direct-labor usage:

| 1,400 | 1,089 | 887 | 801 | 728 | 684 | 600 | 586 |

6. A manufacturer of ceramic products has been awarded a NASA contract to produce ceramic-based heat shields for space vehicles. The contract calls for a total of 20 heat-shield units. If the estimated learning-curve rate is 94 percent and the first unit takes 60 hours to produce, how long will it take to produce the fifth, tenth, and final units?

7. Coast Limited Railways has a car repair yard in Kansas City to repair its own cars. In the six most recent months, Kansas City's car repair workload has been:

Month	Cars
1	83
2	72
3	71
4	90
5	49
6	56

a. Coast Limited headquarters has directed Kansas City to plan for a capacity level that will exceed cumulative demand by no more than half a month's average demand during the six-month planning period. Prepare the capacity plan following the backlogging method of Example 6–2 in the chapter. Explain the positive and negative deviations.

b. What important factors in question a could be analyzed in terms of dollars?

c. Is it necessary that this production planning method be based on *cumulative* demand and planning figures? If it were Coast's policy to divert all excess orders to independent repair yards, would cumulative calculations be suitable? Explain and illustrate with an example.

8. Concrete Products, Inc., makes reinforced concrete structural members (trusses, etc.) for large buildings and bridges. Each order is a special design, so no finished-goods inventories are possible. Concrete members are made by using molds that are bolted onto huge "shake tables." A vibrating action causes the wet concrete to pack, without air pockets, around reinforcing steel in the molds. Concrete Products uses a chase demand strategy of hiring labor to assemble the molds, fill them with concrete, and later disassemble them. If it takes a week to hire and train a laborer, how can Concrete Products make the chase demand strategy work well—that is, what types of labor (capacity) policies would work? Following is a representative sample of recent workloads, in labor-hours, on the shake tables:

Week	Labor-Hours
1	212
2	200
3	170
4	204
5	241
6	194
7	168
8	215
9	225

9. At a fiberglass products company, the dominant product line is fiberglass bathtub and shower units, which sell to the high-quality segment of the market. The company's best employees work in tubs and showers, which are treated as a separate capacity group. Forecast demands for this capacity group are in labor-hours; for the next three months, demand is forecast at 300, 370, and 380 labor-hours. The present inventory is 620 labor-hours' worth of tub and shower units—in all sizes and colors. The plan is to reduce the inventory to 300 after three months, because the slow season is approaching.

a. Prepare a production plan for the next three months that minimizes labor fluctuation.

b. How would the master production schedule differ from the production plan?

10. The production control staff of Quark Electronics (Example 6–3) is preparing alternative trial production plans.

   a. The production rate for a second trial plan is set at 15,300 pieces per week (50 percent greater than in the first trial) for product group 1. The production rates for groups 2 and 3 are unchanged. Calculate labor-hour and machine-hour effects for week 1 only (that is, redo Figure 6–8 using 15,300 pieces for product-group 1). Is the second trial plan feasible, or does it seriously overload capacity?

   b. A third trial production plan is simpler to prepare. This method is based on a single forecast in pieces, which is the composite of the three product-group forecasts. This requires a single average labor rate and a single average machine rate for each shop rather than separate rates for each product group. Assume that for week 1 the composite forecast is for 50,000 pieces and that the shop production rates are:

Rate (pieces per hour)	Shop A	Shop B	Shop C	Shop D
Labor	300	222	650	830
Machine	500	750	2,000	600

   Prepare the trial production plan for week 1 (similar to Figure 6–8). Compare the results of the third trial production plan with those of the first. Where has accuracy been lost in the third plan? In spite of this loss of accuracy, why might the production control chief prefer plan 3 (that is, where has there been a gain in precision)?

11. Gulf Tube and Pipe Company prepares monthly production/capacity plans for three capacity areas, one of which is the pipe-forming, -cutting, and -welding (FCW) processes. The forecast FCW demand for next month is as follows:

Week	Forecast Lineal Feet (000)
1	6,000
2	5,800
3	5,400
4	4,600

The present inventory is 16 million lineal feet.

   a. Devise a production plan following a chase demand strategy that results in an ending inventory of 14 million lineal feet.

   b. Devise a production plan following a level-capacity strategy that results in an ending inventory of 14 million lineal feet.

   c. The following rule of thumb is used for purposes of capacity planning: Two operators are required for every 1 million lineal feet produced. Develop two capacity plans (i.e., work force), one using data from question a and the other using data from question b.

d. Citing data from questions *a* through *c*, explain the contrasting effects on inventories and labor of chase demand and level-capacity strategies.

12. Devise a master scheduling diagram similar to Figure 6–10 but for draftspeople in an engineering firm. Explain your diagram.

13. Devise a master scheduling diagram similar to Figure 6–10, but for a maintenance department. Assume that maintenance includes janitorial crews and repairpeople such as plumbers and electricians, but does not include construction or remodeling personnel. Explain your diagram.

14. Capacity planning is never easy, and seems especially difficult at retail, where demand varies greatly throughout the day. Four retail situations are listed below. Pick any two and write a brief analysis of how each deals with the unpredictability factor in planning capacity (labor). You may need to interview one or more people in a real firm.

Post office   Fast-food restaurant
Motel   Bank

15. At Gulf Tube and Pipe Company, the master scheduler has developed a trial master production schedule. Lately the growing demand for pipe products has strained capacity in the pipe-cutting work center. The work center consists of a single Dynacut cutoff machine with a single-shift daily capacity of 120,000 lineal feet. The master scheduler has been running a rough-cut capacity plan to ensure that the MPS quantities do not overload the Dynacut machine. Engineering has provided the master scheduler with a list of all end-item numbers that require cutoff; those items are starred in the following partial trial MPS:

| End-Item Number | Week | | | | |
	1	2	3	4	5
0263	400	—	—	—	—
0845*	—	300	—	—	300
0997*	300	—	—	300	—
1063	—	200	800	—	—
⋮	⋮	⋮	⋮	⋮	⋮
Total for *-items (000 of lineal feet)	600	680	470	550	590

a. Assuming a five-day-per-week single-shift operation, what does rough-cut capacity planning suggest should be done?

b. Can you tell from the data given what Gulf's production/capacity planning strategy is (i.e., level-capacity or chase demand)? Explain.

16. In general registration at your college, registering for classes probably requires you to pass through several work centers. Which work center would you consider a bottleneck? Do you think the registrar's office would find the rough-cut capacity planning idea useful in planning for that bottleneck work center? Explain. You will probably need to consider what the MPS

would consist of in this case. (If you prefer, you can answer this question using drop-and-add or another administrative procedure instead of general registration.)

17. At Piney Woods Furniture Company, the scarce resource that most concerns the master scheduler is the wood-drying kiln. One product, a cabinet, uses three types of wood, which go through the kiln at different times in the manufacture of the cabinet. A load profile showing the total kiln workload resulting from 1 minimum cabinet order (50 cabinets) follows. The unit of measure is cubic yard-hours, which accounts for size of the drying load and time in the kiln.

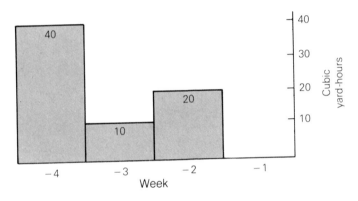

The current MPS includes an order for 1,000 cabinets in week 6 (six weeks from now). Projected kiln workload for all products *other than the cabinet* is as follows for the next six weeks:

			Week			
	1	2	3	4	5	6
Cubic yard-hours	5,000	5,200	5,300	5,800	5,700	6,000

a. Calculate the week-by-week kiln loads (workloads) for the cabinet order. (Assume that week −1 on the load profile means one week prior to the week in which an order is due on the MPS.)

b. If the kiln has a maximum weekly capacity of 6,000 cubic yard-hours, will the MPS overload the kiln? Explain.

c. If the cabinet order is adjustable (the customer would accept a change in delivery date), what MPS changes would you recommend, if any?

18. Pecos, Inc., produces cooking and salad oils in a continuous-process plant. Budgeted annual production is 130,000 gallons. The master production schedule calls for 40,000 gallons of production in the first quarter (January, February, and March). There are 30,000 gallons on hand as of January 1. Two months have passed. Actual production was 16,000 gallons in January

and 13,000 gallons in February. Actual shipments were 10,000 gallons in January and 8,000 in February.

a. Draw a graph showing the budgeted production, master production schedule, actual production, and actual shipments. Use cumulative graphing, and label all lines and points.

b. What is the inventory on hand after two months?

c. Production of oil normally is high in the winter months because raw materials (corn, sunflower seeds, etc.) are plentiful and at their minimum prices. That being the case, is the master scheduler doing a good job?

19. The following graph shows cumulative actual and planned production and shipment data for National Adhesives Corporation, a continuous-process manufacturer of adhesives and related products. Explain what happened in the first four months and the last two months. What action would you suggest the master scheduler take?

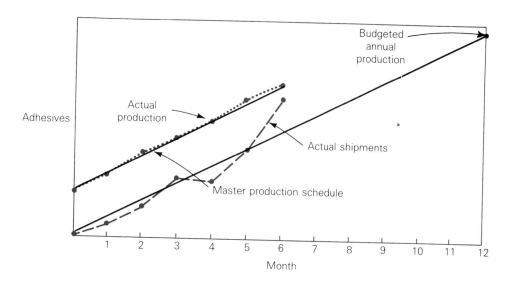

20. Great Lakes Paint Company's major product is a base white paint that is produced in batches continuously year round. Cumulative master scheduling is used and key information is plotted on a cumulative graph. The following data apply to the first six months of this year; beginning inventory was 38,000 gallons:

	Month					
	1	2	3	4	5	6
Master production schedule*	22	20	19	15	15	15
Actual production*	22	21	20	13	13	16
Actual shipment*	20	18	16	15	18	19

*In thousands of gallons

a. Graph the given data in the cumulative graphical format. Label all lines and points.

b. Tell what the inventory on hand is after each month.

c. Explain the master scheduler's actions.

d. Speculate on the causes of the actual production figures in months 3, 4, 5, and 6.

21. Technocratics, Inc., has developed a new type of corrugated aluminum shingle that is highly durable. The shingles are formed 10 at a time (per cycle) on a punch press. Maximum capacity is 2,500 shingles per 24-hour day. In the next 12 months, Technocratics plans to sell 400,000 shingles. Expected demand in the next two months is 28,000 and 30,000. Current inventory is 25,000 shingles. The plan is to build inventory to 50,000 shingles in the next two months so that even a large order can be filled from stock. Punch press operation is easy to learn, and Technocratics is able to hire unskilled people off the street at a low wage to quickly expand production when it needs to. If production were to drop off, employees would be laid off. In the case of a serious machine breakdown, the tooling (dies and fixtures) would be moved to another local company that had agreed to produce the product on its own, identical punch press. Technocratics currently has 12 operators who put in a total of 96 production hours a week. Planned output is 32,000 shingles per month next month at 96 production hours per week.

a. From the given data, what can you tell about the company's business plan?

b. What is the capacity strategy, and what capacity policies exist?

c. Discuss the company's production/capacity plan and master production schedule. Will any labor changes be necessary in the next month or two? In the next year?

CASE STUDY   BRIGHT WAY JANITORIAL SERVICE

Bright Way Janitorial Service has established three categories of capacity:

1. Wet processes (mopping, buffing, etc.).
2. Dry processes (vacuuming/dusting).
3. Glass cleaning.

Those categories were set because they define three separate kinds of employee/equipment processes. Each may be forecast based on historical data. Bright Way uses the forecasts, along with its labor, service, and pricing policies, to arrive at a production/capacity plan for a three-week period by week.

The forecast and production/capacity plan are updated (rolled over) every two weeks. The short forecast interval is suitable because hiring and training require less than two weeks. Updating the production/capacity plan need not be done every week, because there is a staff of irregular employees on call. They serve as a cushion against inaccurate forecasting.

Bright Way has a strategy of seeking "higher-quality" customers, paying a slightly higher wage, and gaining a somewhat more stable work force than its competitors. In support of that strategy it has developed the following capacity policies:

Labor:
  Priority 1—18–22 percent full-time labor, no overtime.
  Priority 2—65–75 percent part-time labor.
  Priority 3—8–12 percent irregular labor.
  Priority 4—20 percent of full-time and part-time staff cross-trained for possible temporary transfer to secondary work category.
  Priority 5—subcontract (make advance agreements) for excess short-term demands, where possible.

Service (responsiveness):
  Priority 1—maintain all schedules for regular customers.
  Priority 2—next-week response to new customers—up to limits of staffing—for routine cleaning, that is, work categories 1 and 2.
  Priority 3—work special cleaning demands into the schedule as soon as possible without disrupting regular schedules.
  Pricing: No pricing incentives. This policy subject to change if competition warrants.

With those policies as a basis, Bright Way's production/capacity plan for the next three weeks is as shown in Exhibit 1. The plan shows forecast labor-hours of demand for each work category and for each week. The forecast labor-hours are assigned to full-time, part-time, and irregular labor. For the entire three-week period, there is no planned need for subcontracting. The totals at the bottom include percentages. These fit the percentage goals that Bright Way has set in its capacity policies.

For example, in week 1, the total forecast demand for category 1 (wet pro-

EXHIBIT 1
Three-Week Group Forecast and Production/Capacity Plan—Bright Way
Janitorial Service

		Labor-Hours, by Week					
		1		2		3	
Work Category	Labor Type	Forecast	Assigned	Forecast	Assigned	Forecast	Assigned
1: "Wet"		1,240		1,160		1,100	
	Full-time		240		240		240
	Part-time		860		860		860
	Irregular		140		60		
	Subcontracted						
2: "Dry"		1,900		2,000		2,260	
	Full-time		400		400		480
	Part-time		1,320		1,320		1,400
	Irregular		180		280		380
	Subcontracted						
3: "Glass"		480		520		480	
	Full-time		120		120		120
	Part-time		360		400		360
	Irregular						
	Subcontracted						
	Totals	3,620		3,680		3,840	
	Full-time		760 (21%)		760 (21%)		840 (22%)
	Part-time		2,540 (70%)		2,580 (70%)		2,620 (68%)
	Irregular		320 (9%)		340 (9%)		380 (10%)
	Subcontracted						
	Change in hours			+60		+160	
	Staffing plan			Hire 2 PT; assign to "glass." Add 20 hours irregular.		Hire 2 FT and 2 PT; assign to "dry." Add 40 hours irregular.	

cesses) is 1,240 labor-hours of business. Janitorial staff assignments for that demand are 240 labor-hours of full-time labor, 860 of part-time labor, and 140 of irregular labor. Since 240 + 860 + 140 = 1,240, the plan meets forecast demand with no need for subcontracting.

Forecast demand for all three work categories in week 1 totals 3,620 labor-hours. To meet that demand without subcontracting, the plan calls for 760 labor-hours full time, 2,540 part time, and 320 irregular. In percentages full-time labor is 21 percent, which falls within the priority 1 goal of 18–22 percent; part-time labor is 70 percent, which is within the priority 2 goal of 65–75 percent; and irregular labor is 9 percent, which is within the priority 3 goal of 8–12 percent.

All priorities are met in week 1. The production plan is to do the full amount of business that the demand forecast indicates is available. The capacity plan that enables demand to be met is the staffing plan at the bottom of Exhibit 1.

In weeks 2 and 3, hiring is called for because forecast demand is on the increase. Since hiring normally is possible in less than two weeks, this plan provides the necessary lead time.

Case Discussion Questions

1. Compared with its competitors, is Bright Way's strategy chase demand or level capacity? Develop a table such as Figure 6–2, with Bright Way's strategy in one column and the more typical janitorial service in the other. Discuss each row in your table.

2. If Bright Way changed to the capacity strategy of its competitors, would capacity planning—and overall management—be simpler or more difficult? Explain.

3. What demand forecasting techniques would you recommend for Bright Way? Why?

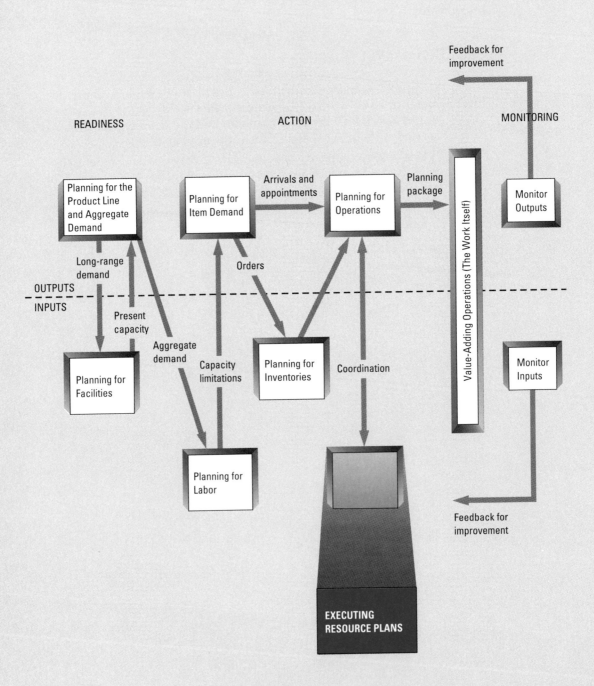

READINESS

ACTION

MONITORING

Feedback for improvement

Planning for the Product Line and Aggregate Demand

Planning for Item Demand

Arrivals and appointments

Planning for Operations

Planning package

Monitor Outputs

Long-range demand

Orders

OUTPUTS

INPUTS

Present capacity

Aggregate demand

Capacity limitations

Planning for Facilities

Planning for Inventories

Coordination

Value-Adding Operations (The Work Itself)

Monitor Inputs

Planning for Labor

EXECUTING RESOURCE PLANS

Feedback for improvement

CHAPTER 7

Purchasing and Materials Management

TRADITIONAL PURCHASING

TOWARD PARTNERSHIPS WITH SUPPLIERS
Tenure of Relationship
Type of Agreement
Number of Sources
Volume of Business
Prices/Costs
Materials Quality
Design
Delivery Frequency/Order Size
Order Conveyance
Delivery Location
Receiving Information
Relationship Openness

PURCHASING POLICIES AND PRACTICES
ABC Analysis
Purchasing and Contracting Procedures
Performance and Compliance: The Tangibility Factor
Value Analysis
Standardization

MATERIALS MANAGEMENT
Make or Buy
Backward Integration versus "Stick to Your Knitting"
Inventory Control

For six chapters we have been in the planning mode. Now we shift to execution—the actions necessary to acquire materials, supplies, equipment, and services. This is one aspect of *executing resource plans,* which is highlighted in the model of operations management (see diagram on the first page of this chapter).

In this chapter we emphasize new thinking about purchasing, which has resulted in a sharp break with past purchasing and overall materials management practices. The shift in thought and practice, which has taken place in numerous well-known companies, is from an adversarial approach toward one's suppliers to a partnership between customer and supplier. Every firm that becomes swept up in the partnership movement experiences turmoil and disruption, but also great opportunity for improving performance and reducing business risk.

And what of the purchasing professional? It's the same thing: turmoil and disruption (initially), but later an opportunity to make a positive impact—and advance a career. Of course, there still are plenty of firms—the majority probably—that so far are untouched by the new thinking. This chapter begins with old-style purchasing, then shifts to the partnership approach. The middle of the chapter explains a few of the better-known purchasing procedures, most of which still apply under the new thinking. The final topic is the role of purchasing in a company's total material management system.

TRADITIONAL PURCHASING

Purchasing departments are typically organized by commodity group. In that system, each buyer is responsible for just one or a few commodities, such as steel, electronic components, paper and supplies, and contracted services (e.g., janitorial and security). In any given week, a buyer may deal with dozens of suppliers and process numerous requisitions and purchase orders. (A *requisition,* prepared in another department, is a request for purchasing to place an order for a certain item.) Reams of data from receiving docks and material users may end up in purchasing for use in evaluating supplier performance. Because supplier performance is often unsatisfactory, purchasing people also keep busy evaluating and taking bids from new suppliers.

The most common problem—or main source of gripes—is that suppliers are notoriously late. Freight haulers compound the problem, and the requisitioner is anxious. Delivery dates or quantities may need to be changed, substitute materials agreed on, other freight methods arranged, orders canceled, or alternate suppliers found. Those problems keep buyers busy with telephones affixed to their ears.

The paperwork burden and constant phone work keep buyers from getting to know their suppliers. Management accepts the situation, rationalizing that "it is not our business to know what happens in the supplier's system." The

FIGURE 7–1

Black Box View of the Supplier's System

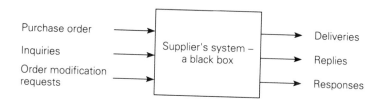

supplier's system, in effect, is treated as a black box (see Figure 7–1). Orders, inquiries about orders, and any requests for order changes enter the box. Order acknowledgments, responses, and eventually the goods or services themselves come out of the box, but what goes on inside remains a mystery.

Over the years, a few companies have bucked the hands-off tendency, encouraging their purchasing professionals to probe the black box. The aggressive, probing buyer may visit a key supplier's plant, study the supplier's production control system, and establish personal relationships with the supplier's personnel. Or information may be obtained by asking the right series of questions over the phone. The following hypothetical exchange is an example:

Buyer: What is the status of my order?
Supplier's Representative: According to my current information, it is on time.
B: What do you mean by current information?
SR: Well, I haven't received a delay notice.
B: Do you receive regular delay reports?
SR: Yes.
B: How often?
SR: Monthly.
B: (mentally noting that month-old delay reports are badly out of date): Could you please check to see where the order is in your shops?
SR: No, I've tried that before. Manufacturing tells me there are just too many orders on the floor to go searching for a particular one.
B: OK. Then could you just check with your master scheduler to see where my order is on your MPS?
SR: MPS?

At this point, it is clear that the supplier's representative is not in the habit of checking with production control or operations. The aggressive buyer will press on and will have scored a coup if the supplier's rep is induced to go to production control for order status information—and succeed in getting it.

TOWARD PARTNERSHIPS WITH SUPPLIERS

The modest activity in past decades in trying to get to know suppliers became a strong movement in the 1980s. Enlightened observers see the old adversarial approach as ineffective. Buying companies distrusted suppliers and changed suppliers often; in response, suppliers did not have a commitment to do their best for a customer, which made their replacement by other suppliers likely.

The current trend away from adversarial relationships is strongest among the bigger industrial companies and major retailers, such as McDonald's and Wal-mart. Some are calling the new approach "partners in profit," and a few com-

FIGURE 7–2
Supplier Relationships

	Adversarial	*Partnership*
1. Tenure	Brief	Long term, stable
2. Type of agreement	Sporadic purchase orders	Exclusive or semiexclusive contracts, usually at least one year
3. Number of sources	Several sources per item for protection against risk and for price competition	One, or a few good suppliers for each item or commodity group
4. Volume of business	Limits on amount of business with any one supplier	High; sometimes supplier dedicates small plant to single customer
5. Prices/costs	High on average; low "buy-in" bids (below costs) can lead to unstable suppliers	Low: scale economies from volume contracts; suppliers can invest in improvements
6. Quality	Uncertain; reliance on receiving inspections	Quality at source; supplier uses statistical process control and total quality management
7. Design specifications	Customer developed	Make use of suppliers' design expertise
8. Delivery frequency/order size	Infrequent, large lots	Frequent (sometimes more than one per day), small lots "just-in-time"
9. Order conveyance	Mail	Long term: contracts. Short term: kanban, phone, fax, or electronic data interchange
10. Delivery location	Receiving dock and stockroom	Direct to production line (user)
11. Receiving information	Packing lists, invoices, count/inspection forms	Sometimes no count, inspection, or list—just monthly bill
12. Openness	Very little; black box	On-site audits of supplier, concurrent engineering design, plant visits by operators

panies are adopting new job and department titles, such as Frito Lay's vice president of supplier development.

The old and new approaches are contrasted in Figure 7–2. Note that the second column describes an extreme set of conditions that add up to adversarial relationships. Few companies have been totally adversarial, but most have been that way to some degree. The 12 items in the figure are discussed next.

Tenure of Relationship

Under the adversarial approach, the normal practice is to change suppliers often. A new supplier's catalog price list might catch a buyer's eye and trigger a switch from the old to the new supplier. For larger-volume (or "big-ticket") purchased items, it is common to request bids from several suppliers at least yearly; the lowest bidder (often not the present supplier) usually gets the contract.

In the partnership approach, the idea is to try *not* to change suppliers. The rule is: Stay with one, in order that it may stay on the learning curve, get to know the customer's real requirements, and perhaps participate with the customer on product and process improvement.

Type of Agreement

In the adversarial approach, sporadic purchase orders for single shipments are the norm, and orders for a single item may rotate among 5 or 10 suppliers. Some "blanket" orders cover multiple shipments over a longer time period, but a blanket order too may go to several suppliers for a single item.

Items that are special, one-time buys will probably always require a purchase order. For regularly used items, however, the trend is toward contracts. Five-year contracts have become widespread in the North American auto industry; one-year contracts are more common in the volatile electronics industry. The contract may be like a blanket order, which does not necessarily commit to a quantity. Some contracts go beyond blanket orders to specify the quantity in fairly precise terms for the next few months and as a forecast for the rest of the year. Also, the contract may tell the supplier, "We don't know exactly how much we'll need, but whatever the need is, we guarantee to buy it from you"—in other words, an exclusive contract. Alternatively, the contract could state that "We guarantee to buy 50 percent from you."

Number of Sources

"Try to obtain several sources for each purchased item." That was a goal that every buyer understood. Government regulations even require it of federal buyers for some classes of material. The reasons have to do with price competition, protection against supplier failure, and—in government and some public-spirited companies—the fairness doctrine: Spread the large purchasing budget over several suppliers.

Multiple sourcing surely does offer short-term price competition. Today's thinking, however, is that over time the practice raises each supplier's costs, because each is denied opportunities for economies of scale. Some believe that multiple sourcing was so widespread in North America and Europe in recent decades that some of the supply base was ruined. That drove buying companies "off shore," primarily to the Far East, in the search for good, low-cost sources.

PRINCIPLE: Cut the number of suppliers to a few good ones.

In reducing the number of suppliers, it does not always make sense to go all the way to sole sourcing. Where technologies are changing rapidly in the supplier base, it's a good idea to maintain cordial relations with each of the suppliers that might come up with the next technical breakthrough. Where there is a serious risk of curtailed supply—for reasons of floods, explosions, strikes, and the like—one approach is to have two suppliers by commodity group but just one by part number. For example, buy business form numbers 1, 3, 5, 7, and so on from supplier A, and buy forms 2, 4, 6, 8, and so on from supplier B. Then, if one supplier has, say, a fire, the other should be able to pitch in.

A 1987 survey of 100 North American companies known to be involved in just-in-time yields some evidence of progress in reducing numbers of suppliers. The average number of sources per company prior to JIT implementation was 1,096. After JIT, the average fell as follows: one year later, 759 sources; two years later, 656 sources, and five years later, 357 sources. On average, the companies cut their number of sources threefold in five years.[1]

Volume of Business

Many large industrial companies have had a policy of not accounting for more than, say, 25 percent of any supplier's total sales. Some supplier companies have had a similar policy; for example, not allowing more than, say, 15 percent of total sales to be with any single customer. The reason is the possible severe impact on a supplier if the customer decides to change suppliers or cancel the business.

Under the partnership approach, a supplier may elect to build a small satellite plant next to a big customer and do up to 100 percent of its business with that customer—in other words, become a dedicated supplier plant but remain independent. Customers sometimes encourage this. Under that concept, a supplier company may grow by building many satellite plants, each serving just one or a small number of nearby customers. Each supplier plant then becomes a close

---

[1] Larry C. Giunipero, "AME Survey Report: A Survey of JIT Purchasing in American Industry," *Target*, Winter 1988, pp. 25–28.

partner with its customer plant, but total risk is spread among many supplier-customer pairs.

PRINCIPLE: Get to know the customer.

Prices/Costs

Price is the dominant basis for selecting a supplier in the adversarial approach. The idea is to find several suppliers capable of providing the desired item and then select the one with the lowest catalog price or bid price. Bidding rather than catalog price is the basis when the item requires some special engineering or design work or the volume is high enough to warrant a special price.

Buyers attempt to play suppliers off one another on price. Sometimes a supplier will "buy in" with a discount or a bid price that is below costs. That supplier then must overcharge on other contracts in order to stay in business. Also, when big customers with clout are able to force suppliers into making recklessly low bids, the suppliers become unstable and financially unable to invest in improvements. That instability, along with frequent changing of suppliers, introduces high change costs for both parties. Thus, while the adversarial approach focuses on getting good prices, it often gets the opposite.

On the other hand, the partnership approach, offering stable high-volume contracts with opportunities for economies of scale, is attractive to suppliers; they have reason to try to improve and do their best for customers.

Materials Quality

When suppliers are distrusted, the customer must have a sizable staff of inspectors at the receiving dock. Incoming freight may have to go into a quality-hold area and await inspection instead of going directly to the user—who perhaps is frantic because the order is late.

Instead of spending so much time inspecting materials, the modern idea is to send a team to the supplier's plant to certify its ability to do any necessary inspection or—better yet—to impose process controls so that inspections will be less necessary.

PRINCIPLE: Make it easy to make/provide the goods or services without error—the first time.

Design

If the customer buys out of a catalog or "off the shelf," the supplier clearly has control of the design specifications. In many cases, however, the customer wants a specially designed product or service. In the adversarial approach, the customer typically does the design work, passes the specs on to the supplier, and expects them to be followed.

That approach has come under attack. The customer company is saying to itself, "We cannot be experts on our suppliers' products and processes, so why try to tell them how to design things?" In the partnership approach, the customer provides essential performance requirements and critical dimensions but tries to make use of the supplier's design expertise.

Delivery Frequency/Order Size

Shipping costs depend partly on whether the volume is great enough to fill a truck (or barge or sea container). Since volume for a certain item traditionally has been split among several suppliers, each supplier must ship less often in order to get full-load freight rates. Thus, it has been normal for customers to have to receive large lots infrequently; many weeks' supply per shipment is common.

Under the partnership approach, ways to permit frequent, small-lot, just-in-time deliveries are developed. The most effective way is to go to large volumes from fewer suppliers.

When suppliers are few but volumes still are small, frequent, small-lot deliveries are made economical by what the auto industry calls *milk runs:* A single truck stops at several suppliers, collecting a small amount from each; when the truck is full, it delivers to one or more customers. Milk runs range from one a week to several loops per day.

Distance need not be a serious problem. One Chrysler milk run, extending from El Paso, Texas, to the Detroit area, takes 56 hours. Small-lot deliveries are even occurring across oceans; for example, a ship departing from a Far Eastern port may carry in a single sea container just a day's worth of several dozen different bulky auto parts; each day another similarly loaded ship departs, and each spends five weeks on the sea, but one arrives at a North American port to off-load every day.

Conventionally, the truck or ship would carry one or more months' supply of a given item per delivery, and would visit a given supplier just once every month or two for a pickup. That is a costly amount of inventory for the supplier to build up for each shipment and a costly amount to dump on the customer. While it may seem that loading and paperwork costs are much greater when pickups and deliveries are daily instead of monthly, that need not be the case. When "partnered" companies, including the freight hauler, get a regular milk run going, they usually are able to greatly simplify the data processing—including invoicing just once a month instead of per delivery and per part number.

PRINCIPLE: Produce and deliver at the customer's use rate (or a smoothed representation of it); decrease cycle interval and lot size.

Order Conveyance

For companies that have converted to frequent, small-lot deliveries, mail is too slow; new, faster methods of transmitting ordering information include phone, facsimile copier, and electronic data interchange (EDI). EDI is a standardized computer-to-computer messaging system open to any company and usable for billing and perhaps funds transfers as well as for ordering.

The National Association of Purchasing Management has found that EDI improves purchasing productivity by reducing paperwork, improving information management, and bettering supplier relationships. Large companies generally use EDI in a *direct transmission* mode—between buyer's and supplier's computers. Small businesses may also reap the benefits of EDI, often using *indirect transmission,* in which a third party maintains the computer network through which buyers and suppliers interact.

Still another communications method is basic kanban: A kanban (identification card) is attached to the container, which is returnable; its return to the supplier is the authorization to forward one more container-full to the customer. Basic kanban is also usable in conjunction with electronic messaging: Standardized returnable containers provide physical discipline and control, while an electronic message or faxed kanban card provides early warning—before the empty container itself is delivered back to the supplier.

Delivery Location

Deliveries have traditionally gone to a single receiving dock and then into receiving stockrooms. Materials may be handled four times: onto the dock for a quick check of contents and quantity; into quality hold in the receiving stockroom for counting and inspection; then to a free-to-use area of the stockroom; and finally to the user or production line.

In the partnership approach, with the supplier quality-certified, materials skip some of those steps. In industry parlance, they go *dock-to-stock,* or better yet *dock-to-line,* which means right to the user on the production line or in the office. Some plants are being remodeled to provide receiving docks and doors around the perimeter of the building so that trucks can deliver close to production lines. In some cases, the driver is authorized to carry or push a dolly of parts through the plant to an interior user location.

Receiving Information

Conventionally, when an order arrives, receiving people verify its correctness: right item, right quantity, and right quality. The supplier's packing list can be checked against the receiving dock's copy of the purchase order. Discrepancies are noted on forms that go to purchasing and accounts payable.

The partnership approach tries to reduce or simplify the paperwork. Ideally there is no packing list, count, or quality inspection. A kanban card or plate on the container identifies the item. The container has egg-crate dividers inside for ease in packing just the right amount into the container. No inspection is necessary, because the supplier and item are certified.

Increasingly, reusable containers are bar coded. Upon receipt, the bar code is wanded, which sends a message to accounts payable authorizing payment.

Some North American plants even skip the notification to accounts payable; they just wait for the suppliers' invoice, which may be sent once a month. Accounts payable sends the invoice to the user, perhaps a line manager; the line manager knows how many products were produced and what purchased materials go into them. If the invoice does not agree with what should have been consumed, the manager advises accounts payable of a discrepancy.

Relationship Openness

The adversarial approach is one of arm's-length relationships. The buyer, in the office or at trade shows, sifts through many suppliers' offerings and finally selects a few; from then on, communication is by mail and fax to the "black box" (except in times of materials scarcity, when the suppliers put their customers "on allocation"—for example, 1,000 Nintendo game sets to this store chain, 1,200 to that one, and so forth).

The partnership approach *requires* the buying company to send people to the supplier's plant now and then. That includes sending operations employees— the people who use the purchased items. The visitors get to know people at the supplier's plant and acquire an understanding of the supplier's culture, skills, processes, nagging problems, and potential sources of misunderstanding, and invite the supplier's people to reciprocate the visit.

Some buying companies actively seek to extend the partnership to the supplier's suppliers—and beyond. A new term used to describe this linked partnership is *supply-chain management*. Sometimes the catalyst for such linkages is a supplier trying to forge partnerships with customers and their customers, which we might call *customer development* or *customer-chain management*.

Buying companies also should do formal audits of the supplier's quality and processes. Failure to visit and perform audits invites misunderstanding, bad feelings, and a return to adversarial relationships. It is perhaps like dating: Follow-up calls keep the interest alive. Or maybe it's like gardening: Till the soil, or weeds will grow.

Throughout this section we have focused on relationships between buyer and seller; to a large extent, these relationships determine how purchasing is accomplished. We obtain additional insight by addressing our next topic, purchasing policies and practices.

PURCHASING POLICIES AND PRACTICES

Purchasing activities are guided by commonsense policies relating to value and kind of item bought. In this section, we consider these policies, first through use of ABC analysis and its influence on common buying procedures. Related topics include measurement and compliance issues, the value analysis method, and the positive benefits of standardization.

ABC Analysis

It makes sense to tightly manage costly materials and loosely manage cheap ones.[2] That logic is the basis of **ABC analysis**, an old and still important tool of materials management.

ABC analysis begins by classifying all stocked items by annual dollar volume, that is, annual demand times cost per unit. Class A items, those needing close control, are the high-dollar-volume group. They may include 80 percent of total inventory cost but only 1 percent of total items bought. Class B is a medium-dollar-volume group—perhaps 15 percent of dollars and 30 percent of items. Class C is the rest—say, 5 percent of dollars and 69 percent of items. Some firms continue with D and perhaps E categories.

Computer processing makes ABC analysis easy to do. Item cost is available in the inventory master file. Any measure of annual usage—such as actual usage last year, actual usage last month times 12, or a forecast—may be used. The computer multiplies item cost by annual usage, giving annual dollar volume. The ABC formula is fed into the computer, and the output is a complete list of items in descending dollar-volume order. The listing is grouped into three parts: A items first, B items second, and C items third.

Examples of how ABC analysis may be used follow (the details will vary from firm to firm):

1. *Purchasing.* Have each purchase order for a class A item signed by the president or chief financial officer, for a class B item by a department head, and for a class C item by any buyer.

2. *Physical inventory counting.* Count A items weekly or daily, B items monthly, and C items annually.

3. *Forecasting.* Forecast A items by several methods on the computer with resolution by a forecasting committee, B items by simple trend projection, and C items by buyer's best guess.

---

[2]This idea of giving an item the degree of attention it deserves is sometimes called the *principle of parsimony* (*parsimony* means *frugality*). The more general principle, widely applicable in society, is the *Pareto principle;* it is named after Vilfredo Pareto (1848–1923), an economist who observed that 90 percent of wealth is in the hands of 10 percent of the population.

4. *Safety stock.* No safety stock for A items, one week's supply for B items, and one month's supply for C items.

ABC dipped a bit in popularity in the 1970s. Experts were saying that fast-dropping computing costs made it economical for a material requirements planning system to give B and C items as much attention as A items; one ordering system could be used for all items. The emergence of just-in-time brings us back to more conventional ABC thinking.

Class A items are the best prospects for the full JIT treatment, because they have the volume to most easily justify frequent small-lot deliveries, perhaps daily. It is no small achievement to switch an item to daily deliveries, since typical delivery intervals/lot sizes in the non-JIT mode are monthly or greater. JIT policies for B and C items are more modest: perhaps weekly deliveries for class B items and quarterly for class Cs.

Actually, many companies have found ways to do much better than that for some Bs and Cs. For example, a sizable number of manufacturing plants now buy all their hundreds of hardware items—screws, washers, bolts, grommets, etc.—from a single supplier. Commonly, that supplier visits the customer at least once a week, goes right out to the factory floor to fill the bins and trays, and just invoices the customer monthly. While each hardware item is class C in annual value, the whole commodity group adds up to class A value, which makes it economical for the supplier to provide that kind of customer service.

A different twist on the same general idea is coming into use in several industries, especially automotive, but also major appliances and large electronic systems: buying completed modules instead of the individual parts. Past practice in automotive assembly, for example, was to buy and receive hundreds of class B parts for instrument panels, doors, and so forth for installation, one by one, on the assembly line. It was a receiving and material handling nightmare.

The current trend is to have a subcontractor—a specialist in instrument panels or doors, for example—deliver completed modules to the assembly plant. While the individual parts are class B, the modules are class A in value, which makes daily deliveries (sometimes several times a day) economical.

ABC applies as well to inventory-intensive wholesaling and retailing as it does to manufacturing. Example 7–1 illustrates ABC for a wholesaler.

EXAMPLE 7–1   ABC ANALYSIS—WHOLESALER

At Universal Motor Supply Company, the buyer has arranged 10 inventory items in order of annual dollar volume. Figure 7–3 shows the ordered list, with dollar volume expressed in percentages. The buyer examines the ordered list to arrive at an ABC classification of the items.

Figure 7–4 shows the 10 items grouped by the buyer into classes A, B, and C. The groupings seem natural: The three B items account for over seven (9.8 ÷ 1.3) times as much annual dollar volume as the five C items; the two A items account for about nine

FIGURE 7–3

Inventory Items in Annual-Dollar-Volume Order—Universal
Motor Supply Company

Stock Number	Annual Demand	Unit Cost	Annual Dollar Volume	Percent
407	40,000	$ 35.50	$1,420,000	59.53%
210	1,000	700.00	700,000	29.35
021	2,000	55.00	110,000	4.61
388	20,000	4.00	80,000	3.35
413	4,400	10.00	44,000	1.84
195	500	36.00	18,000	0.76
330	40	214.00	8,560	0.36
114	100	43.00	4,300	0.18
274	280	1.00	280	0.01
359	600	0.25	150	0.00
Totals			$2,385,290	~100.0%

FIGURE 7–4

ABC Classification—Universal Motor Supply Company

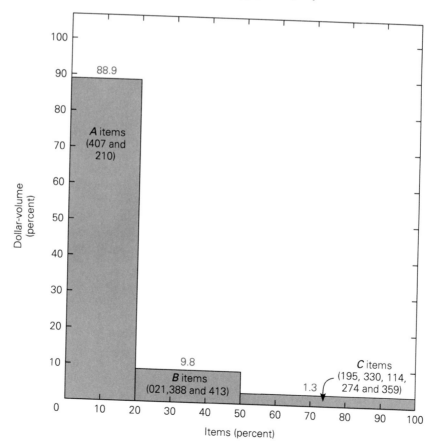

times as much as the three B items. It is clear that A items should receive major attention: Have them delivered often in small quantities, store them in flow racks at or near to the receiving/shipping docks, carefully monitor and control them. Class Bs should receive moderate attention, and class Cs little attention—for example, handle them manually and store them in conventional racks in a remote part of the warehouse.

Purchasing and Contracting Procedures

Besides ABC analysis, there are a few common purchasing practices and terms that business managers should be exposed to. They have to do with arranging the supplier-seller agreement and the terms of that agreement, and they group fairly well into the A, B, and C categories.

Class A Items

A class A item may be an expensive, seldom-ordered item or a low-cost item that is ordered often or in large quantities. Common purchasing measures are:

Soliciting competitive bids on specifications. An *invitation to bid* or a *request for quotation* is mailed to prospective suppliers. The item to be bought is specified in detail; the description may consist of *technical specifications* (physical or chemical properties) and *performance specifications* (mean time until failure, rated output, etc.), and *procedural specifications* (e.g., consultant will conduct an employee attitude survey). Specifications may be necessary because the item is nonstandard or because the buying firm wishes to exclude low-quality suppliers. Also, specifications can provide a sound basis for determining compliance with the buyer's requirements. Engineering often plays a key role in developing specs, and engineering blueprints may be attached. Attorneys may ensure that contractual obligations are legally clear.

Governments, especially the federal government, intermittently buy based on publicly available specs. Regulations require that for many types of purchases the invitation to bid be published in a widely circulated government document.

Certification. Quality-conscious companies often conduct formal studies to quality-certify suppliers and items bought from them. Older approaches, which rank suppliers rather than certify them, are based on external data on prices, delivery timeliness, defect rates, and a few other factors. Certification generally requires evidence of the supplier's use of process control methods, perhaps obtained through on-site visits to the supplier's facility. Quality-certification sometimes is broadly defined to include such factors as quality of design, training, and lead-time or delivery performance. Some certifications, such as Ford's Q1 rating, are highly cherished. Supplier companies proudly advertise their attainment of such levels of excellence.

Negotiation. Where sources of supply are stable, there may be no need to solicit formal bids. Instead, the buying firm may just periodically negotiate with the regular source for better price or delivery terms. Typically, negotiation applies to nonstandard class A goods and services.

Buying down and speculation. Buying down means trying to buy an item with a history of cyclic price swings when its price is down. It is a form of speculative buying. In pure speculation, purchases are made for price reasons rather than for meeting an actual need for the goods.

Hedging. Hedging applies especially to commodities, such as wheat, corn, silver, and lumber. Organized futures markets exist for some commodities. A buyer can pay cash to buy a commodity now and at the same time sell a like amount of a "future" of the commodity. Price changes will mean that losses on one order are offset by gains on the other.

Class B Items

Class B goods and moderate-cost services usually warrant less purchasing effort. This applies to many kinds of standard off-the-shelf goods, such as maintenance, repair, and operating (MRO) supplies, as well as standard services, such as those of a plumber or auto body shop. For *nonstandard* items in the class B cost range, specifications might be necessary, but the expense of soliciting bids is harder to justify than for class A items. Order procedures for the class B category include the following:

Approved supplier lists. Companies like to buy from proven suppliers. The approved supplier list is relied on especially for class B items, though it also is used for class A and class C buying. The approved supplier list may be based on an old-style performance rating or on a full certification study.

Catalog buying. Perhaps the most common purchasing procedure for off-the-shelf (MRO) goods is buying out of current catalogs, sometimes with the help of salespeople. Most buyers have shelves full of suppliers' catalogs for this purpose.

Blanket orders. Where there is an ongoing but varying need for an item—with class B annual volume—a blanket-order contract may be drawn up with a supplier. The blanket order covers a given time period, and deliveries are arranged by sending a simple release notice to the supplier. Price and other matters are covered in the contract.

Systems contract. A systems contract is similar to a blanket order, but it is longer term and more stringently defined. The purchasing department negotiates the systems contract; purchasing then typically becomes a monitor, but not a participant, in ordering. The contract may name certain responsible employees who may order—by mail, phone, or other means—directly from the supplier.

Class C Items

Class C or low-cost items are worthy of little attention by purchasing specialists. Buying such items from a supplier on an approved supplier list provides a measure of control. For many items even that is too much control and red tape, and to avoid these, using departments are provided with *petty cash funds* with which to buy directly and in cash. Until recently, petty cash buying has been restricted to office employees. Now a few progressive North American manufacturers provide each factory employee or improvement team with a petty cash fund, to be used to buy small tools or other devices that can improve performance.

Performance and Compliance: The Tangibility Factor

Buying goods, or *tangibles*, differs from purchasing services, or *intangibles*. The quality of tangibles is physically measurable; the quality of intangibles is not. The distinction has an impact on purchasing practices.

An intangible item, as the designation suggests, is difficult to specify. Without clear, physically measurable specifications, it is more difficult to hold the seller accountable for performance. Intangibility is relative, as Figure 7–5 shows. The top end of the scale represents one extreme—high tangibility. Highly tangible items include simple parts, such as screws, diodes, and switches. Commodities, such as tobacco, iron ore, and bananas, are near the tangible end, but some of their key physical properties may be costly to measure; less tangible "eyeball" judgments on quality may be used to some extent in evaluating commodities. Simple finished goods are a bit less tangible than commodities. For example, books, furniture, and fabrics have several measurable physical properties, but for items of this kind visual inspection for scratches, flaws, and so forth may be as important as physical measurements. Complex finished goods (e.g., autos, ships, and missiles) have thousands of measurable physical properties; yet partly subjective judgments as to their effectiveness (e.g., how well the destroyer protects the fleet) are important.

Procedures for buying these mostly tangible goods are fairly well established. Purchase contracts may be based largely on clear *standards of output*—that is, on physically measurable properties of the end product.

Intangibles, at the bottom end of Figure 7–5, do not have physically measurable properties. Therefore, purchase contracts may be based on input and procedural factors. In a contract with a consultant, input factors may include specifying level of education and years of experience of the consultants sent out on the job; procedural factors may include number of people to be interviewed and number of pages on the final consultant's report. Those do not comprise the quality of the consultant's services, but they are often treated as surrogates for output quality.

Slightly more tangible than ideas is software, such as computer programs and technical manuals. You can count lines of code in a computer program and number of words in a technical manual, and the contract may set limits on such factors. But no one would say that those are measures of quality. However, the

FIGURE 7–5

Tangibility of Purchased Goods

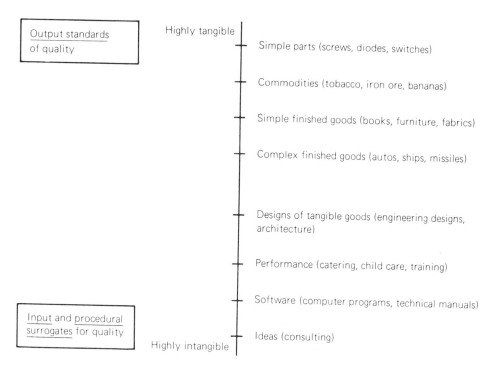

software firm is likely to receive full pay (even for a shoddy job) if it has met the input and procedural contract terms.

Contracting for performance is growing explosively; catering, child care, and employee training are examples. Enterprising college students capitalize on the trend by starting part-time businesses to provide janitorial, yard care, computer dating, and a variety of other services. The end products or outputs are good food, well-adjusted children, requalified employees, clean floors, weed-free lawns, and well-matched dating couples. It is difficult to write standards for those outputs into a contract. Consequently, there has been growing use of measures of compliance such as mean number of customer complaints and opinion polling involving customers, experts, or impartial panels using some form of Likert scale (i.e., a rating scale from 1 to 5, 1 to 7, etc.).

That may seem nearly as objective as measuring the diameter of a shaft with a micrometer. It isn't. The weakness lies in the difficulty of getting a representative sample. A random sample of shafts is easy to get because the shafts have no will and no bias. Selecting people to poll, on the other hand, depends on their willingness to be polled, and there are many possible biases that are hard to control for.

In the center of Figure 7–5 are designs for tangible goods, such as engineering and architectural designs. The output is like software or consulting reports, and the above remarks on the use of input and procedural contract terms apply. But there is a distinct difference: The engineer's or architect's design *becomes a tangible good*. If the bridge collapses or the roof caves in, the engineer or architect may be legally liable. That makes contracting for these services less risky.

We see that the most serious measurement and compliance problems exist in buying performance, software, and ideas. Buying from firms with good reputations (such as those on an approved supplier list) would seem to be one helpful measure. But performance service providers tend to come and go rather than to stay and build clientele and reputation. Software firms and consulting firms are somewhat more stable. Ironically, poor software or consulting is not notably destructive to firms' reputations; the reason is that dissatisfied customers tend not to admit their displeasure (1) because of the risk of defamation suits, since bad quality is difficult to prove, and (2) because dissatisfaction would be an admission of having wasted time and money on poor software or consulting services.

On occasion, however, service providers' failure to perform does not go unnoticed—especially when those providers charge stiff fees for their failure. Consider, for example, the attempted leveraged buyout of UAL Corp. (United Air Lines' parent) that fell through on October 13, 1989. Already reeling from plummeted stock values, UAL shareholders still received a bill for $58.7 million for professional services rendered by the lawyers and bankers hired to complete the deal. Irked by this high price for failure, shareholders and other observers criticized the banks and law firms involved and questioned the wisdom of the UAL Corp. board for its purchase of the services.[3] Thus we see that even large corporations have problems in buying service performance.

Public and corporate officials are increasingly relying on consultants to help them with sticky decisions. Inability to write tough contracts leaves the officials at the consultants' mercy. Fortunately, most consultants are professionally dedicated and motivated to maintain self-respect. Still, contracting for those kinds of intangibles is a challenge for people in the purchasing field.

Value Analysis

Purchasing means spending money. But purchasing professionals also may become involved in projects that offer long-term substantial savings ("making money") for their company. Value analysis projects are of this type.

Value analysis (VA) was developed in the purchasing department of General Electric in 1947. In VA, a team analyzes existing product design specifications with the aim of improving value. In large organizations, file cabinets in purchasing and design may be filled with specs developed years ago. New technology outdates some of the old specifications. Each time such items are reordered, the obsolescence becomes more apparent and purchasing takes the heat

---

[3]"In Failed Bid for UAL, Lawyers and Bankers Didn't Fail to Get Fees," *The Wall Street Journal,* November 30, 1989, p. A1.

for not "buying modern." It is no surprise that VA was developed and promoted by purchasing people. As engineers got more involved, the concepts were extended to include new designs as well as old specs.

In some companies and in the federal government, engineers conduct the analysis, calling it **value engineering (VE)**. While value analysis could be applied to services, it is mostly restricted to goods, especially where material costs and usage rates are high.

The VA step-by-step procedure has been adopted worldwide. The steps (a variation of the scientific method) are:

1. *Select product.* Select a product that is ripe for improvement.

2. *Gather information.* The team coordinator collects drawings, costs, scrap rates, forecasts, operations sheets, and so forth before the team first meets. Team members provide whatever information they have.

3. *Define function.* The team meets and defines each function of the product. A function is defined in two words: a verb and a noun (e.g., "A barrel *contains fluid.*"). Only essential functions are included. Next, the team estimates the present cost of each function. That reveals which functions are costing far too much. (Note: Defining functions in this way is unique and sets VA apart from other cost reduction techniques.)

4. *Generate alternatives.* Team members suggest ideas for new and different ways to accomplish the functions. This is known as *brainstorming*. Ideas are recorded and later culled to a list of manageable size.

5. *Evaluate alternatives.* The team evaluates alternatives based on feasibility, cost and other factors, which cuts the list to one (or a few) good ideas.

6. *Present proposals.* Refine the final alternatives and present them to a management committee as change proposals.

7. *Implement plan.* Translate the approved change proposal into an engineering change order (ECO is a common industry abbreviation), and put it into effect.

In Example 7–2, the description of a real VA study helps show how the procedure works.[4]

EXAMPLE 7–2   **VA PROCEDURE FOR IMPROVING A BEARING HOUSING-SUPPORT**

After selecting a dust-collector valve for value analysis, a VA team, in the information phase, found that the valve assembly was composed of five parts: bearing, left- and right-hand bearing housing support, and left- and right-hand seal. The team reviewed

---

[4]Based on Arthur E. Mudge, *Value Engineering: A Systematic Approach* (New York: McGraw-Hill, 1971), pp. 263–64 (TS168.M83).

FIGURE 7–6
Bearing Housing-Support Undergoing Value Engineering

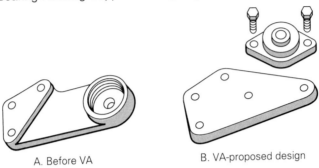

A. Before VA   B. VA-proposed design

Source: Arthur E. Mudge, *Value Engineering: A Systematic Approach*
(New York: McGraw-Hill, 1971), p. 263 (TS168.M83). Used with permission.

the assembly and the five parts and their costs, finally deciding to focus further analysis
on the bearing housing supports; see the sketch in Figure 7–6A.

The pair of housing supports, cast from gray iron, had a direct material and labor cost
of $36. The team noted that the function of the supports was to *locate* the *bearings*, which,
in turn, had the function *support* and *locate* the *main shaft*.

The study centered on those two functions. The team searched a number of bearing
manufacturers' catalogs. All the catalogs included a sealed, self-mounting bearing as a
standard item. When the team's solution to the functions "reduce friction" and "provide
seal" was combined with its solution to the functions "provide support" and "provide
location," the team knew that it had a workable solution.

The team realized that the self-mounting bearing could be mounted on either side of
a common piece of steel plate, as shown in Figure 7–6B. This design cut the total housing
subassembly cost by 33 percent, to $25 per pair. Since only minor engineering changes
were required and no tooling was needed, the annual net savings of about $3,100 began
in the first year.

Impressed by the results of VA and VE in private industry, the Department
of Defense issued VE regulations applicable to all DoD contracts costing more
than $100,000. In 1964, the American Ordnance Association conducted a survey
that randomly sampled 124 successful VE changes in the DoD.[5] The survey
report showed not only impressive cost savings but also, in many cases, collateral
gains in the areas of reliability, maintainability, producibility, human factors,
parts availability, production lead time, quality, weight, logistics, performance,

---

[5]"Reduce Costs and Improve Equipment through Value Engineering," Directorate of Value Engineering, Office of the Assistant Secretary of Defense for Installations and Logistics, January 1967
(TS168.U5).

and packaging. The DoD then implemented a formula for sharing some of the VE savings (usually 20 percent) with contractors; this gave the contractors' VE teams added incentive to squeeze savings out of the design specifications.

A "quick and dirty" brand of value analysis has come into use in recent years. In a plant operating in the just-in-time mode, a problem might arise that threatens to stop production. That summons a buyer or engineer to the shop floor; a foreman and perhaps an operator or two will join in the problem analysis. Blueprints may be marked up and taken immediately to the inside or outside maker of the parts that are causing the problem.

Conducting value analysis "on the fly" in this way requires that blueprints and design specs not be too limiting. Design engineers traditionally have tried to specify every dimension, type of material, finish, and so on, which greatly limits options for producing the item. The nonrestrictive specs concept aims at giving the maker latitude over nonessential design attributes so that easy, cheap ways of making the part may be searched for—and easily changed when someone sees a better way.

The purist might say that making design decisions on the floor should not be called value analysis because the formal steps—defining functions, generating alternatives, and so forth—are bypassed. While that is true, the less formal approach has the advantage of giving more attention to how product design affects producibility, a key element in overall product cost. Also, producibility is a vital concern in just-in-time production in which a production problem can starve later production stages of parts and bring operations to a halt.

Standardization

Industrial **standardization** means settling on a few rather than many sizes, shapes, colors, and so forth for a given part. Value analysis sometimes leads to standardization. But some companies have a permanent standardization committee, often headed by an engineer or buyer.

Lee and Dobler state that "standardization is the *prerequisite* to mass production." They credit Eli Whitney's development of standardization (initially of musket parts) as having triggered the emergence of the United States as the world's dominant mass producer in the first half of the century.[6] The idea is to make not standardized end products but a wide variety of end products from a small number of standardized parts and materials. The cost savings can be substantial. (Standardization is a key to *delayed differentiation*, discussed in Chapter 5.) Fewer items means less purchasing, receiving, inspection, storage, and billing. Internally, fewer different kinds of production equipment and tooling are required, and production of some parts may be relatively continuous and just-in-time—which is efficient—instead of stop-and-go with intermittent delays.

---

[6]Lamar Lee, Jr., and Donald W. Dobler, *Purchasing and Materials Management: Text and Cases,* 3rd ed. (New York: McGraw-Hill, 1977), pp. 54–55 (HD52.5.L4).

The American National Standards Institute (ANSI) is a federation of over 100 organizations that develops industrial standards. After research and debate, ANSI may approve a recommended standard for adoption nationwide. Perhaps the most vexing standardization issue in America is metrics, since the United States is the only nonmetric country among major industrial countries. However, most American companies with good export markets have gone metric on their own.

PRINCIPLE: Cut the number of components in a product or service.

MATERIALS MANAGEMENT

There has been considerable debate on the proper organizational location of the purchasing function and related materials functions. Purchasing people historically were among the first advocates of a strong, centralized **materials management** department or group. The intent was to forge a natural linkage between purchasing and other materials-oriented activities. To that end, some companies created a new vice presidential-level department of materials management to house all the materials functions. In some firms, the department included the complete cycle of material flow, from purchasing and receiving to purchased stores, control of work-in-process inventories, warehousing, shipping, and distribution of finished goods. Materials management departments were especially popular in the 1970s.

Today, a growing number of firms are transferring some of the responsibility for controlling and handling materials to line managers and operating teams, instead of to a staff organization. Thus, some of the materials management departments that were organized in an earlier decade were split up, reduced in size, or otherwise altered in the 1980s.

As examples of some current organizational patterns, Ford's corporate-level department is called *purchasing and supply;* at General Motors, it's *materials management;* at Texas Instruments, the department is called *procurement;* and Westinghouse has a combined department of *purchasing, traffic, and real estate.*[7]

Regardless of how the materials functions are organized, certain key issues remain to be dealt with. Three that we shall treat in this chapter, because they relate to purchasing, are make-or-buy issues, backward integration, and inventory control. They are the next topics.

---

[7]Joseph R. Carter, Ram Narasimhan, and Shawnee K. Vickery, *International Sourcing for Manufacturing Operations,* Monograph no. 3 (Waco, Texas: Operations Management Association, September 1988), p. 27.

Make or Buy

The strategic question of whether to make or buy is often a complex issue. Its basic cost elements, however, reduce to a simple type of break-even analysis, which is illustrated in Figure 7–7.

As the figure shows, if the item is bought, there is no fixed cost. Instead, the total cost, TC, is simply the unit price, P, times demand, D:

$$TC_{buy} = P \times D \qquad (7\text{–}1)$$

If the item is made, there is a fixed cost, FC, of setting up for production. The other element of total cost is the variable cost of production, which equals unit variable cost, V, times demand, D. Then,

$$TC_{make} = (V \times D) + FC \qquad (7\text{–}2)$$

We see in Figure 7–7 that the break-even demand, B, occurs where the total costs are equal. For demand less than B, the total cost to buy is lower; thus, buy is preferred. For demand greater than B, offsetting the fixed cost by the lower unit cost results in a lower cost to make; so, make is preferred. The analysis should be based on annual demand and cost if the item is a stocked one that is

FIGURE 7–7
Make-or-Buy Break-Even Analysis

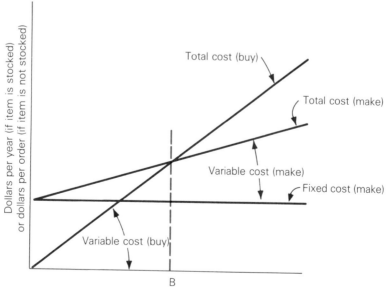

bought year after year. The demand and cost of a single order should be used for a nonstocked item that may or may not be reordered in future years.

Since the total costs are equal at the break-even point, a break-even formula is easily developed. Using B (for break-even demand) instead of D, we have:

$$TC_{buy} = TC_{make}$$

$$P \times B = (V \times B) + FC$$

$$(P \times B) - (V \times B) = FC$$

$$B(P - V) = FC$$

$$B = \frac{FC}{P - V} \qquad (7-3)$$

For example, assume you can buy candles at the store for $1 each. Or you can pay $50 for candle-making apparatus and make your own candles for a unit variable cost (wax, wicks, etc.) of $0.75. What volume is necessary in order to recover your fixed cost, that is, break even?

Solution:

$$B = \frac{50}{1 - 0.75} = \frac{50}{0.25} = 200 \text{ candles}$$

Classical make-or-buy seems simple enough, but what about its overall usefulness? Make-or-buy analysis, like any technique, requires certain assumptions. First, we must assume that make (or buy) is a realistic option. This goes beyond the cost of the candle-making apparatus and into the technical knowledge and other competencies required to be a producer. Do we have such resources? Having to acquire them, perhaps by hiring candle makers or training some existing personnel, will increase fixed costs and thus raise the volume required for break-even.

Second, we must assume that the variable costs associated with making are less than the variable (unit) cost of buying, or we could never reach break-even. What if new technology, simplified production techniques, or other change led to a drop in the buy price? We would have to match the change or see erosion in the economic advantage of making. That is, we would have just acquired another business (candle making) to keep up in. Even if we spent the capital on equipment required for making, could we keep up with candle-making technology? Do we even want to?

Concern over these assumptions seems trivial for the candle-making example. But what if a shopping mall is considering a $10 million capital expenditure for building its own power-generating facilities instead of buying power from the local utility? Now, the issues—such as hiring and retaining competent technical staff, availability and prices of fuel, and so forth—are important indeed, inasmuch as major costs and risks are involved.

The classical make-or-buy approach is fine for small-value items, where entry barriers are low. If in moving from buy to make or from make to buy we don't have to pay much, learn much, change much, or worry much, then a basic make-or-buy analysis is appropriate. Changing our minds later if new tactics are required will entail no substantial economic hardship.

For sourcing decisions that fall outside the simple category, classical make-or-buy must yield to more detailed analysis. Key issues include backward integration.

Backward Integration versus "Stick to Your Knitting"

When materials are scarce or supplier performance is highly inconsistent, panic sets in. In their anxiety, some companies will opt for **backward integration**. This means setting up to make the materials or provide the services formerly bought, or perhaps buying the supplier company and making it a subsidiary. One result is that purchasing may no longer have to scramble to get delivery commitments or to handle problem suppliers. Backward integration is a major financial commitment, and it consumes a lot of managerial energy. When the material shortage evaporates or suppliers upgrade their performance, the company that absorbed another of its suppliers may wish it hadn't.

The authors of an acclaimed 1980 article, "Managing Our Way to Economic Decline," commented on backward integration. Companies with stable, commodity-like products, such as metals and petroleum, often can gain economies and profit improvements through backward integration. The strategy may backfire, however, for companies in technologically active industries. Backward integration "may provide a quick, short-term boost to ROI figures in the next annual report, but it may also paralyze the long-term ability of a company to keep on top of technological change."[8]

Concentrating on doing a few things well and acquiring the rest from outside is popularly known as "sticking to your knitting."[9] This approach, which runs counter to backward integration, has been widely applied to services in recent years. Companies hire caterers to run employee cafeterias and vending machines, janitorial services to clean the premises, contract truckers to haul goods, and consultants to provide advice.

The stick-to-your-knitting viewpoint has its adherents in manufacturing as well, especially in electronics. For example, the strategic plan for the Apple Macintosh plant in Fremont, California, is to focus on assembly. In other words, most of the cost is for purchased materials. Apple controls critical factors, including design and marketing, and lets outside experts—in microprocessors, sheet metal, CRTs, and so forth—produce the parts. Most other successful producers of computers and allied products have adopted a similar strategy.

---

[8] Robert H. Hayes and William J. Abernathy, "Managing Our Way to Economic Decline," *Harvard Business Review*, July–August 1980, pp. 67–77.
[9] That old saw became a buzzword in management circles when a runaway best-selling book gave it a whole chapter. See Thomas J. Peters and Robert H. Waterman, Jr., *In Search of Excellence: Lessons from America's Best-Run Companies* (New York: Harper & Row, 1982), Chapter 10, "Stick to the Knitting."

In the 1980s, the U.S. auto industry, particularly General Motors, began to reassess its long-cherished tradition of backward integration. In the early 1980s, GM was producing 80 percent of the value of its autos in its own plants—at high United Auto Workers wage rates. Ford, which used more outside suppliers, had a comparable figure of only 60 percent.[10]

By 1986, GM was still paying between $300 and $400 more in direct labor and materials costs to build an $11,300 automobile than was Ford.[11] Chrysler's total manufacturing cost advantage over Ford and GM of some $500 per car had been largely attributed to its use of creative component sourcing versus attempting to build the parts itself. The 1986 figures for outside sourcing for the three companies were 70 percent for Chrysler, 50 percent for Ford, and only 30 percent for GM.[12]

Any advantages of stick-to-your-knitting depend on having reliable suppliers. The ideal is for the buyer company to exert control over a few vital factors of the supply channels, leaving the supplier free to innovate and keep up with technologies in its area of manufacturing expertise. Reliable suppliers don't just happen; they must be nurtured.

Inventory Control

A byproduct of sticking to one's knitting is that it simplifies inventory control, by slashing the number and variety of inventory items to be controlled. Combine that with just-in-time methods, which synchronize production so that inventories do not pile up, and you may nearly simplify inventory control out of existence. In fact, in the words of Taiichi Ohno, who was instrumental in developing JIT concepts at Toyota, "If the meaning of production control is truly understood, inventory control is unnecessary."[13] Our discussion of inventory control is in the narrow sense: inventory records, files, and the physical stocks themselves.

Inventory Records and Files

All organizations, except very small ones, need stock records that show what has happened and what current inventory status is. The collection of stock records forms the inventory status file, which may be called the *item master file*—usually a computer file.

Figure 7–8 shows a typical stock record (not computer-formatted). Order quantity and reorder point are shown at the right, and the running balance (stock on hand) is maintained by date in the lower portion. When an issue is

[10]"GM's 'New Alliance' with UAW Is Starting to Look Rather Shaky," *The Wall Street Journal*, June 8, 1982, pp. 1, 18.

[11]"Ross Perot's Crusade," *Business Week*, October 6, 1986, pp. 60–65.

[12]"Chrysler's Next Act," *Business Week*, November 3, 1986, pp. 66–72.

[13]Taiichi Ohno and Tomonori Kumagai, "Toyota Production System" *Proceedings of the International Conference on Industrial Systems Engineering and Management in Developing Countries*, Bangkok, November 1980.

FIGURE 7–8
Stock Record

					STOCK RECORD								

(Stock Record form with the following fields)

Name or description | Stock number | Location

Primary users or uses | Order quantity

| Jan. | Feb. | Mar. | Apr. | May | June | July | Aug. | Sept. | Oct. | Nov. | Dec. | Reorder point |

Monthly usage summary

Date	Orders or allocations	Qty. on order	Receipts	Issues	Balance	Date	Orders or allocations	Qty. on order	Receipts	Issues	Balance

made, an order received, or an allocation or open order (quantity on order) made, the appropriate entry is recorded. In the case of issues, and perhaps allocations, the balance is compared with the reorder point to see if an order is needed.

Unfortunately, stock record accuracy is a real problem for some companies. Computer-based purchasing and production scheduling systems require very high record accuracy, as does the just-in-time system. Ninety-five percent accuracy was commonly recommended for computer-based systems. Actually, even that goal seems loose. In effect, it says, "5 percent wrong records is OK," which is sure to cause people to distrust the entire system. One hundred percent accuracy—zero defects—is the only reasonable goal.

One effect of just-in-time is to greatly improve inventory control—and record accuracy as well—while reducing the number of inventory records and inventory transactions. Conventionally, factories held piles of semifinished inventory (called *work-in-process*) at dozens of stages throughout the entire production process. Each pile of stock had to be controlled and therefore had its own stock record. Every receipt to or issue from the pile required a transaction.

Today, in a JIT plant, some of the piles of stock from stage to stage may be so small (sometimes zero) and so rigidly monitored by simple, visual controls that their computer stock records are eliminated. In eliminating such computer records, the firm "collapses the bill of materials," which names all the parts that become the final product. Some plants that once had 10 and 15 levels in their bills of materials have cut it to just 2: the purchased materials and parts and the final products. In effect, the computerized "bill" ceases to keep track of the intermediate forms of parts.

A related change in recordkeeping is what is known as the **backflush** (or *postdeduct*) method of accounting for stock usage. In the traditional, prededuct method, each issue of materials from stock triggers a transaction to deduct that quantity from the stock record. In the backflush method, the stock record adjustment occurs when the end product is completed and ready for shipment. It is called *backflush* because the method is to "flush" back through the bill of materials for the end product, deducting from stock records each item used up in its production.

Regardless of whether pre- or postdeduct is used, record accuracy is only half of inventory control. The other half is control of the physical stocks themselves.

Physical Inventory Control

Physical inventory control includes (1) the physical inventory count, (2) stockroom security, and (3) tight operational controls. The physical inventory count is the means of finding inaccurate records. Counting is done in natural physical units such as pieces, gallons, yards, boxes, pounds, and, in JIT, standard containers. For accounting purposes, counts are converted to dollars, but for OM purposes of record accuracy and stock security, natural units are sufficient. Count results are compared with item records, and discrepancies call for recounts, correction of records, and sometimes an investigation.

Some advanced JIT factories—those with a total throughput time from front door to back door of just a few days—count mainly to correct record balances to account for material wasted, or scrapped: Stock count minus stock record quantity equals scrap. If scrap is not accounted for, buyers will sometimes fail to order a needed item, because the stock record falsely shows plenty on hand.

Another reason for keeping accurate stock records is that laws require it. The value of the firm's inventory must be made available to various public agencies—and the value is ascertained in an audit by a public accountant. At Harley-Davidson, the motorcycle manufacturer, the just-in-time system subjects plant inventories to such a high degree of disciplined control (in fixed locations and standard containers) that the auditors just assume it to be constant. Still, Harley must keep track of scrap for purchasing reasons.

If a company has an annual shutdown to count everything, it is taking a **complete physical inventory**. Many firms, especially users of computer-based material requirements planning (MRP) or JIT, rely on an alternative called **cycle counting**. Commonly, in MRP, a small fraction of items are cycle-counted each day; some JIT plants count all items weekly, which can be done quickly by counting containers holding standard kanban quantities—no need to count pieces within the containers. One cycle-counting variation is **event-based counting**, one version of which is to count an item whenever there is a stock issue. Still another variation is **stock-location counting**, in which counting moves from one location to another, often finding "lost" items in the process.

Informed opinion a decade ago was that stockrooms should be "closed"— accessible only to material people. While that viewpoint remains strong in wholesaling and retailing (for some good reasons), it has drastically changed in manufacturing. *Open* stockrooms are now popular for two related reasons: One is the effect of just-in-time, which reduces some stocks to the point where they hardly rest long enough to require much control; the other is the strong influence of focused teams who assume "ownership" of their own resources and responsibility for results.

Physical inventory control is also aided by tight operational controls. In the just-in-time system, inventories move quickly; there is no time to count and check records, and there are few stockrooms for which to provide security. Yet inventory control must be at its tightest in a JIT system. The JIT plant gets tight control by buying, producing, and transporting in exact, readily countable quantities. Prior to the JIT movement, it was common for U.S. companies to accept lots as long as they were within ± 10 percent of the requested amount, and production quantities on the shop floor were equally erratic. A growing number of JIT firms, however, expect *zero* deviation—and come close to achieving that goal. More firms *ought* to do the same.

SUMMARY

Purchasing traditionally has operated by commodity groups, with each purchasing agent responsible for one or a few commodities. Relationships between buyer and supplier have often been adversarial and standoffish. The supplier came to be viewed as a black box, the internal workings of which could only be surmised. Some buyers attempted to probe the black boxes through plant visits and other modes of inquiry, but the majority accepted the adversarial relationship as the norm.

Disappointment with supplier performance, such as late deliveries, poor quality, and incorrect quantities, kept purchasing professionals busy searching for and switching to new suppliers. Suppliers had little commitment to do their best, sensing lack of support from customers. With each new prospective supplier would come necessary but time-consuming supplier evaluation procedures, and new startup costs and problems.

In the 1980s, a movement to replace the buyer-supplier adversarial relationship gained momentum. Supplier development programs came into existence as buyers began to view suppliers as "partners-in-profit." Today characteristics of the partnership relationship include longer contracts, more exclusivity in agreements, fewer (but better) suppliers, high volume between buyer and supplier, lower prices, quality at the (supplier) source, supplier-centered design, frequent delivery of small lots, less burdensome order conveyance, delivery to point of consumption (rather than to a receiving inspection), and mutual openness. Visits between buyer and supplier help maintain the open relationship.

Purchasing procedures depend on what is being bought. The ABC method of classifying materials uses annual dollar volume to assign items to one of three classes. High-valued (class A) items are purchased and controlled with more care than medium-valued (class B) items, which in turn are managed more closely than low-valued (class C) goods.

The purchasing of intangibles, such as services, presents special problems for buyers, because the quality of intangibles is difficult to measure. Often the buyer is at the mercy of the seller, and the seller's professionalism and self-respect are the only guarantees for quality.

Value analysis is a procedure that purchasers developed to meet materials needs (functions) with lower-cost materials and designs. Value engineering (VE) emerged as engineers began to influence value analysis efforts. VE has received federal government support in the form of higher profits for contractors able to lower costs through VE studies of government specifications.

Materials management refers to the group of activities related to the complete cycle of material flow through a firm, from selection of sources to warehousing and shipping of finished goods. Some companies that once had a unified materials management organization recently have split it up and reassigned some materials management duties to operating teams.

Classical make-or-buy analysis is an acceptable policy for relatively low-impact materials. Its simplifying assumptions suggest that it not be used for more complex decisions. One historically popular sourcing strategy was backward integration; it calls for making rather than buying materials even if suppliers must be acquired. A recently popular view is to beware of backward integration and "stick to your knitting"; in other words, buy more of the goods and services one needs and concentrate on doing a few things well.

Inventory control depends on files of inventory records, periodic counting of stocks on hand, and physical control of stocks. The computer record contains item identification, keeps a running balance, and may hold other data. The balance helps decide when to reorder and acts as a deterrent to stock misuse. Records are periodically compared to actual stock counts. The cycle-count method, in which a few, or even all, items are counted daily, is a modern alternative to a complete annual count. High record accuracy is vital in MRP and even more so in JIT. However, the lower inventory levels required in those systems tend to make inventory easier to count and control, with fewer records, transactions, and levels on the bill of materials. Policies favoring tight stockroom security—important when stocks are high—have been replaced by "open" stock policies in many JIT plants, as well as in firms in which operating teams are assuming responsibility for managing their own resources.

KEY WORDS

ABC analysis	Certification	Speculation (in buying)
Soliciting competitive bids	Negotiation	Hedging
	Buying down	Approved supplier

Catalog buyer
Blanket orders
Systems contract
Value analysis (VA)
Value engineering
  (VE)

Standardization
Materials management
Backward integration
Backflush
Complete physical
  inventory

Cycle counting
Event-based
  counting
Stock-location
  counting

SOLVED PROBLEM

Consider the following list of parts, their unit costs, and annual requirements:

Part Number	Unit Cost	Annual Demand
M2	$ 20.00	120
A5	2.00	155,000
A7	8,000.00	13
L8	950.00	6
L4	0.30	7,000
A6	10.00	9,400
M9	6,000.00	70
Q2	400.00	240
Z1	0.50	200

Compute the annual value and percentage of total value for each part. Arrange the nine parts into ABC categories. Plot the cumulative percentages in order from the greatest- to least-valued part.

Solution

First, we compute the annual value for each part, obtain the total annual value of materials, and derive the required percentages:

Part Number	Annual Value	Percentage of Total	Cumulative Percentage
M9	$ 420,000	40.61%	40.61%
A5	310,000	29.97	70.58
A7	104,000	10.06	80.64
Q2	96,000	9.28	89.92
A6	94,000	9.09	99.01
L8	5,700	0.55	99.56
M2	2,400	0.23	99.79
L4	2,100	0.20	99.99
Z1	100	0.01	100.00
Sum =	$1,034,300		

Thus, we see that two parts, M9 and A5, account for over 70 percent of the total annual materials value—likely candidates for treatment as A parts. We might

FIGURE 7–9
Cumulative Percentage of Total Annual Inventory Value

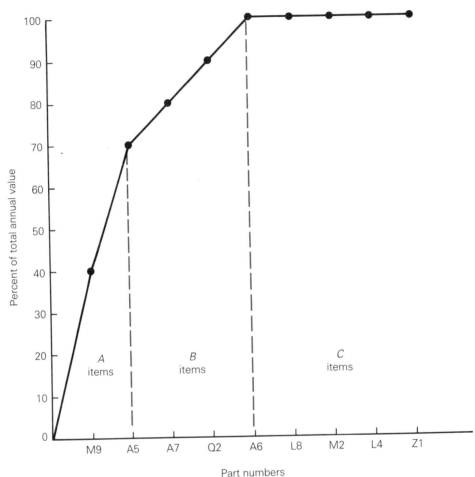

select the next three parts, A7, Q2, and A6, as our class Bs. The remaining items, L8, M2, L4, and Z1, would be the C items. The plot is shown in Figure 7–9.

REFERENCES

Books

Ammer, Dean S. *Materials Management and Purchasing,* 4th ed. Homewood, Ill.: Richard D. Irwin, 1980 (TS161.A42).

Colton, Raymond R., and Walter F. Rohrs. *Industrial Purchasing and Effective Materials Management.* Reston, Va.: Reston Publishing, 1985.

Dobler, Donald W. *Purchasing and Materials Management: Text and Cases,* 4th ed. New York: McGraw-Hill, 1984 (HD39.5.D62).

Leenders, M. R.; H. E. Fearon; and W. B. England. *Purchasing and Materials Management,* 8th ed. Homewood, Ill.: Richard D. Irwin, 1985.

Smolik, Donald P. *Material Requirements of Manufacturing.* New York: Van Nostrand Reinhold, 1983 (TS161.S57).

Wight, Oliver, W. *The Executive's Guide to Successful MRPII.* Englewood Cliffs, N.J.: Prentice-Hall, 1982 (TS161.W5).

Zenz, Gary J. *Purchasing and the Management of Materials,* 5th ed. New York: John Wiley & Sons, 1981 (HD39.5.W47).

Periodicals/Societies

Journal of Purchasing and Materials Management (National Association of Purchasing Management).

Production and Inventory Management (American Production and Inventory Control Society).

Purchasing.

REVIEW QUESTIONS

1. Contrast the black box and the probing buyer approaches to purchasing.
2. In general, how are buyer-supplier relationships changing? Discuss.
3. Explain why the partnership approach favors fewer suppliers.
4. What nontraditional roles does the supplier assume under the partnership approach?
5. How does the partnership approach affect freight and information handling?
6. What is ABC analysis? What are its uses?
7. What are MRO items? How should they be purchased?
8. In what ways does buying intangibles differ from buying tangibles?
9. Is there any similarity between value analysis and standardization? Explain why or why not.
10. What is the materials management concept, and how is it faring today?
11. Why should operating groups have some responsibility for their own materials management activities?
12. Under what conditions would classical (basic) make-or-buy analysis be appropriate?
13. What is backward integration? How does it compare to the concept of "stick to your knitting"? What advantages does the latter have?
14. What does Ohno mean when he states that a true understanding of production control removes the need for inventory control?

15. Under what conditions is the backflush technique most attractive, and why?

16. How can cycle counting effectively replace the complete physical inventory?

PROBLEMS AND EXERCISES

1. The chapter discussion on partnership versus adversarial buyer-supplier relationships examines 12 dimensions on which the relationship might be rated. A number of organizational types are listed below. For each type, identify the relationship's most crucial dimensions. Explain your reasoning.
   a. Aerospace company that is highly project oriented.
   b. Chemical company.
   c. Foundry.
   d. Major accounting firm.
   e. U.S. Navy shipyard.
   f. Private shipyard faced with severe cost problems.
   g. Machine tool manufacturer.
   h. Retail hardware store.
   i. Integrated circuit manufacturer.
   j. Hair-styling salon.

2. You would like to negotiate a long-term (two-year), exclusive contract to sell your automobile repair services to a city government. The city's purchasing agent believes that such a contract would not be in the city's best interests because "free competition wouldn't get a chance to work." Prepare a rebuttal, giving specific ways in which the city might benefit from a contract with you.

3. How do the terms *licensed* and *certified* affect the quality of services rendered by an individual holding either title? Discuss the merits of these measures.

4. John Revere, operations director at CalComp, Inc., a producer of graphics peripheral products, "was given an ultimatum: Shape up the factory or it would be shipped to Singapore" (Bruce C. P. Rayner, "Made in America: CalComp Plots a World-Class Future," *Electronic Business*, August 1, 1988). Among Revere's actions to preserve U.S. operations was his challenge to the team designing the new 1023 model pen plotter: Design it with no more than 20 fasteners (screws, bolts, etc.) bought from no more than 20 suppliers located no farther than 20 miles from the CalComp facility in Anaheim, California.

   How would achievement of these three objectives help keep production in Anaheim? Cite concepts from the chapter in your answer.

5. David N. Burt reports (in "Managing Suppliers Up to Speed," *Harvard Business Review*, July–August 1989, pp. 127–35) that Xerox's copier division was in a cost squeeze and losing market share in the 1970s. Corrective actions included reducing its supplier base from 5,000 to 400 companies. Further,

"it trained suppliers in statistical quality control (SQC), just-in-time (JIT) manufacturing, and total quality commitment (TQC). Under a program of continuous improvement, it included suppliers in the design of new products, often substituting performance specifications for blueprints in the expectation that suppliers should design final parts themselves."

Which of the 12 characteristics of supplier partnership given in the chapter was Xerox following in these actions? Explain.

6. A home remodeling contractor presently subcontracts concrete work, mainly pouring concrete patios. The patios cost an average of $400 each. If the remodeling company were to do the patios itself, there would be an initial outlay of $8,000 for a concrete mixer, wheelbarrows, and so forth, but the cost per patio for labor, materials, and extras would drop to $200.
   a. What is the break-even volume?
   b. Draw and fully label the break-even graph.

7. Othello Corporation has a company uniform that employees may wear if they choose. Othello spends $60 for each new uniform. If Othello made its own uniforms, the variable cost (labor, materials, etc.) would be only $50 each, but it would have to lease a sewing machine for $200 per year.
   a. What number of uniforms per year would be required to break even on the $200 lease cost for the machine?
   b. If 15 new uniforms per year is the projected need, is it better to make or buy uniforms? Explain.
   c. Draw and fully label the break-even graph.

8. A large corporation is considering establishing its own travel department, which would earn commissions on airline tickets. The current cost of airline tickets averages $122 per trip. With an internal travel department earning commissions, it is estimated that the ticket cost would drop to $105 per trip. The salaries and expenses of the travel department would come to $40,000 per year.

   What number of tickets per year would the corporation need to process in order to break even on writing its own tickets instead of buying tickets from an outside agency? If the corporation projects 2,000 trips per year, should it buy or make? Why?

9. Following are eight items in a firm's inventory. Devise an ABC classification scheme for the items. Show which class each item fits into.

Item	Unit Cost	Annual Demand
A	$ 1.35	6,200
B	53.00	900
C	5.20	50
D	92.00	120
E	800.00	2
F	0.25	5,000
G	9,000.00	5
H	15.00	18,000

10. Several examples of uses of ABC inventory classification were discussed in the chapter. Suggest four more uses, and discuss their value.

11. Arrange the following six item numbers into logical A, B, and C classes (put at least one item into each class):

Item Number	Quantity Demanded Last Year	Unit Price
24	2	$ 800
8	10	15,000
37	1,000	0.05
92	3	12
14	80	50
35	20	1.25

12. Arrange the following five item numbers into logical A, B, and C classes (put at least one item into each class):

Item Number	Quantity Demanded Last Year	Unit Cost
109	6	$1,000
083	400	0.25
062	10	10
122	1	280
030	10,000	3

13. Stock records for three inventory items follow:

Stock no.: 3688 Location: B27				Order quantity = 1,000 Reorder point = 680	
Remarks	Purchase/ Manufacture Order No.	Unit Cost	Date	Receipts/ issues	Balance
Adjust for cycle count			2–1 2–17 3–1	– 10 – 400 – 25	1,100 700 675
Order	P-110		3–1 3–15	– 80	595
Receipt	P-110	$50	3–28 4–4 4–20	+ 1,000 – 65 – 100	1,595 1,530 1,430
Adjust for cycle count			5–1	– 5	1,425

Stock no.: 1011 Location: G125				Order quantity = 2,000 Reorder point = 700	
Remarks	Purchase/ Manufacture Order No.	Unit Cost	Date	Receipts/ issues	Balance
Adjust for cycle count			2–1	+2	1,820
			2–10	−500	1,320
			2–18	−700	620
Order	M-88		2–19		
			2-26	−250	370
Back order 30			2–28	−370	0
Receipt	M-88	$2.10	3–2	+2,000	2,000
			3–3	−30	1,970
			3–11	−350	1,620
			3–16	−650	970
			3–20	−500	470
Order	M-110		3–21		
			3–27	−300	170
Receipt	M-110	$2.20	3–30	+2,000	2,170
Adjust for cycle count			4–1	0	2,170

Stock no.: 7092 Location: F62				Order quantity = 20 Reorder point = 4	
Remarks	Purchase/ Manufacture Order No.	Unit Cost	Date	Receipts/ issues	Balance
Adjust for cycle count			2–1	0	15
			2–4	−2	13
			2–9	−3	10
			2–12	−3	7
			2–13	−2	5
Order	P-78		2–18	−1	4
			2–18		
Receipt	P-78	$1,500	2–22	−2	2
			2–23	+20	22
			2–26	−2	20
			2–27	−2	18
Adjust for cycle count			3–1	0	18

    a. What are the average annual demand rates and the average lead times for each item?

    b. For each item, make the computation needed for ABC classification. What class would you expect for each item? Why?

    c. Discuss the firm's physical inventory policies. Include explanation of the cycle-count adjustments for each item.

    d. Explain, if you can, the function of the order quantity and reorder point.

14. Below are four descriptions of inventory *counting* situations. One is an example of good practice; the other three are examples of poor practice. Identify them and explain why they are good or poor. (Note: Pay no heed to the correctness of practices other than counting.)

    a. Allegheny Electric Company is a large electric products wholesaler that carries large stocks. Allegheny uses the counting variation in which class A, B, and C items are counted every time an issue is made.

    b. Shadow Mountain Brass Company, a user of computer-based MRP (material requirements planning), conducts complete physical inventories.

    c. At the Abalone Naval Base, the evening duty officer frequently lets production supervisors into the parts warehouse when they want to return excess materials after hours. The supervisors are supposed to look up the stock locations and put stock away in correct shelves (since stockkeepers don't work the late shifts). The warehouse cycle-counts by the stock-location method.

    d. The Flat Beer Bottling Works cycle-counts materials (such as cans and labels) held in the stockroom using the method of counting after a new order for an item has been received.

15. The purchasing department at OK Industries uses different buying techniques for various items bought. What are two appropriate buying techniques for each of the following items?

    a. Bearings and seals for the factory machinery.

    b. Gear assemblies bought as direct materials in quantities of 8,000 per year.

    c. A special bottle of drafting ink for the company's one draftsperson.

    d. Nails used in the maintenance department.

16. Several types of organizations are listed below, each with different kinds of purchases to make:

Fashions (apparel)
Liquor wholesaler
City government
Major home appliance manufacturer
Electric power company
Furniture manufacturer
Construction contractor

Car rental company
Glass manufacturer
Plastics manufacturer
Computer manufacturer
Food wholesaler
Shipbuilder
Aerospace company

    a. Discuss some key purchasing techniques that would be useful for four of the organization types.

b. Which types of organizations on the list are most likely to be heavily involved in buying intangibles? Explain.

c. Which types of organizations on the list are most likely to use an approved supplier list? Bid solicitation based on specifications? Blanket orders? Explain.

d. Which types of organizations on the list are most likely to use value analysis? Explain.

17. Some years ago, the public school system in Gary, Indiana, contracted with a company to run the Gary schools. The contract featured incentive payments for raising scores on standardized math and verbal tests. What weaknesses do you suppose were present in this contract? Discuss.

18. Value analysis often begins by selecting VA projects from old specifications found in the design engineering files. How is value analysis modified in companies using the just-in-time production system? Why?

19. Following is a list of products to be analyzed by value analysis:

Classroom desk
Mousetrap
Backpack-style book toter
Fireplace grate
Coaster on which to set drinks

Bookends
Electric fan
Bike handlebars
Bike lock
Lamp part shown in the accompanying sketch

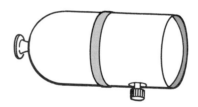

a. Select any four of the above, and define their function or functions in two words as discussed in the chapter.

b. Why is function definition an early and precisely done step in value analysis/value engineering? Explain what this step accomplishes, using some of your examples from question a.

20. Jane A. Doe has just moved to another city and taken a job with a company that manufactures lawn sprinklers, which was exactly the kind of company she had worked for in her prior city of residence. She finds that her new company has three or four times as many different part numbers going into essentially the same models of sprinkler. Is this good or bad? Discuss.

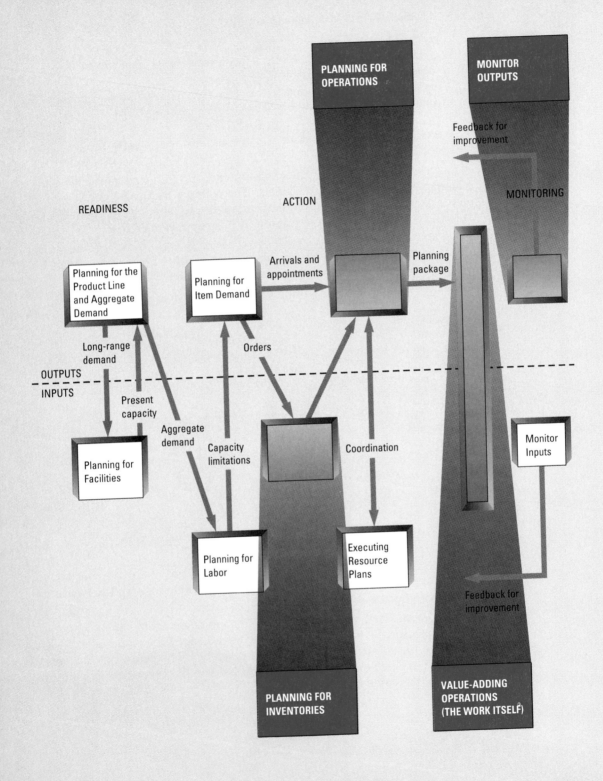

READINESS   ACTION   MONITORING

PLANNING FOR OPERATIONS

MONITOR OUTPUTS

Feedback for improvement

Planning for the Product Line and Aggregate Demand

Planning for Item Demand

Arrivals and appointments

Planning package

Long-range demand

Orders

OUTPUTS

INPUTS

Present capacity

Aggregate demand

Capacity limitations

Coordination

Planning for Facilities

Monitor Inputs

Planning for Labor

Executing Resource Plans

Feedback for improvement

PLANNING FOR INVENTORIES

VALUE-ADDING OPERATIONS (THE WORK ITSELF)

CHAPTER 8

Production-Inventory System Overview

SYSTEM VARIABILITY

INVENTORY SLACKS AND GLUTS

MANAGING THE DELAYS (THE CARRYING COSTS)

Costs of Idle Inventory
Obvious Costs
Semi-Obvious Costs
Hidden Costs
Use of Carrying Cost

DEPENDENT AND INDEPENDENT DEMAND

Material Requirements Planning
Just-in-Time

STALLS, QUEUES, AND BOTTLENECKS

MRP Response
Theory of Constraints
JIT and Other Responses

RELATING INVENTORY TIMING TO QUANTITY

SUCCESS FACTORS

Production and Inventory Control Performance
Inventory Turnover

M ost, if not all, of us walked around in (or on the fringes of) a **production-inventory (PI) system** this morning. Perhaps we were too fixated on getting that first cup of coffee or glass of juice to notice, but our kitchens certainly have all the ingredients of a PI system. *Raw materials*, such as eggs and fresh vegetables; *partially assembled components*, like canned spaghetti sauce; *work-in-process (WIP)*, in the form of casseroles baking or gelatin jelling; and *operating supplies*, like dish towels and sandwich bags, make up the inventory. The cook performs transformation processes, using tools and equipment (knives, blenders, recipes, and coffee pots) to convert the inventory into *finished goods and services*—meals and snacks. That constitutes the production.

We could go on. Determining food budgets, planning meals, procuring inventories, maintaining kitchen tools and equipment, and remembering customer preferences (Johnny doesn't like seeds in his apple) are among the activities that support a smooth-running kitchen PI system.

Beginning to sound complicated? It is. If customers—those who dine—are ever able to say, "That meal was perfect," it won't be for lack of problems that had to be solved. The cook always walks a thin line: right ingredients in the house or not, oven temperature too high or too low, too much or too little salt, food under- or overcooked, courses served too soon or too late. In fact, getting *any* PI system on target—and keeping it there—is a tough job, as we shall see in this chapter. We begin by looking at the root cause of many of the possible problems, variability.

SYSTEM VARIABILITY

A business is like the kitchen, only there are many more things that might go wrong. System *variabilities* cause a lot of the trouble. In any organization, many resources and processes may vary at the same time; the variations can add up and result in extreme mistakes, delays, failures, and total shutdowns. In Figure 8–1, for example, we consider two of the many variations that might occur with purchased materials: variation in delivery time and variation in conformance to a desired specification.

The figure shows the two types of variations plotted over time. Note the "T," which stands for *target*—that is what *should* happen every time. The variabilities are not pluses (goods) and minuses (bads) that cancel out when considered over the long run: One uncooked cake and one burned-to-a-crisp cake do not average

---

*Authors' note: Most of this chapter applies to any kind of activity, not just production. Nevertheless, we stick with the terms *production*, *production-inventory system*, *production control*, and *production control department* simply because those terms are entrenched. Thus we avoid trying to coin new terms, such as *activity control* or *activity-inventory system*, even though they seem to better reflect what we have in mind.

FIGURE 8–1

Variability: Deviation from Target

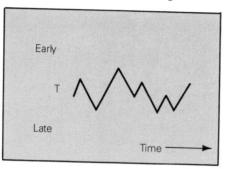

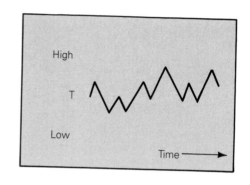

Late or early delivery of material

Material out of specification (bad quality)
on the high side or low side

out to great baking. Variabilities are *all* bads, and their additions only make matters worse. Bad-quality material is not forgiven if delivery is too early.

Consider the following short list:

- Material records showing more or less material than is actually on hand.
- A machine running too fast or too slow, too hot or too cold, etc.
- Machines (computer, punch press, transparency projector—whatever is being used) breaking down randomly.
- An employee (operator or cost accountant, whoever is providing service) overcompensating or undercompensating.
- An employee present or absent (early or late, sometimes doing a task right and sometimes wrong, etc.)
- Yield (percentage of output that is good) varying randomly.

The list could go on; further, any item that could be included in the list results in increasing frustration for customers. Remember from Figure 1–1 that one of the basic customer requirements is *decreasing variability*.

In fact, variability breeds poor performance for other customer wants as well, as Figure 8–2 shows. The graphs show not only bad performance for all five customer wants; they show bad and *variable*—that is, uncertain—performance. Figure 8–2 and our discussion of variability help us reach two conclusions:

1. It is not easy for an organization, especially one with a lot of processes, to perform well in the face of so many interacting sources of variability.
2. It is a formidable challenge to the production-inventory system to plan around or adjust to the sources of variability in order to produce a satisfactory result.

FIGURE 8–2
Variability: Breeding Ground of Customer Uncertainty

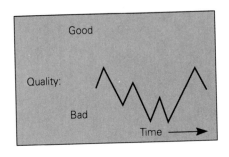

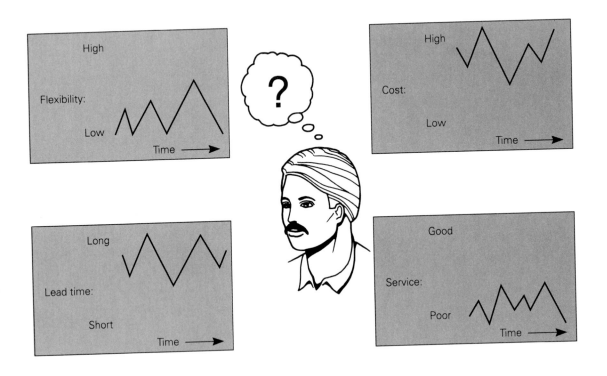

   The remainder of this chapter introduces concepts and terms that are discussed in greater detail in the next six chapters: two chapters on inventory
management that close Part Three and then four chapters (all of Part Four)
on managing different types of operations. We continue by looking at some
basic notions about inventories, responsibilities, system delays, and carrying
costs.

INVENTORY SLACKS AND GLUTS

In manufacturing, it is common for materials to absorb over half of total expenditures. In wholesaling and retailing, the figure is much higher. Control of inventories therefore means control of a major cost.

Controlling inventories does not mean eliminating them. Materials (inventories) are like rivers. They must flow. The rivers are life giving (inventories provide service to customers) and should not dry up; but on the other hand, they should not flood.

At one time, it was thought the "dry-up" and "flooding" costs of inventory could be controlled by professional inventory managers. They cannot be. The main jobs of inventory managers are to keep track of materials and to collect, store, and deliver them. They are inventory caretakers, not controllers of slacks and gluts. Slack and glut problems are *operations* problems, not inventory problems, and they require joint action.

Each of the operations management elements has a role. Buyers and schedulers play a central part. They plan for materials to arrive at just the right time. Ideally, the right time is just in time for use. However, in the case of extreme seasonality of demand, the right time may be well in advance of need: planned buildup of stock to meet the surge of sales.

Plans and timing do not work out if machines break down; thus, machine maintenance plays a role. Long machine setups often make large lots seem necessary, but large lots result in "spiky" arrival of materials, out of phase with material usage rates. Therefore, engineering to cut setup times plays a role. Quality also enters in. If quality is erratic, material will sometimes arrive on schedule but will go directly to the scrap heap or to rework, not into productive use, not toward the ultimate goal: the customer.

Still other functions play roles, but we need not go on. The point is that inventory management cannot be treated in isolation. Inventories grow because of large lots, long setup times, erratic output, and so forth, and thus inventory managers on their own can do little about the amount of inventory on hand. Inventory management is but a part of the greater system that we call the *production-inventory system.*

Inventory management and the PI system as a whole have been reactive in nature. The rule has been: provide for extra inventory as a reaction or response to a wide range of process variabilities. Furthermore, provide ways to reschedule or rearrange priorities in order to get around other variabilities. Progress means relying less on the reactive approach and more on preventing or permanently solving the problems in the first place. People who maintain machines to prevent machine variability, those who cut setup times to pave the way for steady rather than spiky production, and others who act in the *prevention* mode solve problems in advance so reactive solutions are less necessary.

PRINCIPLE: Make it easy to make/provide goods or services without error—the first time.

The PI system and the inventory management function exist, flourish, and are most complex when problems and delays are at their worst and frequency of changes is greatest. Consequently, the costs of managing the delays and changes—the costs of the control system itself—have grown to rival the direct costs of the operations being controlled.[1]

MANAGING THE DELAYS (THE CARRYING COSTS)

Earlier, we said that inventories must flow. That advice becomes doubly important when cost is considered, for cost is like dust—it tends to settle on anything that is sitting around. Rapid flow of materials allows little time for cost (or dust for that matter) to accumulate. Unfortunately, in almost any line of work, materials are mostly in a state of delay or idleness. For example, for every minute that a piece of metal is under a cutting tool, it is likely to spend 5, 10, or even 100 minutes in front of the machine, waiting. When material is idle, it incurs a cost above and beyond its unit price. That cost is called an **inventory carrying cost**.

Office work involves delays and carrying costs too. Office documents undergo little "under-pencil" time compared with the delay time lurking in an in-basket, and jobs on personal computers are usually sitting in a file rather than being worked on. In human services work, the carrying cost includes the cost of clients standing in line.

Costs of Idle Inventory

What do those delays cost? For a client the cost is hard to judge, because most of it is poor-service cost, that is, the cost of the client's involuntary idleness. Likewise, for documents and files the cost of idleness is mostly the cost of slow service to the customer; the costs of storing and carrying the documents and files are minor.

What about materials in a hospital, restaurant, or factory? First, there are the physical costs of holding inventory and the financial costs of having working capital tied up in idle inventory. But those are just the obvious carrying costs—the ones that inventory management writings have always recognized. In recent years, inventory costs have come under closer scrutiny. There is now an awareness of what some call the "hidden inventory." Obvious, semi-obvious, and hidden inventory carrying costs are listed in Figure 8–3.

---

[1]Jeffrey G. Miller and Thomas E. Vollmann, "The Hidden Factory," *Harvard Business Review,* September–October 1985, pp. 142–50.

FIGURE 8–3
Carrying-Cost Elements

Obvious carrying costs:
  Capital cost—interest or opportunity costs of working capital tied up in stock
  Holding cost—stockroom costs of:
   Space
   Storage implements (e.g., shelving and stock-picking vehicles)
   Insurance on space, equipment, and inventories
   Inventory taxes
   Stockkeepers' wages
   Damage and shrinkage while in storage

Semi-obvious carrying costs:
  Obsolescence
  Inventory planning and management
  Stock recordkeeping
  Physical inventory taking

Hidden carrying costs:
  Cost of stock on production floor:
   Space
   Storage implements (e.g., racks, pallets, containers)
   Handling implements (e.g., conveyors, cranes, forklift trucks)
  Inventory transactions and data processing support
  Management and technical support for equipment used in storage, handling, and
    inventory data processing
  Scrap and rework
  Lot inspections

Obvious Costs

In order to be a true inventory carrying cost, a cost must rise with the growth and fall with the reduction of inventory. **Capital cost**, first on the list, clearly qualifies. Businesses frequently attempt to secure bank loans or lines of credit to pay for more inventory. They often use the inventory as collateral for loans.

Only in abnormal situations can a company avoid capital costs. For example, Harley-Davidson people like to crow about the time when they got paid for production *before* they had to pay for the raw materials. On the books, the effect appears as *negative inventory*. (The product was not motorcycles but a subassembly they had contracted to make for another company.) The negative inventory situation arose because of Harley's successful just-in-time efforts: Work sped through the plant—raw materials to finished goods—in a day or two versus the weeks that it would have taken in Harley's pre-JIT days.

Next on the list is **holding cost**, which is mainly the cost of running stockrooms. While the accounting system may consider space and storage implements as fixed costs, they exist only to hold stock; therefore, many or most companies see them as true carrying costs. The other more or less obvious holding costs are insurance, taxes, material department wages, damage, and shrinkage costs.

Semi-Obvious Costs

Semi-obvious carrying costs—the second major category in Figure 8–3—include inventory obsolescence and costs of inventory management and clerical activities. People involved in the latter—inventory planning, stock recordkeeping, and physical inventory counting—do not actually handle stock, and their offices often are some distance away from stockrooms. Perhaps for these reasons, some companies just include those costs as general or factory overhead. Clearly, however, they are inventory carrying costs.

Obsolescence cost is nearly zero when materials arrive just in time for use, but it can be high for companies that buy in large batches and then find that the need for the items has dried up. High-fashion and high-tech electronics companies should be acutely aware of obsolescence as a cost of carrying inventory. Old-line manufacturers, however, might write off obsolete stock only once every 10 years; if so, they may fail to routinely include obsolescence in their calculated carrying-cost rate.

Hidden Costs

Carrying costs tend to be hidden when they co-mingle with other costs. Costs of carrying idle inventory "owned" by operations, that is, stock that has been charged out of stockrooms to operations (factory, sales floor, kitchen, etc.) is the largest hidden-cost component.

Since it is not uncommon for half or more of factory floor space to be used to hold idle in-process inventories in containers and on pallets and racks, those carrying costs can be large. They also can grow because of increased use of costly handling devices: conveyors, automatic storage systems, automatic guided vehicles, and forklift trucks. In the past, most companies failed to include the costs of such factory handling equipment as carrying costs, but increasingly, accountants and operations managers are joining together in pushing a *value-adding* test on conveyors and similar items.[2] If the machine frees an assembler's hands, it helps add value and is a manufacturing cost. But a conveyor that simply spans distance and stores semifinished materials cannot be a manufacturing cost. It is a carrying cost; it literally carries inventory and adds no value to the product.

PRINCIPLE: Cut work-in-process (waiting lines), throughput times, flow distances, and space.

---

[2]John Y. Lee, *Managerial Accounting Changes for the 1990s* (Reading, Mass.: Addison-Wesley Publishing Company, 1987).

Costs of processing inventory transactions also must be scrutinized. They include costs of data-entry terminals, computers, data-entry wages, computer operations, and data processing management. One such cost is for the time that operating employees spend entering inventory usage data into terminals. That cost usually has been charged as a production or service delivery cost—improperly, since it does not add value to the product. More significant are the inventory transaction costs incurred in data processing departments. These have been conveniently bundled into the data-processing departments' total costs, but are—in reality—hidden carrying costs.

One of the major cost-reducing effects of implementing just-in-time is reducing inventory transactions and their processing. Such reductions can be substantial. When Hewlett-Packard's Boise division converted to JIT, it eliminated all work orders. One result was 100,000 fewer computer transactions per month.[3] Since those costs are reducible when inventories are cut, they may be figured in as one more component of the inventory-carrying-cost rate.

Costs of inventory planning, control, and technical support for storage, handling, and data-processing equipment are also carrying costs; however, often they are not treated as such. But they ought to be.

While some companies do consider many of the above as carrying costs, it seems safe to say that virtually none have treated scrap, rework, and inspection costs as carrying costs. Yet they are. Scrap and rework costs are closely related to lot sizes, and large lot sizes generate much or most of the inventories in stock. That is true in processing perishables (throwing out or cutting off rot from food items) and in conventional manufacturing.

Suppose, for example, that fabrication has just completed a lot of 800 gizmo handles. The handles (currently idle inventory) could have any of a number of defects, such as rough finish, scratches, and holes drilled wrong or not drilled at all. An inspector checks for defects, or else defects are discovered at the next process, assembly. For example, the assembler might find that the hole for the shaft has been drilled off center in 10 percent of the handles. Drilling operators are immediately alerted to the problem so they can find the cause and fix it; meanwhile that 10 percent, 80 handles, must be reworked or scrapped. What if the fabrication department made and forwarded handles in lots of 20 instead of 800? The damages would then amount to 10 percent of 20, or just 2 handles, to be reworked or scrapped. The conclusion: Scrap and rework are also carrying costs because they are likely to vary with the amount of idle inventory. In the above example, the amount of idle inventory is the same as the size of the lot (800 or 20).

PRINCIPLE: Produce and deliver at the customer's use rate (or a smoothed representation of it); decrease cycle interval and lot size.

---

[3]Rick Hunt, Linda Garrett, and C. Mike Merz, "Direct Labor Cost Not Always Relevant at H-P," *Management Accounting,* February 1985, pp. 58–62.

Inspection costs merit similar scrutiny. Inspectors converge on large inventory lots like bees to clover patches. The inspectors sort out the bad ones. Some companies avoid large lots by adopting just-in-time techniques, and they avoid large *bad* lots by implementing strict process controls—prevention instead of detection of defects. The tie-in between inspection costs and lot-size quantities is becoming clear, and the conclusion is that even inspectors may be treated as a carrying cost. (We leave it to the reader to speculate on machine repairpeople, parts expediters, and others who respond to work stoppages and stockouts; they are negative inventories, incurring inventory shortage costs. Are those too a type of carrying cost?)

Use of Carrying Cost

Often inventories are such a dominant company cost that virtually every investment proposal has an inventory effect. Therefore, it is important to use a realistic carrying-cost when doing a financial analysis for a proposal.

Traditionally, carrying cost has been stated as an *annual* rate based on the item's value. Older books on inventory management suggested a rate of 25 percent as a good average. Today many North American manufacturers still use 25 percent (or 24 percent—2 percent per month). But that rate is based on the two obvious carrying costs shown in Figure 8–3 and possibly some of the semi-obvious costs.

If all the carrying costs are included, as they should be, what is the proper rate? There are no definitive studies to answer that question. However, the rate surely is at least 50 percent. Indeed, several well-known manufacturers have upped their rates to 50 percent or higher. When more studies have been done to unearth *all* carrying costs, companies will see fit to use higher rates, perhaps as high as 100 percent. To see what 100 percent means, imagine a $50 chair sitting in a stockroom for a year. The owner would be paying another $50 for the chair in the form of the costs of carrying it.

Thinking about moving a machine next to another one to form a cell segment? How much inventory savings are there, and what carrying-cost rate is being used? Suppose the cost of moving the machine is $2,000 and $3,000 of inventory would be eliminated. At a 25 percent rate, the savings are $750 per year (0.25 × $3,000); without doing a discounted cash flow analysis, payback on the investment will take $2\frac{2}{3}$ years ($2,000 ÷ $750 per year), maybe not very attractive. At 100 percent, carrying-cost savings are $3,000 per year and the investment pays for itself in less than a year:

$$\text{Note: Simple payback period} = \frac{\text{Investment cost}}{\text{Annual savings}} \qquad (8\text{–}1)$$

The best-known financial analysis that uses carrying-cost rates is in calculating an *economic order quantity*, a topic that is reserved for Chapter 10. The carrying-cost concept has been introduced here because it is a central cost issue in designing a PI system. Another issue that bears on PI systems is whether demand for an item is dependent on or independent of other items.

DEPENDENT AND INDEPENDENT DEMAND

An item exhibits **dependent demand** when it is to go into or become part of another item. **Component items** go into **parent items**. For example, a tuner is a component that goes into the parent radio receiver. A taco that you buy and eat is an **independent-demand** item; it does *not* go into a parent item (your mouth does not count). The ingredients in the taco, however, are dependent-demand items, since they are components of the parent item.

Sometimes an item appears to be dependent but its parent is unknown. An example is a new tire for sale in a service station. Who knows on what kind of car or truck it will go? The item must be treated as independently demanded. On the other hand, that same tire, if destined for a car in an auto assembly plant, is a dependently demanded component.

The reason for the classification is as follows. The production or delivery schedule for a dependent-demand item matches the demand for the parent; production of the component and parent can be tightly synchronized with little fuss or idle inventory. The schedule for the component is completely accurate relative to the schedule for the parent item or items.

Scheduling the independent-demand item is not so simple. The service station keeps common tires on hand, and this generates a carrying cost. But which common tires and how many of each should be on hand? The station manager can only guess (forecast), and that introduces inaccuracy. To ensure an adequate level of customer service, the manager keeps **buffer stock** (also called *safety stock*) on hand in order to provide protection in the face of forecast inaccuracy.

Retail and wholesale inventories generally are independent-demand items. In factories, service parts (spare or replacement parts) are of that kind, since the parents into which they go are unknown to the producer.

A few decades ago, PI systems were too primitive and data processing too costly for companies to be able to sort out parent-component dependencies. Most parts were ordered based on guesses about how quickly they would be used up, and buffer stock provided protection. Modern PI systems—especially **material requirements planning (MRP)** and **just-in-time (JIT)**—make easy work of planning the dependent demand items. MRP and JIT handle independent demand items, too, but with less precision, since independent demands must be forecast (guessed). Some of the features of MRP and JIT are presented below.

Material Requirements Planning

MRP was perfected in North America in the 1970s. Its first applications were in planning orders for both made and bought component parts needed to meet a known master schedule for final products. At the time of its inception, MRP joined two old techniques with one new one. The old techniques are (1) **bill of materials (BOM) explosion** and (2) **netting**. The "new" technique is **back scheduling**, which means subtracting lead-time requirements from the due date to find the date at which a required item should be started into production or ordered from a supplier.

BOM explosion means breaking down the order for an end product into its primary, secondary, tertiary, components, and so forth, all the way to purchased materials. The purpose is to find out **gross requirements**, that is, how many of each item are needed to produce the ordered quantity of the end product.

Netting comes next: Simply deduct the existing stock balance from the gross requirement to yield the **net requirement**. For example, suppose an end product order is for 100 XYZ tuners, each of which contains 3 JKL resistors. BOM explosion works its way through the product structure to yield a gross requirement for 300 JKL (3 × 100) resistors. If 200 JKLs are already in stock, the net requirement is 300 − 200 = 100. Thus, 100 of the JKLs must be ordered.

At one time, BOM explosion and netting were performed by clerks with calculators and file cards. When unit-record equipment (predecessor of the digital computer) came along, those clerical chores were natural applications. When computers came into use in business, BOM explosion and netting were among the first applications, because they are massive data processing tasks.

Costs of computing and computer memory fell rapidly. Before long, production control and computer experts tacked on the task of calculating order placement time.

This system, with its back-scheduling capability, is called *material requirements planning*. Unlike previous data processing systems, MRP planned inventories as well as production (and purchase) schedules. MRP launched the era of computer-based PI systems.

Just-in-Time

From its origin in Japanese manufacturing, just-in-time (JIT) began to make inroads into Western manufacturing in the early 1980s. Like MRP, JIT plans component parts needed to meet a known master schedule. A key difference is this: MRP feeds a component scheduling system, while JIT provides for component production and deliveries to be triggered by a visual or audible signal instead of schedules.

To illustrate, the MRP approach to ordering eggs for a home would be to calculate on, say, Saturday that you will run out of eggs on Thursday. So, you schedule a buy of one dozen eggs on Wednesday. In contrast, a JIT system might employ three reusable egg containers (each holding a dozen) along with a rule that says when a container is empty, you *may* go for a refill, but when all three are empty, you *must* go refill *without delay*.

Several PI system features are usually present in both MRP and JIT. For example, JIT manufacturers commonly maintain the master schedule, bills of materials, and inventory records in computer files—principally for calculating requirements for purchased items. These same computer applications are also part of MRP.

If full-scale MRP is in use when JIT is launched, there may be some duplication for a while. For example, MRP may schedule or issue a work order notice (buy more eggs on Wednesday), but JIT may overrule the notice (all three egg containers are still full, so no more eggs may be bought). This presents no serious operations problems. Later, after JIT is under way, certain MRP software and data file changes can eliminate the duplication. The result is a PI system that is much simpler *and* cheaper than the full computer-driven MRP system.

A good way of making the transition to JIT is to, little by little, "migrate" blocks of inventory items off the MRP work-order and computer tracking system and onto visual JIT. Some MRP software packages make this kind of transition easy.

Most of the early MRP users enjoyed substantial increases in on-time order completions and reductions in inventories. JIT users gain those benefits as by-products; main goals are quick, flexible response to customer demands; the flexibility comes from quick-change equipment and cross-trained, multiskilled people. Quality improvement and employee involvement are usually so inter-twined with JIT as to be spoken of as additional main goals (or benefits) of just-in-time. Thus, while MRP has a narrow scope—a PI system—JIT touches on a broad range of operations and total company issues, including key customer-service factors.

Thus far, we have considered bare-bones MRP and JIT. One issue that keeps thinkers and tinkerers busy embellishing basic MRP, JIT, and other PI approaches is how to keep work from getting stalled, idled in queues, or stuck in a bottleneck.

STALLS, QUEUES, AND BOTTLENECKS

If you are standing in line waiting to buy a ticket and the ticketing machine or computer breaks down, you are annoyed. So are other people stalled in the growing queue. You are idle inventory at a **bottleneck** process—any process (office, work cell, machine, manager, and so forth) that impedes the flow of work. Generally, we say that demand exceeds capacity at a bottleneck. Repair of the ticketing computer removes the temporary bottleneck in this situation.

When you finally buy your ticket and surrender it to a ticket taker, you may head for the restroom only to find a long queue there. In this case, the bottleneck is "permanent" and stems from failing to plan enough restroom capacity.

Bottlenecks are a serious problem. They are costly, and they drive off cus-tomers. The cause of a bottleneck must be fixed, but that takes time; meanwhile, the PI system must go to work to minimize damages. We shall briefly consider how bottlenecks are dealt with by three types of PI systems: material require-ments planning, theory of constraints, and just-in-time.

MRP Response

How does MRP respond to bottlenecks? The first MRP systems—that is, the computer routines—didn't. Responses to bottlenecks were handled manually. The master scheduler did a rough-cut check on capacity *before* any MRP pro-cessing was done (see *rough-cut capacity planning* in Chapter 6). Production control people on the shop floor juggled jobs in queue at bottleneck machines, split some jobs between two machines, called for overtime, and so forth.

Later, **closed loop-MRP** was developed. In this system, a completion notice is fed to the computer when a job is completed at a work center. The computer calculates an updated job sequence in priority order and issues the new job priority scheme to supervisors every morning. (This is the **production activity control** subroutine of MRP.)

Still later, **manufacturing resource planning (MRPII)** came along. MRPII is a closed-loop system that plans production jobs by the usual MRP method. In addition, MRPII has features for calculating resource needs such as labor-hours, machine-hours, tooling, maintenance service, engineering support, and cash flow.

Typically, MRP and MRPII systems have been based on the assumption of infinite capacity. **Infinite-capacity planning** assumes that machine-hours, labor-hours, and other resources are available to produce the parts required by parent items. However, capacity is actually finite and, in the case of a bottleneck, insufficient; in those cases, the MRP plans are said to be "overstated." But that is not so serious, because the production activity control subroutine can correctively adjust priorities on the shop floor.

Some work has been done to build **finite-capacity planning** into MRP, usually as follows: The computer plans the workload on a certain machine. If the machine capacity is too low—a bottleneck condition—the computer just shoves some of the workload out to the following week's schedule on the machine. Complexities in such systems are enormous, and so MRP with finite-capacity planning has had limited implementation. In the 1980s, however, the finite-capacity planning idea was reborn as a computer software package called *optimized production technology (OPT)*.

Theory of Constraints

Eliyahu Goldratt, developer of OPT, has collaborated with Robert Fox on a newer set of concepts they call the **theory of constraints**.[4] These approaches, which build upon some of the OPT concepts, attempt to schedule and feed work so as to maximize the rate of work flow (and therefore cash flow as well) through bottlenecks or constraints.

One core OPT concept is the distinction between *production or process batches* and *transfer batches*. Cutting transfer batch size allows for movement of portions of a production batch forward to the next work center, instead of waiting until processing is completed on the whole batch. Thus, the next work center receives material for a job and starts it into processing sooner. The idea of small transfer

---

[4]Although OPT-related computer software is still used today (mostly in Europe), the terminology of the theory of constraints (and *synchronous manufacturing,* a newer term intended to incorporate that theory) seems to be fast replacing the OPT terminology. See, for example, M. Michael Umble and M. L. Srikanth, *Synchronous Manufacturing* (Cincinnati: South-Western Publishing Co., 1990) (TS155.U48).

batches has always been a hallmark of JIT production, and Goldratt's emphasis on the point has been helpful to industry.

OPT also calls for increasing production or process batch size, that is, run more of a given high-priority part once it has been set up on the bottleneck machine. The purpose is to cut down on stoppages for machine setup or change-over to a different, lower-priority product, thus making better use of limited capacity.

The theory of constraints also plans for the staging of buffer stocks either before or after certain bottlenecks. Examples include keeping a buffer of already machined parts just past (*after*) a breakdown-prone machine, and keeping a stock of finished items *before* an erratic demand for the item. In other words, provide prudent protection against failure to meet customer demand.

While this is the kind of common sense that most managers would always have understood and practiced, there are two reasons for today's special emphasis on buffer stock policies:

1. In conventional manufacturing, lot sizes were very large. It was common to buy or produce weeks' or months' worth of most items at a time; that meant weeks or months before supplies dwindled to the point where stockout became a concern. In effect, the huge *cycle stocks* (lot-size stocks) did double duty, providing buffer stock protection as well.

   The convenience of using cycle stock as buffer stock disappears as lot sizes and cycle intervals shrink, as they do under the JIT influence. For example, if a dairy makes apple-lemon flavored ice cream every day instead of once a month, it had better think carefully about how much buffer stock to keep on hand. The amount of buffer stock (raw materials, including apple and lemon flavorings, and semifinished product, such as apple-lemon mix) should be based on recent data on fluctuations of demand, yield, on-time deliveries, machine problems, and so forth. While all those variabilities were present when apple-lemon ice cream was made only monthly, the possibility of stockout occurred so seldom that the buffer stock decisions were relatively unimportant, not worth much thought.

2. Some companies, in their pursuit of just-in-time, become sidetracked, and begin to feel that the goal is to eliminate inventory. Most JIT authorities, however, stress that inventory reduction is a lesser benefit (by-product) and that the primary goals are quick, high-quality service to the customer. That often requires prudently placed buffer stock.

We close our discussion of the theory of constraints by noting that it generally treats bottlenecks as permanent, something that must be lived with and worked around. When pushed to increase work flow rate—to meet increased customer demand, for example—those "permanent" bottlenecks must be attacked. When that happens, the theory of constraints must be augmented with solutions from just-in-time, total-quality, and other approaches.

JIT and Other Responses

While MRP/MRPII and the theory of constraints/OPT attempt to employ PI system techniques to plan around existing capacity obstacles, well-run companies are able to keep most of their plants from becoming highly capacity-constrained. It is true that in the early 1980s, when the news media was full of stories about the "productivity crisis," North American industry was indeed in sad shape. It *was* common, even in some highly admired companies, to have large numbers of permanent bottlenecks—chronic conditions of less capacity than demand. Some experts laid the blame on misguided strategies, in which managements milked cash out of their firms and failed to invest in capacity.

It is hard to make any approach work in conditions of chronic capacity constraints. Many firms, especially the most successful, have always understood that. For example, Merck (pharmaceuticals), Milliken (textiles), and most supermarkets plan for a healthy cushion of excess capacity, so as to *prevent* most of the bottleneck problems from arising in the first place. Many others learned their lessons recently and now try to have sufficient resources to be able to schedule them—most of the time—at less than full capacity.

Companies still mired in the mode of permanent bottlenecks can sometimes benefit from PI system treatments (buffering and scheduling around the constraints). But the door is now wide open for using proven measures that are less limited in scope than PI system treatments—ones that incorporate inputs from just-in-time, total-quality management, preventive maintenance, cost accounting, engineering, and marketing. Figure 8–4 provides examples.

Multiple Small Units of Capacity
The first technique in Figure 8–4 recognizes the influence that JIT has in altering the nature of capacity. Instead of a few large units of capacity, JIT encourages multiple small cells, each offering some backup capacity in case another cell falters. Further, since small-cell capacity may be (usually would be) acquired in small units, adding capacity to cope with a bottleneck can be far more affordable than adding capacity in big gulps.

Preference for Profit
The National Association of Accountants, in a survey of its own members, found 78 percent agreed that their accounting systems understated costs and profits on high-volume items and did the opposite for low-volume ones.[5] New costing methods, generally known as *activity-based costing*, help reveal true costs of parts and products. The new costing methods are likely to point out many items in the product line that eat up capacity—and lose money!

Action to cull some of the money-losing and low-profit items can be an effective way to relieve some capacity constraints. In other words, give all high-profit items first priority for capacity, and cull or raise prices on (cutting demand

---

[5]"Outdated Cost-Accounting Systems Call for Activism," *Manufacturing Executives' Report*, November 1989, pp. 1–3.

FIGURE 8–4
Guidelines for Capacity Enhancement

1. Multiple small units of capacity.
2. Preference for profit.
3. Preferred customers.
4. Gaining capacity through quick changeovers.
5. Off-line buffer stock.
6. Gaining capacity through continual improvement.
7. Deliberate temporary bottlenecks to stimulate problem solving.

for) lower-profit items. Formerly, this approach to product and capacity management could not be used with confidence—until ways were found to replace old-style costing with far more precise methods.

Preferred Customers

Just as sensible as the above are approaches that give most-important customers first priority for capacity. For example, a circuit-board producer might have big, exclusive contracts with IBM and Xerox, plus a lot of small-order business. The big contract may require that the board producer *reserve capacity*—a certain number of hours per day or per week—just for the big, important customer. Small-order business then may be scheduled in the unreserved hours. Some suppliers go so far as to pull out people and machines to form a separate unit of capacity dedicated to the big (e.g., IBM or Xerox) contract.

While exclusive contracts once were rare, today's emphasis on partnership with just a few suppliers has made them normal in some industries. The idea of a dedicated unit of capacity also was uncommon in the past, but creating focused cells is a basic element of just-in-time implementation, and the basis for organizing a JIT cell may surely be dedicated service to a certain key customer.

Gaining Capacity through Quick Changeovers

Another JIT tool is concentrated effort to cut product-to-product changeover times. A by-product is reducing losses of capacity to changeovers. Since there are many cases of changeover or setup times being driven down from hours to minutes or seconds, the affected machines could go from being bottlenecks to having comfortable excess capacity. (One tenet of the theory of constraints is to concentrate quick changeover resources on the bottlenecks, but that is often an unnecessary recommendation since the main, widely available resource for quick setup is the mind and common sense of the equipment's operators.)

Off-Line Buffer Stock

A key issue that seems to have been overlooked in writings on the theory of constraints is *location* of buffer stocks. Buried in some of the early books on just-in-time is a pearl of wisdom on the point: Buffer stock needed for a likely but infrequent problem should be kept *in an off-line location*. For example, an Ontario, Canada, manufacturer keeps one day's supply of six sizes of steel blanks in a low-cost, off-line location, because historically the blanking equipment breaks down a few times a year. When it does, someone fetches the buffer stock, and operations carry on—avoiding late deliveries—while the equipment is fixed. If the buffer stock was in line, it would add one extra day of lead time *all year long*, even though it is needed only a few times a year. Furthermore, if in line, it would take up premium space and require constant handling and the usual administrative expenses of work-in-process inventory.

Off-line buffer stock avoids these costs. In addition, off-line stock can be *purified*—subject to 100 percent quality checking to ensure that, if needed, it will be *good* stock. When buffer stock is in line, constantly being used and resupplied in the typical first-in, first-out mode, there is the chance that the buffer stock will be of poor quality—just when it's needed.

Gaining Capacity through Continual Improvement

There are many other new concepts and techniques—especially those associated with employee involvement, total quality, statistical process control, and total preventive maintenance—which act together to continually free up wasted capacity. In other words, in the continually improving firm, capacity problems are continually being solved, and permanent bottlenecks are being converted to temporary ones.

Deliberate Temporary Bottlenecks to Stimulate Problem Solving

Finally, we need to take note of this technique commonly associated with JIT: Cut all inventories between every successive pair of processes to where the customer process sometimes runs out of stock. In other words, deliberately make every process a bottleneck, but not a severe or permanent one; make people feel the pain of a stockout once in a while in order to create the incentive to expose and solve the underlying cause of variability. This is a very aggressive approach to JIT and enforced problem solving; it is not for the faint-hearted.

RELATING INVENTORY TIMING TO QUANTITY

Mrs. X says she always writes eggs on the shopping list when the stock in the refrigerator is down to six. She also says she buys five dozen eggs when she buys. Are those two decisions—timing and quantity of the order—independent? It may seem so, but they are not. Here is why.

Mrs. X has two aims. One is to not tie up too much money and refrigerator space on eggs; a maximum of five dozen is quite enough. The other is to hold down the chance of running out; six eggs as the trigger for restocking, she feels, is just the right amount of protection. What if Mrs. X stayed with six eggs as her **reorder point** but changed her order quantity from five dozen to one dozen? She would find herself *at risk of running out* too often. That is, her egg supply would drop to the six-egg minimum—the danger zone for running out—five times more often than when the order quantity was five dozen. She won't stand for that much risk; she will either go back to a large order quantity or raise her reorder point, say, from six to nine eggs. Either will reduce the long-term frequency (risk) of her running out.

Mrs. X uses common sense, but it applies only for independent-demand items such as eggs (she cannot know when the next need for eggs will arise). In that uncertain situation, her timing for buying eggs is based on reorder points, an approach that calls for a certain amount of idle inventory. She could manage inventories more tightly if she were buying dependent-demand materials for, say, a home business making quilts. In that case, she should buy quilt fabrics (1) only when she books an order or (2) at a rate closely matched to a final-product production schedule.

Any business could follow the reasoning Mrs. X uses in buying eggs: Arrive at a joint policy for determining order quantity and reorder point (timing). Do businesses in fact follow that kind of reasoning? Perhaps some should, particularly wholesalers and retailers, who cannot know when the next demand will arise—the independent-demand case. However, virtually none do; most set order quantities and determine timing or reorder points separately.

To jointly determine order quantity and timing, a business would need a computer package with simulation capability, a type of simulation included in advanced operations management studies. The simulation generally sets risk of stockout at some acceptable percentage and searches for the minimum inventory policy—a total buffer inventory arising from order quantity and reorder point policies—that will protect at that level of risk.

In a well-conceived PI system, the important decisions get most of the attention. Results should show up positively when PI system performance—the next topic—is assessed.

SUCCESS FACTORS

What would a gung-ho, high-performance production control department take pride in? In the late 1970s, it would have been 100 percent on-time completion of work orders. Today, on-time completion of internal work orders takes a back seat to production lead time as the dominant success factor. (But on-time *customer* orders is still a vital success factor.) The reasoning is that production is in better control as the delays are sucked out of the system. Putting it in reverse, if lead time is many weeks, *production is out of control!* Figure 8–5 summarizes the old and the newer concepts of both production control and inventory control.

Production and Inventory Control Performance

Ironically, as lead times fall and production becomes more tightly controlled, the production control department shrinks; fewer expediters and schedulers are needed. For example, when Physio Control (an Eli Lilly company) implemented JIT in the manufacture of defibrillators, work orders were eliminated. The schedule in each of 11 team-built lines (JIT cells) became simply a daily rate, revised monthly. Work-in-process (WIP) inventories plunged to the point where each team-built line kept its own small stocks, and all WIP stockrooms were torn out.

FIGURE 8–5

Performance Measurement in Production and Inventory Management

	Internal Assessment		External Assessment
	Traditional	New	
Production control	Work order completions on time	Production lead time	Annual inventory turnover
Inventory control	Stock record accuracy	Known, invariable quantity of stock and containers in fixed locations between each pair of processess	

Having no scheduling or inventory management to do, the 10-person production control department was abolished, and the 10 people were transferred to other essential jobs, such as supplier development and certification.

In inventory control, perfection has meant 100 percent *stock record accuracy,* which means quantities of stock in the stockrooms that are always in agreement with stock record balances. As lead times and WIP drop, high record accuracy becomes easy to achieve.

PRINCIPLE: Cut work-in-process (waiting lines), throughput times, flow distances, and space.

In advanced JIT plants, all WIP inventory is on the floor, not on shelves in stockrooms. Further, inventory is counted out in exact quantities and placed in a known number of standard kanban containers in predetermined locations throughout the plant. The containers circulate; empties return to preceding work centers for refilling. The quantity of WIP hardly varies from hour to hour and day to day, except by plan. In fact, at Harley-Davidson (an advanced user of kanban), plant inventories are so invariable that the company's auditors have agreed to simply treat the inventory as constant—no need to count and value it every financial period. Counting stock still is done occasionally, if only to find out what the wastage (e.g., scrap) rates are. But counting is simple and quick—just count containers—in the simple, disciplined JIT/kanban system that Harley uses.

In contrast, in conventional large-batch production with long lead times, each item exhibits high variability: from zero stock (or a back-order condition) to thousands of pieces on shelves or in nonstandard containers scattered through-out several locations. Since chances for error are high, including baskets of parts that are simply lost or misplaced, stock counting is a major undertaking and may get done only once a year.

As Figure 8–5 indicates, an emerging concept of inventory control is a known, invariable quantity between each pair of processes. For the PI system as a whole, the new focus is on fast production and stable inventories, with on-time production and high record accuracy as "givens."

Inventory Turnover

Figure 8–5 addresses one more PI issue: *external* assessment of performance. Annual inventory turnover has long been and still is a rather good overall measure—one that accounts for many of the wastes tied up in inventory. Corporate management can use it to assess plant performance, or plant management may use inventory turnover or turnover improvement as one good measure of its own overall performance.

Annual **inventory turnover** is cost of goods sold divided by the value of average inventory. In equation form,

$$T = \frac{CGS}{I}$$

(8–2)

where

$$T = \text{Turnover}$$
$$CGS = \text{Cost of goods sold (annual)}$$
$$I = \text{Average inventory value}$$

To illustrate, assume that a modem costs $30 to produce, is selling at a rate of 1,000 per year, and average inventory is $6,000 worth. What is the inventory turnover? The calculation is as follows:

$$\text{Cost of goods sold (CGS)} = \text{Unit cost} \times \text{Annual sales}$$

$$= \$30 \times 1,000 = \$30,000$$

$$T = \frac{CGS}{I} = \frac{\$30,000}{\$6,000} = 5 \text{ turns per year}$$

The firm is selling its inventory—turning it over—five times per year. Compared with an average of between three and four "turns" for North American industry, that's not bad. (The industry average is much higher in high-volume, continuous production and lower in one-of-a-kind production.) However, some North American plants that used to turn their inventories 3 or 4 times have, through implementing JIT, improved that to 10, 20, 30—even 70 or 80—turns.

A poor turnover—below three—could arise from poorly controlled production in which flow times stretch out over many weeks or months. It could also result when production flow is fast but achieved with high inventories. Thus, turnover is a good measure of *PI system* performance.

It may be useful to calculate turnover by category: raw materials, work-in-process, finished goods, and total inventory. Extending the example of the modem manufacturer, assume that $1,500 of the $6,000 average inventory is finished goods, $1,500 is raw materials, and $3,000 is WIP. Assume further that the cost of labor and overhead to convert raw materials to finished goods is $12,000, which is used in calculating WIP turnover as follows:

$$T_{\text{WIP}} = \frac{\text{Manufacturing costs}}{\text{WIP}} \qquad\qquad (8\text{-}3)$$

$$= \frac{\$12,000}{\$3,000} = 4 \text{ WIP turns per year}$$

To calculate raw material (RM) and finished goods inventory (FGI) turnover, we may assume the price of purchased materials plus purchasing overhead to be $14,000 and the overhead cost to carry finished goods to be $4,000. Then,

$$T_{\text{RM}} = \frac{\text{Purchasing costs}}{\text{RM}} \qquad\qquad (8\text{-}4)$$

$$= \frac{\$14,000}{\$1,500} = 9.3 \text{ RM turns per year}$$

$$T_{\text{FGI}} = \frac{\text{Finished goods overhead costs}}{\text{FGI}} \qquad\qquad (8\text{-}5)$$

$$= \frac{\$4,000}{\$1,500} = 2.7 \text{ FGI turns per year}$$

Some firms also compute a "RIP" turnover, which includes both raw materials and WIP. One company that uses the RIP measure is TRW's Mission Products Division in Texas. The division, one of the more successful JIT converts, improved its RIP turnover from 3 to about 35 per year.

SUMMARY

The production-inventory (PI) system in any business is sure to be plagued by variabilities: arrivals too early or too late; performance too high or too low, too fast or too slow; or machine breakdowns and yields varying randomly over time. The variabilities are undesirable and detract from serving the customer. When added to otherwise poor performance in meeting other customer wants, variability only makes things worse. PI systems try to plan around the variabilities; better PI systems try to eliminate them.

The inventory element of the PI system can be controlled only partially by inventory managers (the material caretakers). Material slacks and gluts are caused by process variabilities and thus must be dealt with by engineers, machine maintainers, quality specialists, and others who have the skills to bring processes under control. Their failures call the PI system into action, but the system costs themselves are high.

With inventory comes inventory carrying costs: capital invested, stockrooms, inventory administration, obsolescence, space, storage and handling gear for factory stock, data processing support, stockroom and handling equipment and support, scrap and rework, and lot inspections. The last six items make up hidden inventory costs and are often co-mingled with other costs categories; only recently have they been seen as inventory carrying costs.

Annual carrying cost is commonly set at 25 percent of the inventory's cost. With hidden costs included, the rate goes as high as 50 or even 100 percent. The rate is important, since in many businesses inventory is a dominant cost that is affected by almost any proposed major change.

Modern PI systems take advantage of the dependence of component parts on demand for the "parent" item the component goes into. Computers can synchronize component schedules with parent-item schedules.

PI systems were manual before decreasing computing costs made computer-based scheduling affordable. Clerical people exploded end-product schedules to yield gross requirements for component parts and then subtracted stock on hand from the gross requirements to obtain net requirements. Computers took over those tasks, and the addition of a routine for back scheduling from the due date to yield an order date resulted in MRP.

Closed-loop MRP added ability to adjust work-order priorities on the shop floor whenever work got stalled or experienced other problems. The approach was needed because the MRP assumption of infinite work center capacity tended to result in overstated plans. The next enhancement—manufacturing resource planning (MRPII)—permitted planning of resource requirements (besides inventory) to support a production schedule.

While MRP/MRPII coordinate production and inventory movements via schedules, just-in-time (JIT) does it via on-the-spot visual signals of an immediate need for more materials. As JIT is superimposed on an existing MRP system, some of the computer routines are reduced or turned off, but basic computerized material recordkeeping and purchasing usually remain. While MRP/MRPII are strictly PI systems, JIT is a broad set of concepts that emphasizes quality and employee involvement.

One of the great challenges to a PI system is coping with capacity bottlenecks and constraints. The MRP/MRPII method is initially to presume infinite capacity and then adjust to bottlenecks by rescheduling affected jobs and by reprioritizing jobs already in process. A newer set of coping approaches is a *theory of constraints,* which aims at maximizing throughput rate and cash flow; its tools include adjusting the sizes of transfer batches and production quantities, and prudent placement of buffer stocks—after an undependable process or before a spikey demand. Today's emphasis on buffer stocks stems from loss of buffering as JIT drives down lot-size (cycle-stock) inventories; too much reduction of inventory is too much exposure to risks and variabilities.

While PI systems provide some help in dealing with capacity constraints, non-PI system approaches offer much more help. The penny-pinching ways of recent decades—failure to invest in capacity—appear to be root causes of the capacity problems. Many good companies today are willing to spend enough to avoid the chaotic conditions that arise when demand exceeds capacity all over the plant. That reduces the fixed bottlenecks and, at the same time, the severity of temporary or floating bottlenecks, particularly if the spending is for multiple smaller units of capacity, which offer mutual backup protection.

Several broad-scope treatments are available for coping with temporary bottlenecks. The new activity-based costing techniques open the door to pinpointing high-profit items and giving them first preference for capacity. The trend toward big, exclusive contracts makes it possible to reserve capacity for the big customers. The many companies engaged in quick changeover projects and many other continual improvements find, as a by-product, that they continually free up wasted capacity, thus easing capacity constraint problems. The "old" JIT technique of putting buffer stock off line allows lead times to be compressed at the same time as risks of stoppages are reduced. Finally, the aggressive JIT approach of drawing down buffer stocks to the pinch point, thus making every process a temporary bottleneck, can drive the pace of improvements, many of which relieve capacity constraints.

PI system performance once was assessed based on on-time work order completions and stock record accuracy. With JIT driving lead times down and inventories down and into exact positions in known quantities, the old perfection criteria are becoming givens. The new measures center around rapid production and inventory stability.

Inventory turnover—the number of times average inventory is "sold" annually—is a good overall way to assess a PI system from an external vantage point. Some JIT plants are driving up annual turnover rates from industry average values of 3 or 4 to rates 10 or 20 times that high.

KEY WORDS

Production-inventory
  (PI) system
Inventory carrying cost
Capital cost
Holding cost
Dependent demand
Component item
Parent item
Independent demand
Buffer stock
Material requirements
  planning (MRP)

Just-in-time (JIT)
Bill of materials (BOM)
  explosion
Netting
Back scheduling
Gross requirement
Net requirement
Bottleneck
Closed-loop MRP
Production activity
  control

Manufacturing
  resource planning
  (MRPII)
Infinite-capacity
  planning
Finite-capacity
  planning
Theory of constraints
Reorder point
Inventory turnover

SOLVED PROBLEMS

1. A print shop often has numerous jobs stacked up before the huge paper slicing machine. Even by running the slicer overtime and with extra shifts, there are days when the slicer cannot keep up with the workload. What is a JIT solution to the problem? What solutions would be consistent with the theory of constraints concept?

Solution

JIT tries to provide "permanent" solutions to capacity problems. In this case, perhaps one or two small, simple paper-cutting machines could provide backup and ease the bottleneck. Other techniques favored under JIT are quick setup to reduce the machine time lost in changing from one size of paper to another; high levels of preventive maintenance on the machine to keep it from breaking down in the middle of a busy day; and high levels of quality control so that the machine's limited capacity will not be eaten up by rework.

Usable theory of constraints concepts include: (1) consolidating similar orders—same paper sizes, for example—into a large production batch, thus minimizing setup frequency, and (2) moving small transfer batches forward from the slicer to the next processes rather than waiting for completion of an entire production run. Both concepts help get more work per day through the bottleneck machine during busy times.

2. One division of J. W., Inc., produces detergent. Its current RIP inventory turnover is 9. Another division, producing a line of electronic timing devices for home and industrial use, has a RIP turnover of 4. Both divisions have about the same annual costs of purchased materials plus cost to convert them to finished goods: $2 million.
   a. What is the average total of raw materials and WIP for each division?
   b. Should the turnovers be used for comparing the two divisions or for some other purpose?

Solution

a. The turnover formula must be inverted from

$$T_{RIP} = \frac{\text{Purchasing and manufacturing costs}}{RIP}$$

to

$$RIP = \frac{\text{Purchasing and manufacturing costs}}{T_{RIP}}$$

Then,

For detergent: RIP = $2,000,000/9 = $222,222

For timers: RIP = $2,000,000/4 = $500,000

b. It is unreasonable to compare turnovers. Detergent is made in a continuous process, which should not give rise to nearly as much idle inventory as in the case of timers. It *is* reasonable to regularly assess the trends in RIP turnover separately for each product. High RIP turnover is an overall sign of improvement in division performance.

REFERENCES

Books

Fogarty, Donald W., and Thomas R. Hoffman. *Production and Inventory Management.* Cincinnati: South-Western Publishing, 1983.

Goldratt, Eliyahu M., and Jeff Cox. *The Goal: Excellence in Manufacturing.* Croton-on-Hudson, N.Y.: North River Press, 1984.

Hall, Robert W. *Attaining Manufacturing Excellence.* Homewood, Ill.: Dow Jones-Irwin, 1987.

———— *Zero Inventories.* Homewood, Ill.: Richard D. Irwin, 1983.

McLeavey, Dennis W., and Seetharama L. Narasimhan. *Production Planning and Inventory Control.* Boston: Allyn & Bacon, 1985 (TS176.M374).

Plossl, G. W., and O. W. Wight. *Production and Inventory Control.* Englewood Cliffs, N.J.: Prentice-Hall, 1967 (HD55.P5).

Schonberger, Richard J. *Japanese Manufacturing Techniques: Nine Hidden Lessons in Simplicity.* New York: Free Press, 1982 (HD70.J3S36).

Vollmann, Thomas E.; William L. Berry; and D. Clay Whybark. *Manufacturing Planning and Control Systems,* 2nd ed. Homewood, Ill.: Richard D. Irwin, 1988.

Periodicals/Societies

Journal of Operations Management (Operations Management Association).

Production and Inventory Management (American Production and Inventory Control Society).

Target (Association for Manufacturing Excellence).

REVIEW QUESTIONS

1. Describe three types of process variabilities. What are their effects on work flow? On customer service?

2. Can material managers control inventory excesses and shortages? Explain.

3. What are capital costs and holding costs?

4. Why have some costs of carrying inventory been semi-obvious or even hidden?

5. What is the meaning of a 35 percent carrying cost? Is it realistic today? Discuss.

6. Give an example of a dependency chain four levels deep (component into parent, which goes into *its* parent, etc., through four levels).

7. Why are buffer stocks more necessary for independent- than for dependent-demand items?

8. Distinguish between a permanent and a temporary bottleneck.
9. How does a PI system determine when to place an order for a component material? List the steps.
10. What is closed-loop MRP?
11. What does MRPII do for overall performance that basic MRP does not?
12. What does the theory of constraints do about bottlenecks?
13. What is a good way of coping with "permanent" bottlenecks?
14. How is JIT supposed to handle bottlenecks?
15. How does lot size affect risk of stockout?
16. When should buffer stock be off line and why?
17. Why is 100 percent on-time completion of work orders inadequate as an indicator of perfection in production control?
18. What is the usefulness of calculating inventory turnover?

PROBLEMS AND EXERCISES

1. Elmo's Burger Shoppe sells $50,000 worth of plain burgers per month. The profit margin is 10 percent. Total inventory on hand averages $12,000. What is the inventory turnover? Should Elmo separately calculate turnovers for purchased materials, WIP, and finished goods?

2. ABC Specialties, Inc., produces a wide variety of office and home products, one of which is a small mail scale. Annual cost of goods sold for the scale is $100,000, which includes $60,000 to purchase raw materials and $35,000 to convert them to finished goods. The average value of recently purchased plastic and metal parts and materials, plus fasteners, is $10,000; the value of partially completed production is $5,000; and the value of completed finished goods is $15,000. Compute separate and total inventory turnovers. Is ABC managing scale production well? Explain.

3. Process variabilities induce firms to carry protective excess inventories; the greater the excess, the greater the inventory carrying costs. Process variabilities also can result in inventory shortages. The greater the shortage, the greater *which* cost? Explain.

4. Iota Company produces bicycle reflectors. Currently Iota buys the main raw material, bags of plastic pellets, in large quantities about three times a year. Its policy is to order another lot when stock on hand falls to five days' worth (the reorder point). Now Iota is considering a just-in-time purchasing approach: small quantities ordered frequently, perhaps as often as every two weeks.

   There is a risk that the supplier will deliver late. Will JIT purchasing increase or decrease the risk? Should the reorder point be changed? Explain.

5. A plant specializing in precision machining is considering buying a numerical control (NC) machine with an installed cost of $200,000. The NC machine can perform multiple metal-cutting operations by successively rotating a mounted metal work piece and selecting cutting tools from a magazine. Thus, it would incorporate operations now done at scattered machine centers and would eliminate idle materials between machine and stockroom. Average inventory reduction from using the NC machine is estimated at $60,000. Also, the single machine will cost less to set up and operate than the present multiple machines—an additional savings of $50,000 per year.
   a. If 20 percent is used as the inventory carrying cost, how quickly can the investment pay for itself (what is the payback period)?
   b. Suggest four more important kinds of savings that are likely but less obvious than savings from materials and direct labor. Recalculate the payback period using a larger, more realistic carrying cost (your best estimate).

6. Find the article cited in note 3 in the chapter. How did Hewlett-Packard's Boise division eliminate 100,000 computer transactions per month?

7. Jack is an assembler at Penrod Pen Company. His job is to pack a gold-plated pen and pencil, plus guarantee card, into a gift box. He puts the completed box on a chute, which feeds a machine that applies an outer wrap. (The chute holds a maximum of five boxes.) As an employee, Jack exhibits normal human failings, especially these:
   (1) Occasionally he drops a pen, pencil, or card and while he searches for it on the floor, the outer-wrap machine runs out of boxes to wrap and stops. Several times the machine has lost 50 to 100 cycles while Jack was searching.
   (2) Every few hours the assembly line is changed to produce a different model of pen and pencil set, which requires a different guarantee card. But Jack often forgets to change to the correct card. (Inspectors discover the error through random sampling.) It is not uncommon to have to tear open as many as 1,000 boxes to rework them, and when that happens an order for an important customer is usually late.
   The supervisor has a solution to Jack's variable performance: *extra inventory.*
   a. Explain exactly how extra inventory can serve as a solution.
   b. Jack has ideas for certain types of fixtures and automatic checkers which, he feels sure, would immediately catch either of his chronic errors. The devices, installed at his end of the feeder chute, would eliminate the need for the extra inventory that his supervisor has proposed. The supervisor weighs the cost of the devices against the savings on inventory carrying costs using Penrod's usual carrying cost rate of 25 percent. Jack feels the rate is too low. Is Jack right? Be specific in your answer.

8. Over-Nite Mail Corporation experienced two serious problems as business grew in the past 18 months: (1) Over 10 percent of its service orders take three days or more for successful delivery; (2) record accuracy—showing

where orders are in its delivery system—is poor; random sampling shows that 30 percent of the records are inaccurate (for example, a log book shows that a piece of mail is in the delivery truck while it is really still in the sorting room). A recent investment in a computerized order tracking system has improved record accuracy to 99.5 percent. Should that give the company a significant competitive edge over competing overnight delivery companies? Explain. In your explanation, describe how the company should measure the effectiveness of its order control system.

9. A plant that produces industrial thermostats has successfully implemented MRPII. One result is that mean production lead time (from raw material to finished goods) has improved modestly, from 9.3 to 8.7 weeks. Two large improvements are: (1) Stock record accuracy has risen from 68 to 99.2 percent, and (2) on-time completion of work orders is up from 60 to 97 percent. Plant management and the consulting company that assisted in the conversion to MRPII are delighted; they claim that inventory control and production control are approaching perfection. They expect the results to stem some of their business losses to domestic and foreign competitors. Are their expectations realistic? Are the inventory and production control really so good? Discuss.

10. Currently the major bottlenecks at a plant that makes electrical fixtures are the paint line and the 600-ton press that stamps out sheet metal parts. Hundreds of different kinds of parts must pass through those processes, and many jobs get stalled in queues before one or both.
    a. What kinds of solutions would be recommended if the theory of constraints concepts were employed?
    b. What are likely to be the main kinds of solutions to these bottleneck problems under JIT?

11. The equipment used in a campus testing service includes order-entry terminals, optical scanning equipment, computers, and printers. At certain times, one or more of the machines has days' worth of jobs queued up. What do you recommend, and why?

12. A producer of decorative brass and stainless steel fixtures has implemented an MRPII system. A newly hired materials manager has just told the plant manager that it would have been far better to have implemented theory of constraints concepts or JIT. Dismayed, the plant manager asks, "But can't we just add theory of constraints or JIT to our present MRPII system?" How should the materials manager respond?

13. Figure 8–1 shows variability in relation to target performance. The point was made in the chapter that positive and negative variations do not cancel one another out. How do these ideas compare with Taguchi's social loss concept (discussed in Chapter 4)?

14. "Customers want increasing flexibility, but they also want decreasing variability." Use material from the chapters you've studied thus far and write a brief essay explaining this statement.

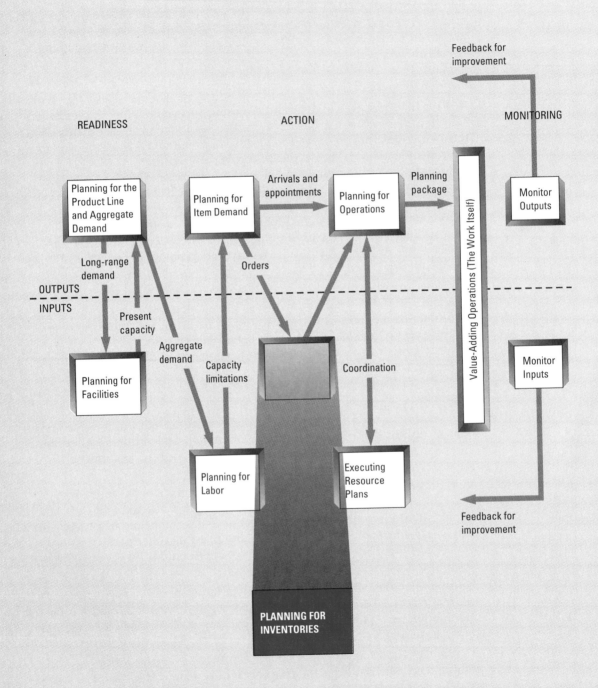

READINESS

ACTION

MONITORING

Feedback for improvement

Planning for the Product Line and Aggregate Demand

Planning for Item Demand

Arrivals and appointments

Planning for Operations

Planning package

Monitor Outputs

Long-range demand

Orders

OUTPUTS

INPUTS

Present capacity

Aggregate demand

Capacity limitations

Coordination

Monitor Inputs

Planning for Facilities

Value-Adding Operations (The Work Itself)

Planning for Labor

Executing Resource Plans

Feedback for improvement

PLANNING FOR INVENTORIES

CHAPTER 9

Inventory Timing: JIT, MRP, and Related Issues

WHAT DRIVES INVENTORY TIMING?

Push versus Pull Systems

Conveyors: Pull or Push?

JIT AND KANBAN

Kanban Signals

Card Systems and Kanban Removal

Kanban in Services

Kanban Applications: A Summary

MATERIAL REQUIREMENTS PLANNING

Basic MRP

MRP Computer Processing

Scheduled Receipts and the Open-Order File

Multiple Parents and Scrap Allowances

Independent Demands for Component Parts

Distribution Requirements Planning

Closed-Loop MRP

Manufacturing Resource Planning (MRPII)

Benefits of MRP and MRPII

REORDER POINT

Perpetual System

Two-Bin System

ROP Calculation

Replenishment Cycle

Periodic System

BUFFER STOCK

Micro-Response Analysis
Physical Control of Buffer Stock
Statistical Safety Stock
Safety Stock in MRP

CASE STUDY: HYGAIN-TELEX

Suppose that a house is being remodeled. A bedroom needs new closet shelves, carpeting, electrical fixtures and wiring, window curtains and blinds, some plaster repair, and two coats of paint. Now, imagine that room if *all* the new materials were to arrive at the same time to be placed inside the room. Work can't get done until the room is cleared.

One solution is to move the materials elsewhere—perhaps store them in the living room until they are needed. But if remodeling is also to be done in the living room, or if people living in the house complain, the materials get moved again. Moving materials around to keep them out of the way is time consuming, and expensive.

The root problem is that most of the materials arrived too soon. The opposite situation, arriving too late, is also bad. No work gets done. The best solution, of course, is for materials to arrive just when they are needed, or just in time.

Unfortunately, most companies do spend a lot of time moving things around and waiting for materials to arrive. Whatever the business—home-remodeling, manufacturing, or income-tax preparation—such waste is caused by the same problem: *poor inventory timing*. Invariably, the results are higher costs of operations, longer lead times, and poor customer service.

There are a number of approaches for averting those bad results of poor inventory timing. In this chapter, we consider the timing features of just-in-time, material requirements planning, and traditional reorder point methods. But first we look briefly at the general issue of what drives inventory timing decisions.

WHAT DRIVES INVENTORY TIMING?

The forces that drive inventory timing decisions seem to fall into two camps: the push system, in which inventory is pushed forward by the provider, and the pull system, in which the user is in command.

Push versus Pull Systems

Imagine a coffee machine that keeps filling cups and setting them aside on a conveyor, regardless of the presence of coffee drinkers. That is a push system. A **push system**, driven by the maker (or provider), pushes out the product without tight connection to rate of use (demand) and user problems.

Of course, coffee machines are not push systems; they respond on demand. In other words, they respond to a "pull" signal from a buyer or user. A **pull system**, driven by the user, pulls the product forward at the rate of use and causes the maker to respond to user problems. (Where possible, the maker responds directly to the user. Sometimes a "middleman"—a provider or supplier—intervenes. The definitions of push and pull apply either way.)

The push system dominates in nearly all types of operations. In services, long lines of people are the inventory pushing forward. In factories, a typical scene is of a conveyor or pallets loaded with idle inventory.

While the push mode seems wasteful, it has been popular for three main reasons:

1. The costs of making a product in advance and carrying it have been grossly underestimated, as the discussion of carrying costs in Chapter 8 indicates.

2. Use and production rates typically are irregular, plagued by assorted variabilities (see Chapter 8). Process variables can be fixed, but the *final* consumers' irregular buying patterns are here to stay. That variability can ripple downward through all stages of operations, which has yo-yo-like effects on capacity and generates overtime and idleness costs.

3. The maker and the user are usually out of touch; that is, the maker does not receive regular communications from the user as to use rate, so the maker just keeps pumping out product.

Sometimes, what appears to be a pull system needs closer inspection. Consider, for example, when a salesperson removes a hamburger from the ramp in a fast-food establishment. That might free a space for the cook to place another burger at the top of the ramp. This sounds like a pull system, but the system is not worthy of being considered "pull" if the ramp is too long. If the ramp is long enough to hold 30 minutes' worth of burgers, they could be cold before they get eaten. Sounds like push, not pull.

In factories, one type of ramp used to move parts forward is called a *flow rack*; conveyors can serve the same purpose. Again, though, if the flow rack or conveyor is long enough to hold several days' worth of stock, it can hardly be considered a pull system. Because of their popularity as inventory movers, conveyors deserve more attention.

Conveyors: Pull or Push?

In most of the world's factories that assemble major appliances, motorcycles, and automobiles, a powered conveyor pulls work from one assembly station to the next and the idle inventory between stations is zero (or, in a few cases, one unit). Such assembly lines may seem to be examples of "pure" pull systems, because when things are going well the conveyor pulls just one unit forward at a time, and when there is a severe problem, the line is stopped. The weakness is that most conveyor-paced lines stop only for severe problems. They fail to respond to individual assemblers' problems, which violates our earlier definition of "pull."

Some JIT users equip their conveyor-paced assembly lines with devices for operating in the true pull spirit: Each assembler has access to a switch for stopping the line or calling for help. When assemblers have that authority—and actually use it—the assemblers come to feel that they are running the line and pulling work forward. Otherwise, a moving chain or belt just pushes work on the assembler. Thus, pull and push reflect, in part, employees' *feelings*—and degree of employee involvement.

Conveyor-paced assembly lines converted so assemblers can use stop, help, and sometimes slowdown switches to pull work forward and control the line are becoming common in a few industries. Included are assembly plants operated by the big automakers, General Electric's dishwasher and refrigerator plants, Harley-Davidson's motorcycle assembly plant, and some of John Deere's farm equipment plants. In those companies, the policy of stopping a line used to be traumatic, but now it is considered a routine, welcome event.

High-speed fill-and-pack lines (packaging foods, drinks, pharmaceuticals, home care products, and the like) are similar to assembly lines for autos and major appliances. Most fill-and-pack lines, however, hold large numbers of idle units on conveyors between processes. JIT requires shortening conveyor lengths and installing stop and help lights that go on automatically or are actuated by the operator when trouble arises.

To summarize a bit: In push systems, the customer and provider are not—or do not *feel*—connected; the provider is the driver and has little choice but to continue to make materials move by shoving more into the system, hoping the customer really wants it. Pull systems, on the other hand, work to close the gap between provider and user, place the user in the driver's seat for controlling the timing of inventory movement, and operate with the goal of reducing wastes associated with idle inventories.

The remainder of the chapter is devoted to the study of inventory timing techniques. We begin with a JIT technique, *kanban*, that exemplifies a pull system.

JIT AND KANBAN

In Chapter 8, we described **just-in-time** not only as a production-inventory (PI) system, but as a broad set of operating concepts. As such, it appears in several chapters of this book. Our focus here, however, is on the inventory timing features of JIT. Because it operates as a pull system, JIT needs some means for a customer to signal the provider that it is time for more work to be sent along the system. That role is filled by *kanban*.

Kanban Signals

The general meaning of **kanban** is a communication or signal from user to maker (supplier), saying "Send me more widgets (or medical records, or customers)." The narrow meaning (from the Japanese) is *card* or *visible record*. Sometimes a written kanban record is required, because kanban is a disciplined technique that must tell exactly what is to be forwarded and in what quantity. In other words, kanban is not meant simply to keep the user busy with more work; its aim is to fill a real need for a specific kind of work. Think of it like this: JIT is a way to provide needed or wanted goods and services and kanbans are communication links that manage JIT. Any signal that communicates a customer's need to the supplier will do, and several types of kanban signals have emerged.

FIGURE 9–1
Verbal and Golf Ball Kanban Signals

Verbal and "Golf Ball" Kanban

Figure 9–1 shows two examples of inexpensive yet effective kanban. The first example is a verbal request, conveyed by intercom, phone, electronic messaging, or even a shout.

The second example in Figure 9–1 is "golf ball" kanban (no joke—several manufacturers use it). Here the user requests more parts from the maker by rolling golf balls down the inclined pipe. The golf balls may be painted different colors, with each color standing for a certain type of part. (There is nothing sacred about using golf balls; anything that will roll or slide will do.)

Verbal and golf ball kanban require an element of human attention. Another version of kanban, automatic kanban, manages itself—without human scrutiny.

Automatic Kanban

Figure 9–2 shows a kind of *automatic kanban,* using a limit switch. Demand from Machine Y is irregular, governed by irregular pulls from further along the process. The switch, positioned in the feed mechanism of Machine Y, provides the pull signal. When piece 2 slides into a position where it blocks the switch, a

FIGURE 9–2

Pull Signals from Limit Switches

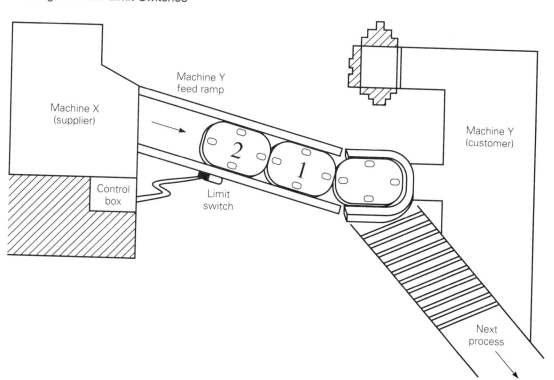

FIGURE 9–3
Kanban Containers at Physio Control Company

signal halts Machine X. When Machine Y pulls the next unit forward for processing, the switch is "tripped" and Machine X gets a signal to provide another piece. In this example, kanban = 2, but of course, that quantity can be changed.

Limit switches, "electric eyes," and other kinds of detectors can be designed to provide kanban management of flexible operations in which work may differ from unit to unit. That includes flexible manufacturing, but also may apply to such automated processes as opening parking lot gates to small cars or huge tractor-trailer rigs, and sorting different-sized packages. In those cases, the automatic kanban devices are not performing the value-adding operations themselves; rather, they are controlling the amount of inventory—and therefore waiting time—in the waiting lines.

Container-as-Kanban

Other potent types of kanban are usable under certain conditions. One type simply uses the container as the signal. That works fine when the container clearly is designed for a certain part and no one would put the wrong part in it. Figure 9–3 shows examples of container-as-kanban. The containers are of a special design used at Physio Control Company of Redmond, Washington. They hold partially assembled heart-monitoring devices. The three-layer container holding three units was designed for Physio's first JIT assembly-and-test line. The single-layer model was designed for Physio's second line and later was put into use on nine more lines (for various models of Physio's line of electronic medical products). All the assembly-and-test lines are composed of about 10 stations arranged close together in a roughly U-shaped configuration. With this arrangement, Physio is able to get by with just one container between stations.

FIGURE 9–3 (concluded)

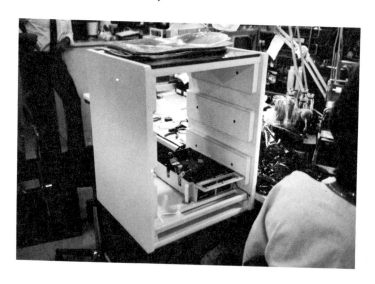

FIGURE 9–4
Kanban Squares in Assembly Operations

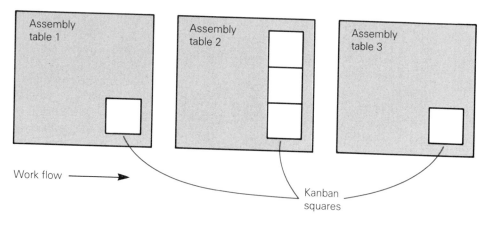

With a single container between stations, Physio's system could be described as kanban = 1. The subject of *how many* kanbans is addressed more clearly in the following discussion.

Kanban Squares

Another popular pull signal is the *kanban square*. It is a space, typically square, on an assembly table, floor, or shelf, and it acts like a kanban container: When empty, it demands to be filled; that is, it authorizes the prior work center to provide another unit to fill the square.

Figure 9–4 shows a three-station assembly line with kanban squares. Assembly tables 1 and 3 each have a single kanban square. Table 2 has three squares, which is good practice if the assembly operation at that table is troublesome. In that case, when assembler 2 needs extra time on a unit, assembler 3 keeps going by using up the units on all three squares. Like limit switch settings, the number of squares at each station is based on the variability of the process.

The ultimate pull system is no square at all. For the example in Figure 9–4, operating with no squares (kanban = 0) would be like a true bucket brigade: Every unit would be active. Setting kanban equal to zero is uncommon, because some "slop" usually must be in the system to allow for human variability. Even robotic assembly lines typically have an idle unit between successive robots; that allows time for a human attendant to rush to the scene when a robot misses or jams, which happens now and then because of variation in part dimensions or location. As problems are solved and causes of variability are eliminated, kanbans may be removed, perhaps allowing attainment of the ideal—kanban and waiting time equal to zero—in some parts of the process.

Card Systems and Kanban Removal

The innumerable kanban variations have their place, and so does the best-known type of kanban, which takes the form of a card. The usual minimal information on the card is part number, name, provider's location, user's location, quantity per container, container number, and total number of containers for that part. While in the original kanban system the card is detachable, today many companies are riveting or otherwise permanently attaching the card to the container. Figure 9–5 illustrates.

We see in the figure that Part A is being made at the work center on the right and used on the left. Three containers, each to hold five units of part A, are shown. At one point in time, two are at the user's stock point and one is at the maker's. When a container-with-card arrives from the maker, the user begins using up the contents. Today it might take an hour to empty a container, tomorrow half a day, or at another time perhaps even a week. But as soon as it is emptied, the container-with-card goes back to the maker (supplier), which is the signal to make and forward another one.

The containers circulate with identifying kanban attached; they circulate rapidly when the use rate is high and slowly when the use rate is low; they stop if there is no demand for a certain part for awhile. In this way, the card method responds to the user's speedups and slowdowns.

The number of containers in the flow is fixed. In Figure 9–5 there are three (kanban = 3). The number of units per container (five in the example) is also fixed. Those numbers are set judgmentally, keeping in mind the JIT dictum of minimal idle inventory and delay.

A good policy is to start with a small number of units per container but with several containers (to keep from running out of stock the first time trouble occurs). Then gradually reduce the number of containers. The supervisor or production team decides to withdraw a container whenever the current number seems excessive. A simple test is: If the user never runs out of part A, there are too many containers; so withdraw one. This technique is often called *kanban removal*, because a kanban is removed from the system each time a container is. Some plants require the maker to end a work shift with all containers full. On certain hectic days, that requires working some overtime. If a work crew *never* has to stay late, there is probably too much stock; time for kanban removal.

Figure 9–5 shows only one part. In practice, the maker usually switches among several different parts and the user probably receives different parts from different makers. When the maker is running part B, the extra containers of part A can keep the user going.

The manual card-container method can be upgraded electronically a step at a time. First convert from manual typing or hand writing of cards to computer printing. Print a new deck of cards at each schedule or design change. The next step is to print bar codes on the cards for items bought from the outside. Upon receipt of container-and-card, wand the bar code. That sends receipt information to accounting and authorizes payment to the supplier.

Some advanced kanban operations, such as Toyota's automobile production, employ a *dual-card kanban* system. *Production kanbans* trigger activities at preceding workstations, while *withdrawal,* or *conveyance kanbans* accompany materials moving from provider to consumer. In a single-card system, one card (or container) serves to authorize both production and conveyance. Toyota and other

FIGURE 9–5

Card (Kanban) System

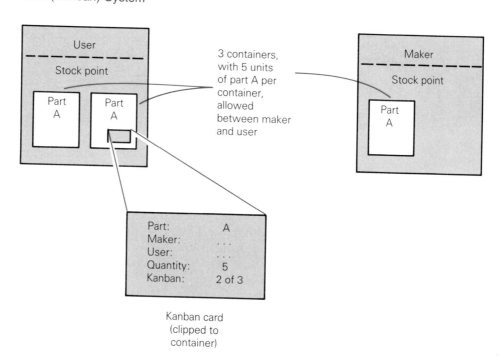

Kanban card
(clipped to
container)

long-time kanban users also make use of a variety of other types of card kanban; they are suitable for specific purposes that are beyond our scope.[1]

Kanban in Services

So far our discussion has focused on goods, but kanban applies to services as well. Some grocery store chains have a policy: If a line gets longer than three customers, open another checkout station. The checkout stations act like assembly stations, each with three "invisible kanban squares" (kanban = 3).

Some manufacturing plants have extended JIT and kanban to office work, especially repetitive, multistep processes such as order entry and accounts payable. One example is Westinghouse's Controls Division, which operates two factories in North Carolina, one in Florida, and one in Puerto Rico. Through JIT, all four plants have reduced production lead times two- to fourfold for a variety of electrical control products.

For one product, however, average lead time just for processing a customer order was *seven weeks*. On average, it took 7 days for the customer to get an order to the Westinghouse sales office, 2 days for sales to interpret and electronically forward the order to the manufacturing division, 7 days for order management to route the order to load planning, 21 days to get the order into the next scheduling cycle, and 12 days for the scheduler to fit the order into the assembly line. Two key changes, however, have cut order-entry lead time to *seven minutes*. First, major customers now have in their personal computers prepackaged information about the product's variations, stated in terms meaningful to Westinghouse assemblers. Second, a customer sends an order message directly to an assembler at a Westinghouse plant; the assembler has broad authority to build, test, and pack the ordered item as well as to acknowledge the order and provide shipping information to the customer.[2]

PRINCIPLE Cut throughput times.

In applying JIT to documents, a good approach is to reorganize people into document flow lines and control the work flow using kanban. For example, the system shown in Figure 9–4 could be used with each kanban square holding a file folder, customer order, or customer invoice packet; or, let each square hold a carrier containing, say *four* packets or folders.

In some cases, the time needed to process each information packet varies widely; for example, one credit check may take 30 seconds, the next, 15 minutes. With such variable task times, too little inventory at each station (for example, kanban = 3 or less) might result in too many stops and delays. Probably the

---

[1]See Yasuhiro Monden, *Toyota Production System* (Norcross, Ga.: Industrial Engineering and Management Press, 1983).
[2]William Barlow, "The Control Division as a Just-in-Time Vendor: A Case Study," *Case Studies of Just-in-Time Implementation at Westinghouse and IBM* (Falls Church, Va.: American Production and Inventory Control Society, 1986), pp. 8–17.

rule should be more flexible, for example: Documents received in the first half of a shift *will* be processed by the end of the second half. This rule would require working overtime on bad days, such as one with many difficult credit-check problems. In effect, the rule in that case would be: At the end of the shift, kanban = 0 for work received during the first half-day.

Such rules are used in only a few companies at this point. Widespread use could yield considerable customer service benefits, since delays in processing documents and related errors are as serious as those in processing goods in factories.

Kanban Applications: A Summary

Table 9–1 summarizes our discussion of pull or kanban methods by type of operation. (A number of exceptions and variations are not listed.)

First on the list is job-order goods. Included are an enormous variety of industrial materials in raw or component form. Kanban is not well suited for custom- or special-design goods unless ordered in large quantity (a large-quantity order may be broken down into kanban-sized units and flowed through via the pull system). However, most custom- and special-design goods are made from standard materials that *can* be ordered, delivered, and produced using kanban containers and cards. Most processes in job shops deal with standard— not special—items.

While kanban is not yet used extensively in the world's industrial job shops, its use surely will increase as more companies become aware of kanban's potential for use with standard components and materials. As industry gets better at designing a greater variety of end products from fewer standard components (discussed in Chapter 3), the potential for kanban will grow. JIT implementation in industry tends to follow this pattern: For more repetitive products, apply kanban as an early step; in job-shop processes, work on setup times and process (quality) control first, and consider kanban later.

In many companies, the more repetitive processes are in final assembly and the job-shop processes are in component fabrication. In fabrication work there are many processes that are not plagued by long setup times or quality problems. For those processes, a firm could profit from implementing kanban as an early step. "Islands of kanban" then are sprinkled around the fabrication shops, eliminating waste and delay at each island (one process feeding another by pull signals). The implementation plan is to gradually link the islands of kanban together into a grand pull system.

The next four entries in Table 9–1 are different kinds of repetitively produced goods. Heavy, low-volume goods rest on kanban squares on the floor; heavy, high-volume goods may be pulled by chain conveyor. Medium- or light-weight, low-volume goods fit on kanban squares on tables; if high-volume, they may be pulled by short lengths of belt conveyor. Operators must have access to help or stop devices and lights so that they are in control of the pulling. Conveyor-driven processes may employ limit switches as the pull method.

The final entry in the table is services on demand, which means human

TABLE 9–1
Pull Methods and Applications

Type of Operation/Examples	Pull Method	Method of Coordinating Make Rate and Use Rate
Job-order and purchase-order goods: raw materials, fabricated components, subassemblies made or bought	Containers holding exact quantities placed in exact locations at make and use points	Exact number of units per container and containers per part number; kanban (card) attached to each container (or special container-as-signal)
Repetitive, heavy, low-volume goods: large computers, line printers, machine tools, test equipment	Kanban squares on floor	Kanban squares on floor; help lights
Repetitive, heavy, medium-volume goods: motorcycles, farm machines, major appliances, autos	Chain conveyor	Stop lights; help lights; limit switches
Repetitive, medium- or lightweight, high-volume goods: assembly of floppy disks, pencils, tape; fill-and-pack of cough drops, cosmetics	Belt conveyor	Short conveyor lengths; little idle stock between stations; stop lights; help lights; limit switches
Repetitive, medium- or lightweight, low-volume goods; electronic and electrical components of all kinds; documents	Kanban squares on tables	Kanban squares on tables; help lights
Service on demand: food service, checkout lines, doctors' offices	"Invisible kanban squares" (policy on maximum line length)	Intercom, phone, or other means of summoning help to keep from exceeding maximum on "squares"

customers waiting to receive an item (ticket, meal, newspaper) or a personal service. The pull technique is the "invisible kanban," which is the same as a maximum line length.

What about the future of kanban? The simple signals are cheap and effective and should gain more widespread use. However, large firms that receive thousands of different parts from outside suppliers or remote plants are gravitating toward electronic transmission—terminal to terminal (or modem to modem).

Is electronic transmission the ultimate kanban? Perhaps. But it does have a problem. JIT is supposed to force a hand-to-mouth mode of replenishment. That is, only when the user empties a container may the maker produce and forward some more. How can the electronic system be made to send the request to the maker at just the right time? There are ways; for example, automatic wanding of a bar code as an empty container goes by. But that requires still another electronic communication system extending back to the maker, perhaps at another site.

When the user can see the item being pulled or that the maker is responsive to a pull signal, kanban works fine. But what if the maker is inflexible, buried in other work, or otherwise far removed in response time? Can there be any coordination between maker and user? Fortunately, there can be: a timing system called *material requirements planning*, the subject of the next section, fits the situation.

MATERIAL REQUIREMENTS PLANNING

Net requirements and timing for any dependent-demand item can be calculated by the **material requirements planning (MRP)** method. The simple calculation, briefly explained in Chapter 8, is elaborated on in several ways in this section. The explanations of MRP techniques also apply to MRPII.

Basic MRP

While MRP is known as a push system, that is an oversimplification. Kanban, if run loosely—for example, kanban = 20 containers—allows the maker to push out product until all containers (here 20) are full, which may take a week. MRP, which usually plans a "push" schedule a week at a time, often includes a production activity control subroutine to adjust the work flow somewhat every day (more on that topic in Chapter 12). Also, MRP can be set to plan everything daily instead of weekly.

It is possible for a process to switch from push to pull as the situation changes. Drink machines, labeled as natural pull systems earlier in this chapter, come to mind. A cola machine in the student lounge might better serve its clientele (and make more sales per day) with the following modification. Three minutes before change of classes, the machine converts itself from pull to push; that is, fills cups with cola and ice and pushes them onto a short conveyor inside the machine. If customers come, as they usually do, they put in their money and get their cola right away; on the few occasions when customers don't come, the cups are dumped. In either case, the machine is set to change back to pull after the conveyor is emptied.

While that is a fanciful example, it helps clarify push and pull and the value of each—or both in tandem. Example 9–1, also for a food product, illustrates basic MRP graphically. Since MRP is easier to grasp graphically than in words, some MRP computer systems even show MRP results in graphical form. Two new terms are introduced: **planned order release**, which is found by back scheduling from the date of need, and **residual inventory**, which is inventory left over when an order is canceled or reduced in quantity.

EXAMPLE 9–1   MRP FOR A CATERER

Imagine that you are a caterer and that you have a master schedule of parties to cater every night for the next two weeks. Your inventory policy is zero inventories (except for incidentals like seasonings). To plan for zero inventories, you consult menus for every food dish to be provided for each catering order in the next two weeks. Menu quantities times number of servings equals gross requirements. Let us say (without showing calculations) that gross requirements for salami are as shown in part A of Figure 9–6. Salami is required in the quantities shown on days 3, 6, 11, and 13.

You normally order salami from a deli two days ahead of time; that is, purchase lead time for salami is two days. Therefore, you plan to release salami orders as shown in part B of Figure 9–6. Each planned order release is two days in advance of the gross requirement shown in part A.

The schedule of planned order releases is correctly timed and in the exact quantities needed. It is a material requirements plan for one of the components that go into the foods to be catered. It is a plan for zero inventory, and is achieved if the deli delivers the salami orders in the planned two days. If deliveries come a day early, inventory builds. Also, if an order of salami arrives on time but a customer cancels the catering order, residual (leftover) inventory builds. Such supply and demand uncertainties create some inventory when MRP is used, but MRP cuts inventory considerably from what it is when the producer (caterer) *plans* to keep components in stock.

FIGURE 9–6
Planned Order Release Determination—Salami

A. Gross Requirement Schedule

Day	1	2	3	4	5	6	7	8	9	10	11	12	13	14
Gross requirements (slices)	—	—	100	—	—	320	—	—	—	—	80	—	510	—

B. Planned Order Releases

Day	1	2	3	4	5	6	7	8	9	10	11	12
Planned order releases (slices)	100	—	—	320	—	—	—	—	—	80	—	510	—

MRP Computer Processing

Clearly MRP is a simple idea. The MRP calculations for salami in Figure 9–6 are easy because there is only a single level of dependency from salami slices to a master schedule of catered food dishes. Now consider the partial **product structure** (also called *bill of materials,* or *BOM*) shown in Figure 9–7. It is a dependent-demand chain having five levels below the end item, an automobile. The end item typically is designated as the *zero* level in a computer file storing a bill of materials. The figure shows raw metal (5) cut into a gear (4), fitted onto a shaft (3), placed in a gear box (2), installed in an engine (1), and assembled into an auto (0).

The timing and quantities of parts to be ordered at each level depend on needs for parts by the parent item directly above. Planned-order-release calculations must cascade, that is, proceed from the first level to the second, to the third, and so on. Cascading calculations are a good reason for using computers, especially for products having thousands of parts.

FIGURE 9–7
Partial Product Structure Showing Dependency Chain

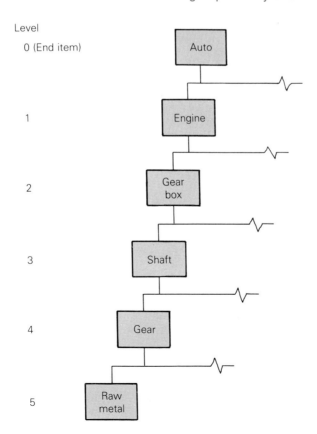

But cascading or **level-by-level** netting is not the only complication. The same raw metal that is cut into a gear might also go into other parent items that ultimately become the vehicle. Further, the raw metal and, perhaps, the gear, shaft, gear box, and engine may go into other parent items that become other types of vehicles. Finally, dependent demands (i.e., demands that descend from parent items) for parts at any level must be combined with independent demands. Independent demands arise, for example, from orders for spare parts (service parts). Computers are needed to total and properly time-phase all those requirements.

Figure 9–8 shows the necessary inputs and outputs of an MRP computer run. The inputs are a master production schedule, an item master file, a bill-of-materials file, and an open-order file. The outputs include a planned-order-release listing, rescheduling notices, and management reports.

Master Production Schedule

The *master production schedule (MPS)* is the action input. The MPS drives MRP with the end-item schedule. In most firms using MRP, the MPS has weekly time buckets (periods) extending a year into the future. The master production schedule normally is updated monthly. As the month passes, the MPS gets increasingly out of date; that is, toward the end of the month some of the scheduled

FIGURE 9–8
MRP Computer Run

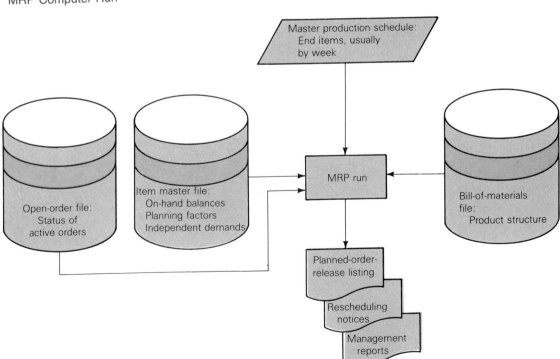

quantities become out of line with orders that marketing is actually booking. The MPS might be updated—say weekly—to correct it. More often, it is left as it is and inaccuracies are dealt with via weekly MRP runs, by component parts schedule changes, and by activity control measures on the shop floor.

Item Master File

The **item master file** holds reference and control data, including on-hand stock balances and planning factors for every component item. The on-hand balance is simply the quantity that is supposed to be in stock; it may be verified periodically by counting what actually is in storage. Posting transactions (receipts, issues, new items, errors, and so forth) to the item master file keeps the balance up-to-date.

The on-hand balance is used by MRP to compute planned orders. First, the system computes gross requirements for a given part. Then it calculates projected stock balances to see if there is a net requirement, which would indicate a need for a planned order; that calculation is calling *netting*. A net requirement is the same as a negative projected stock balance, where:

$$\text{Projected stock balance} = \text{Previous stock balance} \\ - \text{Gross requirements} \\ + \text{Planned and scheduled receipts} \qquad (9\text{--}1)$$

Example 9–2 extends Example 9–1 to allow for an on-hand stock balance. Also, let's change salami into salamite, a hypothetical chemical compound. In keeping with the usual industry practice of scheduling in weeks, gross requirements for salamite are stated as a 14-week rather than 14-day schedule.

EXAMPLE 9–2   **MRP FOR A CHEMICAL PRODUCT**
_____

Let us say that 220 units of salamite is the on-hand balance at time zero (the start of week 1). The gross requirements are as shown in Figure 9–9, but with days changed to weeks. For week 3,

$$\text{Projected stock balance} = \text{Previous balance} - \text{Gross requirements} \\ + \text{Receipts} \\ = 220 - 100 + 0 = 120$$

The positive projected stock balance, 120, shows that there is no need to order. The projected balance stays at 120 in weeks 4 and 5. In week 6,

$$\text{Projected balance} = 120 - 320 + 0 = -200$$

Now the projected stock balance is a negative 200, which is a net requirement. In MRP, a net requirement is covered by a planned order. The planned order quantity is 200, and the planned order release, obtained by back scheduling, is two weeks earlier, since the planned lead time (LT) is two weeks.

Figure 9–9 shows MRP results as a four-row display. This type of display might be available for viewing on a video terminal or as printed output. (The scheduled-receipts row, which is empty in this example, is explained later.)

FIGURE 9–9
MRP Computations—Salamite

Lead time (LT) = 2 Week		1	2	3	4	5	6	7	8	9	10	11	12	13	14
Gross requirements				100			320					80		510	
Scheduled receipts															
Projected stock balance	220	220	220	120	120	120	0 ~~−200~~	0	0	0	0	0 ~~−80~~	0	0 ~~−510~~	0
Planned order releases					200 ↑ LT = 2					80 ↑ LT = 2	510 ↑ LT = 2				

The net requirement of 200 in week 6 is covered by a planned order release of 200 in week 4. A negative stock balance is thus averted; therefore, the −200 is crossed out and replaced by a zero balance. Recomputation of the stock balance in week 6 to account for the planned receipt of 200 is as follows:

$$\text{Projected stock balance} = \text{Previous balance} - \text{Gross requirements} + \text{Receipts}$$
$$= 120 - 320 + 200 = 0$$

The projected balance goes negative twice more, in weeks 11 and 13. Ordering actions cover the net requirements; thus, the negative quantities are crossed out and replaced by zeros.

Planning factors stored in the item master file include lead time, lot size, safety stock, and so forth. Those factors need less updating than stock balances. In Example 9–2, the lead time (LT) of two weeks would have been extracted from the item master file.

So far we have assumed that the planned-order-release quantity is the same as the net requirement. That policy is known as *lot-for-lot* (i.e., production lot size exactly equals "lot" quantity required). Sometimes the item master file specifies a preset order quantity or lot size, Q (for "quantity"). Example 9–3, adapted from Example 9–2, provides for a fixed Q.

Clearly, fixed order quantities compromise the MRP goal of low or zero inventories. The debate over what order-quantity policy to use is reserved for the next chapter.

EXAMPLE 9–3	**MRP FOR A CHEMICAL PRODUCT—FIXED ORDER QUANTITY**

Assume that salamite is produced in a vat that holds 500 units. Even though 500 units is unlikely to be the net requirement, it seems economical to make the salamite in full 500-unit batches. The excess is carried as a stock balance.

Figure 9–10 shows the MRP computations for the case of a fixed order quantity, Q, equal to 500 units. A net requirement of 200 arises when the computed stock balance goes negative by 200 in week 6. The computer covers the net requirement with a planned order two weeks earlier (since LT = 2). The order is for $Q = 500$, the fixed order quantity, which brings projected stock balance in week 6 to +300. The balance drops to 220 in week 11 and to −290, indicating a net requirement, in week 13. To prevent the negative balance in week 13, the computer plans an order for 500. The planned order release is in week 11, which eliminates the negative balance in week 13 and leaves 210 units to spare.

FIGURE 9–10

MRP with Fixed Order Quantity—Salamite

LT = 2 Q = 500															
Week		1	2	3	4	5	6	7	8	9	10	11	12	13	14
Gross requirements				100			320						80		510	
Scheduled receipts																
On hand	220	220	220	120	120	120	300 −200 300	300	300	300	220	220	210 220 −290	210	
Planned order releases					500							500			

Bill-of-Materials File

A **bill of materials (BOM)** is not the kind of bill that demands payment; rather, it is industry's term for a list of component parts that go into a product—often a structured list. The BOM names the parts detailed on the engineer's blueprints.

Like the item master file, the computerized BOM file serves as a reference file for MRP processing. BOMs must be accurately structured and stated in terms of the same end items found on the master production schedule.

The bill-of-materials file keeps track of which component parts and how much of each go into a unit of the parent item. In each MRP run, the computer

(1) calculates planned order timing and quantity for the parent item, (2) consults the BOM file to see what goes into the parent, and (3) translates the parent's planned order requirement into gross requirements for each component. For example, if there are three of a certain component per parent, the gross requirement for that component will be equal to triple the planned order quantity for the parent. (The grand total of gross requirements for the component would also include requirements derived from other parents and from independent demands.) Example 9–4 continues the salamite example to demonstrate the role of the BOM file.

| EXAMPLE 9–4 | **MRP FOR A CHEMICAL PRODUCT WITH TWO LEVELS** |

Planned order releases for salamite have been calculated. The computer consults the BOM file to find what goes into salamite. The first ingredient is a chemical compound known as *sal*. There are two grams of sal per unit of salamite. Therefore, the planned order quantities for salamite are doubled to equal gross requirements for sal. This simple translation of salamite orders into sal needs is shown in Figure 9–11. (The salamite data are from Figure 9–10.)

Projected stock balances and planned order releases may now be calculated for sal as shown in the figure. Then the computer does the same for the next ingredient or component of salamite.

It is cumbersome to develop the master production schedule and forecast MPS requirements if there are a large number of products in the BOM file. For that reason, the BOMs provided by the engineering department—called *engineering bills*—may need to be consolidated. The usual approach is to judiciously combine some engineering bills into *modular bills* and *phantom bills* (or *superbills*). The full approach, called *restructuring the bills of materials*, is often a valued step in MRP implementation; the method is somewhat complicated, however, and is reserved for advanced studies.[3]

As the preceding discussion suggests, MRP computer processing is a crucial activity in MRP-based operations. Commonly, MRP computer runs are weekly; a total regeneration of material requirements is performed, generally over the weekend. A few companies use **regenerative MRP processing** every two or three days or even daily. An alternative to regeneration is **net-change MRP**. Net-change computer software is designed to update only the items that are

---

[3]See Joseph Orlicky, *Material Requirements Planning* (New York: McGraw-Hill, 1975), Chapter 10, "Product Definition" (TS155.8.O74).

FIGURE 9-11

BOM Reference Data and Scheduled Receipts in MRP

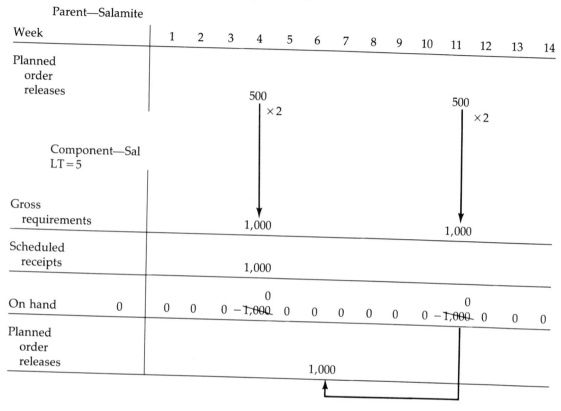

affected by a change in quantity or timing for a related item. Since not all part numbers need be regenerated, net change saves on computer time.

Scheduled Receipts and the Open-Order File

Another MRP factor is scheduled receipts. Returning to Figure 9–11, we see that in week 4 there is a scheduled receipt of 1,000, which is the gross-requirement quantity in week 4. A scheduled receipt represents an **open order** instead of a *planned order*. In this case, an order for 1,000 has already been released, for make or buy, and is scheduled to be delivered in week 4. Since the lead time is five weeks, the order would have been released, opened, and scheduled two weeks ago. (Remember, we're at time zero, the beginning of week 1.)

Let us examine the events that change a planned order into a scheduled receipt. The following sketch is a partial MRP for sal as it might have appeared on Monday morning two weeks ago.

Lead time = 5		1	2	3	4	5	6
Gross							1,000
Scheduled receipts							
On hand	0	0	0	0	0	0	0 ~~1,000~~
Planned order releases		1,000					

Any time a planned order release appears in the first time bucket, action to schedule the order is called for. Therefore, sometime on Monday the scheduler writes up a shop order to make 1,000 grams of sal. The effect of scheduling the order is to remove it from the planned-order-release row and convert it to a scheduled receipt, as follows:

Lead time = 5		1	2	3	4	5	6
Gross							1,000
Scheduled receipts							►1,000
On hand	0	0	0	0	0	0	0
Planned order releases							

On the next MRP run, the scheduled receipt for 1,000 grams will be included. The order is shown as a scheduled receipt each week until the shop delivers the 1,000 grams. (But the order could get canceled or changed in quantity or timing. Also, the shop may successfully produce more or less than the planned quantity of 1,000 grams.)

Referring back to the system flowchart in Figure 9–8, we see that computer processing for MRP makes use of an *open-order file*, which holds data on open orders (scheduled receipts). Each time a scheduler releases a shop order or a buyer releases a purchase order, the order is recorded in the open-order file. (Alternatively, item master file records may contain fields indicating if there is an open order for a given item.) When orders are received (or canceled), they are closed and removed from the file.

One step in a MRP computer run is to evaluate open orders, which can be done after calculating planned order releases. Then the computer checks to see whether quantities and timing for each order in the open-order file are still correct. The check may show that a certain open order is still needed, but perhaps a week later or in a different quantity; or perhaps the order is no longer needed at all. (Order changes are normal, a phenomenon known as *order churn*.) The system issues **rescheduling notices**, which highlight the difference between present requirements and open orders. If the open order is overstated, the shop scheduler or buyer will sometimes ignore a rescheduling notice and allow the order to be completed early or in a quantity in excess of current need, because rescheduling every time there is a new requirement would be too disruptive for the suppliers or shops doing the work. (The disruption resulting from reacting to every rescheduling notice is often called *system nervousness*.)

Multiple Parents and Scrap Allowances

Figure 9–12 is a partial bill of materials for a bicycle. There is enough room to show only a sample of the 300-odd component parts that would go into a bicycle. The complete BOM breaks down into as many levels as are necessary to get to the *purchased* part. Take the breakdown of the front and rear wheels. Each wheel has a tire, an axle assembly, a rim assembly, 28 spokes, and 28 nipples; each spoke is fabricated (cut, bent, and threaded) from 11 inches of raw wire stock. The nipple is a second-level and the wire a third-level purchased item. Both spoke nipples and wire stock appear at two locations in the BOM; they also would occur in the BOMs for other bicycle sizes. The

FIGURE 9–12

Partial Bill of Materials for a Bicycle

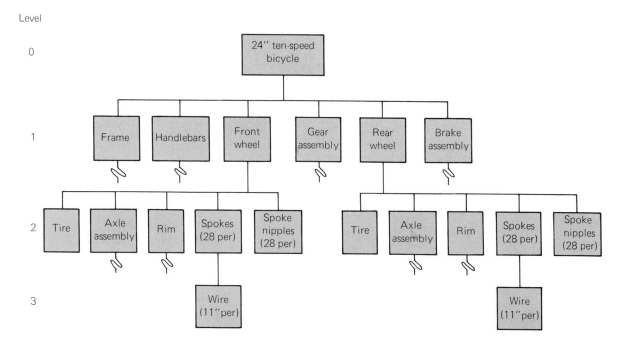

computer is efficient for totaling the quantities needed for parts occurring in multiple locations, which is a step in exploding the BOM. (Before computers and MRP were available, BOM explosion was done with index cards and adding machines.)

Example 9–5 uses some of the bicycle components to show how MRP treats multiple parents and scrap calculations. In the example, netting with scrap allowance included is done as follows:

$$\text{Net requirement} = \frac{\text{Shortage amount}}{1 - \text{Scrap rate}}$$

EXAMPLE 9–5   MRP PROCESSING—BICYCLE SPOKE NIPPLES

Figure 9–13 shows generation of gross requirements for spoke nipples and their translation into planned order releases. Planned order releases for front and rear wheels are given for three sizes of bicycle: 20-inch, 24-inch, and 26-inch. Requirements for wheels would have been derived from master production schedules (level 0) for all bike models.

FIGURE 9–13
MRP Generation of Planned Order Releases—Spoke Nipple Example

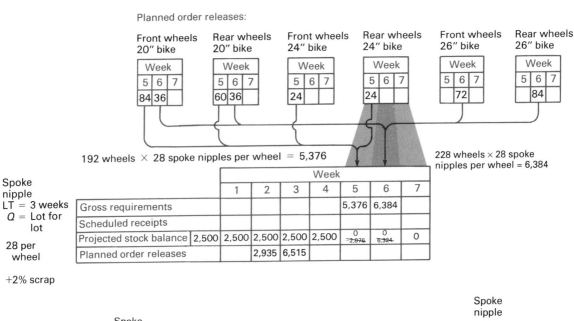

Planned order releases for spoke nipples emerge after higher levels of MRP processing have been completed.

In the figure, orders for more than one parent are consolidated to become gross requirement for a next-lower-level part. The requirement for nipples in week 5 is based on $84 + 60 + 24 + 24 = 192$ wheels. At 28 nipples per wheel, the gross requirement is $192 \times 28 = 5,376$. For week 6, the basis is $36 + 36 + 72 + 84 = 228$ wheels: The gross requirement is 228×28, which equals 6,384. (Front-wheel and rear-wheel planned orders may be unequal, because there may be extra demand for one or the other as service parts, to make up for scrap losses, and so forth.)

The 2,500 nipples on hand at week 0 are projected to stay on hand (in stock) through four weeks. In week 5, 5,376 are needed but only 2,500 are available; there is a projected shortage of 2,876. The possibility of a shortage triggers the following: The MRP program subtracts the purchase lead time (LT), three weeks, from week 5, giving week 2, when an order must be released to avert the shortage in week 5. The lot size is lot-for-lot. Thus, an order is placed for 2,935 units, a quantity sufficient to yield the 2,876 shortage after the 2 percent scrap allowance. The shortage of 6,384 in week 6 is covered by a planned order back-scheduled to week 3. That order quantity is 6,515, again enough to yield the shortage amount after the 2 percent scrap allowance is considered.

Note the treatment of the scrap factor: The planned-order-release amount includes the 2 percent so that the extra amount will be placed on order. Planned receipts do not include it, since 2 percent is expected to be scrapped.

Independent Demands for Component Parts

Independent demands for component parts may be entered into the item master file. The subset of MRP for handling independent demands is often called **time-phased order point (TPOP)**. TPOP requires that the independent demands be forecast since they cannot be computed—there are no parent demands from which to compute.

The main difference between MRP and TPOP is this: *Dependent* demands are *calculated* based on parent-item needs (MRP), while *independent* demands are *forecast* (TPOP). TPOP actually loses its identity when the independent demand is merged with demands derived from MRP; MRP takes over from there. Example 9–6 illustrates the method.

EXAMPLE 9–6   **INDEPENDENT DEMANDS—BICYCLE SPOKES**

For a bicycle manufacturer, most of the gross demands for spokes are dependent demands derived from planned orders for wheels. Some independent demands for spokes come from parts wholesalers and other bicycle manufacturers that do not make their own spokes.

The independent sources do not make their demands known very far in advance. Thus, independent spoke demand is forecast. The most recent forecast for 11-inch spokes is for 800 units. That quantity is used as the forecast for the next 52 weeks. Figure 9–14 shows the 800-per-week projection at the upper left. The upper right shows a dependent demand for 672 spokes in week 5; that demand is derived from MRP processing at the level of the parent item, 24-inch bike wheels.

The two sources of demand merge into gross requirements for spokes. The independent-demand quantities, 800 per period, are extended directly; the single dependent demand of 672 is computed from the planned order of 24 wheels times 28 spokes per wheel. From this point, MRP logic takes over; the figure shows a net requirement in week 6 covered by a planned order release with a fixed quantity of 4,800 a week earlier.

FIGURE 9–14
TPOP—Spoke Example

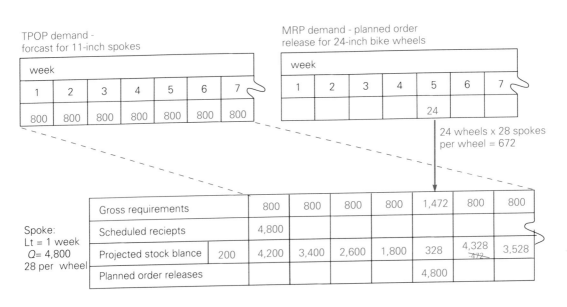

We have seen how TPOP handles independent demands from outside the company. But what about independent demands from *inside*, for example, from company-operated distribution centers? We consider an approach to such demands next.

Distribution Requirements Planning

Traditionally, finished goods inventories in distribution centers have been planned independent of manufacturing. The distribution centers use reorder points, which randomly trigger orders from the manufacturing plants. It makes more sense to fit distribution requirements into master production schedules, a procedure known as **distribution requirements planning (DRP)**.

DRP works in various ways, but one sound approach is to centralize the planning of distribution requirements. Some of the key steps are:

1. Central planning sends historically based demand forecasts (usually weekly, for perhaps a year into the future) to each distribution center.

2. Each distribution center manager adjusts the forecasts based on local factors. Any known large orders or expected demand surges resulting from product promotions are added to the forecast.

3. Forecasts are returned to central planning and totaled. The master scheduler uses the totals as a basis for developing the master production schedule. Some of the requirements will probably be for lower-level components needed in the distribution centers as service parts. In that case, the totals will bypass the MPS and be added directly to gross requirements for the component when the next MRP run is made.

Under DRP, requirements are based on actual forecast needs, not just shelf replenishment. Thus, inventories may be cut even as customer service improves. The manufacturing side of the business operates better as well, because the MPS may be developed based on long-term projections rather than on sudden demands from distribution centers that have found out shelf stock is low.

DRP may be broadened to include planning warehouse space, shipping loads, stock picking, and other distribution activities. The broadened form of DRP is sometimes called distribution *resource* planning.

Closed-Loop MRP

Early MRP systems were "one-way streets," in that they fed plans to production but received no feedback from production as to how well schedules were being met. The advent of **closed-loop MRP** brought file control, rescheduling actions, and production activity control on board. We will see how these three innovations make the street run both ways, after we examine obstacles to staying on schedule.

Obstacles

MRP generates valid schedules in that they are logical extensions of parent demand. But once planned orders are launched, some of the planning factors begin to stray off course.

Lead-time estimates may turn out wrong. This can happen when machines break down, delivery trucks are delayed, goods are damaged, or the power fails.

If one such incident delays the arrival of 1 part number out of, say, 100 that go into an end item, the schedules for all of the remaining 99 will be thrown off.

A second planning factor that can go wrong is quantities. MRP plans for 1,000 of the component part, but 200 may be ruined or fail quality inspection. The order may be on time but short. The other 99 part numbers going into the end item will be affected by the shortage.

A third factor is customer requirements. The master production schedule, which drives MRP, is partly actual customer orders and partly forecast orders. The forecasts may be off by some amount, and customers may change their minds about actual orders. Customers may ask for more or for earlier or later delivery. This changes the MPS, throwing off all component orders.

Finally, the staff may be continually tinkering with product designs and issuing change notices, that is, changing the component parts that go into end items.

File Control

How may valid schedules be maintained in the face of all these changes? First, reference file information must be updated regularly. Notification of design changes goes into the BOM file; changes in scrap rate, lead time, order quantity, and other planning factors go into the item master file; and order completion data go into the open-order file. Finally, regular counts of stockroom inventory ensure that inventory records in the item master file are accurate.

If the information in the files is not kept accurate, factory operatives and people in scheduling and purchasing will lose confidence in the system. The MRP system may continue to churn out advice, but an informal system will actually take over. The MRP systems that have failed to meet expectations usually did so because of shoddy recordkeeping.

Rescheduling Actions

The MRP system's rescheduling notices sometimes are ignored (thereby avoiding "system nervousness"), but at other times require action. A scheduler or buyer might find the old schedule impossible to meet and decide to reschedule part or all of an order—move its due date to a later week. The next computer run would recalculate due dates for all parts affected by the change.

Production Activity Control

After a decision to reschedule has been made, new due dates and quantities go out to the factory and supplier companies. Then the fun begins. How do the new dates and quantities get acted upon by shops and suppliers that, based on the old schedule, have the jobs in progress, perhaps already set up on a machine or in transit on a truck? Many other orders are out in the shops, each requiring work in from 1 to as many as 20 to 30 work centers. The jobs may spend time in queues at each work center. Which jobs get run first? How can you even *find* a given job in order to change its priority?

One way is to tap the pulse of the workplace: know where the work is, what the delays are, and how much is being ruined or scrapped. The usual method is this: As each work center completes a job and sends the work onward, the computer is told *how many* units were sent forward and the date. That information is enough to allow the MRP system to provide each work center with daily notices or priority changes. The completion data fed to the computer and the daily priority reports are part of a loop-closing MRP subroutine known as **production activity control** (more on that topic in Chapter 12).

Manufacturing Resource Planning (MRPII)

Closed-loop MRP closes small loops—those within operations. The operations department also fits into a grand loop that includes capacity planning, marketing, financial planning, and overall business planning. **Manufacturing resource planning (MRPII)** is an extension of basic MRP that closes parts of the grand loop.

MRPII uses the master production schedule to schedule capacity, shipments, tool changes, some design work, and cash flow. It requires several additions to the reference files. One is a bill of labor, which states labor needs, by skill category, to produce a unit of product. The MRPII system can use the bill of labor to project labor shortages. That gives the human resources department advance notice useful in assigning, hiring, and training.

MRPII can also project needs for support staff, including design engineering support in firms in which a customer order normally entails design work on the front end. Some sort of "bill of support labor" is necessary in order for MPRII to provide that kind of projection.

With still more reference data, MRPII can keep track of tool wear and recommend when to replace or resharpen tooling. It can also keep track of machine loads and projected machine capacity shortages, which may call for using alternate machines or arranging to subcontract work to an outside producer.

For financial planning, MRPII treats cash flow almost like materials. The master production schedule is exploded into component parts requirements as usual. Then the system converts planned order releases into cash outflows using unit cost data. Normal delays for bill paying are fed into the computer, and the output is a prediction of future cash outflows. The outflows include payments to suppliers and shippers for bought items and payment of wages, power consumption, and so forth for made items. Budgeting is simple under MRPII. Cash outflows may be projected, by expense category and organizational unit, out to a year or more. The projection may be refined into budgets.

Projected cash outflows also are valuable for predicting excessive needs for cash, for example, in periods of heavy purchasing. Knowing this in advance, the finance department has time to shop around for favorable loans and lines of credit and to consider other options for raising short-term cash. The master production schedule (or shipping schedule) is also converted to cash inflows for projected goods sold. Past rates of payment on accounts receivable are used to project the timing of cash inflows for goods sold. Different price structures may be simulated to see the projected effects on profitability.

As to overall impact, Wight states that, "MRPII results in management finally having *the numbers to run the business.*" And with "everybody using the same set of numbers," MRPII serves as "a company game plan."[4]

Benefits of MRP and MRPII[5]

In the narrow sense, the chief benefit of MRP/MRPII is its ability to generate valid schedules and keep them that way. Valid schedules have broader benefits for the entire company. They include the following, roughly in order of importance:

1. *Improves on-time completions.* Industry calls this *improving customer service,* and on-time completion is one good way to measure it. MRP/MRPII companies typically achieve 95 percent or more on-time completions, because completion of a parent item is less apt to be delayed for lack of a component part.

2. *Cuts inventories.* With MRP/MRPII, inventories can be reduced at the same time that customer service is improved. Stocks are cut because parts are not ordered if not needed to meet requirements for parent items. Typical gains are 20 to 35 percent.

3. *Provides data (future orders) for planning work center capacity requirements.* This benefit is attainable if basic MRP is enhanced by a *capacity requirements planning (CRP)* routine (discussed in Chapter 12).

4. *Improves direct-labor productivity.* There is less lost time and overtime because of shortages and less need to waste time halting one job to set up for a shortage-list job. Reduction in lost time tends to be from 5 to 10 percent in fabrication and from 25 to 40 percent in assembly. Overtime cuts are greater, on the order of 50 to 90 percent.

5. *Improves productivity of support staff.* MRP/MRPII cuts expediting (firefighting), which allows more time for planning. Purchasing can spend time saving money and selecting good suppliers. Materials management can maintain valid records and better plan inventory needs. Production control can keep priorities up-to-date. Foremen can better plan capacity and assign jobs. In some cases, fewer support staff are needed.

[4]Oliver W. Wight, *MRPII: Unlocking America's Productivity Potential* (Williston, Vt.: Oliver Wight Limited Publications, 1981), p. 58 (TS161.W5x).
[5]Data on MRP/MRPII gains are drawn from two sources: Wight, *MRPII,* Chap. 4, and Roger G. Schroeder, John C. Anderson, Sharon E. Tupy, and Edna M. White, "A Study of MRP Benefits and Costs" (Working Paper, Graduate School of Business Administration, University of Minnesota, May 1980).

6. *Facilitates "closing the loop" with total business planning.* That includes planning capacity and cash flow, which is the purpose and chief benefit of MRPII.

Benefits of MRP/MRPII are offset somewhat by its complexity. Considerable time, training, preparation, and discipline make MRP or MRPII yield the promised benefits. The next technique—reorder point—does not offer those benefits, but it is simple.

REORDER POINT

Inventory timing with **reorder point (ROP)** is probably as old as humanity (maybe older, since some animals, such as squirrels, exhibit humanlike behavior in replenishing low stocks). The ROP provides for replenishing stocks when they get down to some low level. Let us look at some of the ROP variations.

Perpetual System

The classic reorder point is a **perpetual inventory system**. Perpetually—every time an issue is made—the stock on hand is checked to see whether it is down to the ROP. If it is, an order is placed. In the small, informal case, the physical stock level itself is perpetually examined. In the more formal case, we examine the balance shown on a stock record.

We create reorder points all around us. We may reorder (go out to get) postage stamps when we are down to three, or another gallon of milk when there is about two inches left in the container. Also, manufacturers build reorder points into their products. For example, desk calendars and boxes of personal checks come with appropriately placed reminders that it is time to reorder. Some tissue manufacturers put small, perforated tabs on one side of the boxes; the customer tears out the tab and then follows ROP-like instructions: "When the tissue level gets down to here, it is time to buy two more boxes." (Notice that the customer is being told not only the reorder point but also that the lot size should be two boxes.)

Two-Bin System

A version of the perpetual reorder point called the *two-bin system* is often used in small stockrooms. Two adjacent storage bins hold a single item, and users are told to withdraw from bin 1 first. The rule is: When the first bin empties, place an order. The second bin contains the ROP, a quantity that covers the lead time for filling the order and allows for some additional buffer or safety stock.

There are many variations. A colored sheet of paper may be inserted in a stack of forms on a shelf to show when the ROP (the second bin) has been reached. Indirect material or free stock, such as washers, screws, and nails, is often placed in trays on assemblers' workbenches; a painted line partway down inside the tray can designate the ROP. Transistors, diodes, and so on are often stored in corrugated boxes on shelves; a small box in the larger box may be used to contain the ROP (the second bin). Figure 9–15 shows some two-bin variations.

FIGURE 9–15
Two-Bin System Variations

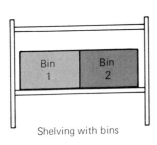

Shelving with bins

Rule: Use from bin 1 first: when empty, reorder

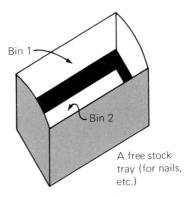

A free stock tray (for nails, etc.)

Rule: When down to black zone, reorder.

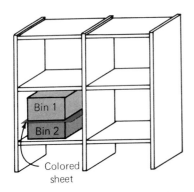

Open shelving (for forms)

Rule: When down to colored sheet, reorder.

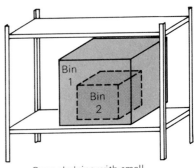

Open shelving with small box inside larger box

Rule: When small box must be broken open, reorder.

The two-bin system works best when a single person is in charge of the stockroom or is in charge of a daily check to see which items are down to the ROP. Otherwise, people will get too busy to note the need for an order; each person can conveniently blame the next one when the second bin is emptied without anyone having reordered.

In firms with partial computer control of inventories, order cards with bar codes can be placed near bin 2. Then, when bin 2 is entered, it is an easy matter to initiate the reorder: Just wand the bar code, which holds identifying data. People are less likely to forget to order when ordering is so simple.

ROP Calculation

The reorder point (the quantity in bin 2) may be set by judgment and experience or by an ROP formula. Judgment would tend to follow the concepts embodied in the basic ROP formula:

$$\text{ROP} = \text{DLT} + \text{SS} = (D)(LT) + \text{SS} \qquad (9\text{–}3)$$

where

ROP = Reorder point

DLT = Demand during lead time

SS = Safety stock (or buffer stock)

D = Average demand per time period

LT = Average lead time

Note that "safety stock" and "buffer stock" mean the same thing. Factory people tend to call it *buffer stock*: a buffer between one machine (or work center) and the next. Retailers and wholesalers tend to prefer *safety stock*: safety against losing a sale. Formal use of a reorder point is more common in retailing and wholesaling than in factories; thus the term used in the formula is *safety stock* (SS).

ROP calculation is simple, but it does require some reliable numbers if it is to be trusted. Recent averages are often used for demand rate and replenishment lead time. Safety stock calculation is treated in more detail later in the chapter; for now, we need only mention that some desired level of customer service determines the safety stock amount. Example 9–7 illustrates.

EXAMPLE 9–7   **ROP CALCULATION—FUEL OIL EXAMPLE**

Assume that a building heated by fuel oil consumes an average of 600 gallons per year and the average lead time is two weeks. Thus,

$$D = 600 \text{ gallons per year}$$

$$LT = 2 \text{ weeks}/52 \text{ weeks per year} = 0.04 \text{ yr.}$$
$$DLT = (D)(LT) = (600)(0.04) = 24 \text{ gallons}$$

Then, if desired safety stock is 40 gallons,

$$ROP = DLT + SS = 24 + 40$$
$$= 64 \text{ gallons}$$

Replenishment Cycle

In Example 9–7, an *average* demand rate of about 24 gallons was calculated based on an *average* replenishment lead time of two weeks. Average values tend to smooth things out, masking the existence of stock outages and inventory peaks. A more realistic picture of ROP replenishment cycles is explained in Example 9–8.

EXAMPLE 9–8   REPLENISHMENT CYCLES FOR DISCRETE DEMAND— RADIATOR CAP EXAMPLE

Radiator caps are issued in discrete units; that is, there cannot be an issue of half a radiator cap. (In contrast, a continuous item, like fuel oil, can be issued in fractions of a gallon.) Figure 9–16 shows two replenishment cycles for radiator caps. The graph shows a stairstep depletion pattern. It also shows early and late order arrivals, including a case in which back-ordering occurs.

In the first cycle, radiator caps are being issued at a slow pace—slower than past average demand, that is. In the fourth time period there is a spurt, and at the end of the period stock on hand drops below the ROP. An order is placed. During lead time, stock issues start out slowly, then speed up in periods 6 and 7. All radiator caps are gone by the beginning of period 7, and orders still come in.

The shaded zone below the zero line indicates orders unfilled because of the stockout condition. Orders accepted when stock is out are said to be **backorders**. They are usually filled first when stock does arrive. In this case, safety stock does not protect. The combination of slow delivery (greater than average actual lead time) and a late spurt in demand causes a stockout.

The second cycle begins when the order arrives in period 7. The order quantity or lot size, Q, brings the stock level up from zero to Q units, and the backorders are immediately filled, dropping the stock level somewhat. Stock depletion is at about an average rate through period 10. In period 11, demand for radiator caps surges. The surge continues into period 12, and it reduces stock to below the ROP. An order is placed.

This time, delivery is faster than average (see actual LT as compared with average LT), and there is little demand during the lead-time period. The result is little use of the DLT quantity and no use of the SS amount. Stock is high when the order quantity, Q, arrives. The order arrival pushes up the stock level to near the maximum possible, which is the ROP plus Q.

FIGURE 9–16
ROP Replenishment Cycles—Radiator Cap Example

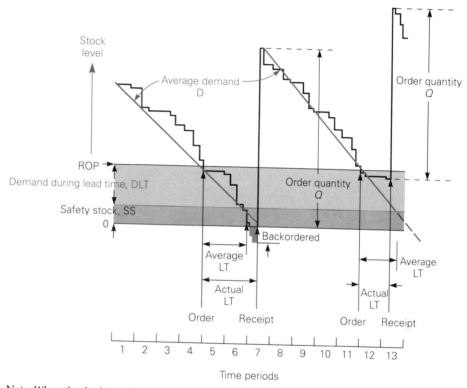

Note: When the depletion line is horizontal, time is passing with no stock depletion; a vertical segment shows a depletion.

Periodic System

The ROP method of replenishment requires perpetual checking of the balance on hand. Why not just check the balance at fixed time intervals? The *periodic system* does just that. The regularity in order intervals makes the periodic system popular with retailers, who often set up a schedule of checking stock levels in slack periods each day, once a week, or perhaps monthly. Grocers, restaurants, gas stations, clothing stores, and auto parts stores are just a few of the many kinds of businesses that favor some type of periodic system.

Often the periodic system of *timing* orders is combined with *maximum-minimum quantity* criteria. For example, a grocery store might periodically reorder laundry soaps, with two days as the order interval. The maximum shelf space, and therefore maximum inventory, for one item—say, Whiter-White Detergent—might be four cases and the desired minimum one case. The periodic system works like this:

1. Check stock of Whiter-White on Monday, Wednesday, Friday, and so on.
2. If shelf stock is below one case, reorder enough to bring the stock as close to four cases as possible without exceeding that amount.
3. If stock is above one case, don't reorder.

Note that the minimum is really a reorder-point *quantity* used in conjunction with the reorder-point interval; the maximum governs what the lot size must be in order to bring up stock to the maximum level.

Regardless of the system used for inventory timing, variabilities in consumption and production rates, disruptions such as accidents or natural disasters, and perhaps some human perception that a stock outage is a sign of poor management all lead to the creation of buffer stocks. We consider that topic next.

BUFFER STOCK

Unfortunately, there has been misunderstanding about the effect that tight production control—such as with JIT—has on inventories. Some critics point out that even well-run JIT plants still have some buffer stock; "Why isn't there zero inventory?" they ask. In one sense, we need the critics, for they remind us to strive to continue reducing inventory. On the other hand, as we pointed out in Chapter 8, inventory is the life blood of production; it should never dry up completely. Buffer stock—a special class of inventory—is like the spare tire in your auto or your homeowner's insurance policy: You hope you don't need it, but you don't dare operate without it. Buffer stock is expensive, however, and needs careful management.

Part of managing buffer stock (covered in other chapters) is treating the underlying problems that generate need for it: poor quality, undependable machines, lack of training, and the like. The other part is controlling the buffer stock itself, which is the topic here.

First, we examine a technique for measuring buffer stock by ratios; the technique is called *micro-response analysis*. Second, we see where to put buffer stock so that it is under firm physical control. Third, we look at a statistical method of setting safety (buffer) stock levels according to customer service policies. Finally, we examine the role of safety stock in an MRP system.

Micro-Response Analysis

Analysis of management system problems often does not easily translate into action at the work center level. **Micro-response analysis** is a way of measuring idle stock in the work centers by using ratios. The method is quite new but seems promising. Among the first large users of micro-response analysis were Emerson Electric Company and Digital Equipment Corporation.

There are three micro-response ratios: lead time to work content, process speed to use rate, and pieces to workstations or operators. For all three the ideal ratio is 1 to 1, but in practice it is typically 5, 10, 100, or 1,000 to 1. What does a ratio of, say, 100 to 1 mean? Examples for each ratio serve to illustrate:

- In a drop-and-add line (at registration for college classes), there is an average of 99 minutes of delay time for a 1-minute transaction to have a form signed. The 99 minutes of delay plus the 1 minute for signature is a ratio of 100 minutes of total lead time to 1 minute of work content (when "value" is added).

- A wire-cutting machine currently is cutting 1,000 pieces of electrical power cord per hour for a certain model of lamp. Lamp assembly, the next process, installs that model of cut cord at only 10 per hour. The ratio or process speed to use rate thus is 1,000 to 10, or 100 to 1.

- A clerk in a purchasing department typically has a stack of 99 invoices in an in-basket and just 1 invoice being worked on. This constitutes a pieces-to-operator ratio of 100 to 1.

In each case, high ratios mean long queues of idle materials (buffer stock) or customers. The micro-response method uses the ratios as a measure of performance in individual work centers or in cells or flow lines. Have supervisors and operators calculate a ratio, post it on a graph in the workplace, and then work to lower it. They cannot do so without making improvements. The types of improvements open to them are unlimited: cut setup times, use kanban squares, have a system for borrowing labor when lines get too long, eliminate disruptive rework by doing it right the first time, keep machines clean, run a machine at the use rate instead of at maximum speed, find a simple method of making an item instead of making it on a costly machine that runs too fast, and so forth.

The ratio is meant to cause people to think about options for improvement. Following an improvement, the new ratio goes up on the graph for all to see. The process continues, one improvement at a time, with 1 to 1 as the ultimate (though sometimes unattainable) goal. It is often a good idea to post "before" and "after" photos or schematic drawings showing reductions in buffer stock as the ratios drop.[6] Use of the ratios is also intended to instill the habit of improvement at the operator level—*kaizen* (from the Japanese)—so improvement becomes primarily a line rather than staff responsibility.

Some firms also use macro-response ratios—for example, total lead time to theoretical minimum—for an entire product. While a macro ratio might be useful for senior managers, micro-response ratios are necessary in order to inspire action at the operator or team level.

---

[6]Examples of use of photos and schematic drawings, as well as more on the micro-response technique, may be found in Richard J. Schonberger, *World Class Manufacturing Casebook: Implementing JIT and TQC* (New York: Free Press, 1987).

Physical Control of Buffer Stock

In Chapter 7, we discussed inventory control; doesn't that discussion apply to buffer stock? The answer is a qualified yes. Things like security and accuracy are important, but for buffer stock there is another somewhat unique concern, one that arises from the dual purpose of buffer stock.

Controlled Floor Stock

Buffer stock serves to smooth irregularities in provider-customer relationships. Kanban containers or squares can provide the cushion needed to accomplish the production-smoothing goal. Because JIT may result in a five- or ten-fold reduction in WIP inventory, there is often room to keep such buffer stock in the work area, near the point of use. The kanban methods—exact number of containers, exact number of units per container, and exact locations for each item at every stock point—provide the discipline needed to make a low-buffer-stock pull system work smoothly.

Off-line Buffer Stock

The second purpose of buffer stock is disaster protection. Buffer stock for that purpose should be kept off line, since it is not needed often. But when, for example, a machine breaks or bad weather disrupts deliveries, such stock is needed to avert a production stoppage. What we want to avoid—and off-line storage helps—is the use of such stock merely because it is handy. That would simply cause the off-line buffer stock to gradually become excess WIP inventory, definitely a step in the wrong direction. If the item is subject to deterioration, the off-line stock should be rotated occasionally.

Segmenting buffer stock into floor stock and off-line disaster stock will probably become a widely used technique. Doing this allows a pull system to be implemented, thus sharply cutting lead times even while retaining protection against disaster.[7] Reductions in total buffer stock can come later, when process improvements justify it.

Controlling Variation in Buffer Stock

The amount of buffer stock between any pair of processes typically goes up and down like a kite in a March wind. With shop-floor terminals for recording inventory transactions, the varying quantity can be determined in real time, which gives an impression of tight control. Still, under today's tougher concept of inventory controls (discussed in Chapters 7 and 8), that is not enough. Kanban further reduces variability of stock among work centers and keeps the micro-response ratio steady except when deliberately reduced as part of a continuing improvement program.

---

[7]Retaining stock for disaster protection off line was an important step in relieving anxieties during JIT implementation at Hewlett-Packard's minicomputer division in Cupertino, California. See Richard Walleigh, "What's Your Excuse for Not Using JIT?" *Harvard Business Review*, March–April 1986, pp. 38–54.

Statistical Safety Stock

In retailing and wholesaling, safety (buffer) stock must be far greater than in dependent-demand situations. Customers must be served, but their demands for a given item tend to be highly variable. Fortunately, demand variability and customer service can be expressed in numbers. Manipulate the two numbers (the desired customer service level and the demand variation level) in a certain way, and the result is a calculated *statistical safety stock*.

Calculation Procedure

The first step is to decide on the desired customer **service level**. Among the various ways of defining service, this one is popular: Service level is the percentage of orders filled from stock on hand; the converse, a failure to deliver from stock, is a **stockout**. Service level (rate) plus stockout rate must equal 100 percent. For example, a planned service level of 0.98 means that customer orders would be filled 98 percent of the time, with a stockout the remaining 2 percent of the time.

Safety stock is calculated from service level by the following formula (assuming independent demands, normally distributed):

$$SS = z \sqrt{LT} \, (SD) \tag{9-4}$$

where

SS = Safety stock

z = Value from normal distribution table (see Appendix A), based on service level

LT = Lead time

SD = Standard deviation of demand

(Note: LT and SD must be stated in the same time units; for example, if SD is calculated based on variability over one-month time periods, LT must be expressed in months.) Example 9–9 illustrates the use of the formula.

EXAMPLE 9-9   **SAFETY STOCK—LOAVES OF BREAD**

Assume that mean demand for bread at your house is 100 slices per week and that demand varies by a standard deviation of 40 slices per week. The desired service level is 97.72 percent. It takes just one day to replenish the bread supply. How much safety stock should you carry? What is the reorder point?

Solution

All data must be in the same time units. Thus, replenishment lead time of 1 day is converted to $\frac{1}{7}$ weeks.

The service level, 0.9772, represents a probability: 0.50 (the left half of the area under the normal curve) plus 0.4772. We look for 0.4772 in Appendix A and find it where $z = 2.00$. Insert the data into the formulas, and solve as follows:

$$SS = z\sqrt{LT}(SD)$$
$$= 2.00\sqrt{1/7}(40) = 30.2 \text{ slices}$$

and, from Equation 9–3:

$$ROP = (D)(LT) + SS$$
$$= (100)(1/7) + 30.2 = 44.5 \text{ slices}$$

Unfortunately, the statistical safety stock method omits factors that affect safety stock. One is the effect of lot size. In Chapter 8, we learned that large lot sizes act as buffer stock; if the lot size is very large, a calculated statistical safety stock will be insignificant (compared with the buffering effects of the large lots) and not worth calculating. Small lot sizes have the opposite effect—it is better to keep larger safety stocks on hand than the calculated statistical quantity.

In retailing and wholesaling, lot sizes normally are moderate, which means that the statistical model is valid enough. Exceptions are hard-to-get items or items from undependable suppliers. In those cases, the main concern may be with variable *supply*, but the statistical model accounts only for variable *demand*.

The same types of limitations restrict use of the statistical model in setting buffer stocks for semifinished factory materials and other dependent-demand items. The big problems are the variabilities in supply (the maker), which the statistical model does not address.

PRINCIPLE: Cut the number of suppliers to a few good ones.

Other miscellaneous factors that affect buffer stock are:

Cost. For very costly items, keep very little (even zero) buffer stock on hand. For low-cost items (washers, paper clips), keep perhaps as much as a year's worth.

Space. If the item is very bulky, keep the buffer stock small; and vice versa.

Consequences of a stockout. Sometimes a wide variety of options, such as substitute items, are available in the event of a stockout; in such cases, keep the buffer stock small.

Obsolescence. In high-tech industries, large buffer stocks mean large obsolescence costs; thus, keep buffer stocks small.

With all these ifs, ands, and buts clouding the safety stock issue, how can the model be effectively used? To answer this question, let us consider a company that takes particular pride in its high service level. Frito-Lay is said to have as the centerpiece of its corporate culture the ability to provide its customers with a 99.5 percent service level.[8] To do that Frito needs dedicated people in its distribution system to assure that deliveries to a store in need are always fast. In other words, Frito must control lead-time variability to ensure that safety stocks are not needed for lead-time reasons. In its distribution centers, Frito would need to calculate demand variability for each product, use it to compute safety stock, and then add safety stock to demand during lead time to yield the reorder point. Of course, Frito-Lay computers would do the calculating of standard deviation of demand, lead time, safety stock, mean demand, demand during lead time, and ROP. Computer listings of ROPs for each product may be scanned by Frito product managers, who may decide to change some of the safety stock and ROPs in light of other safety stock factors such as cost and space.

Safety Stock in MRP

What about safety stocks in MRP? George Orlicky, one of the developers of the MRP method, advises against planning for safety stock at component levels. Instead, he says, provide the protection at the MPS level; since component orders are linked to the MPS, safety stock in the master production schedule provides a balance of safety at all lower BOM levels. Adding more safety stock at component levels tends to unbalance the protection. Worse, it tends to erode people's confidence in MRP, because they know there are component safety stocks to fall back on when MRP plans are not followed.

Still, MRP can be designed to allow for safety stock at component levels, and many MRP-using firms carry some amount of safety stock for certain components. Safety stock is most often used for purchased parts that have long lead times, are hard to get, or are obtainable from only one (perhaps unreliable) source.[9] Safety stock at the MRP component level is illustrated in Example 9–10.

EXAMPLE 9–10   **MRP SAFETY STOCK—BICYCLE SPOKES**

Figure 9–17 (a modification of Figure 9–14) shows gross requirements for spokes translated into planned order releases, with a safety stock allowance.

Safety stock (SS) is given as 2,000, and the stock balance is well below that at week 0. Being below the safety stock is a matter for mild concern but not alarm; after all, safety stock is not worth having around if it is never used.

---

[8]Thomas J. Peters and Robert H. Waterman, *In Search of Excellence* (New York: Harper & Row, 1982), pp. 164–65 (HD70.U5P424).
[9]According to Orlicky, these are legitimate exceptions, but they can be overused. See Orlicky, *Material Requirements Planning*, pp. 78–80.

FIGURE 9–17
MRP with Safety Stock—Spoke Example

Spoke:
LT = 1 week
Q = 4,800
SS = 2,000
28 per wheel

Gross requirements		800	800	800	800	1,472	800	800
Scheduled receipts		4,800						
Projected stock balance	200	4,200	3,400	2,600	6,600 / 1,800	5,128	4,328	3,528
Planned order releases				4,800				

The scheduled receipt of 4,800 in week 1 is to be expected in view of the low on-hand balance. The order for 4,800 spokes would have been released in an earlier period. Receipt of 4,800 and issue of 800 (to cover week 1 gross requirements) leave a projected stock balance of 4,200. The balance drops by 800 in each of the next three weeks. That leaves 1,800 in week 4; since 1,800 is below the 2,000-unit safety stock, an order is planned for receipt in week 4. The lot size, Q, is 4,800, and lead time, LT, is one week. Thus, the planned order release is for 4,800 spokes in week 3, which keeps the projected stock balance from going below the safety stock of 2,000 in week 4.

How would safety stock ever be used when firms plan to always be above it? *Unplanned* events, such as hot orders booked too late to plan for, take care of that.

We close this chapter with a final point about inventory timing systems. Prior to the JIT/kanban era, a common viewpoint was that MRP could—and should—plan and control all of a company's inventory items, even low-cost ones; in other words, there should be one system for everything. That viewpoint should probably be altered today. One possibility is to categorize all inventory items into standard (regular-use) and nonstandard (sporadic-use) items. Put the standard items on a simple pull system, but use MRP software to explode the bills of materials for those items whenever there is a major change. Put the nonstandard items on MRP.

SUMMARY

Growing awareness during the 1980s of the hidden costs of inventory raised the level of concern for better management of those resources. Clearly, poor inventory timing leads to waste. On the other hand, a well-run, tightly connected operations control system helps streamline or even eliminate the need for inventory controls.

In a *pull* system (such as JIT), the customer is the driver—the one giving the signal for materials to move from one process to the next. Close connections between provider-user pairs facilitate pull-system operation. A *push* system is provider or schedule driven; the maker delivers goods according to some plan or to keep busy, not in response to a clear demand signal. Typically, in push systems customers do not have close contact with their providers.

Conveyor-paced systems may be classified as pull systems if assemblers have the means and authority to slow down or stop the line if trouble arises. Without that ability, employees perceive the conveyor as a push device. For high-speed fill-and-pack conveyors, the number of units between workstations on the conveyors is an issue: If there are too many, the connection between adjacent stations is too loose, and the feeder station's problems will not get serious attention. So tighten the line by removing lengths of conveyor.

In JIT systems, the communication linkages that manage materials flow are known as *kanban*, from the Japanese work for *card*. Kanban devices must communicate the need for more materials simply and accurately in a variety of settings; thus, several types of kanban signals exist.

The simplest are verbal and "golf ball" kanbans—shouts or intercom or phone messages, and simple rolling or sliding objects. Work itself may serve as a kanban. Simply moving it gives a signal to providers, visually or by tripping a limit switch. Material containers are used as signals, as are kanban squares on floors or tables (the empty square is a pull signal). In classic kanban, actual cards are used, in a single- or dual-card format. Though originated in manufacturing, kanban is useful in service applications as well.

Kanban puts exact limits on the number of containers and pieces of inventory between any maker and user, and it sets forth exact locations for each. The quantities are small, enabling the user and maker to genuinely feel that their activities are closely coordinated.

In some kanban systems, any kanban containers or squares that are empty at the end of the shift must be filled, which means working overtime on some days. A complete absence of overtime suggests too many kanbans. Therefore, supervisors may remove a kanban so as to create a "constructive" panic that will stimulate action to solve problems.

MRP is a push system; it generates planned orders, which, when executed, authorize producing work centers to make and push product forward.

In MRP, a master production schedule for many periods into the future is exploded into gross requirements for all component parts in the bill of materials. The current stock balance for each part is found in the item master file, and projected stock balances are calculated for each future period. Where a negative projected balance is found, the computer back schedules (offsets for lead time) in order to plan an order in a quantity large enough to prevent the negative balance. Scrap allowances, independent demands for service parts, and safety stock can be included in MRP processing.

Basic MRP just launches orders, but closed-loop MRP provides for production progress data to be fed back to the computer, which then issues any needed rescheduling notices. By prudently acting on the notices, schedulers and buyers can keep make rates and use rates better coordinated with less risk of large residual inventories—more like the pull concept.

An extension of MRP called *time-phased order point (TPOP)* allows for blending independent demands (e.g., for service parts) with calculated demands based on parent-item requirements. Another extension, *distribution requirements planning*, ties demands for distribution inventories to planning for manufacturing inventories.

The unique feature of MRP is not the explosion of bills of materials for items in the master schedule; that was done years before MRP was developed (the method produced a list of shortage items that the reorder point system failed to provide enough of). What is unique is that MRP plans far enough into the future to allow lead time offsetting for ordering parts.

MRP is effective in that it plans for materials to arrive when needed for use, not just to refill a stockroom shelf. MRPII extends MRP into the planning of almost any manufacturing resource, including cash flow, and provides a basis for ties to overall business planning.

The oldest inventory-timing approach is replenishment by reorder point (ROP) methods. In the perpetual system, stock is replenished when it drops to a reorder quantity, the ROP. The ROP equals enough stock to cover average demand over an average lead time, plus some safety stock to protect against nonaverage surges in demand or lengthy lead times. In a periodic replenishment system, reorders are at fixed intervals rather than when stock gets low.

Buffer (safety) stock is wasteful and in need of control. Micro-response analysis employs ratios to show the extent of the waste tied up in buffer stock at the work center level; the ratios may be used to stimulate improvement actions at each work center. Physical control of buffer stock can be achieved off line in controlled stockrooms or on the shop floor with the discipline of kanban.

Statistical safety stock calculation employs standard deviation of demand, desired customer service level (service from stock), and lead time. The formula works where demand uncertainty is the dominant variable, as in retailing and wholesaling. Other businesses involve variabilities in supply, which makes the statistical method less useful.

KEY WORDS

Push system
Pull system
Just-in-time (JIT)
Kanban
Material requirements
  planning (MRP)
Planned order
  release
Residual inventory
Product structure
Level-by-level MRP
  processing
Item master file

Bill of materials (BOM)
Regenerative MRP
Net-change MRP
Open order
Rescheduling notice
Time-phased order
  point (TPOP)
Distribution
  requirements
  planning (DRP)
Closed-loop MRP
Production activity
  control

Manufacturing
  resource planning
  (MRPII)
Reorder point (ROP)
Perpetual inventory
  system
Backorder
Micro-response
  analysis
Service level
Stockout

SOLVED PROBLEMS

1. At Computer Services, Inc., small software jobs start at the chief analyst's desk, where each job is assigned to one of the 10 systems analysts. On the average, a job sits in the chief's in-basket for $7\frac{3}{4}$ hours before the chief starts processing it. Average processing time is 15 minutes. In systems analysis, there typically are 60 active jobs.

   Use the appropriate micro-response ratios to analyze the delay situation at the chief's desk and in systems analysis. Is kanban usable at either work center? Explain.

Solution

Chief—Lead time to work content is the proper ratio:

$$\text{Total lead time} = 7\tfrac{3}{4} \text{ hours delay} + \tfrac{1}{4} \text{ hours work content}$$
$$= 8 \text{ hours}$$

Then,

$$\text{Ratio (lead time to work content)} = 8 \text{ to } \tfrac{1}{4}, \text{ or 32 to 1}$$

Analysts—Pieces to operators is the proper ratio:

$$\text{Number of pieces} = 60 \text{ jobs}$$
$$\text{Number of operators} = 10 \text{ analysts}$$

Then,

$$\text{Ratio (pieces to operators)} = 60 \text{ to } 10, \text{ or 6 to 1}$$

Kanban could be used in several ways. For the chief, the rule could be to have zero jobs in the in-basket (kanban = 0) at the end of the day and stay late, if necessary, to meet the rule. Another possibility is to set kanban equal to 5; if the in-basket ever has more than five jobs, call for help from the most senior analyst.

For the analysts, a general kanban policy is one possibility. For example, set an overall ratio at 2 to 1, with no more than 20 jobs assigned to the 10 analysts. Stay late, borrow programmers for use as analysts, or subcontract work if the ratio gets higher. A rule such as kanban = 2 at each analyst's desk will yield the same overall ratio. It is hard to say whether the overall ratio or kanban = 2 at each analyst's desk would work better.

The result of using kanban is to speed work through in much less total lead time (but the same work content time per job). In the office, kanban forces people to start one job and finish it instead of starting many jobs, switching among them and stretching all of them out.

2. The same extruded plastic case is used for three different colors of highlighter felt-tipped pen, A, B, and C. Demand for each color for the next five weeks is as follows (numbers are in thousands):

	Week				
	1	2	3	4	5
A	10			10	
B	18		18		18
C	8	8	8	8	8

a. What is a plausible reason for demands for A and B to occur in alternate periods whereas demands for C occur in every period?

b. Calculate gross requirements for the plastic case. Then, given an on-hand balance of 70,000 at time 0, a lead time of 2 weeks, a safety stock of 2,000, and an order quantity of 20,000, calculate planned order releases.

Solution

a. Demand for colors A and B appears to come from planned orders for a higher-level parent item—perhaps a package containing both colors of highlighter pen. Color C's demand could be independent—perhaps direct orders from a wholesaler or retailer.

b.

		Week				
		1	2	3	4	5
Gross requirements		36	8	26	18	26
Scheduled receipts				20		16
Projected stock balance	70	34	26	0	2	-24
Planned order releases		20		40		

Explanation: The projected 0 in week 3 is below the safety stock of 2, which requires a planned order of 20 back scheduled by 2 weeks to week 1. The projected −24 in week 5 requires a *double* lot size—40 instead of 20—back scheduled to week 3.

3. A wholesaler's computer records show the following for one of its inventory items:

$$\text{Mean monthly demand} = 8{,}000$$
$$\text{Standard deviation of demand} = 1{,}000 \text{ per month}$$
$$\text{Replenishment lead time} = 1 \text{ month}$$

If the desired service level is 95 percent, what is the statistical safety stock? What is the reorder point?

Solution

The service level, 0.95, represents a probability: 0.50 (the left half of the zone under the normal curve) plus 0.45. We find 0.45 in Appendix A where, by interpolation, $z = 1.645$. Then,

$$SS = z\sqrt{LT}(SD)$$
$$= 1.645\sqrt{1}(1,000)$$
$$= 1,645$$

Next, compute mean demand for the lead time period:

$$DLT = 8,000 \text{ per month} \times 1 \text{ month} = 8,000$$

Then,

$$ROP = DLT + SS$$
$$= 8,000 + 1,645$$
$$= 9,645$$

REFERENCES

Books

Hall, Robert. *Zero Inventories*. Homewood, Ill.: Dow Jones-Irwin, 1983.
Japan Management Association, ed. *Kanban: Just-in-Time at Toyota*. Trans. David J. Lu. Stamford, Conn.: Productivity, Inc., 1986 (originally published in Japanese in 1985) (TS157.T6913).
Monden, Yasuhiro. *Toyota Production System: Practical Approach to Production Management*. Norcross, Ga.: Institute of Industrial Engineers, 1983.
Orlicky, Joseph. *Material Requirements Planning*. New York: McGraw-Hill, 1975 (TS155.8.O74).
Plossl, G. W., and O. W. Wight. *Production and Inventory Control*. Englewood Cliffs, N.J.: Prentice-Hall, 1967 (HD55.P5).
Schonberger, Richard J. *Japanese Manufacturing Techniques: Nine Hidden Lessons in Simplicity*. New York: Free Press, 1982 (HD70.J3S36).
Wight, Oliver W. *MRPII: Unlocking America's Productivity Potential*. Williston, Vt.: Oliver Wight Limited Publications, 1981 (TS161.W5x).

Periodicals/Societies

Journal of Operations Management (American Production and Inventory Control Society).
Journal of Purchasing and Materials Management (National Association of Purchasing Management).
Production and Inventory Management (American Production and Inventory Control Society).
Target (Association for Manufacturing Excellence).

REVIEW QUESTIONS

1. What is the role of the maker or provider under push systems and under pull systems?
2. Why is it desirable for the number of kanbans to be small? Why must it usually be larger than zero?
3. What types of kanban signals might be used to trigger materials movement?
4. Under what circumstances would kanban removal be appropriate?
5. How might kanban be applied to patrons awaiting service?
6. How does MRP differ from MRPII?
7. What is the role of the item master file in MRP?
8. How does an open order differ from a planned order?
9. How does DRP improve on the usual way in which distribution centers are managed?
10. What is the hazard in using the computer and MRP to reschedule whenever any manufacturing variables change?
11. What is closed-loop MRP?
12. Why is the ROP system considered a perpetual system?
13. Given a safety stock, what else is needed to arrive at a reorder point? Explain.
14. Contrast visual and records-based ROP.
15. To what extent can safety stock determinations be computerized? Does it depend on type of industry? Explain.
16. Is the periodic system simpler or more complex than the perpetual system? Explain.
17. What is the purpose of micro-response analysis?
18. How should buffer stock be controlled physically?

PROBLEMS AND EXERCISES

1. Aca-Documents, a copying shop across from a college campus, does many "pick-up-later" jobs. However, customers often return before the jobs have even been started. The manager, Q.R. Smith, sees customers leaving in a huff, taking their jobs to one of the competing shops several blocks away. Smith's analysis reveals that the number of jobs awaiting processing averages 6 but often is 25 or even 40. Equipment is not a major problem, since the shop has six copying machines, ranging in size and speed, behind the counter for pick-up-later jobs. Smith sees labor capacity as the problem, even though part-time student employees are close by and eager to work more hours. Smith employs 30 people, all students working part-time.

    Use micro-response concepts and the ready availability of labor to devise a plan for minimizing job processing delays.

2. An accounts payable office consists of three people. Their work flow includes passing piles of invoices among them in the process of authorizing payment. Recently the average number of invoices on the three desks was 150 and the typical time an invoice spent in the office was 3 days. Select a micro-response ratio, and explain how it might be used to improve the operation. What results migh'. be expected?

3. A high-speed production line fills and packages plastic bottles of shampoo. A conveyor line draws the bottles past 10 workstations, the last being an automatic palletizer of cartons of bottles. The rated speed of the line is 400 bottles per minute, but there are frequent slowdowns and trouble stops. About 8,000 bottles are usually in the line at any given instant, and the production line winds for 1,000 feet through the plant. The new plant manager feels that "no one is really in charge." What clues suggest that the plant manager may be correct? Propose improvements.

4. A manufacturer of X-ray machines presently has partially completed machines scattered around the assembly areas, with only a few actually being worked on by the department's five assemblers. The units accumulate in assembly because parts and subassemblies from other departments arrive whenever the departments happen to complete them.
   a. Is the current system push or pull? Explain.
   b. Suggest an improved system.

5. Four ways to support a pull system are: (1) kanban squares, (2) special-purpose containers, (3) general-purpose containers with kanban (cards) attached, and (4) a powered assembly conveyor with no container or card necessary. Which of the four should be used in each of the following situations? Explain your answers.
   a. A book printer; books are printed and bound in a route through four different departments.
   b. Final assembly of 13-inch TV sets.
   c. Production of vitreous china products (sinks of all sizes, toilets, tubs, etc.); involves molding, glazing, firing in kilns, and so forth.
   d. Repetitive production of several different large, highly polished precision metal parts.
   e. Internal mail delivery in a large office building.

6. The following matrix shows partial MRP data for one component part. Scheduled receipts are missing, as is the planned-order-release row. Lead time is three weeks. A fixed order quantity (rather than lot-for-lot) is used.

	Week					
	0	1	2	3	4	5
Gross requirements		80	80	90	90	90
Scheduled receipts						
Projected stock balance	190	270	190	100	10	80

What fixed order quantity is used? When is a scheduled receipt due in? In what period is there a planned order release?

7. A partial master production schedule and material requirements plans for a bicycle manufacturer are shown in the accompanying figure.
   a. Complete the calculations of gross requirements, projected stock balances, and planned order releases for handlebars and cut tubes.
   b. Recalculate the planned order release given a safety stock of 20 for the handlebars and a scrap allowance of 3 percent for the cut tubing.

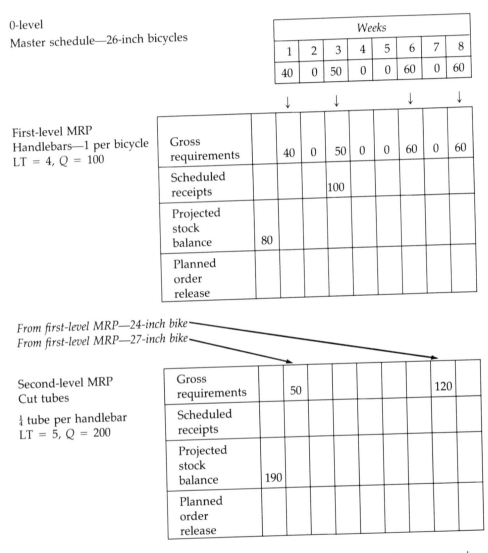

0-level
Master schedule—26-inch bicycles

Weeks							
1	2	3	4	5	6	7	8
40	0	50	0	0	60	0	60

First-level MRP
Handlebars—1 per bicycle
LT = 4, Q = 100

		1	2	3	4	5	6	7	8
Gross requirements			40	0	50	0	0	60	0	60
Scheduled receipts					100					
Projected stock balance	80									
Planned order release										

From first-level MRP—24-inch bike
From first-level MRP—27-inch bike

Second-level MRP
Cut tubes

¼ tube per handlebar
LT = 5, Q = 200

		1	2	3	4	5	6	7	8
Gross requirements			50					120		
Scheduled receipts										
Projected stock balance	190									
Planned order release										

8. Five companies produce and sell irrigation equipment in the same region of the country. Company A has a reorder point system. Company B uses MRP, but only to launch orders. Company C has full closed-loop MRP. Company D uses MRP plus distribution requirements planning. Company E has an MRPII system (including DRP). Discuss each company's likely competitive strengths and weaknesses.

9. Acme Wood Products Corporation makes wooden picture frames. One size is 10″ × 12″ and is made with three finishes: oak stained, walnut stained, and mahogany stained. The parts needed for final assembly and finishing for each frame are two 10-inch and two 12-inch wood pieces and four corner brackets. Inventory planning is by MRP. Lot sizes are 10,000 for wood parts and 5,000 for brackets.

   a. Construct the BOM structure. You need not limit yourself to the given data.

   b. What should go into the item master file? Be as specific as possible given the above data, but you need not limit yourself to these data.

   c. Assume that for every oak-stained frame two walnut-stained and three mahogany-stained frames are made. Also assume that gross requirements for 10-inch wood pieces in the next five weeks are 0, 600, 0, 240, and 300. Compute all parent-item gross requirements based on these gross requirements for the wood pieces (work backward).

   d. Based on the gross requirements information from question c, compute the planned-order-release schedule for 10-inch wood pieces only. Assume a current on-hand balance of zero and a lead time of one week.

10. The following sketch shows the two main parts of a transparent-tape dispenser; molded plastic housing and roll of tape. A master production schedule for the dispenser is shown below the sketch.

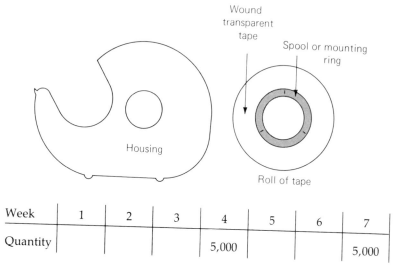

Wound transparent tape

Spool or mounting ring

Housing

Roll of tape

Week	1	2	3	4	5	6	7
Quantity				5,000			5,000

   a. Draw a structured bill of materials for the tape dispenser. Include the main parts and one level of parts below that.

   b. Assume that lead times are one week for the roll of tape and two weeks for the spool (mounting ring). Beginning on-hand balances are 0 for the roll of tape and 3,000 for the spool. Draw the MPS, with MRPs for the roll of tape and the spool below it. (Do *not* include housing and wound transparent tape.) Compute gross requirements, scheduled receipts (if any), on-hand balance, and planned order releases for the roll of tape and the spool. Use lot-for-lot order quantities (*not* fixed order quantities). Show your results in the usual MRP display format.

c. Explain your entries or lack of entries in the scheduled-receipts row for both the roll of tape and the spool.

d. Assume that the rolls of tape are sold separately as well as being a component of the tape dispenser. Make up a forecast of independent (external) demand for rolls of tape for each of the seven time buckets. Merge your forecast of independent demand with the dependent demand from the parent item. Also, assume an on-hand balance of 2,000 for the roll of tape and a scheduled receipt of 4,000 in week 2 for the spool. Recompute the MRPs as in question b. What could explain the quantity 4,000 as a scheduled receipt in week 2?

11. Assume you are employed by a company that makes a type of simple chair (you decide on the chair's design). MRP is to be the method of inventory planning for the chair.

   a. Draw a bill-of-materials structure for the chair. Briefly explain or sketch the type of chair.

   b. Develop an 8- to 10-week MPS for the chair.

   c. Develop MRPs for three or four of the chair's components, with the following restrictions:

   (1) Include level 1 and level 2 components (e.g., a chair arm might be level 1 and the raw material for making it level 2).

   (2) Make your own assumptions about lead times, order quantities, and beginning inventories.

   (3) Include a safety stock for one of the parts.

   Your answer should be realistic; no two students should have the same answer.

12. Repeat problem 11 using a ball-point pen as your product.

13. Select a product composed of fabricated parts (*not* one referred to in the text explanation of MRP or in preceding MRP problems). In *one page*, develop an MPS for the product, plus a level 1 MRP for a major module and a level 2 MRP for a part that goes into the level 1 module.

   a. Develop an 8- to 10-week planning period.

   b. Draw the MPS at the top of your page, with time buckets for the two levels of parts MRPs lined up below it. The material requirements plans for the parts should include four rows: one for gross requirements, one for scheduled receipts, one for projected stock balance, and one for planned order releases. Make up the following data: realistic quantities for the MPS; beginning on-hand balances, lead times, and order quantities for each part (make one order quantity fixed and the other lot-for-lot); and one or more scheduled receipts based on a previous, already released order (be careful about the timing and quantity of scheduled receipts).

   c. For level 1 and level 2 parts, calculate the timing and quantities of gross requirements, scheduled receipts, on-hand balance, and planned order releases. Display results on your charts, and:

   (1) Include a safety stock for one of the parts.

(2) Include a scrap allowance for one of the parts.

(3) Include demands from an external source (rather than from parent planned order releases) for one of the parts.

14. Following are bills of materials for two sizes of kitchen knife. Two parts are common to both knives: rivets and 8-foot wood bars. Also, a 6-inch cut wood block is common to two different parents—handle, left and handle, right—for the medium-size knife. Presently there are no parts of any kind on hand or on order. Order quantities are lot-for-lot rather than fixed. The master schedule for the next seven weeks is as follows:

	Week						
	1	*2*	*3*	*4*	*5*	*6*	*7*
Small knife	0	0	0	0	1,200	0	960
Medium-size knife	0	0	0	800	0	1,200	400

a. What is the first planned order release for rivets? Calculate quantity and week.

b. What is the total number of 4-inch cut wood blocks that should be ordered to cover MPS demand in weeks 1 through 5?

c. How many 8-foot wood bars should be ordered in week 3?

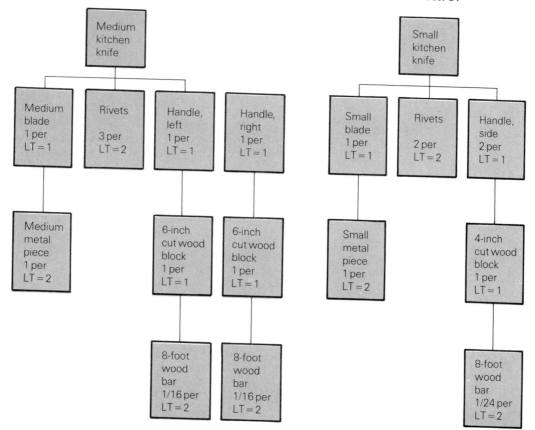

15. The following table shows partial MRP data for one component part. Lead time is two weeks.

		Week				
	0	1	2	3	4	5
Gross requirements		80	0	80	90	90
Scheduled receipts				70		
Projected stock balance	90					

a. If the order quantity is lot-for-lot (just enough to meet requirements), when should there be a planned order release?

b. If safety stock is five units, when should there be a planned order release?

c. If there is a scrap allowance of 10 percent included in planned order releases, what should the planned-order-release quantity be? Assume zero safety stock.

16. Following is a list of inventory items that might be found in various locations in a hospital. For each item, pick what you feel are the two factors that should most influence safety stock for the item. Also, state whether the item should have a high, medium, or low safety stock as measured in weeks' supply. Explain.

Toothpicks
Disposable hypodermic syringes
X-ray film
Coffee cups (pottery)
Daily newspapers (for sale)

Pillows
Rare blood
Aspirin
Soap solution for mopping floors
Prosthetic devices (artificial limbs)

17. A beer distributor reorders when a stock item drops to a reorder point. Reorder points include statistical safety stocks with the service level set at 95 percent. For PBR beer, the forecast usage for the next two weeks is 500 cases and the standard deviation of demand has been 137 cases (for a two-week period). Purchase lead time is one week (a five-day work week).

a. What is the safety stock? How many working days' supply is it?

b. What is the ROP?

c. How many times larger would the safety stock have to be to provide 99 percent service to PBR customers? How many working days' supply does the 99 percent level provide?

d. Statistical safety stock protects against demand variability. What other two factors do you think are especially important influences on size of safety stock for PBR beer? Explain.

18. Brown Instrument Company replenishes replacement (service) parts based on statistical reorder point. One part is a 40-mm thumbscrew. Relevant data for the thumbscrew are:

Planned stockout frequency = Once per year

Planned lead time = 1 week

Forecast for next week = 30

Batch size = 300

Standard deviation of demand = 25 (per week)

a. What is the reorder point? (Hint: Convert planned stockout frequency to service level.)

b. What would the effect on ROP be if lead time were four weeks instead of one? (Just discuss the effect; don't try to calculate it.)

19. An auto muffler shop reorders all common mufflers and the like every Tuesday morning. (Rarely needed mufflers are not stocked.) Two of the biggest-selling models are muffler A and muffler B. Each is ordered if stock is below 3, and enough are ordered to bring the supply up to 10. Under this reordering system, the average inventory of each is about eight. It takes two days to replenish.

   A reorder-point policy with a service level of 90 percent is being considered as a replacement for the present policy. To see whether ROP would reduce costly inventories, the following data are provided:

	Muffler A	Muffler B
Item cost	$7	$39
Daily usage (average)	2	2
Standard deviation of daily usage	1.5	1.5

   a. What kind of reorder policy is the present one? Are there names for it?

   b. What safety stocks and ROPs would there be for mufflers A and B under a perpetual system?

   c. Should the muffler shop go to a perpetual system? Stay with the present system? Devise a hybrid system? Discuss, including pros and cons.

20. One storeroom item has an average demand of 1,200 per year. Demand variability, as measured by standard deviation, is 25 (based on monthly calculations).

   a. If the desired service level is 90 percent and the lead time is 2.5 months, what is the statistical safety stock?

   b. The item is bulky, costs over $1,000 per unit, and is bought from a variety of suppliers. What effects should these factors have on the safety stock? Explain.

21. Star City Tool and Die has been using a certain 2-inch square metal insert at an average rate of 200 per five-day week with a standard deviation of 125. Star City makes the inserts itself on its punch press. Only one day is needed to make more of them.

   a. The insert is so critical that management wants the item to be available (in stock) 99.9 percent of the time. What is the statistical safety stock? What is the statistical reorder point?

   b. The insert has been required for only the past six weeks and is inexpensive to make. Should these factors affect safety stock and reorder point? Explain.

22. Fuel oil is one source of heat in a northern university. Average fuel demand in winter is 6,000 gallons per month. The reorder point is 6,400 gallons; the average lead time is 2 weeks; and the order quantity is 8,000 gallons.
    a. How many orders are there in an average five-month winter season?
    b. What is the demand during lead time? What is the safety stock?
    c. Draw a graph showing three replenishment cycles for the fuel oil. Construct the graph so that:
       (1) In the first cycle, delivery takes more than two weeks (with normal demand during lead time).
       (2) In the second cycle, delivery takes less than two weeks (with normal demand during lead time).
       (3) In the third cycle, lead time is average but demand during the lead-time period is low.
    Note: Since fuel-oil usage for heating is continuous rather than discrete, your line showing actual usage should waver downward rather than follow a downward stairstep pattern.

23. One of the products manufactured by a maker of hand tools is pliers. There are four parts, shown in the accompanying illustration. The status of each part at a given point in time is as shown below the sketch; reference data are also given.

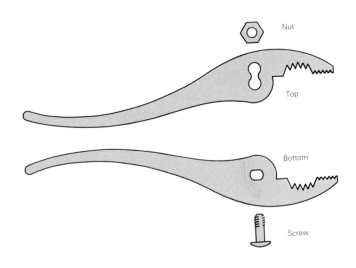

Item	Inventory Status	ROP	Q	LT
Nut	8,000 on hand, none on order	4,000	10,000	10 days
Top	2,200 on hand, none on order	2,000	5,000	10 days
Bottom	3,800 on hand, none on order	2,000	5,000	10 days
Screw	1,700 on hand, 10,000 ordered two days ago	4,000	10,000	5 days
Pliers	2,700 on hand, none on order	3,000	3,000	5 days

For the given data, the following partial table lists required ordering actions and resulting inventory status. Complete the table (determine the correct ordering actions and inventory statuses for the blank cells).

Item	Ordering Actions	Inventory Status
Pliers	Shop order for 3,000 to replenish low (below ROP) stocks.	2,700 in stock
Nut	Release 3,000 from warehouse for pliers shop order.	3,000 on order
Top		
Bottom		
Screw		

CASE STUDY   **HYGAIN-TELEX***

The HyGain-Telex plant in Lincoln, Nebraska, manufactures antennas. It currently has a U.S. Army contract for Model X32 antennas. The contract requires a production rate of 200 Model X32s per day. The contract quantity may be changed quarterly.

Chris Piper, the foreman, is collecting data for a JIT project. Piper has selected the X32 antenna base (not the whip part of the antenna, which is fairly simple) for the JIT project. Exhibit 1 is a photograph of the base.

Manufacture of the X32

There are several stages of manufacture for the X32 base, which is a cylinder 6 inches in diameter and 10 inches high. These are the basic production processes, and their standard times, with which Piper was concerned:

Mold the Lexan plastic base. Some holes are molded into the base by use of core plugs. 2.50 minutes.

Drill and tap (eight operations): Seven drill or tap operations, taking from 0.12 to 1.02 minutes; installing helicoils, 1.82 minutes. (The eight operations include drilling a dozen more holes; half of the drilled and molded-in holes are tapped, and half are installed with helicoils, which are self-threaded inserts—a rather old technology.)

Assemble (epoxy) a "birdcage" (ferrite core, coaxial cable, etc.) inside the Lexan base. 1.78 minutes. (Note: The birdcage is produced as a subassembly, going through 12 operations.)

Foam the assembly. 2.61 minutes.

Paint. 1.82 minutes.

Case topics:

Lead-time-to-work-content ratio.
Pieces-to-workstations ratio.
Distinction between preventive maintenance and setup.
Frequency of delivery.
Kanban.

Statistical process control.
Total preventive maintenance.
Simplifying the schedule.
Partnership with customer.
Cellular manufacturing.

EXHIBIT 1
Base for X32 Antenna

Flow Data

Piper felt that the place to start was between drill-and-tap and assembly. Drill-and-tap ran one shift, and assembly usually ran two shifts. Piper asked L. G. Smith, the industrial engineer, to find out the flow distance between processes, especially those two processes. Smith scaled off the distances on the factory blueprints and came up with a total flow distance of 1,296 feet, which breaks down as follows: from mold to drill-and-tap, 192 feet; from drill-and-tap to tank assembly, 144 feet; from assembly to paint, 480 feet; and from paint to final prep, 480 feet.

Piper wanted to be sure. "Are those prints current?" he asked. Smith assured him that they were. Just to make sure, Piper got a tape measure and checked some of the distances; they were indeed correct.

For flow-time data, Piper went to Raul Nieves, the scheduler. Nieves pointed out that the flow time from molding to final prep had been "as short as about five days for a few lots, but we are quoting six weeks to marketing." Piper asked Nieves to come up with some sort of average. Nieves did so by putting pieces of colored tape on a few molded bases from several lots over the space of three weeks. The average flow time, found by noting how long it took for the taped

EXHIBIT 2
HyGain-Telex—Flowchart

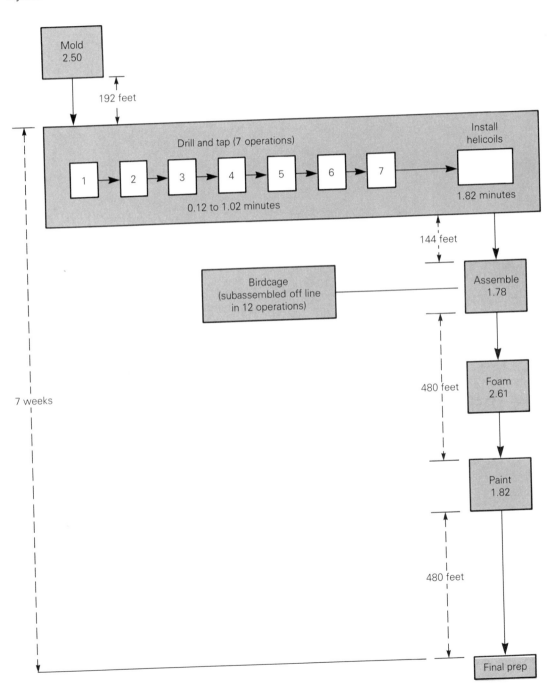

units to get to final prep, was seven weeks. One week of that was the flow time from the start of drill-and-tap to assembly (see Exhibit 2 for summary data).

> *Question 1.* What is the ratio of actual production lead time (or flow time) to work content time from the start of drill-and-tap to final prep? (Note: You will not need to be concerned with the issue of one or two shifts.)

Nieves also provided Piper with scheduling and unit-load data. Scheduling released work packets in lot quantities of 2,000. Drilled and tapped bases were forwarded to assembly by forklift truck, in wire-bound pallets holding about 400 bases. In other words, about five forklift trips were required to move one "packet-release" quantity to assembly.

Problems

At this point Piper called a meeting. Smith and Nieves were there, along with Karen Jones, manager of quality assurance; Bob Crane, an inspector; Doug Atkins, a drill press operator; and Ellie Olson, an assembler. Piper announced that the purpose of the meeting was to "brainstorm what can and maybe can't be done to reduce WIP and flow time" between drill-and-tap and assembly. Piper explained that the purpose was to improve and not look for blame. In that spirit, "please speak frankly."

Piper's first question was directed to Atkins: "Doug, there's no setup time on the drill press that you use for the X32—it's a dedicated tool, right?" Atkins said that it was.

"How about up time on the drill press? Is it reliable?" asked Piper. Atkins replied that the drill press itself was fine but that the tapping head with spindles in the taps was a problem sometimes: "They break or the bushings loosen," which results in off-center taps or a marred surface around the outside. "Then I have to call maintenance to make adjustments or replace the head."

"About how many hours per month are you down waiting for them to make those adjustments or replacements, Doug?" Atkins estimated about five hours.

Ellie Olson was next. "Ellie, do you have any problems with the bases? Quality problems or running out of bases?" Ellie said that sometimes she did have to wait for the fork truck to bring another wire-bound; she estimated six hours of wait time per month.

The quality problems were the biggest headache, Olson felt, and she looked at Bob Crane, the inspector, for corroboration. Crane agreed that the defect rates were high, especially cracks and fractures around the helicoil inserts. Some, "maybe 5 percent," they thought, were minor defects that Crane or Olson let pass. Crane had figures on how many were defective but repairable and defective-scrapped: 2 percent repaired, 4 percent scrapped.

Karen Jones, quality manager, pointed out that their customer, the Army, had been rejecting an average of 7 percent in recent months. "I believe that the majority of the problems can be traced back to drill-and-tap," she stated.

Piper then asked if anyone knew what level of work-in-process (WIP) there was of bases. Nieves said he had just made a rough count; there were six wirebounds full at drill-and-tap and eight and a half full at assembly.

Question 2. If 15 direct labor employees are involved in the production of the Lexan base, what is the ratio of pieces in process to people who could work on them?

JIT Opportunities

At this point, the group began brainstorming on JIT opportunities. Some of the options they discussed were:

1. Setup reduction (adjust and replace spindles/bushings) on the drill presses. To this suggestion, everyone nodded their heads, but no one commented pro or con.
2. Cut transit quantities. Nieves (scheduler) protested: "The fork truck drivers would be making more trips."
3. Adopt kanban. Nieves liked the idea.
4. Use process control charts in drill-and-tap. Everyone thought it was about time to do some of this.
5. Adopt total preventive maintenance. This was Piper's (the foreman's) idea. The others showed little reaction; they seemed not to know what that meant.
6. Put in conveyors. Smith (the I.E.) offered that one; nobody challenged the idea.
7. Slash the buffer stock. Nieves suggested this, pointing out that inventory counting was a headache anyway. Olson was indignant: "I run out of bases too often the way it is."
8. Get rid of the packet-release quantities. Smith suggested this but admitted that he did not know what kind of scheduling might replace the packet-release system.
9. Bring the design engineers in to come up with a better design of the base. Everyone smiled and nodded vigorously.
10. Expand the size of the task force (which they were calling themselves by that time), including a customer (Army) representative. This was Jones's suggestion, which was met by a couple of favorable nods.
11. Move a drill press into the assembly department. This was Smith's idea. Crane (inspector) said that "if we do that I won't have to inspect the bases—and I'm not complaining; it's a boring job."

The meeting broke up with plenty of ideas but no decisions.

Question 3. What should be done? Should all the ideas be implemented? None of them? A different set? What order? To what extent? What time period? What guidance and direction? Discuss each of the eleven options that came out in the brainstorming session.

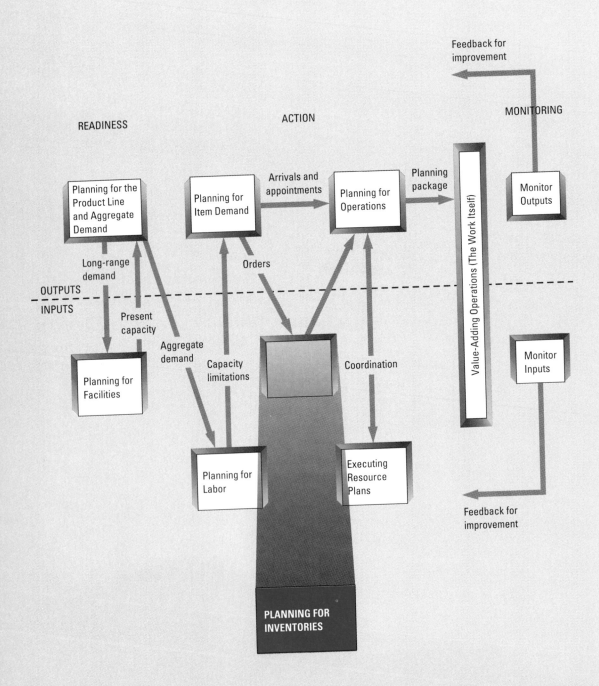

CHAPTER 10

Lot Sizing

LOT SIZING: FUNDAMENTALS

Lot-for-Lot (and Less-than-Lot) Processing
Part-Period Algorithm (PPA)
Economic Order Quantity (EOQ)
EOQ Variations
Concluding Comments

LOT-SIZING UNDER ATTACK

Capturing Lot-Sizing Savings, or Relaxing the Rigidities
Operating Benefits
Reducing Setup Costs
Reducing Order-Processing Costs
The New Economics of Lot Sizing

The natural companion of inventory timing is inventory quantities, or **lot sizing.** At one time, experts argued that lot sizing was less important than the timing issue, for one could order too much or too little and still generally serve the customer. A late order, however, could prove worthless.

The 1980s generated renewed interest in inventory quantities because of the recognition that smaller lot sizes usually equate with reduced lead times. With shorter lead times, response to customer demand is quicker—a competitive advantage. In other words, lot sizes determine lead time, and lead time to *produce* and *deliver* an item is more of a competitive factor than *when* to place an order for it. Before considering lot size reduction, we will first address some basic lot-sizing models and concepts.

PRINCIPLE: Produce and deliver at the customer's use rate (or a representation of it); decrease cycle interval and lot size

LOT SIZING: FUNDAMENTALS

Many lot-sizing methods are in existence. Extremely simple models include fixed-order-quantity, in which a constant order size is used regardless of when the order is placed; and fixed-period-quantity, in which an order is placed every so often, perhaps daily or weekly. In view of the simplicity of these two models, nothing further need be said of them.

We will focus on three models: lot-for-lot, part-period algorithm, and economic order quantity and some of its variations. The section ends with brief general comments on lot sizing.

Lot-for-Lot (and Less-than-Lot) Processing

Lot-for-lot, one of the simplest approaches calls for making just the quantity needed for the "parent" item's demand. In other words, the lot size is the net quantity required in each period; there is no batching of requirements into larger lots. Orders are frequent and order processing costs high, but the idea is to carry no inventory from period to period. Therefore, planned carrying costs are minimized.

From the narrow perspective of a single inventory item, lot-for-lot seems uneconomical because of the high order processing costs. But in some cases, especially as part of a MRP system, lot-for-lot has advantages for the system as a whole. A collection of lot-for-lot orders tends to keep purchasing and fabricating workloads fairly even from period to period. Large lots or batches, on the other hand, tend to cause **lumpy workloads** and uneven demands on capacity. Greater peak capacity is required as Figure 10–1 illustrates.

FIGURE 10–1

Lot-for-Lot versus Batched Ordering

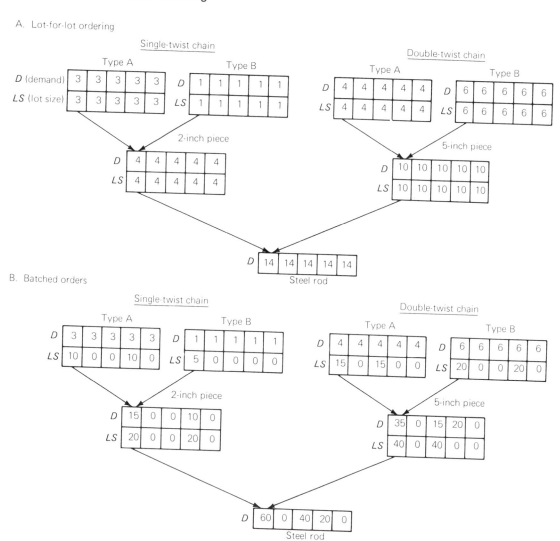

A. Lot-for-lot ordering

B. Batched orders

Figure 10–1A shows a smooth demand pattern for four styles of chain; the smooth demand/production pattern is carried downward through the two levels to the purchased-part level (steel rod). Thus the purchasing/receiving workload (for steel rod) is level and invariable; the workload for cutting 2-inch and 5-inch pieces in the cutting work center is level and invariable; and the workload for making four styles of chain in fabrication work centers is level and invariable. The even workloads may allow the work centers to run at nearly full capacity and with no sporadic overtime.

On the other hand, order batching transforms smooth demands and even loads (workloads) into lumpy ones. Further, the lumpiness is amplified downward through bill-of-materials levels, as shown in Figure 10–1B. At the finished-chain level, batching results in lot sizes varying from 0 to 20. At the cut-piece level, the variation is from 0 to 40, and the steel-rod level, it's from 0 to 60. With uneven workloads, the work center has sometimes too little to do and at other times too much to do.

Lot-for-lot also could be the scheduling rule in a just-in-time operation—temporarily, at least. Bear in mind, however, that the JIT mandate is to keep cutting lot sizes. Thus, a large customer order might be broken up into several sublots, each processed quickly at a work center and quickly sent on to the next, with another sublot hot on its heels.

Large tour groups are handled this way: If a group of 100 college freshmen appear at the library for a tour, the tour guide will break them into, say, five groups of 20, and stagger the start times as the groups tour the building. It is often true that what's good for human customers—in this case, sublot-for-sublot—is also a good way to process widgets in a plant or documents in an office.

In some cases, the JIT ideal—a lot size of one—may ultimately be attained. Sublots or one-unit processing need not raise the cost of order processing, because in the JIT mode, costly order-processing systems are usually replaced by simple visual signals (kanban). Further, handling distances may be compressed by moving equipment into cells.

While lot-for-lot is versatile enough for use in connection with MRP, JIT, or other systems, the part-period algorithm, considered next, was designed particularly for the material requirements planning mode.

Part-Period Algorithm (PPA)

The **part-period algorithm (PPA)** is aimed at minimizing average cost per time period of ordering and carrying inventory for a single item.[1] The algorithm may be applied in either a lumpy or a smoothed demand situation.

A *part-period* is an inventory carrying unit meaning one part carried or held for one period. For example, 12 part-periods can be obtained by carrying one part for 12 periods, two parts for 6 periods, three parts for 4 periods, or any other combination in which the product equals 12. Associated with a part-period is a *carrying cost*—the cost of carrying one part for one period.

PPA uses an *economic part-period (EPP)* factor. The EPP is the number of part-periods required to make carrying costs equal ordering or setup costs. (The reason why it should be economical to equate these costs will be presented in the later discussion of economic order quantities.) Mathematically:

$$EPP = \frac{S}{CC} \qquad (10-1)$$

---

[1]PPA is also known as the *least-total-cost (LTC) method*.

where

$$S = \text{Setup or ordering cost}$$
$$CC = \text{Carrying cost per part per period}$$

PPA calls for placing the first order such that it arrives in the time period of the first (net) requirement. The question is whether this first order should also include requirements for later periods or merely those for the first period. The lot size options are the cumulative period demands throughout the visible planning horizon. In PPA, one more period's demand is added to the order quantity so long as the cumulative part-periods of carried inventory do not exceed the EPP. In other words, the chosen lot size is that whose part-period total most nearly equals, but does not exceed, the EPP.

The chosen lot size covers a certain interval (so many periods) of the planning horizon. The period following the covered interval will require another order, and the PPA routine will repeat. Example 10–1 demonstrates PPA.

EXAMPLE 10–1   PART-PERIOD ALGORITHM

Projected net requirements for the next seven weeks for a certain manufactured part are: 20, 0, 20, 25, 35, 10, 10. If setup cost is $600 per lot, lead time is zero, and carrying cost is $10 per unit per week, what lot size does PPA recommend?

Solution:

1. Calculate EPP:

$$\text{EPP} = \frac{S}{CC} = \frac{\$600}{\$10} = 60$$

2. Calculate cumulative part-periods carried, beginning with the first period, for each lot size option. Stop and back up when EPP is reached. Calculations follow:

Trial Lot Size = Parts Produced in Period 1	Covered Demand Period (week)	Parts Required	Part-Period Calculation	Cumulative Part-Periods
20	1	20	20 parts × 0 weeks carried = 0	0
20	2	0	0 parts × 1 week carried = 0	0
40	3	20	20 parts × 2 weeks carried = 40	40
65	4	25	25 parts × 3 weeks carried = 75	115

The first trial lot size is 20, which covers only the first period's demand. If 20 are made and used in period 1, there is zero inventory to carry; thus, 20 times 0 equals 0 part-periods. The second trial lot size covers a zero-demand period, so there still are zero part-periods to be carried. The third trial lot size adds the demand for period 3. That demand, 20, will be covered by a lot of 40 that is produced in period 1. But the 20 units for period 3 are carried in stock for the entire first and second periods, which equals 20 times 2, or 40 part-periods to be carried. The fourth trial lot size adds another 75 part-periods, calculated by the same logic. The cumulative total becomes 115 part-periods. The EPP, 60, is exceeded by the 115 for the fourth trial lot size. Therefore, select the previous lot size, 40, which covers net requirements for weeks 1 through 3. The whole PPA procedure starts over again at week 4 and yields a second lot size of 70, which covers net requirements for weeks 4, 5, and 6. (Computation of this lot size is reserved as an end-of-chapter problem.)

The results of the PPA calculations are summarized as follows:

				Period			
	1	2	3	4	5	6	7
Net requirements	20	0	20	25	35	10	10
Planned order (lot size)	40			70			*

*Not computed because of lack of net requirements for periods 8 and beyond.

Like lot-for-lot, PPA results in variable lot sizes. Lot size is calculated to equal future projected requirements. With fixed lot size methods, on the other hand, any production in excess of requirements must be carried in inventory until the next demand occurs. The part-period algorithm yields a lot size that roughly minimizes the sum of setup and carrying costs.[2] Fixed lot size models, such as the economic order quantity, *precisely* minimize that sum.

Economic Order Quantity (EOQ)

The **economic order quantity (EOQ)** is one of the oldest tools of management science; a basic EOQ formula was developed by F. W. Harris in 1915. The newer PPA method is actually an offspring of EOQ.

Like PPA, EOQ concerns the inventory costs of a single item. Unlike PPA, however, EOQ does not provide varying lot sizes to match projected variations in demand; instead, EOQ is based on past *average* demand. Recall from Chapter 9 that reorder point (ROP) is also based on past average demand, whereas MRP is based on projected future demand. Historically, EOQ and ROP have been used as a knife-and-fork-like pair, and sometimes they are studied as a set. Actually, EOQ lot sizing may be used with a variety of order-timing methods, and ROP order timing may be used with a variety of lot-sizing models.

Like most models, the basic EOQ makes a few simplifying assumptions. While

[2]Actually, PPA does not *exactly* minimize these costs. The reason is explained in Joseph Orlicky, *Material Requirements Planning* (New York: McGraw-Hill, 1975), pp. 128–29 (TS155.8.074).

the real world never quite matches the assumptions, the matchup sometimes is close enough for the EOQ to be helpful. The assumptions are:

1. Demand is known and constant, without seasonality.
2. Order processing (or setup) costs are known and constant (do not vary with quantity ordered).
3. Cost per unit is constant (no quantity discounts).
4. The entire lot is delivered at one time, instantaneously. This is typical of purchased goods, but not of items produced by the user.
5. The holding cost rate is known and constant. Total holding costs are a linear function and depend on holding cost rate and quantity ordered.

Costs of Inventory

The period inventory costs that EOQ seeks to minimize are of three types: order processing cost, carrying cost, and item cost.

1. Order Processing Cost. In a given time period—say, a year—an item may be reordered once, twice, three times, or more—even daily in some JIT cases. If it is ordered once, the lot size is large enough to cover the whole year's demand; if ordered twice, a half-year's demand is the lot size; and so on.

The costs of processing an order include the clerical costs of preparing the purchase order or shop order. If it is a purchase order, costs of order expediting and processing the invoice are included; if it is a shop order, the main cost may be machine setup cost. As before, let S (for setup) be the average cost of processing an order, Q (for quantity) be the lot size, and D be the forecast of average annual demand for a given item. Then, for the given item:

$$\frac{D}{Q} = \text{Number of orders per year}$$

$$S\left(\frac{D}{Q}\right) = \text{Annual cost of processing orders}$$

Forecast demand, D, could cover a period other than a year. For example, if D represents monthly demand, $S(D/Q)$ equals the monthly cost of processing orders.

2. Carrying Cost. Carrying cost (discussed at length in Chapter 8) is the cost to finance inventory and hold it in storage. Thus, carrying cost increases as number of units in storage increases. If an item is reordered infrequently in large lots, its carrying costs will be large; if ordered often in small lots, its carrying costs will be small.

Total carrying costs per period divided by value of all inventory items yields what is known as the *annual inventory-carrying-cost rate*, I. One rate may be set for all items carried in a given firm. To compute annual carrying cost for a single item, we need the unit cost, C, for the item. Then,

$$IC = \text{Cost to carry one unit for one year}$$

Let us take a look at a few lot-sizing concepts that apply in the typical situation. (Nontypical cases are brought up later.) For any given lot size, Q, annual carrying cost equals annual cost to carry one unit times average number of units in stock, $Q/2$. Symbolically, for a given item we have:

$$IC\left(\frac{Q}{2}\right) = \text{Annual carrying cost}$$

Why is the average inventory equal to $Q/2$? Figure 10–2 illustrates the repetition of EOQ order cycles during the year. Inventory increases from 0 to Q (the EOQ) on receipt of each order. Demands during the order cycle reduce inventory from Q to 0. The average amount of inventory, then, is simply the average of the maximum amount, Q, and the minimum amount, 0, or $Q/2$. (The mathematically inclined might prefer to make the point with a geometrical proof that the triangles labeled I and II in Figure 10–2 are identical.)

3. Item Cost. The annual cost to make an item, or the total price paid for it, is treated as a constant in the basic EOQ model. We pay the same per item regardless of whether it is obtained in small or large lots. The annual item cost, then, is annual demand (D) times unit cost (C).

EOQ Calculations
We may compute a total annual cost by summing the order processing costs, carrying costs, and item costs:

$$\text{Total cost} = TC = \left(\frac{D}{Q}\right)(S) + (IC)\left(\frac{Q}{2}\right) + DC \qquad (10\text{–}2)$$

FIGURE 10–2
EOQ Order Cycles over Time

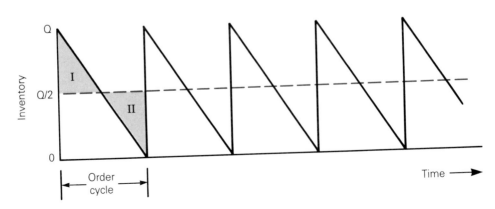

In Figure 10–3, the total annual cost curve is lowest in the center area and increases toward both ends. One component of total cost is carrying cost, which increases along with lot size. The other component, order processing cost, decreases with lot size.

The slope of the tangent to the total cost curve at its minimum is zero. Thus, by taking the derivative of the total cost function with respect to Q and setting it equal to the slope (zero), we obtain an expression for the EOQ:

$$\frac{d(TC)}{d(Q)} = \frac{d\left[\left(\dfrac{D}{Q}\right)(S) + (IC)\left(\dfrac{Q}{2}\right) + (D)(C)\right]}{d(Q)} = 0$$

$$= -\frac{DS}{Q^2} + \frac{IC}{2} = 0$$

Rearranging the terms, we obtain:

$$\frac{DS}{Q^2} = \frac{IC}{2} \tag{10–3}$$

or

$$Q^2 = \frac{2DS}{IC}$$

By taking the square roots of both sides,

$$Q = \sqrt{\frac{2DS}{IC}} \tag{10–4}$$

FIGURE 10–3
Graph of Annual Inventory Cost and Lot Sizes

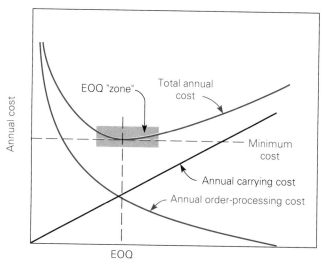

Equation 10–4 is the classic EOQ formula. Graphically, as Figure 10–3 shows, the EOQ occurs at the minimum total annual cost, which is also where annual carrying cost equals annual order processing cost.

Note that the minimum cost is shown in a shaded zone. In that zone, which is fairly large horizontally, total annual cost does not deviate much from the minimum. Thus, in a practical sense EOQ may be thought of as a zone or range of lot sizes, not just the exact EOQ quantity.

Development of input data and use (and misuse) of the basic EOQ model are demonstrated for a small bookstore in Example 10–2.

EXAMPLE 10–2   ECONOMIC ORDER QUANTITY—BOOKSTORE

B. K. Worm, manager of Suburban Books, is thinking of purchasing best-selling titles in economic order quantities. Worm has assembled the following data:

Inventory on hand (books):	
Estimated average last year	8,000
Estimated average cost per book	$10
Average inventory value	$80,000
Annual holding cost:	
Rental: building and fixtures	$7,000
Estimated shrinkage losses	700
Insurance	300
Total	$8,000
Annual capital cost:	
Capital invested (tied up in books)	$80,000
Interest rate	15%
Total	$12,000
Annual carrying cost (Annual holding cost + Annual capital cost):	
$8,000 + $12,000	$20,000
Carrying cost rate, I (Annual carrying cost ÷ Inventory value):	
$20,000/$80,000	0.25
Purchase order processing cost, S:	
Estimate for preparation and invoice handling	$4 per order

Now Worm has the cost data needed to calculate EOQs. He selects his biggest seller as the first book to be ordered by EOQ—*Gone with the Wind*, which is enjoying a burst of renewed popularity in Worm's store. The paperback recently sold at a rate of 80 copies per month and wholesales for $5 per copy. Thus, for the EOQ equation,

$$C = \$5 \text{ per unit}$$

$$D = 80 \text{ units/month} \times 12 \text{ months/year}$$

$$= 960 \text{ units/year}$$

Then,

$$EOQ = \sqrt{\frac{2DS}{IC}} = \sqrt{\frac{2(960)(4)}{0.25(5)}} = \sqrt{\frac{7,680}{1.25}}$$

$$= \sqrt{6,144} = 78 \text{ copies/order}$$

The EOQ, 78 copies, is about one month's supply (78 copies/order ÷ 80 copies/month = 0.98 months/order); it is also $390 worth ($5/copy × 78 copies/order = $390 per order).

Worm's assistant, M. B. Ainsworth, cannot resist pointing out to her boss a fallacy in this EOQ of 78 copies. She puts it this way: "Mr. Worm, I'm not so sure that *Gone with the Wind* is the right book to order by EOQ. The EOQ is based on last month's demand of 80. But demand might be 120 next month and 150 the month after. Also, the average carrying cost rate, *I*, was based mostly on larger hardcover books, which cost more to store. Maybe we should use EOQ only on our stable sellers in hardcover. How about Webster's *New Collegiate Dictionary?*"

EOQ Variations

Variations on the basic EOQ model are available for offsetting some of the limiting assumptions. Three EOQ variations we will consider are carrying cost variations, quantity discounts, and economic manufacturing quantity.

Carrying Cost Variations

Two variations on the basic EOQ treatment of carrying cost warrant some discussion. In the first, annual carrying cost is based on maximum inventory rather than half of the maximum. The second is a variation in which capital cost and holding cost are treated separately rather than together.

In basic EOQ, annual carrying cost equals IC times $Q/2$; in a few situations, however, it is more valid to use IC times Q. The former is proper when a large number of items share the same storage space. In that case, the total storage space needed is *not* based on the sum of the maximum quantities (Qs) for all the items, because it is unlikely that all will be at their maximums at one time. Instead, some items will be low when others are high, and we may assume that space needs are equal to the sum of *half* the maximums ($Q/2$) for all items stored.

IC times Q is proper when only one item is to be stored in a given storage space. In that case, there must be enough space to hold the whole order quantity, Q; since the cost of the space is not shared with other items, annual carrying cost for the given item must be based on maximum inventory. Examples of such items are sides of beef in a walk-in freezer, autos in a parking lot, and fuel in a storage tank. For special items like these, EOQ is derived from annual carrying cost = ICQ; the result is:

$$EOQ_u = \sqrt{\frac{DS}{IC}} \tag{10–5}$$

where the U stands for *unshared* storage space.

The second carrying cost variation separates carrying cost into holding cost plus capital cost. Let H equal the cost of physically holding one unit in storage for one year and iC equal the capital cost per year, where

$$i = \text{Interest rate (or discount rate or cost of capital rate)}$$

$$C = \text{Item's unit cost}$$

Then,

$$\text{Annual carrying cost} = \frac{\text{Annual holding cost} + \text{Annual capital cost}}{2}$$

$$= \frac{H + iC}{2}$$

and

$$EOQ = \sqrt{\frac{2DS}{H + iC}} \tag{10–6}$$

This version of EOQ is a bit more precise than basic EOQ for two reasons. First, it allows an inventory planner to separately estimate H according to the cost of storing an item or items. Second, it provides for item cost, C, to affect only the interest cost of tied-up capital. (The simpler but cruder basic EOQ multiplies C by I, which is a factor that includes holding cost as well as interest cost.)

EOQ with Quantity Discounts

In basic EOQ, periodic item cost is treated as a constant and is omitted. Sometimes, however, the item cost for purchased items varies, stepwise, via *quantity discounts*, or price breaks. Annual item cost then becomes a relevant cost along with annual carrying and order processing costs.

In the quantity-discount situation, an EOQ may be calculated for each price, but the true economic order quantity is the amount that minimizes total annual cost, including item cost. A method for finding the true EOQ is:[3]

1. Calculate EOQs for each price. Reject any EOQ that is not within the allowable quantity range for the price used.
2. For feasible EOQs, calculate total annual cost.
3. Calculate total annual cost at each higher price break.

---

[3] This is not intended to be the most efficient algorithm; we can leave that matter to the computer programmers.

4. Pick the quantity having the lowest total annual cost. This is the true economic order quantity.

Example 10–3 employs the method by continuing the bookstore example.

| **EXAMPLE 10–3** | **EOQ WITH QUANTITY DISCOUNT—BOOKSTORE** |

B.K. Worm, manager of Suburban Books, has applied basic EOQ to *Gone with the Wind*. But Worm didn't allow for quantity discounts. Popular Publications, Inc., offers the following price breaks for *GWTW*:

Quantity Range	Price per Copy
1–48	$5.00
49–96	4.70
97 and up	4.40

Other data, from Example 10–2, are:

$$I = 0.25$$

$$S = \$4 \text{ per order}$$

$$D = 960 \text{ units/year } (12 \times 80)$$

Worm's first step in finding the true economic order quantity is to calculate EOQs for each price:

$$EOQ_5 = \sqrt{\frac{2DS}{IC}} = \sqrt{\frac{2(960)(4)}{0.25(5)}} = \sqrt{6,144} = 78$$

He rejects this EOQ, since it is not within the quantity range, 1 to 48, that applies at the $5.00 price.

$$EOQ_{4.70} = \sqrt{\frac{2(960)(4)}{0.25(4.70)}} = \sqrt{6,536} = 81$$

This EOQ is within the allowable range, 49 to 96, for the $4.70 price, and therefore is feasible.

$$EOQ_{4.40} = \sqrt{\frac{2(960)(4)}{0.25(4.40)}} = \sqrt{6,982} = 84$$

He rejects this EOQ, which is outside the allowable quantity range, 97 and up, for the $4.40 price.

The next step is to compute total annual costs for the feasible EOQ, 81, and at the next higher price break, 97:

Total annual cost = Annual order processing cost +

Annual carrying cost + Annual purchase price

$$= \frac{D}{Q}(S) + IC\left(\frac{Q}{2}\right) + DC$$

$$\text{Total annual cost}_{81} = \frac{960}{81}(4) + 0.25(4.70)\left(\frac{81}{2}\right) + 960(4.70)$$

$$= 47.41 + 47.59 + 4{,}512 = \$4{,}607.00$$

$$\text{Total annual cost}_{97} = \frac{960}{97}(4) + 0.25(4.40)\left(\frac{97}{2}\right) + 960(4.40)$$

$$= 39.59 + 53.35 + 4{,}224 = \$4{,}316.94$$

The true economic order quantity is 97, since its total annual cost $4,316.94, is less than the total of $4,607.00 for a quantity of 81.

FIGURE 10–4
Annual Cost Graph of Lot Sizes with Quantity Discounts

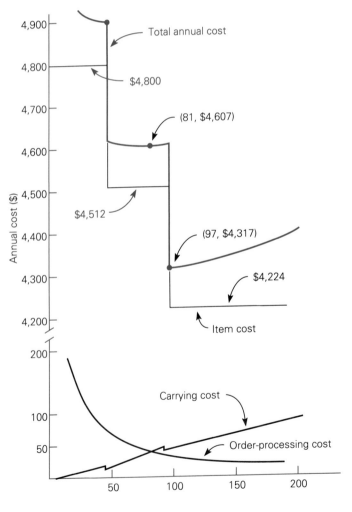

The cost-volume pattern for *Gone with the Wind* has been clarified. Figure 10–4 is Worm's rough sketch of the cost-volume pattern. It shows that annual order-processing cost drops smoothly and is not affected by the quantity discounts. The annual carrying cost line has two small bumps, one at each price break. The annual item cost plunges at each price break, and those effects are dominant in the makeup of total annual cost. The feasible EOQ of 81 at a unit price of $4.70 is not economical compared to the true economic order quantity of 97 at the $4.40 price break.

Economic Manufacturing Quantity

Basic EOQ is suitable for purchased items—an *economic purchase quantity*—in which the whole lot is usually delivered at one time. When an item is made instead of bought, the quantity ordered is available in trickles as it comes off the production line. This complicates figuring average inventory, on which annual carrying cost is based, and results in a modified EOQ formula. The modification may be called an **economic manufacturing quantity (EMQ)** formula. (Note: Purchased items are sometimes delivered in trickles rather than all at once; if so, this EMQ modification would apply.)

The EMQ formula calls for one new term—the production rate, P. P is measured in the same units as D, the demand rate—typically in units per year. P must be greater than D in order for the demand to be covered. $P - D$ is the rate of inventory buildup; that is, producing at rate P and at the same time using at rate D. The difference equals the rate of increase in stock. (Some prefer to use weekly or monthly build and use rates, which work just as well in the EMQ model.)

In developing the model, let us consider a time unit, T. If a lot is made in time, T,

$$I_{max} = Q_{max} = \text{Rate} \times \text{Time} = (P - D)(T)$$

Since Q_{max} is maximum planned inventory and $Q_{max}/2$ is average inventory,

$$\text{Average inventory} = \frac{Q_{max}}{2} = \frac{(P - D)(T)}{2}$$

The extra term, T, may be eliminated by substitution. The time needed to produce a lot, Q, is

$$T = \frac{\text{Quantity}}{\text{Rate}} = \frac{Q}{P}$$

By substitution,

$$\text{Average inventory} = \left(\frac{P - D}{2}\right)\left(\frac{Q}{P}\right) \text{ or } \left(\frac{P - D}{P}\right)\left(\frac{Q}{2}\right)$$

We can express the carrying costs as:

$$CC = (IC)\left(\frac{P - D}{P}\right)\left(\frac{Q}{2}\right)$$

Substituting into Equation 10–3, with the $(P - D)/P$ ratio included at the appropriate point,

$$\frac{DS}{Q^2} = \left(\frac{IC}{2}\right)\left(\frac{P - D}{P}\right)$$

$$Q^2 = \left(\frac{2DS}{IC}\right)\left(\frac{P}{P - D}\right)$$

$$Q = \sqrt{\frac{2DS}{IC}\left(\frac{P}{P - D}\right)}$$

Alternatively,

$$EMQ = \sqrt{\frac{2DS}{(IC)(1 - D/P)}} \tag{10–7}$$

Differences between basic EOQ and EMQ may be shown graphically. Figure 10–5A shows the general pattern of usage and replenishment for basic EOQ. It looks like a ripsaw blade. The vertical line represents the increase in stock that occurs when the whole EOQ is received at one time (*instantaneous replenishment*). The downward-sloping line is the average demand rate, D. Maximum quantity, $Q_{max.}$, is equal to Q, and average quantity, $Q_{ave.}$, is equal to $Q_{max.}/2$.

Figure 10–5B shows the general inventory pattern for EMQ. It looks like a cross-cut saw blade. The upward-sloping solid line represents the rate of inventory buildup, $P - D$; P, the production rate, is shown as a dashed line for reference purposes. The downward-sloping line is the average demand rate, D. Maximum inventory, $Q_{max.}$, is not equal to Q; the stock level never reaches Q because some of Q is being used up (delivered) as it is being produced. $Q_{max.}$ is, instead, equal to $(P - D)(T)$ or $(P - D)(Q/P)$, as was shown earlier, and $Q_{ave.}$ equals half of $Q_{max.}$.

FIGURE 10–5
Basic EOQ and EMQ Replenishment Patterns

A. Basic EOQ pattern of instantaneous
    replenishment

B. EMQ pattern of noninstantaneous
    replenishment

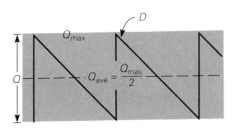
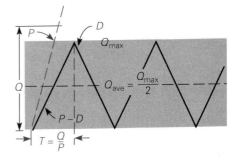

Note that for otherwise equal conditions, EMQ is larger than basic EOQ. Inspection of the EMQ formula shows this to be mathematically obvious, because the factor $1 - D/P$ in the denominator makes the denominator smaller and the EMQ larger. The logical reason is that with EMQ there is less stock to carry since part of Q is used as it is produced; with less to carry, it is economical to produce a bit more per lot.

Concluding Comments

There are more elaborate lot-sizing algorithms than those just discussed. One, the Wagner-Whitin algorithm, is theoretically important in that it has been proved on paper to result in lower total inventory costs than many other models. The problem with some of the models that look good on paper is that they require cost calculations for future periods, which means reaching into the future for a demand forecast. We saw in Chapter 5, however, that forecasting accuracy drops the further into the future one projects.

Ready access to computers allows any of the lot-sizing models to be run *dynamically;* that is, lot sizes can be recomputed every time demand projections change. The effect, however, is unstable planned lot sizes. Ever-changing forecasting signals cause the entire inventory planning and control system to become "nervous." Costs of replanning, rescheduling, and other shuffling of resources outweigh any apparent lot-sizing savings.

For these reasons and others, some experts feel that one lot-sizing method is about as good as another. Historically, the simpler models, such as lot-for-lot, PPA, and basic EOQ, have been preferred by industry.

The preference for simpler models continues today and probably will in the future, judging by the findings of a recent survey. The survey, of firms that provide MRP software to over 25,000 worldwide manufacturing locations, found lot-for-lot to be the most commonly used lot-sizing technique, fixed-order-quantity second, fixed-period-quantity third, and EOQ fourth. The users' rationale for choosing the simple models was found to include: (1) simplicity, (2) employee acceptance, (3) recognition that real-world conditions prevent any savings promised by more complicated optimization models, and (4) realization that lot-sizing is not nearly so important as taking steps to drive lot sizes down.[4]

LOT-SIZING UNDER ATTACK

Today, with just-in-time zealots looking for waste under every rock, some rethinking about lot-sizing models is taking place. Instead of asking, What is the economic lot?, the new question is, What must be changed to move toward

---

[4]Jorge Haddock and Donald E. Hubricki, "Which Lot-Sizing Techniques Are Used in Material Requirements Planning?" *Production and Inventory Management,* Third Quarter 1989, pp. 53–56.

piece-for-piece, or lotless, operations? As we consider that question, we must bear in mind that most of the business world still is not very JIT-minded, and therefore some of the fundamentals of lot-sizing continue to have a useful role.

Our discussion of the pursuit of lotless operations begins with a contrast between a conventional lot-sizing issue and its modern counterpart, then considers some of the benefits and methods of lot-size reduction, and concludes with graphs that illustrate changes in lot-sizing concepts.

Capturing Lot-Sizing Savings, or Relaxing the Rigidities

One issue generally raised in lot-sizing studies is the possible obstacles in the way of capturing the potential savings—in space, money, and staff—from use of a lot-sizing model. We'll take up the "capture" issue here and contrast it with emerging views on overcoming supposed rigidities in the firm.

1. Space

   Conventional concern. Storage space may not be easily converted to other uses. So, if smaller lot sizes reduce total inventory, expected savings on rent, storage racks, and insurance will not be realized easily (but capital costs and inventory taxes *will* be captured immediately).

   New thinking. As lot sizes are continually driven down, more and more space is freed up. Until new uses can be found, the free space should be cordoned off, and no longer charged as an inventory-related cost.

2. Money

   Conventional concern. The business plan may limit the amount of money that can be invested in inventory. Then, if EOQs call for increased lot sizes (thus raising the total capital tied up), management may not allow the EOQs to be adopted.

   New thinking. Don't set arbitrary limits on inventory investment—and *don't* consider increasing any lot sizes. Instead, follow the principle calling for continual reductions in lot size (and therefore inventory investment). That puts pressure where it belongs: on simplifying and reducing costs of processing the larger number of smaller lots (e.g., adopt kanban in order to eliminate some of the order-processing steps, and cut setup times on machines).

3. Staff

   Conventional concern. People who process orders and who set up machines (if machine setup is a separate specialty) may not be easily retrained or reassigned. Then, if fewer orders are placed, expected reductions in order-processing and setup costs will not materialize.

   New thinking. The well-managed firm of the 1980s and 1990s doesn't have its people pigeonholed into narrow job classifications; people take on multiple duties and learn other jobs so that they are versatile. If number of orders is reduced or, more likely, ordering is simplified, buyers and order processors have extra time for more important activities, such as supplier development and certification, or are moved to another area where they are needed. The number of machine setups will *not* be reduced; machine setup times *will* be, thereby increasing setup frequencies and justifying sharp cuts in lot sizes. The attack on setup times will also simplify setups so that operators may take over the task, allowing setup people to be moved to other assignments.

Operating Benefits

For many years, the benefits of smaller lots remained hidden, but today they are obvious. They include:

1. Smaller lots get used up sooner; hence, defective parts are caught earlier. This reduces scrap and rework and allows sources of problems to be quickly caught and corrected—while the evidence of possible causes is still fresh.

2. With small lots, plant floor space to hold inventory may be cut and workstations may be positioned very close together. Then employees can see and talk to one another, learn one another's jobs (which improves staffing flexibility), and function as a team.

3. Small lots allow operations tasks to be closely linked. A problem at one workstation has a ripple effect; subsequent workstations are soon starved of parts to work on. The work team considers one operator's problem the whole team's problem, and joint problem-solving efforts become common practice.

4. Activity control is simplified, and costs of staff support, forklifts, conveyors, racks, control systems, and so forth are reduced.

The benefits become more pronounced as lot size decreases. The limit? An ideal lot size of one. Two important steps in decreasing lot size are reduction of setup costs and reduction of order-processing costs. We must also reexamine our assumptions about how carrying costs affect lot size economics.

Reducing Setup Costs

Cutting setup costs is a key to reducing production lot size. Chapter 3 contained specific guidelines for reducing setup. But just how do high setup costs affect lot sizing?

Setup cost is largely the cost of labor for such preparatory tasks as installing dies, jigs, fixtures, or cutting tools; tearing down, cleaning, sterilizing, and rebuilding food, drug, or chemical processing equipment; or changeover to different parts and tools along a production line. Special setup crews, material handlers, crane and forklift drivers, engineers, plant maintenance employees, and quality control people may be needed to help setup to make a new part. It can take hours or days to complete one setup or production line changeover.

When it costs a lot to set up, it is logical to make quite a few of the parts before setting up again for a different part. The Western tradition is to accept that logic. The goal of lotless production, however, does not accept that thinking. Instead, the idea is to attack the factors that add to setup time so that it becomes reasonable to cut the lot size.

A goal of setup time reduction is a single-digit number of minutes (nine or less) to set up. If that is achieved, the next goal is "one-touch setup," which means virtually no setup time at all.

PRINCIPLE: Cut setup and changeover times.

Reducing Order-Processing Costs

In addition to setup costs, order-processing costs are incurred each time a different part number is to be produced. The kanban system is simple and cheap compared with computer-based order scheduling and control. Kanban ordering along with quick setup makes small production lots economical.

Purchase-order processing costs are the impediment to *buying* in small lots. Kanban sometimes is used for ordering purchased as well as made items. Other methods include use of long-term purchase agreements with the same set of suppliers, transmitting orders by fax or electronic messaging, dealing with nearby suppliers, and using "milk run" freight policies to cut shipping costs. With low-purchase order-processing costs, it is economical to buy in small lots; piece-by-piece buying, however, is quite unfeasible in view of the costs of transporting items from supplier to buyer.

The New Economics of Lot Sizing

Figure 10–3 graphically shows the components of the economic order quantity. With small-lot or lotless production, we see that the graph changes a good deal. Part A of Figure 10–6 is the classical EOQ graph. Part B is the modified graph showing wholesale changes. First, in part B the setup/order processing cost curve has lost its steepness. The cost of ordering frequently in small lots is not much more than ordering infrequently in large lots. Why? Because for made items, setup times have been engineered downward, first to single-digit setup and finally toward one-touch setup. For bought items, kanban has simplified ordering, and stable contracts with a few nearby suppliers have cut the costs of negotiations with suppliers.

The second major change is in carrying cost per year. The cost to carry one unit for one year is modest in part A; the rate is represented (arbitrarily) by a

FIGURE 10–6
Modifying the EOQ Concept

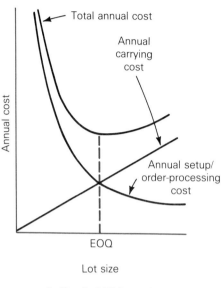

A. Classical EOQ graph

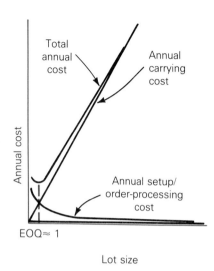

B. EOQ graph modified for
small-lot or lotless production

30-degree angle. In part B, the angle goes up to 60 degrees; the reason is the costs of carrying inventory we have discussed. These costs are most simply stated in the converse form, that is, the benefits of making/buying in small lots and *not* having to carry large inventories are: (1) catching defectives and correcting errors sooner and thereby reducing scrap, rework, and future errors; (2) reducing floor space and moving operators close together so that they may interact; (3) linking processes together (because small lots cut time intervals between process stages) so that each problem is the joint concern of the whole team; and (4) simplified inventory management and costs of staff and equipment. Still another benefit of smaller lots is the avoidance of lumpy workloads in the work centers, discussed earlier in the chapter. Finally, the greatest benefit of all is that small-lot production capability equates with quicker, more flexible response to customer demand.

In sum, the message of Figure 10–6 is that lot sizes should be smaller than the classical EOQ because classical EOQ neglects process benefits of smaller lots (and therefore understates the carrying cost rate). A new EOQ model incorporating the process benefits could be developed. But it is unclear which benefits (or negative costs) would be entered into the equation for such intangibles as better teamwork and quicker customer response. Perhaps because such a question has no easy answer, practical people have not searched for a new EOQ model. Instead, they have simply set forth a goal of piece-for-piece or lotless operations and striven for it by making small improvements month after month and year after year.

SUMMARY

The lot size, or quantity ordered, must be decided each time an order is planned. Several orders may be grouped together (batched) to save on setup and order-processing costs, but that increases inventory carrying costs (holding costs plus capital costs). Also, large orders or batches tend to result in unbalanced or lumpy workloads in production work centers. Thus, lot-for-lot ordering has some advantages.

When setup cost is high, some batching is normal. The part-period algorithm (PPA) is a suitable lot-sizing model for minimizing the sum of annual order-processing and carrying costs given a demand schedule over the planning horizon (as in MRP). PPA lots vary from one order to another; thus, PPA is suitable when demand is lumpy.

Acting on a need for an inventory item generates an order-processing cost, which is mostly the cost associated with equipment setup for manufactured items and the cost of processing purchase orders for purchased goods. In addition to the cost of ordering inventory, there is the cost of having or carrying it. Carrying costs include foregone interest on capital tied up in inventory plus physical holding or storage costs.

A traditional form of lot sizing is the economic order quantity (EOQ). EOQ is like PPA, except that EOQ is based on *average past demand* rather than future demand projection. At the EOQ, annual order-processing costs equal annual carrying costs, and the sum of the two is minimized. Since the sum varies little on either side of the minimum-cost point, the EOQ may be treated as a fairly wide zone. EOQ computation requires four inputs: annual demand, order-processing cost rate, carrying cost rate, and unit cost of the item being ordered.

Variations in the basic EOQ model include: (1) special treatment for items requiring unique storage, (2) separate treatment of holding and capital costs, (3) allowance for quantity discounts, and (4) inclusion of a production-rate minus usage-rate adjustment.

Dynamic lot sizing may be used when "real-world" conditions change, but it tends to result in "nervous" operations. Although simpler lot-sizing models are preferred, there is a growing challenge to the basic assumptions of lot sizing. In particular, the just-in-time ideal is piece-for-piece, or lotless, production.

Operations with smaller lots are beneficial throughout the production process. Benefits include: catching errors and correcting causes sooner, reducing inventory space to put production employees closer together, linking operations more closely so that employees face problems jointly, and simplifying the inventory management system, smoothing workloads, and becoming more flexible and quicker to respond to customer demand.

The new economics of lot sizing favors efforts to reduce lot sizes. The goal is lotless operations, and continuing improvement is the path.

KEY WORDS

Lot sizing
Lot-for-lot
Lumpy workload
Part-period algorithm
(PPA)

Economic order
quantity (EOQ)
Economic
manufacturing
quantity (EMQ)

SOLVED PROBLEMS

1. An eight-week planning horizon for a small manufacturer, containing net demands for a machined part, is shown below. Setup costs are $400 per production run, and weekly carrying costs are $5 per unit. Calculate the economic part-period (EPP), and use part-period analysis (PPA) to determine lot sizes and order release times. Assume a lead time of zero.

Period (week)	1	2	3	4	5	6	7	8
Net requirements	40	30	20	10	15	0	40	30

Solution

Equation 10–1 is used to determine the EPP:

$$\text{EPP} = \frac{S}{\text{CC/week}} = \frac{\$400}{\$5} = 80$$

The PPA method employs a table such as the one in Example 10–1:

Period 1 Trial Lot Size	Covered Period (week)	Demand in Period	Part-Period Calculation	Cumulative Part-Periods
40	1	40	0	0
70	2	30	30 parts × 1 period = 30	30
90	3	20	20 parts × 2 periods = 40	70
100	4	10	10 parts × 3 periods = 30	100

Since 100 > 80, the EPP, period 4 is not included with the lot ordered in period 1. Thus, the lot size of the period 1 order is 90, which covers net demand for periods 1 through 3.

Now start over with period 4:

Period 4 Trial Lot Size	Covered Period (week)	Demand in Period	Part-Period Calculation		Cumulative Part-Periods
				0	0
10	4	10			15
25	5	15	15 parts × 1 period =	15	15
25	6	0	0 parts × 2 periods =	0	135
65	7	40	40 parts × 3 periods =	120	

Since 135 > 80, the demand in period 7 would not be included in the lot ordered in period 4. The lot size of the period 4 order is 25 units, covering demand in periods 4 and 5 (and the zero in period 6). The next period with demand is period 7, so the process is repeated with an order to be released in period 7. (It is left to the student to verify that the lot size for period 7 will be 70 units, covering periods 7 and 8, the remainder of the visible planning horizon.)

2. A manufacturer of industrial solvents has been buying for its own use about 18,000 bottles of solution X4X annually for several years. The cost is $10 per bottle, and $100 is the approximate cost of placing an order for X4X. The firm uses a carrying cost rate of 30 percent. Calculate the economic order quantity (EOQ), the annual ordering cost, and the annual carrying cost for this item.
   What would you expect to occur if lot sizes were made larger than the EOQ? Smaller? (Hint: Base your answer to these questions on Figure 10–3.)

Solution
The EOQ may be found using Equation 10–4:

$$EOQ = \sqrt{\frac{2DS}{IC}}$$

$$= \sqrt{\frac{2(18,000)(\$100)}{(0.3)(\$10)}}$$

$$= \sqrt{1,200,000}$$

$$= 1,095.45 \text{ bottles}$$

Equation 10–2 contains the annual ordering and carrying cost terms. The annual ordering costs are:

$$\text{Annual OC} = \left(\frac{D}{Q}\right)(S) = \left(\frac{18,000}{1,095.45}\right)(\$100) = \$1,643.16$$

The annual carrying costs are:

$$\text{Annual CC} = \left(\frac{Q}{2}\right)(IC) = \left(\frac{1,095.45}{2}\right)(0.3)(\$10) = \$1,643.18$$

Thus, we see that at the EOQ, the annual ordering cost and the annual carrying cost are equal, the very slight difference due to rounding. Figure 10–3 shows the equality of the two costs graphically.

At any lot size other than the EOQ, the total annual cost will increase, as shown by the total cost curve in Figure 10–3. If the lot size were increased, we would expect carrying cost to increase and ordering cost to decrease. A lot size of less than the EOQ will result in a reduced carrying cost but a higher ordering cost.

3. Suppose the firm discussed in problem 2 decides to begin making X4X instead of buying it. An initial estimate of production rate is 150 bottles per day during a production run. The daily usage, assuming 250 workdays per year, averages 72 bottles. The firm elects to continue valuing the X4X at $10 per bottle and, because it is an experienced solvent manufacturer, believes that it can set up to run a lot for approximately $100, the same as it has been costing to place a purchase order.

   a. Calculate the economic manufacturing quantity (EMQ), the annual ordering cost, and the annual carrying cost.
   b. The plant manager thinks the calculated EMQ is much too high. She wants to produce small lots on more of a just-in-time basis. To justify this move, the manager directs that the EMQ be recalculated using a carrying cost rate of 80 percent. What is the recalculated EMQ?
   c. Suppose that after recalculation using the 80 percent rate, the plant manager still thinks the lot size is too large. How can a smaller one be justified?

Solution

a. We use Equation 10–7 to find the EMQ:

$$EMQ = \sqrt{\frac{2DS}{IC(1 - D/P)}}$$

$$= \sqrt{\frac{2(18{,}000)(\$100)}{(0.3)(\$10)(1 - 72/150)}}$$

$$= 1{,}519.11 \text{ bottles}$$

Annual ordering cost is:

$$\text{Annual OC} = \left(\frac{D}{Q}\right)(S)$$

$$= \left(\frac{18{,}000}{1{,}519.11}\right)(\$100)$$

$$= \$1{,}184.90$$

Annual carrying cost is:

$$\text{Annual CC} = (IC)\left(\frac{P - D}{P}\right)\left(\frac{Q}{2}\right)$$

$$= (0.3)(\$10)\left(\frac{78}{150}\right)\left(\frac{1{,}519.11}{2}\right)$$

$$= \$1{,}184.91$$

The annual ordering cost again equals the annual carrying cost, and their total is less than the comparable total for problem 2. Also, note that a larger lot size (about 1,519 units rather than 1,095) is suggested since the firm never has the entire production lot in inventory. As X4X is produced, some of it is consumed.

b. Again using Equation 10–7:

$$EMQ = \sqrt{\frac{2DS}{IC(1 - D/P)}}$$

$$= \sqrt{\frac{2(18,000)(100)}{(0.8)(10)(1 - 72/150)}}$$

$$= 930.26 \text{ bottles}$$

c. The setup time must be reduced. Currently, setup cost is estimated at $100, which could represent about five hours at $20 per hour for setup wages and benefits. In setting up to make solvent, pipes and mixing vessels must be cleaned out. Perhaps the firm could use precleaned pipe lengths and a throwaway liner for the mixing vessel. Quick coupling/uncoupling of pipes may be another promising avenue for improvement.

4. T-Square, Ltd., an engineering firm, uses packages of plastic tape of different patterns, widths, and shading to create layouts and other design drawings. About 2,000 packages are consumed each year. The supplier, an office supply company, offers quantity discounts as follows:

Quantity/Order	Unit price
1–99	$10.00
100–499	9.50
500 and up	9.00

T-Square uses a 35 percent carrying cost rate and spends about $30 placing a tape order. Use the EOQ with quantity discount procedure, as explained in Example 10–3, to determine the appropriate tape lot size.

Solution

First, calculate the EOQ for each of the three price values, rejecting those that do not fall within the allowable quantity range:

$$EOQ_{10.00} = \sqrt{\frac{2(2,000)($30)}{(0.35)($10.00)}} = 185.16 \text{ (Reject—too large)}$$

$$EOQ_{9.50} = \sqrt{\frac{2(2,000)($30)}{(0.35)($9.50)}} = 189.97 \text{ (Feasible)}$$

$$EOQ_{9.00} = \sqrt{\frac{2(2,000)($30)}{(0.35)($9.00)}} = 195.18 \text{ (Reject—too small)}$$

Next, calculate the total annual cost associated with the only feasible EOQ, (approximately) 190 packages, using Equation 10–2:

$$TC = \left(\frac{D}{Q}\right)(S) + (IC)\left(\frac{Q}{2}\right) + DC$$

$$= \left(\frac{2,000}{190}\right)(\$30) + (0.35)(\$9.50)\left(\frac{190}{2}\right) + (2,000)(\$9.50)$$

$$= \$315.79 + \$315.88 + \$19,000.00 = \$19,631.67$$

Now calculate the total cost if the lot size were made equal to the next quantity break point, 500 units in this case:

$$TC = \left(\frac{D}{Q}\right)(S) + (IC)\left(\frac{Q}{2}\right) + DC$$

$$= \left(\frac{2,000}{500}\right)(\$30) + (0.35)(\$9)\left(\frac{500}{2}\right) + (2,000)(\$9)$$

$$= \$120.00 + \$787.50 + \$18,000.00 = \$18.907.50$$

Since the total annual cost of ordering at the best quantity discount value, 500 units, is less than that associated with the EOQ, the more economical lot size for T-square is 500 packages.

REFERENCES

Books

Brown, Robert G. *Materials Management Systems.* New York: John Wiley & Sons, 1977 (TS161.B76).

Orlicky, Joseph. *Material Requirements Planning.* New York: McGraw-Hill, 1975 (TS155.8.O74).

Plossl, G. W., and O. W. Wight. *Production and Inventory Control.* Englewood Cliffs, N.J.: Prentice-Hall, 1967 (HD55.P5).

Vollmann, Thomas E.; William L. Berry; and D. Clay Whybark. *Manufacturing Planning and Control Systems,* 2nd. ed. Homewood, Ill.: Dow Jones-Irwin, 1988.

Periodicals/Societies

Decision Sciences (Decision Sciences Institute).

Journal of Purchasing and Materials Management (National Association of Purchasing Management).

Production and Inventory Management (American Production and Inventory Control Society).

REVIEW QUESTIONS

1. Why does lot-for-lot tend to ease the problem of lumpy workloads?
2. Why are lumpy workloads a problem?
3. What is an advantage of PPA over EOQ?
4. What is a part-period?
5. How does S differ for made versus bought items?
6. Storage costs are semifixed. Should they be included as part of the variable costs of carrying stock? Explain.
7. Explain how order-processing/setup costs and carrying costs relate to lot size.
8. Why omit item cost from basic PPA and EOQ? Why neglect the costs of carrying safety stock?
9. In what sense is the EOQ a zone?
10. What does the EMQ model assume that differs from the basic EOQ model?
11. Why should it take management effort to gain the economies promised by using EOQ?
12. What benefits are associated with smaller lot sizes?
13. Why is setup time reduction important for lot sizing?
14. How may order processing costs be cut, in order to make it economical to buy in small amounts?
15. How does reducing lot size improve quality? Work force communication? Problem solving?
16. Why is construction of the "ultimate" EOQ model, with *all* costs included, an impractical goal?

PROBLEMS AND EXERCISES

1. Door handles for several different models of refrigerators are scheduled by MRP. It costs an estimated $40 to set up for a production run of door handles and $0.20 to carry one handle for one week. Net requirements for the door handles for the next five weeks are 800, 500, 100, 100, and 600.
   a. What is the economic part-period?
   b. Calculate the first lot size using PPA.
   c. Carrying cost is often a rough estimate or average figured for a variety of items. The estimate of $0.20 may not be accurate. Conduct a sensitivity analysis to see whether it makes much difference; that is, recalculate the PPA lot size by using a smaller and a larger carrying cost than $0.20 to see the effects on lot size.
2. In Example 10–1, a planned lot size of 70 is shown for week 4. Verify the correctness of that lot size by making the necessary PPA calculations.

3. The setup cost for producing an electronic component is $100. It costs about $1 to carry one unit for one period. Demands for the next four periods are 120, 80, 0, and 130. Calculate the first lot size using the part-period algorithm. How many periods of demand does it cover?

4. Provincial government uses massive quantities of computer printer paper, which it buys centrally. The purchasing department calculates an economic order quantity based on an assumed carrying cost rate of 30 percent per year. A box of printer paper costs $40, it costs $60 to process an order, and annual demand is for 36,000 boxes of paper.

   a. What is the economic order quantity?

   b. The buyer finds that 10 percent more than the EOQ would be a whole truckload. Should she order the extra 10 percent? Think about this carefully, and explain your answer.

5. Shoes-R-Us, Inc., sells a high-quality line of running shoe. Demand for each of its six models is highly variable. For example, a typical monthly demand pattern for a year (in cases of shoes) looks like this (mean monthly demand is 23):

$$50 \quad 10 \quad 2 \quad 30 \quad 22 \quad 3 \quad 45 \quad 40 \quad 16 \quad 28 \quad 0 \quad 31$$

   With this demand pattern, would it be better to calculate purchase order quantities using PPA or EOQ? Explain.

6. Continental Plate and Boiler Company has one storeroom that holds various sizes of pipe and steelplate. Following are costs and other data associated with pipe and plate buying and storage:

Average inventory on hand	$1.5 million
Purchasing department wages and overhead	$33,000/year
Purchases of pipe and plate	$4.5 million/year
Number of purchase orders processed	500/year
Interest rate	18 percent per year
Depreciation on storeroom and its storage racks	$38,000/year
Overhead and expenses (including taxes and insurance to operate store room)	$10,000/year
Storeroom salaries	$16,000/year

   a. What is the average cost of processing a purchase order (S)?

   b. What is the annual capital cost? Annual holding cost? What is the carrying cost rate (I)?

   c. What are some other, less tangible costs of carrying inventory, and how might those costs affect inventory policy at Continental?

7. Each Chompin' Chicken restaurant buys mixed pieces of frozen precooked chicken from a corporate distribution center for $1 per pound. The cost of placing and handling an order is estimated at $5 and the inventory carrying cost rate at 0.35. The chicken is stored in a special freezer that holds nothing else. If your local Chompin' Chicken restaurant uses 10,000 pounds of frozen chicken per year, what is the economic order quantity? (Be sure to choose the right EOQ formula.)

8. Maple Tree Insurance Company uses 2,000 boxes of staples per year. The boxes are priced at $3 in quantities of 0 to 99 boxes or $2.60 in quantities of 100 boxes or more. If it costs $15 to process an order and the annual carrying cost rate is 0.30, how many boxes should be ordered at one time?

9. A chemical plant consumes sulfuric acid in a certain process at a uniform rate. Total annual consumption is 25,000 gallons. The plant produces its own sulfuric acid and can set up a production run for a cost of $4,000. The acid can be stored for $0.60 per gallon per year. This includes all carrying costs (cost of capital as well as cost to hold in storage). The production rate is so rapid that inventory buildup during production may be ignored.
   a. What is the economic order quantity?
   b. How many times per year should the acid be produced?

10. A cannery buys knocked-down cardboard boxes from a box company. Demand is 40,000 boxes per year. The inventory carrying cost rate is 0.25 per year, and the cannery's purchasing department estimates order processing cost at $20. The box company prices the boxes as follows:

    For a purchase of 100 to 3,999 boxes—$0.60 each (minimum order = 100)
    For a purchase of 4,000 or more boxes—$0.50 each

    a. Determine the economic purchase quantity (EPQ).
    b. Express your EPQ in months' supply, and then in dollars.

11. A company manufactures plastic trays in several models. One model has a forecast annual demand of 16,000. It costs $80 to set up the molding machine (insert mold, adjust, clamp, etc.) to run that model, which is then produced at a rate of 90,000 per year and at a cost of $10 each. Annual carrying cost is estimated at 40 percent.
    a. What is the economic manufacturing quantity?
    b. A pallet holds 20 percent less than the calculated EMQ. Should the company adopt a lot size of one pallet load instead of the calculated EMQ? Explain your answer.

12. A print shop manufactures its own envelopes. Each production run costs $150 to set up and provides envelopes at a production rate of 2,000 per hour. Average usage of the envelopes is 10,000 per month. Envelopes cost $10 per thousand to produce. The annual inventory carrying cost is estimated at 15 percent of average inventory for this item. A working month averages 160 hours.
    a. What is the economic manufacturing quantity for envelopes? How many months' supply is it?
    b. The print shop is thinking of buying the envelopes instead of making them. If the order processing cost is $150 (same as the setup cost), what will the EOQ be? Compare your answer with that in question a. Is the difference large or small? Explain why.
    c. If the production lead time is two days, what is the reorder point?

13. A manufacturer of wooden furniture carries in its warehouse only one type of inventory: lumber. Following are various costs that may or may not be associated with that inventory:

Rent on warehouse	$23,000/year
Wages and salaries, purchasing department	$80,000/year
Inventory taxes	$18,000/year
Cost of capital	14%/year
Value of average inventory on hand	$680,000
Insurance on warehouse contents	$3,500/year
Operating supplies, purchasing department	$1,400/year
Operating budget, production control department	$160,000/year
Expenditures on inventory	$3,400,000/year
Cost of a 12-foot 1" × 4" board	$1
Overhead, purchasing department	$25,000/year
Wages and salaries, warehouse	$48,000/year
Overhead, warehouse	$8,000/year
Miscellaneous expenditures, warehouse	$4,200/year

a. What is the inventory carrying cost rate, I (for the total inventory stored)?

b. What is the average cost of processing a purchase order (S)? Assume that 3,000 purchase orders per year are processed.

c. What is the EOQ for 1" × 4" boards? Assume that 30,000 of these boards are used annually.

d. What is the annual cost of capital invested in 1" × 4" boards? (Ignore safety stock.)

14. An irrigation system manufacturer makes its own pipes from coils of steel strip. Three sizes of pipe—3-inch, 4-inch, and 6-inch—are produced on a rotating schedule on a single production line. Each size is used at a steady rate in assembly. Following are inventory data for the pipes:

Cost to set up for new size of pipe	$130
Cost of capital	12 percent/year
Cost to store one pipe (any size)	$2/year
Manufactured cost of 3-inch pipe	$20/section
Manufactured cost of 4-inch pipe	$22/section
Production rate for pipes (all sizes)	120 sections/day
Usage (demand) rate, same for each size of pipe	90 sections/day
Demands arise during 250 days per year	

a. What is the economic manufacturing quantity for 3-inch pipe? For 4-inch pipe?

b. Assume that each of the three types of pipes is stored in a rack that is made to fit the pipe diameter; that is, a storage rack for one size of pipe may not hold another size (this changes the method of calculating EMQ). What is the EMQ for 3-inch pipe? Explain why this answer differs from that in question *a.*

15. A small company adopts buying by economic order quantities for all items in its stockroom. The EOQs show that many items formerly had been ordered in quantities far larger than their EOQs. The company has one buyer and one enclosed stockroom with one storekeeper.

    a. What savings can the company expect to derive from its EOQ ordering? What potential savings may prove to be difficult to capture?

    b. If the company adopts a full just-in-time effort, including flexible resource policies, how would that affect the answers to the questions posed in part *a?*

16. For the first time, Ordinaire, Inc., has calculated economic order quantities for items carried in stock. The calculations show that for years the supplies stockroom has been ordering quantities that are too large and the direct material stockroom has been ordering quantities that are too small. The comptroller is convinced that adopting the EOQs will save over $100,000 per year in reduced inventory cost. Critique the comptroller's viewpoint. (Hint: What expected savings, if any, may fail to be captured?)

17. Among other things, Marksman Industries makes 10 different models of gun-cleaning rods. Presently, the 10 models are manufactured one at a time, each for about one week's worth of production (average). The schedule is supposed to provide enough of a given model during the week-long production run to satisfy about 10 weeks of consumer demand (since it will not be made again for 10 weeks). The problem is that by the end of the 10-week cycle for a model, expected consumer demand may have changed. By the time of the next production run, Marksman may have run out of a given model or accumulated a large excess. How can Marksman be more responsive to actual consumer demand?

18. Federal Time Corporation makes and sells clocks. Plastic lenses for clock faces are molded in Federal's own facilities. One popular table model has an annual demand of 40,000 clocks. The lens for that clock costs $0.60 to make. Setup to mold the lens, consisting of inserting and clamping the correct die in the injection molding equipment, costs $80 per production run. (Setup time is about four hours.)

    a. Federal has been using EOQ to determine number of lenses per production run. It uses an inventory carrying cost rate of 0.25 and the formula $EOQ = \sqrt{2DS/IC}$. What is the EOQ for this lens?

    b. The plant manager has become convinced that there are benefits in running lenses in much smaller lots than EOQs. The four-hour setup time must be reduced in order to make small lots economical. What kinds of improvements do you think Federal would need in order to achieve single-digit setup? To achieve one-touch setup?

19. Argo Electronics has a subsidiary plant in Wisconsin that produces electronic games and various other products. The plant produces its own circuit boards, which are used at a steady rate on the assembly line. Demand for one type of board is 7,000 per year, and the production rate is 40,000 per year. The standard cost is $6 per circuit board. It costs $200 to set up a production run for that kind of board.

    a. If 0.30 is used as the carrying cost rate, what is the economic manufacturing quantity for circuit boards?

    b. Plant management believes the carrying cost rate should be increased to 0.70. Recalculate the EMQ. Comment on why management should favor a higher carrying cost rate.

20. A well-known phenomenon in the semiconductor industry (making micro-processors and memory chips) is that fast processing of a production lot has a higher process yield than slow processing. (*Process yield* means number of *good* chips from a wafer, i.e., chips that pass electronic tests of quality.) The reason is that the wafers are susceptible to handling, dust, and other kinds of damage that are reduced if the production run is completed and the chips sealed over quickly.

    One semiconductor manufacturer has several models of memory chip to run, one at a time. A production run of a given model normally takes five weeks, but a few small, special runs have been completed in as little as two weeks—with high process yields. How can a manufacturer gain these advantages *all the time* instead of only in special cases?

21. A producer of precision instruments has initiated a just-in-time effort. One of its early achievements was reducing setup time on a milling machine for making a key component part. The old setup cost was $200; now it is $8. As a result, the new economic lot size is only 16 units, whereas the old one had been much higher.

    a. If the company is serious about obtaining full just-in-time benefits, what lot size should be run? Explain.

    b. What was the old EOQ? (Hint: Use the new EOQ along with the ratio of new to old setup cost. No other data are needed.)

Translating Planned Orders into Outcomes

In operations management, orders create activity. Operations, jobs, batches, lots, projects, appointments, and work units reflect the activities that combine to form the end products and services targeted for customers.

In Part Four, we see how activities are planned and controlled—managed—to yield the outcomes that customers want. Chapter 11 examines continuous and repetitive operations. Chapter 12 considers job and batch operations. Large-scale operations such as projects are the focus of Chapter 13. Finally, Chapter 14 looks at the issues of resource assignment and waiting-line operations.

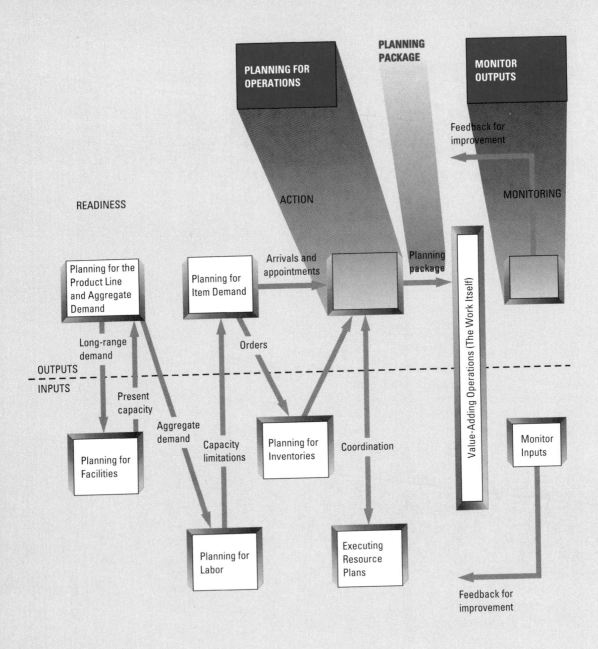

CHAPTER 11

Managing Continuous and Repetitive Operations

Observe the gasoline mileage claim in the window of your new car: 25 highway/19 city. Note also that the owner's manual advises more frequent servicing—oil changes, brake adjustments, filter and belt replacements, and so forth—if the vehicle is to be used predominantly in city traffic. The starts and stops of city driving are bad for the car—they reduce mileage and cause added wear—and worse yet, bad for you: Your time is wasted, both in the stop-and-go traffic and in the extra attention required to keep your car in good working order.

In a similar fashion, stop-and-go, or *irregular*, operations cause extra waste in companies. **Streamlining** operations—smoothing them out into a steady flow, making them run with fewer stops and starts—is the goal in reducing waste. The benefits of steady-flow operations are considerable: high efficiency, low inventory, low labor costs, uniform (consistently high, with proper attention) quality, simple planning and scheduling, shorter throughput times, and few surprises. In short, operations become highly responsive to customers' wants.

Firms with *continuous* or highly *repetitive* operations reap many of those benefits. A central theme in this chapter, however, is that less continuous and less repetitive companies also ought to become more streamlined; they also deserve to share the wealth. In a sense, then, the chapter deals not only with managing the already-streamlined firm, but also with ways for job operations to become more streamlined.

First, we categorize certain industries according to how streamlined they are. Next, we examine process-industry operations with an eye for improving their responsiveness.

STREAMLINED OPERATIONS: A CONTINUUM

To many, the thought of streamlined operations means lines of robots working tirelessly on rivers of moving parts. Indeed, the new Next Computer factory in Fremont, California, lives up to that billing: robotic application of 1,700 dabs of solder to each circuit board, lasers checking to ensure pinpoint accuracy, and component insertion at speeds up to 150 parts per minute—all reflections of the latest in streamlined manufacturing technology. Steve Jobs, creator of the Next workstation, comments, "I'm as proud of the factory as I am of the computer."[1]

The concepts that underlie Next's factory, however, aren't new. Some of history's most skillful entrepreneurs have been people who could cultivate a mass market and keep it supplied with a continuous or repetitive supply of goods and services. Around 1438, the Arsenal of Venice turned out 10 fully armed warships per day. Carpenters fashioned hulls, tarred them, and placed them into canals that carried them through a maze of "assembly-line" stations. Sails, oars, weapons, and supplies were added by craftsmen skilled in each respective trade.

---

[1]Mark Alpert, "The Ultimate Computer Factory," *Fortune*, February 26, 1990, pp. 75–79.

Four and one-half centuries later, John D. Rockefeller's oil wells steadily pumped product into Rockefeller pipelines and rail tanker cars, which forwarded the product to Rockefeller tank farms and retail stations. Also, Andrew Carnegie's steel manufacturing empire included railroads and lake steamers that moved ore to the great furnaces and then the finishing mills of Pittsburgh.

Today, one of the purest examples of streamlined processing may be found in the Western coal fields, where the output of lignite mines goes into trucks that drive a mile or so to giant electric power plants and dump their loads onto conveyors. The conveyors move the coal into furnaces, which convert steam to electric power. The power is "pumped" through wires for immediate consumption by millions of users. Coal, the raw material, is a commodity, as is electric power, the end product.

Perhaps the most quoted accolade to the efficiencies of streamlined operations comes from a pioneer of the automobile industry. Ford Motor Company once transformed commodities such as iron ore into a commodity-like end product, the Model T automobile: "Our production cycle is about 81 hours from the mine to the finished machine in the freight car, or three days and 9 hours."[2] Ford's repetitive-flow mode of manufacture began to unravel when customers started demanding variety: big cars and small ones, luxury models and sporty models with rumble seats. The changing customer tastes had an impact on the producers. The auto industry, from assembly plants to parts makers to steel mills, moved well away from commodity-like product uniformity and turned to *intermittent* production—one model at a time, with long cycle intervals.

The examples of electric power generation and automotive products are presented, on a two-dimensional continuum or matrix, in Figure 11–1.[3] Electric power is in the extreme right corner; this is a **commodity product** made in a **continuous process**. Automotive products are positioned partway up the diagonal, which stretches all the way to **custom products** and **job processing**. A sampling of other industries fills the rest of the diagonal.

Placement of industries on the diagonal is *not* set in concrete, not the natural state. It *is* natural to want to move downward and, perhaps, to the right, because doing so improves most of the indicators of performance in operations management.

At one time, all products—even what we now call *commodities*—were made in the job-processing (or "job-shop") mode. For example, put yourself in Placerville, California, in 1849 during the gold rush. Suppose you have a toothache and are lucky enough to find a dentist in the camp. The dentist says you need a tooth filled. He melts down freshly panned gold from the South Fork River and, by the light of a lamp burning the oil of a muskrat trapped near the same river, he fills your tooth. Fuel and gold are commodities today, produced more

[2]Henry Ford, *Today and Tomorrow* (Garden City, N.Y.: Doubleday, 1926), p. 115.
[3]The original idea for the matrix comes from Robert H. Hayes and Steven C. Wheelwright, "Link Manufacturing Process and Product Life Cycles," *Harvard Business Review*, January–February 1979, pp. 133–40. This version of the matrix is adapted from Sam C. Taylor, Samuel M. Seward, and Steven F. Bolander, "Why the Process Industries Are Different," *Production and Inventory Management*, Fourth Quarter 1981, pp. 9–24.

FIGURE 11–1
Product/Service vs. Process Matrix

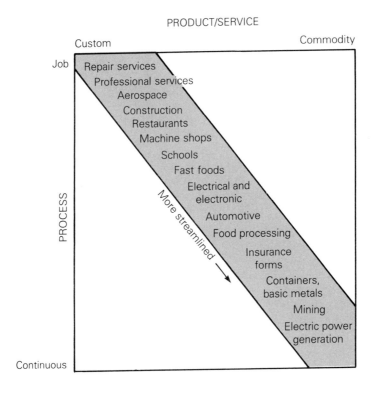

or less continuously. But they were custom products made in the job-shop mode when your hypothetical tooth was filled in 1849.

There are numerous recent examples of industries or companies that have, through improved operations management, moved themselves downward on the process continuum in Figure 11–1. For a prime example, let us return to the automotive industry.

With the exception of Ford's Model T era, the automotive industry's dominant processing mode had been production in lots. Over three decades after the Model T was introduced, Toyota of Japan began developing a system of *synchronized production*, which means synchronizing the stages of manufacturing much like Henry Ford had done. But there was a difference. Toyota's method, unlike Ford's, allowed *mixed-model assembly* and therefore was able to accommodate customers' demands for variety. In Toyota's case the variety is high, because its customers' tastes vary worldwide. (Its Japanese customers can order a particularly large variety of configurations.) As may be seen in Figure 11–2A, Toyota has moved downward toward flow-shop operations without much rightward movement toward commodity products.

Other automobile companies have become more streamlined as well. The movement of Chrysler, downward toward flow-shop, is shown in Figure

FIGURE 11–2
Movement toward Streamlining: Automobile Industry Examples

A. Toyota

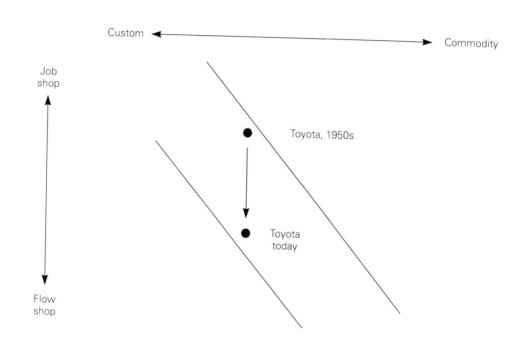

B. Chrysler

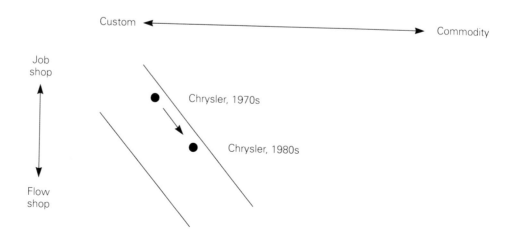

11–2B. Chrysler has also shifted to the right. Since Chrysler's marketplace is mostly North America, not the whole world, Chrysler's strategy has included greatly limiting the model variations available to customers; for example, the highly successful van wagon was initially designed to have only three body styles. Narrowing customer choices makes it easier for providers in Chrysler's supply chain to more closely synchronize their production rates with Chrysler's assembly rates. In other words, there are higher daily volumes of fewer parts, each of which can be made more steadily and repetitively.

Some industries have technological obstacles in the way of streamlined repetitive/continuous flow. The wafer fabrication stage of semiconductor manufacturing is a case in point. Some of the high-tech equipment, especially the diffusion ovens that deposit chemical layers on silicon wafers, was designed to process "boatloads" of wafers at a time (a "boat" might hold 30, 50, or 100 wafers). In attempting to implement JIT, many wafer plants around the world have achieved modest streamlining effects, mainly through use of kanban (Intel's plant in Aloha, Oregon, is completely on kanban). The boat-size loads stand in the way of greater progress. In order to move sharply downward in the process continuum toward flow-shop production, the industry needs a technological breakthrough, namely diffusion ovens that can process one wafer at a time.

As a final example of moving in the flow-shop direction, consider the achievement of a food processing company, the Pepperidge Farms division of Campbell Soup.[4] Pepperidge's problem was the same as most food processors': too many different products, package sizes, and types competing for very few production lines. The schedule for a certain product allowed intervals of days and even weeks between production runs—large lots, or poor service, resulted.

Faster changeovers from production of one product to another would allow *more frequent* production of all items. Pepperidge scoured the world to find equipment that could be quickly changed over. Now the new equipment in one plant permits production of nearly 10 times the number of products per day as the old. With more frequent production—closer to continuous—the company has come closer to synchronizing baking with store sales. Bake-to-store lead times for cookies and breads have been roughly halved; this is a sizable competitive advantage, since the product on the shelf is fresher.

PROCESS INDUSTRIES

Like many companies making widely used consumer products, Pepperidge Farms is generally considered to be in the **process industry.** Actually, many process-industry companies have both continuous and highly repetitive operations. Typically, the front end is process—raw materials start as flows—but the end products emerge as units. In candy factories, for example, sugar, chocolate, water, and other ingredients flow in and cartons of candy bars or boxed candy come

---

[4]"A Smart Cookie at Pepperidge," *Fortune*, December 22, 1986, pp. 67–74.

out. Potatoes, salt, vegetable oil, and so forth flow into a potato chip plant, and cartons of sacked chips emerge. Sugar, water, flavoring, and active ingredients flow into a drug producing plant, and out come boxes of bottled cough medicine.

Clearly, the streamlined flow is the distinguishing feature regardless of whether the output is continuous or repetitive. We turn now to measures of success in process industries.

Key Success Factors

What are the characteristics of responsive continuous and repetitive operations? Figure 11–3 identifies some of the key success factors.

1. *Process design and capital investment.* Most stages from mixing through packaging tend to be quite automated (capital intensive). Some advantages can be gained by having more modern equipment than one's competitors, but it is often more important to keep the equipment in good condition so that the process yield is high and dependable.

2. *Optimal mixtures.* One of the more important uses of linear programming, a mathematical technique, is in determining optimal (best) mixtures of ingredients or other resources in some process industries. For example, most companies that produce dog food, chicken feed, and so on use linear programming. The technique selects the lowest-cost mix of ingredients that will meet nutrition and other standards. Since volumes are usually large, savings of a few cents per pound can be significant.

3. *Rigorous maintenance.* An equipment breakdown idles a whole process, for example, the whole mixing or the whole bottling process in the case of a food or drug company. When the product is perishable, there is further reason for wanting to avoid breakdowns. Perishability is also reason for being unable to use buffer stocks between process stages as protection against breakdowns. In other words, perishability forces more of a just-in-time (stockless) mode of production.

FIGURE 11–3

Success Factors for Process Industries

1. Process design and capital investment.
2. Optimal mixtures.
3. Rigorous maintenance.
4. Close monitoring of the process.
5. Reliability of supply and freight.
6. Fast changeover time.
7. Regularized schedules and linear output.

4. *Close monitoring of the process.* In the process industries, federal law or industrywide standards often govern product quality, purity, and sanitation. Process monitoring must be rigorous to ensure that standards are met and products are safe and salable.

5. *Reliability of supply and freight.* This includes careful selection of a plant site close to markets and supplies of raw materials. Regardless of where the plant is located, the freight haulers bringing in raw material must be reliable, because raw materials are the lifeblood of the process industries. Stockpiling as protection for shaky supply or freight is possible. But most of the process industry produces in such large volumes that even a few days' supply of ingredients can take up too much storage space. "Disaster stock" (see Chapter 9) may be stored offline to keep it from interfering with the continuity and speed of flow.

6. *Fast changeover time.* Nearly all process-industry plants are able to change production lines to run different blends and container sizes. Sometimes it takes several days for a line changeover, which may include completely cleaning out all equipment. The company that can make changes fast has an edge.

7. *Regularized schedules and linear output.* Fast changeovers only improve the economics of running different blends and sizes more frequently. Highly repetitive-continuous production also requires a **regularized schedule**—one in which a certain item is made at regular intervals—and **linear output**, meaning producing the same quantity each time period.

Effects of Competition

The process industry generally has placed its greatest emphasis on items 1 through 5 above; not much attention has been given to items 6 and 7. But competitive pressures are forcing process-industry companies to:

- Seek continuing improvements in items 1 and 2 with increased attentiveness to process-design factors and the emergence of superior process ingredients.
- Step up improvement efforts in items 3 (upgrade to *total preventive maintenance*), 4 (make extensive use of *statistical process control*), and 5 (adopt JIT purchasing).
- Pay heed to items 6 and 7 (fast changeovers, and regularized schedules and linear output).

The competitive pressures are easy to see in the United States and Canada: fast-growing sales of imported beers, wines, chocolates, pens, metals, chemicals, fabrics, and frozen and canned foods.

Other chapters include discussions of process design, total preventive maintenance, statistical process control, JIT purchasing, and quick changeover. Item 7, regularized schedules and linear output, is considered next.

REGULARIZED SCHEDULES AND LINEAR OUTPUT

Despite the razzle-dazzle of new high-technology equipment, improvement in continuous processing and high-volume repetitive operations often hinges on better scheduling and on greater accuracy in providing the scheduled amount (hitting the target) consistently. Proven techniques for accomplishing these and other aims include processing with regularized schedules and linear output. To fully appreciate their usefulness, the negative consequences of irregular schedules and output need to be understood.

Consequences of Irregular Processing

The bar chart in Figure 11–4 represents what a typical process-industry production schedule for item X might look like. Item X is one model or size in a family of products. It might be standard-size 60-watt light bulbs, 8-ounce cans of tomato sauce, type-AAA batteries, rolls of 135 24-exposure, 100-speed color film, twin-bed-size white percale sheets, 3.5-inch Brand Z floppy disks, half-gallon cartons of cherry nut ice cream, six-packs of canned root beer, bottles of

FIGURE 11–4
Schedule, in Work Shifts, for Item X

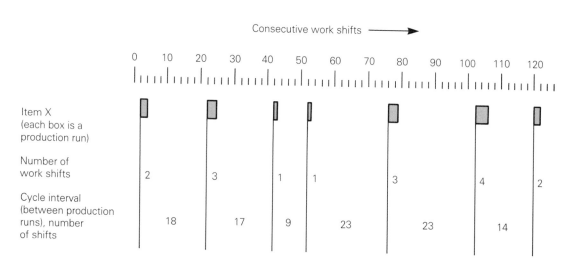

50 decongestant tablets, 100-foot spools of 12-gauge, red-coated copper electrical wire, or 4' × 8' sheets of 3/8" plywood.

Note the tendency to schedule not in pieces or volume, but in work shifts. Now, notice the variabilities. The number of shifts (length) of each production run varies: 2, 3, 1, 1, 3, 4, and 2. The interval *between* production runs also varies: 18 shifts, then 17, 9, 23, 23, and 14. Between production runs, other models of the same basic product occupy the schedule: other types or sizes of light bulbs, canned tomato products, batteries, and so on. Normal sales variations, special marketing promotions, and the end-of-the-month push to meet a sales quota cause demand variability, to which the production schedule must react.

Another source of variability not shown in Figure 11–4 is output. In the process and high-volume assembly industries, the schedule is reasonably definite as to number of shifts but often rough as to units. For example, consider the first bar in Figure 11–4, a production run of two shifts. If Item X is standard 60-watt light bulbs and an average of 10,000 can be produced in a shift, the bar is interpreted as follows: The production run is two shifts, which *might* yield 20,000 bulbs. But the yield varies. If all goes well 20,400 may be produced, but on a poor day only 18,500. Once in a while there will be a serious equipment or raw material failure, and output may be only 8,000. Production of only 8,000 risks a stockout and lost sales; thus, 60-watt bulbs will need to be fitted into the schedule again quite soon. The whole schedule gets adjusted now and then for such reasons.

Overtime or extra shifts are a possibility if the plant is not running at or near full capacity. However, traditional standard accounting systems often press manufacturing to run costly equipment near to full capacity even if inventory builds as a result. Change capacity—close a plant or shut down a production line—if sales fall, but let the *records* show high use of capacity without large cost variances.

To sum up, irregular production intervals, run times, and output release clouds of uncertainty. Since sales is uncertain about how much product to expect from operations, it tries to keep protective—and costly—buffer stocks in the distribution system. The greater costs are at the supplier side: What supplies of all the ingredients should be kept on hand? When and how much should each supplier deliver? How can suppliers ever achieve regular production schedules and thereby hold down *their* wasteful buffer stocks and costs? Irregularities pass backward through all prior stages of supply and production.

Something must be done. There is a crying need for regularity and stability.

Regular-Slot Processing

One fairly easy way to gain some regularity and stability is simply to give the "stars" in the product line regular slots in the schedule. The stars are the models or sizes that sell in some quantity every day and earn a high proportion of total revenue. If they sell every day, the ideal is to make some every day, from 8 to 9 A.M., perhaps. The slots should be equal in hours of run time—changed when the demand rate changes—and should be spaced at regular intervals.

The "superstar"—the number one revenue earner—gets first claim at regular slots in the schedule, followed by some of the "starlets." The regularized portion of the schedule may appear as in Figure 11–5. The example is for three sizes of photographic film (it could also be three—or more—flavors of ice cream, sizes of plywood, etc). Perhaps the manufacturer has a total of 80 film products. The other 77 are fitted into the schedule in the old, irregular fashion.

While the benefits—more predictable needs for ingredients and more pre-dictable deliveries to sales—apply to only 3 out of 80 products, that may represent a sizable percentage of costs and sales dollars, perhaps 15 or 20 percent. That 15 or 20 percent deserves the *very best* management, not av-erage management.

Two points about regular-slot processing deserve further emphasis. First, shorter set-up or changeover times facilitate regular-slot processing. If it takes four hours to change a line over, it might make little sense to schedule a one-hour production run each day, even for a star product. In that case, the star might be given a regular, but less frequent slot, say, once every six shifts.

Second, notice in Figure 11–5 that the 135, 100-speed film (the superstar) is produced for one and one-half shifts out of every ten *and* it is produced on a regular interval of every ten shifts. The 135, 200-speed film is produced for one shift out of every twenty, and the 110 film one shift out of every forty. Those production run lengths and cycle intervals are not set capriciously; together with information about production rates per shift, that schedule should reflect recent average demand for the various film products.

FIGURE 11–5

Three Products with Regularized Schedules

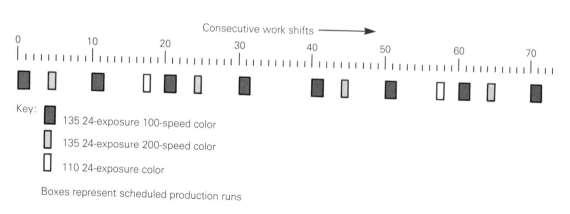

Linear Output with Under-Capacity Scheduling

Regular slots improve predictability, but yield per run still can be quite variable. In many cases, regularizing of schedule slots should be combined with a policy of *linear output*. Some companies call this "making to a number"; that means setting an *attainable* output target, running production until it is achieved, and not allowing overproduction. The technique of setting an attainable schedule quantity is known as **under-capacity scheduling**—scheduling less than full-capacity output. An under-capacity schedule policy generally is set numerically. For example, it might call for scheduling 15 percent under capacity or, as usually stated, 85 percent of capacity. That means that if the schedule calls for 85 units per day, the capacity (measured in number of assemblers, number of assembly-hours, number of machine-operator-hours, or number of machine-hours) should be 100 units per day.

Is this practice wasteful of costly capacity? Not necessarily. When the scheduled quantity is met early—which is most of the time—the practice calls for line employees to fill out the schedule slot in useful pursuits, such as performing preventive maintenance on equipment or some other activity aimed at fixing process variability problems. *Planned* production hours decrease, but so do unplanned stoppages and slowdowns. There should be no loss in output and large gains in predictability of output.

Under-capacity scheduling is illustrated in Example 11–1.

EXAMPLE 11–1   **UNDER-CAPACITY SCHEDULING—COLOR FILM**

The star product of a photographic film manufacturer is 135 24-exposure, 100-speed color film. Yield per eight-hour shift has averaged 6,600 rolls, which is 825 rolls per hour. Production slots are to be evenly spaced in the schedule, and the company wants 6,000 rolls per production run—no more, no less. Is the schedule attainable? What is the underscheduling policy in percentage?

Solution:
The target of 6,000 should be attainable in one eight-hour shift most of the time. In a shift with average problems, the 6,000 rolls would be produced in about $7\frac{1}{4}$ hours (6,000/825 rolls per hour = 7.27 hours). On a bad day with two or three line stoppages, the 6,000 may still get produced—by working right up to the bell. On a very bad day, the 6,000 might be made by working some overtime.

The underscheduling policy is: 6,000/6,600 = 90.9 percent.

What happens if the schedule consistently is not met? More staff or more production lines (more capacity) should be added so that the schedule can be attained regularly. The other option, lowering the schedule quantity, is unappealing because the quantity presumably is what marketing is able to sell.

No matter how attainable the target quantity is supposed to be, it cannot be met every time. A good way to monitor degree of success is with a **linearity index** (which apparently was devised by Hewlett-Packard Company). The index equals 100 percent minus the mean percent deviation, where mean percent deviation is the absolute sum of percentage deviations from schedule quantity divided by number of production runs. Mathematically, it is:

$$L = 100\% - \frac{\Sigma\,|D|}{N}$$

(11–1)

where

L = Linearity index

D = Deviation from schedule quantity
as a percentage of schedule quantity per run

N = Number of production runs

Typically, the index is calculated monthly, and number of production runs, N, equals number of working days in the month. Calculation of the index is more simply illustrated, assuming only one production run per week, in Example 11–2.

EXAMPLE 11–2   CALCULATION OF LINEARITY INDEX

Given

500 units of a certain model of a product are to be run one shift a week, on Mondays. Actual production last month was 500, 490, 510, and 500. Compute the linearity index for the month.

Solution

The deviations from schedule, in units, are 0, −10, +10, and 0. To convert to percent, divide each by the schedule quantity per run, 500. That yields, 0, −2, +2, and 0 percent, respectively. By Equation 11–1 (ignoring minus signs, since the *absolute* sum of deviations is used),

$$L = 100\% - \frac{\Sigma|D|}{N}$$

$$= 100\% - \frac{0\% + 2\% + 2\% + 0\%}{4}$$

$$= 100\% - \frac{4\%}{4}$$

$$= 100\% - 1\%$$

$$= 99 \text{ percent}$$

The linearity index mathematically reflects that any deviation, over or under schedule, is undesirable; both over- and underproduction cause problems for suppliers and uncertainty for users. In Example 11–2, the shortfall of 10 units in week 2 was made up by deliberate overproduction of 10 in week 3 to get back on target. (The index does not reward getting back on target. However, an alternate form of the index, calculated based on a cumulative schedule, *does* encourage getting back on schedule; the cumulative basis might be useful in some cases.) Note too that the index will always be 100 percent if the schedule is met every time.

At some Hewlett-Packard plants, linearity is calculated for every product and every production line every shift every day. The daily results are used to compute a monthly linearity index, which is posted on a graph for all to see.

The linearity index is usable in continuous processes, but it seems to have been first used in repetitive production—our next topic.

REPETITIVE OPERATIONS: IMPROVING RESPONSIVENESS

As was noted, the process industry is usually continuous flow at the start but later ends up in discrete units (packages). Once the product's state changes to discrete units, we call it *repetitive* rather than *continuous*. Of course, a good share of the world's products are discrete from start to finish. In producing discrete units, a worthy goal is to increase the repetitiveness and get away from lots.

Key methods for attaining that goal include more frequent production and transportation and synchronized scheduling. After we address those topics, we conclude the chapter with some ways that benefits of streamlining may be extended to firms with lower volumes and more variety.

Increasing Frequency of Transport and Processing

There are numerous examples of businesses that achieve roughly repetitive operations in final assembly but are far from it in earlier processes. The term *roughly repetitive* allows for variety within limits. In a Mr. Steak restaurant, the cook who grills steaks has a repetitive job, but the steaks vary in size and quality of meat. Routine purchase orders (POs) in a purchasing department are similar. Each PO is slightly different but is basically a repetitive operation. In the first case, the preceding process is in lots, not repetitive—purchased lots of steaks. In the second, both the preceding and next operations are in lots—batches of incoming requisitions (requests to buy) received by internal mail and batches of outgoing mailed purchase orders.

Is there room for improvement? Often there is. If a Mr. Steak restaurant currently receives steaks every three days, improvement would be receiving in smaller (more repetitive) daily amounts. Obvious advantages are less cold storage, better control of aging, and less forecast error. In the case of POs, a modern improvement is electronic communication. Send orders to suppliers electronically via facsimile, one at a time, immediately as needs are known. That gets the supplier working on the order sooner.

Steaks and POs have what are called *shallow* bills of materials. (For grilled steaks there are just two BOM levels: raw and grilled.) Many products with deep BOMs are, like steaks and invoices, roughly repetitive in the last process, final assembly, but not in earlier processes (lower levels on the BOM). Examples are cars, trucks, tractors, and small aircraft. In final assembly, each successive unit may have its own set of options, but the assemblers perform almost the same operations over and over.

For such products, a way to improve operations is to extend the repetitiveness *backward* into subassembly, fabrication, and purchasing. The easy way is to cut transit quantities: smaller loads moved more frequently, ideally with the discipline of kanban. Next, cut lot size and cycle interval between production runs; this often requires reducing setup or changeover times. (When the transit quantity is one unit, that is as repetitive as is possible *for a certain production run or lot.*) These topics were addressed in Chapters 7 through 10 and need no further discussion here.

PRINCIPLE: Produce and deliver at the use rate (or a smoothed representation of it); decrease cycle interval and lot size.

Synchronized Scheduling

As we have seen throughout this chapter, streamlined operations require changes in scheduling. The ultimate is to let a final assembly schedule serve as the schedule for all major assemblies, which in turn would serve as the schedules for fabricated parts, and so on back to purchased parts and beyond. That ideal may be called **synchronized scheduling**. It involves meshing the timing of delivery or production of an item with the use rate of the next item at the next higher process level. Synchronizing delivery with usage is good; synchronizing operations *and* delivery with usage is even better: Make one, deliver one, use one.

As an example of synchronization, consider what happens to a written sales order sent in to a home office for action. Typically, the action is hard to find amid all the order-processing delays: The order may spend two days in central sales, two in accounting for a credit check, three in order filling and packing, and finally one more in shipping. And we should probably add a day for passage through the company mail room between each action activity. The total throughput time in this out-of-synch, snail-paced operation is about 11 days.

One way to synchronize these operations would be requiring each office to process this hour whatever came in last hour—mail service included. That cuts throughput time from 11 days to 7 hours!

As an example of synchronization in a factory, imagine a plant that makes blue jeans. If the schedule for the next two hours calls for the sewing machines (final assembly) to sew stovepipe-cut 28-inch-waist and 30-inch-length jeans, the schedule for the next two hours in the cutting room should call for cutting fabric for the same size and style: Cut one pattern, send it forward, and immediately sew it. If zippers, thread, labels, and rivets are also on the same schedule, the schedule is highly synchronized. While there may still be some idle inventories—because of delivery problems, potential stoppages or defects, and differences in process speeds—there are none resulting from mismatched schedules.

Of course, one way to get synchronization is to relocate far-flung processes into a cell—for example, an order-processing cell in which orders are passed from desk to desk in one room, or a blue jeans cell complete with cutting, sewing, and packaging.

Bands of Synchronization

Synchronized scheduling has not been common practice in industry, but large inventories resulting from mismatched schedules *have* been. A typical obstacle is a long setup time. In order to change size and style of jeans, the sewers may need only to change thread. In contrast, the label makers may need three hours to set up the label-making machine for a different label. In that case, the schedule in the labeling department may call for running two weeks' (10 working days) worth of labels for stovepipe–cut 28-inch-waist and 30-inch-length jeans. Two hours' worth of the labels might get used in the sewing department today, but labels for the next nine working days go into storage, which requires extra handling, inventory transactions, and other costs—and a style change could render them obsolete.

Even in such cases, a subproduct with a long setup time, schedules for the subproduct and all earlier production and purchase stages can be synchronized. In a multilevel product structure, it is possible to have alternate layers of large-lot production, then repetitive or small-lot, then large-lot, then perhaps repetitive for a couple of levels, and so on.

Figure 11–6 depicts the concept for an example in which different models of bicycle are the end products:

Level 0: Schedule is repetitive in final bicycle assembly; all models are assembled daily.

Level 1: Schedule is repetitive in rear wheel subassembly; schedule is synchronized with mix of models in the bicycle assembly schedule at the zero level.

Level 2: Schedule is in large lots in rim fabrication: Produce 20 days' worth of a certain rim size per production run. The reason for the large lot size is an eight-hour die change on the rim-forming machine.

Level 3: Schedule is repetitive in cutting steel strips for rims from steel coil; schedule is synchronized with the mix of models in the repetitive schedules for levels 0 and 1.

Level 4: Schedule is repetitive in slitting coil steel into correct widths for rims; schedule is synchronized with the mix of models in the schedule for levels 0, 1, and 3.

FIGURE 11-6

Bands of Synchronization—Bicycle Manufacturing

Level 0: Repetitive schedule for bicycle final assembly, all models assembled every day	} Synchronized schedule band
Level 1: Repetitive schedule for rear wheel subassembly, synchronized with mix of models in final assembly schedule	
Level 2: Large-lot fabrication of rims: 20 days' worth of each model per run	
Level 3: Repetitive schedule for cutting steel strips for rims, synchronized with mix of models at levels 0 and 1	} Synchronized schedule band
Level 4: Repetitive schedule for slitting coil into rim strips, synchronized with mix of models at levels 0, 1, and 3	

What has been accomplished? Inventory buildup from schedule mismatches occurs between levels 1 and 2 and levels 2 and 3, but the problem is avoided between synchronized levels 0 and 1 and between synchronized levels 3 and 4.

Actually, there is no inventory advantage in synchronizing level 3 to levels 0 and 1. The mismatches among levels 1, 2, and 3 disconnect the final-assembly schedule from level 3. Therefore, at level 3 the models could be run in a different mix or on a different cycle. For example, a two-day cycle could be used instead of every model every day; level 4 may still be synchronized with level 3, thus avoiding inventory buildup there. However, if the die-change problem on the rim-forming machine at level 2 is suddenly solved, all four levels should get right into lock-step schedules with final assembly.

PRINCIPLE: Cut setup and changeover times.

In cases of more complex products and components, product structures can contain dozens of manufacturing stages and levels. Several layers of suppliers and suppliers of suppliers can be involved. (At some lower level the process might be continuous, such as mixed powders and fluids, instead of discrete.) In such cases, the possibilities for synchronizing levels here and there multiply. Each synchronization step eliminates large chunks of waste, cost, and lead time.

There are other advantages. Synchronizing the schedules for slitting at level 4 and cutting at level 3 open the door to use of a simple visual (kanban) system as the dispatching method for level 4—no work orders required. Further, by using kanban, the people in the two levels must learn how to make their processes more dependable; the close linkages in a kanban system reveal each source of process variability and press for a solution.

Mixed-Model Processing

The production schedule interval for the film in Figure 11–5 was shown in work shifts; each perhaps eight hours long. Schedules can be repetitive in much longer, or much shorter, cycle intervals. When a variety of products must be produced and the cycle interval is very short—a day, or a few hours—we might employ **mixed-model processing**.

Consider the irregular, long cycle-interval schedule for products L, M, and N shown in Figure 11–7A. The boxes represent production runs; they vary in duration, as do the intervals between them. For example, in February and March, nearly two months pass between production runs of product N. Suppose that L, M, and N are standard products that enjoy regular, perhaps daily, sales, thus they show good potential for repetitive regularized production.

Figure 11–7B shows a regularized repetitive schedule with a fairly short cycle interval—one day—between repetitions. Let's examine how the mixed-model processing cycle might be determined. Our objectives are to match production to demand with a regularized schedule that gives star products priority status.

Assume that daily sales average 24 Ls, 12 Ms, and 3 Ns, for a total of 39 units.

FIGURE 11–7
Irregular, Repetitive, and Mixed-Model Schedules

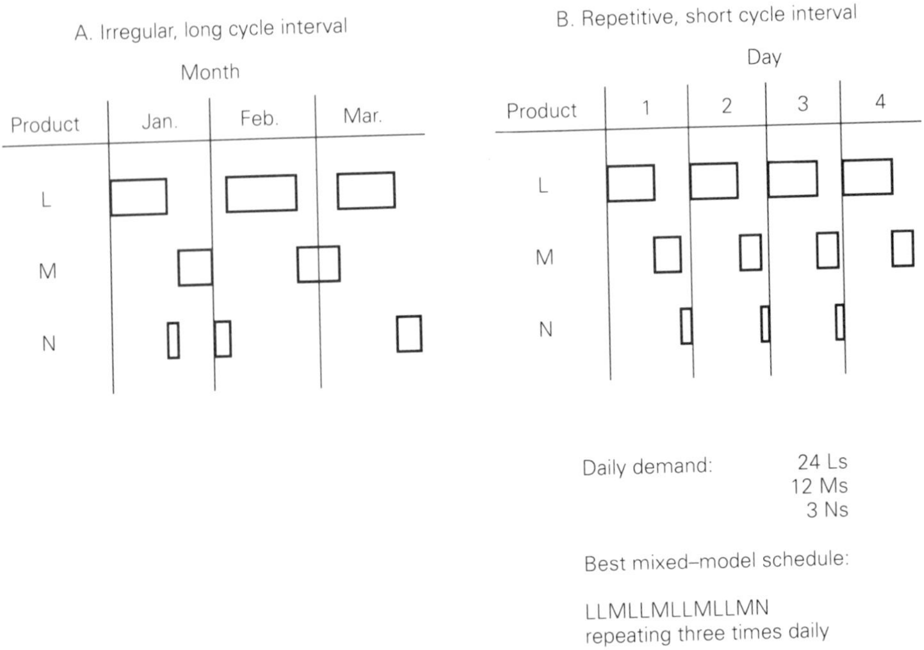

A. Irregular, long cycle interval

B. Repetitive, short cycle interval

Daily demand: 24 Ls
12 Ms
3 Ns

Best mixed-model schedule:

LLMLLMLLMLLMN
repeating three times daily

First, we reduce those requirements to the minimum ratio; dividing each demand amount by 3 yields 8, 4, and 1. Second, we sum the minimum ratios, obtaining the number 13. That becomes the number of units in the repeating processing cycle. That is, every cycle will contain 13 units; 8 will be Ls, 4 will be Ms, and 1 will be N. To meet daily demand, the cycle will repeat 3 times each day. Third, we find the mix of the 13 units that is most repetitive—minimizing the interval between production of each type of product.

This last step might require trial and error, but one or two simple passes will usually suffice. Consider two possible solutions that meet the daily demand requirement:

1. LLLLLLLLMMMMN—Repeat 3 times per day
   Assessment: Not repetitive within cycle; must wait up to 6 units for next L, up to 10 units for next M
2. LLMLLMLLMLLMN—Repeat 3 times per day
   Assessment: Repetitive within cycle, four repeating triplets followed by singleton; maximum wait to next L is 3 units; also, maximum wait to next M is 3 units. (This is the best schedule for this product mix.)

One advantage of going to the lowest-ratio, most-repetitive mix is that it allows providers of component parts to consider low-capacity processes and cheap equipment. Assume that the products L, M, and N in Figure 11–7 are (respectively) 24-, 20-, and 18-inch bicycle wheels, which are made from cut metal strips. If the whole day's requirement of each size is cut in one batch, what cutting equipment is appropriate? A good choice might be a costly, semi-automatic cutting machine that takes an hour to adjust for length changes (setup) but then cuts pieces fast.

On the other hand, if production of each size wheel is spaced out in the lowest-ratio model mix, the need for cut metal strips is also spaced out. Instead of the costly, high-speed cutter, why not use a simple band saw? It is much slower, but it takes virtually no time for a length change, and the low-ratio mixed-model schedule requires many length changes per day. In our example, the band saw would cut two 24-inch strips, one 20-inch strip, two 24s, one 20, two 24s, one 20, two 24s, one 20, and, finally, one 18-inch strip. That 13-unit sequence repeats two additional times throughout the day, exactly matching demand at the next processes, which are rim forming and wheel assembly.

What if the high-speed cutter is already owned and the producer, as part of a continual improvement effort, is changing the schedule from a daily batch to lowest-ratio mix? An attractive option is to treat 24-inch wheels as the star: Set up the high-speed cutter permanently for that length and cut two at a time intermittently throughout the day. This has the advantages of speed, no more one-hour length changes, and perfect "stockless" synchronization with the next process. Buy a band saw, if one is not already owned, to cut the 20- and 18-inch lengths.

The benefit of being able to use cheaper, simpler equipment as a result of low-ratio mixed-model scheduling may seem small, or rarely applicable. Not so! Toyota Motors, which has followed this scheduling and frugal equipment policy (capital expenditure avoidance), perhaps more extensively and longer than any other manufacturer, finds itself with massive retained earnings.

PRINCIPLE: Look for simple, cheap, movable equipment.

Our discussion of producing in mixed models has been limited to scheduling issues and benefits. Mixed-model processing is more complex than our simple examples suggest. Further issues, including how to balance labor on a mixed-model line, are taken up in Chapter 18.

Scope of Application

The techniques of transforming irregular into repetitive, synchronized operations apply not only to high-volume production; they may also be applied to building, say, one ship every two weeks or one passenger aircraft every three days. If each ship or plane is a special order for a different customer, that is only a partial obstacle to repetitive operations. In manufacturing ships and planes, there are always thousands of parts that are the same from unit to unit and therefore unaffected by special orders. Those thousands of *standard* parts may be made to highly repetitive schedules—repeating only every two weeks or every three days—with some levels synchronized with the level directly above. The massive problem of scheduling all those parts thus can be partly simplified, and some flows of parts can be put on kanban.

One of the most pressing needs in operations management is extending benefits of continuous and highly repetitive processing—the "stuff" of this chapter—into job and batch operations. We take up that challenge in the next chapter.

SUMMARY

The efficiencies, quality, and other benefits of repetitive and continuous operations create a worthy goal for any business: Try to streamline operations as much as possible and thereby obtain those advantages. Many of history's fortunes were amassed by entrepreneurs who knew how to streamline flows from one stage of production to the next.

Often, it is possible to become less "job-shop" and more "flow-shop" by reducing transit and production lot sizes. That decreases the time gaps in the production of a given product, making the process more continuous or repetitive. Sometimes a long setup or changeover time impedes use of small, frequent lots, but quick setup techniques or different equipment may be able to remove that obstacle. Another approach is to decrease variety in the product line, which frees up time to make remaining items more often, more continuously, or more repetitively.

Most firms in the process industry—making goods that flow or pour—are plagued by large lots and long cycle intervals just as piece-goods producers are.

The process industry's traditional concerns have been modern, well-maintained equipment for achieving process control and high-volume, low-cost flows; optimal mixtures of ingredients for minimizing raw material cost; and reliable supply and freight. Today, worldwide competition presses for fast equipment changeover, regularized schedules, mixed-model processing and linear output.

In the process and high-volume assembly industries, production intervals typically are irregular. Quantities produced are also irregular, because the tendency is to schedule a definite number of shifts per production run but get a variable yield per shift. One way to avert the high costs of irregularities is to give the star (high-revenue) product regular slots in the schedule and let lesser products fill the gaps.

Often it is good practice to schedule under capacity by some percentage so that a fixed quantity of production is attainable in each run. When the quantity is produced early, employees engage in other useful activities, such as process improvement. Performance may be measured by a linearity index, in which 100 percent linearity means meeting the exact target quantity every time.

Sometimes products start out in continuous flow and later, perhaps in packaging, end up in discrete units produced either irregularly or repetitively. One technique for increasing repetitiveness is more frequent moves and production lots in smaller quantities. Another is to synchronize production schedules from one processing level to the next. Bands of synchronization can be injected at various levels in multilevel product structures. Everywhere that two levels are synchronized eliminates much costly inventory and paves the way for the simplest of scheduling techniques for the lower level: kanban.

A very short cycle repetitive schedule could use mixed-model processing. The shorter the cycle, the better, because short cycles slow the production pace for each model in the mix. Simpler, cheaper, slower equipment may be considered.

Repetitive techniques can apply to both low-volume products, such as airplanes, and high-volume ones, such as telephone sets. Extending benefits of streamlined processing into job and batch operations is a critical need.

KEY WORDS

Streamlined
  operations
Commodity product
Continuous process
Custom product
Job processing

Process industry
Regularized schedule
Linear output
Under-capacity
  scheduling
Linearity index

Synchronized
  scheduling
  (synchronized
  processing)
Mixed-model
  processing

SOLVED PROBLEMS

1. An assembly line currently staffed with 10 assemblers produces an average of 190 units per day. The current sales rate for the product is 200 units per

day. If the company follows a policy of scheduling at 85 percent of capacity, what should it do? (Options include setting a new production rate or changing capacity.)

Solution

The production rate must be 200 units per day—exactly the number being sold. Then 200 is set equal to 85 percent of capacity, and capacity is solved for algebraically:

$$0.85X = 200$$

Then,

$$X = 235.3 \text{ units per day}$$

Since 10 assemblers can produce 190 on the average, we need to know how many assemblers are needed to produce 235.3. Therefore,

$$\frac{10}{190} = \frac{X}{235.3}$$

$$190X = 2{,}353$$

$$X = 12.38, \text{ or } 13 \text{ assemblers}$$

Thus, the company must assign three more assemblers to the production line.

2. The accompanying table shows 22 working days of production against a regularized schedule for a somewhat new product. The schedule rate, seven per day, was set on the 15th of the prior month. It gets changed in mid-month only when actual orders are greatly deviating from plan, as happened on August 22 to 26. Calculate the linearity index.

Date	Working Day	Pack Schedule	Actual Pack	Comments
8–1	1	7	3	No card cages
2	2	7	3	
3	3	7	10	
6	4	7	11	
7	5	7	4	Door latch problems
8	6	7	9	Two people short
9	7	7	9	
12	8	7	1	No drives
13	9	7	5	Rework required
14	10	7	4	Rework required
15	11	7	5	Rework required
16	12	7	6	Rework required
19	13	7	10	
20	14	7	7	
21	15	7	10	
22	16	0	0	No orders
23	17	0	0	No orders
26	18	0	0	No orders
27	19	7	5	
28	20	7	2	
29	21	7	3	
30	22	7	1	

Solution

Step 1: Insert working columns for calculation of absolute deviation (ignore minus signs) and percent deviation:

Working Day	Pack Schedule	Actual Pack	Absolute Deviation	Percent Deviation
1	7	3	4	4/7 = 57%
2	7	3	4	4/7 = 57
3	7	10	3	3/7 = 43
4	7	11	4	4/7 = 57
5	7	4	3	3/7 = 43
6	7	9	2	2/7 = 29
7	7	9	2	2/7 = 29
8	7	1	6	6/7 = 86
9	7	5	2	2/7 = 29
10	7	4	3	3/7 = 43
11	7	5	2	2/7 = 29
12	7	6	1	1/7 = 14
13	7	10	3	3/7 = 43
14	7	7	0	0/7 = 0
15	7	10	3	3/7 = 43
—Omit zero schedule days—				
19	7	5	2	2/7 = 29
20	7	2	5	5/7 = 71
21	7	3	4	4/7 = 57
22	7	1	6	6/7 = 86

Total = 19 working days   Total = 845%

Step 2: Calculate the linearity index (L):

$$L = 100\% - \frac{845\%}{19}$$

$$= 100\% - 44.5\%$$

$$= 55.5\%$$

REFERENCES

Book

Schonberger, Richard J. *World Class Manufacturing: The Lessons of Simplicity Applied.* New York: Free Press, 1986 (HD31.S3385).

Periodical

Assembly Engineering.

REVIEW QUESTIONS

1. What does "streamlining operations" mean?
2. In transforming operations to make them less job-shop and more flow-shop, must there be movement from a custom to a commodity product orientation? Explain.
3. What is regularized processing?
4. What is the advantage in changing from a schedule of making each star product once a day to a minimum-cycle, mixed-model schedule?
5. What kinds of technological obstacles stand in the way of synchronized operations? Give an example other than those in the chapter.
6. In the process industries, what have been the success factors for operations in the past? What are more recent success factors?
7. In continuous operations, production usually is scheduled in shifts rather than units. Does this change under the concept of regularized scheduling?
8. How can a schedule of 5,000 different parts or models be regularized?
9. Explain the linearity index.
10. What, if anything, can be done if the goal is to synchronize schedules for multiple process levels but some processes have very long setup times?
11. How is synchronized production related to mixed-model production?
12. Can the concepts of regularized, synchronized schedules be applied to low-volume production? Explain.

PROBLEMS AND EXERCISES

1. Arrange the following industries on a product-process matrix: motels, shoe manufacturing, processing welfare recipients, shipbuilding, furniture manufacturing. Discuss.
2. In the following industries, which stages of processing are best considered as continuous-flow and which as repetitive? Discuss.
   a. Soft drink manufacturer.
   b. Aspirin tablet producer.
   c. Breakfast cereal producer.
   d. Nursing care for hospitalized patient.
   e. Banking (account maintenance).
3. Modesto Farms operates a high-volume cannery for tomato products: canned whole tomatoes, tomato sauce, tomato paste, and the like. Discuss three vital success factors in the area of manufacturing for this company. Be as specific as you can, even though you have to speculate on the nature of this type of company.
4. Detergent is manufactured in a continuous process through a network of pipes, vessels, and pressure chambers. First, petroleum is distilled into paraffin, which is oxidized and then catalytically hydrogenated under pres-

sure to form fat alcohols. Sulphuric acid is added, and water cools the mixture to yield fat alcohol esters. Bleaching agents and alkalies are injected, and an emerging paste of fat alcohol sulphate is processed through a "spray tower" into finished detergent. Discuss two vital manufacturing success factors for a detergent manufacturer; be as specific as you can.

5. Edsom, Inc., a maker of keyboards for computer products, has a department in which instruction manuals are assembled into three-ring binders and another in which the pages are printed. There are four stages of production for the complete binders:

   a. The print shop slices large sheets of paper to size. It prefers to run as many jobs as possible on a recently acquired heavy-duty slicer, which runs faster than two older model slicers still in the shop. All the slicers require some setup time for any job.

   b. The printshop prints pages for manuals. Because of long setup times, print jobs for manuals compete with other print jobs for slots in the schedule.

   c. A high-speed collator collates the pages. The collator, a dedicated machine in the assembly department, is only used for manuals.

   d. Human assemblers open binders, insert sets of pages, and close binders.
      Elsewhere in the plant, the keyboard assembly line runs to a daily rate and achieves nearly perfect linearity.
      Can the four stages of manual production be synchronized to the assembly rate for the keyboards? Should they be synchronized? Discuss fully, giving an example with sample numbers.

6. Building A delivers several kinds of bulky component parts to building B four miles away. The components are made in three production stages in building A. Setup times on some of the equipment and parts assembly lines have been driven down nearly to zero. Building B houses final assembly and packing, each with negligible setup time from model to model of the family of end products.
   Can the five stages of production in the two buildings, plus the deliveries between, be completely synchronized to the sales rate? Is a fully mixed-model synchronized schedule feasible? Explain.

7. Old English Tea Company blends and packages an average of 8,000 boxes of tea per shift. Eighteen people tend the production line, and the company follows a policy of under-capacity scheduling—scheduling labor at 90 percent of capacity. Demand is down, and the production rate must be reduced to meet the demand of 6,800 boxes per shift. How many people should be added or how many assigned to other work? Assume that labor and output rate are linearly related.

8. A computer software company has one production line that reads programs onto floppy disks and packages the disks. The line has been scheduled at full capacity and has been consuming 30 hours of direct labor per day. Demand recently has fallen from 1,400 to 1,200 packages per day; therefore, now is a good time to convert to under-capacity labor scheduling. (Problems in meeting schedules and resulting lost sales have led to the opinion that

such a policy change is desirable.) Determine the new labor-hour requirements for a policy of 10 percent under-capacity scheduling.

9. Line 1 at the East Texas plant of Feast Frozen Foods has been troublesome. Its average production has been 5,000 12-ounce packages of frozen vegetables per shift, which is equal to average sales. But the variation around that average has been unacceptable. For the 10 shifts last week—a typical week—output was 4,728, 4,980, 5,009, 4,822, 5,860, 5,121, 5,618, 4,899, 4,620, and 4,900.

   About 35 percent of line 1's output consists of Feast's top-selling product, frozen young peas. A production run of peas usually is one shift, but sometimes a half-shift run is scheduled; peas are packaged three or four times per week. The other 65 percent of production is split among 17 other products. Recently, the line 1 crew has been working overtime on about half its shifts. Changing the speeds of the tray-filling and packaging equipment is no problem.

   a. Calculate the linearity for last week.

   b. Recommend a plan for increasing predictability of output on line 1.

10. Faiko Time Company produces grandfather clocks. Customers (mostly retailers) can select from over 100 styles of fine wood and glass outer enclosures, which are made in Faiko's wood and glass shops. In contrast, only three types of clock mechanisms can be ordered; these are assembled in another Faiko shop.

    The past two weeks' production orders have been as follows, in numbers of clocks ordered each day: 8, 9, 5, 7, 7, 9, 7, 4, 6, 10. Can Faiko adopt a workable production plan with a regularized production schedule and linear output? Explain why, why not, or to what extent.

11. A bicycle manufacturer has implemented a schedule of assembling every bike model every day (instead of long production runs for individual models). Can it use the same repetitive daily schedule in making handlebars, frames, and wheel assemblies? If so, can the repetitive schedule extend downward to tires, wheels, and spokes? Can it go further downward to wire extruders that make reels of spoke wire and to the steel plant that makes the commodity steel that is drawn into wire? Discuss the possibilities, obstacles, and benefits.

12. Zeus, Inc., makes three models of personal computers: large, medium, and small. One purchased part is an internal cooling fan: a large fan for the large computer, medium fan for the medium, and small fan for the small. Zeus produces and buys components purely just-in-time. The end-product schedule calls for producing one large, two medium, and four small computers every 10 minutes during the day, and the schedule is frozen for four weeks into the future. Suppliers deliver component parts (such as fans) once a day.

    a. What are the advantages of the daily mixed-model delivery schedule for the fan supplier? (One supplier provides all three sizes.)

    b. During one 5-day period, Zeus has trouble meeting its daily schedule, falling short by 30 units the first day, 5 units on the second, 2 on the

third, 25 on the fourth, and 8 on the fifth. What difficulties does this create for the just-in-time supplier?

c. Zeus's schedule works out to 48 large, 96 medium, and 192 small computers per eight-hour day. What is wrong with the schedule (a possible contributor to the schedule problems described in part b)?

13. Demand for a certain product averages 250 units per day. The product is made and sold in three styles; recently the split among them has been: style one, 60 percent; style two, 30 percent; and style three, 10 percent. Devise a mixed-model schedule with minimum cycle interval for this product line.

14. Find the lowest-ratio mixed-model schedule for four models of typewriter table, where daily market requirements are 6 model Ds, 18 model Es, 12 model Fs, and 24 model Gs.

15. When production volume is high and product variety low, dedicated production facilities may be used to run a streamlined "make-to-a-number" operation. What can be done to streamline production of medium-volume products?

16. In a bank, customers arrive irregularly. Are there any processes in a bank that can "escape" from that basic customer-driven irregularity—and get onto a repetitive schedule? Discuss, including any possible benefits.

17. In a department store, customers arrive irregularly. Are there any processes in a store that are important to customer service but that can be put onto a regularized schedule? If so, what are the benefits?

CASE STUDY   **GETTING READY FOR MIXED-MODEL PRODUCTION AT KAWASAKI MOTORS USA***

Mixed Models in Motorcycle Assembly

In September 1981, a Japanese management team replaced the American plant manager at the Kawasaki motorcycle plant in Lincoln, Nebraska. One goal of the new managers was to convert the main motorcycle assembly line to mixed-model production. The line had been running production lots of at least 200 of each model between line changeovers.

The conversion was expected to take about three months. It required two kinds of exacting preparation:

1. *Identification:* All parts, tools, cartons, racks, and so forth had to be clearly labeled so that an assembler would be able instantaneously to identify and select the right one. With a different motorcycle model next on the conveyor, delay in identifying it and all of the parts and tools to go with it would be intolerable. A color-coding system was devised so that, for example, all items related to a KZ650 motorcycle would be labeled with a gummed red dot. Even the position of the colored dot on the carton, part, or tool had to be precisely designed.

2. *Placement.* Engineers, material controllers, foremen, and assemblers all pitched in to devise exact locations for all parts and tools at workstations along the assembly line. The assembler, on seeing what the next model of motorcycle is, should be able to reach for the correct parts and tools blindfolded. Better racks, containers, and holding fixtures were designed to feed parts and hold tools in the right positions.

The preparations (which today we would refer to as *preautomation*) were successful. On January 1, 1983, the main assembly line converted to fully mixed model production.

At that time, the production volume was at about 200 motorcycles per day. That 200 might consist of the following models: 100 KZ440s, 60 KZ650s, and 40 KZ1000s.

Case topics:
Preautomation.

Mixed-model assembly sequence.

Benefits of mixed-model assembly when sales are falling.

Benefits of setup time reduction on presses.

---

*From the *World Class Manufacturing Casebook: Implementing JIT and TQC.* Copyright © 1987 by Richard J. Schonberger. Reproduced by permission of The Free Press, a Division of MacMillan, Inc.

1. For that mixture, what is the lowest-ratio mixed-model assembly sequence?

2. Would there be any benefits of mixed-model assembly in a period when motorcycle sales were falling and excess bike inventories were building up in the distribution system (as in 1982)?

Mixed Models in Motorcycle Parts Fabrication

Perhaps the main subassembly made in the Lincoln plant is motorcycle frames. The frame parts are formed from steel tube stock, and the parts are welded together into frames.

At one time frame parts were punched out on punch presses in lots of thousands at a time. The large lots were economical, because it typically took half a day or so to move a heavy die into place on a large-size punch press and to get all of the die adjustments and machine controls just right. Part of the setup time was running off trial pieces, inspecting their dimensions, changing settings, running and inspecting a few more, and so forth.

In 1980–1981, the presses were modified for quick die changes and adjustments. Common roller conveyor sections were welded to form a "carousel"

EXHIBIT 1
Carousel Conveyor on Punch Press

around the punch press; all dies were shimmed up so they had standard "shut heights"; and insertion and fastening were simplified. A dozen or more dies could be lined up around the carousel conveyor in the morning, and each die could be quickly and precisely rolled into place during the day in shifting from one frame part model to another (see Exhibit 1). The changes cut average setup time to under 10 minutes (including zero inspection time). Instead of running thousands of a model between setups, it became economical to run in lots of 200, 100, or perhaps 50; while that is not the one-piece-at-a-time mixed-model ideal, it comes close.

But Kawasaki wanted to achieve the ideal: one-touch setup and one-piece-at-a-time production. That was accomplished for high-use frame parts in the summer of 1982. To achieve one-touch setup, large general purpose punch presses were replaced with small special-purpose screw presses. Each screw press has a die permanently built in so that there is no die change time and therefore no setup time—a dedicated machine. The small screw presses apply pressure slowly rather than punch suddenly, but their slowness is more than offset by the zero setup time. With dies exactly positioned, defective parts are much less likely. The screw presses were relocated to the welding shop, where a welder can set up several screw presses to make several different frame parts; as each part is completed, the welder may immediately weld it onto the growing frame. There are no lot-size inventories. Much of the punch press shop has been abolished, since welders now make each part as they go.

3. What kinds of resource costs did Kawasaki reduce through their way of first achieving single-digit setup and then one-touch setup?

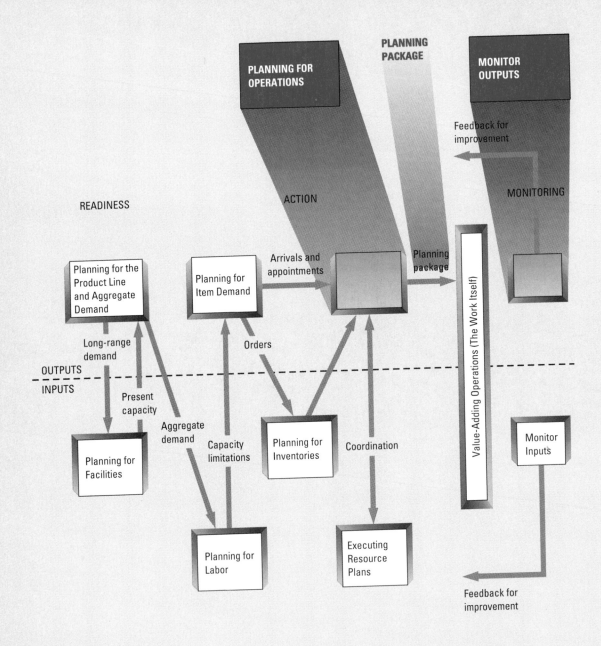

CHAPTER 12

Managing Job and Batch Operations

If all goods and services came from continuous or repetitive operations, management would be much simpler. In reality, much of the world's output stems from *intermittent* operations. This includes nearly all human services, most office work, and industrial job shops; the work itself is called *jobs* or *batches*. Common characteristics of such work include relatively low volumes of a large variety, irregular schedules (often with considerable variation in both run lengths and intervals between runs), jumbled or inconsistent job routings, and scheduling and control nightmares.

Recall from Chapter 11 that streamlining—that is, working toward more repetitive operations—ought to be an ongoing goal. Sometimes, star products can be run often enough to escape treatment as jobs or batches. Also, big jobs or batches may sometimes be chopped into smaller ones and run more often. Despite those efforts, jobs and batches remain, and competitive customer service demands that they receive good management.

Job/batch operations management is well developed, especially in North America. This chapter presents some of the primary techniques; topics include scheduling, loading and control of capacity, activity control, and accountability for results. First, however, we look at some general concerns with intermittent operations.

JOBS AND BATCHES: GENERAL CONCERNS

The immediate goal in performing work is often completion of a **job.** There is typically a defined end point and tangible results: a broken fence board repaired, a directors' meeting plan prepared, 20 tennis rackets strung, or a client visited. A job might yield one, a dozen, or even a few thousand units, and when larger amounts are involved, we refer to the job as a **lot** or *job lot*. A **batch** is a certain type of job, usually a standard run or lot size. Batches often involve mixing ingredients in a process mode, creating a singular batch that is measured by volume or weight: a yard of concrete, a ton of sand, or a gallon of sulfuric acid.

In this chapter, we treat jobs, batches, and lots together, because they require similar management. For convenience, we will use the term *job operations* when referring to any of these types of intermittent processing.

Planning for Responsiveness

In the figure that opens this chapter, we notice that the emphasis falls on the action and control zones, not on the readiness zone. We might accurately surmise that the bulk of attention to managing job operations is devoted to scheduling and control issues—present and near-future concerns. The large variety of work and the inherent schedule variability in job operations create difficulties; improving responsiveness requires flexibility, which in turn calls for rapid information management.

To meet that need, scheduling and control of jobs increasingly rely on computers and advanced communication linkages. In retailing, the point-of-sale terminal captures information about inventories and drives the scheduling of stock replenishment. Service orders may be entered into computers, which schedule jobs and perhaps break them into operations. For example, the operations in a service order or job might be: (1) Record client ID information, (2) record client's description of problem, (3) diagnose problem, and so on.

Factory planning is similar. Advanced factory management systems may include bar code readers at certain "toll gates" around the plant. The work flow is thus monitored at the toll gates, providing data for adjusting job schedules and operation priorities (and also for product costing).

In small firms or informal systems, supervisors do much of the scheduling and controlling. In larger, more formal systems, the function is delegated to a staff organization called the **production control** department (also called *operations control, production planning and control,* or *production scheduling and control department*). The department and its budget—including the budget for data communications and processing—sometimes get as large as the department and budget for operations themselves. When that happens—as it has all too frequently in North America—the tail begins to wag the dog. It is then time to overhaul the system, perhaps with "lean and mean" as the aim.

Actually, complicated and costly scheduling and control systems suggest that insufficient *front-end*, or readiness-zone, attention has been given to job operations. Four (probably interrelated) problems crop up: (1) too many products or technologies under one roof (unfocused plants); (2) too much reliance on the back-end or last-minute scheduling and control activities to cover up or make amends for poor up-front planning (failure to provide flexible facilities); (3) too much scheduling and controlling by staff support groups and not enough by line people; and (4) excess reporting and monitoring of work flows.

Better work-systems design, such as breaking up a large plant into focused factories within the factory, is one possible correction. Another benefit from front-end planning occurs when product and process designs are considered simultaneously. Finally, layout that simplifies work flow by arranging equipment into cells and incorporation of simpler control signals, such as kanban, also help.

Ultimately, whatever the benefits of longer-term planning, continuing improvement and responsiveness in job operations depend on scheduling and controlling—our next topic.

Steps in Scheduling and Controlling Jobs

Referring again to the chapter's opening figure, we see three arrows leading to *planning for operations*. The arrows represent information necessary for job scheduling. The information includes specific order arrivals and customer appointments; requirements for an inventory item; and availability of labor, machines, and other resources.

The arrow emerging from the *planning for operations* box represents the *planning package*, which causes value-adding transformations to begin. To the far right, *output monitoring* is also highlighted. Two concerns are: (1) Is actual output consistent with planned output (i.e., are customers getting what they asked for), and (2) are operations continually improving?

Figure 12–1 shows the flow of order scheduling for both goods and services. Service orders, shown on the left, typically are entered into an *appointment book*, which serves as a *master services schedule*. A client or service order often moves from one department or desk to another. At each move, queues can form. Clients or service orders in queue may be arranged in order of their importance, resulting in a detailed schedule. The general term for detailed scheduling of jobs waiting in a queue is **dispatching**. The term is not widely used in services, except for motor pools and taxi services: If you call a cab, your call is taken by a dispatcher, who assigns you to a cab (or a cab to you).

FIGURE 12–1
Order Scheduling and Control for Services and Goods

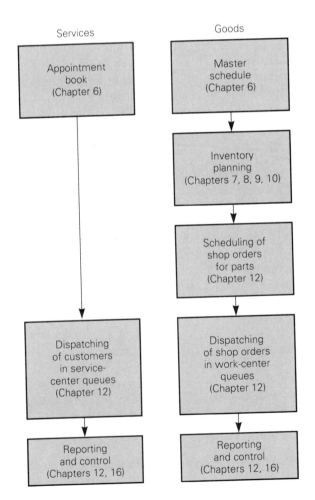

The flow pattern for manufacturing jobs is more complex, as is shown on the right in Figure 12–1. A *master schedule* drives inventory planning, which drives scheduling, dispatching, and control.

In some factories, there are two versions of the flow: one for final assembly and another for production of major modules. The reason is that final assembly often is quick—one day or less— and need not be planned far in advance. In contrast, a major module such as an engine, frame, or housing can take several days or even weeks to produce, and they had better be carefully scheduled well in advance of need.

Of course, major modules go into final assemblies. Thus, the *master assembly schedule* draws on the output of the schedule for major modules, which has a different term—*master production schedule (MPS)*. (In some companies, there is just one master schedule, not separate ones for final assemblies and major modules; in that case, it is likely to be called the *master production schedule*.)

Reporting and control are much alike for services and goods. In both cases, there is concern about getting jobs done on time and without wasting resources.

Jobs and Operations

Figure 12–1 shows that scheduling in manufacturing takes place at three (or more) levels. The top level might be final assemblies; below that comes major modules and then component parts. Can it go still lower? It can—and often does. Production of most component parts is in several steps, called **operations**.

In our discussion of process simplification in Chapter 3, we needed to clarify differences between operations and the processes they created. In a similar fashion, some of the techniques presented in this chapter require understanding of how industry distinguishes between jobs and operations.

Job

A *job* or *batch* (or *lot* or *job lot*) is the whole work activity required to fill a service order or produce a component part. A document concerning the job may be called a *shop order, manufacturing order, work order, job order,* or *service order.*

Operation

An *operation* is one step or task in a job. But more important, each operation requires a new setup. Setups for operations occur in services as well as in goods. It is worth noting that historically, setup times have been a major constraint to managers of job operations. Increasingly, competitive firms place high emphasis on setup reduction—to help reduce or remove the constraint.

PRINCIPLE: Cut setup and changeover times.

There are good reasons for separately planning, scheduling, and controlling each operation. One is that a special setup crew may need to be on hand. Another is that material handlers and handling devices may need to be brought in at just the right time. Still another is that inventory can build up before each operation and may need to be controlled in some way. Finally, and most important, there are usually several jobs queued up at a given work center waiting for an operation to be performed; the priority of processing those jobs must be determined.

Example 12–1 distinguishes between jobs and operations. As is customary in industry, operations are numbered by tens, that is, 10, 20, 30, instead of 1, 2, 3.

EXAMPLE 12–1   **DISTINCTION BETWEEN JOBS AND OPERATIONS— BOOKCASE SHELF**

In bookcase manufacturing, the bookcase appears on the master schedule and is exploded into component parts. One part is a shelf. Making a quantity of the shelf involves planning and controlling one job and several operations. Figure 12–2 shows a job consisting of 10 bookcase shelves. The shelf part number is 777, and the shop order is shown as a five-operation job. We see in the figure five operations and the inventory conditions between them. Operation 10: Withdraw boards from the stockroom. Operation 20: Saw boards. Operation 30: Plane sawed boards. Operation 40: Sand planed boards. Operation 50: Apply finish to sanded boards. The result is 10 finished shelves. They are component parts that go into the next-higher-level item on the bill of materials for the bookshelf order.

Each operation, even stockroom activities, requires setup or get-ready time. After each operation, work-in-process (WIP) inventories form and sit idle for a time. The setups and heaps of WIP require attention. A management specialist called a *dispatcher* assists the wood shop foreman in scheduling and controlling the operations: saw, plane, sand, and finish. But the due date for the whole bookshelf job was set earlier by a scheduler in the production control department.

If we asked 10 experienced managers of job operations what gave them the most headaches, we shouldn't be surprised if all 10 replied: "Scheduling!" We take that up next.

SCHEDULING

In using the word *schedule*, we usually mean a completion time or date and perhaps also a start time. Master schedules state the quantity and the completion day, week, or month, but usually not start times. Detailed scheduling—job by job—at the component level does include start times. Detailed scheduling, simply called *scheduling* in industry, is our concern here (master scheduling was discussed in Chapter 6).

FIGURE 12–2

Job and Operations for 10 Bookcase Shelves

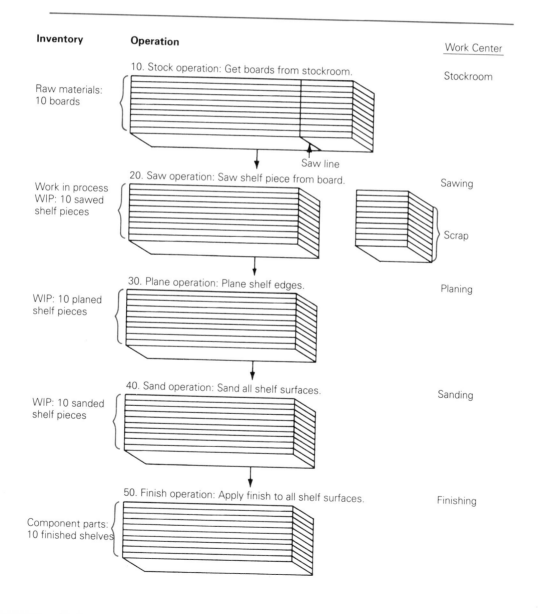

In scheduling a service order or job order, three questions must be answered:

1. When can the job be completed? (Based on standard times)
2. When should the job be completed? (Based on date of customer or parent-item need)
3. When will the job be completed? (Based on realities in production work centers)

It simplifies things if all three questions have the same answer. For example, suppose a patient is undergoing a complete physical examination. An early step is withdrawing specimens of various body fluids. The physician may want the results of laboratory analysis of a certain specimen to be ready at the end of the exam, say, 30 minutes later; that answers question 2—when should it be completed? Perhaps the standard time, adjusted for efficiency and utilization, is also 30 minutes; that answers question 1—when can it be done? Suppose the lab has no higher-priority jobs that would interfere with this lab test; then the job can be expected to be completed in 30 minutes, which answers question 3—when will it be done? Since all three questions have the same answer, it is clear that the lab test should be scheduled to start upon withdrawal of the body fluids and be completed 30 minutes later.

Actually, it is not very likely that a lab can complete its testing as soon as the physician desires the results. A lab is a job shop, and in job shops queues of job orders form and jostle for priority. In repetitive production, in contrast, jobs generally do not compete for the same resources, because problems and other sources of variability have been removed so that jobs flow smoothly from station to station, sometimes without queues of WIP inventory.

Lead-Time Elements

In job operations, lead time to produce or deliver something or provide a service usually contains much more delay time than actual work; that is, the part, client, or document spends far more time idle than being processed. In manufacturing, according to Orlicky,[1] the elements of production lead time for a given part are as follows, in descending order of significance:

1. Queue time.
2. Run time.
3. Setup time.
4. Wait (for transportation) time.
5. Inspection time.
6. Move time.
7. Other.

---

[1]Joseph Orlicky, *Material Requirements Planning* (New York: McGraw-Hill, 1975), p. 83 (TS155.8.O74).

Orlicky and others maintain that queue time (the first element) in metal fabrication shops normally accounts for about 90 percent of total lead time. Other delays—items 3 through 7 in the above list—take up part of the remaining 10 percent, which leaves run time—value-adding operations—with a very small percentage of total lead time.

Run time may be precisely measured using standard time techniques (see Chapter 16). Total lead time, however, is hard to pin down. Accurate estimates of lead times, and therefore accurate schedules, are likely only when work centers are uncongested, because only then may the typical job sail through without long and variable queue times at each work center. One of the scheduler's jobs is to keep things uncongested, that is, without too much work in process.

Work in Process

The WIP problem is attacked directly with just-in-time techniques. But the evils of WIP were receiving attention in Western industry well before JIT found its way across the Pacific. For 20 years or more, production control books and dinner speakers at professional meetings for production control people preached the following benefits of keeping WIP low:

1. *Service.* Low WIP means less queue time and quicker response to customers; also, with less queue time there is less uncertainty in the schedule and customers may be given better status information.

2. *Forecasts.* We know that forecasts are more accurate for shorter periods into the future, that is, for the shorter lead times that result from smaller amounts of WIP.

3. *Production control work force.* Less WIP means less congestion and less need for shop-floor control by expediters and dispatchers.

4. *Floor-space and inventory costs.* These are lower when fewer jobs are in process.

In service to humans, we could add another benefit: Customers are happy when they don't have to wait in long lines (note: the customers *are* the WIP). They get angry and may take their business elsewhere if lines get too long. Manufacturers have it easier, since inanimate parts waiting for machine time are unable to express anger (if they can, we haven't deciphered their language).

Often there is resistance to work-in-process reductions. Some people worry about keeping work centers busy. The operations needed to produce certain parts do not spread evenly over all the work centers. They tend to cluster, overloading some work centers and perhaps underloading others. As the job mix changes, and it often changes quickly, the pattern of over- and underloading changes. The scheduler is under pressure to overload on the average in order to hold down the number of underloaded work centers. Production supervisors get nervous about cost variances when workloads get low.

PRINCIPLE: Cut work in process.

Lead-Time Accuracy

The scheduler seems caught in a bind: Scheduling enough work to keep centers busy means that queue times will grow and make schedules less realistic. Queue time for *an average job* is hard to predict, because the average varies with the changing job mix. Queue time for *a particular job* is even harder to predict, because the job may queue up at several work centers as it completes its routing. Therefore, it is not uncommon for the scheduler to follow a "rule" of adding a fixed number of days for queue time and other delays. Two examples of possible scheduler's rules are:

$$LT = 2N + 4 \qquad (12\text{--}1)$$

$$LT = RT + I + 4 \qquad (12\text{--}2)$$

where

LT = Lead time in days
N = Number of operations in the job
RT = Run time in days
I = Inspection time in days

Equation 12–1 allows two days for each operation plus four days for queue time and other delays. Equation 12–2 is a bit more precise: It specifies a run time and inspection time and then adds four days for queue time and other delays.

A **dynamic scheduling** approach is another possibility. Here queue time includes an extra-time allowance for current or projected shop congestion. A simple measure of shop congestion is the number of open job orders, which the computer can find in the open-order file. (The open-order file is discussed in Chapter 9 in connection with material requirements planning.) Another measure of shop congestion is the number of operations in all open orders. To find number of operations, the computer searches the open-order file and then the routing file, which tells the route taken by an order.

With so much uncertainty and use of "fudge factors" in estimating lead times, is it possible to do a reasonable job of planning and controlling work flows? The answer is yes. In closed-loop material requirements planning, work flows are monitored and schedulers and dispatchers are kept informed. If they find that lead-time estimates, and therefore schedules, are wrong, they can make adjustments.

One way to adjust is to simply change the due date for a job. Advice on the need to change due dates takes the form of *rescheduling notices* from the weekly MRP run. While planned order releases from an MRP run trigger inventory planning (ordering) actions, rescheduling notices trigger scheduling actions. Together those two MRP outputs provide full support for planning and controlling the movement of component parts. A second type of adjustment may be made each day (between weekly MRP runs): A daily dispatch list from the computer tells the dispatcher of the need to change the priorities of work in process in order to meet due dates. (We discuss dispatch lists later.)

Inaccurate lead times have a more severe effect on capacity control. **Capacity**

requirements planning (CRP) is a computer-based extension of MRP in which future work center loads are computed. Accuracy of computed loads may be improved by including some kind of queue-time allowance in lead-time estimates. Allowances based on shop congestion—the dynamic scheduling idea mentioned above—may help. Planning around capacity bottlenecks—the OPT idea—also may be helpful. More accurate load projections permit work center capacity to be planned so there is less need for last-minute capacity control measures.

Backward and Forward Scheduling

For services offered on demand, the usual customer need date is "as soon as possible" (ASAP is the well-known abbreviation). The customer order is scheduled forward from the current date or from the date on which resources are expected to be available.

For services provided by appointment, **backward scheduling** may be used. An example is deliveries of checks and deposit slips from a small bank to a larger bank's computer service center. The service center may require delivery by 9 P.M. each day. If so, schedules for each delivery stop are backward scheduled; that is, operation lead times (times at and between stops) are successively subtracted from 9 P.M. The resulting schedule might appear as shown in the accompanying diagram.

Backward and **forward scheduling** may be used in tandem. A scheduler might be asked to estimate the earliest date on which a job can be completed, which calls for forward scheduling. The date of need could be beyond the calculated earliest completion date; backward scheduling might then be used to determine the scheduled start date.

Goods producers also use both forward and backward scheduling. Generally, manufacturing inventories that are replenished by reorder point (ROP) are forward scheduled. But MRP yields planned order releases that are backward scheduled from the date of the net requirement. Actually, in most MRP systems the planned-order-release date is not the scheduled start *day*. The scheduler is

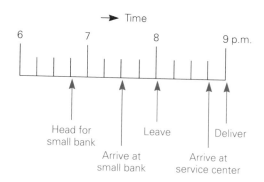

advised by the computer of the (backward-scheduled) start *week* and then determines the start *day*. Example 12–2 illustrates the scheduler's procedure.

EXAMPLE 12–2   SCHEDULING A SHOP ORDER—QUIDCO, INC.

The weekly MRP run at QUIDCO, Inc., shows a planned order in the current time bucket for part number 1005CX. The part is due on Monday of time bucket (week) 3, which is shop calendar date 105 (see Figure 12–3A).

The inventory planner validates the need for the order and the order quantity and timing. He decides that it should be a make rather than a buy order and therefore requests a shop order.

The scheduler finds the part number in the routing file, and the routing and time standards for each operation on a video display terminal. She prepares a shop order

FIGURE 12–3
Generating Shop Order from Current Planned Order Listing

A. MRP listing of planned orders due for scheduling

Week of 90
Orders Planned for Release This Week
QUIDCO Inc.

Part Number	Due Date
0052X	110
0077AX	115
≀	≀
1005CX	105
≀	≀

B. Shop order, backward scheduled

Shop Order Number 9925
Part Number 1005CX   Quantity: 50   Release Date: 92

Operation	Description	Work Center	Setup	Cycle Time	Standard Hours	Finish Date
20	Bend rod	16	4.2	0.05	6.7	99
30	Finish rod	85	0.4	0.18	9.4	102
40	Inspect rod	52				105
					Due Date:	105

using the data from the routing file (see Figure 12–3B). She uses backward scheduling, along with QUIDCO'S "rules" for computing operation lead times:[2]

1. Allow eight standard hours per day; round upward to whole days.
2. Allow one day between operations for move/queue time and other delays.
3. Allow two days to inspect.
4. Release shop order to the stockroom five days before the job is to be started into production.
5. All dates are treated as end of the eight-hour day.

She begins backward scheduling with the due date, 105, in the lower right corner. (A **shop calendar** of consecutively numbered work days, omitting weekends and holidays, is common among manufacturing firms, because it makes computation easy.) That is the finish date for the last operation, inspect. She subtracts two days for inspect and one day between operations, which makes 102 the due date for the finish operation. Finish takes 9.4 standard hours [0.4 + (0.18 × 50 pieces)], which rounds upward to two days. Subtracting that plus one day between operations equals 99 as the due date for the bend operation. Finally, she subtracts one day (6.7 hours rounded upward) for bend, five days for stockroom actions, and one day between operations, which makes day 92 the release date. The scheduler therefore holds shop order 9925 in her *hold-for-release file* on Monday and Tuesday (days 90 and 91) and releases it on Wednesday (day 92).

A week goes by. The inventory planner notifies the scheduler that part number 1005CX has a new need date: the week of 110 instead of 105. (The latest MRP run informed the inventory planner of the later date.) The scheduler recomputes operation due dates as follows:

New job due date = Inspect due date	= Day	110	
Less inspect time	=	2	days
	Day	108	
Less move/queue time	=	1	day
Finish due date	= Day	107	
Less finish time	=	2	days
	Day	105	
Less move/queue time	=	1	day
Bend due date	= Day	104	

The scheduler enters the three new operation due dates into the computer. The computer uses the new dates in printing out a daily dispatch list. Copies of the list go to the three work centers to tell them about the changes in operation due dates.

In this system, the scheduler need not issue paperwork giving initial due dates and then revised due dates, because the computer issues daily dispatch lists giving operation due dates. She does need to assemble a planning package

---

[2]Adapted from Oliver W. Wight, *Production and Inventory Management in the Computer Age* (Boston: CBI Publishing, 1974), pp. 81–82 (TS155.W533). Note that operation lead times are detailed, whereas job-order lead times, discussed earlier (for computing planned order releases), are gross.

that may include job tickets, inspection tickets, and forms on which to record such things as material usage, scrap, and labor changes.

In a manual system, there may not be a daily dispatch list. In that case, the scheduler will need to put due dates on job tickets or other planning-package paperwork. A problem with the manual system is keeping everybody informed of new due dates when schedules change. It can be a paperwork mess.

In the QUIDCO example, a human scheduler performs the backward scheduling. This could be done at a terminal, with the computer handling the calculation chores following the lead-time rules.

Some companies have their MRP systems plan in days rather than weeks. Schedulers then may plan in hours instead of days. That cuts work-in-process inventory further and shortens lead times, which can make the firm stronger financially and competitively. Shop-floor recorders can provide the scheduler with faster feedback on how jobs are doing so that schedule changes can be more responsive.

Scheduling Operating Resources

We have been talking about scheduling jobs and job operations—the ends. At the same time, schedulers must make sure that the right operating resources (means) are there at the right time for the scheduled jobs. The schedules for ends and means must match.

In an earlier era, the tendency was to schedule jobs and operations with little regard for whether resources would be on hand. This was the case in manufacturing for two main reasons:

1. Labor resources were largely unskilled, and labor laws were weak. Companies therefore could adjust labor up or down, on short notice, as job schedules required.
2. Material resources, that is, purchased and made parts, were planned by reorder point, because there was too little data processing power to *schedule* those resources based on future net requirements—today's MRP process. The same was true of reusable resources such as tools, gauges, fixtures, dies, machines, and space.

Over time industry developed ever larger numbers of labor classifications, and moving labor around as job mixes changed became difficult. Scheduling became more complicated. Availability of the right labor skills and other resources had to be considered in scheduling jobs.

MRP systems were developed to provide notices of needs for certain component parts, and the MRP systems were embedded in a broader system that checked on resource availability. Aggregate and rough-cut capacity planning, which can roughly check for resource availability (see Chapter 6), come before the MRP run. Capacity requirements planning, which follows MRP, checks critical resources more precisely. MRPII extends the MRP concept to aid in scheduling labor skills, gauges, tools, dies, machines, and cash flow, all based on explosion of the master production schedule.

Resources sometimes may be scheduled *in advance* of need by making *reservations*. A reservation more clearly defines the resources to be used than does an appointment; in fact, in human services a reservation often amounts to *presale* of a resource, like an airplane seat or hotel room.

A picture is worth a thousand words so they say, and there is a way to represent schedules in pictorial form. It is called a *Gantt chart,* our next topic.

Gantt Scheduling Charts

Henry Gantt's name is attached to a family of widely used scheduling charts. Some common examples appear in Figure 12–4. In the basic **Gantt chart** form—much like Figure 12–4A—vertical divisions represent time and horizontal rows the jobs or resources to be scheduled. Lines, bars, brackets, shading, and other devices mark the start, duration, and end of a scheduled entity. The purpose of the charts, as with any visual aid, is to clarify and thus improve understanding and to serve as a focus for discussion.

The charts in Figure 12–4 are for scheduling three different resource types: equipment, space, and line employees. Each also identifies the jobs to be performed by the resources. Note too that each is a services example. While Gantt's original chart was for the control of repetitive manufacturing, today simpler forms of Gantt charts are more widely used in services, where routings are short and queues have few chances to form.[3]

In goods production, Gantt charts may be usable if:

1. *There are not many work centers.* With many work centers, a carefully developed Gantt display of schedules tends to be a piece of gross fiction, because queuing effects (discussed earlier) make lead times unpredictable. Keeping the chart up-to-date under such conditions would be time consuming and pointless.

2. *Job times are long—days or weeks rather than hours.* One example is a construction project. Drywallers, painters, cement crews, roofers, and so on may each spend several days or weeks at a work site. With such a long job time, a schedule on a Gantt chart will "hold still" and not become instantly out of date as it would with very short jobs.

3. *Job routings are short.* In parts manufacturing, routings can be long. A single job may pass through 5, 10, or even 15 work centers, with unpredictable queue time at each stop. The unpredictability, on display as a Gantt schedule, is not believable and thus not worth displaying. One example in which routings are short and Gantt charts potentially useful is maintenance work. Maintenance is often thought of more as a service- than a goods-oriented activity, even though it is goods that are being maintained. Therefore, maintenance may be expected to benefit from Gantt-charted schedules just as other services do.

---

[3]The original purpose was to display variances from planned production rates in repetitive production.

FIGURE 12–4
Common Forms of Gantt Charts

A. Schedule for machine

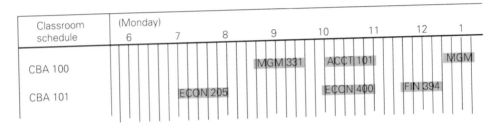

Scheduled summer jobs	M	T	W	T	F	S	S	M	T	W	T	F	S	S	M	T	W	T
Payroll		▓								▓								▓
Accounts recievable				▓								▓						
MRP					▓								▓					

B. Schedule for classrooms

Classroom schedule	(Monday) 6	7	8	9	10	11	12	1
CBA 100				MGM 331	ACCT 101			MGM
CBA 101		ECON 205			ECON 400	FIN 394		

C. Schedule for labor

	Dentist's appointments
Mon. 8.00	Mrs. Harrison
8.30	↓
9.00	J. Peters
9.30	Steve Smith
10.00	
10.30	↓
11.00	

Later in the chapter, we will look at the use of Gantt charts in controlling maintenance jobs.

WORK CENTER LOADING AND CAPACITY CONTROL

A topic of Chapter 6 was capacity planning, which is done early—before and during master scheduling. Now we may discuss **capacity control**, which goes on after work centers are loaded with jobs to make the parts that go into master-scheduled items.

Keeping work centers loaded with work but ensuring that loads do not exceed work center capacity is a day-to-day management problem. The problem applies to work centers of all kinds: The typing pool in an office is a work center; so is the X-ray area in a clinic or hospital and a machine or group of similar machines in a factory. Staff analysts' reports constitute workload for a typing pool; hospital patients generate workload for an X-ray center; and component-parts orders in support of a master production schedule generate workloads for machine centers.

Load is short for **workload**, and **loading** means assigning workload to a work center. Job orders for inventory items create workloads in work centers. Thus, capacity control in work centers comes after inventory planning.

Expediting—A Necessary Evil?

In job operations, loads are likely to be distributed unevenly. For a given work center, loads will vary from week to week. Some work centers will be overloaded and others underloaded. Such loading unevenness may call for short-term capacity adjustments.

The traditional approach is to make capacity adjustments at the last minute because of lack of good information about loadings in future periods. In this older approach, work center loads are calculated for upcoming weeks based only on open orders. (An *open order* is a component-parts order that has been released by production control to the work centers.) No planned (future) orders are included; the traditional planning system simply is not future-oriented. Therefore, work center load reports are incomplete for future time buckets, which means that capacity adjustments cannot be planned very far in advance. Attention is on the current week.

Production control's tendency has been to overload all work centers in the current week. Then expediters pick out the high-priority jobs from all the jobs in queue at each work center and "push" them from one work center to the next.

Lot Splitting

One expediting option is **lot splitting.** For example, a grinding machine might be in the middle of an 18-hour job to produce a lot of 9,000 pieces. An expediter drives up in a forklift truck with a pallet load of castings. Hot job. They need to be ground right away. Stop the machine and run the hot job. That *splits the lot* of 9,000 that was on the machine and necessitates another machine setup once the hot job is finished.

Lot splitting has always been considered, at best, a necessary evil; **expediting** itself has been viewed the same way. Thinking on this matter is changing. The JIT emphasis on quick setup reduces the costs of splitting lots. In fact, when large numbers of machines have been retrofitted for quick setup, lot splitting is no longer expediting; it is just normal practice. The 18-hour lot of 9,000 pieces on the grinding machine perhaps becomes half-hour runs of 250 pieces. Since we are talking about job operations with unsteady demands, those 250-piece runs would be scheduled irregularly as needs arise in the processes that use the ground castings.

Overlapped Production

A close relative of lot splitting is **overlapped production.** Perhaps the hot job *is* the 9,000-piece lot set up and running on the grinding machine. Common practice is to wait 18 hours for all 9,000 to be ground and then move the entire lot to the next process. But this is a hot job! Can't wait 18 hours! The expediter needs some or all of those 9,000 pieces to be moved forward fast.

The expediter has an easy solution: Move small sublots forward to next processes and get them started right away. For example, each time 200 pieces have been ground, hand carry or push them on a wheeled cart to the next work center. The expediter might repeat the action between the next several work centers. The result is a lot that is in overlapped production at two or more work centers at the same time. It resembles assembly-line production, except that the work centers typically are not lined up in close proximity.

It should be noted that when the hot job splits a nonurgent lot, the process is called *lot splitting.* When the split lot *is* the hot job, the action is called *overlapped production.*

While lot splitting can incur extra costs of more setups, overlapped production can incur extra costs of more trips to move small quantities of parts forward. Both can introduce more documents, such as change notices and move tickets.

Countermeasures exist that keep those costs from growing. One is to mount a quick setup effort. Another is to group machines, subassembly stations, and even document-processing work centers into cells. Cells shorten flow distances and make frequent small-lot movements inexpensive, and flows within cells may not require any extra documents. Overlapped production is normal practice wherever cells are formed.

Simplified Handling

Another trend is to reexamine the method of handling. Forklift trucks are everywhere in industrial job shops. They can move loads of thousands of pounds. Since they *can* move very large loads, they *do.* Crates, pallets, and boxes are piled high, and the forklift moves the highly piled loads. In the late 1970s, Western visitors to Japan saw similar industrial job shops that made little use of forktrucks (except on receiving and shipping docks). In the 1980s, forktruck removal became "popular sport" in some Western companies.

The economics work as follows. Forktrucks, with their batteries and high battery-charging costs, are expensive. They require wide aisles, create safety hazards, and run into things and cause damage. If average transport loads are reduced, say, fivefold, simple wheeled carts will usually be strong enough. Wheeled carts moving one fifth of the former load sizes would have to make five times more trips. The total handling cost may be less, however, because of the eliminated direct and indirect costs of the forklifts. Thus, forktruck removal may pay for itself even without the benefits of reduced delays and WIP inventories, which go down nearly fivefold as well.

Reducing Forklift Trucks at Emerson

William Rutledge, executive vice president of Emerson Electric Company, knew what to do about the firm's heavy use of forklift trucks—and the piles of inventory they thrive on. At a company meeting in 1986, he told all his division presidents that henceforth corporate headquarters was charging a license fee for every new forklift: $5 for the first truck, $50 for the second, $500 for the third, and so on. The division presidents *thought* Rutledge was being facetious—but his point was clear!

PRINCIPLE: Deliver at the use rate (or a smoothed representation of it); decrease cycle interval and lot size.

Hand Carrying

Both lot splitting and overlapped production have applications in services. For example, a common expediting approach in services is to hand carry a service order forward instead of the usual procedure of moving a whole batch of documents, medicines, and even clients forward. Delays in getting documents processed—insurance forms, letters of inquiry, and so forth— are notorious. Some of the factory solutions apply, such as organizing cells to shorten distances. Data communications and data processing methods offer another set of solutions.

In sum, the traditional method of controlling capacity—relying on expediters to push or hand-carry hot jobs—was chaotic and costly, and it worsened the problems of long delays and unpredictable completion times for normal, nonurgent jobs. New concepts offer ways to escape partially or fully from that mode of operation. One set of techniques that offers partial escape employs computer processing, discussed next.

Capacity Requirements Planning

Capacity requirements planning (CRP) is a computer-based method of revealing work center loads. A CRP run requires three inputs. One is planned order releases for component parts. Planned order releases are calculated by the computer in an MRP run (see Chapter 9). The second is open orders for component parts. These are orders released by scheduling (or purchasing) in an earlier period and still in process. The third input is routing data that tell which work centers each component-parts order goes through and how long it takes. Both the open-order file and the routing file must be computerized in order to run CRP. (Because of the cost of creating and maintaining valid computer files of routing and operation timing data, most MRP-using firms have not implemented CRP.)

CRP should be applied where it can do the most good: to work centers that have trouble achieving planned output, thus becoming bottlenecks. CRP projections in those work centers can warn of insufficient capacity far enough in advance to do something about it. (There is little sense in asking the computer to run CRP projections for all work centers and for 52 weeks into the future, because the real problems are in the near future and likely only in certain work centers.) Common corrections include training new operators, shifting labor to new jobs, layoffs, subcontracts, and so on. With CRP's potential to alert managers so as to keep work center capacities reasonably close to planned loads, the usual chaotic atmosphere on the shop floor may give way to reasonable order and tranquility. Differences between traditional and CRP load projections are examined next.

Loading to Infinite Capacity

Infinite-capacity loading (presented in Chapter 8) means scheduling job orders without regard for resulting work center loads. Figure 12–5 shows two versions of a visual loading report. Figure 12–5A shows the usual falling-off load projected for a work center in a firm relying only on open orders for parts that are low in the warehouse. The week 0 load is a backlog of parts orders already in the work center; the remaining loads are for parts orders due in this work center after passing through upstream (prior) work centers. The backlog and the week 1 load are shown to be (together) more than double the work center's weekly capacity. That is not a great problem, however, since only a few of the orders are needed for current production, and they will appear on a shortage list. Expediters will see that they are run first. Other orders are for stock replenishment (filling warehouse supplies) and may be safely delayed.

Figure 12–5B shows the up-and-down loading pattern common for work centers in firms that use the computer for inventory planning and CRP-based loading. A line divides open orders—those already released by the scheduler to the shops—from planned orders calculated by the computer to meet future needs. Overloads are shown in weeks 2, 3, and 8. Daily dispatching of more urgent jobs in those weeks can deal with most of the overload problem.

When overloads are severe, the work center scheduler needs help. The master scheduler, who schedules end products but not components, may need to move end-item (end-product) orders on the master production schedule. Moving many end items to an earlier or later period also moves the dates of need for component parts that go into the end items. It may not be easy to trace a component part back to its end items. (That kind of tracing, called *pegging*, sometimes can be performed on the computer by calling up a pegging subroutine of MRP.) Once the linkage has been established, the master scheduler may move an end-item lot and thereby move all the other links in the chain down to the level of the overloaded work center, thus relieving the overloading.

FIGURE 12–5
Infinite-Capacity Loading

A. Manually calculated loads

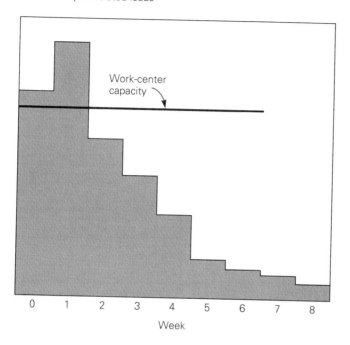

B. Computer-calculated (CRP) loads

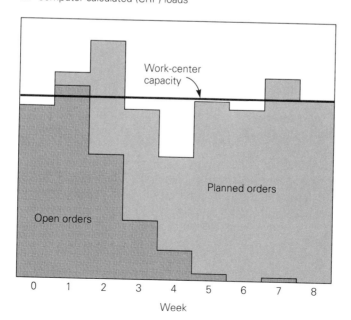

ACTIVITY CONTROL

The workplace is out of control if it is choked with partly completed jobs. That is true for a restaurant, clinic, or bank as well as for a goods producer. In Chapter 6, we studied production/capacity planning and master scheduling, which help to keep an overall balance between workload and capacity, and in the preceding section we considered work center loading concepts. There are two final steps to be taken in the quest for balanced loads in work centers. They involve scheduling and dispatching, which include *input control* of work releases to either gateway or bottleneck work centers (scheduling), *input/output control* over work center loads, and *priority control* of operations in work centers (dispatching). When all else fails, someone may have to expedite an urgent job (expediting was discussed earlier).

These topics comprise *activity control*. Manufacturers may prefer calling it either *production activity control* or *shop floor control*.

Input Control

The first half of the scheduler's job is to set due dates for each operation and a release date for the whole job. The second half is to release orders in trickles so as not to overload the work centers. This is often referred to as **input control**. Two techniques of input control are load leveling and firm planned order.

Load Leveling
The scheduler typically maintains some form of hold-for-release file. The file contains jobs with a mix of priorities. It may also include orders that were due for release on a previous day but were withheld for lack of parts or in order to avoid overloading certain work centers. The scheduler is attempting input **load leveling;** as the term suggests, the purpose is to release a *level load*, which is a mix of orders that neither overloads nor underloads a work center. Input load leveling works well only for *gateway* work centers—those at the input end of the operation sequence. The foundry (producing castings) is a common gateway in metal fabrication; a component sequencing machine (used in printed circuit board assembly) may be a gateway in electronics; and order entry is a gateway in many service businesses.

A scheduler could, with computer help, work up a schedule to level not only gateway but also downstream work centers. But it won't work. Because of variable queue times at later work centers, the later operations would be unlikely to follow the schedule closely enough for the loads to remain level.

Firm Planned Order
The **firm planned order** is a MRP tool that may be used to overrule the automatic rescheduling feature of MRP. That can be helpful in load leveling. A firm planned order may be scheduled earlier than the actual need to get the order into a gateway work center in a slack (underloaded) week. Figure 12–6 illustrates. To

FIGURE 12–6

Firm Planned Order for Load Leveling in Gateway Work Center

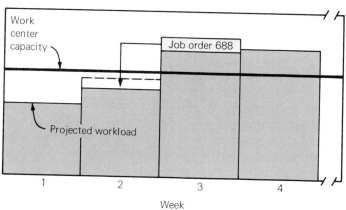

Action taken: Job order 688 is scheduled as a firm planned order in week
2 instead of week 3, its MRP-generated date of need.

invoke the firm planned order, the scheduler instructs the computer to flag a
particular planned order and move it to a given time bucket. In the figure,
planned order 688 is moved from week 3, its calculated date of need, to week
2, which helps level the load imbalance in weeks 2 and 3. The next MRP run
will not reschedule the flagged job back to its need date. It will issue a reschedule
message, which may be ignored.

The firm planned order may also be used to move a job to a later week. There
is no point in going far into the future, however, since conditions will change
the future before it arrives.

Input/Output Control

While the firm planned order technique is best for gateway work centers, the
input/output control technique concerns loads on any work center. An in-
put/output control report shows (1) where work center outputs are too low and
(2) where inputs are too low or too high. The information can suggest actions
such as a need to release more or less work to a problem work center or to
adjust work center capacity by such measures as working overtime.

Figure 12–7 shows a sample input/output report. The report, for work center
111, shows work center performance against the plan for the last three weeks.
The note below the report explains that the planned input is the average of CRP
loads. Raw, unaveraged CRP loads should *not* be entered into the "planned
input" row, because work is not likely to arrive at the same erratic rate that is
projected in the CRP computer run; too many things can happen in preceding
work centers for CRP loads to be valid except as averages.

The bottom half of the report in Figure 12–7 shows actual output; it drops from 725 to 704 to 698. Planned output is not getting done. The result will be a buildup of work-in-process inventory and a negative cost variance (explained in Chapter 16) in work center 111. Later work centers will be delayed because of the low output from work center 111.

The top half of the report shows that the output problems are not all the fault of work center 111. Not enough work is arriving, and the deficiency is growing from −20 to −50 to −60. Prior work centers seem to be bottlenecks to work center 111.

Examination of input/output control reports for all work centers can show where the causal bottlenecks are. Foremen may be able to raise output, for example, by overtime, in those work centers. If actual output is not brought up to planned output, or if actual inputs are chronically low, the master production schedule may need to be changed.

Data for the bottom half of the report may be available in non-MRP as well as MRP firms. Actual output is simply a count of work produced in standard hours. Planned output is the same as planned input in Figure 12–7. But sometimes planned output is set at a higher level than planned input, perhaps to work off a backlog.

The output part of the report is useful with or without the input part. But the input information helps show causes of output deviation and thus may be worthwhile. Getting actual input data requires the firm to keep track of work moved to next work centers, which are data many firms do not normally collect. Thus, new procedures—online computer terminals, for instance—for collecting data on moves between work centers might be necessary.

FIGURE 12–7
Input/Output Control Report

Work center 111	Date: Week ending 94			
Week ending	80	87	94	101
Planned input*	720	720	720	720
Actual input	700	690	710	
Cumulative deviation	− 20	− 50	− 60	
Planned output	720	720	720	720
Actual output	725	704	698	
Cumulative deviation	+ 5	− 11	− 33	

*Calculated by averaging the loads that result from capacity requirements planning for many weeks into the future:

CRP loads | 685 | 730 | 690 | 730 | etc

Average = 720

Priority Control (Dispatching)

Controlling capacity (by input/output control) is only one aspect of work center management. *Priorities* of the jobs and lots flowing through the work centers also must be controlled, because jobs are unlikely to arrive at a work center in an orderly manner. Some jobs arrive earlier than planned and some later, and often there are jobs in queue awaiting their turn. Jobs already behind schedule should be given a higher priority in order to go through first. *Priority rules (dispatching rules)* need to be established, and a dispatcher may be on hand to release the jobs according to the rules. *Priority control* concepts, the daily priority report, and centralized versus decentralized dispatching are discussed next.

Priority

At retail, the priority system is simply *first come, first served.* Customers are considered homogeneous, that is, one is not more important than another. First come, first served runs itself. The retailer need not pay a dispatcher to pick and choose among customers.

Are wholesalers and factories blessed with such simplicity? Yes—if orders can be processed quickly enough, with no queuing or other delays at each work center. If wholesale or factory orders can be filled in, say, a day or less, the company probably will elect just to process orders as they come in; an exception might be an urgent order, which can receive high-priority treatment, such as hand carrying.

Some job shops—wholesalers, offices, labs, and so forth, as well as factories—are striving for delay-free processing, but are still far from it. If it takes many days or weeks to process an order, the orders may need to be sorted by priority. Factors to consider in setting priorities for jobs include:

1. Customer importance.
2. Order urgency.
3. Order profitability.
4. Impact on capacity utilization.

For example, customer orders for items in the U.S. Department of Defense supply system are scheduled to be filled based on a priority composed of two factors. One is urgency. The other, called the *force activity designator,* is the customer's importance. A combat unit deployed in a combat zone is treated as a most important customer. If the unit orders bullets, the order will probably receive a high-urgency factor. The combination of customer importance and urgency yields an overall priority number calculated by computer—probably priority 1 in this case. The supply system has procedures for very fast delivery—say, 24 hours—for priority 1 requisitions; orders with very low priority call for delivery to take a certain number of weeks or months. Note that priority decisions are simplified here because profitability is not a factor; neither is capacity utilization (though it affects the supply system's delivery performance).

Scheduling component parts for end items involves simpler priority decisions than does scheduling the end items themselves. At the component level, orders for the same part are often batched. In batching orders, customer identification is lost, making it hard to schedule parts orders based on end-item profits or customer importance. Therefore, dispatching priorities (for dependent-demand parts) are usually based on order urgency and impact on capacity, not on profitability or customer importance.

Various priority rules have been proposed to aid in dispatching. Some are given in Figure 12–8 and discussed next.[4]

First Come, First Served and Kanban

First come, first served was discussed earlier as the dominant priority rule in retailing. This simple priority rule is often used in industry as well: The first job arriving at a machine or desk is the first job done. First come, first served is also the usual priority rule in kanban: Empty containers with kanban identifiers go back to a provider; the provider fills the containers in order of their arrival.

Shortest Operation Processing Time

Operation processing time means setup time plus run time. In the QUIDCO example (Figure 12–3), the operation processing time for "bend rod" (operation 20) at work center 16 was shown as 6.7 standard hours, of which 4.2 hours was setup time.

The *shortest operation processing time priority rule* is noteworthy because in computer simulations it has been shown to be superior to several others. The simulations show more on-time completions when the rule is used. Even so, few firms have adopted the rule. Instead, more advanced manufacturers, especially MRP users, usually base priority decisions on some measure of relative

FIGURE 12–8
Some Work Center Dispatching Rules

Timing-Based Ruled	*Other Rules*
First come, first served and kanban	Profitability rules
Shortest operation processing time	Cost rules
Longest operation processing time	Preferred customer rules
Earliest operation due date	Work center capacity rules
Earliest operation start date	
Least operation slack	
Critical ratio	
Hot list	

---

[4]These are local priority rules, applied to operations performed at work centers. Global rules, applied to the job as a whole rather than to an operation, may be used for initially scheduling the job. Also, there is a less-precise work center priority system based on the timing of the whole job rather than the operation.

lateness. The next four rules are based on due date and thus measure relative lateness. Each has its adherents among MRP authorities, and all yield about the same good results.

Earliest Operation Due (or Start) Date

The *earliest operation due date* (or *start date) priority rule* simply considers the operation dates for jobs in queue at a work center. First priority goes to the job with the earliest operation due (or start) date.

In MRP firms, job due dates may be updated with each MRP run, typically weekly. The computer may then back schedule from the job due date to recompute operation due (or start) dates. Thus, the operation dates that were assigned before the job was released may change while the job is in the factory, and priorities will then change too.

Least Slack and Critical Ratio

Earliest due (or start) date has a minor flaw: If an eight-hour operation and an eight-day operation each have the same operation due (or start) date, their priorities are equal, but the eight-day operation actually should begin seven days sooner (or end seven days later). Such differences in processing times are accounted for when the *least slack* or *critical ratio priority rule* is used, but extra computations are required.

Slack may be loosely defined as demand time minus supply time. Operation slack is computed as follows:

$$\text{Slack} = \text{Demand (need) time} - \text{Supply (make) time} \qquad (12\text{--}3)$$

or, equivalently,

$$\text{Slack} = \text{Time until operation due date} - \text{Operation lead time} \qquad (12\text{--}4)$$

where

$$\text{Time until operation due date} = \text{Operation due date} - \text{Today's date} \qquad (12\text{--}5)$$

$$\text{Operation lead time} = \text{Queue time} + \text{Processing time} \qquad (12\text{--}6)$$

$$\text{Processing time} = \text{Setup time} + \text{Run time} \qquad (12\text{--}7)$$

Alternatively,

$$\text{Operation lead time} = \text{Operation due date} - \text{Operation start date} \qquad (12\text{--}8)$$

Critical ratio (CR) uses the same data as operation slack, but it is expressed as a ratio as follows:

$$\text{CR} = \frac{\text{Demand (need) time}}{\text{Supply (make) time}} \qquad (12\text{--}9)$$

or, equivalently,

$$\text{CR} = \frac{\text{Time until operation due date}}{\text{Operation lead time}} \qquad (12\text{--}10)$$

The *smaller* the slack or the critical ratio, the more urgent the job. Negative slack or a critical ratio of less than 1.0 signifies a late condition: The operation is due for completion in less than planned operation lead time.

To demonstrate slack and critical ratio, let us assume that on day 101 four jobs are in queue at work center 16, which is the punch press center where metal is punched. Assume the following data (the first shop order, 9925, is from the QUIDCO example of Figure 12–3; recall that operation due dates are derived by back scheduling from the job due date):

Shop Order	Move/Queue Time	Punch Press Processing Time (set up + run)	Operation Due Date
9925	1 day	6.7 hours, or 1 day rounded	Day 99
9938	1 day	15.8 hours, or 2 days rounded	Day 102
9918	1 day	1.8 hours, or 1 day rounded	Day 101
9916	1 day	0.8 hours, or 1 day rounded	Day 105

The slack and critical ratios for the four jobs are given in Figure 12–9, which is roughly in the form of a daily priority report for work center 16. In the figure, slack values show that shop order 9925 is 4 days behind, 9938 and 9918 are each 2 days behind, and 9916 is 2 days ahead; the jobs should be run in work center 16 in that order.

Using critical ratios, shop orders 9938 and 9918 do not have equal priorities, while under least slack they do. The reason can be seen by examining shop order 9918. The numerator (demand time) is zero, and a numerator of zero always yields a critical ratio of zero whether the denominator (supply time) is large or small. The biased result from a zero numerator is not serious; critical ratio is still a worthy priority rule, because you are looking only for a rule of thumb, not mathematical precision.

Hot List and Other Rules

The *hot list* is also known as a *shortage list*, because it lists parts needed but unavailable for a current job. Hot-listed jobs get dispatched first at each work center. The other rules listed in Figure 12–8 are based on profitability, cost, preferred customer, and work center capacity. They are generally more complex than the timing-based rules (and should normally be used in conjunction with

FIGURE 12–9

Daily Priority Report, by Operation Slack and Critical Ratio, for Work Center 16

Shop Order	Demand Time (due date–today)	Supply Time (move/queue + processing)	Operation Slack	Critical Ratio
9925	99–101	1 + 1	−4	−1.0
9938	102–101	1 + 2	−2	0.33
9918	101–101	1 + 1	−2	0.0
9916	105–101	1 + 1	+2	2.0

timing-based rules); elaboration on those kinds of rules is reserved for advanced studies.

Daily Priority Report

The means of setting priorities is less important than the dispatching procedure. A proven procedure, perfected along with MRP, is the daily **priority report** (also called a *dispatch list*). A different priority report goes to each work center every day. Non-MRP firms could produce the report as easily as MRP firms. But without a weekly material requirements planning run to show changes in part need dates, operation priorities on the dispatch list become out of date. Still, some non-MRP firms may find benefits in the dispatch list. The key feature of the priority report is its daily recomputation.

Centralized versus Decentralized Dispatching

In some companies, production control department representatives are assigned to supervisors' offices. Their titles might be "dispatcher" or "shop scheduler." A dispatcher assists in placing higher-priority jobs ahead of lower-priority ones. Related duties include handling blueprints, route sheets, shop orders, job tickets, move tickets, inspection forms, tool orders, material issue forms, and completion forms. Those documents get jobs started and account for their completion at each stage of their routing. Dispatchers are on the scene and can therefore react quickly to delays. One reaction is to assign higher priority to the delayed job at the next work center. Others are to reroute upstream jobs around serious sources of delay, such as a machine breakdown, or to split a lot.

A few companies have a central dispatching group physically located away from shop-floor action. Why centralize? Consider this analogy. In an airport, decentralized air traffic control would amount to putting one air traffic controller on each runway. The controllers would try to communicate with one another via cellular phones. But the results would surely be suboptimal: The peak number of planes handled per hour would be small, or there would be frequent disasters. Thus, air traffic controllers—aircraft dispatchers—are centralized. That way they can coordinate tight scheduling and high peak volumes.

So it is for manufacturers that have centralized dispatching. Major reasons appear to be a need for high-volume production and tight scheduling with little margin for error. Automobile assembly, shoe manufacturing, and large-appliance manufacturing may be among the better candidates for centralized dispatching.

Paperless and Visual Systems

Each of the planning and control topics addressed so far in this chapter puts more paperwork into the system. Will the product or client get lost under piles of paper? Sometimes it seems that way.

Communications and computer technology can be employed to create a *paperless factory*. A few such factories already exist. Data-entry terminals in planning offices, display screens in work centers, bar codes on all parts containers, and bar code readers to track the work flow make it possible. The scheduling and activity control procedures are just as described above. The difference is that the job orders, priority reports, and other notices and files are called up on screens instead of from printed pages.

Another way to deal with paper is the *visual factory*. It is not hard to conceive of this for repetitive or continuous operations. No data screens are needed to tell people what to do when the same work units follow the same flow path, sometimes pulled by conveyors.

Can the scheduling and dispatching paper possibly be eliminated in a job shop? The answer is yes—or at least partly. One documented case is the Hewlett-Packard 9000 computer workstation.[5] H-P calculates that the 9000 series can be produced in 6 million different configurations. All production is to fill customer orders, which are small and in diverse configurations. The H-P plant eliminated job orders, ceased using MRP on the shop floor, and adopted visual kanban. MRP is still used for exploding customer orders into components. The exploded customer order goes to final assembly and is also used in planning orders for purchased parts.

All printed circuit board assembly and major module assembly and testing are triggered visually. Very small amounts—often one unit—of each partially completed item are stored in slots or shelves on racks in the work centers. When a customer orders a certain configuration of the finished item, final assembly pulls major modules (e.g., keyboards, logic units, and power cords) from nearby shelves. That authorizes major module assembly to make one more of each module to refill the emptied shelf spaces. Module assemblers withdraw components, such as circuit boards, from nearby slots. The empty slots authorize test operators to pull untested circuit boards from one rack, test them, and place them in the other rack to fill the emptied slot. The visual authorization to make another item to fill a slot winds back through 11 production stages to the stockroom holding purchased items.

The differences between visual and written work authorization are summarized in Figure 12–10. Note that the written system includes a job order, a pick list, and a priority report. The visual system may require an identification card in the slot, but that is fixed information, not generated for each job; process instructions are also fixed information.

Figure 12–10 includes only work authorization related to a certain job. The visual system, like the written system, may employ other kinds of written information, such as documents that introduce new parts or changes in old parts.

A final point: Often the visual system can be used for some but not all parts and processes. For example, in aircraft production, it would make no sense to keep an extra huge wing in a shelf and then trigger production of the next wing when the shelf empties. A schedule, not an empty shelf, should authorize the production of a wing. The components that go into the wing are another story. Finished units of common struts, fabric pieces, cable lengths, wire assemblies,

---

[5]See cases 2 and 3 in Richard J. Schonberger, *World Class Manufacturing Casebook: Implementing JIT and TQC* (New York: Free Press, 1987).

FIGURE 12–10

Work Authorization in Job Operations

	Visual	*Written*
Semifinished stores	Exact small quantity located next to work center	Large shelf space in stockroom; may be full, partly full, or empty
Material delivery	Empty slot tells line operative to get unfinished part from nearby rack; card in slot identifies locations	Written job order is transformed into "pick list"; tells stockroom what items to pick and deliver to work centers
Dispatching	Emptiest slot is next job	Daily priority report tells work center the order of working on the jobs in queue
Process instructions	In a file at the work center	Part of work package accompanying the job order

and other wing parts *could* be kept in kanban racks near the wing assembly area. Removal of a strut or other piece from a shelf may then visually authorize production of another unit to refill the shelf.

The visual system for job shops and offices is not yet in wide use, but its potential for application is almost limitless. It is a potent technique, because it copes with the explosive growth of overhead costs, especially those of processing written information and of material handling and storage.

REPORTING, CONTROL, AND ACCOUNTABILITY

> The best-laid plans of mice and men
> Oft go awry.[6]

If plans were always successfully carried out, there would be no need for reporting and feedback controls and managerial intervention. But plans do go awry, for two reasons. First, best-laid plans are based on conditions at a given time and always suffer from lack of complete information. Changed conditions and unforeseen events put the original plan out of step with reality. Second, those who carry out the plans are imperfect and sometimes irrational. We cannot count on them to follow plans exactly.

Nevertheless, the best control is still a well-laid plan or, better yet, a well-planned system with plans, procedures, and standards built in. The plan or

---

[6]A popular adaptation of lines from the poem "To a Mouse," 1789, by the Scottish poet Robert Burns. The original lines are:

> The best-laid schemes o' mice an' men
> Gang aft a-gley.

system component that goes awry should be the exception, calling for management action based on feedback or early warning information.

The previous section dealt with control, but a very short-range variety. Activity control decisions are highly task-related. In small organizations, line employees and supervisors make the decisions; in larger ones, production control employees do. In this section, we turn to feedback control based on either periodic historical reports or direct monitoring of the process. Policies, systems, and line performance can be assessed by these means. The overall purpose of controls is not to control people but to establish accountability for good service to the customer.

Control Cycle

Control is cyclic. Plans are fed forward, and measured results are fed back. Sometimes the work itself is fed forward, with plans made obvious by the nature of the work. Feedback information is analyzed, and changes are fed forward. An option is for supervisors to induce compliance with plans—that is, get back on track—instead of changing the plans.

Primary objects of control are the customer's concerns: quality, cost, lead time (or on-time delivery) for the product or service, and flexibility to change. Secondary controls concern usage, waste, and cost of operating resources: labor, materials, machine hours, tools, and space.

We can identify two levels of accountability: direct and indirect. Direct measures for accountability may be put on display in the workplace. Indirect measures are summary reports that go to staff people or upper line managers, who may direct corrective actions.

Control of quality is considered in Chapter 14. Productivity and cost variance standards are discussed in Chapter 16. The following sections examine remaining control topics.

Direct Accountability

In new businesses accountability is mostly direct, residing in the workplace. Large companies tend to have large staff departments, which develop indirect means for accountability. A "back to basics" movement is causing reexamination of the indirect measures. Directly measuring variables in the process and taking immediate action can reduce some of the high costs and delays of indirect accountability.

Statistical process control (discussed in more detail in Chapter 14) is one example of a direct measurement. SPC, like most of the other direct accountability measures, employs visible charts or graphs in the workplace. Visible graphs for SPC, defect rates, yields, scrap, and rework are coming into wide use in industry.

Those are not the kinds of accountability measures that accounting departments generally provide. Robert S. Kaplan, the Arthur Lowes Dickenson Professor of Accounting at Harvard University, believes that the usual accounting measures are no longer adequate. He advocates measures of yield, defects, and rework, which are quality-related, and other measures as well.

Timing and Related Measures

Kaplan notes that "overall performance of an entire factory is judged by its throughput time, [which is] how long from the time an item is first started into production until the time it is shipped, or at least ready to be shipped, to the customer."[7]

Direct accountability for lead time requires formal measurement at regular intervals, such as monthly or quarterly. The overall product lead time should be plotted on a large graph on the main wall in operations. The whole plant is accountable for progress in reducing product lead time, and each improvement goes up on the main graph. One U.S. producer of power supplies for electronic products measures lead times monthly by sampling. A few items are tagged with a date at the first operation (raw material stockroom); when the finished power supply is finally in a shipping box, dates are subtracted to determine lead time. Lead-time graphs are at least as valid in services—even more so if the service is perishable.

A close cousin of lead time is work-in-process (WIP) inventory. Graphs showing current average WIP in each work center and in the whole plant or area are another good direct accountability measure. It is a robust measure, because average WIP cannot drop much (and stay there) unless problems with machines, processes, and procedures are being solved.

Purposes of Visible Graphs

Visible graphs have several purposes. If there really is progress, the people involved can take pride in the visible display of improvements.[8] Further, improvement trends silently call for more of the same—a motivational benefit. Finally, a good assortment of visible graphs can be an excellent tool for communication among operations, support people, management, and visiting customers or suppliers. The graphs may even help draw timid managers and others out of their offices to the source of problems. While it is not natural for a manager to carry a computer report to the floor to use in discussing problems, performance graphs in the workplace are a natural focal point for discussion.

PRINCIPLE: Record and retain output volume, quality, and problem data at the workplace.

---

[7]Kaplan's response to an interviewer's question in H. Thomas Johnson and Robert S. Kaplan, "The Rise and Fall of Management Accounting," *Management Accounting*, January 1987, pp. 22–29.
[8]A description of use of visible performance graphs in a plant assembling minicomputers may be found in Richard C. Walleigh, "What's Your Excuse for Not Using JIT?" *Harvard Business Review*, March–April 1986, pp. 38–54.

Measures of Output

Customers want to deal with firms whose *average* lead time is short; besides the average, they want timely delivery and no delays on each job. There are several ways to measure performance in meeting due dates or schedules and avoiding delays. Figure 12–11 summarizes the contrast between methods usable in job operations and those in continuous/repetitive and project operations.

As the figure shows, in repetitive or continuous operations measuring output simply requires counting units produced (that meet minimum quality standards). The count may be in units per day and the unit of measurement pieces, gallons, yards, or numbers of clients. The count may be transformed into yield or variance from schedule.

In job production, output measurement can be costly and difficult. A parts order may be routed through multiple work centers, with output measured at each. As is shown in Figure 12–11, the measurement may include a *unit count* of clients or documents processed or parts successfully produced (not scrapped). Time of completion is also reported so priorities may be recomputed for upcoming work centers. Periodically—perhaps every two weeks—a report may summarize work moved out (after successful completion) as compared with work moved into each work center. Another report may show job-order *due dates met*, which measures the success for all the work centers put together. Due dates met is also a suitable output measure in simpler job operations involving perhaps only one unit and one work center. Examples are repairing a pair of shoes, papering the walls of a room, performing a lab test, and cooking a meal. *Percent of completion* is a suitable measure where processing time at a given work center is long—days or weeks—and the output is not readily countable. Examples are major overhauls and renovations.

Three kinds of output measures listed in Figure 12–11 for project operations are percent of completion, milestones completed on time, and events completed

FIGURE 12–11
Output Measures, by Type of Operations

Type of Operation	*Output Measures*
Continuous, repetitive, or limited-quantity large scale	Unit count
Job or job-lot	Unit count (work center) Due dates met (job orders) Percent of completion
Project	Percent of completion Milestones completed on time Events completed on time

on time. Those measures are discussed in connection with project management and the PERT/CPM technique in Chapter 13.

Gantt Control Chart

The Gantt chart as a visual aid for scheduling services was discussed earlier, and examples of Gantt charts were given in Figure 12–4. **Gantt control charts** are useful in certain job operations. Renovation, major maintenance, and extensive overhaul work are examples; computer systems analysis and programming may also qualify.

Figure 12–12 shows a Gantt control chart for renovation work. The Gantt chart in Figure 12–12A is an initial schedule for three crews. An arrow at the top of each chart identifies the current day.

Figure 12–12B shows progress made after one day. The shading indicates

FIGURE 12–12

Gantt Control Chart—Renovation Work

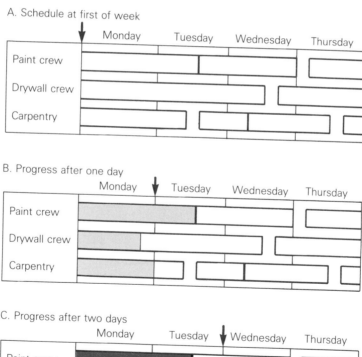

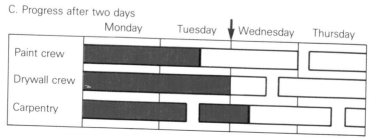

amount of work done, which probably is estimated by the crew chief, in percent of completion. Two thirds of the first paint job was scheduled for Monday, but the paint crew got the whole job done that day. While the paint crew is one half-day ahead of schedule, drywall is one-quarter-day behind. Carpentry did Monday's scheduled work on Monday and is on schedule.

Figure 12–12C for Tuesday shows painting falling behind, drywall on schedule, and carpentry ahead.

Commercially available schedule boards use felt or magnetic strips, pegs, plastic inserts, and the like to block out schedules and to show progress. Such boards are common in construction offices, project managers' headquarters, and maintenance departments. But Gantt control charts are poor for parts fabrication, because parts schedules and work center priorities change too rapidly to make plotting on a schedule board worthwhile.

Average lead time and job lead time or production output are important to the customer—if the price is right. Other direct accountability measures—cost, labor performance, machine utilization, and so forth—are discussed in Chapter 16.

JOB OPERATIONS AND JOB SHOPS IN PERSPECTIVE

In this chapter, we have examined a sophisticated, many-faceted system of managing complex job operations—a system perfected in North America, largely in the 1970s. We would be remiss if we left the impression that it is the best system available. Indeed, in several of this book's chapters, we have emphasized methods of simplifying and streamlining all kinds of operations; job shops are most in need of treatment, since they are the most complex and costly. We'll not repeat the messages from other chapters here; rather, we end this chapter with a real-life summary—see the accompanying box—of what can be done to improve a job shop. The message applies as well to job-oriented offices and, to some extent, to human service operations.

Reforming the Job Shop*

In the summer of 1985 [Schlumberger's Houston Downhole sensors (HDS) Division] was struggling. Operations were costly, chaotic, and falling short of acceptable standards. Customers were dissatisfied. About 15 percent of the logging tools produced by HDS failed on final acceptance test. Most products were built to schedules established far in advance, but on-time delivery was no better than 70 percent. The

*Excerpted from James E. Ashton and Frank X. Cook, Jr., "Time to Reform Job Shop Manufacturing," *Harvard Business Review*, March–April 1989, pp. 106–11. Used with permission.

average lead times exceeded 12 months. Senior management was also dissatisfied. Cost of sales was unacceptably high . . . and the plant was bulging with inventories. WIP alone averaged five months of output.

What explains the chronic and intractable problems afflicting job shops? The answer lies in the manufacturing philosophy. . . . At HDS, most products were batched for final assembly and test in lots that usually represented two or three months' requirements. Therefore, lead times on orders were at least two to three months—and in reality much longer—even though many logging tools could be assembled and tested in two weeks.

So why batch? Because management wanted to be as efficient as possible—with efficiency defined as minimizing direct labor charges. Batching generated short-term savings in virtually every phase of the production process. Setup costs are a good example. Parts needed for final assembly must be "kitted" in a warehouse before arriving at the assembly area. Management believed that pulling kits in large lots, rather than as orders arrived, saved money. Batching also meant that workers had to learn how to assemble and test a product only once per batch. . . . Batching minimized the unit costs of configuring test equipment and debugging completed products. Finally, moving products in large batches was combined with the use of queues to smooth work flows and adjust to ever-present parts shortages. Batching in effect, allowed all the factory's workers to be busy all the time.

In the long term, however, batching becomes a big obstacle to the very efficiencies it seeks to achieve. The long lead-time, large-lot, long-queue philosophy invariably results in split lots, broken setups, lost and defective parts, late deliveries, and large WIP. The results are visible in job shops everywhere: the monthly shipments hockey stick, where a large volume of product leaves the factory at the end of each measurement period; relaxation of quality standards under pressure to make quotas; secret high-rework jobs hidden in WIP; ever-changing production priorities; and daily crises on the shop floor.

We believe the real solution . . . lies in eliminating batching, smoothing, and artificial economies of scale, and organizing a job shop that can quickly and efficiently "change over" from one product to another without incurring large delays and cost penalties.

HDS adopted just such a production philosophy. It emphasizes shorter lead times (down from an average of three months . . . to two weeks today), small to nonexistent queues, low inventories, and quick recognition and correction of defects.

Getting control over the shop floor has allowed us to slash overhead. In the summer of 1985, 520 of the division's 830 employees were salaried or indirect personnel. The overhead count now stands at 220 employees. The largest reductions came from three departments—quality control; shipping, receiving, and warehousing; and production control (expediters, dispatchers)—whose roles diminish as quality and on-time performance improves.

These [and other] dramatic results did not require large capital expenditures. The management team initially cut the capital budget by 50 percent; annual spending has since run at less than half of depreciation. Those results did not require sophisticated computer applications. In fact, we turned off our shop floor computer, adopted a manual floor-control approach, and canceled a $400,000 automation project.

SUMMARY

Job and batch operations, in goods and services, involve handling a diverse, changing mix of small orders. Managing job and service orders requires extensive scheduling, work center loading, expediting, dispatching, reporting, and control.

In goods production, explosion of a master schedule results in job orders for component parts, which are produced in jobs, batches, or lots. In services, customer appointments are like a master schedule. In both cases, jobs are divided into operations—each requiring a setup—which are performed in different work centers. Dispatchers manage jobs in queue at each work center.

Because of variable queues, lead time to complete a job is often a question mark. The more congestion on the floor (WIP, for example), the more uncertain the lead time. Schedulers can help by: (1) controlling releases of orders (input control), (2) employing the firm planned order feature of MRP in order to level workloads in gateway work centers, and (3) using the input/output control report to see which work centers are failing to meet planned outputs.

Appointments and scheduled jobs and operations should dovetail with schedules for operating resources: labor, equipment, tools, materials, and space. In services, it is sometimes helpful to display schedules on visual Gantt charts; Gantt control charts are used to plot status of work, especially in maintenance, construction, computer programming, and so forth.

Hot jobs can be expedited. Expediting techniques include lot splitting, overlapped production, and hand carrying. The extra costs of those actions can be lessened by developing quick setup methods and shortening flow distances through creation of work cells.

Having enough capacity at individual work centers to handle the parts orders routed through them is an old problem. Work center loads that are computed manually are somewhat valid for the near future. But for the load report to be valid, planned orders must be added to open orders. That can be done by computer, using capacity requirements planning (CRP), an extension of MRP. CRP load reports give advance notice of capacity problems so that adjustments need not wait until the last minute.

Scheduling jobs into work centers (called *loading*) is usually done under an assumption of infinite capacity. Rearranging priorities in operations makes the system work; that is, it is the basis for pushing delayed jobs forward. There are several ways to set priorities. First come, first served is common in retailing, but timing—due dates at each operation—is more important as a priority factor within the firm. Earliest operation start (or due) date is a simple way to set priorities. Least slack and critical ratio are also popular. The shop-floor dispatcher (or foreman) follows a daily priority report in assigning work and handling shop documents. Dispatchers sometimes work in a centralized office instead of in the workplace, especially where operations must be tightly coordinated.

Paperless work authorization is possible with computers. Visual kanban-like systems go a step further by eliminating the need for some written work authorizations and flow controls.

Production control systems rely on measurements and reports. Measured results can be plotted on graphs in the workplace for more direct accountability. Customer-oriented measures—quality, lead time, job completions, and so forth—are the graphs' natural focus.

KEY WORDS

Job	Backward scheduling	Infinite-capacity
Lot	Forward scheduling	loading
Batch	Shop calendar	Input control
Production control	Gantt chart	Load leveling
Dispatching	Capacity control	Firm planned order
(dispatcher)	Loading (load,	Input/output control
Operation	workload)	Priority report
Dynamic scheduling	Lot splitting	Statistical process
Capacity requirements	Expediting (expediter)	control
planning (CRP)	Overlapped production	Gantt control chart

SOLVED PROBLEMS

1. The framing department has an order for 20-pound frames. The operations and standard times for producing one frame are:

Operation	Standard Time
Cut	4 hours
Weld	8 hours
Grind	3 hours
Finish	18 hours

a. If it is a hot job, how quickly (in eight-hour days) can it be completed allowing one extra day for material movement and delays?

b. The MRP system sets lead times for component parts by a formula: standard hours times five, plus two weeks, rounded upward to full weeks. What lead time does the MRP system use?

c. The above two answers are far apart, but both are realistic. Explain how a *planned system* can accommodate both.

Solution

a. Total work content = 4 + 8 + 3 + 18 = 33 standard hours
= 4.125 days, rounded up to 5 days

Total "expedited" lead time = 5 + 1 extra day
= 6 days

b. From part *a,*

$$\text{Total hours} = 33 \text{ hours}$$

Then,

$$\text{Lead time} = (33 \text{ hours} \times 5) + 2 \text{ weeks}$$
$$= 165 \text{ hours (or 4.125 weeks)} + 2 \text{ weeks}$$
$$= 6.125, \text{ rounded up to 7 weeks}$$

c. The MRP system must back schedule using normal time estimates. The result is a realistic week of need, seven weeks prior to the week due for the frame order. It is nearly eight times greater than the expedite time of six days, which is to be expected since in job shops work spends most of its total lead time in various kinds of delay. The few hot jobs interrupt the routine ones, causing the latter to be delayed still more. (While that situation has been normal in job shops, simplified operations management systems are eliminating delays in some companies.)

2. Today is day 11 on the shop calendar, and three jobs are in work center 67, as shown in the following table:

Jobs in Work Center 67	Scheduled Operation Start Date	Scheduled Operation Due Date
A	12	18
B	8	16
C	13	17

Calculate critical ratios and operation slack for the three jobs. Arrange the jobs in priority order, and indicate which should be done first.

Solution

From Equations 12–3, 12–4, and 12–5,
Demand time = Operation due date − Today's date

Then,

Job	Demand Time Due − Today	Supply Time (Equation 12–8)	Operation Slack (Equation 12–3)	Critical Ratio (Equation 12–9)
A	18 − 11 = 7	18 − 12 = 6	7 − 6 = +1	7/6 = 1.2
B	16 − 11 = 5	16 − 8 = 8	5 − 8 = −3	5/8 = 0.6
C	17 − 11 = 6	17 − 13 = 4	6 − 4 = +2	6/4 = 1.5

First: B
Second: A
Third: C

REFERENCES

Books

Fitzsimmons, James A., and Robert S. Sullivan. *Service Operations Management*. New York: McGraw-Hill, 1982 (HD9980.5.F55).

Fogarty, Donald F., and Thomas R. Hoffman. *Production and Inventory Management*. Cincinnati, Ohio: South-Western Publishing, 1983.

Fuchs, Jerome H. *The Prentice-Hall Illustrated Handbook of Advanced Manufacturing Methods*. Englewood Cliffs, N.J.: Prentice-Hall, 1988 (TS183.F83).

Plossl, G. W., and O. W. Wight. *Production and Inventory Control: Principles and Techniques*. Englewood Cliffs, N.J.: Prentice-Hall 1967 (HD55.P5).

Wight, Oliver W. *Production and Inventory Management in the Computer Age*. Boston: CBI Publishing, 1974 (TS155.W533).

Periodicals/Societies

Decision Sciences (Decision Sciences Institute), an academic journal.

Production and Inventory Management (American Production and Inventory Control Society).

Operations Management Journal (American Production and Inventory Control Society and Decision Sciences Institute), an academic journal.

REVIEW QUESTIONS

1. Planning for production of goods includes inventory planning and scheduling of shop orders. Why aren't these two functions included in planning for services?

2. How might insufficient attention to front-end or readiness-zone planning harm job operations?

3. Why are setup times such a concern for job operations managers?

4. What is the difference between a job and an operation?

5. Why is it hard to estimate production lead time accurately?

6. Why is it important to minimize work-in-process inventory?

7. Contrast backward and forward scheduling.

8. Explain how a due date for a shop order may be translated into finish dates for each operation in the job.

9. What is the difference between lot splitting and overlapped production?

10. What are some alternatives to expediting in services?

11. How do CRP reports get produced, and what are they used for?

12. When work center workloads are calculated manually in a non-MRP system, why do they end up looking like the bar chart in Figure 12–5A; that is, why the load in week 0 and the tapering-off pattern?

13. In MRP systems, infinite-capacity loading is usual. Does this make the MRP data invalid? Discuss.

14. How do the firm planned order and input/output control help ensure that the right amount of work is released by the scheduler?

15. There are eight timing-based dispatching rules listed in Figure 12–8. How do the last five differ from the first three?

16. Distinguish among scheduling, loading, and dispatching.

17. Why are slack and critical ratio about equal in effectiveness?

18. Who receives the daily priority report (or dispatch list), and what is it used for?

19. When is it wise to do centralized dispatching?

20. Compare the paperless and visual systems.

21. Compare direct and indirect accountability.

PROBLEMS AND EXERCISES

1. A manufacturer of stereo speakers produces five main types of high-quality speaker. The company considers itself a job shop. The single production line produces lots of each type of speaker on an irregular schedule. Price competition has been severe, and the company's profits have eroded. A conglomerate is buying the stereo manufacturer and intends to invest a considerable amount of cash to improve production control and cut production costs. What should the money be invested in?

2. A scheduler at QUIDCO, Inc., is working up a schedule for making 20 of part number 0077AX. The inventory planner advises that the order be released this week, week of day 90, and that the order is due on the week of day 115, when it will be needed to go into a parent item. QUIDCO employs closed-loop MRP.

   a. How would the inventory planner have determined the week due and the week of release? If the inventory planner has determined these dates, doesn't that constitute rescheduling and eliminate the need for the scheduler to do anything? Discuss.

   b. The "A" in the part number signifies a costly item. For A items, the following rules are used for computing operation lead times:
   (1) Allow eight standard hours per day: round upward to whole (eight-hour) days.

(2) Allow *no time* between operations. A items receive priority material handling.

(3) Allow one day to inspect.

(4) Release the job to the stockroom four days before it is to be started into production.

(5) All dates are treated as end of the eight-hour day.

Schedule a shop order for the item, assuming that the part goes through three operations plus inspection. You make up the setup times and operation times such that the schedule will fit between days 90 and 115. Explain.

   c. Compare the operation lead-time rules for part number 0077AX with the rules in Example 12–2 for part number 1005CX. Why should a more expensive item have different lead-time rules? (Hint: WIP has something to do with it.)

   d. A week passes. Inventory planning notifies scheduling that part number 0077AX is now due (to go into a parent item) in the week of day 120 instead of 115. The shop order, along with a planning package (blueprints, job tickets, etc.), has already been released. There is no need to issue new paperwork, because QUIDCO has a computer-produced daily dispatch list for each work center. Least operation slack is the dispatching rule. The scheduler merely gets on a terminal and inputs updated scheduling information. Explain how that information would be used in generating dispatch lists. Also, explain how the dispatch lists serve the purpose of adjusting for the new due date.

3. The maintenance department has two renovation orders that are being scheduled. Order 1 requires these three jobs or tasks: 14 days of wiring, 7 days of drywall work, and 9 days of painting. Order 2 takes 5 days of drywall followed by 6 days of painting.

   a. Draw a Gantt chart showing the workloads (backlogs) for each of the three jobs (wiring, drywall, and paint).

   b. Draw a Gantt chart showing the two orders back scheduled, the first with completion due at the end of day 35 and the second due at the end of day 14.

   c. Draw a Gantt chart with the two orders forward scheduled. In what situation would forward scheduling for these three trades be useful?

4. Open Air Furniture Company makes patio furniture. There are just three work centers: rough saw, finish saw, and assemble.

   Production control keeps track of total workloads for use in short-term scheduling and capacity management. Each week's component-parts orders are translated into machine-hours in rough saw and finish saw and into labor-hours in assembly. Current machine-hour and labor-hour loads are as follows:

	Rough Saw	Finish Saw	Assemble
Current week	270	470	410
Week 2	40	110	100
Week 3	—	40	50
Week 4	—	30	15
Weekly capacity	150	225	190

  a. Discuss probable reasons for the load pattern given for each work center.

  b. Is this the type of firm that is likely to rely heavily on expediting? Explain.

5. Part of a daily open-order file and part of a routing file are shown below (times are in hours):

Daily Open-Order File   **Date: 93**

Part Number	Shop Order Number	Quantity	Work Centers and Dates in Routing Sequence (current location signified by X)					
00112	836	10	11–91	X18–94	40–96	22–100	42–103	—
00810	796	48	11–84	X21–88	18–93	38–95	—	
00901	816	6	X16–88	26–91	12–98	18–100	40–103	—
00904	821	20	21–90	12–92	X18–95	28–98	—	
00977	801	30	21–83	51–86	28–90	X40–94	18–96	16–99
00989	806	18	09–84	40–88	X18–98	13–102	—	
01016	844	4	X12–94	41–98	29–102	18–104	23–107	—

Routing File (only selected part numbers are included)

Part Number	Work Center	Setup Time	Cycle Time
00112	11	—	0.8
	18	2.2	0.2
	40	0.6	1.2
	22	1.1	0.1
	42	5.0	0.7
00810	18	0.5	0.1
00901	18	1.0	2.0
00904	18	3.0	0.6
00977	18	1.5	0.3
00989	18	5.0	1.0
01016	18	1.2	3.1

Note: The complete routing is given only for the first part number.

  a. Using the information in the files, compute the load on work center 18 (WC18) for the weeks beginning on days 94, 99, 104, and 109. Plot the computed totals for each week on a load chart similar to Figure 12–5A and the open-orders part of Figure 12–5B.

b. Backlogs in the recent past for WC18 were:

As of Week	Backlog
79	96 hours
84	97 hours
89	91 hours

In week 94, the WC18 backlog is 70 hours, plus the load calculated in question *a*. (Those results are incomplete, since they are based on only *part* of a daily open-order file—only seven part numbers.) What concerns should the foreman over WC18 have in view of the backlog pattern?

c. Why is it necessary to state rules for computing operation lead times for scheduling purposes but not for loading purposes?

d. Explain how your load chart (from question *a*) could be augmented to include planned orders.

6. The following chart shows projected loads for one work center:

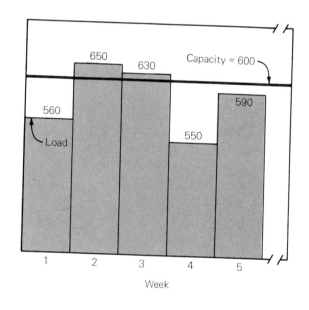

a. What may the scheduler do to help correct the imbalance between load and capacity in some weeks? Discuss, including any limitations or difficulties in correcting the imbalance.

b. How would the load report be produced?

c. Assume that the foreman has set work center output (via planned staffing) at 590 per week for these five weeks. A report after five weeks shows actual output in the five weeks as:

585   590   575   590   585

What may be concluded about the five-week results?

d. A second part of the five-week report shows actual inputs of:

565   650   650   570   600

What should be listed as planned inputs for the period? Now what may be concluded about the five-week results? Discuss fully.

7. On day 280, the daily priority report for the nickel-plating work center includes job number 2228. That job is due out of plating on day 279, and its planned run time is one day. If an additional day is allowed for move and queue time, what is the critical ratio? What is the operation slack? Show your calculation. How should these calculated results be interpreted?

8. Jerrybuilt Machines, Inc., uses the least operation slack priority rule. On shop calendar day 62, the following shop orders will be in work center 30:

Shop Order	Move/Queue Allowance	Operation Time	Operation Due Date
889	2 days	3 days	68
916	2 days	1 day	64
901	2 days	1 day	69

Calculate the slack for each shop order, and arrange your calculated results in list form as they would appear on a daily dispatch list.

9. Two shop orders are in the slitting work center on day 28. Order 888 is due out of slitting on day 32; it requires 1.8 hours of run time. Order 999 is due out of slitting on day 33; it requires 18.0 hours of run time. Determine which job should be run first by calculating critical ratios. Assume that run time is rounded up to whole eight-hour days. Also, assume zero queue time.

10. The following data apply to three shop orders that happen to end up in the same work center on day 120:

Shop Order	Preceding Work Center	Completion Date (day moved to next work center)	Next (current) Work Center	Queue Time plus Run Time in Work Center 17	Date Due Out of Work Center 17
300	28	119	17	3 days	122
310	14	117	17	2 days	123
290	13	118	17	1 day	121

Moves from one work center to another take virtually no time. Calculate critical ratios for the three jobs, and arrange them in priority order, first to last.

11. On day 12, shop order number 222 is in the blanking work center; it requires two days in blanking (including all waits, setups, moves, etc.) and is due out of blanking on day 15. Also on day 12, shop order 333 is in the same work center; it requires three days in blanking and is due out on day 17.

Finally, on day 12, shop order 444 is in the work center; it requires one day and is due out on day 12.

Determine which order should be run first, which second, and which third. Calculate slack for each order to prove your answer. What is the meaning of the slack value you get for order 444?

12. An antenna manufacturer produces in lots. Part of the daily dispatch list on day 314 is shown below for the chrome-plating work center:

Shop Order	Part	Setup Time (standard hours)	Operation Time (standard hours)	Slack (days)
910	AS65	0.5	3.5	−3
914	AS41	2.0	12.0	0
.				
.				
.				
885	AL88	4.5	10.0	+6

a. If shop order 885 is as shown below, what is the critical ratio of the plating operation on day 314 (a Friday)?

Shop Order 885   Part Number AL88   Quantity: 5 loads

Operation	Setup Hours	Total Run Hours	Finish
Cut	1.0	6.0	320
Move			321
Chrome plate	4.5	10.0	323
Trim		8.0	324

b. What rules for computing operation lead times can be detected from shop order 885?

c. On day 315 (Monday morning), inventory planning notifies scheduling that the due date for part number AL88 is now day 319 instead of 324. The chrome-plating operation has not yet been done for the part. What is the new operation slack in the chrome-plating work center? What is the new critical ratio? Is shop order 885 now urgent?

d. On day 315, where are shop orders 910 and 914 likely to be? Base your answer only on the above information.

e. Assume that on day 316 the (partial) daily dispatch list is as follows:

Shop Order	Part Number	Setup Time (standard hours)	Operation Time (standard time)	Slack (days)
898	AL26	1.5	4.0	−4
914	AS41	2.0	12.0	−1
885	AL88	4.5	10.0	−1

Explain what has happened to yield this dispatch list.

  f. Will shop order 885 also appear on the daily dispatch list for the trim work center? Explain.

  g. Is this company likely to use centralized or decentralized dispatching? Explain.

13. An aggressive new chief of production control has developed full computer-based MRP and CRP, plus a wide assortment of feedback reports. The feedback reports include the following, in order of importance according to the PC chief:

> Input/output control report.
>
> Labor efficiency report.
>
> Report of percent of job orders completed on time.
>
> Quality control report of defectives.
>
> Scrap report.
>
> Report of stockroom parts shortage rate.
>
> Miscellaneous minor reports and special audits.

One effect of these reports is that foremen complain about all the paperwork and the continual need to defend their performance as indicated in the reports. Assess the foremen's complaints, and offer your own specific suggestions.

14. A central sales office has seen its expediting (hand-carried orders) increase from 2 to 5 to over 10 percent in the last two years. Nonexpedited orders take at least a week to be processed. Suggest improvements in the priority and order processing system.

15. Following are the ways in which the results in a given organization or program are measured:

Agency, Firm, or Program	Measurement of Results
Library	Books circulated per full-time employee
Highway safety program	Expenditures on safety advertising
Tax service	Cost per tax return prepared
Computer center	Minutes of downtime
Personnel department	Expenditures versus budget
Sales department	Number of clients visited
Hospital	Average length of stay
School lunch program	Average pounds of uneaten food from plates
Antismoking program	Number of antismoking clinics established
School	Student credit hours per full-time equivalent instructor
Maintenance department	Percent of repair orders completed on time
Welding shop	Tons of scrap produced

a. The above list includes customer-oriented output measures and various resource input measures. Which types of measure apply to each item on the list? Explain each answer briefly.

b. Suggest a similar but more customer-oriented type of measure for each item on the list. Explain.

16. Four jobs are on the desk of the scheduler for a firm's minor construction department. Each job begins with masonry, followed by carpentry and wiring. Work-order data are as follows:

Work Order	Estimated Task Time— Masonry	Estimated Task Time— Carpentry	Estimated Task Time— Wiring
58	2 weeks	3 weeks	$1\frac{1}{2}$ weeks
59	1 week	$1\frac{1}{2}$ weeks	1 week
60	3 weeks	2 weeks	3 weeks
61	5 weeks	$\frac{1}{2}$ week	$1\frac{1}{2}$ weeks

a. Prepare a Gantt chart scheduling the four jobs through the three crafts (crafts are rows on your chart). Use first come, first served as the priority rule for scheduling (first *job* first—the *whole* job). Assume that a craft cannot divide its time between two work orders. How many weeks do the four jobs take?

b. Repeat question *a*, but use the shortest job processing time rule instead of first come, first served. Now how many weeks are required?

c. Three weeks pass. The following progress is reported to the scheduler:

Masonry completed on WO 58.

Masonry not started on WO 59, 60, or 61.

Carpentry half completed on WO 58.

Show the progress on a Gantt control chart (using part *a* data).

d. In this problem situation, each shop is fully loaded as the jobs are sequenced and scheduled. It is finite-capacity loading. What is there about minor construction work of this kind that makes scheduling and loading so uncomplicated (relative to job-lot parts fabrication)?

17. The following Gantt chart shows a scheduled project task and progress as of a given date:

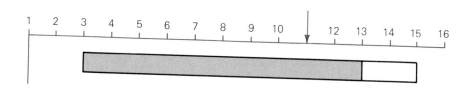

a. What is the present date, and what is the percent of completion for the task? How many days ahead or behind schedule are shown?

b. Redraw the chart as it will look tomorrow if the entire task is completed. How many days ahead or behind schedule does your chart represent?

c. Saturdays and Sundays are not worked and are not identified on the chart. Explain how the dating system treats weekends (and holidays).

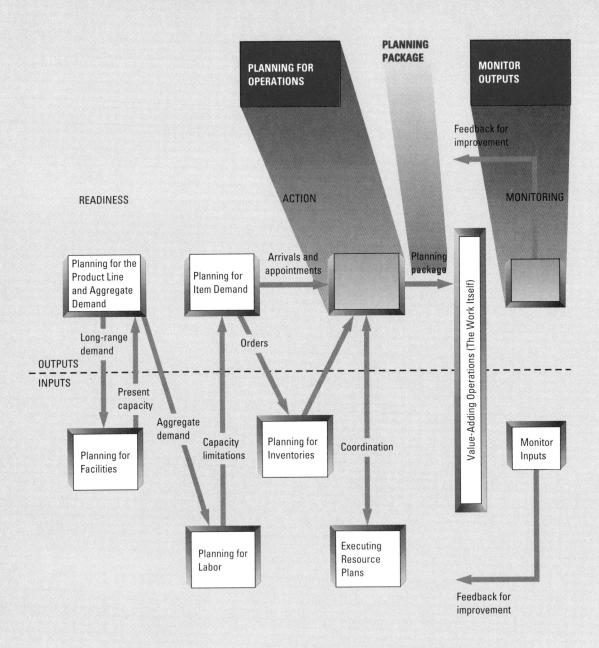

Managing Large-Scale Operations

PERT/CPM

Networks
Project Phases and PERT/CPM Subsystems

PROJECT PLANNING AND SEQUENCING SUBSYSTEM

Work Breakdown Structure
Task Lists, Network Segments, and Whole Networks
Networking Conventions
Alternative Network Forms

TIME-ESTIMATING AND PATH ANALYSIS SUBSYSTEM

Activity Times
Path Analysis
Activity Slack
Negative Slack
Slack-Sort Computer Listing
Network Simulation

PROJECT SCHEDULING SUBSYSTEM

"Crashing" and Time-Cost Trade-Off Analysis
Event Scheduling

REPORTING AND UPDATING SUBSYSTEM

Reporting
Updating

PERT/CPM ENVIRONMENT

COMPRESSING LEAD TIME IN LARGE-SCALE OPERATIONS

This is the third of four chapters on translating planned orders into outcomes. The outcomes that are the subject of this chapter are like jobs and batches, but much larger: large-scale operations generally known as *projects.*

The main characteristics of a **project** are size and complexity. That is, a project consumes a large amount of resources, takes a relatively long time to complete, and usually involves interactions among a number of different organizational units.

The size and complexity of a project translate into a sizeable management planning and control task. Just right for the job is a set of techniques having the abbreviations PERT and CPM. Most of this chapter centers on the hows and whys of PERT/CPM in the management of projects.

PERT/CPM

The **critical path method (CPM)**, a project management tool, was developed by Catalytic Construction Company in 1957. Catalytic developed CPM as a method for improving planning and control of a project to construct a plant for Du Pont Corporation. CPM was credited with having saved time and money on that project and today is well known and widely used in the construction industry.

The **program evaluation and review technique (PERT)** was developed in 1958 by Booz Allen & Hamilton Inc., a large consulting firm, along with the U.S. Navy Special Projects Office. PERT was developed to provide more intensive management of the Polaris missile project. Polaris was one of the largest research and development projects ever undertaken. Nevertheless, it was completed in record time—about four years. PERT got much of the credit and soon was widely adopted in the R&D industry as a tool for intensive project management.

A few early differences between CPM and PERT have mostly disappeared, and it is convenient to think of PERT and CPM as being one and the same, going by the combined term PERT/CPM. The construction industry still calls it *CPM,* and R&D people, *PERT;* a few other terminological differences are noted later.

Networks

A project consists of dozens, or even hundreds or thousands, of related tasks that must be performed in some sequence. PERT/CPM requires the sequence to be carefully defined in the form of a project *network* (see Figure 13–1). The starting and ending nodes are joined by a series of arrows and intermediate nodes that collectively reveal the sequence and relationships of the project tasks.

Networks facilitate project management in at least two ways. First, the im-

FIGURE 13–1
A PERT/CPM Network

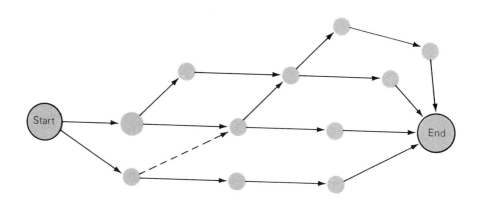

mensity of most projects makes it hard to remember and visualize the day-to-day and task-level activities, but a computerized network model remembers with ease. Second, the network aids in managing a large project as a system, consisting of subprojects (subsystems), sub-subprojects, and so on. For example, two of the successive nodes in Figure 13–1 could represent the start and end nodes of a subproject, for which a separate, more detailed network could be drawn. Alternatively, the network in Figure 13–1 might represent one task in an even larger project.

Although a good deal of attention is devoted to networks in this chapter, keep in mind that the network is only a tool. The project is being managed, not the network.

Project Phases and PERT/CPM Subsystems

PERT/CPM is among the more interesting and written-about management techniques. Actually, in full-scale implementation PERT/CPM is more than a technique; it can become a *management system*. Just as a project network may be viewed as a collection of subprojects or subsystems, PERT/CPM can be thought of in terms of four major subsystems. While most projects are not complex enough to warrant the expense of all four subsystems, very large-scale projects can justify a full, computer-based PERT/CPM system, which includes the following subsystems:

   Project planning and sequencing. This is about the same as the product design and process planning/routing activities in repetitive and job operations.

Time estimating and path analysis. Time estimating for projects is like time estimating in job operations, but path analysis is unique to project operations.

A project scheduling subsystem. Scheduling projects has some elements of both repetitive and job scheduling. But since a project is a self-contained unit of work, scheduling options are looked at differently.

Reporting and updating. Treating the network as a self-contained unit permits intensive project control using the management-by-exception principle.

PROJECT PLANNING AND SEQUENCING SUBSYSTEM

The initial PERT/CPM subsystem addresses network development. In planning jobs, we begin with a bill of materials (BOM); in planning projects, the same is true, but it is labeled a **work breakdown structure** rather than a BOM. The work breakdown structure defines major project modules, secondary components, and so on.

In job production, the sequence of tasks for producing a part is merely listed on a route sheet. In projects, those tasks, or **activities**, are linked to form a network. The project planning and sequencing subsystem of PERT/CPM addresses work breakdown, task listing, and network creation.

Work Breakdown Structure

To illustrate the work breakdown structure, we shall use a familiar example: home construction. (We'll make it a luxury home, since building ordinary houses is so routine as to be more like repetitive than project production.)

A work breakdown structure for building a house is shown in Figure 13–2. Part A is a preferred way to construct a work breakdown structure; the project is broken down into tangible products at levels 2 and 3. Part B is a process-oriented way to draw it—not recommended. The process-oriented chart does not have tangible products whose completion may be assigned to a single manager. Carpentry, for example, is a process that results in several tangible products or parts: forms for footings, the house's frame, finished cabinets, and so forth. Painting, landscaping, and masonry also are found throughout the project and result in several products. When the project is delayed or resources are idled, painters can conveniently blame carpenters, and so forth. If managers are appointed to "honcho" given parts of the project instead of having foremen only for each craft or process, the managers may work to secure cooperation from the various crafts. The idea is to get each craft closely connected to a customer—

FIGURE 13–2

Work Breakdown Structures for a House-Building Project

A. Recommended: Product-oriented work breakdown structure

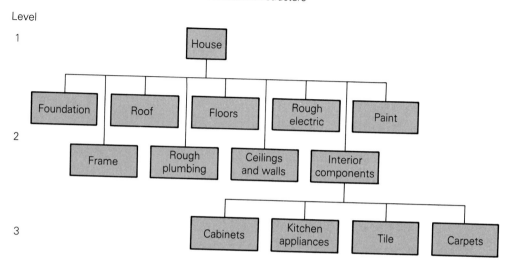

B. Not recommneded: Process-oriented work breakdown structure

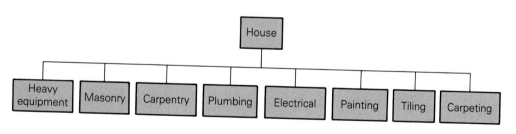

the next craft—in a joint effort to complete a segment of the house correctly with no delays or wasted resources.

PRINCIPLE: Get to know the customer.

Task Lists, Network Segments, and Whole Networks

Figure 13–3 shows how lowest-level products in a work breakdown structure are acted on to produce network segments. Figure 13–3A identifies three products in the house—cabinets, kitchen appliances, and tile—and lists tasks below each product.

FIGURE 13–3
Translating Task Lists into Network Segments

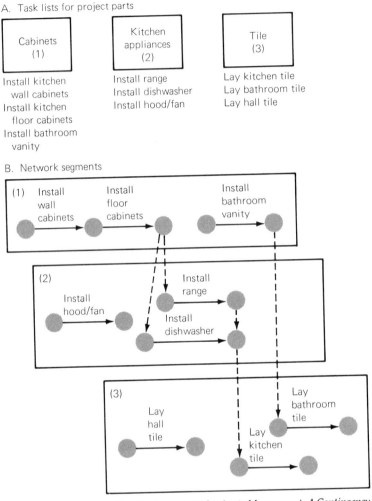

A. Task lists for project parts

| Cabinets (1) | Kitchen appliances (2) | Tile (3) |

Install kitchen
  wall cabinets
Install kitchen
  floor cabinets
Install bathroom
  vanity

Install range
Install dishwasher
Install hood/fan

Lay kitchen tile
Lay bathroom tile
Lay hall tile

B. Network segments

Source: Adapted from Fred Luthans, *Introduction to Management: A Contingency Approach* (Richard J. Schonberger, contributing author)(New York: McGraw-Hill, 1976), p. 88 (HD31.L86). Used with permission.

Without task lists for all the other parts of the house, it is impossible to properly sequence all of the tasks into networks. But Figure 13–3B demonstrates the kind of sequencing logic that must occur. Kitchen wall cabinets go first, since they are easier to install if the lower cabinets are not in the way. Floor cabinets are installed with gaps for the range and dishwasher, which are put in place next. Kitchen tile is laid after the kitchen cabinets and appliances have been installed; if it were laid sooner, it might not butt closely against the cabinets and appliances and also might get marred. Bathroom tile follows the bathroom vanity for the same sort of reason. Since there appears to be no reason why the hood/fan and the hall tile should come either before or after the other tasks shown, they are drawn unlinked to the other tasks (but they will link to tasks not shown when the full network is constructed).

The rectangles numbered 1, 2, and 3 in Figure 13–3B are not essential; they merely show craft groupings. Later, during scheduling, each craft may use Gantt charts to show when its project tasks occur. Note that it would serve no purpose to group all kitchen activities together, all bathroom activities together, and so forth; the kitchen is a room, but it is neither a product to be separately managed nor the responsibility of a separate craft.

More important than the craft groupings in the rectangles are the dashed lines between the rectangles. They signify connections between the task of one craft and the task of the following craft: the all-important maker-customer pair. Task lists and network segments go together to form a whole-project network. Figure 13–4 illustrates. It is a continuation of the house-building example, but further simplified; for example, this house has no tile, carpets, or bathroom vanity.

FIGURE 13–4
Network for House Construction

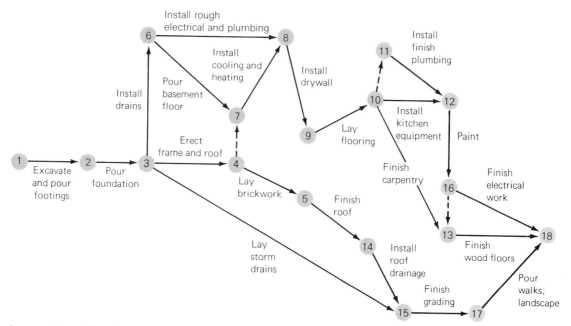

Networking Conventions

A few rules and conventions of networking follow.

1. One Destination. A PERT/CPM network (except segments) has only one start event and one end event. (In Figure 13–4, these are numbered 1 and 18.) To bring this about, all arrows must progress toward the end, and there can be no doubling back or loops.[1] Figure 13–5 shows those two no-no's. In large networks, it is not uncommon to make a few such errors inadvertently, for example, an arrowhead carelessly placed at the wrong end of a line. That results in event numbers going into wrong data fields on computer records, if the network plan is computerized. Most PERT/CPM computer packages detect such errors and print error messages.

2. Event Completion. A network **event** (or *node*) stands for the completion of all activities (or arrows) leading into it. Further, in PERT/CPM logic no activity may begin at an event until *all* activities leading into that event have been completed. For example, consider event 8 in Figure 13–4, completion of rough electrical and plumbling, plus cooling and heating—presumably including an outdoor cooling compressor. We could question that network logic, because it says that the next activity (after event 8), install drywall, depends on completion *even* of the outdoor compressor. In fact, the drywall is intended to cover up only the interior rough

FIGURE 13–5
Networking Errors

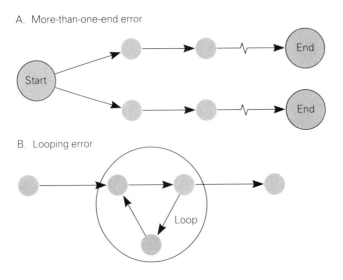

----

[1]However, those two and other options *are* allowed in a PERT/CPM variation called GERT (graphical evaluation and review technique).

work. To reflect that intention, the segment of the network in the event 8 vicinity would need to be drawn differently, with activities relabeled.

Let us generalize to make an important point: Network logic should accurately reflect intended project-flow logic! Typically, managers who spend a little extra time and effort in network creation are rewarded during project implementation.

3. Dummy Activity. A **dummy activity** is a dashed arrow; it takes no time and consumes no resources. Four of the five dummies in Figure 13–3 merely connect subnetworks. They are not essential and may be left out when the full network is drawn.

In Figure 13–4, two of the three dummies, 4–7 and 16–13, are necessary for project logic. Activity 4–7 is there to ensure that both 3–4 and 6–7 precede 7–8 but that only 3–4 precedes 4–5. The logic is as follows. We want cooling and heating to be installed on top of a basement floor (6–7) and through holes drilled in the frame (3–4). We want brickwork to go up against the frame (3–4), but it need not wait for a basement floor (6–7) to be poured. The dummy, 4–7, decouples the two merging and the two bursting activities to correctly show the logic. There is no other way to show it. Dummy activity 16–13 has the same sort of purpose.

Dummy activity 10–11 exists only to avoid confusing the computer—if the network is computerized. The problem is that two different activities occur between events 10 and 12. Most PERT/CPM computer packages identify activities and their direction by predecessor and successor event numbers. For example, dummy activity 10–11 goes *from* 10 *to* 11. The computer knows this because the 10 is read into a predecessor field and the 11 into a successor field in a computer record for that activity. (Each activity gets its own record.) In Figure 13–4 an extra event, 11, creates a dummy activity, 10–11. This ensures that finish plumbing and kitchen equipment will have unique numbers. Three equivalent ways to do this are shown in Figure 13–6.

4. Event Numbering. Most computer software for PERT/CPM does not require that event numbers go from smaller to larger. Larger to smaller (e.g., 16 to 13

FIGURE 13–6

Use of a Dummy Activity

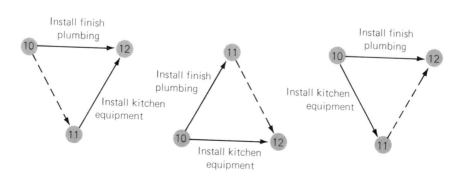

in Figure 13–4) is all right, because the *from* event (16) is entered into the predecessor field in the computer record and the *to* event (13) into the successor field. Thus, the computer has no difficulty keeping the sequence straight.

5. Level of Detail. Every activity in Figure 13–4 could be divided into subactivities. In addition to the burden that more activities impose, however, there is no need to plan for a level of detail beyond what a manager would want to control. On the other hand, there should be enough detail to show when one activity should precede another.

6. Plan versus Actual. The network is only a plan; it is unlikely to be followed exactly. For example, maybe walks and landscapes will get poured (17–18 in Figure 13–4) *before* finish grading (15–17). Or maybe money will run out and finish grading will be cut from the project. Thus, the network is not an imperative, and it is not "violated" when not followed. The network is just a best estimate of how one expects to do the project. A best estimate is far better than no plan at all.

Alternative Network Forms

Networks are *activity*-oriented or *event*-oriented. Descriptions of each type follow.

1. Activity-oriented networks. There are two forms of the activity-oriented network. The first, the **activity-on-arrow (AOA)**, is by far the more common. The activity, or actual passage of time, is signified by the arrow itself; nodes are merely points in time. The other form is called **activity-on-node (AON)**, in which the node or circle represents the activity. Figure 13–7 shows both forms. It is a good idea to pick one form and stick with it; in this book, AOA is the choice.

2. Event-oriented networks. Operating people think in terms of actions, which in PERT are called *activities.* Upper managers are more interested in completions, or *events.* The event-oriented network is created from an activity-oriented network. Its purpose is to give upper managers a basis for reviewing project completions.
   Figure 13–8 shows two forms of event-oriented networks. Figure 13–8A is a portion of the construction project example stated as an event-oriented network. Nodes are drawn large in order to hold event descriptions. Descriptions use present-tense verb forms in activity-oriented networks but past-tense forms in event-oriented networks. For example, "Pour basement floor" in Figure 13–7 becomes "Basement floor poured" in Figure 13–8A. At merge points (nodes where two or more activities converge), the event description can get long and cumbersome. For example, event 8 is "Rough plumbing, cooling, and heating installed."
   Networks for big projects may include tens or even hundreds of thousands

FIGURE 13–7
Activities and Computer Inputs

A. Activity-on-arrow network segment and computer inputs

B. Activity-on-node network segment

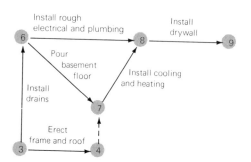

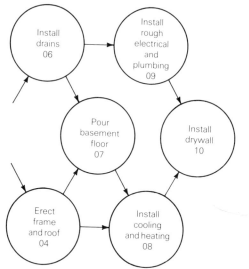

of events. Upper managers surely do not care to review the project event by event. Instead, it is common to create a summary network for upper managers. The summary network may be limited to certain key events, called **milestones.** As an example, events 4 and 10 in Figure 13–8B are shown to be a condensation of a five-event segment, events 4–7–8–9–10, from Figure 13–8A. The best way to construct a milestone chart is to make milestones out of events that signify the end of major project stages. In house construction, most people would think of completion of framing and completion of rough interior work as major stages; these are milestones 4 and 10 in Figure 13–8B.

Some sequential accuracy is lost in condensing a network. For example, milestone event 4 subsumes events 2 and 3 (from Figure 13–4). But in cutting out event 3, two "branches" of the "tree" at that point—branches 3–6 and 3–15— are unceremoniously chopped off, as shown in the following illustration. From an upper-management perspective, however, the inaccuracy is of little concern.

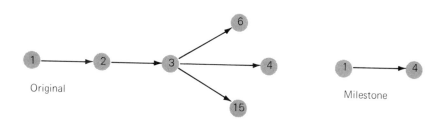

FIGURE 13–8

Events and Milestones

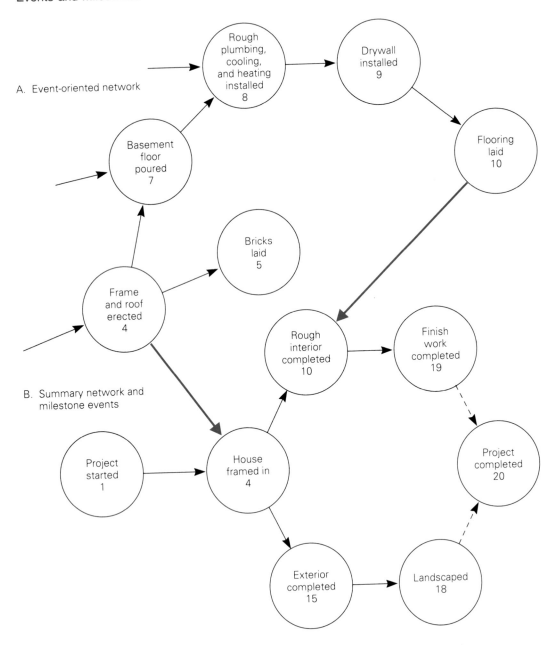

A. Event-oriented network

B. Summary network and milestone events

TIME-ESTIMATING AND PATH ANALYSIS SUBSYSTEM

The second major part of a full-scale PERT/CPM system is the time-estimating and path analysis subsystem. It begins with estimates of the time required to complete each activity in the network. The activity times are the basis of calculations of estimated times to complete any part of the project, the whole project, and amount of **slack** on any activity.

Activity Times

It is harder to accurately estimate times for projects than for repetitive and job operations because of project uncertainty and task variability. Engineered time standards are unlikely for project activities, except for those that tend to recur from project to project. Instead, the project manager obtains technical estimates from those in charge of each project activity. (A *technical estimate* is a type of historical, nonengineered time standard; see Chapter 16.)

The human tendency to pad time estimates in order to arrive at a more attainable goal is somewhat counteracted in construction projects. Typically, enough experience and historical data exist to keep estimators honest. Unfortunately, that is not the case with research and development projects.

R&D projects often include advanced, state-of-the-art activities; historical benchmark data are scarce. Because of this, PERT, the R&D-oriented half of PERT/CPM, was originally designed with a special statistically based routine. PERT project managers asked not for one activity time estimate but for three: a most-likely, an optimistic, and a pessimistic estimate. Next, the three time estimates were converted into most likely times and variances, and the probability of completing any given event by a given date could be calculated.

The apparent logic of the statistical procedure has been confounded in practice by human behavioral problems. First, for an activity never done before it is hard to pry one time estimate out of people, much less three. A request for three estimates may result in drawn-out discussion of the definitions of most likely, optimistic, and pessimistic. Second, the estimators for R&D activities often are scientists, engineers, and other professionals. They tend to be strong-willed and unafraid to withhold their cooperation. If pressed to provide three estimates, they may give meaningless ones such as 5–10–15 or 8–10–12.

For these reasons, the PERT three-time-estimating procedure has mostly fallen into disuse. Today, in both PERT and CPM, a single best estimate is the norm and *best estimate* is defined simply as how long the activity is expected to take under typical conditions and with normal resources.

Path Analysis

The most time-consuming path is the **critical path**. The path is *time*-critical because a delay in completing any of its activities delays the whole project. We continue the house construction exercise to demonstrate path analysis.

The house construction network of Figure 13–4 is reproduced in Figure 13–9, with estimates for each activity added. Path durations are given below the network. Although this network is very small—for illustrative purposes—there are still 17 paths to add up. Computers are efficient at adding path times, and path analysis subroutines are basic in PERT/CPM software.

In the figure, path 12 is critical, at 34 days; it is shown in contrasting color in the network. Several other paths—6, 7, 8, 9, 10, 11, 13, 14, and 15—are nearly critical, at 31 to 33 days. The critical-path and nearly critical-path activities deserve close managerial attention. Other activities have *slack* or *float* time and need not be managed so closely. The more slack, the more flexibility managers have in scheduling activities.

Activity Slack

Calculating slack time by comparing the critical path with noncritical paths seems fairly simple, at least in the networks discussed thus far. However, it becomes tedious—even impossible—for larger, more realistic project networks. Consequently, a three-step algorithm has been developed for finding slack time.

First, we continue with our house construction example to gain an intuitive feel for the concept of slack, especially as it pertains to paths and activities. Second, we use the three-step algorithm to formally calculate slack for activities in a network segment.

In Figure 13–9, paths 7, 11, and 14 take 33 days, or 1 day less than the critical path. This means that relative to the critical path, paths 7, 11, and 14 contain a day of slack (in PERT lingo) or float (in CPM lingo). The day of slack applies not to the whole path but just to certain path activities. Consider path 7 first.

Path 7 is identical to critical path 12 except in the segment from event 3 to event 7. The critical path segment from 3 to 4 to 7 takes four days; the slack path segment from 3 to 6 to 7 takes three days. Activities 3–6 and 6–7 are said to have one day of slack. This means that 3–6 or 6–7 (but not both) could be delayed by one day without affecting the planned project duration. By like reasoning, activity 16–18 on path 11 and activity 10–12 on path 14 have a day of slack.

Slack analysis is complicated when an activity is on more than one slack path segment. Activity 3–6, for example, is on slack path segments 3–6–7 and 3–6–8. Segment 3–6–8 takes four days as compared with eight days for critical path segment 3–4–7–8. It may seem that activities 3–6 and 6–8 have four days of slack and that either could be delayed four days without affecting the planned project duration. But we learned above that activity 3–6, on slack segment 3–6–7, may be delayed no more than one day. Slack on 3–6 is therefore one day, not four days; the larger value is rejected. Activity 6–8, however, does have four days of slack.

The formal calculation of slack time may, in three steps, now be demonstrated for the activities shown in Figure 13–10.

FIGURE 13–9
Path Analysis

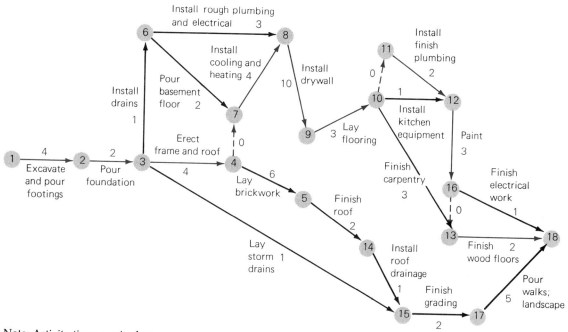

Note: Activity times are in days.

Path Number	Paths	Path Time
1	1–2–3–6–8–9–10–11–12–16–18	29 days
2	1–2–3–6–8–9–10–11–12–16–13–18	30
3	1–2–3–6–8–9–10–12–16–18	28
4	1–2–3–6–8–9–10–12–16–13–18	29
5	1–2–3–6–8–9–10–13–18	28
6	1–2–3–6–7–8–9–10–11–12–16–18	32
7	1–2–3–6–7–8–9–10–11–12–16–13–18	33
8	1–2–3–6–7–8–9–10–12–16–18	31
9	1–2–3–6–7–8–9–10–12–16–13–18	31
10	1–2–3–6–7–8–9–10–13–18	31
11	1–2–3–4–7–8–9–10–11–12–16–18	33
12	1–2–3–4–7–8–9–10–11–12–16–13–18	34 ← Critical path
13	1–2–3–4–7–8–9–10–12–16–18	32
14	1–2–3–4–7–8–9–10–12–16–13–18	33
15	1–2–3–4–7–8–9–10–13–18	32
16	1–2–3–4–5–14–15–17–18	26
17	1–2–3–15–17–18	14

Nearly critical paths (paths 6–11)

Nearly critical paths (paths 13–15)

FIGURE 13–10

Calculating Activity Slack—Summary Table

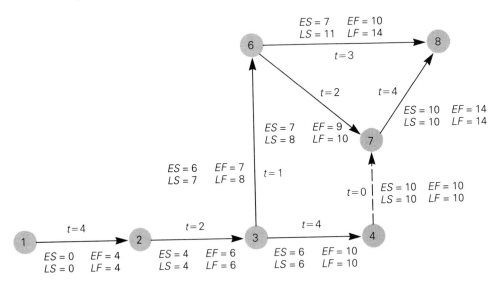

Activity	(LF − EF)	(LS − ES)	Slack	
1–2	(4 − 4)	(0 − 0)	0	Critical activity
2–3	(6 − 6)	(4 − 4)	0	Critical activity
3–4	(10 − 10)	(6 − 6)	0	Critical activity
3–6	(8 − 7)	(7 − 6)	1	
4–7	(10 − 10)	(10 − 10)	0	Critical activity
6–7	(10 − 9)	(8 − 7)	1	
6–8	(14 − 10)	(11 − 7)	4	
7–8	(14 − 14)	(10 − 10)	0	Critical activity

Critical path: 1–2–3–4–7–8
Critical path duration: 14 days

1. Earliest Start and Earliest Finish. Each activity has an **earliest start (ES)** and an **earliest finish (EF)** time, expressed in days for our project. They are deter-mined by a *forward pass* through the network. We begin with activity 1–2 and set its ES to zero, the start of the project. The EF for an activity is equal to its ES plus its duration, t. Thus, the EF for activity 1–2 is:

$$EF_{1-2} = ES_{1-2} + t_{1-2} = 0 + 4 = 4 \text{ (or day 4)}$$

The ES for each successive activity is equal to the largest EF of all predecessor activities. We see that node 2, the origin of activity 2–3, has but one predecessor: activity 1–2. Therefore, the ES for activity 2–3 is equal to the EF for activity 1–2 and has a value of 4. Continuing, we find the EF for activity 2–3 as follows:

$$EF_{2-3} = ES_{2-3} + t_{2-3} = 4 + 2 = 6$$

The remainder of the ES and EF values are shown in Figure 13–10. The largest EF (14 in this case) is taken as the project duration, which is also the duration of the critical path.

2. Latest Start and Latest Finish. Each network activity also has a **latest start (LS)** and a **latest finish (LF)** time, again expressed in days for our project. Values for LS and LF are found by a *backward* pass through the network. Beginning at node 8, we use the project duration ($EF_{7-8} = 14$) as the LF of all activities ending on node 8. Then we find the LS for each activity by subtracting its duration (t) from its LF. For example, the LS for activity 7–8 is

$$LS_{7-8} = LF_{7-8} - t_{7-8} = 14 - 4 = 10 \text{ (or day 10)}$$

and for activity 6–8,

$$LS_{6-8} = LF_{6-8} - t_{6-8} = 14 - 3 = 11$$

As we move backward through the network, each successive activity has its LF defined as the earliest LS of all activities that immediately follow. For example, the LF of activity 3–6 is 8, since 8 is the smaller of the LS values for activities 6–7 and 6–8. Figure 13–10 shows LF and LS values for the remaining activities.

3. Slack Calculation. Slack for each activity is simply $LS - ES$ or $LF - EF$. This is referred to as *total slack*. Another type of slack, free slack, is less important to our discussion and will be left for advanced studies.

Negative Slack

If LS is less than ES, negative slack results. *Negative slack* means the activity is late. Not only is this possible, it is almost the norm—at least for critical path activities. It is so rare for projects to be on time that *The Wall Street Journal* published a front-page story some years ago with headlines proclaiming that a certain large construction project was completed on time. (The project was the domed stadium in Pontiac, Michigan, which also met targeted costs!)

Suppose that in Figure 13–10 the due date had been day 11. For activity 7–8, for example, computations reveal:

$$LS_{7-8} = 11 - 4 = 7$$
$$\text{Slack}_{7-8} = LS_{7-8} - ES_{7-8} = 7 - 10 = -3 \text{ (negative slack)}$$

Each of the other critical path activities would have slack of -3 days, which means the project is three days late while still in the planning stage! Two clear options exist. First, the schedule could be relaxed—push out the due date to 14, for example—to avoid negative slack at the outset. Second—and often the case with large projects—the project could start out late with hopes of catching up.

Slack-Sort Computer Listing

Computers are needed in the path analysis stage of PERT/CPM. The most common computer output is a *slack-sort report* of all project activities. Slack sort means sorting or listing activities in order of their degree of slack. Critical path activities have the least slack and therefore appear first; near-critical activities, usually from more than one path, appear next; and so on.

Figure 13–11 illustrates this, again using the house-building example. In the figure, a line separates each group of activities having common slack times. Note that the early activities have negative slack and are most critical. Bottom-most activities are least critical; the last one, activity 3–15, has +17 days of slack, which means that it may be delayed 17 days without affecting the project due date.

The slack-sorted computer listing helps a manager more than a network does. Indeed, most managers rely on this type of listing and never need to see a network.[2]

FIGURE 13–11
Computer Listing for Path Analysis

Slack-Sorted Activity Report

Activity Number	Description	Time	Earliest Start	Latest Start	Activity Slack	
1–2	Excavate, pour footings	4	0	−3	−3	⎫
2–3	Pour foundation	2	4	1	−3	⎪
3–4	Erect frame and roof	4	6	3	−3	⎪
4–7	Dummy	0	10	7	−3	⎬ Critical
.	.	.	.	.	.	⎪ path
.	.	.	.	.	.	⎪
.	.	.	.	.	.	⎪
13–18	Lay flooring	2	32	29	−3	⎭
3–6	Install drains	1	6	4	−2	
6–7	Pour basement floor	2	7	5	−2	
10–12	Install kitchen equipment	1	27	25	−2	
16–18	Finish electrical work	1	32	30	−2	
10–13	Finish carpentry	3	27	26	−1	
.	.	.	.	.	.	
.	.	.	.	.	.	
.	.	.	.	.	.	
15–17	Finish grading	2	19	24	+5	
17–18	Pour walks and landscape	5	21	26	+5	
3–15	Lay storm drains	1	6	23	+17	

---

[2]Often the listing is event-, rather than activity-oriented; for example, instead of earliest- and latest-start activity times (*ES* and *LS*), there will be time-earliest and time-latest event times (T_E and T_L).

Network Simulation

Calculating critical paths is methodical and easily performed on a computer. Unfortunately, the method treats each path independently of all others. It fails to allow for time variation, which affects all event completion times and the total project duration. It is easy to prove by Monte Carlo simulation that the deterministic critical path time understates the likely project duration.[3] Figure 13–12 illustrates.

FIGURE 13–12
Effects of Variable Activity Times on Project Duration

A. 5-day project

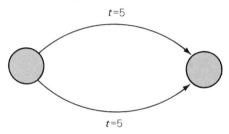

B. 5.4-day project

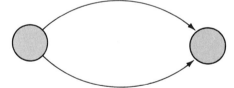

Possible Time Combinations

	Top Path	Bottom Path	Project Duration	
1	4	4	4	
2	4	5	5	
3	5	4	5	
4	5	5	5	
5	4	6	6	Mean = 49/9 = 5.4 days
6	5	6	6	
7	6	6	6	
8	6	5	6	
9	6	4	6	

[3]An explanation is given in A. R. Klingel, Jr., "Bias in PERT Project Completion Time Calculations for a Real Network," *Management Science* 13, no. 4 (December 1966), pp. B-194–201.

The figure presents the simplest possible project network: two activities occurring at the same time. (A single activity is a job; multiple activities going on simultaneously are a key distinguishing feature of a project.) In Figure 13–12A, both paths are critical at five days; thus, it is a five-day project. In Figure 13–12B, the mean or expected task time on each path is still five days. Yet, as the table shows, the simulated mean project duration is 5.4 days. In the table, the variability—four, five, and six days—is simulated by considering all time combinations and allowing equal chances for each time value on each path. For each combination the higher path time is the project duration, which pushes the expected (mean) project duration up to 5.4 days.

If more variability is added, the expected project duration increases further. For example, if the path time is 3, 4, 5, 6, or 7, each equally probable, expected duration by simulation is 5.8 days. If more paths are added, expected project duration also goes up. As a general rule, then, the fatter the network and the more variable the activity times, the more the project duration is in excess of the simple critical path time. This provides a mathematical explanation of why projects tend to be late.

Even though the critical path understates reality, it is widely used for the following reasons:

1. Path addition is cheaper to use than Monte Carlo simulation.
2. Path addition is simpler to understand than Monte Carlo simulation.
3. Activity time estimates are rough anyway, and there are diminishing returns in more rigorous analysis of rough data.
4. It is difficult to know what to do with simulated network data. How should it change project management? When does simulation end?

Despite these reasons, managers should realize that critical path analysis does understate project reality. *Caution* is the key word in its use.

PROJECT SCHEDULING SUBSYSTEM

Project scheduling is PERT/CPM's third major subsystem. After path analysis reveals the project's duration and dates are assigned to project events, it is often true that the projected completion of the final event is beyond the project's scheduled completion date. Management may elect to reduce the expected project duration by spending more on resources, literally buying some project time reduction. A time-cost trade-off analysis shows the numerous options available. This section explains the procedure for selecting from those options a time-cost pair for implementation. Project and work center schedules are also addressed.

"Crashing" and Time-Cost Trade-Off Analysis

Expected project duration may be cut by spending more on resources. The extra expenditures must be applied to critical path activities if the total project duration is to be reduced, or **crashed**. As time is cut on the critical path, new critical paths may emerge. The cost to further reduce the project duration may then involve extra resource costs to reduce activity times on multiple paths. The analysis can get complicated.

If resource costs are inconvenient to collect, the choice of which critical path activity to crash is not clear cut. Crashing an early activity on the critical path may seem wise, because the reduction will apply to other paths that could become critical later; but money spent early is gone. The opposite wait-and-see approach seems wise for another reason: Perhaps some critical path activities will be completed earlier than expected, thus averting the need to crash at all; but if that does not happen, late options for crashing may be few and costly.

When it is convenient to collect resource costs, a technique known as *time-cost trade-off analysis* may be used. The technique is explained with reference to the small network and related time and cost data as given in Figure 13–13. The critical path is B–D–E, eight days long. The cost for that eight-day project is shown to be $390. This plan need not be accepted. More money may be spent— for extra shifts, air freight, and so on— to reduce the time required to complete various tasks. For example, activity A costs $50 to do in three days (normal),

FIGURE 13–13
Network and Time-Cost Data

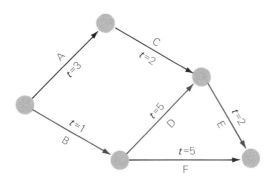

(critical path ——————► is B-D-E at 8 days)

Activity	Normal		Crash		Cost per Day
	Time	Cost	Time	Cost	
A	3	$ 50	1	$100	$25
B	1	40	1	40	—
C	2	40	1	80	40
D	5	100	3	160	30
E	2	70	1	160	90
F	5	90	2	300	70
		$390			

Source: Adapted from Fred Luthans, *Introduction to Management: A Contingency Approach* (Richard J. Schonberger, contributing author) (New York: McGraw-Hill, 1976), p. 378 (HD31.L86). Used with permission.

$75 to do in two days (paying for overtime, perhaps), and $100 to do in one day (paying still more, perhaps for extra shifts).[4] The linear assumption—$25 for each day reduced—may be somewhat erroneous, but it is generally accurate enough for planning purposes.

The method of calculating average cost per day may be expressed as a formula:

$$\text{Cost per day} = \frac{\text{Crash cost} - \text{Normal cost}}{\text{Normal time} - \text{Crash time}} \qquad (13\text{--}1)$$

For activity A, the calculation is

$$\frac{\$100 - \$50}{3 \text{ days} - 1 \text{ day}} = \frac{\$50}{2 \text{ days}} = \$25 \text{ per day}$$

Cost per day for each of the other activities is calculated the same way. Activity B cannot be crashed and thus does not have a cost-per-day entry.

The question is: If it costs $390 to do the project in eight days, what would it cost to do it in seven? If you pick the lowest total in the cost-per-day column, $25 for A, you are wrong. Spending $25 more on A would reduce A from three to two days, but it would not affect the eight-day projection duration. A critical path activity—B, D, or E—must be selected. B is out because its crash time is no better than normal time. The choice between D and E favors D—at an extra cost of $30, as opposed to $90 for E. Thus, doing the project in seven days requires $30 more for a total cost of $420.

The next step is to investigate doing the project in six days. But the above reduction of D to four days results in two critical paths, B–D–E and A–C–E, both seven days long. Reducing the project duration to six days is possible by crashing A and D together at a cost of $55, D and C together at $70, or E alone at $90. The first option is cheapest; thus, it is selected, bringing the total project cost up to $475.

Next, try for five days. After the above step, all paths are critical at six days. The only choice (since B and D are already crashed to their minimum times) is to crash E and F by one day. The added cost is $160, with a total project cost of $635. No further time reductions are possible, since the B–D–E path is fully crashed.

If this were a construction project with a penalty of $100 for every day beyond a six-day project duration, alternative 3 below would look best since it has the lowest total cost, $475.

Alternative	Time	Construction Cost	Penalty Cost	Total Cost	
1	8 days	$390	$200	$590	
2	7	420	100	520	
3	6	475	0	475	← Minimum
4	5	635	0	635	

---

[4]The normal and crash costs are often engineers' or managers' estimates based on current known direct labor and overhead rates; a careful cost accounting estimate may not be necessary. Also, the cost estimates may be incremental rather than full costs.

Time-cost trade-off analysis originated with the CPM people in the construction industry. It remains more suited for use in construction projects than in R&D efforts for at least two reasons. First, costs and times are easier to estimate in construction. Second, the frequent use of late penalties in construction projects serves as extra incentive for managers in construction to consider time-cost trade-off analysis.

In less-certain project environments—R&D, information systems, disaster relief, and so on—the need to crash projects is just as great as in construction. While the time-cost trade-off procedure is generally not appropriate (the cost-uncertainty problem), there now are several excellent approaches for crashing; discussion of them is reserved for the final section in the chapter.

Event Scheduling

Event scheduling—the assigning of dates to events in the final network—follows selection of a time-cost alternative. Final activity times, with holidays and weekends considered, form the basis for event dates. An event-dating subroutine in PERT/CPM software accepts as input the planned date of the first event and computes the others. A typical listing shows time-earliest (TE) and time-latest (TL) to complete each event and event slack ($TL - TE$).

A normal complication in project scheduling is meshing project schedules with work center schedules. Each subcontractor, department, or work center involved in a given project is likely to be in on other projects, jobs, and repetitive operations. Fitting work center activities into project networks *and* fitting project activities into work center schedules is a tricky balancing act.

Figure 13–14 illustrates this concern. The work center, a grading crew, has developed a Gantt chart showing three upcoming activities that are on the PERT/CPM networks for three different projects. The activities are identified in their respective networks (the project managers' schedules) and on the work center schedule, which is the work center manager's concern. Consider activity 9–10 in project X, finish grading of city lot 2012. Obviously the project manager would like the grading crew on the job site at the right time. If activity 9–10 is a critical path activity, any delay on the grading crew's part will affect project X's completion. Any delay will also reflect negatively on the project X manager's performance, especially if late penalties are assessed.

The work center manager, on the other hand, strives for utilization of the work center's resources. After the grading of lot 2012, the work center manager might wish to proceed immediately to lot 8099 to avoid any work center idle time. The manager of project Y would probably have to veto the idea, however, if the predecessor activity for activity 16–17 (lot 8099 grading) has not been completed. Suppose the predecessor activity, shown as 13–16 in the project Y network, is removing a dead tree. Even the work center manager would agree with the project manager's logic: Grading simply cannot begin. Is the grading crew to remain idle for several work days?

Another common problem is when project schedules create demand for work crews to be in two places (perhaps on two projects, each with a different man-

FIGURE 13–14
Decomposition of Network Activities into Work Center Schedules

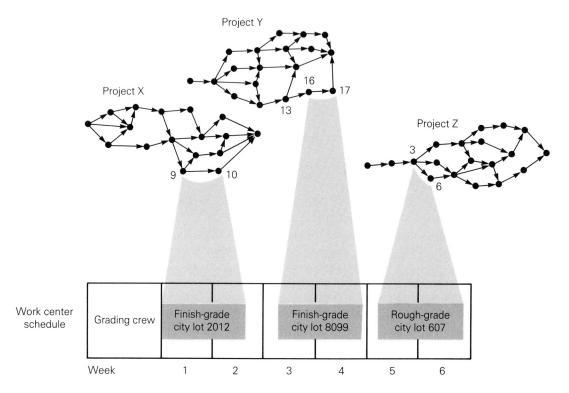

ager) at the same time. Suppose the manager of project Z decides to advance the schedule for activity 3–6, grading of city lot 607 by one week (five workdays). Obviously this will create a problem on the work center schedule during the fourth week. These kinds of conflicts are common and require compromise.

REPORTING AND UPDATING SUBSYSTEM

Reporting and updating is the fourth and final subsystem. It extends PERT/CPM management beyond planning and scheduling and into the project control phase. PERT/CPM control revolves around periodic reports, which generally are issued every two weeks or monthly.

Reporting

Figure 13–15 shows a typical reporting scheme. The partial network at the top of the figure divides into monthly reporting periods. At the end of each reporting

FIGURE 13–15

PERT/CPM Periodic Reporting

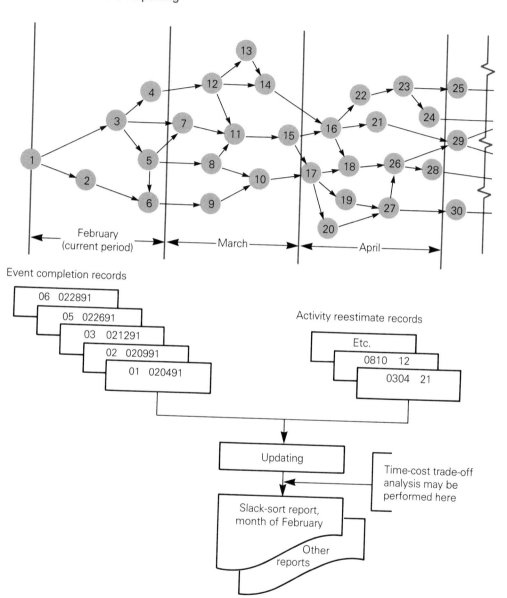

period, event completion data go to the project management office, where they are prepared for entry into the computer. In Figure 13–15, the current month is February and February-planned events 1, 2, 3, 5, and 6 have been completed. A data-entry record is prepared for each; on the first record, for example, an 01 is placed in the event field and the completion date—020491, for February 4, 1991—is entered in another field.

Event 4 was scheduled for February, but no notice of completion has been received. Instead, the project manager has received an activity reestimate notice. The first reestimate record shows the activity 03–04 (without the hyphen) in the key field, and places 21 (days), the new time estimate, in another field. The reestimate pertains to why event 4 has not been completed: Event 3, completed on February 12, plus 21 days for activity 3–4, pushes the planned completion date for event 4 into March. Future activities may also be reestimated, as 08–10 has been in Figure 13–15.

Updating

With event completions and activity reestimates as inputs, the computer updates the PERT/CPM network. A new slack-sort report is produced, showing the new slack status of each activity. The report is like Figure 13–11, except that it gives start and due dates for events. The report tells all parties about the new project schedule for all events. Other reports may be printed—for example, a report listing activities by work center (or department or subcontractor); various resource, budget, and cost reports; and summary (milestone) reports for upper managers. Some of the reports get wide distribution, and in some firms those responsible for activities completed late must explain why.

Replanning is inherent to control. It is possible to rerun a time-cost trade-off analysis each month after the network has been updated, using event completion data and activity reestimates. Without this analysis, the computer will replan (reschedule) all events anyway, but without considering using more or less resources on given activities.

Another major type of replanning is altering the network. Activities may be added or subtracted, and sequence may be changed. All that is required is adding, removing, or changing a few records. The ease of making such changes is a key asset of PERT/CPM, because project uncertainty demands planning flexibility.

PERT/CPM ENVIRONMENT

PERT/CPM is expensive. Fully computerized PERT/CPM may eat up an additional 2 or 3 percent of total project cost, because it is not a replacement for conventional management. Conventional forecasting, scheduling, inventory control, quality control, budgeting, and so forth are still done in each functional area (e.g., department or work center). A project management group and PERT/CPM systems hardware and software are additional costs.

Some organizations have tried out and abandoned PERT/CPM, because it seemed not to pay for itself. In some such cases, the problem is in trying to apply fully computerized PERT/CPM to small-scale projects. Figure 13–16 reemphasizes a point partially made early in the chapter: PERT/CPM consists of distinct and separable subsystems. The figure further suggests that only projects

FIGURE 13–16

Matching PERT/CPM Subsystems to Project Scope

CONTINUUM OF PROJECT CHARACTERISTICS

Small ←————————— Size ————————→ Large
Low ←—————— Uncertainty —————→ High
Low ←——————— Urgency ————————→ High
Low ←——————— Complexity ————————→ High

PERT/CPM
subsystems

1. Plan project and design network	Yes	Yes	Yes	Yes
2. Time estimation and path analysis	No	Yes	Yes	Yes
3. Network scheduling	No	No	Yes	Yes
4. Reporting and updating	No	No	No	Yes

that are grand in scope warrant the full PERT/CPM treatment. At the other extreme, projects of modest scope may justify the expense of only the first subsystem.

Project scope is expressed in Figure 13–16 in terms of four characteristics: size, uncertainty, urgency, and complexity. Size and urgency are self-explanatory. Project uncertainty is of two types:

1. Task uncertainty—doubts about what is to be done.
2. Time uncertainty—doubts about activity time estimates.

Similarly, complexity may be thought of in two ways:

1. Organizational complexity—many organizations involved in the project.
2. Activity complexity—many activities in progress at the same time.

To illustrate, consider the kinds of construction projects managed by a typical (for the United States) Army Corps of Engineers district: dams, manmade lakes, dredging, channel straightening, levees, bridges, and riverbank stabilization, to name a few. The district may have perhaps 100 projects in progress at a given time.

A project such as a major dam may be only moderately urgent and uncertain, but it is likely to be very large and complex. In sum, the project characteristics seem to be far enough to the right in Figure 13–16 to warrant full, computer-based PERT/CPM, including all four subsystems (four "yeses" in the figure). Without computer-based scheduling, reporting, and control, coordinating the many simultaneous activities of the numerous participating organizations might be chaotic.

Most bridge construction jobs are much smaller and less complex. For such intermediate-scope projects, the project engineer probably should design networks, conduct path analysis, and perhaps use a computer to schedule project events, which may include time-cost trade-off analysis (two or three "yeses"). But subsystem 4, reporting and updating, may not be warranted. It is the costliest subsystem to administer—it probably costs a lot more than subsystems 1, 2, and 3 combined. A typical bridge is not so urgent as to require the tight time controls of subsystem 4.

Channeling and riverbank stabilization projects are still less urgent and rarely are large, complex, or uncertain. The project engineer may expend a small amount of time, effort, and cost to accomplish subsystem 1, designing PERT/CPM networks (one "yes," left column of the figure). The benefits—seeing who has to do what and in what order—are large for the modest cost. There seems little reason to perform path analysis and the other subsystems.

In R&D projects, the model seems equally valid. Designing a major aircraft, such as a B-1 bomber, is a project of massive scope—and urgency as well, in view of the capital it ties up. Full PERT/CPM is easily justified. Redesign of a horizontal stabilizer for an existing aircraft, on the other hand, is a modest project; subsystem 1 may be sufficient.

While the logic of this situational approach to the use of PERT/CPM is clear, many managers have not followed it. Attempts to view PERT/CPM as a single indivisible system for use in every project result in disappointment. In such instances, the source of failure is *not* the PERT/CPM technique.

COMPRESSING LEAD TIME IN LARGE-SCALE OPERATIONS

PERT/CPM is aimed at keeping large-scale operations on time. Emphasis is on planning and, sometimes, control, in order to meet scheduled due dates. But what about *compressing* the schedules, that is, shortening the lead time? Companies have always desired to cut lead times on large endeavors, because the working capital tied up can become enormous. In contrast to the tight controls on meeting schedules offered by full-scale PERT/CPM, however, there were, until recently, few techniques and concepts that could be counted on to compress lead times.

Now there is a better array of tools for speeding up large-scale operations. Some are discussed in Chapter 3 on product planning. One of the potent approaches from that chapter is getting R&D people close to their customers and suppliers. The guidelines for effective design can also help; for example, use of standard parts or designs with quality already known reduces the need for new design and design changes (engineering rework).

In construction, design projects, and large-scale production, the **concurrency** concept helps slash lead times: Do some of the later design, construction, or production at the same time and in coordination with the early elements.

Still another concept that applies broadly is organization of cells or teams. The programmer team concept became popular in the 1970s. The fabrication cell—unlike machines grouped to produce a family of components or modules—became important in shipbuilding and aerospace projects in the 1980s.

The extended design and development team, or **design-build team**, also became important in the 1980s. The idea is to fuse product designers with process designers—and, ideally, representatives from purchasing, marketing, quality, finance, operations, the supplier, and the customer. Motorola and NCR have put together such groups and called them *bandit* teams—capable of quick, accurate entry into a market in the expectation of "swiping" the big payoff before competitors have a chance.

In heavy industry, the term **simultaneous engineering** is often used: Get the design engineers in league with the manufacturing engineers and perhaps the engineers of suppliers and key customers in order to ensure close coordination and early problem resolution among the parties involved. The traditional approach, in contrast, was the slow process of passing designs and specs back and forth among departments and out to suppliers and customers, with many tedious error-correction loops and overall bad project performance.

The results of the new approach are gratifying. Design-to-customer cycles typically are reduced by months or even years, costs are less, quality is vastly improved, and customers are more likely to find that the product or service meets their needs.

Quick design is an important competitive factor because, as many observers have noted, product life cycles continue to be shortened. If a company still takes 3, 5, or 10 years to get a new product to market, it is likely to find the market already sopped up by a fleet-footed competitor.

PRINCIPLE: Cut throughput time.

SUMMARY

The program evaluation and review technique (PERT) and the critical path method (CPM) are useful in the management of projects. Both are based on a sequence chart called a *network*.

PERT/CPM consists of four subsystems: designing the network, path analysis, scheduling, and reporting and updating. Designing the network begins with planning project goals; the project plan may be displayed as a work breakdown structure. Task lists are then created and arranged into networks. Networks are activity-oriented for lower managers and event-oriented for high-level managers.

Time estimates may be collected for each network activity. Activity times for each path through the network may be added up, and the sum for the most time-consuming path—called the *critical path*—is the estimated project duration. Path analysis also includes determining slack for each activity. *Slack* is the amount of time that an activity may be delayed without making the whole project late. Negative slack occurs often, especially on the critical path.

The project scheduling subsystem is aimed at determining due dates for each network event. If forward scheduling yields a late project completion time, certain activities may be "crashed." Crashing (cutting activity time) is done by spending more for resources, for example, overtime. Time-cost trade-off analysis yields combinations of project times and costs. One time-cost alternative is selected, and the selected times are the basis for scheduling network events. Finally, organizations having a role in more than one project must fit in the scheduled project tasks so that their capacities will be properly utilized.

The reporting and updating subsystem may come into play after the work begins. Reports are usually monthly or every two weeks. A basic report displays slack time for each activity; it lists most critical activities first, then next most critical activities, and so forth. The reports are valuable for replanning and rescheduling.

Each of the four PERT/CPM subsystems is more costly than its predecessor. All four should be used only if project size, uncertainty, urgency, and complexity are sufficient to justify the cost.

In the 1980s, many companies adopted some version of the extended-design team, which goes by names such as *design-build team, bandit team,* and *simultaneous engineering.* The goals are for all departments, as well as suppliers and customers, to work concurrently to compress project lead time, cut costs, and improve the product in the eyes of the customer.

KEY WORDS

Project	Event	Earliest start (*ES*)
Critical path method	Dummy activity	Earliest finish (*EF*)
(CPM)	Activity-on-arrow	Latest start (*LS*)
Program evaluation	(AOA) network	Latest finish (*LF*)
and review	Activity-on-node	Crash (crashing)
technique (PERT)	(AON) network	Concurrency
Work breakdown	Milestone	Design-build team
structure	Slack (slack time)	Simultaneous
Activity	Critical path	engineering

SOLVED PROBLEMS

1. If there is negative slack of 3 days on the upper path for the network shown:
    a. Will the project be completed on time?
    b. What is the slack on the lower path?
    c. Is there any need for "crashing"? Explain.

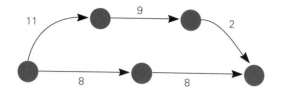

Solution

While the problem may be solved with the aid of *ES/EF/LS/LF* calculations, there is no need to do so for this uncomplicated network (it is uncomplicated in that the upper and lower paths each lead straight from first to last event with no interconnections). Further, avoiding the mechanical *ES/LS/EF/LF* tables forces us to *think* about what the critical path, the project schedule, and slack really mean.

a. Simple addition yields total duration on the two paths:

$$\text{Upper path: } 11 + 9 + 2 = 22 \text{ days}$$
$$\text{Lower path: } 8 + 8 = 16 \text{ days}$$

Since the lower path is less time-consuming, the upper is the critical path. And when there is negative slack on the critical path, that means the project is late—in this case, by 3 days.

b. Since slack on the upper path is -3 and its duration is 22 days, that means that the project's scheduled completion is in 19 days. Since the lower path takes 16 days, and there are 19 days available in the schedule, slack on the lower path is $+3$ days.

c. The top path is late by 3 days and thus must be crashed by 3 days; the bottom path takes 3 days less than the schedule calls for and thus does not need crashing.

2. Figure 13–17 shows a project network with activity times given in weeks.
   a. What are the paths in the network? What is the critical path? Its duration?
   b. Compute the *ES, EF, LS,* and *LF* times and the slack for each activity.
   c. Use the data in the time-cost information table to select appropriate time-cost alternatives for reducing the project duration by:
   (1) One week.
   (2) Two weeks.
   (3) Three weeks.

Solution

a. In this simple network, it is easy to identify all paths. (In more realistic networks, the task becomes impossible to accomplish without a computer.) Paths in this example network are:

1–2–5–6–9	20 weeks' duration	
1–2–6–9	21 weeks' duration	
1–3–7–9	20 weeks' duration	
1–4–7–9	24 weeks' duration	(critical path)
1–4–8–9	23 weeks' duration	

FIGURE 13–17
Example Project Network with Activity Times

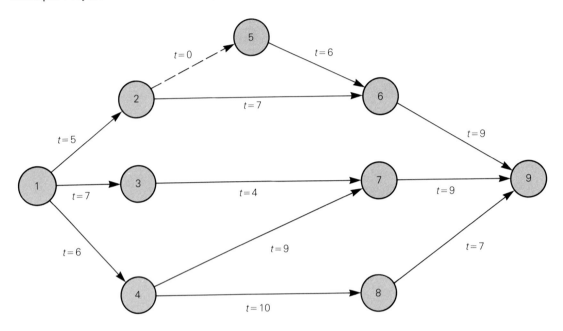

b. The following table contains the information requested in question *b:*

Activity	Duration (weeks)	ES	EF	LS	LF	Slack
1–2	5	0	5	3	8	3
1–3	7	0	7	4	11	4
1–4	6	0	6	0	6	0*
2–5	0	5	5	9	9	4
2–6	7	5	12	8	15	3
3–7	4	7	11	11	15	4
4–7	9	6	15	6	15	0*
4–8	10	6	16	7	17	1
5–6	6	5	11	9	15	4
6–9	9	12	21	15	24	3
7–9	9	15	24	15	24	0*
8–9	7	16	23	17	24	1

Notes: Activity 2–5 is a dummy, required to clarify the network because there are two separate
activities between nodes 2 and 6.
Critical activities, marked with an *, are determined through slack analysis. Recall that $LF - EF =$
$LS - ES =$ Slack.
ES for activity 6–9 is the *larger* of the EF for 2–6 and the EF for 5–6. Of these values (12 and 11,
respectively), 12 governs. The ES for activity 7–9 is determined in the same manner.
LF for activity 1–2 is the *smaller* of the LS for 2–5 and the LS for 2–6. Of these values, 9 and 8, 8 is
used. The LF activity 1–4 is found by comparing the LS values for activities 4–7 and 4–8.

c. The time-cost information for the project is contained in the following table:

Activity	Normal Duration (weeks)	Normal Cost ($)	Crash Duration (weeks)	Crash Cost ($)	Crash Cost ($/week)
1–2	5	800	3	1,100	150
1–3	7	950	3	2,150	300
1–4	6	600	4	1,400	400
2–5	0	—	0	—	—
2–6	7	1,100	5	1,500	200
3–7	4	750	4	750	—
4–7	9	1,600	8	1,800	200
4–8	10	1,000	9	1,300	300
5–6	6	1,300	4	2,200	450
6–9	9	2,000	8	2,500	500
7–9	9	1,500	7	2,000	250
8–9	7	900	5	1,600	350

(1) In order to achieve a one-week project time reduction, one of the critical activities (1–4, 4–7, and 7–9) must be crashed. Of the three, activity 4–7 has the lowest weekly crash cost, $200, and is therefore our selection.

(2) The two-week reduction cannot be found by considering only the *original* critical path. After 4–7 is crashed one week, there are *two* critical paths: 1–4–7–9 and 1–4–8–9. Also, note that 4–7 may not be crashed further. Since both (new) critical paths must be reduced in order to shorten the project, we might consider crashing 7–9 and 4–8 one week each. This costs $250 + $300 = $550, which is cheaper than the $600 cost of crashing 7–9 and 8–9.

Another alternative is to crash activity 1–4, which has the admirable effect of reducing time on *both* of our critical paths. While activity 1–4's crash cost seems high at $400, in this case it is a bargain, since it beats the $550 cost of crashing 7–9 and 4–8. Thus, our choice is to crash activity 1–4.

(3) Again look at activity 1–4. It may be crashed a second week for an additional $400. That should be done to obtain the desired three-week reduction in project duration.

REFERENCES

Books

Goodman, Louis J. *Project Planning and Management.* New York: Van Nostrand Reinhold, 1988 (HD69.P75G65).

Harris, Robert B. *Precedence and Arrow Networking Techniques for Construction.* New York: John Wiley & Sons, 1978 (TH438.H37).

Kerzner, Harold, and Hans Thamhain. *Project Management for Small and Medium Size Business.* New York: Van Nostrand Reinhold, 1984 (HD69.P75K491).

Meredith, Jack R., and Samuel J. Mantel, Jr. *Project Management: A Managerial Approach.* New York: John Wiley & Sons, 1985.

Render, Barry, and R. M. Stair. *Quantitative Analysis for Management,* 3rd ed. Boston: Allyn and Bacon, 1988 (T56.R544).

Roman, Daniel D. *Managing Projects: A Systems Approach.* New York: Elsevier, 1986 (HD69.P75R65).

Wiest, Jerome D., and Ferdinand K. Levy. *A Management Guide to PERT/CPM,* 2nd ed. Englewood Cliffs, N.J.: Prentice-Hall, 1977 (TS158.2.W53).

Periodicals/Societies

Journal of Operations Management (Operations Management Association).

IIE Transactions (Institute of Industrial Engineers).

Project Management Quarterly (Project Management Institute); sometimes catalogued as a monograph series (HD69.P75p76) instead of a periodical.

REVIEW QUESTIONS

1. Why is a process-oriented work breakdown structure not recommended?

2. How is a work breakdown structure translated into a PERT/CPM network?

3. Why must there be dummy activities in networks?

4. Why is the network an incorrect way to display activities (or tasks) occurring in repetitive production?

5. Why has the three-time-estimate (for each activity) procedure proved counter-productive?

6. Why might a project manager prepare both an activity-oriented and event-oriented network for the same project?

7. What is done with time estimates in PERT/CPM?

8. What is the purpose of path analysis in PERT/CPM?

9. What is a critical path?

10. Where and under what conditions is negative slack likely to occur?

11. For what is a slack-sort report used?

12. Why is the deterministic critical path likely to understate the project duration?

13. Why is it often sufficient for a project manager to develop a network but not carry the PERT/CPM technique any further?

14. What data are needed to perform time-cost trade-off analysis, and where are the data obtained?

15. In a time-cost trade-off analysis, why is it necessary to check to see which paths are critical after every change?

16. How are PERT/CPM data translated into scheduled jobs or tasks? Why might those scheduled task dates cause conflict for those who are to do the work?
17. Given the uncertainties inherent in R&D and construction projects, how can PERT/CPM adapt?
18. Why is PERT/CPM costly to administer?
19. What is the design-build team concept, and what are its aims?

PROBLEMS AND EXERCISES

1. Develop a product-oriented work breakdown structure for a nonconstruction project of your choice. (Examples are a market research project, a political campaign, a disaster-relief project, a research and development project, and a large-scale, computer-based information system development.) You may need to speculate about the nature of your chosen project, since most of us have little actual experience in large projects. In addition to drawing the work breakdown structure, explain the nature of your project. Show part of at least three levels on your structure.

2. The R&D group of Home Products Company (HOPROCO) is developing a prototype for a new, gasoline-powered lawn mower. The project is to be managed using PERT/CPM. Project activities include all design, manufacturing, and testing for the single prototype mower. The mower engine is to be designed and made by another firm, an engine manufacturer. All other major modules are to be designed and made by HOPROCO's employees.

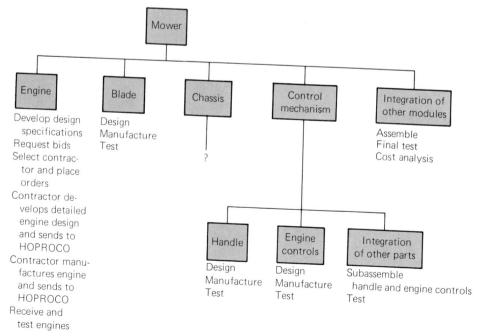

a. A partial work breakdown structure and task lists for the mower are shown above. One module, the chassis, has not been broken down into major parts and task lists. Your assignment is to do this. You must decide, as best you can, what major parts the chassis would need to include. Then decide on tasks for each major part. Note that the work breakdown structure is product-oriented, except for an integration activity whenever there is a need to combine other modules or parts.

b. Some of the beginning and ending activities for the mower project are shown as a partial PERT/CPM network. Network activities are taken from the task lists in the WBS. Complete the network. (Note: Engine-design data are needed before certain HOPROCO tasks can begin. You must determine where this is the case and draw the network that way.)

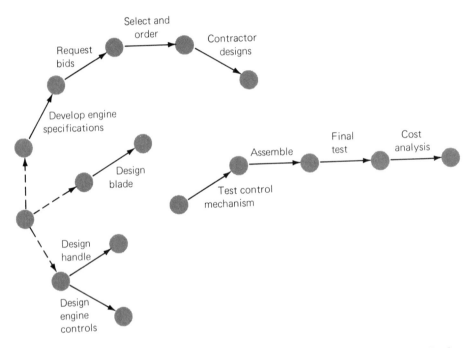

c. Some of the dummy activities in your network are not needed. Redraw portions of the network to show elimination of all unnecessary dummy activities.

3. Explain the purpose of activity 16–13 in Figure 13–4.

4. You and several others have been appointed as a planning committee by the president of your social organization. Your committee has decided that in order to obtain additional funds for operating expenses, you will produce a play or a variety show. You have been asked to submit a plan for the next meeting. The plan is to include all the activities or tasks that will have to be accomplished up to the opening of the show. Publicity, tickets, printed programs, and so on, as well as staging for the production, should be part

of the plan. The committee has already decided that the scenery will be constructed in a member's garage and that the costumes will be rented.

To facilitate presentation of the plan, draw a network diagram of about 30 activities. Include brief descriptions of the activities.

5. A manufacturer of tape and record players buys turntables from outside contractors. A new contract is to be awarded for a new style of turntable. The company has developed an activity-on-node network for the turntable project. The accompanying network includes an initial contract for turntable development and a second contract (assuming that the turntable tests are OK) for production. Redraw the network in the activity-on-arrow form.

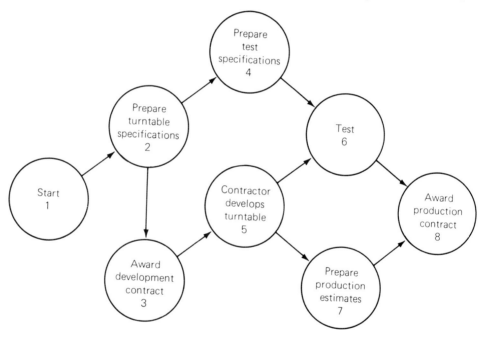

6. The manager for a project to develop a special antenna system is preparing a PERT-based project plan. Data for the plan are as follows:

Activity Number	Description	Expected Time (days)
1–2	Design frame	4
1–3	Procure mechanism	5
2–4	Procure parts	1
3–4	Dummy	0
3–7	Determine repair requirements	4
4–6	Assemble	2
4–7	Hire maintenance crew	3
6–7	Test	1

  a. Draw the network.
  b. Compute and indicate the critical path.
  c. Compute slack times for all activities assuming that the project is scheduled for completion in the number of days on the critical path.
  d. Five working days have passed, and status data have been received, as follows:
    (1) Activity 1–2 was completed in five days.
    (2) Activity 1–3 was completed in four days.
    (3) Activity 4–6 has been reestimated at four days.
    Based on the data, recompute the critical path and slack on all of the remaining project activities. (Assume no change in scheduled project completion dates.)

7. Aeropa, Inc., has a contract to develop a guided missile. A PERT/CPM network and activity times are given in the following illustration. Times are in weeks.

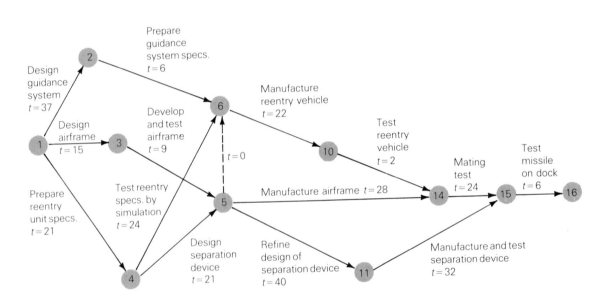

  a. Compute ES, LS, EF, LF, and slack for each activity. Assume that slack = 0 on the critical path. Identify the critical path activities and the critical path duration.
  b. Draw a condensed event-oriented network with only five milestone events. The five events should be designated: 1. Start. 5. Shell specs completed. 6. Guidance specs completed. 14. Modules completed. 16. Missile tested.
       Put activity times on the arrows between your events. Compute ES, LS, EF, LF, and slack for each activity. Verify that the critical path duration is the same as in question a. What activity time goes on arrow 1–6? Explain the difficulty in deciding on a time for this activity.
  c. Assume the following project status at the end of week 50:

Activity	Actual Duration
1–2	39
1–3	17
1–4	20
2–6	7
3–5	9
4–5	28
4–6	20

No other activities have been completed.

Develop a slack-sorted activity report similar to Figure 13–11 for the project as of the end of week 50. What is the new projected project duration?

8. Figure 13–12 shows a simulation of a simple network with equally possible activity times of 4, 5, or 6. In discussing the figure, it was stated that expected project duration increases to 5.8 for the five equally probable activity times—3, 4, 5, 6, and 7. Verify the figure 5.8.

9. A network consists of two activities that occur at the same time. Each is expected to take one, two, or three weeks to complete, and the probabilities of each possible time are 1/3, 1/3, and 1/3. What is the expected project duration based on the critical path? What is it based on PERT simulation?

10. A network consists of two activities that occur at the same time. Each is expected to take one or two months to complete, and the probabilities of each possible time are 1/2 and 1/2.

   a. What is the expected project duration based on the critical path? What is it based on PERT simulation?

   b. What would the expected project duration be using PERT simulation if the network had three instead of two activities, each with equally probable activity times of one or two months?

11. The following data have been collected for a certain project:

Activity		Normal		Crash	
Predecessor Event	Successor Event	Time (days)	Cost ($)	Time (days)	Cost ($)
1	2	6	250	5	360
2	3	2	300	1	480
2	4	1	100	1	100
2	5	7	270	6	470
3	4	2	120	1	200
4	5	5	200	1	440

   a. Draw the network.

   b. Compute and indicate the critical path and the normal project cost.

   c. Compute slack time for each activity in the network, using 12 days as
   the project due date.
   d. Perform time-cost trade-off analysis, crashing down to the minimum
   possible project duration. Display each time-cost alternative.

12. Normal and crash data for the accompanying network are given below.
   Compute all time-cost options. Which is best if there is a $40-per-day penalty
   for every day beyond a seven-day project duration?[5]

	Normal		Crash	
Activity	Days	Cost	Days	Cost
A	3	$ 50	2	$ 100
B	6	140	4	260
C	2	25	1	50
D	5	100	3	180
E	2	80	2	80
F	7	115	5	175
G	4	100	2	240
		$610		$1,085

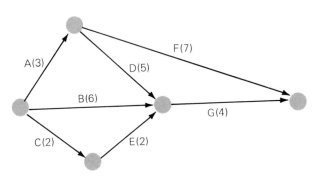

13. a. For the accompanying network, what is the critical path and expected
   project duration? What is the second most critical path and its duration?

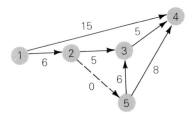

   b. What can the largest time value for activity 3–4 be to ensure that it is not
   a critical path activity? (Ignore the present time of five days for that activity
   in answering the question.)

[5]Adapted from J. S. Sayer, J. E. Kelly, Jr., and M. R. Walker, "Critical Path Scheduling," *Factory*,
July 1960.

14. *a.* For the accompanying network, if there is a positive slack of $+6$ on the upper path, what is the slack on the lower path?

   b. If the slack is -4 on the upper path, what is the slack on the lower path?

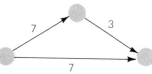

15. *a.* For the accompanying network, if there is slack of $+5$ on the lower path, what is the slack on the upper path?

   b. If there is slack of $+1$ on the upper path, what is the slack on the lower path?

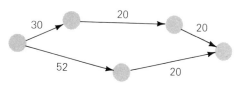

16.

Activity	Normal		Crash	
	Time	Cost	Time	Cost
1–2	2	$10	1	$15
2–3	6	8	5	18
2–4	2	15	1	21
2–5	8	30	6	52
4–3	2	7	2	7
3–5	3	21	1	33
1–5	8	20	5	41

   a. For the accompanying time-and-cost table, what is the least costly way to reduce the project time by one day? (You may wish to draw the network for better visualization of the problem.)

   b. What is the least costly way to reduce the expected project duration (i.e., "crash" the project) by three days?

17.

Activity	Normal		Crash	
	Time	Cost	Time	Cost
1–2	6	$100	5	$205
1–4	17	200	12	600
2–3	5	100	4	190
3–4	5	150	3	360
5–3	6	80	5	185
5–4	8	300	7	360

   a. For the accompanying network and time-and-cost table, what is the least costly way to reduce ("crash") the project by one day?

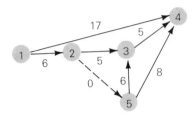

b. What is the fastest the project could be done if you used crash times?

18. A number of project types are listed below, ranging from small and simple to grand. As indicated in Figure 13–16, modest projects warrant only the first PERT/CPM subsystem, whereas grand projects justify all four subsystems; in-between projects warrant subsystems 1 and 2 or subsystems 1, 2 and 3. Decide which subsystems should apply for each project listed. Explain each.

Computer selection and installation for company of 200 employees.

Moving the computer facility for a large bank to a new building in a major city.

Moving the computer facility (same size as the bank's) to a new building at a major university.

Community project to attract new industry in three large, abandoned factory buildings (town of 10,000 people).

Five-year overhaul of a nuclear submarine.

Implementing MRP in a manufacturing company of 1,000 employees.

New-product development and testing (including market research) for a major food company.

Moving an army division from one closed-down post to a new one in another state.

Planning a national sports championship event.

Building a 500-room hotel in Lincoln, Nebraska.

Building a 500-room hotel in Manhattan.

19. The accompanying network segments are all part of the same home construction project. Where is a dummy activity needed, and why?

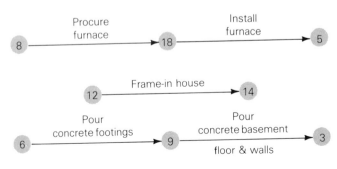

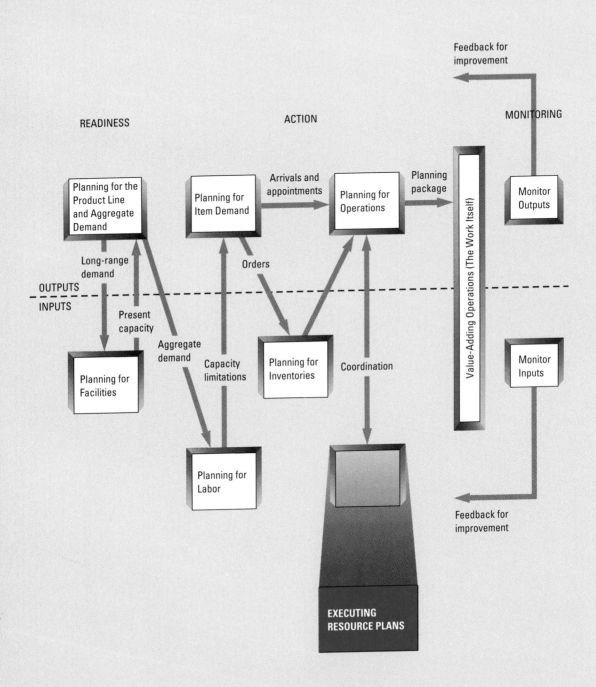

READINESS

ACTION

MONITORING

Feedback for improvement

Planning for the Product Line and Aggregate Demand

Planning for Item Demand

Arrivals and appointments

Planning for Operations

Planning package

Monitor Outputs

Long-range demand

OUTPUTS

INPUTS

Orders

Value-Adding Operations (The Work Itself)

Present capacity

Planning for Facilities

Aggregate demand

Capacity limitations

Planning for Inventories

Coordination

Monitor Inputs

Planning for Labor

EXECUTING RESOURCE PLANS

Feedback for improvement

CHAPTER 14

Managing Assignment and Waiting-Line Operations

A common dilemma, in nearly any line of work, is trying to provide high levels of service and yet stay lean on resources. Assign too few resources, and customers or jobs will sometimes have to wait; that is, *queues* will form. Adding resources will solve that problem but creates another: resource idleness.

In factories, lack of enough resources results in queues of parts or jobs stacked up before machines and causes delays in forwarding the work to the next process and, ultimately, the final customer; sometimes the queues melt, leaving idleness at the next process. The problem is usually worse when the work itself is a human customer, possibly an angry one waiting in a long queue. Further, human customers tend to arrive for service in random, highly uneven patterns, which makes it more difficult to assign the right amount of resources to the service center.

While one way to treat the problem is to even out the work flow, in this chapter we look at the opposite kind of treatment: assigning resources to meet customer demand. Waiting-line models and simulation, two aids for resource assignment, receive particular attention. The techniques are most usable when arrivals are random and uneven, as with human clients and certain kinds of nonhuman phenomena, such as machine breakdowns.

RESOURCE ASSIGNMENT ISSUES

Earlier chapters (especially Chapters 5 and 6) treated capacity planning and resource scheduling under an assumption of adequate "get ready" time—that is, enough time to develop a plan for resources *after* demand becomes known. This chapter considers the special issues for the many cases in which the demand is unknown until very late in the planning cycle.

Consider the demand pattern shown in Figure 14–1. It is labeled a "roller-coaster workload," a pattern typical in copying centers, tax advice offices, high-way toll facilities, college registrars' offices, concert ticket takers, hotel desks, hospital delivery rooms, and any kind of repair center. The top part of the figure graphically illustrates how customer or job arrivals might follow a roller-coaster pattern from month to month or week to week. Close examination of each time period, perhaps even a day, as is shown, reveals a compressed roller-coaster pattern. We might expect an even more compressed "thrill ride" if we were to look at single hours during a given day.

The peaks and valleys on the roller coaster's path cannot be known and fully planned for in advance. Draw a horizontal line across the graph to represent the resources assigned, and the result will be waiting lines where the vertical bar (workload) is above the line and resource idleness where the bar falls short of the line.

Waiting-line conditions must be managed to some extent; but first those doing the managing need to have some understanding of basic characteristics of waiting lines, which we take up next.

FIGURE 14–1

Roller-Coaster Workloads

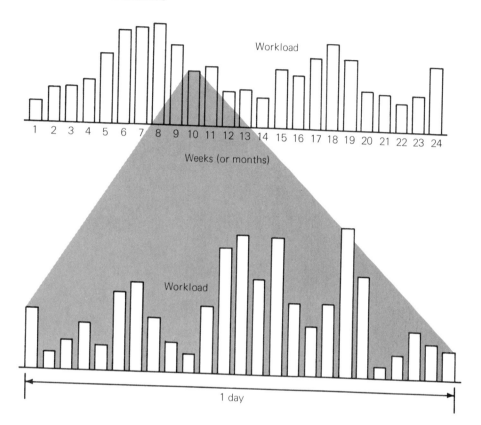

Channels and Stages

A waiting line may be simple, involving only one *server* (or *channel*) and one *stage* of service. A single stoplight on the main highway through a very small village acts as such a server (serving to regulate traffic flow). If the village were to grow and install more stoplights on the highway, autos would pass through what is called a *multistage* waiting line, where each light is a stage. Autos also sometimes get into what is known as a *multichannel* (or *multiserver*) waiting-line situation. An example is a toll station with several lanes from which the driver may choose. The lanes are channels, each offering the same service (taking tolls). People applying for various kinds of licenses may pass through a multichannel, multistage waiting line: The applicant enters one of the application lines, gets processed, and then joins one of the payment lines.

Figure 14–2 shows sketches of these four types of service facilities and waiting-line patterns: single-channel, single-stage; single-channel, multistage; multi-channel, single-stage; and multichannel, multistage. Distinguishing among the

FIGURE 14–2
Service Facilities and Waiting-Line Patterns

A. Single channel, single stage

B. Single channel, multistage

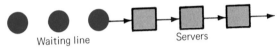

C. Multichannel, single stage

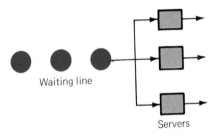

D. Multichannel, multistage

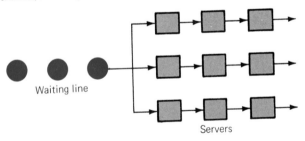

four types is necessary in **queuing analysis**, because there are mathematical formulas for each one. The first step is to find which type applies so as to select the right formula. The four types are not so important in **simulation** of waiting lines, which can be applied to many combinations of arrival, waiting, and service patterns.

Timing Factors

In the operation of a service facility, customers or jobs arrive, wait in line for a time (no wait, if the line is empty), receive service, and leave. Two key timing factors are the frequency distribution of arrivals and the frequency distribution of service times.

In the simplest case, arrivals are evenly spaced and service times are constant. If the evenly spaced arrivals are more frequent than the constant serving rate, the system is unstable. The customer flow must slow down or the service must speed up; otherwise, the waiting line grows without limit (instability). If arrivals are less frequent than the service rate, the system is stable, with zero customer waiting time. The service facility will, however, be idle some of the time: Merely subtract the constant service time from the constant time between arrivals to get the idleness per cycle.

Usually arrivals are unevenly spaced and service times vary, which makes customer waiting and service facility idleness harder to determine. That is where queuing formulas or simulation methods can be helpful.

If a facility operates continuously, it gets into a **steady-state** condition, in which the *average* waiting line stays stable. On the other hand, many facilities do not run continuously. Some spend most of their operating lives in a state of startup and shutdown, perhaps never reaching steady state. Other facilities have substantial startup and shutdown periods, with steady state in between. Still others, including some production lines that begin each day with empty machines, may come up to steady-state operation rather quickly. Study of steady-state conditions can be fairly simple, as compared with study of mixtures of startup, steady-state, and shutdown conditions.

When human customers rather than production job orders are in the waiting lines, the concept of steady-state operation is more complicated. Arrival rates of customers for food service, copier service, entertainment, and so forth seem to change all the time. We may divide mealtimes into 15-minute periods and look for a different set of steady-state variables (waiting lines and service-facility idleness) for each period. But it is very costly to collect, analyze, and make and implement decisions for the larger number of cases that result from so fine a time division.

A final timing factor is human reaction to waiting lines. Some customers *balk* at entering a waiting line that seems too long, and some *renege* or leave a line that is moving too slowly. The server's reaction to a long line often is to speed up and to a short or empty line to slow down. Those tendencies further complicate the study of waiting lines.

Despite the difficulties, waiting lines are common and must be studied, for unless properly managed, they waste resources through either excessive waiting or idleness. We now turn our attention to mathematical queuing models and simulation.

QUEUING FORMULAS

A simple, precise way to perform a waiting-line study is to use queuing formulas, most of which require only two inputs:

1. Mean arrival rate in units arriving per time period; the Greek letter *lambda*, λ, is the symbol.

2. Mean service rate in units served per time period; the Greek letter *mu*, μ, is the symbol.

Queuing formulas have been developed for each of the four queuing patterns shown in Figure 14–2. We examine only the first—single channel, single stage. A few queuing formulas for that pattern are given in Figure 14–3.

Formulas Depending on Means Only

Equations 14–1 and 14–2 in Figure 14–3 are for computing the percentage of time the service facility is busy and idle, respectively. Percentage of time busy, known as **utilization rate**, is the mean arrival rate, λ, divided by the mean service rate, μ. When the server (service facility) is not busy, it is idle. The **idleness rate** is 1 minus the utilization rate, λ/μ. For example, if customers arrive at a mean rate of 8 per hour and the service facility can serve them at a mean rate of 10 per hour, utilization rate and idleness rate are:

$$U = \frac{\lambda}{\mu} = \frac{8}{10} = 0.8, \text{ or } 80\%$$

$$I = 1 - \frac{\lambda}{\mu} = 1 - 0.8 = 0.2, \text{ or } 20\%$$

FIGURE 14–3
Queuing Formulas for a Single-Channel, Single-Stage Service Facility

Not dependent on probability distributions
Utilization of server:

$$U = \frac{\lambda}{\mu} \tag{14–1}$$

Idleness of server

$$I = 1 - \frac{\lambda}{\mu} \tag{14–2}$$

Poisson-distributed arrival rate and service rate
Mean waiting time in queue:

$$T_q = \frac{\lambda}{\mu(\mu - \lambda)} \tag{14–3}$$

Mean time in system (in-queue + in-service):

$$T_s = \frac{1}{\mu - \lambda} \tag{14–4}$$

Mean number in queue:

$$N_q = \frac{\lambda^2}{\mu(\mu - \lambda)} \tag{14–5}$$

Mean number in system (in-queue + in-service):

$$N_s = \frac{\lambda}{\mu - \lambda} \tag{14–6}$$

Probability of n customers in system (in-queue + in-service):

$$P_n = \left(1 - \frac{\lambda}{\mu}\right) \left(\frac{\lambda}{\mu}\right)^n \tag{14–7}$$

Poisson-distributed arrival rate and constant (c) service rate
Mean waiting time in queue:

$$T_q(c) = \frac{\lambda}{2\mu(\mu - \lambda)} \tag{14–8}$$

Mean number in queue:

$$N_q(c) = \frac{\lambda^2}{2\mu(\mu - \lambda)} \tag{14–9}$$

Rate of service, μ, means rate of service *when customers are there*. It is the standard production rate. We are not concerned about whether the rate is based on an engineered or a nonengineered time standard. (See discussion of time standards and their reciprocal, standard production or output rates in Chapter 16.) But some timing method is necessary in order to find out what μ is. A simple way is to use a wristwatch to time a few customer service cycles and average the times; we divide the result, the average time per customer, into 1.0 to yield mean (average) customers per time unit, μ. For example, suppose service times for six customers are 5, 7, 5, 6, 4, and 9 minutes. The average is:

$$\frac{5 + 7 + 5 + 6 + 4 + 9}{6} = \frac{36}{6} = 6 \text{ minutes per customer}$$

Then, mean service rate is

$$\mu = \frac{1}{6.0 \text{ minute/customer}} \times \frac{60 \text{ minutes}}{1 \text{ hour}} = 10 \text{ customers per hour}$$

Rate of arrivals, λ, is simply a count of number of arrivals divided by the time over which they are counted. For example, suppose a 3-hour study is taken of customer arrivals and 24 customers are counted. The mean rate of arrivals is:

$$\lambda = \frac{24 \text{ customers}}{3 \text{ hours}} = 8 \text{ customers per hour}$$

Utilization and idleness rates are based only on the means, λ and μ. The pattern of variability distribution around the means makes no difference. The formulas apply for any (or no) variability pattern or distribution. Not so for the formulas discussed next.

Formulas Using Poisson-Distributed Arrival and Service Rates

The second group of queuing formulas in Figure 14–3 is also solved using only λ and μ. But the results are true only if variability about the means forms a particular probability distribution: the Poisson distribution.[1]

Equation 14–3 shows how to calculate mean queue time, T_q. Equation 14–4 is for mean time in the system, T_s, which includes both queue time and service

[1]It is usually stated that arrival-*rate* distribution must be Poisson and that service-*time* distribution must be exponential. However, an exponential probability distribution of service times (times to serve customers) transforms into a Poisson probability distribution of service rates (number of customers served per time period—when the facility is busy). Since the queuing formulas use mean rates rather than mean times, the exponential distribution of times need not be discussed here.

time. If customers arrive at a mean rate of 8 per hour and can be served at a mean rate of 10 per hour,

$$T_q = \frac{\lambda}{\mu(\mu - \lambda)} = \frac{8}{10(10 - 8)} = \frac{8}{(10)(2)} = \frac{8}{20}$$

$= 0.4$ hours, or 24 minutes of waiting time per customer

$$T_s = \frac{1}{\mu - \lambda} = \frac{1}{(10 - 8)} = \frac{1}{2}$$

$= 0.5$ hours, or 30 minutes in the system per customer

Equations 14–5 and 14–6 are for calculating mean number in the queue, N_q, and mean number in the system, N_s. Again for $\lambda = 8$ and $\mu = 10$,

$$N_q = \frac{\lambda^2}{\mu(\mu - \lambda)} = \frac{8^2}{(10)(10 - 8)} = \frac{64}{20}$$

$= 3.2$ customers waiting

$$N_s = \frac{\lambda}{\mu - \lambda} = \frac{8}{10 - 8}$$

$= 4$ customers in system

Equation 14–7 is for calculating the probability, P_n, of any given number, n, of customers in the system. For example, the probability of four customers in the system of $\lambda = 8$, $\mu = 10$ is:

$$P_n = \left(1 - \frac{\lambda}{\mu}\right)\left(\frac{\lambda}{\mu}\right)^n$$

$$P_4 = \left(1 - \frac{8}{10}\right)\left(\frac{8}{10}\right)^4 = (1 - 0.8)(0.8)^4$$

$= 0.082$, or 8.2%

We know from the earlier calculation of N_s that 4 is the mean number of customers in the system but the probability that there will be exactly 4 customers is only 0.082.

Formulas Using Poisson-Distributed Arrival and Constant Service Rates

Two formulas are given in Figure 14–3 for the case of Poisson arrival rates with constant service rates. Equation 14–8 is for mean waiting time, $T_q(c)$, and Equation 14–9 is for mean number in the queue, $N_q(c)$. Constant service rates are increasingly likely as more services become mechanized in our society. For $\lambda = 8$ and $\mu = 10$,

$$T_q(c) = \frac{\lambda}{2\mu(\mu - \lambda)} = \frac{8}{(2)(10)(10 - 8)}$$

$$= 0.2 \text{ hours, or } 12 \text{ minutes per customer}$$

$$N_q(c) = \frac{\lambda^2}{2\mu(\mu - \lambda)} = \frac{8^2}{(2)(10)(10 - 8)}$$

$$= 1.6 \text{ customers waiting}$$

Imposing a constant service rate makes a big difference. T_q and N_q for Poisson arrival and service rates were calculated earlier as 24 minutes' waiting time and 3.2 customers waiting. Those figures are twice as large as $T_q(c)$ and $N_q(c)$. A constant service time reduces waits a great deal (but does not eliminate them as long as arrivals are variable).

The simplicity and power of the queuing formulas, as well as some of their limitations, are brought out in Example 14–1.

EXAMPLE 14–1   QUEUING—PLUMBING SERVICE

At present, the plumbing breakdown crew can easily handle plumbing trouble calls. The logbook shows trouble calls coming in at an average of 1 call every 100 minutes; thus, the mean arrival rate, λ, is 1/100, or 0.01 calls per minute. The dispatcher's logbook also shows that the average plumbing repair takes 33 minutes; that is a mean service rate, μ, of 1/33, or 0.03 repairs per minute. Thus, the service rate, 0.03, is three times as fast as the arrival rate, 0.01.

That is good service, but it means the crew is busy only one-third of the time. That should be obvious, but for those who like formulas we can use Equation 14–1 to calculate "busyness" or utilization rate for the repair crew:

$$\text{Utilization rate} = \frac{\lambda}{\mu} = \frac{0.01}{0.03} = 0.33, \text{ or } 1/3$$

The plumbing repair crew is not really idle the other 67 percent of the time; it has some shop cleanup and tool upkeep work to do between trouble calls. But should well-paid journeyman plumbers be sweeping floors and honing tools? The maintenance manager does not think so. (Is he right?)

The maintenance manager wants to reduce the plumbing crew size so that things will be reversed; that is, keep the crew busy 67 percent of the time and "idle" only 33 percent of the time. His plan is to cut the crew size in half, thereby doubling service time; this halves the wage expense. The manager feels the change should hardly affect service since mean service rate will still be 50 percent faster than mean arrival rate, which may be proven by using an inversion of the utilization rate formula.

Since utilization rate, U, $= \lambda/\mu$, then $\mu = \lambda/U$. Since $\lambda = 0.01$ and desired utilization rate, U, $= 0.67$,

$$\mu = \frac{\lambda}{U} = \frac{0.01}{0.67} = 0.015$$

As the manager thought, mean service rate, μ, at 0.015 is 50 percent faster than mean arrival rate, λ, at 0.01.

Is the maintenance manager correct in believing that service will hardly be affected? Further use of queuing formulas may help to answer the question.

Solution

Service responsiveness to trouble calls may be measured by average trouble-call waiting time, which is the mean time that trouble-call orders sit on the dispatcher's desk waiting, in queue, for a plumbing crew to return from previous trouble-call work. Service also may be measured by the average number of jobs waiting in the queue.

The manager computes average (mean) time in queue, T_q, and average (mean) number in queue, N_q.

For the present size of plumbing crew, $\lambda = 0.01$ trouble calls per minute and $\mu = 0.03$ repairs per minute. Therefore, by equations 14–3 and 14–5, respectively,

$$\text{Mean time in queue} = T_q = \frac{\lambda}{\mu(\mu - \lambda)}$$

$$= \frac{0.01}{(0.03)(0.03 - 0.01)}$$

$$= 16.67 \text{ minutes per job}$$

$$\text{Mean number in queue} = N_q = \frac{\lambda^2}{\mu(\mu - \lambda)}$$

$$= \frac{(0.01)^2}{(0.03)(0.03 - 0.01)}$$

$$= 0.17 \text{ jobs}$$

The manager wants to cut crew size in half, which cuts service rate, μ, from 0.03 to 0.015. Arrival rate, λ, stays at 0.01. For this proposed level of staffing,

$$\text{Mean time in queue} = T_q = \frac{\lambda}{\mu(\mu - \lambda)}$$

$$= \frac{0.01}{(0.015)(0.015 - 0.01)}$$

$$= 133.33 \text{ minutes per job}$$

$$\text{Mean number in queue} = N_q = \frac{\lambda^2}{\mu(\mu - \lambda)}$$

$$= \frac{(0.01)^2}{(0.015)(0.015 - 0.01)}$$

$$= 1.33 \text{ jobs}$$

Now the manager may compare service levels. Cutting the crew size in half increases mean waiting time from $T_q = 16.67$ minutes per job to $T_q = 133.33$ minutes per job, which is an eightfold increase in waiting time—a large deterioration in service. At the same time, mean number of plumbing jobs waiting for a crew goes up from $N_q = 0.17$ jobs to $N_q = 1.33$ jobs, also an eightfold increase. The maintenance manager believed that cutting crew size in half would have little effect on service. The queuing analysis proves him wrong.

Perhaps the manager should perform additional analysis. The wage reduction might justify the crew cuts even though service worsens. In problems in which a cost may be placed on waiting time, the sum of wages and waiting time costs could be compared for various crew sizes. (This type of analysis is shown later in a simulation example.) Since costs of waiting for a plumbing crew are hard to estimate, the manager is probably stuck with comparing service-*time* data and wage-*cost* data.

Also, the manager must consider under-capacity scheduling to ensure that there is enough time for maintenance of plumbing equipment and necessary quality assurance activities. At the very least, training time will be needed. Thus, something less than full crew utilization is desirable.

Realities Affecting Queuing

The previous problem shows the efficiency of queuing formulas: The casual observer sees a jumble of job arrivals, queue variability, and service time variability; yet a few trivial calculations reduce it all to easy-to-comprehend responsiveness statistics. Further, it is not only the calculations that are simple. There are but two items of input data: λ and μ. Those means may be computed based on sample cases from a dispatcher's logbook.

For all this efficiency there are two major requirements or limitations in queuing formulas. First is the Poisson probability distribution requisite, which merits further discussion.

Are plumbing trouble calls and service rates sufficiently Poisson for the above solution to be valid? The trouble calls probably are. "Natural" arrival rates, such as "arrival" of breakdowns of mechanical devices, are most likely to follow the idealized Poisson distribution. Any time people get into the act, their habits and proclivities tend to distort the natural Poisson pattern: balking at entering a long queue and reneging or leaving a queue that is moving too slowly. But potential trouble spots for plumbing breakdowns are wash basins, sewer systems, water pipes, and so forth. They are mechanical entities; there is little human distortion, and so the breakdown frequencies are largely Poisson.

Plumbing service rate distributions seem more subject to distorting human influences. The natural Poisson shape, shown in Figure 14-4A, has a tail extending (skewed) to the right. But the plumbers would feel pressure not to allow the tail to go so far; that is, during a very time-consuming plumbing repair, a queue of other trouble calls may form. The dispatcher may then put pressure on the plumbers to get done and move on to the next case. Most of us are quite capable of working far faster than we normally do, at least for short spurts of time. The plumbers are likely to do just that in response to queuing pressure. The distribution is no longer perfect Poisson but is crunched from the left, as in Figure 14-4B.

Sometimes there is an opposite effect. Say that the plumbers are on a minor job and know there are no backlogged trouble calls. Their reaction might be to stretch out the job. (Stretching out work to fill the available time is a phenomenon

FIGURE 14–4
Distortions of Service Rate Distributions

A.

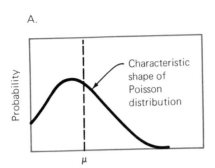

B.

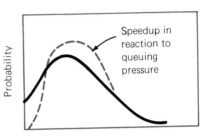

C.

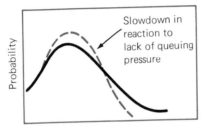

D.

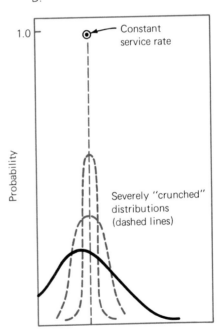

popularly—or unpopularly—known as *Parkinson's law*.) The Poisson curve becomes crunched from the right, as in Figure 14–4C.

Figure 14–4D shows the effect of crunching on both the right and the left. With the stretching out of short jobs and the compressing of long ones, the distribution narrows and grows taller. The limit occurs where distribution (variability) disappears and gives way to a constant service rate. That rate is the single circled point, with probability equal to 1.0.

When dealing with humans—customers, servers, or both—queuing formulas clearly will give inaccurate results. Even so, it can be argued that the queuing calculations can be helpful. They show the *limit* on queue length and waiting time.

For example, in a travel agent's office, if customers arrive at a mean of two per hour and the agent can handle a mean of three per hour, the mean waiting time by queuing formula is:

$$T_q = \lambda/[\mu(\mu - \lambda)] = 2/[3(3 - 2)]$$

$$= 0.67 \text{ hours, or 40 minutes}$$

Of course, some customers will wait for awhile and then renege or will not wait at all (balk). Therefore, the agent should expect that mean waiting time will be *less than* 40 minutes (probably a good deal less). If the travel agent can speed up the mean serving rate to four per hour—say, by adding a word processor—the mean waiting time computation is:

$$T_q = 2/[4(4 - 2)] = 0.25, \text{ or 15 minutes}$$

Now the agent should expect mean waiting time to be less than 15 minutes, since the calculated time of 15 minutes is an upper limit. That is much better service. While neither 40 minutes nor 15 minutes is accurate, the queuing results show a large improvement in service when the word processor is used. That may be enough to convince the agent to buy the work processor.

A second limitation of queuing formulas is that they be based on a steady-state condition. A repair system may close down at the end of the day without ever having achieved steady state. If so, it is startup and the **transient state** that are of interest. Queuing formulas do not apply to transient conditions, because λ is changing all the time. In such cases, Monte Carlo simulation, discussed next, is an alternative.

SIMULATION

Simulation means imitation. As a tool in waiting-line analysis, simulation means imitating a waiting line by use of numbers. On the other hand, queuing formulas do not imitate a waiting line; rather, they make simplifying assumptions so that summary waiting-line data can be easily solved for.

The purpose of waiting-line simulation is to enhance decision making in *real* situations. Another popular kind of simulation applies to *realistic* situations and has education as its purpose. Examples are physical simulations that help train drivers and pilots, and simulation games (e.g., management games) that provide students with realistic experience in making decisions.

Real waiting lines change all the time. Simulation captures the changes with streams of numbers that stand for customers or orders and their progress through a service facility. Computer graphics software may then convert the numbers to a service facility in action on a screen. Whether graphics capability is present or not, the simulation produces summary numbers on maximum, minimum, and average waiting-line and service usage.

One would have to watch real waiting lines for a long time in order to find out the same thing. With the aid of computers, a waiting-line simulation can represent a long time period—hundreds of simulated years if so desired—at rather small expense. The cost is low, at least, in comparison with trial and error on real waiting lines. Even if a simulation is run for a short time, say a few simulated hours or days, a computer may be needed to handle the many numbers necessary to represent the changing flows through the waiting lines and the service facility. We consider arrivals and service times next using the **Monte Carlo simulation** method—named after the famous European gambling mecca.

Monte Carlo Simulation

Monte Carlo simulation takes time and is messy compared to the mathematical simplicity of queuing formulas. But Monte Carlo simulation is versatile; it can capture repair time distributions distorted by repairpeople's proclivities, and it can deal with startup as well as steady-state conditions in a repair system.

Monte Carlo simulation follows the five-step procedure shown in Figure 14–5. The whole purpose of the simulation, testing out options for managing a service facility, is contained in the last three steps: Conducting simulations of different options (step 3), which produces output statistics (step 4), which are analyzed in order to make a decision (step 5). But those steps are often the easy part. Usually, the real work is in building the model on which to run tests.

Building the Monte Carlo Model
Building the model may require gathering representative data on customer arrivals and service times at a confusing, active work site, although in some cases records in a logbook can provide the needed input data; this is step 1 in Figure 14–5.

Step 2 is condensing the data into two probability distributions, one for arrivals and the other for service times. The method is to divide the data into several equal classification intervals, tote up the frequency (of arrivals or service times) in each interval, and express the frequencies as percentages. Center values of each interval represent the whole interval in the resulting probability distributions. We may see how this works in Example 14–2.

FIGURE 14–5
Monte Carlo Simulation Analysis Procedure

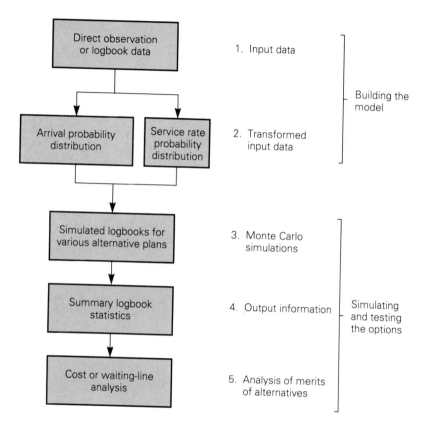

EXAMPLE 14–2   BUILDING A MONTE CARLO SIMULATION MODEL— A SHOESHINE STAND

A shoeshine stand currently has a staff of one. During the peak period, 9:30 A.M. to 11:30 A.M., customers often have to wait, but some are too impatient to do so. What if the proprietor were to add staff, use an electric buffer, smooth the flow of customer arrivals by taking appointments, or take other actions to alleviate the waiting problem? Monte Carlo simulation offers a way to see the effects of such actions. The first step is to build a model of shoeshine customers and service times, a two-step procedure.

1. Gather arrival and service-time data. We observe the shoeshine stand for three days from 9:30 A.M. to 11:30 A.M. We record customer arrivals and times to complete shoe shining and plot them on time charts, Figure 14–6. Checking the charts, we see that the three days are mostly alike and arrivals are spread out over the 120-minute periods. Numbers of arriving customers look similar enough from minute to minute and day to day to use all the data in a simulation. (If days and minutes should have differing arrival

FIGURE 14–6
Customer Arrival and Service-Time Data on Time Charts

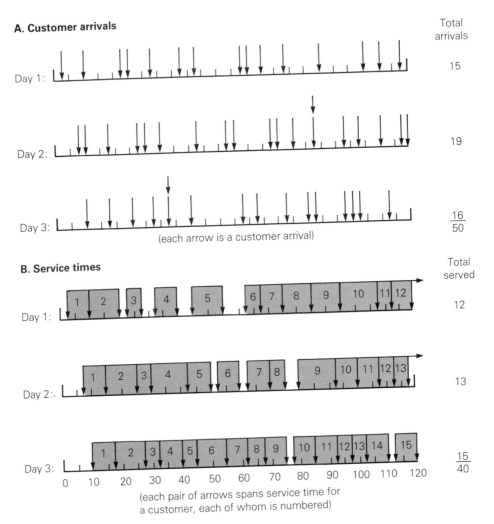

A. Customer arrivals

Day 1:   15

Day 2:   19

Day 3:   16
                                                                         ——
                    (each arrow is a customer arrival)   50

Total arrivals

B. Service times

Day 1:   12

Day 2:   13

Day 3:   15
     0   10   20   30   40   50   60   70   80   90 100 110 120   ——
                                                                         40
              (each pair of arrows spans service time for
              a customer, each of whom is numbered)

Total served

patterns, the study could be divided into parts, such as first half-hour of the day, second half-hour, and so forth; then separately simulate for each part.)

The total number of customers served is only 40 (Figure 14–6B), as compared with 50 customers counted as arrivals (Figure 14–6A). The 10-customer difference includes 8 customers who refused to wait in line (lost business) and 2 customers whose shoes were still being shined at the end of the 120-minute periods in days 1 and 2. (We were careful to count even those persons who approached the shoeshine stand but turned away upon seeing a waiting line.)

From Figure 14–6, we could find the utilization rate of the server, maximum and average waiting lines, and so on, but that would serve no purpose. We gather the data in order to transform them—get the data into a form that will permit simulations for comparing present and proposed service options.

2. Transform data into probability distributions. We see from Figure 14–6 that time between arrivals, or **interarrival time (IAT)**, varies from 0 (two arrivals at the same time) to 17.5 minutes (which occurs once on day 3, between minute 45 and minute 62.5 in Figure 14–6A). The service time to shine one customer's shoes varies from 5 to 12.5 minutes.

Our next task is to capture and condense the variability into probability distributions, first for interarrival times; see Figure 14–7. We divide the data into four classification intervals and count the number of occurrences (frequency) in each; midpoints of each

FIGURE 14–7
Developing an IAT Probability Distribution

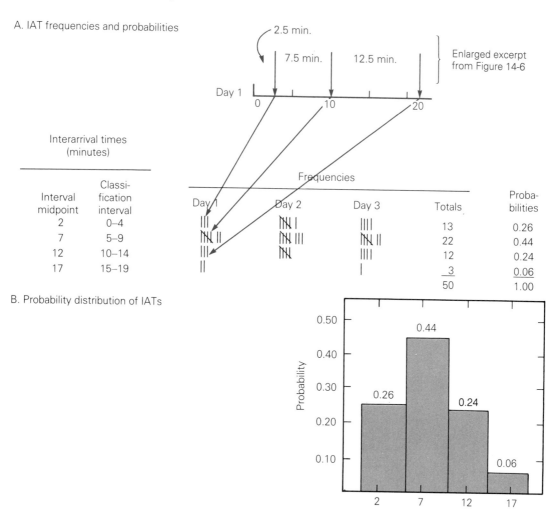

A. IAT frequencies and probabilities

B. Probability distribution of IATs

interval—2, 7, 12, and 17—represent the whole interval. (Division into five or six narrower intervals would work as well.)

Tally marks indicate frequencies. The arrows in the figure show how this is done for the first three arrivals that were entered on the time chart in Figure 14–7A. The first customer arrived 2.5 minutes after the observer began watching, so 2.5 minutes is the first IAT (interarrival time); one tally mark goes in the 0–4 row, since 2.5 minutes falls within that classification interval. The second customer arrived 7.5 minutes after the first. Since 7.5 falls within interval 5–9, a tally goes in the 5–9 row. The third customer arrived 12.5 minutes after the second, and a tally goes in the 10–14 row.

The tallies are shown separately for each day but are then totaled for all three days. Dividing the interval totals—13, 22, 12, and 3—by the grand total of 50, we get the probabilities in the final column in Figure 14–7A.

Figure 14–7B shows the probabilities for each of the four interval midpoints as a bar

FIGURE 14–8
Developing a Service-Time Probability Distribution

A. Service-time frequencies and probabilities

| Service times (minutes) | | Frequencies | | | | Proba- bilities |
Interval midpoints	Classi- fication interval	Day 1	Day 2	Day 3	Totals	
5	4–6.9	|||	||||	|||||	12	0.30
8	7–9.9	||||	|||||		||||| |||	18	0.45
11	10–12.9	|||||	|||	||	10	0.25
					40	1.00

B. Probability distribution of service times

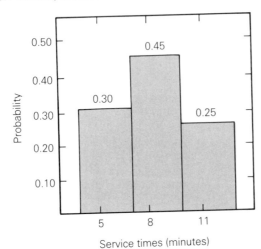

chart. The bar chart format is not necessary for simulation purposes, but it is a useful visual aid.

We follow the same procedure for service times. The result is the service time frequency data and probability distribution in Figure 14–8. Since service times may be parts of minutes, the classification intervals allow for decimal parts. In contrast, the intervals for arrivals are in whole numbers only, since there cannot be a part of a customer. The smallest service time interval is set at 4–6.9, with 5 as the midpoint, since every shoeshine in Figure 14–6B took at least five minutes.

Conducting the Simulation

A Monte Carlo simulation makes use of random numbers, which are manipulated by already-prepared IAT and service-time probability distributions to yield simulated arrivals and service times. As a preparatory step, the probabilities must be expressed as number ranges, sometimes called *Monte Carlo number ranges*. The number ranges should cover the same span of numbers as the table of random numbers—for example, both from 00 to 99 or 000 to 999.

Using our shoeshine stand data, Example 14–3 illustrates the creation of Monte Carlo number ranges and simulation of arrivals and service times (step 3 of the 5-step simulation analysis procedure in Figure 14–5). Included in the example are a simulated logbook and summary information (step 4 of the 5-step procedure). The simulation maintains present service conditions: the proprietor only, with no electric buffers and no appointment system. Random numbers are taken from a table of uniformly distributed random numbers, Appendix C.

EXAMPLE 14–3   **MONTE CARLO SIMULATION—A SHOESHINE STAND**

Figure 14–9B is a small simulation of the shoeshine stand. Interarrival and service-time distributions are taken from Figures 14–7 and 14–8. Monte Carlo number ranges mirror the probabilities: In Figure 14–9A, the probability 0.26 for an IAT of 2 yields a Monte Carlo number range from 00 to 25; the next probability, 0.44, takes in the range of 44 digits from 26 to 69; and so forth.

3. *Conduct simulation.* Figure 14–9B makes use of the part A data, plus random numbers from Appendix C. The first random number, 27 (in column 2), is used to represent the IAT for customer 1. Since 27 falls within Monte Carlo range 26–69 in the IAT table in Figure 14–9A, the IAT is 7. Arrows drawn between Figures 14–9A and 14–9B show these steps. The second random number, 39 (in column 6), is used to represent service time for customer 1. Since 39 falls within Monte Carlo range, 30–74 in the service time table in Figure 14–9A, the service time is 8 (see arrows).

Columns 4, 5, and 8 in Figure 14–9B represent what an observer would see at the shoeshine stand: Column 4 gives the arrival time for each customer. It is simply the cumulative sum of the IATs in column 3. Column 5 is the time service starts. Service does not always begin when the customer arrives, because some customers must wait. In this simulation customers 2, 3, 5, 6, 7, 8, 9, and 10 must wait (the waiting time is the

FIGURE 14–9
Monte Carlo Simulation—Shoeshine Stand

A. Monte Carlo number ranges

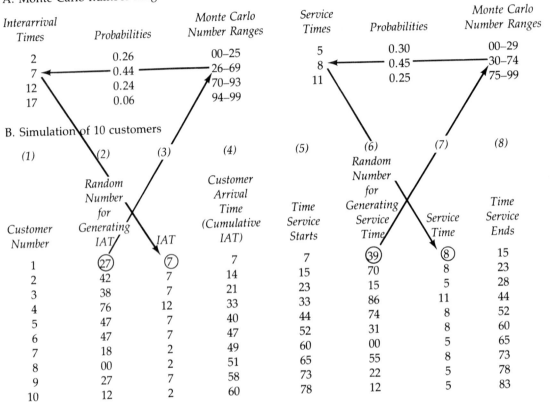

Interarrival Times	Probabilities	Monte Carlo Number Ranges	Service Times	Probabilities	Monte Carlo Number Ranges
2	0.26	00–25	5	0.30	00–29
7	0.44	26–69	8	0.45	30–74
12	0.24	70–93	11	0.25	75–99
17	0.06	94–99			

B. Simulation of 10 customers

(1) Customer Number	(2) Random Number for Generating IAT	(3) IAT	(4) Customer Arrival Time (Cumulative IAT)	(5) Time Service Starts	(6) Random Number for Generating Service Time	(7) Service Time	(8) Time Service Ends
1	27	7	7	7	39	8	15
2	42	7	14	15	70	8	23
3	38	7	21	23	15	5	28
4	76	12	33	33	86	11	44
5	47	7	40	44	74	8	52
6	47	7	47	52	31	8	60
7	18	2	49	60	00	5	65
8	00	2	51	65	55	8	73
9	27	7	58	73	22	5	78
10	12	2	60	78	12	5	83

difference between the times in columns 4 and 5). Column 8 is the completion time for each shoeshine. It is the start time (column 5) plus the service time (column 7).

To see when the next shine may start, look at the time service ends for earlier customers. For example, the first customer's shine starts at minute 7, takes eight minutes, and ends at minute 15. Customer 2 arrives at minute 14 but must wait until customer 1 leaves at minute 15. Therefore, to get a start time in column 5, compare the previous end time with the arrival time for the current customer.

Useful summary information may be extracted from the simulation, as explained next.

4. *Extract information.* Common information from a Monte Carlo waiting-line simulation includes maximum and average waiting-line length, average waiting time per customer, and percent idleness or utilization of the service facility. All these statistics come from columns 4, 5, and 8 of the simulation in Figure 14–9B. Those columns, plus three more columns of working figures and summarized information, are given in Figure 14–10.

Columns 5, 6, and 7 in Figure 14–10 show number of customers waiting, customer waiting time, and service facility idleness. The first customer arrives after the facility has been idle for seven minutes. The second arrives in minute 14 and waits one minute until customer 1 departs in minute 15. Customers 3, 5, and 6 also find a customer ahead of

FIGURE 14–10

Summary Information from Simulation

(1) Customer Number	(2) Customer Arrival Time	(3) Time Service Starts	(4) Time Service Ends	(5) Number of Customers Waiting	(6) Customer Waiting Time	(7) Time of Idleness in Service Facility
1	7	7	15			7
2	14	15	23	1	1	
3	21	23	28	1	2	
4	33	33	44			5
5	40	44	52	1	4	
6	47	52	60	1	5	
7	49	60	65	2	11	
8	51	65	73	3	14	
9	58	73	78	3	15	
10	60	78	83	3	18	
Totals				15	70	12

Maximum waiting line = 3 customers

$$\text{Mean waiting line} = \frac{15 \text{ customers waiting}}{10 \text{ customer arrivals}} = 1.5 \text{ customers}$$

$$\text{Mean waiting time} = \frac{70 \text{ minutes waiting}}{10 \text{ customers}} = 7.0 \text{ minutes}$$

$$\text{Idleness rate} = \frac{12 \text{ minutes idle}}{83 \text{ minutes simulated}} = 0.145 \text{ or } 14.5\% \text{ idleness}$$

them when they arrive. Customer 7 arrives at minute 49, but customer 5 does not leave until minute 52, so customers 6 and 7 are waiting at the same time. Each of the other calculations follows the same logic.

The summary information at the bottom of Figure 14–10 tells us that the maximum waiting line is 3 customers; the mean waiting line, 1.5 customers; and the mean waiting time, 7.0 minutes. The idleness rate is found by dividing 12 minutes of idleness by the 83 minutes in the simulation, which equals 14.5 percent idleness.

The simulation of a shoeshine stand was simplified for illustrative purposes. A real simulation usually would take longer and generate more and better information. Also:

1. A 10-customer, 83-minute simulation is very short. The simulation period should last 120 minutes, which is the peak period of operation for the shoeshine stand. To have confidence in the final waiting-line

and idleness statistics, we should run the simulation on a computer, which permits simulating for hundreds or thousands of days. With many days of simulation, the effects of an unusual selection of random numbers wash out.

2. With a longer simulation, we get more data. Then we may narrow the classification intervals. The interval midpoints for the IAT and service time distributions in Figures 14–7 and 14–8 were set rather far apart (i.e., 2, 7, 12, and 17 for the IAT distribution) because of limited data for narrower intervals.

3. As was noted at the outset, a purpose of simulation is to test various conditions, such as adding staff. Reruns of the simulation with different IAT or service time distributions are among the options we may try. Special computer simulation languages (such as SIMSCRIPT, GPSS, GASP, Q-GERTS, and SLAM) and graphics simulation packages are useful in testing a variety of options, including customer balking and reneging.

Simulation for System Improvement

Having seen how a simulation model is developed, we now turn to practical uses of the procedure. Example 14–4 is long—but even the simplest Monte Carlo simulations always are.

EXAMPLE 14–4   MONTE CARLO SIMULATION—REPAIR CREW SIZES

At Echo Engine Company, a serious problem is malfunction and breakdown of the powered conveyor sections that feed various parts to the engine assembly line. Conveyor failure shuts down the given feeder line, idling its work crew. Crew size is nearly the same on each feeder line, and Echo uses a flat $50 per hour as the cost of feeder-line idleness.

A four-hour parts inventory is stockpiled at the end of each feeder line. If any feeder line is idle for more than four hours, the parts stockpile is used up, idling the whole assembly line; the cost of assembly-line idleness is $1,000 per hour. A partial layout sketch of the assembly and feeder lines is shown in Figure 14–11.

Echo's maintenance department employs one mechanic whose main job is to repair and adjust conveyors. The mechanic's wage is $10 per hour, time and a half ($15) for overtime. Overtime is scheduled for any maintenance not completed during the eight-hour workday.

Echo operates only one production shift per day, but an evening skeleton crew builds up parts so that the four-hour parts inventories are fully restored by the next morning. That way the regular day-shift production crews are not paid for any overtime.

FIGURE 14–11

Layout Sketch of Echo Engine Plant

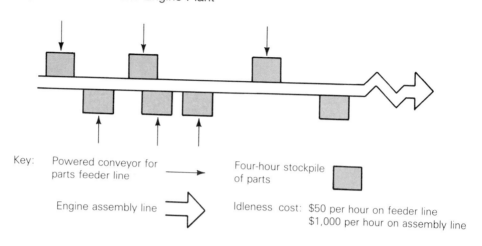

Key: Powered conveyor for
       parts feeder line

       Engine assembly line

Four-hour stockpile
of parts

Idleness cost: $50 per hour on feeder line
                 $1,000 per hour on assembly line

The question is: Is one mechanic enough?

Solution

Monte Carlo simulation clearly seems preferable to queuing formulas for the following reasons:

1. Because of distorting human influences, breakdown and service rate probability distributions are not likely to be Poisson, which is necessary when queuing formulas are used. Monte Carlo simulation is usable with any probability distribution.

2. The system starts fresh each day with empty queues, and average queues grow as the day progresses. Queuing formulas require steady-state queue conditions, but Monte Carlo can capture transient conditions.

Step 1: Input data. The conveyor repairperson also acts as a dispatcher, and keeps a thorough trouble-call logbook. A page from the logbook is shown in Figure 14–12A.

Step 2: Transformed input data. The logbook has enough data for computing arrival time and service time probability distributions. To the logbook in Figure 14–12A we add two columns of working figures: an interarrival time (time between arrivals) column and a repair time column. The working figures are shown in Figure 14–12B, just to the right of the raw data in the repair logbook. Interarrival time (IAT) is determined by successive subtraction of trouble-call times. The first trouble call after the 8:00 A.M. opening time is at 8:50; 8:50 minus 8:00 is 50 minutes, the IAT. Repair time for call 1 is 9:10 minus 8:50, which is 20 minutes. Each of the other IAT and repair time working figures is similarly calculated.

Next, transform the working figures into frequency distributions. To do this, segment the continuous distributions into intervals; 10-minute intervals will suffice. Then tally the number of working figures that fall into each interval. This produces the frequency distributions in Figure 14–12C. Arrows in the figure show the tallies for trouble-call 1. The 50-minute IAT falls within the interval 50–59, so one tally is entered in the 50–59

FIGURE 14–12

Developing IAT and Service-Time Frequency Distributions

A. Logbook entries

B. Working figures

Date	Trouble Call Number	Trouble Call Time	Service Started	Service Completed	IAT (minutes)	Repair Times (minutes)
3/12	1	8:50	8:50	9:10	(50)	(20)
	2	9:25	9:25	10:35	35	70
	3	9:55	10:35	10:53	30	18
	4	10:20	10:53	11:20	25	27
			Lunch 12:00–1:00			
	5	1:05	1:05	1:05	45	45
	6	1:14	1:50	2:35	9	45
	7	3:00	3:00	3:25	106	25
	8	4:00	4:48	5:10	60	22

C. IAT and service-time frequencies

	Frequencies	
Interval	IAT	Repair Times
0–9	|	
10–19		|
20–29	|	||||
30–39	||	
40–49	|	||
50–59	|	
60–69	|	
70–79		|
80–89		
90–99		
100–109	|	
110–119		

row under IAT frequencies. The 20-minute repair time falls within the interval 20–29, so one tally is entered in the 20–29 row under repair time frequencies. The rest of Figure 14–12C is determined similarly.

For only eight trouble calls—one day's worth—the frequency distribution table is sparse. We must gather and tally trouble-call data for a number of days so that we may capture the full range of variability in the frequency distributions. Let us assume that a total of 100 trouble calls is tallied and that the resulting frequency distributions are as shown in Figure 14–13A.

Step 3: Monte Carlo simulations. Figure 14–13B is extended from Figure 14–13A. The midpoints in B are midpoints for each interval in A, and the probabilities in B are the number of tallies in A divided by the total of 100 tallies in the sample. Now we state the probabilities as ranges of two-digit Monte Carlo numbers from 00 to 99. The sizes of the

FIGURE 14–13

Transformed Trouble-Call and Service-Time Data—Echo Engine Company

A. Frequency distribution

Interval	Distribution IAT	Service Time
0–9	||||	|
10–19	ⅢⅡ ||	Ⅲ |
20–29	Ⅲ Ⅲ Ⅲ	Ⅲ Ⅲ Ⅲ |
30–39	Ⅲ Ⅲ Ⅲ Ⅲ |||	Ⅲ Ⅲ Ⅲ Ⅲ Ⅲ |||
40–49	Ⅲ Ⅲ Ⅲ ||	Ⅲ Ⅲ Ⅲ Ⅲ Ⅲ |||
50–59	Ⅲ Ⅲ |||	Ⅲ Ⅲ Ⅲ
60–69	Ⅲ Ⅲ	Ⅲ |||
70–79	Ⅲ |	||||
80–89	|||	||
90–99	|	|
100–109	|	|
	100	100

B. Probabilities and Monte Carlo number ranges

	IAT		Service Time	
Interval Midpoint	Probabilities	Monte Carlo Number Ranges	Probabilities	Monte Carlo Number Ranges
5	0.04	00–03	0.01	00
15	0.07	04–10	0.06	01–06
25	0.15	11–25	0.16	07–22
35	0.23	26–48	0.23	23–45
45	0.17	49–65	0.23	46–68
55	0.13	66–78	0.15	69–83
65	0.10	79–88	0.08	84–91
75	0.06	89–94	0.04	92–95
85	0.03	95–97	0.02	96–97
95	0.01	98	0.01	98
105	0.01	99	0.01	99
	1.00		1.00	

Monte Carlo number ranges are proportional to the probabilities; for example, 00–03 comprises 4 of the 100 numbers, which is proportional to the probability 0.04.

Now we make a simulated logbook by drawing random numbers from Appendix C and fitting them into the Monte Carlo ranges. The first random number in the upper left corner of the table is 42; 42 fits into IAT range 26–48, representing the midpoint 35 (see Figure 14–13B). Therefore, the first trouble call occurs at 00 (beginning of shift) plus 35, that is, the 35th minute. The next lower random number, 55, is used to simulate the service time; the 55 fits into service time range 46–68, representing 45. Therefore, the first simulated trouble call takes 45 minutes to repair.

Those numbers go into columns 3, 4, 7, and 8 of Figure 14–14A, which is a simulation of 20 trouble calls with one repairman at Echo Engines. Column 5 contains trouble-call arrival times, which are cumulative interarrival times (from column 4). The IAT for trouble call 2 is 25, which means 25 minutes between call 1 and call 2. Therefore, since call 1 arrived in minute 35, call 2 arrives in 35 + 25 = 60.

Column 9, time service completed, is simply time service started (column 6) plus service time (column 8). For the first call, service time is completed at 35 + 45 = minute 80.

Column 6, time service started, is the same as trouble-call arrival time (column 5) when there is no waiting line of trouble calls. That is the case for call 1. Call 2 arrives in minute 60, but we see from column 9 that call 1 is still in service until minute 80. Thus, call 2 has to wait. The wait is 80 − 60 = 20 minutes, which is entered in column 10, feeder-line idleness waiting for repairperson.

Column 11, repairperson overtime (after 480th minute), may contain entries only at the end of the day—if overtime is needed. In this simulation, overtime is not needed in day 1, when there is only one repairperson. In day 2, overtime is needed for the last three trouble calls (18, 19, and 20), since all three are completed later than the 480th minute.

Column 12, assembly-line idleness for repair (of feeder line) over 30 minutes, occurs in day 2 for calls 16 through 20. Feeder-line idleness for call 16 is 40 minutes (column 10), which is 10 minutes longer than the 30-minute stockpile of feeder-line parts. When feeder-line parts are gone, the whole assembly line stops.

In Figure 14–14B, the simulation data are applied to two repairpeople, but only for the busiest repair day, day 2. The random-number and IAT columns are omitted in Figure 14–14B, and a new column (number 5) is added to show which repairperson the job is assigned to.

In Figure 14–14B, call 12 is assigned to repairperson 2, who leaves at minute 210 and returns at minute 245. Meanwhile, trouble call 13 comes in at minute 225, so the call is assigned to repairperson 1. Skipping down to call 17, we see that it comes in at minute 335, when both repairpeople are out. Repairperson 1 returns first, at minute 340, so he gets call 17. Call 17 had to wait $340 - 335 = 5$ minutes, which is entered as feeder-line idleness (column 8). Overtime is not needed.

Step 4: Summary logbook statistics. Summary idleness and overtime totals are shown for day 2 in Figure 14–14A and 14–14B. The results are no surprise: Feeder-line idleness while waiting for a repairperson is drastically cut from 490 minutes for one repairperson to 10 minutes for two. And, of course, the 70 minutes of feeder-line idleness in day 1 and the 320 minutes' assembly-line idleness in day 2 are cut to zero with two repairpeople. Overtime is also reduced to zero with two repairpeople.

The two-day, 20-call simulation is too short to be precise. Let us assume that the simulation is continued for 100 days and for one, two, and three repairpeople. Idleness and overtime data for the 100-day simulation may be averaged. Assume that the averaged data are:

One Repairperson

Feeder-line idleness	130 minutes/day
Overtime	110 minutes/day
Assembly-line idleness	50 minutes/day

Two Repairpeople

Feeder-line idleness	3 minutes/day
Overtime	0 minutes/day
Assembly-line idleness	0 minutes/day

Three Repairpeople

Feeder-line idleness	0 minutes/day
Overtime	0 minutes/day
Assembly-line idleness	0 minutes/day

Step 5: Cost analysis of repairperson alternatives. Total costs for each repairperson alternative are the sum of regular and overtime repairperson wages and the cost of feeder-line and assembly-line idleness. Not relevant are the wages of production employees

and feeder-line idleness during service; they are constant—not related to number of repairpeople. Relevant average daily costs are determined below.

The regular wage rate was given at $10 per hour per repairperson. For an eight-hour day, wage costs are:

For one repairperson: 1 repairperson × $10/hour × 8 hour = $80/day
For two repairpeople: 2 repairpeople × $10/hour × 8 hours = $160/day
For three repairpeople: 3 repairpeople × $10/hour × 8 hours = $240/day

Overtime wages are time and a half, or $15 per hour. Simulated overtime per day, from step 4 above, is 100 minutes for one repairperson, zero for two repairpeople, and zero for three repairpeople. Therefore, the daily cost for one repairperson is:

$$\frac{110 \text{ minutes/day}}{60 \text{ minutes/hour}} \times \$15/\text{hour} = \$27.50/\text{day}$$

Feeder-line idleness cost was given as $50 per hour. Simulated feeder-line idleness per day, from step 4, above, is 130 minutes for one repairperson, 3 minutes for two repairpeople, and 0.0 minute for three repairpeople. Daily costs are:

For one repairperson:

$$\frac{130 \text{ minutes/day}}{60 \text{ minutes/hour}} \times \$50/\text{hour} = \$108.33/\text{day}$$

For two repairpeople:

$$\frac{3 \text{ minutes/day}}{60 \text{ minutes/hour}} \times \$50/\text{hour} = \$2.50$$

For three repairpeople:

$$\frac{0.0 \text{ minutes/day}}{60 \text{ minutes/hour}} \times \$50/\text{hour} = \$0.00/\text{day}$$

Assembly-line idleness was given as $1,000 per hour. Simulated assembly-line idleness, from step 4 above, is 50 minutes for one repairperson and zero time for two and three repairpeople. The daily cost for one repairperson is:

$$\frac{50 \text{ minutes/day}}{60 \text{ minutes/hour}} \times \$1,000/\text{hour} = \$833.33/\text{day}$$

The four types of daily costs are totaled in Figure 14–15 for the three staffing options. Comparing total costs helps us decide on the best staffing policy.

In Figure 14–15, the total average cost per day for two repairpeople is $162.50. That is over $75 per day less than the next lowest cost, $240.00 for three repairpeople. The wage cost alone for three repairpeople is $240 per day, considerably more than the total daily cost for two repairpeople. The $75-per-day saving, when extended to a 250-day year, is a saving of $18,750 per year. On the basis of costs alone, two repairpeople is clearly the best staffing policy. An additional advantage of two (and three) repairpeople over one is that output on the engine line is more predictable and uniform when feeder-line breakdowns can be repaired with no waiting time. Of course, the very idea of maintaining a 30-minute buffer stock for each feeder line is questionable. We should try to cut that stock and keep cutting it. A good preventive maintenance program to keep the equipment running justifies cutting the buffer stock.

FIGURE 14–14
Simulation of Trouble Calls and Repairs—Echo Engine Company

A. One repairperson

(1) Day Number	(2) Trouble-Call Number	(3) Random Number for Generating IAT	(4) IAT	(5) Trouble-Call Arrival Time: Cum. IAT	(6) Time Service Started	(7) Random Number for Generating Service Time	(8) Service Time	(9) Time Service Completed	(10) Feeder-Line Idleness Waiting for Repair-person (minutes)	(11) Repair-person Overtime (minutes after 480th minute)	(12) Assembly-Line Idleness for Repair over 30 Minutes (minutes)
1	1	42	35	35	35	55	45	80	20		
	2	24	25	60	80	82	55	135	30		
	3	56	45	105	135	48	45	180			
	4	95	85	190	190	86	65	255			
	5	49	45	235	255	41	35	290	20		
	6	95	85	320	320	78	55	375			
	7	84	65	385	385	40	35	420			
	8	80	65	450	450	12	25	475			
2	9	84	65	65	65	01	5	70			
	10	25	25	90	90	46	45	135			
	11	83	65	155	155	69	55	210			
	12	78	25	210	210	43	35	245			
	13	07	15	225	245	00	5	250	20		
	14	55	45	270	270	17	25	295			
	15	22	25	295	295	57	45	340			
	16	02	5	300	340	70	55	395	40		
	17	28	35	335	395	86	65	460	60	55	30
	18	04	15	350	460	95	75	535	110	75	80
	19	89	75	425	535	92	75	610	110	75	80
	20	30	35	460	610	86	65	675	150	65	120
								Day 2 totals:	490	195	320

B. Two repairpeople

(1) Day	(2) Trouble-Call Number	(3) Trouble-Call Arrival Time	(4) Time Service Started	(5) Which Repairperson Is Assigned to Trouble Call	(6) Service Time	(7) Time Service Completed	(8) Feeder-Line Idleness Waiting For Repairperson (minutes)	(9) Repairperson Overtime (minutes after 480th minute)
2	9	65	65	1	5	70		
	10	90	90	2	45	135		
	11	155	155	1	55	210		
	12	210	210	2	35	245		
	13	225	225	1	5	230		
	14	270	270	2	25	295		
	15	295	295	1	45	340		
	16	300	300	2	55	355		
	17	335	340	1	65	410	5	
	18	350	355	2	75	430	5	
	19	425	425	1	75	500		
	20	460	460	2	65	525		
				Day 2 totals:			10	0

FIGURE 14–15
Total Costs for Three Staffing Options—Echo Engine Company

| Number of Repairpeople | Wages | | Idleness | | Total Average Daily Cost |
	Regular	Overtime	Feeder Line	Assembly Line	
1	$ 80.00	$27.50	$108.33	$833.33	$1,049.16
2	160.00	0.00	2.50	0	162.50
3	240.00	0.00	0.00	0	240.00

Realities Affecting Simulation

The chief limitation of Monte Carlo simulation is cost. Monte Carlo simulation is as time consuming—to set up and run, generally on a microcomputer—as queuing formulas are time saving. But Monte Carlo can be as realistic as one cares to make it—and cares to pay for. Despite its cost, the technique can pay large dividends.

In the Echo Engine Company example, the saving, with two repairpeople instead of one, amounts to $18,750 per year. The cost to set up and run the simulation is a pittance compared to that. But let us not become overly ecstatic. In some cases, the maintenance chief and production chief together would be able to correctly decide the optimal number of repairpeople—*without benefit of simulation* and without the cost.

The astute manager is able to recognize when a good decision may be based purely on judgment and when simulation or other analysis is called for. What kind of manager can recognize these things? The answer is, in part, the manager who thoroughly understands waiting-line phenomena. Further, the best way to understand waiting lines is probably *not* by experience and personal observation; that would provide only limited exposure, even in a lifetime. Those who best understand waiting lines are those who have studied many cases—in fairly short periods of time—as students, for example.

It may be true that study is rarely a worthy substitute for the real thing. Let us examine why, in the case of waiting lines, study may well be superior to the real thing.

A valuable lesson for the student of simulation is learning how waiting lines are affected by different arrival and service-time distributions. Those distributions may be wide or narrow, close together or far apart, and in many combinations.

Arrival- and Service-Time Conditions: A Closing Note

In the Echo Engine Company example, the service-time and arrival-time distributions look a lot alike. Figure 14–16A shows one superimposed on the other.

With the two distributions overlapping so much, we may expect long waiting lines, which is exactly what happened in the simulation. By making computations based on data from Figure 14–12, we can show that the mean service time is 47.8 and mean interarrival time 43.4 minutes. When people arrive faster than they can be served, the long-run consequence is waiting lines that grow infinitely! But Echo Engine prevents this by stopping the arrivals after one eight-hour shift each day. Then the machines awaiting repair are fixed during overtime so that none are waiting the next morning.

With so great a potential for waiting lines, simulation begins to pay for itself. The reason is that it is quite impossible to guess, even if you are experienced, how long the waits will be, how much overtime pay is likely, and how much assembly-line shutdown cost there will be.

Now look at Figure 14–16B. The IAT distribution has been moved 30 minutes to the right; its mean is at 73.4, which means breakdowns occur at 73.4-minute intervals, on average. Time to repair still averages 47.8 minutes—much faster. We should surmise, *without simulating*, that long queues of machines waiting for service are unlikely to form. Overtime costs should be very low, perhaps

FIGURE 14–16

Arrival- and Service-Time Distributions—Echo Engine Company

A. Greatly overlapped (Echo engines)

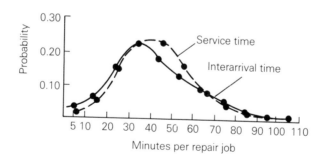

B. Moderately overlapped

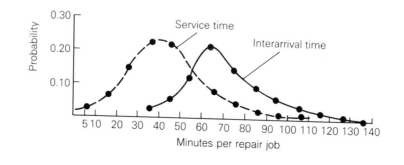

FIGURE 14–17
Arrival- and Service-Time Conditions and Effects

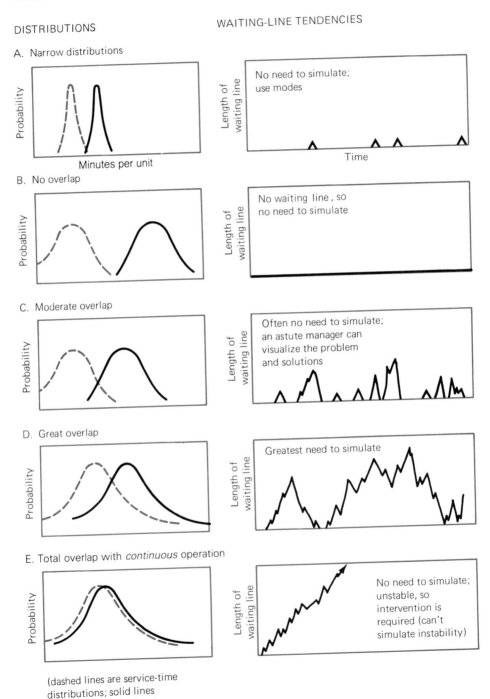

(dashed lines are service-time
distributions; solid lines
are arrival distributions)

negligible. So stick with one repairperson (and be prepared to find other work for that person to do in slack periods). And don't bother to conduct a simulation.

Figure 14–17 shows the effects of five general arrival and service-time conditions. It illustrates the two cases discussed previously: great overlap (case D) and moderate overlap (case C) between interarrival time and service-time distributions. It also includes three other cases: narrow distributions, no overlap, and "total" overlap with continuous operation.

For case A, narrow distributions, there is no point in simulating. The distributions are too narrow. It is practical to act as though interarrival and service times were not distributed at all. In other words, find the modes of these very narrow distributions—the most frequently occurring interarrival time and service time; then treat the modes as single-valued estimates. That way, decisions on staffing and scheduling are simple—often self-evident.

For case B, the probability distributions are wide but do not overlap. Without overlap, there are no interactions or chances of waiting lines, so there is nothing to simulate. A good management decision may be to cut staff in order to avoid staff idleness and allow a small amount of waiting time.

Case E is nearly total overlap with *continuous* operation; that means no stops at the ends of shifts to allow queues to empty out. The *pattern* of growth could be simulated; this might seem valuable in order to learn about waiting-line behavior in the startup phase. But it usually would not be worth doing, because the conditions leading to an infinite queue are unstable. Management is likely to quickly intervene to reduce such instability—add staff, for example. The condition would scarcely last long enough to gather data to simulate it.

We have seen that four of the five cases in Figure 14–17 do not seem to call for Monte Carlo simulation. Considering the cost of simulation, that is good news!

Managers of service units are not likely to find a lot of uses for Monte Carlo simulation. They should, however, find many uses for a thorough understanding of waiting-line phenomena.

SUMMARY

Resource assignment has two major concerns: appropriate response to customer demand and finding the right mix of resources to do so. The resource assignment task is difficult in service centers because the workload pattern is usually irregular—not unlike a roller coaster. The manager, attempting to meet demand and yet control resource costs, must deal with waiting lines when customer arrivals bunch up (heavy demand) or idle resources (when demand slacks off).

A simple waiting line is the single-channel, single-stage line, but other numbers of channels (lines) and stages (servers) can occur. One way to study waiting lines is to gather arrival and service-time data and then create a model of the waiting-line patterns for different levels of use of server capacity (often number of servers on hand).

One approach is to use simple queuing formulas to predict average waiting times, number waiting, and server utilization. The formulas just require entry of mean arrival rate and mean service rate. But they yield valid data only if arrival rates are Poisson distributed and service rates are Poisson distributed or constant. Poisson is the normal pattern. But *human* customers tend to balk when lines look too long and to leave if they move too slowly; these tendencies push the arrival pattern away from Poisson. Similarly, Poisson service rates often do not hold up for human servers, because servers tend to speed up when lines are long and slow down when lines are short. These human tendencies cause waiting to decrease and server utilization to rise. Finally, the queuing formulas do not work out unless average arrival and service rates are stable—what is called the *steady state*.

For all those limitations, queuing formulas can at least predict an upper limit on average waiting, which can help managers decide on service capacity. Also, when the arrivals or the service performed are more mechanical and less human, the formulas can indeed work well.

In studying startup (nonsteady-state) conditions and nonstandard arrival and service-rate patterns, a more difficult waiting-line analysis technique applies: Monte Carlo simulation. It requires keeping records on arrivals and service times, translating them into probability distributions, simulating by matching random numbers against probability distributions, and extracting output information on waiting and server utilization. Put a price on the waiting times and on the servers, and management can better decide on how to manage the lines and the servers.

Computers are usually used to generate random numbers and simulate many time periods to yield reliable average statistics. Because of the cost of Monte Carlo simulation, it is not often used. But a student can find it valuable to run many types of simulation exercises, because these offer insights on what happens to waiting lines under varying combinations of arrival and service rates. Actually running a simulation for service center management purposes is most valuable when the arrival and service-rate distributions greatly overlap, creating hard-to-protect waiting patterns.

KEY WORDS

Queuing analysis
Simulation
Steady state

Utilization rate
Idleness rate
Transient state

Monte Carlo
  simulation
Interarrival time (IAT)

SOLVED PROBLEMS

1. A motel desk clerk spends an average of 2.5 minutes checking a guest into the motel. Between the hours of 1 P.M. and 5 P.M., an average of 20 guests arrive each hour. Assuming Poisson-distributed arrivals and service times, describe the queue behavior. If the service time were a constant 2.5 minutes, what would the average queue length and time in line be?

Solution

First, calculate a working figure, the service rate, μ. It is the reciprocal of the service time:

$$\mu = \frac{1}{2.5} = 0.4 \text{ guest per minute, or 24 guests per hour}$$

Now proceed with the formulas shown in Figure 14–3:

$$\text{Utilization} = U = \frac{\lambda}{\mu} = \frac{20}{24} = 0.833, \text{ or } 83.3\%$$

$$\text{Idleness} = I = 1 - U = 1 - 0.833 = 0.167, \text{ or } 16.7\%$$

$$\text{Average number in line or queue} = N_q = \frac{\lambda^2}{\mu(\mu - \lambda)}$$

$$= \frac{20^2}{24(24 - 20)} = \frac{400}{96} = 4.167 \text{ guests}$$

$$\text{Average waiting time in line} = T_q = \frac{\lambda}{\mu(\mu - \lambda)}$$

$$= \frac{20}{24(24 - 20)} = \frac{20}{96} \quad \begin{array}{l} 0.2083 \text{ hours,} \\ \text{or 12.5 minutes} \end{array}$$

$$\text{Average number in system} = N_s = \frac{\lambda}{\mu - \lambda}$$

$$= \frac{20}{(24 - 20)} = \frac{20}{4} = 5.0 \text{ guests}$$

$$\text{Average time in system} = T_s = \frac{1}{\mu - \lambda}$$

$$= \frac{1}{(24 - 20)} = \frac{1}{4} = 0.25 \text{ hours, or 15 minutes}$$

$$\text{Average time in queue (constant service)} = T_q(c) = \frac{\lambda}{2\mu(\mu - \lambda)}$$

$$= \frac{20}{48(24 - 20)} = \frac{20}{192}$$

$$= 0.1042 \text{ hours, or 6.25 minutes}$$

$$\text{Average number in queue} = N_q(c) = \frac{\lambda^2}{2\mu(\mu - \lambda)}$$

$$= \frac{400}{48(24 - 20)} = \frac{400}{192} = 2.083 \text{ guests}$$

Thus, the assumption of constant service rate reduces average queue length and waiting time by 50 percent.

2. You have observed waiting-line conditions at the parking application window at the campus police office. You've built the following model, complete with Monte Carlo number ranges, that is representative of waiting and service behavior over 100 10-minute periods (assume a 10-minute service time):

Applicant Arrivals per 10-Minute Period	Frequency	Monte Carlo Number Ranges
0	10	00–09
1	70	10–79
2	20	80–99

 a. Conduct a simple Monte Carlo simulation using these six random numbers: 79, 35, 92, 24, 82, and 3. Use your simulated data to find the total customer delay time, assuming there is just one application window.

 b. Repeat, assuming two application windows. Is customer service improved much? Explain.

Solution

Construct simulated logbooks. Formats for simulation logbooks vary, depending on what the problem calls for. Formats that will work in this case are as follows:

a.

10-Minute Period	Random Number	Arriving Applicant(s)	Applicant Receiving Service	Applicant Waiting
1	79	1	1	None
2	35	2	2	None
3	92	3, 4	3	4
4	24	5	4	5
5	82	6, 7	5	6, 7
6	3	None	6	7

Summary: Applicants 4, 5, and 6 wait 10 minutes each; applicant 7 waits 20 minutes. Total applicant waiting time is 50 minutes.

b.

10-Minute Period	Random Number	Arriving Applicant(s)	Applicant Served, First Window	Applicant Served, Second Window	Applicant Waiting
1	79	1	1	None	None
2	35	2	2	None	None
3	92	3, 4	3	4	None
4	24	5	5	None	None
5	82	6, 7	6	7	None
6	3	None	None	None	None

Conclusion: Two service windows greatly improve service: They reduce applicant waiting time from 50 minutes to zero for the 60-minute simulation.

REFERENCES

Books

Banks, Jerry, and John S. Carson II. *Discrete-Event System Simulation.* Englewood Cliffs, N.J.: Prentice-Hall, 1984 (T57.62.B35).

Cooke, William P. *Quantitative Methods for Management Decisions.* New York: McGraw-Hill, 1985 (T57.6.C658).

Fabrycky, W. J.; P. M. Ghare; and P. E. Torgersen. *Applied Operations Research and Management Science.* Englewood Cliffs, N.J.: Prentice-Hall, 1984 (T57.6.F3).

Markland, Robert E. *Topics in Management Science,* 2nd ed. New York: John Wiley & Sons, 1983 (T56.M275).

Rubinstein, Reuven Y. *Monte Carlo Optimization, Simulation, and Sensitivity of Queuing Networks.* New York: Wiley, 1986 (QA298.R79).

Solomon, Susan L. *Simulation of Waiting-Line Systems.* Englewood Cliffs, N.J.: Prentice-Hall, 1983 (T57.9.S64).

Periodicals/Societies

Decision Sciences (Decision Sciences Institute).

Interfaces.

Management Science (The Institute of Management Science).

REVIEW QUESTIONS

1. What makes resource assignment difficult in service centers? What are the two major problems with *any* resource assignment task?

2. What is a waiting-line channel? A waiting-line stage? How many channels and stages are permitted in using the queuing formulas given in this chapter?

3. What is meant by *steady state?* By *transient state?* How do these terms relate to the use of queuing formulas?

4. In using queuing analysis, are the data to be entered into the formulas hard or easy to obtain? Explain.

5. If human servers (who change their work speed all the time) are replaced by mechanical servers, what changes should be made in conducting a queuing analysis?

6. In studying a waiting line, why does it make a difference whether the customer and server are human or nonhuman?

7. What are some key advantages and disadvantages of queuing formulas?

8. Why are Monte Carlo simulations run over and over again in a single waiting-line study?

9. In using Monte Carlo simulation, are the data to be used easy or hard to obtain? Explain.

10. Why do a Monte Carlo simulation? How can management use the results?

11. How can a random number represent (simulate) an arrival at a service center or represent serving time?

12. What happens to the waiting time when the average arrival rate is nearly as great as the average serving rate? Answer the question first assuming Poisson distributions and second assuming a rigid appointment system and a mechanical (constant) server.

13. Under what combinations of arrival time and service-time distributions is it not very useful to do a Monte Carlo simulation. Why?

14. Why may a *student* of waiting-line analysis perhaps gain a better understanding of waiting lines and server utilization than an experienced service-center manager?

15. What options are open to the service-center manager when waiting lines are too long?

PROBLEMS AND EXERCISES

1. At an entry station along the Mexican border, state agents check to see that people on foot are not bringing in fruits, vegetables, and so forth that could house undesirable creatures like the Mediterranean fruit fly. It takes an average of 75 seconds to check each person, but there is a good deal of variability around that average. The slow afternoon hours on Tuesday, Wednesday, and Thursday have average arrivals of a person on foot every 95 seconds. The bureau's policy is to have an average of three people waiting to be checked—and to call for another checker whenever that average is exceeded for any appreciable length of time. Can one checker handle the arrivals on Tuesday, Wednesday, and Thursday afternoons? Explain.

2. Metro Pollution Control moves about the city with a mobile unit checking auto emissions. They block the road, stop all cars, and attach an exhaust-sampling device. There are two new exhaust-sampling devices on the market. One has a fixed test time: one minute. The other has a variable time; the manufacturer claims that the mean test time is 0.85 minutes. If cars arrive at the road block at an average rate of 40 per hour, which is better for minimizing the citizens' total delay for the check? Does your answer change if there are only 10 cars per hour? Explain.

3. Which of the following are queuing situations in which our simple set of queuing formulas—single channel, single server—is *not* adequate (would require more advanced queuing formulas)? Explain.

   Ships entering a busy port, seeking tugboats and then a berth.

   Trains coming on different tracks to switch onto the one track crossing Royal Gorge.

Airplanes getting into a holding pattern above Chicago's O'Hare field, then seeking a passenger gate.

Long-distance telephone call routing systems that search for open communications channels.

4. Voters arrive at a precinct polling place at a mean rate of 60 per hour during the peak 5 P.M. to 8 P.M. period. Their mean voting rate is 61 per hour through just 1 voting booth.

a. Though the line is long, there is virtually no balking or reneging by new arrivals. (Those who make the effort to drive to the polls apparently are committed enough to wait through the lines.) What statistical distribution of arrivals seems likely? Why?

b. The service rates seem to approximate a Poisson distribution. (The distribution is "crunched" on the left slightly because voters are hurrying a bit.) Calculate the mean waiting time in queue and the mean number in queue. Discuss the results.

c. The precinct captain has the authority to enforce a time limit of under one minute for a voter to finish voting. If the captain were to enforce the time limit, the voting time would be approximately constant at 0.9 minutes, because few voters take much less than that. What, then, would be the mean waiting time in queue and the mean number in queue? Explain your results—as compared with those in question b.

d. For question b, draw arrival and service time distributions on a single graph, as in Figure 14–17. Do the same for question c. Explain your results from parts b and c by referring to the graphs.

5. Plastic parts for medical syringes are manufactured in a completely automated molding plant. It is presently a one-shift (eight hours a day) operation; that is, there are no production people, only maintenance crews. Maintenance policies need to be reviewed, by type of machine. The review begins with the molding-machine crew.

a. Molding machines break down at a mean rate of five per day. When a machine breaks down, the molding-machine crew is sent to fix it. The mean repair time is 45 minutes. Refer to the queuing formulas in Figure 14–3, and use two that you feel would yield especially useful statistics for setting maintenance policies. Perform the calculations, and explain their value.

b. Is it reasonable to use queuing rather than Monte Carlo simulation in question a? Explain.

c. If a preventive maintenance (PM) program is established, molding-machine breakdowns will be expected to decrease from five to four per day. The PM crew will get its budget and staff from decreases in the repair crews; the smaller molding-machine repair crew will then require 60 minutes of mean repair time (instead of 45 minutes, as in question a). Is the PM program worthwhile? Base your answer on queuing analysis.

6. An automobile engine plant has four engine assembly lines. On each line, the head is found not to fit properly to the engine block on an average of 1 engine every 30 minutes. Those that don't fit are reworked at the end of

the day by operators on the line where the defect occurred, and the problem is corrected in an average of 25 minutes. Note that the 30 and 25 are just averages within probability distributions; the actual distributions for the four lines are as follows (whole distributions are represented by just a few time values):

Time Interval (in minutes) between Engine Problems:	20	25	30	35	40
Probabilities of each time interval on line 1	0.10	0.20	0.40	0.20	0.10
Probabilities of each time interval on line 2	0.05	0.20	0.50	0.20	0.05
Probabilities of each time interval on line 3	0.10	0.20	0.40	0.20	0.10
Probabilities of each time interval on line 4	0.05	0.10	0.70	0.10	0.05

Rework Time (in minutes)	15	20	25	30	35
Probabilities of each rework time value on line 1	0.10	0.20	0.40	0.20	0.10
Probabilities of each rework time value on line 2	0.10	0.20	0.40	0.20	0.10
Probabilities of each rework time value on line 3	0.05	0.20	0.50	0.20	0.05
Probabilities of each rework time value on line 4	0.05	0.10	0.70	0.10	0.05

You have chosen to use Monte Carlo simulation as an aid in scheduling labor on *one* of the rework lines. Which line is the best candidate for Monte Carlo simulation, and why? (Hint: Examine the interactions between time interval and rework time for each line.)

7. The following figures summarize the last 100 hours of service-call requests for the typewriter maintenance department, including translation of frequencies into Monte Carlo numbers. Four random numbers are also shown:

Calls per Hour	Frequency	Monte Carlo Numbers	Random Numbers
0	5	00–04	06 80 49 17
1	40	05–44	
2	55	45–99	

Do a Monte Carlo simulation of service calls using the four random numbers. Assume you have two repairpersons to send on calls. What is the total idle time for repairpersons assuming a fixed one-hour service time for each job?

8. A group of similar machines require servicing. Preventive maintenance is neither feasible nor economical. Therefore, the problem is to hire the number of repairpeople that will result in minimizing the sum of the costs of machine idle time and the repairpeople's wages. Solve the problem using Monte Carlo simulation; limit your analysis to about 100 simulated hours. Comment on the validity of your simulation.

Data for solution:

Idle machine time is estimated to cost the company $35 per hour.

The daily wage for one repairperson is $36.

Historical data on breakdown frequencies and repair times are as follows:

Breakdowns per Hour	Frequency	Probability
0	1,025	0.854
1	156	0.130
2	19	0.016
3 or more	0	0.000
	1,200	1.000

Hours Spent on Repair	Frequency	Probability
2 or less	0	0.000
3	72	0.072
4	178	0.178
5	281	0.281
6	307	0.307
7	115	0.115
8	47	0.047
9 or more	0	0.000
	1,000	1.000

Suggestion: Set up a simulated logbook. Try simulating one repairperson; show the resulting waiting-time costs plus wages for a given number of simulated hours. Then try the same thing for two repairpeople, and so on, until the optimal hiring policy is apparent. (No two people should get the same results.)

9. The following table shows the results of a Monte Carlo simulation. Time is in hours. (Assume the simulation began at hour 00 and ended at hour 32.)

Customer Number	Arrival Time	Service Time	Departure Time
1	10	3	13
2	13	5	18
3	17	2	20
4	21	6	27
5	25	5	32

a. What is the average amount of waiting time per eight-hour day if there is just one server?

b. What would the total waiting time be if two customers could be served at once?

10. The following table shows the results of a Monte Carlo simulation:

Customer Number	Arrival Time	Service Time	Departure Time
1	1		13
2	13		18
3	17		20
4	21		27
5	25		32

If there is one server, what should be the total of the now empty service-time column? What would be the total customer waiting time?

11. The following table shows the results of a Monte Carlo simulation. The simulated time period is 32 hours, or 4 working days (from hour 00 to hour 32), and there is a single server.

Customer Number	Arrival Time	Service Time	Departure Time
1	10	3	13
2	13	5	18
3	15	2	20
4	21	6	27
5	23	5	32

What is the total waiting-time cost for the simulated period if the cost of customers waiting is $3.00 per hour? What would the cost be if there were two servers instead of one?

12. A factory has two truck docks. Trucks sometimes have to get into a queue to await their turn in one of the docks. There is talk about adding a third dock to hold down this queuing. A Monte Carlo simulation has been done. Results are as follows for one 15-truck simulation run:

Truck	Arrival Minute	Enters Dock	Service Time	Leaves Dock
1	30	30	35	65
2	32	32	28	60
3	48	60	30	90
4	62	65	41	106
5	64	90	40	130
6	88	106	43	149
7	95	130	75	205
8	110	149	41	190
9	110	190	50	240
10	142	205	37	242
11	170	240	40	280
12	195	242	68	310
13	199	280	52	332
14	208	310	30	240
15	242	332	58	390

The plant manager feels that there should be enough dock space so that the *average* wait for dock space is less than 30 minutes. Should the third dock be built? Prove your answer by applying the same simulation to a third dock.

13. Global Trade Center, a massive office complex, retains its own elevator maintenance staff so that elevator breakdowns may be repaired promptly. Problems occur when several elevators break down at the same time. A Monte Carlo simulation of breakdowns and service times is being performed based on logbook data. Simulated breakdowns and repair times, along with the random numbers used in their generation, are as follows:

Breakdown Number	Random Number	Minutes between Breakdowns	Random Number	Repair Minutes
1	29	50	95	60
2	01	10	55	40
3	97	130	80	50
4	54	80	66	40
5	19	40	95	60
6	08	20	12	10
7	27	50	15	20
8	71	90	89	50
9	36	60	58	40
10	17	40	49	30
11	00	10	95	60
12	03	10	21	20
13	92	120	72	40
14	62	80	66	40
15	48	70	64	40

a. Complete the Monte Carlo simulation by setting up a simulated logbook. (The instructor may direct that part of the class base the simulation on the first eight breakdowns, others on the first nine, others on the first ten, and so on.) Assume the repair crew can work on only one elevator at a time. What is the mean number of elevators that are out of service?

b. Determine the average number of minutes that an out-of-service elevator waits for repair to begin.

c. Determine the percentage of utilization (percentage of the time busy) for the elevator repair crew.

d. The busy period for Global Trade Center's elevators is the 10-hour period from 7:30 A.M. to 5:30 P.M. Is your simulation of 15 (or fewer) breakdowns adequate to provide statistics good enough for the maintenance manager to make staffing decisions? Explain.

e. To the best of your ability, reconstruct Monte Carlo number ranges and probabilities that fit the breakdown and service-time data for the given 15 simulated breakdowns. Also, estimate mean time between breakdowns and mean time to repair. With the difference in means, how do you explain the average waiting time statistic you obtained in question b?

14. Repeat questions *a*, *b*, and *c* in problem 13, except assume that two repair crews are available.

15. The maintenance staff of the local office of Aquarius Computers completes trouble-call maintenance at the rate of about three per day, but the exact number of completions varies above and below three. Jobs not completed on one day are delayed until the next. The pattern of variability, taken from maintenance logbooks, is as follows:

Daily Job Completion Rate	Probability
1	0.05
2	0.15
3	0.50
4	0.20
5	0.10

The same logbooks also contain enough data to show the frequency of trouble calls per day:

Daily Number of Trouble Calls	Probability
0	0.12
1	0.16
2	0.18
3	0.25
4	0.20
5	0.09
	1.00

a. Use Monte Carlo simulation to determine the average number of jobs delayed until the next day. Simulate for 10 days only. (Each student should get a different answer based on different random numbers.)

b. What other useful statistics may be obtained from your simulation? Provide two other such statistics, and explain their significance.

c. Could queuing formulas be used in this problem? Discuss fully.

16. Following are service center situations in which queuing formulas or Monte Carlo simulation *could* be used. For each situation, what would be the value *to management* (if any) in doing a waiting-line study using either method? Explain.

Light bulbs burn out at random in a large building, and maintenance gets calls to replace them.

Sears, Roebuck operates small appliance repair centers around the country.

The San Francisco–Oakland Bay Bridge has a large number of manned toll booths.

An attorney's office has 30 attorneys who receive large numbers of clients, all on an appointment basis.

17. Sometimes queuing formulas yield fairly accurate information on average waiting time for receiving a service. Other times, queuing formulas are less accurate, and we resort to a more expensive Monte Carlo simulation. Of the following six situations, for which would the queuing formulas be reasonable, and which one would you use? For which situations would Monte Carlo simulation be preferable? Explain your answers.

(1) A public health nurse is inoculating large numbers of people for a new strain of Asian flu. There is one helper to make sure sleeves are rolled up and so on.

(2) Airline passengers returning from a foreign country line up to go through customs.

(3) Thread breakages occur periodically on any of 500 spinning machines in a fabric mill, and the breakage automatically turns on a flashing light to summon a repairperson.

(4) Students make copies on a self-service copier in their dormitory.

(5) Customers bring telephone sets to the phone center for repairs.

(6) Season ticket holders arrive at the metropolitan dome for a sports event and line up to have their tickets taken.

18. Human customers line up for all kinds of services in our society. Name *four* actions that management can take to hold down the waiting lines. Explain.

19. Suppose Dr. Sawbones schedules office appointments at 20-minute intervals beginning at 9 A.M. and continuing until 4 P.M. If you have an appointment at 11 A.M., will the doctor actually see you at 11 A.M.? Explain. Will Dr. Sawbones be able to leave for home at 4:20 P.M., when the last appointment is supposed to be over? Explain. If appointment systems don't always work, why use them at all? Think of your visit to Dr. Sawbones in forming your response.

20. You and your significant other have dinner reservations at a posh (and expensive) restaurant. Your reservation is for 8 P.M. Will you be seated at 8 P.M.? Why or why not? If you think not, would you visit the restaurant again? How does the concept of "reasonable waiting time" fit when people are physically in the queue?

Areas for Continuing Improvement

Continuing improvement ought to be a way of life throughout organizations. Certain activities stand out as prime targets for improvement if streamlined operations, and thus better service to customers, are to be obtained. We examine those in Part Five.

Perhaps foremost is quality, the subject of Chapter 15. Better ways to manage performance, standards that reflect contemporary needs, and their effects on productivity are considered in Chapter 16. In Chapter 17 we take up maintenance, which in some industries is a key to readiness and customer responsiveness. Facilities deployment, emphasizing location, layout, handling, and transportation, is the topic of Chapter 18. Finally, in Chapter 19, we examine some topics that promise to affect the way future operations are managed.

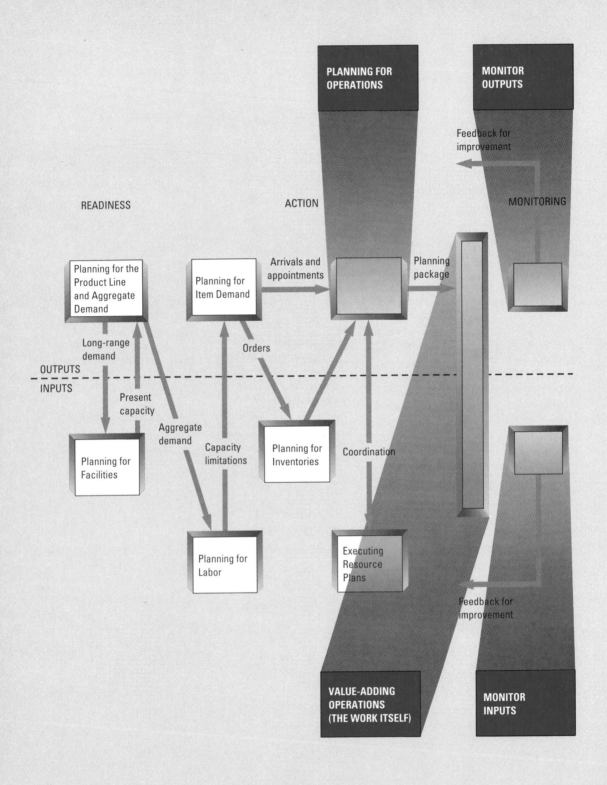

CHAPTER 15

Quality Control and Improvement

QUALITY IMPROVEMENT—AT THE SOURCE

TQ Guidelines
Time-Quality Connection
Role of Quality Department

THE PROCESS FOCUS

Processes: Description and Performance
Special and Common Causes
Process Example
Process Control and Capability
Quality Goals and Continual Improvement

PROCESS IMPROVEMENT CYCLE

Variables and Attributes
Variables Inspection: An Example
Upgrading the Process
What Was Improved?

CONFORMANCE TO SPECIFICATIONS

Run Diagram
$\bar{X}$ and R Charts
Overview of Process Control and Improvement

PROCESS CONTROL FOR ATTRIBUTES

The p Chart
The c Chart

LOW-VOLUME PROCESS CONTROL AND IMPROVEMENT

FROM COARSE TO FINE PROCESS ANALYSIS

Process Analysis Sequence
Pareto Analysis
Fishbone Chart
Scatter (Correlation) Diagram

LOT INSPECTION

QUALITY OF SERVICE—SOME FINAL REMARKS

CASE STUDY:
AMERICAN CERAMIC AND GLASS PRODUCTS
CORPORATION

Modern quality management puts process improvement and quality control on a pedestal. In this chapter, we see how, by focusing on processes, we get quality—of goods and services. An impressive set of process analysis and control techniques is the driving force. The fall-back position (since process controls are not always used) is to rely on inspection of the product or service itself, perhaps by sampling inspection. Before examining the techniques, we put responsibility for quality and process improvement where it belongs—at the source.

QUALITY IMPROVEMENT—AT THE SOURCE

A. V. Feigenbaum stated in *Total Quality Control* that "the burden of proof for quality rests with the makers of the part."[1] Today, we may state that even more strongly—and make it action-oriented: The *responsibility for* quality rests with the makers of the part or providers of the service. In other words, in total quality control, today usually shortened to **total quality (TQ)**, primary responsibility for quality resides in operations.

TQ Guidelines

What should operations people *do* to carry out their primary responsibility for quality? The answer, diagrammed in Figure 15–1, is in three parts, which repeat in circular fashion:

 I. *Process control.* Build quality into the process:
   1. Design a capable and fail-safe (error-proof) process (fail-safing is sometimes called by its Japanese name, *pokayoke*), and keep all resources in perfect condition. A capable process is one that is designed or built to be able to meet specified quality levels. In machine-oriented processes, fail-safing might consist of automatic checking and adjustment devices.
   2. If the process cannot be made fail-safe, next best is self-inspection (which, of course, introduces chances of human error) and correction. For this to be effective, it is necessary to:
      a. Give each employee authority to correct a mistake on the spot (placate on angry customer), or stop production (even a whole production line) to avoid making a bad product.
      b. Make every work group responsible for correcting its own errors and defects; avoid passing problems on to a separate rework or complaint group.

---

[1]A. V. Feigenbaum, *Total Quality Control: Engineering and Management* (New York: McGraw-Hill, 1961).

FIGURE 15–1
Actions for Quality

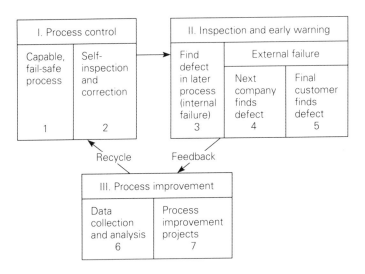

II. *Inspection and early warning.* When the process cannot be fully controlled, we're in trouble—pushed into the poor practice of *inspection* at a later process. Since delayed detection is costly and damaging, let's not compound the error by allowing long feedback delays as well. Strive for quick and specific feedback on the problem—an early warning system tapping the following error discovery points.

3. Inspection in a later process in the same organization.
4. Inspection within the next company.
5. Inspection and use by the final customer.

III. *Process improvement.* Process improvement requires collection and use of data about process problems. This requires:

6. Training supervisors and operators in how to measure quality, collect quality data, and analyze quality statistics in order to isolate causes.
7. Formally organizing operators, supervisors, and experts into process improvement projects to apply data analysis and problem-solving techniques. Projects include making deficient processes capable and fail-safe; thus we return to step I.

Time-Quality Connection

The *time* element makes a difference in the execution of each of the elements of Figure 15–1. If operations is under heavy pressure for output, quality gets slighted: there is not enough time for training, inspection, on-the-spot correction, feedback and consultation with people in earlier processes, data collection and analysis, and improvement projects.

Ensuring that there is time for quality requires intelligent *scheduling* and *pacing*. A modern viewpoint is that labor and equipment should be *underscheduled* in order to provide time for the many activities that bring about quality. While the work pace should be brisk, it should not be so hectic as to drive employees into error through haste; strive for a pace that keeps people busy but allows them to do the job right the first time.

While many firms find it necessary to provide more time for human involvement in quality, they are striving for less delay time in the flow of the work itself. This is the quick-response or just-in-time mode, which aims for delay-free movement of the work (or the customer) forward from process to process, as well as quick feedback of data about problems. The best approach is to organize employees and equipment the way the work flows so that the customer (next process) is very near or adjacent. To borrow from a page in Western Electric's classic handbook on quality control, "It is an axiom in quality control that the time to identify assignable causes is while those causes are active." Further, "Delay may mean that the cause of trouble is harder to identify, and in many cases cannot be identified at all."[2] In other words, anything that reduces delays is a powerful technique for quality control and process improvement.

PRINCIPLE: Make it easy to make/provide the goods or services without error—the first time.

Role of Quality Department

With "quality at the source," is there a need for a quality department? Usually there is, except in small firms. However, under the influence of total quality (which is thriving, even in less-developed countries) the quality assurance department's role is changing.

Humdrum inspection is down, though not out. Before quality was seen as everyone's job, inspectors bore the load. There never were enough inspectors, so the QA department also selected which processes would be inspection points. Manufactured parts might have sat around for hours or days until an inspector came along and declared them quality parts. Similarly, human clients sometimes have had to wait for an inspector—often a supervisor—to approve the service (e.g., authorize payment on a check).

Under total quality, a main and all-important job of the QA department is training, because there are so many people to train and QA staffers have the knowhow to do it. Rather than resisting the sudden change, some QA people

---

[2]*Statistical Quality Control Handbook*, 2nd ed. (Indianapolis: AT&T Technologies, 1956), p. 217.

may welcome their new role, since it includes activities that are of higher status than inspection:

- Helping to set quality specifications.
- Training everyone in quality control and improvement.
- Paving the way for implementation of ideas for quality improvement.
- Evaluating supplier quality for purposes of selecting suppliers.
- Leading quality certification audits at supplier sites.
- Auditing quality in their own company.

Usually, the QA department still needs to check on service delivery and customers' reactions to it, conduct some final product tests, and inspect incoming materials not yet certified at the source. In some cases, regulations (or policies) make it difficult to get out of the inspection mode. Nevertheless, some firms or plants have virtually eliminated inspection:

- At Kodak's copier division, the number of inspectors fell from 25 to zero.[3]
- At Kelly Air Force Base in Texas, 171 teams have been formed to focus on quality improvement. According to Rodney House, assistant to the base commander, "Inspection has always been a separate operation by certified personnel. We are now trending toward production workers' doing their own inspection and we will certify a limited number of them for it."[4]

THE PROCESS FOCUS

When inspectors looking at products give way to operators responsible for processes, it's a different world. It's a world of work populated by "operator-owners," who understand that guarding the door to keep bad products away from customers is not enough; customers want a good deal more. The set of tools operator-owners have for controlling and improving processes turns out to have positive effects on delivery, timeliness, output, aesthetics, and safety, as well as product and service quality.

The old days of trying to control and improve each of these process outcomes independently, perhaps by different sets of people, often in vain, are gone. Today, we see the need for better understanding of how closely they are linked, and how use of a few good tools of control and improvement can exert leverage

---

[3]William W. Davis, Dale P. Esse, and Donald L. Teringo, "Successfully Communicating Can Pay High Dividends," *Quality Progress*, July 1987, pp. 36–39.
[4]"When You Discover Things You Don't Like to Hear About," *Industry Week*, April 17, 1989, p. 54.

on a broad group of those outcomes. Before studying the tools, we must examine just what it is that makes up the entity called a *process* and causes processes to misperform.

Processes: Description and Performance

A **process** is a unique set of elements from the *seven Ms,* which are:

Materials (raw materials or components).

Manpower (the human factor).

Methods (product and process design and operating procedures).

Machines (tools and equipment used in the process).

Measurement (techniques and tools used to gather data on process performance).

Maintenance (the system of providing care for process variables).

Management (policy, work rules, and environment).

All of the Ms are not always apparent in a process. Some services, for example, involve little or no materials. In other cases, maintenance might blend with methods and measurement.

Furthermore, a process changes over time. If one data-entry operator replaces another, a new process is created even though all other elements remain the same. Buying materials from a different supplier, substituting one lathe for another, and switching from one optical scanner to another for measuring process output are other examples of shifting from one process to a second. Obviously the more variables that are allowed to change, the more difficult it becomes to determine their individual effects on process performance.

Special and Common Causes

Any process has some inherent variation due to *chance* or **common causes.** Other variation is due to *assignable* or **special causes,** such as an incorrect tool setting or a server not following procedures. An objective of quality control is to identify when an assignable cause exists so that the process can be fixed. This requires separating assignable causes from chance causes, because chance causes are expected. Remember, special-cause variation is assignable to a *specific* source.

That does not mean that nothing can be done about chance causes. In fact, improvement of the process aims at reducing the range of variability of chance causes. This is a key way of coping with the **variation stackup** problem: two or more parts, ingredients, or processes marginally within spec that produce a bad result when put together.

Francis and Gerwels state that W. Edwards Deming's "enormous contribution to management theory" is his recognition "that the responsibility for improvement could be assigned according to the type of variation": Those working in the system have the job of finding and eliminating special causes; those managing the system work on eliminating common causes, which are tougher to pin down and may involve spending money.[5]

The idea of segmenting responsibility in this way is powerful—and still new to many companies. Nevertheless, some firms have taken it even further: Don't limit operating people's responsibilities to special causes; in a mature employee involvement situation, operators will have ideas for dealing with common causes as well—ideas such as changing a design, a supplier, a form, or a training procedure.

George Box gives several examples, including this one: A friend mentioned that his department secretary said, "Don't ever circulate stuff through the campus mail. They take forever to get it delivered." But Box suggests that, if campus mail really is a problem, the best way to solve it may be to make up a team of the department secretary, mail sorter, and mail deliverer.[6] The team might find a special cause for the delay; on the other hand, it may want to design and recommend a new system (e.g., change the delivery routes, mailing envelopes, or address designators) that eliminates a number of common causes.

Process Example

An example, production of 3-inch-long bolts (Figure 15–2), illustrates the concept of process performance. The process is made up of ingredients from each of the seven Ms and creates bolts with several quality characteristics. A *quality characteristic* is a performance output of the process that created the product or service.

Input from the customer (next process) can indicate which quality characteristics are important enough to place under tight, formal controls. For a simple product like our machine bolt, customer-critical characteristics might be length, diameter, and thread depth. Each may be represented by a frequency distribution. The distribution in Figure 15–2 represents but one characteristic—bolt length.

The distribution of bolt lengths resembles the normal probability function, which is typical of the physical dimensions of many products. Further, the distribution will have a certain central tendency and a specific variability or dispersion. The mean and standard deviation are commonly used to denote central tendency and variation. In studying just these two numbers, we are studying the process as a whole. This is a simple, cheap, effective method of understanding the process so that it may be improved.

---

[5]A. E. Francis and John M. Gerwels, "Building a Better Budget," *Quality Progress*, October 1989, pp. 70–75.
[6]George Box, "When Murphy Speaks—Listen," *Quality Progress*, October 1989, pp. 79–84.

FIGURE 15–2

The Process Focus: Contributing Variables and Performance

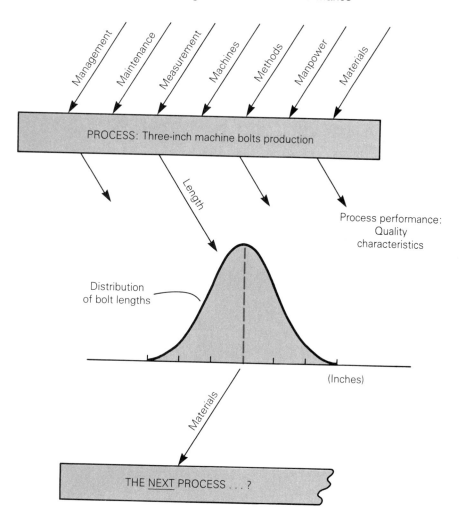

Process Control and Capability

The complex interaction of process variables that results in performance is more easily understood using two key concepts: process control and process capability. Since process control must exist before there can be meaningful process capability analysis, we consider control first.

Process Control

In our bolt example, we have been considering the characteristic *length*. The target is to produce bolts that are 3 inches long. The distribution of bolt lengths in Figure 15–2 shows, however, that not all the bolts are 3 inches long; the lengths vary. *Reduction of variation* in bolt lengths—or in any other process performance characteristic, for that matter—is a fundamental quality improvement goal.

In the case of our bolts, we may find that lengths are around 2.9 inches for an hour, around 3.1 inches for the next hour, then 2.9 inches for the following hour, and so on. Figure 15–3A shows how the length distributions might look. Suppose investigation reveals that a different method of cutting the steel bars was used every other hour, leading us to suspect cutting technique as the cause of the differences. That is a *special* cause of variation. Correction of the cutting

FIGURE 15–3
Bolt Length Process Output

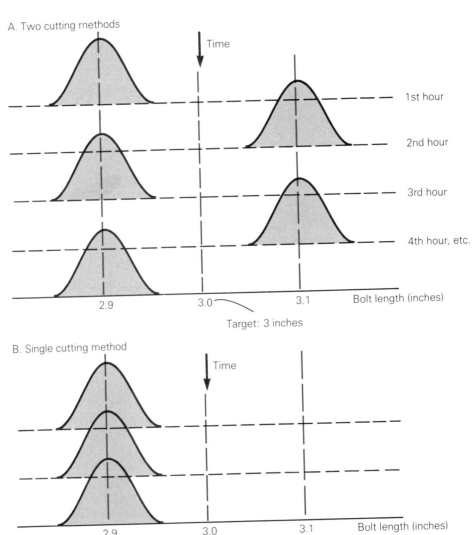

FIGURE 15–3   (concluded)

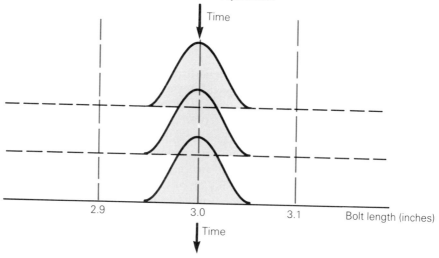

C. Single cutting method with bar-stock feed adjustment

problem—by deciding on one or the other method, for instance—could resolve the apparent difference in lengths, but will it result in better bolts? Obviously several other questions remain.

First, assume we select the cutting method that led to bolts of about 2.9 inches and use only this. Since one of the seven Ms, methods, has been changed, we have a new process. Figure 15–3B shows how the new process performance might appear. Continued measurement, say, for several hours, could convince us that we had solved the special variation problem. Bad assumption! The bolt averages are short of the target of 3 inches. Another specific, and easily correctable, cause of variation exists: increasing the feed of barstock into the cutting tool by 0.1 inch (perhaps by moving a stop block). That creates yet another new process, one that produces bolts with a length much closer to our target of 3 inches.

Figure 15–3C shows the length distribution after fixing the second special cause of variation. If no other special variation exists, the process output is operating in control. The main benefit of statistical control is predictability, for process performance will not vary over time so long as process control is maintained. The bolt length output will be (predictably), as shown in Figure 15–3C, hour after hour, day after day.

But what about "good" bolts? Up to this point we have talked about process performance, its specific and common variations, and statistical process control. Quality depends on what the customer wants the characteristic (length, in this case) to be, as well as on what the process is capable of delivering. The concept of process capability addresses the merger, or resolution, of customer expectations and process performance.

We have just done step one of a process capability study—which is to get to a state of process control. We did so by removing causes of specific variation. Since capability analysis deals only with common variation, removing specific variation is always the first step. Now let's see what process capability is all about.

Process Capability

The total common variation of a performance distribution such as those in Figure 15–3 is equal to about six standard deviations. We use the lowercase Greek letter σ (sigma) to represent one standard deviation. Let us assume that bolt length distribution has a σ value of 0.005 inches. Thus, the entire process width is approximately 6×0.005 inches, or 0.030 inches. The larger the value of σ, of course, the greater will be the process spread of 6σ. It is common to refer to 6σ as the *inherent capability* of the process, a term that makes no claim as to the **process capability**, that is, ability of the process to meet customer needs. Inherent capability refers only to the natural width, or variation, in process output.

Customer needs (and therefore producers' goals) may be stated in formal terms as *specifications*—specs, for short. A spec has two parts: a nominal value and tolerances. In our bolts, 3 inches is the nominal, or target, value. Suppose we have a tolerance of 0.020 inches on either side of 3.000 inches. The complete spec for bolt length would appear as:

$$3.000 \pm 0.020 \text{ inches}$$

Specs shouldn't just happen; rather, they should reflect customer needs. But just as the inherent process capability, 6σ, was ignorant of specifications, so are specs ignorant of process capability.

Thus, we have the merging of two traditional antagonists of quality management. First are the statistical aspects of the process, its capability and location, or its performance; they are, historically, part of the terminology of quality control statisticians. Second are the specifications, needs, or customer demands; they stem from the engineering and/or marketing functions—assuming the two can agree with each other long enough to debate the statisticians. Basically, proponents of the statistical and the customer-oriented points of view have not communicated very well. In some sectors that problem is being set to rest through use of the **process capability index, C_{pk}**. C_{pk} shows the position of the process relative to the target spec value. Thus, it merges the historical statistics and engineering/marketing views of quality management. When spoken, C_{pk} becomes "seepy kay"; it shows how much capability is "seeping" out of the process. So if you like to use memory joggers, call it the "seepy capability" index.

To compute C_{pk}, we need statistics on the historical behavior of the process, namely the mean and the standard deviation. Since the mean and standard deviation of processes are usually unknown, we must estimate them. We estimate the mean by drawing a series of samples from the process and measuring the individual values of the quality characteristic of interest (in our example, length). For each sample, we compute a sample average and range. The average of all the sample averages, or the grand average, goes by the symbol $\bar{\bar{X}}$. The average of the sample ranges is $\bar{R}$.

We use $\overline{\overline{X}}$ as an estimate for the true process mean. We use $\overline{R}$ in a procedure for estimating the true value of the process standard deviation, σ, assuming that the process performance is approximately normally distributed. The procedure is:

$$\hat{\sigma} = \overline{R}/d_2 \qquad\qquad (15\text{--}1)$$

where

$\hat{\sigma}$ = Estimate for σ

d_2 = Conversion factor, found in quality control tables (explained in Example 15–2); it is a function of the sample size

The formula for C_{pk} is:

$$C_{pk} = \frac{Z_{min}}{3} \qquad\qquad (15\text{--}2)$$

where Z_{min} is the smaller of

$$\frac{(\text{Upper spec limit} - \overline{\overline{X}})}{\hat{\sigma}} \qquad \text{or} \qquad \frac{(\overline{\overline{X}} - \text{Lower spec limit})}{\hat{\sigma}}$$

Consider what the index might reveal: Z_{min} and C_{pk} *could* be negative. That happens when $\overline{\overline{X}}$ is above the upper spec limit or below the lower one, which means the process average isn't even inside the spec limits. Something *must* be done to fix the process, get $\overline{\overline{X}}$ "between the goal posts," and make C_{pk} positive— and the larger the better:

- If C_{pk} just equals 1.0, the process just (barely) meets specs.
- If C_{pk} is less than 1.0 (but positive), only part of the process output is meeting specs; again, some process fixing is needed.

Some companies require their suppliers to show C_{pk} values of at least 1.33 (an arbitrary but popular indicator of "okay" performance). There are ways to push the index up to 1.33 and higher. One is to improve $\overline{\overline{X}}$—get the process average closer to the target spec (it could be off-center simply because a scale or gauge is not calibrated correctly). The second is to improve $\hat{\sigma}$; in other words, decrease the process variation. That might require spending some money, say, to replace bearings or control air-borne particulates. The third is to widen the spec limits ("goal posts"), which is clearly ridiculous. Continual improvement— ever better service to the customer—requires *narrowing* spec limits periodically, not widening them.

Quality Goals and Continual Improvement

The statement that a *goal* is continual improvement at first appears to be a contradiction. What about getting a process in control and then capable? What about satisfying the customer? What if we achieve all those objectives and are then able to maintain this performance? Isn't that enough? Haven't we met the goals if we work hard to correct a process? Doesn't continuing improvement seem to be the sort of thing that people with no goals would preach? In short, doesn't the old proverb "If it ain't broke, don't fix it!" apply?

These are questions that have popped up in many an organization when somebody suggests a goal of continual improvement. Many quality professionals, engineers, sales reps, and others can attest to the historical difficulty of *meeting* specifications, let alone trying to improve. Unfortunately, relaxed tolerances, slipshod measurements, and other failures are all too common. Customers are fed up. If your company can't produce quality, another will. Quality is a competitive weapon.

If the goal is continual improvement, does it make sense to set spec limits? It does. Quality specs help in process comprehension. Suppliers and consumers must know how the spec was set, its relation to process output, where in the process it is assured or controlled, and when it might be reviewed or tightened. Specs also serve as milestones of performance—platforms upon which to launch improvement efforts. Success in meeting a spec also is evidence of ability to improve. In behavioral psychology terms, meeting a spec is a reward, and a motivator too. It's a motivator, that is, if continual improvement—continual reduction of variability around the process target—is clearly the goal.

With that goal, the motivated operator or team needs techniques. We examine a few of the very good ones in the next sections.

PROCESS IMPROVEMENT CYCLE

Improving a product or service means going through successive cycles of measuring, controlling for consistency, and improving the process. These cycles should never end, but the amount of measurement may decrease over time and the measurement procedure should become simpler. The whole process should improve. This can mean fewer complaints and returns, less scrap, less labor content, fewer equipment failures, better tooling, and, of course, better quality of the item or service itself.

Process improvement is a matter of attacking variation in process output. The many variabilities in processes can be reduced to just three classes. One is item-to-item or customer-to-customer variability: A dimension differs slightly from one item to the next; one customer differs from the next. The second is variation of a characteristic within a piece or a human customer: variation of diameter along the length of a bolt; right and left shoe sizes not the same. The third is variation occurring over time: As a tool wears from usage, a machine's dimension may become greater; a provider of human services is full of smiles and cheer in the morning and a tired, stressed-out grouch late in the day.

Variables and Attributes

Each of these classes of variation may be measured or simply judged as to presence or absence. To see the difference, consider the excess plastic, called "flash," that must be trimmed off plastic parts coming out of an injection-molding machine. Process improvement might begin with collecting and weighing the flash for every piece, which is known as **variables inspection**.

Another kind of variation review, **attribute inspection**, is simpler. It doesn't require a measurement, just a yes-or-no, go-or-no-go, judgment. The battery tester with a red zone and a green zone provides an attribute check. We do not care to measure the voltage. Similarly, we test a night light by putting it into a socket and flipping the switch. It either lights or it doesn't; we are not taking a reading of footcandles. A table setting in a fancy restaurant may be checked by the headwaiter. If one fork or glass is out of place, the headwaiter judges the table setting to be defective. Diameters of ball bearings could be checked by rolling them across a hole-filled surface. Those that fall through are too small; no one needs to measure their diameters.

Attribute inspection is not powerful, since a yes-no judgment yields little information about the process. In contrast, measurement of a variable tells us *how* good the process is. Although variables inspection is usually better, attribute inspection has the advantage of being easy to do and has its place as a process control technique.

Variables Inspection: An Example

Let's return to the example of measuring flash scraped off plastic parts. If the weight of flash per piece trends up or down, or there are a few pieces with a great amount of flash (or none at all), that shows inconsistency. The injection-molding process is out of control.

Bringing it under control means searching for a special cause. Perhaps the machine is experiencing heat buildup, which might explain an increasing amount of flash. Perhaps the hopper gets low on raw materials now and then, which might explain an extreme value. Or maybe the person running the machine has a bad habit, like adjusting the timer once in awhile instead of leaving it alone; that could also explain an extreme value.

Whatever the special cause, the object is to find and eliminate it; then verify the finding and correction by weighing more pieces. When consistency has been attained, there will still be piece-to-piece variation arising from common causes. Once the process is in control, we may want to cut back on the number of pieces checked. Perhaps weighing flash for a sample of five pieces every hour will be enough to see if the process is staying in control.

Upgrading the Process

While a process is in control, it's time to think about improving it. Note that *control* refers to process consistency, not quality. Improving the quality of the process requires a good idea and a management decision to carry it out. For our injection molding example, some possibilities for reducing flash are to improve the mold, install a more precise device to measure out raw material, or buy a better grade of raw plastic pellets. Or maybe it's the operator: one who is consistent all right, but consistently poor as a molding machine operator, even after being fully trained. The answer may be to transfer that person to another job and bring in someone else to run the molding machine.

Regardless of which improvement is made, the process has to be rechecked—every piece weighed for awhile—to ensure consistency. In fact, maybe the inspection itself can be improved; perhaps the weighing could be automatic, which saves money on human inspection, avoids human inspector error, and makes 100 percent inspection (every piece) possible for the long run. Automated 100 percent inspection can be a powerful quality control tool—one that in some companies has been instrumental in producing strings of defect-free end products numbering into the hundreds of thousands and even millions.

Repeat the cycle, and keep repeating it. We strive to eliminate every source of variation. We can never quite achieve perfection. But we keep trying.

What Was Improved?

In improving the injection-molding process, was product quality improved? No. We did not mention the plastic part being made or its specifications; it was the flash, or waste, that was the center of attention. Cutting the flash lowered the product cost by reducing material wasted. Labor per unit to check for and trim off flash may have been reduced too. Perhaps product quality improved as a byproduct of reducing the amount of flash. For example, if heat buildup was avoided as a way to reduce flash, the plastic piece may also have ended up with a smoother finish or more uniform dimensions. The point is that the technique is for controlling and improving the *process.*

Now we change the example a bit to make quality of the product the foremost concern.

CONFORMANCE TO SPECIFICATIONS

Assume the specifications for the injection-molded part call for an outer diameter of 5.0, plus or minus 0.05, centimeters. The 5.0 cm. is the target dimension, and the plus or minus 0.05 cm. is the tolerance. What kind of quality control technique should be used? The answer is to do just about what was described for controlling and reducing flash. This time we examine the use of the run diagram and process control chart. The following sections demonstrate several phases of process measurement and improvement.

Run Diagram

Example 15–1 shows the use of the **run diagram,** which is just a running plot of measurements, piece-by-piece, as the process continues.

EXAMPLE 15–1   RUN DIAGRAM—INJECTION-MOLDED PARTS

Specifications: Outer diameter $= 5.00 \pm 0.05$ cm.

Quality control objective: Continually improve quality and productivity and continually reduce fraction of injection-molded parts that do not meet the specifications, that is, do not stay within the tolerances (plus or minus 0.05 cm.). Pursuit of the objective takes us through a six-phase cycle of improvement and then repeats.

Phase 1: Operator measures every piece; plots results on a run diagram. Figure 15–4 shows outer diameters of 30 pieces plotted on the run diagram. Pieces 7 and 23 look way out of line, and there is also a trend downward. The process is out of control—inconsistent.

Phase 2: Operator and supervisor look for special causes; correct them (may need to call maintenance, engineering, etc., for help). The operator *knows* why the diameters are decreasing: heat buildup (same thing mentioned earlier as possible causes of excess flash). Maintenance is called in to work on the thermostat. The supervisor suspects the cause of bad pieces 7 and 23: impurities in the raw material. The solution is to put a sheet of clear plastic over the containers of plastic pellets so that passersby will not think the open box is a trash receptacle.

Phase 3: New run diagram. Figure 15–5 shows 30 more measures. They look consistent, so there is no longer any need to measure every piece. Most of the diameters are greater than 5.0 cm., the specification, but that is not yet the concern.

(Phases 4 through 6 are discussed in Example 15-2.)

FIGURE 15–4

Run Diagram—Outer Diameters of 30 Pieces

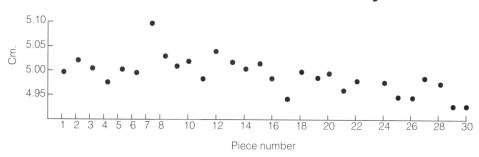

Piece number

FIGURE 15–5

Run Diagram—Outer Diameters of 30 More Pieces

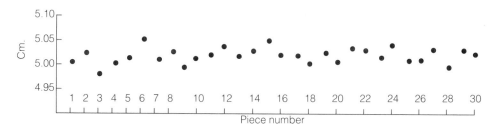

Piece number

$\overline{X}$ and R Charts

Example 15–2 continues Example 15–1 and takes us through use of two types of **process control charts**. The first, the $\overline{X}$ chart, contains the means of small sample measurements; the means are plotted as the process goes on. Its companion, the **R chart**, is a plot of the ranges within each of the same samples.

EXAMPLE 15–2 $\overline{X}$ AND R CHARTS—INJECTION-MOLDED PARTS

Phase 4: Use sampling and control charts. Figure 15–6 gives mean diameters and ranges for 20 samples. The sample size is four pieces, and a sample is drawn and plotted hourly. The means tell whether the diameters are abnormally high or low. The ranges tell whether the consistency is still OK. Note: The range is simply the highest minus the lowest of the four measures in a sample. (Standard deviation is a better measure of consistency, but it takes more calculations. The range has been used instead in process control charting, because it is simple and quick.)

Now some calculations are necessary in order to create control charts. Results of some

FIGURE 15–6
Measurements for Designing $\overline{X}$ and R Charts

Sample Number	Date	Measurements (cm.) x_1	x_2	x_3	x_4	Mean $(\overline{X})$	Range (R)
1	10/10	5.01	5.00	5.03	5.06	5.025	0.06
2		4.99	5.03	5.03	5.05	5.025	0.06
3		5.03	5.04	4.99	4.94	5.000	0.10
4		5.05	5.03	5.00	5.01	5.022	0.05
5		4.97	5.04	4.96	5.00	4.992	0.08
6		4.97	5.00	4.99	5.02	4.995	0.05
7		5.06	5.00	5.02	4.96	5.010	0.10
8		5.03	4.98	5.01	4.95	4.992	0.08
9	10/11	5.05	5.03	5.05	4.98	5.028	0.07
10		4.99	5.03	5.01	4.96	4.998	0.07
11		4.98	5.05	5.05	4.94	5.005	0.11
12		4.95	5.04	4.99	4.99	4.992	0.09
13		5.00	5.05	5.01	4.97	5.008	0.08
14		4.96	5.03	5.05	5.00	5.010	0.09
15		5.08	5.01	5.02	4.96	5.018	0.12
16		5.02	4.98	5.04	4.95	4.998	0.09
17	10/12	5.02	4.99	4.99	5.04	5.010	0.05
18		4.99	5.00	5.05	5.05	5.022	0.06
19		5.03	5.02	5.01	4.96	5.005	0.07
20		5.02	5.04	5.04	5.04	5.040	0.02
Totals						100.195	1.50

of the calculations are given in Figure 15–6. The mean, $\overline{X}$, is the simple average of the four units in the sample. Thus, for sample 1,

$$\overline{X}_1 = \frac{\Sigma x}{n} = \frac{5.06 + 5.00 + 5.03 + 5.01}{4} = 5.025$$

The range, R, is the largest minus the smallest of the four units in each sample. For sample 1, the largest is 5.06 and the smallest is 5.00. Thus,

$$R_1 = 5.06 - 5.00 = 0.06$$

We also need to know $\overline{R}$, the average (mean) range of the 20 sample ranges. Finally, we must compute the *grand average*, $\overline{X}$, which is the average of the 20 sample averages. The values $\overline{X}$ and $\overline{R}$ become the center lines on a control chart for averages and another for ranges. The calculations follow:

$$\overline{\overline{X}} = \frac{\Sigma \overline{X}}{k} = \frac{100.195}{20} = 5.010 \text{ cm.}$$

$$\overline{R} = \frac{\Sigma R}{k} = \frac{1.50}{20} = 0.075 \text{ cm.}$$

where k is the number of samples or subgroups (in this case, 20).

The next step is calculating control limits. The *central limit theorem*, usually covered in statistics studies, applies. Since we plot sample averages rather than individual piece measurements, we are actually dealing with a distribution of sample averages. The standard deviation of this distribution of sample averages, or simply *standard error*, depends on the size of the samples. We compute the standard error as:

$$\sigma_{\overline{x}} = \frac{\sigma}{\sqrt{n}}$$

The central limit theorem also tells us that (for our purposes) the distribution of sample averages will be approximately normal regardless of the population from which the samples were taken. Thus, a plot of all possible sample averages should approach the familiar bell shape of the normal curve. Further, we know that approximately 99.72 percent of all sample averages should fall within three standard errors of the mean of the distribution of sample averages—that is, *if* our process is within a state of statistical control.

Process control limits are typically—but not always—set at three standard errors above and below the center line. Although a bit of a misnomer, these are commonly referred to as *three-sigma limits*. In practice, however, the standard error is not calculated; approximations are used to obtain control limits. The most frequently used factors for $\overline{X}$ and R charts are shown in Table 15–1. The table is derived from the basic mathematics of the normal distribution and the distribution of ranges.[7]

Control limits for the chart for sample averages (the $\overline{X}$ chart) are:

$$\text{Upper control limit (UCL}_{\overline{x}}) = \overline{\overline{X}} + (A_2)(\overline{R})$$

$$\text{Lower control limit (LCL}_{\overline{x}}) = \overline{\overline{X}} - (A_2)(\overline{R})$$

---

[7]The tables are based on an assumed normal distribution.

TABLE 15–1
Process Control Chart Factors

Sample (or Subgroup) Size (n)	Control Limit Factor for Averages ($\overline{X}$ Charts) (A_2)	UCL Factor for Ranges (R Charts) (D_4)	LCL Factor for Ranges (R Charts) (D_3)	Factor for Estimating Process Sigma ($\hat{\sigma} = \overline{R}/d_2$) ($d_2$)
2	1.880	3.267	0	1.128
3	1.023	2.575	0	1.693
4	0.729	2.282	0	2.059
5	0.577	2.115	0	2.326
6	0.483	2.004	0	2.534
7	0.419	1.924	0.076	2.704
8	0.373	1.864	0.136	2.847
9	0.337	1.816	0.184	2.970
10	0.308	1.777	0.223	3.078

Earlier we determined that $\overline{\overline{X}} = 5.010$ and $\overline{R} = 0.075$. Thus, the control limits are:

$$\text{UCL}_{\overline{x}} = 5.010 + (0.729)(0.075) = 5.010 + 0.055 = 5.065$$

$$\text{LCL}_{\overline{x}} = 5.010 - (0.729)(0.075) = 5.010 - 0.055 = 4.955$$

For the R chart, we use $\overline{R}$ as the center line. The three-sigma limits are determined with the D_4 and D_3 factors from Table 15–1, using sample size $n = 4$:

$$\text{UCL}_R = (D_4)(\overline{R}) = (2.282)(0.075) = 0.171$$

$$\text{LCL}_R = (D_3)(\overline{R}) = (0)(0.075) = 0$$

The control chart limits have nothing to do with specification (tolerance) limits, which *should not be drawn on control charts.* Remember: Control charts are for averages and ranges *of a multipiece sample.* Specification limits, on the other hand, apply to one-at-a-time (piece-by-piece) measures.

The initial test for statistical process control is to look for sample plots outside the control limits. Such a plot suggests a process out of (statistical) control—that is, inconsistent. In such cases, we again search for a special cause, remove it, and resume sampling to build new control charts.

Now draw the $\overline{X}$ and R charts (see Figure 15–7), and plot the 20 samples on the charts. Since all points are within the control limits on both charts, the process appears to be in control; that is, the charts tell us what the consistency of the process is: "The control chart is the process talking to us."[8]

Phase 5: Cease sampling. If control charts continue to show that the process is in control, there may be no need to keep it up. However, measurement and plotting on control charts should still be done on an audit basis occasionally in order to ensure that the process does not stray out of control. There are exceptions, of course. If defectives absolutely cannot be tolerated—such as checking radiation levels in containers of materials coming out of a nuclear power plant—inspection must continue. But in that case, quality

---

[8]I. W. Burr, *Engineering Statistics and Quality Control* (New York: McGraw-Hill, 1953).

FIGURE 15-7

$\overline{X}$ and R Charts, Including Plotted Data

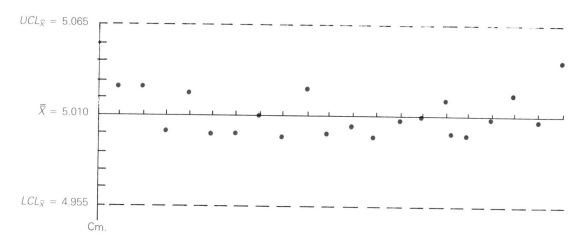

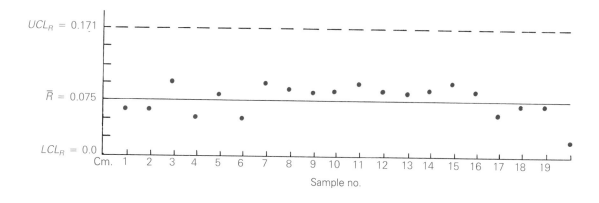

control probably would never be relaxed to sampling; instead, measuring 100 percent of items—perhaps automatically—and plotting on run diagrams would remain in force.

Phase 6: Improve the process. This is *not* the same as removing a special cause of inconsistent quality (e.g., defective thermostat or raw material contamination). It is a wholesale improvement, usually requiring an improved grade of raw material, mold, fixtures, tools, or equipment—or, possibly, a design change.

Finally, the issue of meeting design specifications arises. Figure 15–8 charts all 80 x values from Figure 15–6. The first, 5.01 cm., exceeds the 5.00-cm. specification target, but it is within the +0.05-cm. tolerance range. A total of 75 of the 80 xs are inside and five (circles) are outside the spec limits: In sample 1, x_4 is 0.01 cm. too large; in sample 3, x_4 is 0.01 cm. too small; in sample 7, x_1 is too large; in sample 11, x_4 is too large; and in sample 15, x_1 is too large. Five out of 80 off-spec parts is a defective rate of 6.25 percent, which seems poor. Perhaps management will choose to place a high priority on improving the process.

What if the process is improved to the point where *no* parts are off-spec? That is

FIGURE 15–8

Injection-Molded Parts, 80 Individual Diameters

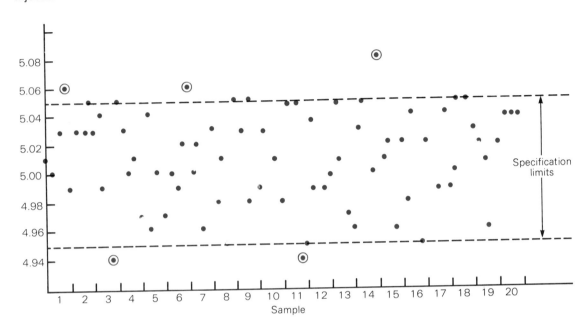

theoretically impossible; some fraction, however small, will be off-spec if the process continues long enough. But the question doesn't matter anyway. Continual improvement calls for getting within spec and then going further by reducing the range of variability of the process itself. At issue is the urgency of making the next improvement; it depends on the present percent off-spec and on defect rates as compared with competitors'.

Each process improvement calls for a new round of run diagrams and control charts, because the improvement may introduce some new inconsistency. A special cause of the inconsistency must be rooted out before the next round of process improvement.

Overview of Process Control and Improvement

The control and improvement phases we have just gone through may now be summarized, with comments about their purposes. The phases are:

1. Operator measures every piece and plots results on a run diagram. The purpose is to see if the process is in control, that is, is consistent.

2. Operator and supervisor look for special causes of inconsistency and correct them. The purpose is not to control the *level* of quality but to make sure the quality is steady with only common variation from common causes.

3. Repeat phase 1 to see that the change has truly erased the inconsistency.

4. Relax the frequency of measurement. Take small samples (such as 4, 5, or 6 pieces), and average the results. Plot on $\overline{X}$ and R charts. The $\overline{X}$ chart plots the mean level of quality. The R chart plots the range of variability within a sample, which is the consistency check. As long as no points are plotted above upper or below lower control limit on both charts, the process is presumed to be in control. Determine capability.

5. Cease sampling, but reintroduce it periodically to see that the process has not strayed out of control.

6. Improve the process, first to achieve lower defect (off-spec) rates and second to decrease the range of process variability. An improvement may require approval of funds for better resources or designs. Management will be more eager to spend the money if customers are complaining. Once the process has been improved, repeat the above phases.

Behind this six-phase procedure is what Juran calls "the precious habit of improvement." Get the process consistent, then improve it; get it consistent, then improve it; and so forth. Keep it up for the life of the process.

The reader might wonder why it is necessary to bring the process under control before improving it. One reason is that special causes are severe, and it is urgent to correct them. A second reason is that trying out new ideas for improving the process—new chemical formulations, new fixtures, new source of raw materials—may yield phony results if special causes are still present. For example, using a higher grade of plastic bead to reduce flash may not work if the thermostat on the injection-molding machine is defective. The flash may actually worsen and make it seem like the new raw materials are the cause.

Thus, process control is the first order of business. William E. Conway, a quality consultant and trainer, notes that "Engineers and chemists then become innovative, creative toward improvement, once they see that the process is in statistical control. They sense that further improvement is up to them."[9]

PROCESS CONTROL FOR ATTRIBUTES

Attribute process control operates a bit differently from variables measurement. For one thing, there cannot be a piece-by-piece run diagram in attribute inspection, because the fraction or percent defective out of a sample is the logical unit of analysis. That is, collect a few, check them, and plot the fraction defective; collect a few more, check, plot; and so forth. Plotted points go on a chart with

---

[9]Cited in W. Edwards Deming, *Quality, Productivity, and Competitive Position* (Cambridge, Mass.: MIT, Center for Advanced Engineering Study, 1982), p. 121.

an upper control limit and a lower control limit. The chart is called a *p* **chart**, for percent defective, or a *c* **chart**, for number of defects per unit.

The *p* Chart

Despite its weaknesses, attribute process control has its uses, as is shown in Example 15–3 using the *p* chart method.

EXAMPLE 15–3   **ATTRIBUTE INSPECTION—LIGHT BULBS**

Manufacture of a light bulb entails many operations and hundreds of process variables that could be inspected for. For example, measure the width of filament-wire samples, or test the strength of glass bulbs by applying measured degrees of force to the glass. But a likely final test of samples of completed bulbs is a simple attribute inspection: Apply current, and reject those that do not light—or are cracked or improperly mounted.

Phase 1: In control charting for attributes, the first step is to develop *p* charts. First, choose the sample size, number, and frequency. Frequent sampling—every half hour or hour in some cases—provides better process control than infrequent sampling. Attribute sample size is usually somewhere between 50 and a few hundred.

In this case, the sample size, *n*, is 200 light bulbs; samples are taken once a day for 20 days ($k = 20$). Figure 15–9 summarizes the collected data.

Phase 2: Now the *p* chart calculations are made. Like the $\overline{X}$ and *R* charts, the *p* chart has control limits $\pm 3\sigma$ from the center line. The *p* chart is based on the binomial statistical distribution (instead of the normal distribution). *Binomial* means two numbers, which is fitting since an attribute can have only two degrees of quality: good or defective. The formula for σ in the binomial distribution is:

$$\sigma = \sqrt{\frac{\overline{p}(1 - \overline{p})}{n}}$$

where

$\overline{p}$ = Average (mean) fraction defective (or percent defective)

n = Number in each sample

Therefore, the control limits, at 3σ from the center line, $\overline{p}$, are:

$$\text{UCL} = \overline{p} + 3\sqrt{\frac{\overline{p}(1 - \overline{p})}{n}}$$

$$\text{LCL} = \overline{p} - 3\sqrt{\frac{\overline{p}(1 - \overline{p})}{n}}$$

The average fraction defective, $\overline{p}$, is total defectives divided by total items inspected, where total items inspected equals number of samples, *k*, times sample size, *n*:

$$\overline{p} = \frac{\text{Total defectives found}}{kn}$$

FIGURE 15–9

Attribute Inspection Data for Designing a *p* Chart

Sample Number	Number of Defective Lights	Fraction Defective
1	4	0.020
2	1	0.005
3	6	0.030
4	3	0.015
5	8	0.040
6	10	0.050
7	7	0.035
8	3	0.015
9	2	0.010
10	2	0.010
11	6	0.030
12	12	0.060
13	7	0.035
14	9	0.045
15	9	0.045
16	6	0.030
17	2	0.010
18	4	0.020
19	5	0.025
20	1	0.005
Total	107	

An alternative form of the formula is:

$$\bar{p} = \frac{\text{Total percent defective}}{k}$$

Since 107 defectives were found (from Figure 15–9),

$$\bar{p} = \frac{107}{(20)(200)} = 0.027$$

The control limits are:

$$\text{UCL} = \bar{p} + 3\sqrt{\frac{\bar{p}(1 - \bar{p})}{n}}$$

$$= 0.027 + 3\sqrt{\frac{(0.027)(1 - 0.027)}{200}}$$

$$= 0.027 + 0.034 = 0.061$$

$$\text{LCL} = 0.027 - 0.034 = -0.007 \text{ or } 0.0$$

(The control limit may not be negative.)

Figure 15–10 shows the resulting *p* chart. As is proper, the data used in its construction are plotted back on the chart. All points are within the control limits. If there were a

FIGURE 15–10

Trial and Final p Chart for Attribute Inspection

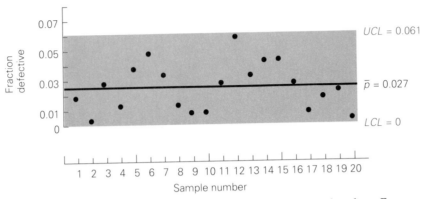

point out of control, a search for a special cause would be undertaken. For example, the machine that bonds the base to the globe may be set to apply too little of the bonding agent. Changing the machine settings may clear up the problem.

Sometimes the special cause is found in an earlier process. For example, the metal base may be bent out of shape in handling. More care in handling could make the process consistent.

Phase 3: Cease sampling. There probably is no need to continue sampling, since the process is in control. But inspection should resume on an audit basis from time to time to ensure that the process does not stray away from control.

Phase 4: Improve the process. This usually requires a management decision to spend money for a better raw material, an equipment improvement, or some other process upgrade.

Phase 5: Repeat.

The c Chart

A single control chart, the c chart, is used in statistical process control when inspection consists of counting the number of defects found on a surface area or unit. There are far fewer uses for c charts than for $\overline{X}$, R, or p charts. The best applications of c charts seem to be in producing sheets of a basic product: glass, film, steel, plastics, paper, and fabric. Some products in a more finished state may also be suitable for c charts: a keg of nails, an aircraft wing, or a ship's hull. Scratches, bubbles, and breaks per sheet, per surface, or per 10 lineal yards are examples of ways of counting defects in such products.

The basis for the c chart is the Poisson statistical distribution rather than normal or binomial. In Poisson, the formula for standard deviation, σ, is very simple:

$$\sigma = \sqrt{c}$$

where $\bar{c}$ = average (mean) number of defects per surface area. Thus, the control limits at 3σ are:

$$\text{UCL} = \bar{c} + 3\sqrt{\bar{c}}$$

$$\text{LCL} = \bar{c} - 3\sqrt{\bar{c}}$$

The center line, $\bar{c}$, is the sum of the defects found on the sampled surface areas (or units) divided by the number of samples, k (k should be at least 25):

$$\bar{c} = \frac{\Sigma c}{k}$$

Design, inspection, correction for consistency, and process improvement with use of c charts follow the same general steps as for p charts.

LOW-VOLUME PROCESS CONTROL AND IMPROVEMENT

The process improvement cycle that we have just examined can become an ingrained routine in higher-volume operations. Low-volume operations, such as a pure job shop or a human services provider, are more complicated. While the improvement cycle generally applies, as well as variations of process control charting, assuring quality in the low-volume case is more prevention than cure:

1. Run diagrams and conventional control charts are important for the *suppliers* of raw materials, parts, tools, and equipment. The purchasing department should try to select suppliers of goods and services who are willing to certify "quality at the source" and demonstrate that they use TQ techniques.

2. A high level of training and equipment, tool, and die maintenance is important to prevent errors caused by human lapses or mechanical defects.

3. Tradespeople in a job shop should be treated as craftspeople who naturally take pride in good workmanship; similarly, service employees should be recognized for efforts to treat clients with kindness, respect, and care. In both cases, good results come from following accepted procedures (there is even a right and a wrong way to pound a nail). Use of gauges and other measurement devices and of performance standards are often part of the craftsperson's or service employee's training.

4. In small-lot manufacturing, controlling a process often centers around the operator doing a *first-piece inspection* using a proper gauge. If the piece is not within tolerances, adjust the machine. Then do another first-piece inspection. When the process succeeds in making a good piece, inspection may cease until the *last piece*. Gauge the last one and, if it is good, presume that the process did not stray off course,

Improvement team at Atlanta's West Paces Ferry Hospital discusses a Pareto chart. Hospital Corporation of America, the parent company, is overseeing development of quality improvement teams in each of its hospitals.

The same Pareto chart just being drawn, as well as a preliminary fishbone chart.

for example, the tool did not lose its sharp edge. A widespread but less effective practice is to do the first-piece inspection but skip the last-piece inspection.

For some firms, checking first and last pieces from a small or medium-size run is not enough. The **precontrol chart** is an attractive alternative; it requires only a bit more checking and is simple to use.

The precontrol chart is bounded by an upper specification limit (USL) and a lower specification limit (LSL). (Note: Spec limits, unlike control limits, are *not* statistical controls.) Within the USL and LSL are lines setting off three zones: Two outer red zones each include about 2 percent of the total space, two yellow zones account for 23 percent each, and an innermost green zone takes in the remaining 50 percent. After machine setup and production startup, plotting on the chart begins. The operator measures each piece and plots each measurement on the chart until five consecutive pieces are in the central green zone. Then, at random times during production, the operator measures and plots two pieces. The rules are:

1. It is safe to continue producing if both plot in the green or one is green and one yellow.

2. Stop, adjust the process, and start over (continuous measurement until five straight are in the green) if both are yellow or either is red.

This is called *precontrol* because it only concerns meeting spec, the first quality goal. Precontrol can and should be embedded in an improvement cycle; its aim is not to play games with the specification limits but rather to improve designs of processes and products, materials, training, coordination, and other factors affecting quality. In cases where precontrol is in use in high-volume production, it may be wise to switch over to conventional process control charts.

For very low volumes (too low even for precontrol), special versions of control charts are available and growing in use. They plot measures for different parts on the same chart and still retain the ability to assess statistical control. Most versions use *deviation* from a target spec value as the measure to be plotted.[10]

In businesses that make use of flexible automation, the craftsperson becomes more of a machine programmer than an operator. Similarly, some service employees spend more time monitoring and entering data into service machines (such as automatic bank tellers and vending machines) than with clients. With less chance for checking identical pieces or getting immediate client feedback, the TQ concept of controlling the process becomes even more vital. Product and service designers, equipment designers and makers, machine maintainers, and raw material buyers will then have nearly all of the job of making sure that the process is capable of making good products.

---

[10]An excellent source is Davis R. Bothe, "SPC for Short Production Runs," prepared for the U.S. Army Armament Munitions and Chemical Command by the International Quality Institute, Inc., Northville, Mich., 1988.

FROM COARSE TO FINE PROCESS ANALYSIS

Run diagrams and process control charts are fine-grained tools for process improvement. They are used to control just one characteristic of the process—that is, one characteristic per chart. Which one is worthy of that special treatment? A good deal of coarse analysis and sifting of data is needed to find out. The coarse-grained analysis tools include the *process flowchart, Pareto analysis,* and *fishbone charts.* In this section, we examine the use of those tools in showing where to use run diagrams and control charts and, sometimes, still another tool, the *scatter diagram.*

All those tools, except for the run diagram, were labeled as "elemental statistical method" by Ishikawa (see discussion in Chapter 4). The term elemental means *for use by line operations people.* Statisticians in a quality department may turn their attention to the intermediate and advanced statistical methods listed by Ishikawa.

Process Analysis Sequence

The **process flowchart** comes first in a process improvement project. It identifies the operations in a production process and their sequence. Pareto analysis, used to identify which operations are major and which minor, is second. The third step is the fishbone chart, which keys in on a major factor needing improvement; the fishbone chart identifies subfactors and sub-subfactors. Fourth are run diagrams and control charts, which provide data on out-of-control factors. Fifth and last is the scatter diagram, which is used to check potential causes of error in processes in which error causes are not obvious. While other steps or techniques could be used in a process improvement, these five are a solid core group, which are collectively referred to as **statistical process control (SPC).**

Usually an initial round of coarse Pareto and fishbone analysis is followed by one or more rounds of finer-grained Pareto and fishbone charting. The analysis is fine enough when a problem's solution reveals itself or the problem has been defined well enough to gather useful data to plot on run diagrams, control charts, or scatter diagrams. In some cases, only two or three of the five steps are necessary. In tougher cases, the full five-step sequence, with recycling of Pareto-fishbone, is needed (additional tools are beyond the scope of this book). The sequence is summarized as follows:

1. Process flowchart.
2. Pareto analysis. ◀┐ (Recycle)
3. Fishbone chart. ──┘
4. Run diagrams and control charts.
5. Scatter diagram.

While steps 4 and 5 are especially suited for products with physically measurable quality characteristics, steps 1, 2, and 3 are for anybody in any line of work. A smattering of banks, insurance companies, and governmental offices began training their employees in use of them in the late 1980s. Step 4 has already been discussed, and we will save step 1, the process flowchart, for discussion in Chapter 16 as a methods study technique. Steps 2, 3, and 5 come next.

Pareto Analysis

Pareto analysis helps separate the important few from the trivial many. (ABC analysis, discussed earlier as an inventory management technique, is one type of Pareto analysis.) Pareto analysis, as used in process improvement, goes like this:

1. Identify the factors affecting process variability or product quality.
2. Keep track of how often a measurable defect or nonconformity is related to each factor.
3. Plot the results on a bar chart, where length of a bar stands for (or is proportional to) the number of times the causal factor occurs. More serious causes (longest bars) are positioned to the left of less serious ones.

Figure 15–11 is a sample **Pareto chart** for a certain product being supplied to an important customer. The process flow (which could be shown on a process flowchart) is from raw materials, to fabrication of component parts, to subassemblies, to final assembly, to delivery. The Pareto chart shows that by far the greatest number of critical errors—about 85 percent—are made in delivering the finished product to the customer and in raw materials. The process improvers will want to focus their efforts on those two factors and save the other three for a later round of improvement. (Note: This Pareto analysis is simplified for illustrative purposes. Usually there are more than five sources of problems on the chart.)

Fishbone Chart

The **fishbone chart** is so named because it looks like the skeleton of a fish. (It is also called an *Ishikawa diagram,* after its developer, Kaoru Ishikawa, or *cause-and-effect diagram.*) The central spine represents an important process or quality characteristic. Primary bones connecting to the spine are main contributors, and secondary bones are secondary contributors.

Figure 15–12 shows a fishbone chart for a quality-of-service characteristic: on-time truck deliveries of goods in the right amount, which is the spine. That characteristic was identified in the earlier Pareto analysis as a trouble spot. Four main contributors are shown: trucking, packing, shipping documents, and con-

FIGURE 15–11
Pareto Chart—Occurrences of Errors in Providing a Product to a Customer

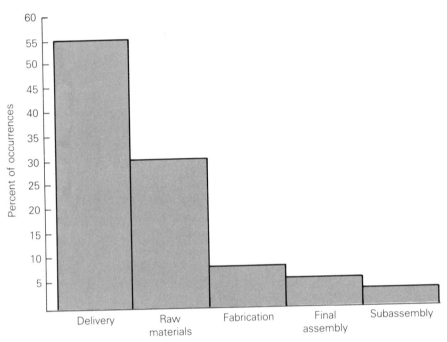

tainer labeling. Each main cause is influenced by secondary causes. For example, trucking quality is influenced by four secondary factors, each shown as small bones: latest traffic and road conditions, truck maintenance, leave at right time, and driver knows route.

Generally the chart is produced by the people who know the process: trucker, packer, material handler, material controller, supervisor. The group may then post the chart in the shipping area and begin thinking about or working on controlling and improving each process factor.

The group examines each end point on the fishbone chart. Have any solutions to problems been revealed in the detail on the end points in Figure 15–12? It seems not. Further rounds of Pareto-fishbone are needed for some end points; run diagrams or process control charts may be suitable for others.

For example, the end points "leave at right time" and "quantity in container" are easy to measure numerically. Sample measures of each could be plotted on $\overline{X}$ and R charts. A word of caution: Controlling the problem—e.g., using control charts—is for when you can't *solve* the problem. Consider, for example, the sub-bone "quantity in container." Companies with that problem have found a solution: egg-crate-like partitions in the container as a simple visual control on the container quantity, such that it is hard *not* to have the right, planned quantity

FIGURE 15–12

Fishbone Chart—Delivery of Goods by Truck

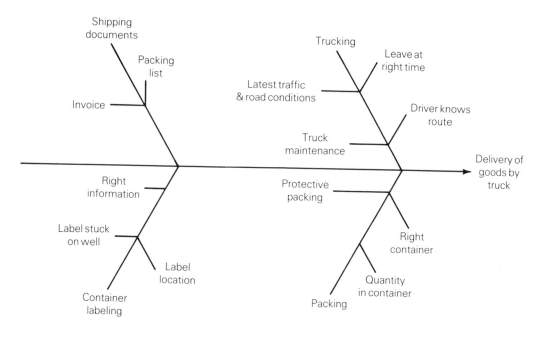

in it. For small parts, a precision scale can be used for precisely weigh-counting the container quantity.

How about the subfactor "leave at right time?" Should it be control charted? Perhaps not. "Right time" might depend on road traffic, weather, load consolidation, and other factors. Further Pareto analysis just for that factor may be the next step, then another fishbone chart, and then perhaps some action on better timing of departures.

At least one factor, truck maintenance, is far too coarse and nonspecific for action. Two or more further rounds of Pareto-fishbone may get to the nub of the truck maintenance problem. Most of the other factors—invoice, protective packing, and so on—require perhaps one more round of Pareto-fishbone.

What happens when the analysis group feels the breakdown is fine enough? There may be 50 or 100 detailed problem causes that need attention. Clearly all of them should not require separate process control charts or scatter diagram analysis. In fact, for all but a few, the solution is likely to be a change in equipment, procedure, materials, or design. (Example: To ensure correct label location, have the packer use a template that makes a "window" for the label to appear in at a measured distance from two corners of the box.) Only a few of the problem causes will merit data collection using control charts or scatter diagrams. In other words, most process improvement should *not* involve formal measurement and statistical analysis.

Scatter (Correlation) Diagram

A **scatter**, or **correlation**, **diagram** is used to plot effects against experimental changes in process inputs. The correlation coefficient (discussed in Chapter 5 as a demand-forecasting tool) may be calculated, although the strength of the correlation is often obvious just by looking at the diagram.

Scatter diagrams are most useful when the process is complex and causes of error are not well understood or obvious. That tends to rule out our previous simple example of deliveries by truck. As a more realistic example, suppose that samples of rubber inner tubes are tested by blowing them up. In a previous process the formed tubes are cured in ovens, with the cure time varied experimentally. A scatter diagram—see Figure 15–13—is used to show the correlation between cure time and strength. Each point on the diagram represents one tube; cure time is a point's horizontal location and strength its vertical location. The points seem to follow an upward but bending pattern. Natural conclusions are: (1) Tube strength correlates well with cure time, since there is a definite clustering of points about the curving dashed line and (2) tube strength increases with cure time up to a point, after which further cure time does no more good and may even be harmful. Next, look for other factors that might correlate with tube strength.

The scatter diagram approach is particularly useful for chemical, biological, metallurgical, paint, and similar complex processes. The approach is less useful for simple standard processes, where most cause-effect relationships are already well known. For example, a carpenter already knows that two nails in a board provide more strength than one; so, there is no point in plotting number of nails on a scatter diagram.

FIGURE 15–13
Scatter Diagram—Cure Time for Inner Tubes

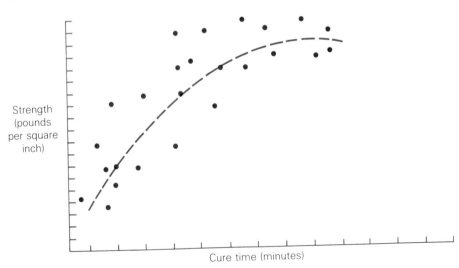

LOT INSPECTION

Lot inspection takes place well after production and therefore is not used for control. As the term implies, it is lots (or samples from lots) that are inspected. A lot is generally large, perhaps hundreds or thousands of units. The lot to be inspected may be an incoming shipment of raw materials, a completed production order for parts or end items, or an impending shipment of finished goods. One purpose is to remove the bad parts from the lot; industry calls this *sorting*. When sampling inspection is used, the main purpose is to find out if the lot is good enough to let it go forward or bad enough to stop it.

Lot inspection has been derogatorily called the "death certificate" approach: Sort out the bad ones and sign their death certificates—too late to save them. Clearly process control, controlling while the product is being made, is a better way. But all too often process control does not take place, particularly when the item comes from another company, a supplier that has not become part of the customer's quality improvement effort. Lot inspection then comes into use, often on the customer's receiving dock.

Sometimes 100 percent of the lot is checked. That may be necessary for a new part or a new supplier, when suspicion is high that something is wrong with the process that made the parts, or when it is vital for all parts to meet the specification.

Manufacturers can sometimes automate inspection so that 100 percent of items are automatically checked, sometimes with advanced *vision systems*. A fail-safe variation is when the machine not only checks its work but also automatically adjusts itself—or, sensing something is wrong, shuts itself off and turns on a blinking red light.

Sampling inspection, which is probably more common than 100 percent inspection, is often called *acceptance sampling:* Accept the lot if the sample is good. Sampling can be nearly as effective as 100 percent inspection, because the inspector may become fatigued or bored and make judgmental errors if 100 percent of a large lot must be checked.

In lot-sampling inspection, the sample size is often set using statistical tables. Then the inspector tries to select a random or *stratified sample*, one in which pieces are drawn from the back, middle, front, top, and bottom strata in a pile (not just selected from an area of the lot dictated by the maker).

If a bad sample is found, the whole lot is presumed unacceptable. Then, in some cases, every piece in the lot is inspected so that all bad ones may be removed and replaced with good ones. That is called a *100 percent rectifying inspection*. In the case of cheap items, the rejected lot may be discarded, melted down and reprocessed, or sold as scrap or seconds.

Sometimes the only way to properly inspect an item is to destroy it—referred to as **destructive testing** (e.g., running a car into a wall to see how the bumper holds up). Of course, destructive testing is always done on a sampling basis. Like statistical process control, lot inspection may be for variables or attributes, but acceptance inspection for attributes is more common. Sets of sampling tables—for attribute and variable inspection—are available in many quality control handbooks and textbooks. Use of the tables is easily learned on the job and thus is not considered further here.

One management issue that *is* worth consideration here is an economic (cost) issue—what we might call *the acceptance sampling paradox.* The sampling tables are constructed in such a way that for larger lots, the percent sampled from the lot gets smaller. Thus, industry's tendency has been to delay sampling until a large lot accumulates. The paradox is that accumulating large lots is itself wasteful and costly—directly contrary to the just-in-time ideal of making and forwarding items in small amounts at the customer's use rate. The powerful JIT viewpoint is leading some companies in the direction of sampling from smaller lots, or better yet, switching to process control and abandoning acceptance sampling entirely.

QUALITY OF SERVICE—SOME FINAL REMARKS

Most operations management concepts and techniques apply more or less equally to services and goods. Is that the case for the process analysis and improvement techniques? Yes and no.

The problem definition tools—process flowchart, Pareto, and fishbone—are particularly good for pinpointing problem causes in the less-structured world of human services and the office. For example, the end bones of a fine-grained fishbone chart point to causes, which often suggest solutions; an actual statistical data analysis may not be necessary or useful.

Many characteristics of quality in services *are* statistically measurable, however. What is the cook-down weight of a hamburger patty? How many trees survive after planting? How many pages must be reprinted or retyped? How many tax forms contain errors? For those kinds of service characteristics, run diagrams and process control charts are usable.

The statistical tools can also be used in human services work, though there are some special problems. One is the subjectivity of human services. Are you happy? Satisfied? Full? Cured? Getting a response is not hard, but getting a statistical measure of responses can be. Numeric scales are one way to transform the customer's feelings into a statistic.

Another problem is eliciting a response. The client or customer is not like a tangible good. The client won't stay still and submit to measures of any kind. A response must be asked for. The percentage willing to respond varies. Also, what about the client's mood? The mood bias tends to wash out if the sample is large. Still, there often is a problem in getting a *representative* sample.

Consider, for example, a rest area alongside a major highway. The highway department may place questionnaires in the rest area to solicit opinions about the quality of restrooms, tourist brochures, state roads, state police, and so on. Travelers' opinions may be measured in numbers, perhaps on a scale of 1 to 7, just as a micrometer might measure diameters of from 1 to 7 centimeters. Should the data then be plotted on statistical process control charts? Probably not. Process control charts suggest high precision when the collected data are themselves imprecise. If plotted on control charts, the data may show the process out of control—but the reason could just be that a motorcycle gang filled out a disproportionate number of questionnaires in one time period, truckers caught in a storm filled out a large number in another period, and so forth. The idea is to control the process while it is occurring, but the measurement of the process is too flawed for control charting to be effective. The questionnaire data are helpful but, in this case, not reliable in the control charting mode.

In sum, we may conclude that process improvement works well in services, even though some of the techniques do not work perfectly.

SUMMARY

With a *small* quality department playing a facilitator's role, quality improvement and total quality (TQ) begin at the source, the maker of the item or provider or the service. Further, TQ calls for process control—at every process—instead of relying on inspection of lots and placating angry customers, giving people the time and training to do the job right the first time, and giving them authority to slow or stop production if necessary to avoid bad output. Process controls should be built into the process itself and, as a backstop, there must be a good way of getting feedback from users on their satisfaction with quality.

Modern quality management takes a process focus. Operations processes are complex, consisting of materials, manpower, methods, machines, measurement, maintenance, and management. Process performance yields quality characteristics. Study of distributions of quality characteristics is at the heart of process analysis.

Process variation may be common or special; the latter must be removed in order to achieve statistical process control. A process that is in control is predictable. After process control is obtained, process capability analysis is used to compare process performance to desired customer specifications. Buyers use capability index values to rate suppliers' production. Work continues on capable processes; reduction of the remaining (common) variation is a goal of continual quality improvement. It ultimately copes with the tolerance stackup problem: two or more parts marginally within spec that produce a bad result when joined or mixed together.

There is a well-established cycle of process improvement that may yield direct quality improvement, reduction of waste, higher labor productivity, or other benefits. First, measure every piece to see if the variability is normal. If there is an abnormal trend or extreme values, look for a special cause and eliminate it. Then measure every piece for a time to ensure that the process really has been brought under control. If so, it may make sense to reduce to sampling instead of 100 percent inspection and then perhaps cease inspecting altogether, except for an occasional check, or perhaps automate inspection so that 100 percent inspection will make sense. The last step is to improve the process, which may require spending funds on better equipment, materials, tools, designs, and so forth.

Critical process characteristics may be monitored using process control procedures: Measure small samples (such as four, five, or six pieces) and plot them on process control charts: an $\overline{X}$ chart reflecting sample means and an R chart for variability within samples. Each chart has an upper control limit and a lower control limit typically set three standard deviations away from the mean. From then on, plot all sample means and ranges on the charts. Assume that the process is in control if all points stay between control limits; look for a special cause, and fix it if a point strays outside the limits.

A variation of the process control and improvement technique is checking for the existence or absence of a desirable attribute. This is a yes-or-no judgment, not a measurement of a variable. Take a number of sizable samples, and see what percent in each sample lacks the attribute, that is, is defective. The mean of those percents defective becomes the center line on a control chart. The chart is used in much the same way $\overline{X}$ and R charts are used. Another type of attribute inspection requires counting *number* of defects per unit (instead of percents of pieces defective); the mean number goes on a c chart with control limits in place. Low volume production calls for small-lot charting methods, or else a high level of craftsmanship, plus first- and last-piece inspection.

Other process improvement techniques include the process flowchart, Pareto analysis, fishbone chart, and scatter diagram. The process flowchart identifies each step in the process for analysis as to cause of error. Pareto analysis arranges the causes on a bar chart from most to least frequent. The most frequent are the factors to be given the most attention. On the fishbone chart, a main quality characteristic serves as the spine bone on a drawing resembling a fish's skeleton. Secondary and tertiary bones represent factors that contribute to that quality characteristic. The chart helps focus attention on causes of defects, which may then be plotted on run diagrams and control charts to isolate out-of-control factors. The scatter diagram correlates experimental changes in process inputs (amount of water added, time of cure, etc.) with test results. It shows which set of inputs is best.

Less adequate than process control—but sometimes necessary anyway—is lot inspection. Every piece in a lot may be inspected, or the lot may be sample inspected. Where sampling is used, the sampling plan may be made statistically correct by using sampling tables or formulas. Accepted lots are passed along (minus the bad ones found in the sample). Rejected lots are often subjected to a 100 percent rectifying inspection, which means inspecting every piece in the lot and replacing bad ones with good ones. The acceptance sampling paradox is that the tables allow smaller percent sample sizes from larger lots, but larger lots are contrary to the frugal ideals of just-in-time.

All the process analysis and improvement methods work in services as well as goods production. Process flowcharts, Pareto, and fishbone analysis are especially potent tools: They require no measurement, and services are sometimes hard to measure. For service features that are countable, standard control charts can be valuable. When customer impressions are expressed on a numerical scale, the scale values may be useful by themselves but are not precise enough to use in formal process control charts.

KEY WORDS

Total quality (TQ)
Common cause
Special cause
Variation stackup
Process capability
  index, C_{pk}
Variables inspection
Attribute inspection
Run diagram

Process control chart
$\overline{X}$ chart
R chart
p (percent-defective)
  chart
c (number-defective)
  chart
Precontrol chart

Process flowchart
Statistical process
  control (SPC)
Pareto chart
Fishbone chart
Scatter (correlation)
  diagram
Destructive testing

SOLVED PROBLEMS

1. Connector leads for electronic ignition components are produced to a specification of 8.000 ± 0.010 cm. The process has been studied, and the following values have been obtained:

$$\text{Process average} = \overline{\overline{X}} = 8.003 \text{ cm.}$$

$$\text{Standard deviation (estimate)} = \hat{\sigma} = 0.002 \text{ cm.}$$

Calculate:

a. The inherent process capability
b. The capability index C_{pk}

Solution

a. Inherent process capability $= 6 \times \hat{\sigma}$

$$= 6 \times 0.002 \text{ cm.}$$

$$= 0.012 \text{ cm.}$$

b. Capability index $C_{pk} = \dfrac{Z_{min}}{3}$

where Z_{min} is the smaller of

$$\frac{\text{USL} - \overline{\overline{X}}}{\hat{\sigma}} = \frac{8.010 - 8.003 \text{ cm.}}{0.002 \text{ cm.}} = \frac{0.007 \text{ cm.}}{0.002 \text{ cm.}} = 3.5$$

or

$$\frac{\overline{\overline{X}} - \text{LSL}}{\hat{\sigma}} = \frac{8.003 - 7.990 \text{ cm.}}{0.002 \text{ cm.}} = \frac{0.013 \text{ cm.}}{0.002 \text{ cm.}} = 6.5$$

Therefore

$$Z_{min} = 3.5$$

$$C_{pk} = \frac{3.5}{3} = 1.167$$

The value of C_{pk}, although greater than one, would not satisfy some buyers in today's marketplace. Process improvement to increase the value of C_{pk} is needed.

2. Samples of 180 units are drawn from production in order to construct a p chart. For the following 16 samples of percentages defective, develop a p chart. Is the chart satisfactory for use on the production line? Explain.

Sample	Percent Defective	Sample	Percent Defective	Sample	Percent Defective	Sample	Percent Defective
1	2	5	1	9	6	13	4
2	5	6	0	10	2	14	3
3	5	7	2	11	7	15	2
4	3	8	2	12	1	16	3

Solution
Step 1: Calculate center line, UCL, and LCL.

$$\bar{p} = \frac{\text{Total percent defective}}{k}$$

$$= \frac{2 + 5 + 5 + 3 + 1 + 0 + 2 + 2 + 6 + 2 + 7 + 1 + 4 + 3 + 2 + 3}{16}$$

$$= \frac{48}{16} = 3\%, \text{ or } 0.03$$

$$\text{UCL} = \bar{p} + 3\sqrt{\frac{\bar{p}(1 - \bar{p})}{n}}$$

$$= 0.03 + 3\sqrt{\frac{0.03(0.97)}{180}}$$

$$= 0.03 + 0.038$$

$$= 0.068$$

$$\text{LCL} = \bar{p} - 3\sqrt{\frac{\bar{p}(1 - \bar{p})}{n}}$$

$$= 0.03 - 0.038$$

$$= -0.08, \text{ or } 0.0$$

Step 2: Develop a chart and plot the 16 data points on it:

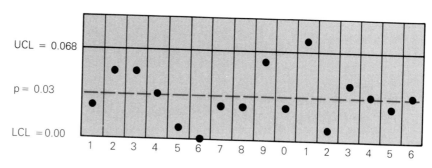

The chart is *not* satisfactory. Sample 11 is above the UCL, which indicates that the process is unstable, out of statistical control. Look for a special cause, eliminate it, and try again.

3. I.B. Poorly's quality problem is bad health. I.B. has developed a Pareto chart showing the incidence of each of several indicators of bad health (see the following diagram). The most frequently recurring problem is weight over what is recommended for I.B.'s height.

    I.B. has made weight the spine of a fishbone chart. For the end points, suggest one reasonable use of process control charting and one of further Pareto analysis.

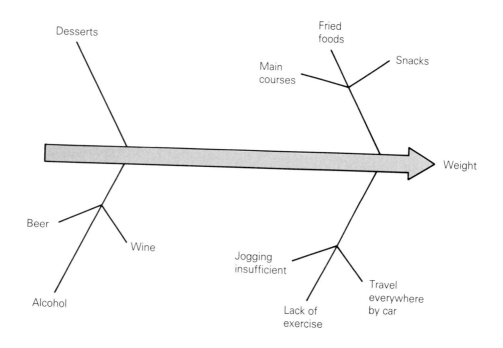

Solution

Process control charting could be used to plot percentage of days of the month that I.B. succumbs to snacks—a p chart. The chart could be useful in showing whether I.B.'s snacking habits change one way or the other. If a change in habits is shown, I.B. may want to take action.

Pareto analysis could be used for the end point, "jogging insufficient." A sample chart is shown below. Such a chart can provide concrete data on types of jogging insufficiencies. The dominant insufficiency in the sample is "skipped entirely." That knowledge may be enough to convince I.B. of a corrective solution or may lead I.B. to do a finer fishbone analysis, with "skipped entirely" as the spine and main bones indicating reasons for skipping (e.g., bad weather and working late).

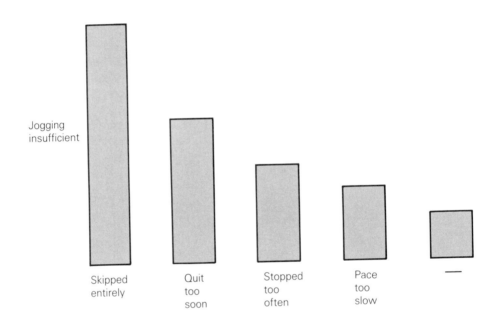

REFERENCES

Ishikawa, Kaoru. *Guide to Quality Control.* Tokyo: Asian Productivity Organization, 1972 (TS156.G82).

Juran, J. M., Frank M. Gryna, Jr., and R. S. Bingham, Jr., eds. *Quality Control Handbook,* 3rd ed. New York: McGraw-Hill, 1974 (TS156.Q3J8).

Statistical Quality Control Handbook, 2nd ed. (Indianapolis: AT&T Technologies, 1956).

REVIEW QUESTIONS

1. Under total quality what is the role of the line employee? Of the QA department staff?

2. What is the most advanced form of process control, and why? What is the role of feedback from users of a producer's product?

3. What is a process? How might process performance be described in terms of quality characteristics?

4. Differentiate between process control and process capability. In your response address specifications, common variation, and special variation.

5. What C_{pk} index should a company strive for? Explain.

6. Should reduction of all process output variation be a goal? Why or why not?

7. What are the roles of run diagrams and process control charts in process improvement? What are the similarities and differences?

8. Do specifications and tolerances play a role in process improvement? Explain fully.

9. Does process improvement mean the same thing as quality improvement? Are process improvement techniques restricted to improving product quality? Discuss.

10. In control charting for variables, why are there two kinds of charts ($\overline{X}$ and R charts)?

11. Compare and contrast $\overline{X}$, R, p, and c charts and their uses.

12. Compare the effectiveness of process control with that of lot inspection.

13. How is a fishbone chart constructed, and what is it used for?

14. How is Pareto analysis used in process control or process improvement?

15. How is a scatter diagram used in process control or process improvement?

16. Does the precontrol chart lead to process improvement? Explain.

17. How does improving processes in services differ from that in goods production?

PROBLEMS AND EXERCISES

1. Fix-M-Up, Inc., is a small chain of stores that clean and repair typewriters, photocopiers, and other office equipment. Define a process for the company along the lines of that discussed in the chapter for the manufacture of 3-inch bolts. Prepare a list of quality characteristics you might wish to use if you were considering using Fix-M-Up as the maintenance contractor for your company's office equipment.

2. A food processing company has large tanks that are cleaned daily. Cleaning includes the use of packaged detergents, which dissolve in a solution inside the tanks. Detergent packages are purchased with a fill-weight specification of 12.00 ± 0.08 oz.

   A vendor representative claims that his company uses statistical process control and will promise an inherent process capability of 0.20 oz. for the fill-weight specification. The vendor's brochure says nothing else about the process except that the "advertised" weight of the detergent packages is 12 oz.

   a. Should the food processor buy detergent from this vendor? Why or why not?
   b. If the vendor had control chart evidence that its fill-weight process was in fact centered at 12.00 oz. and was in a state of statistical control, how would your answer to question *a* change?
   c. Suppose the vendor is a reliable supplier of other products and can reasonably be expected to improve the detergent-packaging process. What advice would you offer to the food processor on seeking alternate suppliers? What advice would you offer the vendor regarding the relationship with the food processor?

3. Plug-N-Go, Ltd., makes valve covers to a diameter specification of 0.500 ± 0.020 cm. The normally distributed process is in control, centered at 0.505 cm., and has an inherent process capability of 0.024 cm. The process distribution is as follows:

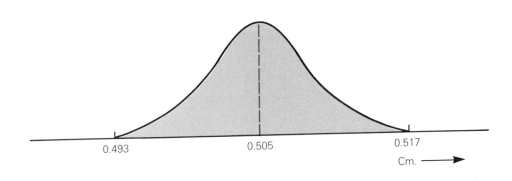

| 0.493 | 0.505 | 0.517 |

Cm. ⟶

   a. Calculate the process capability index C_{pk}.
   b. Should Plug-N-Go be concerned about reducing the variation in the diameter process output? Why or why not?

4. Suppose the valve cover process in problem 3 is in control but centered at 0.510 cm. The inherent process capability and the diameter specification are as given in problem 3. The process would appear as:

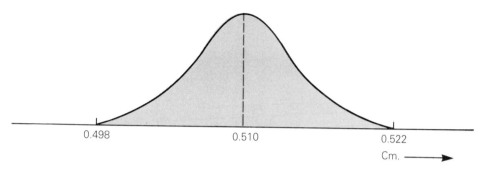

0.498   0.510   0.522

Cm. ⟶

   a. Calculate C_{pk}.

   b. Use Appendix A (areas under the normal curve) to determine what proportion, if any, of the valve covers would fall outside the specifications.

   c. What action, if any, should Plug-N-Go take regarding the valve cover process?

5. Sixteen-ounce chunks of longhorn cheese are packaged by a cheese processor. Quality control has designed $\overline{X}$ and R charts: $\overline{X}$ is at 16.09 ounces, with $UCL_{\overline{X}} = 16.25$ and $LCL_{\overline{X}} = 15.93$; $\overline{R}$ is at 0.376 ounces, with $UCL_R = 0.723$ and $LCL_R = 0$.

   a. What sample size, n, would have been used? (It may be calculated.)

   b. Although the cheese packages are labeled as 16-ounce chunks, $\overline{\overline{X}} = 16.09$. What is a reasonable explanation for the difference?

6. Hypodermic needles are subjected to a bend test, and the results, in grams, are to be plotted on $\overline{X}$ and R charts. A suitable number of samples have been inspected. The resulting $\overline{\overline{X}}$ is 26.1, and the resulting $\overline{R}$ is 5.0.

   a. For $n = 8$, calculate the control limits for the control charts.

   b. What should be done with the data calculated in question *a*?

   c. Assume that process control charts have been developed for the above data and that the operator has been using the charts regularly. For one sample of hypodermics, $\overline{X} = 26.08$ and $R = 0.03$. Should there be an investigation for a special cause? Explain.

7. Random samples, each with a sample size of six, are periodically taken from a production line that manufactures one-half-volt batteries. The sampled batteries are tested on a voltmeter. The production line has just been modified, and a new quality control plan must be designed. For that purpose, 10 random samples (of 6 each) have been taken over a suitable period of time; the test results are as follows:

Sample Number	*Tested Voltages*					
	V_1	V_2	V_3	V_4	V_5	V_6
1	0.498	0.492	0.510	0.505	0.504	0.487
2	0.482	0.491	0.502	0.481	0.496	0.492
3	0.501	0.512	0.503	0.499	0.498	0.511

4	0.498	0.486	0.502	0.503	0.510	0.501
5	0.500	0.507	0.509	0.498	0.512	0.518
6	0.476	0.492	0.496	0.521	0.505	0.490
7	0.511	0.522	0.513	0.518	0.520	0.516
8	0.488	0.512	0.501	0.498	0.492	0.498
9	0.482	0.490	0.510	0.500	0.495	0.482
10	0.505	0.496	0.498	0.490	0.485	0.499

a. Compute and draw the appropriate process control chart(s) for the data.

b. What should be done next? Discuss.

8. Current loss in a circuit is being measured, and the means of sample measurements are plotted on a process control chart. Most of the means fall below the lower control limit—less current loss than before. What is the implication of this on such factors as pricing, marketing, purchasing, production, training, design, and control charts?

9. A manufacturer of coat hangers has decided what constitutes a defective hanger. Samples of 200 hangers have been inspected on each of the last 20 days. The numbers of defectives found are given below. Construct a p chart for the data. What should be done next? Explain.

Day	Number Defective	Day	Number Defective
1	22	11	21
2	17	12	21
3	14	13	20
4	18	14	13
5	25	15	19
6	16	16	24
7	12	17	14
8	11	18	8
9	6	19	15
10	16	20	12

10. OK-Mart, a chain retailer, contracts with Electro Corporation to manufacture an OK brand of photo flashbulb. OK-Mart states that it wants an average quality of 99 percent good flashbulbs, that is, 99 percent that actually flash. Electro's marketing manager states that their goal should be for 99.9 percent to flash (better than OK-Mart's stated goal). After production begins at Electro, sampling on the production line over a representative time period shows 0.2 percent defective.

a. Where should the center line be drawn on a process control chart? Why?

b. What, if anything, needs to be done about the differences between goals and actual quality?

11. Guarantee Seed Company applies process control charting to germination rates on its line of seeds. For one new type of seed, the inspection plan is to pull out samples of 100 seeds from bags before they are fastened shut and test them to determine the germination rate. After production starts up, 5 samples of 100 are drawn, containing 1, 3, 3, 3, and 5 seeds that will not germinate. Calculate the center line and upper and lower control limits for a process control chart that plots germination rates. (Note: Usually 20 or more samples are taken to produce the charts, but in this problem use only 5 to simplify calculations.)

12. Process control charts are being constructed in a pottery manufacturing firm. Thirty pottery samples are taken, and the mean percentage of pottery samples that fail a strength test is 0.02, which becomes the center line on a p chart. Control limits are put in place, and the 30 defect rates are plotted on the chart. Two of the 30 fall above the upper control limit, but all 30 are less than the major customer, a department store, requires. Explain the situation. What should be done?

13. Redraw the following chart. Fill in your chart to show the type of inspection for process control that is suitable for each of the products on the left. Briefly explain each of your answers.

	Run Diagram	$\bar{X}$ and R Chart	p Chart	c Chart
Alcoholic content in beer batches				
Billiard balls—ability to withstand force in a destructive test				
Vibration of electric motor right after a process improvement				
New electronic component				
Number of fans that do not turn when plugged in				
Percent of lenses having a scratch				
Number of scratches per table surface				

14. Orville's Ready-Pop Popcorn is packaged in jars. The jars are supposed to contain a certain quantity of popcorn, and the fill-machine operator inspects for quantity using statistical process control. Which of these three process control charting methods—$\bar{X}/R$, p, and c charts—could or could not be used for process control of this product? Explain.

15. Explain why each of the above three process control inspection techniques could be used in inspecting tabletops.

16. American Pen and Pencil (AmPen) has had most of the market for ball-point pens, but now it is under great pressure from a competitor whose product is clearly superior. AmPen operators have identified several quality problems, including viscosity of ink, which is affected by the temperature of the mixing solution; purity of powdered ink and amount of water; the ball-point assembly, which is affected by diameter of ball, roundness of ball, and trueness of the tube opening into which the ball goes; and strength of the clip, which is affected by the thickness of the metal and the correctness of the shape after stamping.

   a. Draw a fishbone chart for these ball-point pen factors. How should the chart be used?

   b. An inspection procedure at the ink-mixing stage reveals that 80 percent of bad samples are caused by impurities, 15 percent by wrong temperature, and 5 percent by wrong amount of water. Draw a Pareto chart. How should it be used?

17. A waiter is trying to determine the factors that increase tips. Some of his ideas are how long it takes to serve, how many words he speaks to a table of patrons, how long it takes the kitchen to fill the order, time between taking away dishes and bringing the check, and how far the table is from the kitchen.

   a. Arrange these few factors into a *logical* fishbone chart. Explain your chart.

   b. Which of the factors is likely to plot on a scatter diagram as an upside-down U? Explain.

18. A group of mathematics instructors and students is developing a fishbone chart on how to improve the average math score on the Scholastic Aptitude Test (SAT). So far the chart is as shown below; only the primary bone, "materials and machines," is filled out.

   a. Fill out the rest of the primary bones with reasonable cause and subcause arrows.

   b. Suggest three actions to be taken next.

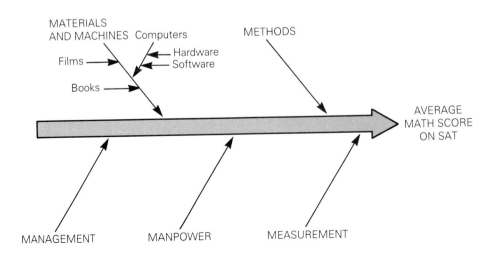

19. Following is a scatter diagram showing inches of deviation from the correct length of wooden blinds and humidity in the shop.
    a. What does the shape of the scattered points indicate?
    b. Sharpness of the saw blade is known to also affect the correctness of blind length. Make a drawing of how the scatter for those two factors (sharpness and deviation of length) would probably look.

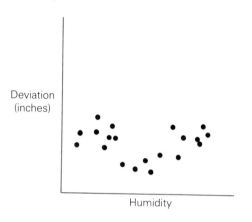

20. A listing of products/services follows. Select two from each column, and do the following:
    a. For each of your four selections, decide on two attributes and/or variables that you think are most suitable for inspection. Explain your reasoning.
    b. Discuss whether a formal statistical sampling method or an informal inspection method is more sensible for each selection.

Column 1	*Column 2*
Telephone	Auto tire mounting
Ball-point pen	Bookbinding
Pocket calculator	Data entry
Dice	Proofreading
Space heater	Wallpaper hanging
Electric switch	Library reference
Glue	services
Bottle of cola	Nursing care
Watch	Food catering
Handgun	Cleanliness of dishes
Light bulb	Bank teller service
	Roadside rest stop

21. An office furniture manufacturer (which employees 1,000 people) is planning to adopt a total quality program. Following are some characteristics of its present production system:
    (1) There is a quality assurance department of 50 people, including 30 inspectors.

(2) Rejected products discovered at the end of final assembly are sent by conveyor to a rework area staffed by 120 people.

(3) All purchased raw materials and parts are inspected on the receiving docks using MIL-STD-105D (a formal lot-inspection procedure).

(4) All direct laborers are paid by how much they produce, which is measured daily.

What changes would you suggest?

AMERICAN CERAMIC AND GLASS PRODUCTS CORPORATION*

The American Ceramic and Glass Products Corporation employed approximately 13,000 people, each of its three plants employing between 4,000 and 5,000 of this total. About three quarters of its sales volume came from standard glass containers produced on highly automatic equipment; the balance of the company's sales were of specialized ceramic and glass items made in batches on much less automated equipment. John Parr, production manager for American Ceramic and Glass Products, had just completed a trip that covered eight states, seven universities, and three major industrial centers. The purpose of his trip was to recruit personnel for American's three plants. He felt that his trip had been extremely successful. He had made contacts that would, he hoped, result in his firm's acquiring some useful and needed personnel.

Parr was anxious to hire a capable person to head up the inspection and quality control department of the largest of American's plants, located in Denver, Colorado. The position of chief of inspection and quality control had just been vacated by George Downs, who had taken an indefinite leave of absence due to a serious illness. There was little chance that Downs would be able to resume any work duties within a year and a substantial chance that he would never be capable of working on a full-time basis. During the 10 years that Downs was chief of inspection and quality control, he had completely modernized the firm's inspection facilities and had developed a training program in the use of the most modern inspection equipment and techniques. The physical facilities of Downs's inspection department were a major attraction for visitors to the plant.

THOMAS CALLIGAN

During his trip, Parr interviewed two men who he felt were qualified to fill Downs's position. Although each appeared more than qualified, Parr felt that a wrong choice could easily be made. Thomas Calligan, the first of the two men, was a graduate of a reputable trade school and had eight years of experience in the inspection department of a moderately large manufacturing firm (approximately 800 employees). He began working as a production inspector and was promoted to group leader within two years and chief inspector two years later. His work record as a production inspector, as a group leader, and as chief inspector was extremely good. His reason for wishing to leave the firm was "to seek better opportunities." He felt that in his present firm he could not expect further promotions in the near future. His firm was known for its stability, low

---

*Adapted from Robert C. Meier, Richard A. Johnson, William T. Newell, and Albert N. Schrieber, *Cases in Production and Operations Management,* © 1982, pp. 8–18. Reprinted by permission of Prentice-Hall, Inc., Englewood Cliffs, N.J.

employee turnover, and slow but assured advancement opportunities. His superior, the head of quality control, was recently promoted to this position and was doing a more than satisfactory job. Further, he was a young man, only 32 years old.

JAMES KING

James King, the second of the two men being considered by Parr, was a graduate of a major southwestern university and had about five years of experience. King was currently employed as head of inspection and quality control in a small manufacturing firm employing 300 people. His abilities exceeded the requirements of his job, and he had made arrangements with his employer to do a limited amount of consulting work for noncompeting firms. His major reason for wanting a different position was a continuing conflict of interests between himself and his employer. King did not wish to make consulting his sole source of income, but he felt that his current position was equally unsatisfactory. He believed that by working for a large firm he would be able to fully use his talents within that firm and thus resolve conflict between his professional interests and the interests of his employer.

King's work record appeared to be good. He had recently been granted a sizable pay increase. King, like Calligan, began his career as a bench inspector and was rapidly promoted to his current supervisory position. Unlike Calligan, King viewed his initial position of bench inspector primarily as a means of financing his education and not as the beginning of his lifetime career. King was 31 years old.

ROLE OF INSPECTION AND QUALITY CONTROL

Major differences between the two men centered on their philosophies on the role of inspection and quality control in a manufacturing organization. Calligan's philosophy was:

> Quality is an essential part of every product. . . . It is the product development engineer's function to specify what constitutes quality and the function of quality control to see that the manufacturing departments maintain these specifications. . . . Accurate and vigilant inspection is the key to controlled quality.

When asked how important process control was in the manufacture of quality products, he stated,

> Process control is achieved primarily through the worker's attitude. If a firm pays high wages and provides good working conditions, they should be able to acquire highly capable workers. . . . A well-executed and efficient inspection program will, as it has done in my firm, impress the importance of quality on the employees and motivate high-quality production. In the few cases when quality lapses do occur,

an efficient inspection program prevents defective products from leaving the plant. . . . Any valid quality control program must hold quality equal in importance to quantity. . . . Quality records must be maintained for each employee and be made known to both the employee and his or her immediate superiors. Superior quality should be a major consideration in recommending individuals for promotion or merit pay increases.

King's philosophy paralleled that of Calligan only to the extent that "quality was an essential part of every product." King made the following comments on his philosophy toward inspection and quality control:

If quality is properly controlled, inspection becomes a minor function. The more effective a quality control system becomes, the less inspection is required. . . . The key to quality control is process control, and inspection serves only as a check to assure that the process controls are being properly administered. . . . An effective inspection scheme should locate and pinpoint the cause of defects rather than place the blame on an often-innocent individual. A good rejection report will include the seeds from which a solution to future rejections can be developed. . . . One sign of an unsatisfactory quality control system is a large, impressive inspection program.

King was asked what steps he would take to develop such a program if he were to be offered and accept the job of chief of inspection and quality control in the Denver plant. He answered:

I would design and install a completely automatic inspection and process control system throughout the plant. By automatic I do not mean a mechanical or computer-directed system, but rather a completely standardized procedure for making all decisions concerning inspection and process control. The procedures would be based on a theoretically sound statistical foundation translated into layperson's terminology. The core of the program would be a detailed inspection and quality control manual.

When asked how long this might take, King continued,

I constructed a similar manual for my present employer in a period of less than 12 months and had the whole process operating smoothly within 18 months after beginning work on the task. Since your firm is somewhat larger, and accounting for my added experience, I would estimate it to take no longer than two years and hopefully significantly less time. . . . As previously stated, I would place major emphasis on process control and would minimize inspection by applying appropriate sampling procedures wherever possible. . . . Employee quality performance should be rated on the basis of process control charts rather than on the basis of final inspection reports. The employee should be trained and encouraged to use these charts as his chief tool toward achieving quality output.

King further stated that one of the reasons for his desire to find a new employer was that he had developed the quality control program in his present firm to the point where it was no longer offering him any challenge. He further stated that he felt this situation would recur at American Ceramic and Glass Products but that, because of the size of the firm, he could direct his attention to bigger and more interesting problems rather than be required to seek outside consulting work to satisfy his need for professional growth.

When asked what his real interests were, King stated, "Application of statistical concepts to the nonroutine activities of a manufacturing organization." He cited worker training, supplier performance, and trouble shooting as areas of interest. King submitted several reports that summarized projects that he had successfully completed in these or related areas.

This was the extent of information that Parr had on each of the two individuals he felt might best fill the position vacated by Downs.

DISCUSSION QUESTIONS

1. What should be the role of the chief of inspection and quality control?

2. What was Calligan's philosophy toward quality control?

3. What was King's philosophy toward quality control?

4. Under what conditions would you expect Calligan and King, respectively, to be most effective?

5. Which of the two candidates, if either, should be selected for the position of chief of the inspection and quality control department? Explain your choice.

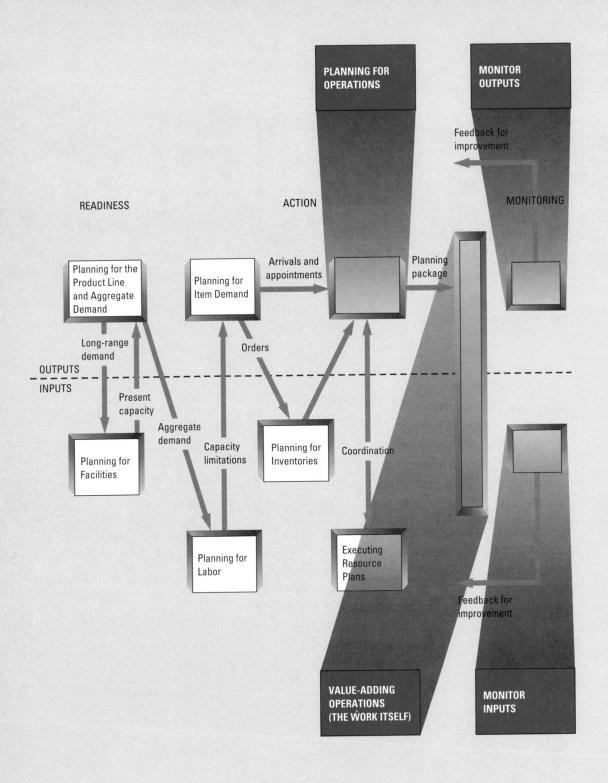

Productivity, Measurement, and Standards

Labor Utilization
Labor Efficiency
Labor Productivity
Productivity Reporting in Perspective

TIME STANDARDS AND THEIR USES

Importance of Time Standards
Coordination and Scheduling
Under-Capacity Scheduling of Labor
Analysis of Operations

TIME STANDARDS TECHNIQUES

Engineered and Nonengineered Standards
Requisites of an Engineered Standard
Time Study
Work Sampling Standards
Predetermined Standards
Standard Data
Historical Standards and Technical Estimates

HUMANITY AND FAIRNESS ISSUES

Tasks, Jobs, and Service to Customers
Responses to Variability
Fair Pay

CASE STUDY: LAND AND SKY WATERBED COMPANY

 At first glance, **productivity** is a simple measure. Economists and engineers say that it is outputs divided by inputs. Closely related is a widely used accounting method that subtracts actual cost inputs from standard cost outputs to yield a productivity measure known as **cost variance**. But wait a minute. What is an output? What is an input? And how are they measured?

Productivity actually has never been a simple concept, nor has it been easy to measure; that is especially true inasmuch as productivity has a growing list of meanings and uses. These days we even speak of the productivity of professional athletes—and that can get a little complicated. Magic Johnson, stellar guard of the Los Angeles Lakers, scores over 20 points and "dishes out" over 10 assists per game. He's productive—per number of minutes played and, probably, per dollar that he's paid; those are two ways to measure a player's productivity. The National Basketball Association might prefer to measure Magic's productivity in the number of fans who come to see him (and his team) per game, for the Lakers tend to fill arenas wherever they play.

Let's take another example: a postal service. Several combinations of ways to measure productivity come to mind: number of pieces or pounds or amount of postage value processed divided by number of employees, employee hours, or total expenses over a certain period.

The consistency in all those productivity measures is that they stay within the standard definition, outputs divided by inputs. In fact, that is what this chapter is all about: how to continually improve the ratio of outputs over inputs. Of course, it is also about how to meaningfully measure the outputs and inputs. Viewpoints have been changing enough on that topic that portions of many accounting, management, and engineering textbooks are in need of extensive revision.

We begin the chapter with a direct plunge into the matter of why the business world is rethinking its measures of productivity and performance, and the close connection between upheavals taking place in operations management and management accounting. The remainder of the chapter treats some of the traditional (and still dominant) measures and techniques; they include efficiency and utilization, as well as tried-and-true methods and time standards techniques.

BOTTOM LINE FOR OPERATIONS MANAGEMENT

The new and old views about productivity are summarized below, followed by more extensive discussion:

- *New productivity: Broad and integrated*—On the output side, the focus is on whole products and subproducts. On the input side, all operating costs are included and most are directly charged to products ("contained" rather than "allocated" costs).

- *Old productivity: Narrow and fractionated*—On the output side, emphasis is on performing operations (not whole products). On the input side, the focus is on direct labor of individuals and functional groups.

As has been suggested, three major business functions have a hand in changing the productivity measurement system: Operations managers must be satisfied with the productivity data, because they are the main users of it: for performance appraisal, recognition, reward, and motivation for continual improvement. Measuring outputs and inputs has required the expertise of industrial engineers, who are labor and process measurement experts; and accountants, who are cost determination experts. Let us take a close look at these experts' handiwork: the classic cost-variance system.

Cost Variance

For years, best business practice has called for use of periodic cost variances as a control on productivity. The system sums up standard cost and actual cost for all work completed in a period. Standard cost represents the output of the period—what the output should cost using "normal" amounts of direct labor, materials, and so forth; the input is the actual cost—actual payroll, material, and other expenditures. Periodic reports, which go to each operating manager, list cost variances: standard cost minus actual cost. If actual cost is higher than standard cost, a negative cost variance results, and the pressure is on operations to do better.

More specifically, the cost-variance report is segmented into subcategories, including labor cost variance and material cost variance. A negative labor variance suggests that the direct labor force should work more diligently; a negative material variance means it should work more carefully so as not to "scrap" so much material.

Misplaced Blame

The modern view is that far too much blame—for cost, scrap, rework, delays, and so forth—has been heaped on direct labor. In fact, today direct labor averages less than 15 percent of operating cost—and more like 1 or 2 percent in a few cases. A century ago, when direct labor was over 50 percent of cost on average, emphasis on labor variances made more sense. Today, overhead costs are typically at least five times higher than direct labor, but the cost-variance system leaves overhead uncontrolled.

There are other reasons, besides the dramatic percentage reduction in direct labor, for questioning the classic cost-variance measurement system. One is the realization that quality, not just output, is a key to competitive advantage. Another is the wholesale reorganization of resources that has been taking place in many industries: away from fragmented and toward product- or customer-focused. This paves the way to simpler, more meaningful measures of performance. A third is the blurring of job responsibilities: Operators are assuming first responsibility for quality, good workplace organization, upkeep of equipment, data collection and diagnosis, problem solving, and, sometimes, interviewing and training new employees. Formerly, those activities were treated as indirect labor, supervision, and overhead.

Data Collection

Still another disadvantage of conventional productivity systems is the extensive data required to feed them. For example, some systems require data on when an operator starts and completes each different job, and commonly the operator works on several jobs every day; time not working (stoppages for lack of parts, breakdowns, etc.) thus can be deducted, which yields a refined measure of direct-labor productivity, or labor *efficiency*. To collect all that data, many companies have installed data-entry terminals all over the operating area.

The new outlook, favoring lumping together all operating costs, no longer requires operators to report what they are working on or when they are stopped. It is sometimes possible to get by with just an exception report—daily or less often. For example, at a Westinghouse plant in North Carolina, employee salaries are automatically charged directly to the miniplants they are assigned to (the plant had undergone extensive reorganization into several product-focused miniplants); once a week supervisors simply turn in an exception report noting any absenteeism or overtime hours.[1]

Better Measures

The need for better productivity measures is clear. Some improved measures are already in use. Here are three examples:

1. *Schlumberger Corp., Houston Downhole Sensors Division.* One new measure is *total* spending per unit of production, rather than just direct labor expenditures per unit. Another is product *completions* per dollar of input. Formerly, the firm (like almost every other firm) counted all semi-finished production as productivity, which caused bloated inventories and extremely long flow times, including time at rest in stockrooms.[2]

2. *Square D Corporation (primary product line: circuit breakers).* The company's plants have been converting to an incentive pay system, often called **gain-sharing**, in which everyone receives a share of the value of productivity increases; the measure of output is *good* units *packed out* (i.e., packed for immediate shipment to fill a customer order). Previously, most employees were covered by a conventional individ-

---

[1]S. S. Cherukuri, "Westinghouse Electric Corporation Asheville's Focused Factories Make a Difference—the 'Village' Concept," *Target*, Fall 1988, pp. 30–32.

[2]J. E. Ashton and N. Holmlund, "Relevant Managerial Accounting in the Job Shop Environment," *Manufacturing Review*, December 1988, pp. 230–35.

ual incentive plan, which paid each operator for production above "standard." Since each operator's production went into a stockroom, defective production was usually not discovered until much later, too late to identify which operator it came from; thus, operators could receive incentive pay even for defects.

3. *Harley-Davidson Motor Company*. New measures include motorcycles per employee and conversion cost per motorcycle.[3] Formerly, Harley—like most other companies—computed productivity separately for every one of its many work centers and departments. Overall measures for a whole motorcycle were not meaningful for any single operations manager, because each managed a different process and was separated from the next process—the internal customer—by stockrooms full of inventory. Harley's advanced JIT system, including reorganization into product-focused cells, has connected the operations closely in time (stockrooms for semi-finished production have been eliminated); the effect of an improvement in any operation shows up clearly and directly in the new overall measures of performance for a whole motorcycle.

Simple, Accurate, Strong

As the three examples above illustrate, today's trend is to replace weak, complex measures of productivity and performance with strong, simple ones. The new measures are strong in that they are directed toward end products and sub-products—what customers buy—whereas older measures allowed any output, whether customers wanted it or not, to qualify as productivity. The new measures are more accurate, in that the aim is to include not just direct labor but all operating costs; and the strong trend toward focusing resources by type of product or customer makes it easier to measure the inputs accurately. Employees are likely to be supportive of measures that are truly customer-oriented, with simple-to-determine accuracy.

We have considered productivity, old and new, in general terms. Now we turn to specifics: the emergent cause-control system, as well as ways to improve its predecessor, the classic cost-variance system.

CONTROLLING CAUSES OF COST

If companies abandon detailed cost measurements and substitute overall measures, such as Harley-Davidson's conversion cost per motorcycle, aren't there some risks? Won't it be all too easy for shirkers to escape detection, for poor performance to be hidden?

---

[3]John A. Saathoff, "Maintaining Excellence through Change," *Target*, Spring 1989, pp. 13–20.

The solution to these concerns is a multifaceted system of controlling the *causes* of cost. The cause-control system relies on frequent measurements of non-cost factors, which are usually plotted on large wall charts. The measures are of three types:

1. *Product and component, or customer, specific*—Lead time, flow distance, space, work-in-process inventory, on-time completions, yield, nonconformities, scrap, rework, returns, and claims.

2. *Process specific*—Changeover and get-ready time, micro-response ratios, process check sheets, and process control charts.

3. *Activities, recognition, rewards, celebration*—Present improvement projects, present training programs, completed projects, completed training, number of suggestions, appreciation letters from customers, awards won, plaques, photos of recognition ceremonies, and so forth.

Visual Controls

This system is visual, located where the work is performed, usually "owned" by operating people, and up to date. Controlling causes in this way is, in the words of H. Thomas Johnson, "unlike the distant, often distorted financial echoes of those causes that appear in traditional cost and performance reports."[4] The full system of visual measures includes all of the factors listed in Chapter 1 (Figure 1–1) as "customer requirements," namely, quality, cost, lead time, flexibility, variability, and service.

Examples of the visual system are shown in the photographs in Figure 16–1, which come from Milliken and Company. Milliken, a large, privately held textile and chemical producer, has charts of these kinds throughout all of its offices and plants—one of the reasons why Milliken was a winner of the 1989 Baldrige National Quality Award.

In the cause-control system, cost ceases to be used for controlling productivity. The on-the-spot visual signboard system controls the causes, and productivity improvement (as well as improvement in quality, lead time, etc.) follows.

That does not mean that costs are no longer measured; they are. Regulatory agencies require data such as the value of inventories and statements of profit and loss, but those reports require only a fraction of the data needed for a full-blown cost-variance system. The overall cost data needed for periodic profit and loss accounting will, of course, prove the value of the cause controls.

---

[4]H. Thomas Johnson, "A Blueprint for World-Class Management Accounting," *Management Accounting*, June 1988, p. 23–30.

FIGURE 16–1
Visual Management at Milliken and Company

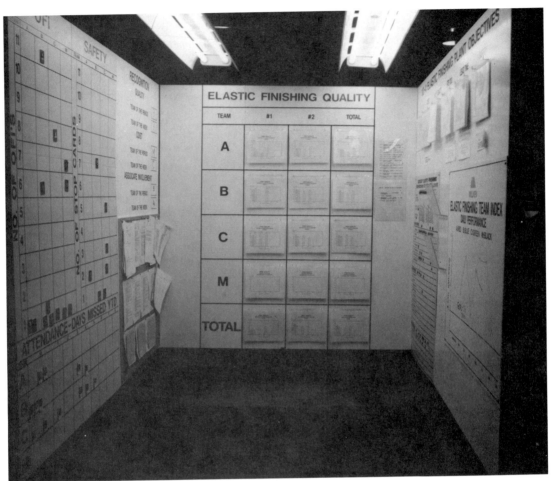

Improving the Old System

While the visual cause-control system appears to be the choice of leading-edge firms, many other companies are looking for ways to salvage some of their traditional productivity measures by correcting some of their weaknesses.

One weakness, the fixation on direct labor, is reduced when operators assume responsibility for quality, data collection, and other duties usually handled by "overhead" people. More of the factors included in the productivity measures thus come under the control of operators, and the size of the overhead group and its cost shrink.

PRINCIPLE: Record and retain output, volume, quality, and problem data at the workplace.

Another weakness, the focus on producing "anything" (even off-quality output), is greatly reduced when operations is successful in slashing lead times; this ties operations more closely in time to real customer demands. Related to this is the movement of people and equipment into product-focused groupings, which makes any measure of productivity more focused on what the customer is paying for.

Despite these improvements, the old productivity measures retain the weaknesses of being periodic, delayed, staff-directed, and not cause-oriented.

Cost of Products and Services

The changes taking place in productivity measurement are closely related to another issue: improving the accuracy of product costing. The National Association of Accountants found that 78 percent of practicing accountants participating in a survey believe that their firms' costing system understates cost (and overstates profit) on low-volume items and does the opposite for high-volume items.[5] Cost accounting inaccuracies can hurt a productivity improvement effort. For example, a team working on high-volume products might be immensely successful in improving productivity, but the cost system falsely shows the products to be money-losers; another team providing special services (low-volume outputs) may be doing poorly on productivity improvement, yet the cost system credits them, falsely, for big contributions to company profits.

Costs are important in operations management for other purposes as well, including aiding in the make-or-buy decision and evaluating changes in methods. If the costs are biased, however, they will do more harm than good.

The inaccuracy of cost data is owed mainly to the difficulty of allocating overhead (which, as has been mentioned, is usually huge) to goods and services. One point of view calls for relying on experienced estimates in allocating over-

---

[5]"Outdated Cost-Accounting Systems Call for Activism," *Manufacturing Executive's Report*, November 1989, pp. 1–3.

head. Ashton and Holmlund claim that such estimates should be *"better* than the estimates usually used . . . following accounting overhead allocation procedures."[6] Some of those holding this viewpoint call for just doing a cost audit as needed and entirely halting the costly system of periodic product cost reporting. (Profit and loss accounting must remain, but it does not require data on each specific product.)

Others would prefer to improve overhead allocation by use of new **activity-based costing (ABC)** methods. The weakness that ABC aims to correct is the widespread practice of allocating overhead by direct labor. In that system, if overhead averages 500 percent of direct labor, then every dollar of direct labor expended on a certain product receives five dollars of overhead.

Briefly, the ABC method attempts to assign overhead to a product only where there is actual overhead "activity" in support of that product. The ABC analysis team searches for simple activity cost "drivers." A simple example is allocating operating overhead (supervision, engineering, maintenance, scheduling, etc.) based on lead time. The reasoning is that if a product is in process for five days (lead time = 5), the product probably actually receives five days of overhead cost; if another product zips through in just one day, it is scarcely seen or handled by overhead people and therefore should receive proportionately less overhead cost—in this case, only one fifth as much.

Although cost and cost-variance methods of productivity management have roots in the accounting field, the conventional system usually also has additional measures for certain of the operating resources that create the costs. Those measures—including resource utilization and labor efficiency and productivity—are associated with industrial engineering and *scientific management*, key concepts of which are considered in the remainder of the chapter.

PRODUCTIVITY AND SCIENTIFIC MANAGEMENT

The first organized approach to improving the productivity of *labor* arose in the United States at the turn of the century from the work of the pioneers of scientific management—Frederick W. Taylor, Frank and Lillian Gilbreth, and others. Their approach was to standardize the labor element of production: standard *methods* and standard *times*. Nonstandard labor practices were simply too expensive and wasteful.

The scientific management movement was a period of transition. On the one hand, scientific management could be thought of as the last phase of the Industrial Revolution. Earlier phases concerned invention, mechanization, standardization of parts, division of labor, and the factory system. Machines and parts were standardized, and labor was divided into narrow specialties. Prior to scientific management, however, labor productivity was controlled more by su-

---

[6]J. E. Ashton and N. Holmlund, "Relevant Managerial Accounting in the Job Shop Environment," *Manufacturing Review*, December 1988, pp. 230–35.

pervisors' skill than by design. Taylor's and the Gilbreths' techniques for methods study (or motion study) and time study extended science into the realm of the line employee. U.S. Supreme Court Justice Louis Brandeis named the approach "scientific management."

While putting the finishing touches on the Industrial Revolution, scientific management ushered in the beginnings of the modern manufacturing era. Since the United States was the birthplace of scientific management, it enjoyed the first benefits. Methods and standards programs spread rapidly in U.S. manufacturing firms between 1900 and 1950, which may help explain the phenomenal growth of industrial output in the United States in the first half of the century.

Is Taylorism Outdated?

Some writers have said that rejection of Taylorism is one reason for Japan's industrial success. That is nonsense. While Frederick W. Taylor did hold some views about supervision and the employees that today are considered odd, his main contribution was methods study and time standards—and the industrial engineering profession. The Japanese are the most fervent believers in industrial engineering in the world. At Toyota even the foreman is often an IE, or studying to become one. In the just-in-time approach, problems surface, and then people apply methods-study (and quality-improvement) concepts to solve the problems. Time standards are widely used in Japanese industry not to measure and report on performance but to plan how long to expect a job to take, assign the right amount of labor, and compare methods. Taylor declared that his "whole object was to remove the cause for antagonism between the boss and the men who were under him."*

*Frederick W. Taylor, *The Principles of Scientific Management* (New York: Harper & Row, 1911), pp. 20–28.

Methods and time standards programs are not limited to manufacturing. Beginning in the 1940s, they began to find their way into hospitals, food service, hotels, transportation, and other services. So carefully industrially engineered is the McDonald's hamburger that Levitt calls it "the technocratic hamburger."[7] In many industries, it has been hard to compete without good methods design and labor standards.

Scientific management is not without its critics. Labor unions often have resisted time standards. Some believe that under work measurement a person

---

[7]Theodore Levitt, "Production-Line Approach to Service," *Harvard Business Review*, September–October 1972, pp. 41–52.

is treated like a microcomputer memory chip. At the first sign of performance deterioration, the chip is discarded and replaced; it's just not cost effective to attempt to repair or recycle it. Often the ultimate plan is to replace the entire memory system, and even the computer itself, with faster memory and more powerful equipment.

Employees see themselves as "memory chips" and automated operations as the "new computers." For many, the reality is even worse than our analogy, for unlike memory chips, people are not a cheap resource. It is little wonder that so many employees resist workplace improvements. To them, increased productivity is just another excuse for taking away their jobs.

The problem is clear: Productivity is essential for survival. Increased automation *is* part of the solution, but often there are ample opportunities to improve on existing human work *before* spending on automation. The classic methodology for improvement is **methods study**.

METHODS STUDY

Formal methods-study techniques are based on the scientific method, a general method of inquiry. The steps in one version of the scientific method are: define problem, collect data, generate alternatives, evaluate alternatives and choose, implement and measure results (output), and repeat to correct and/or improve.

Let us see how Taylor, the Gilbreths, and the other pioneers of scientific management translated the scientific method into a procedure for methods study. We will also see that the scientific method is consistent with the theme of continuing improvement. Figure 16–2 illustrates the procedures.

Methods-Study Procedures

Methods study begins with task selection (step 1 in Figure 16–2). It may be a present task that seems inefficient or has never been studied before, or it may be a new task.

Steps 2 and 3 often feature *before* and *after* comparisons. Collected data go onto a flowchart showing the present method—the "before" condition. Then an "after" flowchart is developed to show a better method.

The before and after methods are described in symbols as well as words. Five flowcharting symbols were standardized by the American Society of Mechanical Engineers (ASME), which provided aid and encouragement in the formative years of scientific management. The ASME symbols are accepted throughout the world. The five symbols and their meanings are:

FIGURE 16–2
Methods Study and Scientific Method

Scientific Method	*Methods Study*
1. Define problem	Select a present task for methods improvement (or a new task for methods development).
2. Collect data	Flowchart present method (the *before* chart), or synthesize a flowchart for a new task.
3. Generate alternatives	Apply questioning attitude, principles of motion economy, etc., to arrive at alternative method and flowchart the method (the *after* chart).
4. Evaluate alternatives and choose	Evaluate new method via savings in:
	Cost Delays
	Time Transportation
	Effort Transportation
	Storages distances
	Choose the best method.
5. Implement and measure results	Implement—in training employees and in job planning.
	Measure results in terms identified in step 4.
6. Repeat as required	Repeat present study if measured results are not satisfactory; or repeat procedure with new study—another task selected for improvement.

Operations are productive; *moves, holds,* and *inspections* less so; and *delays* not at all. Putting it differently, operations *add value;* the others do not.

Methods analysts develop a better method by applying the "questioning attitude." Also, like newspaper reporters, methods analysts embrace Kipling's six honest serving men:

> I keep six honest serving men
> (They taught me all I knew);
> Their names are what and why and when
> and how and where and who.
>
> Rudyard Kipling
> The Elephant's Child

Principles of methods improvement are also useful. Frank and Lillian Gilbreth were early developers of such principles.[8] Ralph Barnes elaborated on the Gilbreths' work in developing "principles of motion economy." Others have offered further refinements. For example, Mundel provides a list of "general principles,"

---

[8] F. B. Gilbreth and L. M. Gilbreth, *Fatigue Study* (New York: Sturgis and Walton, 1916). The book was written by Lillian Gilbreth.

which attempt to incorporate the human factor. Study of the human factor is a subfield of industrial engineering known as **ergonomics**.[9]

Mundel's general principles are grouped under four headings: elimination, combination, rearrangement, and simplification. Under those headings are principles that concern better posture; danger; natural, sweeping motions as opposed to choppy, irregular ones; and the physiology of effort. The idea is that much of the potential for productivity gain is found in the labor-machine interface, and this calls for attention to human comfort and emotions as well as physical efficiency.

Step 4 in Figure 16–2 is evaluating alternatives and choosing the new method based on cost or other criteria. Cost analysis is itself often costly, and cost estimates for untried methods can be inaccurate. Therefore, other criteria are often used as surrogates for cost: time, effort, storage, delays, transportation, and transportation distances. Historically, quality was *not* one of those criteria, because the methods study typically treated a minimum level of quality as a given.

Step 5 is implementing the chosen method, mainly for use in training and job planning. Sometimes the industrial engineer's chosen method must be "signed off" by the foreman and perhaps also by quality control, safety, production control, human resources, and a labor-union steward.

Results are measured in units identified in step 4. If results are unsatisfactory, study steps 1 through 4 are repeated, perhaps with extra diligence. If results from step 5 *are* satisfactory, there is the chance that complacency may set in and the improvement effort may stop. There is *always* another task needing improvement. Thus, step 6 is *always* required—that is, if continuing methods improvement is a genuine goal.

The six steps in methods study may be applied to small, medium, or large units of work. In fact, the history of methods study began with motion study of employees confined to the workbench and gradually grew. Variations on the six-step process were developed for studying whole workstations, and then work that crosses work center and departmental lines.

Figure 16–3 presents four such variations—from study at the level of the workbench to the machine to the work area to the whole plant; the focus shifts from hand motions to operator and machine to mobile employee to product flow. The first level is described next.

Motion Study

Frank Gilbreth is the father of **motion study**, which began as a laboratory approach to analyzing basic hand and body motions. In fact, basic motions such as reach and grasp are known as **therbligs**; the word "therblig" is "Gilbreth" spelled backward (except for the *th*). It was sensible for Gilbreth to focus on highly repetitive short-cycle manual motions. Even small gains can yield large

[9]Marvin E. Mundel, *Motion and Time Study: Improving Productivity*, 5th ed. (Englewood Cliffs, N.J.: Prentice-Hall, 1978), pp., 172–173 (T60.7.M86).

FIGURE 16-3

Four Levels of Methods Study

Type	Application	Flowchart
Motion study	Manual task at workbench or desk	Left-and-right-hand chart
Operator-machine analysis	Machine tending at workplace	Operator-machine chart
Employee analysis	Task involving mobile employee	Process flowchart (employee-oriented)
Product analysis	Product flow	Process flowchart (product-oriented)

benefits, and the analysis is not complicated by costly machines, operator travel, or irregular activities.

The left-and-right-hand chart is suitable for before-and-after analysis. A goal is to keep both hands busy, because an idle hand is like half an idle employee. Example 16-1 illustrates.

EXAMPLE 16-1   LEFT- AND RIGHT-HAND CHART—BOLT-WASHER-NUT ASSEMBLY

One repetitive task in a certain firm is to make a bolt-washer-nut assembly. The present method is under study using the left-and-right-hand charting method.

Figure 16-4 charts the present method. The summary at the bottom of the flowchart shows mostly low-productive and nonproductive elements, that is, seven moves, six holds, two delays, and no inspections. A workbench sketch commonly goes with the left-and-right-hand chart, because a poor workbench design impedes productivity.

Figure 16-5 charts the proposed method based on improved workbench design, the principles of methods improvement, and the concept of quality at the source. To accomplish the quality objective, it is necessary for the assembler to inspect his or her own work.

The summary in Figure 16-5 shows elimination of all holds and delays. There are seven more moves, but the proposed method produces two assemblies every cycle versus one per cycle under the present method. The proposed method clearly increases productivity. Also, it provides smoother, more natural motions and shorter hand-travel distances; the proposed method may be less tiring. Finally, bad assemblies go no further in the production process. They are stopped at the source by placement in reject bins. A "quick toss" by the assembler saves much later grief for the customer—the next process.

If the results of the motion study appear disputable, it may be worth the extra effort to measure elements in time units. Also, having the results in minutes permits conversion into dollars so that operating savings may be compared with the costs of new-methods development and implementation. The comparison should also recognize that the proposed method may eliminate inspection at a later stage.

FIGURE 16–4
Left- and Right-Hand Chart for Bolt-Washer-Nut Assembly, Present Method

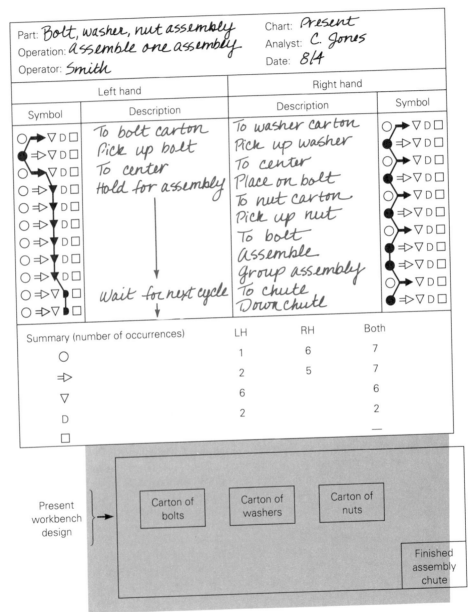

Part: Bolt, washer, nut assembly		Chart: Present
Operation: assemble one assembly		Analyst: C. Jones
Operator: Smith		Date: 8/4

Left hand		Right hand	
Symbol	Description	Description	Symbol
○ ⇒ ▽ D □	To bolt carton	To washer carton	○ ⇒ ▽ D □
○ ⇒ ▽ D □	Pick up bolt	Pick up washer	○ ⇒ ▽ D □
○ ⇒ ▽ D □	To center	To center	○ ⇒ ▽ D □
○ ⇒ ▽ D □	Hold for assembly	Place on bolt	○ ⇒ ▽ D □
○ ⇒ ▽ D □		To nut carton	○ ⇒ ▽ D □
○ ⇒ ▽ D □		Pick up nut	○ ⇒ ▽ D □
○ ⇒ ▽ D □		To bolt	○ ⇒ ▽ D □
○ ⇒ ▽ D □		Assemble	○ ⇒ ▽ D □
○ ⇒ ▽ D □	Wait for next cycle	Group assembly	○ ⇒ ▽ D □
○ ⇒ ▽ D □		To chute	○ ⇒ ▽ D □
○ ⇒ ▽ D □		Down chute	○ ⇒ ▽ D □

Summary (number of occurrences)		LH	RH	Both
○		1	6	7
⇒		2	5	7
▽		6		6
D		2		2
□				—

Present workbench design →   Carton of bolts   Carton of washers   Carton of nuts

Finished assembly chute

FIGURE 16–5

Left- and Right-Hand Chart for Bolt-Washer-Nut Assembly—Proposed Method

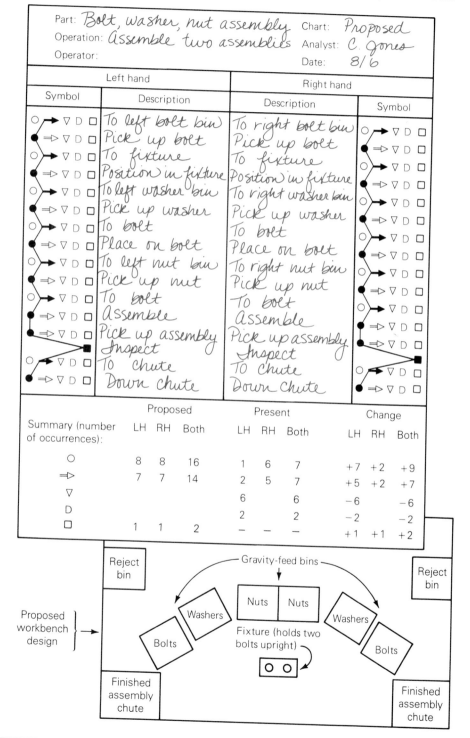

Part: Bolt, washer, nut assembly   Chart: Proposed
Operation: Assemble two assemblies   Analyst: C. Jones
Operator: Date: 8/6

Left hand		Right hand	
Symbol	Description	Description	Symbol
○ ▷ ▽ D □	To left bolt bin	To right bolt bin	○ ▷ ▽ D □
● ▷ ▽ D □	Pick up bolt	Pick up bolt	● ▷ ▽ D □
○ ▷ ▽ D □	To fixture	To fixture	○ ▷ ▽ D □
● ▷ ▽ D □	Position in fixture	Position in fixture	● ▷ ▽ D □
○ ▷ ▽ D □	To left washer bin	To right washer bin	○ ▷ ▽ D □
● ▷ ▽ D □	Pick up washer	Pick up washer	● ▷ ▽ D □
○ ▷ ▽ D □	To bolt	To bolt	○ ▷ ▽ D □
● ▷ ▽ D □	Place on bolt	Place on bolt	● ▷ ▽ D □
○ ▷ ▽ D □	To left nut bin	To right nut bin	○ ▷ ▽ D □
● ▷ ▽ D □	Pick up nut	Pick up nut	● ▷ ▽ D □
○ ▷ ▽ D □	To bolt	To bolt	○ ▷ ▽ D □
● ▷ ▽ D □	Assemble	Assemble	● ▷ ▽ D □
● ▷ ▽ D □	Pick up assembly	Pick up assembly	● ▷ ▽ D □
○ ▷ ▽ D ■	Inspect	Inspect	○ ▷ ▽ D ■
○ ▷ ▽ D □	To chute	To chute	○ ▷ ▽ D □
● ▷ ▽ D □	Down chute	Down chute	● ▷ ▽ D □

	Proposed			Present			Change		
Summary (number of occurrences):	LH	RH	Both	LH	RH	Both	LH	RH	Both
○	8	8	16	1	6	7	+7	+2	+9
⇒	7	7	14	2	5	7	+5	+2	+7
▽				6		6	−6		−6
D				2		2	−2		−2
□	1	1	2	—	—	—	+1	+1	+2

Proposed workbench design →

Reject bin

Gravity-feed bins

Nuts   Nuts

Washers   Washers

Bolts   Fixture (holds two bolts upright)   Bolts

Reject bin

Finished assembly chute

Finished assembly chute

PRINCIPLE: Arrange the workplace to eliminate search time.

Operator-Machine Analysis

When the employee is a machine tender instead of a tool user, we worry about the productivity of the machine as well as of the person, since a machine is a costly resource. An operator-machine-time chart may be used to record present (before) and proposed (after) methods for work involving one or more operators and machines. For example, a two-person crew might sort, wash, dry, and iron sheets in a hospital laundry. A five-column operator-machine-time-chart could be set up to record activities and durations, one column for the first crew member, one for the second, one for the washer, one for the dryer, and one for the ironing machine. A workplace layout normally accompanies the chart. Time saving is the basis for comparing the new method with the old.

Employee Analysis

The activities of a mobile employee may be studied by the process **flowchart,** another Gilbreth contribution. It employs four process flow symbols: circle, arrow, large D, and square, which were discussed earlier. The inverted triangle, representing "hold" or "store," is not used in employee analysis because you do not store a person. The process flowchart also is used in product analysis.

Product Analysis

Product analysis is much like employee analysis, except all five flowcharting symbols are used. The symbols and the product analysis flowchart are used in Example 16–2, in which a "a product" of the accounting department—expense vouchers—is the focus.

EXAMPLE 16–2   **PROCESS FLOWCHART—"THE EXPENSE-ACCOUNT EXPRESS"[10]**

Intel Corporation has "rediscovered" the process flowchart and uses it extensively in both its paperwork and its goods production operations. For example, Intel's expense-account processing steps were reduced from 25 to 14, as is shown in the before-and-after charts of Figure 16–6. The accounts-payable clerk took over the cash-receipts clerk's job of checking the employee's past expense accounts (steps 8, 10, and 11). This eliminated

---

[10]Adapted from Jeremy Main, "Battling Your Own Bureaucracy," in *Working Smarter,* by the Editors of *Fortune* (New York: Viking press, 1982), pp. 88–89 (HC110.152W67).

FIGURE 16-6
Process Flowchart

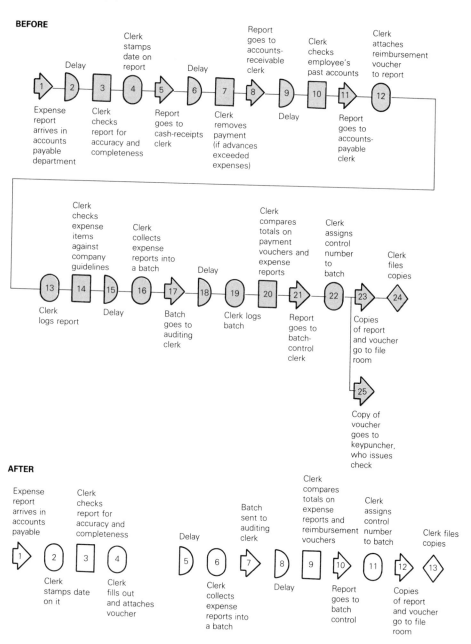

Source: *Fortune* Art Dept.

steps 5 and 7. There was no need for an accounts-receivable clerk to check the employee's past expense accounts, since another department had already done that; steps 8, 10, and 11 were eliminated. Checking items against company guidelines (step 14) was done away with; it seemed more trouble than it was worth. Logging batches (step 19) was found to be unnecessary. Four delays (steps 2, 6, 9 and 18) were eliminated. Those changes cut time to process expense accounts from weeks to days.

For expenses under $100, the employee now just fills out a petty-cash voucher and collects right away from the cashier. After these and other simplifications, the accounts-payable department cut its staff from 71 in 1980 to 51 in April 1981.

Work Sampling and Other Methods-Analysis Tools

Methods analysis makes use of other tools besides flowcharting. Systems flow-charting and program flowcharting are similar tools in the computer industry. Material handling and plant/office layout, discussed in Chapter 18, are special-purpose process analysis techniques. Capital budgeting/engineering economy techniques are used mainly to evaluate facilities proposals, but they are also used to compare manual methods with automated facilities. Linear program-ming, queuing, simulation, and other management science models are also useful in process analysis. We examine some of those tools in other chapters.

One bedrock analysis tool that differs substantially from the flowcharting tools is **work sampling**, which is useful for both process and time-standards analysis. It is like the "before" flowchart in that it shows what is happening at present. The work-sampling study yields data on percentage of idle or delay time.[11] Further, the study can be designed with idleness broken down into categories, thereby showing process bottlenecks. Example 16–3 illustrates.

EXAMPLE 16–3   **WORK SAMPLING—PATHOLOGY LAB**

The director of Midtown Pathological Labs is concerned. Costs are going up rapidly; the staff has plenty to do, yet is often idled by assorted problems. The director decides to probe the sources of delay by conducting a one-week work-sampling study. Of special interest are lab equipment failures, supply shortages, delays waiting for instructions, excessive coffee breaks, and lab technicians absent from the work area. The director prepares a work-sampling data sheet that includes those five categories of delay (plus an "other" category); she also works up a schedule for taking 100 sample observations (20 per day).

The schedule and completed form are shown in Figure 16–7. The results—the staff

---

[11]In fact, work sampling used to be known as *ratio delay*, a term proposed by R. L. Morrow, an early U.S. user of the technique. (L. H. C. Tippett developed the method in England in the 1920s.) Later, the editor of *Factory* magazine, recognizing its usefulness in time-standards as well as delay analysis, proposed the more general term *work sampling*. See Ralph M. Barnes, *Work Sampling* (New York: John Wiley & Sons, 1957), pp. 8–10 (T60.T5B3).

"not working" 35 percent of the time—confirm the director's impression of serious delay problems. The breakdown into categories of delay yields insight into causes.

The management system can be blamed for the first 18 percent of nonworking time. Equipment failure (3 percent), supply shortages (6 percent), and wait for instructions (9 percent) are failures to provide technicians with resources for keeping busy.

The 13 percent of delay for coffee breaks is an employee problem. Authorized coffee breaks are a 15-minute morning break and a 15-minute afternoon break. This amounts to 30 minutes or, in percent of an 8-hour day,

$$\frac{30 \text{ min}}{8 \text{ hr.} \times 60 \text{ min./hr.}} = 0.0625 \approx 6\%$$

The coffee-break abuses may be dealt with immediately. The data on resource shortages do not offer a solution, but they do tip off the director on where to look.

FIGURE 16–7

Work-Sampling Data Sheets—Midtown Pathological Labs

SCHEDULE OF OBSERVATION TIMES				
Mon.	Tues.	Wed.	Thurs.	Fri.

| 8:01 |
| 8:13 |
| 9:47 |
| 9:59 |
| 10:12 |
| 10:59 |
| 11:16 |
| 11:32 |
| 1:00 |
| 1:15 |
| 1:19 |
| 2:52 |
| 2:55 |
| 2:56 |
| 2:57 |
| 3:02 |
| 3:29 |
| 3:37 |
| 4:07 |
| 4:32 |

WORK-SAMPLING FORM		
Category of Activity	Observations (tallies)	Percentages
Working	ＴＨＴ ＴＨＴ ＴＨＴ ＴＨＴ ＴＨＴ ＴＨＴ ＴＨＴ ＴＨＴ ＴＨＴ ＴＨＴ ＴＨＴ ＴＨＴ ＴＨＴ (65)	65%
Not working:		
• Equipment failure	||| ③	3%
• Supplies shortage	ＴＨＴ	⑥	6%
• Wait for instructions	ＴＨＴ |||| ⑨	9%
• Coffee break	ＴＨＴ ＴＨＴ ||| ⑬	13%
• Out of area	|| ②	2%
• Other	|| ②	2%
Total	100	100%

Besides delay statistics, work sampling yields the complement, utilization rate. As we have seen, utilization rate (65 percent in the example) means "busyness," that is, hours busy divided by hours available. But most of us are very busy at times and not so busy at others. This means that to avoid bias, the analyst doing work sampling must take care to do the study in a representative time period (representative of average conditions if that is the goal of the study; representative of very busy conditions if peak conditions are being examined; etc.).

There are other types of bias to guard against. Seven guidelines are:

1. Conduct the study over a number of days or weeks so that results will not be biased by a single unusual day.

2. Make instantaneous observations so that the employee doesn't glide into another activity, leaving the analyst a choice of which one to record.

3. Vary the route of travel if the study goes to several work areas to guard against having employees in one area alert employees in the next area that the observer is coming.

4. Observe at random intervals so that employees may not come to expect and prepare for the observer's arrival at set intervals.

5. Tell the employees what you are doing, and emphasize the goal of improving resource support—to prevent hostility and deliberate attempts to foul up the study.

6. When in doubt, ask the employee what the observed activity is—to avoid judgmental bias.

7. Take a large enough sample to yield convincing results. (Probably 100, the sample size in Figure 16–7, is not enough. Statistical guidelines are available in many industrial engineering books.)

BUSY AND PRODUCTIVE RESOURCES

Walk into a drugstore when it is moderately busy, and what do you see? A clerk in the cameras and film department flitting back and forth taking care of three customers; one cashier up front ringing up a customer's purchases, and another cashier trying hard not to look idle and bored; customers bumping into each other in the cold remedies aisle while most other aisles are empty. The cameras and film clerk is *busy*, and working very *efficiently* as well. One cashier is busy, the other *idle*. The space around cold remedies is highly *utilized*, whereas most of the rest of the store isn't even justifying the power to keep the lights on.

We have identified some common, noncost ways of evaluating the productivity of various resources. Terms like *efficiency*, *busyness* and *idleness*, and *utilization* can be used loosely; they also have precise meanings and can be measured numerically. Examples follow, first for equipment and other nonhuman resources; then for people.

Machine Utilization

A general formula for **utilization** of labor or machines is:

$$\text{Utilization rate} = \frac{\text{Time in use}}{\text{Time available}} \tag{16–1}$$

Machine utilization reports, expressing Equation 16–1 as a percentage, are common in larger companies. For some equipment, 40 hours—one shift operation—is used as available hours per week. Sometimes two or more shifts are the basis. Data for the reports sometimes can be collected automatically by timers in the machine, vehicle, conveyor line, or data terminal.

The machine utilization report has at least two purposes. First, it serves as a check on how well the plant and the company plan in advance for the right machine capacity. Second, trends in machine utilization suggest when more capacity will be needed so that equipment may be ordered in advance.

Figure 16–8 shows utilization for a machine already over 100 percent on a one-shift basis; that means the machine is run on overtime, extra shifts, or weekends, which may require payment of overtime wages. The company might have seen the trend months earlier so that another or a larger machine was put on order and is due in soon.

With today's mood of questioning virtually everything in operations management, the machine utilization report has come under fire. Harley-Davidson

FIGURE 16–8
Machine Utilization Trend Report

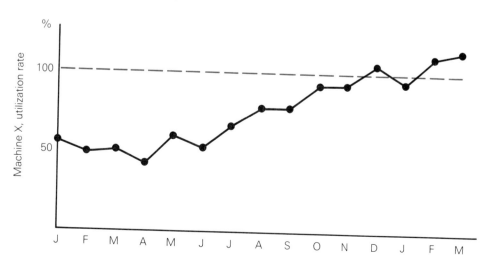

has simply eliminated machine utilization reports. Why? Because the reports can cover up certain faults and result in treating symptoms, not real problems. Some potential weaknesses in machine utilization reports or the way the reports are used include:

High utilization can be achieved by disposing of slow machines and running all jobs on new, fast machines. But old, slow machines are valuable when considering moving machines into cells or other focused zones within a building.

Utilization may include "bad" time, such as production of scrap and rework, machine slowdowns, and setup or changeovers. If capacity is added when equipment is engaged in such ineffective activities, habits of accepting bad performance set it.

High utilization may be achieved by running very large lots, which produce unneeded inventories.

Utilization reports can encourage dabbling in peripheral products to keep machines busy; over time, the facility becomes unfocused.

Utilization is usually measured in hours, when the real concern should be utilization of dollars (return on investment).

Finally, and perhaps most importantly, 100 percent utilization is not even desirable. For example, no computer center wants its mainframe to be 100 percent utilized, because the effect would be long backlogs, interminable delays in getting jobs run, and squabbling for priority among anxious customers.

Other Resource Utilization Measures

Besides machine utilization, some firms, especially larger ones, measure and report on space utilization. The reports express space-in-use as a percentage of total space, which may be broken down by type of space or type of use. Colleges and universities generally report based on several room-use categories, which in the United States are specified by the Department of Education.

Use of information resources can also be measured. Typically the measure is frequency of use rather than percentage of time in use. For example, records and files may be archived based on a certain standard of use or nonuse and disposed of completely in the next phase of records/file control. (*Migration* is a common term for moving information from active storage to archives to disposal.) These are common techniques of records management.

There are many other measures of resource utilization. For example, for the labor resource, it is common to keep track of absences resulting from illness, jury duty, military duty, labor union activities, tardiness, and so forth—all of which eat into productive time. Measures of materials utilization might include scrap, theft, deterioration, obsolescence, and misplacement—all of which hinder productive use of materials. Some of the same kinds of measures may be applied to tools, space, and information.

Labor Utilization

The machine utilization formula, Equation 16–1, also works for the human resource.

Assume, for example, that in a 2,400-minute (40-hour) week a six-person office group spends 2,000 minutes at work on an assortment of 38 jobs (such as letters and reports). The utilization rate, from Equation 16–1, is

$$\text{Utilization} = \frac{\text{Time working}}{\text{Time available for work}}$$

$$= \frac{2,000}{2,400} = 0.83, \text{ or } 83\%$$

And what about the other 400 minutes of the 2,400-minute week? We should not be too quick to label it *idleness*. That time may actually be used for worthwhile activities such as cross training or problem solving.

Labor Efficiency

Human labor is a unique resource that is not merely *utilized*. Unlike the non-human kind (e.g., equipment and materials), the human resource has a will; it can choose to work at a "normal" pace or much faster or slower than that. Later, we shall see how to find out what normal—or *standard*—pace is. For now, we'll examine one of the uses of **standard time**.

Formal production control systems generally include a periodic report of **efficiency** by employee, work center, and department. Labor efficiency is determined in one of two ways:

$$\text{Efficiency} = \frac{\text{Standard time per unit}}{\text{Actual time per unit}} \text{ or, simply, } \frac{\text{Standard time}}{\text{Actual time}} \quad (16\text{--}2)$$

$$\text{Efficiency} = \frac{\text{Actual units per time period}}{\text{Standard units per time period}} \text{ or, simply, } \frac{\text{Actual units}}{\text{Standard units}}$$

$$(16\text{--}3)$$

Note that the two versions are mathematically equivalent; each is an inversion of the other.

To illustrate the formulas, assume that 440 actual units are produced in a 40-hour week and 400 is the standard output per week. Using Equation 16–3,

$$\text{Efficiency} = \frac{440 \text{ units/week}}{400 \text{ units/week}}$$

$$= 1.10, \text{ or } 110\%$$

To use Equation 16–2, the data must be converted to time per unit. Since there are 2,400 minutes in a 40-hour week,

$$\text{Standard time} = \frac{2{,}400 \text{ minutes/week}}{400 \text{ units/week}}$$

$$= 6 \text{ minutes/unit}$$

and

$$\text{Actual time} = \frac{2{,}400 \text{ minutes/week}}{440 \text{ units/week}}$$

$$= 5.45 \text{ minutes/week}$$

Then, by Equation 16–2,

$$\text{Efficiency} = \frac{6 \text{ minutes/unit}}{5.45 \text{ minutes/unit}}$$

$$= 1.10, \text{ or } 110\%$$

Sometimes Equation 16–2 is adapted to cover a number of jobs over a fixed reporting period. As Equation 16–4 shows, the numerator becomes the total standard time for all jobs worked on in the period and the denominator is actual time spent on the jobs:

$$\text{Efficiency} = \frac{\text{Total standard time for all jobs done}}{\text{Actual direct labor time on those jobs}} \qquad (16\text{–}4)$$

Returning to our office example, assume that the 38 jobs completed in the week represent 1,900 standard minutes of work content (for the six people, that averages 50 minutes per job or 8.3 minutes of each employee's time). The six employees report 2,000 actual direct-labor minutes on those 38 jobs. Then, by Equation 16–4,

$$\text{Efficiency} = \frac{1{,}900}{2{,}000}$$

$$= 0.95, \text{ or } 95\%$$

Labor Productivity

We saw earlier in the chapter that labor productivity can be measured using cost as the basis; a simpler way, using time as the basis, has the following formula:

$$\text{Productivity} = \frac{\text{Standard time for all work done}}{\text{Time available for work}} \qquad (16\text{–}5)$$

In our office example,

$$\text{Productivity} = \frac{1{,}900}{2{,}400} = 0.79, \text{ or } 79\%$$

Also, it happens that

$$\text{Productivity} = \text{Efficiency} \times \text{Utilization} \qquad (16\text{--}6)$$

So,

$$\text{Productivity} = 0.95 \times 0.83 = 0.79, \text{ or } 79\%$$

Productivity Reporting in Perspective

Reports on resource productivity tend to proliferate and get out of hand, sometimes to the point where as much is spent on reporting as on paying for the resources. For example, in a Tektronix plant producing portable oscilloscopes, a study revealed that all the labor reporting—data entry, computer costs, error correction, etc.—was costing as much as the total payroll the labor reports were supposed to control! Needless to say, Tektronix canceled the labor reporting, which eliminated about 35,000 computer transactions per month.[12]

It is staff organizations, such as purchasing, human resources, and inventory control, that generate resource reports. They are *input*-oriented—below the dashed line in the chart that opens the chapter—and they exist only for serving above-the-line operations, which are output- and customer-oriented. But preservation, growth, and power instincts can conflict with the mandate to provide only the resources necessary for operations to use in serving customers. Those instincts tend to result in too much resource management and too many reports. When large organizations fall on hard times, regaining economic health may include cutting staff employees and many of their reports. The tens of thousands of jobs lost in the North American financial services industry in 1989–1990 serve as a reminder.

Thus far in this chapter, we have considered cost and non-cost approaches to productivity management. Next we examine a key source of data for these approaches, namely, the time standard.

TIME STANDARDS AND THEIR USES

Methods study comes first. Time study follows. Why? Because it is unproductive to set a time standard on a poor method. In launching a methods and standards program, however, some firms may reverse the process, first covering all tasks with time standards—perhaps "quick and dirty" ones, later turning to methods studies and then refining time standards based on the improved methods.

---

[12]Peter B. B. Turney and Bruce Anderson, "Accounting for Continuous Improvement," *Sloan Management Review*, Winter 1989, pp. 37–47.

Importance of Time Standards

Work is simply a form of exertion. But a unit of work (such as a job, task, or project) is defined more specifically, including the *time* taken to perform it. Sometimes work time is estimated in advance. For example, in a two-person operation, if person B must wait for person A to finish a job, B will want an advance estimate of how long A's job will take. Time estimates are also useful in planning labor needs and labor costs as well as for motivational purposes.

To summarize, we have identified three purposes of time standards (time estimates): scheduling and coordination, analysis of operations, and motivating for productivity. We discussed the latter earlier in the chapter. In the remainder of this section, we examine the two other purposes of time standards, and also the concept of under-scheduling labor.

Coordination and Scheduling

The primary use of time standards is in coordination and scheduling. Actually, by definition, a schedule is a time standard, with proper adjustments for efficiency and utilization; that is, the time between the scheduled start and the scheduled finish of a task equals:

Standard time—the time it should take under normal assumptions
    . . . adjusted downward for a fast employee or upward for a slow employee.
    . . . adjusted downward for less than 100 percent labor utilization (i.e., for expected idleness).

Mathematically, scheduled output for a given time period is:

$$\text{Scheduled output} = \frac{\text{Efficiency} \times \text{Utilization}}{\text{Standard time per unit}} \qquad (16\text{--}7)$$

or

$$\text{Scheduled output} = \text{Standard units per time period} \qquad (16\text{--}8)$$
$$\times \text{Efficiency} \times \text{Utilization}$$

where

$$\text{Utilization} = \frac{\text{Time working}}{\text{Time available for work}} \qquad (16\text{--}9)$$

A useful inversion of Equation 16–7 is:

$$\text{Scheduled time} = \frac{\text{Standard time per unit}}{\text{Efficiency} \times \text{Utilization}} \qquad (16\text{--}10)$$

which may also be expressed as:

$$\text{Scheduled time} = \frac{\text{Standard time per unit}}{\text{Productivity rate}} \qquad (16\text{--}11)$$

Utilization goes up when employees are kept busy and provided with proper tools, materials, well-maintained equipment, and so forth. The scheduled time for a job that is done more than once may be cut as utilization is improved. It is up to management to provide the right resources needed to keep employees busy.

Where coordination demands are light, formal scheduling of work units may be unnecessary. But there is nearly always at least a vague time plan for starting and finishing an upcoming task. This plan is an *implied* time standard. For example, in the service sector implied time standards are at least in the back of people's minds for all work assignments. On the other hand, for most factory work, a *real* (not implied) standard typically is used, especially for repetitive production.

Under-Capacity Scheduling of Labor

Current thinking on labor scheduling favors a schedule that is attainable on most days. The concept is called **under-capacity scheduling** (of labor). A simple way to implement it is to base scheduled output, as determined by Equation 16–7 or 16–8 on fewer hours than are in the full work shift.

Consider, for example, a 480-minute (8-hour) work shift. Suppose the plan is to underschedule labor by 10 percent, that is, schedule for 10 percent less than 480 minutes, or for 432 minutes. Personnel are present and paid for 480 minutes, but scheduled output is based on 432 minutes.

On the average day, the crew completes the required number of units in 432 minutes. In the remaining 48 minutes of the shift, the crew performs preventive maintenance, holds problem-solving meetings, splits up into project teams with engineers or buyers, engages in training activities, and so forth. On a good day, they complete direct labor in less than 432 minutes and thus have more than 48 minutes for support activities. On a bad day, they work the entire shift; every once in a while, they may even need to work overtime in order to get scheduled production out.

Under-capacity scheduling was not necessary in the past when one work center typically was separated from the next by hours' or even weeks' worth of material. With so much excess stock in the system, labor was scheduled to produce a certain amount, but overproduction and underproduction were normal from day to day; the schedule was really just an average. Today, with many firms eliminating the excess stocks between processes, each work center must turn out an exact, planned quantity—just in time. Otherwise, there will be epidemics of work stoppages for lack of parts.

The next category of uses for time standards is analysis of operations. Again, real rather than implied standards are required.

Analysis of Operations

One important group of analytical uses of time standards consists of staffing, budgeting, and estimating/bidding. Staff (labor) needed is the product of units forecasted and standard time per unit. Budgeting for staff goes one step further; staff needed times wage rate equals staff budget.

The staff component of an estimate or bid is computed the same way as the staff component of a budget. Accurate bidding is a key to success in contract-oriented businesses such as construction. Accurate cost estimating is important in such work, because pricing is based on estimated cost plus profit margin. Physicians, attorneys, and consultants also often operate this way.

Another analytical use of time standards is evaluating alternative methods and equipment, which usually involve some labor costs. The labor component of operating cost is based on standard time per unit of output, with adjustments for efficiency and utilization. The labor component of maintenance cost is based on standard time to repair, with appropriate adjustments.

Analysis of operations comes before the work itself. The third use of time standards, motivating for productivity, applies while the work is underway.

Having examined the uses of time standards, we now explore techniques of determining them.

TIME STANDARDS TECHNIQUES

Some of the common uses for time standards that we have studied, as well as some of the abuses (discussed later), relate to the techniques for developing time standards. As Figure 16–9 shows, the techniques are of two types; engineered and nonengineered. In this section, we first discuss the differences between the two types and then examine what is required in order to consider a standard to have been engineered. Next, we see a detailed explanation of the two most prevalent techniques, time study and work sampling. Finally, we briefly discuss the remaining techniques listed in Figure 16–9.

Engineered and Nonengineered Standards

Four techniques may result in engineered time standards. Engineered standards are prepared at some expense following the scientific methods of the industrial engineer. Two of the engineered techniques require direct observation. They are stopwatch time study, a well-known approach, and work sampling, presented earlier as a process analysis technique. Predetermined and standard data techniques, on the other hand, make use of already-prepared tables of time

FIGURE 16–9

Techniques for Setting Time Standards

Technique	Source of Times	Timing Role of Analyst
Engineered		
1. Time study	Stopwatch (or film)	Direct observation: Record times for several cycles of the task; judge and record pace.
2. Work sampling	Percent of study period busy at given task divided by number of units produced	Direct observation: Randomly check employee status; keep tallies of employee activities and pace; obtain production count.
3. Predetermined	Table look-up	Define task in basic body motions; look up time values in basic motion tables.
4. Standard data	Table look-up	Define task in small, common elements (e.g., pound nail); look up time value in standard-data tables.
Nonengineered		
5. Historical (statistical)	Past records on actual task times	Determine arithmetic mean and/or other useful statistics.
6. Technical estimate ("guesstimate")	Experienced judgment	Experienced person estimates times, preferably after breaking task into operations.

values; since a real employee is not involved, they are sometimes called *synthetic time standards*.

Two techniques are listed in Figure 16–9 as nonengineered. The first, historical or statistical, is based on past records rather than on controlled study. The second is the technical estimate, or "guesstimate,"[13] which comes from subjective judgment rather than recorded statistics.

Requisites of an Engineered Standard

The expense of an engineered time standard is worthwhile if precision is needed; for example, in highly repetitive processes, where small gains add up fast. The following steps lead to an engineered standard:

1. Clearly specify the method.
2. Obtain time values via a proper sampling procedure or from validated tables.

---

[13]It is also known as WAG or a SWAG, common abbreviations for slightly salty terms that some readers may be familiar with.

3. Adjust for employee pace.

4. Include allowances for personal, rest, and delay time.

Each step adds precision. A precise time standard is associated with a known standard method (ideally an improved or engineered method). One way to get precise time values is to use direct observation and a proper sampling procedure; direct observation is avoided by use of a "synthetic" time value from validated tables. Where direct observation is used, the time value should be adjusted for employee pace; but validated tables for time values have built-in pace adjustments. Finally, the pace-adjusted time is further adjusted by adding reasonable allowances for employees' personal and rest time and for unavoidable delay.

The nonengineered techniques control for *none* of the above four factors of precision. (Even the first four techniques in Figure 16–9 are worthy of the term *engineered* only if they are precisely developed following the four steps.) In the following discussions, we see how the steps apply for each technique.

Time Study

The most direct approach to time standards is timing an employee who is performing the task. A stopwatch is the usual timing device, but motion picture film or videotape also works.[14] **Time study** is best for shorter-cycle tasks. The cost of having an analyst at the worksite and timing a proper number of cycles of the task tends to rule out time study for longer-cycle tasks. The four time-study steps are explained next and illustrated in solved problem 3 in this chapter.

1. Select Task and Define Method. Time study begins with selection of a task to study. There are choices to be made here. For example, packing and crating a large refrigeration unit consists of packing the unit into a carton, placing the carton on a pallet, building a wooden crate around the carton and pallet, stenciling, and steelstrapping. A single time study of the whole series of tasks is one possibility. Alternatively, separate time studies could be done for each major task; but each of those involves lesser tasks, which could be separately time studied. Pounding a single nail into a crate could be the task chosen for study.

Once the task has been chosen, the analyst defines the method. This involves dividing the task into elements that are easy to recognize and to time. The definition must clearly specify the actions that constitute the start and the end of each element, which is how the analyst knows when to take each stopwatch reading.

2. Cycle Time. Tools of the time-study analyst include a clipboard, a preprinted time-study data sheet, and a stopwatch. The watch is mounted on the clipboard. Before timing, the analyst observes for a while to be sure the operator is following the prescribed method.

---

[14]Film analysis was common in the World War II era. Any idea that might help with the war effort had a good chance of being funded at that time, and industrial film labs seemed to have the potential to help increase productivity. Today few firms use film techniques.

In the timing phase, the analyst records a stopwatch reading for each element. Several cycles of the task should be timed so that effects of early or late readings can be averaged out. Multiple cycles also provide a better basis for judging pace and observing unavoidable delays and irregular activities. Comments on irregularities are entered in a "remarks" section on the data sheet.

The number of cycles to time could be calculated based on the statistical dispersion of individual element readings. However, most firms pay more attention to the cost of multiple cycles than to the statistical dispersion of readings. For example, General Electric has established a table as a guide to the number of cycles.[15] The table calls for timing only 3 cycles if the cycle time is 40 minutes or more, but it calls for timing 200 cycles if the cycle time is as short as 0.1 minutes. Since 200 cycles at 0.1 minutes adds up to only 20 minutes of observer time, the 200-cycle study may cost less to do than the 3-cycle study of a 40-minute task.

The result of timing is an average **cycle time (CT)**—a raw time value.

3. Pace Rating. If the analyst times a slow person, the average cycle time will be excessive (*loose* is the term usually used); if a faster person is timed, the CT will be tight. To avoid loose or tight standards, the analyst judges the employee's pace during the study. The **pace rating** is then used mathematically to adjust CT to yield a **normal time**. This is called **normalizing** or **leveling**. The normal pace is 100 percent; a 125 percent pace is 25 percent faster; and so on.

Pace rating is the most judgmental part of setting time standards. But it need not be pure guesswork. Films are available from the American Management Association and other sources for training in pace rating. The films show a variety of factory and office tasks. The same task is shown at different speeds, and the viewer writes down the apparent pace for each speed. The projector is shut off, and the viewer's ratings are compared with an "answer key." The correct answers have been decided upon by experts or measured by film speed.

Expert opinion has been channeled to some extent. There are two widely accepted benchmarks of normal (100 percent) pace. One, for hand motions, is dealing 52 cards into 4 equal piles (bridge hands) in 30 seconds. The other benchmark is walking on a smooth, level surface, without load, at three miles per hour. These concepts of normal extrapolate to many other manual activities.

Most people can become good enough at pace rating to be able to come within ± 5 percent of the "correct" ratings. It is easier to rate a person who is close to normal than one who is very slow or fast. Because of this, it is a good idea for the analyst to try to find a "normal" employee to observe in doing a time study (or work-sampling study). Sometimes pace rating is "omitted" by preselecting an employee who is performing at normal; the omission is illusory, since the rating is done in the employee selection step.

4. Personal, Rest, and Delay (PR&D). The normalized time per unit is not the standard time. We can't expect a person to produce at that normal rate hour

---

[15]Benjamin W. Niebel, *Motion and Time Study*, 7th ed. (Homewood, Ill.: Richard D. Irwin, 1982), p. 337; also see a more elaborate table from Westinghouse on the same page (T56.N48).

after hour without stopping. Personal time (drinking fountain, rest room, etc.) must be allowed. Rest time, such as coffee breaks, must also be permitted. There may also be unavoidable delays to include in the time standard.

Personal and rest time may be set by company policy or union contract. The rest (fatigue) allowance may be strictly a coffee-break allowance; this is common with clerical employees. In industrial shops, the rest or fatigue allowance may be job dependent. For example, for tasks performed in a freezer or near a furnace, the fatigue allowance may be as high as 50 percent.

Unavoidable delay could be set by contract or policy. More often, it is task dependent. Unavoidable delays may result from difficulty in meeting tight tolerances, from material irregularities, and from machine imbalances when an operator runs more than one machine. Interruptions by foreman, dispatcher, material handler, and so on may also qualify. Strictly speaking, an unavoidable delay is one inherent in the method. Under that strict interpretation, delays caused by foremen or staff would be considered avoidable delays and excluded from the unavoidable delay allowance. Those delays (like material or tool shortages and machine breakdowns) may be avoided by better management of resources. Unavoidable delays are sometimes determined by a work-sampling study in which occurrences of various types of delay are tallied.

The allowances are usually combined as a percentage, referred to as the **personal, rest, and delay (PR&D) allowance** (or PF&D, where F stands for "fatigue"). The combined allowance is then added to the normalized time, resulting in a standard time.

Work Sampling Standards

In Example 16–3 we looked at work sampling as a technique for determining labor utilization and delay rates. Work sampling for setting a time standard requires one extra piece of data: a *production count*, that is, a count of units produced or customers served during the study period. Cycle time (CT), then, is:

$$\text{Cycle time} = \frac{\text{Percent of time on task} \times \text{Total minutes in study period}}{\text{Production count}}$$

$$(16\text{–}12)$$

As in time study, cycle time is transformed into standard time by normalizing for employee pace and adding a PR&D allowance.

Solved problem 4 in this chapter shows work sampling applied to time standard determination. The problem also discusses some of the reservations that might arise in practical applications.

Predetermined Standards

Predetermined time standards really are only part-way predetermined. The predetermined part is the tables of time values for basic motions. The other part is properly selecting basic-motion time values in order to build a time standard for a larger task.

Basic-motion tables were Frank Gilbreth's idea, but it took some 35 years of effort by many researchers to develop them. The best-known tables are those of the MTM (Methods-Time Measurement) Association.[16] Others include the Work-Factor, Brief Work-Factor, and Basic Motion Timestudy (BMT) systems. Our limited discussion focuses on **Methods-Time Measurement**.

MTM and other synthetic techniques have several advantages:

1. No need to time; the data are in tables.
2. No need to observe; the standard may be set before the job is ever performed and without disrupting the employee.
3. No need to rate pace; the time data in the table were normalized when the tables were created.

A disadvantage of MTM is the great amount of detail involved in building a standard from the tables. Basic MTM motions are tiny; motions are measured in **time measurement units (TMUs)**, and one TMU is only 0.0006 minutes. A 1.0-minute cycle time equals 1,667 TMUs. One MTM motion usually takes 10 to 20 TMUs; thus, about 80 to 160 basic motions would be identified in the 1.0-minute period. Although much training is required of the analyst to achieve that detail, MTM is perceived as a fair approach to time standards and is widely used.

The MTM Association has developed tables for the following types of basic motions: reach; move; turn and apply pressure; grasp; position; release; disengage; eye travel and eye focus; body, leg, and foot motions; and simultaneous motions. Most of the tables were developed by film analysis.

One of the tables, the reach table, is shown in Figure 16–10. From the table we see, for example, that reaching 16 inches to an "object jumbled with other objects in a group so that search and select occur" takes 17 TMUs. That motion, abbreviated as an *RC16* motion, takes about 0.01 minutes or less than a second.

In an MTM study, the analyst enters each motion on *a simultaneous motion (SIMO) chart*, which is a left-and-right-hand chart. The total TMUs on the chart are converted to minutes. The total is the rated (leveled) time, not the cycle time, because 100 percent pace is built into the tables. Add a PR&D allowance, and you have the standard time.

Standard Data

Standard-data standards, like predetermined (e.g., MTM) standards, are synthetically produced from tables. But standard-data tables are for larger units of work. An example is the flat-rate manuals used in the auto-repair industry.[17] Flat-rate tables list times for repair tasks such as "Replace points" and "Change oil."

---

[16] The tables were originally developed by H. B. Maynard and associates. See Harold B. Maynard. G. J. Stegemerten, and John L. Schwab, *Methods-Time Measurement* (New York: McGraw-Hill, 1948) (T60.T5M3).

[17] Auto manufacturers produce such tables for repairs on new cars. Flat-rate manuals for older cars, which take more time to repair, are available from independent companies. Best known are the Chilton manuals.

FIGURE 16–10
Reach Table for MTM Analysis

Length of Reach in Inches	Time in TMUs[a]				Hand in Motion (TMU)		Case and Description
	Case A	Case B	Case C or D	Case E	A	B	
³/₄ or less	2.0	2.0	2.0	2.0	1.6	1.6	A—Reach to object in a
1	2.5	2.5	3.6	2.4	2.3	2.3	fixed location or to
2	4.0	4.0	5.9	3.8	3.5	2.7	object in other hand
3	5.3	5.3	7.3	5.3	4.5	3.6	or on which the
4	6.1	6.4	8.4	6.8	4.9	4.3	other hand rests
5	6.5	7.8	9.4	7.4	5.3	5.0	B—Reach to single
6	7.0	8.6	10.1	8.0	5.7	5.7	object in location
7	7.4	9.3	10.8	8.7	6.1	6.5	that may vary
8	7.9	10.1	11.5	9.3	6.5	7.2	slightly from cycle to
9	8.3	10.8	12.2	9.9	6.9	7.9	cycle
10	8.7	11.5	12.9	10.5	7.3	8.6	C—Reach to object
12	9.6	12.9	14.2	11.8	8.1	10.1	jumbled with other
14	10.5	14.4	15.6	13.0	8.9	11.5	objects in a group so
16	11.4	15.8	17.0	14.2	9.7	12.9	that search and
18	12.3	17.2	18.4	15.5	10.5	14.4	select occur
20	13.1	18.6	19.8	16.7	11.3	15.8	D—Reach to a very
22	14.0	20.1	21.2	18.0	12.1	17.3	small object or
24	14.9	21.5	22.5	19.2	12.9	18.8	where accurate grasp
26	15.8	22.9	23.9	20.4	13.7	20.2	is required
28	16.7	24.4	25.3	21.7	14.5	21.7	E—Reach to indefinite
30	17.5	25.8	26.7	22.9	15.3	23.2	position to get hand in position for body balance, next motion, or out of way

[a]One time measurement unit (TMU) represents 0.00001 hour.
Source: MTM Association for Standards and Research. Copyrighted by the MTM Association for Standards and Research. No reprint permission without written consent from the MTM Association, 16-01 Broadway, Fair Lawn, New Jersey 07410.

If precise time study, work sampling, or MTM is the basis for the tables, the standard data may be considered to be engineered. It is normal for a firm to keep time standards on file, and it is just one more step to assemble standards from the files into standard-data tables. The next step is to assemble standard data for a whole trade or industry. This has been done in auto repair and other common trades, notably machining and maintenance trades.[18]

---

[18]The standard-data tables come in several levels. Basic motions (e.g., MTM) are the most detailed level. Next come combinations of basic data (e.g., MTM Association's general-purpose data), such as a joint time for reach-grasp-release. Then come elemental standard data for common elements, like gauging and marking. Standard data for still larger units of work are at the level of whole tasks, such as those of auto repair mechanics or electricians.

Variable working conditions and lack of common methods from firm to firm may compromise the built-in precision of standard data. Still, standard data are a powerful tool in that they bring time standards down to the level of the planner, the supervisor, and the operator. Experts create the tables, but we all can use them.

Historical Standards and Technical Estimates

Nonengineered techniques—historical and technical estimates—are far more widely used than engineered techniques, and rightly so. Most of our work (or play) is variable, and the cost to measure it with precision is prohibitive. Still, explicit time estimates help improve management, and nonengineered techniques serve the purpose. Historical standards and technical estimates are simple to develop and need not be explained further.

HUMANITY AND FAIRNESS ISSUES

Scientific management is a two-edged sword, one edge sharp and the other dull. The sharp edge raises productivity; the dull one leaves wounds and scars.

More specifically, the sharp edge gets its results as follows. Methods study chops work into narrow, easy-to-perform tasks. The concept has long been known as *division of labor*. As the theory goes, even unskilled, low-paid labor can perform such tasks with acceptable quality. Each task is timed so that just the right amount of labor may be assigned. The low labor costs are passed on to the customer in the form of lower prices and satisfactory goods and services. Apparently no "dull edge" thus far.

Chopped-up, well-timed tasks leave little time for "fun and games" on the job. Further, when jobs are put on time standards, employees may complain about a faster work pace, or "speedup." The employer's rightful response is that fun and games are for *after* work and that time standards do not force an unreasonable pace. Most employees can only agree with this viewpoint.

Still, there *are* negative human effects. Narrow tasks created by methods study are unrewarding to employees. Quick, visible gains in productivity may be eroded by longer-term alienation resulting from boredom and lack of challenge. The firm's chief resource, its people, may suffer. Degradation of employees is reflected in degradation of goods and services for customers.

Further, scientific management is often tied to the firm's method of judging performance and determining pay. It is not easy to do so in a way that is fair or, perhaps even more crucial, *perceived* as fair, by all employees.

Employers have long sought solutions to the human problems associated with the application of methods and time standards. The most promising approaches, past and present, lie in putting variety and meaning back into the task or job. Closely related is the need to make sure that the reward system will recognize task differences and the many ways in which employees can serve their employers and customers. Those issues—tasks, jobs, customer service effects, and the reward system—are considered next.

Tasks, Jobs, and Service to Customers

The design of work and work systems has evolved through three phases. First was scientific management, which focused on the task itself. Next came job design, which aims at improving the job and therefore the life of a jobholder. Today's approach, emphasized throughout this book, is on service to the next and final customer—and related feelings of satisfaction by the server. A review of the three phases follows.

Tasks
Division of labor, performed scientifically using methods-study techniques, yields a well-engineered task. Consider the task of scraping food leavings off a stainless steel tray into a garbage can. Is that task also a job—that is, can the firm define it as a job and hire someone to do just that task over and over? The answer is yes. Such narrow tasks *are* sometimes treated as a whole job.

Jobs
If all jobs were developed like the plate-scraping one, wouldn't work life be intolerable? A collection of concepts now called **job design** attempts to avoid such a fate for working people.

Best known among the job design ideas are job enlargement and job enrichment. *Job enlargement* dates back to the 1950s, when Thomas Watson, founder of IBM, promoted the effort out of his strong belief in providing people with meaningful work. Job enlargement means expanding the number of tasks included in a person's job; it offers horizontal variety. *Job enrichment*, a later development with roots at Texas Instruments and AT&T, expands on the job enlargement idea. Enlargement means more tasks; enrichment means more meaningful, satisfying, and fulfilling tasks or responsibilities; for example, an enriched job may entail use of mental and interpersonal skills.

In the late 1960s and early 1970s, a few manufacturers began experimenting with a team approach to assembly that might be called *nonlinear assembly*. Volvo and Saab in Sweden were among the first to try it. In this approach, assembly lines are replaced by assembly areas, and assemblers become team members who are no longer isolated at spots along an assembly line. Team members are cross-trained, and the team has a daily or weekly production quota or standard to meet. Sometimes teams are leaderless and do their own interviewing to fill vacancies. The team may have responsibility for the quality or operability of the end product (and even packaging, shipping, and office work, as in the case of one General Foods pet food plant in Topeka).

Nonlinear assembly is aimed at restoring task variety, social interaction, commitment, and motivation. But this approach has caught the fancy of only a few companies. Part of the reason may be the higher training costs and greater variability (lessened dependability) of output. Training costs are high because methods are less well defined and jobs less specialized. Variability of output can lead to factory coordination problems.

Customers

If the factory or office is not well coordinated, the firm can hardly do a good job of meeting customer needs. An assortment of techniques presented throughout this book, especially those associated with JIT and TQ, are aimed squarely at customer needs. How do those techniques affect task efficiency and job satisfaction? The question has been partly answered in earlier chapters and need only be summarized and expanded upon a bit here.

A central concept of TQ is process capability. That means specifying a set of process standards that exceed customer requirements, then ensuring that the process is capable of meeting those specs. Do tight customer requirements and process standards unduly restrict the creativity of the employee? Not at all; product and process standards merely direct the employee's creativity in the right direction—toward even better response to the customer. Also, standards create discipline over the many little things that tend to vary or go wrong in order to free the employee to focus on the big issues.

A chief feature of JIT is tight coupling of operations—few or no delays. That requires exacting knowledge of how long it takes to perform each task. Standard methods and standard times therefore are important modern aids.

Just-in-time does not allow performing tasks well in advance of need. Operators must be cross-trained for mastery of several kinds of jobs so that they can move to where the work is. That includes moving from direct labor to indirect work, such as fetching material, helping install equipment, and pushing a broom. Restrictive work rules must be relaxed. The cross-training and movement from job to job provide task variety as well as job enlargement.

PRINCIPLE: Cross-train for mastery of more than one job.

Other central TQ and JIT concepts deal with line-centered responsibilities for quality, delivering work to the next process without delay, and process improvement. Technical competence in maintaining one's own equipment is required, as is the ability to keep records and analyze process data in the cause of continuing process improvement. In other words, the production operative has a considerably enriched job as well.

The point has perhaps been made: Efficient designs of tasks, fulfilling designs of jobs, and effective designs of operations to serve the customer are not in conflict. Modern approaches, aiming squarely at customer needs, can benefit from traditional scientific management and offer greater fulfillment to jobholders.

The next issue pertains to the scope of application of scientific management. Specifically, can time standards be applied fairly even to variable tasks?

Responses to Variability

Time standards seem well suited to repetitive tasks. They may seem poorly suited for variable tasks such as those typical in the service sector. Actually, a better way of putting it is that time standards should be applied differently to variable tasks. Four key differences between standards for variable tasks and repetitive tasks are detailed next.

   1. *For variable tasks, nonengineered time standards are often more suitable.* Engineered standards are costly and, for a job just received and about to begin, there is not enough time to develop more than a technical estimate. But variable jobs may be made up of tasks that have been done before; engineered standards may already exist, perhaps as standard data.

   2. *For variable tasks, variance from standards should be reported less often.* Nonengineered standards will sometimes be unfairly high or low. High and low estimates may cancel out over a suitable reporting period. That allows efficiency reporting to be used fairly, but only if times for many jobs are aggregated over the reporting period.

   Example: The U.S. Air Force Logistics Command, which operates very large job shops for aircraft repair, compares accumulated standard times against accumulated clock hours for most of its repair-shop crews (and calculates efficiency using Equation 16–4). The reporting period of two weeks is long enough to include perhaps hundreds of task time standards, most of which are technical estimates.

   3. *When a task covered by a time standard includes variable operations, don't use it to compare employees unless all employees encounter the same mix of operations.*

   Example: Most college libraries use computers to produce catalog cards. A cataloging aide with book in hand enters data about a new book at a terminal, and the data are transmitted to a central library cataloging service center. The center's computer database is searched to find (in the United States) a Library of Congress catalog number for the book. For the search to be successful, the cataloging aide must enter the right data. This can be difficult, for example, for foreign-language books, musical compositions, and government documents.

   One college library set a monthly standard rate (historical) of 300 books per cataloging aide. The standard rate was deeply resented, because some aides arrived early in the morning in order to fill their carts with easy books, which allowed them to easily exceed 300 books per month. Some of the aides who liked the challenge of the tough books actually looked worse when the monthly report came out. The solution: Distribute books to cataloging aides at random each morning. That way, each receives about the same variety of types of book over a period of months.

   4. *For variable tasks, limit the uses of time standards.* For example, in one effort to set time standards on lawyers' tasks, the sole purpose was to straighten out a staffing mess. The lawyers worked in 36 program offices of the U.S. Department of the Interior, and it was hard to assign the proper number of lawyers to each office.

The department hired a consultant to help define work units and set standards.[19] The basic work unit was a *matter* (not a case, because matters often did not result in cases). Fifty-nine varieties of matters were defined, and secretaries kept records on the time lawyers spent on each matter. The results were fairly consistent throughout the United States, and the average times served as historical (nonengineered) standards for use in staffing decisions; that is, in a given office each matter could be forecast (by trend projection, etc.) and multiplied by standard time to yield labor-hours, which converted into staff needs.

Professional work like that of a lawyer is not only variable but often seen as something of an art and resistant to standardization. The lawyers in this example cooperated because the limited purpose—better staffing—was made clear. Probably there would have been no cooperation had the purpose been to judge efficiency or even to schedule lawyers' tasks.

Fair Pay

Tying pay directly to output or efficiency seems fair to some people, and direct wage incentives are still common in some industries, such as fruit and vegetable picking and old-line manufacturing. This section ends with a brief discussion of some common incentive-pay approaches. First, however, we examine the general issue of fair pay more closely.

Concepts of Fair Pay

Differing concepts of fair pay may explain why direct wage incentives are common in only a few industries. Figure 16–11 helps put fair pay into perspective.

One concept of fair pay is that everyone should be paid the same, and minimum-wage laws are a means of bringing that about. Pay by time worked is a second fair-pay concept, and a popular one. Pay by job content also seems fair, especially in large organizations where unequal pay for the same work would be a visible problem; evaluating job content has been a major function in larger human resources departments. A fourth concept of fair is pay based on output against standards, often called **incentive pay**. A pure incentive is simply a piece rate; for example, a berry picker's piece rate might be $1 per bucket. But laws (such as the United States wage-and-hour laws) require that piece-rate earnings not fall below the minimum wage, based on hours worked.

Another popular system is **measured daywork**, which is only nominally an incentive-pay system. In measured daywork, standard output serves as a target that methods engineers, trainers, and supervisors help the employee attain. The employee who cannot attain it is moved to another position or advised to seek work elsewhere.

---

[19]Part of the consultant's story is told in Mundel, *Motion and Time Study*, pp. 485–94.

FIGURE 16–11
Concepts of Fair Pay

What Is Fair Pay?	*Who Subscribes To This?*
1. **Everyone paid the same** Rationale: We are all created equal; we are all products of our environments and partners in society. Means: High minimum wage applied equally to all.	Organized labor Socialists
2. **Pay by the hour (or week, month, year)** Rationale: Though we are products of our environment, society's work must be done, and work is most easily measured in time units. Means: Have employees punch time clocks, and reprimand them for tardiness.	Supervisors (easy to figure out pay) Organized labor (employees like to "put in their time"—or their time and a half)
3. **Pay according to job content** Rationale: It is not the person who should be paid but the position; "heavy" positions should be paid heavily, "light" positions lightly. Means: Job evaluation, using job ranking/classfication, point plan, factor comparison.	Personnel managers (requires a large pay-and-classification staff) Bureaucrats (seems rational and impersonal; fits concept of rank or hierarchy)
4. **Pay according to output** Rationale: Though we are products of our environment, society's work must be done, and work should be measured in output (not merely time on the job). Output efficiency is based on a count of actual units produced as compared to a standard. Means: Piecework, incentive pay, profit sharing.	Industrial engineers Economists
5. **Pay according to supply and demand** Rationale: Society's messiest jobs must be done too, and greater pay for less desirable jobs is necessary to attract employees. Means: Let the labor market function (or list jobs needing to be done, and set pay according to willingness to do each job—The *Walden II* method).	Some economists (e.g., those advocating below-minimum wages for teenagers) B. F. Skinner (see his book *Walden II*)
6. **Pay for knowledge** Rationale: Pay system should encourage learning so employees can take "ownership" of their processes and of improving customer service. Means: Extra pay for passing tests of mastery of more skills and knowledge.	A growing number of some of the best-known companies

The last concept in Figure 16–11 (not necessarily a complete list) is **pay for knowledge**, which has burst on the scene so recently that it was not even mentioned in the third edition of this book. A parallel trend is reduction of job classifications. For example, a number of North American automobile assembly plants have negotiated contracts with their unions that reduce job classifications from as many as 300 or 400 to as few as two (e.g., assembler and technician). In return for agreeing to such reductions in "work rules," the company offers extensive training—and more pay for skills learned. The companies feel they need multiskilled employees who are versatile enough to move to where the work is and to be involved in process improvement. Employees tend to feel they need to become multiskilled for *work-life security*, which reflects a longer-range view than *job security*.

We opened this chapter by pointing out that productivity is a complex topic in a state of change and revision. We have just seen that pay is complex and in flux as well, and that pay for productivity is just one of several ways of judging the fairness of a pay system.

SUMMARY

Productivity is in a state of change—except for the basic components of measuring it: outputs compared with inputs. The traditions of productivity measurement date back to scientific management, which emerged at the turn of the century as a final phase of the Industrial Revolution. Its main ingredients are methods study, process design, and time standards.

One use of time standards is determination of standard labor cost, which when compared with actual labor cost yields labor variance. Labor variance, material variance, and total cost variance are the core of periodic accounting-based productivity measurement, which is entrenched in much of industry. A weakness is that there has been too much emphasis on direct labor productivity; too much also on mere outputs, as opposed to meeting customers' needs.

Companies are addressing the weaknesses by moving resources into groups focused on whole products provided just in time with total quality, costing the outputs of the whole rather than the parts, putting up cause-control charts throughout the operating areas, and extensively training employees to become multiskilled problem solvers. Inasmuch as most operating costs become "contained" in the focused groups, complex operation-by-operation cost collection may no longer be needed.

Still, good product cost information *is* needed in order to make good decisions, for example, on alternate processes or on make-versus-buy. Improvements in product costing are forthcoming through use of activity-based costing techniques.

These new concepts of productivity management are still far from dominant. Traditional methods improvement and time standards are still in wide use and likely to continue to play several important roles.

Methods improvement follows the scientific method: Select a task, collect data on it, analyze the data leading to alternative methods, evaluate the alternatives, and implement the chosen one. Repeat the procedure as part of a continuing improvement program. Data collection and documenting the improved method are done on before-and-after flowcharts. Another tool, work sampling, can yield data on labor or facility utilization and show percentages of time in various categories of work or delay.

Time standards are necessary for coordinating and scheduling, analyzing operations, and motivating employees for improvement. Accurate time standards, for example, facilitate under-capacity labor scheduling, which allows time for important indirect work activities. Time standards also play key roles in determination of efficiency, utilization, and productivity values. They are a valuable means of fostering self-motivation among employees.

There are six basic techniques for setting time standards: stopwatch time study, work sampling, predetermined standards, standard-data time standards, historical standards, and technical estimates. Engineered (high-precision) standards require controls on methods, time measurement, employee pace, and allowances for personal, rest, and delay time.

Finally, care must be taken to ensure that productivity improvement does not dehumanize jobs, for this could lead to longer-term degradation of performance. Fortunately, an assortment of techniques that focus on meeting customer needs (JIT and TQ, for example) also show promise for putting meaning back into people's work lives. For example, knowledge-based pay, a concept that has become popular in just the last few years, provides employees with new opportunities to develop, grow, and make themselves more valuable to present or future employers.

KEY WORDS

Productivity
Cost variance
Gain-sharing
Activity-based costing
  (ABC)
Methods study
Ergonomics
Motion study
Therbligs
Flowchart
Work sampling
Utilization

Standard time (time
  standard)
Efficiency
Under-capacity
  scheduling
Time study
Cycle time (CT)
Pace rating
Normal time
Leveling (normalizing)
Personal, rest, and
  delay (PR&D)

Methods-time
  measurement (MTM)
Time measurement
  unit (TMU)
Standard data
Job design
Incentive pay
Measured daywork
  system
Pay for knowledge

SOLVED PROBLEMS

1. At Metro Gas and Electric, the productivity of each of five functional departments involved in billing (for power consumption and other sales to commercial, industrial, and residential customers) is reported monthly. The main measure in the report is cost variance, which is based on cost of billings processed as compared with standard cost. An improvement team has concluded that the variance system generally fails to lead to improved performance. What changes should they recommend?

Solution

The first step is to reorganize the five departments into a few focused cells; for example, separate cells for commercial, industrial, and residential customers—and perhaps separate cells for power usage and for other sales. That will contain most of the operating costs within each focused cell.

Other steps include posting cause-control charts in every cell, upgrading the skill levels of every employee (perhaps including pay for knowledge), and using activity-based costing to more accurately find the costs and track cost trends for processing bills in each cell.

2. Gate City Tire Company sells and installs tires, some by appointment and the rest to drop-in customers. Appointments are carefully scheduled so that (1) the customer may be told when the car will be ready and (2) installers are kept busy. The manager knows that under normal conditions a four-tire installation takes about 20 minutes. The time varies depending on the installer's speed (efficiency) and the delay (utilization) encountered. Gate City follows the concept of under-capacity scheduling: For an 8-hour paid shift, the company schedules 7.3 hours of tire installing.

During the 7.3 hours of assigned work, efficiency has been found to be 90 percent; it is low because the present crew lacks experience. Utilization, again during the 7.3 assigned hours, is 80 percent. Delays arise from tool break-downs, parts shortages, special customer requests, and two authorized 15-minute coffee breaks; these, plus miscellaneous delays, account for the 20 percent nonutilization time.

Regardless of expected daily output, each daily job may be separately scheduled. For example, the third job of the day, a phoned appointment, is assigned to Jeff, who has been only 80 percent efficient. But the manager expects no delays for lack of materials, tool breakdowns, or other problems, and it is not near coffee-break time; thus, he expects utilization on this job to be 100 percent.

a. Calculate the current scheduled daily output.

b. What is the scheduled installation time of the third job of the day, assuming Jeff is given the job?

Solution

a. Scheduled output $= \dfrac{7.3 \text{ hours} \times 60 \text{ minutes/hour}}{20 \text{ minutes/installation}} \times 90\%$ efficiency

$\times\ 80\%$ utilization

$= 15.768$, or approximately 16 installations per day

b. The scheduled installation time, from Equation 16–10 is:

$$\text{Scheduled time} = \frac{20 \text{ minutes/installation}}{80\% \times 100\%} = 25 \text{ minutes}$$

3. The proposed bolt-washer-nut assembly method of Figure 16–5 was approved, and a time-study analyst was assigned to develop a time standard for the task. After observation, the analyst has reduced the task to four timable elements (as opposed to the 16 elements that were defined for detailed methods study). Six cycles are timed[20] by the continuous stopwatch method, and each element is pace rated. Calculate the standard time.

Solution

The time-study data sheet is shown in Figure 16–12. The analyst reads the stopwatch in hundredths of a minute and does not insert decimal points until after the last computation. The stopwatch begins at zero and runs continuously for 7.55 minutes. Continuous readings are entered below the diagonal line, and elemental times are then computed by successive subtraction.

Average cycle time (CT) is the sum of elemental times divided by 6; for element 2, CT is divided by 5 because one irregular elemental time was thrown out. The average goes below the diagonal line in the CT column. Pace ratings are in the rating factor (RF) column, with decimal points not included. Normalized time

---

[20]For a short-cycle task like bolt-washer-nut assembly, it would take less than an hour to time, say, 30 cycles, and this would improve reliability. The six-cycle example thus is less than ideal.

FIGURE 16–12

Time-Study Data Sheet—Bolt-Washer-Nut Assembly

Element	Cycles						CT	RF	NT	Remarks
	1	2	3	4	5	6				
1. Get bolts and place in fixture	12 / 12	10 / 116	13 / 240	11 / 349	16 / 468	10 / 656	72 / 12	110	13.2	
2. Get washers and place on bolts	14 / 26	16 / 132	15 / 255	14 / 363	93 / 561	14 / 670	73 / 14.6	100	14.6	5th cycle: Blew nose
3. Get nuts and assemble onto bolts	75 / 101	86 / 218	77 / 332	82 / 445	79 / 640	78 / 748	477 / 79.5	95	75.5	
4. Drop assemblies down chutes	05 / 106	09 / 227	06 / 338	07 / 452	06 / 646	07 / 755	40 / 6.7	100	6.7	

Total normalized time   110.0
× PR&D allowance + 100%   111.25%
Standard time   122.375, or 1.22 minutes/unit

Note: CT is sometimes called the *select time* (ST); NT is sometimes called the *leveled time* (LT) or *rated time* (RT).

(NT) equals CT times RF. The NT column adds up to 110, or 1.10 minutes per cycle.

The firm has a PR&D allowance negotiated with the labor union. It provides 3 percent personal time (e.g., blow nose), two 15-minute rest (coffee) breaks, and 2 percent unavoidable delay allowance. (These are minimum allowances; the contract allows rest time to be set higher for highly fatiguing work, and the delay allowance may be set higher for tasks involving abnormal delays.)

The two 15-minute breaks convert to percentages of an 8-hour, or 480-minute, day by:

$$\frac{30 \text{ minutes}}{480 \text{ minutes}} = 0.0625, \text{ or } 6.25\%$$

$$\text{Total PR\&D allowance} = 3\% + 6.25\% + 2\%$$

$$= 11.25\%$$

The final computation is multiplying the total normalized time by the PR&D allowance of 11.25 percent plus 100 percent (which is mathematically the same as adding 11.25 percent of the total normalized time). The result is the standard time of 1.22 minutes per unit.

4. The director of Midtown Pathological Labs conducted a one-week work-sampling study of the lab staff. The results were that the staff was working 65 percent of the time. The director also tallied the type of work task observed. The lab performs two major types of analysis and a host of miscellaneous analyses. The director found that the 65 percent work time was divided as follows:

Serum-blood tests (standard tests) in chemistry lab	30%
Whole-blood tests (complete blood count) in hematology lab	25
Miscellaneous tests in either lab	10
Total work time	65%

There are two lab technicians in the chemistry lab and one in hematology.

At the end of the study, the director found that 48 serum tests and 32 whole-blood tests had been performed. Her estimates of operator pace are 90 percent for serum tests and 105 percent for whole-blood tests. Midtown has a PR&D allowance of 13 percent.

With these data, calculate a time standard for both the serum test and the whole-blood test. Discuss the precision and fairness of the resulting standards and any effects on capacity planning.

Solution

Serum test:

$$\text{Cycle time} = \frac{0.30 \times 5 \text{ days} \times 480 \text{ min./technician-day} \times 2 \text{ technicians}}{48 \text{ tests}}$$

$$= 30 \text{ minutes per test}$$

$$\text{Standard time} = \text{CT} \times \text{RF} \times (100\% + \text{PR\&D})$$

$$= 30 \times 90\% \times 113\%$$

$$= 30.51 \text{ minutes per test (per technician)}$$

Whole-blood test:

$$\text{Cycle time} = \frac{0.25 \times 5 \text{ days} \times 480 \text{ minutes/technician-day}}{32 \text{ tests}}$$

$$18.75 \text{ minutes}$$

$$\text{Standard time} = \text{CT} \times \text{RF} \times (100\% + \text{PR\&D})$$

$$= 18.75 \times 105\% \times 113\%$$

$$= 22.25 \text{ minutes per test}$$

Are these precise (engineered) time standards? The technicians in the chemistry lab don't think theirs is. They point out to the director that their method is to run the serum tests in batches and as a two-person team. There could be one or many samples in a batch, but the time to run a batch does not directly depend on the number of samples in it. The time standard for serum testing is imprecise, indeed, invalid, because the work-sampling study was not precise as to method.

The hematology technician has a milder objection: A mere 25 observations of the whole-blood testing were extrapolated into an assumed 600 minutes of testing time during the week. While the sample size seems rather small, the technician and the director decide that the standard time of 22.25 minutes per test is usable for short-term capacity adjustments. These include scheduling overtime, using part-time help, and subcontracting to other labs.

For example, on a given day, perhaps 30 blood samples will arrive and require testing in hematology. At 22.25 minutes per test, the workload is 22.25 × 30 = 667.5 minutes of testing. Since an 8-hour day is only 480 minutes, the director had better tell the technician to plan on some overtime that evening. Part-time help and subcontracting are other options.

REFERENCES

Books

Caruth, Donald L. *Work Measurement in Banking,* 2nd ed. Boston: Bankers Publishing, 1984 (HG1616.W6C37).

Kazarian, Edward, A. *Work Analysis and Design for Hotels, Restaurants, and Institutions,* 2nd ed. Westport, Conn.: AVI Publications, 1979 (TX911.K36).

Konz, Stephan, A. *Work Design: Industrial Ergonomics,* 2nd ed. Columbus, Ohio: Grid, 1983 (T60.8.K66).

Konz, Stephan A. *Facilities Design.* New York: Wiley, 1985 (TS177.K66).

Krick, Edward V. *Methods Engineering: Design and Measurement of Work Methods.* New York: John Wiley & Sons, 1962 (T56.K7).

Maynard, Harold B., G. T. Stegemerten, and John L. Schwab. *Methods-Time Measurement.* New York: McGraw-Hill, 1948 (T60.T5M3).

Niebel, Benjamin W. *Motion and Time Study,* 8th ed. Homewood, Ill.: Richard D. Irwin, 1988 (T56.N48).

Salvendy, Gavriel. *Handbook of Industrial Engineering.* New York: John Wiley & Sons, 1982 (T56.23.H36).

Periodicals/Societies

Industrial Engineering (Institute of Industrial Engineering).

Journal of Systems Management (Association for Systems Management) (paperwork management and systems analysis).

REVIEW QUESTIONS

1. What is the primary way of measuring productivity?
2. Why have some managers and accountants questioned the value of the cost-variance system?
3. What is meant by the phrase "control causes of cost"?
4. In methods study, what information is included in a before-and-after comparison?
5. How are principles of motion economy (or methods improvement) used?
6. Which flowcharting symbols are used in each of the four types of methods study? Explain.
7. How do work sampling studies reveal deficiencies in the management system?
8. How can labor efficiency and utilization be allowed for in scheduling? How is productivity allowed for?
9. How can wages be based on time standards given minimum-wage laws?
10. When is a nonengineered time standard not good enough?
11. In a stopwatch time study, how many cycles should be timed before calculating the average (CT) values? Why?
12. How can work-sampling data yield CT values?
13. Why isn't the CT the time standard?
14. Which of the PR&D factors are task dependent? Explain.
15. In what sense is pace rating unfair? Fair?
16. What is the difference between predetermined standards and standard data?
17. Why do employees tend to prefer synthetically set standards?
18. How can labor standards be fair if tasks are variable?
19. Is it fair to pay based on amount of work produced? Why or why not?
20. What is under-capacity scheduling? Why would it be used?
21. How does pay for knowledge help drive productivity improvement?

PROBLEMS AND EXERCISES

1. The president of Universal Service Corp. is concerned. His company is in serious financial trouble, even though its cost system—roughly the same system most other firms use—shows that labor costs have been going down significantly for months. How would you advise the president?
2. Name the four most important visual performance charts—for control of causes—in each of the following cases:
   a. A movie theater chain.
   b. A long-running play.

    c. A home-building construction company.

    d. A custom spray-painting plant.

3. Figure 16–2 lists a number of ways to evaluate new methods: cost, time, effort, storage, delays, transportation, transportation distances. Explain how each type of evaluation data may be determined from flowcharts. Refer to one or more of the types of flowcharts discussed in the chapter in your explanations.

4. L&L Landscape Services is expanding into new lines of relatively diverse services, including building decks, pools, patios, gardens, and living sculpture. The expansion requires L&L's employees to receive training in these new service lines. To make time for training, L&L uses under-capacity scheduling of labor. Ninety percent of each 40-hour workweek is scheduled for each employee. Pay is for the full 40 hours.

    a. For a six-person crew, how many direct-assignment hours are available each week?

    b. Suppose it rains for several consecutive days and L&L gets behind schedule. What might the firm do if available assignment hours are not enough to cover labor-hour needs?

    c. Should L&L try to have all employees learn each new service, or should it have each employee trained in only one or two of them? Explain.

    d. Suppose L&L's pay scale averages $11 per hour. How much is the under-capacity scheduling costing each week? Do you think the costs are justified?

5. Find a screw-together type of ball-point pen. Take it apart, and set the pieces before you. Imagine you are an assembler in a factory that makes this type of pen. Develop a left-and-right-hand chart for your method of assembly. Now develop an "after" flowchart for an improved method—which may use a special workbench, feed trays, chutes, fixtures, and so on. You may wish to include a workbench sketch. Evaluate the extent of improvement.

    a. How long, in your estimation, would it take to assemble a pen using your improved method?

    b. How would you set a time standard for this assembly? List the steps in setting such a standard. What is your estimate of daily pen production?

    c. Assuming under-capacity scheduling of labor with 88 percent of time available for assignment, how will this affect your response to question *b*?

6. The present method of reading gas meters (on a successful call) is shown below (an employee analysis chart).

    a. The gas company is considering a requirement that all gas meters be located outside or be visible through a window. Draw a new process flowchart for meter reading for the proposed new meter locations. Develop a summary of the improvements.

    b. What other improvements exist that are not shown on the summary? What are the disadvantages of the new method?

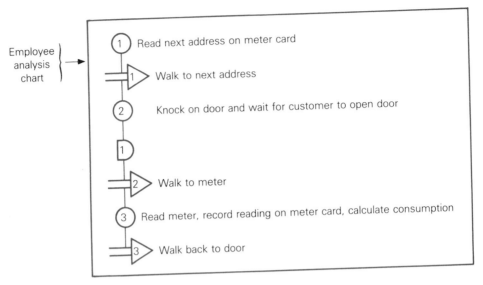

7. The present method of billing, weighing, and stenciling sacks is shown in the accompanying illustration. Develop a process flowchart for a proposed new, improved method. Include a summary of the improvements.

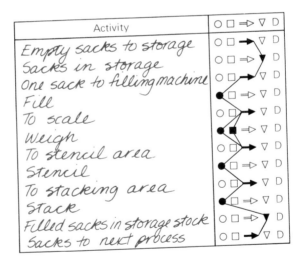

8. The accompanying chart shows five days of actual on-the-job activities of a seamstress who sews decorator pillows together. (Ten minutes is used as the smallest time increment so that time values can be read off the chart easily.) You are to conduct a 50-observation work-sampling study, taking your observations from the chart instead of from on-site observation.

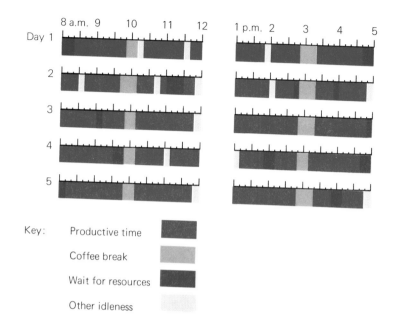

a. As a first step in conducting the study, you will need a schedule of 50 random observation times. You will find a list of two-digit random numbers in Appendix C. Select 50 of those numbers, and devise a method of translating them into 50 clock times between 8:00 A.M. and 12:00 P.M. and between 1:00 and 5:00 P.M. for a 5-day study period. Show your 50 random numbers and 50 times.

b. Develop a tally sheet, and conduct the work-sampling study. The desired end result is percentage of time in four activity areas: productive time, coffee break, wait for resources, and other idleness.

c. The unavoidable-delay component of the PR&D allowance is to be based on the wait-for-resources element of the work-sampling study in question b. The rest component is set at two 15-minute coffee breaks per day, and personal time is set by company policy at 5 percent. What is the total PR&D allowance?

d. Explain the difference between the time allowed for coffee breaks and the time taken as revealed by the work-sampling data.

e. During the 5-day study period, the seamstress completed 760 pillows. You, the analyst, judged her pace during the study period. Your pace rating is 90 percent. Calculate the standard time. Express the standard in pieces per day (standard production rate).

f. Discuss possible weaknesses or sources of bias in the work-sampling study. Is the time standard engineered?

g. What should be the primary uses of this time standard? Explain.

h. What, if any, steps would you take concerning quality?

i. How would you change your results if only 720 pillows were acceptable?

9. A salesperson has an order for 1,000 candles in the shape of an athletic team's mascot. Production control assembles the following data from the candlemaking shop, to be used in setting a price (direct cost and overhead plus markup):

Cycle time	20,000 TMUs
Allowance for personal time and unavoidable delay	9%
Authorized break time	20 minutes per day

Recent candlemaking statistics are:

Total clock hours for candlemakers	350 hours
Standard hours' worth of candles produced	380 hours

   a. What standard time should be used in computing direct cost?
   b. If there are two employees in candlemaking, how many hours should be scheduled for them to complete the order for the 1,000 special candles?
   c. Assume the candle order has been finished and took 190 hours to complete. What rate of efficiency did the crew attain?

10. The director of a social agency is preparing next year's budget. The agency's caseload averaged 42 clients per day last year, but it has been increasing at an annual rate of 15 percent. The director and caseworkers agree that it takes 3.5 hours to handle each client properly.
   a. How many caseworkers should be requested as the staff component of next year's budget assuming the 15 percent increase in caseload? Assume that caseworkers work an average 250 days per year (which allows for vacation days, sick days, etc.) at 8 hours per workday.
   b. What kind of time standard is the agency using? Is there any way to improve this?
   c. What other reasonable uses exist for the time standard?

11. Assume your boss is foreman of the packing and crating department and has just sent you the following memo: "The president wants all shops, including ours, covered by time standards. I'd like you to do a preliminary study to see if reasonable time standards can be set for our type of work. Everything we pack is of a different size. So how can we have standard times?"
   a. Respond to the boss's memo.
   b. What technique for setting time standards is best for this type of work? Explain.

12. In an automobile plant, a time standards analyst finds that the average cycle time for mounting tires onto rims is 3.6 minutes. If the personal, rest, and delay allowance is 14 percent and the pace rating 105 percent, what is the standard time?

13. An MTM analyst predicts that installing a cord on a proposed new telephone set will take 4,250 TMUs.

a. What is the standard time in minutes if the shop allows a 20 percent PR&D allowance?

b. How can the analyst set a standard on a *proposed* telephone set? Doesn't the item have to actually exist? Discuss.

14. An employee in an electronics plant is using a lugging machine to attach a connector onto the end of a wire. (The machine automatically kicks the wire into a chute once the connector has been attached.) The following data are provided by a time study analyst. Stopwatch readings are in hundredths of a minute and cumulative from element to element and cycle to cycle.

	Cycle				
Job Element	1	2	3	4	Pace Rating
Cut length of wire	21	48	74	103	100
Insert into lugger and press start button	30	58	86	112	90

a. What is the standard time? Assume a personal time allowance of 5 percent, a delay allowance of 3 percent, and two 20-minute coffee breaks per 8-hour day.

b. What would be the advantage in using methods-time-measurement (MTM) instead of stopwatch time study?

15. A work sampling study has been conducted for the job of spray-painting a set of parts. The job consists of mounting the parts on hangers, then spraying them. The PR&D allowance is 20 percent. The analyst's tally sheet is shown below:

Job: Spray painting					
Time period: Five 8-hour days					
Activities Sampled	Tallies		Total	Work Count	Pace Rating
1. Mount	THL THL THL THL THL THL		30	20	110
2. Spray	THL THL THL THL THL THL THL THL THL THL		50	20	120
3. Nonwork	THL THL THL THL		20		
Total			100		

a. What is the cycle time for each task?

b. What is the rated time for each task?

c. What is the standard time for each task?

d. What is the value of the data on nonwork time? How could the data be improved to make them more useful?

16. A supervisor has done a work-sampling study of a subordinate, a clerk-typist. The purpose was to set time standards for typing letters and retrieving letters on file. Therefore, those two tasks were tallied on the work-sampling tally sheet, along with a miscellaneous category for all other clerk-typist activities. The complete tally sheet is as follows:

Subject: Typist
Tasks: Typing letters and retrieving letters on file
Dates: November 29–December 10 (10 working days)
Analyst: Clerical supervisor

Activities Sampled	Tallies	Total	Percentage	Work Count	Pace Rating
1. Type letters	ⅢⅢ ⅢⅢ ⅢⅢ ⅢⅢ ⅢⅢ ⅢⅢ ⅢⅢ ⅢⅢ ⅢⅢ ⅢⅢ ⅢⅢ ⅢⅢ ⅢⅢ ⅢⅢ ⅢⅢ ⅢⅢ	80	40%	60	90
2. Retrieve letters	ⅢⅢ ⅢⅢ ⅢⅢ ⅢⅢ ⅢⅢ ⅢⅢ	30	15	150	80
3. Miscellaneous	ⅢⅢ ⅢⅢ ⅢⅢ ⅢⅢ ⅢⅢ ⅢⅢ ⅢⅢ ⅢⅢ ⅢⅢ ⅢⅢ ⅢⅢ ⅢⅢ ⅢⅢ ⅢⅢ ⅢⅢ ⅢⅢ ⅢⅢ ⅢⅢ	90	45	—	—
Totals		200	100%		

a. PR&D allowance is 12 percent. Compute cycle time, rated time, and standard time for each task.
b. Discuss the possible uses of these time standards.
c. Comment on the fairness and/or validity of these time standards. Are they engineered?

17. An insurance company mailroom prepares all of the company's premiums and letters for mailing. A time study has been done on the job of enclosing premium statements in envelopes. Continuous stopwatch data are given below; the readings are in hundredths of minutes:

	Cycle							Performance Rating
Job Element	1	2	3	4	5	6	7	
Get two envelopes	11		55		105		151	105
Get and fold premium	22	41	65	83	116	135	162	115
Enclose in envelope and seal	29	48	73	97	123	143	169	95

a. Develop a time standard, providing 15 percent for allowances.
b. Assume that the premiums and letters are of various sizes and shapes. The get-and-fold element takes much longer if the item is large and requires several more folds than are needed if the item is small. Therefore, the time standard could be unfair to some of the employees it covers. Suggest some situations in which the standard would be unfair. Suggest some options for making it fair.
c. Assume there is an irregular element: At every 25th envelope, 25 envelopes are wrapped with a rubber band and placed in a box. This element

was timed once, and the elemental time was 15 with a performance rating of 90. With this added factor, recompute the time standard from question *a*.

18. Wabash Airways calculates that a flight attendant needs two minutes to fully serve a meal to a passenger on one of its aircraft; that is, the standard time is two attendant-minutes per meal.
    a. If 2 flight attendants are assigned to an aircraft with 80 passengers on board and serve all of them in a flight having 1 hour of serving time, what is their efficiency.
    b. If the flight attendants are utilized (busy) 90 percent of the time (not counting when they are strapped in for takeoff and landing), what is their productivity?
    c. If a new jumbo aircraft seats 600 passengers, how many flight attendants are needed for a flight with 100 minutes of serving time?

19. At the Transcona Plating Company, all metal-plating jobs are covered by time standards. Last week the company did 850 standard hours' worth of plating jobs. Total clock time for production employees was 1,000 hours that week, and their actual hours of direct labor (hours allocated to actual plating jobs) was 800.
    a. What is the efficiency rate?
    b. What is the utilization rate?
    c. What is the productivity rate?

20. Following is a list of tasks on which time standards/estimates may be set. Suggest a suitable technique or techniques for setting a time standard for each task, and explain your choice.
    Mowing grass.
    Soldering connections in small electronic components.
    Drafting (design drawing).
    Typing and filing.
    Overhauling or adjusting carburetors.
    Cooking in fast-food restaurant.
    Computer programming.
    Installing auto bumpers on car assembly line.

21. "Equal pay for equal work" was the hot pay issue in an earlier era. Now it's "Equal pay for comparable work." With which concept(s) of fair pay (from Figure 16–11) does the comparable-work idea seem most consistent? Explain.

| CASE STUDY | **LAND AND SKY WATERBED COMPANY*** |

Land and Sky Waterbed Company of Lincoln, Nebraska, was the fourth largest waterbed company in the United States and the largest in the Midwest. Land and Sky (L&S) was founded in 1972 by two brothers, Ron and Lynn Larson. The brothers remain as co-owner/managers. One of the brothers is responsible for research and development. (Outside R&D consultants are called on for assistance sometimes.)

The total work force, including office staff, is 67. The oldest employee is the vice president, Jim Wood, a psychology graduate in his mid-30s. Wood has played a major role in developing the scheduling, inventory, quality, and employee payment system at L&S.

THE PRODUCT LINE

L&S produces two lines of waterbed mattresses and liners in standard sizes (king, queen, double, super single, and twin). L&S also manufactures special made-to-order mattresses for other frame manufacturers. The Land and Sky label goes on the higher-quality gold and bronze bed sold exclusively to franchised dealers. L&S produces another brand called the Daymaker. It is sold without advertising as a "commodity" product. The Daymaker is available to any dealer.

There is a trade group for the waterbed industry, but the group has not yet achieved consensus on standard dimensions for king size, queen size, and so forth for the soft-sided foam frame. Therefore, more than 60 sizes must be built to order. Also, some customers make beds to their own dimensions before checking to see what mattress size they can readily obtain. L&S will accept special orders for such unusual sizes, but the price will be high and the order will take thirty days to be filled.

L&S also makes two kinds of soft-sided frames, which make a waterbed look like a conventional bed with box spring and ordinary mattress ("a waterbed that appeals to older people," according to Jim Wood). One kind is made of rigid

Case topics:	Pay incentive for quality
Self-discovery of JIT	Frequency of deliveries from
Make-to order JIT	key suppliers
Off-line subassembly	Evolving from a small to a large
Pay for knowledge/multifunctional	business
employees	

*From the *World Class Manufacturing Casebook: Implementing JIT and TQC.* Copyright © 1987 by Richard J. Schonberger. Reproduced by permission of The Free Press, a Division of Macmillan, Inc.

foam and is cheap and easy to make. The other kind, L&S's own unique design, has a plastic rim built in and is called Naturalizer 2000; the rim keeps the foam from breaking down.

COMPETITIVE CLIMATE

Since waterbed manufacturing is not highly technical and is quite labor-intensive, competitors spring up all over. Low-wage countries like Taiwan are becoming tough competitors.

L&S markets its product line throughout the United States and Canada. An Australian producer makes to L&S's specifications under a licensing agreement. (Jim Wood now wishes that L&S had set up its own Australian subsidiary, rather than licensing the Australian manufacturer.) The European market for waterbeds is still too small to bother with.

There are two main market outlets. The older outlet is the small waterbed retailer, many of whom tend to be less experienced in the ways of the business world and therefore unstable. Recently waterbeds have become popular enough for a second major market outlet to emerge: old-line furniture stores. The two market types place very different demands on the waterbed manufacturer. The small waterbed retailer wants "instant" delivery response. The old-line furniture store plans orders carefully in advance and does not expect delivery right away, but does drive a hard bargain on price. L&S has developed a quick-response production system aimed at filling orders faster than the competition. Most orders can be shipped within 48 hours, and same-day production and shipment is possible (but not cost effective). With the emergence of price-conscious furniture stores as a second major market, L&S has instituted procedures that tightly control material storage costs, labor costs, and costs of scrap and defects.

One complicating factor is that a few retailers are unsophisticated in their ordering. For example, one retailer phoned in a large order specifying the quantity but not which models he wanted. When asked which models, he said, "Just send about what I have ordered before." That was not of much help, because prior orders had come in at different times for different models.

Some inventory of finished waterbeds is kept in bonded public warehouses in different regions of the country so orders in those regions may be filled quickly.

THE PLANT

L&S is in an industrial park, housed in three noncustom metal buildings arranged in a U-shaped configuration. Building 1—at one leg of the U—houses the sales and administrative offices with a shipping and receiving warehouse in the back. Building 2, forming the bottom of the U, is the main manufacturing and quality-check area. Building 3—the other leg of the U—is for fiber baffle production and assembly, liner production, and injection-molding and assembly of soft-sided frames. A parking lot in the center of the U is also used for vinyl storage.

ASSEMBLY

Producing the Waterbed

Vinyl Processes. The waterbed begins as a roll of vinyl. It is cut to size by hand. (A $20,000 cutting machine had been used, but it broke down often and also yielded too much scrap.) The next steps are to install valves and corner seam panels using special machines. Then the vinyl sheets go to machines that fuse the corners together by high-frequency radio waves. Last, the ends and sides are sealed (see Exhibit 1).

Baffle Installation. High-quality waterbeds contain a fiber baffle that keeps the water from "making waves" when in use. Research and development at L&S has come up with a baffle made of polyurethane fiber that reduces the "wave time" from twenty-five to three seconds. L&S considers fusing of the side and end seams on the mattress especially important, and the best operators are assigned that operation. One outside observer watching the job estimated that the two operators were working at about 140 percent of normal pace.

Responsiveness

Total throughout time for these steps in making the waterbed is 35 minutes. The daily output is about 450 waterbed units.

One way that L&S holds down production lead time is by performing early stages of manufacture—such as cutting the vinyl, installing valves, and fusing corners—before knowing exactly what the model mix is. Later the same day, late-arriving orders are totaled by product type, and final model-mix instructions go out to the shop floor. Some of the options that are determined "at the last minute" are (1) the number that are to be top-of-the-line beds with fiber baffles and (2) the number that are to have the L&S label or the Daymaker commodity label.

1. In what sense do the assembly operations sound like just-in-time production? (No one at L&S had ever heard of JIT at the time of the case.) What JIT improvements do you suggest for assembly?

SUBASSEMBLIES AND ACCESSORIES

Baffles (a subassembly) and frames and liners (accessories) are scheduled so as to avoid stockouts. The items are made as follows:

Fiber baffles. Baffles are machine-cut—on the cutting machine originally bought for $20,000 to cut vinyl. Then holes are drilled around the edges of a stack of fiber sheets, and vinyl ties are threaded through

EXHIBIT 1
Sealing Ends and Sides

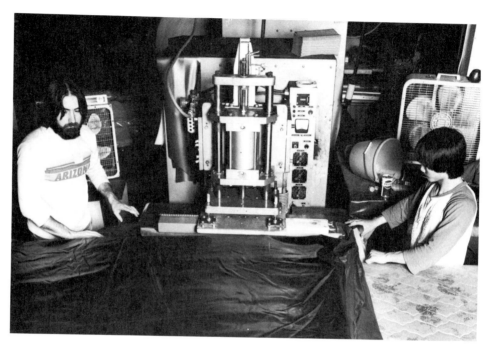

the holes to hold the stack together for storage and transport (the idea
for vinyl ties was developed after glue and plastic hooks failed).

Soft-sided frames. Frames are injection-molded and assembled. L&S has
patented a plastic rim insert, for which it spent $250,000 on research
and development; the insert lends support and adds life to the foam
in the frame.

Cardboard-reinforced bottom liner. The bottom liners were developed by
L&S to make it faster and easier for the customer to set up the waterbed (it cuts setup time by about 20 percent). The liners have been
on the market for about seven months. Retailers love this feature, because the liner is reusable—a good sales point; the bottom liners sell
for $16 to $20 at retail.

2. What could be done about subassembly and accessories manufacture
to mold them into more of a JIT relationship with their "customers"
(assembly and final pack and ship)?

PAY SYSTEM

In July 1982, L&S converted from a straight hourly pay plan to a piece-rate
system having the following features:

Base piece rate. The base piece rate depends on the assigned job (e.g.,
$0.20 per bed).

Achievement raise. An operator gets a 5 percent bonus on top of base rate for each additional machine that the operator learns to run. A few operators have learned to run 10 or 12 machines and therefore get 50–60 percent more than the base piece rate. The bonus buys flexibility for the company. Typically an operator who can run just 2 or 3 machines averages $5–$7 per hour, while one who can run 12 machines might earn $9–$11 per hour. Jim Wood stated that other companies send people home when a machine is down; here "we put them on another machine."

Quality bonus. Operators get a bonus of 25 percent of total pay per period for zero errors. The bonus decreases for each error found: one or two errors, 20 percent; three errors, 15 percent; four errors, 10 percent; five errors, 5 percent, and six or more errors, 0 percent. The owners were initially dubious about the 25 percent bonus (Jim Wood's idea). Previously the bonus was 15 percent. Their feeling was, "Why pay a large bonus for what the employees are supposed to do anyway?" But they agreed to give the plan a try and were very pleased with the results. The error rate had been about 5 percent (5 out of 100 beds). It was down to about 0.5 percent by October. Some of the better operators were achieving zero error rates.

Error penalty. The operator has to pay a penalty of $0.65 for every error discovered by quality control inspectors. Errors are easily traced back to the operator responsible, because each operator has an employee number that is attached to the bed when the operator is working on it. If the operator notifies quality control of an error by marking it, then the penalty is only $0.25. Plans are in motion to make the penalty zero for an admitted error; that way there will be no temptation to try to sneak one by the inspector. Inspection is much more efficient and valid when operators mark their own errors.

Quality control does the bookkeeping for the entire piece-rate and quality incentive system. QC people record daily production and quality performance data for each employee. All information is maintained on the computer.

LABOR POLICIES

Waterbeds are a somewhat seasonal product, which makes staffing difficult. The peak seasons are March–April–May and August–September–October. L&S will not build inventory just to keep operators busy. Competition from other waterbed manufacturers is fierce, especially the Taiwanese manufacturers of liners. A low-inventory policy is a competitive necessity. Therefore, in the slack season operators are laid off. Layoffs are strictly by productivity, not seniority.

Since bed materials are too large for one person to handle easily, operators usually work in pairs; pairings are generally by comparable skill levels. If one operator is tardy or absent, the partner must keep busy on lower-pay work and forego the chance for piece-rate bonuses—a sacrifice that the operator is sure to complain about. Therefore, policies on absenteeism and tardiness are rigid: Absenteeism usually means automatic termination.

> 3. In what ways does the pay and labor system stand in the way of, or further, quicker response?

QUALITY CONTROL AND WARRANTIES

Quality control visually inspects each bed. Inspectors check surfaces for blemishes, check seams, check valves, and so forth. Once in a while the inspector will blow up a bed with air like a balloon in a more thorough leak check. Water is not used to test beds, because it leaves a residual odor.

If no blemishes or defects are found, L&S ships the bed to the retailer with a five-year warranty. Beds with a flaw are sold as blems at a lower cost and with a three-year warranty.

> 4. Critique the L&S approach to quality control.

PURCHASING AND INVENTORY CONTROL

In the waterbed business, material costs are a good deal higher than payroll costs. Thus materials are tightly controlled.

There are rather few manufacturers of vinyl, a key raw material, and vinyl suppliers require a 30-day lead time. Vinyl suppliers ship to L&S by a regular purchase-order schedule, and any schedule changes require about 30 to 60 days' advance notice. Therefore demand forecasting is important for L&S. One of the owners does the forecasting, which is based on seasonal factors and past sales.

Other materials are reordered by a visual reorder-point method. When stock looks low based on the projected manufacturing schedule, an order is placed. The safety stock is typically about two and a half days' supply.

Average raw material inventory is typically two to three weeks' worth. In other words, inventory turns 20 times a year or more. That is partly a matter of necessity. Fiber must be stored indoors, but since it is bulky and there simply is not space to store more, it is maintained at a two-and-a-half-day inventory level. Fiber orders are delivered twice a week in semitrailer loads of 8,000 pounds.

The main purchased material is vinyl in large rolls. Since vinyl is waterproof and may be stored cheaply outdoors, L&S orders larger lots of vinyl than it does for other materials. Vinyl is received about three times a month, 40,000 pounds at a time.

Purchasing and traffic (shipping) are under the management of a single individual, Mr. Bergman. Purchasing buys from at least two sources, which provides protection in case one supplier should shut down—a serious matter, since

L&S's inventories are kept so low. On occasion, purchased parts have been delayed to the point where vinyl rolls are gone; then the operators do what they can with scrap materials, after which they perform other duties or shut down and go home.

Finished goods are stored in the warehouse for a short time prior to loading onto an outbound truck.

A complete physical inventory of finished goods and raw materials is taken every four weeks.

5. What are some ways to improve purchasing procedures?

6. How can L&S protect itself from the miseries that plague most Western companies as they grow large?

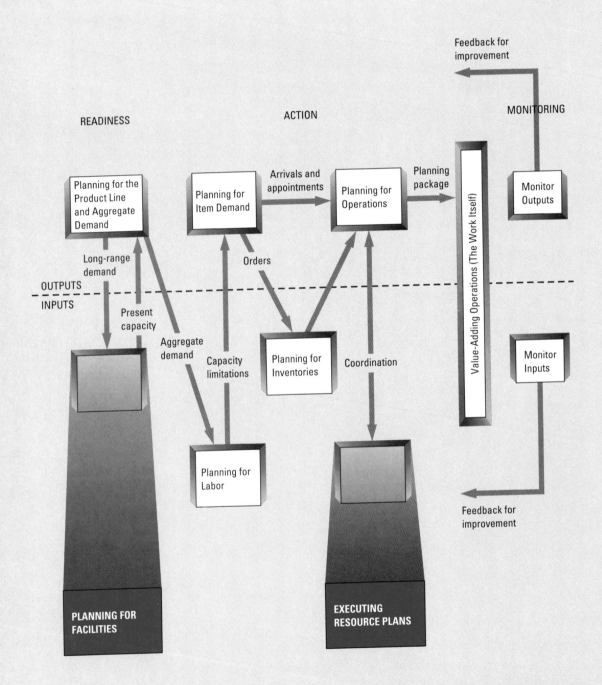

READINESS

ACTION

MONITORING

Feedback for improvement

Planning for the Product Line and Aggregate Demand

Planning for Item Demand

Arrivals and appointments

Planning for Operations

Planning package

Value-Adding Operations (The Work Itself)

Monitor Outputs

Long-range demand

Orders

OUTPUTS
INPUTS

Present capacity

Aggregate demand

Capacity limitations

Planning for Inventories

Coordination

Monitor Inputs

Planning for Labor

Feedback for improvement

PLANNING FOR FACILITIES

EXECUTING RESOURCE PLANS

Maintenance Management

TOTAL PREVENTIVE MAINTENANCE

THE MAINTENANCE ENVIRONMENT

Operator-Centered Maintenance
Maintenance Department

PERIODIC MAINTENANCE

Preventive Maintenance
Derating
PM Time

GROUP REPLACEMENT

Failure Patterns
Light Bulb Example

STANDBY EQUIPMENT

Machine Failures: The Poisson Distribution
Example of Standby Equipment Analysis
Expected-Value Concept

CASE STUDY: SWANBANK FROZEN FOODS

"What a day! The boss didn't finish the meeting until 6:15—only 45 minutes to get home, walk and feed the dog, shower, drink a V8, brush my teeth, and so on. Big date at 7:00. Oops! What's this? Car's low-fuel warning light is on. Got to stop for gas. Quick phone call to move date back 15 minutes.

"Garage door opener still broken, got to get around to fixing that someday. Ditto for mailbox; mail wet again. Oh no! Forgot to replenish supply of dog food and V8 juice. Oh well, I'll settle for coffee, hope Fido is understanding. No clean dishes! Where's the dog leash? If only I'd put it in the same place each time I finished with it. I'll improvise—like MacGyver does each week—and use an old shoelace. Another phone call, another 15-minute delay.

"At last, the shower. What! No clean towels? Now, what to wear? Shoes look a mess, why can't I remember to clean and shine them when I take them off? Can't find the iron. One more phone call, 'No, really, I'm not standing you up. It's just that today the little things are getting to me. I'll be ready in 30 minutes, I promise.' "

We've all had days when—like our friend in the preceding paragraphs—the "little things" get to us. A second look, however, reveals that at least some of the little things could be avoided with a bit more attention to readiness. Having things ready for use when they are needed prevents many of the kinds of problems one faces when in a hurry to do something important. A fundamental part of that readiness is maintenance, and a fundamental object of maintenance is readiness—ready to use when needed.

Businesses are no different. When hurrying to serve an important customer there is no time for lost or misplaced tools, broken or dirty equipment, or even sloppy appearances. Unfortunately, business has not made maintenance a high-priority concern. Its neglect in North American industry throughout the 1960s, 1970s, and early 1980s adds up to big problems with much of industry's productive equipment: bent shafts, broken-off adjustment cranks and knobs, stripped threads, worn bearings, grime- and chips-clogged gears, and machine surfaces pocked from a thousand hammer blows.

In offices and human services (which are more labor- than machine-intensive), maintenance of equipment usually is not a severe problem. Lack of readiness, however, is. Consider, for example, how often you stand waiting while your server tries to find a pen or pencil to record an order or a sale. Inability to find a needed form or implement in typically disorganized, messy work environments is an all too common problem. It is poor maintenance of the workplace.

Today's emphasis on responsiveness to customers mandates strong renewed attention to maintenance and readiness throughout the organization. A broad-based program that stresses problem prevention—*total preventive maintenance*—is the answer.

TOTAL PREVENTIVE MAINTENANCE

Short on glamour and visibility, maintenance has been susceptible to the budget-cutter's ax. Maintenance budgets, especially for **preventive maintenance (PM)**, were cut. Dependability of quality and output suffered as a result. Some of the leading fast-food chains are notable exceptions; for example, at McDonald's spills, dirt, and other messes are cleaned up fast—a part of everyone's job.

Since equipment users were not maintenance conscious, equipment makers devoted little attention to designing equipment for **maintainability.** A current exception is the highly competitive copier industry. Copier operators rarely have strong technical skills; nevertheless, they are given the job of keeping their machines making good copies. Copier manufacturers have responded by designing the machines so they are easy to service, with easy-open doors and panels, easily removable rolls and brushes, displays that flash a problem-location icon, and so forth.

Today in industry there is a renewed emphasis on maintenance, but without large budget increases. The approach, called **total preventive maintenance (TPM)** or, sometimes, *total productive maintenance,* is operator centered. The idea is for the operator to feel a sense of *ownership* of the machine and the process. The maintenance department then becomes a "backstop," handling more technical machine diagnoses, performing overhauls, and conducting audits. The goals of TPM may be summed up thus:

> Preventive maintenance, yes.
>
> Overhauls, yes.
>
> Breakdowns, no.

Those goals and the TPM concept are gradually catching on in industry, positively affecting the total maintenance environment, considered next.

THE MAINTENANCE ENVIRONMENT

Maintenance is the third of the four stages in the life cycle of operating resources. The stages are diagrammed below:

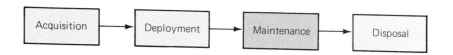

Maintenance means keeping operating resources in good working order. Plant, equipment, and tools usually come to mind, but work force and materials must also be maintained (training people, properly storing materials). A problem in managing repair crews is uncertainty about when breakdowns will occur. Similarly, a problem in maintaining people's health and well-being—via food, health, entertainment, and other services—is uncertainty about when people will "break down" and come in for service. The problems of running a service center with that kind of uncertainty were treated in Chapter 14. Here we stay with traditional maintenance topics, such as preventive maintenance, repairs, group replacement, and standby equipment.

Operator-Centered Maintenance

Like many support functions, maintenance was turned over to specialists. They resided in the maintenance department, usually at least a room away from the equipment they were to maintain and the space they were to keep tidy. Specializing the function seemed to be a way of saving money: Hire low-wage custodians for shop and office cleanup; hire fairly low-wage people to tighten belts, oil machines, and perform other preventive maintenance tasks; and hire a few high-wage people for equipment repair—because the cost to train operators to fix their machines was assumed to be prohibitive.

Such savings are deceptive. If someone else cares for my equipment and workspace, I become sloppy. My keyboard fills with foreign matter, which causes poor performance, greater need for maintenance, and shorter life. The same goes for desktops, electronic displays, copiers, milling machines, extruders, furnaces, automobiles, and so on. By relying on outside experts for repairs, I never come to understand my equipment very well. I become incapable of making even simple repairs. When the equipment fails—as it often does with an uncaring operator—I wait for help and may cease being productive while I wait. Further, I do not recognize symptoms of deterioration—declining quality, for example.

The case for operator-centered maintenance is strong. It becomes stronger as a plant moves toward just-in-time operations. With JIT, a breakdown at one work center soon causes a work stoppage for lack of parts, clients, documents, and so on at the next ones. The person running the equipment needs to care for it and to be capable of doing at least some of the repairs as well. Speed is important. Waiting for someone from maintenance may take too long. The operator who feels some kinship with the machine is also more likely to try to get the machine improved (make it fail-safe) so the same problem will not recur.

Operator-centered maintenance is the core concept in the TPM approach. One of the earlier TPM efforts in North America was at Harley-Davidson, the motorcycle manufacturer, where TPM was one element of the company's successful JIT/TQ campaign. In Harley's Milwaukee engine and transmission plant, maintenance tasks were transferred to machine operators. Machine lubrication came first. Maintenance people spent months training the operators: where the lubricants go, what lubricants to use, and how often. Color-coding aids (grease from the orange barrel goes in the orange fittings) and check sheets were developed. Operators found fittings that had *never* been greased. The next phase was for maintenance to train operators to do simple machine checks and repairs, such as tightening and changing drive chains, replacing motors, and replacing oil seals.

Operator-centered maintenance is sure to become still more common with automation and robotics. Are operators turned out on the street when machines take over? Some are, but there is still a need for a sizable staff to keep the machines running. Hitachi operates a production line producing videotape recorders with about 80 robot and hard-automated workstations. Several people are on hand to maintain the equipment and fix machines when a red trouble light goes on. They do not work for a maintenance department; they are former assemblers retrained to do equipment maintenance and trouble shooting.

Maintenance Department

Even with a high degree of employee involvement in maintenance, there still is a need for a maintenance department. The department might have not only the pure maintenance functions, but also the other three stages in the life cycle of operating resources (acquisition, deployment, and disposal). The organization structure could look like Figure 17–1.[1] The three major sections are *analysis* (planning) on the left; *design* (engineering) in the middle; and *operations* on the right.

Common to the functions shown in Figure 17–1 is the mission of providing for an *efficient* working environment at *reasonable cost.* The TPM concept strives for *both* efficiency and low cost by having operators perform certain maintenance tasks during stoppages and lulls. Also, maintenance can be performed before quitting on days when scheduled output has been completed early; since JIT does not allow overproduction, maintenance is an ideal filler.

In the more traditional approach to maintenance, efficiency and cost were viewed as trade-offs. Some of the conditions that lead to a trade-off viewpoint

FIGURE 17–1

Organization of a Maintenance Department

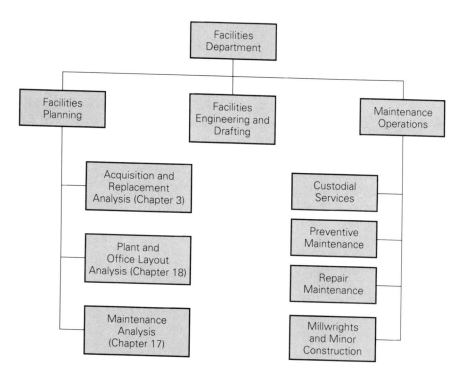

[1]A variety of other maintenance facilities organization structures may be found in James A. Murphy, ed., *Plant Engineering Management* (Dearborn, Mich.: Society of Manufacturing Engineers, 1971), Chapter 2 (TS184.P435x).

are likely to be present for the foreseeable future; therefore, trade-off analysis receives attention later in this chapter.

Figure 17–1 shows four types of maintenance operations: custodial services, preventive maintenance (PM), repairs (including overhauls), and millwrights and minor construction. The first two fall into the category of **periodic maintenance.** Repairs and millwrights/minor construction are **irregular maintenance.** In the maintenance field, much of management's attention has been on the proper mix of periodic and irregular maintenance. The sections of this chapter on group replacement and standby equipment include ways to analyze the mix of periodic and irregular maintenance.

The millwright shop has tradespeople who move and install machines and other facilities (originally in a mill). But machines and work centers often are not so difficult to move as to require trained millwrights. Flexible equipment not bolted or dug into the building structure can be a real asset.

PRINCIPLE: Look for simple, cheap, movable equipment.

Repair employees are skilled, well-paid tradespeople. They need to know more than how to tighten nuts onto bolts. Their troubleshooter role requires diagnostic skills as well as breadth of technical skills. In fact, in some companies the diagnostic role of maintenance troubleshooter overlaps a good deal with that of the quality technician or engineer. Both strive to eliminate machine variability. Only their tools differ: The quality technician gauges the produced part to judge the performance of the process; the maintenance technician gauges the machine (its vibration, the chemistry of its lubricants, and so forth).

In fact, a nice maintenance department career ladder, with increasing skills and wage rates, is from custodianship to preventive maintenance to repair and overhaul or to millwright and minor construction. The steps of the ladder are arranged in just that way in Figure 17–1.

The maintenance department may be viewed as a minifactory. As such, it has a full operations management system. Of course, the minifactory shares many resources with the parent organization. The parent usually supplies the maintenance department with such services as personnel, purchasing, and methods and time standards.

PERIODIC MAINTENANCE

Repair maintenance is usually a necessity, but periodic maintenance is discretionary. Though it may not *have* to be done, periodic maintenance has appeal for at least two reasons:

1. Periodic maintenance can be scheduled to coincide with the availability of someone to perform it. Repairs can come in bunches, overwhelming the repair staff. (Remember those "little things" that can go wrong?)

2. Periodic maintenance tends to forestall work stoppage. Repair crews feed on adversity: breakdowns and stoppages.

Custodial work, one type of periodic maintenance, is usually housed in the maintenance department. This may be changing somewhat. In some companies, the TPM concept includes having machine operators and assemblers clean their own areas. Standards of cleanliness and neatness usually are very high, partly to ensure that quality and machine operation are not compromised by dirt and grime. Also, appearance is important to customers.

Preventive Maintenance

Preventive maintenance (PM) is the more issue-laden aspect of periodic maintenance. There are three types of PM:

PM based on calendar time—maintenance at regular intervals.

PM based on time of usage—maintenance after a set number of operating hours. (This is often called **predictive maintenance**, since the idea is to do the maintenance before the predicted time of failure or wearout.)

PM based on inspection—any maintenance that seems prudent as revealed by planned inspections.

In the TPM approach, the machine operator often has a PM checklist taped to the machine, and the first task at the start of a work shift is to check everything on the list. Production begins only after everything is right.

Among the most ardent believers in the PM concept are aircraft people. In aircraft maintenance, PM is everything; waiting for a failure is intolerable, because if a failure occurs there may be nothing left to fix. The well-traveled B-52 is one shining example of success of the PM concept in aircraft. Even more remarkable is the DC-3, over half a century old. (The military version, the C-47, was affectionately known as the "Gooney Bird.") A few hundred of these venerable aircraft are still logging mileage, thanks to the thoroughness of aircraft PM practices coupled with good design.

The strong commitment to PM for aircraft extends backward to design of the product for maintainability. Airframe manufacturers try to design maintainability into their aircraft in order to have a chance at government contracts. Preventive maintenance of aircraft is largely based on time of usage. Flight logs recording hours of usage are the basis for thorough overhauls and replacements. PM based on inspection is also important. Pilots and ground crews have inspection checklists for routine maintenance. Also, critical components are periodically torn down for interior inspections; the U.S. Air Force refers to this as *IRAN*—inspect and repair *as* necessary—*maintenance.*

Most auto owners do a small amount of PM based on time of usage; examples are oil changes, grease jobs, and tuneups. The number of recent-model cars in auto graveyards provide mute testimony to the poor job that many of us do in preventively maintaining our cars. In the face of this is some evidence that applying airplane-style maintenance to automotive vehicles can yield impressive results. For example, the average life of United Parcel Service's big brown delivery trucks is 22 years, and long-haul UPS trucks often run over 2 million miles. UPS achieves those results by following a rigorous PM regimen, including daily cleaning, checking, and adjusting.

A good PM program requires records. A maintenance history is needed for each piece of equipment. This permits study of breakdown frequency and causes; the findings provide the basis for improving PM procedures. (Lack of a simple maintenance recordkeeping system for the auto owner surely contributes to poor auto maintenance. Another factor is that consumers have never made it known to auto manufacturers that they care about maintainability.)

Derating

People who overwork (or overplay) may suffer hypertension, heart disease, or ulcers. The doctor says, "Slow down. Get more rest. Learn to relax." A machine is not much different. If it is to run right when its owner wants it to, it must not be run too hard, and time must be taken to check and fix it.

The allied TPM principle is to run machines and production lines at speeds (or loads) lower than their rated capacity or under better than usual operating conditions. The principle, known as **derating,** is an old one. Sadly, in many companies, managers several hierarchical levels away from the equipment read the numbers and press for maximal speeds and loads. Often those distant managers have no operating experience and fail to see the risks.

The risks are that the equipment's moving parts will wear, overheat, and clog with chips and metal filings, producing increasing amounts of defective product. The machines will become breakdown prone. The defects and breakdowns will raise costs, place a large obstacle—uncertainty—in the way of JIT implementation, and make it hard to deliver good quality and dependable service to the customer. Next comes decreased sales revenue, lower budgets, and even less PM.

Besides derating, TPM requires sufficient time to check and fix machines.

PM Time

When machines are run day and night, PM people have trouble getting time to check the equipment, tighten, oil, replace components, clean, and so forth. Then machines malfunction and wear out for lack of proper care. TPM calls for setting aside time each day for PM.

Some companies—Toyota and Ford, for example—go so far as to insert mini-shifts for preventive maintenance before and after production shifts. Under one such plan there is a four-hour maintenance shift, then an eight-hour production shift, then a four-hour maintenance shift, then an eight-hour production shift, and so on. Companies following this or a similar plan believe they get about the same amount of production in two shifts as they otherwise would in three, because the two production shifts run full blast with no breakdowns. A whole shift of direct labor may be saved. The number of maintenance people may be unchanged; they just work different hours.

But what about massive equipment in such industries as paper making, sheet coating and extruding, and steel making? Steel making is a special case: Can't shut down a steel furnace for daily maintenance because of the very high cost of heating it up. Except for such special cases, however, there is mounting evidence that a daily maintenance shutdown, even if only for one hour, makes sense.

At one U.S. particle-board plant, the massive mix-mold-bake-cool line was run 24 hours a day, 7 days a week, except for 1 hour of maintenance weekly. For lack of regular maintenance, the line produced a large amount of scrap and defective particle board. When asked why they don't shut down for some maintenance every day, the reply was, "We have startup problems." The general manager of several Brazilian particle-board plants heard that story and offered this comment: "We *do* shut down for maintenance every day, and we *don't* have startup problems." In other words, by having to face the problems of startup every day, they learned how to make startup an easy routine.

The tendency to want to run machines full speed day and night, with no maintenance time, is strongest in the case of very expensive machines: The counter viewpoint is: Don't our most expensive machines deserve our *best* care rather than our worst? The viewpoint that question expresses is gaining a foothold in industry, primarily in support of quality and JIT campaigns, both of which press for dependability.

For all its advantages, PM can be overdone. Preventing all failures is commendable for aircraft, but that is too expensive for most other kinds of equipment; *some* breakdowns must be allowed. Management pays the bills and therefore must make choices as to the level of preventive versus repair maintenance. Cost analysis is possible in the case of certain replaceable components: Find the cost of **group replacement** (which means replacing a whole group of components at periodic intervals) versus the cost of replacing individual machines as they fail. Another kind of cost analysis concerns standby equipment. Keeping standby equipment on hand for use in case of breakdown of primary equipment is akin to preventive maintenance; that is, the standby equipment keeps the work going when there is a breakdown. Group-replacement analysis and standby-equipment analysis are considered in the following two sections.

GROUP REPLACEMENT

Replacement (or trade-in) of a machine is a capital acquisition problem. When to replace machine *components* is a maintenance problem, which we take up here.

For a few kinds of components, replacement is based on wear and tear. Tires are of this type. For many kinds of components, however, sudden failure is a greater problem than wear-out. Examples include electronic components, relays, light bulbs, shoelaces, and, to a considerable extent, bearings. Where a number of the same type of component are in use, one should consider group replacement as opposed to replacing individual components as they fail.

Failure Patterns

Finding the cost of group replacement requires data on the failure pattern for the component. Three examples of a *general* failure probability pattern over component operating life are shown in Figure 17–2. Each represents the failure pattern for a different type of machine or machine system. A variety of components of each machine could be the cause of sudden failure.

Three zones are identified in the figure. The first is the **infant mortality zone**. Such early failure may result from improper assembly or from rough handling or shipping. The probability of infant mortality can sometimes be reduced by preuse or by "burning in" components or the whole machine before shipment. Apple burns in its Macintosh computers for 24 hours prior to shipment. Sometimes burn-in of the end-product can be reduced or eliminated by burning in components at component-parts suppliers' plants—"quality at the source." Many electronics companies demand this of their suppliers.

If a component survives the infant mortality period, the chances of failure tend to be low for a time. Failures occur randomly and for diverse reasons. This is the normal operating period.

After that, the component enters the *wear-out zone.* In that zone the probability of failure raises sharply, peaks, and then falls to zero at maximum product life. In both the normal operating period and the wear-out zone, failure probability can sometimes be reduced by derating.

FIGURE 17–2
Probability of Failure over Component Operating Life

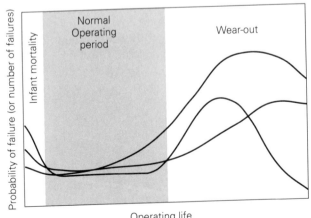

The shape of the curve for a given machine or machine system must be discovered by testing. For a certain machine component, the manufacturer or a trade association may do the testing and publish the results. Otherwise, the maintenance department may run its own tests, as illustrated in the following discussion.

Light Bulb Example

Example 17–1 compares two policies on light bulb replacement. One is to allow light bulbs to last as long as they will before replacing them. In this policy, a few fail in infant mortality, a few more fail at random for various reasons, and the rest (probably the majority) fail in the wear-out zone.

In the second policy, bulbs are not left in their sockets long enough for wear-out. Instead, all bulbs are replaced at regular intervals (periodic maintenance) partway through their normal life expectancy. This second preventive policy, called *group replacement*, requires failure-rate data.

EXAMPLE 17–1	GROUP VERSUS INDIVIDUAL LIGHT BULB REPLACEMENT

At present, light bulbs in building C are replaced as they fail. Whoever notices a failure phones the trouble-call desk, maintenance department. The trouble-call dispatcher sends someone to change the light bulb. The average cost is $3.30 per bulb, including labor.

An alternative policy is the preventive one of replacing all building C bulbs at regular intervals (group replacement). For building C the group-replacement policy would cost $1 per bulb, including labor. There are 1,000 light bulbs in building C. Therefore each group replacement would cost $1,000. What replacement policy is optimal?

Solution

When light bulb failure data are not given, we need to run an experiment. Place bulbs in 1,000 sockets in building C. It is not practical to let the building go dark, so all failures are replaced during the experiment. The experimental results are shown in Figure 17–3.

It appears in Figure 17–3 that the experiment has been run long enough to achieve a nearly **steady state**: that is, all new bulbs put in at the beginning of the year have been replaced and their replacements have been replaced; the mix of bulbs is now a more uniform mix of ages, and the steady-state failure rate is about 310 per month (a rough

FIGURE 17–3
Experimental Failure Data

Month	1	2	3	4	5	6	7	8	9	10	11	12
Failures during month	46	150	218	360	520	353	387	240	260	330	301	310

average of failures in recent months, e.g., in the last three months). Actually, there is no need to run the experiment long enough to achieve a steady state unless a new type of bulb is being used or the building is new. In an existing building the light bulb failure rate prior to the experiment would have been steady state.

Cost of present policy: The steady-state condition applies to the present replace-as-they-fail policy. Its cost is:

$$310 \text{ bulbs/month} \times \$3.30/\text{bulb} = \$1,023 \text{ per month}$$

Cost of group-replacement policy: The cost of group replacement every month is:

$$
\begin{array}{lll}
\text{Group cost: } 1,000 \text{ bulbs} \times & \$1.00/\text{bulb} = & \$1,000/\text{month} \\
\text{Failure cost: } 46 \text{ bulbs} \times & \$3.30/\text{bulb} = & \underline{152/\text{month}} \\
& \text{Total cost} & \$1,152/\text{month}
\end{array}
$$

The cost of group replacement every two months is:

$$
\begin{array}{lll}
\text{Group cost:} & & \$1,000/2 \text{ months} \\
\text{Failure cost: } (46 + 150) \times \$3.30 = & & \underline{647/2 \text{ month}} \\
& \text{Total cost} & \$1,647/2 \text{ month} \\
& = & \$823/\text{month}
\end{array}
$$

The cost of group replacement every three months is:

$$
\begin{array}{lll}
\text{Group cost:} & & \$1,000/3 \text{ month} \\
\text{Failure cost: } (46 + 150 + 218) \times \$3.30 = & & \underline{1,366/3 \text{ month}} \\
& \text{Total cost} & \$2,366/3 \text{ month} \\
& = & \$789/\text{month}
\end{array}
$$

The cost of group replacement every four months is:

$$
\begin{array}{lll}
\text{Group cost:} & & \$1,000/4 \text{ month} \\
\text{Failure cost: } (46 + 150 + 218 + 360) \times \$3.30 = & & \underline{2,554/4 \text{ month}} \\
& \text{Total cost} & \$3,554/4 \text{ month} \\
& = & \$888/\text{month}
\end{array}
$$

The costs have begun to turn upward; this suggests that we have found the optimum (lowest cost on a U-shaped cost curve). It is $789 per month for group replacement every three months. That beats the $1,023 per month for replacing the bulbs as they fail, so group replacement every three months is the optimum among the policies considered.

Does Example 17–1 explore all the issues in group replacement? It does not. What about the cost of interruptions for those components that fail? For light bulbs, the cost may be small. If the components were critical, the cost of interruptions would add a new layer of complexity to the problem. Common sense suggests, however, that where failures are costly, group replacement is even more attractive.

STANDBY EQUIPMENT

Society depends increasingly on technology. We are at the mercy of machines. They break down, and lives are lost, not to mention profits. Sometimes the consequences of breakdowns are severe enough to justify spares. Spares, or standby facilities, provide comforting backup at some price, and they are an alternative to paying for a high level of maintenance in order to reduce the chance of breakdowns.

Indeed, one computer manufacturer, Tandem Computers, has made a profitable market for itself by selling a computer that actually is up to 16 processors operating in parallel. Their "fault-tolerant" computer appeals to customers for whom downtime is a crisis or even a life-threatening disaster. Tandem's largest market is in large fund transfers, as between the Federal Reserve and large banks. Shop-floor manufacturing uses are its second largest market, followed by monitoring hospital patients, power stations, and so forth.

Machine Failures: The Poisson Distribution

When large numbers of identical machines exist, there is a simplified way to analyze standby policies. The method uses our knowledge about patterns of machine failure. Studies show that machine failures per unit of time are random variables that tend to follow the Poisson probability distribution. The shape of the Poisson is based on a mathematical function, and the complete shape can be developed by simply entering the mean number of failures per time unit into the Poisson general formula.

A characteristic shape of the distribution is shown in Figure 17–4. We see

FIGURE 17–4
Poisson Probability Distribution

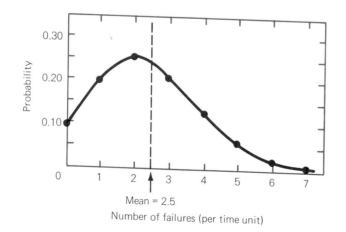

Mean = 2.5

Number of failures (per time unit)

that there is some chance of zero failures per time unit (for example, per day), but, of course, there can be no chance of negative failure per time unit. Poisson distributions rise to a peak probability and then taper off (are skewed) to the right. There is a 50 percent chance that in the given time period the number of failures will be less than the mean (2.5 per time unit in Figure 17–4) and also a 50 percent chance that the number of failures will exceed the mean.

Example of Standby Equipment Analysis

Sometimes the merits of standby equipment may be judged by a cost analysis. Example 17–2 illustrates a type of cost analysis that employs the Poisson probability distribution.

EXAMPLE 17–2   **STANDBY "SCOPES" AND POISSON-DISTRIBUTED FAILURES**

A large electronics manufacturer does testing with "scopes" at each of 100 assembly and testing stations. When a scope breaks down, testing is halted at one station for one day (the time it takes to get the scope repaired). The company estimates the cost of disruption and idleness at $100 for each day that a scope is down. That cost is $200 if two scopes are down, $300 if three scopes are down, and so forth. One way to avert the downtime cost is to keep spare scopes on hand. It costs about $50 per day to own and maintain each spare.

If scope breakdowns are random and average three per day, how many spare scopes should be maintained?

Solution
The mean number of scope failures is known to be three per day. From that figure, the probabilities of any other number of failures per day can be calculated or looked up in a table or graph. The calculations (and tables and graphs) are based on the Poisson formula:

$$P(n) = \frac{e^{-\lambda}\lambda^n}{n!}$$

where

n = Number of failures per time unit

λ = Mean number of failures per time period = 3 scopes/day

e = 2.7183

$P(n)$ = Probability of n failures per time unit

For example, zero scope failures per day has the probability

$$P(0) = \frac{2.7183^{-3} \times 3^0}{0!} = \frac{1}{(1)(2.7183)^3} = \frac{1}{(20.086)} = 0.050$$

FIGURE 17–5

Calculating Optimal Number of Standby Machines—Tabular Approach

Number of Spares	n: P(n):	0 0.050	1 0.150	2 0.224	3 0.224	4 0.168	5 0.101	6 0.050	7 0.022	Daily Cost of Curtailed Testing	Daily Cost of Spares	Total Cost per Day
0		0	$100	$200	$300	$400	$500	$600	$700	$290.10	$ 0	$290.10
1			0	100	200	300	400	500	600	196.20	50	246.20
2				0	100	200	300	400	500	117.30	100	217.30
3					0	100	200	300	400	60.80	150	210.80 ←
4						0	100	200	300	26.70	200	226.70

*Based on $\lambda = 3$ failures per day.

One scope failure per day has the probability.

$$P(1) = \frac{2.7183^{-3} \times 3^1}{1!} = \frac{3}{(1)(20.086)} = 0.150$$

Appendix B is an abbreviated table of *cumulative* Poisson probabilities. Find the *individual* probabilities by successive subtraction. For example, in the case of $\lambda = 3$ scopes per day, go to the row where $\lambda = 3.0$. Then, where $n = 0$, note that $P(0) = 0.050$. For $P(1)$, find 0.199 in the column where $n = 1$; subtract 0.050 from 0.199 and get 0.149, which (allowing for rounding error) is the same as the 0.150 that we obtained mathematically. Next, subtract 0.199 from 0.423 and get 0.224, which is $P(2)$; and so forth.

Calculating the optimal number of spare scopes requires a number of steps. Figure 17–5 simplifies the bookkeeping. The calculation procedure in the table follows the expected-value concept. For example, for the first row, zero spares, expected cost of failures is:

$$E_F = \$100(0.150) + \$200(0.224) + \$300(0.224) + \$400(0.168)$$
$$+ \$500(0.101) + \$600(0.050) + \$700(0.022)$$
$$= \$15 + \$44.8 + \$67.2 + \$67.2 + \$50.5 + \$30.0 + \$15.4$$
$$= \$290.10$$

Calculate each row similarly. Stop when the total cost bottoms out and begins to rise. That identifies the optimal policy. In this case, it is to provide three spares at a total cost of $210.80 per day.

The standby and group-replacement methods have been around for many years, but we should be cautious about their apparent logic. The costs of downtime are many; some are not obvious or easy to measure, and estimating too low can yield a decision to allow the downtime. Today, companies increasingly are simply adopting the view that downtime is bad. In practice, that view translates into a policy of forcing downtime to decrease. That makes us look more favorably on group replacement and standby equipment.

PRINCIPLE: Seek to have plural rather than singular work stations, machines, cells and flow lines for each product, service, or customer.

Expected-Value Concept

The solution to Example 17–2 employed the **expected-value** concept, which deserves further comment. Expected value is a weighted average. It is the sum of all "payoffs" (in Example 17–2, cost of failures) times respective probabilities.[2] The probabilities must add up to 1.0, which accounts for all possible payoffs.

The expected-value concept is useful only for probability-distributed input data and only when records are good enough to yield the probabilities. In maintenance, where breakdowns tend to be probabilistically distributed random events, the expected-value concept can be useful. This is especially true since good recordkeeping on equipment and component failures has become accepted practice in well-run maintenance organizations.

Elsewhere in this book, input data mostly are more narrowly distributed, and single-valued estimates (rather than expected values) suffice.[3]

SUMMARY

Despite a historical lack of glamour, maintenance is being increasingly recognized as a necessity for competitive organizations. The interests of improved customer service increase the need for total preventive maintenance (TPM).

Maintenance and cleanliness of work space should be largely the operator's responsibility. If we leave maintenance to outsiders, we get sloppy, never understand our equipment, run it roughly, and have frequent breakdowns. Operator-centered maintenance is especially necessary in a JIT plant, where breakdowns are so disruptive, and as an ingredient in TQ, since quality cannot be good if machines don't work right. Further, it is natural to retrain operators to be machine maintainers when robotics and automation are introduced.

Good upkeep on equipment is made easier when equipment is designed for maintainability. Then machine operators can be active in keeping their machines in operation, with backup support by the maintenance department. The department may house facilities acquisition, deployment, and disposal as well as

---

[2]Some readers may be aware of an application of the expected-value concept in the behavioral sciences: Vroom's expectancy model. In Vroom's model,

$$\text{Motivation} = \Sigma[(\text{Valence})(\text{Expectancy})]$$

One can see that valence is about the same as value or payoff and expectancy is about the same as probability. Substituting the alternative terms on the right side of the equation, we have $\Sigma[(\text{Payoff})(\text{Probability})]$, which is the general form of the expected-value model.

[3]A point of terminology for those students who have studied decision theory: Use of single-valued estimates is known in decision theory as a condition of *assumed certainty*; use of probabilistic input data is a condition of *assumed risk* (or, by some authors *assumed uncertainty*).

maintenance. Maintenance planning centers on choices between periodic and irregular maintenance. Periodic maintenance ranges from routine custodianship to well-planned preventive (and predictive) maintenance (PM) to group-replacement and standby equipment policies. Custodianship can and often should be employee centered, but with careful management oversight.

PM (preventive maintenance) expands to TPM in support of JIT/TQ goals. TPM includes operator-centered maintenance; calls for setting aside time for PM each day; and recommends derating, which means running machines at less than rated capacity in order to avoid degradation of performance and premature wear-out. Effective PM also requires good records. Group-replacement and standby equipment decisions sometimes require cost analysis.

Group replacement may apply to any large group of identical components that fail (rather than wear out). The analyst considers costs of two replacement options. One is replacing components as they fail on a trouble-call basis. The second is replacing all components at periodic intervals, plus trouble-call replacements between periods. Data inputs are (1) the unit costs of each type of replacement and (2) the historical pattern of component life. The latter may be a failure probability distribution or actual numbers of failures per time unit as found in a live test.

Standby equipment analysis applies to large groups of machines rather than components. Failures of such groups of machines tend to follow the Poisson probability distribution. If the maintenance manager knows the average number that fail per time period, the probabilities of any other number of failures per time period may be found using Poisson tables or formulas. The probability of any number of out-of-service machines may be multiplied by the cost of lost service. The other factor is the cost of keeping standby machines on hand to avoid lost service. A minimum-cost standby policy is sought.

KEY WORDS

Preventive maintenance (PM)	Periodic maintenance	Group replacement
Maintainability	Irregular maintenance	Infant mortality zone
Total preventive maintenance (TPM)	Predictive maintenance	Steady state
	Derating	Expected value

SOLVED PROBLEMS

1. A process control system contains 100 identical diodes, each costing $0.10. Electronic Service Providers, Inc. (ESP), which holds the maintenance contract for the control system, is searching for a low-cost replacement policy for the diodes, which are prone to failure. ESP has gathered its own failure data by starting up the control system with 100 new diodes and recording their op-

erating lives; each failed diode was replaced during the data collection period. The data, collected over 5,000 hours of operation, are as follows:

Operating hours	500	1,000	1,500	2,000	2,500	3,000	3,500	4,000	4,500	5,000
Number of diodes replaced during period	18	10	8	10	37	49	54	56	57	53

ESP also has estimated that its labor and overhead cost to replace a single diode is $4.90, but is only $1.90 if all 100 are replaced at one time. What is the best replacement policy?

Solution

Replacing single diodes: The failure data show what appear to be steady-state conditions from about 3,500 hours on. The average failures replaced during steady state are 55 [(54 + 56 + 57 + 53)/4 = 55]. ESP calculates the cost, per 500 hours of operation, of replacing single diodes as:

$$55 \text{ diode failures per 500 hours} \times \$5.00 = \$275$$

Note: The cost of each failure, $5.00, is based on $0.10 for the diode plus $4.90 for labor and overhead.

Group replacement every 500 hours: Cost of replacing all 100 diodes every 500 hours, plus all failures during that 500 hours, is:

Group cost:	100 diodes × ($0.10 + $1.90)	= $200
Failure cost:	18 failed diodes × $5.00	= $ 90
	Total cost per 500 hours	= $290

Group replacement every 1,000 hours:

Group cost:	100 diodes × ($0.10 + $1.90)	= $200
Failure cost:	(18 + 10) failed diodes × $5.00	= $140
	Total cost for two 500-hour periods	= $340
	Cost per 500 hours = $340/2	= $170

Group replacement every 1,500 hours:

Group cost:	100 diodes × ($0.10 + $1.90)	= $200
Failure cost:	36 failed diodes × $5.00	= $180
	Total cost for three 500-hour periods	= $380
	Cost per 500 hours = $380/3	= $127

Group replacement every 2,000 hours:

Group cost:	100 diodes × ($0.10 + $1.90)	= $200
Failure cost:	46 failed diodes × $5.00	= $230
	Total cost for four 500-hour periods	= $430
	Cost per 500 hours = $430/4	= $108

Group replacement every 2,500 hours:

$$\begin{aligned}
\text{Group cost:} \quad & 100 \text{ diodes} \times (\$0.10 + \$1.90) && = \$200 \\
\text{Failure cost:} \quad & 83 \text{ failed diodes} \times \$5.00 && = \underline{\$415} \\
& \text{Total cost for five 500-hour periods} && = \$615 \\
& \text{Cost per 500 hours} = \$615/5 && = \$123
\end{aligned}$$

Since costs have begun to rise, it appears that the lowest-cost policy has been found: Group replacement every 2,000 hours, plus replacement of any failures during that period. According to ESP's data, that policy's cost is about $108 per 500 hours, which is far better than the $275 cost for individual replacements.

2. Given:

Current number of units of an identical machine = 20
Cost to own and maintain a spare unit = $7 per hour
Mean number of failures per hour = 2

Cost of downtime:
$10 per hour for one unit out of service
$30 per hour for two units out of service
$60 per hour for three units out of service
$100 per hour for four units out of service
$150 per hour for five or more units out of service

If breakdowns of the units are random, how many standby units should there be?

Solution

The following table aids in solution. To get the row of probabilities, $P(n)$, go to Appendix B. Use the row in which $\lambda = 2$, since the mean number of failures per hour is 2. The probability of zero failures, 0.135, is taken from the $n = 0$ column. The other probabilities require successive subtraction. For example, the 0.090 is obtained by subtracting the value in the $n = 3$ column from the value in the $n = 4$ column: $0.947 - 0.857 = 0.090$.

Number of Standbys	$P(n)$	0	1	2	3	4	5	6	7	Hourly Cost of Downtime	Hourly Cost of Standbys	Total Cost per Hour
	n:	0	1	2	3	4	5	6	7			
	$P(n)$:	0.135	0.271	0.271	0.180	0.090	0.036	0.012	0.004			
0		0	$10	$30	$60	$100	$150	$150	$150	$38.44	$ 0.00	$38.44
1			0	10	30	60	100	150	150	19.51	7.00	26.51
2				0	10	30	60	100	150	8.46	14.00	22.46 ←
3					0	10	30	60	100	3.10	21.00	24.10

Sample cost calculation: For zero number of standbys, use the expected-value method to find the hourly cost of downtime: Multiply cost by probabilities across the entire row, from $n = 0$ to $n = 7$:

$$0.135(0) + 0.271(10) + 0.271(30) + 0.180(60) + 0.090(100)$$
$$+ 0.036(150) + 0.012(150) + 0.004(150) = \$38.44 \text{ per hour}$$

The optimum number of standbys is 2, since that policy yields the lowest cost per hour, $22.46.

REFERENCES

Books

Cordero, S. T. *Maintenance Management Handbook.* Englewood Cliffs, N.J.: Fairmont Press, 1987.

Mann, Lawrence, Jr. *Maintenance Management*, rev. ed. Lexington, Mass: Lexington Books, 1983.

Nakajima, Seiichi. *Introduction to TPM: Total Productive Maintenance.* Cambridge, Mass.: Productivity Press, 1988 (originally published in Japanese in 1984).

Tomlingson, Paul D. *Industrial Maintenance Management*, 8th ed. Chicago: McLean Hunter, 1989 (658.202T659).

Wireman, Terry. *Preventive Maintenance.* Englewood Cliffs, N.J.: Reston, 1984.

Periodicals

Plant Engineering (includes plant maintenance).

REVIEW QUESTIONS

1. Name two ways in which TPM differs from conventional maintenance.
2. Who should be responsible for upkeep of machines and workspace? Explain.
3. What effect do automation and robotics have on the maintenance function?
4. "If it ain't broke, don't fix it" is a common colloquial phrase, but it is contrary to the PM philosophy. Which is right, and why?
5. What are three keys to a successful PM program?
6. What is the infant mortality problem? Do burn in or derating help with it? Explain.
7. Where can you get failure probability data for individual components or products?
8. In group-replacement analysis, group replacement may be every period,

every two periods, every three, and so on. Why wouldn't the cost *per period* always be less the longer the interval between replacements?

9. How do you get the average number of failures per day in order to calculate the cost of replacing components as they fail?

10. What are the costs and savings in maintaining standby machines?

11. The Poisson distribution simplifies data analysis in the standby machine method. Why doesn't Poisson also apply in group-replacement analysis?

PROBLEMS AND EXERCISES

1. To what extent do commerical semi-truck drivers get involved in PM and repairs to their equipment? (You may need to interview someone.) Do you think their involvement is enough?

2. To what extent do copy machine operators get involved in cleaning and maintaining their own machines (clean glass; clean rollers; resupply with fluids, papers, etc.)? In *repairing* their machines? (You may need to interview someone.) Is their involvement adequate?

3. Every maintenance *operation* requires facilities *planning* (see Figure 17–1). A number of maintenance operations are as follows:

> Replace ceramic tiles in a floor.
>
> Mop floors.
>
> Repair power outage.
>
> Change oil and grease equipment.
>
> Change extrusion heads—simply unscrew dirty one and screw on clean one—as they randomly clog up (in a factory full of plastics extrusion lines, each with an extrusion head to form the plastic).
>
> Replace drive belts, bearings, and so on as they fail (among large group of various machines on factory floor).
>
> Repaint walls.
>
> Maintain spare motors for bank of spinning machines.
>
> Remodel president's office.
>
> Repair shoes (shoe repair shop).

   a. Name one or more analysis techniques (if any) that apply to each maintenance operation.

   b. List the data inputs necessary for conducting the analysis. (Note: Some of the analysis methods are presented in other chapters.) Two completed examples follow:

Maintenance Operation	Analysis Technique	Data Inputs
Rearrange office equipment	Layout analysis (Chapter 18)	Flow data (types and volume) Relationship data
Prepare platform with utility hookups for new equipment	None	

4. With computers (microprocessors) now in common use as automobile control devices, they sometimes serve a preventive maintenance purpose. A dash panel could be used to input into a computer every maintenance operation performed on the car, and mileage data could be entered into the computer automatically. A screen could then recommend preventive maintenance whenever a program determines a need.
   a. To what extent is this idea in use *right now*? What are some obstacles in the way of implementing or improving on such a PM system?
   b. What are some important items of historical data that would need to be programmed into the auto's computer? Where would such data come from? Explain.
   c. Large numbers of nearly identical autos are sold, which provides a sizable potential database for gathering failure and wear-out data. For almost any type of factory machine there is a smaller potential database; that is, there are far fewer "copies" of the same machine. Yet good factory PM is based on good failure records. How can good records be developed for factory machines?

5. Think of a consumer product that advertisers tout as being especially *maintainable*. Distinguish between the maintainability and reliability of the product.

6. Name two industries in which maintainability is especially important, and two in which it is especially unimportant. Discuss. What can maintenance managers do about the maintainability of the facilities in their firms?

7. Joe Black is head of the maintenance operations division of the plant engineering department at Wexco., Inc., Rumors have been flying around his division. The buzzing is regarding the company's plan to launch a new program called "Operator Ownership." The program is aimed at the problem of machine undependability and would place more responsibility for machine performance on the machine operators—a step backwards, in the minds of Black and his subordinates.

   Part of the worry is that operator ownership is budget cutting—that is, slashing the maintenance budget—in disguise, which equals losses of jobs in maintenance operations. Black also harbors natural concerns regarding losses of personal prestige and power.

   Are those worries really justified? Discuss.

8. There are 50 filter traps in the cooling system of a nuclear power plant. Monitor lights warn an attendant when a filter clogs up, and the attendant alerts the maintenance department. It costs $100 in labor and downtime to remove plates and clean out the filter. Maintenance can remove plates and clean out all 50 filters at the same time for a labor-and-downtime cost of $800.

   The maintenance department has collected some experimental data on filter-clogging frequencies. The experiment began with 50 clean traps and ran for 6,000 hours. Results are:

Operating hours	1,000	2,000	3,000	4,000	5,000	6,000
Number of clogged filters replaced during period	1	3	5	6	6	6

   What is the optimal maintenance policy?

9. A refinery has 50 identical pumps installed in various places. Replacing the seal in the pump motor is a delicate task requiring a visit from a maintenance engineer of the pump company, which is situated in another city. The cost of the trip is $200. The cost of replacing one seal is $20. The refinery has used the 50 pumps for 10 quarters ($2\frac{1}{2}$ years), which is the amount of time the plant has been in service. Pump seals have been replaced as they failed. Following is the failure history for the 10 quarters:

Quarter	1	2	3	4	5	6	7	8	9	10
Seal failures	0	1	1	2	3	3	2	4	3	3

   Analyze the merits of a group-replacement policy.

10. Duncan aviation maintains a fleet of Lear jets. The fleet requires 30 identical jet engines installed in the planes. Spare engines are ready to go in Duncan's hangars in case of malfunction of an engine in one of the planes. The spares cost $500 a week to keep on hand. If a plane is idled for lack of a good engine, the cost (lost net revenue) is about $2,000 per week. If an average of two engines per week fail, what is the correct number of spares?

11. Another refinery also has 50 identical pumps installed in various places. When a pump fails, the product flow rate drops, but the refining continues. The estimated average cost of reduced flow rate when a pump is down is $1,000 per day. If a spare pump is on hand when one goes down, the spare can be installed quickly enough so that flow-rate losses are negligible. It costs $60 per day to own and maintain one spare pump. The maintenance manager estimates that one pump per day fails on the average. How many spare pumps should be maintained?

12. Here are three situations in which standby machine analysis *might* be used. Comment on the suitability of standby analysis in each case.
    (1) Spare fluorescent tubes in case one burns out in an auditorium.

(2) Spare memory cards (identical ones) in case one fails in one of a large number of microcomputers used in an electronic test equipment center.

(3) Spare pizza ovens in case one (of many) fails in a large take-out/eat-in pizza place.

13. Hewlett-Packard pays its janitors, guards, and food service people the same wage as its product assembly people, yet the product assembly people have higher status. At one H-P division, the division manager intends to begin rotating assembly people into the lower-status positions, and vice versa. But she wonders how the assemblers will react when asked to "push a broom." From what you have learned about responsibility for maintenance, do you think this rotation plan is a step in the right direction? Explain. What else might be done?

14. Captain Henry Harrison has spent much of his career in Navy shipyards. In the last 10 years, he has held three positions of authority over shops that build and repair ships. He has been a firm believer in conducting frequent inspections of shop facilities and is a stickler for having everything neat, clean, and painted. Some people think Captain Harrison spends too much time on this. What do you think?

CASE STUDY   SWANBANK FROZEN FOODS

Swanbank is a major North American frozen food producer. Its Forbes, North Carolina, plant produces between 280,000 and 320,000 frozen dinners per day. Each year the schedule is cut back in the spring, in advance of reduced summer sales, and raised again in the fall.

In 1983 Jerry Hanks, plant manager at Forbes, inaugurated a just-in-time effort. Hanks's JIT task force has progressed as far as goal setting, and one goal was to set a daily production rate for each product (type of dinner) and meet it everyday.

At that time, setting even a modest rate and hitting it daily was not remotely possible. The normal problems of undependable deliveries of ingredients and packaging materials could perhaps be resolved. Internal problems in food preparation, mixing, cooking, aluminum tray stamping, and material handling also seemed solvable. The big problems were in final assembly and packaging. This case study concerns only that stage of production.

FILL AND PACK

Final assembly and packaging consisted of three high-speed fill-and-pack lines located side by side in a large area stretching lengthwise from the main factory area through two plant additions. The lines were 600 to 850 feet long and conveyor driven. Filling nozzles, chutes, gravity drop devices, and mechanical pushers deposited cooked food items into aluminum tray compartments at early workstations along the line. Automatic cartoners, corrugated box packers, and palletizers were at the end of the line.

The lines were by no means fully automated. A crew of 50 to 60 people, classified as direct labor and supervision, tended a line. Their normal jobs were to load trays and kettles of cooked ingredients into hoppers. Their abnormal jobs were to manually keep production going whenever nozzles clogged up and jamups occurred on the line.

The company had always taken pride in the high speed at which its tray-filling lines were designed to run, about 270 trays per minute. However, with trays moving at that speed past many fill stations, through long and not always straight and level lengths of conveyor, and into temperamental cartoning and packing equipment, slight misalignments could result in spectacular jamups. Trays and their contents could fly into the air and quickly litter the floor and cover the equipment with gravy, peas, and apple cobbler. In such instances, the nearest line crew member would rush to hit a stop button. Then crew members would roll in trash barrels, push carts, and other apparatus so they could manually fill and forward stalled trays and dispose of ruined ones.

A line stop could also sometimes summon technicians from maintenance. Their job was to fix the cause. Often the cause was minor and fixable within a few minutes by a line supervisor or maintenance technician already present at lineside. Filling equipment was also frequently adjusted to correct for spilling of food portions into the wrong tray compartment, which tended to happen

EXHIBIT 1
Distribution of Durations of Stop Times

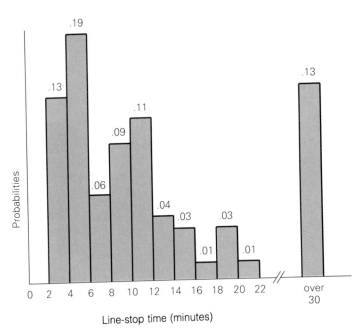

frequently because of the fast line speeds. Those adjustments often could be done "on the fly."

Records kept by line supervisors revealed that the mean stoppage time per shift was 3 hours and the mean number of stops per shift was 26. Exhibit 1 is a distribution of the duration of stoppages per shift. The distribution summarizes a sample of stoppages over 50 shifts. It shows that the vast majority of stoppages were short; in fact, 58 percent were 12 minutes or less. Just 13 percent were over 30 minutes and these incorporated just one instance each of several different stoppage durations, such as 39, 41, . . . , 93, 171, . . . minutes. The longest stoppage in the 50 shifts sampled was 3 hours 17 minutes.

The high incidence of stoppages affected design of the line. Between each pair of fill stations, the conveyor length usually was long enough to hold a few dozen trays. Then, whenever the line stopped, the extra trays could be processed manually. Over the years, the conveyors lengthened as line speeds were increased.

When a line stoppage incident included under- or overfilling, spillover, or damaged containers, the bad product went into trash barrels. The average trash rate had been 5 percent.

Unfortunately, although the trash contained food, no one—company people, local charities, welfare agencies, or farm groups—could come up with an economical way to salvage the good food. The waste was bulldozed under at the local landfill. The average cost of one trashed unit was $0.38, of which $0.015 was container and packaging material (usually just an aluminum tray, since most stoppages came before cartoning).

WORK PACE

When the line was running full speed, line crew members were not hard pressed to keep up. Most people who watched the line for awhile would estimate that perhaps half the crew size, say, 30 people, could keep up with the line. With half a crew, each person would have to tend two geographically separated stations, but even with walk time from one to the next, it appeared that they should have been able to keep up; for example, dump a fresh kettle of gravy into a feeder tank, walk to the next station, load a tray of veal cutlets into the magazine of a feeder machine, walk back to gravy, and repeat.

Hanks summed up the crew size and work pace issue this way: "Half of the line crew are on hand because the equipment doesn't run right." Indeed, the leisurely pace of the line crew could swiftly change to frenzy, and it often did—whenever the line stopped. Manual processing around the bottleneck was fast and furious. During longer stoppages, say, 20 minutes or more, line crews would run out of partially filled trays and then have to stop. They stayed idle until maintenance technicians and line supervisors could fix the problem and restart the line.

The unionized labor force was accustomed to this hurry-and-then-wait work life. Hanks and the JIT team anticipated the need for an education effort, but not big problems with labor, in the upcoming JIT conversion effort.

WORK SHIFTS AND PRACTICES

Most of the year the Forbes plant operated five days a week with two work shifts per day. A $2\frac{1}{2}$ hour changeover and cleanup shift followed each work shift. Product changes, chicken to beef or ravioli to lasagna, for example, generally occurred at the end of each shift. The shift schedule was as follows:

First work shift	5:30 A.M.–2:00 P.M.
Changeover/cleanup	2:00 P.M.–4:30 P.M.
Second work shift	4:30 P.M.–1:00 A.M.
Changeover/cleanup	1:00 A.M.–3:30 A.M.

Average line output per shift varied, depending partly on what product the line was producing. Some products, such as spaghetti dinners, were run at a slower speed than, say, fried shrimp dinners. The main cause of variable line output, however, was amount of line stoppage during a shift. Over one three-week period, output on line 3 was as shown in Exhibit 2.

EXHIBIT 2
Ouptut on Line 3 over Three-Week Period

Day	1	2	3	4	5	6	7	8	9	10	11	12	13	14	15
Output (000 trays packed)	95	102	123	100	87	103	57	85	113	103	68	107	60	102	108

CLEANUP AND LINE CHANGEOVER

A five-person maintenance crew performed cleanups. About half the crew worked on disengaging filling equipment from the chain conveyor and reengaging equipment for use on the next shift. The other half began the task of shoveling, scraping, and push-brooming the litter of food and containers. Large piles went into garbage cans; smaller scatterings near the conveyor were pushed into a trough centered below the conveyor.

The crew started with fill-and-pack line 1, then went to line 2, then 3. As soon as line 1 was torn down and prep-cleaned, part of the crew, in rubber hip boots, began hosing down everything on that line. Hosing was in the direction of the central trough, where it drained into a filtering system. The filtered matter *was* recovered; it was containered and sold as feed to chicken growers.

As hosers moved to line 2, technicians wheeled the next set of filling machines to line 1 and attached and adjusted them for the next production run. The hose crew moved to line 3 and the setup technicians to line 2. Filling equipment to be used from one shift to the next stayed connected but was flushed in place. Hosing included detergent wash-down after the late shift but water only following the first shift.

As production lines started up, the maintenance crew moved to other areas. One remaining task was to completely flush and steam-clean the filling equipment just removed from the three lines. That was done in a separate steam room.

EQUIPMENT MAINTENANCE

The filling machines were about 20 years old but had been ingeniously designed for quick and easy attach/detach from the rotary conveyor line shaft, and they were built to last. A strong corporate manufacturing engineering group (in another city) that had designed the equipment had dwindled to just a few people over the years.

The filling equipment in the steam room was cleaned—and that was all. There was no time for mechanical checking or other maintenance. In fact, throughout the Forbes plant there was a notable lack of preventive maintenance. Lines were lubricated daily by someone from maintenance, but not thoroughly. Old-timers recalled when there had been good PM in the Forbes plant and throughout the company, but PM programs had been pruned by company budget cutters. As PM dwindled, the plant's mode of operation evolved to, in Jerry Hanks's words, "run until it breaks."

The JIT task force was very much aware of the need to reinstall PM. The challenge was to do it without appreciably increasing payroll and other costs.

DISCUSSION QUESTIONS

1. Is the equipment maintenance problem severe? Support your answer

with data and facts, if available. Consider possible causes of problems other than equipment troubles.

2. What are the Forbes plant's three biggest problems, in rank order? Are they interrelated or mostly independent? Discuss.

3. Devise a PM plan, including tasks, schedules, and labor needs, that will not appreciably raise costs. Discuss the benefits of the plan and its prospects for working.

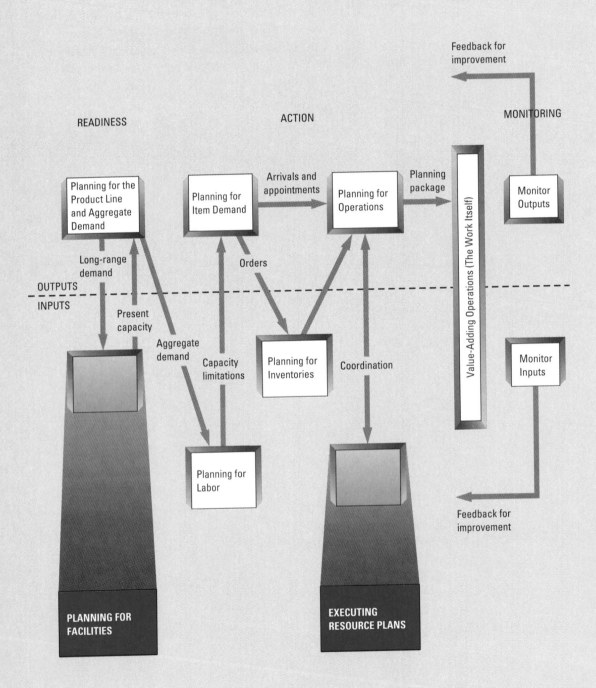

READINESS   ACTION   MONITORING

Feedback for improvement

Planning for the Product Line and Aggregate Demand

Planning for Item Demand

Arrivals and appointments

Planning for Operations

Planning package

Value-Adding Operations (The Work Itself)

Monitor Outputs

Long-range demand

OUTPUTS

INPUTS

Present capacity

Orders

Aggregate demand

Capacity limitations

Planning for Inventories

Coordination

Monitor Inputs

Planning for Labor

PLANNING FOR FACILITIES

EXECUTING RESOURCE PLANS

Feedback for improvement

Facilities Deployment: Location, Layout, Handling, and Transportation

HANDLING AND TRANSPORTATION

Handling Concepts
Handling Analysis
Containerization

SUPPLEMENT: STEPPING-STONE METHOD AND VOGEL'S APPROXIMATION METHOD

Realtors say there are three important factors in buying a house: location, location, and location. That's true of plenty of businesses, too. But a good *location* doesn't guarantee success. It is also important to have an efficient, appealing *layout* of furnishings and equipment inside the building.

The buildings, furnishings, and equipment are **facilities**, and their positioning is called **deployment**. We seek to deploy facilities in order to hold down costs of external *transportation* and internal *handling*—and, of course, to provide better service to customers. These terms—*facilities deployment, location, layout, transportation,* and *handling*—are the discussion topics of this chapter. The first facility issue is size and type.

DEPLOYMENT STRATEGY: WHAT TO BUILD

North American shoppers have plenty of where-to-buy choices. Pick up a catalog and phone in your order, for instance. In the United States, your choice might be Spiegel, the leading direct-mail-only retailer. Since catalog sales constitute Spiegel's operating mode, its facility requirements are for warehouses and order-taking offices, which are efficient space users as compared with retail stores. Spiegel's three distribution warehouses, in the Chicago area, occupy 4.6 million square feet.

If you prefer walk-in shopping, you might opt for—and pay for—the hushed, nicely appointed atmosphere of, say, Saks Fifth Avenue. Saks's strategy is to operate just a few fine stores in order to retain a sense of exclusivity.

If you are price-conscious, on the other hand, you are prepared to overlook the jammed aisles and plain decor of a discount store. The discounters' strategy is to saturate the landscape with stores, and support them with a network of well-stocked warehouses.

High- and low-end retail strategies have been more or less as described above for decades. Product lines, marketing, and operating strategies are fairly predictable, and so are the kinds and numbers of facilities they build. It's been the same in factories, government agencies, fast-food restaurants, groceries, and many other businesses. Is anything new going on?

Yes. For example, while space must stay fairly stable within a category of store, warehouse space responds to new operations management concepts. Wal-Mart, a major seller of Pampers and Luvs disposable diapers, has teamed up with the maker, Procter and Gamble, to bypass Wal-Mart warehouses. Point-of-sale data go by satellite from the Wal-Mart store to a P&G factory which ships a new order of diapers directly to a store.

Many other retailers, as well as factories buying from other factories, have been adopting similar tactics to bypass distribution warehouses. The impact is that companies are cutting down on warehouse sizes and numbers, while users are experiencing fewer run-outs of stock. Facilities planners have to keep adjusting old ratios of warehouse space per sales dollar.

Various other new management concepts are also altering long-standing facilities practices. Both warehouse space and factory holding areas shrink as a result of product design practices that reduce numbers of parts (see Chapter 3) and purchasing policies that cut numbers of suppliers (Chapter 7).

At the same time, frequent deliveries of smaller lots just in time for use sometimes requires more receiving docks and doors. At a Ford assembly plant in Wixom, Michigan, the four walls of the building are liberally punctuated with receiving doors, which allow hundreds of deliveries per day right to points of use on the long automobile assembly line.

Ford, and the many other firms that strive for just-in-time deliveries, also seek (but don't always find) suppliers that are nearby rather than across a continent or an ocean. That affects plant location decisions in that suppliers are urged to operate satellite plants close to major customers.

Use of kanban inside a factory (Chapters 8 and 9) eliminates stockrooms of semifinished parts. A kanban policy in human services is one that limits waiting lines; while that policy reduces space needed for waiting, it may require extra space for more service channels and facilities, which operate or are idle depending on customer load.

Rework, scrap, and "quality-hold" areas, as well as complaint departments, shrink or disappear as companies push quality responsibility back to the provider (Chapters 4 and 15). Getting focused (mentioned in several chapters and discussed at greater length in this one) has profound effects on how facilities are laid out.

We need not go on. The point is that companies electing to get on the path of improvement in operations will find their physical facilities greatly affected. Facility deployment decisions do not stand alone. That is worth remembering as we take up deployment topics in more detail in the remainder of the chapter, beginning with location decisions.

LOCATION

Good companies tend to change or augment their location strategies slowly. Holiday Inn had a rural location strategy for many years but then added urban locations; it now operates fine hotels downtown in several major cities around the world. McDonald's, on the other hand, began with an urban strategy but expanded into low-population centers. Sears has been converting retail outlets in smaller communities into catalog sales stores, preferring to operate retail stores in larger cities.

We may see similar patterns for whole industries. Meat packers used to be in cities where labor and markets were, but they decentralized and moved closer to the cattle and hogs. This resulted in not only lower animal shipping costs but lower-cost labor in the plants. In the cities, hospitals and clinics that once were dispersed now tend to cluster. High-tech electronics companies also cluster—in California's Silicon Valley and near Boston, Phoenix, Austin, Portland, the

The clustering provides a "critical mass" of talent. Further, part of "smokestack America" has moved to the Sun Belt, not so much for sun as for cheap, nonunion labor.

Facility location is strategically important for many businesses and much less so for a few (for example, a consultant). However, in the case of communities competing for a new plant—or trade school, prison, or trucking terminal—the location decision might be the *only* one that matters. Also, location decisions usually are interesting. Consider, for example, some of the events of the mid-1980s in the automobile industry.

Tangibles versus Intangibles

The recession of the early 1980s was felt heavily in North America's industrial heartland, and almost every sign of new jobs in the region provoked heavy competition among cities and states. Chrysler-Mitsubishi's decision to locate its Diamond-Star automobile plant in Bloomington–Normal, Illinois, was the major economic news item for central Illinois in 1985 and 1986. By early 1987, other new supplier plants had been announced and several existing plants were eagerly seeking supplier contracts with Diamond-Star. The benefits had been felt throughout Illinois long before Diamond-Star assembled its first automobile.

In 1986, officials from Fuji Heavy Industries and Isuzu Motors toured many of the sites previously visited by Chrysler-Mitsubishi. Fuji-Isuzu was looking for a location for a new, $480 million Subaru-Isuzu auto-truck plant that would employ 1,500 people in its first phase. Cities in Arkansas, Illinois, Indiana, Kentucky, and Missouri were mentioned as potential sites. State and local officials once again threw out the red carpets, spruced up the incentive packages they had shown earlier to Chrysler-Mitsubishi, and waited.

Kentucky and Illinois locations were rumored to be at a disadvantage because the Japanese were seeking to broaden their political base. Toyota was building a plant at Georgetown, Kentucky, and the Diamond-Star plant would be in Illinois. Mazda Motors already had a plant underway near Detroit; Honda had one in Marysville, Ohio; Toyota and GM were partners in the NUMMI automobile plant in Fremont, California; and Nissan had a car-truck plant in Smyrna, Tennessee. Another state meant more influence in Congress. The eventual location for the Subaru-Isuzu plant? Lafayette, Indiana.

Do political considerations dictate plant location decisions.? Most observers would say no but admit that politics is one variable. Lafayette undeniably had most, if not all, of what Subaru-Isuzu wanted in a location. Just as undeniable, however, is the reality that business location decisions are partly based on intangible and even emotional factors: good recreation, educational facilities, housing, and even fishing or scenery. Cost factors weigh heavily in the location decision as well. All the data, cost and non-cost, can be confusing. Various rating systems are available to reduce the confusion.

Rating Alternative Locations

One such rating system is in use at United Technologies, Inc., a large industrial corporation. The first of three steps is to comparatively rate the importance of a large number of location factors. Figure 18–1 is an abbreviated example (many more factors could be included in a location study).

The figure shows that each of 14 factors (A through N) is compared with each other one; ratings are inserted on the matrix. Take, for example, the intersection

FIGURE 18–1
Evaluation Matrix for Relative Weighting of Location Factors*

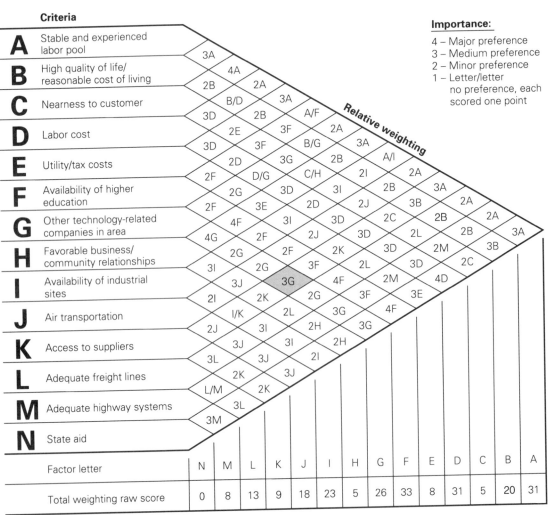

*Not a comprehensive list.
Source: Adapted from Eugene Bauchner, "Making the Most of Your Company's Resources," *Expansion Management*, 1989 Directory, pp. 20–25.

of factors G and K, "other technology-related companies in area" and "access to suppliers." The rating in the diamond-shaped box is 3G. Checking the "importance" scale, we see that 3 means "medium preference"—in this case, a medium preference of G over K.

The bottom row in Figure 18–1 contains total weighting raw scores. Those scores reflect type of facility. By studying the scores, we might be able to guess what kind of facility this matrix represents. Availability of higher education (F) is number one in importance; nearness to customer (C) and access to suppliers (K) are near the bottom. Could the facility be a design center?

Step 2 in United Technologies' system is to rate the locations under consideration against the location factors—A through N in this case. Figure 18–2A is

FIGURE 18–2
Rating Prospective Locations

A. Rating Locations by Factors

Factor	Red	Yellow	Green	Locations Orange	Blue	Purple	White
F. Higher education	10	5	4	7	8	6	9
G. Other technology-related companies	6	5	4	7	8	9	10
A. Stable, experienced labor pool	6	5	4	7	8	9	7
D. Labor cost	9	6	7	4	8	10	5
E. Utility/tax cost	7	6	5	3	8	10	9
J. Air transporation	10	6	5	8	9	7	4

B. Weighted Location Scores

Factor	Red	Yellow	Green	Locations Orange	Blue	Purple	White
F. Higher education (33)	330	165	132	231	264	198	297
G. Other technology companies (26)	156	130	104	182	208	234	260
A. Stable, experienced labor (31)	186	155	124	217	248	279	217
D. Labor cost (31)	279	186	217	124	248	310	155
E. Utility/tax cost (8)	56	48	40	24	64	80	72
J. Air transporation (18)	180	108	90	144	162	126	72
Total weighted score	1,187	792	707	922	1,194	1,227	1,073
Ranking	3	6	7	5	2	1	4

Source: Adapted from Eugene Bauchner, "Making the Most of Your Company's Resources," *Expansion Management*, 1989 Directory, pp. 20–25.

a partial matrix (listing just 6 of the 14 factors) showing the results of this step for seven locations; in a real study real names rather than colors would be on the matrix. We see that location Red gets the highest rating, 10, on factor F, higher education. In fact, all of location Red's ratings (for the factors shown) are fairly high. But these are not the final ratings. A third stage is needed.

The third matrix, Figure 18–2B, combines ratings from the first and second steps. Location Red got 10 points for higher education, and higher education was rated 33 in importance; 10 times 33 is 330, which goes into the upper-left corner in Figure 18–2B. The rest of the matrix gets the same treatment, column totals are added, and total weighted scores are compared. Location Purple is the winner with 1,227 points; locations Blue and Red are not far behind.

Sometimes, in facility location, transportation costs dominate above all other factors. If so, separate analysis of transportation cost is needed.

Transportation Cost Analysis

The **simplex method** of linear programming, which is widely taught and perhaps familiar to the reader, *may* be used in the study of transportation costs. But there is a simpler method called the **transportation method**. The difference is that the transportation method is limited to a single, homogeneous resource (that must be moved in quantity from multiple sources to multiple destinations), while the simplex method is suitable for a single, homogeneous resource *or* a variety of unlike resources (e.g., different resource inputs transformed into various resource outputs or products).

The transportation method is in two steps. First, we need an initial feasible transportation routing—a routing pattern that fulfills demand and uses up supply. Second, we improve the initial solution until the optimum is reached. Alternative techniques for developing initial and optimal solutions are as follows:

Initial-solution techniques:
1. **Northwest-corner rule.**
2. **Vogel's approximation method (VAM).**

Optimal-solution techniques:
1. **Stepping-stone method.**
2. **Modified distribution method (MODI).**

The chapter supplement discusses VAM and stepping-stone. Example 18–1, presented next, includes northwest-corner in showing the use of the transportation method in location planning and in finding optimal transportation routings once locations have been set.

EXAMPLE 18–1   **TRANSPORTATION METHOD FOR LOCATING A PRINTING PLANT IN THE HAWAIIAN ISLANDS**

Basic problem. The *Island Explorer*, a newspaper serving the Hawaiian Islands, is presently printed in two plants. One plant is in Honolulu on the island of Oahu, and the other is in Hana on the island of Maui. The two printing plants serve readers in the six major islands: Oahu, Maui, Hawaii, Kauai, Molokai, and Lanai.

Printing capacity has become insufficient at Honolulu and Hana. Honolulu's capacity is 300 pallets of newspapers per week and Hana's is 100 pallets per week. Demands are: Oahu, 275 per week; Maui, 60 per week; Hawaii, 60 per week, Kauai, 50 per week; Molokai, 30 per week; and Lanai, 20 per week. Total demand, 495, exceeds capacity, 400, by 95 pallets per week, which are lost sales.

The publisher has decided to locate a third printing plant at either Hilo on Hawaii or Lihue on Kauai.[1] A transportation cost analysis is needed to support the location decision.

Additional problem data—Hilo location. Figure 18–3 is a map of the island region. The arrows between islands in Figure 18–3A show all possible routes—and air transportation costs—from printing plants to destinations if the new plant is located at Hilo. No arrows lead into Oahu, Maui, and Hawaii because the Honolulu, Hana, and Hilo plants can provide newspapers to readers on their own islands at zero air transportation cost.

For analyzing a plant at Lihue instead of Hilo, Figure 18–3B applies. It shows three arrows leading into Hawaii instead of into Kauai.

Transportation matrix—Hilo location. The transportation matrix in Figure 18–4, for the Hilo option, shows quantities to be transported from each source to each destination; it also gives transportation costs above the slash (/) in each matrix cell. The upper left or "northwest"-corner cell, for example, represents the route from Honolulu to the island of Lanai, with a transportation cost of $7 per pallet. Demands for the three destinations are shown at the bottom of the three destination columns: 20, 30, and 50. Supply of the three sources, at the right in the three source rows, is the net transportable capacity of each. Net capacities, computed below, are based on the logic that each printing plant services its own island:

$$\text{Honolulu net transportable capacity} = \text{Honolulu gross capacity—Oahu demand}$$
$$= 300 - 275 = 25$$
$$\text{Hana net transportable capacity} = \text{Hana gross capacity—Maui demand}$$
$$= 100 - 60 = 40$$
$$\text{Hilo net transportable capacity} = \text{Capacity shortage—Hawaii demand}$$
$$= 95 - 60 = 35$$

The calculation for Hilo is based on having a gross capacity just sufficient to meet the gross capacity shortage, 95, that was mentioned at the outset.

Supply and demand are totaled in the lower right corner of Figure 18–4. Both equal 100 pallets per week.

Initial solution—Hilo location. A feasible solution following the northwest (NW)-corner rule is developed in Figure 18–5. We begin by making an allocation to the NW-corner cell, Honolulu–Lanai. The most that can be allocated is 20, which is Lanai's entire requirement; this leaves five more units available from Honolulu, which goes into the adjacent cell to the right, Honolulu–Molokai. Molokai needs 25 more units, which it gets from the cell below, Hana–Molokai. This leaves 15 more available from Hana, which goes into the cell to the right, Hana–Kauai. Kauai needs 35 units more, which it gets from the cell below, Hilo–Kauai. All rim requirements are now met; the solution is feasible. (An equally simple initial solution could be developed from the SW, NE, or SE corners; the NW corner has no particular significance.)

---

[1] A note on pronunciation to those unfamiliar with the lingual heritage of the 50th state: Pronounce *every* letter of a Hawaiian word. Thus, *Kauai* is pronounced *kah-ōō-ah-ēē*.

FIGURE 18–3
Map Showing Transportation Routes and Costs

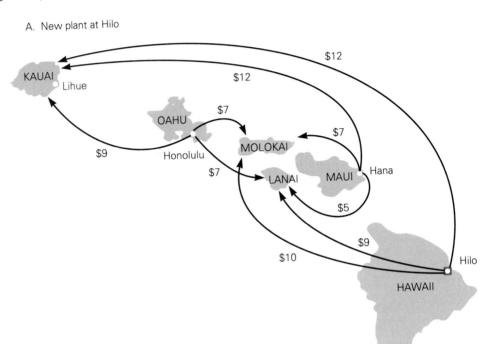

A. New plant at Hilo

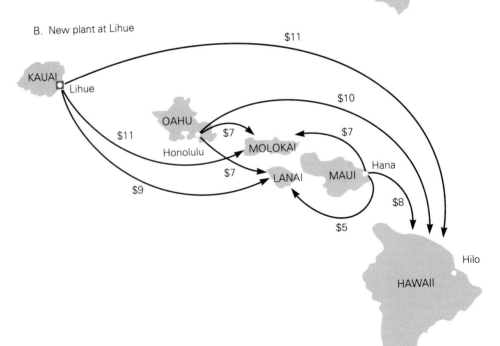

B. New plant at Lihue

Note: Transportation costs are per pallet of newspapers.

FIGURE 18–4
Transportation Matrix—Hilo Location

Sources	Lanai	Molokai	Kauai	Supply
Honolulu	7	7	9	25
Hana	5	7	12	40
Hilo	9	10	12	35
Demand	20	30	50	100 / 100

FIGURE 18–5
NW-Corner Initial Solution—Hilo Location

Sources	Lanai	Molokai	Kauai	Supply
Honolulu	7 / 20 →	7 / 5 ↓	9	25
Hana	5	7 / 25 →	12 / 15 ↓	40
Hilo	9	10	12 / 35	35
Demand	20	30	50	100 / 100

The total weekly transportation cost for the NW-corner solution is $950 per week, as calculated below:

Honolulu–Lanai	$ 7 × 20 =	$140 per week
Honolulu–Molokai	7 × 5 =	35 per week
Hana–Molokai	7 × 25 =	175 per week
Hana–Kauai	12 × 15 =	180 per week
Hilo–Kauai	12 × 35 =	420 per week
	Total	$950 per week

The NW-corner solution usually can be improved. Improvements would aim, for example, at avoiding the $12 cells (to Kauai from Hana and from Hilo) in favor of low-cost cells such as the $5 Hana-to-Lanai cell, which was not used in the NW-corner solution. Improvements *could* be found by trial and error. Better yet, use the stepping-stone or MODI methods, which may be computerized.

Optimal solution—Hilo location. After all improvements have been taken, we have an optimal solution. The optimum for the Hilo location is given in Figure 18–6. The total weekly transportation cost for the optimal solution is as follows:

Honolulu–Kauai	$ 9 × 25 =	$225 per week
Hana–Lanai	5 × 20 =	100 per week
Hana–Molokai	7 × 20 =	140 per week
Hilo–Molokai	10 × 10 =	100 per week
Hilo–Kauai	12 × 25 =	300 per week
	Total	$865 per week

The improved solution, at $865 per week, is $85 per week less than the NW-corner solution, at $950 per week. Now we must see whether it is more economical to build at Lihue.

Additional problem data—Lihue location. The publisher has decided that if the plant goes up in Lihue, it will be built with five pallets per week of excess capacity, which will allow for projected expansion to the small island of Niihau near Kauai. But Niihau is not included in the current transportation cost analysis.

Transportation matrix—Lihue location. The excess capacity at Lihue results in an unbalanced transportation problem: Supply exceeds current demand by five pallets per week. The transportation method still works, but only after demand is artificially adjusted upward to equal supply—that is, by adding a dummy column with a dummy demand of five in the transportation matrix. (In the reverse situation, demand greater than supply, we add a dummy row with the required extra supply to the matrix.)

Figure 18–7 shows the adjusted matrix. The demands, including the dummy demand of 5, total 115 pallets per week. The supply (capacity) for Lihue is set at 50 in order that supply be equal to demand. The dummy's transportation cost are set at zero, because it costs nothing to ship to a dummy destination.

Optimal solution—Lihue location. The optimal solution is shown in Figure 18–8. The

FIGURE 18–6
Optimal Transportation Solution—Hilo Location

Sources	Destinations: Lanai	Molokai	Kauai	Supply
Honolulu	7	7	9 / 25	25
Hana	5 / 20	7 / 20	12	40
Hilo	9	10 / 10	12 / 25	35
Demand	20	30	50	100 / 100

FIGURE 18-7

Transportation Matrix with Dummy Destination—Lihue Location

			Destinations			
		Lanai	Molokai	Hawaii	Dummy	Supply
Sources	Honolulu	7	7	10	0	25
	Hana	5	7	8	0	40
	Lihue	9	11	11	0	50
	Demand	20	30	60	5	115 / 115

chapter supplement demonstrates how to arrive at this solution using the stepping-stone method. If the *Island Explorer* builds at Lihue, $925 per week is the expected transportation cost.

Assessment. The Hilo location has an optimal transportation cost of $865 per week. For the Lihue location, the optimal transportation cost is $925 per week, which is $60 or 6.9 percent more. We would expect the Lihue solution to cost more because Hawaii's demand is 60 when the plant is built at Lihue. That is 10 units more than Kauai's demand of 50 in the Hilo solution. In other words, the total to be shipped from the three sources to the three destinations is 110 (not counting the dummy demand) if the plant is at Lihue but 100 if the plant is at Hilo.

FIGURE 18-8

Optimal Solution—Lihue Location

			Destinations			
		Lanai	Molokai	Hawaii	Dummy	Supply
Sources	Honolulu	7	7 / 25	10	0	25
	Hana	5 / 20	7 / 5	8 / 15	0	40
	Lihue	9	11	11 / 45	0 / 5	50
	Demand	20	30	60	5	115 / 115

In Example 18–1, the Hilo site has the advantage in transportation cost. Does that mean the facility will be located at Hilo? Well, maybe—unless other costs, such as labor and construction, don't tilt the decision the other way. Also, the whim of the chief executive officer or president could change the decision, or politics could intervene. Systematic analysis is valuable in any case, in that it reduces a lot of data to a few numbers, which may be used to at least influence the final choice. As we shall see next, gamesmanship also can play a role in location strategies.

Preemptive Strategy

If you are a bridge player, you know that a preemptive bid is a very high opening bid made when one has few points. The purpose is to raise the stakes enough to discourage competitors from making their own bids, even though they may have more points. A similar strategy occurs in locating businesses or adding production capacity. A grocery chain, hotel, or pizza franchise may decide to open its next facility in a sparsely populated location in the hope of discouraging competitors. Manufacturers also sometimes follow facility strategies partly aimed at deterring competition. For a giant manufacturer selling nationwide, many locations for added capacity may be acceptable. Sometimes just an announcement (which itself can even be a bluff) of an intent to add capacity *somewhere* may convince a competitor not to do likewise because overcapacity in the industry—with resulting lower profit expectations—might result. And yes, it is called a *preemptive strategy* in business and industry just as it is in the game of bridge.

Regardless of location, or even of the strategy used to make location decisions, deployment continues by looking *inside* facilities, at *facility layout.*

LAYOUT

At precisely 12 noon, the entire insurance staff—nearly 500 clerks, technicians, and managers—piled their personal belongings on office chairs and said good-bye to fellow employees. Pushing the chairs along crowded corridors, crisscrossing and colliding at intersections, all 500 made their way to newly assigned work areas.[2]

That's the sound of moving day at Aid Association for Lutherans (AAL), an insurance company. But this moving day was different. Departments and sections weren't just changing offices; the organization structure itself was on the chopping block. The 500 employees were shaken out into 15 focused teams in two tiers. The top tier is five groups, each serving insurance agents in a different

---

[2]John Hoerr, "Work Teams Can Rev Up Paper-Pushers, Too," *Business Week*, November 28, 1988, pp. 64–72.

region. Within each group are three bottom-tier teams of 20 to 30 people, one team for new policies, one for claims, and a third for services.

We've talked about this through the whole book: the advantages of creating focused cells, flow lines, and teams—focusing all resources, actually. Now, in the second-to-last chapter, we zero in on the geographical side of focus—and the lack of it. Getting the geography right inside a facility is called *layout planning*. Our discussion includes the effects of environment on layout and re-layout, customer and employee considerations, types of layouts, steps in planning layouts, a layout planning example, and other contemporary layout issues.

Layout and Re-layout

New facilities require new layouts. Existing facilities occasionally get out of date and require re-layout. Type of operating environment affects facility layout; we'll consider just four operating environments: mechanized production lines, labor-intensive production lines, job or batch production, and labor-intensive services.

In mechanized production lines, original layout planning had better be good because of the high cost of repositioning large machinery and related facilities. In a petrochemical plant, for example, the layout of tanks, chambers, valves, pipes, and other equipment is so much a part of the plant itself that major re-layout may never be feasible. In steel manufacturing the cost of major re-layout is also enormous, and steel plants may close rather than retool and re-layout to improve efficiency, meet pollution control regulations, and so on. Retooling of automated transfer lines in the auto industry is undertaken every few years, but the *layout* of retooled machines changes infrequently. In each of these examples, the initial layout choices restrict the firm's ability to respond to major changes in product line or technology for years to come.

Assembly lines (the manual, not the robotic kind) are less fixed. Assemblers and their tools are mobile. Thus, initial layout planning is not so critical; the focus is on re-layout, which has its own costs. These include costs of planning, line balancing, retraining, and rearranging benches, storage facilities, material handling aids, and large pieces of equipment.

Job and batch production often entail large machines and storage and handling aids. Re-layout may be attractive, however, because the equipment used tends to be general purpose, loosely coupled, and movable. A pump manufacturer in South Carolina has constructed a plant with very thick concrete floors so that heavy equipment can be moved anywhere. A Japanese manufacturer has put its machines on casters for easy re-layout; see the photo in Figure 18–9. These kinds of preparation for re-layout are important; otherwise the need to change and continually improve may be thwarted. Symptoms of the need include bottlenecks, backtracking, overcrowding, poor utilization of capacity (including space), poor housekeeping, missed due dates, too much temporary storage, and a high or growing ratio of total lead time to actual work content.

Labor-intensive services tend to undergo frequent re-layout. Office employees may begin to "wonder where my desk will be on Monday morning." The desk may be across town in newly rented office space. Physical obstacles are few;

FIGURE 18–9
Machine on Casters

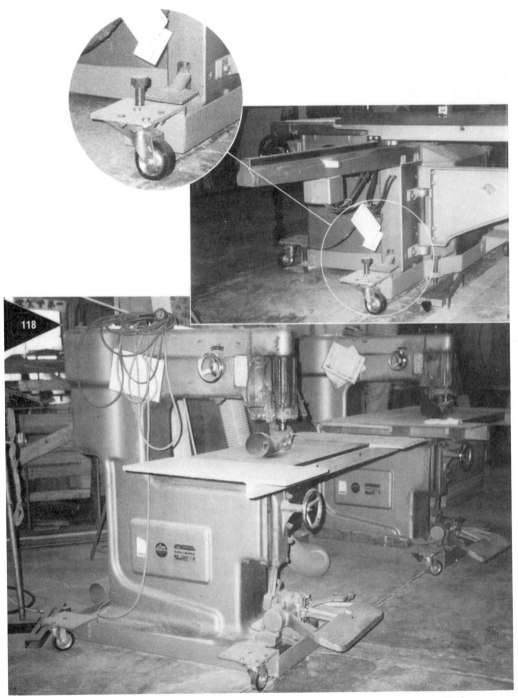

most offices can move overnight if telephone hookups can be arranged. With few physical problems, office re-layout commonly focuses on people and work climate.

Employees and Customers in Layouts

Perhaps people and work climate should be central concerns in *all* cases, not just in the service sector. In keeping with the theme of this book, improving customer service, let us see how layout affects people's attitudes toward their customers.

As small organizations grow, they typically put similar facilities and functions together: personnel people in the personnel department, sheet-metal equipment and people grouped into the sheet-metal shop, and so forth. The problem is, the customer, the next process, is a long distance from the maker or provider. Good service and quick response demands that many of the common groupings—called **process layouts**—be broken up.

Drill presses may be plucked out of a drill-press area and stuck into a cell making a family of parts. A stamping machine may be pulled from a stamping department and moved to where it can make and feed a single part right to a using station on a production line. The photo in Figure 18–10 shows just that: a stamping machine that makes junction box brackets at the *point of use* in a General Electric dishwasher plant.

The same concepts apply in processing documents and human clients. Human resource specialists and their desks and file cabinets may be moved next to foremen's offices, into the marketing department, or wherever there are customers—that is, other employees in need of human services. Alternatively, the entire human resource department could be located near the employee cafeteria in order to make it convenient for employees to stop in.

Until recently plant layout, and often office layout as well, was approached in a rather mechanical way. The emphasis was on location of machines, desks, tool rooms, storage racks, and cafeterias. Of course, where machines and desks go, so go people. In recognition of this, the term *plant organization* is sometimes used instead of *plant layout*. We will stick with the traditional term, *layout*, in this book, but with the realization that human organization structures change when physical resources are moved.

Layout Types

There are four types of layout. One, the process layout, has already been mentioned. Here facilities are arranged into process groups. Putting like facilities together may facilitate tool and maintenance support, utility hookups, control of fumes and heat, and removal of chips. Putting people with like functions together provides a climate for mutual support and learning, as well as in-depth skill development. Job operations, for either goods or services, generally have process layouts.

FIGURE 18–10
Point-of-Use Manufacturing

Because like functions are grouped together, some refer to process layouts as **functional layouts**. Regardless of the name, the process layout has the weakness of putting distance between provider and customer.

Product-oriented layout, or **product layout**, the second type, means laying out facilities along product-flow lines, with the customer (next process) next to the provider. The result is a **production line**.

The product layout and the production-line method of manufacturing are not new. Here, for example, is a description of a production line for equipping ship galleys at the Arsenal of Venice in about 1438.[3]

> And as one enters the gate there is a great street on either hand with the sea in the middle, and on one side are windows opening out of the houses of the arsenal, and the same on the other side, and out came a galley towed by a boat, and from the windows they handed out to them, from one the cordage, from another the bread, from another the arms, and from another the balistas and mortars, and so from all sides everything which ws required, and when the galley had reached the

[3]This description is from Pero Tafur, *Travels and Adventures* (London: G. Routledge & Sons Ltd., 1926) pp. 1435–39; R. Burlingame, *Backgrounds of Power* (New York: Charles Scribner's Sons, 1949).

end of the street all the men required were on board, together with the complement of oars, and she was equipped from end to end. In this manner there came out ten galleys full armed, between the hours of three and nine. I know not how to describe what I saw there, whether in the manner of its construction or in the management of the workpeople, and I do not think there is anything finer in the world.

A third type is the **cellular layout**. The idea is to arrange workstations and machines into cells that process families of parts that follow similar flow paths. Included are a number of subconcepts: parts deliberately designed to have as many common features as possible, high-use tools and data located within the cell, cross-trained cell operators, and the cellular layout itself. A cellular layout actually is about the same as a product layout, although most people think of product layouts (production lines) as handling only one or just a few products instead of a family. Cellular layout became one of the more important operations management concepts in the 1980s.

In the fourth type, the **fixed-position layout** (or simply **fixed layout**), the product itself is fixed and the facilities must come to it. Construction is a good example. Another is the manufacture of oversized vehicles and heavy equipment—items too large to be easily moved—such as aircraft and locomotives.

Mixed layouts—two or more layout types in a single facility—are common, if not the norm. An apt example is a restaurant that sets up a buffet brunch line on Sundays. The patron has the choice of going through the buffet line or sitting down and ordering from the menu. A patron entering the restaurant may be thought of as raw materials; a patron leaving is finished goods. The operations are to transform an empty patron into a full one. The two types of patrons are processed through two types of facilities layout. The buffet customer goes through a product or cellular layout (hard to narrow it down to one or the other). It is like an assembly line. The menu customer receives service in a fixed layout: Menu, waiter, food, drinks, and check come to the fixed position.

Figure 18–11 is a sketch of such a restaurant, identifying the product layout and fixed layout. It also shows that the restaurant includes a process layout—in the kitchen. There foods, not patrons, are the products being transformed. The process areas include grill, salad area, range, dessert area, ovens, freezer, and pantry. Arrows show the jumbled flow patterns.

Compared with a single-layout facility, a mixed-layout facility is more difficult to plan, more costly to equip, and more troublesome to maintain. But it may be easier to keep busy because it serves a wider variety of customers or products.

U-Shaped Layouts

The main feature of both production lines and work cells is the close proximity of workstations, speeding up the flow and reducing in-process inventory. Another feature of both *should* be layout of stations into a U. Although the U shape is commonly associated with work cells, little has been written about the benefits

FIGURE 18–11

Mixed Layout in a Restaurant

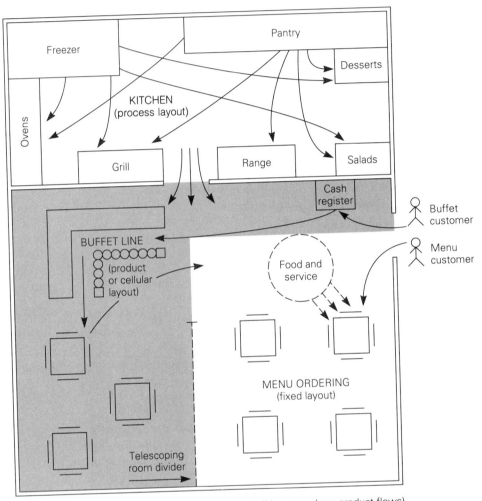

(solid arrows show product flows)

of U-shaped production lines. At least five advantages—for cells or lines—result from U-shaped layout:

1. *Staff flexibility and balance.* The U shape allows one person to tend several work centers—adjacent or across the U—since walking distance is not great, and it allows more options for balancing the work among operators. As demand picks up, more labor can be added until every station has an operator.

2. *Teamwork.* Getting all staff into a cluster is necessary for teamwork and joint problem solving. As we know, a major benefit of just-in-time production is that lack of backup stock forces problem solving

and quality improvement. Operators who are starved of parts form a natural team who must use their heads to solve problems and get production going again. It can't work well if employees are strung out along long lines or dispersed and separated by walls of inventory.

3. *Rework.* Separate rework lines have been common practice. Now they are bad form. Rework should return to the original maker so the maker cannot evade responsibility for product quality. When the line bends around itself, if bad products are found at the end of the line, there is less distance to span in returning them to the right station for rework.

4. *Passage.* A long, straight line interferes with travel of people and vehicles. We do not like supermarket shelving to be too long. People protest when a superhighway cuts a neighborhood in half. A long, straight production line is a similar imposition.

5. *Material and tool handling.* In labor-intensive cells or production lines, the same person who takes away products at the end of one leg of the U can bring back parts to load in at the end of the other leg. The principle is, keep the delivery path for parts and tools short. In unmanned cells, put a robot in the center and assign it to change tools and load and unload machines. In fully or partly automated production lines making small products, run an automated guided vehicle around the inside of the loop delivering full tubs of parts and taking away empties.

There are cases where these advantages of the U shape do not apply. For example, with a high degree of automation and few parts or tools to be handled, the teamwork and handling benefits are absent. Also, a line processing wide sheets of steel, aluminum, glass, and so on perhaps should run straight, because transfer between machines is simpler if there are no changes in direction.

Layout Features

Some of the distinguishing features of the primary layout types are shown in Figure 18–12. It lists eight resource factors and the ways in which each is commonly treated for each layout type.

The first factor, facilities arrangement, states the main differences among the layout types. They have already been discussed.

Type of production is the second factor. Process layout is dominant in job and batch operations; product layout is typical in repetitive and continuous operations. The JIT mandate is to identify all items that have the potential for more or less repetitive operations and to organize product layouts for those items. Cellular layout is suitable for small lots of first one part in a family and then another. Fixed layout is common in construction and industrial projects and for production of large-scale products (e.g., missiles and dynamos). Fixed layout is also found where special human services are provided. For example,

FIGURE 18–12
Resources and Layouts—Common Characteristics

Resource Factors	Types of Layout		
	Process-Oriented	*Product or Cellular*	*Fixed Position*
1. Facilities arrangement	Facilities grouped by specialty	Facilities placed along product-flow lines	Facilities arranged for ease of movement to fixed product
2. Type of operations	Job and batch	Continuous and repetitive	Construction and industrial projects; large-scale products, special human services
3. Cost of layout/ re-layout	Moderate to low	Moderate to high	Moderate to low
4. Facility utilization	Usually low	High	Moderate
5. Type of production facilities	General purpose	Special purpose	Mostly general purpose
6. Handling equipment	Variable path	Fixed path	Variable path
7. Handling distance	Long	Short	Moderate
8. Employee skill level	Skilled	Unskilled	Unskilled to skilled

the resources come to the client or customer in surgery, grooming, feeding, and home TV repair.

Cost of layout/re-layout is third. In process layout machines, desks, and the like generally are not tightly linked; thus, process layout usually is not costly. For a product or cellular layout, the cost is high if pieces of equipment are closely interlinked as in automated lines; the cost may be moderate if production is more labor intensive, that is, where one person hands work to the next. Fixed layout of a construction site requires temporary parking and storage space for operating resources, which usually are not costly. Fixed layout for goods production and for special human services may take more than just parking space; it may require a well-equipped bay for assembling a missile or aligning wheels, or a well-equipped operating room. The layout cost can be low if the facilities are mainly general-purpose hand tools, but can be higher (moderate) if special lighting, holding fixtures, work pits, and so forth are involved.

Fourth is facility utilization. In process layouts, facilities tend toward low utilization. That is not desirable, but it is typical because the job mix changes all the time and different jobs use different facilities. High facility utilization—little idleness—is a goal of product layout. Line balancing helps achieve it. Fixed layouts tend to have moderate facility utilization because the product mix is not very diverse.

The fifth factor is type of production facilities. Process layouts usually hold standard, general-purpose machines, hand tools, handling aids, and so forth.

Special-purpose facilities are worth spending money on if the volume is high, as it normally is with product or cellular layouts. In fixed layouts, special products call for some special-purpose facilities, such as an overhead crane or a mounting fixture, but most of the facilities will be general purpose since production volume is not high.

Sixth is handling equipment. In process layouts, variable-path equipment—hand-carry or on wheels—provides needed handling flexibility. Fixed-path handling equipment—conveyors, elevators, chutes, and so on—helps cut handling time in product layouts. Variable-path handling equipment is used in fixed layouts because a variety of resources come to the site from different places.

Seventh is handling distance. Long distances occur in process layouts. In product and cellular layouts, the opposite is true. In fact, a purpose is to tightly cluster the facilities in order to *cut* distance and handling time. Fixed layouts are in between. The product stays put, but the resources do not flow to the product by fixed routes; resources move to the product from various locations over moderate handling distances.

The eighth factor is employee skill level. In process layouts, employees tend to be skilled. Stenographers, machinists, plumbers, computer operators, nurses, and accountants fit the category. In industry, such employees historically were organized by craft (e.g., by the American Federation of Labor). If the skill is based on higher education or apprenticeship, the pay tends to be high; if based on vocational training, the pay tends to be moderate or low. Employees along product layouts are usually hired without a particular skill. Such employees may become adept at installing rivets or molding or soldering connections, but they are classed as unskilled because they are easily replaced from an unskilled labor market. Historically they are the type of assembly-line employees who were organized into the Congress of Industrial Organizations (CIO). Their pay may be minimum wage in smaller, nonunion shops, although under Walter Reuther's presidency CIO members gained respectable pay levels. In fixed layouts, skilled craftspeople, such as carpenters and welders, often work alongside unskilled laborers, such as shovelers or riveters.

While there are many more operating-resource factors that could be discussed, these eight are enough to show the basic nature of each layout type. Figure 18–12 is not intended as an if-then analysis device; that is, we would not conclude that if people are skilled, facility utilization is low, and so on, then a process layout should be developed. There are better ways to plan the right kind of layout. We consider some of them next.

Layout Planning Steps

In a complex layout situation, hundreds or thousands of jobs may be in progress at any given time. Repetitive, job, and project work may be included, with products and resources delivered to work centers via many routings.

When routes are so diverse, does it matter how work areas are arranged in a building? Yes, it does. Dominant flow patterns—from makers to customers—

are probably there among the apparent jumble of routings. Layout analysis helps find those patterns.

One layout principle is to arrange work areas in order of dominant flow. A goal is to get production or resources into, through, and out of each work center in minimum time at reasonable cost. The less time products/resources spend in the flow pattern, the less chance they have to collect labor and overhead charges and the faster the immediate and final customers are served.

Other factors besides flows may be important. If so, the nonflow factors may be combined with flow data. The combined data will suggest how close work areas should be to one another, and a rough layout can be developed. The next step is to determine the space requirements for a rough layout. The last step in layout planning is to fit the rough layout into the available space, that is, the proposed or existing building. Several layout plans may be developed for managers to choose from.

The layout planning steps just described are listed in Figure 18–13, along with planning aids usable in each step.

Layout Planning Example

Example 18–2 demonstrates the layout planning steps. The method and some of the tools were developed by Muther, who calls the approach **systematic layout planning (SLP)**.[4] SLP is a practical approach that is widely referenced and used. Though developed in an earlier era, SLP works well in support of a modern, customer-oriented approach to layout.

FIGURE 18–13
Layout Planning—Steps and Possible Tools

Steps	*Possible Tools*
1. Analyze product (resource) flows.	Flow diagram From-to chart
2. Identify and include nonflow factors, where significant.	Activity-relationship (REL) chart Combined REL chart
3. Assess data and arrange work areas.	Activity arrangement diagram
4. Determine space arrangement plan.	Space relationship diagram
5. Fit space arrangement into available space.	Floor plan Detailed layout models

---

[4]Richard R. Muther, *Systematic Layout Planning* (Boston: Cahners, 1973), pp. 3-1–3-8 (TS178.M87).

EXAMPLE 18-2   **LAYOUT PLANNING—GLOBE COUNTY OFFICES**[5]

The main contact that Globe County citizens have with county offices is in registering and licensing vehicles. Many people complain because the three county offices involved have not consolidated their services. On busy days there are waiting lines at all three offices. Many vehicle owners must visit all three, and it is not uncommon for a citizen to find out, after shuffling forward for awhile, that it is the wrong line.

The elected officials who run the three offices have decided to jointly undertake consolidation. Mr. Ross, a consultant, has been hired to conduct layout analysis using SLP.

Ross's analysis reveals 12 activities to be located in the available space, four of which have significant flows: three service counters, plus the office copier (see Figure 18–14). The space requirements are based on careful measurement of desks, files, and so forth, plus use of widely available industry space standards (e.g., 300 square feet per auto in a parking lot).

Flow Analysis. For those four activities, Ross gathers flow data, which he enters on a *from-to chart* (which resembles the distance chart found on many road maps), as shown in Figure 18–15A. Numbers above the diagonal represent flows of patrons *from* one

FIGURE 18–14

Major Work Areas—County Offices

Activity	Space Requirements (square feet)
1. County assessor's office	
a. Management	600
*b. Motor vehicle—counter	300
c. Motor vehicle—clerical	240
d. Assessors	960
2. County clerk's office	
e. Management	840
f. Recording and filing—counter	240
g. Recording and filing—clerical	960
*h. Motor vehicle—counter-clerical	960
3. County treasurer's office	
i. Management	420
*j. Motor vehicle—counter-clerical	1,600
4. Support areas	
*k. Mail and copier	240
l. Conference room	160
Total	7,520

*Significant flows.

[5]This is adapted from a real case. Thanks go to Ross Greathouse of Greathouse-Flanders Associates, Lincoln, Nebraska, for providing original case data.

FIGURE 18–15

Flow Volume (people per day)—County Offices

A. From–to chart

To From	Clerk 1.	Assessor 2.	Treasurer 3.	Copier 4.	Totals 5.
Motor vehicle counter –clerk 1.		A 100	B 250	D 30	380
Motor vehicle counter –assessor 2.	C 20.		A 100	D 10	130
Motor vehicle counter –treasurer 3.	C 40				40
Copier 4.	D 30	D 10			40
Totals	90	90	350	40	590

B. Conversion to vowel
ratings on bar chart

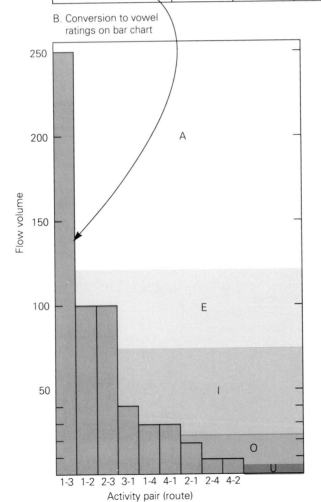

Note: Types of product flow:

A   Patrons licensing newly
    purchased vehicles.
B   Patrons licensing same–
    owner vehicles.
C   Patrons to wrong office–
    backtrack to correct office.
D   Round trips to copier.

Key:

A   for abnormally high flow
E   for especially high flow
I   for important flow
O   for ordinary flow
U   for unimportant moves
    of negligible flow volume

FIGURE 18–16
Combined Activity Relationship (REL) Chart—County Offices

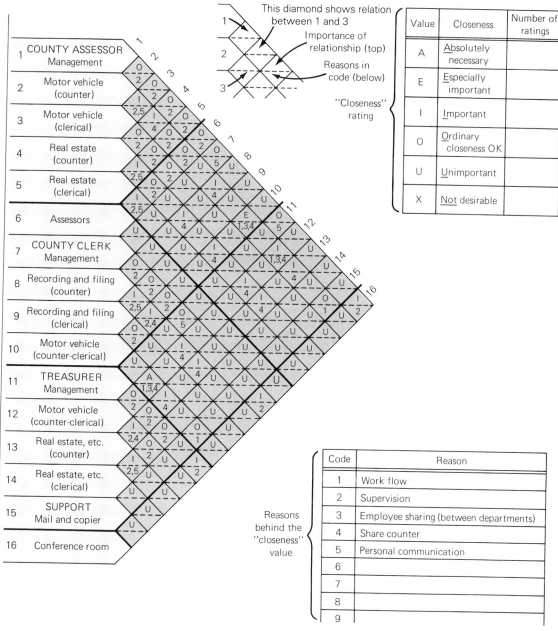

Source of REL chart form: Richard Muther and Associates, Kansas City, Missouri. Used with permission.

FIGURE 18–17
Activity Arrangement Diagram—County Offices

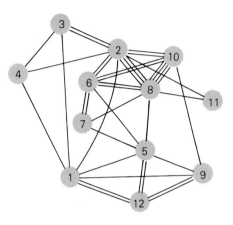

FIGURE 18–18
Space Relationship Diagram—County Offices

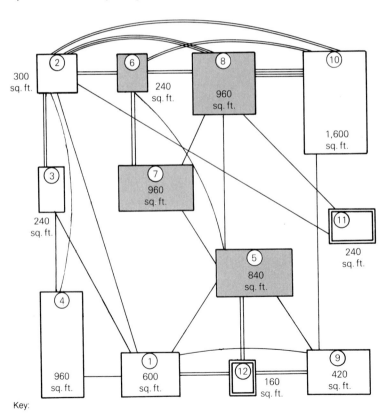

Key:

| Numbers 2, 6, 8, and 10 are service-counter activities. | County assessor activities are 1-4. | County treasurer activities are 9-10. | County clerk activities are shaded. | Shared activities are double-bordered. |

activity *to* another; numbers below the diagonal reflect backtracking by patrons who find themselves in the wrong office, and also round trips to and from the copiers.

Figure 18–15B is a conversion chart, which Ross develops for displaying from-to data in order of descending flow volume. Ross then judgmentally inserts horizontal lines that divide the flow-volume bars into five zones, labeled A, E, I, O, and U, which are the standard SLP symbols for flow volume.

Nonflow Factors. Next, Ross lists nonflow factors, such as need for employees to be near to their supervisor, and rates them using the same five vowel designators. He combines flow and nonflow factors on an activity relationship (REL) chart, as shown in Figure 18–16.

The REL chart is easy to interpret. The single A in the chart indicates that it is *absolutely* necessary for customer service people in the clerk and treasurer offices to be close together. Reasons why are work flow (1), employee sharing among departments (3), and share counter (4). The same reasons apply to the E—for *e*specially important—in the box connecting customer service people in the clerk and assessor office.

Activity Arrangement. Now Ross converts the combined REL chart to an activity arrangement diagram, which shows the arrangement of all activities but without indicating requirements for space, utilities, halls, and so on (see Figure 18–17). In this diagram, number of lines between activities stands for flow volume: Four lines corresponds to an A rating on the REL chart, three lines stands for an E rating, and so forth. Distances between circles are set according to desired degree of closeness, as much as possible.

FIGURE 18–19

Possible Final Layout—County Offices

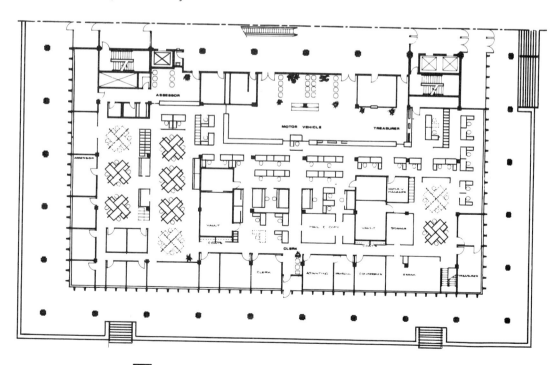

FIRST FLOOR SOUTH PLAN

Activities 2, 6, 8, and 10, at the core, are all service counter activities, which earlier ratings showed should be placed close together.

Space Arrangement. Ross's next-to-last chart, shown in Figure 18–18, injects the space data from Figure 18–14. The result is a diagram that is in the generally rectangular shape of the space into which the activities must fit; activity blocks are sized according to space needed. The space relationship diagram may be regarded as a rough layout.

Layout into Available Space. Finally, Ross is ready to draw some final layouts, complete with walls, halls, aisles, and other needed elements. Figure 18–19 is an example of one of Ross's final layouts.[6]

The Globe County Offices example is fairly simple. In large, complex layouts, analysis within each activity area could include the full SLP treatment—that is, all the SLP steps. In later steps, various two- and three-dimensional models—manual or computer graphic—may be manipulated to produce workable layout options.

In the Globe County example, we also glossed over all the trial and error usually involved in some of the diagramming; by trial and error, we mean drawing after drawing, or erasure after erasure.

Computer Assistance in Layout

Some of the drudgery—and erasing—can be avoided by using computer software in the *search* phase of layout planning. One program, called CORELAP (*co*mputerized *rel*ationship *la*yout *p*lanning), uses closeness ratings from the REL chart (e.g., Figure 18–16) as inputs. It produces a single layout of rectangular-shaped departments; department lengths and widths are set forth in advance. The CORELAP algorithm maximizes common borders for closely related departments. CORELAP is flexible enough to be used for either office or plant layout.

Another program, called CRAFT (*c*omputerized *r*elative *a*llocation of *f*acilities *t*echnique), requires an existing layout as an input. Its job is to improve the layout. CRAFT uses flow (from-to) data but not nonflow (REL-chart) data. Its main purpose is to minimize material handling cost, which is a dominant concern in *plant* layout. CRAFT is usually not well suited for *office* layout, in which other matters besides work flow are important.[7]

---

[6]While Figure 18–19 is an actual layout of county offices, all the preceding parts of this example were mock designs.

[7]Copies of the programs are available as follows: CORELAP from Engineering Management Associates of Boston, and CRAFT from the IBM Share Library System. Enhanced versions of these programs are announced frequently.

Open Layouts

One of the special influences on office layout is the **open-office concept**, which was a phenomenon in the 1960s and became commonplace in the 1970s. The open-office idea eliminates many floor-to-ceiling walls and deemphasizes compartmentalization of people. Open-office layouts are thought to foster communication and provide flexibility for easy re-layout. Modular office furniture and movable, partial-height partitions aid in achieving these goals.

Open offices in Japan, where the concept is deeply ingrained, often are truly wide open. In North America, in contrast, there has been some emphasis on maintaining a degree of privacy and cutting noise. Interior designers use wall carpeting, sound-absorbent panels, acoustical screens, fabric-wrapped desktop risers, and free-standing padded partitions. Office landscaping (use of plants) is also commonplace.

In addition to interior design consultants, layout planning expertise is available from architectural firms and firms specializing in layout. Interior designers are likely to focus on appearance, atmosphere, light, and acoustics, mostly in offices (especially offices in which the public is met frequently). Layout specialists are more engineering-oriented and likely to direct their efforts to material-flow factors; they tend to work mostly on factory layouts, where function rather than appearance is the main concern. Architects are helpful for new construction or major remodeling.

In factories evolving to JIT production, it is valuable to have problem-solving specialists close to where the production problems occur. Consequently there is a strong trend toward moving engineers and technical support people out of offices and onto the factory floor. The usual result is a large room containing machines and assembly benches intermingled with alcoves for engineers' desks; we might think of it as the open factory-office. Hewlett-Packard plants have long been arranged in such a pattern.

LINE BALANCING

After a product or cellular layout has been developed, the task assignments must be balanced, that is, divided up equally among employees. Dividing the work is called **line balancing**. (Note: Balancing the *machines* assigned to the line also must be done, but that is fairly cut and dried: Buy or design machines that all have about the capacity needed; put in two machines instead of one where necessary to get needed capacity; slow down machines that run too fast, or turn them on and off intermittently; and so forth.)

Some products can be made either in a fixed layout or a product/cellular layout. Of course, line balancing applies only to the latter case. If an invoice is paid or a personal computer, oscilloscope, or printer is made at a single station—**autonomous operations**—there is no balancing among stations as there would be with **progressive operations**, where items being worked on are passed from station to station. Also, lines may be balanced for making one product or model, the simple case, or for mixed models.

Line-Balancing Concepts

Line balancing is not easily reduced to simple models or algorithms; there are simply too many choices, given the flexibility and variability of humans. Employees can run one machine or several, push a broom or wield a paintbrush between machine cycles, handle machine setup and inspection duties or leave those chores for special crews, speed up or loaf, stay at their work or wander off, fix broken equipment and suggest improvements or leave it up to the specialists, file documents or sit around waiting for file clerks to do it. How can balance be designed into a process with those uncertainties? The answer is: One can design only a roughly balanced line. Supervisors and the work group itself need to fine-tune it, and redo it often as customer demand rates change.

The designer in charge of rough line balancing is often an industrial engineer, since the IE is the keeper of the time standards and methods-study data. If the production line is to provide a unit of work every 3.5 minutes, the IE wants to give precisely a 3.5-minute task to each employee or workstation (two or more employees could share the task at a workstation). That 3.5 minutes is the **cycle time**. Perhaps time standards show that the total **work content time** to make one unit is 35 minutes. Then, with each task taking 3.5 minutes, there must be 10 workstations. (A 1969 line-balancing survey found that 3.5 minutes and 10 stations or employees were the medians for the American firms surveyed.)[8]

For a piece having 35 minutes of work content, the **throughput time** or production lead time is unlikely to be 35 minutes. Handling among stations and various delays may add time. Also, there may be small buffer stocks between some processes. For example, most high-volume conveyor-driven, or *paced*, production lines making TVs, cameras, videocassette players, keyboards, and so forth have several units between stations. If there are two idle units between stations for every one being worked on, the throughput time is 3 times 35 minutes, or 105 minutes; that is, a unit gets 3.5 minutes of work at station 1, then waits for 7 minutes, then gets 3.5 minutes more work at station 2, then 7 minutes' wait time, and so on, through 10 stations. Raw material enters every 3.5 minutes and completed units emerge every 3.5 minutes, but each unit spends 105 minutes in the system. The **production rate** is 17.14 units per hour.

The concepts of cycle time, production rate, throughput time, and work content can be confusing but must be understood. If you get your needed production rate, say, 17 per hour, with just 35 instead of 105 minutes of throughput time, you are far more efficient: less inventory, less floor space, less time until discovery of errors, faster response to change (design and demand changes), closer dependency and better atmosphere for teamwork, and close connection between each provider and customer. As a production line ages, a goal should be to *cut throughput time,* as well as cycle time, in order to decrease waste and improve efficiency. Therefore, designs should be flexible, and rebalancing or adjusting the balancing should go on continually.

With these points in mind, let us take a look at line-balancing methods used

[8]M. Lehman, "What's Going on in Product Layout?" *Industrial Engineering*, April 1969, pp. 41–45.

by IEs in the rough balancing stage. Most begin with a precedence diagram. With data from the diagram, line balancing proceeds by trial and error, heuristics, algorithms, or mathematical models.[9] Computer packages are available for some of the algorithms and models.

In this chapter, we look at a manual heuristic line-balancing procedure. Then we consider a fine-tuning method called "watching the lights." The manual heuristic method begins with a precedence diagram, discussed next.

Precedence Diagram

The **precedence diagram** charts the work elements and their required sequence. To get the work elements, the entire process is divided into tasks and subtasks. This *division of labor* is carried down to where a task is assignable to a single person.

One popular type of precedence diagram shows the earliest stage of production where each work element may be done. Element durations, numbers, and sometimes descriptions go on the diagram; arrows show which elements must come before which others.

Example 18–3 demonstrates the precedence diagram. The assembly task is clothing a male doll. In real doll-making, all of the work elements for such assembly would probably be done by a single assembler, because the element times are very short. But for the sake of illustration, we shall assume progressive rather than autonomous assembly. Precedence diagramming can allow for a variety of special restrictions, but this example is kept simple.

| EXAMPLE 18–3 | PRECEDENCE DIAGRAM FOR LINE BALANCING—DOLL ASSEMBLY[10] |

A toy company is coming out with a new male doll. The doll is to be clothed on an assembly line, with different items of clothing put on at different stations. The company wants a balanced assembly line.

Methods engineers have broken up the whole job into 13 separate items of clothing, each of which is a work element, with element times as follows:

Element	Element time t (in 0.01 minutes)
1. Put on undershorts	10
2. Put on undershirt	11
3. Put on left sock	9

---

[9]A heuristic is a search procedure that may give an optimal (best) solution to a problem but offers no guarantee of doing so. If it can be proven that an exact solution exists, the method becomes an algorithm rather than a heuristic search procedure.

[10]Adapted from Theodore O. Prenting and Nicholas T. Thomopoulos, *Humanism and Technology in Assembly Line Systems* (Rochelle Park, N.J.: Spartan Books, 1974), pp. 131–32 (TS178.4P73).

	Element	Element time t (in 0.01 minutes)
4.	Put on right sock	9
5.	Put on slacks	22
6.	Put on shirt	42
7.	Put on left shoe	26
8.	Put on right shoe	26
9.	Put on belt	30
10.	Insert pocket items (wallet, keys, and handkerchief)	20
11.	Put on tie	63
12.	Put on coat	32
13.	Put on hat	6
	Total work content time, Σt	306

FIGURE 18–20

Precedence Diagram—Clothing a Doll

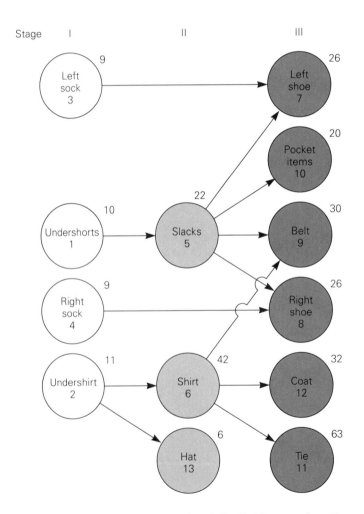

Source: Theodore O. Prenting and Nicholas T. Thomopoulos, *Humanism and Technology in Assembly Line Systems* (Rochelle Park, N.J.: Spartan Books, 1974), p. 132 (TS178.4.P73). Used with permission.

Solution

Using the elemental data, the engineers develop the precedence diagram shown in Figure 18–20. Work elements are in the circles and element times are beside the circles. The four elements under stage I have no predecessors and can be started anytime. No elements may begin until their predecessors have been completed.

In a column, work elements are independent of one another. Three elements—left sock, right sock, and hat—have lateral flexibility; that is, they may be moved one column to the right without disturbing precedence restrictions. With these kinds of flexibility, a large number of combinations of workstation layout sequences can satisfy precedence restrictions.

Precedence diagrams are a bit like the activity-on-node networks used in PERT/CPM (see Chapter 13). A difference is that the precedence diagram does not have a single start and a single end point, as does the PERT/CPM network. The reason is that assembly lines keep running rather than starting and ending at finite points in time, as projects do. Also, the precedence diagram is not a final plan; it just shows sequence limitations (the numbered stages in Figure 18–20). The PERT/CPM network is a final sequence plan.

Line-Balancing Analysis

Once the precedence diagram has been completed, actual line balancing may begin. A perfectly balanced line has zero balance delay, which means no wait time at any workstation. **Balance delay**, d, is:

$$d = \frac{nc - \Sigma t}{nc} \tag{18–1}$$

where

n = Number of workstations
c = Cycle time
Σt = Total work content time for one unit

A manual heuristic line-balancing method is shown in Example 18–4, again using the doll assembly.

EXAMPLE 18–4   **MANUAL HEURISTIC LINE BALANCING— DOLL ASSEMBLY**

Total work content, Σt, for the doll assembly is 306 hundredths of a minute (see data given in Example 18–3). A first step in line-balancing analysis is breaking Σt into its prime numbers. There are five prime numbers:

$$306 = 1 \times 2 \times 3 \times 3 \times 17$$

For a balanced line, the cycle time must equal the product of some combination of these prime numbers. However, a cycle time shorter than the *longest* single work element time is not feasible (unless a way can be found to divide the element into two distinct elements). The combinations yield 12 possible cycle times:

$$
\begin{aligned}
c_1 &= 2 \times 3 \times 3 \times 17 = 306 & c_7 &= 17 \\
c_2 &= 3 \times 3 \times 17 = 153 & c_8 &= 3 \times 3 = 9 \\
c_3 &= 2 \times 3 \times 17 = 102 & c_9 &= 3 \times 2 = 6 \\
c_4 &= 3 \times 17 = 51 & c_{10} &= 3 \\
c_5 &= 2 \times 17 = 34 & c_{11} &= 2 \\
c_6 &= 2 \times 3 \times 3 = 18 & c_{12} &= 1
\end{aligned}
$$

Now we want to see how many workstations, n, we would end up with in a balanced line. To find out, we simply divide cycle times into the total work content, 306:

$$
\begin{aligned}
n_1 &= \frac{\Sigma t}{c_1} = \frac{306}{306} = 1 \text{ station} \\[6pt]
n_2 &= \frac{\Sigma t}{c_2} = \frac{306}{153} = 2 \text{ stations} \\[6pt]
n_3 &= \frac{\Sigma t}{c_3} = \frac{306}{102} = 3 \text{ stations} \\[6pt]
n_4 &= \frac{\Sigma t}{c_4} = \frac{306}{51} = 6 \text{ stations}
\end{aligned}
$$

Note: Six or more stations would be poorly balanced, since the minimum cycle time is 0.63 minutes, which is the time it takes to install the tie on the doll, element 11. Thus, there are just three feasible perfectly balanced options: n_1 through n_3.

The choice of number of stations may be dictated by the production schedule. Assume the schedule calls for 400 dolls per day and there is one shift of 400 working minutes. The required cycle time, then, is $400/400 = 1.00$ minutes per doll. Option n_3, which has a cycle time of 1.02 minutes and calls for 3 stations, is almost perfect.

To develop a plan for a well-balanced line with three stations, we begin by rearranging the precedence diagram, Figure 18–20, into a table, Figure 18–21. Columns A, B, and D in the table are taken directly from the precedence diagram. Column C shows elements that could just as well be performed in a later stage. Column E sums the element times for each stage, and Column F cumulatively sums the times for the three stages.

Now, we inspect for ways to achieve a well-balanced line, which must have three stations, each with work content close to 102. We can see from Figure 18–21 that the cumulative sum of stages I and II is close at 109. A way to reduce it closer to 102 presents itself: Move element 13, with a time of 6, from stage II to stage III. This reduces the time for stages I through II to 103, which is very close to the 102 that would give perfect balance.

Moving element 13 to stage III increases the stage III sum from 197 to 203. Now we want to split stage III into two stations, with cycle times close to 102, the ideal. To find a set of work element times whose sum is close to 102 or 101, it is efficient to begin by adding the larger numbers. Adding elements 11 and 12—63, and 32—gives 95; adding 6, the time for element 13, gives us 101. The remaining four elements—7, 10, 8, and 9—total 102.

Figure 18–22 gives us the nearly perfect solution, with station times of 103, 102, and 101. This means that one doll may be clothed every 103 hundredths of a minute, not counting transit time between stations. Station 1's capacity is fully used each cycle; station 2 wastes 0.01 minutes per cycle; and station 3 wastes 0.02 minutes per cycle. The waste

FIGURE 18–21
Tabular Form of Precedence Relationships in Assembling Clothes

(A) Column Number in Precedence Diagram	(B) Element Number	(C) Remarks	(D) Element Time, (t)	(E) Sum of Element Times	(F) Cumulative Sum of Times
I	3	→ II	9		
	1		10		
	4	→ II	9		
	2		11	39	39
II	5		22		
	6		42		
	13	→ III	6	70	109
III	7		26		
	10		20		
	9		30		
	8		26		
	12		32		
	11		63	197	306

FIGURE 18–22
Improved Line-Balancing Solution for Assembling Clothes

(A) Column Number in Precedence Diagram	(B) Element Number	(C) Remarks	(D) Element Time, (t)	(E) Sum of Element Times	(F) Cumulative Sum of Times	
I	3		9			↑
	1		10			
	4		9			Station
	2		11			1
II	5		22			
	6		42	103	103	↓
III	7		26			↑
	10		20			Station
	9		30			2
	8		26	102	205	↓
	13	From Stage II	6			↑
	12		32			Station
	11		63	101	306	3
						↓

or underuse of capacity for the whole assembly line is the balance delay, which, by Equation 18–1 is:

$$d = \frac{nc - \Sigma t}{nc} = \frac{(3 \times 103) - 306}{3 \times 103}$$
$$= \frac{309 - 306}{309} = \frac{3}{309} \approx 1\%$$

Note that fewer than three stations is not feasible, since the precedence diagram, Figure 18–20, shows several sequences that include all three stages (for example, 1 to 5 to 7). It is feasible to have four or five stations, but it seems unlikely that either would cut the balance delay below 1 percent, because the resulting cycle times would not be products of primes. Therefore, we select n_3, and the analysis ceases.

The heuristic method yields good but not necessarily optimal results, and development of optimizing algorithms and models continues. A variety of line-balancing computer software is available, easing the computational burden and gaining in acceptance. Still, manual heuristic and trial-and-error line balancing are widespread.

Mixed-Model Line Balancing

Line-balancing algorithms have also been developed for **mixed-model assembly lines**, in which more than one model of a product is made on the same line. For example, in a mixed-model doll clothing line male dolls, female dolls, large dolls, small dolls, and so forth may be clothed in a mixed sequence. Our example above was of a single-model line, since there was only one type of male doll.

Mixed-model line-balancing involves (1) determining the sequence of products (model numbers) moving down the line and (2) balancing the line. Some line-balancing methods allow for restrictions and special conditions: subassembly lines that feed main lines, distance and direction requirements, safety needs, special groupings of elements, zoning restrictions, maximum and minimum conveyor speeds, and so forth.

Example 18–5 illustrates some of the factors involved in mixed-model line balancing.

EXAMPLE 18–5   **MIXED MODELS—BORING HOLES IN PUMP HOUSINGS**

A machine center bores holes in pump housings. It used to take twice as long to set up and run a lot of large pump housings as it did small housings. After a vigorous improvement effort, the setup times are now nearly zero for either size of housing. With negligible setup times, it seems reasonable to run mixed models down a mini-production line composed of machines that bore the holes.

The schedule calls for 22 large (L) and 88 small (S) pump housings per day. Run times are 12 minutes per large unit and 2 minutes per small unit. What cycle of mixed models will produce the scheduled quantity with balanced production?

Solution

Model sequence:	L	S	S	S	S	L	S	S	S	S	
Operation time:	12	2	2	2	2	12	2	2	2	2	. . .
			20					20			

This cycle takes 20 minutes and repeats 22 times per day. The production requires $20 \times 22 = 440$ minutes out of a 480-minute workday, which leaves 40 extra minutes for problem solving, equipment care, and so forth.

Fine-Tuning: "Watching the Lights"

Manual heuristic line-balancing *seems* precise and accurate. It isn't. A good typist can type twice as many words per minute as an average one. Similarly, a good welder, solderer, or painter can work twice as fast as an average one. In a line balance based on standard pace, the fast people will not have enough to do and the slow ones will have trouble keeping up. Fine-tuning is needed. The supervisor or operating team will see who the slow ones are and can fine-tune by reassigning some work elements from slower to faster people. A novel method called "watching the lights" serves to make fine-tuning a bit easier.

It is fairly common for trouble lights to be mounted above production lines to alert troubleshooters and supervisors when there is a slowdown or line stoppage. Typically, a red light signals shutdown and a yellow signals trouble. Yellow lights may also aid in fine-tuning the line balancing. Here is how it works:

1. A new production schedule is issued, rough line balancing takes place, and work begins.

2. Anyone who has trouble keeping up will turn on the yellow light frequently. Those who have no trouble keeping up will *not* turn on their yellow lights. The message to the supervisor and team is clear: Take a few small duties away from those with too much to do and reassign them to those whose lights have not been coming on. When everyone's yellow lights are coming on at about the same frequency, the line is balanced, and no one is pushed into making errors out of haste.

3. With the line balanced, yellow lights no longer suggest line imbalance—they indicate trouble. For the remaining days or weeks of the schedule, the problem signaled by a yellow light is recorded so that there are good data for problem solving.

When industry veterans first hear about this approach, they tend to be dubious or full of questions: "But some people will have much more to do than others. Is that fair? Won't the faster operators complain? Or won't they deliberately go slow and push the yellow button in order to avoid getting more tasks to do?"

The first question is not so hard. It is true that the fast people will end up with more tasks to do, but surely that is *more* fair, not less. The system should not mask the abilities of the fast employees, nor should it unduly pressure the slower ones. There *will* be complaints from some of the faster people. The complaints may be resolved in two ways:

1. Give the faster employees bonuses, incentive pay, merit wage increases, or other rewards.

2. Evolve a performance appraisal approach that rewards for problem solving, quality control, and work improvement. These activities focus on innovativeness, leadership, and communication skills. Make sure that enough labor is available to make it possible to meet the schedule every day and on most days still allow time for problem solving, quality control, work improvement, and maintenance.

Throughout our discussion of layout, including line balancing, the concern for movement of materials, tools, and equipment has played a big part. We now examine handling and transportation in greater detail.

HANDLING AND TRANSPORTATION

In one respect, *transportation* and *handling* systems are to be avoided, for they add cost but not value. Yet they are needed to some degree in order for work to move through operations and out into customers' hands. While layout concerns flow and nonflow factors, the flow factors are dominant in handling and transportation. In this section we examine handling concepts and analysis, and containerization—one of the techniques for reducing handling while goods are being moved.

Handling Concepts

A well-established practice that is supposed to hold down handling cost is the **unit-load concept.** The idea is simple: Avoid moving piece by piece and instead accumulate enough pieces to move them as a unit load. Examples are truckloads and rail-car loads between plants, and a loaded pallet, skid, drum, tote box, hand truck, and carton within a facility.

While the unit-load idea has dominated thinking for years, it is now being questioned. The new idea is the opposite: *Avoid* accumulating enough pieces to move them as a unit load; instead, try to move them *piece by piece* so there is *no* extra stock in a state of idleness and no delay for building up a load.

Actually, the unit-load and piece-by-piece viewpoints can converge. If process layouts are broken up and work centers grouped into production cells or lines, handling distances collapse. Without distances to span, the economical unit-load size is pushed downward and may approach one piece.

Using several small, dispersed machines instead of a supermachine is a way to cut handling distances. Multiple small machines can be located close to where material comes from and goes to, that is, in a production line or cell.

Of course, there always will be some distances to span and therefore some handling costs. Careful analysis can reduce the costs.

Handling Analysis

Handling analysis requires two basic steps: (1) analyzing resource flows—materials, plus other resources requiring handling (e.g., tools and mail)—and (2) prescribing handling methods. If the first step is done well, the second is relatively easy.

Data collected on each product or resource may be plotted on a **distance-quantity (DQ) chart**—or, if products/resources are dissimilar, on a **distance-intensity (DI) chart**. *Intensity of flow,* a measure developed by Muther, equals quantity times transportability. *Transportability* is an artificial measure that may include size, density or bulk, shape, risk of damage, condition, and (sometimes) value of the given item.[11]

The DQ or DI chart helps show the types of handling methods needed. Figure 18–23 serves as a guide. Four quadrants are shown in the figure. A low distance, high-volume product would plot in the first quadrant, which suggests *complex handling* equipment, such as conveyors. Low-distance, low-volume calls for *simple handling,* such as hand-carry and the other items in the second quadrant. High-distance, low-volume calls for *simple transport* equipment—any of the types of *vehicles* in the third quadrant. High-distance, high-volume, in the fourth quadrant, suggests poor layout; handling distances are too great. If re-layout is not practical right away, the need is for *complex transport* equipment, such as a railroad.

The solid line cutting through the chart makes another distinction. Above the line are fixed-path types of handling equipment; below it are variable-path types. It is well to be cautious about investing in the fixed-path variety, because it may be too costly to relocate or modify fixed equipment when needs change. It is common to enter a plant of average age and see unused remnants of an overhead conveyor or pneumatic tube system up in the rafters. Automatically guided vehicles and self-guiding order pickers, popularized in the 1960s, were something of a breakthrough. They have fixed-path advantages, but it is cheap to change their route: Simply paint a new white line on the floor for those that optically follow a line, or embed a new wire in the floor for those that sense a magnetic field generated by a current-carrying wire.

Some equipment has both handling and storage functions. One example is carousel systems, which are rotatable racks holding small parts, tools, documents, dry cleaning, and so forth. Another example, the automatic storage/retrieval system, consists of rows of racks with automated, perhaps com-

---

[11]A method for determining transportability may be found in Richard Muther, *Systematic Handling Analysis* (Management and Industrial Research Publications, 1969) (TS180.M8).

FIGURE 18–23

DQ or DI Chart Indicating Preferred Handling Methods

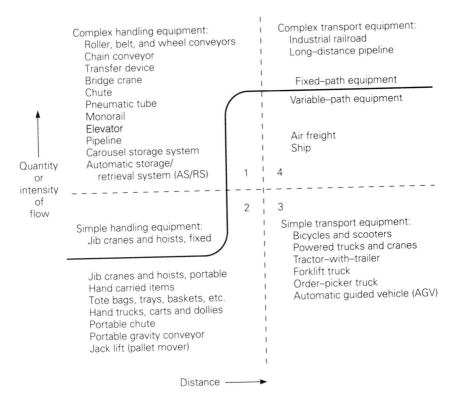

puter-controlled devices to put away and later select baskets or pallets of stock. Both types of equipment were widely installed in North America in the late 1970s and the 1980s. More recently, many companies have been figuring out ways to dismantle some of them, because the racks conflict with the goal of *avoiding* storage. The AS/RS is fine in distribution centers, but when used for storing work-in-process inventories, it is usually a symptom of coordination problems. An exception is a newer type of "mini" AS/RS, which is small enough to be placed at the location where parts or tools are made or used; see photo.

Forklift trucks are also losing favor as a means of handling in-process materials. If machines are close together, as in cells or product layout, materials may be moved by hand, conveyor, transfer device (transfer between adjacent stations), robot, or chute.

After the analyst picks out general types of handling equipment, it is time for detailed study, considering cost, reliability, maintainability, and adaptability. Vendors of material handling equipment may help with the detailed design and then submit bids.

The equipment in quadrant 4 and some in quadrant 3 of Figure 18–23 serves a transportation as well as a handling function. Such equipment tends to be costly enough to warrant special cost analyses; the transportation method, presented earlier, may fit this need.

Mini automatic storage/retrieval system being installed next to plastic-injection molding machine in South Korean factory. With mini AS/RS, the "owner" of the inventory is the machine operator, not a central stock room. Courtesy of Dorner Mfg. Corp., Hartland, Wisc.

Containerization

Design of containers, which once was haphazard, has come to be viewed as critical for effective handling and transportation. The goals are to protect the goods, ensure exact counts, and simplify loading and unloading.

The Automobile Industry Action Group's containerization task force hopes to agree on standard reusable collapsible containers for auto parts (see the example in Figure 18–24), usable by competing suppliers and auto assembly plants. The containers avoid throw-away materials, especially cardboard, which cuts costs by a surprisingly large amount—over $50 per car already, according to the manager of one auto assembly plant. Other industries are also plunging into containerization, but mostly with each firm doing its own.

The new containers often are designed to hold an exact, easily verifiable quantity, perhaps through use of partitions or "egg-crate" molded bottoms or inserts. That helps solve a chronic problem. Outside suppliers would deliberately ship too much, hoping to be paid for the excess, or, where the supplier had a stock shortage, ship less than the ordered quantity. The bad habits of over- and undershipment led to costly delays to count every piece upon receipt—and also generated ill will. The new designs allow for just counting containers, not pieces; or not counting at all, except on an audit basis. JIT makes containerization all the more necessary, since it lowers inventories and available storage space to the point where receipt of too little or too much can't be tolerated.

On a larger scale, containerization includes semitrailers or large seagoing cargo boxes that can also move by rail or be trucked. Cargo boxes avoid costly handling of diverse small crates and boxes.

FIGURE 18–24
Reusable Collapsible Container

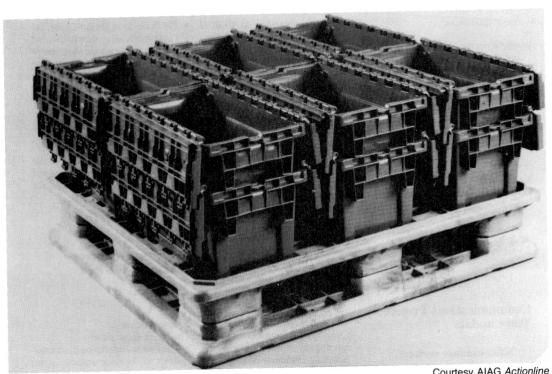

Courtesy AIAG *Actionline*

JIT shippers load the cargo boxes with small amounts of multiple components, called *kits*, rather than loading a huge lot of just one item into the box. Some North American plants use the transport-kit technique to receive just one day's supply of mixed parts every day from across an ocean!

SUMMARY

Deployment of operating facilities is a strategic concern. It includes location, layout, handling, and transportation. Minimizing handling, which adds cost but not value, is a goal at all levels of deployment.

Location decisions involve intangible as well as tangible factors. Communities compete vigorously to attract jobs. Markets, labor, taxes, supply sources, transportation costs, and political and social forces are among the factors considered in location decisions. Various rating schemes are available to assist in reducing reams of location data to a ranking of each alternative location. A preemptive strategy is to announce pending capacity addition, seeking to deter competitors from taking similar actions.

The transportation method is useful in assisting with facility location decisions and determining shipment patterns from existing facilities. The model is set up as a from-to matrix, with each matrix cell representing one transportation route with its own unit transportation cost. Quantities available at each supply point (capacities) and needs at each destination (demands) are shown as matrix rim or boundary constraints.

An initial solution may be obtained by the northwest-corner method or Vogel's approximation method (VAM). Solution improvement, using the stepping-stone method, for example, is an iterative procedure designed to yield an optimal transportation pattern, that is, one that meets demand and allocates supply at minimal costs.

Deployment of facilities within buildings is referred to as *layout*. A goal is to minimize distances over which materials must be moved. Additional targets include minimizing space and in-process inventories and getting related activities into close proximity. Major types of layout include process (or functional), product, cellular, and fixed. Process layouts group together similar skills, machines, processes or functions—grinding machines in a grinding shop, for example. Weaknesses of process layout are long flow lines, excessive handling among the process areas, separation of providers from their customers at the next process, and long throughout times.

Process layouts are being broken up into product or cellular designs, where work moves short distances between unlike processes. In fixed layout, work is not mobile; thus, resources do the moving. For example, people take machines and tools with them when they move around a large aircraft being assembled.

Systematic layout planning (SLP) is a useful approach that usually begins with product and quantity analysis. Next, from-to charts show flow volumes for products or resources that move in quantity while activity relationship charts address nonflow factors. The charted data are used to construct activity arrangement diagrams that lead, in turn, to space relationship diagrams showing work area requirements for each activity. Finally, the activities are fit onto a floor plan, and the layout is complete. SLP may be partially computer assisted and is suitable for offices as well as plants. Interior design—furnishings, plants, acoustics, lighting, color, signs, fabrics, counters, landscapes, and so on—has become important in office layout. Thus, interior designers tend to rely more on art than on systematic layout analysis.

Balancing workstation capacity is a primary concern in production-line layout. Line balancing usually begins by dividing a job into work elements or tasks and showing the task sequence on a precedence diagram. In a manual heuristic method, precedence diagram data yield a nearly balanced line, specifying cycle time and number of workstations. A perfectly balanced line has zero balance delay, or full utilization at each workstation while the line is running.

Line balancing is more difficult in mixed-model situations. Sequencing becomes critical, and a work cycle may call for mixed sequences of several short-cycle-time models along with one long-cycle-time model. The work cycle repeats. Fine-tuning is required with any line balance. By "watching the lights," supervisors and operators may adjust workloads away from those who turn on their yellow trouble lights most often.

The primary aim of handling analysis is to minimize handling costs; thus, it is a crucial part of all deployment activities. Unit loading and sophisticated handling systems have been desirable, but modern thinking is that no handling is the best handling. Although this ideal is impossible, handling systems are being dismantled in favor of simpler methods for moving smaller lots over shorter distances. Layout improvement reduces the need for handling.

Systematic handling analysis starts with distance-quantity (or distance-intensity) data that suggest the type of handling equipment: simple handling, complex handling, simple transport, or complex transport. Finally, specific handling equipment is selected. Variable-path equipment is more adaptable. Small-scale handling problems may be solved by feasibility study, but large-scale problems warrant full systematic analysis.

The use of standard containers with dividers to hold an exact quantity is increasing. Containerization reduces losses and amount of handling. The precise quantities per container eliminate time-consuming receiving counts and foster the precision called for in JIT purchasing.

KEY WORDS

Facilities
Deployment
Simplex method (linear programming)
Transportation method
Northwest-corner rule
Vogel's approximation method (VAM)
Stepping-stone method
Modified distribution (MODI) method
Process (functional) layout

Product layout
Production line
Cellular layout
Fixed (fixed-position) layout
Systematic layout planning (SLP)
Open-office concept
Line balancing
Autonomous operations
Progressive operations

Cycle time
Work content time
Throughput time
Production rate
Precedence diagram
Balance delay
Mixed-model assembly
Unit-load concept
Distance-quantity (DQ) chart
Distance-intensity (DI) chart

SOLVED PROBLEMS

1. Zappo Electronics produces microcomputers at three factories and distributes them to three central warehouse distribution centers for subsequent distribution throughout the marketing channels. The three factories (row constraints) have supply capacities and the three warehouses have processing capabilities (destination demand) as shown below. All boundary values are in hundreds and represent monthly volume capacity. Unit transportation costs for each transportation route are as shown. Solve this transportation problem so as to minimize monthly transportation costs.

Transportation Data—Zappo Electronics

Warehouses (destinations)

Factory	A	B	C	Capacity (supply)
I	7	8	11	30
II	4	6	5	25
III	3	10	2	40
Demand →	15	38	42	95 / 95

Solution

The initial solution, obtained by the northwest-corner method, is shown below. The test for degeneracy (see the supplement to this chapter) requires $(S + D - 1)$ "filled" cells. Substituting the value 3 for both S and D, we find that 5 filled cells are required. Since the solution does contain five filled cells, it is not degenerate. The total transportation costs associated with this solution are $45,300 per month.

Northwest-Corner Solution—Zappo Electronics

Warehouses (destinations)

Factory	A	B	C	Capacity (supply)
I	7 / 15 OUT	8 / 15	11	30
II	4 / IN	6 / 23	5 / 2	25
III	3	10	2 / 40	40
Demand →	15	38	42	95 / 95

Next, we use the stepping-stone method to test for optimality. The northwest-corner-solution shows four empty transportation routes, or cells, to be tested: I-C, II-A, III-A, and III-B.

Evaluation of cell I-C is as follows:

Cell	Unit		Rate		Cost Change
I-C	+1	×	$11	=	$ 11
I-B	−1	×	8	=	−8
II-B	+1	×	6	=	6
II-C	−1	×	5	=	−5
			Net change	=	$+4

Tests for other empty cells are shown in abbreviated form.

For cell II-A:

$$\text{II-A} \rightarrow \text{II-B} \rightarrow \text{I-B} \rightarrow \text{I-A}$$
$$+4 \quad\quad -6 \quad\quad +8 \quad\quad -7 = \$ - 1$$

For cell III-A:

$$\text{III-A} \rightarrow \text{III-C} \rightarrow \text{II-C} \rightarrow \text{II-B} \rightarrow \text{I-B} \rightarrow \text{I-A}$$
$$+3 \quad\quad -2 \quad\quad +5 \quad\quad -6 \quad\quad +8 \quad\quad -7 = \$ + 1$$

For Cell III-B:

$$\text{III-B} \rightarrow \text{III-C} \rightarrow \text{II-C} \rightarrow \text{II-B}$$
$$+10 \quad\quad -2 \quad\quad +5 \quad\quad -6 = \$ + 7$$

Since cell II-A has a negative improvement index, the initial solution to our transportation problem is *not* optimal. Use of the transportation route from factory II to warehouse A lowers transportation costs. To bring the cell into the solution, however, we must let one of the cells currently in the (initial) solution go out. Cell II-A is labeled as the *IN*coming cell and cell I-A as the *OUT*going cell. I-A is selected as the *OUT*going cell by: (1) identifying the path used to evaluate the incoming cell, (2) identifying the cells—in this path—that made a *negative* contribution to the improvement index, and (3) selecting the cell from the resulting set with the smaller(est) *shipped* value.

The second solution to our problem is shown below. It was obtained by: (1)

Second Solution, Stepping-Stone Method—Zappo Electronics

placing the *OUT*going cell's shipment into the *IN*coming cell, (2) leaving all cells that were *not* in the path used to evaluate cell II-A as they were, and (3) using the rim constraints to complete the solution.

Next, we apply the degeneracy test $(S + D - 1)$ to the second solution. The five filled cells indicate that this new solution is not degenerate. Its total transportation costs are $43,800. The lower costs were expected, since we moved 1,500 units into cell II-A at a savings of $1 per unit (the improvement index for cell II-A was $ - 1$). The initial solution costs ($45,300) less $1,500 yields $43,800. Certainly this second solution is better. It should, however, be subjected to the optimality test before it is accepted.

The four empty cells are evaluated.

For cell I-A:

$$\begin{array}{cccc} \text{I-A} \rightarrow & \text{I-B} \rightarrow & \text{II-B} \rightarrow & \text{II-A} \\ +7 & -8 & +6 & -4 = \$ + 1 \end{array}$$

For cell I-C:

$$\begin{array}{cccc} \text{I-C} \rightarrow & \text{I-B} \rightarrow & \text{II-B} \rightarrow & \text{II-C} \\ +11 & -8 & +6 & -5 = \$ + 4 \end{array}$$

For cell III-A:

$$\begin{array}{cccc} \text{III-A} \rightarrow & \text{III-C} \rightarrow & \text{II-C} \rightarrow & \text{II-A} \\ +3 & -2 & +5 & -4 = \$ + 2 \end{array}$$

For cell III-B:

$$\begin{array}{cccc} \text{III-B} \rightarrow & \text{III-C} \rightarrow & \text{II-C} \rightarrow & \text{II-B} \\ +10 & -2 & +5 & -6 = \$ + 7 \end{array}$$

All the empty cells have positive improvement indices; thus, the second solution is optimal. We conclude that Zappo can ship its microcomputers from its three factories to its three warehouses for $43,800 per month.

2. The five departments of a warehouse with their approximate square-footage requirements and activity relationships are as follows:

Department	Area (square feet)	Activity Relationships
1. Materials scheduling	1,000	
2. Packaging and crating	1,500	
3. Materials control supervisor	500	
4. Shipping and receiving	3,000	
5. Warehouse (storage)	6,000	
Total (square feet)	12,000	

  a. Develop an activity arrangement diagram based on the REL chart data
  b. Develop a space relationship diagram for the five departmental areas.
  c. Fit the five departments into a 100-foot by 150-foot building, and try to
     maintain 10-foot aisles between departments.

Solution

a. Activity arrangement diagram:

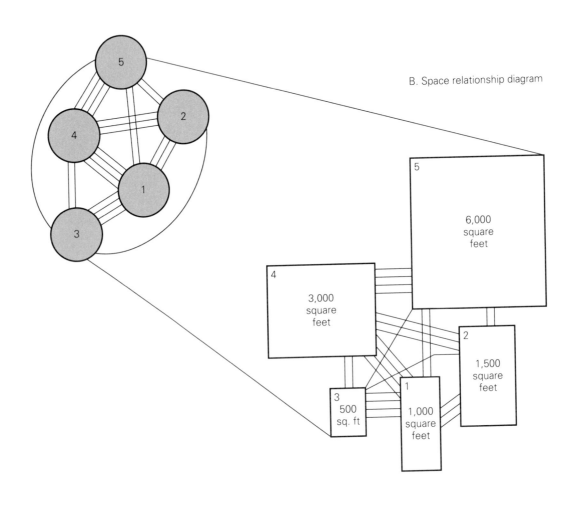

B. Space relationship diagram

  c. Following is a sample departmental layout in a 100-foot-by-150-foot building,
     maintaining 10-ft aisles. (Note: Department 1 has more space than required;
     all others have the required amount.)

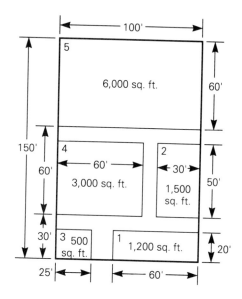

3. Consider the following elemental precedence diagram (element times are in units of 0.01 minutes):

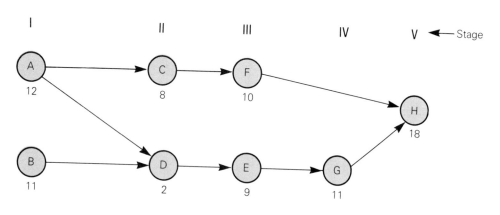

a. What would be the cycle time for a line with one workstation (autonomous production)?

b. What would be the maximum daily capacity of such a line assuming 420 minutes of work time per day?

c. What is the shortest possible cycle time?

d. Assuming we used this shortest cycle time, what would daily line capacity be?

e. Plan a balanced line for the assembly operation using a cycle time of 0.29 minutes. Compute the balance delay for your solution. What will be the approximate capacity of the line assuming a 420-minute workday?

f. Try to reduce the balance delay in your solution to question *e* by adjusting element assignments. What effect would you hope to obtain regarding cycle time? Compute the balance delay and the approximate daily capacity assuming a 420-minute workday.

g. The solution in question *f* cuts balance delay. In what ways, if any, does that benefit the customer.

Solution

a. With one workstation, the sum of the element times would be a reasonable estimate for the cycle time. In this case, the sum is 0.81 minutes.

b. With 420 minutes of available work time per day, the maximum capacity possible with a cycle time of 0.81 minutes would be:

$$420/0.81 = 519 \text{ units}$$

c. The shortest possible cycle time equals the time of the longest element, or 0.18 minutes. We would not necessarily want to use this as the cycle time, but it is possible to do so.

d. If we were using 0.18 minutes as the cycle time, again assuming a 420-minute workday, the maximum capacity would be:

$$420/0.18 = 2{,}333 \text{ units}$$

e. Cycle time = 0.29 minutes

Precedence relationship table:

(A) Element Stage	(B) Element Letter	(C) Remarks	(D) Element Time	(E) Sum of Element Times	(F) Cumulative Sum of Element Times
I	A		12	23	23
	B		11		
II	C	→ III	8	10	33
	D		2		
III	E		9	19	52
	F	→ IV	10	11	63
IV	G		11	18	81
V	H		18		

By assigning the elements in stage I to the first workstation, stages II and III to the second, and stages IV and V to the third, we arrive at the following balance:

Station	Element	Element Time	Cumulative Station Work Time	Station Idle Time
1	A	12	12	
	B	11	23	6
2	C	8	8	
	D	2	10	

Station	Element	Element Time	Cumulative Station Work Time	Station Idle Time
	E	9	19	
	F	10	29	
3	G	11	11	0
	H	18	29	
				0

Total idle time $\overline{6}$

$$\text{Balance delay } \frac{(3 \times 29) - 81}{87} = 0.069, \text{ or } 6.9\%$$

$$\text{Capacity} = 420/0.29 = 1,448 \text{ units per day}$$

f. Station 1 in the solution for question e has 0.06 minutes of idle time, so we might begin by moving element D to station 1, raising the work time from 0.23 to 0.25 minutes. Next, we could assign elements C, E, and G to station 2, resulting in a work time of 0.28 minutes. The remaining elements, F and H, would be assigned to station 3; it too will have a total work time of 0.28 minutes.

Since 0.28 minutes is the largest amount of work time in a station (for stations 2 and 3, in this case), we could have a cycle time of 0.28 minutes. The slight reduction, from 0.29 minutes in question e, might be desirable. As we see below, we will have a lower balance delay and will be capable of slightly greater capacity. The balance appears as follows:

Station	Element	Element Time	Cumulative Station Work Time	Station Idle Time*
1	A	12	12	
	B	11	23	
	D	2	25	3
2	C	8	8	
	E	9	17	
	G	11	28	0
3	F	10	10	
	H	18	28	
				0

Total idle time $\overline{3}$

$$\text{Balance delay } \frac{(3 \times 28) - 81}{84} = 0.036, \text{ or } 3.6\%$$

$$\text{Capacity} = 420/0.28 = 1,500 \text{ units per day}$$

*Based on a cycle time of 0.28 minutes.

g. The solution in question f raises daily line capacity slightly from the 1,448 units found in question e to 1,500 units. Rebalancing to achieve 1,500 per day—and producing at that rate—is worthwhile only if sales are 1,500 per day; if sales are less, the excess production will just go into storage, which will add an unnecessary cost and ultimately forces a price rise. The point is that the production line should be run at the customers' buying rate and balanced accordingly. Sales rates usually change every few weeks, requiring that the supervisor work on rebalancing and reassigning people every few weeks.

REFERENCES

Books

Apple, James M. *Plant Layout and Material Handling,* 3rd ed. New York: Ronald Press, 1977 (TS155.A58).

Coyle, John J.; Edward J. Bardi; and Joseph L. Cavinato. *Transportation,* 2nd ed. St. Paul, Minn.: West Publishing, 1986 (HE151.C88).

Hales, H. Lee. *Computer Aided Facilities Planning.* New York: Marcel Dekker, 1984 (TS177.H35).

Konz, Stephan A. *Facility Design.* New York: John Wiley & Sons, 1985 (TS177.K66).

Kulwiec, Raymond A., ed.-in-chief. *Materials Handling Handbook,* 2nd ed. New York: John Wiley & Sons, 1985 (TS180.M315).

Molnar, John. *Facilities Management Handbook.* New York: Van Nostrand Reinhold, 1983 (TH151.M59).

Steele, Fritz. *Making and Managing High-Quality Workplaces: An Organizational Ecology.* New York: Teachers College Press, 1986 (HF5547.2.S74)

Taff, Charles A. *Management of Physical Distribution and Transportation,* 7th ed. Homewood, Ill.: Richard D. Irwin, 1984.

Wineman, John D., ed. *Behavioral Issues in Office Design.* New York: Van Nostrand Reinhold, 1986 (HF5547.2.B43).

Periodicals/Societies

Factory Management.
Industrial Engineering (Institute of Industrial Engineers).
Material Handling Engineering.
Material Management Pacesetter (International Materials Management Society).
Modern Materials Handling.
Office.
Today's Office.

REVIEW QUESTIONS

1. What is facilities deployment? Is the deployment process over after locations are chosen? Explain.

2. Identify tangible and intangible factors that might be considered in location decisions.

3. What can a community or state do to attract business or industry?

4. How can the transportation method be used in location planning? If plants are already located, might there be further use for the transportation model? Explain.

5. Can a northwest-corner solution ever be optimal? Explain.

6. In a transportation method problem, what happens if demand exceeds supply? What if supply exceeds demand?

7. What is a preemptive capacity deployment strategy? How does such a strategy affect competition?

8. What is layout? Distinguish among four major layout types.

9. What kinds of products are produced in fixed layouts? Why?

10. In what kinds of industry does the layout plan have far-reaching consequences? Explain.

11. How is the handling system related to layout?

12. Why is the U-shaped layout well suited for cells or flow lines?

13. How does office layout planning differ from plant layout planning?

14. What are some "interior design" variables? How are they related to the concept of layout?

15. What is the origin of the data that go on the combined activity relationship chart?

16. How are degrees of closeness shown on the activity arrangement diagram? What determines sizes of blocks on the diagram?

17. What has to be done to the space relationship diagram to convert it to the final layout?

18. What is the open-office concept? Is it desirable in all offices? Explain.

19. Define (a) cycle time, (b) work content time, (c) throughput time, and (d) production rate.

20. What is meant by a mixed-model line? Are there any special problems associated with balancing a mixed-model line? Explain.

21. What does "watching the lights" refer to? How can it lead to increased productivity?

22. Is it a good idea to transport in unit loads? Discuss.

23. What are the advantages of variable-path handling equipment?

24. Explain the role of containerization in modern operations management.

PROBLEMS AND EXERCISES

1. What are the current location strategies for the following industries?

Carpeting	Furniture
Movie theaters	Bottling

Petroleum refining   Electric power generation

Boxing and packing materials   Plastic molding

2. Find out what you can about the U.S. Motor Carrier Deregulation Act of 1980. How has that act affected handling or location strategies (or both) in North American industry? Discuss.

3. "Our approach to the labor union is to run from it." That is one auto parts executive's explanation of why they had nonunion plants in small, remote rural towns around the country. How do you think that strategy will be affected by the automakers' determination to get daily deliveries from their suppliers? Discuss.

4. Recyclation, Inc., has three aluminum can collection stations located around the metropolitan area. Trucks periodically haul the cans to either of two can-crush facilities; one is referred to as the East facility, the other as the West facility. A third can-crush facility is to be set up, and two alternative sites—a North and a South site—are being considered. The average weekly volume of cans available from the three collection sites is given below, along with the can-crushing capacities of the two present and the two proposed sites. The costs of transportation from each collection site to each can-crush site are also given.

Collection Sites	Supply (loads per week)	Routes From	To	Transportation Costs per Load
1	3	1	E	$8
2	8	1	W	4
3	6	1	N	3
		1	S	7
		2	E	5
		2	W	5
		2	N	7
		2	S	3
		3	E	1
		3	W	3
		3	N	3
		3	S	5

Can-Crush Sites	Capacity (loads per week)
East	5
West	7
North	6
South	6

a. Develop the minimum transportation cost solution if the new plant is built at the North site. Use NW-corner and stepping-stone.

b. Develop the minimum transportation cost solution if the new plant is built at the South site.

c. Which site is preferable, North or South? Discuss in terms of transportation and possible nontransportation factors. Do all can-crush sites operate at full capacity? Explain.

5. In a large woodshop, tubs of sawdust accumulate in three locations (sawdust is sucked to those locations via a vacuum system with tubes going to each machine). Several times daily the tubs are grabbed by a forktruck and taken to be dumped at chutes located at two sides of the building. Transportation cost works out at $1 per 200 feet removed. A third dump chute is to be installed at one of two locations in order to cut move distance. The accompanying floor plan shows the layout with distances. Squares show where sawdust builds up in tubs; solid circles are present chutes; and dashed circles are alternative locations for a new chute.

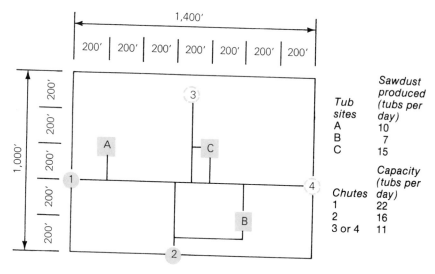

a. Create a transportation matrix for the sawdust-movement problem assuming that a new chute is installed at site 3.

b. Develop the minimum-cost solution for your matrix from question a.

c. Create a transportation matrix for the sawdust-movement problem assuming that a new chute is installed at site 4.

d. Develop the minimum-cost solution for your matrix from question c.

e. Compare the results from questions b and d. Discuss the need for the chute at either location.

6. Continental Tractor Company machines engine-block castings in three different plants. The castings come from two of the company's foundries, but the supply has become inadequate. A third foundry, at either Toronto or Rock Island, is to begin casting the tractor engines. Its capacity is to be just enough to make up for the capacity shortage.

The transportation method is being used to analyze transportation costs for the two sites. Transportation costs, demands, and capacities are as follows:

Foundries	Plant	Transportation Cost (per casting)	Supply (castings)
A	1	$10	Foundry A—80/week
B	1	3	Foundry B—100/week
Toronto	1	5	
Rock Island	1	9	
A	2	7	Demand (castings)
B	2	11	Plant 1—40/week
Toronto	2	6	Plant 2—90/week
Rock Island	2	3	Plant 3—110/week
A	3	8	
B	3	5	
Toronto	3	9	
Rock Island	3	7	

a. Use the transportation method to solve for the minimum transportation cost using Toronto as the foundry site.

b. Use the transportation method to solve for minimum transportation cost using Rock Island as the foundry site.

7. Ten thousand TV tubes per month are produced at three different plants; they go to 5 assembly locations having a total demand of 11,000 tubes per month. Set up these data into a transportation matrix, complete with *all* rows and columns that would be needed to work the problem. What other data are needed? What decisions would be aided by the solution to the problem?

8. For each of the following types of industry, suggest which types of layout (process, product, cellular, fixed, and mixed) are likely to apply. Some types may have more than one likely type of layout. Explain your choices briefly.

Auto assembly	Military physical exams
Auto repair	Small airplane manufacturing
Shipbuilding	Small airplane overhaul and repair
Machine shop	Large airplane overhaul and repair
Cafeteria	Shoe manufacturing
Restaurant	Shoe repair
Medical clinic	Central processing of insurance forms
Hospital	Packing and crating

9. Draw a layout of a dentists' office (group practice with three dentists). Label the areas as to whether they are process, product, cellular, or fixed. Explain.

10. In a bicycle assembly plant, there are five separate shops: (1) Front wheels are built; (2) rear wheels are built with brake and gear assemblies installed;

(3) tires are mounted on wheels; (4) sprocket, seat, handlebars, and pedal assembly are mounted on the frame; (5) wheels are assembled to frame, cables and hand brakes are attached, and the bike is tested and packed. Three sizes of bicycle are made in rotation, with 500 as the average lot size.

a. What kind of layout does this appear to be? Sketch it.

b. Resketch the plant layout to provide a layout for streamlined just-in-time production.

11. Develop an REL chart for a large discount or department store that you are familiar with. (You may need to visit the store for firsthand information.) Use the store's different departments as activities. Is the REL chart likely to be helpful in layout or relayout of such a store? How about a flow diagram or a from-to chart? Explain.

12. Automatic Controls Corporation is building a new plant. Eight departments are involved. As part of a plant layout analysis, the activity relationships and square-footage needs for the departments are shown on the following combined REL chart (combined flow analysis and nonflow analysis):

Activity	Area (square feet)
1. Shipping and receiving	600
2. Stockroom	1,500
3. Fabrication	800
4. Assembly	700
5. Paint	500
6. Tool crib	300
7. Cafeteria	600
8. Offices	1,200
Total	6,400 square feet

Code	Reasons
1	Personal contact
2	Paperwork contact
3	Product/resource flow
4	Use same equipment/tools
5	Possible fumes

    a. Develop an activity arrangement diagram based on the REL chart data.

    b. Develop a space relationship diagram for the eight departmental areas.

    c. Fit the eight departments into a 100-foot-by-80-foot building in as close to an optimal layout as you can. Include aisles between departments on your layout.

    d. How necessary is the combined REL chart in this case? If it were not included in the analysis, what would the analysis steps be? Explain. (Hint: Note the pattern of reasons for relationships.)

13. Pharmaco, Inc., manufacturer of a drug line in liquid and tablet form, is considering moving to a new building. Layout planning is in process. The following data have been collected on material movements in the drug manufacturing process:

	Unit Loads per Month	Move Distances (feet) in Present Building
Raw-material movements:		
Receiving to raw-material storage		180
1. Powder in drums	800	
2. Powder in sacks on pallets	1,100	
3. Liquid in drums	100	
4. Controlled substance (heroin) in cans in cartons	10	
5. Empty bottles in cartons on pallets	8,000	
6. Water piped into granulating and liquid mixing (gallons)	3,000	
In-process movements:		
Raw-material storage to granulating		410
7. Powder in drums	800	
8. Powder in sacks	1,000	
9. Controlled substance in cans	50	
Raw-material storage to liquid mixing		300
10. Powder in sacks	100	
11. Liquid in drums	100	
12. Controlled substance in cans	10	
13. Granulating to tableting (granules in drums)	1,500	290
14. Tableting to fill and pack (tablets in tubs)	6,000	180
15. Liquid mixing to fill and pack (gallons piped)	4,000	370

	Unit Loads per Month	Move Distances (feet) in Present Building
16. Raw-material storage to fill and pack (empty bottles)	8,000	260
17. Fill and pack to finished storage (cartons of bottles and of tablet packs on pallets)	10,000	320

a. Convert the given flow-volume data to a vowel-rating scale; that is, identify which activity pairs (routes) should be rated A, E, I, O, and U.

b. Develop an activity arrangement diagram.

c. The layout planners see little need for a from-to chart or an REL chart. Explain why.

d. One option is to call off the move to the new building and update the material handling system in the present building. Develop a DQ chart using data for the present building. From your DQ chart, draw some conclusions about types of handling methods (equipment) that seem suitable for the present building.

14. As a first step in a line-balancing analysis, the following precedence diagram has been developed.

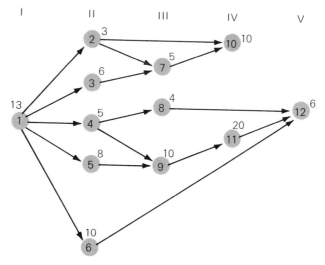

a. Calculate Σt. Now calculate all the possible cycle times and numbers of stations that could be used in a perfectly balanced assembly line.

b. Which of the options developed in question *a* are not worth pursuing further? Why?

c. Balance the line as best you can, and calculate the resulting balance delay.

15. The following precedence diagram has been developed for circuit breaker assembly:

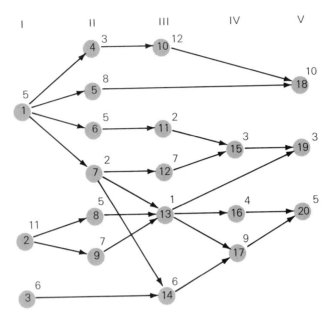

a. Calculate all the possible cycle times and numbers of stations that could be used in a perfectly balanced assembly line.

b. Balance the line as best you can for six stations. Explain. Calculate the resulting balance delay.

16. The processing of worker's compensation claim forms in a state office is being organized as a production line. Work elements have been divided as far as possible and have been organized into the following precedence diagram:

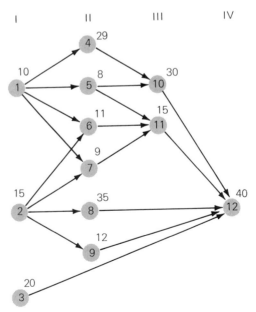

 a. Calculate all combinations of cycle time and number of stations that would result in zero balance delay.
 b. Which combinations (from question *a*) are not reasonable for further analysis? Explain.
 c. Balance the line for five stations and again for six stations. Which is better? Why?

17. Crow's Eye Foods, Inc., has patent rights to a special type of segmented dish for perfect warming of foods in a microwave oven. The dish permits Crow's to launch a new line of frozen breakfasts. Crow's kitchens are planning for the first breakfast: two strips of bacon, one egg, and two slices of buttered toast.
 a. Develop a precedence diagram for use in balancing the production line for this breakfast. Make your own (reasonable) assumptions about work elements and element times. Explain your diagram.
 b. Determine all sets of cycle time and number of stations that would result in a balanced line.
 c. Balance your line.

18. The woodshop building of E-Z Window Company is undergoing major relayout in order to reduce backtracking and decrease flow distances. A flow diagram of the frame-manufacturing operation and an REL chart for nonflow factors in the operation follow:
 a. Construct a from-to chart based on flow diagram data. What is the meaning of the notation that quantities are in "unit loads?" Explain by referring to a few examples on the chart.
 b. What proportion of total flow on your from-to chart represents backtracking? How does that proportion depend on your chosen order of listing

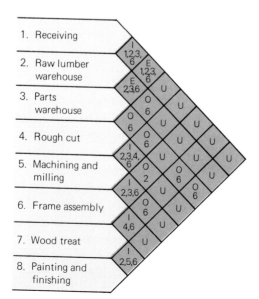

Code	Reason
1	Share records
2	Share employees
3	Share supervision
4	Share portable equipment (frame racks and saws)
5	Isolate together for reasons of fumes
6	Personal and paperwork coordination

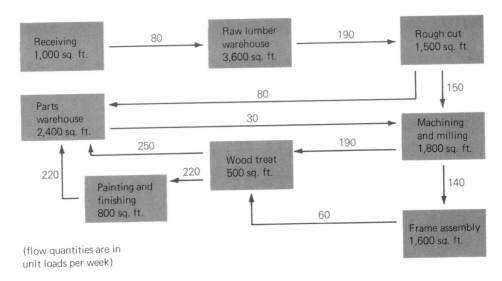

(flow quantities are in
unit loads per week)

activities on the chart? What does your chosen order of listing activities imply about the final layout arrangement?

c. Convert the flow volume data in your from-to chart to a vowel-rating scale; that is, identify which activity pairs (routes) should be rated A, E, I, O, and U.

d. Combine your vowel-rating data representing flow volumes with the nonflow-factor vowel ratings on the REL chart. Express the result in a new, combined REL chart.

e. Convert your combined REL chart into an activity arrangement diagram.

f. Develop a space relationship diagram for the eight activity areas.

g. Fit the eight activity areas into a square building without allowances for aisles, and so on. Make your layout as nearly optimal as you can.

h. Based on distances between departments in your layout in question g, develop a DQ chart. From your DQ chart, draw some general conclusions about the types of handling methods (equipment) that seem suitable.

19. A production line assembles two models of hair dryer: standard (S) and deluxe (D). Each S requires 4 minutes of assembly time and each D 12 minutes. Marketing sells twice as many Ss as Ds. Develop a mixed-model sequence for the two dryers. Make it as well balanced as possible. What is the cycle time, and how many times can it repeat in a 480-minute day?

20. Parts A and B must be heat treated. The heat-treat time for part A is 5 minutes; for part B, it is 10 minutes. The schedule calls for 36 As and 12 Bs per day. Develop a balanced mixed-model sequence for the two parts. How many hours will it take to produce the scheduled amount?

21. Acme Corporation has invested $5 million in storage and handling gear: $1 million in pallet racks, $1 million in an operatorless wire-guided vehicle delivery system, $1 million in carousel storage (three carousels), $1 million in an AS/RS, and $1 million in a transporter (moving parts from person to person in production cells and lines).

Evaluate these five handling/storage systems. Rank them in worst-to-best order for a plant pursuing just-in-time production with continual improvement. Explain.

22. Use Vogel's approximation method (VAM) to:
    a. Solve the Hilo location problem (Figure 18–4).
    b. Solve the Lihue location problem (Figure 18–7).

23. Suppose Recyclation, Inc. (see problem 4), is adding a new collection site (number 4) in a rapidly growing suburb on the Northeast side of the city. The new site will be able to supply seven loads per week. Because of the projected population growth throughout the metropolitan area, Recyclation plans to operate both new can-crush facilities—that is, both the North and the South—in addition to the original East and West facilities. The costs of transportation from the number 4 collection site to the four can-crunch facilities are:

From	To	Transportation Cost per Load
4	E	$ 4
4	W	12
4	N	1
4	S	13

Transportatin costs for other routes are given in problem 4. Use Vogel's approximation method to develop the minimum transportation cost solution.

SUPPLEMENT

CHAPTER 18	STEPPING-STONE METHOD AND VOGEL'S APPROXIMATION METHOD

STEPPING-STONE METHOD

The stepping-stone method leads to an optimal solution to a transportation problem. Stepping-stone begins with an initial feasible solution, as Example S18–1 (using data from Example 18–1) demonstrates.

EXAMPLE S18–1	STEPPING-STONE METHOD—LIHUE LOCATION

Initial solution—Lihue location. An initial feasible solution using the NW-corner rule is shown in Figure S18–1. The total weekly transportation cost for the NW-corner solution is $965, as calculated below:

Honolulu–Lanai	$ 7 × 20 =	$140 per week
Honolulu–Molokai	7 × 5 =	35 per week
Hana–Molokai	7 × 25 =	175 per week
Hana–Hawaii	8 × 15 =	120 per week
Lihue–Hawaii	11 × 45 =	495 per week
Lihue–Dummy	0 × 5 =	0 per week
	Total	$965 per week

FIGURE S18–1
Initial Solution, NW-Corner Method—Lihue Location

NW-corner is subject to improvement. For Lihue, we will manually improve the NW-corner solution using the stepping-stone method. While computers usually perform these calculations, there are insights to be gained from manual calculations.

Optimal solution—Lihue location. Stepping-stone begins with a degeneracy test. The solution is degenerate if the number of cells in it ("filled" cells, that is) is not equal to 1 less than the number of sources (S) plus destinations (D), or $S + D - 1$. In this case, there are six filled cells resulting from the NW-corner method, and $S + D - 1 = 3 + 4 - 1 = 6$. The number of filled cells equals $S + D - 1$, so the initial solution is not degenerate. If it were, the solution would have to be modified slightly in order to proceed with the stepping-stone method.

Next, we test empty cells. The test determines whether the solution can be improved—that is, whether the total transportation cost can be reduced—by transferring some units into an empty cell. But supply-and-demand restrictions ("rim conditions") must be maintained.

The first empty cell to test is Honolulu–Hawaii. Suppose that one pallet-load is transferred to that cell. That added unit creates an imbalance, which requires a series of corrections, as shown in Figure S18–2. The pallet-load can be transferred from Hana in the Hawaii column; this keeps the total in the column at 60, but it drops the total in the Hana row from 40 to 39. The correction is to add one unit to the Hana–Molokai cell, which brings the Hana row back up to 40 but also raises the Molokai column total from 30 to 31. The correction is to subtract one unit from the Honolulu–Molokai cell; this brings Molokai back to 30 and also drops the Honolulu row total back to 25 (recall that one unit was added to Honolulu–Hawaii in the first step, which raised the Honolulu row total to 26). In Figure S18–2A, the four steps—adding one, subtracting one, adding one, and subtracting one—are shown connected by arrows. The rectangular circuit of pluses balanced by minuses in affected rows and columns preserves rim values.

FIGURE S18–2

Stepping-Stone Revisions—Lihue Location

A. Testing the Honolulu-Hawaii cell

Cell	Units		Rate		Cost change
Honolulu-Hawaii	+1	×	$10	=	+$10 per week
Hana-Hawaii	−1	×	$8	=	−$8 per week
Hana-Molokai	+1	×	$7	=	+$7 per week
Honolulu-Molokai	−1	×	$7	=	−$7 per week
Net change				=	+$2 per week

FIGURE S18–2 *(continued)*

B. Testing the Honolulu-dummy cell

	Lanai	Molokai	Hawaii	Dummy	Supply
Honolulu	7 / 20	7 / 5 −1	10 /	0 / +1	25
Hana	5 /	7 / 25 +1	8 / 15 −1	0 /	40
Lihue	9 /	11 /	11 / 45 +1	0 / 5 −1	50
Demand	20	30	60	5	115 / 115

Cell	Units		Rate		Cost change
Honolulu-Dummy	+1	×	$0	=	$0 per week
Lihue-Dummy	−1	×	$0	=	$0 per week
Lihue-Hawaii	+1	×	$11	=	+11 per week
Hana-Hawaii	−1	×	$8	=	−$8 per week
Hana-Molokai	+1	×	$7	=	+$7 per week
Honolulu-Molokai	−1	×	$7	=	−$7 per week
Net change				=	+$3 per week

The effect on transportation cost is calculated and shown at the bottom of Figure S18–2A. Adding one unit in the Honolulu–Hawaii cell increases transportation cost by $10 per week; Hana–Hawaii cuts cost by $8 per week; and so forth. The net change is +$2 per week. This is a higher cost, so the test fails. Honolulu–Hawaii should remain an empty cell; no newspapers should be sent via that route.

The next empty cell is Honolulu–Dummy. The test is shown in Figure S18–2B. This test requires pluses and minuses in six rather than four cells: a minus offsetting every plus in three rows and three columns. There is no other way to preserve rim values and thus satisfy both supply and demand.

The test starts by adding one unit to the Honolulu–Dummy cell. Next, we subtract one unit from Lihue–Dummy and add one unit to Lihue–Hawaii. Why not add to Lanai or Molokai instead of to Hawaii? A simple reason is that we want to test only one empty cell at a time, and adding Lihue–Lanai or Lihue–Molokai, which are empty, would confound our test of the empty Honolulu–Dummy cell. To conduct a pure test of only one cell at a time requires that all other cells involved in the test already be filled.[1]

---

[1]Lee offers a picturesque explanation of the rule that only filled cells must be used to support the test of an empty cell:

When we walk into a Japanese garden, we often see a beautiful pond. There are water lilies, goldfish, frogs and dragonflies. Then, no doubt, we will notice a set of stepping-stones going across the pond. We can go across the pond if we carefully step on these stones. [In] the stepping-stone method . . . we evaluate all the empty cells by carefully stepping on the occupied cells. We should always remember that if we step on an empty cell, we shall be in the water, screaming, "help!"

Sang M. Lee, *Linear Optimization for Management* (Princeton, N.J.: Petrocelli-Charter, 1976), p. 261 (HD20.5.L39).

FIGURE S18–2 (continued)

C. Testing the Hana-Lanai cell

	Lanai	Molokai	Hawaii	Dummy	Supply
Honolulu	7 20 −1	7 +1	5 10	0		25
Hana	5 +1	7 25 −1	8 15	0		40
Lihue	9	11	11 45	0 5	50
Demand	20	30	60	5 115	115

Cell	Units		Rate		Cost change
Hana-Lanai	+1	×	$5	=	+$5 per week
Honolulu-Lanai	−1	×	$7	=	−$7 per week
Honolulu-Molokai	+1	×	$7	=	+$7 per week
Hana-Molokai	−1	×	$7	=	−$7 per week
	Net change			=	−$2 per week

After adding one unit to the Lihue–Hawaii cell, we subtract one unit from Hana–Hawaii, add one unit to Hana–Molokai, and subtract one unit from Honolulu–Molokai. These steps keep the Lihue row at 50, the Hawaii column at 60, the Hana row at 40, the Molokai column at 30, and the Honolulu row at 25. The net change, calculated below Figure S18–2B, is +$3 per week; therefore, the test fails.

We test the Hana–Lanai cell as shown in Figure S18–2C. Adding a unit to the cell saves $2 per week, so the test passes. If moving one unit into the Hana–Lanai cell saves $2, moving three units would save $6, moving seven units would save $14, and so forth. (Costs are linearly related to quantities in linear programming.) When an empty-cell test saves any money, you want to move maximum units into that cell to save maximum dollars. The maximum here is 20 units, because 20 is the limit that may be subtracted from the "minus" cells without going negative. It is the Honolulu–Lanai cell that limits the quantity moved: Honolulu–Lanai is at 20 in Figure S18–2C and is reduced to zero (emptied) in the improved solution of Figure S18–2D. Each of the other cells tested in Figure S18–2C was also changed by 20 units (up or down).

Below the Figure S18–2D matrix are cost calculations for the new solution. The new cost is $925 per week. That is $40 less than the NW-corner initial cost of $965—which we would expect, since 20 units were moved at a savings of $2 each.

Whenever units are moved within a matrix, cell testing begins all over again. Conditions have changed, and cells previously tested might test out differently.

Thus, we turn again to the first cell, Honolulu–Lanai. We need not retest the cell, since it was emptied for good reason in the test in Figure S18–2C. We need not retest the Honolulu–Hawaii and Honolulu–Dummy cells either, because inspection shows that

FIGURE S18–2 *(continued)*

D. Improved transportation solution

	Lanai	Molokai	Hawaii	Dummy	Supply
Honolulu	7	7 25	10	0 +1	25
Hana	5 20	7 5	8 15	0	40
Lihue	9	11	11 45	0 5	50
Demand	20	30	60	5	115 / 115

New cost

Honolulu-Molokai:	$7	×	25	=	$175 per week
Hana-Lanai:	$5	×	20	=	$100 per week
Hana-Molokai:	$7	×	5	=	$35 per week
Hana-Hawaii:	$8	×	15	=	$120 per week
Lihue-Hawaii:	$11	×	45	=	$495 per week
Lihue-Dummy:	$0	×	5	=	$0 per week

$925 per week

E. Testing the Hana-dummy cell

	Lanai	Molokai	Hawaii	Dummy	Supply
Honolulu	7	7 25	10	0	25
Hana	5 20	7 5	8 15 −1	0 +1	40
Lihue	9	11	11 45 +1	0 5 −1	50
Demand	20	30	60	5	115 / 115

Cell	Units		Rate		Cost change
Hana-Dummy	+1	×	$0	=	$0 per week
Lihue-Dummy	−1	×	$0	=	$0 per week
Lihue-Hawaii	+1	×	$11	=	+$11 per week
Hana-Hawaii	−1	×	$8	=	−$8 per week
	Net change			=	+$3 per week

FIGURE S18–2 *(concluded)*

F. Testing the Lihue-Lanai cell

	Lanai	Molokai	Hawaii	Dummy	Supply
Honolulu	7	7 / 25	10	0	25
Hana	5 / 20 / −1	7 / 5	8 / 15 / +1	0	40
Lihue	9 / +1	11	11 / 45 / −1	0 / 5	50
Demand	20	30	60	5	115 / 115

Cell	Units		Rate		Cost change
Lihue-Lanai	+1	×	$9	=	+$9 per week
Hana-Lanai	−1	×	$5	=	−$5 per week
Hana-Hawaii	+1	×	$8	=	+$8 per week
Lihue-Hawaii	−1	×	$11	=	−$11 per week
	Net change			=	+$1 per week

G. Testing the Lihue-Molokai cell

	Lanai	Molokai	Hawaii	Dummy	Supply
Honolulu	7	7 / 25	10	0	25
Hana	5 / 20	7 / 5 / −1	8 / 15 / +1	0	40
Lihue	9	11 / +1	11 / 45 / −1	0 / 5	50
Demand	20	30	60	5	115 / 115

Cell	Units		Rate		Cost change
Lihue-Molokai	+1	×	$11	=	+$11 per week
Hana-Molokai	−1	×	$7	=	−$7 per week
Hana-Hawaii	+1	×	$8	=	+$8 per week
Lihue-Hawaii	−1	×	$11	=	−$11 per week
	Net change			=	+$1 per week

testing them would include exactly the same cells and transportation costs that were in the earlier tests of those cells.

Hana–Dummy is the next cell to test. The test result, in Figure S18–2E, is a net change in cost of +$3 per week; the test fails.

The last two tests are Lihue–Lanai and Lihue–Molokai. Both result in a $1 greater cost and therefore fail (see Figures S18–2F and S18–2G).

There are no more empty cells to test. The solution in Figure S18–2D, costing $925 per week, is optimal. If the *Island Explorer* builds at Lihue, $925 is the expected transportation cost.

If a nonoptimal solution is degenerate, there are not enough filled cells to be able to test all of the empty ones. The correction is to place a very small quantity into one or more empty cells to eliminate the degeneracy. The small quantity is designated ε (the Greek letter *epsilon*). The transportation cost for the cell times the quantity, ε, equals zero because ε is so small; therefore, ε does not alter the cost structure but only helps with the solution. There is no good rule for selecting the proper empty cell in which to place ε. You can try a spot and see whether it works out; if not, try another.

The use of ε was actually devised for computer-based solutions. Putting ε into a degenerate matrix allows the computer to proceed with the normal transportation algorithm. (The computer treats ε as equaling the lowest character in the computer's collating sequence.)

Sometimes we want to leave out certain transportation routes. For example, fishermen between Maui and Lanai may object to the noise of a predawn airplane transporting newspapers from Hana. Perhaps one hotheaded fisherman may decide to shoot at the plane. The newspaper may avoid the risk of being hit by excluding Hana as the source of newspapers to Lanai. In the transportation method, it is simple to ensure that the Hana–Lanai cells end up empty: Use the value ∞ (symbol for *infinity*) as the transportation cost in that cell (the symbol M, for *maximum* cost, is sometimes used).

VOGEL'S APPROXIMATION METHOD

Vogel's approximation method (VAM) may be used instead of the NW-corner method to arrive at an initial solution to a transportation problem. If the problem is being worked manually rather than by computer, we care about efficiency, and VAM is more efficient. The NW-corner method ignores route transportation costs, but VAM considers them and thereby zeroes in on the solution more quickly. VAM will not always yield an optimal initial solution, but generally it reduces the required number of iterations—using the stepping-stone method, for example—to reach optimality.

As with the NW-corner method, we first determine whether or not the problem is balanced and add a dummy source or destination if required. The remaining steps of the VAM are:

1. For each row and each column, calculate a penalty number. This number is the difference between the two *cheapest* routes available in the row or column and is the minimum "penalty" that one must pay for not using the cheapest available transportation route in that row or column. Transportation route unit costs are used to make this determination. If there are not at least two available routes, a penalty number may not be calculated; a dash (-) indicates this. If two routes (or cells) have the same "cheapest" cost, use a zero for the penalty number. There will be $(S + D)$ values, including any dashes, in each set of penalty numbers.

2. Select the largest penalty number from the set; the number indicates where maximum cost savings are available. This largest penalty number could be either a row penalty or a column penalty.

3. Enter the row or column associated with the largest penalty number, and identify the cheapest transportation route (cell) in that row or column.

4. Determine the maximum amount that can be shipped in the route identified in step 3 by comparing available (row) capacity with remaining (column) demand. The smaller of these two numbers is the maximum amount that can be shipped in the selected route; assign that amount to the route. This assignment will either satisfy demand in a column or allocate capacity for a row, making it impossible to calculate further penalties for the column or row.

5. Return to step 1; that is, the process repeats until no further penalties can be calculated for any row or column.

6. When no further penalties can be calculated, use the rim (boundary) constraints to make final cell assignments.

7. Test the solution for optimality. If not optimal, improve the solution by using, for example, the stepping-stone method.

The VAM procedure is illustrated in Example S18–2.

EXAMPLE S18–2 VOGEL'S APPROXIMATION METHOD (VAM)

In Figure S18–3, a simple transportation problem, demand amounts are shown above the matrix and capacities at the left, so that penalty numbers may extend to the right and below the figure. Shipment assignments are already shown in Figure S18–3; rationale is provided in the following solution, which employs the steps identified earlier:

1. The first set of penalty numbers—3 for column 1, 5 for column 2, 2 for row 1, and 4 for row 2—are obtained by computing the differences in the costs associated with the two cells in each row and column. Penalty numbers are shown below and to the right of the solution matrix.

FIGURE S18–3
VAM Example

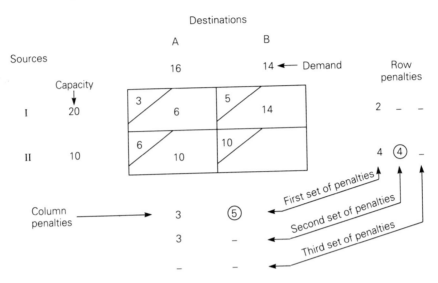

2. The largest penalty number in the first set is 5, which comes from column 2.

3. Enter column 2 and identify the cheapest route. It is the route from source I to destination B.

4. By comparing the 20 units available from source I with the 14 units demanded by destination B, we find the smaller to be 14, which is the maximum amount that may be shipped in that route. After assigning 14 units to that route, we see that all of destination B's demand is satisfied. The source-II-to-destination-B route must be empty, making further penalties in column 2 impossible to calculate. Further, since there are no longer at least two *available* routes in row 1—one of the two having just been used—we cannot calculate penalties for row 1 either. Although we see (by inspection in this simple problem) that the source-I-to-destination-A route must be used, there is no remaining penalty associated with row 1.

5. Calculate a second set of penalties using the procedure described in step 1. They consist of a 3 for column 1, a dash (no penalty can be calculated) for column 2, a dash for row 1, and a 4 for row 2.

6. The 4 associated with row 2 is the largest penalty number in the second set.

7. Enter row 2 and locate the cheapest cell: from source II to destination A.

8. The maximum that can be shipped from source II to destination A is 10 units. (Remember: Compare available source capacity with remaining destination demand, and select the smaller.) Assign 10 units to this cell.

9. After assigning 10 units to the source II-to-destination-A route, we find that no further penalties can be calculated.

10. Rim constraints require a final assignment of 6 units in the route from source I to destination A.

11. Calculate an improvement index for the one empty cell (II-B) to test the solution for optimality using the stepping-stone method.

$$\text{II-B} \rightarrow \text{II-A} \rightarrow \text{I-A} \rightarrow \text{I-B}$$
$$+10 \quad -6 \quad +3 \quad -5 = \$ + 2$$

The positive improvement index indicates that the solution is optimal.

CHAPTER 19

A Look Ahead

"Is it going to rain tomorrow? Should I carry an umbrella?"

"Hm, I wonder what's going to happen in the job market in my specialty."

"When will solar energy be in widespread use?"

"What's for dinner, Mom?"

Regardless of nationality, occupation, or age, humans share a desire to somehow get a jump on tomorrow, or an hour from now—to find out what's going to happen. We want to know what lies ahead. The future fascinates us.

LIMITING FATE

The future also can be a pain. The prudent person—certainly the competent operations manager—works to reduce the pain by limiting the bad things that might happen in the future. Preparation and projection are two of the keys.

Each chapter (until this one) has been introduced with our functional model of operations—the one with the time axis going down the center. In Chapter 2 we noted that things in the present (the right side on the time axis) go smoother when early and midrange planning (the left side and the middle, respectively) are done well. In other words, good preparation helps us gain control and predictability. When preparation is lacking, *anything* could happen, especially anything *bad*.

Preparation comes in many forms, such as having flexible resources, keeping off-line buffer stock, and projecting past demand patterns. Or, simply, *looking around*.

Looking Ahead by Looking Around

Want to know what your firm ought to do in the future? Look around for the companies that are leaders today; they're doing it now. Find out where those firms are going; that's where the rest of the pack will be heading tomorrow. Look around for the offices with cross-trained employees who spend time in quality improvement teams; that's where tomorrow's offices are heading. Seek out the manufacturers with quick machine setups, short throughput times, and low in-process inventories. Look around for the suppliers of high and increasing quality, low and decreasing costs, and excellent service. Look around for the businesses with a loyal and growing base of clients.

Does all this sound like a lazy consultant's advice? It isn't. Today's leading companies have come off years of stagnation and are taking giant steps toward **world-class excellence**. They are resisting the satisfaction that comes with goal attainment, because world-class performance benchmarks are on a sharp incline. Just to stay even, they realize the need for buying into the notion of never-ending improvement. To them, world-class operations means ever better service to customers. Chapter 1 offered 17 principles for doing this, and the other chapters filled in with the necessary methods and concepts.

Preparing for the future by looking around wouldn't have worked well in earlier times—at least not in operations management. Innovative, leading-edge firms were probably marketing-driven, or maybe R&D-driven, but not OM-driven, because OM was in a state of little change and few improvements.

We've seen some of the evidence of remarkable OM achievements in companies that are on the world-class express. The chapter-ending case study, "Becoming World Class at K2 Corporation," demonstrates how quickly the results pour in once a firm sets its mind to getting on that express; the case also raises a few what-next, looking-ahead issues.

In addition, we've seen how OM affects and is affected by changes elsewhere in the firm: Design is out of isolation and teaming up with operations; management accounting's new thrust is operating-level controls on causes of cost; and supplier-designer-operations-marketing teams are becoming commonplace. Indeed, one distinguishing feature of world-class companies is that organizational units are teaming up, recognizing one another as customers, and affording the same courtesy to fellow internal customers as they do the traditional external ones.

What's Important: Changing Viewpoints

The world-class bandwagon doesn't just roll down Main Street or traverse Interstate 80—it jumps oceans.

There is a lag effect. Businesses in one country (Japan) raised performance levels and sent their products across the Pacific, where they created havoc for a while in the United States. The United States and Canada caught on after a few years and worked the same magic. Western Europeans, who take plenty of justifiable pride in their business expertise, peeked across the Atlantic and said, "Whoa! Japan's miracle must not be cultural. Even the North Americans are doing it."

The lag effect is starkly illustrated in Figure 19–1, which shows some results of a three-continent survey called the *Manufacturing Futures Project*. The study was carried out by research teams in Boston University; INSEAD, Fountainebleau, France (involving 12 European countries); and Waseda University, Tokyo, Japan.

Note the close similarity of the U.S. and Japanese lists: Eight of the ten items are on both lists. Note also the dissimilarity of the European list: Six of its items don't appear at all on the U.S. and Japanese lists. Further, four of those six are cost items, reflecting, we believe, the way that North American companies *used to* think. Cost was everything; little thought was given to such customer cares as quick response (manufacturing and supplier lead time) and flexibility (setup time and cross-training).

We view these lists of performance measures as a snapshot in time: the year of the survey is 1987. Since we are in an era of rapid change and continual improvement, no doubt the three lists would be quite different today. We think, for example, that the European list today would be much like the U.S. and Japanese lists were in 1987.

FIGURE 19–1

Most Important Measures of Performance in U.S., Japanese, and European Manufacturing Companies (rank-ordered)

United States	*Japan*	*Europe*
1. Incoming quality	Manufacturing lead time	Outgoing quality
2. Inventory accuracy	Direct labor productivity	Unit manufacturing cost
3. Direct labor productivity	In-process inventory turnover	Material cost
4. Manufacturing lead time	Incoming quality	Overhead cost
5. Supplier lead time	Supplier lead time	On-time deliveries
6. Setup time	Indirect labor productivity	Incoming quality
7. In-process inventory turnover	Material yield	Direct labor productivity
8. Material yield	Finished goods inventory turnover	Material yield
9. Outgoing quality	Inventory accuracy	Unit labor cost
10. Indirect labor productivity	Absenteeism	Forecast accuracy

Source: Adapted from Jeffrey G. Miller et al., "Closing the Competitive Gap—The International Report of the Manufacturing Futures Project" (Boston: Boston University Manufacturing Round Table, 1988).

We can only guess what the same kind of a survey would show for service-sector firms. Today, the business press is filled with stories about service firms newly caught up in time-based competition, customer commitment, quality, and employee involvement.[1] It seems as though service firms are not far behind manufacturers in emphasizing the "right" things.

HOT TOPICS FOR THE 1990s AND BEYOND

We have seen that the notion of pleasing customers grew in importance in operations management in the 1980s. That surely will continue. But what are the other, or related, looming hot topics for the current decade and beyond? It's important to try to find out, and thus be prepared.

There is no shortage of people willing to offer general predictions and comment on what needs to be done to correct the world's ills. We need only to sift through the predictions and sort out the effects on operations management.

Our own rather random search identifies seven hot topics: flexibility and responsiveness, training, employee rights, "right-sizing," company statesman-

---

[1]See, for example, Leonard L. Berry, David R. Bennett, and Carter W. Brown, *Service Quality: A Profit Strategy for Financial Institutions* (Homewood, Ill. : Dow Jones-Irwin, 1989); Jaclyn Fierman, "Fidelity's Secret: Faithful Service," *Fortune*, May 7, 1990, pp. 86–92; and Bill Saporito, "Retailing's Winners & Losers," *Fortune*, December 18, 1989, pp. 69–80.

ship, environmentalism, and internationalism. While each of the seven is a broad business and societal issue, our discussion focuses on OM impacts.

Flexibility/Responsiveness

Flexibility is a basic customer want—so identified in Chapter 1. We've given some emphasis to the topic in other chapters—for example, Chapter 3 had a section on quick setup and several chapters discussed reducing lead time.

Besides being a basic want, flexibility is, in some experts' opinions, the next global competitive battleground. For example, several publications coming out of Boston University's Manufacturing Futures Project express that belief.[2] Dixon, Nanni, and Vollmann, of the Boston University team, define the battleground in eight dimensions under four headings, as shown in Figure 19–2.[3] The four general categories associated with flexibility are quality, products, service, and cost.

Regarding the first category, the report says that firms need to be flexible on

FIGURE 19–2

A Defintion of Manufacturing Flexibility Grounded in Terms of Competitive Advantage

Quality-Associated Flexibility Dimensions

Material: Ability to accommodate variation in the quality of purchased materials.

Output: Ability to make products with different quality requirements.

Product-Associated Flexibility Dimensions

New Product: Ability to introduce new products.

Modification: Ability to modify existing products.

Service-Associated Flexibility Dimensions

Delivery: Ability to change the current production and/or delivery schedule to accommodate unanticipated needs.

Volume: Ability to vary aggregate production volume from period to period.

Mix: Ability to manufacture a variety of products within a fixed period without major modification of existing facilities.

Cost-Associated Flexibility Factors

Factor: Ability to modify the mix of resources (materials, labor, and capital) used in the production processes.

Source: J. Robb Dixon, Alfred J. Nanni, and Thomes E. Vollmann, *The New Performance Challenge: Measuring Operations for World-Class Competition* (Homewood, Ill.: Dow-Jones-Irwin, 1990), p. 152 (HF5549.5.P35D59). Used with permission.

---

[2]An early report on that theme is found in Arnaud De Meyer, Jinichiro Nakane, Jeffrey G. Miller, and Kasra Ferdows, "Flexibility: The Next Competitive Battle," *Manufacturing Roundtable Research Report Series* (Boston: Boston University School of Management, February 1987).

[3]J. Robb Dixon, Alfred J. Nanni, and Thomas E. Vollmann, *The New Performance Challenge: Measuring Operations for World-Class Competition* (Homewood, Ill: Dow Jones-Irwin, 1990) (HF5549.5.P35D59).

quality: what goes in and what comes out. That does not conflict with the goal of continual quality improvement; rather, it is saying we should find uses even for lower-quality materials and serve markets with varying quality for varying tastes (and pocketbooks).

According to the table's developers, each flexibility factor is strategically essential. In other words, it's not enough to have the right concepts and techniques for flexible introduction of new products or modification of old ones (we presented some in Chapter 3). The need for that flexibility must be seen strategically in order to move the firm to use the techniques.

Training, Training, Training

The many firms that already are achieving some world-class results in operations could not have done so without a strong commitment to training. Operations managers, experts, and line employees have to learn about statistical process control, quick changeover, and total preventive maintenance concepts; otherwise, there's no way that SPC, quick setup, and total preventive maintenance will ever get started. (So it is with all of the other OM tools for moving in the world-class direction.)

But training cannot be a one-time shot. On October 3, 1989, Robert W. Galvin, chairman of Motorola Corporation, addressed the 5th National Quality Forum in New York City. In describing Motorola's emphasis on *continual* training, Galvin suggested that executives plan to work for ten months a year, spend one month in training programs, and enjoy one month on vacation. Business demands, he continued, might cut into vacation time but shouldn't be allowed to cut into training.[4]

Motorola backs up that kind of talk with money and time: It devotes a hefty 2.8 percent of its payroll to employee training.[5] Motorola is also one of a small but growing number of large firms to have established impressive new training centers. Motorola's is called the *Manufacturing Management Institute*; Honeywell, Inc., has a *Quality College*; and Square D Corporation has a 10-campus *Vision College* dedicated to customer service, quality as a way of life, and personal accountability.[6]

Until fairly recently, these companies, like most others in North America, spent very little on managerial training—and virtually nothing on first-line employee training. The high visibility given to these new commitments to training in the most respected firms is perhaps the best way to awaken others. Companies could get by with little training in the past, simply because there wasn't much new to be learned. That, of course, is no longer the case, especially in operations management.

Read on. The next hot topic also is training-related.

---

[4]Galvin's speech, along with others presented at the Forum, are available on videotape from the American Society for Quality Control, 310 West Wisconsin Ave., Milwaukee, Wisconsin 53203.
[5]Susan Dentzer, "The Maypo Culture," *Business Month*, November 1989, pp. 26–34.
[6]Barbara Dutton, "An Interview with Jerre L. Stead," *Manufacturing Systems*, April 1990, pp. 36–43.

Employee Rights

"If they fire me, I'll sue!" In the more litigation-happy parts of North America, that kind of statement defines the new pugnacious attitude of some employees, an attitude encouraged by certain court decisions.

Employee rights in the past were basically civil rights: no discrimination on the basis of sex, color, age, or religious preference. The expanded view goes something like this: When an employee has invested part of his or her life in an employer, it obligates the employer to treat the employee like an investor.

Without getting any more deeply into the related arguments, let's see what this shift in employee rights means to operations management. We believe that world-class OM concepts help protect the "employee-investor" and at the same time help the firm stay on the continual improvement course.

The "low-class" firm always has candidates that seem to deserve firing. But the real reasons for this are poor employee-hiring practices, company instability (shifts into totally different kinds of business that require different human skills), and failure to train and develop people's many talents. Rarely is it really a "bad employee" problem.

The world-class firm continually trains its people, develops their talents, and provides a high degree of stability and security. The security is based on the financial health of working for a competitive employer who knows how to attract and keep loyal customers. For the employee, it is not so much job security as work-life security. Jobs change along with new products and technologies; continual training and retraining protect past company investments in the employee. Thus, the employer hates to lose any employee.

Right-Sizing

The problem of company instability became acute in the 1980s. Some of it—personnel cuts and divestitures of what were referred to as *non-performing assets*—was necessary. Some were survival measures, and were directly attacking organizational waste in the form of nonvalue-adding activities. Sometimes the aims were to achieve a clearer company and work-unit focus, and to streamline operations in order to enhance quality, cut throughput times, and improve customer service. Those are themes emphasized throughout this book.

At other times the cost cutting was aimed at improving the fortunes of certain investors, but at the expense of destroying some of the enterprise and leaving the remainder with inadequate resources. Rampant downsizing has too often been ruinous.

Will troubled firms be able to do any better in the 1990s? Perhaps so, if they follow a more even-handed *right-sizing* approach. Explained in Figure 19–3, right-sizing's "rules" are aimed at getting rid of waste without suffering severe losses. The rules call for eliminating nonvalue-adding activities, putting quality first, questioning everything, teaming up, tapping people's common sense in the cause of simplification, communicating goals and aims, and retraining people

FIGURE 19–3

Six Rules for Right-Sizing

1. *Cut unnecessary work.* Eliminate nonvalue-adding activities. Cut out procedures, reviews, reports, and approvals that don't directly advance operations.
2. *Put quality first.* We've addressed this point throughout the book. Basically, doing it right the first time *does* reduce workloads. Customers like it that way, too.
3. *Bust your paradigms.* Question long-held assumptions about why things are done as they are. Work teams accomplish this much more effectively than individuals working alone. The objective (and the result) is, again, less activity waste.
4. *Empower people.* The most vital resource for work simplification ideas must be tapped. For managers, the key words are *decentralize* and *delegate.* For employees, accept more responsibility for job decision making.
5. *Communicate.* "Improve your communications" is perhaps the most frequently dispensed advice in the history of business consulting (a characteristic that makes it no less important). People need to know what the aims are. Fewer "junk" reports certainly help emphasize the important ones that remain.
6. *Take care of the survivors.* Even if people complain about bureaucracy and paper-shufflers, personnel cuts *are* demoralizing. Often, survivors need retraining.

Source: Ronald Henkoff, "Cost Cutting: How to Do It Right," *Fortune,* April 9, 1990, pp. 40–49.

who survive the staff reductions. Most of these items are familiar, having been emphasized in this book.

One company that seems already to be putting right-sizing to work is H. J. Heinz. The accompanying box, taken intact from a feature story in *Fortune,* reviews how the change in thinking came about at Heinz.

Reducing the Bile Factor at Heinz

Anthony J. F. O'Reilly, chief executive of Heinz since 1979, realizes that a company, much like a plastic bottle of ketchup, can be squeezed only so much. Even at Heinz, one of industry's most successful cost cutters, downsizing has its limits.

In the eighties, O'Reilly closed factories, laid off workers, and revved up production lines with enviable results. Gross profit margins swelled from 33% to 39% of sales, and Heinz posted average earnings increases of 15% per year in a decade when the processed-food industry was bedeviled by sluggish growth, merciless competition, and bitter takeover battles.

But O'Reilly now realizes that his sharp pencil, while financially successful, alienated workers, interfered with the quality of the products, and left the company still wasting millions of dollars a year on unnecessary work. His solution: Stop squeezing and start changing. Concentrate on quality, not cost.

Under the company's total quality management (TQM) effort, introduced two years ago, teams of workers are re-examining virtually everything Heinz does—from the way it packages French fries to the way it conducts market research. O'Reilly figures that TQM can save the company $250 million over the next three years, mostly by eliminating waste and rework.

The Dublin-born O'Reilly, 53, is a former star rugby player who owns six provincial newspapers in England, an outdoor advertising agency in France, and a recently acquired stake in Waterford Wedgewood, the crystal and china maker. He spoke about Heinz's cost and quality control with *Fortune's* Ronald Henkoff:

- *The cost-cutting imperative.* We feel the spear of the marketplace in our back. We are extremely conscious of the vulnerability of even our greatest brands. All it takes is a modest shortfall in volume or a modest hiccup in cost control and we become exposed to earnings loss very quickly. We are in a business where, in most sectors, the volume increase is 1% per year. That's pretty chilling.

- *The emphasis on quality.* We want to secure our cost reductions from something we never concentrated on before—the price of nonconformance. That is, the need to get things right the first time. So we've begun to question our entire system, our entire manufacturing processes right across the spectrum. The thing I like about TQM is that it's more Socratic than surgical.

- *The removal of waste.* There is an enormous amount of redundancy in every corporation. For example, we've reduced from five to one the number of market research services we use. Market research is an area of exotica, where everyone has a set of numbers that flatters his particular perceptions. We just said: One bible is called for in this case.

- *The focus on service.* We've realized that Weight Watchers, which we own, is not based on cost structures. It's based on service satisfaction. That's an enormous shift for us. When people decide to come to a Weight Watchers class, cost is not their primary concern. The question is how can we, for example, harness the power of the computer to provide them with a complete statement of their goals, their weight loss, and their caloric intake over the last week?

- *The bile factor.* Over the years the relentless pressure of cost cutting had created within Heinz a mounting feeling of bile. The notion that when people on high exhort you to cut costs, they're talking about cutting your costs, not theirs, bred distaste. There was a ever-increasing feeling of hostility among the employees. Fewer people do more work. Layoffs create a degree of insecurity because workers wonder if 50 people were cut last year and 100 this year, how many will go next year?

- *The empowering of workers.* Working in teams creates a great sense of interdependence. Jobs are now substantially more sophisticated, interesting, and exciting. Instead of staring mindlessly at a moving belt of peas or carrots or bottles or whatever, workers are now able, for example, to work the computerized photo-imaging machinery that controls the labeling line.

The advent of TQM has greatly elevated the dignity of the worker at Heinz. In the past there was very little consultation with employees. That led to a natural sense of human irritation, a sense that "at least they could have bloody well asked me about that. After all, I've done this particular job for 20 years."

■ *The future.* If we are going to make this company grow to match the expectations of the stock market—that is, 10% to 12% growth a year—we have to do it by doing better what we do best. Henry J. Heinz, our founder, had a marvelous phrase that I think exactly describes TQM: "doing common things uncommonly well." One hundred twenty years later, I couldn't put it any better myself.

Company Statesmanship

The public has plenty of cause for accusing business leaders of sacking and pillaging the economic landscape. But perhaps the more statesmanlike attitude of Heinz's CEO reflects a general shift in approach. It could be that our business executives are rediscovering that preserving and building existing capacity, brand names, customers, and employee talents is the sure way to create wealth. The firm that operates under such thinking sees its interests as coinciding well with those of society.

Heinz is by no means alone in looking more statesmanlike: Baldrige Quality Award winners Motorola and Milliken have "gone public" with aggressive quality campaigns. In a dramatic gesture, Motorola announced that all of its U. S. suppliers who are eligible for the Baldrige prize would be required to seek it. As many as 364 suppliers told Motorola they would apply in 1990; others said they would submit plans for entering the competition in a later year.[7] The few suppliers that are refusing will no longer be doing business with Motorola.

Milliken and Company, which is privately held, has, for several years, been coaxing and cajoling its suppliers, freight haulers, customers—and anyone else who will listen—to actively join the quality crusade. Just one of several ways Milliken does this is by sponsoring periodic "sharing rallies." They usually are two- or three-day events in which high-level executives from other companies come to Milliken to share plans, anecdotes, and accomplishments. The same executives return the next year to tell how well they followed through on their plans, and what comes next.

One of this text's authors was an invited speaker for one such rally, which was sponsored by Milliken's Decorative Fabrics Business Unit. Other invited participants—mainly CEOs and presidents—were from several dozen key customers in furniture manufacturing and a few dozen of their customers in furniture retailing. Over the three days, speakers from one company after another stepped to the rostrum and spilled out competitive secrets to blood rivals in the audience. The stories had to do with commitments to quality, next-process-as-

---

[7]Michael A. Verespoj, "An Ultimatum for Suppliers," *Industry Week*, February 19, 1990, pp. 23–26.

customer, quick response, employee training and problem-solving, supplier partnerships, dedicated freight carriers, visual "signboard" controls in the workplace, and related topics.

Environmentalism

The public can only cheer about these moves toward quality by leading companies. We all cheer some more when business leaders get serious about protecting the environment.

Environmentalism has generally been way down the list at strategy-making time in North American companies; that's because it wasn't on the shopping lists of many consumers. Three-Mile Island, Love Canal, Chernobyl, Bopal, and Prince William Sound have jolted enough of us that environmentalists may become the majority rather than a fringe movement in the 1990s and beyond.

Further, under *glasnost* and its rippling effects, the citizens of Eastern Europe—and the world—learned the truth about ruined lakes, rivers, forests, land, and air—outside and inside industrial facilities, too. Feelings of outrage caused Eastern and Western Europeans—probably the majority of them—to quickly line up to pledge allegiance to the "greens," which is the name of a worldwide grassroots environmental movement (and also, in some countries, a political group).

Insulated North Americans are a bit behind. Nevertheless, recycling now has a strong foothold, new waste management companies have popped up like tulips in the spring, and industry is scrambling.

Edgar Woolard, Jr., chairman of E.I. du Pont de Nemours & Company, sees the environmental issue as "a knife with two edges. . . . One edge is vulnerability, and one edge is opportunity."[8] Du Pont is familiar with the vulnerability edge, for nearly all of its products—chemicals, oils, plastics, coal, and fibers—face some threat from environmentalists. On the opportunity side, Du Pont has found that by taking care of its own environmental problems, it has become expert at dealing with such concerns, and that expertise is very much in demand around the world. In short, there's money to be made in helping others establish and maintain clean operations. Mr. Woolard predicts that Du Pont's environmentally sound products coupled with its environmental protection services could account for up to $8 billion of its annual revenues by 1995.

McDonalds, 3M, Procter & Gamble, Amoco, Apple, and Pacific Gas & Electric are among other companies that have recently embarked on collaborative efforts with environmentalist groups—former adversaries in many cases—covering a variety of product and process improvements. In late 1989, an *ad hoc* group of institutional investors controlling some $150 billion of assets asked companies to subscribe to a set of guidelines referred to as the Valdez Principles, named after Exxon's 1989 Alaskan oil spill. Basically, companies were asked to use resources wisely, cut waste from operations, market safe products, and take

---

[8]Ruth Simon, "Dirty Chemicals In, Clean Water Out," *Forbes*, March 19, 1990, pp. 56–60.

responsibility for past harm.[9] In 1990, this and similar environmental proposals were up for a vote at many corporate annual meetings.

To the employee, all this environmental ferment means changes in habits and mindsets. Managers and work teams will have to develop a keen awareness of customers' new concerns: The customer now wants environmental protection, not just good products, services, and prices. Many of the customers are internal—next process—and they are likely to want an environmentally safe and healthy environment in their workplaces, as well as in their communities.

A main OM effect of these trends is that environmental issues will be prominent on the agendas of quality improvement teams, quality circles, and other such problem-solving groups. Progress in environmental improvement will be tracked on large wall charts. Management will get it from both sides: outside customers and inside customers.

Internationalism and Global Competition

The strong new global concern about the environment tends to support Professor Theodore Levitt, author of a classic 1983 article, "The Globalization of Markets."[10] Levitt's point that customers around the world want the same things has been both acclaimed and ridiculed. Those who ridicule it say instead that markets are becoming more localized, fractionated, and diverse. If so, business and industry will have to spend most of its energy on quick-change flexibility, and little of it on standardization and volume operations.

It now seems clear that political, trade, and economic alliances among nations—especially "Europe 1992"—are creating huge new mass markets. To the extent that those markets demand the same thing—the Levitt view—companies will be able to put together massive dedicated facilities that drive down costs and drive up quality, mostly following classical economy-of-scale concepts. We say "mostly," because there is a newly important variable to factor in: Life cycles for goods and services are being squeezed down to where both high-volume and niche-product providers must continually and quickly bring out new products and sign off on old ones. Old notions about facility designs—monumental machines and fixed-cubicle offices—fall by the wayside.

It seems appropriate to be ending this book with remarks about global impacts on operations management. The little picture—what every employee can do to meet the needs of the next process—gets bigger and bigger as the chains of customers lengthen. Customer-driven OM extends vertically to encompass many linked up supplier-customer pairs, often—indeed, increasingly—crossing country borders and spanning oceans. Final users may be scattered around the globe. But they still have the same basic wants: better quality, lower costs/prices, shorter

---

[9]David Kirkpatrick, "Environmentalism: The New Crusade," *Fortune*, February 12, 1990, pp. 44–55.
[10]Theodore Levitt, "The Globalization of Markets," *Harvard Business Review*, May–June 1983, pp. 92-102.

lead times, greater flexibility, less variability, and better service. Operations management is in the thick of providing all of these.

SUMMARY

Humans have a fascination with the future. We exhibit a natural curiosity about things yet to come. For businesses, attempts to predict, prepare, and project are driven by the desire to be more competitive by offering more responsive service to customers.

There are now enough examples of world-class operations that one can gain some insight as to what the future holds by looking around at what the leading companies are doing today. In world-class firms, OM is on a course of continual improvement—moving toward even more streamlined operations, greater internal teamwork, linkages with suppliers, elimination of waste, and above all, better service to customers—internally as well as externally.

Operations managers ought to be deeply involved in meeting challenges of the future. Gone are the days when the production or operations function could remain buried within a company, avoiding contact with customers, suppliers, and other functional areas of the organization.

The broadened range of continual improvement concepts must be accompanied by altered measures of performance. Surveys taken in 1987 of manufacturers in Japan, the United States, and Europe are revealing. U.S. firms listed nearly the same top-ten important measures as Japan—a highly customer-oriented list. Europe's top ten were more conventional, dealing mostly with internal costs and problems. As the new OM knowledge and thinking spreads, and as world competition forces change, it seems likely that companies everywhere will evolve to a more customer-oriented set of beliefs about what performances are important.

Besides pleasing customers, other "hot topics" need to be threaded into OM planning. Some observers feel that one of the emerging hot topics—possibly the next major weapon of global competition—is flexibility, which has quality, product, service, and cost dimensions. Flexibility-enhancing techniques such as quick setup are fine, but they won't be used to the fullest until business leaders see the strategic importance of driving for increased flexibility.

To get the necessary human commitment to improve, there is growing awareness of the need to step up the training effort. Several leading companies have established training institutes aimed at training all employees (usually for several days a year) for their entire work lives.

Employee rights, including the right to a job, is another hot topic. World-class companies invest enough in training and employee development that they rarely feel the desire to fire anyone, and the stabilizing effect of world-class OM concepts helps prevent losses of business and jobs.

The business instability of the 1980s, in contrast, caused many firms to get into a cost-cutting, downsizing spiral. Unfortunately, too many companies rid themselves of competitively essential resources. A new term for the 1990s is *right-sizing*, the aims of which include elimination of *causes* of costs along with the costs themselves. It also puts premiums on quality, changing ways of thinking, empowering people, better communications, and concern for survivors of company lay-offs. Companies like Heinz are pleased with results of right-sizing efforts and plan to continue them.

A related hot topic is company statesmanship. Examples include using OM-driven world-class concepts to provide security to employees and other stakeholders (avoiding rampant downsizing) and taking the quality message public, as Motorola and Milliken—Baldrige Quality Award winners—have done so dramatically.

Statesmanlike companies also will want to pay attention to environmental protection, which must include inside health and safety as well as making the external environment clean and safe. This is in companies' interests, because their internal and external customers, shocked by major industrial accidents as well as by progressive deterioration of environments in Eastern Europe, are increasingly demanding it. Plenty of companies (Du Pont, for example) see business opportunities in developing goods and services that help clean and preserve the environment.

Global environmentalism is but one aspect of global competition, which is the final hot topic that we consider. New customers—and new competitors—are changing the way the world does business. Global marketing of standard, high-quality goods and services seems realistic to some, especially considering the new mass markets that arise as trade barriers disappear. Other people argue that markets are becoming more differentiated. Regardless of that debate, OM offers tools and techniques for competitively responding: linking up of pairs of suppliers and customers regardless of where they are in the world, responsiveness to model-mix changes, and equipment and methods that adapt well to frequent changes in the product/service line.

KEY WORD

World-class excellence

REFERENCES

Books

Dertouzos, Michael L., Richard K. Lester, and Robert M. Solow. *Made in America: Regaining the Productive Edge.* Cambridge, Mass.: The MIT Press, 1989 (HC110.152M34).

Dixon, J. Robb, Alfred J. Nanni, and Thomas E. Vollmann. *The New Performance Challenge: Measuring Operations for World-Class Competition.* Homewood, Ill.: Richard D. Irwin, Inc., 1990 (HF5549.5.P35D59).

Naisbitt, John, and Patricia Aburdene. *Megatrends 2000: Ten New Directions for the 1990s.* New York: Wm. Morrow & Co., 1990 (HN59.2.N343).

Schonberger, Richard J. *Building a Chain of Customers: Linking Business Functions to Create the World-Class Company.* New York: The Free Press, 1990 (HD58.9.S36).

Shetty, Y. K., and Vernon M. Buehler, Eds. *Competing Through Productivity and Quality.* Cambridge, Mass.: Productivity Press, 1988 (HC110.I52C655).

Periodicals

Looking to the future is a popular activity. Many reputable business, economic, and scientific periodicals publish articles on the subject.

REVIEW QUESTIONS

1. How does flexibility decrease the need to rely on forecasting?
2. What is meant by the advice to look ahead by looking around?
3. How can a company that has achieved world-class excellence be identified?
4. Why should operations managers communicate with suppliers? With customers?
5. How similar—or different—are European, Japanese, and North American firms in their understanding of world-class excellence?
6. What dimensions might be included in a multifaceted view of flexibility? What operations management concepts or techniques support all dimensions of flexibility?
7. How is industrial training likely to change in the years to come?
8. What does the emerging "hot topic" of employee rights mean for the operations manager?
9. What is "right-sizing?" What are the rules for applying right-sizing?
10. What are the key points in Heinz's right-sizing program?
11. Assuming everything is kept legal, how might normal operations damage a company's reputation?
12. Explain how company statesmanship can coincide with OM's agenda for world-class excellence.
13. Why should operations managers take on more responsibility for a clean and safe environment?
14. How can environmental concern become a business and OM opportunity?
15. What might operations managers do to position themselves to deal with global markets or differentiated markets?

| CASE STUDY | **BECOMING WORLD CLASS AT K2 CORPORATION*** |

Scott Doss had just described the rapid progress he and his fellow maintenance technicians had made over the last three months in lowering setup times on the mold-presses used in forming ski bottoms. He went on to speculate on further improvements:

> Everyone on the team is looking ahead to the day when we can have a mold prestaged, maybe with removable plates—whatever—with molds already on; slide this one out and slide the next one in that's already been plugged in, preheated and ready to go. What we've concentrated on so far are things where we don't have to remove the bolts—where we just change the profile. . . . In the future basically anything is possible.

With faster mold changeovers, schedulers were starting to plan smaller lots that could be run more often with better response to the customer. Lot sizes on the presses had been weeks' or months' worth in the past, but Doss expressed the hope that "we get, in the next couple of years, to the point where we could change day to day if we had to."

Doss's employer is K2 Corporation, a manufacturer of high-quality snow skis. K2, which has been in the ski-manufacturing business for nearly three decades, became a subsidiary of Anthony Industries Co. in 1986. K2's main plant and headquarters is located on Vashon Island, across Puget Sound from Seattle. K2's current annual sales volume is $60 million, which is about 10 percent of the world market for skis. Total company employment is 500 people.

SPOTLIGHT ON MANUFACTURING

In the fall of 1987, K2 hired consultant Peter Scontrino to study K2's compensation plan for hourly employees. At that time, about 35 percent of the company's hourly workers were paid on a piece-based incentive system. Mr. Scontrino learned that K2 managers favored extending that plan to cover more job classifications. Scontrino, however, believed that the company should shelve the incentive system and move toward a gain-sharing plan. He recommended Richard J. Schonberger's book, *World Class Manufacturing*, as background reading for K2 managers.

Before long the K2 management team had developed plans for its own "world-class manufacturing" system, which included gain-sharing, along with just-in-time production, total quality control, employee involvement, and total preventive maintenance. Implementation of the plan was swift, including the following improvements by late summer 1988:

- The former inventory of plastic top-edge strips was about 150,000 pieces—a 2½ weeks' supply. Still, with 22 different size/color combina-

---
*This case is based on research conducted by Richard J. Schonberger in August 1988.

tions, it was not uncommon to be out of one that was needed. Now the inventory is about 20,000 and there are no stockouts. The machine operator runs a kanban quantity of 300 strips only when a green card is in one of the 22 slots in a nearby rack; otherwise the slot holds a red card. Material control people insert the green or red kanbans each morning based on how much of each part is on hand in the mold-press room. The operator, who has duties elsewhere, runs the strip cutter only when green cards are present. (The operator had to quit producing for six weeks while the large inventory was being whittled down.)

- The steel-edge crew (which bends and welds "cracked" steel to metal tail protectors to form a one-piece steel-edge assembly) has reduced its flow time from four days to six hours, its lot size from 450 to 150 pieces, and its inventory from 50 carts (20,000 pieces) to a maximum of 11 carts. The maximum is controlled by 11 kanban squares among the machines on the floor. Each operator has line-stop authority. Implementation was done in one day, but it took almost a week to work the steel inventory down by halting receipts from the local supplier (who provides the material already punched.)

- Setup time on mold-presses making K2's foam-core type of ski bottom has been reduced from 30 minutes to as little as 5 minutes.

- Setup time on mold-presses for K2's premier braided-fiber type of ski bottom has been reduced from two weeks to as little as ten hours at zero capital cost. The setup reduction effort included providing each operator with a set of the right tools; rewiring electrical panels; checking first skis at the bench instead of in the lab; using uniform, easy-to-adjust, shorter bolts (requiring fewer turns); installing setting rails; using air equipment with Allen socket heads; putting T-handles on Allen wrenches; using stacked shims; and painting each machine as it is converted. Ten of the 50 presses were converted during summer 1988, with the rest due for conversion by year's end.

- In rough-base finishing, molded ski bottoms go through seven wet-sanders and four grinders, which had been grouped into three separate work centers; now they are merged into a flow line operated by an 11-person team. Formerly 60 to 90 carts—three or four weeks' worth—of skis were crammed into the rough-finishing room. Now carts come direct from molding for nearly immediate processing (no work orders); the buffer stock is only about ten carts, or three to four hours' worth, so feedback to molding on quality problems is fast. See "before" and "after" photos in Figure 19-4.

- Lead time to produce a set of graphics (designs that go on the tops of the skis) has been cut from one week to one shift or less.

- Changeover time on the silk-screening lines (five of them) has been reduced from 25 minutes to as little as 5 minutes.

- The room housing the single large piece of equipment (designed in-house) that joins ski tops to bottoms formerly was fronted by a queue

FIGURE 19–4
Skis in Rough Base Finishing at K2 Corp.

A. Three to four weeks' worth of skis—before world-class manufacturing emphasis

B. Three to four hours' worth of skis—after world-class manufacturing emphasis

of about 150 carts; it is now more like 7 carts (a typical cart holds 150 skis).

- Skis formerly spent about three weeks in finishing; now they zip through in only one shift.

- Rework in finishing had been 50 to 60 percent; it is now down to about one-half of 1 percent. At the same time, attainable plant capacity has increased from under 2,000 good pairs per day to about 2,500 per day. The quality and capacity improvements occurred during the turmoil of hiring 100 new people and bringing them up to proper skill level.

- Inventory of the basic raw material, uniglass, has been reduced from $225,000 to $41,000.

- In 1986 there were some 300 carts (about 50,000 skis) on the floor; now it is perhaps 20 carts.

- In many parts of the plant work orders and completion reporting by bar-coding have been eliminated, along with sending material into stock and performing storekeeping on it. Jeff Bardsley, production and inventory control planner, states that he had been spending up to eight hours a day on the computer. "Now I'm out on the floor, and I can see what the real problems are." Lead times on some items were reduced from three weeks to four days.

- At Vashon for meetings in August 1988, K2's sales representatives from all over the world were enthused by what they saw in the factory. Some expressed the view that K2 is now the standard against which the best in the industry would have to be measured.

WHAT'S NEXT?

With such a string of impressive—and quick—accomplishments, a nagging notion in the back of some people's minds at K2 is what's next? And how do we keep up the enthusiasm and create a sustained work culture of continual improvement?

Discussion Questions

1. Is it reasonable for K2 people to expect much more improvement? Sustained improvement?

2. Outline a strategic plan for operations management at K2 for the next five years.

APPENDIX A

Areas under the Normal Curve

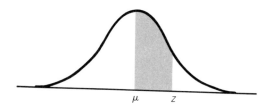

Example

The area between the mean (μ) and the point one standard deviation above the mean ($z = 1.00$) is 0.3413, or 34.13 percent of the total area under the curve. The area between $z = -1.00$ and $z = 1.00$ is $0.3413 + 0.3413 = 0.6826$.

TABLE A–1
Areas of Standard Normal Distribution

Z	0.00	0.01	0.02	0.03	0.04	0.05	0.06	0.07	0.08	0.09
0.0	0.0000	0.0040	0.0080	0.0120	0.0160	0.0199	0.0239	0.0279	0.0319	0.0359
0.1	0.0398	0.0438	0.0478	0.0517	0.0557	0.0596	0.0636	0.0675	0.0714	0.0753
0.2	0.0793	0.0832	0.0871	0.0910	0.0948	0.0987	0.1026	0.1064	0.1103	0.1141
0.3	0.1179	0.1217	0.1255	0.1293	0.1331	0.1368	0.1406	0.1443	0.1480	0.1517
0.4	0.1554	0.1591	0.1628	0.1664	0.1700	0.1736	0.1772	0.1808	0.1844	0.1879
0.5	0.1915	0.1950	0.1985	0.2019	0.2054	0.2088	0.2123	0.2157	0.2190	0.2224
0.6	0.2257	0.2291	0.2324	0.2357	0.2389	0.2422	0.2454	0.2486	0.2518	0.2549
0.7	0.2580	0.2612	0.2642	0.2673	0.2704	0.2734	0.2764	0.2794	0.2823	0.2852
0.8	0.2881	0.2910	0.2939	0.2967	0.2995	0.3023	0.3051	0.3078	0.3106	0.3133
0.9	0.3159	0.3186	0.3212	0.3238	0.3264	0.3289	0.3315	0.3340	0.3365	0.3389

(continued)

TABLE A–1
(*concluded*)

Z	0.00	0.01	0.02	0.03	0.04	0.05	0.06	0.07	0.08	0.09
1.0	0.3413	0.3438	0.3461	0.3485	0.3508	0.3531	0.3554	0.3577	0.3599	0.3621
1.1	0.3643	0.3665	0.3686	0.3708	0.3729	0.3749	0.3770	0.3790	0.3810	0.3830
1.2	0.3849	0.3869	0.3888	0.3907	0.3925	0.3944	0.3962	0.3980	0.3997	0.4015
1.3	0.4032	0.4049	0.4066	0.4082	0.4099	0.4115	0.4131	0.4147	0.4162	0.4177
1.4	0.4192	0.4207	0.4222	0.4236	0.4251	0.4265	0.4279	0.4292	0.4306	0.4319
1.5	0.4332	0.4345	0.4357	0.4370	0.4382	0.4394	0.4406	0.4418	0.4429	0.4441
1.6	0.4452	0.4463	0.4474	0.4484	0.4495	0.4505	0.4515	0.4525	0.4535	0.4545
1.7	0.4554	0.4564	0.4573	0.4582	0.4591	0.4599	0.4608	0.4616	0.4625	0.4633
1.8	0.4641	0.4649	0.4656	0.4664	0.4671	0.4678	0.4686	0.4693	0.4699	0.4706
1.9	0.4713	0.4719	0.4726	0.4732	0.4738	0.4744	0.4750	0.4756	0.4761	0.4767
2.0	0.4772	0.4778	0.4783	0.4788	0.4793	0.4798	0.4803	0.4808	0.4812	0.4817
2.1	0.4821	0.4826	0.4830	0.4834	0.4838	0.4842	0.4846	0.4850	0.4854	0.4857
2.2	0.4861	0.4864	0.4868	0.4871	0.4875	0.4878	0.4881	0.4884	0.4887	0.4890
2.3	0.4893	0.4896	0.4898	0.4901	0.4904	0.4906	0.4909	0.4911	0.4913	0.4916
2.4	0.4918	0.4920	0.4922	0.4925	0.4927	0.4929	0.4931	0.4932	0.4934	0.4936
2.5	0.4938	0.4940	0.4941	0.4943	0.4945	0.4946	0.4948	0.4949	0.4951	0.4952
2.6	0.4953	0.4955	0.4956	0.4957	0.4959	0.4960	0.4961	0.4962	0.4963	0.4964
2.7	0.4965	0.4966	0.4967	0.4968	0.4969	0.4970	0.4971	0.4972	0.4973	0.4974
2.8	0.4974	0.4975	0.4976	0.4977	0.4977	0.4978	0.4979	0.4979	0.4980	0.4981
2.9	0.4981	0.4982	0.4982	0.4983	0.4984	0.4984	0.4985	0.4985	0.4986	0.4986
3.0	0.4986	0.4987	0.4987	0.4988	0.4988	0.4989	0.4989	0.4989	0.4990	0.4990
3.1	0.4990	0.4991	0.4991	0.4991	0.4992	0.4992	0.4992	0.4992	0.4993	0.4993
3.2	0.4993	0.4993	0.4994	0.4994	0.4994	0.4994	0.4994	0.4995	0.4995	0.4995
3.3	0.4995	0.4995	0.4995	0.4996	0.4996	0.4996	0.4996	0.4996	0.4996	0.4997
3.4	0.4997	0.4997	0.4997	0.4997	0.4997	0.4997	0.4997	0.4997	0.4998	0.4998
3.5	0.4998	0.4998	0.4998	0.4998	0.4998	0.4998	0.4998	0.4998	0.4998	0.4998
3.6	0.4998	0.4998	0.4999	0.4999	0.4999	0.4999	0.4999	0.4999	0.4999	0.4999
3.7	0.4999	0.4999	0.4999	0.4999	0.4999	0.4999	0.4999	0.4999	0.4999	0.4999
3.8	0.4999	0.4999	0.4999	0.4999	0.4999	0.4999	0.4999	0.5000	0.5000	0.5000
3.9	0.5000	0.5000	0.5000	0.5000	0.5000	0.5000	0.5000	0.5000	0.5000	0.5000

The Poisson Distribution— Cumulative Probabilities

$$P(n) = \frac{e^{-\lambda}\lambda^n}{n!}$$

Where, for a given period of time,

λ = Mean number of events expected to occur
n = Actual number of events observed
$P(n)$ = Probability of observing exactly n events
e = Base of the natural logarithms, approximately 2.7183

Example

For $\lambda = 0.1$

		Cumulative Probability
$P(0) = \dfrac{e^{-0.1}(0.1)^0}{0!} = 0.905$		0.905
$P(1) = \dfrac{e^{-0.1}(0.1)^1}{1!} = 0.090$		0.995
$P(2) = \dfrac{e^{-0.1}(0.1)^2}{2!} = 0.005$		1.000

TABLE B–1
The Poisson Distribution—Cumulative Probabilities

λ	n = 0	1	2	3	4	5	6	7	8	9	10
					P(n)						
0.02	0.980	1.000									
0.04	0.961	0.999	1.000								
0.06	0.942	0.998	1.000								
0.08	0.923	0.997	1.000								
0.10	0.905	0.995	1.000								
0.15	0.861	0.990	0.999	1.000							
0.20	0.819	0.982	0.999	1.000							
0.25	0.779	0.974	0.998	1.000							
0.30	0.741	0.963	0.996	1.000							
0.35	0.705	0.951	0.994	1.000							
0.40	0.670	0.938	0.992	0.999	1.000						
0.45	0.638	0.925	0.989	0.999	1.000						
0.50	0.607	0.910	0.986	0.998	1.000						
0.55	0.577	0.894	0.982	0.998	1.000						
0.60	0.549	0.878	0.977	0.997	1.000						
0.65	0.522	0.861	0.972	0.996	0.999	1.000					
0.70	0.497	0.844	0.966	0.994	0.999	1.000					
0.75	0.472	0.827	0.959	0.993	0.999	1.000					
0.80	0.449	0.809	0.953	0.991	0.999	1.000					
0.85	0.427	0.791	0.945	0.989	0.998	1.000					
0.90	0.407	0.772	0.937	0.987	0.998	1.000					
0.95	0.387	0.754	0.929	0.984	0.997	1.000					
1.00	0.368	0.736	0.920	0.981	0.996	0.999	1.000				
1.1	0.333	0.699	0.900	0.974	0.995	0.999	1.000				
1.2	0.301	0.663	0.879	0.966	0.992	0.998	1.000				
1.3	0.273	0.627	0.857	0.957	0.989	0.998	1.000				
1.4	0.247	0.592	0.833	0.946	0.986	0.997	0.999	1.000			
1.5	0.223	0.558	0.809	0.934	0.981	0.996	0.999	1.000			
1.6	0.202	0.525	0.783	0.921	0.976	0.994	0.999	1.000			
1.7	0.183	0.493	0.757	0.907	0.970	0.992	0.998	1.000			
1.8	0.165	0.463	0.731	0.891	0.964	0.990	0.997	0.999	1.000		
1.9	0.150	0.434	0.704	0.875	0.956	0.987	0.997	0.999	1.000		
2.0	0.135	0.406	0.677	0.857	0.947	0.983	0.995	0.999	1.000		
2.2	0.111	0.355	0.623	0.819	0.928	0.975	0.993	0.998	1.000		
2.4	0.091	0.308	0.570	0.779	0.904	0.964	0.988	0.997	0.999	1.000	
2.6	0.074	0.267	0.518	0.736	0.877	0.951	0.983	0.995	0.999	1.000	
2.8	0.061	0.231	0.469	0.692	0.848	0.935	0.976	0.992	0.998	0.999	1.000
3.0	0.050	0.199	0.423	0.647	0.815	0.916	0.966	0.988	0.996	0.999	1.000
3.2	0.041	0.171	0.380	0.603	0.781	0.895	0.955	0.983	0.994	0.998	1.000
3.4	0.033	0.147	0.340	0.558	0.744	0.871	0.942	0.977	0.992	0.997	0.999
3.6	0.027	0.126	0.303	0.515	0.706	0.844	0.927	0.969	0.988	0.996	0.999
3.8	0.022	0.107	0.269	0.473	0.668	0.816	0.909	0.960	0.984	0.994	0.998
4.0	0.018	0.092	0.238	0.433	0.629	0.785	0.889	0.949	0.979	0.992	0.997
4.2	0.015	0.078	0.210	0.395	0.590	0.753	0.867	0.936	0.972	0.989	0.996
4.4	0.012	0.066	0.185	0.359	0.551	0.720	0.844	0.921	0.964	0.985	0.994
4.6	0.010	0.056	0.163	0.326	0.513	0.686	0.818	0.905	0.955	0.980	0.992
4.8	0.008	0.048	0.143	0.294	0.476	0.651	0.791	0.887	0.944	0.975	0.990
5.0	0.007	0.040	0.125	0.265	0.440	0.616	0.762	0.867	0.932	0.968	9.986

TABLE B–1
(*continued*)

λ	n = 0	1	2	3	4	5	6	7	8	9	10
5.2	0.006	0.034	0.109	0.238	0.406	0.581	0.732	0.845	0.918	0.960	0.982
5.4	0.005	0.029	0.095	0.213	0.373	0.546	0.702	0.822	0.903	0.951	0.977
5.6	0.004	0.024	0.082	0.191	0.342	0.512	0.670	0.797	0.886	0.941	0.972
5.8	0.003	0.021	0.072	0.170	0.313	0.478	0.638	0.771	0.867	0.929	0.965
6.0	0.002	0.017	0.062	0.151	0.285	0.446	0.606	0.744	0.847	0.916	0.957
6.2	0.002	0.015	0.054	0.134	0.259	0.414	0.574	0.716	0.826	0.902	0.949
6.4	0.002	0.012	0.046	0.119	0.235	0.384	0.542	0.687	0.803	0.886	0.939
6.6	0.001	0.010	0.040	0.105	0.213	0.355	0.511	0.658	0.780	0.869	0.927
6.8	0.001	0.009	0.034	0.093	0.192	0.327	0.480	0.628	0.755	0.850	0.915
7.0	0.001	0.007	0.030	0.082	0.173	0.301	0.450	0.599	0.729	0.830	0.901
8.0	0.000	0.003	0.014	0.043	0.100	0.192	0.314	0.454	0.594	0.718	0.817
9.0	0.000	0.001	0.006	0.021	0.055	0.116	0.207	0.324	0.456	0.588	0.707
10.0	0.000	0.000	0.002	0.009	0.028	0.066	0.129	0.219	0.332	0.457	0.582

Two-Digit Random Numbers

TABLE C–1

Two-Digit Random Numbers—Uniform Distribution

42	27	11	61	64	20
55	39	37	71	35	78
24	42	25	60	61	78
82	70	68	68	28	08
56	38	62	42	05	47
48	15	21	40	25	78
95	76	15	43	63	18
86	86	96	50	43	17
49	47	10	94	14	22
41	74	33	33	28	76
95	47	92	56	95	95
78	31	27	77	66	63
84	18	88	65	46	81
40	00	61	17	82	53
80	00	85	42	64	44
12	55	13	20	74	16
84	27	50	45	97	19
01	22	40	81	36	10
25	12	07	98	82	74
46	12	83	52	30	42
83	02	73	53	18	07
69	18	16	09	93	65
78	22	36	94	45	32
43	18	05	33	44	45
07	34	46	30	49	10
00	50	31	12	42	88
55	34	73	61	96	44
17	39	51	92	64	44
22	81	84	00	95	32
57	00	21	12	36	96
02	20	12	50	71	82
70	15	52	75	67	60
28	36	84	20	73	23

(continued)

TABLE C–1
(*concluded*)

86	60	52	37	46	79
04	34	33	73	42	91
95	35	13	16	75	03
89	14	24	19	29	82
92	46	72	35	17	81
30	28	74	35	87	67
86	31	84	29	75	89
13	21	48	73	40	73
38	87	98	23	72	43
02	42	81	84	08	38
72	22	79	60	26	26
16	05	14	42	74	74
70	03	63	58	32	12
45	45	96	64	49	83
05	38	40	89	75	32
29	24	05	17	03	53
20	87	26	88	06	18

Answers to Selected Problems and Exercises

Note to the student: Generally, answers given here are "check" answers to most even-numbered and occasional odd-numbered problems and exercises, serving only to guide your solution and thought procedures. Full rationale is not provided. Where multiple responses are sought, one or two example answers are suggested. Essay items are omitted. For each item, answers are preceded by a brief problem identifier in parentheses.

Chapter 1

2. (Arbor Nurseries) Principles 2, 10, 14, and 16. The nature of the question shows that Arbor is already following principle 1.

4. (Company examples) Examples include McDonalds, the North American farmer, and Swatch watches.

6. (Deere) Very up to date. Direct support for principles 1 and 10. Indirect support for others, especially 2.

8. (Western manufacturing) Western companies have been structured along functional specialties. Line people aren't heard from. Solutions include assigning hot-shots to multifunctional or cellular teams.

Chapter 2

2. (Strategy shapers)
   a. Regional.
   b. Global (early 1950s; an early test of United Nations' peacekeeping resolve).
   c. Primarily local (the South), but regional (U.S.) to some extent.
   d. Regional.

4. (First City Bank)
   a. Attract/retain small-account customers.
   b. Principle 16 (plural machines); secondarily, principle 1.

6. (Consolidated Enterprises) Fiberglass—job; snowblowers and lawnmowers—repetitive; thread—continuous.

8. (Development of OM) In repetitive operations, development costs are amortized over large output quantities so marginal costs are low.

10. (Long- vs. short-range forecasting) Long-range needed in capital intensive industries; short-range usually adequate in labor intensive ones, especially those with relatively low-level skill requirements.

12. (Business capacity) Production planning. Example: A firm may define full capacity as output from a five-day, two-shifts-per-day (80-hour) week, or it might prefer a six-day, ten-hour-per-day (60-hour) week. Desire to

use or avoid overtime pay, a goal of free weekends for employees, or a strategy of not producing goods simply for storage in a warehouse (make-to-stock) are among the many factors that help define planned capacity. Actual operating capacity often deviates from planned capacity.

14. (Competitive) Customer expectations increase. Standard products, exact schedules, and precise methods—all OM concerns—allow for high quality, timely delivery, and so forth.

16. (Outputs, Inputs, and OM Functions)
UPS Inputs: adjustable capacity—delivery employees, packing materials and supplies; fixed capacity—trucks, planes, parcel-sorting rooms. Outputs: on-time delivery, damages. OM functions: Examples include readiness-zone planning for facilities and equipment (e.g., planes and trucks), action-zone labor planning, and monitoring-zone measurement of timeliness and damage.

Fire department Inputs: adjustable capacity—employees, consumable firefighting supplies and gear, public education materials; fixed capacity—stations, trucks, communications equipment. Outputs: incidence of fires, response time, human and property casualties. OM functions: Examples include readiness-zone planning for facilities and special equipment (e.g., jaws of life), action-zone operations and labor (e.g., schedules and training), and monitoring-zone measurement of response time and fire prevention results.

Chapter 3

2. (Telephone system innovations) Examples 1948, transistor—breakthrough; 1954, silicon transistor—refinement; 1957, man-made satellite (Sputnik)—breakthrough; 1970, communications satellite (one of many)—refinement.

6. (IBM) Guidelines 2, 10, and 11 stand out.

8. (Role playing) Examples
Dietician: Don't call for out-of-season fruits and vegetables; fashion designer: Don't request skins of rare animals; architect: Don't specify nonstandard fixture or materials; portfolio manager: Don't advertise hard-to-get assets.

10. (Mazda) Myopia and overspecialization.

12. (GMF Robotics) Example
Prudent managers are reaping benefits of streamlined manual processes without having to incur the expense and uncertainties of automation.

14. (Justify robot) Example
Cost: the robot itself; benefit: greater machining precision.

16. (Preautomation) Items b, c, e, and f.

18. (Robotic assembly) Second item (*b*).

20. (Rocky Mountain Tech) Quality circles are a good idea for the basketball team but not for the ski team.

22. (Prison Production) Move machines out of functional machine shops and into work cells or flow lines.

Chapter 4

8. (Fail-safing)
   a. Place alarm clock on pillow when bed is made each morning.
   b. Keep pocket or desk appointment calendar.
   c. Reset trip odometer at each gas fill-up, then always refill when odometer gets near 400 miles. (One of your authors does just that!)

9. (Tolerance stackup—goods) Engine blocks: cylinder diameter = 3.000 ± 0.005 cm. tolerance; piston diameter = 2.995 ± 0.005 cm. tolerance. Combining a 3.005 cylinder with a 2.990 piston would be within spec, but a very loose fit!

10. (Tolerance stackup—services) Career counseling meeting: Counselor arrives 10 minutes early; student arrives 10 minutes late—neither far off target, but together a poor result.

Chapter 5

2. (Forecasting in organizational types)
   Examples
   Type 1—highway construction; Type 2—air conditioning contractor; Type 3—tractor manufacturer; Type 4—small appliance manufacturer.

4. (County Hospital) Group totals: actual = 2,729; forecast = 2,580; error = +149; percent error = 5.8.

6. (Metro Auto Sales) Examples
   Rolling forecast mode and group forecasting mode.

8. (Service part) MAD = 2.6; SD = 3.5; MAPE = 14.86.

10. (Computer logons) Approximately 13,500 logons.

12. (Public defender's office)
    a. A longer time span smooths the data more.
    b. June-centered moving average = 130. Index = 120/130 = 0.92.
    c. True seasonality of caseload and "best" time span for forecasting.

14. (Computer media)
    a. 178; (1) +9, (2) −12; 160.
    b. 173.
    c. Yes, 160 differs considerably from 173.

17. (Huckleberry Farms)
    a. 501.5, applicable to next month.
    b. Three months.
    c. 509.1, applicable to January of next year.
    d. $\alpha = 0.5$ is best of values tested.
    e. 3-quarter M.A. = 1,546; 3-year M.A. = 5,952; quarterly E.S. = 1,574; annual E.S. = 6,079.

18. (Seal-Fine Sash)
    a. 972—applicable to next quarter.
    b. Four quarters.
    c. 1,536—applicable to winter next year.
    d. $\alpha = 0.5$ is best of values tested.

20. (Smith's Kitchens)
    a. "Rough" association, lead time is about 18 months.
    b. New hires appear to lead by one month.
    c. $Y = 60.9 + 0.13X$.
    d. $r = 0.27$

22. (Acme Manufacturing)
    a. Approximately 35.
    b. New hires appear to lead by one month.
    c. $Y = 56.4 - 4.7X$; next month = 38; two months away = 33.
    d. $r = 0.86$.

Chapter 6

2. (IBM) Retraining and reassignment are major tools. That is easier when very talented people are hired in the first place. Aggressive development of new products and services ensures that there will be a place to go when older lines fade away.

4. (Bright Way) With a chase-demand strategy, Bright Way becomes more like its competitors. It would rely more on a transient work force for adjustable capacity, so there would be less need to plan capacity far ahead. New management problems would be in the labor area; hiring/firing, scheduling, and foremanship concerns.

6. (Ceramic products) Fifth unit = 51.97 hours; Tenth unit = 48.85 hours; Twentieth unit = 45.92 hours.

8. (Concrete products)
   a. Have six operators and use shortened workweeks as needed. If contracts prevent that, use part-time personnel.
   b. Have five operators and use overtime (or subcontracting if reliable concrete specialists can be found) as required.

10. (Quark Electronics)
    a. Labor hour shortage for week 1 (all shops) = 74 hours. Week 1 machine hour shortages: shop A = +20; shop B = +5; shop C = −15; shop D = +3.
    Plan appears *not* feasible as a single-shift plan, although more weeks should be considered before final determination.
    b. Labor hour shortage by shop: shop A = +7; shop B = +25; shop C = −3; shop D = −20.
    Machine hour shortage by shop: shop A = −20; shop B = −33; shop C = −11; shop D = −17.

14. (Capacity planning—retail) General concerns: Where skill requirements are higher and

seasonal demand variations exist, the capacity planning problems increase.

18. (Pecos, Inc.)
    b. 30,000 + 29,000 − 18,000 = 41,000 gallons.
    c. Yes.

20. (Great Lakes Paint Co.)
    b. Month   0 1 2 3 4 5 6

    Inventory
    on hand   38 40 43 47 45 40 37
    c. Master scheduler cut MPS quantities because shipments dropped in months 2, 3, and 4.

Chapter 7

6. (Home Remodeling)
   a. Breakeven = 40 patios.

8. (Travel department)
   Breakeven = 2,353 tickets/year. Travel department should buy rather than "make."

10. (ABC uses) Example: Make or buy analysis/decisions
    A items—done by executive committee; B items—done by product or materials manager; C items—done by inventory planner.

12. (ABC classes)

Item Number	Dollar Usage Last Year	Class
030	$30,000	A
109	6,000	B
all others		C

14. (Inventory counting)
    a. Poor. b. Poor. c. Good. d. Very poor.

16. (Organizational purchasing) Examples
    b. The city is heavily involved in buying intangibles; examples include consultants' services and software.
    c. Approved supplier lists: all except liquor wholesaler.
    Bid solicitation: city government and larger manufacturers (for selected items).
    Blanket orders: High-volume standard items going into fashions, home

appliances, electric power, glass, plastics, computers, ships, aerospace.

18. (VA in JIT companies) JIT requires on-the-spot problem solving, including any design changes. For value analysis to be done "on the fly," specifications should be held to a minimum, or focus on just "performance" specs.

20. (Jane Doe—Standardization) Bad. A lack of standardization is shown.

Chapter 8

2. (ABC Specialties, Inc.)

   $T_{RM} = 6$. $T_{WIP} = 7$. $T_{FG} = 0.33$ $T_{Total} = 3.3$

   Management is about average for North American industry.

4. (Iota Co.) Increase the risk. Inventory stock level will fall to minimum level every two weeks instead of three times per year. The large order quantities have been serving as buffer stock. Buffer stock component of reorder point needs to be increased—more buffer for greater risk; thus, reorder point should be increased.

6. (HP) Simplified product costing, eliminated work orders, reduced need for accounting, and reduced buffer inventories.

8. (Over-Nite Mail Order Tracking) Even 100 percent record accuracy doesn't solve the real problem—the very high percentage of late orders. Real order control involves *getting rid* of delays, not just being able to instantly find out what is causing the delay. Customers don't want to have to worry about why an order is late.

10. (Bottlenecks in paint factory)
    a. Theory of constraints recommends longer production runs when setups are troublesome and smaller transfer lot sizes to keep the product moving.
    b. JIT recommends cutting setup times so small lots—produced more frequently—are the economical choice as well as the customer-oriented choice. Also, focus is on high quality and preventive maintenance every day.

14. (Flexibility and variability) Flexibility is responsiveness; it allows providers to do more things with shorter changeover times. Variability is inconsistency in output, something customers do not want.

Chapter 9

2. (Accounts Payable Office—Micro Response) Pieces-to-persons ratio is 50:1. Plot this ratio on large chart and work to reduce it, plotting reductions for all to see.

4. (X-ray machines)
   a. Push: Components are pushed onto final assembly.
   b. Convert to pull system, perhaps using kanban squares.

6. (Partial MRP data—FOQ) The fixed-order quantity is 160. A scheduled receipt is due in week one and a planned order release is scheduled for week two.

10. (Tape dispenser)
    b. Planned order release schedule is: Roll of tape: 5,000 in week 3 and 5,000 in week 6; Spool: 2,000 in week 1 and 5,000 in week 4.
    c. Planned receipts for rolls of tape are due in weeks 4 and 7, and for spools in weeks 3 and 6. Planned receipts do not become scheduled receipts, however, until orders are placed.

14. (Kitchen knives)
    a. Order 2,400 rivets in week 2.
    b. Order 2,400 blocks in week 3.
    c. Order 130 wood bars in week 3.

16. (Hospital—Safety stock factors) Example X-ray film: Safety stock factors are high cost and obsolescence, so keep safety stock low. (But need rapid replenishment source—medical supply company or other medical facilities—in case of urgent high demand.)

18. (Brown Instrument Co.—ROP)
    a. ROP = 81.4.
    b. Both DLT and SS would increase.

20. (Service level and safety stock)
    a. SS = 51.
    b. All three factors should lower the safety stock.

22. (Fuel oil—ROP)
    a. About 3.75 orders per winter.
    b. DLT = 3,000 gallons; SS = 3,400 gallons.

Chapter 10

2. (EPP) From Example 10–1, the EPP is 60; for lot size = 70, part periods = 55; for lot size = 80, part periods = 85 (85 > 60, so lot size = 70).

4. (Provincial government)
   a. EOQ = 600 boxes.
   b. Yes, the EOQ must be used as a zone, not as a point.

6. (Continental Plate and Boiler Co.)
   a. S = $66 per order.
   b. Annual capital cost = $270,000; annual holding cost = $64,000; carrying cost rate (I) = 0.22.
   c. Refer to factors in Chapter 10 and Chapter 8 (Figure 8–3).

8. (Maple Tree Insurance) At $3.00, EOQ = 258 boxes—not feasible; at $2.60, EOQ = 277 boxes—feasible.

10. (Cannery) At $0.60, EPQ = 3,266—feasible (total annual costs = $24,490); at $0.50, EPQ = 3,577—not feasible.
    Total annual costs at order quantity of 4,000 = $20,450. The correct order quantity—4,000—will last about 1.2 months and is $2,000 worth.

12. (Print shop)
    a. EMQ = 157,400.
    b. EOQ = 154,900 (small difference since production rate is much larger than demand rate).
    c. ROP = 1,000 plus any desired safety stock.

14. (Irrigation system)
    a. 3-inch EMQ = 2,306 pipe sections; 4-inch EMQ = 2,246 sections.
    b. 3-inch EMQ = 1,631 pipe sections.

18. (Federal Time Corporation)
    a. EOQ = 6,532 lenses.
    b. Single-digit setup: Equip molding machines with tables to hold dies at usage

height; use rollers or air cushions to make it easier to slide dies into position.

20. (Semiconductors—small lots) By always running in small lots; cut setup times to make that easier.

Chapter 11

2. (Continuous vs. repetitive processing) Examples
   a. Soft drinks: Syrup processing (flavoring, sweetening, coloring, etc.) is continuous; bottling or canning is repetitive.
   b. Nursing care: Electronic monitoring of patient's heartbeat is continuous; hourly charting of temperature is repetitive.

4. (Detergent manufacturing)
   • Process design and capital investment; much automation and extensive process engineering.
   • Reliability of supply; firm, long-term contracts with suppliers and dependable transportation (e.g., an owned, or controlled pipeline).

8. (Computer software—under-capacity scheduling) 1,400 (0.9)/30 = 42 packages per labor hour. For 1,200 packages/day, labor requirements = 1,200/42 = 28.6 hours per day.

10. (Faiko Time Co.) Faiko should regularize mechanism assembly to about 7 per day (for example, 4 of type A, 2 of B, and 1 of C); check demand every two weeks and adjust schedule as required. Enclosures are less amenable to regularizing. Still, perhaps there is dominant demand for one type and it should get regularized production.

12. (Zeus, Inc.—Mixed models)
    Full cycle (10 minutes) production ratio L:M:S: = 1:2:4.
    a. Ten-minute cycle SMSMSLS, challenges supplier to match it, possibly with simpler dedicated equipment.
    b. Supplier should slow down as Zeus slows down—and use excess labor for training and improvement projects.
    c. Zeus' schedule is "too full." A policy of under-capacity scheduling is needed so

targets can be met almost every day; for example, try L:M:S = 44:88:172 units per day.

14. (Typewriter table—Mixed model) Model ratios D:E:F:G = 1:3:2:4. The most repetitive mixed-model sequence is GEFGEFGEDG, six times/day.

16. (Repetitive scheduling in bank) Yes, check and deposit processing are examples.

Chapter 12

2. (QUIDCO, Inc.)
   a. MRP calculations show week of need. Scheduler still decides the *day* of release, and may release orders earlier or later than specified in order to level work center loads.
   c. The costly part (0077AX) has no allowances for handling time, which consumes carrying costs but adds no value. Thus, foremen and dispatchers try to move that part along ASAP.

4. (Open Air Furniture Company)
   a. Current workloads exceed capacity by a considerable margin in all three work centers, suggesting that some of the load is backlog from last week's orders. Centers are probably overloaded with the hope that expediters will pull along the "hot" jobs.
   b. Yes.

6. (Work center load imbalance)
   a. If the work center is a gateway, leveling techniques may be used, perhaps firm planned orders. In extreme cases, the master scheduler may be asked to adjust the MPS.
   b. Computer processes open order file, accumulating loads by time bucket for each work center. Next, the same thing is done for the planned orders via CRP software. The combination produces the load report.
   c. Actual output averages 585 per week, five less than planned.
   d. Actual input averages 607 per week. The work center is accumulating an input

backlog; it is performing at substandard efficiency.

8. (Jerrybuilt Machines, Inc.) Order list: 916 slack = −1; 889 slack = +1; 901 slack = +4.

10. (Critical ratios—priority ordered) Order list: 300 CR = 0.67; 290 CR = 1.00; 310 CR = 1.50.

12. (Antenna Manufacture—production activity control)
    a. CR = 4.5.
    b. (1) Allow 8 standard hours per day, round up to whole day. (2) Allow 1 day for a move if it is called out on a shop order.
    c. Slack = 1; CR = 1.5. No, 885 is not urgent.
    d. Shop order 910 will have been plated and in—or on its way to—the next work center. Order 914 will still be in plating (it is a 14-hour job).
    g. Decentralized.

14. (Central sales office) Reorganize to permit all orders to be processed as fast as hand carry is now. Break up the central order-processing department and create cells for families of orders. Use under-capacity scheduling of labor to allow all orders to get processed most days. Maybe a fax machine would also help.

Chapter 13

3. (Dummy activity) Dummy activity 16–13 assures that both 12–16 and 10–13 precede 13–18 but that only 12–16 precedes 16–18.

6. (Antenna system)
    b. Critical path: 1–3–7 = 9 days.

    c.

Activity	Slack
1–3	0
3–7	0
all others	1

    d. Critical path: 1–2–4–6–7 = 11.

10. (Critical path and network simulation)
    a. Expected duration (deterministic) = 1.5 months; expected duration (simulation) = 1.75 months.

    b. Expected duration (deterministic) = 1.5 months; expected duration (simulation) = 1.88 months.

12. (Crashing the network)
    Critical path: A–D–G = 12 days.
    - Cost (normal) $610 + $200 (penalty) = $810.
    - Cut to 11 days by crashing D by 1 day, total cost = $810.
    - Cut to 10 days by crashing D another day, total cost = $810.
    - Cut to 9 days by crashing A & G by 1 day, add one back to D for a total cost of $850.
    - May also cut to 8 days ($910) or to 7 days ($1,000).

14. (Slack calculations)
    a. Critical path = 10; scheduled project duration = path time + slack = 10 + 6 = 16. Slack on lower path = 16 − 7 = 9.
    b. Scheduled duration = +6; slack on lower path = −1

16. (Time-cost trade-off)
    a. Critical path: 1–2–3–5 = 11 days; Activity 1–2 costs $5 to reduce 1 day.
    b. Reduce 1–2 by 1 day, 2–5 by 1 day, and 3–5 by 2 days.

18. (PERT subsystems) Examples
    - Implementing MRP in a manufacturing company of 1,000 employees: moderate size, moderate complexity, moderate uncertainty, low urgency; subsystem 1 only.
    - New product development and testing including market research for a major food company: moderate size, high uncertainty (R&D always is), moderate complexity, and low urgency; subsystems 1, 2, and 3.

Chapter 14

2. (Metro Pollution Control) Second device is better; customer system time is 1.96 minutes. With 10 cars/hour, still second device (0.99 minutes system time).

4. (Voters in queuing analysis)
    a. Poisson.
    b. T_q = 59.0 min./voter; N_q = 59 voters.

c. Mean service rate = 66.7 voters/hr.; $T_{q(c)}$ = 4 min. $N_{q(c)}$ = 4 voters.

6. (Auto engine plant) Line 1 has the most variability in both time interval and rework time distributions. The two variabilities interact extensively, which causes problems in operations. Line 1 is the best candidate for Monte Carlo simulation.

9. (Monte Carlo simulation—interpretation)
   a. In the four-day study period, three hours of waiting time occurred (18 − 17 = 1 and 27 − 25 = 2), so the average is 0.75 hours/day.
   b. With two servers, there is no waiting time.

10. (Monte Carlo simulation—tabular results) Sum of service times = 30 hours and total waiting time = 3 hours.

12. (Truck docks—Monte Carlo simulation) With two docks, the mean wait is 44 minutes, but with three docks the mean wait is 4.2 minutes; so build the third dock.

14. (Global Trade Center—Monte Carlo simulation, 2 crews)
   a. Total minutes out of service = 610, and the study period = 900 minutes, so mean number of elevators out = 610/900 = 0.68.
   b. Average waiting time = 10 minutes/15 repairs = 0.67 minutes/repair.
   c. Crew utilization rate = 600/1,800 = 0.33 or 33 percent.

16. (Value of waiting-line analysis) The light-bulb replacement and attorney's office are *not* good candidates, but the appliance repair and toll booths are.

18. (Actions to decrease waiting lines) Examples
   • Appointment systems.
   • Lower pricing for slack demand periods.
   • Addition of servers during high demand periods.

Chapter 15

2. (Food processing company)
   a. Total tolerance band is 0.16 oz.; vendor's inherent capability (0.20 oz.) is not good enough, so don't buy.

b. No change. The vendor's problem is excess variation in process output; a change in location and process control can't change that fact.
   c. Advise *both* to work together to determine and remove cause of excess variability.

4. (Plug-N-Go—Process capability)
   a. C_{pk} = 0.833.
   b. About 0.62 percent of the valve covers are out of spec.
   c. Two actions: First, *always* strive to reduce variation in process output; second, shift process downward toward spec nominal of 0.50 cm.

6. (Hypodermic needles)
   a. $UCL_{\bar{X}}$ = 27.96 grams; $LCL_{\bar{X}}$ = 24.24 grams; UCL_R = 9.32 grams; LCL_R = 0.68 grams.
   b. Create trial control charts, plot sample averages and ranges, test for process control. If in control, put process to use; if not, determine special causes, eliminate, and repeat trial control charts.
   c. R is below the *LCL* so there is more process consistency than is expected (out of control). Investigate to determine the cause and then try to replicate it—permanently. Remember: Being out of control is not necessarily bad, as shown in this case.

8. (Circuit current loss) Circuit current losses are lower than before, so some process improvement has occurred. The job is to find out why and make the improvement permanent. Most likely, factors of design, purchasing, production and/or training are responsible for the process output improvement. Pricing and marketing might incorporate improvement in advertising. Again, we see that being out of control sometimes is *good news*.

10. (OK-Mart & Electro Corp).
   a. Center line on p chart is at 0.2%—the actual process average.
   b. Process improvements are needed; then sample again with new charts.

12. (Pottery manufacturing) Process is out of control (inconsistent). Special causes of process variation need to be identified and

eliminated. Stop production if corrective action isn't immediately apparent.

14. (Orville's Popcorn—choice of control charting method) Variables charts, X-bar and R, are superior to attributes charts. Here, measurements can easily be taken, so variables charts are the proper choice.

16. (AmPen)
    a. Fishbone chart categorizes causes of error, alerts people to cause-effect relationships.
    b. Pareto chart shows relative importance of problems or defects; here, the impurity problem dramatically overshadows the others, and it should be the first problem attacked.

20. (Attributes and variables) Examples
    • Telephone: Attributes—does it ring? does it convey sound?
      Variables—physical dimensions of components.
      The attributes are easy to evaluate; the physical dimensions would require some measurement equipment. Customers would find the attributes more meaningful and would assume the variables are suitable for assembly.
    • Dice: Attributes—are the dots clearly visible? are there any chips?
      Variables—distribution of weight.
      Again, the attributes are easily determined, but the weight distribution requires some precisely calibrated equipment.
    • Library reference services: Attributes—proportion of reference requests filled. Variables = time taken to fill requests. Here, both are easy to obtain. A simple charting system would suffice.

Chapter 16

2. (Visual performance charts—cause-control) Example
   Home-builder: on-time completions, scrap, rework, and training completion records.

4. (L & L Landscaping)
   a. $(0.9)(40)(6) = 216$ hours.
   b. First, L & L can make use of the 24 hours not regularly scheduled; next, overtime

and subcontracting are options. Finally, client rescheduling (changing the master schedule) might be required.
   c. It is better if all employees learn the new services; scheduling flexibility and capacity planning are easier. Also, people get more from their jobs.
   d. Costs are $(24)(\$11) = \$264$/week.

6. (Meter reading—methods improvements)
   a. Savings: two transportations, one operation, and one delay.
   b. Advantages: (1) avoid interrupting customers, (2) shorter walk for readers, and (3) more complete meter reading. Disadvantages: (1) cost of moving meters and (2) pathways through customers yards—some might object.

9. (Candle—work sampling standards)
   a. C.T. = 12.00 minutes; S.T. = 13.58 minutes/candle (assuming a 480-minute work day).
   b. Need to schedule 208.5 hours.
   c. Efficiency = 119 percent.

10. (Social service agency)
    a. 21 employees.
    b. Historical.

12. (Auto plant—time standards) $3.6 \times 1.14 \times 1.05 = 4.31$ minute/wheel.

14. (Lugging machine—standard time)
    a. S.T. = 0.314 minute/piece.
    b. MTM data are already normalized, so pace rating is unnecessary.

16. (Typing—work sampling) Assuming a 480-minute work day:
    a. Typing: C.T. = 32.00 minutes; R.T. = 28.80 minutes; S.T. = 32.26 minutes.
       Retrieving: C.T. = 4.80 minutes; R.T. = 3.84 minutes; S.T. = 4.30 minutes.
    b. Uses include staffing, scheduling, and evaluating equipment and methods.
    c. Yes, they are engineered. If biases (such as easy vs. hard job assignments) are controlled, the standards could be used for personnel evaluation.

18. (Wabash Airways)
    a. Efficiency = 133 percent.
    b. Productivity = 119.7 percent.
    c. 12 attendants.

20. (Setting time standards) Examples
    - Soldering connections; time study or predetermined standards.
    - Computer programmers; historical standards.

Chapter 17

2. (Copy machines) Operators do a considerable amount of maintenance and minor repair work; cleaning glass and rollers, adding toner and other fluids, and clearing paper jams. Major repairs and PM (predictive, usually) is performed by service technicians—especially for large models.

4. (PM for automobiles)
    a. Considerable usage data exists. Obstacles center around getting owners to accept the maintenance recommendations.
    b. Wear-out and failure data for components and replacement parts would need to be input into car's computers at some regular interval, say when new tires or filters are installed.
    c. Factory machines are usually operated intensively at rather uniform operating conditions; not the case for automobiles.

6. (Maintainability) Computers and projectors are examples of products that require a high degree of maintainability. Removable panels allow easy access to compartments where frequent repairs are needed (e.g., lamp compartment on projectors).
    Maintainability is less important where downtime costs are low, e.g., lawn and garden equipment and small kitchen appliances.

8. (Cooling system filter traps) *Individual:* Steady-state clogging rate is about 6 per 1,000 hours. Cleaning costs would be ($100) (6) = $600 per 1,000 hours. *Group:* Best policy is group replacement every 3,000 hours at a cost of $567 per 1,000 hours.

10. (Duncan Aviation) Best number of spares is three; cost is $1,938 per week. Remember: The Poisson distribution will yield engine breakdown probabilities.

12. (Standby machine analysis)
    1. Fluorescent tubes—not suitable; minor costs are involved.

2. Memory cards—suitable; don't overstudy, just keep some spares.
3. Pizza oven—not suitable; spare ovens aren't very practical.

14. (Captain Henry Harrison) The good captain's approach is sound. A clean workplace reduces search time, prevents accidents, improves machine operation, and improves morale of personnel.

Chapter 18

2. (Motor carriers) JIT operations have caused more carriers to offer "as requested" delivery times. Willingness of truckers to serve customers' needs may slow the movement to locate supplier plants adjacent to customers.

4. (Recyclation, Inc.)
    a. Total cost for North site = $59.
    b. Total cost for South site = $48.
    c. Choose South site. Since crush capacity exceeds can supply, all sites will not operate at 100 percent capacity.

6. (American Tractor Company—foundry location)
    a. Total cost Toronto location = $1,390.
    b. Total cost Rock Island location = $1,210.

8. (Types of layout) Examples
    - Auto assembly: product
    - Shipbuilding: fixed
    - Shoe repair: process
    - Hospital: mixed

10. (Bicycle assembly plant)
    a. Process layout

12. (Automatic Controls Corp.)
    d. The combined REL chart is not very necessary. The large number of "3 codes" suggest that product/resource flow is a dominant factor. Proceed directly from the from-to chart to the activity-arrangement diagram.

14. (Line-balancing analysis) Time in minutes:
    a. Task time sum = 100 minutes. Possible cycle time/number of stations pairs: 100/1, 50/2, 25/4, 20/5, 10/10, 5/20, 4/25, 2/50.
    b. The last three are not feasible since there are only 12 work elements. The first three are feasible only if multiple stages can be

performed at a single workstation, since two segments in the precedence diagram require five stages.

c. With a cycle time of 20 minutes, a six-station solution would yield a balance delay of 17 percent.

16. (Worker's compensation claims office)
    a. Task time sum = 234 minutes; prime numbers are 2, 3, 3, and 13.
    c. Five station balance is better since its balance delay (10 percent) is less than the balance delay of the six-station solution (13 percent).

19. (Hair-drier—mixed models) Sequence: S S D,

cycle time = 4 + 4 + 12 = 20 minutes; repeats 24 times in a 480-minute work day.

20. (Heat treating—mixed models) Five hours will be required.

22. (Island Explorer—VAM solutions)
    a. Hilo location, first solution optimal; assignment sequence: 25 units assigned to Honolulu–Kauai; 20 units assigned to Hana–Lanai; 20 units assigned to Hana–Molokai; 10 units assigned to Hilo–Molokai; 25 units assigned to Hilo–Kauai. Costs are $865 per week.
    b. Lihue location, first solution optimal; costs are $925/week.

Glossary

ABC (inventory) analysis Materials classification system in which all stocked items are classified by annual dollar volume. The high-value "A" items receive close control; medium-value "B" items get intermediate control; low-value "C" items receive lowest priority.

Activity Basic unit of work in a project.

Activity-based costing (ABC) A method of costing whereby a job, product, or service is assigned overhead costs only if overhead activity is actually expended in support of it; replaces the old methods of allocating overhead costs—typically in proportion to direct labor costs.

Activity-on-arrow network A PERT/CPM network form in which activities are shown as arrows.

Activity-on-node network A PERT/CPM network form in which activities are shown as nodes.

Adaptive smoothing Technique for automatic adjustment of time-series smoothing coefficients based on some function of forecast error, commonly the tracking signal.

Adjustable capacity Adjustable resources (as opposed to relatively fixed plant and equipment resources)—labor, aggregate materials, and tools.

Aggregate demand Long- and medium-range demand expressed in collective terms rather than broken down by type of product or service or specific model.

Aggregate demand forecast Forecast for whole-product or capacity groups; long- or medium-term focus.

Aggregate inventory Total rather than specific materials and tools.

Appointment book A master schedule for the provision of services; a statement of the services to be provided.

Approved supplier A supplier given preferential treatment in purchasing decisions by earning high ratings on quality, delivery, price, and service.

Attribute inspection Inspection requiring only a yes-no, pass-fail, or good-bad judgment.

Automatic storage and retrieval system (AS/RS) Automated equipment, such as racks, bins, forklifts, and computerized location records, collectively designed to hold and retrieve inventory.

Autonomous operations The assignment of all work on certain products to a single workstation; work is not passed from station to station.

Backflush A post-deduction method of accounting for component stock usage at the time of end-product completion. Uses BOM explosion to identify quantity of components to deduct from inventory record balances.

Backorder An order accepted when stock is out; usually filled when stock arrives.

Back-scheduling Subtracting lead time (or throughput time) from an order due date to find the time when the order should be started into production or ordered from a supplier.

Backward integration Setting up to provide goods or services formerly purchased; (sometimes) buying a supplier company, making it a subsidiary.

Backward scheduling See **Back-scheduling.**

Balance delay Ratio of waiting or idle time to total available time—per cycle—in an assembly line.

Batch A kind of job that involves a mixture of ingredients; a single unit of output, but measured by volume.

Batch processing A type of processing in which ingredients are mixed in separate batches.

Bill of labor Labor requirements (type and quantity) for an end-item product or service; analogous to a BOM.

Bill of materials (BOM) Product structure for an assembly; shows required components and their quantity at each level of fabrication and assembly.

Bill of materials (BOM) explosion Breaking an order for end products down into major, secondary, tertiary, and so forth components for the purpose of finding gross requirements for all component items.

Blanket orders A contract covering purchase of relatively low-cost items for which there is continuous but varying need; specifies price and other matters, but delivery is usually triggered by simple "release" orders issued as required.

Bottleneck Workstation or facility for which demand exceeds service capacity.

Buffer stock Inventory maintained to provide customer service in the face of demand and production uncertainty; also known as *safety stock.*

Buying down Attempting to buy an item with historical price swings at a time when the price is down.

c **chart (number-defective chart)** A process control chart for attributes showing the number of defective items in each sample.

Capacity control Keeping work centers busy but not overloaded; takes place after work center loading and may include input/output control.

Capacity planning Planning for adjustable resources such as labor, equipment, usage, and aggregate inventory, typically over a medium-term (a few weeks to about 18 months) planning horizon.

Capacity requirements planning (CRP) A computer-based method of revealing work center loads; determines labor and machine resources needed to achieve planned outputs.

Capital cost Cost (e.g., interest rate) of borrowing money.

Carrying cost The cost, above and beyond unit price, to carry or hold an inventory item in a state of idleness.

Catalog buying Purchasing from current supplier catalogs; the common purchasing procedure, for example, for off-the-shelf maintenance, repair, and operating (MRO) items.

Cell A group of maker-customer pairs, created by drawing people and machines from functional areas and placing them in the same work area to reduce movement distances, inventory, and throughput time and improve coordination.

Cellular layout A layout in which workstations and machines are arranged into cells that provide families of goods or services that follow similar flow paths; very similar to product layout.

Certification Formal approval of a supplier as a source for purchased goods and services; typically bestowed after a supplier exhibits process control, design and delivery standards, and other desirable traits.

Changeover time The time it takes to change the setup on a machine, production line, or process in order to produce a new product or service; the required time for start up; also called *setup time.*

Chase demand (strategy) A capacity management strategy in which sufficient capacity is maintained to meet current demand; capacity levels "chase" (respond to) demand fluctuations.

Closed-loop MRP An MRP system with feedback loops aimed at maintaining valid schedules; includes file control, rescheduling actions, and production activity control.

Commodity product An undifferentiated product.

Common cause Cause for common variation in process output (after specific or assignable causes have been removed).

Common variation Variation remaining in process output after all special variation has been removed; may be thought of as the natural variation in a process that is in statistical control.

Complete physical inventory An actual count of all inventory items.

Component item An item that "goes into" the assembly of the parent item; for example, a bulb is a component of a flashlight.

Computer-integrated manufacturing (CIM) Computer assistance or direct control of manufacturing from product and process design to scheduling to production and material handling; may include FMS, CAD, CAE, and CAPP.

Concurrency Technique for reducing lead times in projects by doing design and production of later stages at the same time and coordinated with earlier activities.

Continuous operations Perpetual production of goods that flow; may include production of one batch after another.

Continuous process See **Continuous operations.**

Correlation coefficient A measure of the degree of association between two or more variables.

Cost variance Productivity measure computed by subtracting actual costs of inputs from standard costs of outputs for a given operating unit or job.

Crash (crashing) Reducing the time requirement for an activity by adding resources; crashing critical activities reduces project time.

Critical path The path (activity sequence) through a project network that is estimated to consume the most time.

Critical path method (CPM) A network-based project management technique initially used on construction projects; about the same as PERT.

Custom product A highly differentiated, unique, special-purpose, or one-of-a-kind product.

Customer The next process (where the work goes next).

Cycle counting An inventory counting plan in which a small fraction of items are counted each day; an alternative to complete physical inventory.

Cycle interval The time interval (minutes, hours, days, or weeks) between when a certain product or service is made or delivered until the next time it is made or delivered.

Cycle time (CT) Raw average time for completion of one cycle or element of a repeating operation; may also be called *select time (ST)* in time study.

Cyclical pattern Recurring pattern in a time series; generally each occurrence spans several years.

Delayed differentiation Retaining standard forms or parts further along the assembly sequence; waiting as long as possible to transform common- or general-purpose items into special-purpose parts.

Demand forecasting Estimating future demand for goods and services.

Demand management Recognizing and managing all demands for products and services to ensure that the master schedule is as desired.

Dependent demand Demand that results from demand for a parent item; for example, demand for mower blades is dependent on demand for mowers.

Deployment Positioning of resources; includes location, layout, handling, and transportation.

Derating Running a machine or production line at less than "rated" or maximum capacity to forestall breakdowns, deteriorating quality, and early wearout.

Design-build team Team consisting of product design and process development people, whose aim is a producible product design.

Design review A check on engineering designs to ensure satisfaction of customers' requirements and producibility.

Destructive testing Product inspection that destroys the product's usefulness, rendering it unfit for sale; may be used, for example, in inspecting a sample of flashbulbs.

Dispatcher A person whose responsibility is to release jobs into work centers or, sometimes, resources to jobs.

Distance-intensity (DI) chart   A chart showing intensity of flow (for dissimilar products or resources) on one axis and distance to be moved on the other; indicates preferred handling methods.

Distance-quantity (DQ) chart   Like a DI chart, except used for similar products and resources; the axes are quantity to be moved and distance to be moved.

Distinctive competency   A strength that sets an organization apart from its competition.

Distribution requirements planning (DRP)   Incorporation of distribution requirements into master production schedules; requirements are based on actual forecast needs, not just shelf replacement.

Dummy activity   A PERT/CPM network activity that consumes no time or resources; used to clarify a network diagram.

Dynamic scheduling   Job scheduling that includes an extra-time allowance for current or projected shop congestion; requires accurate open-order file to determine congestion value for work centers.

Earliest finish (EF)   The earliest possible time at which a project activity may be completed; EF equals ES plus activity duration (t).

Earliest start (ES)   The earliest possible starting time for a project activity; if an activity has multiple predecessors, its ES is equal to the latest predecessors' EF.

Early supplier involvement   A program for getting a supplier's personnel involved early in new development or changes affecting items the supplier provides.

Economic manufacturing quantity (EMQ)   A variation of the EOQ model incorporating acquisition of a lot over the production time rather than all at once; applicable, for example, when goods are made rather than bought.

Economic order quantity (EOQ)   The (fixed) quantity to be ordered in each order cycle that will minimize total inventory costs.

Efficiency   Standard time divided by actual time or actual output (units) divided by standard output (units).

Engineering changes (ECs)   Formal changes in product or process design that alter bills of materials, routing, or production technique.

Ergonomics   Study of a work environment with emphasis on human physiological concerns; efforts to "fit the job to the person" are examples of ergonomics in practice.

Event   Point signifying completion of one or more project activities and sometimes the beginning of others; consumes no time or resources but merely marks a point in time.

Event-based counting   An inventory counting technique in which counting occurs whenever there is an inventory event, such as a stock issue.

Expected value   A weighted average usable when there is a chance of more than one outcome or "payoff"; the summation of each payoff, expressed as a number, times its probability of occurrence.

Expediting (Expediter)   Actions aimed at pulling hot production or purchase orders through more quickly; expediters also called *parts chasers*.

Exponential smoothing   A form of weighted moving average forecasting that (in single form) uses a single smoothing coefficient to assign an "aged" weight to each period of historical data.

Facilitator   An individual with overall responsibility for formation and training of quality circle members.

Facilities   See **Fixed capacity.**

Fail-safing   Designing a process to be incapable of allowing an error to be passed on to the next process.

Finite-capacity planning   Workload planning methods that consider the limited (finite) capacity of workstations and assign work accordingly.

Firm planned order   An MRP tool for overriding the automatic rescheduling feature of MRP; useful for getting a job into a gateway work center at a convenient time, even if different from the calculated order due date.

Fishbone chart   A chart resembling the skeleton of a fish in which the spine bone represents the major cause of quality problems and connecting bones contributing causes; reveals cause-effect linkages. (Also known as *cause-effect diagram* and *Ishikawa diagram*.)

Fixed capacity Plant and equipment that are generally fixed and unalterable for months to years.

Fixed-position layout A facility layout in which the product is kept in one place and facilities come to it; examples include construction and production of very large-scale items.

Flexible manufacturing cell (FMC) Cluster of machines capable of producing a whole part or family of parts.

Flexible manufacturing system (FMS) Machine work cell controlled by a local micro or mini computer and assisted by one or more robots; produces a whole part or family of parts.

Flowcharts A family of forms used in data collection and analysis in a methods study.

Focus forecasting A form of simulation-based forecasting; involves selection of the most accurate of several forecasting models as the basis for the next forecast.

Focused factory Concept that stresses doing one or a few things well at a given plant.

Forecast error For a given time period, actual demand minus forecast demand.

Forward scheduling Beginning with current date or expected start date, adding throughput (lead) time, thus arriving at a scheduled order completion date.

Gain-sharing An incentive pay system in which everyone receives a share of the value of productivity increases.

Gantt control chart A chart used to control certain types of jobs with stable priorities, for example, renovation and major maintenance.

Gantt scheduling chart A widely used scheduling chart with horizontal rows representing jobs or resources to be scheduled and vertical divisions representing time periods.

Gross requirements The total amount of each component needed to produce the ordered quantity of the end product.

Group-based capacity planning Creating aggregate capacity plans with product and service groups or families as core requirement components and a cross-trained labor force available for assignment.

Group replacement Replacing a whole set of components, whether bad or not, at planned intervals; an alternative to a replace-as-they-fail policy.

Hedging A form of purchasing that offers some protection from price changes; applies especially to commodities and includes trading on futures markets.

Holding cost An element of carrying cost; generally associated with stockroom costs, insurance, inventory taxes, and damage or shrinkage during storage.

Idleness rate Percentage of time that a facility is idle; computed as 1 minus the utilization rate.

Incentive pay Pay based on work output; in its purest form, a piece rate.

Independent demand Demand for items that do not go into parent items; generally, independent demand is forecast and dependent demand is calculated.

Infant mortality Early-life failure of a component or product; often caused by improper assembly or rough handling.

Infinite-capacity loading Scheduling jobs without regard for resulting work center loads. See also **Infinite-capacity planning.**

Infinite-capacity planning A workload planning system that assumes the availability of resources required to provide needed parts and services and assigns work accordingly; relies on an activity control subroutine to adjust priorities when bottlenecks arise.

Input control Control of work releases to gateway or bottleneck work centers.

Interarrival time Time between arrivals of customers or work in waiting-line operations.

Inventory carrying cost See **Carrying cost.**

Inventory turnover Annual cost of goods sold divided by value of average inventory.

Irregular maintenance   Unscheduled repairs, machine installations (millwright work), and minor construction.

Item demand   Demand broken down into specific types or models of products or services.

Item master file   An inventory file containing records for each component and assembly; holds on-hand balances, planning factors, and independent demand data.

Job   A task with an end point, usually resulting in something tangible; the whole work activity required to fill a service order or produce a component.

Job design   The function of fitting tasks together to form a job that can be assigned to a person; emphasis is on creating useful jobs that people can and want to do; job enlargement and job enrichment are associated with theories of job design.

Job-shop process   Intermittent production, frequently one at a time; characterized by extreme variation in output and process.

Just-in-time (JIT) production   A system of managing operations with little or no delay time or idle inventories between one process and the next.

Kanban   A communication or signal from the user to the maker (or supplier) for more work; from the Japanese word for "card" or "visible record."

Latest finish (LF)   The latest possible completion time for a project activity to avoid project delay; if the activity has multiple successor activities, its LF equals the successors' earliest LS.

Latest start (LS)   The latest possible starting time for a project activity to avoid project delay; LS = LF − Activity duration (*t*).

Lead time   See **Throughput time.**

Leading indicator   A variable that correlates with demand one or more periods later, giving some signal of magnitude and direction of pending demand change.

Learning curve   Graphical representation of the economy of scale concept: Greater volume yields lower unit cost; the curve plots resource utilization as a function of lot quantity.

Level-by-level MRP processing   The MRP way of calculating planned order release quantities and dates—top (zero) level of the BOM first, then subsequent lower levels; ensures complete capture of all requirements.

Level capacity (strategy)   A capacity management strategy that seeks to retain a stable or constant amount of capacity.

Leveling (normalizing)   In setting time standards, adjusting the raw cycle time to reflect the pace (level of effort) of the person observed, which yields the leveled (normalized) time.

Line balancing   A procedure for dividing tasks evenly among employees at workstations in a product or cellular layout; also known as *assembly-line balancing.*

Linear output   Production of the same quantity each time period.

Linearity index   A measure of the success in attaining targeted production or processing quantities; mathematically, it is 100 percent minus the mean percent deviation from scheduled production quantity.

Load leveling   Scheduler's attempt to release a mix of orders that neither overloads nor underloads work centers.

Load profile   Future work center capacity requirements for open and planned orders.

Loading (load, workload)   Assigning workload to a work center.

Lot   Large purchase or production quantity of the same item; often has its own identifying number.

Lot-for-lot   The simplest approach to lot sizing; the period order quantity is simply the net quantity required in each period.

Lot size   Quantity of an item produced, serviced, or transported at one time.

Lot sizing   Planning order quantities.

Lot splitting   Splitting a lot quantity into more than one sublot, traditionally for expediting reasons: Stop (split up) a current lot already on a machine so a hot job can replace it. Under JIT, lot splitting is more or less normal practice (not expediting), especially if a lot can be split among several of the same type of machine or workstation.

Lumpy workload (demand)   Highly variable pattern of workload (demand).

Maintainability   Features that make equipment or products easy to maintain.

Manufacturability   See **Producibility.**

Manufacturing resource planning (MRPII)   A comprehensive planning and control system that uses the master production schedule as a basis for scheduling capacity, shipments, tool changes, design work, and cash flow.

Master planning   Broadly, matching aggregate demand with capacity; narrowly, steering the firm's capacity toward actual item demands that materialize over time.

Master production schedule (MPS)   Master schedule for product-oriented company.

Master schedule   A statement of what the firm plans to produce (products) and/or provide (services), broken down by product model or service type.

Material requirements planning (MRP)   A computer-based system of planning orders and tracking inventory flows.

Materials management   Management functions related to the complete cycle of materials flow; sometimes collected into one department.

Mean absolute deviation (MAD)   A measure of forecast model accuracy; the sum of absolute values of forecast errors over a number of periods divided by the number of periods.

Mean absolute percent error (MAPE)   Measure of forecast model accuracy; the average of the absolute error to demand ratio over a number of periods converted to a percentage.

Measured daywork (MDW) system   A nominal incentive-wage system in which standard output serves as a target for an employee.

Methods study   Procedure for improving the way work is done; follows the scientific method of inquiry.

Methods-time-measurement (MTM)   Procedure for developing synthetic time standards by referring to tables of standards for basic motions.

Micro-response analysis   A method for measuring idle work in work centers by using ratios of lead time to work content, process speed to use rate, and pieces to workstations or operators; process improvements are reflected in smaller ratios.

Milestone   A key event in a project; one type of upper management-oriented network consists solely of milestones.

Mixed-model assembly lines   Assembly lines on which more than one model of a product is made.

Mixed-model production (mixed-model assembly)   Production schedule that is repetitive in short cycles; conducive to supplying some of each needed model each day closely in line with customer requirements.

Model   A likeness (mental, graphic, mathematical, or procedural) of a reality.

Modified distribution method (MODI)   A technique for achieving solution optimality in transportation problems.

Monte Carlo simulation   A simulation technique using probability distributions and random numbers to represent events such as arrivals and service times; used to imitate operations to promote better understanding and decision making.

Motion study   Methods improvement approach focusing on basic hand and body motions called *therbligs*.

Moving average   In forecasting, the mean or average of a given number of the most recent demand amounts, which becomes the forecast for the next (first future) period; the procedure repeats each period by dropping the oldest and adding the newest demand.

Multiple regression/correlation   A mathematical model allowing for investigation of a number of causal variables in order to determine their simultaneous effect on a predicted variable such as demand.

Negotiation   A form of purchasing without competitive bidding, typically in a stable supply situation; usually applies to high dollar-volume items produced to a buyer's specs.

Net-change MRP processing   MRP processing system in which only those records that have changed since the last run are updated.

Net requirement   For an item, its gross requirement minus stock on hand.

Netting   A procedure for determining the net requirement for an item.

Normal time   Time for accomplishment of a work task after the cycle time has been adjusted to reflect pace rating. See also **Pace rating.**

Northwest-corner rule   A method for finding an initial solution for a transportation problem; makes assignments to transportation routes along the upper-left-corner to lower-right-corner diagonal of the problem matrix; ignores transportation route costs.

Numerically controlled (NC) machine   A machine that performs tasks in response to a preprogrammed digital instructions (numeric codes) on punched tape or in a computer program.

Open-office concept   An office arrangement plan that eliminates most floor-to-ceiling walls, stresses use of modular furniture and movable, partial-height partitions, and deemphasizes compartmentalization of people.

Open order   An order that has been placed but not completed.

Operation   Part of a job; one step or task, which requires a new setup, often at a different work center.

Operations   The operating end of the business, where resources are transformed into goods and services.

Operations management   Direction and control of operations; includes self-management, expert management, team management, and formal manager management; aims are improvement of transformations and allied processes.

Order entry   Organizational acceptance of an order into the order processing system; includes credit checks, customer documentation translation into production terms, stock queries, and order number assignment.

Order promising   Making a commitment to a customer to ship or deliver an order.

Overlapped production   Condition in which a lot is in production at two or more work centers at the same time, typically because some of the lot is rushed forward on a "hot" basis; normal practice within work cells.

***p* chart (percent-defective chart)**   A process control chart for attributes showing the proportion or fraction defective in each sample.

Pace rating   Judging the pace of the subject of a time-standards study, where 100 percent is considered normal; yields a factor used in normalizing or leveling the raw cycle time.

Parent item   For a component, its next higher-level assembly; the part into which a component goes.

Pareto chart   A chart showing items in any population grouped by category from most to least frequently occurring.

Part-period algorithm (PPA)   A lot-sizing method designed to minimize the average cost per time period for ordering and carrying a single inventory item.

Pay for knowledge   Remuneration system in which employees are paid more for acquiring additional skills and greater knowledge.

Periodic maintenance   Regularly scheduled custodial services and preventive maintenance.

Perpetual inventory system   A system in which every issue from inventory triggers a check on on-hand stock to see if the reorder point has been reached.

Personal, rest, and delay (PR&D) allowance   Amount of time added to normal time to yield standard time; accommodates personal needs and unavoidable delay when setting time standards.

Planned order (planned order release)   Anticipated order placement; indicated by item, date, and quantity.

Preautomation   What must be done to the work space to make the work possible for a machine to do; basically concentrates on propinquity and precision.

Precedence diagram   A chart showing a repetitive job broken into sequenced flow lines; used in assembly-line balancing.

Precontrol chart A quality-monitoring chart composed of three colored zones that encompass specification (not control) limits; measures of quality are plotted, and the zones they fall into tell the operator what action to take.

Predictive maintenance A form of preventive maintenance performed after a set amount of operating time—prior to predicted failure or wear-out.

Preventive maintenance (PM) Any actions, including adjustments, replacements, and basic cleanliness, that forestall equipment failure; may be based on calendar time, time of usage, or faults revealed in an inspection.

Priority report A (typically) daily list of job priorities sent to a work center; also called a *dispatch list.*

Process A unique set of interrelated elements that act together to determine performance; categories from which the specific elements are taken include manpower, materials, methods, machines, measurement, maintenance, and management.

Process capability In general, a statement of the ability of process output to meet specifications; inherent capability is the width (approximately six standard deviations) of the distribution of process output.

Process control A condition signifying that all special or assignable variation has been removed from process output; only common or chance variation remains; also known as *statistical control.*

Process control chart Statistical control chart on which to record samples of measured process outputs; the purpose is to note whether the process is statistically stable or changing, so that adjustments can be made as needed.

Process flowchart See **Flowcharts.**

Process industry An industry that produces goods that flow, pour, or mix together; also called *continuous-flow process industry.*

Process (functional) layout A layout type in which similar facilities and functions are grouped together in one place, usually meaning that all people working in these functional areas are also grouped together.

Producible or producibility Easy to make without error and undue cost with present or planned equipment and people; a desirable product design characteristic.

Product layout A type of facility layout in which facilities are placed along product flow lines, with the customer (next process) next to the provider.

Product planning Developing lines of goods and services.

Product structure See **Bill-of-materials (BOM).**

Production activity control Keeping work on schedule on the shop floor, using progress information (feedback), which is compared with schedules; sometimes employs daily priority report, which gives priority to latest work.

Production control Directing or regulating the flow of work through the production cycle, from purchase of materials to delivery of finished items.

Production-inventory (PI) system A planning and control system governing work flow, schedules, and material movements.

Production line Multiple sequential processes arranged into one grand process to produce a product or narrow family of products.

Production/operations management (POM) See **Operations management.**

Production plan Total planned production, or production rate; unspecific as to product model or type of service.

Production rate Pace of production output, expressed in units per time period.

Productivity In general, output divided by input; specifically, efficiency times utilization, which is (also) standard time for work done divided by time available for the work.

Program evaluation and review technique (PERT) A network-based project management technique originally developed for R&D projects; about the same as CPM.

Progressive operations Production in which material being worked on is passed from workstation to workstation; alternative to autonomous production.

Project A large-scale, one-of-a-kind endeavor; generally employs large amounts of diverse resources.

Pull system A system in which the user "pulls" work from the maker or provider by some kind of signal (called *kanban*); pull signals should be issued at rate of actual usage.

Push system A system in which the maker "pushes" work forward into storage or onto the next process with little regard for rate of use; rate of pushing out the work often is preset by schedule.

Quality assurance In general, the activities associated with making sure that the customer receives quality goods and services; often, the name given to a department charged with carrying out these responsibilities.

Quality characteristic A process performance (output) property of a product or service deemed important enough to control.

Quality control circle (quality circle) A small work group that meets periodically to discuss ways to improve quality, productivity, or the work environment.

Quality cost Costs of preventing defects, checking process output, and paying for the results of defective output; more broadly, the loss to society of any deviation from target.

Queuing analysis A study of a waiting-line system using a series of formulas appropriate to the assumptions (e.g., service and arrival distributions) and description (channels and stages) of the particular system.

R **chart (ranges chart)** A process control chart for variables; shows range of each sample, that is, within-sample variation.

Random events In a time series, patternless occurrences—such as jumps or drops in demand—for which there is no apparent cause.

Regenerative MRP processing A mode of MRP processing in which all material requirements are regenerated on each run (usually weekly).

Regularized schedule A schedule in which certain items are produced at regular intervals.

Reorder point (ROP) Quantity of on-hand inventory that serves as a trigger for placement of an order.

Repetitive operations Producing the same item or providing the same service over and over.

Rescheduling notice A notice (usually from an MRP system) that an order for a component part needs to be rescheduled; stems from a change in due dates or quantities for one or more parent items.

Residual inventory Inventory left over when an order is canceled or reduced in quantity.

Resource requirements planning (RRP) A gross check to see if items in the master schedule will overload a scarce resource; also known as *rough-cut capacity planning* on the trial master schedule.

Rolling forecast A forecast that is redone at intervals, typically dropping oldest data and replacing it with most recent data.

Rough-cut capacity planning Conversion of an operations plan into capacity needs for key resources; the purpose is to evaluate a plan before trying to implement it.

Routings Path from work center to work center that work follows in its transformation into a finished part or end product; standard routings may be kept in records.

Run diagram A running plot of measurements of some process or quality characteristic, piece by piece as a process continues.

Scatter (correlation) diagram A plot of effects (e.g., quality changes) against experimental changes in process inputs.

Seasonal index Ratio of demand for a particular season to demand for the average season.

Seasonality (seasonal variation) Recurring pattern in a time series; occurring within one year and repeating annually.

Service level Percentage of orders filled from stock on hand.

Setup time See **Changeover time.**

Shop calendar A scheduling calendar with workdays as sequentially numbered days; sometimes numbered 000 to 999.

Simplex method (linear programming) A mathematical optimization model; may be used to obtain a "first pass" solution to some operations problems.

Simulation Manipulation of numbers or movable objects to represent an action or operation; used to test an operations plan.

Simultaneous engineering Inclusion of supplier, process, and manufacturing engineers early in product design stages; results in shorter lead times, better quality, and better coordination.

Slack (slack time) The amount of time an activity may be delayed without delaying the project schedule; usually changes as the project progresses.

Small-group improvement activities (SGIAs) *Ad hoc* groups or project teams formed from operations people to address improvements.

Social loss (of bad quality) A concept introduced by Genichi Taguchi stating that there is a cost imparted to society whenever process output deviates from the target.

Soliciting competitive bids Inviting prospective suppliers to bid (offer a price) on a contract to provide goods or services according to specifications.

Special cause variation A type of variation in process output that can be traced to a specific cause such as a fault or malfunction, removal of which removes the variation.

Specification Process output description commonly in two parts: the target (nominal) and the tolerances.

Speculation (speculative) buying Purchasing to get an attractive price rather than because of need.

Standard data Tables of time-standard values used to construct synthetic standards.

Standard deviation (SD) A measure of dispersion in a distribution; equal to the square root of the variance; in forecasting, defined as the square root of the mean-square error.

Standard time The time a person is expected to take to complete a task; the normal time plus an allowance factor.

Standardization Settling on a few rather than many sizes, shapes, colors, and so forth for a given part.

Statistical process control (SPC) Collection of process analysis techniques including process flowchart, Pareto analysis, fishbone chart, run diagram, control chart, and scatter diagram.

Steady state In waiting lines, a condition of stable average queues, usually achieved after running the system long enough to "wash out" startup conditions.

Stepping-stone method A technique for finding the optimal solution in transportation problems.

Stock location counting A form of physical inventory control in which counting moves from one location to another, often finding "lost" items in the process.

Stockout Failure to deliver from stock upon receipt of a customer order.

Strategy A basic type of plan with far-reaching effects; a foundation for more specific plans.

Streamlined operations Steady-flow operations with few delays, stops, starts, or storages.

Synchronized schedules (synchronized processing) Processing with schedules in which the timing of delivery or production of a component is meshed with the use rate of the parent item.

Systematic layout planning (SLP) A multistep approach to layout planning based on flow and relationship data.

Systems contract A contract with a supplier for a defined set of items, often allowing orders to be placed by line managers without going through the purchasing department.

Theory of constraints Approach to operations that attempts to schedule and feed work so as to maximize work flow rate (and therefore cash flow as well) through bottlenecks and constraints.

Therbligs The 17 basic units of work motion, first set forth by Frank and Lillian Gilbreth; examples include grasp, move, release, select, and position.

Throughput time Elapsed time, including all delays, to transform resources into goods or services; same as *lead time*.

Time fence   A point on a company's planning horizon that separates the firm portion (typically the near future) from the tentative portion (more distant future).

Time measurement unit (TMU)   A time unit in MTM analysis: 1 TMU = 0.0006 minutes, or 0.00001 hours.

Time-phased order point (TPOP)   A subset of MRP for handling independent demand items.

Time series   A sequential set of observations of a variable taken at regular intervals over time.

Time standard   See **Standard time.**

Time study   A direct approach for obtaining the cycle time to be used in setting a time standard; obtained by stopwatch or film analysis.

Tolerance stackup   See **Variation stackup.**

Total preventive maintenance (TPM)   A full agenda of procedures that improve dependability of equipment, with emphasis on maintaining equipment before it breaks down; bestows primary responsibility for PM on equipment operator.

Total quality (TQ)   Comprehensive program for managing to ensure quality throughout an organization; includes planning and design, supplier and manufacturing interface, self-inspection for control, and continual improvement in customer service through process monitoring and feedback; places primary responsibility for quality at the source (i.e., the maker or provider).

Total quality control (TQC)   See **Total quality.**

Total quality management (TQM)   See **Total quality.**

Tracking signal   Typically, the cumulative deviation in a time series divided by the MAD; used as a limit to trigger adjustment in smoothing coefficients in adaptive smoothing models.

Transient state   Time period in which a queuing system exhibits unstable arrival and service rates, such as startup and shutdown phases.

Transportation method   A linear optimization mathematical model useful in solving transportation problems; views the problem as a transportation matrix containing sources (rows) and destinations (columns).

Trend   A long-term shift, positive or negative, in the value of a time series; also known as *slope.*

Under-capacity (labor) scheduling   Scheduling labor at less than full capacity output; allows schedule to be met on most days and allows times for operators to work on quality and maintenance.

Unit load concept   A concept calling for accumulation of enough pieces to "make a complete load" before moving any pieces.

Utilization   Ratio of time in use to time available.

Utilization rate   In queuing systems, the percentage of time that the system is busy; computed as the arrival rate divided by the service rate.

Value analysis   Examination of existing product design specifications with the aim of lowering cost; typically centered in the purchasing department.

Value engineering   Same as *value analysis,* but typically centered in the engineering organization.

Variables inspection   A test in which measurements of an output (quality) characteristic are taken.

Variation stackup   The output that results when two or more components at extreme edges within tolerance (specification) limits are assembled or mixed together; often the result is an assembly, batch, or service that is out of specification limits.

Vogel's approximation method (VAM)   A method for determining an initial solution to transportation problems; considers transportation route costs.

Work breakdown structure (WBS)   Product-oriented list and definition of major modules and secondary components in a project.

Work cell   See **Cell.**

Work content time   Time required to make a complete assembly or perform a job; usually the sum of the times of all tasks needed.

Work in process (WIP)   Partly completed work that is either waiting between processes or is in process.

World-class excellence Category of companies that compete successfully on a global basis; those companies are dedicated to continual improvement in all facets of operations, especially in service to customers.

$\overline{X}$ **chart (averages chart)** A process control chart for variables inspection showing the sample averages for a number of samples or subgroups and thus revealing between-sample variations.

Zero defects (ZD) Proposed as the proper goal of a quality program; an alternative to the past practice of setting an acceptable quality (defect) level.

Index